Constitutional Law in Context

Third Edition

Volume 1

Michael Kent Curtis
WAKE FOREST UNIVERSITY SCHOOL OF LAW

J. Wilson Parker
WAKE FOREST UNIVERSITY SCHOOL OF LAW

Davison M. Douglas
WILLIAM & MARY SCHOOL OF LAW

Paul Finkelman
ALBANY LAW SCHOOL

William G. Ross
SAMFORD UNIVERSITY, CUMBERLAND SCHOOL OF LAW

CAROLINA ACADEMIC PRESS
Durham, North Carolina

Copyright © 2003, 2006, 2011
Michael Kent Curtis, J. Wilson Parker,
Davison M. Douglas, Paul Finkelman,
and William G. Ross
All Rights Reserved

ISBN: 978-1-59460-811-7
LCCN: 2010934323

Carolina Academic Press
700 Kent Street
Durham, North Carolina 27701
Telephone (919) 489-7486
Fax (919) 493-5668
www.cap-press.com

Printed in the United States of America

Summary of Contents

List of Charts and Diagrams	vii
Table of Cases	ix
Table of Authorities	xxvii
Permissions	xxxiii
A Timeline of American Constitutional History	xxxv
Justices of the U.S. Supreme Court	lxxi

Chapter 1 • An Introduction to American Constitutional Law	3
I. The Articles of Confederation	5
II. The Constitution of the United States of America	6
III. The Constitution: Institutions, Powers, and Limits	20
IV. What Is *Constitutional* Law?	21
V. On Reading the Constitution	32
VI. A Problem for Constitutional Analysis: The Clinton Impeachment	40
Chapter 2 • National Power: Article I and the Powers and Limits of Congress	61
I. Implied Congressional Power: Its Nature and Extent	64
II. The Commerce Clause: A Delegated Power	97
III. Ducking the Issue: Statutory Construction as a Means of Avoiding Constitutional Interpretation	218
IV. Other Delegated Sources of National Power: The Power to Spend, the War Power, and the Treaty Power	225
Chapter 3 • Limits on Federal Power: The Federal Structure, the 10th Amendment, and State Sovereign Immunity	247
I. National Power and State Power: The 10th Amendment	249
State Intergovernmental Immunity and the 10th Amendment	252
II. National Power and State Power: State Sovereign Immunity	284
III. The Rehnquist Court	304
Chapter 4 • Powers and Limits of the Federal Courts	309
I. Federal Judicial Review	311
II. Congressional Control over Federal Judicial Review	357
III. Justiciability	364

Chapter 5 · The Role of the President ... 437
I. The Scope of Executive Power ... 439
II. The President as Commander-in-Chief ... 465
III. Appointments and the Separation of Powers ... 476
IV. Executive Privilege: Judicial Immunities ... 479

Chapter 6 · Limits on State Power: Preemption, the Dormant Commerce Clause, and the Privileges and Immunities Clause ... 507
I. Preemption ... 509
II. The Dormant Commerce Clause ... 540
III. The Privileges and Immunities Clause of Article IV ... 610
IV. Special Considerations: The World Trade Organization and the North American Free Trade Agreement ... 620

Chapter 7 · The Incorporation of the Bill of Rights ... 625
I. Introduction ... 627
II. Application of the Bill of Rights to the States: 1791–1833 ... 637
III. From *Barron* to the Adoption of the 14th Amendment: The Pre-Civil War Background ... 640
IV. The Drafting of the 14th Amendment ... 661
V. Applying Methods of Interpretation to the 14th Amendment's First Section ... 684
VI. Reconstruction and the Initial Judicial Response ... 686
VII. The Bill of Rights and Incorporation after *Slaughter-House* ... 709
VIII. Incorporation: Approaches, Effects, and Further Thoughts ... 730
IX. The Warren Court ... 732
X. A Short Note on Political Transformation: 1948–2008 ... 737
XI. The Roberts Court and Incorporation ... 742

Chapter 8 · Substantive Due Process ... 785
I. Introduction ... 787
II. A Model of Substantive Due Process Analysis ... 796
III. Liberty and Economic Rights ... 799
IV. The Origins of Substantive Protection for Non-Economic Rights ... 834
V. Liberty and Sexual Privacy ... 844
VI. Liberty and the Family ... 912
VII. Liberty and Sexual Autonomy: Restrictions on Private Sexual Behavior ... 926
VIII. Liberty and the "Right" to Die ... 967
IX. The Takings Clause ... 986

Index ... 1011

List of Charts and Diagrams

Chapter 2

Commerce Clause Graphic Portrayals

Neither congress nor the states have legislated	98
Congress and the states legislate exercising concurrent powers	99
Preemption	100
Congress legislates and turns power over to the states by providing that each state's rule shall become the federal rule	101
Affirmative constitutional limitations on federal commerce power	102
Truism view of the 10th Amendment	102
Dual sovereignty view of the 10th Amendment	103

Chapter 4

The American Judicial System: A Graphic Portrayal	312
Independent and Adequate State Ground: Appeal or Petition for Certiorari from State Court to U.S. Supreme Court	356

Chapter 6

Dormant Commerce Clause: Two Types of Analysis	544
Analylsis of Article IV, § 2 Privileges and Immunities Claim	613
Dormant Commerce Clause	614
Article IV Privileges and Immunities Clause	614

Chapter 7

Approaches to Application of the Bill of Rights to the States: A Graphic Portrayal	730

Chapter 8

Substantive Due Process Analysis: Harm and Trait	797
Full Model of Substantive Due Process Analysis	800

Table of Cases

Primary cases are printed in bold and the page number is also bold. Note cases and cases discussed in notes by the authors have the page numbers indicated, but are not in bold. Page numbers are not listed for cases that are cited in primary cases and in note cases.

A.L.A. Schechter Poultry Corp. v. United States, 295 U.S. 495 (1935), 191, 441

Abbott Laboratories v. Gardner, 387 U.S. 136 (1967), 430

Ableman v. Booth, 62 U.S. (21 How.) 506 (1859), 349

Adair v. United States, 208 U.S. 161 (1908), 141, 148, 191

Adamson v. California, 332 U.S. 46 (1947), 626, 635, 716, 720, 725, 727, 756, 917

Addyston Pipe Steel Co. v. United States, 175 U.S. 211 (1899), 127

Adkins v. Children's Hospital, 261 U.S. 525 (1923), 143, 157, 820, 837, 874, 885, 917, 918, 984

Aetna Health Care v. Davila, 542 U.S. 200 (2004), 536

Agins v. Tiburon, 447 U.S. 255 (1980), 991, 997, 998, 1003

Agostini v. Felton, 521 U.S. 203 (1997), 306

Aguilar v. Felton, 473 U.S. 402 (1985), 306

Air Courier Conference of America v. American Postal Workers Union, AFL-CIO, 498 U.S. 517 (1991), 430

Akron v. Akron Center for Reproductive Health, Inc., 462 U.S. 416 (1983), 869, 885

Alden v. Maine, 527 U.S. 706 (1999), 247, 273, 284–286, 302, 303, 305, 527, 743

Alexander v. Louisiana, 405 U.S. 625 (1972), 729

Allen v. Wright, 468 U.S. 737 (1984), 404, 412, 423

Allgeyer v. Louisiana, 165 U.S. 578 (1897), 131, 788, 809, 837, 984

Altria Group, Inc. v. Good, 129 S. Ct. 538 (2008), 539

American Power Light Co. v. SEC, 329 U.S. 90 (1946), 441

American Trucking Associations, Inc. v. United States Environmental Protection Agency, 195 F.3d 4 (D.C. Cir. 1999), 437, 439, 440, 444

American Yearbook Co. v. Askew, 339 F. Supp. 719 (M.D. Fla.1972), 603

Americans United for Separation of Church and State, Inc. v. United States Dep't of Health Education and Welfare, 619 F.2d 252 (3rd Cir. 1980), 386, 395, 396, 400, 413

Anderson v. Dunn, 19 U.S. (6 Wheat.) 204 (1821), 266

Andrus v. Allard, 444 U.S. 51 (1979), 995, 1002, 1009

Apodaca v. Oregon, 406 U.S. 404 (1972), 729, 771

Aptheker v. Secretary of State, 378 U.S. 500 (1964), 891

Arizona v. California, 373 U.S. 546 (1963), 462

Arlington Heights v. Metropolitan Housing Dev. Corp., 429 U.S. 252 (1977), 424, 579

Armstrong v. United States, 364 U.S. 40 (1960), 1003, 1009

Asbell v. Kansas, 209 U.S. 251 (1908), 588, 589

Ashby v. White (Eng. Q.B. 1702), 301

Ashcraft v. Tennessee, 322 U.S. 143 (1944), 719

Ashwander v. Tennessee Valley Authority, 297 U.S. 288 (1936), 365
Association of Data Processing Service Organizations, Inc. v. Camp, 397 U.S. 150 (1970), 429
Atkin v. Kansas, 191 U.S. 207 (1903), 603, 816
Atlantic Coast Line R.R. Co. v. Georgia, 234 U.S. 280 (1914), 554
Austin v. New Hampshire, 420 U.S. 656 (1975), 617
Bacchus Imports, Ltd. v. Dias, 468 U.S. 263 (1984), 546, 547
Baehr v. Lewin, 852 P.2d 44 (1993), 960
Bain Peanut Co. of Tex. v. Pinson, 282 U.S. 499 (1931), 842
Baker v. Carr, 369 U.S. 186 (1962), 368, 370, 376, 377, 380, 392, 393, 579, 734
Baker v. Nelson, 191 NW.2d 185 (Mn. 1971), aff'd. 409 U.S. 810 (1972), 960
Baker v. Vermont, 744 A.2d 864 (Vt. 1998), 961
Baldwin v. Fish Game Comm'n of Montana, 436 U.S. 371 (1978), 614, 615, 617, 782, 947
Baldwin v. G.A.F. Seelig, Inc., 294 U.S. 511 (1935), 547, 569, 575, 576, 585–589, 599
Baltimore Ohio R.R. Co. v. Baugh, 149 U.S. 368 (1893), 267
Bank of Augusta v. Earle, 38 U.S. 519 (1839), 683
Bank of Columbia v. Okely, 17 U.S. (4 Wheat.) 235 (1819), 712
Bank of the State v. Cooper, 10 Tenn. 599 (1831), 983
Barrett v. United States, 668 F. Supp. 339 (S.D.N.Y. 1987), 384
Barron v. Mayor and City Council of Baltimore, 32 U.S. (7 Pet.) 243 (1833), 625, 637
Barrows v. Jackson, 346 U.S. 249 (1953), 428
Bartemeyer v. Iowa, 85 U.S. 129 (1874), 984
Bates v. Dow Agrosciences LLC, 544 U.S. 431 (2005), 537
Beer Co. v. Massachusetts, 97 U.S. 25 (1877), 988
Benton v. Maryland, 395 U.S. 784 (1969), 729, 757, 771

Berea College v. Kentucky, 211 U.S. 45 (1908), 365
Berman v. Parker, 348 U.S. 26 (1954), 1005
Bessette v. People, 193 Ill. 334 (1901), 812
Bibb v. Navajo Freight Lines, Inc., 359 U.S. 520 (1959), 571
Bivens v. Six Unknown Named Agents of Federal Bureau of Narcotics, 403 U.S. 388 (1971), 381, 383, 412, 490, 493, 495
Blake v. McClung, 172 U.S. 239 (1898), 614
Blatchford v. Native Village of Noatak, 501 U.S. 775 (1991), 288, 290
BMW of North America, Inc. v. Gore, 517 U.S. 559 (1996), 833
Board of Regents of State Colleges v. Roth, 408 U.S. 564 (1972), 925
Board of Trade v. Olsen, 262 U.S. 1 (1923), 207
Board of Trustees of the University of Alabama v. Garrett, 531 U.S. 356 (2001), 303
Board of Trustees v. Scott, 125 Ky. 545 (Ky. 1907), 941
Bolling v. Sharpe, 347 U.S. 497 (1954), 770, 774, 845, 975, 985
Bond v. Floyd, 385 U.S. 116 (1966), 734
Borden's Farm Products Co. v. Baldwin, 293 U.S. 194 (1934), 827
Boumediene v. Bush, 553 U.S. 723 (U.S. 2008), 468, 476
Bowen v. Kendrick, 487 U.S. 589 (1988), 397, 399
Bowers v. Hardwick, 478 U.S. 186 (1986), 36, 355, 773, 786, 790, 869, 888, 923, 926, 927, 929, 937, 938, 940, 942, 943, 945, 951, 952, 968
Bowles v. Willingham, 321 U.S. 503 (1944), 176
Bowman v. Chicago Northwestern Ry. Co., 125 U.S. 465 (1888), 585, 588, 589
Bowsher v. Synar, 478 U.S. 714 (1986), 444, 478
Boyd v. United States, 116 U.S. 616 (1886), 846, 850
Boynton v. Virginia, 364 U.S. 454 (1960), 175
Bradwell v. Illinois, 83 U.S. (16 Wall.) 130 (1873), 634, 880, 908

Brandenburg v. Ohio, 395 U.S. 444 (1969), 734

Brause v. State, 21 P.3d 357 (Alaska 2001), 960

Breithaupt v. Abram, 352 U.S. 432 (1957), 968

Brents v. Morgan, 299 S.W. 967 (Ky. App. 1927), 941

Brooks v. United States, 267 U.S. 432 (1925), 160, 161, 175

Brown-Forman Distillers Corp. v. New York State Liquor Authority, 476 U.S. 573 (1986), 599

Brown v. Board of Education (Brown I), 347 U.S. 483 (1954), 27, 31, 347, 349, 885, 935, 962, 965

Brown v. EPA, 521 F.2d 827 (9th Cir. 1975), 277

Brown v. Maryland, 25 U.S. (12 Wheat.) 419 (1827), 342

Brown v. Mississippi, 297 U.S. 278 (1936), 715

Browning-Ferris Industries of Vermont, Inc. v. Kelco Disposal Inc., 492 U.S. 257 (1989), 730

Buck v. Bell, 274 U.S. 200 (1927), 785, 838, 842, 861

Buck v. Kuykendall, 267 U.S. 307 (1925), 586

Buckley v. Valeo, 424 U.S. 1 (1976), 62, 226, 228, 232, 478, 501

Bunting v. Oregon, 243 U.S. 426 (1917), 820

Burbank v. Lockheed Air Terminal, Inc., 411 U.S. 624 (1973), 584

Burch v. Louisiana, 441 U.S. 130 (1979), 729

Burton v. United States, 196 U.S. 283 (1905), 365

Bush v. Lucas, 462 U.S. 367 (1983), 382

Butz v. Economou, 438 U.S. 478 (1978), 484, 487, 493, 495, 496

C A Carbone v. Town of Clarkstown, 511 U.S. 383 (1994), 592

Calder v. Bull, 3 U. S. 386 (1798), 787, 793, 983

Califano v. Goldfarb, 430 U.S. 199 (1977), 908

California Coastal Comm'n v. Granite Rock Co., 480 U.S. 572 (1987), 533

California Div. of Labor Standards Enforcement v. Dillingham Constr., N. A., Inc., 519 U.S. 316 (1997), 608

California Retail Liquor Dealers Assn. v. Midcal Aluminum, Inc., 445 U.S. 97 (1980), 228

Callan v. Wilson, 127 U.S. 540 (1888), 725

Caminetti v. United States, 242 U.S. 470 (1917), 136, 138

Campbell v. State, 11 Ga. 353 (1852), 641

Camps Newfound/Owatonna, Inc. v. Town of Harrison, 520 U.S. 564 (1997), 606

Canadian N. R. Co. v. Eggen, 252 U.S. 553 (1920), 614, 615

Cantwell v. Connecticut, 310 U.S. 296 (1940), 716, 891

Carey v. Population Services International, 431 U.S. 678 (1977), 929, 936

Carlson v. Green, 446 U.S. 14 (1980), 382

Carter v. Carter Coal Co., 298 U.S. 238 (1936), 61, 144, 162, 191, 232, 260

Carter v. Virginia, 321 U.S. 131 (1944), 561

Case v. Bowles, 327 U.S. 92 (1946), 260, 261

Chambers v. Florida, 309 U.S. 227 (1940), 719

Champion v. Ames (The Lottery Case), 188 U.S. 321 (1903), 61, 129, 130, 135, 138, 139, 160, 175

Chapman v. United States, 365 U.S. 610 (1961), 847

Chappell v. Wallace, 462 U.S. 296 (1983), 382, 385

Chastleton Corporation v. Sinclair, 264 U.S. 543 (1924), 827

Cheff v. Schnackenberg, 384 U.S. 373 (1966), 725

Cherokee Nation v. Georgia, 30 U.S. (5 Pet.) 1 (1831), 343

Chevron, U.S.A., Inc. v. Natural Resources Defense Council, Inc., 467 U.S. 837 (U.S. 1984), 534

Chicago Grand Trunk Ry. Co. v. Wellman, 143 U.S. 339 (1892), 365

Chicago Southern Air Lines, Inc. v. Waterman S.S. Corp., 333 U.S. 103 (1948), 482

Chicago, Burlington, Quincy Railroad Co. v. Chicago, 166 U.S. 226 (1897), 710, 711, 723

Chirac v. Chirac, 15 U.S. (2 Wheat.) 259 (1817), 238
Chisholm v. Georgia, 2 U.S. (2 Dall.) 419 (1793), 284, 287, 294, 296, 339
Christensen v. Harris County, 529 U.S. 576 (2000), 534
Cipollone v. Liggett Group, Inc., 505 U.S. 504 (1992), 523, 529, 539
Citizens for Equal Protection v. Bruning, 290 F. Supp.2d 1004 (D.C. Neb. 2005), 962
City of Boerne v. Flores, 521 U.S. 507 (1997), 305
City of Los Angeles v. Alameda Books, 535 U.S. 425 (2002), 781
City of Los Angeles v. Lyons, 461 U.S. 95 (1983), 310, 387, 405, 412, 430
City of Philadelphia v. New Jersey, 437 U.S. 617 (1978), 507, 583
Civil Rights Cases, 109 U.S. 3 (1883), 172, 173, 181, 189, 634, 690, 706
Clark Distilling Co. v. Western Maryland Railway Co., 242 U.S. 311 (1917), 136
Cleburne v. Cleburne Living Center, Inc., 473 U.S. 432 (1985), 951
Cleveland Board of Education v. LaFleur, 414 U.S. 632 (1974), 911, 913, 915
Clinton v. City of New York, 524 U.S. 417 (1998), 437, 462
Clinton v. Jones, 520 U.S. 681 (1997), 47, 48, 437, 479, 497, 505, 506
Cloverleaf Creamery v. Minnesota, 289 N.W.2d 79 (Minn. 1979), 544, 596
Cohens v. Virginia, 19 U.S. (6 Wheat.) 264 (1821), 187, 309, 335, 336, 341
Cole v. Arkansas, 333 U.S. 196 (1948), 720
Colegrove v. Green, 328 U.S. 549 (1946), 368, 387
Coleman v. Thompson, 501 U.S. 722 (1991), 527
Collector v. Day, 78 U.S. 113 (1870), 147
College Savings Bank v. Florida Prepaid Postsecondary Education Expense Board, 527 U.S. 666 (1999), 285, 302, 304, 305
Collins v. Harker Heights, 503 U.S. 115 (1992), 971
Columbus Greenville Ry. Co. v. Miller, 283 U.S. 96 (1931), 365
Commonwealth v. Aves, 35 Mass. 193 (1836), 653
Commonwealth v. Bonadio, 415 A.2d 47 (Pa. 1980), 943
Commonwealth v. Campbell, 117 S.W. 383 (Ky. 1909), 940
Commonwealth v. Poindexter, 118 S.W. 943 (Ky. 1909), 939
Conn. Dep't of Pub. Safety v. Doe, 538 U.S. 1 (2003), 612, 750, 858, 865, 949, 951, 952
Consolidated Edison Co. v. National Labor Relations Board, 305 U.S. 197 (1938), 178
Cook v. Pennsylvania, 97 U.S. 566 (1878), 608
Cooley v. Board of Wardens, 53 U.S. (12 How.) 299 (1851), 61, 117, 118, 122, 123, 550, 551, 581, 592, 607
Cooper v. Aaron, 358 U.S. 1 (1958), 309, 348, 349, 357
Coppage v. Kansas, 236 U.S. 1 (1915), 802, 819, 917
Corfield v. Coryell, 6 F. Cas. 546 (C.C.E.D. Pa. 1823), 611, 640, 680, 683, 697, 702, 705, 766, 787, 926
Coronado Coal Co. v. United Mine Workers, 268 U.S. 295 (1925), 149
County of Sacramento v. Lewis, 523 U.S. 833 (1998), 948
Coyle v. Oklahoma, 221 U.S. 559 (1911), 255
Craig v. Boren, 429 U.S. 190 (1976), 310, 424, 425, 432
Crandall v. Nevada, 73 U.S. (6 Wall.) 35 (1868), 699
Crist v. Bretz, 437 U.S. 28 (1978), 771
Crowell v. Benson, 285 U.S. 22 (1932), 366, 904
Cruzan v. Director, Mo. Dept. of Health, 497 U.S. 261 (1990), 873, 967, 969, 970, 986
CSX Transp., Inc. v. Easterwood, 507 U.S. 658 (1993), 530, 532
Currin v. Wallace, 306 U.S. 1 (1939), 574
Curtin v. Benson, 222 U.S. 78 (1911), 996
DaimlerChrysler Corp. v. Cuno, 547 U.S. 332 (2006), 403
Dartmouth College v. Woodward, 17 U.S. 518 (1819), 341

Davidson v. City of New Orleans, 96 U.S. 97 (1878), 728

Davis v. Passman, 442 U.S. 228 (1979), 382, 495

Day-Brite Lighting v. Missouri, 342 U.S. 421 (1952), 829

De Jonge v. Oregon, 299 U.S. 353 (1937), 715, 716, 755, 828

Dean Milk Co. v. City of Madison, 340 U.S. 349 (1951), 507, 546, 549, 559, 573, 576, 577, 581, 582, 611

DeFunis v. Odegaard, 416 U.S. 312 (1974), 310, 426, 432

Department of Agriculture v. Moreno, 413 U.S. 528 (1973), 951

Department of Revenue of Kentucky v. Davis, 553 U.S. 328 (2008), 609

District of Columbia v. Clawans, 300 U.S. 617 (1937), 725

District of Columbia v. Heller, 128 S. Ct. 2783 (2008), 626, 742, 753, 769, 778

District of Columbia v. John R. Thompson Co., 346 U.S. 100 (1953), 176

Doe v. Bolton, 410 U.S. 179 (1973), 612, 858, 865

Dolan v. City of Tigard, 512 U.S. 374 (1994), 1009

Doremus v. Board of Education, 342 U.S. 429 (1952), 393

Douglas v. California, 372 U.S. 353 (1963), 735

Dred Scott v. Sandford, 60 U.S. (19 How.) 393 (1857), 25, 340, 343, 510, 625, 633, 643, 645, 696, 764, 792, 896, 965, 983, 986

Dudgeon v. United Kingdom, 45 Eur. Ct. H. R. (Sir. A) (1981), 948, 950

Duncan v. Louisiana, 391 U.S. 145 (1968), 626, 630, 635, 721, 722, 756, 763, 772, 779

Dunn v. Blumstein, 405 U.S. 330 (1972), 614

Durousseau v. United States, 10 U.S. (6 Cranch) 307 (1810), 361

Eakin v. South Dakota State Cement Comm'n, 183 N.W. 651 (S.D. 1921), 600

Eastern Enterprises v. Apfel, 524 U.S. 498 (1998), 1007

Edwards v. California, 314 U.S. 160 (1941), 550, 587

EEOC v. Wyoming, 460 U.S. 226 (1983), 266, 267, 269

Eisenstadt v. Baird, 405 U.S. 438 (1972), 427, 428, 785, 856, 859, 861, 868, 876, 891, 905, 911, 917, 923–925, 929, 936, 945, 955

Eisner v. Macomber, 252 U.S. 189 (1920), 717

Elk Grove Unified Sch. Dist. v. Newdow, 542 U.S. 1 (2004), 777

Elkison v. Deliesseline, 8 F. Cas. 493 (C.C.D.S.C. 1823), 117

Employers' Liability Cases, 207 U.S. 463 (1908), 134, 191, 282

Engel v. Vitale, 370 U.S. 421 (1962), 733

English v. General Elec. Co., 496 U.S. 72 (1990), 530

EPA v. Brown, 431 U.S. 99 (1977), 277

Erie R.R. Co. v. Tompkins, 304 U.S. 64 (1938), 267, 607

Euclid v. Ambler Realty Co., 272 U.S. 365 (1926), 913, 989, 998, 1001, 1003

Everson v. Board of Education, 330 U.S. 1 (1947), 716

Ex parte Bollman, 8 U.S. (4 Cranch) 75 (1807), 449

Ex parte Henderson, 11 F. Cas. 1067 (C.C.D. Kent. 1878), 245

Ex parte McCardle, 74 U.S. (7 Wall.) 506 (1869), 309, 359, 360, 362

Ex parte Merryman, 17 F. Cas. 144 (C.C.D. Md. 1861), 449

Ex parte New York, 256 U.S. 503 (1921), 288

Ex parte Watkins, 28 U.S. 193 (1830), 733

Ex parte Yerger, 75 U.S. (8 Wall.) 85 (1869), 362

Ex parte Young, 209 U.S. 123 (1908), 284, 285, 291, 293

Exxon Corp. v. Governor of Maryland, 437 U.S. 117 (1978), 593, 598

Fahey v. Mallonee, 332 U.S. 245 (1947), 441

Fairchild v. Hughes, 258 U.S. 126 (1922), 365

FCC v. Beach Communications, 508 U.S. 307 (1993), 785, 831

Federal Energy Regulatory Commission (FERC) v. Mississippi, 456 U.S. 742 (1982), 276

Federal Maritime Commission v. South Carolina State Ports Authority, 535 U.S. 743 (2002), 303

Federal Trade Comm. v. Mandel Bros., Inc., 359 U.S. 385 (1959), 175

Feiner v. New York, 340 U.S. 315 (1951), 576

Feres v. United States, 340 U.S. 135 (1950), 381, 383

Ferguson v. Skrupa, 372 U.S. 726 (1963), 858, 865, 917, 919

Fernandez v. Wiener, 326 U.S. 340 (1945), 260

Ferri v. Ackerman, 444 U.S. 193 (1979), 499

Fidelity Fed. Sav. Loan Ass'n v. de la Cuesta, 458 U.S. 141 (1982), 526, 532, 533

First English Evangelical Lutheran Church v. County of Los Angeles, 482 U.S. 304 (1987), 996

Fiske v. Kansas, 274 U.S. 380 (1927), 723, 828

Fitzgerald v. Porter Memorial Hospital, 523 F.2d 716 (7th Cir. Ind. 1975), 770

Fitzpatrick v. Bitzer, 427 U.S. 445 (1976), 293, 305

Flast v. Cohen, 392 U.S. 83 (1968), 309, 366, 388, 390, 397–399, 402, 403, 435

Fleming v. Page, 50 U.S. 603 (1850), 662

Fletcher v. Peck, 10 U.S. (6 Cranch) 87 (1810), 340–342, 983

Florida Lime Avocado Growers, Inc. v. Paul, 373 U.S. 132 (1963), 581

Florida Prepaid Postsecondary Education Expense Board v. College Savings Bank, 527 U.S. 627 (1999), 285, 302, 304, 305

Foster v. Florida, 537 U.S. 990 (2002), 956

Foster-Fountain Packing Co. v. Haydel, 278 U.S. 1 (1928), 601–602, 587

Foster-Milburn Co. v. Chinn, 137 Ky. 834 (Ky. 1910), 941

Foucha v. Louisiana, 504 U.S. 71 (1992), 986

Freightliner Corp. v. Myrick, 514 U.S. 280 (1995), 523, 531

Frontiero v. Richardson, 411 U.S. 677 (1973), 790

Frothingham v. Mellon, 262 U.S. 447 (1923), 389, 391, 393, 394, 397, 400

Fry v. United States, 421 U.S. 542 (1975), 254, 265, 304

FTC v. Ruberoid Co., 343 U.S. 470 (1952), 461

Gade v. National Solid Wastes Management Ass'n., 505 U.S. 88 (1992), 532

Garcia v. San Antonio Metropolitan Transit Authority, 469 U.S. 528 (1985), 86, 193, 247, 249, 262, 263, 299, 304, 533, 872

Geer v. Connecticut, 161 U.S. 519 (1896), 237

Geier v. American Honda Motor Company, Inc., 529 U.S. 861 (2000), 507, 521, 522, 535

General Motors Corp. v. Tracy, 519 U.S. 278 (1997), 593

General Oil Co. v. Crain, 209 U.S. 211 (1908), 291

Geofroy v. Riggs, 133 U.S. 258 (1890), 244

Gibbons v. Ogden, 22 U.S. (9 Wheat.) 1 (1824), 61, 97, 103, 104, 113, 117, 130, 132, 133, 135, 148, 159, 160, 163, 166, 167, 173, 174, 178, 190, 191, 251, 254, 258, 259, 262, 342, 542, 550, 576, 742, 816

Gibbs v. Babbitt, 214 F.3d 483 (4th Cir. 2000), 224

Gideon v. Wainwright, 372 U.S. 335 (1963), 721, 723, 734

Gitlow v. New York, 268 U.S. 652 (1925), 635, 714, 828, 836

Glucksberg v. Washington, 521 U.S. 702 (1997), 758, 763, 770, 786, 790, 902, 953, 967, 969, 970

Godcharles v. Wigeman, 113 Pa. 431 (1886), 806, 812

Goldberg v. Kelly, 397 U.S. 254 (1970), 924

Goldblatt v. Hempstead, 369 U.S. 590 (1962), 991, 993, 997, 998, 1001, 1009

Golden v. Zwickler, 394 U.S. 103 (1969), 407

Goldman v. Weinberger, 475 U.S. 503 (1986), 386

Gonzales v. Carhart, 550 U.S. 124 (2007), 785, 892, 897

Gonzales v. Oregon, 546 U.S. 243 (2006), 218, 777

Gonzales v. Raich, 545 U.S. 1 (2005), 62, 199, 218, 306

Gooch v. United States, 297 U.S. 124 (1936), 160

Goodridge v. Dept. of Public Health, 798 N.E.2d 941 (2003), 961

Goshen v. Stonington, 4 Conn. 209 (1822), 983

Graham v. Richardson, 403 U.S. 365 (1971), 721, 733

Granholm v. Heald, 544 U.S. 460, (2005), 507, 557

Great Atlantic Pacific Tea Co. v. Cottrell, 424 U.S. 366 (1976), 547, 581

Great Falls Mfg. Co. v. Attorney General, 124 U.S. 581 (1888), 365

Great Northern Life Ins. Co. v. Read, 322 U.S. 47 (1944), 292

Gregory v. Ashcroft, 501 U.S. 452 (1991), 275

Griffin v. California, 380 U.S. 609 (1965), 723, 735, 828

Griffin v. Illinois, 351 U.S. 12 (1956), 735

Griswold v. Connecticut, 381 U.S. 479 (1965), 427, 428, 431, 432, 721, 728, 735, 770, 785, 789, 848, 855, 857, 859–861, 865, 868, 870, 873, 883, 891, 911, 913, 915–917, 922–925, 929, 934, 936, 945, 955, 983, 985

Grosjean v. American Press Co., 297 U.S. 233 (1936), 828

Gryczan v. State, 942 P.2d 112 (Mont. 1997), 926

Gulf, Colorado Santa Fe Ry. Co. v. Ellis, 165 U.S. 150 (1897), 805

Gundling v. Chicago, 177 U.S. 183 (1900), 814

Guy v. Mayor and City Council of Baltimore, 100 U.S. 434 (1880), 625, 637

H.P. Hood Sons, Inc. v. Du Mond, 336 U.S. 525 (1949), 546, 585, 586

Hackensack Meadowlands Development Comm'n v. Municipal Sanitary Landfill Auth., 316 A.2d 711 (N.J. Super. Ch. 1974), rev'd, 348 A.2d 505 (N.J. 1975), 584

Hadacheck v. Sebastian, 239 U.S. 394 (1915), 993, 1001, 1002

Hamdan v. Rumsfeld, 548 U.S. 557 (2006), 236, 476

Hamdi v. Rumsfeld, 542 U.S. 507 (2004), 468, 475

Hamilton v. Kentucky Distilleries Warehouse Co., 251 U.S. 146 (1919), 234

Hammer v. Dagenhart, 247 U.S. 251 (1918), 61, 128, 135, 139, 147, 160, 161, 163, 191, 251, 260, 788, 789, 819

Hans v. Louisiana, 134 U.S. 1 (1890), 284, 288, 298, 305

Harlow v. Fitzgerald, 457 U.S. 800 (1982), 483, 493, 496

Harper v. Virginia Board of Elections, 383 U.S. 663 (1966), 935

Harris v. McRae, 448 U.S. 297 (1980), 869, 884

Hawaii Housing Authority v. Midkiff, 467 U.S. 229, (1984), 1005

Healy v. The Beer Institute, 491 U.S. 324 (1989), 599

Heart of Atlanta Motel, Inc. v. United States, 379 U.S. 241 (1964), 184, 189, 195, 203, 207, 217, 264

Heckler v. Mathews, 465 U.S. 728 (1984), 413

Heim v. McCall, 239 U.S. 175 (1915), 603

Heimgaertner v. Benjamin Electric Mfg. Co., 128 N.E.2d 691 (Ill. 1955), 829

Hein v. Freedom from Religion Foundation, Inc., 551 U.S. 587 (2007), 309, 395, 398, 399

Heller v. Doe, 509 U.S. 312 (1993), 750

Helvering v. Davis, 301 U.S. 619 (1937), 226, 228, 229

Helvering v. Gerhardt, 304 U.S. 405 (1938), 266, 275

Hennington v. Georgia, 163 U.S. 299 (1896), 553

Herb v. Pitcairn, 324 U.S. 117 (1945), 353

Herndon v. Lowry, 301 U.S. 242 (1937), 715, 828

Herring v. State, 46 S.E. 876 (Ga. 1904), 933

Hess v. Port Authority Trans-Hudson Corporation, 513 U.S. 30 (1994), 221

Hicklin v. Orbeck, 437 U.S. 518 (1978), 618

Hillsborough County v. Automated Medical Laboratories, Inc., 471 U.S. 707 (1985), 532, 533

Hines v. Davidowitz, 312 U.S. 52 (1941), 524, 530, 533

Hipolite Egg Co. v. United States, 220 U.S. 45 (1911), 135, 138, 160, 161

Hodel v. Irving, 481 U.S. 704 (1987), 1009

Hodel v. Virginia Surface Mining Reclamation Assn., Inc., 452 U.S. 264 (1981), 184, 193, 223, 276

Hoke v. United States, 227 U.S. 308 (1913), 135, 138, 160

Holden v. Hardy, 169 U.S. 366 (1898), 128, 728, 804, 809, 810, 813, 814

Hope Clinic v. Ryan, 195 F.3d 857 (7th Cir. 1999), 896

Hopkirk v. Bell, 7 U.S. (3 Cranch) 454 (1806), 238

Houston v. Moore, 18 U.S. (5 Wheat.) 1 (1820), 520, 745

Houston, East and West Texas Ry. Co. v. United States (The Shreveport Rate Case), 234 U.S. 342 (1914), 128

Hudson Distributors, Inc. v. Eli Lilly Co., 377 U.S. 386 (1964), 175

Hughes v. Alexandria Scrap Corp., 426 U.S. 794 (1976), 585

Hughes v. Oklahoma, 441 U.S. 322 (1979), 546, 547, 549, 558, 597, 604, 609

Humphrey's Executor v. United States, 295 U.S. 602 (1935), 478, 494

Hunt v. Washington State Apple Advertising Comm'n, 432 U.S. 333 (1977), 597

Hurtado v. California, 110 U.S. 516 (1884), 710, 712, 713, 756, 771, 788

In re Ayers, 123 U.S. 443 (1887), 291

In re Custody of Smith, 969 P.2d 21 (Wa. 1998), 197, 242, 244, 288, 314, 949

In re Debs, 158 U.S. 564 (1895), 140, 788

In re House Bill No. 147, 48 P. 512 (Colo. 1897), 806

In re Marriage Cases, 43 Cal. 4th 757 (Cal. 2008), 962, 963, 965

In re Oliver, 333 U.S. 257 (1948), 720, 723

In re Rahrer, 140 U.S. 545 (1891), 61, 122, 259, 551

In re Ross, 140 U.S. 453 (1891), 242, 246

In re Sealed Case, 838 F.2d 476 (D.C. Cir. 1988), 478

In re Turner, 24 F. Cas. 337 (C.C.D. Md. 1867), 694

In re Winship, 397 U.S. 358 (1970), 729

Industrial Union Dept., AFL-CIO v. American Petroleum Institute, 448 U.S. 607 (1980), 441

Ingraham v. Wright, 430 U.S. 651 (1977), 925

INS v. Chadha, 462 U.S. 919 (1983), 270, 444, 463, 471

Insular Cases (Downes v. Bidwell, 182 U.S. 244 (1901), 242

Int'l Paper Co. v. Ouellette, 479 U.S. 481 (1987), 526

Ivanhoe Irrigation Dist. v. McCracken, 357 U.S. 275 (1958), 229

J.W. Hampton, Jr., Co. v. United States, 276 U.S. 394 (1928), 440, 443, 502

Jacobellis v. Ohio, 378 U.S. 184 (1964), 935

Jacobson v. Massachusetts, 197 U.S. 11 (1905), 813, 814, 839, 857, 861, 968

Jaffee v. United States, 663 F.2d 1226 (3rd Cir. 1981), 384

Johnson v. Eisentrager, 339 U.S. 763 (1950), 475

Johnson v. Haydel, 278 U.S. 16 (1928), 587

Johnson v. M'Intosh, 21 U.S. 543 (1823), 342

Johnson v. Tompkins, 13 F. Cas. 840 (C.C.E.D. Pa. 1833), 745

Jones v. Clinton, 1994 U.S. Dist. LEXIS 5739 (1994), 47, 48, 437, 479, 497, 505, 506

Jones v. Rath Packing Co., 430 U.S. 519 (1977), 533, 584

Jones v. United States, 529 U.S. 848 (2000), 62, 209, 218, 306

Kaiser Aetna v. United States, 444 U.S. 164 (1979), 991, 995, 997, 1009

Kane v. New Jersey, 242 U.S. 160 (1916), 547

Kassel v. Consolidated Freightways Corp., 450 U.S. 662 (1981), 507, 561, 569

Katz v. United States, 398 U.S. 347 (1967), 867, 932

Katzenbach v. McClung, 379 U.S. 294 (1964), 62, 176, 179, 184, 189, 191, 195, 203, 207, 217, 258

Kelo v. City of New London, 545 U.S. 469 (2005), 1004

Kentucky v. Dennison, 65 U.S. 66 (1861), xli

Kentucky v. Wasson, 842 S.W.2d 487 (Ky. 1992), 309, 355, 356, 786, 926, 927, 937

Kentucky Whip Collar Co. v. Illinois Central R.R. Co., 299 U.S. 334 (1937), 160

Kerrigan v. Comm'r of Pub. Health, 289 Conn. 135 (Conn. 2008), 963, 966

Keystone Bituminous Coal Association v. Debenedictis, 480 U.S. 470 (1987), 988

Kidd v. Pearson, 128 U.S. 1 (1888), 149

Kimel v. Florida Board of Regents, 528 U.S. 62 (2000), 285, 302, 304, 305

Kinsella v. Krueger, 351 U.S. 470 (1956), 242

Klopfer v. North Carolina, 386 U.S. 213 (1967), 721, 723

Knoxville Iron Co. v. Harbison, 183 U.S. 13 (1901), 806, 810

Korematsu v. United States, 323 U.S. 214 (1944), 896

Kovacs v. Cooper, 336 U.S. 77 (1949), 256

Kramer v. Union Free School District, 395 U.S. 621 (1969), 861, 891

Laird v. Tatum, 408 U.S. 1 (1972), 414, 429

Lane County v. Oregon, 74 U.S. (7 Wall.) 71 (1869), 254, 299

Lawrence County v. Lead-Deadwood School Dist., 469 U.S. 256 (1985), 229

Lawrence v. Texas, 539 U.S. 558 (2003), 37, 763, 764, 772, 786, 790, 944, 964

Lead Industries Assn., Inc. v. EPA, 647 F.2d 1130 (D.C. Cir. 1980), 440

Leary v. United States, 395 U.S. 6 (1969), 254, 258

Lehnhausen v. Lake Shore Auto Parts Co., 410 U.S. 356 (1973), 832

Leisy v. Hardin, 135 U.S. 100 (1890), 122, 550

Levy v. Louisiana, 391 U.S. 68 (1968), 735

Lewis v. BT Investment Managers, Inc., 447 U.S. 27 (1980), 546, 548, 597

Lewis v. Harris, 188 N.J. 415 (N.J. 2006), 962

Lewis v. United States, 445 U.S. 55 (1980), 747

License Cases (Thurlow v. Massachusetts), 46 U.S. (5 How.) 504 (1847), 119, 133, 607

Lichter v. United States, 334 U.S. 742 (1948), 441

Linda R.S. v. Richard D., 410 U.S. 614 (1973), 422

Little v. Barreme, 6 U.S. 170 (1804), 468, 469

Liverpool, N.Y. Phila. Steamship Co. v. Commissioners of Emigration, 113 U.S. 33 (1885), 365

Livingston v. Moore, 32 U.S. (7 Pet.) 469 (1833), 641

Lochner v. New York, 198 U.S. 45 (1905), 128, 141, 591, 594, 635, 710, 735, 774, 785, 788, 807–809, 837, 843, 848, 849, 855, 859, 867, 874, 885, 917, 932, 975, 984, 990, 1002

Loretto v. Teleprompter Manhattan CATV Corp., 458 U.S. 419 (1982), 991, 993, 995, 1009

Lovell v. Griffin, 303 U.S. 444 (1938), 828

Loving v. United States, 517 U.S. 748 (1996), 440, 442, 443, 502, 924, 942

Loving v. Virginia, 388 U.S. 1 (1967), 732, 770, 861, 887, 911, 916, 917, 924, 929, 935, 942, 957, 985

Low v. Rees Printing Co., 41 Neb. 127 (1894), 779, 812

Lucas v. South Carolina Coastal Council, 505 U.S. 1003 (1992), 786, 990, 1004, 1008

Lujan v. Defenders of Wildlife, 504 U.S. 555 (1992), 402, 414, 428

Luther v. Borden, 48 U.S. (7 How.) 1 (1849), 367

Lyng v. Int'l Union, 485 U.S. 360 (1988), 832

Mabee v. White Plains Publishing Co., 327 U.S. 178 (1946), 258

MacDonald, Sommer Frates v. Yolo County, 477 U.S. 340 (1986), 1009

Maher v. Roe, 432 U.S. 464 (1977), 868

Maine v. Taylor, 477 U.S. 131 (1986), 545, 546, 549, 592, 593, 609

Malloy v. Hogan, 378 U.S. 1 (1964), 721, 723, 758, 771

Mandeville Island Farms, Inc. v. American Crystal Sugar Co., 334 U.S. 219 (1948), 207

Mapp v. Ohio, 367 U.S. 643 (1961), 721, 723, 732, 758, 763, 850

Marbury v. Madison, 5 U.S. (1 Cranch) 137 (1803), 30, 132, 183, 271, 309, 312, 313, 315, 319, 328, 329, 331, 340, 349, 376, 480, 481, 488, 489, 493, 495, 496, 503, 633, 747, 764, 791, 851, 986

Martin v. City of Struthers, 319 U.S. 141 (1943), 849

Martin v. Hunter's Lessee, 14 U.S. (1 Wheat.) 304 (1816), 147, 259, 267, 309, 330–332, 335, 336, 340, 358

Maryland v. Wirtz, 392 U.S. 183 (1968), 191, 193, 253, 256, 259, 261, 263, 267, 300

Massachusetts v. Mellon, 262 U.S. (11 Pet.) 447 (1923), 365, 400, 429

Massachusetts v. United States, 435 U.S. 444 (1978), 229, 231, 813

Maxwell v. Dow, 176 U.S. 581 (1900), 635, 710, 711, 716, 723–725

McCarroll v. Dixie Greyhound Lines, Inc., 309 U.S. 176 (1940), 556

McCreary County v. ACLU, 545 U.S. 844 (2005), 404

McCulloch v. Maryland, 17 U.S. (4 Wheat.) 316 (1819), 35, 61, 68, 69, 79, 82, 87, 89, 91–93, 130, 132, 146, 161, 163, 208, 215, 227, 249, 250, 259, 268, 299, 335, 340, 341, 773, 814, 828, 844

McDonald v. Chicago, 2010 U.S. LEXIS 5523 (U.S. June 28, 2010), 626, 635, 730, 741, 753, 790

Medtronic, Inc. v. Lohr, 518 U.S. 470 (1996), 536, 537

Meek v. Pittenger, 421 U.S. 349 (1975), 306

Memoirs v. Massachusetts, 383 U.S. 413 (1966), 733

Metropolitan Washington Airports Authority v. Citizens for the Abatement of Aircraft Noise, Inc., 501 U.S. 252 (1991), 501

Meyer v. Nebraska, 262 U.S. 390 (1923), 713, 763, 770, 785, 788, 820, 828, 835, 836, 846, 848, 849, 854, 860, 861, 911, 913, 917–919, 921, 929, 985

Michael H. v. Gerald D., 491 U.S. 110 (1989), 772, 786, 869, 920, 921, 926

Michigan Organization for Human Rights v. Kelly, No. 88–815820 (CZ) Wayne Cnty Cir. Ct., July 9, 1990), 943

Michigan v. Long, 463 U.S. 1032 (1983), 309, 351, 355–357

Miller v. California, 413 U.S. 15 (1973), 195

Miller v. Schoene, 276 U.S. 272, (1928), 786, 988–990, 993

Miller v. Texas, 153 U.S. 535 (1894), 755

Milwaukee v. Illinois, 451 U.S. 304 (1981), 607

Mima Queen and Child v. Hepburn, 11 U.S. (7 Cranch) 290 (1813), 342

Minersville School District v. Gobitis, 310 U.S. 586, (1940), 935

Minneapolis S. L. R. Co. v. Bombolis, 241 U.S. 211 (1916), 771

Minnesota Rate Cases (Simpson v. Shepard), 230 U.S. 352 (1913), 550, 576

Minnesota v. Barber, 136 U.S. 313 (1890), 575

Minnesota v. Clover Leaf Creamery Co., 449 U.S. 456 (1981), 507, 544, 595, 596, 608

Minnesota v. National Tea Co., 309 U.S. 551 (1940), 353

Minor v. Happersett, 88 U.S. (21 Wall.) 162 (1875), 634

Mintz v. Baldwin, 289 U.S. 346 (1933), 576

Miranda v. Arizona, 384 U.S. 436 (1966), 735

Missouri v. Holland, 252 U.S. 416 (1920), 62, 221, 224, 236, 244, 300

Mistretta v. United States, 488 U.S. 361 (1989), 441–443, 502

Mitchell v. Forsyth, 472 U.S. 511 (1985), 385

Mitchell v. Helms, 530 U.S. 793 (2000), 306

Monroe v. Pape, 365 U.S. 167 (1961), 731

Moore v. East Cleveland, 431 U.S. 494 (1977), 786, 868, 912, 921, 922, 924, 930, 933, 934, 970

Moore v. Illinois, 55 U.S. (14 How.) 13 (1852), 684

Moore v. Mead's Fine Bread Co., 348 U.S. 115 (1954), 175

Moose Lodge No. 107 v. Irvis, 407 U.S. 163 (1972), 413

Morehead v. New York, 298 U.S. 587 (1936), 144, 157, 820

Morrison v. Olson, 487 U.S. 654 (1988), 444, 477

Morrissey v. Brewer, 408 U.S. 471 (1972), 124, 130, 132, 809

Motor Vehicle Mfrs. Assn. of United States, Inc. v. State Farm Mut. Automobile. Ins. Co., 463 U.S. 29 (1983), 528

Mugler v. Kansas, 123 U.S. 623 (1887), 809, 814, 984, 987, 989, 990, 993, 997–999, 1001, 1002

Mulford v. Smith, 307 U.S. 38 (1939), 260

Muller v. Oregon, 208 U.S. 412 (1908), 141, 804, 817, 908

Munn v. Illinois, 94 U.S. 113 (1877), 147, 788, 801, 830, 919, 984, 987, 1002

Murray's Lessee v. Hoboken Land Improvement Co., 59 U.S. (18 How.) 272 (1856), 711

Muscarello v. United States, 524 U.S. 125 (1998), 743

Myers v. United States, 272 U.S. 52 (1926), 448, 478

NAACP v. Alabama, 357 U.S. 449 (1958), 424, 849, 850, 916

NAACP v. Button, 371 U.S. 415 (1963), 849

Nashville, C. St. L. R. Co. v. Alabama, 128 U.S. 96 (1888), 554

National Broadcasting Co. v. United States, 319 U.S. 190 (1943), 441

National Labor Relations Board v. Fainblatt, 306 U.S. 601 (1939), 162

National Labor Relations Board v. Jones Laughlin Steel Corp., 301 U.S. 1 (1937), 151, 152, 161, 169, 175, 183, 184, 187, 192, 196, 201, 207, 209, 211, 260, 819, 826

National League of Cities v. Usery, 426 U.S. 833 (1976), 193, 247, 249, 253, 257, 263, 269, 300, 304, 603

Nat. Abortion Federation v. Gonzales, 437 F.3d 278 (2d Cir. N.Y. 2006), 902

Near v. Minnesota, 283 U.S. 697 (1931), 714, 715, 716, 828

Nebbia v. New York, 291 U.S. 502 (1934), 820, 834, 919

New Energy Co. v. Limbach, 486 U.S. 269 (1988), 558

New Orleans v. Dukes, 427 U.S. 297 (1976), 596

New State Ice Co. v. Liebmann, 285 U.S. 262 (1932), 209, 266, 604, 728, 772, 782

New York Central Securities Corp. v. United States, 287 U.S. 12 (1932), 441

New York Times Co. v. Sullivan, 376 U.S. 254 (1964), 428, 733, 734

New York v. Miln, 36 U.S. 102 (1837), 61, 116

New York v. United States, 326 U.S. 572 (1946), 217, 272, 275–277, 279, 282, 304, 305, 441, 932, 990

New York v. United States, 505 U.S. 144 (1992), 217, 272, 275–277, 279, 282, 304, 305, 441, 932, 990

Nixon v. Condon, 286 U.S. 73 (1932), 828

Nixon v. Fitzgerald, 457 U.S. 731 (1982), 437, 479, 483, 497, 498

Nixon v. Herndon, 723 U.S. 536 (1927), 828

Nixon v. Sirica, 487 F.2d 700 (D.C. Cir. 1973), 482

Nixon v. United States, 506 U.S. 224 (1993), 50, 309, 376, 437, 479, 486, 494, 500, 503

Nollan v. Cal. Coastal Comm'n, 483 U.S. 825 (1987), 993,994,1003

Nordlinger v. Hahn, 505 U.S. 1 (1992), 832

Norfolk S. Ry. v. Shanklin, 529 U.S. 344 (2000), 532

North American Co. v. SEC, 327 U.S. 686 (1946), 259

Northeastern Fla. Chapter, Associated Gen. Contractors of America v. Jacksonville, 508 U.S. 656 (1993), 404

Northern Securities Co. v. United States, 193 U.S. 197 (1904), 162, 813

Norwich Gas Light Co. v. Norwich City Gas Co., 25 Conn. 19 (Conn. 1856), 703

Nunn v. State, 1 Ga. 243 (Ga. 1846), 641, 745

O'Gorman Young, Inc. v. Hartford Fire Ins. Co., 282 U.S. 251 (1931), 998

Oklahoma Tax Comm'n v. Jefferson Lines, Inc., 514 U.S. 175 (1995), 609

Oklahoma v. United States Civil Service Comm'n, 330 U.S. 127 (1947), 229, 477, 483, 488

Olmstead v. United States, 277 U.S. 438 (1928), 846, 932, 934

O'Neil v. Vermont, 144 U.S. 323 (1892), 711, 727

Opinions of the Justices to the Governor, 363 N.E. 2d 251 (Mass. 1977), 366

Oregon v. Hass, 420 U.S. 714 (1975), 939

Oregon v. Henry, 732 P.2d 9 (Or. 1987), 309, 350, 355, 356

Oregon v. Kennedy, 456 U.S. 667 (1982), 352

Oregon Waste Systems, Inc. v. Department of Environmental Quality of Ore., 511 U.S. 93 (1994), 558

O'Shea v. Littleton, 414 U.S. 488 (1974), 406, 410, 413

Otis v. Parker, 187 U.S. 606 (1903), 813
Palazzolo v. Rhode Island, 533 U.S. 606 (2001), 1004
Palko v. Connecticut, 302 U.S. 319 (1937), 626, 630, 635, 714, 716, 717, 719, 723, 724, 756, 763, 772, 852, 860, 884, 890, 916, 918, 920, 923, 930, 985
Panama Refining Co. v. Ryan, 293 U.S. 388 (1935), 441
Parden v. Terminal R. of Ala. Docks Dep't, 377 U.S. 184 (1964), 290, 302
Parham v. J.R., 442 U.S. 584 (1979), 968
Paris Adult Theatre I v. Slaton, 413 U.S. 49 (1973), 934, 935
Parker v. Brown, 317 U.S. 341 (1943), 574
Passenger Cases (Smith v. Turner), 48 U.S. (7 How.) 283 (1849), 175
Patterson v. Kentucky, 97 U.S. 501 (1879), 814
Paul v. Davis, 424 U.S. 693 (1976), 774, 918
Paul v. Virginia, 75 U.S. (8 Wall.) 168 (1869), 611, 617, 686
Penn Central Transportation Co. v. New York, 438 U.S. 104 (1978), 989, 991, 992, 1003
Pennell v. San Jose, 485 U.S. 1 (1988), 1003
Pennhurst State School and Hospital v. Halderman, 451 U.S. 1 (1981), 228
Pennsylvania Coal Co. v. Mahon, 260 U.S. 393 (1922), 988, 991, 992, 995, 997, 1008, 1009
Pennsylvania v. Union Gas Co., 491 U.S. 1 (1989), 285, 305
Pennsylvania v. West Virginia, 262 U.S. 553 (1923), 587, 604
People v. Carolene Products Co., 177 N.E. 698 (Ill. 1931), 827
People v. Onofre, 415 N.E.2d 936 (N.Y. 1980), 943
Perez v. United States, 402 U.S. 146 (1971), 62, 179, 184, 195, 201, 203, 206, 223
Permoli v. Municipality No. 1 of New Orleans, 44 U.S. (3 How.) 589 (1845), 641
Perpich v. Department of Defense, 496 U.S. 334 (1990), 748
Petit v. Minnesota, 177 U.S. 164 (1900), 810
Phalen v. Virginia, 49 U.S. (8 How.) 163 (1850), 130
Pierce v. Society of Sisters, 268 U.S. 510 (1925), 715, 770, 820, 828, 835, 846, 849, 854, 861, 911, 913, 917, 921, 929, 933, 985
Pike v. Bruce Church, Inc., 397 U.S. 137 (1970), 560, 567, 581, 586, 594, 597, 598, 602
Planned Parenthood v. Ashcroft, 462 U.S. 476 (1983), 888
Planned Parenthood v. Casey, 505 U.S. 833 (1992), 763, 785, 790, 869, 870, 892, 899, 905, 947, 952, 953, 970, 983, 985
Planned Parenthood Federation of America v. Ashcroft, 320 F.Supp. 957 (N.D.Ca. 2004), aff'd, 435 F. 3d 1163 (9th Cir. 2006), rev'd, Gonzales v. Carhart, 550 U.S. 124 (2007), 899, 905
Plaut v. Spendthrift Farm, Inc., 514 U.S. 211 (1995), 501
Plessy v. Ferguson, 163 U.S. 537 (1896), 140, 347, 737, 874, 885, 886
Plyler v. Doe, 457 U.S. 202 (1982), 951, 952
Poe v. Ullman, 367 U.S. 497 (1961), 430, 431, 728, 770, 785, 844, 852, 913, 914, 917–919, 924, 972, 974, 982, 983
Pointer v. Texas, 380 U.S. 400 (1965), 721, 723, 771
Polish National Alliance of U.S. v. NLRB, 322 U.S. 643 (1944), 178
Pollock v. Farmers' Loan Trust Co. (Pollock I), 157 U.S. 429 (1895), 139-141
Pollock v. Farmers' Loan Trust Co. (Pollock II), 158 U.S. 601 (1895), 139-141
Powell v. Alabama, 287 U.S. 45 (1932), 714, 715, 723
Powell v. McCormack, 395 U.S. 486 (1969), 83, 309, 369, 380, 432, 481
Powell v. State, 510 S.E.2d 18 (Ga. 1998), 926
Presser v. Illinois, 116 U.S. 252 (1886), 710, 711, 755
Prigg v. Pennsylvania, 41 U.S. (16 Pet.) 539 (1842), 507, 510, 511
Prince v. Massachusetts, 321 U.S. 158 (1944), 861, 911, 913, 916, 929
Principality of Monaco v. Mississippi, 292 U.S. 313 (1934), 266, 298
Printz v. United States, 521 U.S. 898 (1997), 247, 249, 272, 273, 286, 305

Prize Cases, 62 U.S. 635 (1863), 468, 470
Prudential Ins. Co. v. Benjamin, 328 U.S. 408 (1946), 560
PruneYard Shopping Center v. Robins, 447 U.S. 74 (1980), 1002, 1009
Radovich v. National Football League, 352 U.S. 445 (1957), 175
Railroad Co. v. Husen, 95 U.S. 465 (1877), 589
Railroad Comm'n Cases, 116 U.S. 307 (1886), 984
Railroad Retirement Bd. v. Alton R.R. Co., 295 U.S. 330 (1935), 191
Railway Express Agency, Inc. v. New York, 336 U.S. 106 (1949), 857
Raines v. Byrd, 521 U.S. 811 (1997), 462
Rapanos v. United States, 547 U.S. 715 (2006), 224
Rasul v. Bush, 542 U.S. 466 (2004), 475
Ray v. Atlantic Richfield Co., 435 U.S. 151 (1978), 584
Raymond Motor Transportation, Inc. v. Rice, 434 U.S. 429 (1978), 563, 564, 566–569, 571, 585
Redrup v. New York, 386 U.S. 767 (1967), 195
Reeves, Inc. v. Stake, 447 U.S. 429 (1980), 507, 548, 600
Regents of the University of California v. Bakke, 438 U.S. 265 (1978), 436
Reid v. Colorado, 187 U.S. 137 (1902), 588
Reid v. Covert, 354 U.S. 1 (1957), 62, 239
Reno v. Condon, 528 U.S. 141 (2000), 305
Rewis v. United States, 401 U.S. 808 (1971), 219
Reynolds v. Sims, 377 U.S. 533 (1964), 841
Rice v. Santa Fe Elevator Corp., 331 U.S. 218 (1947), 532, 533, 537, 584
Riegel v. Medtronic, Inc., 552 U.S. 312 (2008), 536
Riley v. State, 78 P.2d 712 (Okla. Crim App. 1938), 842
Rizzo v. Goode, 423 U.S. 362 (1976), 406, 407, 410, 413
Robbins v. Shelby County Taxing Dist., 120 U.S. 489 (1887), 607
Roberts v. United States Jaycees, 468 U.S. 609 (1984), 774, 933

Robinson v. California, 370 U.S. 660 (1962), 723, 785, 843
Rochin v. California, 342 U.S. 165 (1952), 774, 785, 843, 845
Roe v. Wade, 410 U.S. 113 (1973), 64, 434, 612, 736, 785, 790, 798, 855, 857, 858, 868–871, 873, 875–878, 883, 884, 886–889, 891, 892, 894, 896, 905, 910–913, 916–918, 923, 930, 932, 933, 935, 936, 945, 952, 955, 978, 985
Romer v. Evans, 517 U.S. 620 (1996), 949, 951–953, 966
Roth v. United States, 354 U.S. 476 (1957), 733
Ruckelshaus v. Monsanto Co., 467 U.S. 986 (1984), 1009
Ruppert v. Caffey, 251 U.S. 264 (1920), 234
Sabri v. United States, 541 U.S. 600 (2004), 215
Saenz v. Roe, 526 U.S. 489 (1999), 635, 691, 755
San Diego Gas Electric Co. v. San Diego, 450 U.S. 621 (1981), 992
Sanitary District v. United States, 266 U.S. 405 (1925), 259
Santa Clara County v. Southern Pacific Rw. Co., 118 U.S. 394 (1886), 788
Santa Cruz Fruit Packing Co. v. NLRB, 303 U.S. 453 (1938), 259
Schechter Poultry Corp. v. United States, 295 U.S. 723 (1935), 191, 441, 789, 820
Scheuer v. Rhodes, 416 U.S. 232 (1974), 385, 484, 489
Schilb v. Kuebel, 404 U.S. 357 (1971), 729
Schlesinger v. Reservists Committee to Stop the War, 418 U.S. 208 (1974), 389, 395, 396, 412
Schneider v. New Jersey, 308 U.S. 147 (1939), 576
Schnurman v. United States, 490 F.Supp. 429 (E.D. Va. 1980), 384
Scott v. Negro Ben, 10 U.S. (6 Cranch) 3 (1810), 342
Scranton v. Wheeler, 179 U.S. 141 (1900), 995
Seagram Sons, Inc. v. Hostetter, 384 U.S. 35 (1966), 600
SEC v. Ralston Purina Co., 346 U.S. 119 (1953), 175

Second Employers' Liability Cases, 223 U.S. 1 (1912), 134, 282
Seminole Tribe of Florida v. Florida, 517 U.S. 44 (1996), 285, 286, 293
Semler v. Oregon State Board of Dental Examiners, 294 U.S. 608 (1935), 831
Shapiro v. Thompson, 394 U.S. 618 (1969), 615, 891
Sheldon v. Sill, 49 U.S. (8 How.) 441 (1850), 358, 363
Sherbert v. Verner, 374 U.S. 398 (1963), 891
Shoemaker v. United States, 147 U.S. 282 (1893), 265
Sierra Club v. Morton, 405 U.S. 727 (1972), 414
Siler v. Louisville Nashville R.R. Co., 213 U.S. 175 (1909), 365
Silkwood v. Kerr-McGee Corp., 464 U.S. 238 (1984), 532
Simon v. Eastern Kentucky Welfare Rights Organization, 426 U.S. 26 (1976), 422
Singer v. United States, 380 U.S. 24 (1965), 724
Singleton v. Wulff, 428 U.S. 106 (1976), 426
Skinner v. Oklahoma, 316 U.S. 535 (1942), 785, 789, 840, 841, 845, 848, 850, 857, 861, 911, 913, 929, 975, 985
Slaughter-House Cases, **83 U.S. (16 Wall.) 36 (1873)**, 34, 626, 634, 636, 686, 690, 691, 706, 709, 710, 717, 754, 755, 764, 769, 780, 787, 788, 791, 801, 837, 840, 984, 985
Sligh v. Kirkwood, 237 U.S. 52 (1915), 589
Smith v. Doe, 538 U.S. 84 (2003), 949
Smith v. Reeves, 178 U.S. 436 (1900), 288
Snyder v. Massachusetts, 291 U.S. 97 (1934), 715, 724, 756, 867, 884, 922, 923
Solid Waste Agency of Northern Cook County v. United States Army Corps of Engineers, 531 U.S. 159 (2001), 62, 220
Somerset's Case, 98 Eng. Rep 499 (K.B. 1772), 516
Sosna v. Iowa, 419 U.S. 393 (1975), 615
South Carolina State Highway Department v. Barnwell Bros., Inc., 303 U.S. 177 (1938), 550, 585, 597, 828
South Dakota v. Dole, 483 U.S. 203 (1987), 62, 227, 232, 292

Southern Pacific Company v. Arizona, 325 U.S. 761 (1945), 507, 549
Southern Pacific Terminal Co. v. Interstate Commerce Com., 219 U.S. 498 (1911), 434
Southern R. Co. v. United States, 222 U.S. 20 (1911), 127, 134
Spalding v. Vilas, 161 U.S. 483 (1896), 484
Sperry v. Florida ex rel. Florida Bar, 373 U.S. 379 (1963), 260
Sporhase v. Nebraska ex rel. Douglas, 458 U.S. 941 (1982), 224, 546, 547, 549
Springer v. United States, 102 U.S. 586 (1881), 140
Stafford v. Wallace, 258 U.S. 495 (1922), 152, 207
Stanford v. Kentucky, 492 U.S. 361 (1989), 971
Stanley v. Georgia, 394 U.S. 557 (1969), 857, 860, 931, 932, 934
Stanley v. Illinois, 405 U.S. 645 (1972), 925
State Bd. of Equalization of Cal. v. Young's Market Co., 299 U.S. 59 (1936), 561
State v. Kennedy, 666 P.2d 1316 (Or. 1983), 356
State v. Manuel, 20 N.C. 144 (1838), 652
State v. Morales, 826 S.W.2d 201 (Tex. App. 1992), 948, 951
State v. Nelson, 11 A.2d 856 (Ct. 1940), 430
State v. Newsom, 27 N.C. 250 (1844), 652
State v. Reid, 1 Ala. 612 (Ala. 1840), 62, 239, 588
State v. Tidyman, 30 Or. App. 537 (1977), 356
State v. Worth, 52 N.C. 488 (1860), 633, 659, 662
Steffel v. Thompson, 415 U.S. 452 (1974), 431
Stenberg v. Carhart, 530 U.S. 914 (2000), 892, 893, 896, 897, 905
Steward Machine Co. v. Davis, 301 U.S. 548 (1937), 226, 230, 231
Stewart v. Kahn, 78 U.S. 493 (1871), 234
Stone v. Miss., 101 U.S. 814 (1880), 988
Stowel v. Zouch, 75 Eng. Rep 536 (C.P. 1569), 518
Strauss v. Horton, 46 Cal. 4th 364 (Cal. 2009), 963
Stromberg v. California, 283 U.S. 359 (1931), 714, 828

Sturges Burn Mfg. Co. v. Beauchamp, 231 U.S. 320 (1913), 141
Sturges v. Crowninshield, 17 U.S. (4 Wheat.) 122 (1819), 86, 520
Sullivan v. Little Hunting Park, Inc., 396 U.S. 229 (1969), 428
Supreme Court of New Hampshire v. Piper, 470 U.S. 274 (1985), 616, 617, 620
Supreme Court of Virginia v. Friedman, 487 U.S. 59 (1988), 507, 615
Sweezy v. State of New Hampshire, 354 U.S. 234 (1957), 849
Swift and Co. v. United States, 196 U.S. 375 (1905), 127
Swift v. Tyson, 41 U.S. (16 Pet.) 1 (1842), 511
Tahoe-Sierra Pres. Council, Inc. v. Tahoe Regional Planning Agency, 535 U.S. 302 (2002), 1004
Terry v. Ohio, 392 U.S. 1 (1968), 353, 860
Testa v. Katt, 330 U.S. 386 (1947), 282
Texas v. Morales, 826 S.W.2d 201 (Tex. App. 1992), 943
Texas v. White, 74 U.S. (7 Wall.) 700 (1869), 254
The Antelope, 23 U.S. (10 Wheat.) 66 (1825), 342
The Emily and the Caroline, 22 U.S. (9 Wheat.) 381 (1824), 342
The Merino, 22 U.S. (9 Wheat.) 391 (1824), 342
The Orono, 18 F. Cas. 830 (C.C.D. Mass. 1812), 464
The St. Jago de Cuba, 22 U.S. (9 Wheat.) 409 (1824), 342
Thompson v. City of Louisville, 362 U.S. 199 (1960), 365, 938
Thompson v. Utah, 170 U.S. 343 (1898), 725
Thornburgh v. American College of Obstetricians Gynecologists, 476 U.S. 747 (1986), 885, 933, 934
Thornhill v. Alabama, 310 U.S. 88 (1940), 773
Thornwell v. United States, 471 F. Supp. 344 (D.D.C. 1979), 384
Toomer v. Witsell, 334 U.S. 385 (1948), 586, 587, 617, 620
Torcaso v. Watkins, 367 U.S. 488 (1961), 733
Touby v. United States, 500 U.S. 160 (1991), 441
Transportation Union v. Long Island R. Co., 455 U.S. 678 (1982), 264, 265, 270
Troxel v. Granville, 530 U.S. 57 (2000), 920
Truax v. Raich, 239 U.S. 33 (1915), 62, 199, 200, 205, 214–216, 218, 306
Turner Broad. Sys. v. FCC, 520 U.S. 180 (1997), 189, 751
Turner v. Safley, 482 U.S. 78 (1987), 924
Twining v. New Jersey, 211 U.S. 78 (1908), 710, 715, 717, 718, 725, 756, 837
Tyler v. Judges, 179 U.S. 405 (1900), 365
U.S. R.R. Retirement Bd. v. Fritz, 449 U.S. 166 (1980), 831
U.S. Term Limits, Inc. v. Thornton, 514 U.S. 779 (1995), 61, 81, 82, 275, 464
U.S. v. Curtiss-Wright Export Co., 299 U.S. 304 (1936), 232
Union Pacific R. Co. v. Botsford, 141 U.S. 250 (1891), 860, 890
United Building Construction Trades Council v. Mayor and Council of Camden, 465 U.S. 208 (1984), 617
United Haulers Association, Inc. v. Oneida-Herkimer Solid Waste Management Authority, 550 U.S. 330 (2007), 507, 591
United States v. Baltimore Ohio R.R. Co., 333 U.S. 169 (1948), 175
United States v. Brandt, (The Medical Case) 2 Trial of War Criminals Before the Nuremberg Military Tribunals Under Control Council Law No. 10 (1949), 384, 386
United States v. Burr, 25 F. Cas. 187 (C.C.D. Va. 1807), 482, 485, 503
United States v. Butler, 297 U.S. 1 (1936), 225, 227–229, 231, 260, 820
United States v. California, 297 U.S. 175 (1936), 257–261
United States v. Carolene Products Co., 304 U.S. 144 (1938), 785, 826, 827, 975
United States v. Causby, 328 U.S. 256 (1946), 991
United States v. Central Eureka Mining Co., 357 US. 155 (1958), 998
United States v. Classic, 313 U.S. 299 (1941), 88, 227

United States v. Colgate Co., 250 U.S. 300 (1919), 603

United States v. Comstock, 130 S. Ct. 1949 (2010), 81

United States v. Concentrated Phosphate Export Ass'n, 393 U.S. 199 (1968), 435

United States v. Coombs, 37 U.S. 72 (1838), 207

United States v. Cruikshank, 92 U.S. 542 (1876), 707, 710, 743, 755

United States v. Curtiss-Wright Export Corp., 299 U.S. 304 (1936), 232

United States v. Darby, 312 U.S. 100 (1941), 62, 158, 162, 166, 168, 175, 178, 184, 191, 207, 253, 254, 258, 260, 264, 789

United States v. DeWitt, 76 U.S. 41 (1870), 215

United States v. E.C. Knight Co., 156 U.S. 1 (1895), 127, 140, 149, 167, 191, 788

United States v. General Motors Corp., 323 U.S. 373 (1945), 448

United States v. Harris, 106 U.S. 629 (1883), 181, 183

United States v. Hays, 515 U.S. 737 (1995), 404

United States v. Jackson, 390 U.S. 570 (1968), 254, 258

United States v. Johnson, 481 U.S. 681 (1987), 383, 475

United States v. Jones, 109 U.S. 513 (1883), 62, 209, 218, 306

United States v. Klein, 80 U.S. (13 Wall.) 128 (1872), 363

United States v. Locke, 529 U.S. 89 (2000), 531

United States v. Lopez, 514 U.S. 549 (1995), 36, 180, 181, 183, 187, 188, 195, 203, 207, 209, 214, 219, 221, 223, 280, 306

United States v. Mazurie, 419 U.S. 544 (1975), 442

United States v. McCullagh, 221 F. 288 (D. Kan. 1915), 237

United States v. Miller, 307 U.S. 174 (1939), 283, 744, 746, 777

United States v. Mitchell (D.C. Crim. No. 74-110), 479

United States v. Morrison, 529 U.S. 598 (2000), 36, 62, 180, 181, 203, 207, 209, 221, 223, 306, 777, 780

United States v. Nixon, 418 U.S. 683 (1974), 50, 309, 376, 437, 479, 486, 494, 500, 503

United States v. O'Brien, 391 U.S. 367 (1968), 734

United States v. Padelford, 76 U.S. (9 Wall.) 531 (1870), 363

United States v. Perkins, 116 U.S. 483 (1886), 494

United States v. Peters, 9 U.S. (5 Cranch) 115 (1809), 349

United States v. Pewee Coal Co., 341 U.S. 114 (1951), 448

United States v. Raines, 362 U.S. 17 (1960), 427, 428

United States v. Richardson, 418 U.S. 166 (1974), 388, 395, 396

United States v. Riverside Bayview Homes, Inc., 474 U.S. 121 (1985), 222

United States v. Rock Royal Co-Operative, Inc., 307 U.S. 533 (1939), 161

United States v. Salerno, 505 U.S. 317 (1987), 750

United States v. Shauver, 214 F. 154 (E.D. Ark. 1914), 237

United States v. Sprague, 282 U.S. 716 (1931), 260, 742

United States v. Stanley, 483 U.S. 669 (1987), 309, 381, 924, 934

United States v. SCRAP, 412 U.S. 669 (1973), 413, 414

United States v. Texas, 143 U.S. 621 (1892), 61, 128, 133, 301

United States v. Universal C.I.T. Credit Corp., 344 U.S. 218 (1952), 220

United States v. Virginia, 518 U.S. 515 (1996), 184, 908, 924, 942

United States v. W.T. Grant Co., 345 U.S. 629 (1953), 434

United States v. Women's Sportswear Mfg. Ass'n, 336 U.S. 460 (1949), 175

United States v. Wrightwood Dairy Co., 315 U.S. 110 (1942), 178

Vacco v. Quill, 521 U.S. 793 (1997), 969

Valley Forge Christian College v. Americans United for Separation of Church and State, Inc., 454 U.S. 464 (1982), 386, 395, 400, 413

Vance v. Bradley, 440 U.S. 93 (1979), 596, 832

Varnum v. Brien, 763 N.W.2d 862 (Iowa 2009), 786, 963, 964

Veazie Bank v. Fenno, 75 U.S. (8 Wall.) 533 (1869), 138, 160

Veazie v. Moor, 55 U.S. (14 How.) 568 (1852), 148

Vieth v. Jubelirer, 541 U.S. 267 (2004), 386

Village of Arlington Heights v. Metropolitan Housing Development Corp., 429 U.S. 252 (1977), 424, 579

Village of Belle Terre v. Boraas, 416 U.S. 1 (1974), 868, 911–913, 915

Vitek v. Jones, 445 U.S. 480 (1980), 925, 968

Wabash, St. Louis Pacific Rw. Co. v. Illinois, 118 U.S. 557 (1886), 788

Walker v. Birmingham, 388 U.S. 307 (1967), 734

Walker v. Sauvinet, 92 U.S. 90 (1876), 710, 711

Wallace v. Chappell, 661 F.2d 729 (9th Cir. 1981), 382, 385

Ward v. Maryland, 79 U.S. (12 Wall.) 418 (1871), 614, 617, 620

Ware v. Hylton, 3 U.S. (3 Dall.) 199 (1796), 238

Warth v. Seldin, 422 U.S. 490 (1975), 310, 415, 422, 427, 579

Washington v. Glucksberg, 521 U.S. 702 (1997), 758, 763, 770, 786, 790, 902, 953, 967, 969, 970

Washington v. Harper, 494 U.S. 210 (1990), 968

Washington v. Texas, 388 U.S. 14 (1967), 721, 723

Weaver v. Palmer Bros. Co., 270 U.S. 402 (1926), 817

Webster v. Reproductive Health Services, 492 U.S. 490 (1989), 869, 870, 873, 882, 884

Weeks v. United States, 245 U.S. 618 (1918), 175

Welton v. Missouri, 91 U.S. 275 (1876), 546, 607, 608

West Coast Hotel Co. v. Parrish, 300 U.S. 379 (1937), 144, 151, 820, 849, 855, 874, 885, 918, 919, 984

West Lynn Creamery, Inc. v. Healy, 512 U.S. 186 (1994), 608

West v. Kansas Natural Gas Co., 221 U.S. 229 (1911), 587

West Virginia Board of Education v. Barnette, 319 U.S. 624 (1943), 935

Whitman v. American Trucking Associations, Inc., 531 U.S. 457 (2001), 437, 439, 440, 444

Whitney v. California, 274 U.S. 357 (1927), 770, 780, 828

Wickard v. Filburn, 317 U.S. 111 (1942), 62, 165, 169, 175, 177, 178, 184, 188, 191, 196, 201, 212, 217, 223, 258, 261, 264, 542, 789

Wieman v. Updegraff, 344 U.S. 183 (1952), 849

Williams v. Florida, 399 U.S. 78 (1970), 729, 771

Williamson v. Lee Optical of Oklahoma, Inc., 348 U.S. 483 (1955), 785, 829

Willson v. Black-Bird Creek Marsh Co., 27 U.S. (2 Pet.) 245 (1829), 607

Wolf v. Colorado, 338 U.S. 25 (1949), 758, 846

Wolman v. Walter, 433 U.S. 229 (1977), 306

Woodruff v. Parham, 75 U.S. (8 Wall.)123 (1869), 607

Woods v. Miller Co., 333 U.S. 138 (1948), 234

Worcester v. Georgia, 31 U.S. (6 Pet.) 515 (1832), 343

Wyeth v. Levine, 129 S. Ct. 1187 (2009), 539

Wynehamer v. People, 13 N.Y. 378 (1856), 983

Yakus v. United States, 321 U.S. 414 (1944), 441

Yick Wo v. Hopkins, 118 U.S. 356 (1886), 842, 952

Youngberg v. Romeo, 457 U.S. 307 (1982), 968

Younger v. Harris, 401 U.S. 37 (1971), 432, 607

Youngstown Sheet Tube Co. v. Sawyer, 343 U.S. 579 (1952), 437, 444, 445, 454, 467, 481, 486, 501–503

Table of Authorities

Ackerman, Bruce, *Taxation and the Constitution*, 99 Colum. L. Rev. 1 (1999), 140
Ackerman, Bruce, *We The People: Transformations* (1998), 156, 825
Amar, Akhil Reed, *Architexture*, 77 Ind. L. Rev. 671 (2002), 37
Amar, Akhil Reed, *The Bill of Rights: Creation and Reconstruction* (1998), 686, 721
Amar, Akhil Reed, *The Bill of Rights and the Fourteenth Amendment*, 101 Yale L. J. 1193 (1992), 721
Avins, Alfred, ed., *The Reconstruction Amendments' Debates: The Legislative History and Contemporary Debates in Congress on the 13th, 14th, and 15th Amendments*(1967), 665
Aynes, Richard L., *Constricting the Law of Freedom: Justice Miller, the Fourteenth Amendment, and the Slaughter-House Cases*, 70 Chi.-Kent L. Rev. 627 (1994), 706
Aynes, Richard L., *On Misreading John Bingham and the Fourteenth Amendment*, 103 Yale L. J. 57 (1993), 721
Bailey, Fred Arthur, *Free Speech and the Lost Cause in the Old Dominion*, 103 Va. Mag. Hist. and Bio. 237 (1995), 709
Balkin, Jack M.,*Abortion and Original Meaning*, 24 Const.Comm. 291 (2007) 28
Balkin, Jack M. and Sanford Levinson, *Understanding the Constitutional Revolution*, 87 Va. L. Rev. 1045 (2001),28
Barnett, Randy E., *New Evidence of the Original Meaning of the Commerce Clause*, 55 Ark. L. Rev. 847 (2003), 115
Barnett, Randy E., *The Original Meaning of the Commerce Clause*, 68 U. Chi. L. Rev. 101, 112–125 (2001), 214
Basler, Roy P., ed., *The Collected Works of Abraham Lincoln*(1953),22-23,
Berger, Raoul, *Government by Judiciary: The Transformation of the Fourteenth Amendment* (1977),721
Berger, Raoul, *Incorporation of the Bill of Rights in the Fourteenth Amendment: A Nine-Lived Cat*, 42 Ohio. St. L. Rev. 435 (1981), 721
Black, Charles L., Jr., *Structure and Relationship in Constitutional Law* (1986), 34
Blackstone, William, Sir, *Commentaries on the Laws of England* (1765-1769), 242, 297, 314, 323, 374, 517, 655,743, 749,758, 764,778, 779,781, 792, 794, 924, 932, 943,
Blight, David W., *Race and Reunion, the Civil War in American Memory* (2001), 738
Bobbitt, Philip, *Constitutional Fate: Theory of the Constitution* (1982), 34
Bonauto, Mary L., *Goodridge in Context*, 40 Harv. Civil Rights-Civil Liberties L. Rev. 1, 39–40 (2005), 962
Bond, James E., *No Easy Walk to Freedom: Reconstruction and Ratification of the Fourteenth Amendment* (1998), 686
Bork, Robert, *Neutral Principles and Some First Amendment Problems*, 47 Ind. L. J. 1 (1971), 855
Branch, Taylor, *Pillar of Fire: America in the King Years, 1963–65*(1998),171

Brown, Ernest J., *Book Review,* 67 Harv. L. Rev. 1439 (1954), 115
Chemerinsky, Erwin, *Constitutional Law: Principles and Policies* (2nd ed. 2002),363
Church, William, *The Eastern Enterprises Case: A New Vigor for Judicial Review,* 2000 Wis. L. Rev. 547 (2000), 1007
Congressional Globe, see *Globe*
Cooley, Thomas. *Constitutional Limitations,* 746
Corwin, Edward. *Liberty Against Government* (1948), 983
Crosskey, William Winslow, *Charles Fairman, Legislative History and the Constitutional Limits on State Authority,* 22 U. Chi. L. Rev. 1 (1954),721
Crosskey, William Winslow, *Politics and the Constitution in the History of the United States* (1953), 114
Curtis, Charles, *A Better Theory of Legal Interpretation,* 3 Vand. L. Rev. 407 (1950), 34
Curtis, Michael Kent, *The 1859 Crisis Over Hinton Helper's Book, The Impending Crisis: Free Speech, Slavery, and Some Light on the Meaning of the First Section of the Fourteenth Amendment,* 68 Chi.-Kent L. Rev. 1113 (1993), 662
Curtis, Michael Kent, *Book Review,* 42 Am. J. Leg. Hist. 417 (1998), 156
Curtis, Michael Kent, *Conceived in Liberty: The Fourteenth Amendment and the Bill of Rights,* 65 N.C. L. Rev. 889 (1987), 686
Curtis, Michael Kent, *Free Speech, "The People's Darling Privilege"* (2000), 314,n1, 326
Curtis, Michael Kent, *Further Adventures of the Nine Lived Cat: A Response to Mr. Berger on Incorporation of the Bill of Rights,* 43 Ohio. St. L. J. 89 (1982), 721
Curtis, Michael Kent, *Historical Linguistics, Inkblots, and Life After Death: The Privileges or Immunities of Citizens of the United States,* 78 N.C. L. Rev. 1071 (2000), 661
Curtis, Michael Kent, *No State Shall Abridge: The Fourteenth Amendment and the Bill of Rights* (1986), 632, 661
Curtis, Michael Kent, *Resurrecting the Privileges or Immunities Clause and Revising the Slaughter-House Cases Without Exhuming Lochner: Individual Rights and the Fourteenth Amendment,* 38 Bost. Coll. L. Rev. (1996), 34, 685-686
Curtis, Michael Kent, *The Bill of Rights as a Limitation on State Authority: A Reply to Professor Berger,* 16 Wake Forest L. Rev. 45 (1980), 721
Defoe, Daniel, *A Plan of the English Commerce* (1728), 115
Dew, Charles B., *Apostles of Disunion: Southern Secession Commissioners and the Causes of the Civil War* (2001), 709
Douglas, Davison, *Jim Crow Moves North: The Battle Over Northern School Segregation (1865-1964)* 27-28
Dworkin, Ronald, *Comment,* in Antonin Scalia, *A Matter of Interpretation: Federal Courts and the Law* (1997), 28
Ellis, Elmer, *Public Opinion and the Income Tax, 1860–1900,* 27 Miss. Valley Hist. Rev. 225 (1940), 139
Epstein, Richard, *History Lean: The Reconciliation of Private Property and Representative Government,* 95 Col. L. Rev. 523 (1995), 986
Epstein, Richard, *Takings: Private Property and the Power of Eminent Domain* (1985), 986
Fairman, Charles, *Does the Fourteenth Amendment Incorporate the Bill of Rights?: The Original Understanding,* 2 Stan. L. Rev. 5 (1949), 721, 726, 728
Fallon, Richard H. Jr., *A Constructivist Coherence Theory of Constitutional Interpretation,* 100 Harv. L. Rev. 1189 (1987), 34
Farber, Daniel A., *Public Choice and Just Compensation,* 9 Const. Comm. 331 (1985), 1109
Farrelly, David G., *Harlan's Dissent in the Pollock Case,* 24 So. Cal. L. Rev. 175 (1951), 140

Fehrenbacher, Don E., *The Dred Scott Case: Its Significance in American Law and Politics* (1978), 655
Finkelman, Paul, *The Constitution and the Intentions of the Framers: The Limits of Historical Analysis*, 50 U. Pitt. L. Rev. 349 (1989), 64
Finkelman, Paul, *The First American Constitutions: State and Federal*, 59 Tex. L. Rev. 1141 (1981), 115-116
Flack, Horace, *The Adoption of the Fourteenth Amendment* (1908), 720
Fleming, Walter L., ed., *Documentary History of Reconstruction: Political, Military, Social, Religious, Educational and Industrial, 1865 to 1906* (1966), 662, n*
Forbath, William E., *Law and the Shaping of the American Labor Movement*,(1991), 141
Fried, Charles. *Order and Law: Arguing the Reagan Revolution—A Firsthand Account* 81–84 (1991).949-950
Gallagher, Gary W., and Alan T. Nolan, eds., *The Myth of the Lost Cause and Civil War History* (2000), 709
Gerhardt, Michael, *"Clinton v. Jones,"* Encyclopedia of the American Constitution (2000), 506
Gillman, Howard, *The Constitution Besieged: The Rise and Demise of Lochner Era Police Powers Jurisprudence* (1993), 799
Gilreath, Shannon, *The Constitutional Status of Gay Marriage* (2010), 960
Gilreath, Shannon. *Sexual Politics: The Gay Person in America Today* (2006), 962
Globe 35(2)(Binhgam), 655
Globe 36(1), 659
Globe 38(1), 661
Globe 39(1), 26, 27, 666, 668, 670, 672+678
Globe 42(1), 27, 682
Goebel, Julius, Jr., *Ex Parte Clio*, 54 Col. L. Rev. 450 (1954),115
Goldsmith, Jack, *The Terror Presidency: Law and Judgment Inside the Bush Administration* (2007), 468
Gould, Stephen Jay, *Carrie Buck's Daughter*, 2 Const. Comm. (1985), 839
Graber, Mark A., *Desperately Ducking Slavery: Dred Scott and Contemporary Constitutional Theory*, 14 Const. Comm. 271 (1997), 655
Graham, Howard Jay, *Everyman's Constitution: Historical Essays on the Fourteenth Amendment, the "Conspiracy Theory," and American Constitutionalism* (1968), 971
Hamilton, Alexander, John Jay, and James Madison, *The Federalist* (1788), 43,44, 197, 280, 287, 294-295, 379,
Hamilton, Alexander, *Report on Public Credit* (1790), 65
Hamilton, J.G. de Roulhac, *Reconstruction in North Carolina* (1914), 688
Harbaugh, William H., *The Writings of Theodore Roosevelt*, (1967), 819
Harrington, James, *The Art of Lawgiving* (1659), 21
Hart, Henry M., *Book Review, Politics and the Constitution*, 67 Harv. L. Rev. 1439 (1954), 115
Hart, H. L. A., *The Concept of Law* (1961), 34
Helper, Hinton, *The Impending Crisis of the South: How to Meet It* (1860), 659, 661, 662
Hobbes, Thomas, *Leviathan* (1651), 792
Holmes, Oliver Wendell, *Book Review*, 14 Am. L. Rev. (1880), 24
Huhn, Wilson, *The Five Types of Legal Argument* (2002), 34, 38
Irons, Peter, *The Courage of Their Convictions* (1988),927
Kaczorowski, Robert J., *The Politics of Judicial Interpretation: The Federal Courts, Department of Justice and Civil Rights, 1866–1876* (1985), 706

Kammen, Michael G., *A Machine That Would Go of Itself: The Constitution in American Culture* (1986),140

Klarman, Michael J., -Brown, Originalism, and Constitutional Theory, *81 Va., L. Rev. 847 (1995),* 27

Klarmen, Michael J., *The Plessy Era, 1988 S. Ct. Rev. 1365 (1998),* 31

Lessig, Larence, Fidelity and Constraint, *65 Fordham L. Rev. 1365 (1997),* 33-34

Leuchtenburg, William E., The Supreme Court Reborn: The Constitutional Revolution in the Age of Roosevelt *(1995),* 158

Lincoln, Abraham. Collected Works of Abraham Lincoln 268 *(Roy P. Basler, ed., 1953),* 347

Lincoln, Abraham. Speeches and Writings, 1832–1858: Speeches, Letters, and Miscellaneous Writings: The Lincoln-Douglas Debates *(Don E. Fehrenbacher ed., 1989),* 343 n*, 346 n.*,

Linde, Hans A. First Things First: Rediscovering the States Bills of Rights, *9 U. Balt. L. Rev. 379 (1980),* 629

McConnell, Michael W., Originalism and the Desegregation Decisions, *81 Va. L. Rev. 947 (1995),* 27

Nelson, Grant S., and Robert J. Pushaw, Jr. Rethinking the Commerce Clause: Applying First Principles to Uphold Federal Commercial Regulations but Preserve State Control Over Social Issues, *85 Iowa L. Rev. 1 (1999),* 115

Nelson, William E. The Fourteenth Amendment: From Political Principle to Judicial Doctrine *(1988),* 686

Newman, Roger K. Hugo Black: A Biography *(1994),* 719

New York Law Journal, Oct 26. 1990, p 1. Pg 897, 936

Paul, Arnold M. Conservative Crisis and the Rule of Law: Attitudes of Bar and Bench, 1887–1895 *(1960)*,139

Pennoyer, Sylvester. A Reply to The Foregoing, *29 Am. L. Rev. 856 (1896),* 141

Perry, Michael J. We the People: The Fourteenth Amendment and the Supreme Court *(1999),* 34

Popper, Karl. The Open Society and Its Enemies *(1966),* 804

Posner, Richard. Sex and Reason, *(1992),* 950

Powe, Lucas A., Jr. The Warren Court and American Politics *(2000),* 732

Prather, H. Leon, Sr. We Have Taken A City A Centennial Essay, *in David S. Cecelski & Timothy B. Tyson, eds., Democracy Betrayed: The Wilmington Race Riot of 1898 and Its Legacy 15 (1998),* 709

Presser, Stephen B., Congressional Testimony re: "The Background and History of Impeachment" *(Nov. 9, 1998),* 40

Rauch, Basil. The Roosevelt Reader *(1957),* 143

Reagan, Ronald, Excerpt from the Second Inaugural Address of President Ronald Reagan, 180

Rehnquist, William H. Observation: The Notion of a Living Constitution, *54 Tex. L. Rev. 693 (1976),* 795

Revesz, Richard L. Rehabilitating Interstate Competition: Rethinking the "Race-to-the-Bottom" Rationale for Federal Environmental Regulation, *67 N.Y.U. L. Rev. 1210 (1992),*224

Rice, Charles E. Flimflam Under the 14th, *Wall St. J. (July 31, 1985),* 359

Riekhof & Sykuta. Regulating Wine by Mail, *27 Regulation, No. 3, pp. 30, 31 (Fall 2004),* 558

Roberts, Thomas E., An Analysis of Tahoe-Sierra and Its Help and Hindrance in Understanding the Concept of Contemporary Regulatory Taking, *24 U. Haw. L. Rev. 417, 425 (2003),* 1004

Roosevelt, Franklin D. The Constitution of the United States Was a Layman's Document, Not a Lawyer's Contract, *(September 17, 1937),* 153

Roosevelt, Franklin D. The Roosevelt Reader: Selected Speeches, Messages, Press Conferences, and Letters of Franklin D. Roosevelt *(Basil Rauch, ed. 1957),* 143

Roosevelt, Theodore. Theodore Roosevelt: An Autobiography *(1913),* 819

Roosevelt, Theodore. Writings *(William H. Harbaugh, ed., 1957),* 139

Rosenman, Samuel, ed. 6 The Public Papers and Addresses of Franklin D. Roosevelt *(1941,* 155

Ross, Michael A. Justice Miller's Reconstruction: *The Slaughter-House Cases,* Health Codes, and Civil Rights in New Orleans, 1861–1873, *64 J. S. Hist. 649 (1998),* 690

Ross, William G. A Muted Fury: Populists, Progressives, and Labor Unions Confront the Courts, 1890–1937 *(1994), 143*

Schneider, Richard. Special Considerations: The World Trade Organization and the North American Free Trade Agreement *(2002),* 620

Schwartz, Bernard. 2 The Bill of Rights, A Documentary History *(1971),* 250, 271,632 note*

Scott, Sir Walter. Guy Mannering *(1815),* 28

Smith, James Morton. Freedom's Fetters: The Alien and Sedition Laws and American Civil Liberties *(1956),* 314

"Southern Manifesto", The. *102 Cong. Rec. 4515–16 (1956),* 348

Story, Joseph. Commentaries on the Constitution of the United States *(1833),* 93, 162, 260, 295, 485, 492, 500

Sunstein, Cass. General Propositions and Concrete Cases (With Special Reference to Affirmative Action and Free Speech), *31 Wake Forest L. Rev. 369 (1996),* 33

Ten Broek, Jacobus. Equal Under Law *(1965),* 721

Thompson, E.P. The State Versus Its Enemies, *in E.P. Thompson,* Writing by Candlelight *(1980),* 729

Tocqueville, Alexis De. Democracy in America *(Henry Reeve trans., 1838),* 21, 22, 241, 729, 791

Treanor, William Michael. The Original Understanding of the Takings Clause and the Political Process, *95 Col. L. Rev. 782 (1995),* 1009

Tribe, Laurence. Testimony Before the Constitution Subcommittee of the Committee on the Judiciary *(1988),* 49

Tucker, St. George. A Dissertation on Slavery: With a Proposal for the Gradual Abolition of It in the State of Virginia *(1796),* 655

Tussman, Joseph & tenBroek, Jacobus. The Equal Protection of the Laws, *37 Calif. L. Rev. 341 (1949),* 796 note *

Twain, Mark. Life on the Mississippi *(1883),* 169

Urofsky, Melvin I. Myth and Reality: The Supreme Court and Protective Legislation in the Progressive Era, *Yearbook 1983, Sup. Ct. Hist. Soc. (1983),* 141

Urofsky, Melvin I. State Courts and Protective Legislation during the Progressive Era: A Reevaluation, *72 J. of Am. Hist. 63 (1985),* 141

Van Alstyne, William W. A Critical Guide to *Ex Parte McCardle* 15 Ariz. L. Rev. 229 (1973), 359

Van Alstyne, William W. A Critical Guide to *Marbury v. Madison,* 1969 Duke L.J. 1 (1969), 329, note 1

Warren, Charles. The Supreme Court in United States History, 1789–1835 *(1925, 1935, 1937), 330 note 2, 336*

Weaver, James. A Call to Action *(1892), 801*

Westin, Alan Furman. The Supreme Court, the Populist Movement and the Campaign of 1896, *15 J. Politics 3 (1953), 140*

Wharton, Vernon. The Negro in Mississippi, 1865–1890 *(1947), 687*

Wiecek, William M. The Sources of Antislavery Constitutionalism in America, 1760–1848 *(1977), 721*

Wildenthal, Bryan H. The Lost Compromise: Reassessing the Early Understanding in Court and Congress on Incorporation of the Bill of Rights in the Fourteenth Amendment, *61 Ohio St. L.J. 1051 (2000), 706*

Wildenthal, Bryan H. The Road to *Twining:* Reassessing the Disincorporation of the Bill of Rights, *61 Ohio St. L.J. 1457 (2000), 721*

Will, George F. A Labored Ruling on Pornography, *Greensboro Record (1982), 358*

Wolfenden Report. Report of the Committee on Homosexual Offenses and Prostitution *(1963), 943.*

Woodward, C. Vann. Tom Watson: Agrarian Rebel *(1938), 709*

Yoo, Christopher, Symposium: Presidential Power in Historical Perspective: Reflections on Calabresi and Yoo's The Unitary Executive, *Univ. of Penn. Journal of Con. Law, (Feb 2010), 467*

Young, Ernest A. State Sovereign Immunity and the Future of Federalism, *Sup. Ct. Rev. 42-7 (1999), 509*

Zietlow, Rebecca, Congress and Individual Rights *163*

Zietlow, Rebecca, Enforcing Equality: Congress, The Constitution, and The Protection of Individual Rights *(2006), 165*

Permissions

Balkin, Jack M. & Levinson, Sanford. *Understanding the Constitutional Revolution*, 87 Va. L. Review 1045, 1066–73 (2001). Copyright 2001 by the Virginia Law Review Association, Jack M. Balkin, and Sanford Levinson. Reprinted by permission of rightsholders via the Copyright Clearance Center.

Curtis, Michael Kent. *Albion Tourgee* in the *American National Biography*, edited by John Garraty. Copyright 1999 by the American Council of Learned Societies. Used by permission of Oxford University Press.

Curtis, Michael Kent. Book Review of *We the People: Transformations*, 42 American Journal of Legal History. 417 (1988), reprinted with the permission of the publisher and the author.

Curtis, Michael Kent. *Free Speech: The People's Darling Privilege: Struggles for Freedom of Expression in American History* (Duke University Press, 2000), reprinted by permission.

Emerson, Thomas. *The System of Freedom of Expression* (© 1970 by Thomas I. Emerson). Used by permission of Random House, Inc.

Gillman, Howard. *The Constitution Besieged: The Rise and Fall of Lochner Era Jurisprudence*, 76–77, 114–116 (Duke University Press, 1993), reprinted with the permission of the Duke University Press.

Huhn, Wilson. *The Five Types of Legal Argument*, 152–156 (Carolina Academic Press, 2002), reprinted with the permission of the publisher and author.

Irons, Peter. *The Courage of Their Convictions: Sixteen Americans Who Fought Their Way to the Supreme Court*, 393–396 (© 1988, Peter Irons) reprinted with the permission of The Free Press, A Division of Simon & Schuster Adult Publishing Group and the author.

Kalven, Harry, The New York Times Case: A Note on "the Central Meaning of the First Amendment" Supreme Court Review (© 1964, University of Chicago Press), reprinted with the permission of the University of Chicago Press.

Linde, Hans. *Clear and Present Danger Re-examined: Dissonance in the Brandenburg Concerto*, 22 Stan. L. Rev. 1163 at 1171 and 1174 (1970), reprinted with the permission of the Stanford Law Review.

Popper, Karl. *The Open Society and its Enemies* Vol. 2, 124–125 (Princeton University Press 1966), reprinted with permission of the Princeton University Press.

Urofsky, Melvin I and Finkelman, Paul. "Justices of the U.S. Supreme Court", in *A March of Liberty: A Constitutional History of the United States*, 2 vols. pp. A 28–A 36, (New York: Oxford University Press, 2002) reprinted with permission of the publisher.

Wharton, Vernon. *The Negro in Mississippi (1865–1890)*, 187, 185, 191 (University of North Carolina Press, 1947), reprinted with the permission of the publisher.

Writte, Jr., John, *The Essential Rights and Liberties of Religion in the American Constitutional Experiment*, 71 Notre Dame Law Review, 371, 377–388 (1996), © Notre Dame Law Review, University of Notre Dame. Reprinted with permission.

The authors would also like to thank LEXIS-NEXIS Group and West Group for granting permission to access electronic forms of the case law material used in this book from LEXIS and Westlaw. The cases have been obtained with the permission of LEXIS-NEXIS Group and West Group. Copyrights to any original material held by LEXIS-NEXIS, a division of Reed Elsevier Inc. and West Group. No copyright is claimed as to any part of the original work prepared by a government officer or employee as part of that person's official duties.

A Timeline of American Constitutional History

Constitutional law can best be understood in light of American history. The following chronology will give you some historical context. It is designed to be a supplement to your reading of the cases. You should review the chronology now, and also refer to it as you read cases from different time periods throughout the course. If you review the chronology periodically during the semester, it will deepen your understanding of the cases.

Timeline of American Constitutional History

1215: The Magna Carta imposes restrictions on the English monarch, establishing the principle that no person is above the law.

1454–55: Gutenberg prints a Bible using moveable type. The advent of type creates printed books.

1492–1600s: Various European countries explore the New World, making claims on the land under various theories that they developed to legitimize European settlement of Indian lands.

1514–17: Spanish begin to import Africans to the New World colonies to serve as slaves.

1517: The Protestant Reformation begins. Within a few decades, most churches of northern Europe, including the Church of England, have withdrawn from papal jurisdiction and have been placed under civil authority.

1607: English colonists land at Jamestown, Virginia, marking the first permanent English settlement in North America.

1619: The first blacks come to Virginia as indentured servants, but by 1640 slavery has taken root in Virginia.

1620: The Pilgrims land in the Mayflower at Plymouth Rock, adopting a compact for self-government.

1640: The English Revolution begins; Charles I is tried and beheaded in 1649.

1649: The English Levellers propose an Agreement of the People with expanded parliamentary franchise and limitations on the power of government (including Parliament) in the interest of individual liberty.

1680: John Locke's *The Second Treatise of Government* challenges absolute monarchy.

1687: Sir Isaac Newton publishes *Philosophiae Naturalis Principia Mathematica* in which he sets out his laws of motion and gravity.

1688–89: The English "Glorious Revolution" establishes the primacy of Parliament over the Crown.

1689: Parliament passes the English Bill of Rights. The Bill of Rights declares that levying money for the use of the Crown without the consent of Parliament is illegal; that it is the right of subjects to petition the King, and all prosecutions for such petitioning are illegal; that the freedom of speech and debates or proceedings in Parliament ought not to be impeached or questioned in any court or place out of Parliament; that excessive bail ought not to be required, nor excessive fines imposed, nor cruel and unusual punishments inflicted; and that parliaments ought to be held frequently. The Bill of Rights was an act of Parliament, so it could be repealed by subsequent Parliaments. It limited the power of the King, not Parliament.

First printed newspapers; printed news sheets existed earlier during the English revolution of the 1640s.

1735: The jury acquits journalist John Peter Zenger in New York on the charge of seditious libel. The case is an early landmark in "freedom of the press." Zenger's counsel had argued that writing the truth about political affairs is one of the privileges of freeborn Englishmen and is not a crime.

1754: In anticipation of a war with France, Benjamin Franklin proposes the Albany Plan of Union which would have established a "Grand Council" of representatives of all the Colonies.

1761: Writs of Assistance Case. James Otis, in the Massachusetts colony, challenges writs of assistance (general search warrants that allowed searches without specifying in advance the person or place to be searched). Otis argues even if authorized by Parliament the writs are illegal because "An Act Against the Constitution is void."

1763: The French and Indian War ends; Britain issues Proclamation of 1763 to stop colonists from settling west of the Appalachian Mountains. This is the first of a number of new laws and regulations that create conflict between Britain and the colonies, and ultimately lead to the American Revolution.

1765: Parliament passes the Stamp Act. Widespread protests against "taxation without representation" unify the colonies in their conflict with Britain. The Stamp Act Congress meets in New York. Delegates from nine colonies protest the Stamp Act and plan concerted action against the policies of Parliament. Congress asserts that it is "the undoubted right of Englishmen, that no taxes be imposed on them but with their own consent, given personally or by their representatives."

Parliament passes the "Quartering Act" which allows the British Army to use privately owned buildings to house troops.

1772: In *Somerset v. Stewart* the Court of Kings Bench in London frees a slave brought into England by his master, establishing the principle that slavery could not exist on English soil.

1773:	The Boston Tea Party. In response to a tax on tea, the Sons of Liberty dump hundreds of pounds of tea into the Boston Harbor.
1774:	In response to the Boston Tea Party, Parliament passes the Intolerable Acts, which deprive Massachusetts of self-government.
1775:	American Minutemen meet English Redcoats at Lexington and Concord. The American Revolution begins with "the shot heard round the world."
1776:	The *Declaration of Independence* of the colonies from Great Britain: "We hold these truths to be self-evident: that all men are created equal; that they are endowed, by their Creator, with certain unalienable rights; that among these are life, liberty, and the pursuit of happiness. That to secure these rights, governments are instituted among men, deriving their just powers from the consent of the governed; that whenever any form of government becomes destructive of these ends it is the right to the people to alter or abolish it...."
1776–90:	The first state constitutions are adopted. They vary greatly: all but two have a religious test for office holding, some have broad adult male suffrage, many allow free blacks to vote, and some have property requirements for voting. New Jersey allows women to vote (but the state abrogates this right in the early 1800s).
1781:	Surrender of British forces at Yorktown, Virginia ends most military hostilities in the Revolution. The states ratify the *Articles of Confederation*, the first American federal constitution for the thirteen new states.
1783:	The Treaty of Paris ends the American Revolution.
1787:	The Constitutional Convention in Philadelphia proposes the United States Constitution. It is ratified in 1788 after heated Federalist-Anti-Federalist debate. James Madison, Alexander Hamilton, and John Jay write pro-union editorials, now known as *The Federalist Papers*.
	Meeting under the Articles of Confederation, the Congress passes the Northwest Ordinance, which sets up a system of government for territories as a prelude to statehood. The Ordinance also bans slavery in the area north of the Ohio River.
1789:	George Washington is inaugurated as the first President of the United States. The First Congress convenes; the Bill of Rights is proposed; and Congress enacts the Judiciary Act of 1789, which creates the federal courts.
1791:	The Bill of Rights is ratified by the requisite number of states.
	Congress establishes the First Bank of the United States; Washington signs the bank bill into law over the protest of James Madison and Thomas Jefferson who claim that Congress has no power to create a bank.
1793:	Congress enacts the first Fugitive Slave Law. The Supreme Court decides *Chisholm v. Georgia*, which allows citizens of one state to sue the government of another state.
	Eli Whitney invents a gin to remove seeds from cotton, which revives the moribund institution of slavery by making the production of cotton in the South much more profitable.
1798:	The 11th Amendment is ratified, effectively overruling *Chisholm v. Georgia* which had allowed a citizen of one state to sue another state.

	The Sedition Act criminalizes "false and malicious" criticisms of the President or Congress (but not of the Vice President). As construed, it reaches false opinions as well as false facts.
1800:	Jeffersonian Republicans defeat the Federalists to win majorities in both houses of Congress for the first time. The Federalist Party never again wins control of either house of Congress and disappears by 1815.
1801:	Thomas Jefferson is elected President by the House of Representatives after tying Aaron Burr in Electoral College votes. This leads to the adoption of the 12th Amendment in 1804. The Sedition Act expires and President Jefferson pardons violators.
1801–24:	Marshall Court's expansive nationalist phase.
1803:	*Marbury v. Madison*: The Court in an opinion by Chief Justice John Marshall articulates the principle of judicial review, by which the Supreme Court passes on the constitutionality of acts of Congress. The Court declares a section of the Judiciary Act of 1789 unconstitutional.
	The Louisiana Purchase doubles the territory of the United States.
1807:	Robert Fulton's *Clermont* proves steam to be a practical source of power for river craft.
	New Jersey abolishes property and tax-paying qualifications for voting but only for *white males*. (Maryland follows in 1810.)
1808:	Congress bans the African Slave Trade.
1811:	The charter of the Bank of United States expires and is not renewed because Jeffersonian Republicans control Congress and the presidency.
1812–15:	A second war with England. After the treaty of peace is signed, but before word reaches Louisiana, American troops under the command of Andrew Jackson win the Battle of New Orleans.
1813:	Organization of the Boston Manufacturing Company to produce cotton cloth in Waltham, Massachusetts. The United States is beginning to evolve from a commercial and agricultural nation into an industrial one.
1816:	*Martin v. Hunter's Lessee*: The Court reviews and reverses a decision of a state supreme court interpreting a matter of federal law.
	President Madison successfully urges Congress to establish the Second Bank of the United States with a twenty year charter. In supporting the new bank, Madison waives all constitutional objections to the bank.
1817–25:	New York state builds the Erie Canal. It connects the Great Lakes to the Hudson River which in turn flows into the Atlantic Ocean.
1819:	*McCulloch v. Maryland*: The Court upholds the power of Congress to establish a Bank of the United States and offers an expansive interpretation of the powers of the national government.
	The Panic of 1819, the nation's first depression since the Constitution was adopted, leads to hostility to the Bank of the United States, which calls in loans in the wake of the panic.
1819:	*Dartmouth College v. Woodward*: The Court uses the Contract Clause to provide a constitutional foundation for the protection of corporations from arbitrary interference by states.

1820: The Missouri Compromise prohibits slavery in all federal territory above 36 degrees 30 minutes (north and west of Missouri); territory south of that latitude remains open to slavery.

1821: New York state abolishes its property qualification for voting for white males over the opposition of conservatives like Chancellor James Kent. New York retains its property qualification for black male voters. During the next two decades, most states will drop property qualifications for white voters, while Pennsylvania, Tennessee, and North Carolina take the vote away from black men.

1824: *Gibbons v. Ogden*: In a very popular opinion, Chief Justice Marshall strikes down a steamboat monopoly in New York with a broad definition of commerce.

After no candidate receives a majority of the Electoral College votes, John Quincy Adams is elected President by the House of Representatives. Andrew Jackson, who won the most popular and electoral votes, complains that he lost the election because of a corrupt bargain between Adams and the man who ran fourth, Henry Clay.

1824–33: Marshall Court's defensive or more cautious phase.

1828: Congress passes the "Tariff of Abominations," raising import duties on most goods far beyond what is needed to raise revenue for the nation.

Andrew Jackson is elected President.

1830: The first 13 miles of the Baltimore and Ohio Railroad opens, initiating railroad passenger travel in the United States. President Jackson vetoes the "Maysville Road Bill" asserting that Congress has no power to finance a road built entirely within one state (Kentucky), even though the road is part of the larger National Road, which crosses many state lines.

1831: William Lloyd Garrison publishes the first issue of the radical abolitionist periodical, the *Liberator*. In Virginia, Nat Turner leads the bloodiest slave revolt since the colonial period.

Chief Justice Marshall decides that the Cherokee Nation has no standing to sue in a federal court in *Cherokee Nation v. Georgia*. The decision sets the stage for the Indian Removal.

1832: *Worcester v. Georgia*: The Court rejects Georgia's claim to sovereignty over Indian lands, but the United States Government refuses to enforce the ruling.

South Carolina issues an "Ordinance of Nullification," declaring it will not allow the new tariff of 1832 to be enforced in the state, even though that tariff substantially reduced the rates from the 1828 levels. President Jackson responds with his "Proclamation to the People of South Carolina" warning them not to challenge the national government in this manner. In 1833, Congress passes the "Force Bill" authorizing the President to use the military to enforce the laws. South Carolina rescinds its nullification of the tariff, but in a last moment of defiance, nullifies the "Force Bill."

President Jackson vetoes the bill to recharter the Bank of the United States, declaring that despite the Court's decision in *McCulloch v. Maryland*, he finds the law to be unconstitutional.

1833:	*Barron v. Baltimore*: The Court holds that the guarantees of the Bill of Rights limit only the federal government, not the states; President Jackson orders the Secretary of the Treasury to remove federal deposits from the Bank of the United States. After two Secretaries refuse to comply, Roger B. Taney, as acting Secretary, follows President Jackson's instructions.
1835:	Roger Taney is appointed Chief Justice by Andrew Jackson, replacing John Marshall (1801–35). The Taney Court lasts from 1835 until 1864.
	The American Anti-slavery Society calls for the immediate abolition of slavery and it sends anti-slavery publications to the Southern elite. Men break into the Charleston post office and burn the abolitionist publications. The New York postmaster embargoes abolitionist publications. Mobs attack abolitionists in various Northern cities.
	In his 7th Annual Message to Congress, Andrew Jackson urges removal of the Indians living east of the Mississippi.
1836:	Gag rule: The House of Representatives bans reading or discussion of petitions for abolition of slavery.
	American women attending the World's Anti-Slavery Convention in London are refused permission to speak and are allowed to attend only if they sit behind a screen. They vow to have a women's rights convention when they return to America, leading to the Seneca Falls Convention in 1848.
1837:	Elijah P. Lovejoy, anti-slavery editor, is killed defending his newspaper press from an anti-abolitionist mob in Alton, Illinois.
	Charles River Bridge v. Warren Bridge Co.: Chief Justice Taney offers an interpretation of the Contract Clause of the Constitution, allowing a state to charter a new bridge that harms the interest of an existing company.
	The nation suffers the Panic of 1837, a major depression, in part caused by Jackson removing federal deposits from the Bank of United States.
1841:	Dorr's Rebellion in Rhode Island results in the final elimination of property restrictions on the right to vote.
1842:	*Prigg v. Pennsylvania*: The Court upholds the Fugitive Slave Law of 1793 despite its lack of procedural protections for free blacks who might be wrongly seized as fugitive slaves. At the same time, the Court strikes down Pennsylvania's "personal liberty law," which had required that a state judge hold a hearing before anyone could remove a black from the state as a fugitive slave.
1844:	The electric telegraph is inaugurated for commercial use.
	James K. Polk, Democrat, is elected President; Henry Clay, Whig, is defeated.
	Frederick Douglass, an escaped slave, publishes *Narrative of the Life of Frederick Douglass*. He goes on to work with the Underground Railroad, to co-found and edit an abolitionist newspaper, the *North Star* (1847–1860), and to serve as United States ambassador to Haiti after the Civil War.
1845:	United States annexes Texas.
1846:	The United States wins vast new territory in the Mexican War. But the new territory reopens conflicts over the extension of slavery to new territories.

1848: Seneca Falls Women's Rights Convention begins movement for women's suffrage and other women's rights.

1850: The Compromise of 1850 brings California into the Union as a free state; it bans the public sale of slaves in the District of Columbia; it allows slavery in the remaining territory acquired in the war with Mexico (the Mexican Cession); and it settles a boundary dispute between Texas and New Mexico. The most important provision is the Fugitive Slave Law of 1850, which creates a new system for returning fugitive slaves that involves using federal marshals, the army, the navy, and newly appointed federal commissioners in every county. The law has harsh penalties for people who help fugitive slaves and does not allow alleged slaves to testify at hearings on their status.

1851–61: Numerous protests, riots, and rescues involving fugitive slaves. Two major cases, *Ableman v. Booth* (1859) and *Kentucky v. Dennison* (1861), go to the Supreme Court. In *Ableman*, the Court upholds the constitutionality of the new law and rejects the idea that a state can interfere with the implementation of the law. In *Dennison*, decided after seven states had seceded, the Court held that the federal government cannot force a state governor to remand a fugitive from justice to another state.

1852: *Cooley v. Board of Wardens*: The Court recognizes the states' ability to regulate areas of local concern in the absence of federal legislation.

Harriet Beecher Stowe publishes *Uncle Tom's Cabin*. The book is a national best seller, but is banned in most of the slave states.

1854: With the Kansas-Nebraska Act, Congress repeals part of the Missouri Compromise by allowing slavery in federal territories north and west of Missouri. The Act allows settlers in these territories to decide the issue of slavery under a theory known as "popular sovereignty."

The Anti-Nebraska Movement, in response to the new law, soon leads to the creation of the Republican Party, founded to oppose the expansion of slavery into the territories.

1857: *Dred Scott v. Sandford*: The Court rules that Congress lacks the power to outlaw slavery in federal territories and that even free blacks cannot be citizens of the United States. Every justice on the Court writes an opinion.

Hinton Helper publishes the *Impending Crisis*, an indictment of slavery. Members of the Republican Party use the book as a campaign document. Southern states treat circulation of the book as a crime.

A typesetting machine is created and exhibited.

1859: John Brown raids the federal arsenal at Harpers Ferry in order to begin a slave-manned guerilla war in the South. Daniel Worth, a minister, is prosecuted in North Carolina for circulating the *Impending Crisis* among whites. Worth is charged under a North Carolina statute that bans circulation of books tending to make free Negroes or slaves discontent with their condition.

Charles Darwin publishes *Origin of Species*.

1860: North Carolina Supreme Court affirms Worth's conviction; Abraham Lincoln's election as a Republican President, on a platform opposing further

	expansion of slavery, leads South Carolina to secede and it is quickly followed by six other states in the South.
1861:	The Confederate attack on Fort Sumter begins the Civil War. Four more states leave the Union.
1862:	Homestead Act provides 160 acres of free land to settlers who cultivate it.
	Morrill Act permits Congress to provide land to states for the establishment of colleges.
1863:	The Emancipation Proclamation frees only the slaves residing in states "in rebellion against the United States."
1864:	National Banking Act provides the framework for a national banking system.
1865:	Confederate General Robert E. Lee surrenders to Union General Ulysses S. Grant at Appomattox. Five days later President Lincoln is assassinated.
	Andrew Johnson becomes President after Lincoln's assassination.
	The 13th Amendment is ratified. Congress and the nation face the question of the return of Southern states to the Union and to representation in Congress. The 13th Amendment, by its implied repeal of the clause by which slaves counted as 3/5ths of a person for purposes of representation in the federal House of Representatives and the Electoral College, raises the prospect that the South, having lost the war, might return to political power on the backs of disenfranchised Americans of African descent.
	Former slave states begin to pass harsh "Black Codes" that limit the legal, social, and political rights of blacks.
	The first African American is licensed to practice before the U.S. Supreme Court.
1865–77:	Reconstruction. A White and Black Republican coalition rules the South. Ultimately, Republicans and blacks are driven from power by political terrorism. The "Jim Crow" era is later entrenched by racist laws requiring segregation in various aspects of public and private life.
1866:	Congress passes the Civil Rights Act of 1866, basing its authority on the new 13th Amendment. Questions about the constitutionality of the law under the 13th Amendment, together with concerns about the repression of civil liberty in the South before the Civil War, lead Congress to propose the 14th Amendment.
	Mendel publishes his path breaking study on genetics.
1867:	Alaska (admitted as the 49th state in 1959) is purchased from Russia.
	The Patrons of Husbandry is organized and starts the farmer's protest movement known as the Granger Movement.
	Kansas holds a state referendum on whether to enfranchise blacks, women, or both. Lucy Stone, Susan B. Anthony, and Elizabeth Cady Stanton traverse the state speaking in favor of women's suffrage. Both black suffrage and women's suffrage are voted down.
1868:	President Johnson is impeached, but the Senate fails by one vote to convict and remove him from office.

The 14th Amendment is ratified by the requisite number of states. Susan B. Anthony and Elizabeth Cady Stanton bitterly oppose the Amendment because § 2 reduces a state's congressional representation *only* if it restricts the voting rights of *males*.

1869: The first transcontinental railroad is completed.

Ex Parte McCardle: The Court seemingly recognizes the power of Congress to control the appellate jurisdiction of the federal courts, at least in the facts of that case.

The Wyoming Territory grants women's suffrage, the first jurisdiction to do so since New Jersey abolished women's suffrage early in the century.

1870: The 15th Amendment is ratified by the requisite number of states, giving the right to vote to black men, but not to women.

Victoria Woodhull addresses the Judiciary Committee of the House of Representatives arguing that women have the right to vote under the 14th Amendment and asking for congressional enforcement. A divided Judiciary Committee issues a negative report.

1870–1900: Alexander Graham Bell patents the telephone.

The last three decades of the 19th century are known as the Gilded Age because of the rise of great and ostentatious concentrations of wealth. During this time period, great corporations are organized and businesses are merged and consolidated into larger units. Laissez faire economics and limited government are strong ideologies, but this is also an era of some reform legislation such as the Sherman Anti-trust Act and the Interstate Commerce Act. All Presidents during this time period are Republican except for Grover Cleveland, a conservative Democrat.

1872: The Amnesty Act restores political privileges to most citizens of the late Confederacy who had sworn allegiance to the United States and then fought against it; widespread violence begins restoration of "white supremacy" in the South.

In Rochester, New York, Susan B. Anthony registers and votes, contending that the 14th Amendment gives her that right. Several days later she is arrested for voting illegally. At Anthony's trial, the judge does not allow her to testify that she believed that she had the right to vote, directs the jury to enter a verdict of guilty, and fines her $100. She refuses to pay, yet the judge releases her.

1872–76: Attack on and eventual overthrow of Reconstruction in the South.

1873: *Slaughter-House Cases*: The Court, in a 5–4 decision, narrowly construes the Privileges or Immunities Clause of the 14th Amendment. Following the decision, the Court holds one after another of the guarantees of the Bill of Rights do not limit the states.

Bradwell v. State: Following the approach of *Slaughter-House* to the Privileges or Immunities Clause of the 14th Amendment, the Court upholds Illinois ban on women practicing law, ruling law practice is not a privilege of national citizenship. No equal protection claim is made.

Minor v. Happersett: The Court unanimously rules that citizenship does not give women the right to vote under the Privileges or Immunities Clause of the 14th Amendment; therefore, women's political rights are under the jurisdiction of each individual state. Mrs. Minor's husband had to sue on her behalf since married women, like children, could not file suit on their own.

1876: The Centennial Exposition in Philadelphia exhibits the economic progress of the nation since 1776.

1877: The "Compromise of 1877" effectively ends Reconstruction. Republicans get the Presidency in a contested election. Federal troops are withdrawn from the South.

Munn v. Illinois: The Court upholds a state regulation of grain elevators against claims that the regulation violates due process and rights to private property.

Railroad strikes occur across the nation. Industrial warfare marks the late 19th and early 20th centuries. Speculative panics, business failures, and substantial unemployment occurred from 1873 to 1878, 1882 to 1885, and 1893 to 1897.

The phonograph is invented.

Thomas A. Edison builds the first central electric power station, located in New York City.

1879: *Reynolds v. United States*: The Court upholds prosecutions of Mormons for practicing polygamy in accordance with their religious beliefs. In 1890 the Mormon Church renounces polygamy and by the end of the decade Congress returns most of the property taken from the Church.

1881: Congress passes the Chinese Exclusion Act, which eliminates Chinese immigration for a decade.

1883: The Pendleton Act establishes the federal civil service.

Civil Rights Cases: The Court, over Justice Harlan's dissent, strikes down the Civil Rights Act of 1875, which prohibited racial discrimination in public accommodations. The Court holds that Congress lacks power under the 13th Amendment to pass such a statute and that Congress's power under the 14th Amendment is limited to "state action."

1886: *Wabash, St. Louis & Pacific Rw. Co. v. Illinois*: The Court limits state power to regulate the intra-state rates charged by railroads.

Santa Clara County v. Southern Pacific Rw. Co.: The Court holds 14th Amendment's protection of "persons" includes corporations.

The American Federation of Labor (AFL) is organized under the leadership of Samuel Gompers.

1887: Interstate Commerce Commission is created, an early effort in federal regulation.

1890: The Sherman Antitrust Act forbids monopolies and combinations in restraint of trade.

1891: The Judiciary Act of 1891 transfers most federal appellate jurisdiction from the Circuit Courts to the newly established Courts of Appeals. The legislation also abolishes "circuit riding" by Supreme Court justices.

1892: The People's Party (also know as the Populist Party) is organized. Protesting farmers and others nominate General James B. Weaver for President.

	The party's 1896 platform favors direct election of Senators, a progressive income tax, initiative and referendum, government ownership of railroads, employment of labor on public works in times of depression, and other "radical" measures.
1893:	Chicago's "World's Fair" illustrates the use of electricity for illumination and power.
	The Panic of 1893 strikes the nation and is the worst depression to date in United States history.
1894:	Workers at Pullman Railroad Car plant strike, leading to a sympathy strike by railroad workers. President Cleveland sends federal troops to Chicago to break the strike on the grounds that it is interfering with the United States mail. During the strike, federal courts issue injunctions against the railroad union, its leaders, and locals, and forbid communication between locals. The Court upholds this exercise of federal authority in *In re Debs* (1895).
1895:	Booker T. Washington, President of the Tuskegee Institute, makes his "Atlanta Compromise" speech. He urges blacks to accept their inferior social position for the present and to strive to raise themselves through vocational training and economic self-reliance.
	U.S. v. E.C. Knight Co.: The Court embraces a narrow reading of the Commerce Clause, and holds the Sherman Act does not reach a sugar manufacturing monopoly because manufacturing is not commerce.
	The Court holds that the federal income tax is unconstitutional in two decisions in *Pollock v. Farmer's Loan and Trust Co.*
1896:	A motion picture is commercially exhibited for the first time.
	Plessy v. Ferguson: The Court, over Justice Harlan's dissent, upholds a Louisiana statute requiring racially segregated railway cars.
	William Jennings Bryan runs for President as candidate of both the Democratic and Populist parties. He attacks the tight fiscal policies of Congress in his famous "Cross of Gold Speech." He is defeated in a watershed election by the Republican, William McKinley.
1897:	*Allgeyer v. Louisiana*: The Court unanimously holds that the right to make contracts is protected by the Due Process Clause of the 14th Amendment. "Freedom of Contract" and "substantive due process" will mark the "*Lochner* Era" in the Court's jurisprudence; it lasts until 1937.
1898:	A successful war with Spain establishes the United States as a colonial empire as the nation acquires Puerto Rico and occupies the Philippines. The war also leads to the annexation of Hawaii (admitted as the 50th state in 1959).
1899:	Thorstein Veblen publishes *The Theory of the Leisure Class*. Sigmund Freud publishes *The Interpretation of Dreams*.
1900:	William McKinley decisively defeats Williams Jennings Bryan in a rematch of the 1896 presidential election. McKinley's new running mate is Theodore Roosevelt, a hero of the Spanish-American War and a leading progressive reformer.
	Maxwell v. Dow: The Court, in an opinion written by Justice Peckham, soon to be the author of *Lochner v. New York*, rules that the criminal jury

trial guarantee of the 6th Amendment does not limit the states. The Court warns that the application of the Bill of Rights to the states would threaten state sovereignty.

1901: Theodore Roosevelt becomes President after McKinley's assassination. Roosevelt's presidency is often seen as the beginning of the Progressive Era.

1902: Oregon becomes the first state to establish primary elections for the nomination of candidates in general elections.

1903: *Champion v. Ames*: The Court holds that Congress may use its commerce power to ban interstate movement of lottery tickets.

"Muckraking" articles by Ida Tarbell and Lincoln Steffens in national magazines expose business and governmental corruption.

Orville and Wilbur Wright fly an airplane at Kitty Hawk, North Carolina.

W.E.B. Du Bois publishes *The Souls of Black Folk*, criticizing Booker T. Washington's willingness to forfeit social justice for economic progress.

1904: *Northern Securities Company v. United States*: The Court upholds the use of the Sherman Anti-Trust Act to break up the James J. Hill-J.P. Morgan railroad monopoly. Justice Holmes dissents, arguing that every consolidation is not a restraint of trade.

Dorr v. United States: The Court holds that the Constitution does not "follow the flag" and that it is therefore permissible to try someone in the Philippines without a jury, and that in general, Bill of Rights guarantees do not necessarily apply to overseas territories.

Oregon becomes the first state to adopt the initiative and referendum for the enactment of legislation.

1905: *Lochner v. New York*: The Court, in a 5–4 decision, strikes down a state law limiting hours of work for bakers. It asserts that the law violates liberty of contract said to be secured by the Due Process Clause of the 14th Amendment. Critics of the *Lochner* decision and other decisions striking down Progressive Era reform legislation urge restraints on judicial review.

Albert Einstein publishes a paper setting out his theory of relativity.

1906: Congress passes the Pure Food and Drug Act.

1907: William James publishes *Pragmatism, A New Name for Some Old Ways of Thinking*. James' philosophy affects legal thinkers, including Oliver Wendell Holmes, Jr.

1908: *Muller v. Oregon*: The Court upholds an Oregon statute limiting the number of hours that women can work. The case is seen as a great victory for Progressives. It was argued by Louis D. Brandeis, "the People's Lawyer," who presented the Court with massive statistical evidence on the harm to women from overwork. This type of "sociological" evidence is known as a "Brandeis Brief."

Japan and U.S. reach a "Gentlemen's Agreement" pursuant to which Japan agrees to voluntarily limit the number of its citizens emigrating to the United States.

1909: Henry Ford introduces the "Model T," a car mass-produced by assembly-line methods.

	The National Association for the Advancement of Colored People (NAACP) is formed.
1912:	In 1908, after serving out McKinley's term and winning election on his own, Theodore Roosevelt retires from the Presidency, but in 1912 he opposes the re-election bid of his hand-picked successor, William Howard Taft. When Roosevelt loses the Republican nomination, he runs on the Progressive Party (also called the "Bull Moose" Party). Roosevelt divides the Republican vote, setting the stage for the Democrat, Woodrow Wilson, to win the election. Socialist Party candidate Eugene V. Debs receives nearly a million votes.
1913–21:	Woodrow Wilson serves as President; Progressive Era ends with the end of Wilson's second term.
1913:	The Income Tax Amendment (the 16th) is adopted.
	The Federal Reserve Act revamps the American banking structure.
	Alice Paul organizes a woman's suffrage parade in Washington, D.C., on the day of Woodrow Wilson's inauguration.
1914:	The Panama Canal is opened.
	Congress enacts the Clayton Antitrust Act, which forbids a tendency to monopolize commerce.
	Congress establishes the Federal Trade Commission.
1916:	Jeannette Rankin, a Republican from Montana, is elected to the House of Representatives and becomes the first woman to serve in Congress.
1917–18:	U.S. in World War I.
1917:	Socialist Party presidential candidate Eugene Debs is convicted and imprisoned for an anti-war speech. His conviction is upheld by the Supreme Court in 1919.
	Members of the National Woman's Party picket the White House. Alice Paul and 96 other suffragists are arrested and jailed for "obstructing traffic." When they go on a hunger strike to protest their arrest and treatment, they are force-fed.
1918:	The House of Representatives passes a resolution in favor of a woman's suffrage amendment. The resolution is defeated by the Senate.
	Hammer v. Dagenhart: The Court, in a 5–4 decision, holds that Congress may not prohibit movement in commerce of articles made by child labor.
1919:	Adoption of the 18th Amendment inaugurates nationwide "Prohibition," which lasts until 1933. In 1933, the 21st Amendment repeals the 18th.
	The 19th Amendment to the Constitution granting women the vote is adopted by a joint resolution of Congress and sent to the states for ratification.
	Schenck v. United States: The Court articulates a constricted view of free speech under Justice Holmes' "clear and present danger test." In his dissent in *Abrams v. United States* (1919), Holmes, joined by Brandeis, reshapes the test as a much more speech-protective one.
	The U.S. Senate refuses to ratify peace treaty that would have made the United States a member of the newly formed League of Nations.

1920: The Senate again rejects United States membership in the League of Nations.

The Woman's Suffrage Amendment (the 19th) is ratified.

A radio station in Pittsburgh inaugurates commercial radio broadcasting in the United States.

The decade of the 1920s, known as the "Roaring Twenties," marks the end of the Progressive Era and its various reforms. Anti-trust enforcement declines, as does the strength of labor unions. There is a wave of mergers and the rise of public utility holding companies. Farmers suffer throughout the decade as farm prices decline. The decade ends with the onset of the Great Depression in October 1929. Republicans control the White House from 1921 until 1933 with the presidencies of Harding, Coolidge, and Hoover.

1921: The Budget and Accounting Act provides for a centralized federal budget system.

1923: *Meyer v. Nebraska*: The Court invalidates, as a violation of the "liberty" of the Due Process Clause of the 14th Amendment, a state statute prohibiting the teaching of foreign languages in schools. The case shows the *Lochner* Court's recognition of personal as well as economic rights as "liberty."

At the behest of Chief Justice Taft, Congress establishes what later becomes known as the Judicial Conference of the United States, which provides a system for administration and oversight of the federal judicial system by senior federal judges.

1924: Congress passes a law extending United States citizenship to all Native Americans.

The National Origins Act, the most important immigration statute of the 20th century, limits annual immigration to 2 percent of each nationality as of the 1890 census, an effort to limit certain "undesirable" ethnic groups in the United States.

1925: *Gitlow v. New York*: The Court assumes that the federal guarantees of free speech and press limit the states. Beginning of incorporation of the 1st Amendment into the 14th as a limit on the states.

Scopes "Monkey Trial" is held in Tennessee; a teacher is fined for teaching evolution.

The Judiciary Act of 1925 eliminates most automatic appeals to the U.S. Supreme Court and makes most of the Court's appellate jurisdiction discretionary through the *certiorari* process.

1927: Charles A. Lindbergh, alone in the *Spirit of St. Louis*, makes the first New York-Paris nonstop flight.

The Jazz Singer, with Al Jolson, demonstrates partially talking movies.

Whitney v. California: Justice Brandeis, in a concurring opinion, crafts a modern rationale for free speech: that evil words should be answered with counter-speech, unless immediate circumstances prevent an opportunity for discussion.

1929: Wall Street's crash ends prosperity. The Great Depression begins. Widespread unemployment, bank failures, business and personal bankruptcy, and foreclosure of mortgages on homes and farms sweep the nation.

John Maynard Keynes, an English economist and monetary expert, departs from classical laissez-faire economic concepts to endorse a government public-works program to promote employment during recessions. His theories, known as Keynesian economics, are among the most influential economic formulations of the 20th century. He advocates spending programs, such as those of the New Deal—but on a more extensive scale, to maintain high national income. His chief work, *The General Theory of Employment, Interest and Money* (1936), advocates active government intervention in the market and, during recessionary times, deficit spending and easier monetary policies to stimulate business activity. In times of prosperity Keynes advocates paying down the national debt.

1930: President Hoover appoints Charles Evans Hughes to be Chief Justice, replacing William Howard Taft (1921–30); he also appoints Owen J. Roberts to the Court, replacing Edward Sanford (1923–30).

1931: *Near v. Minnesota*: The Court holds an injunction involving future issues of libelous or scandalous newspapers to be an invalid prior restraint.

1932: President Hoover appoints Benjamin N. Cardozo to the Court, replacing Oliver Wendell Holmes, Jr. (1902–32).

Franklin Roosevelt is elected President and will ultimately serve until 1945. Roosevelt's New Deal is characterized by a far more activist federal government, including public works projects instituted to give work to the unemployed, regulation of banks and federal deposit insurance, regulation of the stock market, and regulation of agricultural production. The National Labor Relations Act guarantees workers the right to form labor unions and to engage in collective bargaining. The New Deal also pioneers reforms such as unemployment insurance, social security, and national legislation setting minimum wages and maximum hours. During this time, Congress enacts a progressive income tax with high rates for upper brackets.

Norris-LaGuardia Anti-Injunction Act curtails the extent to which courts can issue injunctions to bar strikes and interfere with other labor union activities.

1934: Congress enacts the Federal Declaratory Judgment Act.

1935–36: The Supreme Court imperils the New Deal by invalidating eight federal economic regulatory statutes, including the National Industrial Recovery Act (*Panama Refining Co. v. Ryan* and *Schechter Poultry Corp.* v. *United States*); the Agricultural Adjustment Act (*United States v. Butler*); and the Bituminious Coal Conservation Act (*Carter v. Carter Coal*). Several of the cases rely upon a highly restrictive interpretation of the commerce power.

1936: President Roosevelt is re-elected in a landslide, carrying 46 of 48 states. Democrats win enormous majorities in both houses of Congress.

1937: *Palko v. Connecticut*: The Court explains selective incorporation of guarantees of the Bill of Rights into the 14th Amendment as a limit on the states.

President Roosevelt proposes legislation to permit him to appoint up to six additional justices to the Supreme Court. The Senate Judiciary Committee tables this so-called "court packing" measure after it encounters widespread opposition.

President Roosevelt appoints Hugo L. Black to the Court, replacing Willis Van Devanter (1910–37).

In several landmark decisions, the Court upholds the constitutionality of important New Deal legislation. The cases include *National Labor Relations Board v. Jones & Laughlin Steel Corp.* (using an expansive definition of interstate commerce to uphold far-reaching regulation of labor-management relations); *Steward Machine Co. v. Davis* (using an expansive definition of the taxing power to uphold the unemployment compensation features of the Social Security Act); and *Helvering v. Davis* (using an expansive definition of the General Welfare Clause to uphold the old-age benefits provisions of the Social Security Act). Meanwhile, the Court interred the doctrine of economic due process in *West Coast Hotel v. Parrish*. These decisions signaled the so-called "Judicial Revolution of 1937.

1938: Congress enacts a national minimum wage.

The Congress of Industrial Organizations (CIO) secedes from the AFL. It becomes a vigorous independent labor organization that seeks to unionize previously unorganized industrial workers.

President Roosevelt appoints Felix Frankfurter to the Court, replacing Benjamin Cardozo (1932–38), and Stanley F. Reed, replacing George Sutherland (1922–38).

United States v. Carolene Products: The Court holds that economic regulation typically will be judged by a rational basis standard. Footnote 4 suggests a higher level of scrutiny in at least some cases involving civil rights, civil liberties, and discrete and insular minorities.

Promulgation of the Federal Rules of Civil Procedure.

1939: President Roosevelt appoints William O. Douglas to the Court, replacing Louis Brandeis (1916–39), and Frank Murphy, replacing Pierce Butler (1922–39).

1940: *Minersville School District v. Gobitis*: The Court upholds the expulsion of Jehovah's Witness schoolchildren from school for refusing to salute the American flag.

1941: The Federal Communications Commission authorizes the first commercial television stations. On December 7, Japan attacks Pearl Harbor. The United States officially enters World War II.

President Roosevelt promotes Justice Harlan Fiske Stone to Chief Justice, replacing Charles Evans Hughes (1910–16, 1930–1941 as Chief Justice), and appoints James F. Byrnes to the Court, replacing James McReynolds (1914–41), and Robert H. Jackson, who takes Stone's Associate seat.

United States v. Darby: The Court unanimously overrules *Hammer v. Dagenhart* and allows Congress to ban the interstate transportation of items made in violation of the Fair Labor Standards Act.

1942: The federal government forcibly removes 120,000 Japanese-Americans living on the West Coast (approximately two thirds of whom are American citizens) from their homes and relocates them in internment camps.

Wickard v. Filburn: The Court unanimously adopts a very deferential aggregate impact test for determining scope of federal commerce power.

Skinner v. Oklahoma: The Court invalidates a state criminal eugenics law (mandatory sterilization for larceny but not for embezzlement) as violating the Equal Protection Clause. The Court subjects a statute that involves the "fundamental" right of procreation to heightened scrutiny.

1943: Race riots in Detroit and Harlem leave many dead or injured.

President Roosevelt appoints Wiley B. Rutledge to the Court, replacing James Byrnes (1941–42).

West Virginia Board of Education v. Barnette: The Court holds that the refusal of Jehovah's Witness schoolchildren to salute the American flag is protected by the guarantee of freedom of speech.

1944: President Roosevelt, though quite ill, is elected to an unprecedented fourth term.

Korematsu v. United States: The Court upholds forced "re-location" and detention of Japanese Americans into internment camps, although the Court at the same time announces that racial classifications are inherently suspect.

NBC broadcasts the first network newscast.

1945: President Roosevelt dies, replaced by Harry Truman, who is re-elected in 1948.

Germany surrenders on May 8. Japan surrenders on August 14 after the United States drops the first atomic bombs used in wartime on Hiroshima and Nagasaki.

The United Nations Charter is adopted at San Francisco.

President Truman appoints Harold H. Burton to the Court, replacing Owen Roberts (1930–45).

Southern Pacific v. Arizona: The Court holds that an Arizona statute that prohibits long trains from operating within the state violates the dormant commerce clause as an undue burden on interstate commerce.

1946: The Cold War begins. After World War II, Soviet troops remain in Eastern Europe and establish pro-Soviet regimes.

President Truman appoints Frederick M. Vinson to be Chief Justice, replacing Harlan Stone (1925–46, 1941–1946 as Chief Justice).

Administrative Procedure Act establishes rule-making procedures for executive departments and independent governmental agencies.

1947: The Marshall Plan for the economic reconstruction of Europe is introduced. The plan marks the first major United States offensive in the "Cold War".

Jackie Robinson integrates Major League Baseball by playing for the Brooklyn Dodgers.

Adamson v. California: The Court, in a 5–4 decision, refuses to apply the privilege against self-incrimination to the states. In dissent, Justice Black advocates total incorporation of the Bill of Rights, relying on his reading of the historical record.

The Taft-Hartley Act, passed over President Truman's veto, curtails the powers of labor unions. Its provisions include prohibition of secondary boycotts and the closed shop, and it increases the legal liability of labor unions for their actions.

1948: Whitaker Chambers accuses Alger Hiss of giving State Department documents to the Soviet Union. Hiss is convicted of perjury in 1949.

President Truman issues an Executive Order integrating the military and advocates federal civil rights legislation. Angered by the pro-civil rights stand of the national Democratic party, Southern Democrats bolt the party and nominate Governor Strom Thurmond of South Carolina as the States' Rights Party candidate for President. The Dixiecrat revolt marks the beginning of the end of the solidly Democratic South.

The Universal Declaration of Human Rights, drafted by a commission chaired by Eleanor Roosevelt, is promulgated by the General Assembly of the United Nations.

1949: China becomes communist.

Federal prosecutors bring criminal charges against 11 top leaders of the United States Communist Party; they are convicted under the Smith Act and sentenced to prison.

President Truman appoints Thomas C. Clark to the Court, replacing Frank Murphy (1940–49), and Sherman Minton, replacing Wiley Rutledge (1943–49).

1950: The United Nations (with most troops supplied by the United States) enters the Korean War.

Senator Joseph McCarthy (R.-Wis.) charges that Communists have infiltrated the State Department. McCarthy will eventually accuse many prominent Americans of assisting the Soviet Union, including General George Marshall.

1951: *Dennis v. United States*: The Court upholds several Smith Act convictions. The plurality opinion uses the "gravity of the evil discounted by its improbability" test.

Ethel and Julius Rosenberg are convicted for transferring atomic secrets to the Soviet Union. They were executed in 1953.

1952: *Youngstown Sheet & Tube Co. v. Sawyer* (The Steel Seizure Case): The Court prevents the President from seizing control of the steel industry during the Korean War.

Beauharnais v. Illinois: The Court, in a 5–4 decision, upholds Illinois' group libel law.

Dwight Eisenhower, Republican and World War II hero, is elected President. He captures several Southern states.

1953: Francis Crick and James Watson publish an article explaining the structure of DNA.

President Eisenhower appoints Earl Warren to be Chief Justice, replacing Frederick Vinson (1946–53). The Warren Court, which lasts until 1969, will expand protection for free speech and the rights of those accused of crimes and will strike down government-imposed racial discrimination. The Court will also apply most of the still unincorporated Bill of Rights guarantees to the states.

The Korean War ends with a truce that retains the division of Korea between a Communist North and a pro-western South.

1954:	The United States Senate censures Joseph McCarthy.
	President Eisenhower appoints John M. Harlan to the Court, replacing Robert Jackson (1941–54).
	Brown v. Board of Education: The Court unanimously holds that racial segregation of public schools violates the Equal Protection Clause of the 14th Amendment. The Court repudiates *Plessy's* "separate but equal" standard for education.
	After the *Brown* decision is announced, White Citizens' Councils are organized in much of the South to oppose school desegregation. President Eisenhower takes no public position on *Brown*.
1955:	The Montgomery bus boycott begins when Rosa Parks refuses to comply with a local segregation ordinance. Martin Luther King leads the boycott which eventually succeeds and helps trigger a broader civil rights movement.
	Williamson v. Lee Optical: The Court unanimously rejects heightened Equal Protection scrutiny for most purely economic regulation.
1956:	President Eisenhower appoints William J. Brennan to the Court, replacing Sherman Minton (1949–56).
	A drug company patents the oral contraceptive (birth control) pill.
	92 of the 106 southern members of Congress sign a "Southern Manifesto" which labels the *Brown* decision "a clear abuse of judicial power" and commends those "States which have declared the intention to resist forced integration."
	Congress enacts legislation that inaugurates the interstate highway system.
1957:	President Eisenhower sends federal troops to help desegregate the public schools in Little Rock, Arkansas.
	Roth v. United States: The Court holds that obscenity is not protected by the 1st Amendment because it is "utterly without redeeming social value." However, all sexual content is not deemed to be obscene.
1958:	The Soviet Union launches Sputnik 1, the first earth satellite. The United States launches its first satellite, Explorer 1, three months later.
	President Eisenhower appoints Potter Stewart to the Court, replacing Harold Burton (1945–58).
1959:	The microchip is invented. Xerox introduces the plain paper copier.
1960:	John Kennedy, age 43, is elected President, defeating the incumbent Vice President, Richard Nixon.
	The "Sit-in" Movement begins when four black college students in Greensboro, North Carolina, refuse to move from a Woolworth lunch counter when denied service. By September 1961, more than 70,000 students, whites and blacks, have participated in sit-ins to protest racial discrimination at lunch counters.
1960s:	The Court rules that most of the remaining provisions of the Bill of Rights (those not yet incorporated) limit the states.
1961:	*Mapp v. Ohio*: The Court holds in a 5–4 decision that the federal exclusionary rule, by which evidence seized in violation of the 4th Amendment is typ-

ically deemed inadmissible, limits the states. For all practical purposes, this begins a process through which the Court federalizes much state criminal procedure by nationalizing nearly every criminal procedural provision of the Bill of Rights by 1969. The right to indictment by a grand jury is a notable exception.

United States sends advisors to South Vietnam, becoming involving in a war between North and South Vietnam that will claim 58,000 American lives by 1973.

The first humans travel in outer space.

1962: The publication of Rachel Carson's *Silent Spring* helps to launch the environmental movement.

President Kennedy appoints Byron R. White to the Court, replacing Charles Whittaker (1957–62) and Arthur J. Goldberg, replacing Felix Frankfurter (1939–62).

The first microcomputer appears.

Baker v. Carr: The Court recognizes that an Equal Protection challenge to mal-apportioned state legislative districts is justiciable, holding that the issue is not a "political question." In 1964, the Court announces its "one man, one vote" standard in *Reynolds v. Sims*.

Engel v. Vitale: The Court invalidates a state sponsored school prayer as a violation of the Establishment Clause. Constitutional amendments to reverse the *Engel* decision are proposed in Congress, but fail.

1963–73: The United States assumes an ever larger role in the Vietnam War.

1963: Photographs of the use of fire hoses and police dogs on black citizens in Birmingham, Alabama, many of whom are children, outrage much of the nation and lead to growing support for federal civil rights legislation. Martin Luther King, Jr., leads a March on Washington in support of such legislation and delivers his "I Have a Dream" speech from the steps of the Lincoln Memorial.

Lyndon Johnson assumes the presidency following the assassination of President Kennedy.

The publication of Betty Friedan's *The Feminine Mystique* contributes to the rise of the modern women's movement.

1964: Congress, with the urging of President Johnson, enacts the Civil Rights Act of 1964, the most sweeping civil rights legislation in American history. The Act prohibits both race and sex discrimination in public accommodations and employment. Democratic support for civil rights transforms the South from an overwhelmingly Democratic region to a predominately Republican one. On signing the bill Johnson tells his aide Bill Moyers that he has delivered the South to the Republican Party for my generation and your generation.

The FBI continues aggressive wiretapping of Martin Luther King, Jr., based on allegations that he associates with certain people alleged to be Communists. The FBI uses material gathered on King to attempt to discredit him.

In Mississippi and elsewhere, civil rights demonstrators are threatened, beaten, and murdered for their efforts on behalf of racial integration and the right of black people to vote.

George Wallace, who had run strong races in the Democratic primaries in Indiana, Michigan, and Maryland, demands that the Democratic party repeal the Civil Rights law and warns of an "uprising" comparable to the attack on Reconstruction. Wallace promises that a conservative movement will "take charge of one the parties in the next four years." Wallace keeps electors pledged to Johnson off the Alabama ballot and eventually throws Alabama's electors to Republican Barry Goldwater, who opposed the 1964 Civil Rights Bill.

President Johnson wins a term of his own in a landslide, receiving a record 61 percent of the vote in his defeat of the Republican candidate, Barry Goldwater. Democrats win huge majorities in both houses of Congress. Johnson's strong support for civil rights contributes to the growing rejection of the Democratic Party by many southern whites. President Johnson launches a "War on Poverty," emphasizing jobs for the poor and a variety of new social programs, including federal aid to education, Medicare, Medicaid, and Food Stamps. Johnson's War on Poverty will soon become a casualty of the massive escalation of America's war in Vietnam. Widespread protests against the Vietnam War eventually cause Johnson not to seek re-election in 1968.

After an alleged attack on an American ship by the North Vietnamese, Congress approves the Tonkin Gulf Resolution, which authorizes the President to take whatever action is necessary to protect American forces serving in South Vietnam. The House vote is 418 to 0 and the Senate vote is 98–2.

Heart of Atlanta Motel v. United States: The Court upholds the public accommodation section of the Civil Rights Act of 1964 based on the commerce power.

New York Times v. Sullivan: The Court holds that the 1st Amendment requires that a public official suing for defamation must prove actual malice (intentional falsity or reckless disregard of the truth).

1965: *Griswold v. Connecticut*: The Court upholds the right of married couples to use birth control devices under a 14th Amendment right to privacy.

Martin Luther King leads a Selma-to-Montgomery march for voting rights. The national media broadcasts images of "Bloody Sunday," a violent attack by local law enforcement on the marchers. These images, as well as news of the brutal murder of a white minister who had joined the marchers, contribute to the enactment of the Voting Rights Act of 1965.

Race riots in the Watts section of Los Angeles last for six days and leave 34 dead and $200 million in property damage.

Malcolm X is assassinated. One year later, Stokely Carmichael will coin the phrase, "Black Power," during a civil rights march in Mississippi, signaling a new phase in the Civil Rights Movement.

Immigration and Nationality Act removes tight restrictions on immigration from Asia, Africa, and South America.

The United States sharply escalates its military presence in Vietnam.

President Johnson appoints Abe Fortas to the Court, replacing Arthur Goldberg (1962–65).

1966: *Miranda v. Arizona*: The Court holds that police may not conduct interrogations of criminal suspects after arrest unless they are aware of their constitutional rights. Starting with Richard Nixon's appointments to the Court and in subsequent years, including 2010, the Court repeatedly limits the *Miranda* rule, but so far has not overruled it.

1967: *Loving v. Virginia*. The Court finds the Virginia state ban on interracial marriage violates Equal Protection and Due Process Clauses of the 14th Amendment.

Race riots in Newark, New Jersey, leave 26 dead and 1,500 injured; race riots in Detroit leave more than 40 dead, 2,000 injured, and 5,000 homeless.

President Johnson appoints Thurgood Marshall to the Court replacing Tom Clark (1949–67). Marshall is the first black justice in the nation's history.

Democrats Carl B. Stokes of Cleveland and Richard G. Hatcher of Gary, Indiana, become the first black mayors of major American cities.

1968: Assassins kill Martin Luther King and Robert Kennedy.

Earl Warren announces his intention to resign as Chief Justice. President Johnson nominates sitting justice Abe Fortas for Chief Justice, but withdraws the nomination following a Senate filibuster led by Republicans and Southern Democrats. Fortas resigns from the Court in 1969 following allegations of financial impropriety arising from investigations made during his nomination.

Richard Nixon is elected President, defeating the Democrat, Vice President Hubert H. Humphrey, in a very close contest. Democrats retain control of both houses of Congress. George Wallace runs as the candidate of the American Independent Party and receives 46 electoral votes. President Nixon calls for the appointment of strict constructionists to the Supreme Court and a greater comparative role for states in the federal system. President Nixon will appoint two new justices during his first two years and four new justices during his first term.

Rep. Shirley Chisholm (D-NY) becomes the first black woman elected to Congress.

Green v. New Kent County School Board: The Court unanimously rejects a "freedom of choice" school desegregation plan and calls for a desegregation plan that promises to engage in actual racial mixing in the public schools.

United States v. O'Brien: The Court holds that burning a draft card as a political protest is not protected "speech."

Duncan v. Louisiana: The Court holds that the right to a jury trial is fundamental to the American scheme of justice and incorporates that right in the 14th Amendment's Due Process Clause as a limit on the States.

Jones v. Alfred H. Mayer Co.: The Court reverses the *Civil Rights Cases*' narrow construction of Congressional power under the 13th Amendment and holds that the 13th Amendment can justify a statutory prohibition on racial discrimination in private housing.

1969: The Stonewall Riots in New York City mark the beginning of an activist gay rights movement.

Four months into his term, with more than half a million U.S. troops in Vietnam, President Nixon announces that the United States will gradually withdraw military forces from Vietnam. The process takes three and a half years.

The first human, Neil Armstrong of the United States, walks on the moon.

President Nixon appoints Warren E. Burger as Chief Justice, replacing Earl Warren (1953–69).

Brandenberg v. Ohio: The Court articulates a modern form of the clear and present danger test.

1970: President Nixon appoints Harry A. Blackmun to the Court after two failed nominations, replacing Abe Fortas (1965–69).

Lorna Lockwood of Arizona becomes the first woman chief justice of a state supreme court.

President Nixon sends U.S. troops into Cambodia in order to destroy bases that are being used to support Communists in Vietnam. Congress does not authorize the action, but provides funding. The incursion exacerbates anti-war protests., striking critics as an expansion of the war.

The computer floppy disk is invented.

The first Earth Day reflects growing environmental activism.

1971: The 26th Amendment lowers the voting age to eighteen.

Congress rescinds the Tonkin Gulf Resolution, but continues to provide funding for the war in Vietnam.

President Nixon appoints Lewis F. Powell, Jr., to the Court, replacing Hugo Black (1937–71), and William Rehnquist, replacing John Harlan (1955–71).

New York Times v. United States: The Court holds that an injunction preventing the publication of the Pentagon Papers is an invalid prior restraint.

Reed v. Reed: Using rational basis language, the Court begins the era of heightened scrutiny for gender discrimination and voids an Idaho statutory preference for men in the administration of estates ("rational basis with bite").

Swann v. Charlotte-Mecklenburg County Bd. of Education: The Court unanimously approves busing as a permissible remedy for school segregation. Anti-busing amendments to the Constitution are proposed in Congress, but fail.

Lemon v. Kurtzman: The Court holds that a statute must satisfy three criteria in order to withstand a constitutional challenge under the Establishment Clause: (1) the statute must have a secular legislative purpose; (2) its principal or primary effect must be one that neither advances nor inhibits religion; and (3) it must not foster an excessive government entanglement with religion.

President Nixon ends the convertibility of the dollar into gold.

1972: President Nixon opens diplomatic relations with communist China.

Burglars break into the Democratic National Headquarters in the Watergate complex in Washington, D.C. The burglars, it turns out, were hired by the Committee to Re-elect the President (Nixon). A subsequent cover-up will eventually topple the Nixon presidency.

President Nixon wins re-election in a 49-state landslide over the Democrat, George McGovern. Democrats retain control of both houses of Congress.

Congress approves the Equal Rights Amendment and sends it to the states for ratification.

Ms. Magazine begins publication.

Sony introduces the video recorder and the VCR.

Furman v. Georgia: The Court, in a 5–4 decision, voids existing death sentences, concluding that they are the product of procedures that violate Due Process. In 1976, the Court approves newly adopted procedures in *Gregg v. Georgia*, thereby permitting the resumption of the death penalty.

Moose Lodge No. 107 v. Irvis: The Court begins a restrictive view of state action with the adoption of a "nexus" requirement between a private actor's wrongful act and the government.

1973: On January 27, the United States and North Vietnam sign a peace treaty that ends U.S. military participation in the Vietnam war.

President Nixon fires special prosecutor Archibald Cox, who is investigating the Watergate break-in and cover-up.

Conflict between President Nixon and Congress over presidential impoundment of funds authorized by Congress for expenditure.

War Powers Resolution, passed over President Nixon's veto, requires President to inform Congress of use of military forces abroad and to obtain authorization for continuation of their use.

The federal government establishes the Internet to link American University and government computers.

Frontiero v. Richardson: Four justices of the Court conclude that gender discrimination should receive strict scrutiny; three justices say the Court should wait for the ratification of the Equal Rights Amendment to resolve the issue.

Roe v. Wade: The Court holds that a limited right to abortion is protected under the 14th Amendment Due Process Clause.

Miller v. California: The Court agrees on a test for pornography that is easier for prosecutors to meet. The plurality test requiring that material be utterly without redeeming social value in order to be labeled obscene is replaced with a test that the allegedly obscene material must lack "serious literary, artistic, political, or scientific value." The Court also rejects the requirement that prurience and patent offensiveness must be judged by a national standard. Local standards are sufficient.

San Antonio Independent School District v. Rodriguez: The Court, in a 5–4 decision, rejects an equal protection challenge to a state school funding statute, ending the Warren Court's heightened scrutiny of many statutes adversely affecting the poor.

1974:   The House Judiciary Committee votes articles of impeachment against President Nixon.

United States v. Nixon: The Court unanimously orders President Nixon to surrender White House tapes bearing on the Watergate scandal, rejecting the President's claim of executive privilege. Facing eroding support, even within his own party, President Nixon resigns. Gerald Ford assumes the presidency.

1975:   President Ford appoints John P. Stevens to the Court, replacing William O. Douglas (1939–75).

Warth v. Seldin: The Court narrows standing, imposing stricter limits.

On April 30, the South Vietnamese government collapses. North Vietnam conquers South Vietnam and unites North and South under a Communist government. All remaining U.S. diplomats and advisors leave Vietnam. The United States provides political asylum for more than one hundred thousand Vietnamese.

1976:   Jimmy Carter is elected President.

National League of Cities v. Usery: The Court, in a 5–4 decision, overrules precedent and holds that the 10th Amendment prohibits the application of the Fair Labor Standards Act to state employees. The Court suggests that the 10th Amendment is an affirmative limitation on federal legislative power.

Craig v. Boren: The Court holds that gender discrimination against males violates the Equal Protection Clause. The Court resolves the debate over the appropriate level of scrutiny in gender cases with the introduction of intermediate scrutiny.

Washington v. Davis: The Court holds that racially disproportionate impact alone is insufficient to prove a violation of the Equal Protection Clause.

Bishop v. Wood: The Court accepts a restrictive state law definition of property as a trigger for the protections of procedural due process.

Virginia State Bd. of Pharmacy v. Virginia Citizens Consumer Council, Inc.: The Court recognizes commercial speech as coming within the protection of the 1st Amendment.

1977:   *Maher v. Roe*: The Court begins a retreat from *Roe v. Wade* by recasting *Roe* as protecting the right not to be "unduly burdened" in making a decision to terminate a pregnancy.

1978:   *Regents of University of California v. Bakke*: The Court invalidates a racial quota-based affirmative action plan while splitting on the appropriate level of scrutiny to be applied in affirmative action cases.

1979:   Jerry Falwell founds the Moral Majority, a political action group composed of politically conservative Christians.

Iran overthrows the Shah and institutes an Islamic government. On November 4, Iran seizes the U.S. embassy and holds 52 Americans hostage, demanding that the United States return the former Shah to Iran for prosecution. The hostage crisis undermines support for the Carter presidency. The hostages are released on January 20, 1981, after the inauguration of Ronald Reagan.

1980: Ronald Reagan is elected President, defeating incumbent Jimmy Carter. Reagan wins the election by promising smaller government, lower taxes, and a tough stand with the Soviet Union.

Reeves, Inc. v. Stake: The market participant exception is recognized as a limit to the scope of the dormant commerce clause.

1981: AIDS is recognized as a disease; by 1994, AIDS would be the leading cause of death for Americans aged 25–44.

President Reagan appoints Sandra Day O'Connor to the Court, the Court's first female justice, replacing Potter Stewart (1958–81).

Michael M. v. Superior Court: The Court holds that a statute imposing criminal liability when a man has intercourse with a woman under age 18 (but not imposing liability on a woman who has intercourse with a man under age 18) does not violate the Equal Protection Clause. The Court finds the statute is sufficiently related to a legitimate state objective.

Kassell v. Consolidated Freightways Corp.: The Court strikes down an Iowa statute banning double-long tractor-trailers in an opinion noted for differing approaches to the dormant commerce clause.

1981–86: Tax reform acts sharply reduce rates on earned income, leaving little difference between the highest and lowest rates, and reduce taxes on dividends and capital gains.

1982: The extended deadline for ratification of the Equal Rights Amendment expires as opponents, particularly in the South, mobilize and lobby legislatures to vote no.

Plyler v. Doe: The Court uses "rational basis with bite" to void a statute denying public education to the children of illegal aliens.

1983: *Michigan v. Long*: The Court makes it easier to review (and reverse) state court decisions dealing with federal constitutional questions when state constitutional grounds are also mentioned in the opinion.

City of Los Angeles v. Lyons: The Court announces a restrictive interpretation of "ripeness" that means lower federal courts are less likely to be able to issue injunctions against future unconstitutional police behavior. The Court finds no case or controversy present in a suit for injunctive relief brought by a motorist who alleged that he had suffered unconstitutional excessive force in the past and that there was a pattern of such conduct.

INS v. Chadha: The Court holds that a legislative veto of executive action on questions "legislative in character" violates constitutional requirements.

1984: Geraldine Ferraro, (D-N.Y.), becomes the first woman to be nominated for Vice President by a major political party. President Reagan is re-elected in a 49-state landslide over Democrat Walter Mondale.

Lynch v. Donnelly: In a Pawtucket, Rhode Island, creche case, the Court signals a retreat from the *Lemon* Establishment Clause test to a more deferential one that examines governmental coercion or endorsement of religion.

1985: A CD-ROM is developed that can put 270,000 pages of text on a single disk.

Garcia v. SAMTA: The Court, in a 5–4 decision, overrules *National League of Cities* and rejects the 10th Amendment as an affirmative limitation on federal legislative power.

American Booksellers v. Hudnut: The 7th Circuit holds that an ordinance seeking to ban pornography that is not obscene under the *Miller v. California* test (on the ground that it produces subordination of women) violates the 1st Amendment.

1986: *Bowers v. Hardwick*: The Court, in a 5–4 decision, rejects a substantive Due Process challenge to a state sodomy law. The Court upholds the law as applied to consensual homosexual activity that took place in a private home.

President Reagan elevates William H. Rehnquist to Chief Justice, replacing Warren Burger (1969–86), and appoints Antonin Scalia to Rehnquist's associate seat.

1986–87: Iran-Contra scandal, involving the Reagan Administration's failure to secure congressional authorization for sale of weapons to Iran in return for Iran's help in connection with the freeing of hostages in Lebanon.

1988: George Bush is elected President, defeating Democrat Michael Dukakis.

The market share of the "Big 3" television networks drops below 50% for the first time due to the growth of cable television, a trend that has continued.

Nearly 1.4 million illegal aliens meet a deadline for applying for amnesty under a new United States Immigration and Naturalization Service policy.

New Energy Co. of Indiana v. Limbach: The Court reaffirms its Dormant Commerce Clause jurisprudence by holding that state acts that discriminate against interstate commerce are unconstitutional.

After the unsuccessful nominations of Robert Bork and Douglas Ginsburg, President Reagan appoints Anthony Kennedy to the Court, replacing Lewis Powell (1971–87).

Non-Communist governments are formed in Poland and Hungary.

1989: The Tianamen Square crackdown on pro-democracy demonstrators in China is broadcast throughout the world.

Non-Communist government is formed in East Germany after Berlin Wall is torn down; Germany re-unites in 1990. Non-Communist governments are formed in Czechoslovakia and Romania.

Texas v. Johnson: The Court holds a Texas statute unconstitutional as applied to punish flag burning as a political protest.

City of Richmond v. Croson: In a fragmented opinion, the Court invalidates the City of Richmond's minority contractor set-aside program, distinguishes between specific and societal discrimination, and announces strict scrutiny as the appropriate level of review for challenges to state affirmative action plans.

1990: President Bush signs the Americans With Disabilities Act, barring discrimination against the disabled.

President Bush vetoes a civil rights bill that sought, in effect, to reverse several recent Supreme Court decisions that had interpreted various civil rights statutes narrowly. Two years later, Congress enacted the Civil Rights

Restoration Act of 1991 which accomplished similar goals as the prior legislation. This time, President Bush signs the legislation.

President Bush appoints David H. Souter to the Court, replacing William Brennan (1956–90).

Cruzan v. Director, Missouri Dept. of Health: The Court articulates a "clear and convincing" standard as the requirement for the termination of life support for a woman in a permanent vegetative state. The Court speaks in terms of "liberty interests" rather than "fundamental rights," and appears to use "rational basis with bite" rather than strict scrutiny.

Employment Div., Dept. of Human Resources of Oregon v. Smith: The Court holds that infringements on religious practices by statutes of general application are not prohibited by the Free Exercise Clause.

1991: President Bush appoints Clarence Thomas to the Court, replacing Thurgood Marshall (1967–91).

The United States and its allies wage the Persian Gulf War, liberating Kuwait from Iraqi control in only two months. President Bush's commitment of troops had been authorized by congressional resolution in 1990.

The Soviet Union dissolves, its constituent parts emerging as independent countries. Yugoslavia dissolves as well, with great violence in Serbia, Croatia, and Bosnia.

The VCR becomes the fastest selling domestic appliance in history.

Dowell v. Oklahoma: The Court ends the school desegregation era with a ruling that school boards that have achieved unitary status have no further duty to overcome school segregation that results from segregated housing patterns.

1992: Bill Clinton is elected President with 43% of the popular vote. Incumbent George Bush receives 38% of the popular vote while Reform Party candidate Ross Perot captures 19%.

Five days of rioting in Los Angeles, following the acquittal of police officers for the videotaped beating of Rodney King, leaves more than 50 dead and 2,300 injured, and an estimated $1 billion in property damage.

Carol E. Moseley Braun (D-Ill.) is the first African-American woman elected to the United States Senate.

President Clinton appoints Ruth Bader Ginsburg to the Court, replacing Byron White (1962–93).

R.A.V. v. St. Paul: The Court holds that even speech that is not protected by the 1st Amendment cannot be regulated in a manner that reflects content or viewpoint discrimination.

Planned Parenthood v. Casey: The Court rejects calls for a reversal of *Roe v. Wade* in a fragmented series of plurality opinions, but allows much regulation under an "undue burden" standard.

Lee v. Weisman: The Court sidesteps calls to overrule the *Lemon* test and voids school-sanctioned prayer at graduation ceremony as coercive.

International Society for Krishna Consciousness, Inc. v. Lee: A closely divided Court continues a trend begun during the early 1980s of limiting the scope of "traditional public forums" and upholding "reasonable" regulation in non-public fora. The Court upholds a ban on solicitation at an airport, but rejects a ban on literature distribution.

New York v. United States: The Court continues its *National League of Cities-Garcia* dispute over the nature of the 10th Amendment as it invalidates part of a federal environmental statute that requires the states to engage in a certain type of regulation pertaining to the disposal of hazardous wastes.

1993: Islamic fundamentalist terrorists bomb the World Trade Center in New York. In Waco, Texas, a 51-day siege conducted by the FBI and the Bureau of Alcohol, Tobacco, and Firearms of an armed compound controlled by a religious cult called the Branch Davidians ends with 82 deaths.

Congress enacts the Religious Freedom Restoration Act in response to the Court's decision in *Employment Div., Dept. of Human Resources of Oregon v. Smith* (1991). The Act requires strict scrutiny of governmental statutes of general application that infringe the free exercise of religion. In 1997, in *City of Boerne v. Flores*, the Court will hold that Congress lacks power under Section 5 of the 14th Amendment to enact the Religious Freedom Restoration Act.

World Wide Web Usage explodes. By 1999, 150 million people will log on every week.

While homosexuality remains a grounds for discharge, President Clinton announces a "don't ask, don't tell" policy for homosexuals in the United States military. Significant numbers of servicemen and women who disclose their sexual orientation will be discharged pursuant to this policy.

Shaw v. Reno: The Court uses strict scrutiny to invalidate North Carolina congressional districts that had been drawn to facilitate the election of minority candidates for Congress, and coincidentally helped to elect more Republicans.

President Clinton appoints Ruth Bader Ginsburg to the Supreme Court, replacing Byron R. White.

1994: President Clinton appoints Stephen Breyer to the Court, replacing Harry Blackmun (1970–94).

Republicans win majorities in both houses of Congress for the first time since 1952, ending the longest period of single-party rule in U.S. history. Republicans run on a platform called the "Contract with America," which promises to reduce the size of the federal government and return power to the states.

White supremacist Byron De La Beckwith is convicted of the 1963 murder of Medgar Evars in Jackson, Mississippi, by a racially integrated jury. He had been tried twice in 1964, but all-white juries had deadlocked both times.

The United States government privatizes the Internet.

J.E.B. v. Alabama: The Court extends the ban on the use of peremptory challenges to include jurors struck because of their gender as well as because of their race.

1995: Timothy McVeigh bombs the federal building in Oklahoma City to protest against the federal government. The bombing leaves 168 dead.

O.J. Simpson is acquitted of the 1994 murders of Nicole Simpson and Ron Goldman after spending $6 million on his defense.

United States v. Lopez: The Court, in a 5–4 decision, declares that an Act of Congress banning possession of guns near a school exceeds congressional power under the Commerce Clause.

Adarand Constructors, Inc. v. Pena: The Court, in a 5–4 decision, establishes strict scrutiny as the standard for all affirmative action programs.

U.S. Term Limits v. Thornton: The Court invalidates an amendment to the Arkansas Constitution which precludes persons who have served a certain number of terms in the United States Congress from having their names placed on the ballot for election to Congress.

1996: Congress passes and President Clinton signs welfare reform legislation that tightens eligibility requirements for the receipt of welfare benefits. Congress enacts, but President Clinton vetoes, legislation imposing a federal ban on "partial birth" abortions.

Romer v. Evans: The Court invalidates a Colorado constitutional amendment that would have prohibited localities from protecting homosexuals under laws that prohibit discrimination based on sexual orientation. The Court uses what appears to be "rational basis with bite" Equal Protection analysis to invalidate the amendment.

United States v. Virginia: The Court invalidates a ban on female admissions to VMI. The decision raises the possibility of a new level of scrutiny for gender.

Hopwood v. Texas: The United States Court of Appeals for the 5th Circuit holds that the use of race as a factor in university admissions is unconstitutional. The Supreme Court declines to consider the case.

1997: *Washington v. Glucksberg*: The Court holds that a Washington state statute's ban on physician-assisted suicide for terminally ill patients does not violate the Due Process Clause of the 14th Amendment. The Court emphasizes the nation's history, legal traditions, and practices which it says demonstrate that the Anglo-American common law has disapproved of assisting suicide for 700 years.

Clinton v. Jones: The Court rules that a sitting president may be sued civilly during his term for acts which occurred before he assumed office.

Printz v. United States: The Court, in a 5–4 decision, strikes down provisions of the Brady Handgun Violence Prevention Act as violating the concept of "dual sovereignty" implicit in the structure of the Constitution and reinforced by the 10th Amendment. Significantly, the Act's provisions, which required state officials to conduct record checks of gun buyers, were within the scope of the Commerce Clause, but nonetheless were held to violate state sovereignty.

Reno v. ACLU: In the Communications Decency Act, Congress banned sending patently offensive, indecent, or obscene materials by computer to persons under 18 years of age. The Court held these were content-based restrictions on speech and that the ban on offensive or indecent materials was unconstitutionally overbroad.

1998: Revelations of President Clinton's sexual affair with White House intern Monica Lewinsky dominate the news and lead to events that culminate in Clinton's December impeachment by the House of Representatives.

American embassies in Kenya and Tanzania are bombed by terrorists.

Searchers unsuccessfully comb western North Carolina mountains for alleged abortion clinic bomber John Rudolf.

Clinton v. City of New York: The Court strikes down legislation giving the president a line item veto.

1999: President Clinton is acquitted on impeachment charges after a Senate trial.

Two students kill 13 of their classmates at Columbine High School in Colorado, fueling a national debate over guns and violence in American society.

Florida begins a voucher program, providing public funds for use by students to attend private schools if their "home" school fails to meet certain criteria.

NATO bombs Serbian positions in effort to end ethnic violence in Kosovo, leading to Serbian retreat and NATO occupation.

Alden v. Maine: The Court, in another 5–4 decision, continues its expansive view of federalism, exemplified by *United States v. Printz*. The Court had previously ruled that the 11th Amendment prohibits states from being sued in *federal* court without their permission. In *Alden*, it holds that the doctrine of sovereign immunity means that Congress (when acting pursuant to its Article I powers) cannot provide a cause of action against states in *state* court either.

Saenz v. Roe: The Court invokes the Privileges or Immunities Clause of the 14th Amendment to strike down California's refusal to pay new residents the same welfare given to longer term California residents, if the California welfare was a higher rate of welfare than they had received in their previous state. The lower rate prevailed until they had resided in California for one year.

2000: Vermont becomes the first state to allow same-sex couples to enter into civil unions. The Vermont legislature passed "An Act Relating to Civil Unions" after the Vermont Supreme Court ruled in December 1999 that denying the benefits of marriage to same-sex couples violated the Vermont constitution. The Act conferred the legal benefits and responsibilities of marriage, but not the name.

Scientists announce a complete mapping of the human genome, raising the possibility of dramatic advances in genetic engineering.

Bush v. Gore: The Supreme Court renders a decision that stops the recount of votes in Florida, insuring the presidential election of George W. Bush over incumbent Vice President Al Gore

United States v. Morrison: The Court holds in a 5–4 decision that the federal Violence Against Women Act exceeds congressional power under the

Commerce Clause, rejecting extensive findings showing the aggregate effect of such violence on commerce.

Kimel v. Florida Board of Regents: The Court holds in another 5–4 decision that the federal Age Discrimination in Employment Act cannot be applied to prohibit age discrimination by the states. Neither the Commerce Clause nor the 14th Amendment can justify the statute. Sovereign immunity prevents enforcement under the Commerce Clause and enforcement under the 14th Amendment is barred because the elderly are not a protected class under the 14th Amendment's Equal Protection Clause.

Boy Scouts of America v. Dale: The Court overturns a New Jersey statute requiring Boy Scouts to admit gay leaders, basing its decision on the 1st Amendment right of association.

2001: George W. Bush announces that the White House will no longer ask the American Bar Association to evaluate nominees for the federal judiciary, a practice dating to the Eisenhower administration.

United States Senator James Jeffords (R-Vt.) leaves the Republican Party, giving control of the Senate to the Democrats. Republicans retain control of the House of Representatives.

The economy enters a recession, ending the longest period of economic expansion in U.S. history (since 1991).

Al-Qaida terrorists hijack and crash 2 airliners into the World Trade Center in New York and an airliner into the Pentagon. Approximately three thousand persons die. A 4th hijacked airliner crashes into the Pennsylvania countryside following a passenger revolt against the hijackers.

Allied forces invade Afghanistan in an effort to eradicate the bases of Osama bin Laden and the Al-Qaida terrorist network. The war displaces the Taliban regime that had given shelter to the terrorists.

Five people die after unwitting exposure to envelopes containing anthrax, raising fears of bio-terrorism.

Enron Corporation, a Texas energy-trading company, files the largest bankruptcy in American history amid charges of corrupt accounting practices and manipulation of electric rates causing huge increases in certain states. Discovery of accounting irregularities subsequently causes other large corporations to collapse and contributes to the continued downward spiral of the U.S. economy.

Board of Trustees of the University of Alabama v. Garrett: The Court continues its 5–4 split over federalism. The majority rules that states are immune from employment claims for damages under the Americans With Disabilities Act. Sovereign immunity prevents liability under the Commerce Clause and liability under the Equal Protection Clause is barred because the disabled are not a protected class under the Equal Protection Clause.

Nguyen v. Immigration and Naturalization Service: The Court rejects an Equal Protection challenge to an immigration law that makes it easier for an illegitimate child born overseas to become an American citizen if the mother is an American than if the father is an American.

2002: *Zelman v. Simmons-Harris*: The Court upholds the city of Cleveland's school voucher program that allows parents to use government-provided vouchers at religious schools.

Atkins v. Virginia: The Court bans the execution of the mentally retarded as a violation of 8th Amendment.

Federal Maritime Commission v. South Carolina Ports Authority: The Court extends state sovereign immunity for lawsuits brought by individuals under statutes based on the Commerce Clause. Immunity now extends beyond actions in federal and state courts to include actions in federal executive agencies.

Republican Party of Minnesota v. White (5–4): The Court holds that the 1st Amendment prevents states from restricting judicial candidates from announcing their views on specific issues during their election campaigns.

2003: The United States and its allies invade and occupy Iraq and depose the dictator Saddam Hussein after Congress authorizes military action in 2002 in response to President Bush's warnings that Iraq has "weapons of mass destruction." No weapons of mass destruction are found. Insurgents, opposed to the United States' occupation and the new Iraqi government, wreak havoc throughout the country.

Grutter v. Bollinger (5–4): The Court upholds the use of an affirmative action program at the University of Michigan Law School, while striking one down at the university's undergraduate campus. *Gratz v. Bollinger* (5–4).

Lawrence v. Texas: Five members of the Court overrule *Bowers v. Hardwick* and strike down a criminal sodomy law that applies only to single sex couples, finding it a violation of the right to privacy found in the due process clause of the Fourteenth Amendment. Justice O'Connor also strikes the statute down, but on equal protection grounds only.

The Supreme Judicial Court of Massachusetts decides *Goodridge v. Dept. of Public Health* and declares that prohibiting gay marriage violates the state constitution's "common benefits" clause. The court rejects a legislative compromise that would have created civil unions for same-sex couples and orders that marriage licenses be issued on May 17, 2004. The first same-sex marriage in the United States takes place May 17, 2004, in Cambridge, Massachusetts. As of July, 2005, eighteen states have amended their constitutions to expressly ban same-sex marriage in *Goodridge's* wake.

2004: George W. Bush defeats John Kerry in the presidential election. Republicans firmly retain control of both houses of Congress as Democrats lose seats in each.

2005: *Gonzales v. Raich* (6–3): The Court upholds the power of the federal government to use the Interstate Commerce Clause to prevent California from legalizing the personal use of medicinal marijuana pursuant to the state's Compassionate Use Act of 1996.

Justice Sandra Day O'Connor resigns from the Supreme Court after twenty-four years. Chief Justice William Rehnquist dies in office after thirty-three years. George W. Bush nominates and the Senate confirms Judge John G. Roberts, Jr., (R-Md.), of the United States Court of Appeals for the D.C. Circuit to replace Chief Justice Rehnquist. Bush nominates Judge Samuel

Alito, (R-N.J.), of the United States Court of Appeals for the Third Circuit to replace Justice O'Connor.

The Canadian Parliament passes a statute approving gay marriage throughout Canada. The statute follows judicial victories in challenges brought under the Canadian constitution that had legalized gay marriage in certain provinces and that had ruled that the Parliament had authority to pass such a statute. Canada joins the Netherlands (2000), Belgium (2003), and Spain (2005) as major countries recognizing gay marriage. Several European countries and New Zealand have civil union statutes.

Connecticut becomes the first state to allow civil unions for same-sex couples by action of the legislature without prior litigation and a judicial decree.

Terrorists bomb London transportation system.

2007: *Parents Involved in Community Schools v. Seattle School District No. 1*: Court prohibits assignment of students to public schools solely for the purpose of achieving racial integration. *Gonzales v. Carhardt*: the Court upholds a congressional statute without a health exception, banning "partial birth abortion." The decision effectively overrules prior precedent and reflects a shift in the Court after Justice O'Connor's resignation and her replacement by Justice Alito.

Great Recession begins. Unemployment reaches nearly ten percent by 2010.

2008: *District of Columbia v. Heller*: The Court holds that the Second Amendment protects an individual's right to possess firearms for private use in federal enclaves.

Boumediene v. Bush: The Court holds that the Military Commissions Act of 2006 unconstitutionally suspended *habeas corpus*.

Financial crisis generates legislation to provide massive federal funds to "bail out" financial institutions.

Barack Obama, a Democrat, becomes the first African-American elected to the presidency. Democrats increase their majority in the Senate and take control of the House for the first time in fourteen years.

2009: President Obama appoints Sonia Sotomayor to the Supreme Court, replacing David H. Souter.

2010: Congress enacts a comprehensive program of federal health care.

President Obama appoints Elena Kagan to the Supreme Court, replacing John Paul Stevens.

Citizens United v. Federal Elections Commission: The Court invalidates federal law prohibiting for profit non-media corporations and labor unions from paying with corporate or union treasury funds for broadcasting ads about candidates in federal election campaigns when the ads are run within sixty days of a general election or within thirty days of a primary. The decision substantially overrules *McConnell v. Federal Election Commission* (2003) which had upheld the McCain-Feingold campaign reform act against a facial challenge. The decision is another indication of a shift in the Court after the resignation of Justice O'Connor.

McDonald v. *Chicago*: In a 5–4 decision, the court holds that an individual right to bear arms is incorporated as a limit on the states. Justice Thomas concurs basing incorporation on the Privileges or Immunities Clause.

Justices of the U.S. Supreme Court

Reprinted with permission from Melvin I. Urofsky and Paul Finkelman, *A March of Liberty: A Constitutional History of the United States*, 2 vols. (New York: Oxford University Press, 2002), pp. A 28–A 36.

THE NUMBER (1) indicates the Chief Justice; the other numbers show the order in which the original members of the Court were appointed, and then the order of succession. For example, if we follow the number (4) we see that James Wilson was succeeded first by Bushrod Washington, then by Henry Baldwin, and so on.

Many of those who have served on the nation's highest court have either not been well served by biographers or have been outright ignored. There are good sources for biographical and analytical essays on these, and in fact on all the justices. The most recent scholarship is contained in the essays in Melvin I. Urofsky, ed., *The Supreme Court Justices: A Biographical Dictionary* (1994). Leon Friedman and Fred L. Israel, eds., *The Justices of the United States Supreme Court, 1789–1978: Their Lives and Major Opinions* 5 vols. (1969–1980) is still useful, and also has some of the more important opinions.

Appointed by George Washington

(1) *John Jay* (1745–1829); Federalist from New York; served 1789–1795; resigned.

(2) *John Rutledge* (1739–1800); Federalist from South Carolina; appointed 1789; resigned 1791, without ever sitting.

(3) *William Cushing* (1732–1810); Federalist from Massachusetts; served 1789–1810; died.

(4) *James Wilson* (1742–1798); Federalist from Pennsylvania; served 1789–1798; died.

(5) *John Blair* (1731–1800); Federalist from Virginia; served 1789–1796; resigned.

(6) *James Iredell* (1751–1799); Federalist from North Carolina; served 1790–1799; died.

(2) *Thomas Johnson* (1732–1819); Federalist from Maryland; served 1791–1793; resigned.

(2) *William Paterson* (1745–1806); Federalist from New Jersey; served 1793–1806; died.

(1) *John Rutledge* (1739–1800); Federalist from South Carolina; unconfirmed recess appointment in 1795.

(5) *Samuel Chase* (1741–1811); Federalist from Maryland; served 1796–1811; died.

(1) *Oliver Ellsworth* (1745–1807); Federalist from Connecticut; served 1796–1800; resigned.

Appointed by John Adams

(4) *Bushrod Washington* (1762–1829); Federalist from Pennsylvania and Virginia; served 1798–1829; died.

(6) *Alfred Moore* (1755–1810); Federalist from North Carolina; served 1799–1804; resigned.

(1) *John Marshall* (1755–1835); Federalist from Virginia; served 1801–1835; died.

Appointed by Thomas Jefferson

(6) *William Johnson* (1771–1834); Republican from South Carolina; served 1804–1834; died.

(2) *Henry Brockholst Livingston* (1757–1823); Republican from New York; served 1806–1823; died.

(7) *Thomas Todd* (1765–1826); Republican from Kentucky; served 1807–1826; died.

Appointed by James Madison

(5) *Gabriel Duvall* (1752–1844); Republican from Maryland; served 1811–1835; resigned.

(3) *Joseph Story* (1799–1845); Republican from Massachusetts; served 1811–1845; died.

Appointed by James Monroe

(2) *Smith Thompson* (1768–1843); Republican from New York; served 1823–1843; died.

Appointed by John Quincy Adams

(7) *Robert Trimble* (1776–1828); Republican from Kentucky; served 1826–1828; died.

Appointed by Andrew Jackson

(7) *John McLean* (1785–1861); Democrat (later Republican) from Ohio; served 1829–1861; died.

(4) *Henry Baldwin* (1780–1844); Democrat from Pennsylvania; served 1830–1844; died.

(6) *James Moore Wayne* (1790–1867); Democrat from Georgia; served 1835–1867; died.

(1) *Roger Brooke Taney* (1777–1864); Democrat from Maryland; served 1836–1864; died.

(5) *Philip Pendleton Barbour* (1783–1841); Democrat from Virginia; served 1836–1841; died.

Appointed by Martin Van Buren

(8) *John Catron* (1786–1865); Democrat from Tennessee; served 1837–1865; died.

(9) *John McKinley* (1780–1852); Democrat from Kentucky; served 1837–1852; died.

(5) *Peter Vivian Daniel* (1784–1860); Democrat from Virginia; served 1841–1860; died.

Appointed by John Tyler

(2) *Samuel Nelson* (1792–1873); Democrat from New York; served 1845–1872; resigned.

Appointed by James K. Polk

(3) *Levi Woodbury* (1789–1851); Democrat from New Hampshire; served 1845–1851; died.

(4) *Robert Cooper Grier* (1794–1870); Democrat from Pennsylvania; served 1846–1870; resigned.

Appointed by Millard Fillmore

(3) *Benjamin Robbins Curtis* (1809–1874); Whig from Massachusetts; served 1851–1857; resigned.

Appointed by Franklin Pierce

(9) *John Archibald Campbell* (1811–1889); Democrat from Alabama; served 1853–1861; resigned.

Appointed by James Buchanan

(3) *Nathaniel Clifford* (1803–1881); Democrat from Maine; served 1858–1881; died.

Appointed by Abraham Lincoln

(7) *Noah Haynes Swayne* (1804–1884); Republican from Ohio; served 1862–1881; resigned.

(5) *Samuel Freeman Miller* (1816–1890); Republican from Iowa; served 1862–1890; died.

(9) *David Davis* (1815–1886); Republican (later Democrat) from Illinois; served 1862–1877; resigned.

(10) *Stephen Johnson Field* (1816–1899); Democrat from California; served 1863–1897; resigned.

(1) *Salmon P. Chase* (1808–1873); Republican from Ohio; served 1864–1873; died.

Appointed by Ulysses S. Grant

(4) *William Strong* (1808–1895); Republican from Pennsylvania; served 1870–1880; resigned.

(6) *Joseph Philo Bradley* (1803–1892); Republican from New Jersey; served 1870–1892; died.

(2) *Ward Hunt* (1810–1886); Republican from New York; served 1873–1882; resigned.

(1) *Morrison Remick Waite* (1816–1888); Republican from Ohio; served 1874–1888; died.

Appointed by Rutherford B. Hayes

(9) *John Marshall Harlan* (1833–1911); Republican from Kentucky; served 1877–1911; died.

(4) *William Burnham Woods* (1824–1887); Republican from Georgia; served 1880–1887; died.

Appointed by James A. Garfield

(7) *Stanley Matthews* (1824–1889); Republican from Ohio; served 1881–1889; died.

Appointed by Chester Arthur

(3) *Horace Gray* (1828–1902); Republican from Massachusetts; served 1881–1902; died.

(2) *Samuel M. Blatchford* (1820–1893); Republican from New York; served 1882–1893; died.

Appointed by Grover Cleveland (First Term)

(4) *Lucius Quintus Cincinnatus Lamar* (1825–1893); Democrat from Mississippi; served 1888–1893; died.

(1) *Melville Weston Fuller* (1833–1910); Democrat from Illinois; served 1888–1910; died.

Appointed by Benjamin Harrison

(7) *David Josiah Brewer* (1837–1910); Republican from Kansas; served 1889–1910; died.

(5) *Henry Billings Brown* (1836–1913); Republican from Michigan; served 1891–1906; resigned.

(6) *George Shiras, Jr.* (1832–1924); Republican from Pennsylvania; served 1892–1903; resigned.

(4) *Howell Edmunds Jackson* (1832–1895); Democrat from Tennessee; served 1893–1895; died.

Appointed by Grover Cleveland (Second Term)

(2) *Edward Douglass White* (1845–1921); Democrat from Louisiana; served 1894–1910; promoted to chief justice.

(4) *Rufus Wheeler Peckham* (1838–1909); Democrat from New York; served 1895–1909; died.

Appointed by William McKinley

(10, now 8) *Joseph McKenna* (1843–1926); Republican from California; served 1898–1925; resigned.

Appointed by Theodore Roosevelt

(3) *Oliver Wendell Holmes, Jr.* (1841–1935); Republican from Massachusetts; served 1902–1932; resigned.

(6) *William Rufus Day* (1849–1923); Republican from Ohio; served 1903–1922; resigned.

(5) *William Henry Moody* (1853–1917); Republican from Massachusetts; served 1906–1910; resigned.

Appointed by William Howard Taft

(4) *Horace Hannon Lurton* (1844–1914); Democrat from Tennessee; served 1909–1914; died.

(7) *Charles Evans Hughes* (1862–1948); Republican from New York; served 1910–1916; resigned.

(1) *Edward Douglass White* (1845–1921); promoted from associate justice; served 1910–1921; died.

(2) *Willis Van Devanter* (1859–1941); Republican from Wyoming; served 1910–1937; resigned.

(5) *Joseph Rucker Lamar* (1857–1916); Democrat from Georgia; served 1911–1916; died.

(9) *Mahlon Pitney* (1858–1924); Republican from New Jersey; served 1912–1922; retired.

Appointed by Woodrow Wilson

(4) *James Clark McReynolds* (1862–1946); Democrat from Tennessee; served 1914–1941; retired.

(5) *Louis Dembitz Brandeis* (1856–1941); Democrat from Massachusetts; served 1916–1939; retired.

(7) *John Hessin Clarke* (1857–1945); Democrat from Ohio; served 1916–1922; resigned.

Appointed by Warren G. Harding

(1) *William Howard Taft* (1857–1930); Republican from Ohio; served 1921–1930; resigned.

(7) *George Sutherland* (1862–1942); Republican from Utah; served 1922–1938; retired.

(6) *Pierce Butler* (1866–1939); Democrat from Minnesota; served 1922–1939; retired.

(9) *Edward Terry Sanford* (1865–1930); Republican from Tennessee; served 1923–1930; died.

Appointed by Calvin Coolidge

(8) *Harlan Fiske Stone* (1872–1946); Republican from New York: served 1925–1941; promoted to chief justice.

Appointed by Herbert Hoover

(1) *Charles Evans Hughes* (1862–1948); Republican from New York; served 1930–1941; retired.

(9) *Owen Josephus Roberts* (1875–1955); Republican from Pennsylvania; served 1930–1945; resigned.

(3) *Benjamin Nathan Cardozo* (1870–1938); Democrat from New York; served 1932–1938; died.

Appointed by Franklin D. Roosevelt

(2) *Hugo Lafayette Black* (1886–1971); Democrat from Alabama; served 1937–1971; retired.

(7) *Stanley Forman Reed* (1884–1980); Democrat from Kentucky; served 1938–1957; retired.

(3) *Felix Frankfurter* (1882–1965); Independent from Massachusetts; served 1939–1962; retired.

(5) *William Orville Douglas* (1898–1980); Democrat from Connecticut; served 1939–1975; retired.

(6) *Frank Murphy* (1890–1949); Democrat from Michigan; served 1940–1949; died.

(4) *James Francis Byrnes* (1879–1972); Democrat from South Carolina; served 1941–1942; resigned.

(1) *Harlan Fiske Stone* (1872–1946); promoted from associate justice; served 1941–1946; died.

(8) *Robert Houghwout Jackson* (1892–1954); Democrat from New York; served 1941–1954; died.

(4) *Wiley Blount Rutledge* (1894–1949); Democrat from Iowa; served 1943–1949; died.

Appointed by Harry S. Truman

(9) *Harold Hitz Burton* (1888–1964); Republican from Ohio; served 1945–1958; retired.

(1) *Frederick Moore Vinson* (1890–1953); Democrat from Kentucky; served 1946–1953; died.

(6) *Tom C. Clark* (1899–1977); Democrat from Texas; served 1949–1967; retired.

(4) *Sherman Minton* (1890–1965); Democrat from Indiana; served 1949–1956; retired.

Appointed by Dwight D. Eisenhower

(1) *Earl Warren* (1891–1974); Republican from California; served 1953–1969; retired.

(8) *John Marshall Harlan II* (1899–1971); Republican from New York; served 1955–1971; retired.

(4) *William Joseph Brennan, Jr.* (1906–1997); Democrat from New Jersey; served 1956–1990; retired.

(7) *Charles Evans Whittaker* (1901–1973); Republican from Missouri; served 1957–1962; retired.

(9) *Potter Stewart* (1915–1985); Republican from Ohio; served 1958–1981; retired.

Appointed by John F. Kennedy

(7) *Byron Raymond White* (1917–2000); Democrat from Colorado; served 1962–1993; retired.

(3) *Arthur Joseph Goldberg* (1908–1990); Democrat from Illinois; served 1962–1965; resigned.

Appointed by Lyndon B. Johnson

(3) *Abe Fortas* (1910–1982); Democrat from Tennessee; served 1965–1969; resigned.

(6) *Thurgood Marshall* (1908–1993); Democrat from New York, served 1967–1991; retired.

Appointed by Richard M. Nixon

(1) *Warren Earl Burger* (1907–1995); Republican from Minnesota; served 1969–1986; retired.

(3) *Harry Andrew Blackmun* (1908–1999); Republican from Minnesota; served 1970–1994; retired.

(2) *Lewis Franklin Powell, Jr.* (1907–1998); Democrat from Virginia; served 1972–1987; retired.

(8) *William Hubbs Rehnquist* (1924–2005); Republican from Arizona; served 1972–1986; promoted to chief justice.

Appointed by Gerald Ford

(5) *John Paul Stevens* (1920–); Republican from Illinois; served 1975–2010; retired.

Appointed by Ronald Reagan

(9) *Sandra Day O'Connor* (1930–); Republican from Arizona; served 1981–2006; retired.

(1) *William Hubbs Rehnquist* (1924–2005); promoted from associate justice; served 1986–2005; died.

(8) *Antonin Scalia* (1936–); Republican from Ohio and Virginia; served 1986–.

(2) *Anthony M. Kennedy* (1936–); Republican from California; served 1988–.

Appointed by George Bush

(4) *David Hackett Souter* (1939–); Republican from New Hampshire; served 1990–2009; retired

(6) *Clarence Thomas* (1948–); Republican from Georgia; served 1991–.

Appointed by William Clinton

(7) *Ruth Bader Ginsburg* (1933–); Democrat from New York; served 1993–.

(3) *Stephen G. Breyer* (1938–); Democrat from Massachusetts; served 1994–.

Appointed by George W. Bush

(1) *John G. Roberts, Jr.* (1955–); Republican from Maryland; served 2005–.

(9) *Samuel A. Alito, Jr.* (1950–); Republican from New Jersey; served 2006–.

Appointed by Barack Obama

(4) *Sonia Sotomayor,* (1954–); Democrat from New York; served 2009–.

(5) *Elena Kagan,* (1960–); Democrat from Massachusetts; served 2010–.

Constitutional Law
in Context

Chapter 1

An Introduction to American Constitutional Law

Contents

I.	The Articles of Confederation	5
II.	The Constitution of the United States of America	6
III.	The Constitution: Institutions, Powers, and Limits	20
IV.	What Is *Constitutional* Law?	21
V.	On Reading the Constitution	32
	A. Types of Constitutional Arguments	34
	B. Goals for Reviewing the Types of Constitutional Arguments	38
	C. Exercises	39
VI.	A Problem for Constitutional Analysis: The Clinton Impeachment	40

Chapter 1

An Introduction to American Constitutional Law

I. The Articles of Confederation

The Second Continental Congress drafted the Declaration of Independence in 1776 and then turned its attention to drafting a document that would provide a structure for the new federal constitutional order. Most states had already adopted their own constitutions by the time the Congress had finished the Articles of Confederation in 1777. The state constitutions commonly provided for three distinct branches of government: the legislative, the executive, and the judicial. Many gave the legislatures broad authority. For example, the Delaware Constitution of 1776 gave the legislature "all ... powers necessary for the legislature of a free and independent State," while the Georgia Constitution of 1777 provided that "The house of assembly shall have power to make such laws and regulations as may be conducive to the good order and well-being of the State." The state constitutions typically had either a Bill of Rights or extensive listings of the rights their citizens possessed against the new state government.

The Articles of Confederation (1777) stated that "The said States hereby severally enter into a firm league of friendship with each other, for their common defence." While the league was to be "perpetual," the entity created was somewhere between a military alliance and a nation. While state governments were given open-ended grants of authority, the national government had only those powers "expressly delegated" in the Articles. The Congress was not given the power to tax individuals or to draft troops. In both instances, Congress could only send requests to the state legislatures, which had the power to tax and to raise militias. While states had executives and judiciaries, the Articles created neither a president nor a national court system. Each state had one vote in a unicameral legislature. Finally, while the Articles could be amended, any amendments had to be approved unanimously.

No attempt was made to regulate slavery, which at the time was legal in all 13 states. Only "free inhabitants" were entitled to travel interstate and enjoy the "privileges and immunities of free citizens in the several States." (An effort by several southern states to insert the word "white" before "free inhabitants" was defeated.) States were required to provide militia to the national government "in proportion to the number of white inhabitants in such State."

While the new continental government was able to win the American Revolution, the postwar era saw a period of economic upheaval. States printed their own paper money, states allowed the repudiation of debts, and the national government continued to have difficulties raising revenues. A convention convened in 1787 to address the shortcomings of the Articles and propose amendments. Its leaders quickly decided to abandon the Articles and their requirement of unanimity and set out to create a document that would give the United States a new, stronger national government.

II. The Constitution of the United States of America[1]

We the People of the United States, in Order to form a more perfect Union, establish Justice, insure domestic Tranquility, provide for the common defence, promote the general Welfare, and secure the Blessings of Liberty to ourselves and our Posterity, do ordain and establish this Constitution for the United States of America.

ARTICLE I

SECTION 1. All legislative Powers herein granted shall be vested in a Congress of the United States, which shall consist of a Senate and House of Representatives.

SECTION 2. [1] The House of Representatives shall be composed of Members chosen every second Year by the People of the several States, and the Electors in each State shall have the Qualifications requisite for Electors of the most numerous Branch of the State Legislature.

[2] No Person shall be a Representative who shall not have attained to the Age of twenty five Years, and been seven Years a Citizen of the United States, and who shall not, when elected, be an Inhabitant of that State in which he shall be chosen.

[3] {Representatives and direct Taxes shall be apportioned among the several States which may be included within this Union, according to their respective Numbers, which shall be determined by adding to the whole Number of free Persons, including those bound to Service for a Term of Years, and excluding Indians not taxed, three fifths of all other Persons.}[2] The actual Enumeration shall be made within three Years after the first Meeting of the Congress of the United States, and within every subsequent Term of ten Years, in such Manner as they shall by Law direct. The Number of Representatives shall not exceed one for every thirty Thousand, but each State shall have at Least one Representative; and until such enumeration shall be made, the State of New Hampshire shall be entitled to chuse three, Massachusetts eight, Rhode-Island and Providence Plantations one, Connecticut five, New York six, New Jersey four, Pennsylvania eight, Delaware one, Maryland six, Virginia ten, North Carolina five, South Carolina five, and Georgia three.

[4] When vacancies happen in the Representation from any State, the Executive Authority thereof shall issue Writs of Election to fill such Vacancies.

[5] The House of Representatives shall chuse their Speaker and other Officers; and shall have the sole Power of Impeachment.

---

1. The Constitution and all Amendments are presented in their original form. Items which have since been amended or superseded are bracketed and footnoted.

2. The part of this clause relating to the mode of apportionment of representatives among the several States has been affected by the 13th Amendment's abolition of slavery—eliminating "all other persons"—and by §2 of the 14th Amendment, and as to taxes on incomes without apportionment by the 16th Amendment.

SECTION 3. [1] The Senate of the United States shall be composed of two Senators from each State, {chosen by the Legislature thereof,}[3] for six Years; and each Senator shall have one Vote.

[2] Immediately after they shall be assembled in Consequence of the first Election, they shall be divided as equally as may be into three Classes. The Seats of the Senators of the first Class shall be vacated at the Expiration of the second Year, of the second Class at the Expiration of the fourth Year, and of the third Class at the Expiration of the sixth Year, so that one third may be chosen every second Year; {and if Vacancies happen by Resignation, or otherwise, during the Recess of the Legislature of any State, the Executive thereof may make temporary Appointments until the next Meeting of the Legislature, which shall then fill such Vacancies.}[4]

[3] No Person shall be a Senator who shall not have attained to the Age of thirty Years, and been nine Years a Citizen of the United States, and who shall not, when elected, be an Inhabitant of that State for which he shall be chosen.

[4] The Vice President of the United States shall be President of the Senate, but shall have no Vote, unless they be equally divided.

[5] The Senate shall chuse their other Officers, and also a President pro tempore, in the Absence of the Vice President, or when he shall exercise the Office of President of the United States.

[6] The Senate shall have the sole Power to try all Impeachments. When sitting for that Purpose, they shall be on Oath or Affirmation. When the President of the United States is tried, the Chief Justice shall preside: And no Person shall be convicted without the Concurrence of two thirds of the Members present.

[7] Judgment in Cases of Impeachment shall not extend further than to removal from Office, and disqualification to hold and enjoy any Office of honor, Trust or Profit under the United States: but the Party convicted shall nevertheless be liable and subject to Indictment, Trial, Judgment and Punishment, according to Law.

SECTION 4. [1] The Times, Places and Manner of holding Elections for Senators and Representatives, shall be prescribed in each State by the Legislature thereof; but the Congress may at any time by Law make or alter such Regulations, except as to the Places of chusing Senators.

[2] The Congress shall assemble at least once in every Year, and such Meeting shall {be on the first Monday in December,}[5] unless they shall by Law appoint a different Day.

SECTION 5. [1] Each House shall be the Judge of the Elections, Returns and Qualifications of its own Members, and a Majority of each shall constitute a Quorum to do Business; but a smaller Number may adjourn from day to day, and may be authorized to compel the Attendance of absent Members, in such Manner, and under such Penalties as each House may provide.

[2] Each House may determine the Rules of its Proceedings, punish its Members for disorderly Behaviour, and, with the Concurrence of two thirds, expel a Member.

[3] Each House shall keep a Journal of its Proceedings, and from time to time publish the same, excepting such Parts as may in their Judgment require Secrecy; and the Yeas

---

3. This clause has been affected by clause 1 of the 17th Amendment.
4. This clause has been affected by § 2 of the 17th Amendment.
5. This clause has been affected by § 2 of the 20th Amendment.

and Nays of the Members of either House on any question shall, at the Desire of one fifth of those Present, be entered on the Journal.

[4] Neither House, during the Session of Congress, shall, without the Consent of the other, adjourn for more than three days, nor to any other Place than that in which the two Houses shall be sitting.

SECTION 6. [1] {The Senators and Representatives shall receive a Compensation for their Services, to be ascertained by Law, and paid out of the Treasury of the United States.}[6] They shall in all Cases, except Treason, Felony and Breach of the Peace, be privileged from Arrest during their Attendance at the Session of their respective Houses, and in going to and returning from the same; and for any Speech or Debate in either House, they shall not be questioned in any other Place.

[2] No Senator or Representative shall, during the Time for which he was elected, be appointed to any civil Office under the Authority of the United States, which shall have been created, or the Emoluments whereof shall have been increased during such time; and no Person holding any Office under the United States, shall be a Member of either House during his Continuance in Office.

SECTION 7. [1] All Bills for raising Revenue shall originate in the House of Representatives; but the Senate may propose or concur with Amendments as on other Bills.

[2] Every Bill which shall have passed the House of Representatives and the Senate, shall, before it become a Law, be presented to the President of the United States; If he approve he shall sign it, but if not he shall return it, with his Objections to that House in which it shall have originated, who shall enter the Objections at large on their Journal, and proceed to reconsider it. If after such Reconsideration two thirds of that House shall agree to pass the Bill, it shall be sent, together with the Objections, to the other House, by which it shall likewise be reconsidered, and if approved by two thirds of that House, it shall become a Law. But in all such Cases the Votes of both Houses shall be determined by yeas and Nays, and the Names of the Persons voting for and against the Bill shall be entered on the Journal of each House respectively. If any Bill shall not be returned by the President within ten Days (Sundays excepted) after it shall have been presented to him, the Same shall be a Law, in like Manner as if he had signed it, unless the Congress by their Adjournment prevent its Return, in which Case it shall not be a Law.

[3] Every Order, Resolution, or Vote to which the Concurrence of the Senate and House of Representatives may be necessary (except on a question of Adjournment) shall be presented to the President of the United States; and before the Same shall take Effect, shall be approved by him, or being disapproved by him, shall be repassed by two thirds of the Senate and House of Representatives, according to the Rules and Limitations prescribed in the Case of a Bill.

SECTION 8. [1] The Congress shall have Power To lay and collect Taxes, Duties, Imposts and Excises, to pay the Debts and provide for the common Defence and general Welfare of the United States; but all Duties, Imposts and Excises shall be uniform throughout the United States;

[2] To borrow Money on the credit of the United States;

[3] To regulate Commerce with foreign Nations, and among the several States, and with the Indian Tribes;

---

6. This clause has been affected by the 27th Amendment.

[4] To establish an uniform Rule of Naturalization, and uniform Laws on the subject of Bankruptcies throughout the United States;

[5] To coin Money, regulate the Value thereof, and of foreign Coin, and fix the Standard of Weights and Measures;

[6] To provide for the Punishment of counterfeiting the Securities and current Coin of the United States;

[7] To establish Post Offices and post Roads;

[8] To promote the Progress of Science and useful Arts, by securing for limited Times to Authors and Inventors the exclusive Right to their respective Writings and Discoveries;

[9] To constitute Tribunals inferior to the supreme Court;

[10] To define and punish Piracies and Felonies committed on the high Seas, and Offences against the Law of Nations;

[11] To declare War, grant Letters of Marque and Reprisal, and make Rules concerning Captures on Land and Water;

[12] To raise and support Armies, but no Appropriation of Money to that Use shall be for a longer Term than two Years;

[13] To provide and maintain a Navy;

[14] To make Rules for the Government and Regulation of the land and naval Forces;

[15] To provide for calling forth the Militia to execute the Laws of the Union, suppress Insurrections and repel Invasions;

[16] To provide for organizing, arming, and disciplining, the Militia, and for governing such Part of them as may be employed in the Service of the United States, reserving to the States respectively, the Appointment of the Officers, and the Authority of training the Militia according to the discipline prescribed by Congress;

[17] To exercise exclusive Legislation in all Cases whatsoever, over such District (not exceeding ten Miles square) as may, by Cession of particular States, and the Acceptance of Congress, become the Seat of the Government of the United States, and to exercise like Authority over all Places purchased by the Consent of the Legislature of the State in which the Same shall be, for the Erection of Forts, Magazines, Arsenals, dock-Yards, and other needful Buildings;—And

[18] To make all Laws which shall be necessary and proper for carrying into Execution the foregoing Powers, and all other Powers vested by this Constitution in the Government of the United States, or in any Department or Officer thereof.

SECTION 9. [1] The Migration or Importation of such Persons as any of the States now existing shall think proper to admit, shall not be prohibited by the Congress prior to the Year one thousand eight hundred and eight, but a Tax or duty may be imposed on such Importation, not exceeding ten dollars for each Person.

[2] The Privilege of the Writ of Habeas Corpus shall not be suspended, unless when in Cases of Rebellion or Invasion the public Safety may require it.

[3] No Bill of Attainder or ex post facto Law shall be passed.

[4] {No Capitation, or other direct, Tax shall be laid, unless in Proportion to the Census or Enumeration herein before directed to be taken.}[7]

---

7. This clause has been affected by the 16th Amendment.

[5] No Tax or Duty shall be laid on Articles exported from any State.

[6] No Preference shall be given by any Regulation of Commerce or Revenue to the Ports of one State over those of another: nor shall Vessels bound to, or from, one State, be obliged to enter, clear, or pay Duties in another.

[7] No Money shall be drawn from the Treasury, but in Consequence of Appropriations made by Law; and a regular Statement and Account of the Receipts and Expenditures of all public Money shall be published from time to time.

[8] No Title of Nobility shall be granted by the United States: And no Person holding any Office of Profit or Trust under them, shall, without the Consent of the Congress, accept of any present, Emolument, Office, or Title, of any kind whatever, from any King, Prince, or foreign State.

SECTION 10. [1] No State shall enter into any Treaty, Alliance, or Confederation; grant Letters of Marque and Reprisal; coin Money; emit Bills of Credit; make any Thing but gold and silver Coin a Tender in Payment of Debts; pass any Bill of Attainder, ex post facto Law, or Law impairing the Obligation of Contracts, or grant any Title of Nobility.

[2] No State shall, without the Consent of the Congress, lay any Imposts or Duties on Imports or Exports, except what may be absolutely necessary for executing its inspection Laws: and the net Produce of all Duties and Imposts, laid by any State on Imports or Exports, shall be for the Use of the Treasury of the United States; and all such Laws shall be subject to the Revision and Controul of the Congress.

[3] No State shall, without the Consent of Congress, lay any Duty of Tonnage, keep Troops, or Ships of War in time of Peace, enter into any Agreement or Compact with another State, or with a foreign Power, or engage in War, unless actually invaded, or in such imminent Danger as will not admit of delay.

ARTICLE II

SECTION 1. [1] The executive Power shall be vested in a President of the United States of America. He shall hold his Office during the Term of four Years, and, together with the Vice President, chosen for the same Term, be elected, as follows.

[2] Each State shall appoint, in such Manner as the Legislature thereof may direct, a Number of Electors, equal to the whole Number of Senators and Representatives to which the State may be entitled in the Congress: but no Senator or Representative, or Person holding an Office of Trust or Profit under the United States, shall be appointed an Elector.

[3] {The Electors shall meet in their respective States, and vote by Ballot for two Persons, of whom one at least shall not be an Inhabitant of the same State with themselves. And they shall make a List of all the Persons voted for, and of the Number of Votes for each; which List they shall sign and certify, and transmit sealed to the Seat of the Government of the United States, directed to the President of the Senate. The President of the Senate shall, in the Presence of the Senate and House of Representatives, open all the Certificates, and the Votes shall then be counted. The Person having the greatest Number of Votes shall be the President, if such Number be a Majority of the whole Number of Electors appointed; and if there be more than one who have such Majority, and have an equal Number of Votes, then the House of Representatives shall immediately chuse by Ballot one of them for President; and if no Person have a Majority, then from the five highest on the List the said House shall in like Manner chuse the President. But in chusing the President, the Votes shall be taken by States, the Representation from each State

having one Vote; A quorum for this Purpose shall consist of a Member or Members from two thirds of the States, and a Majority of all the States shall be necessary to a Choice. In every Case, after the Choice of the President, the Person having the greatest Number of Votes of the Electors shall be the Vice President. But if there should remain two or more who have equal Votes, the Senate shall chuse from them by Ballot the Vice President.}[8]

[4] The Congress may determine the Time of chusing the Electors, and the Day on which they shall give their Votes; which Day shall be the same throughout the United States.

[5] No Person except a natural born Citizen, or a Citizen of the United States, at the time of the Adoption of this Constitution, shall be eligible to the Office of President; neither shall any Person be eligible to that Office who shall not have attained to the Age of thirty five Years, and been fourteen Years a Resident within the United States.

[6] {In Case of the Removal of the President from Office, or of his Death, Resignation, or Inability to discharge the Powers and Duties of the said Office, the Same shall devolve on the Vice President, and the Congress may by Law provide for the Case of Removal, Death, Resignation or Inability, both of the President and Vice President, declaring what Officer shall then act as President, and such Officer shall act accordingly, until the Disability be removed, or a President shall be elected.}[9]

[7] The President shall, at stated Times, receive for his Services, a Compensation, which shall neither be increased nor diminished during the Period for which he shall have been elected, and he shall not receive within that Period any other Emolument from the United States, or any of them.

[8] Before he enter on the Execution of his Office, he shall take the following Oath or Affirmation:—"I do solemnly swear (or affirm) that I will faithfully execute the Office of President of the United States, and will to the best of my Ability, preserve, protect and defend the Constitution of the United States."

SECTION 2. [1] The President shall be Commander in Chief of the Army and Navy of the United States, and of the Militia of the several States, when called into the actual Service of the United States; he may require the Opinion, in writing, of the principal Officer in each of the executive Departments, upon any Subject relating to the Duties of their respective Offices, and he shall have Power to grant Reprieves and Pardons for Offences against the United States, except in Cases of Impeachment.

[2] He shall have Power, by and with the Advice and Consent of the Senate, to make Treaties, provided two thirds of the Senators present concur; and he shall nominate, and by and with the Advice and Consent of the Senate, shall appoint Ambassadors, other public Ministers and Consuls, Judges of the supreme Court, and all other Officers of the United States, whose Appointments are not herein otherwise provided for, and which shall be established by Law: but the Congress may by Law vest the Appointment of such inferior Officers, as they think proper, in the President alone, in the Courts of Law, or in the Heads of Departments.

[3] The President shall have Power to fill up all Vacancies that may happen during the Recess of the Senate, by granting Commissions which shall expire at the End of their next Session.

SECTION 3. He shall from time to time give to the Congress Information of the State of the Union, and recommend to their Consideration such Measures as he shall judge

---

8. This clause has been superseded by the 12th Amendment.
9. This clause has been affected by the 25th Amendment.

necessary and expedient; he may, on extraordinary Occasions, convene both Houses, or either of them, and in Case of Disagreement between them, with Respect to the Time of Adjournment, he may adjourn them to such Time as he shall think proper; he shall receive Ambassadors and other public Ministers; he shall take Care that the Laws be faithfully executed, and shall Commission all the Officers of the United States.

SECTION 4. The President, Vice President and all civil Officers of the United States, shall be removed from Office on Impeachment for, and Conviction of, Treason, Bribery, or other high Crimes and Misdemeanors.

ARTICLE III

SECTION 1. The judicial Power of the United States, shall be vested in one supreme Court, and in such inferior Courts as the Congress may from time to time ordain and establish. The Judges, both of the supreme and inferior Courts, shall hold their Offices during good Behaviour, and shall, at stated Times, receive for their Services, a Compensation, which shall not be diminished during their Continuance in Office.

SECTION 2. [1] The judicial Power shall extend to all Cases, in Law and Equity, arising under this Constitution, the Laws of the United States, and Treaties made, or which shall be made, under their Authority;—to all Cases affecting Ambassadors, other public Ministers and Consuls;—to all Cases of admiralty and maritime Jurisdiction;—to Controversies to which the United States shall be a Party;—to Controversies between two or more States; {—between a State and Citizens of another State;}[10]—between Citizens of different States;—between Citizens of the same State claiming Lands under Grants of different States; and between a State, or the Citizens thereof, and foreign States, Citizens or Subjects.

[2] In all Cases affecting Ambassadors, other public Ministers and Consuls, and those in which a State shall be Party, the supreme Court shall have original Jurisdiction. In all the other Cases before mentioned, the supreme Court shall have appellate Jurisdiction, both as to Law and Fact, with such Exceptions, and under such Regulations as the Congress shall make.

[3] The Trial of all Crimes, except in Cases of Impeachment, shall be by Jury; and such Trial shall be held in the State where the said Crimes shall have been committed; but when not committed within any State, the Trial shall be at such Place or Places as the Congress may by Law have directed.

SECTION 3. [1] Treason against the United States, shall consist only in levying War against them, or in adhering to their Enemies, giving them Aid and Comfort. No Person shall be convicted of Treason unless on the Testimony of two Witnesses to the same overt Act, or on Confession in open Court.

[2] The Congress shall have Power to declare the Punishment of Treason, but no Attainder of Treason shall work Corruption of Blood, or Forfeiture except during the Life of the Person attainted.

ARTICLE IV

SECTION 1. Full Faith and Credit shall be given in each State to the public Acts, Records, and judicial Proceedings of every other State. And the Congress may by general Laws prescribe the Manner in which such Acts, Records and Proceedings shall be proved, and the Effect thereof.

---

10. This clause has been affected by the 11th Amendment.

SECTION 2. [1] The Citizens of each State shall be entitled to all Privileges and Immunities of Citizens in the several States.

[2] A Person charged in any State with Treason, Felony, or other Crime, who shall flee from Justice, and be found in another State, shall on Demand of the executive Authority of the State from which he fled, be delivered up, to be removed to the State having Jurisdiction of the Crime.

[3] {No Person held to Service or Labour in one State, under the Laws thereof, escaping into another, shall, in Consequence of any Law or Regulation therein, be discharged from such Service or Labour, but shall be delivered up on Claim of the Party to whom such Service or Labour may be due.}[11]

SECTION 3. [1] New States may be admitted by the Congress into this Union; but no new State shall be formed or erected within the Jurisdiction of any other State; nor any State be formed by the Junction of two or more States, or Parts of States, without the Consent of the Legislatures of the States concerned as well as of the Congress.

[2] The Congress shall have Power to dispose of and make all needful Rules and Regulations respecting the Territory or other Property belonging to the United States; and nothing in this Constitution shall be so construed as to Prejudice any Claims of the United States, or of any particular State.

SECTION 4. The United States shall guarantee to every State in this Union a Republican Form of Government, and shall protect each of them against Invasion; and on Application of the Legislature, or of the Executive (when the Legislature cannot be convened) against domestic Violence.

ARTICLE V

The Congress, whenever two thirds of both Houses shall deem it necessary, shall propose Amendments to this Constitution, or, on the Application of the Legislatures of two thirds of the several States, shall call a Convention for proposing Amendments, which, in either Case, shall be valid to all Intents and Purposes, as Part of this Constitution, when ratified by the Legislatures of three fourths of the several States, or by Conventions in three fourths thereof, as the one or the other Mode of Ratification may be proposed by the Congress; Provided that no Amendment which may be made prior to the Year One thousand eight hundred and eight shall in any Manner affect the first and fourth Clauses in the Ninth Section of the first Article; and that no State, without its Consent, shall be deprived of its equal Suffrage in the Senate.

ARTICLE VI

[1] All Debts contracted and Engagements entered into, before the Adoption of this Constitution, shall be as valid against the United States under this Constitution, as under the Confederation.

[2] This Constitution, and the Laws of the United States which shall be made in Pursuance thereof; and all Treaties made, or which shall be made, under the Authority of the United States, shall be the supreme Law of the Land; and the Judges in every State shall be bound thereby, any Thing in the Constitution or Laws of any State to the Contrary notwithstanding.

[3] The Senators and Representatives before mentioned, and the Members of the several State Legislatures, and all executive and judicial Officers, both of the United States

---

11. This clause has been superseded by the 13th Amendment.

and of the several States, shall be bound by Oath or Affirmation, to support this Constitution; but no religious Test shall ever be required as a Qualification to any Office or public Trust under the United States.

ARTICLE VII

The Ratification of the Conventions of nine States, shall be sufficient for the Establishment of this Constitution between the States so ratifying the Same.

* * *

ARTICLES IN ADDITION TO, AND AMENDMENT OF, THE CONSTITUTION OF THE UNITED STATES OF AMERICA, PROPOSED BY CONGRESS, AND RATIFIED BY THE SEVERAL STATES, PURSUANT TO THE FIFTH ARTICLE OF THE ORIGINAL CONSTITUTION[12]

AMENDMENT I (1791)

Congress shall make no law respecting an establishment of religion, or prohibiting the free exercise thereof; or abridging the freedom of speech, or of the press; or the right of the people peaceably to assemble, and to petition the government for a redress of grievances.

AMENDMENT II (1791)

A well regulated militia, being necessary to the security of a free state, the right of the people to keep and bear arms, shall not be infringed.

AMENDMENT III (1791)

No soldier shall, in time of peace be quartered in any house, without the consent of the owner, nor in time of war, but in a manner to be prescribed by Law.

AMENDMENT IV (1791)

The right of the people to be secure in their persons, houses, papers, and effects, against unreasonable searches and seizures, shall not be violated, and no warrants shall issue, but upon probable cause, supported by oath or affirmation, and particularly describing the place to be searched, and the persons or things to be seized.

AMENDMENT V (1791)

No person shall be held to answer for a capital, or otherwise infamous crime, unless on a presentment or indictment of a grand jury, except in cases arising in the land or naval forces, or in the militia, when in actual service in time of war or public danger; nor shall any person be subject for the same offense to be twice put in jeopardy of life or limb; nor shall be compelled in any criminal case to be a witness against himself, nor be deprived of life, liberty, or property, without due process of law; nor shall private property be taken for public use, without just compensation.

AMENDMENT VI (1791)

In all criminal prosecutions, the accused shall enjoy the right to a speedy and public trial, by an impartial jury of the state and district wherein the crime shall have been com-

---

12. The first ten amendments were ratified December 15, 1791, and form what is known as the "Bill of Rights."

mitted, which district shall have been previously ascertained by law, and to be informed of the nature and cause of the accusation; to be confronted with the witnesses against him; to have compulsory process for obtaining witnesses in his favor, and to have the assistance of counsel for his defense.

AMENDMENT VII (1791)

In suits at common law, where the value in controversy shall exceed twenty dollars, the right of trial by jury shall be preserved, and no fact tried by a jury, shall be otherwise reexamined in any court of the United States, than according to the rules of the common Law.

AMENDMENT VIII (1791)

Excessive bail shall not be required, nor excessive fines imposed, nor cruel and unusual punishments inflicted.

AMENDMENT IX (1791)

The enumeration in the Constitution, of certain rights, shall not be construed to deny or disparage others retained by the people.

AMENDMENT X (1791)

The powers not delegated to the United States by the Constitution, nor prohibited by it to the states, are reserved to the states respectively, or to the people.

AMENDMENT XI (1798)

The judicial power of the United States shall not be construed to extend to any suit in law or equity, commenced or prosecuted against one of the United States by citizens of another state, or by citizens or subjects of any foreign state.

AMENDMENT XII (1804)

The electors shall meet in their respective states and vote by ballot for President and Vice-President, one of whom, at least, shall not be an inhabitant of the same state with themselves; they shall name in their ballots the person voted for as President, and in distinct ballots the person voted for as Vice-President, and they shall make distinct lists of all persons voted for as President, and of all persons voted for as Vice-President, and of the number of votes for each, which lists they shall sign and certify, and transmit sealed to the seat of the government of the United States, directed to the President of the Senate;—The President of the Senate shall, in the presence of the Senate and House of Representatives, open all the certificates and the votes shall then be counted;—the person having the greatest number of votes for President, shall be the President, if such number be a majority of the whole number of electors appointed; and if no person have such majority, then from the persons having the highest numbers not exceeding three on the list of those voted for as President, the House of Representatives shall choose immediately, by ballot, the President. But in choosing the President, the votes shall be taken by states, the representation from each state having one vote; a quorum for this purpose shall consist of a member or members from two-thirds of the states, and a majority of all the states shall be necessary to a choice. And if the House of Representatives shall not choose a President whenever the right of choice shall devolve upon them, before the fourth day of March next following, then the Vice-President shall act as President, as in the case of the death or other constitutional disability of the President. The person having the greatest number of votes as Vice-President, shall be the Vice-President, if such number be a majority of the whole number of electors appointed, and if no person have a majority, then from the two highest numbers on the list, the Senate shall choose the Vice-President; a quorum for the purpose shall consist of two-thirds of the whole number of Senators, and a majority of the whole number shall be necessary to a choice. But no person constitutionally ineligible to the office of President shall be eligible to that of Vice-President of the United States.

AMENDMENT XIII (1865)

Section 1. Neither slavery nor involuntary servitude, except as a punishment for crime whereof the party shall have been duly convicted, shall exist within the United States, or any place subject to their jurisdiction.

Section 2. Congress shall have power to enforce this article by appropriate legislation.

AMENDMENT XIV (1868)

Section 1. All persons born or naturalized in the United States, and subject to the jurisdiction thereof, are citizens of the United States and of the state wherein they reside. No state shall make or enforce any law which shall abridge the privileges or immunities of citizens of the United States; nor shall any state deprive any person of life, liberty, or property, without due process of law; nor deny to any person within its jurisdiction the equal protection of the laws.

Section 2. Representatives shall be apportioned among the several states according to their respective numbers, counting the whole number of persons in each state, excluding Indians not taxed. But when the right to vote at any election for the choice of electors for President and Vice President of the United States, Representatives in Congress, the executive and judicial officers of a state, or the members of the legislature thereof, is denied to any of the male inhabitants of such state, being twenty-one years of age, and citizens of the United States, or in any way abridged, except for participation in rebellion, or other crime, the basis of representation therein shall be reduced in the proportion which the number of such male citizens shall bear to the whole number of male citizens twenty-one years of age in such state.

Section 3. No person shall be a Senator or Representative in Congress, or elector of President and Vice President, or hold any office, civil or military, under the United States, or under any state, who, having previously taken an oath, as a member of Congress, or as an officer of the United States, or as a member of any state legislature, or as an executive or judicial officer of any state, to support the Constitution of the United States, shall have engaged in insurrection or rebellion against the same, or given aid or comfort to the enemies thereof. But Congress may by a vote of two-thirds of each House, remove such disability.

Section 4. The validity of the public debt of the United States, authorized by law, including debts incurred for payment of pensions and bounties for services in suppressing insurrection or rebellion, shall not be questioned. But neither the United States nor any state shall assume or pay any debt or obligation incurred in aid of insurrection or rebellion against the United States, or any claim for the loss or emancipation of any slave; but all such debts, obligations and claims shall be held illegal and void.

Section 5. The Congress shall have power to enforce, by appropriate legislation, the provisions of this article.

AMENDMENT XV (1870)

Section 1. The right of citizens of the United States to vote shall not be denied or abridged by the United States or by any state on account of race, color, or previous condition of servitude.

Section 2. The Congress shall have power to enforce this article by appropriate legislation.

AMENDMENT XVI (1913)

The Congress shall have power to lay and collect taxes on incomes, from whatever source derived, without apportionment among the several states, and without regard to any census of enumeration.

AMENDMENT XVII (1913)

[1] The Senate of the United States shall be composed of two Senators from each state, elected by the people thereof, for six years; and each Senator shall have one vote. The electors in each state shall have the qualifications requisite for electors of the most numerous branch of the state legislatures.

[2] When vacancies happen in the representation of any state in the Senate, the executive authority of such state shall issue writs of election to fill such vacancies: Provided, that the legislature of any state may empower the executive thereof to make temporary appointments until the people fill the vacancies by election as the legislature may direct.

[3] This amendment shall not be so construed as to affect the election or term of any Senator chosen before it becomes valid as part of the Constitution.

AMENDMENT XVIII (1919)

{Section 1. After one year from the ratification of this article the manufacture, sale, or transportation of intoxicating liquors within, the importation thereof into, or the exportation thereof from the United States and all territory subject to the jurisdiction thereof for beverage purposes is hereby prohibited.

Section 2. The Congress and the several states shall have concurrent power to enforce this article by appropriate legislation.

Section 3. This article shall be inoperative unless it shall have been ratified as an amendment to the Constitution by the legislatures of the several states, as provided in the Constitution, within seven years from the date of the submission hereof to the states by the Congress.}[13]

AMENDMENT XIX (1920)

[1] The right of citizens of the United States to vote shall not be denied or abridged by the United States or by any state on account of sex.

[2] Congress shall have power to enforce this article by appropriate legislation.

AMENDMENT XX (1933)

Section 1. The terms of the President and Vice President shall end at noon on the 20th day of January, and the terms of Senators and Representatives at noon on the 3d day of

---

13. Repealed by § 1 of the 21st Amendment.

January, of the years in which such terms would have ended if this article had not been ratified; and the terms of their successors shall then begin.

Section 2. The Congress shall assemble at least once in every year, and such meeting shall begin at noon on the 3d day of January, unless they shall by law appoint a different day.

Section 3. If, at the time fixed for the beginning of the term of the President, the President elect shall have died, the Vice President elect shall become President. If a President shall not have been chosen before the time fixed for the beginning of his term, or if the President elect shall have failed to qualify, then the Vice President elect shall act as President until a President shall have qualified; and the Congress may by law provide for the case wherein neither a President elect nor a Vice President elect shall have qualified, declaring who shall then act as President, or the manner in which one who is to act shall be selected, and such person shall act accordingly until a President or Vice President shall have qualified.

Section 4. The Congress may by law provide for the case of the death of any of the persons from whom the House of Representatives may choose a President whenever the right of choice shall have devolved upon them, and for the case of the death of any of the persons from whom the Senate may choose a Vice President whenever the right of choice shall have devolved upon them.

Section 5. Sections 1 and 2 shall take effect on the 15th day of October following the ratification of this article.

Section 6. This article shall be inoperative unless it shall have been ratified as an amendment to the Constitution by the legislatures of three-fourths of the several states within seven years from the date of its submission.

AMENDMENT XXI (1933)

Section 1. The eighteenth article of amendment to the Constitution of the United States is hereby repealed.

Section 2. The transportation or importation into any state, territory, or possession of the United States for delivery or use therein of intoxicating liquors, in violation of the laws thereof, is hereby prohibited.

Section 3. This article shall be inoperative unless it shall have been ratified as an amendment to the Constitution by conventions in the several states, as provided in the Constitution, within seven years from the date of the submission hereof to the states by the Congress.

AMENDMENT XXII (1951)

Section 1. No person shall be elected to the office of the President more than twice, and no person who has held the office of President, or acted as President, for more than two years of a term to which some other person was elected President shall be elected to the office of the President more than once. But this article shall not apply to any person holding the office of President when this article was proposed by the Congress, and shall not prevent any person who may be holding the office of President, or acting as President, during the term within which this article becomes operative from holding the office of President or acting as President during the remainder of such term.

Section 2. This article shall be inoperative unless it shall have been ratified as an amendment to the constitution by the legislatures of three-fourths of the several states within seven years from the date of its submission to the states by the Congress.

AMENDMENT XXIII (1961)

Section 1. The District constituting the seat of government of the United States shall appoint in such manner as the Congress may direct:

A number of electors of President and Vice President equal to the whole number of Senators and Representatives in Congress to which the District would be entitled if it were a state, but in no event more than the least populous state; they shall be in addition to those appointed by the states, but they shall be considered, for the purposes of the election of President and Vice President, to be electors appointed by a state; and they shall meet in the District and perform such duties as provided by the twelfth article of amendment.

Section 2. The Congress shall have power to enforce this article by appropriate legislation.

AMENDMENT XXIV (1964)

Section 1. The right of citizens of the United States to vote in any primary or other election for President or Vice President, for electors for President or Vice President, or for Senator or Representative in Congress, shall not be denied or abridged by the United States or any state by reason of failure to pay any poll tax or other tax.

Section 2. The Congress shall have power to enforce this article by appropriate legislation.

AMENDMENT XXV (1967)

Section 1. In case of the removal of the President from office or of his death or resignation, the Vice President shall become President.

Section 2. Whenever there is a vacancy in the office of the Vice President, the President shall nominate a Vice President who shall take office upon confirmation by a majority vote of both Houses of Congress.

Section 3. Whenever the President transmits to the President pro tempore of the Senate and the Speaker of the House of Representatives his written declaration that he is unable to discharge the powers and duties of his office, and until he transmits to them a written declaration to the contrary, such powers and duties shall be discharged by the Vice President as Acting President.

Section 4. Whenever the Vice President and a majority of either the principal officers of the executive departments or of such other body as Congress may by law provide, transmit to the President pro tempore of the Senate and the Speaker of the House of Representatives their written declaration that the President is unable to discharge the powers and duties of his office, the Vice President shall immediately assume the powers and duties of the office as Acting President.

Thereafter, when the President transmits to the President pro tempore of the Senate and the Speaker of the House of Representatives his written declaration that no inability exists, he shall resume the powers and duties of his office unless the Vice President and a majority of either the principal officers of the executive department or of such other body as Congress may by law provide, transmit within four days to the President pro tempore of the Senate and the Speaker of the House of Representatives their written declaration that the President is unable to discharge the powers and duties of his office. Thereupon Congress shall decide the issue, assembling within forty-eight hours for that purpose if not in session. If the Congress, within twenty-one days after receipt of the latter written declaration, or, if Congress is not in session, within twenty-one days after Congress is required to assemble, determines by two-thirds vote of both Houses that the President is unable to discharge the powers and duties of his office, the Vice President shall continue to discharge the same as Acting President; otherwise, the President shall resume the powers and duties of his office.

AMENDMENT XXVI (1971)

Section 1. The right of citizens of the United States, who are 18 years of age or older, to vote, shall not be denied or abridged by the United States or any state on account of age.

Section 2. The Congress shall have the power to enforce this article by appropriate legislation.

AMENDMENT XXVII (1992)

No law, varying the compensation for the services of Senators and Representatives, shall take effect, until an election for Representatives shall have intervened.

III. The Constitution: Institutions, Powers, and Limits

1. Read the Constitution and Amendments 1–17, 19, 22, 24 and 26. Make a list of the governmental institutions that are created or recognized as already existing by the Constitution. What are the powers of each institution? How do these powers compare to those of the government created by the Articles?

2. Identify provisions that limit the exercise of power. What entity is being limited? Who are the intended beneficiaries of these limitations (e.g., states, the national government, individuals)?

3. Match the provisions that confer or limit power with the institutions, officials, and persons that the provisions primarily address. You might set this information up as a chart organized at least in part by the federal government, divided into the branches of government, and the states.

Re-read the Constitution and the listed Amendments in an attempt to answer the following questions. With reference to each question below list all the provisions you find in the Constitution that seem to bear on the question. Make note of the specific part of the Constitutional text involved, e.g., Art. I, §9, cl. 3.

4. What are the purposes of the Constitution? Does the document list them? Where does it do so?

5. List guarantees of liberty in the original Constitution.

6. What, if any, provision does the Constitution make with reference to slavery?

7. Consider the following hypothetical:

A member of Congress advocates commission of a crime during a speech in Congress. Assume that the advocacy is not protected by the 1st Amendment. She is prosecuted. Is there any provision of the Constitution that she might rely on? What if she defames a private person during a speech in Congress? Is she liable in damages assuming the tort law of the District of Columbia provides that the defamatory statement is actionable?

8. What provisions does the Constitution make with reference to commerce? Does it establish a common market in the United States (a free trade zone in which state tariffs and protectionist measures are prohibited)? What provisions are involved?

9. Suppose the President secretly sells some weapons to a foreign power and then sends the proceeds of the sale to another country to assist in putting down a rebellion. No congressional legislation is passed regarding either the sale or the payment of the funds to the foreign country. Are there provisions of the Constitution that may bear on this question?

10. If the Vice President were impeached and convicted, could the President prevent his removal by pardon?

11. If a state law conflicts with a federal law within the power of Congress, which prevails?

12. What, if any, provision does the Constitution make with reference to judicial review of congressional legislation?

13. A state passes term limits for members of Congress. Are the term limits constitutional? What sections of the Constitution apply?

IV. What Is *Constitutional* Law?

The word "constitution" comes from the root word "constitute," meaning to establish or set up. In this broad sense the *constitution* of a nation consists of those fundamental understandings, customs, institutions, and laws that establish how political power will be exercised in a society. In this broad sense virtually all societies have a constitution, whether or not they have a specific document called a constitution. The study of a constitution could take into account all of the factors listed above.

Some political thinkers have discussed constitutional arrangements in the broadest sense. For example, 17th century English political philosopher James Harrington believed that the character of a government was determined by the distribution of wealth in a society and how the legal system reinforced that distribution. In essence, he argued that the consolidation of economic wealth led to the concentration of political power in the political system and that the dispersal of economic wealth led to a more broadly representative or republican system. Harrington thought of land as the primary source of wealth and, when he wrote, he was probably largely correct. James Harrington, *The Art of Lawgiving*, ch. 1 (1659).

In the 1830s, Alexis de Tocqueville wrote *Democracy in America*, a book that described the basic arrangements that constituted American democracy including the federal Constitution, state constitutions, the President, the Congress, and the judiciary. But he did not stop there. He considered civil and criminal jury trials (which he said put a strong democratic element into the judicial system). He also discussed state laws that had eliminated the institution of primogeniture—inheritance of all property by the eldest son:

> But the law of descent [inheritance] was the last step to equality.... It is true that these laws belong to civil affairs; but they ought, nevertheless, to be placed at the head of all political institutions, for whilst political laws are only the symbol

of a nation's condition, [laws of inheritance] exercise an incredible influence upon its social state.... When the legislator has once regulated the law of inheritance, he may rest from his labor.... When framed in a particular manner, this law unites, draws together, and vests property and power in a few hands; its tendency is clearly aristocratic. [Formed o]n opposite principles ... it divides, distributes, and disperses both property and power.... [I]t gradually reduces or destroys every obstacle, until by its incessant activity the bulwarks and influence of wealth are ground down to the fine and shifting sand which is the basis of democracy.

Alexis de Tocqueville, *Democracy in America*, 29–30 (Henry Reeve translation, 1838).

Any document that reflects or establishes fundamental ideas to which citizens appeal and that continues to shape political arrangements through time is a constitutional document in the broad sense. The Declaration of Independence is such a document; it contains the nation's pronouncement that governmental power is justified by the consent of the governed and that all people are created equal and endowed with "unalienable" rights.

A central concern of constitutional analysis (using *constitutional* in its broadest sense) is locating where *sovereignty*, or ultimate political power, resides. In an absolute monarchy, it resides in the King (or Queen). In England at the time of the American Revolution, sovereignty resided in Parliament or, more accurately, the King in Parliament. The Magna Carta and the English Bill of Rights were understood to limit the power of the Crown. But the power of Parliament was not limited by any formal document. Still, the English could and would criticize actions by Parliament as "unconstitutional," meaning that they violated basic historical understandings that underlay the establishment of the British government. In the end, however, Parliament had the final word. There was no written constitution or enforceable understanding that limited its power.

Central to the American Revolution was the idea of popular sovereignty, that ultimate political power resided in "the people." Determining exactly who "the people" are, and how direct their influence must be, has been a source of conflict throughout American history. Still, the idea of popular sovereignty helped American democracy evolve toward a more truly popular government. The Declaration of Independence sounded the basic theme:

> We hold these truths to be self-evident, that all men are created equal, that they are endowed by their Creator with certain unalienable rights, that among these are life, liberty, and the pursuit of happiness. That to secure these rights, governments are instituted among men, *deriving their just powers from the consent of the governed.*

People do not always agree, of course, as to what the fundamental values reflected in constitutional documents mean. Did the Declaration mean only that all *white men* were created equal or that all *people* were? Did the idea that legitimate governmental power must be based on the consent of the governed mean that women should have the vote, or even that all free, adult men should vote?

In the Lincoln-Douglas debates, both Abraham Lincoln and Stephen Douglas discussed and appealed to the Declaration as a fundamental founding document. Here is Lincoln's assessment:

> I think the authors of that notable instrument [the Declaration of Independence] intended to include *all* men, but they did not intend to declare all men equal *in all respects.* They did not mean to say all were equal in color, size, intellect, moral

developments, or social capacity. They defined with tolerable distinctness, in what respects they did consider all men created equal — equal in "certain inalienable rights, among which are life, liberty, and the pursuit of happiness." This they said, and this they meant. They did not mean to assert the obvious untruth, that all were then actually enjoying that equality, nor yet, that they were about to confer it immediately upon them. In fact they had no power to confer such a boon. They meant simply to declare the *right*, so that the *enforcement* of it might follow as fast as circumstances should permit. They meant to set up a standard maxim for free society, which should be familiar to all, and revered by all; constantly looked to, constantly labored for, and even though never perfectly attained, constantly approximated, and thereby constantly spreading and deepening its influence, and augmenting the happiness and value of life to all people of all colors every where. The assertion "that all men are created equal" was of no practical use in effecting our separation from Great Britain; and it was placed in the Declaration, not for that, but for future use. Its authors meant it to be, thank God, it is now proving itself, a stumbling block to those who in after times might seek to turn a free people back into the hateful paths of despotism. They knew the proneness of prosperity to breed tyrants, and they meant when such should re-appear in this fair land and commence their vocation they should find for them at least one hard nut to crack.

2 *Collected Works of Abraham Lincoln* 405–06 (R. Basler, ed. 1953).

Connected to the broad idea of a constitution is a somewhat narrower one. A constitution in this sense is the basic *document* that establishes how governmental power is to be set up. In the United States we have a federal Constitution and state constitutions as well. The American theory is that our constitutions emanate from the people and are legitimate because of popular assent. The federal Constitution took effect only upon ratification by the people (through ratifying conventions) of nine states. Of course the right to vote for representatives to these conventions was severely restricted by modern standards. Still, suffrage was broad in comparison to England at the same time. Many state constitutions still require that amendments or new constitutions be submitted to a vote of the people. The framers of the federal Constitution used the idea of popular sovereignty to explain why a ratified new Constitution could replace the Articles of Confederation, even though the framers had clearly departed from the provision the Articles had established for their amendment.

Not all of our constitutional principles (even in the narrow sense) are explicitly set out in the federal Constitution. A prime example of the variety of sources which constitute the American constitutional order is found in the right to vote. While acknowledged, it is not set out *as such* anywhere in the text of the Constitution. Indeed, the main body of the original Constitution assumes that the states, and not the federal government, will be the primary regulators of voting. Article I, §2 provided that voters for the federal House shall have the qualifications set for voters for the most numerous branch of the state legislature. Senators were chosen by state legislatures until the 17th Amendment was ratified in 1913. Article I, §4 provides that the time, places, and manner of electing Senators and Representatives will be set by the state legislatures, though Congress was given a right to alter these rules. Greater national regulation of the right to vote, as a matter of federal *constitutional law*, began with various amendments to the Constitution, starting with the 14th in 1868. To the extent that we now recognize a right to vote secured by the federal Constitution, the recognition stems from judicial decisions drawing on the Constitution's amendments, its structure and history, and on its historic recognition by various state constitutions and statutes.

In our American tradition, a Constitution established "by the people" implies that the Constitution limits governmental power—legislative, judicial, and executive. According to this theory, since the Constitution comes from the highest authority—the people—all elected and appointed officials should follow it. "Popular sovereignty" refers to the theory that the people are the ultimate authority. Elected and appointed officials are merely those persons the people have temporarily invested with political power and legal authority. Article VI, § 3 requires that presidents, congressmen, federal and state judges, governors, and state legislators take an oath to uphold the Constitution. The requirement shows that they are expected to follow the fundamental instructions given them in the Constitution.

Traditionally, most constitutional law books are composed of decisions of the Supreme Court that interpret the text of the Constitution. However, the constitutional system consists of both the federal government and state governments, and each government in turn consists of an executive, a legislature, and a judiciary. "Constitutional law" is practiced daily in the operations of the executive and legislative branches of government, whether or not a case is ever filed. It occurs when people in these branches consider the effect the Constitution has on their decisions.

Governmental actors, who interpret the Constitution, live in a specific time and place, within a specific culture. The federal Constitution is a document that arose in a specific historical context, as did its later amendments and its judicial interpretations. Understanding constitutional law requires some understanding of historical context. This book provides historical context for some Supreme Court decisions and constitutional amendments. We hope the reader will recall that context is always a factor, whether we allude to it or not.

Oliver Wendell Holmes commented on the relation between context and legal doctrine:

> The life of the law has not been logic: it has been experience. The seed of every new growth within its sphere has been a felt necessity. The form of continuity has been kept up by reasonings purporting to reduce every thing to a logical sequence; but that form is nothing but the evening dress which the newcomer puts on.... The important phenomenon is ... the justice and reasonableness of a decision, not its consistency with previously held views. No one will ever have a truly philosophic mastery over the law who does not habitually consider the forces outside of it which have made it what is. More than that, he must remember that as it embodies the story of a nation's development through many centuries, the law finds its philosophy not in self consistency, which it must always fail in so long as it continues to grow, but in history, and the nature of human needs.

Oliver Wendell Holmes, *Book Review*, 14 Am. Law. Rev. 233–35 (1880).

Holmes' dichotomy is too stark. The life of the law has been both logic and experience. One traditional logical form is the syllogism. This form of argument consists of a major premise, a minor premise, and a conclusion that necessarily follows from the premises. For example:

Major premise: oral contracts to convey real property are unenforceable.

Minor premise: A's contract to convey Blackacre to B was oral.

Conclusion: A's contract to convey Blackacre to B is unenforceable.

Constitutional rules (and our basic understanding of them) also arise out of practical struggles. The rule provides, at least for a time, the major premise in the syllogism of constitutional analysis that will in fact be used in deciding cases. But words are not mathematical symbols and the context of the dispute is often crucial. Even without constitutional amendment, social transformations inevitably lead us to understand constitutional principles, rules and facts in a new light. Principles begin to have new meanings or new applications. (This is one view, but, of course, there are others.) The major premise (the rule) may change or the minor premise (the understanding of the facts) may change as the context changes. So too our understanding of the meaning of words changes over time. So entirely new conclusions arise. Examples of this phenomenon are the Court's decisions about the legal status of women and of blacks. Consider the Equal Protection Clause of the 14th Amendment. The principle accepted by some leading proponents of the Amendment and later by the Court was that irrational and invidious discrimination violates equal protection. At first some leading supporters of the Amendment, and the Court, did not understand racial segregation or laws limiting the career opportunities of women to be irrational and invidious.

One could translate the logical structure of the racial analysis described above in various ways. This would be one way:

> Major premise: Only invidious and irrational racial distinctions violate the Equal Protection Clause.
>
> Minor Premise: Legally mandated racial segregation of railway cars (or schools) is not irrational and invidious.
>
> Conclusion: Legally mandated racial segregation of railway cars or schools does not violate the Equal Protection Clause.

Eventually, this idea would harden into a mechanical rule: legally mandated racial segregation does not violate the Equal Protection Clause. Segregation of schools is legally mandated racial segregation. Therefore, such segregation does not violate the Equal Protection Clause. (Of course, such an understanding of the meaning of the 14th Amendment was never universal and some of the framers of the Amendment would have rejected it.) Over time, the dominant view of race and racial segregation began to change. Though the principle remained the same (that invidious and irrational classifications violated the Equal Protection Clause), the changed understanding of race and state-imposed racial classifications produced a new rule.

There are other ways that the meaning of the Constitution can change. Amendments change the meaning of the Constitution. *Dred Scott v. Sandford* (1857) held that descendants of slaves (including free black citizens entitled to vote in Northern states) could never be citizens of the United States. That rule was changed by the first sentence of § 1 of the 14th Amendment: "All persons born or naturalized in the United States are citizens of the United States...."

A reading of the Constitution might change because of the need to recognize the transforming effect of an amendment on other parts of the Constitution. As originally understood by its framers, the 14th Amendment did not impose any limits on the ability of states to limit the right to vote, except that if a state excluded males over 21 from voting it should have its representation reduced. At least some leading framers did not see the right to vote as fundamental. After all, women had fundamental rights and they could not vote. But constitutional amendments prohibiting discrimination in the right to vote based on race and sex, prohibiting the poll tax in federal elections, and prohibiting age qualifications for those above 18 years of age might be seen as requiring a new synthesis. (Expansion of the right to vote in state laws and constitutions also contributed to a new understanding.)

An earlier interpretation may also be seen as mistaken or it might change because shifts in political power produce shifts in interpretation by newly appointed Justices.

Constitutional provisions contain *principles*, and people at the time, including framers ratifiers, and members of the public, have *expectations* as to how those principles will function to produce legal rules. Scholars, including notably Professor Jack Balkin, have made a distinction between principles and expected applications, as did some lawyers, legislators, and judges in the 19th century.

Should the *principle* of a constitutional provision be distinct from the *expected legal application* people had for it in 1791 or 1868? Should it be distinct from widely accepted social practices and legal rules at the time? Or should the expected application in 1868, for example, be the same as the legal meaning of the principles of the 14th Amendment today?

Senator Howard presented the proposed 14th Amendment to the Senate on behalf of the Committee that drafted it. He quoted the Equal Protection and Due Process Clauses, and he identified a principle: "This abolishes all class legislation in the States and does away with the injustice of subjecting one caste of persons to a code not applicable to another." Similarly, Congressman Stevens, another leading Republican, saw the principle of the Equal Protection Clause as a ban on irrational discrimination.

Though a number of Republicans opposed distinctions based on color, many accepted some segregation and some racial distinctions. Some endorsed gender equality, but many assumed the discriminations against married women were reasonable.

The Senate that proposed the Amendment had racially segregated galleries—a progressive step since Americans of African descent were now permitted in the Senate galleries. And the 39th Congress that proposed the 14th Amendment had provided tax support for segregated schools in the District. Segregated schools were another progressive development, since before black children had no tax supported schools in the District. At the time the 14th Amendment was passed and sent to the states in 1866 and when it was ratified in 1868, bans on interracial marriage existed in most states. In Congress in 1866, a leading Republican rejected the claim that a guarantee of equality would invalidate the ban on interracial marriages. He said the ban treated all equally since blacks could not marry whites, but whites also could not marry blacks. In the campaign of 1866 a leading Republican denied that the 14th Amendment would upset his state's bans on interracial marriages. On the other hand, the Congress in 1865 outlawed segregation on railroad cars in the District of Columbia.

In 1868, married women were often denied basic civil rights, including the right to contract, to sue in their own names, to control of their earnings, and the right to vote. Though reform had begun in some states, the inferior status of married women was quite common in the states at the time of the 14th Amendment. Congressman Stevens apparently believed that so long as all married women were treated alike, there was no denial of equality. Discussing the right to vote, Senator Howard said, "by the law of nature ... women and children were not regarded as the equals of men." *Globe*, 39 (1) 2767 (1866).

If a judge seeks to follow original intent or original understanding of a part of the constitutional text, should the judge follow the principle of Equal Protection embraced by leading framers—no caste system or no invidious and irrational discrimination—but follow it in light of our modern understanding of the social facts (women and men are equal, most gender discriminations are irrational; segregation based on race fosters a caste system and is irrationally discriminatory)?

Or should the judge follow the expected legal application of the principle accepted by many people in 1866–68? Should the principle be reduced to the expected application, or are the principle and and the expectations of the framers of the 17th Amendment in 1866–1868 distinct questions?

If the principle and expected application at the time of enactment and ratification are distinct and we follow our generally held contemporary understanding of social facts, then it is impossible to be true to *both* the framers' principle and their expected legal application.

On this issue consider the views of Congressman Monroe speaking in Congress in 1871. Monroe said "every free constitution" had evolved in similar ways. Free governments had a "natural growth," a growth that did not come only from amendment or change of the letter or spirit. "It is not the intrusion of new principles, but it is the more extended application of old ones. Principles have commonly a much wider application than we suspect."

> A new application of a well-known principle, whether in morals, in science, or in the organic law of the land, takes us by surprise ... yet it is only what is required by the most logical consistency. When we first study the constitution of a free country we think of its principles only as applicable to that state of society and to those needs of the people which then exist and with which we are familiar. But, in time, new circumstances arise, new social conditions appear, and minds will then be found who will propose to include the new phenomena under the old rule. This will startle many as an innovation, as a violation of the constitution, whereas it may be only the application of known and admitted principles to new circumstances. *Globe*, 42(1) 370 (1871).

At least some framers and ratifiers may have expected one legal application at the time of ratification and another in the future. In discussing slavery, Abraham Lincoln insisted that the principle of the Declaration of Independence that all people are created equal was different from its expected immediate application. He thought the framers expected the application of the principle to evolve and expand over time. On the other hand, Stephen A. Douglas, in the famous debates with Lincoln, and Chief Justice Roger Taney in the *Dred Scott Case*, insisted that the Declaration should be understood in light of the practice of slavery at the time and in light of its immediate expected application.

In the 39th Congress that proposed the 14th Amendment, Congressman Plants said, "without any formal amendments the Constitution has changed and will continue to change, with the ever-changing wants of the people." Like the "unwritten British constitution and the written Bible," Plants said that the Constitution was "precisely what the prevailing sentiment makes it by interpretation." *Globe*, 39th Cong. 1st Sess. 1011 (1866). Plants had an optimistic view of the future. "All laws founded on caste will be repealed. All races and sexes will be enfranchised.... The prejudices of today will die out, and truth and justice resume the seats so long usurped by error and wrong." *Globe*, 39(1) at 1015 (1866).

For a scholarly debate on the original meaning and school segregation, see Michael W. McConnell, *Originalism and the Desegregation Decisions*, 81 Va. L. Rev. 947 (1995) (finding the *Brown v. Board of Education* decision consistent with original understanding and relying heavily on evidence from later congressional debates in 1875) and Michael J. Klarman, Brown, *Originalism and Constitutional Theory: A Response to Professor McConnell*, 81 Va. L. Rev. 947 (1995) (finding *Brown* an expansion of the original meaning of the 14th Amendment). For struggles over school segregation in the North, see, Davison M. Douglas, *Jim Crow Moves North: The Battle over Northern School Segregation, 1865–1954* (2005).

For a case that suggests that the understanding of constitutional principles does *not* change with changed understanding of social facts, consider *Goeseart v. Cleary* (1948). That case upheld a Michigan statute that forbad women from working as bartenders unless they were the wife or daughter of the male owner. The owner was not required to be present. The Court's majority upheld the statute in an opinion written by Justice Frankfurter:

> Michigan could, beyond question, forbid all women from working behind a bar. This is so despite the vast changes in the social and legal position of women. The fact that women may now have achieved the virtues that men have long claimed as their prerogatives and now indulge in vices that men have long practiced, does not preclude the States from drawing a sharp line between the sexes, certainly, in such matters as the regulation of the liquor traffic. The Constitution does not require legislatures to reflect sociological insight, or shifting social standards....

The case is no longer the law. Gender classifications now get substantially heightened scrutiny.

Under current law, the gender discrimination in the Michigan law would be found a violation of Equal Protection.

There are two questions, one descriptive and one normative: 1. Does the understanding of the application of the Constitution change over time? 2. Should it change over time? The first question is a factual matter. The second is not. For an article arguing for the principle-application distinction, see, e.g., Jack Balkin, *Abortion and Original Meaning*, 24 Const. Comm. 291, 293, 295–97 (2007); cf., Ronald Dworkin, *Comment* in Antonin Scalia, *A Matter of Interpretation: Federal Courts and the Law* 119 (1997).

Understanding historical context—the eras of constitutional law—is crucial because different eras are characterized by different understandings of social facts and the application of constitutional principles. The reasoning may be formally logical. But new dominant understandings produce new premises and lead to new conclusions. During a lawyer's working life, many legal rules are treated as settled. The argument is over the meaning of the facts or how the rule applies to a set of facts. But law is also often changing, through new statutes or new interpretations. A lawyer sensitive to social context and social change is a wiser lawyer, a better counselor.

> A lawyer without history or literature is a mechanic, a mere working mason; if he possesses some knowledge of these, he may venture to call himself an architect.
>
> —Sir Walter Scott, *Guy Mannering* (1815).

Consider the following analysis by Jack M. Balkin and Sanford Levinson, taken from *Understanding the Constitutional Revolution*, 87 Va. L. Rev. 1045, 1066–1073 (2001).

How Constitutional Revolutions Occur: A Theory of Partisan Entrenchment

> The most important factor in understanding how constitutional revolutions occur, and indeed, how judicial review works, particularly in the twentieth century, is a phenomenon we call partisan entrenchment. To understand judicial review one must begin by understanding the role of political parties in the American constitutional system. Political parties are among the most important institutions for translating and interpreting popular will and negotiating among various interest groups and factions. Political parties are both influenced by and pro-

vide a filter for the views of social movements. Both populism and the Civil Rights Movement influenced the Democratic Party, for example, which, in turn, accepted some but not all of their ideas. The same is true of the popular insurgency that accounted for much of Senator Barry Goldwater's support in 1964, which became the base for the ultimate takeover of the Republican Party by conservatives rallying around Ronald Reagan.

When a party wins the White House, it can stock the federal judiciary with members of its own party, assuming a relatively acquiescent Senate. They will serve for long periods of time because judges enjoy life tenure. On average, Supreme Court Justices serve about eighteen years. In this sense, judges and Justices resemble Senators who are appointed for 18-year terms by their parties and never have to face election. They are temporally extended representatives of particular parties, and hence, of popular understandings about public policy and the Constitution. The temporal extension of partisan representation is what we mean by partisan entrenchment. It is a familiar feature of American constitutional history. Chief Justice John Marshall kept Federalist principles alive long after the Federalist Party itself had disbanded. William O. Douglas and William Brennan, two avatars of contemporary liberalism, promoted the constitutional values of the Democratic party for decades, just as William Rehnquist has for thirty years now proved to be a patient but persistent defender of the constitutional values of the right wing of the Republican Party.

Partisan entrenchment is an especially important engine of constitutional change. When enough members of a particular party are appointed to the federal judiciary, they start to change the understandings of the Constitution that appear in positive law. If more people are appointed in a relatively short period of time, the changes will occur more quickly. Constitutional revolutions are the cumulative result of successful partisan entrenchment when the entrenching party has a relatively coherent political ideology or can pick up sufficient ideological allies from the appointees of other parties. Thus, the Warren Court is the culmination of years of Democratic appointments to the Supreme Court, assisted by a few key liberal Republicans.

Partisan entrenchment through presidential appointments to the judiciary is the best account of how the meaning of the Constitution changes over time through Article III interpretation rather than through Article V amendment. In some sense, this is ironic, because the original vision of the Constitution did not even imagine that there would be political parties. Indeed, the founding generation was quite hostile to the very idea of party, which was associated with the hated notion of "faction." This vision collapsed no later than 1800; among other things, the 12th Amendment is a result of that collapse and the concomitant recognition of the legitimacy of political parties. A key function of political parties is to negotiate and interpret political meanings and assimilate the demands of constituents and social movements; as such, parties are the major source of constitutional transformations. They are also the major source of attempts to maintain those transformations long enough for them to become the new "conventional wisdom" about what the Constitution means.

But presidents cannot appoint just anyone to the federal judiciary or to the Supreme Court. The Senate, which may be controlled by a different political party, must advise and consent. This means that judges—and particularly Supreme Court Justices—tend to reflect the vector sum of political forces at the time of their confirmation. That is why Dwight D. Eisenhower appointed a Catholic Democrat, William Brennan, rather than a conservative Republican in 1956. And it is also why although Harry Blackmun and Antonin Scalia were both Republicans who were appointed by Republican Presidents, they turned out so differently. Blackmun was appointed in 19[70], when liberalism was still quite strong. Although the Democrats had lost the White House in 1968, they still retained control of Congress. Two Southern nominees were rejected by the Democratic Senate before President Nixon nominated the far more centrist Harry Blackmun, a close friend of Chief Justice Burger from Minnesota.

Scalia, on the other hand, was appointed in 1986. Not only had President Reagan been triumphantly reelected in 1984, but Republicans also continued to control the Senate. Scalia, who had in effect been auditioning for the Supreme Court since his appointment to the Court of Appeals for the District of Columbia, easily won unanimous confirmation in spite of his refusal to discuss even *Marbury v. Madison* (1803) with the Senate Judiciary Committee. There is little doubt that Robert Bork would have made it to the Court had he been nominated in these glory days of the Reagan Revolution, before the 1986 elections that returned the Senate to Democratic control (and the discovery that Reagan and renegades like Oliver North had traduced the law in the so-called "Iran-Contra" scandal). Following the 1986 elections, however, Democrat Joseph Biden, and not a senior Republican, headed the Senate Judiciary Committee. That meant, among other things, that extended hearings would take place, with ample opportunity for Bork's opponents to elaborate the reasons for their position and to generate widespread popular opposition to the former Yale professor. Ultimately, of course, Justice Powell's successor was not Bork, but, rather, Anthony Kennedy. It should occasion no surprise that Scalia, who faced a Senate controlled by Republicans, has turned out to be more conservative than Kennedy, who had to run the gauntlet of a Democratic Senate.

To be sure, judges and Justices grow and develop over time, though, we strongly suspect, there is less "growth" and "development" than is suggested by the ideologically-freighted reassurance that one often hears that Justices are ruggedly independent and have thoroughly unpredictable views. Indeed, there may be reason to think that Justices are less likely to change in part because they remain significantly isolated in Washington, D.C., and are too often surrounded by adoring clerks and other admirers who reinforce their existing structures of belief. Still, it would be foolhardy to deny that Justices' views sometimes do change, along with the rest of the country. But their starting points are the forces at work when they are confirmed. And those starting points are particularly important in assessing the development of their careers. Presidents will sometimes make "mistakes" like William Brennan and David Souter, both of whom turned out to be considerably more liberal than the Presidents who appointed them hoped would be the case. But this is a familiar feature of democratic politics. People often make mistakes in electing or appointing people who turn out to be more conservative or liberal than originally predicted.... The only difference is that judges and Justices serve longer, so mistakes are much costlier to the appointing party.

Furthermore, we must remember that the parties are not ideological monoliths. There are many contending factions within a party at any point in time, and a president may have sound political reasons for favoring one faction over another given the balance of forces at the time of confirmation. Moreover, the ideological centers of the major parties shift over time; as already noted, the Republican Party today is far more conservative than it was in 1968 or in 1975, the date of Gerald Ford's appointment of John Paul Stevens. Thus, we can expect that even if one party nominates most of the Justices in a particular period, there will be ideological fractures among those Justices, with later appointees, almost by definition, being more "representative" of current party positions than appointments made years before, when the political constellations might have been quite different. That Harry Blackmun was a more or less centrist Republican in 19[70] did not prevent him from being accurately perceived, two decades later, as one of the Court's leading liberals. The same is obviously true of Stevens. Of Nixon's four appointees, the only one who turned out to be strongly conservative in terms of the parameters of our own era is Rehnquist, whose name Nixon seems quite literally not to have known when he appointed him. The selection of Rehnquist — a relatively anonymous Justice Department lawyer at the time — along with Lewis Powell — a courtly Southern Democrat and former President of the American Bar Association — seems in many ways an effort simply to fill the vacancies left by Justices John Marshall Harlan and Hugo Black with appointees who would be easily confirmable and thus allow Nixon to move on to other issues about which he cared far more.

In addition to the fact that parties are themselves pluralistic, one must also take into account that presidents have a relatively short-term time horizon when making appointments. They attempt to influence certain issues that are most salient to them at the time. When genuinely new issues of constitutional interpretation arise, former allies may disagree heatedly about how to resolve them. For example, the harbingers of the "Roosevelt Revolution" — Justices Black, Douglas, Frank Murphy, Stanley Reed, and Frankfurter — were all appointed between 1937 and 1940 largely to legitimize Franklin Roosevelt's New Deal policies. Roosevelt had no reason to be disappointed: All of them opposed strict — some would say any — review of ordinary social and economic legislation, and all of them agreed that the federal government should be given immense regulatory power. Yet in later years when the focus of attention shifted to civil liberties and civil rights — a concern much less important to Roosevelt — they differed strongly, indeed bitterly, among themselves. Reed, for example, was basically opposed to *Brown v. Board of Education* (1954), acquiescing in the Court's decision only after being assured that the consequences of enforcement would be relatively minimal. And, of course, the feuds between Felix Frankfurter and Hugo Black over the degree of judicial deference in civil liberties cases were legendary.

Professor Michael Klarman has also commented on the role that individual values play in the Court's decisions. In *The Plessy Era*, 1998 Supreme Court Review 303, 306 (1998), he argued that

> in light of the general indeterminacy of traditional legal sources, the Court's constitutional interpretations are likely to reflect the personal values of the Justices. Those values, in turn, are likely to be broadly reflective of popular opinion, because the Justices are part of contemporary culture. This is not to say, of course, that the Court precisely mirrors public opinion; it plainly does not. Court decisions invalidating school prayer or criminal prohibitions on flag burning, as well as protecting the procedural rights of criminal defendants, plainly have contravened majority opinion. Yet these countermajoritarian decisions simultaneously

reveal the limits of the potential gap between public opinion and judicial outcomes. The Court did not invalidate school prayer until after the demise of the nation's unofficial Protestant establishment. The Court did not revolutionize criminal procedure until after the civil rights revolution, the War on Poverty, and revulsion against totalitarian excesses had altered popular attitudes toward criminal defendants. And the Court did not invalidate flag burning prohibitions until after a dramatic post-World War II transformation in popular conceptions of free speech.

Moreover, many of the Court's most countermajoritarian decisions have involved issues upon which a gap exists between elite opinion, as represented by the Justices, and mass opinion, as represented in legislation.

An exaggerated skepticism might see the law as merely a partisan instrument. We count on the law to protect our liberties. Judges who believe the law should not be a partisan instrument would presumably be more likely to resist partisan applications. Might extreme cynicism, to the extent that it is widely accepted, undermine the ideal that the law should not be a partisan device—should not be a device used to punish political opponents and to protect political allies?

In sum, the study of American Constitutional Law involves the examination of how all three branches of the federal government have interpreted the Constitution and have responded to the social problems presented during various eras. A major focus is on understanding the Supreme Court's opinions. These opinions articulate rules about the relationship among the three federal branches (separation of powers), the relation of the federal government to the states (federalism), and the relation of government to citizen (individual liberties). How previous generations have confronted constitutional crises may provide perspective on the unforeseen challenges of the future.

V. On Reading the Constitution

The starting point for understanding the American Constitution is to read the text. As you read the text, note the contrast between some provisions which are very precise and some provisions which are open-ended and vague. Some provide detailed and specific standards that seem automatically applicable. (The president must be at least thirty-five years of age.) Some require greater reasoned judgment in their application. (No state shall make or enforce any law which denies to any person in its jurisdiction the equal protection of the laws.)

The Constitutional Convention was divided by conflicting interests: free state vs. slave state; big state vs. small state; commercial interests vs. agricultural interests. As you read the Constitution, note the provisions which are vague. One commentator has labeled such provisions "incompletely specified agreements;" such provisions allow people to agree on general principles without agreeing in advance as to how the general principle will apply to a specific factual setting:

> Incompletely specified agreements thus have important social uses. Many of their advantages are practical. They allow people to develop frameworks for decision and judgment despite large-scale disagreements. At the same time, they help produce a degree of a social solidarity and shared commitment. People who are able to agree on political abstractions—freedom of speech, equal protection of

the laws, freedom from unreasonable searches and seizures—can also agree that they are embarking on shared projects. These forms of agreement can help *constitute* a democratic culture. It is for the same reason that they are so important to constitution-making.

Cass Sunstein, *General Propositions and Concrete Cases,* 31 Wake Forest L. Rev. 369, 371 (1996).

Drafters of statutes or constitutions write rules for future application. They delegate authority to future decision makers, in some cases allowing them more discretion, and in other cases less. Congress has discretion to raise or lower income tax rates and to decide how much different income groups should pay in taxes. It may provide for the punishment of certain crimes, but it may not pass ex post facto laws. Drafters of constitutional provisions are limited both by the inability to foresee all future situations to which their provisions will apply and by the difficulty of reaching agreement on how myriad situations should be dealt with.

Applying the law involves classification. But while the concepts by which the law classifies may have a clear central meaning, decision makers confront more difficult problems of interpretation as one moves from clear or paradigm cases to more remote ones. This is so because of the impossibility of explicitly and specifically providing for all future cases. Not even legislators can imagine all possible cases that will arise under a statute, and even if they could, it would probably be impossible to secure an agreement on how these cases should be decided. Obviously a longer document can be much more specific than a shorter one. The United States Constitution is a much shorter document than the United States Code.

Another problem with interpreting a constitution written in the past is translating its provisions so as to apply them to the contemporary world. A literal translation from one language to another may not convey the author's meaning. An assumption that 18th and 19th century words have contemporary meanings may distort the original meaning. The problem of translation of 18th century constitutional provisions to a 21st century context is extraordinarily complex. Lawrence Lessig suggests there are two steps. "The first is to locate a meaning in an original context; the second is to ask how that meaning is to be carried to a current context." *Fidelity and Constraint*, 65 Fordham L. Rev. 1365, 1372–73 (1997). The problem is complex because one must consider not only how those who gave us constitutional provisions would have understood their application in their own time, but also how their principles should be applied in a world that has been transformed from that of the 18th, 19th, or 20th centuries.

Chief Justice Marshall said that the commerce power of Congress applied to those transactions that affected more than one state. Wheat production for local use on a farm in Virginia may in 1787 have affected only Virginia. But as transportation has evolved and as markets for food have become national and international, wheat production in Virginia, or anywhere else, clearly affects more than one state.

The 4th Amendment protects persons, houses, papers, and effects from unreasonable searches and seizures. As written, it protects persons and their property. Wiretaps and electronic surveillance did not exist when the Amendment was written. Should the 4th Amendment apply to these investigative techniques? At first, the majority of the Supreme Court held the Amendment did not apply. Justice Brandeis dissented. He said the Amendment was designed to protect privacy, not simply property. As Professor Lessig has commented,

> To that end, given the technologies of the late eighteenth century, [the framers and ratifiers of the 4th Amendment] selected the means [they] did. But as the

technologies of invasion have changed, Brandeis said, so too should the techniques of protection change. The 4th Amendment ... had to be translated to give citizens in the twentieth century the sort of protection that the Framers gave citizens in the eighteenth.

Lessig, 65 Fordham L. Rev. at 1379.

One response to those who advocate less mechanical methods of interpretation is that if change is required, the Constitution has provisions for amendment. Amendments are quite difficult to enact because of the type of supermajority required. The original Constitution was drafted and ratified by a narrow segment of the population. If provisions of the Constitution disadvantage or fail to protect groups that were excluded from the original process, is it problematic that democracy requires that they now must convince a supermajority to amend these provisions?

It is also true, however, that other branches of government can institute changes short of constitutional amendment. Congress and state legislatures have sometimes responded to the failure of the Court to protect rights by passing legislation. For example, when the Illinois Supreme Court ruled that women could not become lawyers, and the U.S. Supreme Court upheld that result, the legislature of Illinois passed a statute allowing women to practice law and to engage in all professions but the military.

For discussions of problems of drafting and interpretation, see, e.g., H. L. A. Hart, *The Concept of Law*, 125–26 (1961) and Charles Curtis, *A Better Theory of Legal Interpretation*, 3 Vand. L. Rev. 407 (1950). The literature on constitutional interpretation is vast. For additional thought provoking explorations, see, e.g., Richard H. Fallon, Jr., *A Constructivist Coherence Theory of Constitutional Interpretation*, 100 Harv. L. Rev. 1189 (1987); Wilson Huhn, *The Five Types of Legal Argument* (2002); and Michael J. Perry, *We the People: The Fourteenth Amendment and the Supreme Court* (1999).

A. Types of Constitutional Arguments

We have prepared this discussion to help you in your study of methods of constitutional argument. The concepts set out here are influenced by two major books on types of constitutional arguments: Philip Bobbitt, *Constitutional Fate* (1982) and Charles L. Black, Jr., *Structure and Relationship in Constitutional Law* (1986). It may help you to see how these arguments have been used in another context—whether the 14th Amendment requires the states to obey the guarantees of the federal Bill of Rights. For a discussion of that question, see Michael Kent Curtis, *Resurrecting the Privileges or Immunities Clause and Revising the Slaughter-House Cases Without Exhuming Lochner: Individual Rights and the Fourteenth Amendment*, 38 Boston College L. Rev. 1, 19–36 (1996).

In the following discussion we describe some basic types of constitutional argument. To see the type of argument being made (textual, structural, from precedent, historical, or policy) ask yourself where the argument starts, what are its premises. Textual arguments typically start by looking intensively at words of the text. Structural arguments look first at the type of arrangement or governmental structure the Constitution contemplates. Historical arguments typically begin with a look at history, etc. If you believe that the arguments sometimes appear in hybrid or mixed form, you are correct. However, often one type of argument predominates.

1. *An argument from text*. This method seeks to find the meaning and operation of provisions of the Constitution by looking at the meaning of the words of the text. What

is the plain meaning of the words to an ordinary speaker of English? What is the accepted legal meaning? One resource for analysis is a dictionary. Should the dictionary be one in use at the time the text at issue was drafted? The reasoning tends to move from a detailed examination of the particular words of the Constitution to a conclusion about how a particular legal problem is to be resolved.

2. *An argument from context* (an intra-textual argument). The contextual argument focuses on the use of words in other parts of the Constitution to throw light on the clause under consideration. In *McCulloch v. Maryland* (1819), a case dealing with federal power to establish a national bank, Chief Justice Marshall argues that necessary in the "necessary and proper" clause means useful or conducive to, not absolutely necessary. He points to another section of the Constitution where the words "absolutely necessary" are used to argue that had the framers meant absolutely necessary in the Necessary and Proper Clause they would have used those exact words as they did elsewhere.

3. *An argument from structure and relationship.* This argument does not focus on the meaning of particular constitutional words or texts, but rather looks at the broader objects or purposes of the Constitution and asks how the Constitution must be interpreted to achieve those purposes. The focus is on how the constitutional machinery needs to work in order to achieve constitutional objectives.

   Charles Black, in his book *Structure and Relationship in Constitutional Law*, argues that the decision in *McCulloch v. Maryland* is mainly one based on structure. May the state tax the Bank of the United States? Marshall answers no. He reasons that the overall structure created by the Constitution establishes the necessary relation between the states and the federal government. To allow a part, a single state, to frustrate the will of the whole by destroying a congressionally chartered bank is contrary to the way the governmental structure established by the Constitution was intended to function.

4. *An argument from precedent.* By precedent we mean a judicial decision. Here the argument runs from the fact that an analogous case has been decided in a particular way in the past to the conclusion that the case under consideration should be decided based on the "rule" contained in the prior case. For example, in 1833 the Court held in *Barron v. Baltimore* that the Bill of Rights was not a limitation on the states, but only on the national government. Thus, the Court held that the Takings Clause of the 5th Amendment did not limit the states. It supported this decision by the argument that none of the generally phrased limitations in the Constitution were designed to limit state or local government. *Barron* did not cite a single case, so it made no argument from precedent. The next case involved the right to civil jury trial guaranteed by the 7th Amendment. The Court argued from the rule of *Barron* to the conclusion that the 7th Amendment did not limit the states. That was an argument from precedent.

   There is another factor you should understand in the use of precedent: the era in which the case was decided. Precedent based on a type of analysis that has subsequently been repudiated by the Court is typically not controlling, even though the case has not been formally overruled. At the very least, it is entitled to diminished weight. Similarly, a later constitutional amendment may undermine earlier precedent. The trend of modern decisions can also be used to undermine prior inconsistent precedent. If three of the four propositions a case stands for have been undermined, that fact may make the fourth proposition less persuasive. Sometimes the result of prior cases can be and is re-interpreted so that the outcome is compatible with current doctrine.

5. *An argument from history.* Here the argument often runs from the historical problem that the constitutional provision was addressing to a conclusion as to how a particular case should be decided. For an example, consider the Establishment Clause of the 1st Amendment, "Congress shall make no law respecting an establishment of religion...." Some Supreme Court Justices argue that the framers of the Establishment Clause were well aware of the fact that governmentally-mandated religious doctrine had often led to sectarian strife and persecution during the 17th and 18th centuries. Therefore, for these Justices, the main purpose of the Establishment Clause was to prevent the state from endorsing or mandating religion.

We list six types of historical argument. They are not entirely distinct from one another.

   a. *Original intent.* The claim that a constitutional question should be decided in accordance with the "intent of the framers" is a type of historical argument. The framers of the Constitution are (typically) those members of the Constitutional Convention. The framers of a constitutional amendment are (typically) those members of Congress who proposed it. One might also look at the intent of the ratifiers in the states or the intent of the people they represent. Establishing the "original intent" of the framers is a difficult matter because there are so many framers and so few typically speak to the issue. This problem has led some to propose instead that we look at the views of "leading proponents."

   b. *Original meaning.* This method suggests that we seek to find the meaning of a constitutional provision by looking at how the words it uses would have been commonly understood at the time it was proposed and adopted. This view pays less attention to "intent" (which is difficult to ascertain) and more to actual words. For example, dictionary definitions from the time, and how people then used the words, are considered highly relevant.

   c. *Larger historical context and grievances that led to the proposal.* One way of understanding a constitutional provision is to study the larger historical context in which it was produced and the social or political problems the provision sought to address. Sometimes prior cases can be used to show what a constitutional amendment was designed to change.

   d. *History as experience leading to practical wisdom.* Often the Court reviews history for the light it throws on the decisions it faces. One approach is the use of history as showing what should be avoided—history as negative precedent (using precedent in the broad sense of an appeal to the past). For example, in *United States v. Morrison* (2000) and *United States v. Lopez* (1995), some dissenting Justices reviewed the history of the collision between the Court's restrictive interpretation of the Commerce Clause and New Deal legislation. They concluded that the Court's narrow construction of congressional power was a mistake that should not be repeated. In gender discrimination cases, Justices sometimes refer to the history of past discrimination against women and the Court's decisions upholding such discrimination. Again, history is used, at least in part, to show what should be avoided.

   e. *History as a tradition used to limit broad constitutional phrases (such as "liberty" in the Due Process Clause).* In *Bowers v. Hardwick* (1986), the Court points to a long history of condemnation of homosexual sodomy to justify its decision that the right of consenting adults to engage in consensual sodomy in the privacy of the home is not constitutionally protected. In *Lawrence v. Texas* (2003), the Court overruled *Bowers* and criticized the historical analysis used by the *Bowers* majority.

    f. *The arc of history as revealed by the text of the Constitution.* Professor Akhil Amar has suggested still another use of history: the arc of history. This analysis focuses, for example, on the unfolding progress of liberty and equality as revealed by the evolving text of the Constitution. Examples include the addition of the Bill of Rights; the abolition of slavery; the expansion of suffrage to include black men, then women, and then those eighteen years of age or older; an Amendment permitting a progressive income tax; and the abolition of the poll tax in federal elections. Akhil Reed Amar, *Architexture*, 77 Ind. L.J. 671, 685–86 (2002).

6. *An argument from ethical aspirations.* The Constitution and founding documents such as the Declaration of Independence contain ethical aspirations. The Constitution announces the goal of promoting the "General Welfare" and securing the "Blessings of Liberty." The Declaration says "all men are created equal" and are "endowed by their Creator" with "certain unalienable Rights" including "Life, Liberty, and the Pursuit of Happiness" and that "to secure these Rights Governments are instituted among Men, deriving their just Powers from the Consent of the Governed...." The Court may cite the ethical aspirations reflected in such language as a guide to interpretation of a particular provision.

7. *An argument from public policy.* Here the argument is that a certain interpretation is necessary to promote some social good. Arguments from policy do not depend on interpretation, for example, of text, history, or precedent. Of course, all these categories are sometimes less distinct in the real world.

* * *

Some of these methods of construction are primarily intrinsic, that is they mainly look within the four corners of the document—e.g., text and context. Some are mainly extrinsic—e.g., history and policy.

Obviously the Court can make more than one type of argument in favor of a particular result. Indeed, the strongest briefs and court opinions are often those that successfully combine several types of argument. Interpretation is most difficult when the methods of interpretation point in opposite directions. It is easiest when all support the same result. Conflict between types of argument has led some scholars to suggest a hierarchy of constitutional arguments.

Professor Richard Fallon suggests a "constructivist coherence theory of interpretation." He suggests that the various types of constitutional argument, while distinct, are sufficiently interconnected; so, a constitutional interpreter can often construct a coherent argument in which the five types he identifies (text, historical intent, theory, precedent, and value) reciprocally influence each other and point toward the same result. When this is not the case, Fallon suggests a hierarchy be used to address "the commensurability problem"— the problem of the comparative weight to be given to different types of argument when they conflict and how the different types fit together to produce a result. In the case of conflict, Fallon suggests a hierarchy in which a clear text controls. The intent of the framers "occupies a second slot in the hierarchy;" arguments from theory are third, followed by arguments from precedent and finally by what he calls arguments from value. Though Fallon's terminology differs somewhat from that suggested here, he is considering similar problems to those involved in the types of constitutional argument we suggest. Richard

H. Fallon, Jr., *A Constructivist Coherence Theory of Constitutional Interpretation*, 100 Harv. L. Rev. 1189, 1244–46 (1987).

Professor Wilson Huhn suggests a different method of resolving conflicts between types of argument. Again his categories (text, intent, precedent, tradition, and policy) are somewhat different from those suggested here and are designed to apply to all kinds of legal analysis, not just constitutional analysis.

> [W]hen the different types of legal argument were introduced, I suggested that each type of argument serves a different fundamental value of our system of laws. Textual analysis makes the law objective. Reference to the intent of the drafters of the law shows respect for the principle of popular sovereignty. Following precedent ensures stability in the law. Adhering to tradition promotes social cohesion. And policy arguments allow the law to adjust to new situations and ensure that the consequences of the legal determination will be consistent with the underlying purposes of the law....
>
> The resolution of cross-type conflict—and the solution to the commensurability problem—lies in balancing the values that each of the different types of argument serve. It is not possible to create a rigid hierarchy of types of arguments. There is a rough sense that the arguments should be ranked in the order they are listed: text, intent, precedent, tradition, and policy. Certainly many judicial opinions proceed in that order. However, the existence of a rigid hierarchy could not explain why, for example, when text conflicts with intent, the text controls in some cases, and the intent of the drafters controls in other cases. Each conflict must be evaluated in the context of the particular case.
>
> The resolution of cross-type conflicts is more nuanced and complex than can be explained by either a foundational or hierarchical approach. Cross-type conflicts are resolved by balancing the policies that are served by the different kinds of legal arguments. For example, in cases where the court finds that the need for objectivity and clarity outweighs the need to conform to societal expectations, then text will prevail over tradition. In a case that pitted precedent against policy, Cardozo balanced "consistency and certainty" against "equity and fairness," and found that the latter prevailed....
>
> Each type of legal argument has particular virtues and vices which vary from case to case and from field to field. The solution that I propose to the "commensurability problem" is that judges implicitly weigh not only the internal strength of an argument on its own terms, but also the external strength of the type of argument as measured by the underlying values of objectivity, popular will, consistency, societal coherence, flexibility and justice, in the context of the particular case. The persuasiveness of any legal argument is a function of both its internal (intra-type) and its external (cross-type) strength.

Wilson Huhn, *The Five Types of Legal Argument* 152–56 (2002).

B. Goals for Reviewing the Types of Constitutional Arguments

- As you read the following cases, look for types of arguments. Do particular types of arguments tend to appear more often in certain types of cases? Once precedent is well established, the Court looks more to precedent and less to text, structure, history, and policy, except perhaps when it reconsiders precedent.

- Be aware of these types of argument when they appear in court decisions.
- Should any one of these types of argument control another when they conflict? Is there a hierarchy of constitutional arguments?
- When might you be more likely to use a particular type of argument?
- Consider what to do if precedent is against you. Do you automatically give up or are there other types of arguments you might make? What arguments might suggest that the precedent should be changed?

C. Exercises

1. Assume a state statute prohibits obscuring the letters or numbers on vehicle license plates. It reads as follows:

> *Alteration, Disguise, or Concealment of Numbers.* Any operator of a motor vehicle who shall willfully cover or cause to be covered, or alter or add to or cut off any part or portion of a registration plate or the numbers or letters thereon, shall be guilty of a misdemeanor.

The state places the slogan "First in Freedom" on the license plates in addition to the numbers and letters that identify the vehicle. Could a motorist who thought the state was not First in Freedom cover up the slogan with black masking tape? Does covering up a non-identifying slogan fall within the statute's prohibition of obscuring the letters and numbers? Is there a conflict between the purpose of the statute and its wording?

If the conduct violates the statute, should the act of obscuring the slogan (but not the identifying letters and numbers) be treated as protected expression under the 1st and 14th Amendments? Government can make no law "abridging the freedom of speech." Is covering the slogan with tape within the "freedom of speech?"

Sometimes the plain meaning of the text, its history and purpose, sound public policy, and other factors bearing on the decision will all point in one direction. But sometimes they will not, creating a situation where an individual judge's hierarchy of values is more likely to be determinative.

2. Assume that the constitution of a state, ratified in 1858, provided that "jurors shall be chosen randomly from a list of all persons who are qualified to vote in the county in which a session of court requiring jurors shall be held." This provision was still in effect in 1923. In 1920, the 19th Amendment to the United States Constitution was ratified. It provides that the

> right of citizens of the United States to vote shall not be denied or abridged by the United States or by any State on account of sex.

Women could not vote in the state before the 19th Amendment. After the Amendment, the state continues to select only male jurors. This practice is challenged in 1923 as a violation of the *state* constitution by a group of women voters who reside in the state. The women allege that they want to serve as jurors and that they possess all requisite qualifications. The case is brought in state court and the only issue raised is whether, in light of the fact that women are now voters, the state constitution should be interpreted to require that they be allowed also to serve as jurors. Decide the case based on the state constitutional provision mentioned in this hypothetical. Explain your theory of interpretation that underlies your decision and acknowledge any theory that you reject and explain why you do so. Can you use different types of constitutional argument—text, history, structure, ethical aspirations, etc.? Is the text relevant? Is Professor Lessig's idea of "translation" relevant? Is original intent relevant? What would original intent mean in these circumstances? Is original meaning relevant? Is history? Should a federal claim that the 19th Amendment made women jurors as well as voters be successful?

VI. A Problem for Constitutional Analysis: The Clinton Impeachment

The impeachment of President William J. Clinton involved constitutional law even though there was never a court case. Congressional removal of a duly elected president is obviously a profound alteration of the political order. It is also a constitutional decision of the highest order. The House of Representatives continually referred to the Constitution as it decided whether any of the various allegations made against Clinton justified Articles of Impeachment. The Senate similarly consulted the Constitution as it tried Clinton on the Articles. The eventual acquittal in the Senate allowed Clinton to remain in office. Decisions made during both the House and Senate proceedings will be appealed to as precedent during some future impeachment crisis.

Below are remarks by two law professors, Stephen Presser and Laurence Tribe, who testified before the House Judiciary Committee on whether or not Clinton had committed any offenses which called for impeachment under the standards set out in the Constitution. The historic and current understanding is that decisions on whether to impeach and convict are solely for Congress. As you read the testimony, note the nature of the various arguments each makes. How many different types of argument can you recognize? Which type of argument do you find the most persuasive? Whose conclusion do you find to be the most compelling?

Testimony of Stephen B. Presser, Raoul Berger Professor of Legal History, Northwestern University School of Law, Before the Constitution Subcommittee of the Committee on the Judiciary, United States House of Representatives, Hearing on "The Background and History of Impeachment," November 9, 1998.[1]

I appear at the request of the Committee to discuss the history of impeachment, and the meaning of the Constitutional phrase "high Crimes and Misdemeanors."

The Constitution, as you know, provides in Article II, §4, that "The President, Vice President, and all civil Officers of the United States, shall be removed from Office on impeachment for, and Conviction of Treason, Bribery or other high Crimes and Misdemeanors."... I think I can be of most service to the subcommittee if I examine the question of what "Treason, Bribery or other high Crimes and Misdemeanors" means by asking what the phrase would have meant to the Constitution's framers. In order to understand this we need to try to place the impeachment remedy in the context of the framers' assumptions about how the Constitution would work, and what would make it work best....

---

1. The remarks have been edited and the footnotes have been renumbered.

The debates over the 1787 Constitution are filled with discussion about how virtue was to be secured in the new government, in all three branches. It is in this context that impeachment must be understood. Impeachment was believed by the framers to be a vital device intended to guarantee that the president and other federal officials would act with integrity. Indeed, it was a device designed to ensure that the president and other federal officials would do what they were supposed to do, because they would know that they would face removal if they did not. This becomes clear when we examine the contemporary record.

I will rely, for most of my testimony, on the text of the Constitution, and on the most important contemporary exposition of the Constitution, *The Federalist Papers*, the series of essays on the Constitution written by James Madison, Alexander Hamilton, and John Jay, in the years 1787–88, immediately following the drafting of the Constitution at the Philadelphia Convention. *The Federalist* is universally acknowledged to be the most important contemporary exposition of the federal Constitution. But it is more than a powerful contemporary account. It is, in many ways, a work exploring timeless political truths. To this day, it is regarded as the most important American work in political science.

Thomas Jefferson praised the book as "the best commentary on the principles of government which ever was written." James Madison, one of *The Federalist*'s three authors, suggested in 1825 that *The Federalist* was "the most authentic exposition of the text of the federal Constitution, as understood by the Body which prepared and the authority which accepted it." The fact that the third and the fourth Presidents were thus so fulsome in praise of *The Federalist* suggests that they agreed with *The Federalist*'s views of how the Presidency and how the impeachment process was to operate.

One very clear indication of what was intended with regard to impeachment is provided in *Federalist* 64, one of the few numbers written by John Jay, who was to become the first Chief Justice of the United States. Jay is discussing the treaty power, and is responding, in particular, to critics of the Constitution who argued that the President and the Senate were given too much discretion in committing the new nation to treaties with other nations. Jay notes that the presidential power of making treaties—perhaps the most important foreign policy power which the president has discretion to exercise—is important because it relates to "war, peace, and commerce," and that it should not be delegated "but in such a mode, and with such precautions, as will afford the highest security that it will be exercised by men the best qualified for the purpose, and in the manner most conducive to the public good." Jay goes on to explain that the means of picking the president—indirectly through the electoral college—is calculated so that the president will be a person noted for integrity, virtue, and probity, and that the original indirect means of selecting Senators—through the state legislatures—was to assure the same for the Senators.

Jay makes plain that when a president fails to live up to the requirement of trust, honor, and virtue that is necessary to meet his treaty-making and other executive responsibilities—if, in short, he is not an honorable or virtuous person who will perform his duties in the interest of the people—impeachment is available to remove him. When Jay addresses the requisite integrity for Presidents and Senators, he states:

> With respect to their responsibility, it is difficult to conceive how it could be increased. Every consideration that can influence the human mind, such as honor, oaths, reputations, conscience, the love of country, and family affections and attachments, afford security for their fidelity. In short, as the Constitution has taken [through the indirect election of Senators and Presidents] care that they

shall be men of talents, and integrity, we have reason to be persuaded that the treaties they make will be as advantageous as, all circumstances considered, could be made; and so far as the fear of punishment and disgrace can operate, that motive to good behaviour is amply afforded by the article on the subject of impeachments.

Virtue, probity, and honor were so important in the executive, as Jay's remarks indicate, that it is no surprise that the framers assumed that the first President of the United States would have to be George Washington. He was the greatest national hero, he was given the lion's share of the responsibility for securing independence, and then as now was regarded as the father of his country. His reputation for integrity, virtue, and honor was unparalleled. George Washington, the national epitome of virtue and honor, was, in short, precisely the kind of executive *Federalist* 64 contemplates.

Federalist 64 thus tells us about the requisite character of federal officials, and is persuasive authority for believing that when it becomes clear that the president has committed acts which raise grave doubts about his honesty, his virtue, or his honor, impeachment is available as a remedy. This is further supported by the text of the Constitution itself, where it provides in article I, §3, that the punishments which are to be imposed following impeachment by the house and conviction by the Senate are "removal from Office, and *disqualification to hold and enjoy any Office of honor, Trust or Profit* under the United States." The kind of a person who would be impeached was believed to be one without honor and who thus could not be trusted. The fear was that such a person, if allowed an office offering the opportunity to profit, would use his office for personal ends and not for the good of the people. Impeachment, then, is all about deciding whether a particular official can be trusted to act with disinterested virtue, or whether an official will put his own needs or desires above his Constitutional duties.

It is for this reason—that impeachment is a remedy against those who would betray their oaths to uphold the Constitution and would instead seek personal advantage—that the framers chose to describe, although not to limit impeachable offenses, by including and using as an analogy "Treason and Bribery." "Treason" is defined in [Article III, §3 of] the Constitution itself as "levying War against [the United States], or in adhering to their Enemies, giving them Aid and Comfort." The essence of Treason, then, is that it involves a betrayal of one's obligation to one's own people, by making war against them, or by adhering to their enemies. Similarly, "Bribery" involves a betrayal of virtue and a refusal to exercise disinterested judgment in the interests of the people in order to serve the interests of someone else—someone who wrongly and corruptly buys what should only belong to the people. In both cases the wrongdoer, the traitor or the person bribed, turns from his duty and puts his own interests ahead of those who trusted in him.

This suggestion that impeachment, in essence, is about a fundamental betrayal of trust, finds further support in the limited records that we have of the Constitutional Convention. On August 20, 1787, the Committee of Detail presented a proposal that would have made federal officers "liable to impeachment and removal from office for neglect of duty, malversation,[2] or corruption." Somewhat later, however, on September 8, 1787 the Con-

---

2. *Black's Law Dictionary* defines "malversation," as "In French law, this word is applied to all grave and punishable faults committed in the exercise of a charge or commission (office), such as corruption, exaction, concussion, larceny." *Black's Law Dictionary* 865 (5th ed., 1979). "Concussion," according to *Black's* is "In the civil law, the unlawful forcing of another by threats of violence to give something of value." *Id.*, at 264.

vention had before it a revised text that would have limited impeachment only to those cases involving "Treason & bribery." George Mason, of Virginia, thought this too limiting, and argued:

> Why is the provision restrained to Treason & bribery only? Treason as defined in the Constitution will not reach many great and dangerous offences. [Warren] Hastings [the administrator of the East India Company and Governor-General of Bengal whom Edmund Burke led an effort to impeach for corruption] is not guilty of Treason. Attempts to subvert the Constitution may not be Treason as above defined—As bills of attainder which have saved the British Constitution are forbidden, it is the more necessary to extend: the power of impeachments.

Mason then moved to add after the word "bribery" the words "or maladministration." James Madison, one of the authors of *The Federalist*, and the man most commonly described at the "Father" of the Constitution, objected on the grounds that "maladministration" was too elusive. "So vague a term," he said, "will be equivalent to a tenure during pleasure of the Senate." To meet Madison's objection, and to make clearer that more than Senatorial whim was required for removal, Mason "withdrew 'maladministration' and substitute[d] 'other high crimes & misdemeanors,'" which was then accepted and became the Constitutional text we now seek to interpret.

The colloquy between Mason and Madison is the only evidence we have from the debates at the 1787 Constitutional convention at Philadelphia, but it appears to suggest that more than mere maladministration, something approaching "great and dangerous offences," or an "[a]ttempt to subvert the Constitution" is required. Those who emphasize the awful consequences of impeachment, and the propriety of its use only for offenses that strike at the heart of American government can find support in Mason's words. But it must be understood what Mason and the other framers believed the needs of the state were, and what American government was all about. The essence of the new republic was that ours was to be a "government of laws and not of men," and that our laws and our legal doctrines were not to be tossed aside at whim for personal or partisan political purposes. For a president to be impeached, then, he must have committed some grave offence which is contrary to his oath to uphold the Constitution and laws of his country; he must have put his interests above the Constitution and the laws.

The distinction between mere "maladministration" and the betrayals of the Constitution with which impeachment was supposed to be concerned is also the subject of some rumination by another one of *The Federalist*'s authors, Alexander Hamilton. In *Federalist* 79, Hamilton warns against using "inability," a term similar in meaning to "maladministration,"[3] as a trigger for impeachment because "[a]n attempt to fix the boundary between the regions of ability and inability would much oftener give scope to personal and party attachments and enmities than advance the interests of justice or the public good."[4] Impeachment, then, is a remedy for, and is not to be used as a tool of, per-

---

3. The meaning of maladministration may be somewhat elusive. *Black's Law Dictionary* defines it as "This term is used interchangeably with misadministration, and both words mean 'wrong administration.'" *Black's Law Dictionary, supra* note 13, at 861. The Concise Oxford Dictionary defines "maladministration" as "Faulty administration," H.W. Fowler and F.G. Fowler, eds., *The Concise Oxford Dictionary of Current English* 693 (3rd ed. 1944).

4. ... In *Federalist* 79 Hamilton is discussing impeachment of judges, which he suggests can occur whenever there is "malconduct." He draws no distinction between the criterion for impeachment of judges and those for the president, however, and thus the "malconduct" to which he refers is most likely the same kind discussed in *Federalist* Nos. 64 and 65 which deal with impeachment of the president. There are some who have sought to suggest that the criteria for impeaching a judge ought to

sonal or party ambition or enmity; impeachment is to be used to further "justice" and "the public good." Again, the essence of what's impeachable appears to be an unjust turning against public duties, an attempt to work an "injustice" and to betray one's duties to the public—in short, to act contrary to one's oath to uphold the Constitution and laws of the Country.

The words "high crimes or misdemeanors" similarly suggest the anti-public oath-abjuring characteristics of what ought to constitute an impeachable offense. A "high" crime or misdemeanor is distinguishable from run of the mill crimes or misdemeanors in that it requires proof of an "injury to the commonwealth—that is, to the state and to its constitution." An impeachable act, then, must be one that involves injury to the state, one that, as Mason suggested, subverts the Constitution. In the United States, of course, acts which consciously seek to undermine the nature of our rule by settled laws and processes are just such an injury to the state, such a subversion of our Constitution.

There are many ways such an undermining or subversion can take place. Accordingly, the framers believed that "high Crimes and Misdemeanors," if the impeachment provisions were to serve their purposes of keeping the executive and judiciary faithful to their Constitutional trust, could be broadly construed. Thus, Alexander Hamilton, in *Federalist* 65, where he discusses the judicial function of the Senate in trials of impeachments, broadly defines impeachment as a remedy generally available to correct wrongdoing. "The subjects of [the Senate's impeachment] jurisdiction are those offenses which proceed from the misconduct of public men, or, in other words, from the abuse or violation of some public trust." Hamilton, as did some of the other framers noted above, supplied some limitation on the impeachment power when he wrote that impeachable offenses "relate chiefly to injuries done immediately to the society itself." Hamilton even observed—presciently, given recent events in our case—that when an impeachment proceeding was underway it will seldom fail to agitate the passions of the whole community, and to divide it into parties more or less friendly or inimical to the accused. In many cases it will connect itself with the pre-existing factions, and will enlist all their animosities, partialities, influence, and interest on one side or on the other; and in such cases there will always be the greatest danger that the decision will be regulated more by the comparative strength of parties than by the real demonstrations of innocence or guilt.

Hamilton believed that the Senate, supposedly further removed from the people through election by state legislatures and not by the people themselves, would be better able to put raw partisan political concerns aside, and make objective determinations on the guilt or innocence of one impeached. Since the Senate is no longer thus insulated from popular election, it is doubly important that both the House and the Senate try to approach the impeachment of the president in as objective a manner as possible. Given the breadth of the possible definition of "high Crimes and Misdemeanors," and, as Hamilton noted, the inevitable involvement of partisan politics, it is no wonder that there is division in this body and in the nation generally about what constitutes an impeachable offense. If we are able to set aside partisan politics, however, we can fix with some certainty the nature of the acts against the state and the Constitution which the framers would have regarded as coming within the phrase "high Crimes and Misdemeanors."

At the time the framers were inserting the phrase "high Crimes and Misdemeanors" into the Constitution they had a wealth of English experience with those words to draw on, and it appears clear that the framers intended and understood that the phrase "high

---

be different from the criteria for impeaching a president, but there is no clear indication of a difference either in the Constitution or in the *Federalist*.

crimes and misdemeanors" was to be interpreted according to the meaning it was given by English Common Law. As Justice Joseph Story was later to write, "The only safe guide in such cases must be the common law, which is the guardian at once of private rights and public liberties."

Raoul Berger, in his book on impeachments, has given us a handy summary of some of the impeachment proceedings brought in England before the framing of our Constitution, proceedings described as involving all or part of the phrase "high Crimes and Misdemeanors." These included the proceedings brought against the Earl of Suffolk (1386), who "applied appropriated funds to purposes other than those specified;" the Duke of Suffolk (1450), who "procured offices for persons who were unfit and unworthy of them; [and who] delayed justice by stopping writs of appeal (private criminal prosecutions) for the deaths of complainants' husbands;" Attorney General Yelverton (1621), who "committed persons for refusal to enter into bonds before he had authority so to require; [and who also was guilty of] commencing but not prosecuting suits;" Lord Treasurer Middlesex (1624) who "allowed the office of Ordinance to go unrepaired though money was appropriated for that purpose [and who] allowed contracts for greatly needed powder to lapse for want of payment;" the Duke of Buckingham (1626) who "though young and inexperienced, procured offices for himself, thereby blocking the deserving; [who] neglected as great admiral to safeguard the seas; [and who] procured titles of honor to his mother, brothers, kindred;" Justice Berkley who "reviled and threatened the grand jury for presenting the removal of the communion table in All Saints Church; [and who] on the trial of an indictment ... 'did much discourage complainants' counsel' and 'did overrule the cause for matter of law;'" Sir Richard Burney, Lord Mayor of London (1642), who "thwarted Parliament's order to store arms and ammunition in storehouses;" Viscount Mordaunt (1660), who "prevented Tayleur from standing for election as a burgess to serve in Parliament; [and who] caused his illegal arrest and detention;" Peter Pett, Commissioner of the Navy (1668) who was guilty of "negligent preparation for the Dutch invasion; [and who was responsible for] loss of a ship through neglect to bring it to mooring;" Chief Justice North "[who] assisted the Attorney General in drawing a proclamation to suppress petitions to the King to call a Parliament;" Chief Justice Scroggs (1680), who "discharged a grand jury before they made their presentment, thereby obstructing the presentment of many Papists; [and who] arbitrarily granted general warrants in blank;" Sir Edward Seymour (1680) who "applied appropriated funds to public purposes other than those specified;" and the Duke of Leeds (1695) who "as president of the Privy Council accepted 5,500 guineas from the East India Company to procure a charter of confirmation."

One way of characterizing all of this English experience is to say, as Joseph Story did, that "lord chancellors and judges and other magistrates have not only been impeached for bribery, and acting grossly contrary to the duties of their office, but for misleading their sovereign by unconstitutional opinions and for attempts to subvert the fundamental laws, and introduce arbitrary power." The English cases lend further support to the notion derived from *The Federalist* and the text of the Constitution that impeachable offenses, "high Crimes and Misdemeanors" if you will, are acts that are inconsistent with the obligations and duties of office, are acts that involve putting personal or partisan concerns ahead of the interests of the people, and are acts which demonstrate the unfitness of the man to the office.

The Constitution, *The Federalist*, and the English common law experience give a very good general idea of what was meant by the Constitution's impeachment clauses. The meaning of "high Crimes and Misdemeanors" is thus capable of being understood as it was to the framers. It is important also to understand, however, that it is impossible to fix with certainty the complete enumeration of impeachable offenses, and it is impossible to escape the fact that the Constitution vests complete and unreviewable discretion with regard to impeachment and removal in Congress. Hamilton recognized this too:

> This [the trial of impeachments] can never be tied down by such strict rules, either in the delineation of the offense by the prosecutors [The House of Representatives] or in the construction of it by the judges [the Senate], as in common cases serve to limit the discretion of courts in favor of personal security. There will be no jury to stand between the judges who are to pronounce the sentence of the law and the party who is to receive or suffer it. The awful discretion which a court of impeachments must necessarily have to doom to honor or to infamy the most confidential and the most distinguished characters of the community forbids the commitment of the trust to a small number of persons [and so it is placed in the hands of the entire Senate].

All of this and more, of course, has led earlier students of impeachment to believe that the phrase "high Crimes and Misdemeanors" does not necessarily encompass only criminal acts, but is a general term to refer to any kind of misuse of office that the Congress finds intolerable. Indeed, Gerald Ford's famous suggestion that "high Crimes and Misdemeanors" means anything the House of Representatives wants it to mean, reflects the essential notion that the Constitution confers broad discretion on this House to make up its own mind about what kinds of conduct should lead to an impeachment proceeding. It is more than a little presumptuous, then, for me or any other law professor—or even 400 history professors—to tell you how you should define "high Crimes and Misdemeanors"—the oath you took to uphold the Constitution requires you to make that determination for yourselves, because the maintenance of the quality of the Executive which the Constitutional structure demands is part of your job.

It should be remembered, after all, that the Constitution, while it gives you discretion to determine whether a particular act or series of acts amounts to grounds for impeachment, requires you to move forward to impeach if you determine there are such acts. The language of Article II, §4 is imperative: "The President, Vice President, and all civil Officers of the United States, shall be removed from Office on impeachment for, and Conviction of Treason, Bribery or other high Crimes and Misdemeanors." Once you determine that impeachable acts have been committed, you have no choice—if the Constitution is to function as the framers' understood—you must impeach, leaving the decision on removal to the Senate. In the exercise of your discretion, though, as we have seen, there are some guidelines from the text of the Constitution, from the contemporary exposition in *The Federalist*, in the debates over the impeachment provision, and in the examples from English practice: impeachable offenses are those that demonstrate a fundamental betrayal of a public trust; they are those that suggest the federal official under investigation has deliberately failed in his duty to uphold the Constitution and laws he was sworn to enforce; and they are those which suggest that the official does not possess the virtue or character necessary to maintain the faith of the people in his honesty and wisdom. This is a determination to be made by the peoples' representatives in the House of Congress closest to the people themselves—you.

But perhaps it would not be untoward of me, in light of what I have tried to suggest about the Framers' understanding, briefly to consider the charges so far levied against President Clinton, and to express an opinion about whether they rise to the level the framers thought necessary. As this is written, there are two formulations of these charges that have come before you. The first is from Judge Starr's report to you, and the other is by the Committee's chief investigator, David Schippers.

Judge Starr submitted what he believed to be "substantial and credible information" regarding eleven impeachable offenses....

Your Chief Investigative Counsel, Mr. Schippers, based on the referral from Judge Starr, recast Judge Starr's evidence into fifteen purportedly impeachable offenses, including that 1) The President may have been part of a conspiracy with Monica Lewinsky and others to obstruct justice by providing false and misleading testimony under oath in a civil deposition and before a grand jury, withholding evidence, and tampering with prospective witnesses, 2) The President may have aided, abetted, counseled, and procured Monica Lewinsky to file and caused to be filed a false affidavit in the case of *Jones v. Clinton*, 3) The President may have aided, abetted, counseled, and procured Monica Lewinsky to obstruct justice by filing a false affidavit, 4) The President may have engaged in misprision of felonies by taking affirmative steps to conceal Monica Lewinsky's felonies in connection with her submission of a false affidavit, 5) The President may have testified falsely under oath in his deposition in *Jones v. Clinton* regarding his relationship with Ms. Lewinsky, 6) The President may have given false testimony under oath before the federal grand jury on August 17, 1998, regarding his relationship with Ms. Lewinsky, 7) The President may have given false testimony under oath in his deposition in *Jones v. Clinton* regarding his statement that he could not recall being alone with Ms. Lewinsky and minimizing the number of gifts they had exchanged, 8) The President may have testified falsely in his deposition concerning conversations with Ms. Lewinsky about her involvement in the *Jones* case, 9) The President may have endeavored to obstruct justice by engaging in a pattern of activity calculated to conceal evidence from the judicial proceedings in *Jones v. Clinton* regarding his relationship with Monica Lewinsky, 10) The President may have endeavored to obstruct justice in *Jones v. Clinton* by agreeing with Ms. Lewinsky on a cover story, by causing a false affidavit to be filed by her, and by giving false and misleading testimony in his deposition, 11) The President may have endeavored to obstruct justice by helping Ms. Lewinsky obtain a job in New York at a time when she would have given evidence adverse to Mr. Clinton if she had told the truth in the *Jones* case, 12) The President may have testified falsely under oath in his deposition in *Jones v. Clinton* concerning his conversations with Vernon Jordan, 13) The President may have endeavored to obstruct justice and engage in witness tampering in attempting to coach and influence the testimony of Betty Currie before the grand jury, 14) The President may have engaged in witness tampering by coaching prospective grand jury witnesses and by telling them false accounts intending that the witnesses would repeat these before the grand jury, and 15) The President may have given false testimony under oath before the federal grand jury on August 17, 1998.

[I]f true, these allegations show a pattern of conduct, extending over many months, on the part of the President, of deception, of lying under oath, of concealing evidence, of tampering with witnesses, and, in general, of obstructing justice by seeking to prevent the proper functioning of the courts, the grand jury, and the investigation of the Office of Independent Counsel. These offenses, if true, would undoubtedly amount to criminal interference with the legal process, but more to the point, they would demonstrate that the President had failed to live up to the requirements of honesty, virtue, and honor which the framers of the Constitution and the authors of *The Federalist* believed were essential for the Presidency. These offenses, if true, would bear a clear resemblance to many of the English precedents of impeachment for interfering with orderly processes of law, for tampering with the grand jury, and for seeking to use one's office for personal rather than public ends. These offenses, if true, would show that President Clinton engaged in a pattern of conduct which involved injury to the state and a betrayal of his Constitutional duties, because President Clinton would have thereby abused his office for personal gain and betrayed the ideal that ours is a government of laws and not of men.

If these allegations are true, then the President, instead of carrying out his oath of office to uphold the Constitution and faithfully to execute the laws, sought instead to subvert the judicial process specified in Article III, and, in order to protect himself from an adverse judgment in the *Jones* proceeding, sought to frustrate the laws designed to protect Ms. Jones and others like her. There are those who will argue before you that what the President did was simply to lie about his private sexual conduct. It should be remembered, however, that the essential allegation in *Jones v. Clinton* was that the President misused his governmental office (then as Governor of Arkansas) to attempt to procure sexual favors from Ms. Jones, and the allegations of impeachable offenses of the President now before you all flow from efforts of the President to suppress the truth in the course of *Jones v. Clinton*. It should also be remembered that Judge Starr expanded his investigation to include the facts regarding Ms. Lewinsky because Judge Starr believed that he could discern a pattern of interference with judicial proceedings on the part of the President which Judge Starr had before encountered in the Whitewater investigation. Judge Starr's inquiry, after all, has never been about sex, it has been about abuse of power, obstruction of justice and other impeachable offenses.

There may still be further allegations of impeachable offenses from Judge Starr to come before you, but looking only to the allegations made by Judge Starr and by your Chief Investigator detailed above, there is more than enough to require you to move forward now. These allegations concern conduct by the President in which he allegedly ignored his Constitutional obligations to take care that the laws be faithfully executed, and instead used his august position to frustrate enforcement of the law. If these allegations are true, then the President has acted in a manner against the interests of the state and he has sought to subvert the essence of our Constitutional government—that ours is a government of laws and not of men. If these allegations are true, then the President has engaged in conduct that can only be described as corrupt, and corrupt in a manner that the impeachment process was expressly designed to correct.

For many people, apparently, the allegations against the President can still be characterized as "lying about sex," and it is difficult for many people to believe that such conduct is anything but a private matter, far removed from Constitutional procedures or requirements. The President is accused of much more than "lying about sex," of course, as Judge Starr and Mr. Schippers have made plain. It is appropriate to note in passing, however, that our legal tradition has never made any distinction about the content of matters that might involve perjury, obstruction of justice, or tampering with witnesses. No person and least of all no President, who is sworn faithfully to execute all the laws, can pick and choose over which matters he will be truthful and which he will not, particularly when he is under oath.

An oath, and the virtue of one swearing to it, perhaps lightly regarded by many today, were not so lightly regarded at the time of the Constitution's framing. Our best evidence of this is George Washington's statements in his famous "Farewell Address." The "Farewell Address" is the first President's "one outstanding piece of writing," and is regarded as comparable in importance to Thomas Jefferson's Declaration of Independence, Alexander Hamilton's financial plan, or James Madison's journal of the proceedings of the Constitutional Convention. Like the Declaration, Hamilton's ideas about the importance of Commerce and Manufacturing, or the Constitutional Convention, Washington's Farewell

Address offers a valuable and authentic glimpse into what the framers considered vital for the new Republic they were founding. In that Farewell Address, in one of its most important passages, the man whom the framers designated as their First President, asked "[W]here is the security for property, for reputation, for life, if the sense of religious obligation desert the oaths which are the instruments of investigation in courts of justice?" Somewhat later in the address Washington added:

> It is substantially true, that virtue or morality is a necessary spring of popular government. The rule, indeed, extends with more or less force to every species of free government. Who that is a sincere friend to it can look with indifference upon attempts to shake the foundation of the fabrick?

Washington, the Platonic Form of an American President, believed that the oath taken in court was a fundamental security for all that was held dear in American Society. He believed that those who took their oaths in vain were eroding the foundation of American government, and that they had lost the virtue which he believed essential to sustain freedom and popular sovereignty. Even if all President Clinton had done were to lie under oath in a judicial proceeding, the first President would have believed that President Clinton was engaged in an effort to "shake the foundation of the fabrick" of our Constitutional scheme. It is clear, based on this, that George Washington would have recommended President Clinton's impeachment, and this would likely have been the view of Madison, Hamilton, Jefferson, and Mason as well.

The allegations against President Clinton amount to much more than lying under oath, however. I think that the framers' view of the Constitution means that if these allegations are true, then the oath that you took to support the Constitution requires you to impeach the President.

Prepared Statement of Laurence H. Tribe, Tyler Professor of Constitutional Law, Harvard University Law School, before the House Committee on the Judiciary, Subcommittee on the Constitution, November 9, 1998

Defining "High Crimes and Misdemeanors": Basic Principles

I am honored to have been invited to appear before this Subcommittee of the House Judiciary Committee to shed whatever light I can on the vitally important topic of "The Background and History of Impeachment."... I have understood my assignment to be ... to analyze how the Constitution requires Congress to approach the threshold issue of deciding what constitutes an "impeachable" offense. Because so much has been written, and so much more has been said, about this topic, I have chosen to focus my comments on the basic principles that I believe should guide us in this endeavor, rather than to essay yet another detailed compilation of excerpts from the records of the 1787 Constitutional Convention, from accounts of the state ratification debates, from *The Federalist Papers*, from the commentaries of Blackstone and Story, from the 1974 Staff Report of the House Judiciary Committee on "Constitutional Grounds for Presidential Impeachment," and the like.

I begin with this historical note: Nearly a quarter of a century ago, the work of the House Judiciary Committee under the leadership of Representative Peter Rodino, in seeking to define impeachable offenses when dealing with a Republican President, set the stage on which the House Judiciary Committee under the leadership of Representative Henry Hyde plays out today's sober drama in dealing with a Democratic President. So too, what the Judiciary Committee does today in attempting to define impeachable offenses will set the stage on which future struggles over the possible impeachment of presidents to come, including presidents yet unborn, will be waged. Indeed, how this Subcommittee and ultimately the House of Representatives (and possibly the Senate) define impeachable offenses in this proceeding will play an important role not only on those occasions, hopefully rare, when the nation again focuses its energies and its attention on the possible impeachment and removal of a sitting president, but in the day-to-day life of the republic....

For this reason, it would be short-sighted indeed for any witness before this body, or for any member of Congress, to approach the task of defining "high crimes and misdemeanors" from a narrowly result-oriented perspective. To put it bluntly, anyone who would raise the bar on what constitutes an impeachable offense simply in an effort to save President Clinton, whether for partisan reasons or in a spirit of genuine patriotism, may live to regret the abuses by future presidents that might be unleashed were we to establish a precedent making it too difficult—more difficult than the Constitution, rightly understood, contemplated—to remove a president whose misuse of the awesome powers of that office endangers the republic. And, conversely, anyone who lowers the bar on what constitutes an impeachable offense simply in an effort to "get" President Clinton, whether for partisan reasons or in a spirit of equally genuine patriotism, may live to regret the abuses by future congresses, and the resulting incapacity of future presidents, that might just as easily be unleashed were we to establish a precedent making it too easy—easier than the Constitution contemplated—to remove a president simply because, as in a parliamentary system, the legislature has come to disagree profoundly with his or her public policies or personal proclivities and has thus lost confidence in the President's leadership.

For these reasons, and because I—like many others who have expressed grave doubts about the propriety of using the impeachment device to deal with what President Clinton is alleged to have done—hold no brief for the President's behavior and regard it as both inexcusable and worthy of condemnation, I believe the situation in which we find ourselves contains powerful, built-in safeguards—safeguards that ought to function well to prevent all people of good will from artificially making the category of impeachable offenses too narrow or too broad. Not knowing whose ox might be gored in the long run by an error in either direction, anyone who takes the task ahead with the seriousness its nature demands will necessarily proceed under what the philosopher John Rawls famously described as a veil of ignorance that can help us all go forward in a manner sufficiently focused on the long run and insulated against the temptations of short-term rewards and punishments.

With that preface, I turn to the principles that I believe ought to guide the search for the appropriate definition of impeachable offenses.

1. Because Congress has the last word in defining what constitutes an impeachable offense, it is more important, not less, that Congress get it right. It appears to be common ground that judicial review would be unavailable to check the House or the Senate in their definitions of high crimes and misdemeanors under Article II, §4 of the Constitution. The Supreme Court held in *Nixon v. United States*(1993)—in a case involving former federal judge Walter Nixon—that Article I, §3, clause 6, which says "[t]he Senate shall have the sole Power to try all Impeachments," precludes Supreme Court review of whether the Senate, rather than sitting as a jury of 100, may instead delegate the task of hearing and reporting evidence to a committee. It would almost surely follow that Article I, §2, clause 5, which says "[t]he House of Representatives ... shall have the sole Power of Impeachment," precludes Supreme Court review of whether the House has proceeded on a definition of impeachable offenses that is too lax or too strict. Nor is it at all plausible

that the Chief Justice, who under Article I, § 3, clause 6, "shall preside" when the "President of the United States is tried," would control the Senate's definition of an impeachable offense.

Thus, Congress is essentially on its own in this vital realm. But that is not to say that the deliberately political process of impeachment that the framers left unpoliced by judicial overseers is not bound by the Constitution—by what it says as to impeachable offenses, and by what it means by what it says. Article VI provides that all Senators and Representatives "shall be bound by Oath or Affirmation, to support this Constitution." That duty is not relaxed whenever the judiciary is not on guard; it is heightened. Any solace that members of either the House or the Senate may sometimes take, in voting for a measure of contested constitutionality, that the Supreme Court will step in and save them from constitutional error if they are wrong—solace that I have elsewhere argued is inappropriate even when judicial review is in fact available to conduct just such a rescue mission—is manifestly unavailable here. Err here, and live forever with the consequences, for no judge will appear as a deus ex machina to set the constitutional system straight. Thus, the statements sometimes heard to the effect that an impeachable offense is whatever the House and Senate say it is are true only in the most cynical and constitutionally faithless sense. If those statements mean that Congress can "get away with murder" in this sphere, they are literally correct. But there are consequences to be suffered from defying the Constitution, even if those consequences do not include being reversed by judges. And if those statements about impeachable offenses being a content-less category, a mere mirror for the preferences of members of the House and Senate, mean that Congress simply is not constrained by the Constitution in this matter, then those statements are flatly false. Congress is indeed constrained, even if the only enforcer of that constraint is its own conscience.

This first principle has one significant corollary. When we say it is important that Congress get it right, and even more important because no court stands guard to keep the balance true, we should realize that we are speaking not simply of the Senate, whose task it is to try impeachments brought to it by this body, but of the House as well. Some have suggested that, because it will fall to the Senate, in any case where this body returns a bill of impeachment, to make a final judgment as to whether something the House deems impeachable is in fact impeachable, the House is somehow relieved of the full burden of having to decide the issue for itself. Passing the buck to the Senate—impeaching because one thinks what the accused official did might well be deemed impeachable—would be a profoundly irresponsible breach of the duty laid upon this body by Article I.

The prospect of a trial in the United States Senate, regardless of which federal officer is in the dock, cannot be equated with the prospect of an ordinary trial, civil or criminal, in the courts of Law. When the Senate is enlisted to perform this unique task, not even delegating part of its work to a committee can obscure the inevitable distraction from the Senate's normal and proper functions in the lawmaking process. And when the Senate is asked to perform this task in the special case of a sitting President, both the distractions from its legislative role and the consequences for the nation as a whole, internationally as well as domestically, are monumental. The one occasion on which the Senate sat in judgment on a President, in the trial of Andrew Johnson, provided just a foretaste of the far greater distractions and divisions that such a trial in the modern era would entail, whatever its outcome.

This is not to say that the House should shrink from impeaching a president where impeachment is called for; it is to say, however, that the consequences of passing the matter off to the Senate in order to send a message of disapproval or otherwise to avoid seeming to condone presidential misbehavior are far too grave to make that an acceptable option. If members of this body believe the president should be censured, mechanisms to achieve that end are available. If members believe the president should be criminally prosecuted, that remains an option after he leaves office. But allowing uncertainty over whether these other modes of accountability will be brought to bear in a timely and effective way to tempt one into voting to impeach where there has been no high crime or misdemeanor, taking refuge in the confidence that the Senate will not muster the requisite two-thirds vote to convict, would set a horrific precedent—and would punish the entire nation in order to administer punishment to the President. I would urge every member to focus not on what we should do to Bill Clinton but on what impeaching Bill Clinton would do to the country—and to the Constitution. To that end, it is vital that the House get it right, and not rely on the Senate to come to the rescue.

2. Getting it right means taking seriously exactly what the Constitution says on the subject, as well as the context in which the Constitution says it. When we look at the words of Article II, §4, telling us the offenses for which Presidents or any other civil officers of the United States may be impeached and, on conviction, removed from office, we encounter the curious phrase—familiar today only because we have all been steeped in this business for some time—"high Crimes and Misdemeanors." To take those words and their context seriously, it is essential that we not stop with the easy observation that they are theoretically capable of various definitions, that they have fuzzy boundaries, that not everybody agrees exactly on what they mean, and that they might indeed mean big crimes and little ones. Neither writing a constitution nor reading and applying one is a merely theoretical exercise. Yes, those words could mean any of a number of things, but the fact that this is the case with many, perhaps all, constitutional provisions does not give us license simply to fill in the meanings we find most pleasing.

We deal in the Impeachment Clause with one of the Constitution's architectural cornerstones. It identifies a key feature of the Constitution's structure, and of the form of government the Constitution created. As I, and many others, have argued in other settings, constitutional provisions of this structural sort are the least likely candidates for translation into open-textured, highly fluid, norms and ideals. Unlike the Constitution's command that no state deprive anyone of "liberty" without "due process of law," for example—a command that is famously flexible and whose content has evolved, many of us think quite properly, with the changing times—the provision stating the circumstances in which federal officials, including Presidents, may be impeached, convicted, and removed from office ought to be given as fixed and firm a reading as the logic of the situation permits. The basic criteria for what makes something a "high crime" or "misdemeanor" in the impeachment context should not be permitted to "morph" with the ebb and flow of attitude and opinion—although, of course, as times change the set of acts that might represent abuses of power or assaults upon the state might change as well.

Some, though not I, think that at least the criteria for what makes something fit into a given constitutional category should be constant over time for every part of the Constitution, properly construed; for them, it should be true a fortiori for the Impeachment Clause. For the rest of us, the important point is that the clause defines not simply the rights of individuals but the very design of the government on which we must, in the end, rely to defend those rights. To raise or to lower the impeachment bar as time goes on is to move the nation closer to an imperial presidency or to a parliamentary system, depending entirely on which way the impeachment winds are blowing. But those are not changes we should make casually or as the accidental byproducts of steps taken for entirely different reasons. If it is a parliamentary system people want, or something closer to such a system than we have had for two centuries, then amending the Constitution to achieve such a system or an approximation thereto is the only constitutionally proper course. Weakening the presidency through watering down the basic meaning of "high Crimes and Misdemeanors" seems a singularly ill-conceived, even a somnambulistic, way of backing into a new—and, for us at least, untested—form of government.

What, then, did "high Crimes and Misdemeanors" mean when those words were inserted into the Constitution? The surrounding text gives us more than a slight clue, for the words are embedded in the larger phrase, "Treason, Bribery, or other high Crimes and Misdemeanors." The word "other" is a dead giveaway: high crimes and misdemeanors are offenses that bear some strong resemblance to the flagship offenses listed by the framers—treason and bribery. That the framers' choice of words here was entirely deliberate is most clearly shown by the fact that, when it came to the very different question of which offenses would be subject to interstate extradition, the framers began with the categories "treason, felony, or high misdemeanor," but ended by replacing the phrase "high misdemeanor" with the phrase "other crime," which evidently seemed more appropriate in a constitutional provision—Article IV, §2, clause 2—dealing not with abuse of power or subversion of the constitutional order but with ordinary common-law or statutory crime. That alone should tell us that reading Article II's reference to "high Crimes and Misdemeanors" as some sort of shorthand for major and minor criminal offenses, or even as shorthand for felonies—that is, for the most serious crimes—would be a mistake. When the Constitution's authors meant to identify a particularly serious category of crime, they knew just how to do it. Thus, not only does the Interstate Extradition Clause speak of persons "charged in any State with Treason, Felony, or other Crime," but the Privilege from Arrest Clause speaks of congressional immunity from arrest during attendance of a congressional session "in all Cases, except Treason, Felony and Breach of the Peace." Article I, §6, clause 1. And the Grand Jury Clause of the 5th Amendment guarantees "a presentment or indictment of a Grand Jury," with certain military exceptions, whenever a person is "held to answer for a capital, or otherwise infamous crime."

It follows that "high Crimes and Misdemeanors" cannot be equated with mere crimes, however serious. Indeed, it appears to be all but universally agreed that an offense need not be a violation of criminal law at all in order for it to be impeachable as a high crime or misdemeanor. A President who completely neglects his duties by showing up at work intoxicated every day, or by lounging on the beach rather than signing bills or delivering a State of the Union address, would be guilty of no crime but would certainly have committed an impeachable offense. Similarly, a President who had oral sex with his or her spouse in the Lincoln Bedroom prior to May 23, 1995 (the date on which D.C. Code Ann. 22-3502 was repealed), or in a hotel room in Georgia, Louisiana, or Virginia at any time, would be guilty of a felony but surely would have committed no impeachable offense.

And that brings us back to the word "other." What distinguishes certain offenses as "high Crimes and Misdemeanors" must be not the fact that serious crimes are involved but the fact that those offenses are similar, in ways relevant to what the devices of impeachment and removal are for, to treason and bribery. But that in turn means that, like treason and bribery, high crimes and misdemeanors, as terms of art, must refer to major offenses against our very system of government, or serious abuses of the governmental power with which a public official has been entrusted (as in the case of a public official who accepts a bribe in order to turn his official powers to personal or otherwise corrupt ends), or grave wrongs in pursuit of governmental power (as in the case of someone who subverts democracy by using bribery or other nefarious means in order to secure government office and its powers, or in order to hold onto such office once attained). And, sure enough, even a cursory examination of the precise history of the phrase "high Crimes and Misdemeanors," and of the path that phrase took as it found its way from 14th century England into the Constitution of the United States in the summer of 1787, confirms that understanding of what the words meant.

3. Getting it right requires paying close attention to the historic evolution of the Impeachment Clause. The story is a lengthy one, but its relevant elements can be set forth briefly. The Constitutional Convention wrestled with various formulations of the grounds for impeaching and removing federal officials, starting out with phrases that focused on the abuse or non-use of official power—phrases like "malpractice and neglect of duty" and oscillating between variants that would have precluded impeachment and removal altogether in the case of the President, and variants that leading delegates such as James Madison feared would reduce the President to a creature of the legislature.

By late July 1787, the Committee of Detail had settled on "treason, bribery, or corruption" instead of "malpractice and neglect of duty," and shortly thereafter the reference to "corruption" was dropped. On September 8, George Mason of Virginia objected that "treason and bribery" was too narrow. That pair of words nicely captured the possibility that sufficiently grave assaults on the state, like high treason, might be carried out by a public official not through misuse of his official powers but in a traitorous sort of moonlighting—shades of Aaron Burr come to mind, and of Jonathan Fassett, the Vermont assemblyman impeached by a state legislature in the colonial period for leading a mob that attempted to shut down a county court. What, then, was missing? Not, apparently, room to multiply the examples of conduct injurious to the state but not involving abuse of official power. For Mason's proposed remedy for the narrowness he perceived was the addition of the term "maladministration," a term clearly limited to conduct involving improper use of the powers entrusted to a public official. Mason's argument for adding maladministration to treason and bribery was straightforward: There might be "attempts to subvert the Constitution" that would not fit the definitions of treason or of bribery but would nonetheless imperil the republic.

James Madison did not disagree with Mason's reason for going beyond treason and bribery; he objected only to Mason's proposed solution in the notion of maladministration. And he objected not because he thought that notion too narrow, believing that conduct other than abuse of power should be impeachable, but because he feared that the breadth and vagueness of Mason's proposed addition would reduce the Executive to serving "during the pleasure of the Senate." Mason then countered with an alternative borrowed directly from 14th century England: "other high crimes and misdemeanors against the State," which passed without debate (at least without debate recorded by Madison) by a vote of 8–3. Immediately thereafter, "State" was replaced by "United States," which was in turn dropped without explanation by the Committee of Style when, on September 12, it reported the final language of the Impeachment Clause: "Treason, Bribery, or other high Crimes and Misdemeanors."

There is no evidence that the deletion of the phrase "against the United States" was meant to do anything but eliminate a redundancy; the deletion appears to have been not substantive but stylistic, inasmuch as the very concept of "high Crimes and Misdemeanors," which when first used as early as 1386 denoted political crimes against the state, contained within its four corners the requirement that the system of government itself be the target of the wrong. Blackstone notes that the use of the word "high" in the context of treason implied not simply a more significant offense—as in the notion of a major rather than a minor crime—but, rather, an injury to the crown, distinguishing it from "petit treason," which involved betrayal of a private person. For sufficiently grave abuses of official power—abuses entailing encroachment on the prerogatives of another branch of government or usurpations of the power of popular consent and representation—serious injury to the state seems implicit in the abuses themselves. But such injury to the state or, what amounts to the same thing, to the constitutional structure, may in exceptional cases be brought about by means other than an abuse of power entrusted to a public official. The judge or private citizen who lends support to an enemy engaged in an attack on the nation, or who leads a private mob in an attempted coup, does not abuse official power but threatens grave injury to the state, either in an act of treason or in what is surely "[an]other high Crime[] and Misdemeanor[]."

Although in the English practice impeachment was not even restricted to officeholders, much less to official misdeeds, and although the English practice did not limit penalties to removal from office and disqualification from further officeholding, the American colonies, and later states, reacted against the enormous concentration of power in the legislature that borrowing these features of parliament's impeachment authority would entail. Influenced by the writings of John Adams and others, American states transformed impeachment by restricting it to officeholders, limiting it essentially to official misdeeds, and confining the punishment to removal and disqualification.

Against this background, it apparently did not occur to the framers or ratifiers that some sufficiently monstrous but purely private crimes against individuals might require impeachment and removal of the criminal in order to safeguard the government and the people it serves. The ratification debates, like the debates at the Constitutional Convention, focused solely on high offenses against the state and on grave abuses of—or gravely culpable failures to use—official power. Thus, when Vice President Aaron Burr killed Alexander Hamilton in a duel in July 1804, leading to Burr's indictment for murder in New York and New Jersey, Burr served out his term, which ended in early 1805, without any inquiry in the House of Representatives as to whether his murder of Hamilton might be an impeachable offense. Indeed, rather than urging their colleagues in the House to consider returning a bill of impeachment, eleven U.S. Senators wrote to the governor of New Jersey asking him to end the prosecution of the flamboyant Vice President, so as "to facilitate the public business by relieving the President of the Senate from the peculiar embarrassments of his present situation, and the Senate from the distressing imputation thrown on it, by holding up its President to the world as a common murderer."

Today, I would suppose, the specter of being governed by "a common murderer"—and of the United States being held up to the world as a nation so governed—would lead at least some students of the English and colonial history to question whether the remedy of impeachment and removal must be withheld even from the most heinous of crimes, at least when committed by a sitting President, simply because the crime in question involved no abuse of presidential power and did not in itself endanger the nation as a polity. There may well be room to argue that the very continuation in office of a President who has committed a crime as heinous as murder, and who under widely accepted practice is deemed immune to criminal prosecution and incarceration as long as he holds that office, would itself so gravely injure the nation and its government that such a President's decision not to resign under the circumstances amounts to a culpable omission and thus an abuse of power and that, in any event, the fact that such a President's continuation in office was itself gravely injurious to the nation would transform his remaining in office, if not the murder he committed, into an impeachable offense.

4. Exceptions to the general rule that an impeachable offense must itself severely threaten the system of government or constitute a grievous abuse of official power or both must not be permitted to swallow that rule. Both the text and the context we have examined, and the history of the phrase the framers used, preclude any casual movement from something like the example of murder committed by a sitting President to any broad notion that all serious crimes—say, felonies involving the administration of justice—are impeachable even if they are not committed through an abuse of the official powers entrusted to the alleged criminal, and even if their commission does not genuinely threaten the nation and its system of government.

It is always possible to argue, when confronted by a serious crime, that the system would crumble if everyone followed the wrongdoer's example. If everyone took President Richard Nixon's allegedly false filing of tax returns under oath, including backdating of documents, as a model to emulate, the nation's tax system, and thus its defenses, would crumble. Yet there was no realistic basis to suppose that the Nixon example would start any such stampede, and the simple proposition that, if all did as Nixon had done, the consequences would be catastrophic did not mislead the House Judiciary Committee into treating the President's alleged tax evasion as an impeachable offense: By a vote of 26–12, the Committee soundly declined to treat it as such. Similarly, it is important to see the fallacy in the alluring argument that every instance of perjury, or of witness tampering, or of conspiracy to suppress evidence relevant to a civil proceeding or to a grand jury, significantly injures the legal system itself and thus the nation because, if everyone did it, the system obviously could not function. It is no doubt true that, if perjury and witness tampering became the order of the day, our government would be severely hurt. But if that were the test—if an offense became impeachable even when it entailed no abuse of the offender's official position and caused no grave injury to the nation provided one could argue that such injury would ultimately occur if the offense became not exceptional but universal—then the carefully crafted safeguards against legislative hegemony and presidential weakness hammered out at the Constitutional Convention would amount to nothing. Find a sitting President guilty of some offense that, if universalized, would bring down the system—or maneuver the President into committing some such offense—and one would, under the hypothesized test, have a solid basis for removing that President from office. These "sky is falling" arguments disrespect not only the Constitution's text and history; they disrespect common sense.

5. The Take Care Clause and the Presidential Oath of Office cannot properly be invoked so as to make the President of the United States more vulnerable to impeachment, conviction, and removal from office than other federal officials. We have already seen that the commission of a crime, whether state or federal, is neither a sufficient nor a necessary element of an impeachable offense. Indeed, the words "high Crimes and Misdemeanors" had little or nothing to do with the criminal law at the time they were incorporated into Article II of our Constitution; the term "misdemeanor" was not even employed in the criminal context, where it now connotes a minor offense, until centuries after the English period from which the framers borrowed it.

All of that is true, some say, but the presidency is unique. The President alone takes a special oath whose every word is prescribed by the Constitution, an oath "faithfully to execute the Office of President of the United States and ... to the best of [his or her] Ability, preserve, protect and defend the Constitution of the United States." Article II, §1, clause 8. Beyond that oath, the President is enjoined by Article II, §3, clause 1 to "take Care that the Laws be faithfully executed." Thus, if the President should commit a federal crime—not, it might be noted, a crime like murder, which typically violates only state law—he or she will have failed to carry out the duty imposed by the Take Care Clause and, in a sense, will have violated his or her oath "faithfully to execute" the office.

Candor requires the concession that, for anyone who has not thought carefully about the Impeachment Clause and the consequences of this way of reading it, this line of argument has a beguiling simplicity and a down-to-earth appeal. But if this argument were to carry the day, it would follow that President Nixon should indeed have been impeached for filing a false tax return, and that Presidents generally are in the unique position of being subject to impeachment and removal whenever it becomes possible to pin a federal offense—any federal offense—on them. Yet it simply cannot be the case under our Constitution that removing a sitting President should be easier, not harder, than removing a Vice President, a cabinet officer, or a sitting federal judge. After all, the Constitution itself expressly recognizes the special gravity of what we do when we even try, much less remove, a President: It puts the Chief Justice of the United States in the chair to preside over the trial, something it does not do when any other federal officer, including the Vice President, is impeached and put on trial in the Senate. And, beyond this express recognition of how much is at stake, there is the brute fact that only when we put the President on trial are we placing one federal branch in a position to sit in judgment on another, empowering the Congress essentially to decapitate the Executive Branch in a single stroke—and without the safeguards of judicial review. Neither of the other two branches of the national government is embodied in a single individual, so the application of the Impeachment Clause to the President of the United States involves the uniquely solemn act of having one branch essentially overthrow another. Moreover, in doing so, the legislative branch essentially cancels the results of the most solemn collective act of which we as a constitutional democracy are capable: the national election of a President. To suggest that, having deliberately rejected parliamentary supremacy at the founding of our republic, we should now embrace a theory that would make the President the most vulnerable of all federal officials to the drastic remedy of impeachment and removal—truly the political equivalent of capital punishment—is preposterous.

None of this is to say that the Take Care Clause is unimportant, or that presidential abuse that rises to an impeachable level might not take the form of a violation of that clause. Of course it might. Certainly, a President who ordered the IRS to stop collecting federal income taxes for six months as part of his reelection campaign, or the FDA to stop enforcing the laws against marijuana use because he was philosophically opposed to the regulation of marijuana or because he was widely known to have used it as a youth and feared accusations of hypocrisy, would have committed an impeachable high crime or misdemeanor of the most dramatic sort by shredding his obligation to execute the laws of the country. But that is a far cry from what occurs if a President personally violates several related federal criminal laws in the course of trying to cover up an embarrassing sexual affair, without turning any executive agency into an instrument of the president's wrongful conduct or otherwise abusing the powers of the presidency or working grave injury to the nation and its government.

Applying These Principles

It may be useful to contrast the conclusion that presidential misconduct even involving such offenses as perjury may, depending upon the circumstances, involve no abuse of official power and no serious harm to the system of government and hence no impeachable offense, with the potentially impeachable offenses that might have been uncovered—and might yet be uncovered—in the areas of inquiry with which the Office of Independent Counsel began its investigations of President Clinton more than four years ago. Thus, it remains theoretically possible that the President might be found to have committed impeachable offenses if there were convincing proof that he was personally connected to the allegations involved in "Filegate," where it is said that the White House procured some 400 FBI files on members of the Reagan and Bush administrations. Clearly, a president who deliberately uses an executive agency to seek "dirt" on political opponents is abusing presidential power to undermine the political processes established by the Constitution and thereby cause the most serious injury to our constitutional system. There might even be circumstances in which a president, by deliberately looking the other way with a wink and a nod while lower executive officials performed such nefarious work while maintaining maximum plausible deniability for their chief, would have committed an impeachable violation of the Take Care Clause.

Similarly, if President Clinton were responsible for the abuses alleged in Travelgate, in which seven members of the White House travel office were fired in 1993 apparently to make room for a distant cousin of the President, one might at least make a forceful argument that, despite the absence of serious harm to the nation as a whole, such corrupt misuse of presidential power would be so close to bribery that it too should qualify as a high crime and misdemeanor. So too if President Clinton had induced the Pentagon or The White House to break the ordinary hiring rules for that agency in order to find a sinecure for a young intern in exchange for her willingness to file a false affidavit.

But none of these things, and nothing truly comparable, has been alleged against President Clinton. Even if, for example, he arranged a job for the young woman in question at a private firm in the expectation that she would then be less likely to contradict his denial of any improper sexual affair, neither an abuse of presidential power as such, nor conduct demonstrably injurious to the nation, would have occurred, and impeachment would accordingly be improper.

The strongest case for identifying an impeachable offense in the allegations currently pending against the President is probably to be found in the claim that he committed perjury before the grand jury or obstructed its work not simply to avoid personal embarrassment and indictment for a private wrong (in the form of prior false statements under oath in a civil deposition into which the President felt he had been trapped), but to avoid a constitutional check by staving off impeachment—even if the impeachment he sought to avoid would in fact have been unwarranted. If it could be shown that President Clinton deliberately sought to usurp the impeachment power of Congress—part of which had been delegated through the Independent Counsel Act to the grand jury in this matter—by preventing the referral called for in that Act from containing a full account of his own prior conduct, then at least the outlines of a high crime or misdemeanor might be visible. But attributing to the President such a constitution-subverting program, rather than the more straightforward effort to minimize embarrassment and reduce the risk of criminal indictment, seems implausible and indeed unfair. And, even assuming such an impeachment-triggering scheme, the threat of substantial harm to the nation that would be required to establish a high crime or misdemeanor is nowhere to be found.

Applying the principles set forth in this statement, therefore, I would be hard pressed to find in anything that has been alleged against President Clinton thus far a defensible basis to impeach and remove a president from office. What other options might be available to Congress in these circumstances, where the President himself has conceded that he behaved indefensibly, is beyond the scope of this statement. So too is the question whether, if indeed the public is tired of this whole matter and believes that the President has been made to suffer enough for his sins, Congress has some sort of obligation to let the matter rest.

One thing is clear in the latter regard: Anyone who insists that Congress has the converse obligation—an obligation, having taken up the impeachment cudgels and begun to wield them in a setting that might on reflection prove ill-suited to such drastic remedies, to pursue this course to the bitter end—is mistaken. Just as ordinary prosecutors have discretion not to push their power to the outer limits, and not to take to trial someone they believe it would serve no useful purpose to pursue further, so too the House of Representatives, entrusted by Article I, §2, clause 5, with the "sole Power of Impeachment," has discretion—even more clearly than does the average prosecutor—to cease and desist rather than pressing on. Article II, §4 contains only one mandatory provision: It mandates that the President or any other federal officer "shall be removed from Office on Impeachment for, and Conviction of, Treason, Bribery, or other high Crimes and Misdemeanors." If the Senate convicts, there is no room for clemency; the convicted offender must be removed. But that is the only "must" in the picture.

Some argue that, at least if something that might technically fit the definition of a high crime or misdemeanor is believed to have been committed by the President, the House has a "duty" under the Constitution to impeach the president and hand him over to the Senate for trial. But there is no more in the Constitution to support that argument than there is to support the argument that, having begun a formal impeachment inquiry, the House must see the matter through. The Constitution, in this matter as in many others, leaves ample room for judgment, even for wisdom, in the deployment of power. What it leaves no room for is the impeachment of a president who has not committed "Treason, Bribery, or other high Crimes and Misdemeanors."

Chapter 2

National Power: Article I and the Powers and Limits of Congress

Contents

I.	Implied Congressional Power: Its Nature and Extent	64
	A. Implied Powers and the Nature of the Union	64
	The Controversy over the Bank of the United States	64
	McCulloch v. Maryland	69
	B. The Nature of the Union Revisited	81
	U.S. Term Limits, Inc. v. Thornton	82
II.	The Commerce Clause: A Delegated Power	97
	A. Graphic Portrayals: The Modern View of the Commerce Clause	97
	Affirmative Limits and 10th Amendment Charts	101
	B. The Marshall Court's Interpretation of the Commerce Clause	103
	Gibbons v. Ogden	104
	The Controversy over "Original Meaning"	114
	Slavery and Federal Power	116
	C. The Preemptive Effect of the Commerce Clause Revisited	116
	Note: *New York v. Miln*	116
	Cooley v. Board of Wardens	118
	In re Rahrer	122
	D. The Limited View of the Commerce Clause during the Late 19th and Early 20th Centuries	124
	Champion v. Ames (The Lottery Case)	130
	Houston, East & West Texas Railway Company v. United States	133
	Hammer v. Dagenhart	135
	E. Populist and Progressive Discontent	139
	The Income Tax of 1894: The *Pollock* Decisions and the Political Response	139
	Progressives Respond to "Judicial Activism"	141
	F. The New Deal: Political Realignment and the Commerce Clause	143
	1. Shall the Court Defer to Congress?	144
	Carter v. Carter Coal Co.	144
	The Roosevelt Court Plan: The Court Changes Direction	151
	"The Constitution of the United States Was a Layman's Document, Not a Lawyer's Contract"	153
	A Theory Regarding Constitutional Change	156
	2. The Emergence of a New (or Old?) View of the Commerce Clause	158

	United States v. Darby	158
	Note: *Congress and Individual Rights*	163
	Wickard v. Filburn	165
	An Excerpt from Mark Twain's *Life on the Mississippi*: "Perplexing Lessons"	169
G.	The Commerce Clause and the Great Society	170
	Heart of Atlanta Motel v. United States	171
	Katzenbach v. McClung	176
H.	Dual Federalism and the Commerce Clause: The Rehnquist Revolution	179
	Note: *Perez v. United States*	179
	Excerpt from the Second Inaugural Address of President Ronald Reagan	180
	United States v. Morrison	181
	Gonzales v. Raich	199
III.	Ducking the Issue: Statutory Construction as a Means of Avoiding Constitutional Interpretation	218
	Jones v. United States	218
	Solid Waste Agency of Northern Cook County v. United States Army Corps of Engineers	220
IV.	Other Delegated Sources of National Power: The Power to Spend, the War Power, and the Treaty Power	225
A.	The Taxing and Spending Power	225
	Buckley v. Valeo	226
	South Dakota v. Dole	227
B.	The War Power	232
	Woods v. Miller Co.	234
C.	The Treaty Power	236
	Missouri v. Holland	236
	Reid v. Covert	239

Chapter 2

National Power: Article I and the Powers and Limits of Congress

In this chapter, we explore national power under the Constitution. We will also return to the themes of interpretation with which we began. Four large themes run through this material:

1. The development of constitutional ideas of national power through American history.

2. The power of Congress over commerce and present rules for determining the scope of that power.

3. Determining how a decision about the exercise of power (for example, over commerce) is allocated between the Congress and the Court. (A major device to separate those areas where the Court substantially defers to the judgment of Congress and those where it exercises more active judicial review is the level of scrutiny. You will see that rational basis scrutiny leaves very wide discretion to Congress. Strict scrutiny is used when the Court engages in much more independent judicial review.)

4. The use of types of constitutional interpretation (text, context, structure, precedent, history, ethical aspirations, and policy) in cases we are considering.

In addition, we will seek to identify the underlying tensions that shape the decisions we are studying.

Hypothetical Case

Consider the following hypothetical case as you read and discuss the material on the Commerce Clause. This approach begins with a problem and then provides material from which you can search for solutions. Starting with a problem and then analyzing legal authorities is the way practicing lawyers typically approach problems.

The following problem involves federal legislation to secure the right to an abortion. (This statute would be of substantial importance if the Court rejects the limited right to an abortion currently protected under the right of privacy.) Its proponents contend it is authorized pursuant to the Commerce Clause. Legislation much like that discussed in this question has been before Congress. Is the proposed legislation constitutional?

As you read the cases in this section, consider how Courts of different eras would have approached this problem. After you finish all of the material bearing on national power over commerce, we suggest you return to this problem and write out an answer.

A BILL to protect the reproductive rights of women. Be it enacted by the Senate and House of Representatives of the United States of America in Congress assembled,

SECTION 1. SHORT TITLE.

This Act may be cited as the "Freedom of Choice Act of 2006."

SECTION 2. RIGHT TO CHOOSE.

(a) In General. Except as provided in subsection (b), a State may not restrict the right of a woman to choose to terminate a pregnancy—

(1) before fetal viability; or

(2) at any time, if such termination is necessary to protect the life or health of the woman.

(b) Medically Necessary Requirements. A State may impose requirements medically necessary to protect the life or health of women referred to in subsection (a).

* * *

Assume that *Roe v. Wade* has been overruled and that the "Freedom of Choice Act of 2006" is enacted by Congress and signed by the President. Assume further that the effect of the Act will be to override some state anti-abortion laws. A doctor is convicted under a state anti-abortion law after performing an abortion that would be protected under the federal law. His conviction is affirmed by the state supreme court in spite of the doctor's claim that his conduct is protected by the federal statute. Assume that the case is currently pending in the United States Supreme Court.

Comment on the constitutionality of this bill. In particular, consider:

A) Does Congress have the power to pass the Act under the Commerce Clause? Explain.

B) What, if any, relevance does the 10th Amendment have to this question?

C) If the statute is constitutional, what is its effect on the doctor's conviction?

I. Implied Congressional Power: Its Nature and Extent

A. Implied Powers and the Nature of the Union

The Controversy over the Bank of the United States

In December of 1790, Secretary of the Treasury Alexander Hamilton proposed that Congress establish a national bank. Congress quickly passed a bill, over the objections of Rep. James Madison. Madison argued that Congress lacked the constitutional power to incorporate a bank. President Washington had been a delegate to the Constitutional Convention, but he was unsure whether this bill was constitutional. Madison's opposition troubled Washington, who asked members of his cabinet to comment on the bank bill. This debate raised interesting questions about original intent and textual interpretation. This debate is explored in the following excerpt from Paul Finkelman, *The Constitution and the Intentions of the Framers: The Limits of Historical Analysis*, 50 U. Pitt. L. Rev. 349 (1989) (footnotes deleted).

Constitutional Interpretation and the Bank of the United States

At the Philadelphia convention James Madison proposed that Congress be given the power "to grant charters of incorporation in cases where the Public good may require them.".... Such a power was important because at the time no state had general incorporation laws. The formation of a corporation at this time required a special act of the legislature.... The delegates in Philadelphia had no reason to believe that in the future corporations created by the laws of one state would be legally able to conduct business in another state. Thus, federal power to grant charters of incorporation seemed like a good idea. However, when the Committee of Style reported its draft of the Constitution to the entire convention, in early September, the powers of Congress did not include granting charters of incorporation.

When the convention debated the entire committee report, Benjamin Franklin moved to give Congress the power to build canals where necessary for the public good. Madison amended Franklin's motion to give the United States the authority "to grant charters of incorporation where the interest of the U.S. might require" it....

Rufus King of Massachusetts opposed Madison's motion. King "thought the power unnecessary." Furthermore, King felt that such a provision would produce interstate conflict as states and localities competed for federal charters. Specifically, King argued that such a power would be used by the citizens of New York and Philadelphia for "the establishment of a Bank." James Wilson, who came from Philadelphia, and who would one day sit on the Supreme Court, said that he did not think that the power to incorporate a bank in one city would "excite prejudices" and political partisanship in other cities. Wilson was a founding director of the Bank of North America which had been incorporated in Philadelphia in 1781. [Nevertheless,] by a vote of three states for and eight against, the convention defeated Franklin's original motion giving Congress the power to build canals [and grant charters of incorporation]....

In 1790, Secretary of the Treasury Alexander Hamilton asked Congress to charter the Bank of the United States, to be located as King had predicted, in Philadelphia. In his *Report Relative to a Provision for the Support of Public Credit*, Hamilton argued that a national bank was necessary for a smoothly functioning economy. Hamilton presented his report to Congress just three years after the constitutional convention. The Senate unanimously endorsed Hamilton's proposal. Almost half of the senators in 1790–91 had been delegates to the convention. One of the senators voting for Hamilton's plan was Rufus King, the man who, as a delegate to the Philadelphia convention in 1787, had opposed giving Congress the power to create banks.

[In the House of Representatives] James Madison of Virginia vigorously opposed the bank. Most of the arguments against the bank, as well as the arguments of those who supported the bank, focused on the meaning of the "necessary and proper" clause of the Constitution and the proper methods of constitutional "construction." Supporters of the bank argued that Congress had implied powers to carry out the functions of government specifically stated in the Constitution. Opponents denied this. Indeed, central to Madison's opposition was the argument that the power to create a bank might be "convenient" but that it was not a "necessary and proper" function of the government....

Madison told the House that "[i]n controverted cases, the meaning of the parties to the instrument, if to be collected by reasonable evidence, is a proper guide." He argued that "contemporary and concurrent expositions are a reasonable evidence of the meaning of the parties." Finally, he relied on the debates in the various state ratifying conventions to show that the "contemporary expositions" were for narrow construction of the ambiguous clauses of the Constitution, and that neither under the "necessary and proper" nor the "general welfare" clauses could the bank's constitutionality be sustained.

Madison predicated these arguments on what is the first appeal to the specific intentions of the framers of the Constitution in the nation's history. [He] told the House that "a power to grant charters of incorporation had been proposed in the General Constitutional Convention and rejected."

The response of the House to Madison's intentionalist arguments is revealing. Most of the other congressmen who spoke on the bank simply ignored the argument, in part because ... they did not know what actually happened in Philadelphia. Fisher Ames, of Massachusetts, for example, noted Madison's assertion that the Constitution must be "interpreted by contemporaneous testimony" and that Madison's "opinion is entitled to peculiar weight" because "[h]e was a member of the Convention which formed" the Constitution. Nevertheless, Ames went on to reject Madison's position and to support the bank.

One congressman who was equipped to answer Madison's intentionalist arguments was Elbridge Gerry of Massachusetts, who had represented his state at the Philadelphia convention. For the most part Gerry relied on the standards laid down by Blackstone, including the assertion that "the fairest and most rational method to interpret the will of the legislator is by exploring his intentions at the time when the law was made by signs the most natural and probable; and these signs are either the words, the context, the subject-matter, the effect and consequence, or the spirit and reason of the law." According to Blackstone, this was to be done "not so much" by examining "the grammar" of a statute as by the "general and popular use" of the words of the statute. This approach led Gerry to conclude that the Constitution authorized broad congressional powers for the regulation of the economy, including the creation of a bank....

This debate, less than four years after the Philadelphia convention, reveals the weakness of an intentionalist argument. The debates show that a textualist approach was the one most favored by the first Congress under the new Constitution. Madison's attempt to use his insider's knowledge of the convention gained him nothing. It is perhaps for this reason that he never again used intentionalist arguments of this sort in his extraordinarily long political career. Despite Madison's opposition, by a vote of 39 to 20, the House approved the bank. Five of the bank's supporters had been at the Philadelphia Convention, but so had three of its opponents.

While unable to persuade the House, Madison's opposition at least troubled President Washington. The President had, of course, also been at the Philadelphia convention, but he was unsure whether he ought to sign the bank bill. Washington sought the advice of three of his cabinet officers, Edmund Randolph, Thomas Jefferson, and Alexander Hamilton.

Attorney General Edmund Randolph, who had attended the convention throughout the summer, opposed the bank on textual grounds. He argued that the meaning of the Constitution should "be decided on by the import of its own expressions." He acknowledged that some opposition to the bank was based on what had been discussed "in the federal convention on the subject," but he did not find this argument compelling because it was dangerous to let "an almost unknown history ... govern the construction" of the Constitution....

Secretary of State Thomas Jefferson also opposed the bank on constitutional grounds. Jefferson had been America's ambassador to France in 1787 and was not at the Philadelphia convention or the Virginia ratifying convention. Nevertheless, it is hard not to think of Jefferson as a founder, if not a framer. In his opinion to Washington, Jefferson made a blatantly intentionalist argument, reminding the President "that the very power now proposed as a means, was rejected as an end, by the Convention which formed the constitution." Jefferson conceded that the bank would be convenient for the collection of taxes, but he argued that "the Constitution allows only the means which are 'necessary,' not those which may be 'convenient,' for effecting the enumerated power." He argued that "a little difference in the degree of convenience, cannot constitute the necessity which the constitution makes the ground for assuming any non-enumerated power." ...

Hamilton, who had attended the Philadelphia convention only sporadically, argued in favor of the bank in his *Opinion on the Constitutionality of the Bank of the United States*.... Hamilton acknowledged that the convention rejected a proposal to allow Congress to finance the construction of canals, but he refused to say that this rejection also applied to the power of granting charters of incorporation. Rather, he claimed that neither by "authentic document, or even by accurate recollection" could anyone determine whether the convention considered and rejected giving Congress the power to incorporate banks. He would only admit that "some affirm that it was confined to the opening of canals and obstructions in rivers; others, that it embraced banks; and others, that it extended to the power of incorporating generally." Hamilton simply asserted that "whatever may have been the nature of the proposition or the reasons for rejecting it" was irrelevant, and "whatever may have been the intentions of the framers of a constitution," it was "incumbent to interpret that Constitution according to the usual & established rules," which meant by common law analysis of the text. Hamilton in effect rejected the notion that the intentions of the framers were relevant, less than four years after the Constitution had been written. Instead, he argued that the government possessed "implied as well as express powers," and that the power to create a bank was one of the former. He argued that congressional power to create a bank was implied by Congress' power to collect taxes and regulate trade. He similarly argued for a broad interpretation of the word "necessary" in the "necessary and proper" clause....

Despite the opposition of three important fellow Virginians — Madison, Randolph, and Jefferson — after much soul-searching, Washington signed the bill, accepting Hamilton's argument that the bank was necessary for the proper functioning of the government.

The history of the bank does not end in 1791, with Washington's signature on the bill. The initial charter of the bank was for twenty years. In 1811, the Congress refused to recharter the bank, partly on grounds of public policy and partly because many in Congress doubted the constitutionality of the bank....

In 1814, Congress passed legislation rechartering the bank. In January 1815, James Madison, now President Madison, vetoed this bill because he felt it did not "answer the purposes of reviving the public credit, of providing a national medium of circulation, and of aiding the Treasury" in collecting taxes. In his veto message, Madison made it clear that he was not rejecting the bill on constitutional grounds. Indeed, Madison declared he was

> [w]aiving the question of the Constitutional authority of the Legislature to establish an incorporated bank as being precluded in my judgment by repeated recognitions under varied circumstances of the validity of such an institution in acts of the legislative, executive, and judicial branches of the Government, accompanied by indications, in different modes, of a concurrence of the general will of the nation.

Madison, it seems, was willing to modify his understanding of the Constitution because of the "repeated recognitions" by others of the constitutionality of the bank. This suggests that James Madison, the "father of the Constitution," either could no longer be certain what the intentions of the framers had been in 1787, or more likely, that he did not believe those intentions could possibly govern the nation over a quarter of a century later. It also suggests that the "father of the Constitution" intended the nation's frame of government to be a "living Constitution." ...

Eleven months later [in] his annual message [Madison] declared that "the probable operation of a national bank will merit consideration." The man who had so strenuously argued against the constitutionality of the bank in 1791 was now asking Congress to create such a bank. Madison's position was endorsed by Thomas Jefferson who had also opposed the bank on constitutional grounds in 1791.

Congress quickly endorsed Madison's call for a new bank. The bill to incorporate the bank was introduced by the chairman of the House Committee on Currency, John C. Calhoun, of South Carolina. This future strict constructionist found no constitutional objections to the bank. With relative ease the Congress, in 1816, chartered the Second Bank of the United States. This was possible because in 1816 the former opponents of the bank now favored it.

In 1819, in *McCulloch v. Maryland*, Chief Justice John Marshall gave his stamp of approval to the bank, with a powerful argument in favor of expansive congressional power. Marshall, it should be noted, was not at the Philadelphia convention but was a delegate to the Virginia ratification convention where he supported the Constitution. This opinion says little, however, about the specific intentions of the framers. He did, however, talk about the general intentions of those who framed the Constitution and wrote the "necessary and proper clause" of Article I:

> It must have been the intention of those who gave these powers, to insure, as far as human prudence could insure, their beneficial execution. This could not be done by confiding the choice of means to such narrow limits as not to leave it in the power of Congress to adopt any which might be appropriate, and which were conducive to the end. This provision is made in a constitution intended to endure for ages to come, and consequently, to be adapted to the various crises of human affairs. To have prescribed the means by which government should, in all future time, execute its powers, would have been to change, entirely, the character of the instrument, and give it the properties of a legal code. It would have been an unwise attempt to provide, by immutable rules, for exigencies which, if foreseen at all, must have been seen dimly, and which can be best provided for as they occur.

We should expect the story of the bank to end here with Marshall declaring that the statute creating the Second Bank of the United States was indeed constitutional. But there was one more twist. In 1832, Congress passed a bill extending the charter of the bank. But this time America had a president who did not support the bank. Asserting that the statute creating the bank did in fact violate the Constitution, Andrew Jackson vetoed the bill. Echoing Madison's and Jefferson's 1791 opposition to the bank, Jackson conceded that the bank was "in many respects convenient for the Government and useful to the people" of the United States. But, he argued, convenience did not make the bank constitutional.

Unlike those who opposed the bank in 1791, Jackson did not believe that the chartering of a bank was inherently unconstitutional. He agreed with proponents of the bank that, under certain circumstances, Congress had "unlimited and uncontrollable" power to create a bank. Jackson noted that Congress might constitutionally charter a bank in Washington, D.C., because the Constitution gave Congress exclusive jurisdiction over the federal city. To this extent, Jackson seemed to be willing to ignore the intentions of the framers of the Constitution about banks or other corporations.

Jackson did not believe, however, that the law chartering the Second Bank of the United States had been constitutional in 1816, when it was adopted. This was because the bank had too many "powers and privileges" and was a "monopoly." Jackson reasoned that if the 1816 charter was unconstitutional, then the extension of the charter was also unconstitutional. Even without the benefit of *Madison's Notes*, Jackson concluded that the Bank recharter was "unauthorized by the Constitution, subversive of the rights of the States, and dangerous to the liberties of the people." Thus, he vetoed the recharter bill. His Vice President, John C. Calhoun, who had supported the chartering of the Second Bank of the United States in 1816, applauded this result.

Jackson did more than just veto the recharter bill. He also decided to remove from the bank all funds owned by the United States government. Such an action threatened the entire economy, and Jackson's Secretary of the Treasury, Louis McLane, refused to comply with the order. Jackson therefore appointed a new Treasury Secretary, William J. Duane, but he too refused to remove the deposits, because he also felt that such an act would hurt the economy. Finally, Jackson found a man who would do his bidding. That man was Roger B. Taney. When Taney removed the government deposits, the bank began to call in loans and restrict credit, thus setting in motion the forces that helped cause the Panic of 1837. In 1835, before the panic erupted, Jackson rewarded Taney for his loyalty by appointing him to succeed John Marshall as Chief Justice of the United States. For the next twenty-nine years, Taney would help determine what the Constitution meant.

The history of the bank demonstrates that the intentions of the framers are not easily determined. In 1790–91, five former convention delegates, Madison, Gerry, Randolph, Hamilton, and Washington, and a major figure in the founding, Jefferson, could not agree on what they had intended three years earlier, or if those intentions still mattered. Two and a half decades later, Madison and Jefferson had changed their minds. They now accepted the constitutionality of the bank which, in Madison's case, means that he no longer believed that the framers intended to prevent Congress from chartering banks, or, more likely, that he no longer felt bound by his intentions as a framer. But, where Madison and his immediate successors found the bank constitutional, Jackson did not. Successive Chief Justices also disagreed. Marshall declared the bank constitutionally sound; Taney helped dismantle it as Treasury Secretary.

* * *

1. Review Article I, §§ 8, 9, and 10 and the 10th Amendment.
2. Identify the arguments Chief Justice Marshall makes to support his conclusion.
3. How does the question of the scope of national power bear on the question of the powers reserved to the states? What parts of the text of the Constitution particularly bear on this problem?

McCulloch v. Maryland
17 U.S. 316 (1819)

Marshall, C.J., delivered the opinion of the court.

[In 1816, Congress passed a statute incorporating the second Bank of the United States. The provision for the first Bank of the United States, established during the Washington administration, had lapsed. In 1818, the general assembly of Maryland passed an act taxing the notes of the Bank. McCulloch, the cashier of the Bank's branch in Baltimore, refused to pay the tax. Maryland filed suit to force payment.]

[1] In the case now to be determined, the defendant, a sovereign state, denies the obligation of a law enacted by the legislature of the Union, and the plaintiff, on his part, contests the validity of an act which has been passed by the legislature of that state. The constitution of our country, in its most interesting and vital parts, is to be considered; the conflicting powers of the government of the Union and of its members, as marked in that constitution, are to be discussed; and an opinion given, which may essentially influence the great operations of the government. No tribunal can approach such a question without a deep sense of its importance, and of the awful responsibility involved in its decision. But it must be decided peacefully, or remain a source of hostile legislation, perhaps, of hostility of a still more serious nature; and if it is to be so decided, by this tribunal alone can the decision be made. On the supreme court of the United States has the constitution of our country devolved this important duty.

[2] The first question made in the cause is—has congress power to incorporate a bank? It has been truly said, that this can scarcely be considered as an open question, entirely unprejudiced by the former proceedings of the nation respecting it. The principle now contested was introduced at a very early period of our history, has been recognized by many successive legislatures, and has been acted upon by the judicial department, in cases of peculiar delicacy, as a law of undoubted obligation.

[3] It will not be denied, that a bold and daring usurpation might be resisted, after an acquiescence still longer and more complete than this. But it is conceived, that a doubtful question, one on which human reason may pause, and the human judgment be suspended, in the decision of which the great principles of liberty are not concerned, but the respective powers of those who are equally the representatives of the people, are to be adjusted; if not put at rest by the practice of the government, ought to receive a considerable impression from that practice. An exposition of the constitution, deliberately established by legislative acts, on the faith of which an immense property has been advanced, ought not to be lightly disregarded.

[4] The power now contested was exercised by the first congress elected under the present constitution. The bill for incorporating the Bank of the United States did not steal upon an unsuspecting legislature, and pass unobserved. Its principle was completely understood, and was opposed with equal zeal and ability. After being resisted, first, in the fair and open field of debate, and afterwards, in the executive cabinet, with as much persevering talent as any measure has ever experienced, and being supported by arguments which convinced minds as pure and as intelligent as this country can boast, it became a law. The original act was permitted to expire; but a short experience of the embarrassments to which the refusal to revive it exposed the government, convinced those who were most prejudiced against the measure of its necessity, and induced the passage of the present law. It would require no ordinary share of intrepidity, to assert that a measure adopted under these circumstances, was a bold and plain usurpation, to which the constitution gave no countenance. These observations belong to the cause; but they are not made under the impression, that, were the question entirely new, the law would be found irreconcilable with the constitution.

[5] In discussing this question, the counsel for the state of Maryland have deemed it of some importance, in the construction of the constitution, to consider that instrument, not as emanating from the people, but as the act of sovereign and independent

states. The powers of the general government, it has been said, are delegated by the states, who alone are truly sovereign; and must be exercised in subordination to the states, who alone possess supreme dominion. It would be difficult to sustain this proposition. The convention which framed the constitution was indeed elected by the state legislatures. But the instrument, when it came from their hands, was a mere proposal, without obligation, or pretensions to it. It was reported to the then existing congress of the United States, with a request that it might "be submitted to a convention of delegates, chosen in each state by the people thereof, under the recommendation of its legislature, for their assent and ratification." This mode of proceeding was adopted; and by the convention, by congress, and by the state legislatures, the instrument was submitted to the people. They acted upon it in the only manner in which they can act safely, effectively and wisely, on such a subject, by assembling in convention. It is true, they assembled in their several states—and where else should they have assembled? No political dreamer was ever wild enough to think of breaking down the lines which separate the states, and of compounding the American people into one common mass. Of consequence, when they act, they act in their states. But the measures they adopt do not, on that account, cease to be the measures of the people themselves, or become the measures of the state governments.

[6] From these conventions, the constitution derives its whole authority. The government proceeds directly from the people; is "ordained and established," in the name of the people; and is declared to be ordained, "in order to form a more perfect union, establish justice, insure domestic tranquillity, and secure the blessings of liberty to themselves and to their posterity." The assent of the states, in their sovereign capacity, is implied, in calling a convention, and thus submitting that instrument to the people. But the people were at perfect liberty to accept or reject it; and their act was final. It required not the affirmance, and could not be negatived, by the state governments. The constitution, when thus adopted, was of complete obligation, and bound the state sovereignties.

[7] It has been said, that the people had already surrendered all their powers to the state sovereignties, and had nothing more to give. But, surely, the question whether they may resume and modify the powers granted to government, does not remain to be settled in this country. Much more might the legitimacy of the general government be doubted, had it been created by the states. The powers delegated to the state sovereignties were to be exercised by themselves, not by a distinct and independent sovereignty, created by themselves. To the formation of a league, such as was the confederation, the state sovereignties were certainly competent. But when, "in order to form a more perfect union," it was deemed necessary to change this alliance into an effective government, possessing great and sovereign powers, and acting directly on the people, the necessity of referring it to the people, and of deriving its powers directly from them, was felt and acknowledged by all. The government of the Union, then (whatever may be the influence of this fact on the case), is, emphatically and truly, a government of the people. In form, and in substance, it emanates from them. Its powers are granted by them, and are to be exercised directly on them, and for their benefit.

[8] This government is acknowledged by all, to be one of enumerated powers. The principle, that it can exercise only the powers granted to it, would seem too apparent, to have required to be enforced by all those arguments, which its enlightened friends, while it was depending before the people, found it necessary to urge; that principle is now universally admitted. But the question respecting the extent of the powers actually granted, is perpetually arising, and will probably continue to arise, so long as our system shall exist. In discussing these questions, the conflicting powers of the general and state gov-

ernments must be brought into view, and the supremacy of their respective laws, when they are in opposition, must be settled.

[9] If any one proposition could command the universal assent of mankind, we might expect it would be this—that the government of the Union, though limited in its powers, is supreme within its sphere of action. This would seem to result, necessarily, from its nature. It is the government of all; its powers are delegated by all; it represents all, and acts for all. Though any one state may be willing to control its operations, no state is willing to allow others to control them. The nation, on those subjects on which it can act, must necessarily bind its component parts. But this question is not left to mere reason: the people have, in express terms, decided it, by saying, "this constitution, and the laws of the United States, which shall be made in pursuance thereof, shall be the supreme law of the land," and by requiring that the members of the state legislatures, and the officers of the executive and judicial departments of the states, shall take the oath of fidelity to it. The government of the United States, then, though limited in its powers, is supreme; and its laws, when made in pursuance of the constitution, form the supreme law of the land, "anything in the constitution or laws of any state to the contrary notwithstanding."

[10] Among the enumerated powers, we do not find that of establishing a bank or creating a corporation. But there is no phrase in the instrument which, like the articles of confederation, excludes incidental or implied powers; and which requires that everything granted shall be expressly and minutely described. Even the 10th amendment, which was framed for the purpose of quieting the excessive jealousies which had been excited, omits the word "expressly," and declares only that the powers "not delegated to the United States, nor prohibited to the states, are reserved to the states or to the people"; thus leaving the question, whether the particular power which may become the subject of contest, has been delegated to the one government, or prohibited to the other, to depend on a fair construction of the whole instrument. The men who drew and adopted this amendment had experienced the embarrassments resulting from the insertion of this word in the articles of confederation, and probably omitted it, to avoid those embarrassments. A constitution, to contain an accurate detail of all the subdivisions of which its great powers will admit, and of all the means by which they may be carried into execution, would partake of the prolixity of a legal code, and could scarcely be embraced by the human mind. It would, probably, never be understood by the public. Its nature, therefore, requires, that only its great outlines should be marked, its important objects designated, and the minor ingredients which compose those objects, be deduced from the nature of the objects themselves. That this idea was entertained by the framers of the American constitution, is not only to be inferred from the nature of the instrument, but from the language. Why else were some of the limitations, found in the 9th section of the 1st article, introduced? It is also, in some degree, warranted, by their having omitted to use any restrictive term which might prevent its receiving a fair and just interpretation. In considering this question, then, we must never forget that it is a *constitution* we are expounding.

[11] Although, among the enumerated powers of government, we do not find the word "bank" or "incorporation," we find the great powers, to lay and collect taxes; to borrow money; to regulate commerce; to declare and conduct a war; and to raise and support armies and navies. The sword and the purse, all the external relations, and no inconsiderable portion of the industry of the nation, are entrusted to its government. It can never be pretended, that these vast powers draw after them others of inferior importance, merely because they are inferior. Such an idea can never be advanced. But it may with great reason be contended, that a government, entrusted with such ample powers, on the due execution of which the happiness and prosperity of the nation so vitally de-

pends, must also be entrusted with ample means for their execution. The power being given, it is the interest of the nation to facilitate its execution. It can never be their interest, and cannot be presumed to have been their intention, to clog and embarrass its execution, by withholding the most appropriate means. Throughout this vast republic, from the St. Croix to the Gulf of Mexico, from the Atlantic to the Pacific, revenue is to be collected and expended, armies are to be marched and supported. The exigencies of the nation may require, that the treasure raised in the north should be transported to the south, that raised in the east, conveyed to the west, or that this order should be reversed. Is that construction of the constitution to be preferred, which would render these operations difficult, hazardous and expensive? Can we adopt that construction (unless the words imperiously require it), which would impute to the framers of that instrument, when granting these powers for the public good, the intention of impeding their exercise, by withholding a choice of means? If, indeed, such be the mandate of the constitution, we have only to obey; but that instrument does not profess to enumerate the means by which the powers it confers may be executed; nor does it prohibit the creation of a corporation, if the existence of such a being be essential, to the beneficial exercise of those powers. It is, then, the subject of fair inquiry, how far such means may be employed....

[12] But the constitution of the United States has not left the right of congress to employ the necessary means, for the execution of the powers conferred on the government, to general reasoning. To its enumeration of powers is added, that of making "all laws which shall be necessary and proper, for carrying into execution the foregoing powers, and all other powers vested by this constitution, in the government of the United States, or in any department thereof." The counsel for the state of Maryland have urged various arguments, to prove that this clause, though, in terms, a grant of power, is not so, in effect; but is really restrictive of the general right, which might otherwise be implied, of selecting means for executing the enumerated powers. In support of this proposition, they have found it necessary to contend, that this clause was inserted for the purpose of conferring on congress the power of making laws. That, without it, doubts might be entertained, whether congress could exercise its powers in the form of legislation....

[13] But the argument on which most reliance is placed, is drawn from that peculiar language of this clause. Congress is not empowered by it to make all laws, which may have relation to the powers conferred on the government, but such only as may be "necessary and proper" for carrying them into execution. The word "necessary" is considered as controlling the whole sentence, and as limiting the right to pass laws for the execution of the granted powers, to such as are indispensable, and without which the power would be nugatory. That it excludes the choice of means, and leaves to congress, in each case, that only which is most direct and simple.

[14] Is it true, that this is the sense in which the word "necessary" is always used? Does it always import an absolute physical necessity, so strong, that one thing to which another may be termed necessary, cannot exist without that other? We think it does not. If reference be had to its use, in the common affairs of the world, or in approved authors, we find that it frequently imports no more than that one thing is convenient, or useful, or essential to another. To employ the means necessary to an end, is generally understood as employing any means calculated to produce the end, and not as being confined to those single means, without which the end would be entirely unattainable. Such is the character of human language, that no word conveys to the mind, in all situations, one single definite idea; and nothing is more common than to use words in a figurative sense. Almost all compositions contain words, which, taken in their rigorous sense, would convey a meaning different from that which is obviously intended. It is essential to just con-

struction, that many words which import something excessive, should be understood in a more mitigated sense—in that sense which common usage justifies. The word "necessary" is of this description. It has not a fixed character, peculiar to itself. It admits of all degrees of comparison; and is often connected with other words, which increase or diminish the impression the mind receives of the urgency it imports. A thing may be necessary, very necessary, absolutely or indispensably necessary. To no mind would the same idea be conveyed by these several phrases. The comment on the word is well illustrated by the passage cited at the bar, from the 10th section of the 1st article of the constitution. It is, we think, impossible to compare the sentence which prohibits a state from laying "imposts, or duties on imports or exports, except what may be *absolutely* necessary for executing its inspection laws," with that which authorizes congress "to make all laws which shall be necessary and proper for carrying into execution" the powers of the general government, without feeling a conviction, that the convention understood itself to change materially the meaning of the word "necessary," by prefixing the word "absolutely." This word, then, like others, is used in various senses; and, in its construction, the subject, the context, the intention of the person using them, are all to be taken into view.

[15] Let this be done in the case under consideration. The subject is the execution of those great powers on which the welfare of a nation essentially depends. It must have been the intention of those who gave these powers, to insure, so far as human prudence could insure, their beneficial execution. This could not be done, by confiding the choice of means to such narrow limits as not to leave it in the power of congress to adopt any which might be appropriate, and which were conducive to the end. This provision is made in a constitution, intended to endure for ages to come, and consequently, to be adapted to the various *crises* of human affairs. To have prescribed the means by which government should, in all future time, execute its powers, would have been to change, entirely, the character of the instrument, and give it the properties of a legal code. It would have been an unwise attempt to provide, by immutable rules, for exigencies which, if foreseen at all, must have been seen dimly, and which can be best provided for as they occur. To have declared, that the best means shall not be used, but those alone, without which the power given would be nugatory, would have been to deprive the legislature of the capacity to avail itself of experience, to exercise its reason, and to accommodate its legislation to circumstances....

[16] So, with respect to the whole penal code of the United States: whence arises the power to punish, in cases not prescribed by the constitution? All admit, that the government may, legitimately, punish any violation of its laws; and yet, this is not among the enumerated powers of congress. The right to enforce the observance of law, by punishing its infraction, might be denied, with the more plausibility, because it is expressly given in some cases....

[17] Take, for example, the power "to establish post-offices and post-roads." This power is executed, by the single act of making the establishment. But, from this has been inferred the power and duty of carrying the mail along the post-road, from one post-office to another. And from this implied power, has again been inferred the right to punish those who steal letters from the post-office, or rob the mail. It may be said, with some plausibility, that the right to carry the mail, and to punish those who rob it, is not indispensably necessary to the establishment of a post-office and post-road. This right is indeed essential to the beneficial exercise of the power, but not indispensably necessary to its existence. So, of the punishment of the crimes of stealing or falsifying a record or process of a court of the United States, or of perjury in such court. To punish these offences, is certainly conducive to the due administration of justice. But courts may exist, and may decide the causes brought before them, though such crimes escape punishment.

[18] The baneful influence of this narrow construction on all the operations of the government, and the absolute impracticability of maintaining it, without rendering the government incompetent to its great objects, might be illustrated by numerous examples drawn from the constitution, and from our laws. The good sense of the public has pronounced, without hesitation, that the power of punishment appertains to sovereignty, and may be exercised, whenever the sovereign has a right to act, as incidental to his constitutional powers. It is a means for carrying into execution all sovereign powers, and may be used, although not indispensably necessary. It is a right incidental to the power, and conducive to its beneficial exercise.

[19] If this limited construction of the word "necessary" must be abandoned, in order to punish, whence is derived the rule which would reinstate it, when the government would carry its powers into execution, by means not vindictive in their nature? If the word "necessary" means "needful," "requisite," "essential," "conducive to," in order to let in the power of punishment for the infraction of law; why is it not equally comprehensive, when required to authorize the use of means which facilitate the execution of the powers of government, without the infliction of punishment?

[20] In ascertaining the sense in which the word "necessary" is used in this clause of the constitution, we may derive some aid from that with which it is associated. Congress shall have power "to make all laws which shall be necessary and proper to carry into execution" the powers of the government. If the word "necessary" was used in that strict and rigorous sense for which the counsel for the state of Maryland contend, it would be an extraordinary departure from the usual course of the human mind, as exhibited in composition, to add a word, the only possible effect of which is, to qualify that strict and rigorous meaning; to present to the mind the idea of some choice of means of legislation, not strained and compressed within the narrow limits for which gentlemen contend.

[21] But the argument which most conclusively demonstrates the error of the construction contended for by the counsel for the state of Maryland, is founded on the intention of the convention, as manifested in the whole clause....

[22] 1st. The clause is placed among the powers of congress, not among the limitations on those powers. 2d. Its terms purport to enlarge, not to diminish the powers vested in the government. It purports to be an additional power, not a restriction on those already granted. No reason has been, or can be assigned, for thus concealing an intention to narrow the discretion of the national legislature, under words which purport to enlarge it. The framers of the constitution wished its adoption, and well knew that it would be endangered by its strength, not by its weakness. Had they been capable of using language which would convey to the eye one idea, and, after deep reflection, impress on the mind, another, they would rather have disguised the grant of power, than its limitation. If, then, their intention had been, by this clause, to restrain the free use of means which might otherwise have been implied, that intention would have been inserted in another place, and would have been expressed in terms resembling these. "In carrying into execution the foregoing powers, and all others," &c., "no laws shall be passed but such as are necessary and proper." Had the intention been to make this clause restrictive, it would unquestionably have been so in form as well as in effect.

[23] The result of the most careful and attentive consideration bestowed upon this clause is, that if it does not enlarge, it cannot be construed to restrain the powers of congress, or to impair the right of the legislature to exercise its best judgment in the selection of measures to carry into execution the constitutional powers of the government. If

no other motive for its insertion can be suggested, a sufficient one is found in the desire to remove all doubts respecting the right to legislate on that vast mass of incidental powers which must be involved in the constitution, if that instrument be not a splendid bauble.

[24] We admit, as all must admit, that the powers of the government are limited, and that its limits are not to be transcended. But we think the sound construction of the constitution must allow to the national legislature that discretion, with respect to the means by which the powers it confers are to be carried into execution, which will enable that body to perform the high duties assigned to it, in the manner most beneficial to the people. Let the end be legitimate, let it be within the scope of the constitution, and all means which are appropriate, which are plainly adapted to that end, which are not prohibited, but consist with the letter and spirit of the constitution, are constitutional....

[25] But were its necessity less apparent, none can deny its being an appropriate measure; and if it is, the decree of its necessity, as has been very justly observed, is to be discussed in another place. Should congress, in the execution of its powers, adopt measures which are prohibited by the constitution; or should congress, under the pretext of executing its powers, pass laws for the accomplishment of objects not entrusted to the government; it would become the painful duty of this tribunal, should a case requiring such a decision come before it, to say, that such an act was not the law of the land. But where the law is not prohibited, and is really calculated to effect any of the objects entrusted to the government, to undertake here to inquire into the degree of its necessity, would be to pass the line which circumscribes the judicial department, and to tread on legislative ground. This court disclaims all pretensions to such a power....

[26] After the most deliberate consideration, it is the unanimous and decided opinion of this court, that the act to incorporate the Bank of the United States is a law made in pursuance of the constitution, and is a part of the supreme law of the land....

[27] It being the opinion of the court, that the act incorporating the bank is constitutional; and that the power of establishing a branch in the state of Maryland might be properly exercised by the bank itself, we proceed to inquire—

[28] 2. Whether the state of Maryland may, without violating the constitution, tax that branch? That the power of taxation is one of vital importance; that it is retained by the states; that it is not abridged by the grant of a similar power to the government of the Union; that it is to be concurrently exercised by the two governments—are truths which have never been denied. But such is the paramount character of the constitution, that its capacity to withdraw any subject from the action of even this power, is admitted. The states are expressly forbidden to lay any duties on imports or exports, except what may be absolutely necessary for executing their inspection laws. If the obligation of this prohibition must be conceded—if it may restrain a state from the exercise of its taxing power on imports and exports—the same paramount character would seem to restrain, as it certainly may restrain, a state from such other exercise of this power, as is in its nature incompatible with, and repugnant to, the constitutional laws of the Union. A law, absolutely repugnant to another, as entirely repeals that other as if express terms of repeal were used.

[29] On this ground, the counsel for the bank place its claim to be exempted from the power of a state to tax its operations. There is no express provision for the case, but the claim has been sustained on a principle which so entirely pervades the constitution, is so intermixed with the materials which compose it, so interwoven with its web, so blended with its texture, as to be incapable of being separated from it, without rending it into shreds. This great principle is, that the constitution and the laws made in pursuance

thereof are supreme; that they control the constitution and laws of the respective states, and cannot be controlled by them. From this, which may be almost termed an axiom, other propositions are deduced as corollaries, on the truth or error of which, and on their application to this case, the cause has been supposed to depend. These are, 1st. That a power to create implies a power to preserve. 2d. That a power to destroy, if wielded by a different hand, is hostile to, and incompatible with these powers to create and to preserve. 3d. That where this repugnancy exists, that authority which is supreme must control, not yield to that over which it is supreme.

[30] These propositions, as abstract truths, would, perhaps, never be controverted. Their application to this case, however, has been denied; and both in maintaining the affirmative and the negative, a splendor of eloquence, and strength of argument, seldom, if ever, surpassed, have been displayed.

[31] The power of congress to create, and of course, to continue, the bank, was the subject of the preceding part of this opinion; and is no longer to be considered as questionable. That the power of taxing it by the states may be exercised so as to destroy it, is too obvious to be denied. But taxation is said to be an absolute power, which acknowledges no other limits than those expressly prescribed in the constitution, and like sovereign power of every other description, is entrusted to the discretion of those who use it. But the very terms of this argument admit, that the sovereignty of the state, in the article of taxation itself, is subordinate to, and may be controlled by the constitution of the United States. How far it has been controlled by that instrument, must be a question of construction. In making this construction, no principle, not declared, can be admissible, which would defeat the legitimate operations of a supreme government. It is of the very essence of supremacy, to remove all obstacles to its action within its own sphere, and so to modify every power vested in subordinate governments, as to exempt its own operations from their own influence....

[32] The argument on the part of the state of Maryland, is, not that the states may directly resist a law of congress, but that they may exercise their acknowledged powers upon it, and that the constitution leaves them this right, in the confidence that they will not abuse it....

[33] The people of a state, therefore, give to their government a right of taxing themselves and their property, and as the exigencies of government cannot be limited, they prescribe no limits to the exercise of this right, resting confidently on the interest of the legislator, and on the influence of the constituent over their representative, to guard them against its abuse. But the means employed by the government of the Union have no such security, nor is the right of a state to tax them sustained by the same theory. Those means are not given by the people of a particular state, not given by the constituents of the legislature, which claim the right to tax them, but by the people of all the states. They are given by all, for the benefit of all—and upon theory, should be subjected to that government only which belongs to all....

[34] That the power to tax involves the power to destroy; that the power to destroy may defeat and render useless the power to create; that there is a plain repugnance in conferring on one government a power to control the constitutional measures of another, which other, with respect to those very measures, is declared to be supreme over that which exerts the control, are propositions not to be denied. But all inconsistencies are to be reconciled by the magic of the word *confidence*. Taxation, it is said, does not necessarily and unavoidably destroy. To carry it to the excess of destruction, would be an abuse, to presume which, would banish that confidence which is essential to all government. But

is this a case of confidence? Would the people of any one state trust those of another with a power to control the most insignificant operations of their state government? We know they would not. Why, then, should we suppose, that the people of any one state should be willing to trust those of another with a power to control the operations of a government to which they have confided their most important and most valuable interests? In the legislature of the Union alone, are all represented. The legislature of the Union alone, therefore, can be trusted by the people with the power of controlling measures which concern all, in the confidence that it will not be abused. This, then, is not a case of confidence, and we must consider it is as it really is.

[35] If we apply the principle for which the state of Maryland contends, to the constitution, generally, we shall find it capable of changing totally the character of that instrument. We shall find it capable of arresting all the measures of the government, and of prostrating it at the foot of the states. The American people have declared their constitution and the laws made in pursuance thereof, to be supreme; but this principle would transfer the supremacy, in fact, to the states. If the states may tax one instrument, employed by the government in the execution of its powers, they may tax any and every other instrument. They may tax the mail; they may tax the mint; they may tax patent-rights; they may tax the papers of the custom-house; they may tax judicial process; they may tax all the means employed by the government, to an excess which would defeat all the ends of government. This was not intended by the American people. They did not design to make their government dependent on the states....

[36] In the course of the argument, *The Federalist* has been quoted; and the opinions expressed by the authors of that work have been justly supposed to be entitled to great respect in expounding the constitution. No tribute can be paid to them which exceeds their merit; but in applying their opinions to the cases which may arise in the progress of our government, a right to judge of their correctness must be retained; and to understand the argument, we must examine the proposition it maintains, and the objections against which it is directed. The subject of those numbers, from which passages have been cited, is the unlimited power of taxation which is vested in the general government. The objection to this unlimited power, which the argument seeks to remove, is stated with fulness and clearness. It is, "that an indefinite power of taxation in the latter (the government of the Union) might, and probably would, in time, deprive the former (the government of the states) of the means of providing for their own necessities; and would subject them entirely to the mercy of the national legislature. As the laws of the Union are to become the supreme law of the land; as it is to have power to pass all laws that may be necessary for carrying into execution the authorities with which it is proposed to vest it; the national government might, at any time, abolish the taxes imposed for state objects, upon the pretence of an interference with its own. It might allege a necessity for doing this, in order to give efficacy to the national revenues; and thus, all the resources of taxation might, by degrees, become the subjects of federal monopoly, to the entire exclusion and destruction of the state governments."

[37] The objections to the constitution which are noticed in these numbers, were to the undefined power of the government to tax, not to the incidental privilege of exempting its own measures from state taxation. The consequences apprehended from this undefined power were, that it would absorb all the objects of taxation, "to the exclusion and destruction of the state governments." The arguments of *The Federalist* are intended to prove the fallacy of these apprehensions; not to prove that the government was incapable of executing any of its powers, without exposing the means it employed to the embarrassments of state taxation. Arguments urged against these objections, and these apprehensions,

are to be understood as relating to the points they mean to prove. Had the authors of those excellent essays been asked, whether they contended for that construction of the constitution, which would place within the reach of the states those measures which the government might adopt for the execution of its powers; no man, who has read their instructive pages, will hesitate to admit, that their answer must have been in the negative.

[38] It has also been insisted, that, as the power of taxation in the general and state governments is acknowledged to be concurrent, every argument which would sustain the right of the general government to tax banks chartered by the states, will equally sustain the right of the states to tax banks chartered by the general government. But the two cases are not on the same reason. The people of all the states have created the general government, and have conferred upon it the general power of taxation. The people of all the states, and the states themselves, are represented in congress, and, by their representatives, exercise this power. When they tax the chartered institutions of the states, they tax their constituents; and these taxes must be uniform. But when a state taxes the operations of the government of the United States, it acts upon institutions created, not by their own constituents, but by people over whom they claim no control. It acts upon the measures of a government created by others as well as themselves, for the benefit of others in common with themselves. The difference is that which always exists, and always must exist, between the action of the whole on a part, and the action of a part on the whole—between the laws of a government declared to be supreme, and those of a government which, when in opposition to those laws, is not supreme.

[39] But if the full application of this argument could be admitted, it might bring into question the right of congress to tax the state banks, and could not prove the rights of the states to tax the Bank of the United States.

[40] The court has bestowed on this subject its most deliberate consideration. The result is a conviction that the states have no power, by taxation or otherwise, to retard, impede, burden, or in any manner control, the operations of the constitutional laws enacted by congress to carry into execution the powers vested in the general government. This is, we think, the unavoidable consequence of that supremacy which the constitution has declared. We are unanimously of opinion, that the law passed by the legislature of Maryland, imposing a tax on the Bank of the United States, is unconstitutional and void.

[41] This opinion does not deprive the states of any resources which they originally possessed. It does not extend to a tax paid by the real property of the bank, in common with the other real property within the state, nor to a tax imposed on the interest which the citizens of Maryland may hold in this institution, in common with other property of the same description throughout the state. But this is a tax on the operations of the bank, and is, consequently, a tax on the operation of an instrument employed by the government of the Union to carry its powers into execution. Such a tax must be unconstitutional.

[42] JUDGMENT.—[I]t is the opinion of this court, that the act of the legislature of Maryland is contrary to the constitution of the United States, and void....

McCulloch v. Maryland: Questions

1. How does Chief Justice Marshall use history in this case? How does he use the debate over the first Bank of the United States? Is there a tension between following original purposes and the argument that we must never forget that it is a constitution that we are expounding?
2. What structural arguments does Marshall make? How does Marshall use the argument that the Constitution was established by the people, not by the states?

3. Identify the textual arguments Marshall makes. What canons of construction does he invoke? Are they an accurate guide to the intent of the framers?
4. Identify policy arguments in the opinion. Does Marshall argue that his interpretation leads to sound results and that the opposite interpretation would lead to disaster?
5. How are arguments from precedent used in Marshall's opinion?
6. Some specific arguments:
   a. What is the significance of Marshall's statement that "we must never forget it is a *constitution* we are expounding"?
   b. Marshall argues that if Congress goes beyond its limits, it is the duty of the Court in a case requiring a decision on the issue to declare the act unconstitutional. But, he argues, where the act is not prohibited and is calculated to effectuate the general objects entrusted to government, the Court would invade the sphere of the legislature if it were to strike the act down. What basic concept is Marshall invoking here? What type of argument is this?
7. The merits of the decision in *McCulloch:*
   a. What are the basic tensions that shape decisions about implied powers of Congress? What problems arise if no implied powers are allowed? What potential problems exist if Congress can do anything that is convenient for the exercise of its express powers? What problems exist if the Court simply defers to congressional judgment on the question of implied powers? What problems arise if the Court reads implied powers very narrowly?
   b. Does Marshall provide a test derived from the Constitution to determine when Congress has exceeded its implied powers under the Constitution? When are laws appropriate and plainly adapted to a legitimate end within the scope of the Constitution? To what extent, if at all, is it a test courts can enforce?
   c. Does *McCulloch* provide any real limitations? John Taylor, a close political ally of Thomas Jefferson, thought it did not. He said:

   "Taverns are very necessary or convenient for the offices of the army.... But horses are undoubtedly more necessary for the conveyance of the mail and for war, than roads ... and therefore the principle of implied power of legislation will certainly invest Congress with a legislative power over horses. In short, this mode of construction completely establishes the position, that Congress may pass any internal law whatsoever in relation to things, because there is nothing with which war, commerce and taxation may not be closely or remotely connected."

8. How might Congress seek to exercise powers not entrusted to the national government under the pretext of executing congressional powers? Would it be necessary to examine congressional motives to make such a decision? Are there problems connected with examining motives? Must Congress legislate primarily for a commercial purpose? Or could it legislate under the Commerce Clause to enforce morality, to end racial discrimination, or to preserve the right to abortion so long as the law affects some commerce-connected activity?
9. The second issue in *McCulloch* involves a state's ability to tax the federal government. Is Marshall's rule—that states may *never* tax federal instrumentalities—broader than the Constitution requires?
   a. Are the states protected from federal invasion of their appropriate sphere because all states are represented in Congress? Should that fact mean that protec-

tion of the sphere allocated to the states from federal invasion is essentially a political question, beyond the supervisory power of the Court?

b. Are there reasons why the Court should be especially sensitive to state encroachment on the sphere and powers of the national government?

The Court broadly interpreted the Necessary and Proper Clause in *United States v. Comstock*, 560 U.S. ___ (2010), which upheld a federal statute allowing federal district judges to order the civil confinement of mentally ill and sexually dangerous federal prisoners beyond their prescribed release date. In his opinion for the Court, Justice Breyer explained that "five considerations, taken together," provided Congress with authority to enact the statute, 28 U.S.C. §4248.

First, the Court explained that "the Necessary and Proper Clause grants Congress broad authority to enact federal legislation" and that the statute was "rationally related to the implementation of a constitutionally enumerated power" insofar as Congress has the power to create federal crimes and to build and regulate prisons. Second, the Court relied upon "the long history of federal involvement in this area," describing the statute as "a modest addition to a set of federal prison-related mental-health statutes that have existed for many decades." Third, the Court held that the federal government, as custodian of prisoners, "has the constitutional power to ... protect nearby (and other) communities from the danger federal prisoners may pose." Fourth, the Court found that "the statute properly accounts for state interests" and attempts to accommodate them by requiring the Attorney General to encourage the state in which a prisoner was domiciled or tried to assume custody of the prisoner. Accordingly, the Court found no violation of the 10th Amendment. Finally, the Court determined that the statute was sufficiently narrow in its scope because it applied only to a small fraction of federal prisoners. The Court explained that its decision was not intended to foreclose challenges based upon other constitutional grounds, including due process or equal protection.

Justices Thomas and Scalia dissented on the ground that "[n]o enumerated power in Article I, §8 expressly delegates to Congress the power to enact a civil-commitment regime for sexually dangerous persons, nor does any other provision in the Constitution vest Congress or the other branches of the Federal Government with such a power." In particular, they argued that "[t]he fact that the Federal Government has the authority to imprison a person for the purpose of punishing him for a federal crime ... does not provide the Government with the additional power to exercise indefinite civil control over that person." Contending that the Court's five-part test lacked support in the text of the Constitution and in precedent, Justice Thomas complained that the Court's decision "comes perilously close to transforming the Necessary and Proper Clause" into a federal police power.

B. The Nature of the Union Revisited

U.S. Term Limits, Inc. v. Thornton: Background

1. Review Article I, §2, cl. 2; Article I, §3, cl. 3; and the 10th Amendment.
2. What types of constitutional arguments (arguments from text, context, history, structure, precedent, and policy) are made in the case? Be able to identify the arguments made and to categorize them based on type.

3. This decision, like many more that you will read, is decided by a 5–4 margin. Do you think that the majority and dissent have a fundamental disagreement that extends beyond the specifics of this case? What might it be? Which decision do you think is more well-reasoned? Whose treatment of *McCulloch v. Maryland* is more persuasive, Justice Stevens' or Justice Thomas'? Is one interpretation "correct" and one "incorrect"?

4. Briefs and oral arguments show how lawyers craft arguments in constitutional cases. They often combine the various types of constitutional arguments. In particular, reading opposing briefs shows how lawyers rely on and attempt to distinguish precedent.

Briefs and transcripts of oral arguments are available for recent cases on Westlaw and Lexis. The citations for the *Term Limits* case follow, but will not be given for subsequent cases. For crucial older cases, briefs and the transcript (or summary for older cases) of the oral argument are available in the series entitled *Landmark Briefs and Arguments of the Supreme Court of the United States*. Substantial excerpts from briefs can also be found in the *U.S. Reports, Lawyer's Edition*.

Lexis has this service going back to the 1979–80 term. Westlaw has party briefs and oral argument transcripts going back to the 1990–91 term and amicus briefs going back to the 1995–96 term. For those cases that Westlaw has available, it provides hotlinks from the opinion to the briefs and usually to the transcript of the oral argument. If there is not a hotlink, access the Supreme Court Oral Argument directory. Lexis also has hotlinks from the "full text" opinion to briefs and the transcript of the oral argument. The links are at the end of the opinion text under "references." Lexis and Westlaw also have directories for the ABA Supreme Court Preview, which often contains useful information about a case.

Each brief is listed separately in Westlaw:

Brief for Petitioners U.S. Term Limits, Inc., 1994 WL 444704 (U.S., Aug. 16, 1994)

Brief for Respondent Thornton, 1994 WL 570304 (U.S., Oct. 17, 1994)

Reply Brief for Petitioners U.S. Term Limits, Inc., 1994 WL 646175 (U.S., Nov. 16, 1994)

All briefs are found at one cite for Lexis and then identified and accessed separately within the cite:

1993 U.S. Briefs 1456 (*U.S. Term Limits, Inc. v. Thornton*)

The oral arguments are found at individual cites on both databases:

Oral Argument, 1994 WL 714634 (*U.S. Term Limits, Inc. v. Thornton*)

1994 U.S. TRANS LEXIS 169 (*U.S. Term Limits, Inc. v. Thornton*)

Recordings of oral arguments for all cases since 1995 and selected earlier cases are available from the Oyez Project, found at http://www.oyez.org.

U.S. Term Limits, Inc. v. Thornton
514 U.S. 779 (1995)

[Majority: Stevens, Breyer, Souter, Ginsburg, Kennedy. Concurring: Kennedy. Dissenting: Thomas, Rehnquist (C.J.), O'Connor, Scalia.]

Justice Stevens delivered the opinion of the Court.

The Constitution sets forth qualifications for membership in the Congress of the United States. Article I, §2, cl. 2, which applies to the House of Representatives, provides:

> No Person shall be a Representative who shall not have attained to the Age of twenty five Years, and been seven Years a Citizen of the United States, and who shall not, when elected, be an Inhabitant of that State in which he shall be chosen.

Article I, § 3, cl. 3, which applies to the Senate, similarly provides:

> No Person shall be a Senator who shall not have attained to the Age of thirty Years, and been nine Years a Citizen of the United States, and who shall not, when elected, be an Inhabitant of that State for which he shall be chosen.

Today's cases present a challenge to an amendment to the Arkansas State Constitution that prohibits the name of an otherwise-eligible candidate for Congress from appearing on the general election ballot if that candidate has already served three terms in the House of Representatives or two terms in the Senate. The Arkansas Supreme Court held that the amendment violates the Federal Constitution. We agree with that holding. Such a state-imposed restriction is contrary to the "fundamental principle of our representative democracy," embodied in the Constitution, that "the people should choose whom they please to govern them." *Powell v. McCormack* (1969). Allowing individual States to adopt their own qualifications for congressional service would be inconsistent with the Framers' vision of a uniform National Legislature representing the people of the United States. If the qualifications set forth in the text of the Constitution are to be changed, that text must be amended.

I. At the general election on November 3, 1992, the voters of Arkansas adopted Amendment 73 to their State Constitution. Proposed as a "Term Limitation Amendment," its preamble stated:

> The people of Arkansas find and declare that elected officials who remain in office too long become preoccupied with reelection and ignore their duties as representatives of the people. Entrenched incumbency has reduced voter participation and has led to an electoral system that is less free, less competitive, and less representative than the system established by the Founding Fathers. Therefore, the people of Arkansas, exercising their reserved powers, herein limit the terms of the elected officials.

The limitations in Amendment 73 apply to three categories of elected officials.... Section 3, the provision at issue in these cases, applies to the Arkansas Congressional Delegation. It provides:

> (a) Any person having been elected to three or more terms as a member of the United States House of Representatives from Arkansas shall not be certified as a candidate and shall not be eligible to have his/her name placed on the ballot for election to the United States House of Representatives from Arkansas.
>
> (b) Any person having been elected to two or more terms as a member of the United States Senate from Arkansas shall not be certified as a candidate and shall not be eligible to have his/her name placed on the ballot for election to the United States Senate from Arkansas....

On November 13, 1992, respondent Bobbie Hill, on behalf of herself, similarly situated Arkansas "citizens, residents, taxpayers and registered voters," and the League of Women Voters of Arkansas, filed a complaint in the Circuit Court for Pulaski County, Arkansas, seeking a declaratory judgment that § 3 of Amendment 73 is "unconstitutional and void."...

On cross-motions for summary judgment, the Circuit Court held that § 3 of Amendment 73 violated Article I of the Federal Constitution....

[T]he Arkansas Supreme Court affirmed....

II. [T]he constitutionality of Amendment 73 depends critically on the resolution of two distinct issues. The first is whether the Constitution forbids States from adding to or altering the qualifications specifically enumerated in the Constitution. The second is, if the Constitution does so forbid, whether the fact that Amendment 73 is formulated as a ballot access restriction rather than as an outright disqualification is of constitutional significance. Our resolution of these issues draws upon our prior resolution of a related but distinct issue: whether Congress has the power to add to or alter the qualifications of its Members.

Twenty-six years ago, in *Powell* we reviewed the history and text of the Qualifications Clauses in a case involving an attempted exclusion of a duly elected Member of Congress. The principal issue was whether the power granted to each House in Art. I, §5, to judge the "Qualifications of its own Members" includes the power to impose qualifications other than those set forth in the text of the Constitution. In an opinion by Chief Justice Warren for eight Members of the Court, we held that it does not. Because of the obvious importance of the issue, the Court's review of the history and meaning of the relevant constitutional text was especially thorough. We therefore begin our analysis today with a full statement of what we decided in that case.

THE ISSUE IN *POWELL*. In November 1966, Adam Clayton Powell, Jr., was elected from a District in New York to serve in the United States House of Representatives for the 90th Congress. Allegations that he had engaged in serious misconduct while serving as a committee chairman during the 89th Congress led to the appointment of a Select Committee to determine his eligibility to take his seat. That Committee found that Powell met the age, citizenship, and residency requirements set forth in Art. I, §2, cl. 2. The Committee also found, however, that Powell had wrongfully diverted House funds for the use of others and himself and had made false reports on expenditures of foreign currency. Based on those findings, the House after debate adopted House Resolution 278, excluding Powell from membership in the House, and declared his seat vacant.

Powell and several voters of the District from which he had been elected filed suit seeking a declaratory judgment that the House Resolution was invalid because Art. I, §2, cl. 2, sets forth the exclusive qualifications for House membership. We ultimately accepted that contention, concluding that the House of Representatives has no "authority to exclude any person, duly elected by his constituents, who meets all the requirements for membership expressly prescribed in the Constitution." In reaching that conclusion, we undertook a detailed historical review to determine the intent of the Framers. Though recognizing that the Constitutional Convention debates themselves were inconclusive ... we determined that the "relevant historical materials" reveal that Congress has no power to alter the qualifications in the text of the Constitution.

POWELL'S RELIANCE ON HISTORY. [W]e concluded in *Powell* that "on the eve of the Constitutional Convention, English precedent stood for the proposition that 'the law of the land had regulated the qualifications of members to serve in parliament' and those qualifications were 'not occasional but fixed.'"

Against this historical background, we viewed the Convention debates as manifesting the Framers' intent that the qualifications in the Constitution be fixed and exclusive. We found particularly revealing the debate concerning a proposal made by the Committee of Detail that would have given Congress the power to add property qualifications. James Madison argued that such a power would vest "'an improper & dangerous power in the Legislature,'" by which the Legislature "'can by degrees subvert the Constitution.'" ...

The Framers further revealed their concerns about congressional abuse of power when Gouverneur Morris suggested modifying the proposal of the Committee of Detail to grant Congress unfettered power to add qualifications.... We found significant that the Convention rejected both Morris' modification and the Committee's proposal.

We also recognized in *Powell* that the post-Convention ratification debates confirmed that the Framers understood the qualifications in the Constitution to be fixed and unalterable by Congress. For example, we noted that in response to the antifederalist charge that the new Constitution favored the wealthy and well-born, Alexander Hamilton wrote: "'The truth is that there is no method of securing to the rich the preference apprehended but by prescribing qualifications of property either for those who may elect or be elected. But this forms no part of the power to be conferred upon the national government.... The qualifications of the persons who may choose or be chosen, as has been remarked upon other occasions, are defined and fixed in the Constitution, and are unalterable by the legislature.'" We thus attached special significance to "Hamilton's express reliance on the immutability of the qualifications set forth in the Constitution."

The exercise by Congress of its power to judge the qualifications of its Members further confirmed this understanding. We concluded that, during the first 100 years of its existence, "Congress strictly limited its power to judge the qualifications of its members to those enumerated in the Constitution."

As this elaborate summary reveals, our historical analysis in *Powell* was both detailed and persuasive. We thus conclude now, as we did in *Powell*, that history shows that, with respect to Congress, the Framers intended the Constitution to establish fixed qualifications.

POWELL'S RELIANCE ON DEMOCRATIC PRINCIPLES. In *Powell*, of course, we ... noted that allowing Congress to impose additional qualifications would violate that "fundamental principle of our representative democracy ... 'that the people should choose whom they please to govern them.'"

Our opinion made clear that this broad principle incorporated at least two fundamental ideas. First, we emphasized the egalitarian concept that the opportunity to be elected was open to all. We noted in particular Madison's statement in *The Federalist* that "'[u]nder these reasonable limitations [enumerated in the Constitution], the door of this part of the federal government is open to merit of every description, whether native or adoptive, whether young or old, and without regard to poverty or wealth, or to any particular profession of religious faith.'" ...

Second, we recognized the critical postulate that sovereignty is vested in the people, and that sovereignty confers on the people the right to choose freely their representatives to the National Government. For example, we noted that "Robert Livingston ... endorsed this same fundamental principle: 'The people are the best judges who ought to represent them. To dictate and control them, to tell them whom they shall not elect, is to abridge their natural rights.'" ...

POWELL'S HOLDING. Petitioners argue somewhat half-heartedly that the narrow holding in *Powell*, which involved the power of the House to exclude a member pursuant to Art. I, §5, does not control the more general question whether Congress has the power to add qualifications. *Powell*, however, is not susceptible to such a narrow reading. Our conclusion that Congress may not alter or add to the qualifications in the Constitution was integral to our analysis and outcome....

III. Our reaffirmation of *Powell*, does not necessarily resolve the specific questions presented in these cases. For petitioners argue that whatever the constitutionality of additional qualifications for membership imposed by Congress, the historical and textual materials discussed in *Powell* do not support the conclusion that the Constitution prohibits additional qualifications imposed by States. In the absence of such a constitutional prohibition, petitioners argue, the 10th Amendment and the principle of reserved powers require that States be allowed to add such qualifications.

Before addressing these arguments, we find it appropriate to take note of the striking unanimity among the courts that have considered the issue. None of the overwhelming array of briefs submitted by the parties and amici has called to our attention even a single case in which a state court or federal court has approved of a State's addition of qualifications for a member of Congress. To the contrary, an impressive number of courts have determined that States lack the authority to add qualifications.... Courts have struck down state-imposed qualifications in the form of term limits.... Prior to *Powell*, the commentators were similarly unanimous. See, e.g., 1 Story §627 (each member of Congress is "an officer of the union, deriving his powers and qualifications from the constitution, and neither created by, dependent upon, nor controllable by, the states").... This impressive and uniform body of judicial decisions and learned commentary indicates that the obstacles confronting petitioners are formidable indeed.

Petitioners argue that the Constitution contains no express prohibition against state-added qualifications, and that Amendment 73 is therefore an appropriate exercise of a State's reserved power to place additional restrictions on the choices that its own voters may make. We disagree for two independent reasons. First, we conclude that the power to add qualifications is not within the "original powers" of the States, and thus is not reserved to the States by the 10th Amendment. Second, even if States possessed some original power in this area, we conclude that the Framers intended the Constitution to be the exclusive source of qualifications for members of Congress, and that the Framers thereby "divested" States of any power to add qualifications.

The "plan of the convention" ... draws a basic distinction between the powers of the newly created Federal Government and the powers retained by the pre-existing sovereign States. As Chief Justice Marshall explained, "it was neither necessary nor proper to define the powers retained by the States. These powers proceed, not from the people of America, but from the people of the several States; and remain, after the adoption of the constitution, what they were before, except so far as they may be abridged by that instrument." *Sturges v. Crowninshield* (1819).

This classic statement by the Chief Justice endorsed Hamilton's reasoning in *The Federalist* No. 32 that the plan of the Constitutional Convention did not contemplate "an entire consolidation of the States into one complete national sovereignty," but only a partial consolidation in which "the State governments would clearly retain all the rights of sovereignty which they before had, and which were not, by that act, exclusively delegated to the United States." ... The text of the 10th Amendment unambiguously confirms this principle....

As we have frequently noted, "[t]he States unquestionably do retain a significant measure of sovereign authority. They do so, however, only to the extent that the Constitution has not divested them of their original powers and transferred those powers to the Federal Government." *Garcia v. San Antonio Metropolitan Transit Authority* (1985).

SOURCE OF THE POWER. Contrary to petitioners' assertions, the power to add qualifications is not part of the original powers of sovereignty that the 10th Amendment reserved to the States. Petitioners' 10th Amendment argument misconceives the nature of the right at issue because that Amendment could only "reserve" that which existed before. As Justice Story recognized, "the states can exercise no powers whatsoever, which exclusively spring out of the existence of the national government, which the constitution does not delegate to them.... No state can say that it has reserved what it never possessed."

Justice Story's position thus echoes that of Chief Justice Marshall in *McCulloch v. Maryland* (1819) [where] the Court rejected the argument that the Constitution's silence on the subject of state power to tax corporations chartered by Congress implies that the States have "reserved" power to tax such federal instrumentalities. As Chief Justice Marshall pointed out, an "original right to tax" such federal entities "never existed, and the question whether it has been surrendered, cannot arise." In language that presaged Justice Story's argument, Chief Justice Marshall concluded: "This opinion does not deprive the States of any resources which they originally possessed."

With respect to setting qualifications for service in Congress, no such right existed before the Constitution was ratified.... [T]he Framers envisioned a uniform national system, rejecting the notion that the Nation was a collection of States, and instead creating a direct link between the National Government and the people of the United States.... As Justice Story observed, each Member of Congress is "an officer of the union, deriving his powers and qualifications from the constitution, and neither created by, dependent upon, nor controllable by, the states.... Those officers owe their existence and functions to the united voice of the whole, not of a portion, of the people." Representatives and Senators are as much officers of the entire union as is the President. States thus "have just as much right, and no more, to prescribe new qualifications for a representative, as they have for a president.... It is no original prerogative of state power to appoint a representative, a senator, or president for the union."

We believe that the Constitution reflects the Framers' general agreement with the approach later articulated by Justice Story. For example, Art. I, §5, cl. 1 provides: "Each House shall be the Judge of the Elections, Returns and Qualifications of its own Members." The text of the Constitution thus gives the representatives of all the people the final say in judging the qualifications of the representatives of any one State. For this reason, the dissent falters when it states that "the people of Georgia have no say over whom the people of Massachusetts select to represent them in Congress."

Two other sections of the Constitution further support our view of the Framers' vision. First, consistent with Story's view, the Constitution provides that the salaries of representatives should "be ascertained by Law, and paid out of the Treasury of the United States," Art. I, §6, rather than by individual States.... Second, the provisions governing elections reveal the Framers' understanding that powers over the election of federal officers had to be delegated to, rather than reserved by, the States. It is surely no coincidence that the context of federal elections provides one of the few areas in which the Constitution expressly requires action by the States, namely that "[t]he Times, Places and Manner of holding Elections for Senators and Representatives, shall be prescribed in each State by the legislature thereof." This duty parallels the duty under Article II that "Each State shall appoint, in such Manner as the Legislature thereof may direct, a Number of Electors." Art II., §1, cl. 2. These Clauses are express delegations of power to the States to act with respect to federal elections.

This conclusion is consistent with our previous recognition that, in certain limited contexts, the power to regulate the incidents of the federal system is not a reserved power of the States, but rather is delegated by the Constitution. Thus, we have noted that "[w]hile, in a loose sense, the right to vote for representatives in Congress is sometimes spoken of as a right derived from the states, ... this statement is true only in the sense that the states are authorized by the Constitution, to legislate on the subject as provided by §2 of Art. I." *United States v. Classic* (1941).

In short, as the Framers recognized, electing representatives to the National Legislature was a new right, arising from the Constitution itself. The 10th Amendment thus provides no basis for concluding that the States possess reserved power to add qualifications to those that are fixed in the Constitution. Instead, any state power to set the qualifications for membership in Congress must derive not from the reserved powers of state sovereignty, but rather from the delegated powers of national sovereignty. In the absence of any constitutional delegation to the States of power to add qualifications to those enumerated in the Constitution, such a power does not exist.

THE PRECLUSION OF STATE POWER. Even if we believed that States possessed as part of their original powers some control over congressional qualifications, the text and structure of the Constitution, the relevant historical materials, and, most importantly, the "basic principles of our democratic system" all demonstrate that the Qualifications Clauses were intended to preclude the States from exercising any such power and to fix as exclusive the qualifications in the Constitution.

Much of the historical analysis was undertaken by the Court in *Powell*. There is, however, additional historical evidence that pertains directly to the power of States. That evidence, though perhaps not as extensive as that reviewed in *Powell*, leads unavoidably to the conclusion that the States lack the power to add qualifications.

THE CONVENTION AND RATIFICATION DEBATES. The available affirmative evidence indicates the Framers' intent that States have no role in the setting of qualifications. In *Federalist Paper* No. 52, dealing with the House of Representatives, Madison ... explicitly contrasted the state control over the qualifications of electors with the lack of state control over the qualifications of the elected:

> The qualifications of the elected, being less carefully and properly defined by the State constitutions, and being at the same time more susceptible of uniformity, have been very properly considered and regulated by the convention. A representative of the United States must be of the age of twenty-five years; must have been seven years a citizen of the United States; must, at the time of his election be an inhabitant of the State he is to represent; and, during the time of his service must be in no office under the United States. Under these reasonable limitations, the door of this part of the federal government is open to merit of every description, whether native or adoptive, whether young or old, and without regard to poverty or wealth, or to any particular profession of religious faith....

In light of the Framers' evident concern that States would try to undermine the National Government, they could not have intended States to have the power to set qualifications....

We find further evidence of the Framers' intent in Art. 1, §5, cl. 1, which provides: "Each House shall be the Judge of the Elections, Returns and Qualifications of its own Members." ... If the States had the right to prescribe additional qualifications—such as property, educational, or professional qualifications—for their own representatives, state law would provide the standard for judging a Member's eligibility.... The judging of questions concerning rights which depend on state law is not, however, normally assigned to federal tribunals....

We also find compelling the complete absence in the ratification debates of any assertion that States had the power to add qualifications....

In short, if it had been assumed that States could add additional qualifications, that assumption would have provided the basis for a powerful rebuttal to the arguments being advanced. The failure of intelligent and experienced advocates to utilize this argument must reflect a general agreement that its premise was unsound, and that the power to add qualifications was one that the Constitution denied the States.

CONGRESSIONAL EXPERIENCE. Congress' subsequent experience with state-imposed qualifications provides further evidence of the general consensus on the lack of state power in this area. In *Powell*, we examined that experience and noted that during the first 100 years of its existence, "Congress strictly limited its power to judge the qualifications of its members to those enumerated in the Constitution." ...

We recognize, as we did in *Powell*, that "congressional practice has been erratic" and that the precedential value of congressional exclusion cases is "quite limited." ...

DEMOCRATIC PRINCIPLES. Our conclusion that States lack the power to impose qualifications vindicates the same "fundamental principle of our representative democracy" that we recognized in *Powell*, namely that "the people should choose whom they please to govern them."

As we noted earlier, the *Powell* Court recognized that an egalitarian ideal—that election to the National Legislature should be open to all people of merit—provided a critical foundation for the Constitutional structure. This egalitarian theme echoes throughout the constitutional debates. In *The Federalist* No. 57, for example, Madison wrote:

> Who are to be the objects of popular choice? Every citizen whose merit may recommend him to the esteem and confidence of his country. No qualification of wealth, of birth, of religious faith, or of civil profession is permitted to fetter the judgment or disappoint the inclination of the people....

Similarly, we believe that state-imposed qualifications, as much as congressionally imposed qualifications, would undermine the second critical idea recognized in *Powell*: that an aspect of sovereignty is the right of the people to vote for whom they wish. Again, the source of the qualification is of little moment in assessing the qualification's restrictive impact.

Finally, state-imposed restrictions, unlike the congressionally imposed restrictions at issue in *Powell*, violate a third idea central to this basic principle: that the right to choose representatives belongs not to the States, but to the people.... [T]he Framers, in perhaps their most important contribution, conceived of a Federal Government directly responsible to the people, possessed of direct power over the people, and chosen directly, not by States, but by the people. The Framers implemented this ideal most clearly in the provision, extant from the beginning of the Republic, that calls for the Members of the House of Representatives to be "chosen every second Year by the People of the several States." Art. I, § 2, cl. 1. Following the adoption of the 17th Amendment in 1913, this ideal was extended to elections for the Senate. The Congress of the United States, therefore, is not a confederation of nations in which separate sovereigns are represented by appointed delegates, but is instead a body composed of representatives of the people. As Chief Justice John Marshall observed: "The government of the union, then ... is, emphatically, and truly, a government of the people. In form and in substance it emanates from them. Its powers are granted by them, and are to be exercised directly on them, and for their benefit." *McCulloch v. Maryland* (1819).

The Framers deemed this principle critical when they discussed qualifications. For example, during the debates on residency requirements, Morris noted that in the House, "the people at large, not the States, are represented." Similarly, George Read noted that the Framers "were forming a Nati[ona]l Gov[ernmen]t and such a regulation would correspond little with the idea that we were one people." ...

Consistent with these views, the constitutional structure provides for a uniform salary to be paid from the national treasury, allows the States but a limited role in federal elections, and maintains strict checks on state interference with the federal election process. The Constitution also provides that the qualifications of the representatives of each State will be judged by the representatives of the entire Nation. The Constitution thus creates a uniform national body representing the interests of a single people.

Permitting individual States to formulate diverse qualifications for their representatives would result in a patchwork of state qualifications, undermining the uniformity and the national character that the Framers envisioned and sought to ensure....

STATE PRACTICE. Petitioners attempt to overcome this formidable array of evidence against the States' power to impose qualifications by arguing that the practice of the States immediately after the adoption of the Constitution demonstrates their understanding that they possessed such power. One may properly question the extent to which the States' own practice is a reliable indicator of the contours of restrictions that the Constitution imposed on States, especially when no court has ever upheld a state-imposed qualification of any sort. But petitioners' argument is unpersuasive even on its own terms. At the time of the Convention, "[a]lmost all the State Constitutions required members of their Legislatures to possess considerable property." Despite this near uniformity, only one State, Virginia, placed similar restrictions on members of Congress, requiring that a representative be, inter alia, a "freeholder." Just 15 years after imposing a property qualification, Virginia replaced that requirement with a provision requiring that representatives be only "qualified according to the constitution of the United States." Moreover, several States, including New Hampshire, Georgia, Delaware, and South Carolina, revised their Constitutions at around the time of the Federal Constitution. In the revised Constitutions, each State retained property qualifications for its own state elected officials yet placed no property qualification on its congressional representatives.

The contemporaneous state practice with respect to term limits is similar. At the time of the Convention, States widely supported term limits in at least some circumstances.... Despite this widespread support, no State sought to impose any term limits on its own federal representatives. Thus, a proper assessment of contemporaneous state practice provides further persuasive evidence of a general understanding that the qualifications in the Constitution were unalterable by the States.

In sum, the available historical and textual evidence, read in light of the basic principles of democracy underlying the Constitution and recognized by this Court in *Powell*, reveal the Framers' intent that neither Congress nor the States should possess the power to supplement the exclusive qualifications set forth in the text of the Constitution....

V. The merits of term limits ... have been the subject of debate since the formation of our Constitution, when the Framers unanimously rejected a proposal to add such limits to the Constitution. The cogent arguments on both sides of the question that were articulated during the process of ratification largely retain their force today. Over half the States have adopted measures that impose such limits on some offices either directly or indirectly, and the Nation as a whole, notably by constitutional amendment, has imposed a limit on the number of terms that the President may serve. Term limits, like any other qualification for office, unquestionably restrict the ability of voters to vote for whom they wish. On the other hand, such limits may provide for the infusion of fresh ideas and new perspectives, and may decrease the likelihood that representatives will lose touch with their constituents. It is not our province to resolve this longstanding debate.

We are, however, firmly convinced that allowing the several States to adopt term limits for congressional service would effect a fundamental change in the constitutional framework. Any such change must come not by legislation adopted either by Congress or by an individual State, but rather—as have other important changes in the electoral process—the Amendment procedures set forth in Article V....

Justice Kennedy, concurring.

I join the opinion of the Court.

[I]t is well settled that the whole people of the United States asserted their political identity and unity of purpose when they created the federal system. The dissent's course of reasoning suggesting otherwise might be construed to disparage the republican character of the National Government, and it seems appropriate to add these few remarks to explain why that course of argumentation runs counter to fundamental principles of federalism....

A distinctive character of the National Government, the mark of its legitimacy, is that it owes its existence to the act of the whole people who created it. It must be remembered that the National Government too is republican in essence and in theory....

It might be objected that because the States ratified the Constitution, the people can delegate power only through the States or by acting in their capacities as citizens of particular States. But in *McCulloch v. Maryland* (1819), the Court set forth its authoritative rejection of this idea: "The Convention which framed the constitution was indeed elected by the State legislatures. But the instrument ... was submitted to the people.... It is true, they assembled in their several States—and where else should they have assembled? No political dreamer was ever wild enough to think of breaking down the lines which separate the States, and of compounding the American people into one common mass. Of consequence, when they act, they act in their States. But the measures they adopt do not, on that account, cease to be the measures of the people themselves, or become the measures of the State governments."

The political identity of the entire people of the Union is reinforced by the proposition, which I take to be beyond dispute, that, though limited as to its objects, the National Government is and must be controlled by the people without collateral interference by the States....

[T]here exists a federal right of citizenship, a relationship between the people of the Nation and their National Government, with which the States may not interfere. Because the Arkansas enactment intrudes upon this federal domain, it exceeds the boundaries of the Constitution.

Justice Thomas, with whom the Chief Justice, Justice O'Connor, and Justice Scalia join, dissenting....

I dissent. Nothing in the Constitution deprives the people of each State of the power to prescribe eligibility requirements for the candidates who seek to represent them in Congress. The Constitution is simply silent on this question. And where the Constitution is silent, it raises no bar to action by the States or the people.

I. Because the majority fundamentally misunderstands the notion of "reserved" powers, I start with some first principles. Contrary to the majority's suggestion, the people of the States need not point to any affirmative grant of power in the Constitution in order to prescribe qualifications for their representatives in Congress, or to authorize their elected state legislators to do so.

I-A. Our system of government rests on one overriding principle: all power stems from the consent of the people. To phrase the principle in this way, however, is to imprecise about something important to the notion of "reserved" powers. The ultimate source of the Constitution's authority is the consent of the people of each individual State, not the consent of the undifferentiated people of the Nation as a whole.

The ratification procedure erected by Article VII makes this point clear. The Constitution took effect once it had been ratified by the people gathered in convention in nine different States. But the Constitution went into effect only "between the States so ratifying the same."...

When they adopted the Federal Constitution, of course, the people of each State surrendered some of their authority to the United States (and hence to entities accountable to the people of other States as well as to themselves)....

In each State, the remainder of the people's powers—"[t]he powers not delegated to the United States by the Constitution, nor prohibited by it to the States," Amdt. 10—are either delegated to the state government or retained by the people. The Federal Constitution does not specify which of these two possibilities obtains; it is up to the various state constitutions to declare which powers the people of each State have delegated to their state government. As far as the Federal Constitution is concerned, then, the States can exercise all powers that the Constitution does not withhold from them. The Federal Government and the States thus face different default rules: where the Constitution is silent about the exercise of a particular power—that is, where the Constitution does not speak either expressly or by necessary implication—the Federal Government lacks that power and the States enjoy it.

These basic principles are enshrined in the 10th Amendment....

To be sure, when the 10th Amendment uses the phrase "the people," it does not specify whether it is referring to the people of each State or the people of the Nation as a whole.... [I]t would make no sense to speak of powers as being reserved to the undifferentiated people of the Nation as a whole, because the Constitution does not contemplate that those people will either exercise power or delegate it. The Constitution simply does not recognize any mechanism for action by the undifferentiated people of the Nation. Thus, the amendment provision of Article V calls for amendments to be ratified not by a convention of the national people, but by conventions of the people in each State or by the state legislatures elected by those people. Likewise, the Constitution calls for Members of Congress to be chosen State by State, rather than in nationwide elections. Even the selection of the President—surely the most national of national figures—is accomplished by an electoral college made up of delegates chosen by the various States, and candidates can lose a Presidential election despite winning a majority of the votes cast in the Nation as a whole. See also Art. II, § 1, cl. 3 (providing that when no candidate secures a majority of electoral votes, the election of the President is thrown into the House of Representatives, where "the Votes shall be taken by States, the Representatives from each State having one Vote"); Amdt. 12 (same).

In short, the notion of popular sovereignty that undergirds the Constitution does not erase state boundaries, but rather tracks them.... As Chief Justice Marshall put it [in *McCulloch v. Maryland* (1819)], "[n]o political dreamer was ever wild enough to think of breaking down the lines which separate the States, and of compounding the American people into one common mass."...

If we are to invalidate Arkansas' Amendment 73, we must point to something in the Federal Constitution that deprives the people of Arkansas of the power to enact such measures.

I-B. The majority disagrees that it bears this burden. But its arguments are unpersuasive.

I-B-1. The majority begins by announcing an enormous and untenable limitation on the principle expressed by the 10th Amendment. According to the majority, the States possess only those powers that the Constitution affirmatively grants to them or that they enjoyed before the Constitution was adopted....

The majority's essential logic is that the state governments could not "reserve" any powers that they did not control at the time the Constitution was drafted. But it was not the state governments that were doing the reserving. The Constitution derives its authority instead from the consent of the people of the States. Given the fundamental principle that all governmental powers stem from the people of the States, it would simply be incoherent to assert that the people of the States could not reserve any powers that they had not previously controlled....

The majority ... seeks support for its view of the 10th Amendment in *McCulloch v. Maryland* (1819). But this effort is misplaced.... *McCulloch* observed that the Amendment "leav[es] the question, whether the particular power which may become the subject of contest has been delegated to the one government, or prohibited to the other, to depend on a fair construction of the whole [Constitution]." *McCulloch* did not qualify this observation by indicating that the question also turned on whether the States had enjoyed the power before the framing. To the contrary, *McCulloch* seemed to assume that the people had "conferred on the general government the power contained in the constitution, and on the States the whole residuum of power." ...

For the past 175 years, *McCulloch* has been understood to rest on the proposition that the Constitution affirmatively barred Maryland from imposing its tax on the Bank's operations. For the majority, however, *McCulloch* apparently turned on the fact that before the Constitution was adopted, the States had possessed no power to tax the instrumentalities of the governmental institutions that the Constitution created. This understanding of *McCulloch* makes most of Chief Justice Marshall's opinion irrelevant; according to the majority, there was no need to inquire into whether federal law deprived Maryland of the power in question, because the power could not fall into the category of "reserved" powers anyway.

[T]he only true support for its view of the 10th Amendment comes from Joseph Story's 1833 treatise on constitutional law. Justice Story was a brilliant and accomplished man, and one cannot casually dismiss his views. On the other hand, he was not a member of the Founding generation, and his *Commentaries on the Constitution* were written a half century after the framing. Rather than representing the original understanding of the Constitution, they represent only his own understanding....

I-B-2. The majority also sketches out what may be an alternative (and narrower) argument. Again citing Story, the majority suggests that it would be inconsistent with the notion of "national sovereignty" for the States or the people of the States to have any reserved powers over the selection of Members of Congress. The majority apparently reaches this conclusion in two steps. First, it asserts that because Congress as a whole is an institution of the National Government, the individual Members of Congress "owe primary allegiance not to the people of a State, but to the people of the Nation." Second, it concludes that because each Member of Congress has a nationwide constituency once he takes office, it would be inconsistent with the Framers' scheme to let a single State prescribe qualifications for him.

Political scientists can debate about who commands the "primary allegiance" of Members of Congress once they reach Washington.... But the selection of representatives in Congress is indisputably an act of the people of each State, not some abstract people of the Nation as a whole....

II. I take it to be established, then, that the people of Arkansas do enjoy "reserved" powers over the selection of their representatives in Congress.... [W]e may not override the decision of the people of Arkansas unless something in the Federal Constitution deprives them of the power to enact such measures.

The majority settles on "the Qualifications Clauses" as the constitutional provisions that Amendment 73 violates. Because I do not read those provisions to impose any unstated prohibitions on the States, it is unnecessary for me to decide whether the majority is correct to identify Arkansas' ballot-access restriction with laws fixing true term limits or otherwise prescribing "qualifications" for congressional office. As I discuss in Part A below, the Qualifications Clauses are merely straightforward recitations of the minimum eligibility requirements that the Framers thought it essential for every Member of Congress to meet. They restrict state power only in that they prevent the States from abolishing all eligibility requirements for membership in Congress....

II-A. ... The Qualifications Clauses do prevent the individual States from abolishing all eligibility requirements for Congress....

If the people of a State decide that they would like their representatives to possess additional qualifications, however, they have done nothing to frustrate the policy behind the Qualifications Clauses. Anyone who possesses all of the constitutional qualifications, plus some qualifications required by state law, still has all of the federal qualifications. Accordingly, the fact that the Constitution specifies certain qualifications that the Framers deemed necessary to protect the competence of the National Legislature does not imply that it strips the people of the individual States of the power to protect their own interests by adding other requirements for their own representatives....

This conclusion is buttressed by our reluctance to read constitutional provisions to preclude state power by negative implication. The very structure of the Constitution counsels such hesitation. After all, § 10 of Article I contains a brief list of express prohibitions on the States. Many of the prohibitions listed in § 10, moreover, might have been thought to be implicit in other constitutional provisions or in the very nature of our federal system. Compare, e.g., Art. II, § 2, cl. 2 ("[The President] shall have Power, by and with the Advice and Consent of the Senate, to make Treaties") and Art. I, § 8, cl. 5 ("The Congress shall have Power ... [t]o coin Money") with Art. I, § 10, cl. 1 ("No State shall enter into any Treaty" and "No State shall ... coin Money"); see also Art. VI, cl. 2 (explicitly declaring that state law cannot override the Constitution). The fact that the Framers nonetheless made these prohibitions express confirms that one should not lightly read provisions like the Qualifications Clauses as implicit deprivations of state power.

The majority responds that "a patchwork of state qualifications" would "undermin[e] the uniformity and the national character that the Framers envisioned and sought to ensure." Yet the Framers thought it perfectly consistent with the "national character" of Congress for the Senators and Representatives from each State to be chosen by the legislature or the people of that State. The majority never explains why Congress' fundamental character permits this state-centered system, but nonetheless prohibits the people of the States and their state legislatures from setting any eligibility requirements for the candidates who seek to represent them....

II-B. Although the Qualifications Clauses neither state nor imply the prohibition that it finds in them, the majority infers from the Framers' "democratic principles" that the Clauses must have been generally understood to preclude the people of the States and their state legislatures from prescribing any additional qualifications for their representatives in Congress. But the majority's evidence on this point establishes only two more modest propositions: (1) the Framers did not want the Federal Constitution itself to impose a broad set of disqualifications for congressional office, and (2) the Framers did not want the Federal Congress to be able to supplement the few disqualifications that the Constitution does set forth. The logical conclusion is simply that the Framers did not want the people of the States and their state legislatures to be constrained by too many qualifications imposed at the national level. The evidence does not support the majority's more sweeping conclusion that the Framers intended to bar the people of the States and their state legislatures from adopting additional eligibility requirements to help narrow their own choices.

I agree with the majority that Congress has no power to prescribe qualifications for its own Members. This fact, however, does not show that the Qualifications Clauses contain a hidden exclusivity provision. The reason for Congress' incapacity is not that the Qualifications Clauses deprive Congress of the authority to set qualifications, but rather that nothing in the Constitution grants Congress this power. In the absence of such a grant, Congress may not act. But deciding whether the Constitution denies the qualification-setting power to the States and the people of the States requires a fundamentally different legal analysis....

II-C. In addition to its arguments about democratic principles, the majority asserts that more specific historical evidence supports its view that the Framers did not intend to permit supplementation of the Qualifications Clauses. But when one focuses on the distinction between congressional power to add qualifications for congressional office and the power of the people or their state legislatures to add such qualifications, one realizes that this assertion has little basis....

II-C-1. To the extent that the records from the Philadelphia Convention itself shed light on this case, they tend to hurt the majority's case. The only evidence that directly bears on the question now before the Court comes from the Committee of Detail, a five-member body that the Convention charged with the crucial task of drafting a Constitution to reflect the decisions that the Convention had reached during its first two months of work....

The [draft by the Committee on Detail] is an extensive outline of the Constitution. Its treatment of the National Legislature is divided into two parts, one for the "House of Delegates" and one for the Senate. The Qualifications Clause for the House of Delegates originally read as follows: "The qualifications of a delegate shall be the age of twenty five years at least. and citizenship: and any person possessing these qualifications may be elected except [blank space]." The drafter(s) of this language apparently contemplated that the Committee might want to insert some exceptions to the exclusivity provision. But rather than simply deleting the word "except"—as it might have done if it had decided to have no exceptions at all to the exclusivity provision—the Committee deleted the exclusivity provision itself. In the document that has come down to us, all the words after the colon are crossed out.

The majority speculates that the exclusivity provision may have been deleted as superfluous. See ante. But the same draft that contained the exclusivity language in the House Qualifications Clause contained no such language in the Senate Qualifications Clause. See 2 Farrand 141. Thus, the draft appears to reflect a deliberate judgment to distinguish between the House qualifications and the Senate qualifications, and to make only the former exclusive. If so, then the deletion of the exclusivity provision indicates that the Committee expected neither list of qualifications to be exclusive....

II-C-2. Unable to glean from the Philadelphia Convention any direct evidence that helps its position, the majority seeks signs of the Framers' unstated intent in the Framers' comments about four other constitutional provisions. But even if the majority's reading of its evidence were correct, the most that one could infer is that the Framers did not want state legislatures to be able to prescribe qualifications that would narrow the people's choices. However wary the Framers might have been of permitting state legislatures to exercise such power, there is absolutely no reason to believe that the Framers feared letting the people themselves exercise this power.

In any event, none of the provisions cited by the majority is inconsistent with state power to add qualifications for congressional office....

II-C-3. In discussing the ratification period, the majority stresses two principal data. One of these pieces of evidence is no evidence at all—literally. The majority devotes considerable space to the fact that the recorded ratification debates do not contain any affirmative statement that the States can supplement the constitutional qualifications....

But the majority's argument cuts both ways. The recorded ratification debates also contain no affirmative statement that the States cannot supplement the constitutional qualifications....

II-C-4. [S]tate practice immediately after the ratification of the Constitution refutes the majority's suggestion that the Qualifications Clauses were commonly understood as being exclusive. Five States supplemented the constitutional disqualifications in their very first election laws, and the surviving records suggest that the legislatures of these States considered and rejected the interpretation of the Constitution that the majority adopts today.

As the majority concedes, the first Virginia election law erected a property qualification for Virginia's contingent in the Federal House of Representatives. What is more, while the Constitution merely requires representatives to be inhabitants of their State, the legislatures of five of the seven States that divided themselves into districts for House elections added that representatives also had to be inhabitants of the district that elected them. Three of these States adopted durational residency requirements too, insisting that representatives have resided within their districts for at least a year (or, in one case, three years) before being elected....

III. It is radical enough for the majority to hold that the Constitution implicitly precludes the people of the States from prescribing any eligibility requirements for the congressional candidates who seek their votes. This holding, after all, does not stop with negating the term limits that many States have seen fit to impose on their Senators and Representatives. Today's decision also means that no State may disqualify congressional candidates whom a court has found to be mentally incompetent, who are currently in prison, or who have past vote-fraud convictions. Likewise, after today's decision, the people of each State must leave open the possibility that they will trust someone with their vote in Congress even though they do not trust him with a vote in the election for Congress....

The voters of Arkansas evidently believe that incumbents would not enjoy such overwhelming success if electoral contests were truly fair—that is, if the government did not put its thumb on either side of the scale. The majority offers no reason to question the accuracy of this belief. Given this context, petitioners portray § 3 of Amendment 73 as an effort at the state level to offset the electoral advantages that congressional incumbents have conferred upon themselves at the federal level....

[T]oday's decision reads the Qualifications Clauses to impose substantial implicit prohibitions on the States and the people of the States. I would not draw such an expansive negative inference from the fact that the Constitution requires Members of Congress to be a certain age, to be inhabitants of the States that they represent, and to have been United States citizens for a specified period. Rather, I would read the Qualifications Clauses to do no more than what they say. I respectfully dissent.

II. The Commerce Clause: A Delegated Power

Overview: This section begins our study of the Commerce Clause. Basically, there are two large approaches to congressional power under the Commerce Clause that you will see in what follows. One is basically an empirical and economic approach. It asks whether the activity is commercial and affects more than one state or if congressional regulation is reasonably related to the regulation of commercial activity. If the answer is yes, Congress has the power to regulate the activity under the Commerce Clause. In today's increasingly integrated world, this approach provides very broad power to Congress to regulate commerce. The other approach is more formal and definitional. It seeks to limit congressional power in various ways.

A court's choice of one or the other approach involves more than the interpretation of the words "regulate Commerce ... among the several states." Behind these two approaches lie many other issues, including judicial attitudes towards federalism, the preference for a laissez faire versus a more regulated form of capitalism, and attitudes regarding the effect of government policies on different economic and racial groups. The decision in *Gibbons v. Ogden* (1824) provided substantial support for an empirical economic approach (yet also contained seeds of a more restrictive approach). Decisions since *Gibbons* have varied. During the late 19th and early 20th centuries, the Court often employed a formal and definitional approach to the commerce power as a result of which a number of congressional statutes were struck down. The New Deal Court and the Warren Court employed the most unalloyed form of empirical economic analysis. The current Court has returned to at least some more formal limits on congressional power.

The text:

Article I, §8 [1] Congress shall have Power ... [3] to regulate Commerce ... among the several states....

A. Graphic Portrayals: The Modern View of the Commerce Clause

Five diagrams follow. The first four diagrams represent examples of possible relations between congressional regulation of commerce and state regulation. The diagrams are designed to show the relation between state and federal power in four imaginable Commerce Clause situations. Most of these are extreme examples that do not exist in today's world. That is, it is not the case that neither Congress nor the states pass regulations (diagram 1), or that Congress pre-empts all state laws that are within the potential reach of federal commerce power (diagram 3), or that Congress, in effect, turns all commercial regulation over to the states by removing any prohibition on state laws in the area of conditionally exclusive federal power (diagram 4).

The Commerce Power:
Theoretically Possible Allocations of Federal and
State Power under Current Doctrine

In diagram 1, neither Congress nor the state has legislated. The circumference of the dark top circle represents the universe of potential federal commerce power. The circumference of the lighter bottom circle represents the universe of all potential state power — without any assistance from congressional legislation. The circles overlap to show the relationship between state and federal power.

The top crescent of the upper circle (marked *CE*) is an area from which states are *Conditionally Excluded* from legislating — that is, an area where states may not legislate without authority from Congress. For example, the Commerce Clause in its dormant state forbids states from reserving business opportunities to in-state residents. By legislation, however, Congress can lift the ban imposed by the Dormant Commerce Clause. (As you will see, there may be other applicable constitutional limitations in Article IV, § 2 that forbid such preferences.) The top crescent shows the negative effect of the Commerce Clause in its dormant state — that is where Congress has not legislated. The bottom part of the lower circle (marked ESP) is the area of *Exclusive State Power*. This area contains reserved state powers and is, by definition, beyond potential federal power. A federal law requiring state employees to administer a federal program (e.g., to do background checks on gun buyers) by the view of the current Court invades the area of exclusive state power. The center of the diagram shows an area of concurrent power where (in the absence of conflict between federal and state legislation) both states and the federal government could legislate on the same subject at the same time.

1. Neither congress nor the states have legislated. The federal system produces an area of conditionally exclusive federal power, of concurrent federal and state power, and of exclusive state power

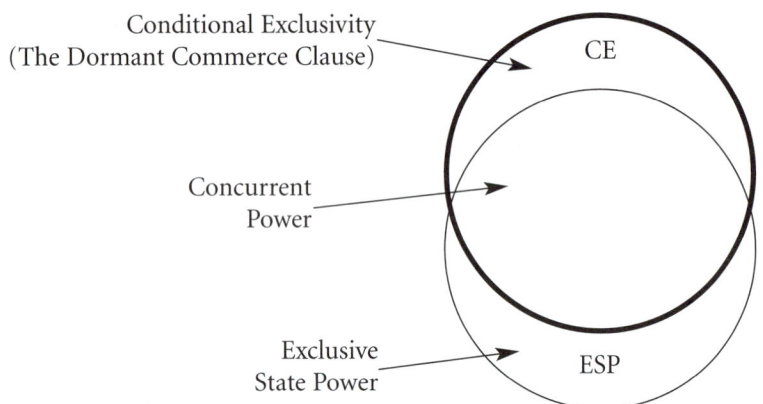

Legend:
- ⭕ Potential Federal Power over Commerce
- ○ Potential State Power without Congressional Legislation to add to it
- CE Federal Power is "Conditionally Exclusive" i.e. exclusive unless Congress gives it up
- ESP Exclusive State Power

In diagram 2 both Congress and the states have legislated in the area of concurrent power. For example, assume that Congress sets emission standards for automobiles, but explicitly allows states to impose more stringent standards. Such state standards would neither contradict nor frustrate the congressional regulation and hence would be a legitimate exercise of concurrent state power over the subject of auto emissions. (On the other hand, if a state regulation does contradict or frustrate congressional regulation, the federal law pre-empts the concurrent state regulation pursuant to the Supremacy Clause. For example, if a state imposed an automobile emission standard less stringent than the federal standard, such standard would frustrate the federal regulation and hence would be pre-empted.)

2. Congress and the states legislate exercising concurrent powers

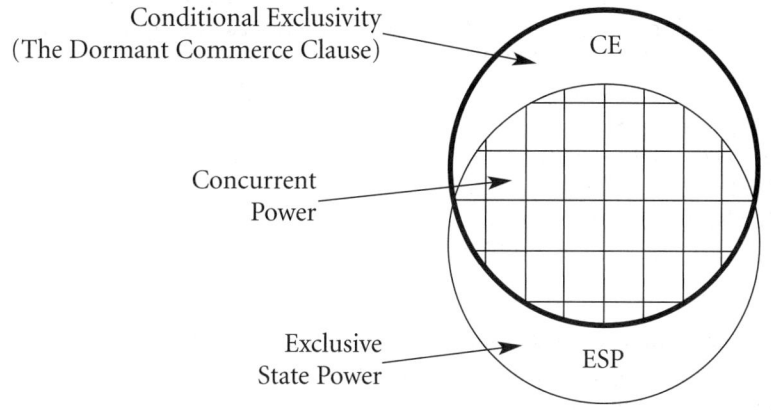

Legend:
- O   Potential Federal Power over Commerce
- O   Potential State Power without Congressional Legislation to add to it
- CE   Federal Power is "Conditionally Exclusive" i.e. exclusive unless Congress gives it up
- ESP   Exclusive State Power
- ||| Federal Legislation
- **|||**   Preemptive Federal Legislation
- =   State Legislation

In diagram 3, Congress has legislated and asserted as much exclusive power as it can. It has now fully occupied and pre-empted the area of concurrent power. The bold line of potential federal power that describes the upper circle has now become an area where federal pre-emptive power is actually exercised. Congress has legislated and declared that states may not legislate on the subject. All that would be left to the state would be the zone of exclusive state power at the bottom of the bottom circle—marked ESP.

3. The Commerce Clause: Congress Legislates And Asserts As Much Exclusive Power As It Can — Preemption

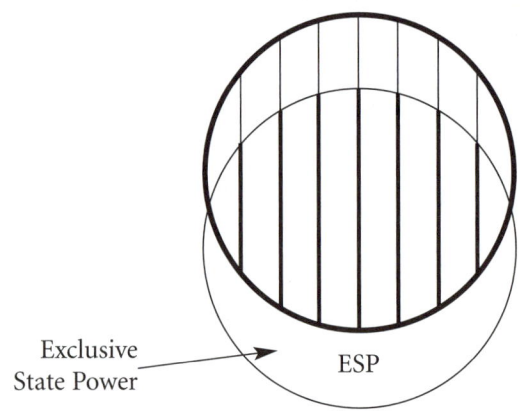

Legend:
- ○ Potential Federal Power over Commerce
- ○ Potential State Power without Congressional Legislation to add to it
- CE Federal Power is "Conditionally Exclusive" i.e. exclusive unless Congress gives it up
- ESP Exclusive State Power
- ||| Federal Legislation
- ||| Preemptive Federal Legislation
- ═ State Legislation

In diagram 4, Congress has taken the opposite course. It has, in effect, turned over to the states all the commercial regulation it can in what was the area of conditional exclusivity. It has done so by adopting the states' rule (whatever they may be) as its own. The crescent at the top of the federal power circle in diagrams 1 and 2 had excluded state power because there was no federal action allowing it (the area of the negative effect of the Dormant Commerce Clause). Because Congress has now provided that state law will govern the subject in this area, this crescent has now become a domain where the state can exercise power. (The diagram assumes the state has now legislated in this area.) The state has also legislated in the area of concurrent power, which it can effectively do in any case so long as there is no conflict with federal law. Because in this case there is no federal legislation, this center area where the circles of potential federal and state power can overlap is now also occupied only by state power. Here again the diagram assumes the state has chosen to legislate in this area. Of course, the area of exclusive state power remains one that can be occupied only by the state.

4. Congress legislates and turns power over to the states by providing that each state's rule shall become the federal rule. The diagram assumes the states have legislated as broadly as possible.

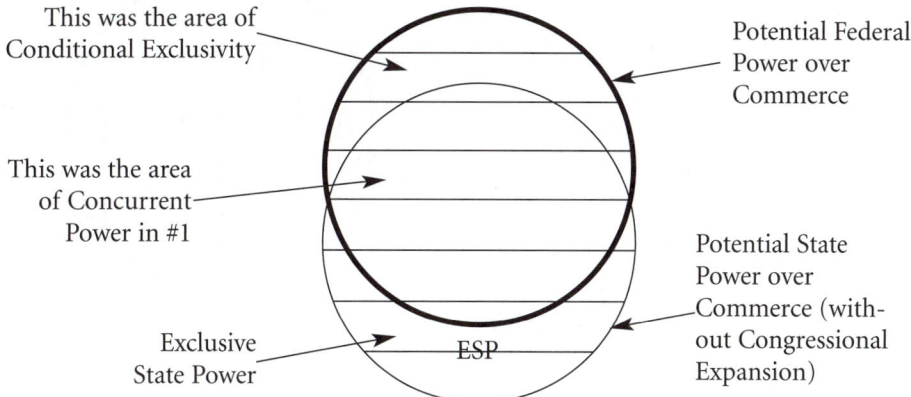

Legend:
- ◯ Potential Federal Power over Commerce
- ◯ Potential State Power without aid of Congressional Legislation
- ≡ Exercised State Legislative Power includes power added by Congress

Affirmative Limits and 10th Amendment Charts

Two Types of Limits on Federal Power

Limits on the federal commerce power can come from affirmative constitutional limitations or from the 10th Amendment. For example, the 1st Amendment affirmatively limits the exercise of federal power that would otherwise be permissible. While Congress has the power under the Commerce Clause to prevent the interstate shipment of various products, it may not ban the interstate shipment of books because they advocate socialism. Enforcement of such a ban would violate the 1st Amendment. In diagram 5, the circle represents the full scope of federal power pursuant to the Commerce Clause. The shaded portion of the circle represents the affirmative limitations that constitutional provisions such as the 1st Amendment impose on Congress's commerce power. Thus, because of these affirmative constitutional limitations, Congress cannot exercise all of the federal power granted it by the Commerce Clause.

**Diagram 5
Affirmative Constitutional Limitations
on Federal Commerce Power**

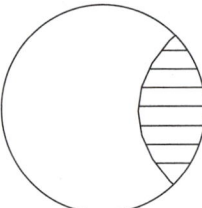

Legend:

Entire area inside circle:
federal power over commerce

Lined area inside circle:
affirmative constitutional limitations on
federal power

The 10th Amendment also constrains federal power depending on one's view of how the Amendment should be interpreted. There are two competing views of the 10th Amendment that we will consider. The first view is sometimes called the truism (or tautology) view. The truism view contends that the 10th Amendment is limited to its text — the states retain only those powers not given to the federal government. Under this view, if the only limit on federal power were the 10th Amendment, then Congress could exercise all of its constitutionally delegated commerce power because the 10th Amendment places no independent limit on federal power. In diagram 6, the circle represents the full scope of federal power. Under this view, only that which is outside the circle is reserved to the states pursuant to the 10th Amendment. As a practical matter, advocates of this interpretation of the 10th Amendment argue that the political process adequately protects the role of the states.

**Diagram 6
Truism View of the
10th Amendment**

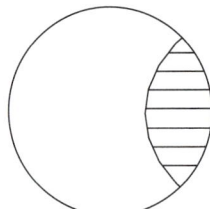

Legend:

Entire area inside circle:
federal power over commerce

Lined area inside circle:
affirmative constitutional limitations on
federal power

Entire area outside circle:
powers reserved to states by
10th Amendment

A contrary view sees the 10th Amendment as reflecting a structural, dual sovereignty view of the Constitution. Under this view, the 10th Amendment functions as an affirmative limit on federal power (much as the 1st Amendment does) or, put another way, the amendment reflects the fact that the basic structure of the Constitution limits federal power so as to protect state sovereignty. Advocates of this interpretation of the 10th Amendment see an essential role for the judiciary in protecting states from what they see as federal intrusions into state sovereignty. Under this dual sovereignty view of the 10th Amendment, the amendment limits federal power in much the same way as does the 1st Amendment. Diagram 7 illustrates this view of the 10th Amendment.

Diagram 7
Dual Sovereignty View of
the 10th Amendment

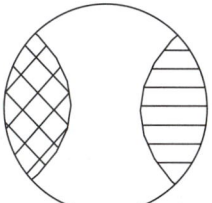

Legend:

Entire area inside circle:
federal power over commerce

Lined area inside circle:
affirmative constitutional limitations on federal power

Entire area outside circle plus cross-hatched area inside circle:
powers reserved to states by 10th Amendment

B. The Marshall Court's Interpretation of the Commerce Clause

Gibbons v. Ogden: Background

A state statute might conflict with federal power in two ways: it might directly violate the Constitution or it might violate a federal statute enacted pursuant to a delegated power. Most cases that involve a conflict between a state statute and the Constitution involve specific constitutional provisions held to limit state power. For example, a state statute requiring public school segregation would conflict with the Equal Protection Clause of the 14th Amendment. In the case of the Commerce Clause, the Court currently holds that the simple grant of power to Congress to regulate commerce sometimes functions as a negative restraint on state power. As you read *Gibbons*, note how the Court deals with each of these possible conflicts between the New York statute and federal power.

Gibbons v. Ogden
22 U.S. 1 (1824)

[The New York legislature gave Robert R. Livingston and Robert Fulton the exclusive right to operate steamboats within New York waters. The New York law authorized the Chancellor of the New York Chancery Court to enjoin any other person from navigating New York waters with steamboats. Ogden alleged that Livingston and Fulton had assigned the right to navigate the waters between Elizabethtown, New Jersey, and the city of New York to John R. Livingston, and John R. Livingston had in turn assigned the right to Ogden. Ogden further alleged that Gibbons was operating two steamboats, called the *Stoudinger* and the *Bellona*, between New York and Elizabethtown, in violation of the monopoly privilege possessed by Ogden. Ogden sought an injunction to restrain Gibbons from infringing his New York monopoly steamboat privilege. Gibbons answered that his boats were duly enrolled and licensed to conduct the coasting trade, pursuant to a 1793 act of Congress. Gibbons claimed the right, by virtue of the licenses, to navigate the waters between Elizabethtown and the city of New York. He also claimed that the New York statute was a regulation of commerce exclusively entrusted to the federal government.

The New York court sustained the injunction prohibiting the operation of Gibbons' boats. It rejected the claim that the monopoly was inconsistent with the United States coasting license. It also rejected the contention that the New York law was a regulation of commerce reserved exclusively to Congress and held that New York could legislate unless Congress enacted inconsistent legislation.]

Mr. Chief Justice Marshall delivered the opinion of the Court.

The appellant contends that this decree is erroneous, because the laws which purport to give the exclusive privilege it sustains, are repugnant to the constitution and laws of the United States.

They are said to be repugnant—

1st. To that clause in the constitution which authorizes Congress to regulate commerce....

[The Constitution] contains an enumeration of powers expressly granted by the people to their government. It has been said, that these powers ought to be construed strictly. But why ought they to be so construed? Is there one sentence in the constitution which gives countenance to this rule? In the last of the enumerated powers, that which grants, expressly, the means for carrying all others into execution, Congress is authorized "to make all laws which shall be necessary and proper" for the purpose. But this limitation on the means which may be used, is not extended to the powers which are conferred; nor is there one sentence in the constitution, which has been pointed out by the gentlemen of the bar, or which we have been able to discern, that prescribes this rule. We do not, therefore, think ourselves justified in adopting it. What do gentlemen mean, by a strict construction? If they contend only against that enlarged construction, which would extend words beyond their natural and obvious import, we might question the application of the term, but should not controvert the principle. If they contend for that narrow construction which, in support of some theory not to be found in the constitution, would deny to the government those powers which the words of the grant, as usually understood, import, and which are consistent with the general views and objects of the instrument; for that narrow construction, which would cripple the government, and render it unequal to the object for which it is declared to be instituted, and to which the powers given, as fairly understood, render it competent; then we cannot perceive the propriety of this strict construction, nor adopt it as the rule by which the constitution is to be expounded. As men, whose intentions require no concealment, generally employ the words which most directly and aptly express the ideas they intend to convey, the enlightened patriots who framed our constitution, and the people who adopted it, must be understood to have employed words in their natural sense, and to have intended what they have said. If, from the imperfection of human language, there should be serious doubts respecting the extent of any given power, it is a well settled rule, that the objects for which it was given, especially when those objects are expressed in the instrument itself, should have great influence in the construction....

The words are, "Congress shall have power to regulate commerce with foreign nations, and among the several States, and with the Indian tribes."

The subject to be regulated is commerce; and our constitution being, as was aptly said at the bar, one of enumeration, and not of definition, to ascertain the extent of the power, it becomes necessary to settle the meaning of the word. The counsel for the appellee would limit it to traffic, to buying and selling, or the interchange of commodities, and do not admit that it comprehends navigation. This would restrict a general term, applicable to many objects, to one of its significations. Commerce, undoubtedly, is traffic, but it is something more: it is intercourse. It describes the commercial intercourse between nations, and parts of nations, in all its branches, and is regulated by prescribing rules for carrying on that intercourse. The mind can scarcely conceive a system for regulating commerce between nations, which shall exclude all laws concerning navigation, which shall be silent on the admission of the vessels of the one nation into the ports of the other, and be confined to prescribing rules for the conduct of individuals, in the actual employment of buying and selling, or of barter.

If commerce does not include navigation, the government of the Union has no direct power over that subject, and can make no law prescribing what shall constitute American vessels, or requiring that they shall be navigated by American seamen. Yet this power has been exercised from the commencement of the government, has been exercised with the consent of all, and has been understood by all to be a commercial regulation. All America understands, and has uniformly understood, the word "commerce," to comprehend navigation. It was so understood, and must have been so understood, when the constitution was framed. The power over commerce, including navigation, was one of the primary objects for which the people of America adopted their government, and must have been contemplated in forming it. The convention must have used the word in that sense, because all have understood it in that sense; and the attempt to restrict it comes too late.

If the opinion that "commerce," as the word is used in the constitution, comprehends navigation also, requires any additional confirmation, that additional confirmation is, we think, furnished by the words of the instrument itself.

It is a rule of construction, acknowledged by all, that the exceptions from a power mark its extent; for it would be absurd, as well as useless, to except from a granted power, that which was not granted — that which the words of the grant could not comprehend. If, then, there are in the constitution plain exceptions from the power over navigation, plain inhibitions to the exercise of that power in a particular way, it is a proof that those who made these exceptions, and prescribed these inhibitions, understood the power to which they applied as being granted.

The 9th section of the 1st article declares, that "no preference shall be given, by any regulation of commerce or revenue, to the ports of one State over those of another." This clause cannot be understood as applicable to those laws only which are passed for the purposes of revenue, because it is expressly applied to commercial regulations; and the most obvious preference which can be given to one port over another, in regulating commerce, relates to navigation. But the subsequent part of the sentence is still more explicit. It is, "nor shall vessels bound to or from one State, be obliged to enter, clear, or pay duties, in another." These words have a direct reference to navigation.

The universally acknowledged power of the government to impose embargoes, must also be considered as showing, that all America is united in that construction which comprehends navigation in the word commerce. Gentlemen have said, in argument, that this is a branch of the war-making power, and that an embargo is an instrument of war, not a regulation of trade....

When Congress imposed that embargo which, for a time, engaged the attention of every man in the United States, the avowed object of the law was, the protection of commerce, and the avoiding of war. By its friends and its enemies it was treated as a commercial, not as a war measure....

The word used in the constitution, then, comprehends, and has been always understood to comprehend, navigation within its meaning; and a power to regulate navigation, is as expressly granted, as if that term had been added to the word "commerce."

To what commerce does this power extend? The constitution informs us, to commerce "with foreign nations, and among the several States, and with the Indian tribes."

It has, we believe, been universally admitted, that these words comprehend every species of commercial intercourse between the United States and foreign nations. No sort of trade can be carried on between this country and any other, to which this power does not extend. It has been truly said, that commerce, as the word is used in the constitution, is a unit, every part of which is indicated by the term.

If this be the admitted meaning of the word, in its application to foreign nations, it must carry the same meaning throughout the sentence, and remain a unit, unless there be some plain intelligible cause which alters it.

The subject to which the power is next applied, is to commerce "among the several States." The word "among" means intermingled with. A thing which is among others, is intermingled with them. Commerce among the States, cannot stop at the external boundary line of each State, but may be introduced into the interior.

It is not intended to say that these words comprehend that commerce, which is completely internal, which is carried on between man and man in a State, or between different parts of the same State, and which does not extend to or affect other States. Such a power would be inconvenient, and is certainly unnecessary.

Comprehensive as the word "among" is, it may very properly be restricted to that commerce which concerns more States than one. The phrase is not one which would probably have been selected to indicate the completely interior traffic of a State, because it is not an apt phrase for that purpose; and the enumeration of the particular classes of commerce, to which the power was to be extended, would not have been made, had the intention been to extend the power to every description. The enumeration presupposes something not enumerated; and that something, if we regard the language or the subject of the sentence, must be the exclusively internal commerce of a State. The genius and character of the whole government seem to be, that its action is to be applied to all the external concerns of the nation, and to those internal concerns which affect the States generally; but not to those which are completely within a particular State, which do not affect other States, and with which it is not necessary to interfere, for the purpose of executing some of the general powers of the government. The completely internal commerce of a State, then, may be considered as reserved for the State itself.

But, in regulating commerce with foreign nations, the power of Congress does not stop at the jurisdictional lines of the several States. It would be a very useless power, if it could not pass those lines. The commerce of the United States with foreign nations, is that of the whole United States. Every district has a right to participate in it. The deep streams which penetrate our country in every direction, pass through the interior of almost every State in the Union, and furnish the means of exercising this right. If Congress has the power to regulate it, that power must be exercised whenever the subject exists. If it exists within the States, if a foreign voyage may commence or terminate at a port within a State, then the power of Congress may be exercised within a State.

This principle is, if possible, still more clear, when applied to commerce "among the several States." They either join each other, in which case they are separated by a mathematical line, or they are remote from each other, in which case other States lie between them. What is commerce "among" them; and how is it to be conducted? Can a trading expedition between two adjoining States, commence and terminate outside of each? And if the trading intercourse be between two States remote from each other, must it not commence in one, terminate in the other, and probably pass through a third? Commerce among the States must, of necessity, be commerce with the States. In the regulation of trade with the Indian tribes, the action of the law, especially when the constitution was made, was chiefly within a State. The power of Congress, then, whatever it may be, must be exercised within the territorial jurisdiction of the several States. The sense of the nation on this subject, is unequivocally manifested by the provisions made in the laws for transporting goods, by land, between Baltimore and Providence, between New York and Philadelphia, and between Philadelphia and Baltimore.

We are now arrived at the inquiry—What is this power?

Power Defined

It is the power to regulate; that is, to prescribe the rule by which commerce is to be governed. This power, like all others vested in Congress, is complete in itself, may be exercised to its utmost extent, and acknowledges no limitations, other than are prescribed in the constitution. These are expressed in plain terms, and do not affect the questions which arise in this case, or which have been discussed at the bar. If, as has always been understood, the sovereignty of Congress, though limited to specified objects, is plenary as to those objects, the power over commerce with foreign nations, and among the several States, is vested in Congress as absolutely as it would be in a single government, having in its constitution the same restrictions on the exercise of the power as are found in the constitution of the United States. The wisdom and the discretion of Congress, their identity with the people, and the influence which their constituents possess at elections, are, in this, as in many other instances, as that, for example, of declaring war, the sole restraints on which they have relied, to secure them from its abuse. They are the restraints on which the people must often rely solely, in all representative governments.

Conclusion

The power of Congress, then, comprehends navigation, within the limits of every State in the Union; so far as that navigation may be, in any manner, connected with "commerce with foreign nations, or among the several States, or with the Indian tribes." It may, of consequence, pass the jurisdictional line of New York, and act upon the very waters to which the prohibition now under consideration applies.

But it has been urged with great earnestness, that, although the power of Congress to regulate commerce with foreign nations, and among the several States, be co-extensive with the subject itself, and have no other limits than are prescribed in the constitution, yet the States may severally exercise the same power, within their respective jurisdictions. In support of this argument, it is said, that they possessed it as an inseparable attribute of sovereignty, before the formation of the constitution, and still retain it, except so far as they have surrendered it by that instrument; that this principle results from the nature of the government, and is secured by the 10th Amendment; that an affirmative grant of power is not exclusive, unless in its own nature it be such that the continued exercise of it by the former possessor is inconsistent with the grant, and that this is not of that description.

The appellant, conceding these postulates, except the last, contends, that full power to regulate a particular subject, implies the whole power, and leaves no residuum; that a grant of the whole is incompatible with the existence of a right in another to any part of it.

Both parties have appealed to the constitution, to legislative acts, and judicial decisions; and have drawn arguments from all these sources, to support and illustrate the propositions they respectively maintain.

The grant of the power to lay and collect taxes is, like the power to regulate commerce, made in general terms, and has never been understood to interfere with the exercise of the same power by the State; and hence has been drawn an argument which has been applied to the question under consideration. But the two grants are not, it is conceived, similar in their terms or their nature. Although many of the powers formerly exercised by the States, are transferred to the government of the Union, yet the State governments remain, and constitute a most important part of our system. The power of taxation is indispensable to their existence, and is a power which, in its own nature, is capable of residing in, and being exercised by, different authorities at the same time. We are accustomed to see it placed, for different purposes, in different hands. Taxation is the simple operation of taking small portions from a perpetually accumulating mass, susceptible of almost infinite division; and a power in one to take what is necessary for certain purposes, is not, in its nature, incompatible with a power in another to take what is necessary for other purposes. Congress is authorized to lay and collect taxes, to pay the debts, and provide for the common defence and general welfare of the United States. This does not interfere with the power of the States to tax for the support of their own governments; nor is the exercise of that power by the States, an exercise of any portion of the power that is granted to the United States. In imposing taxes for State purposes, they are not doing what Congress is empowered to do. Congress is not empowered to tax for those purposes which are within the exclusive province of the States. When, then, each government exercises the power of taxation, neither is exercising the power of the other. But, when a State proceeds to regulate commerce with foreign nations, or among the several States, it is exercising the very power that is granted to Congress, and is doing the very thing which Congress is authorized to do. There is no analogy, then, between the power of taxation and the power of regulating commerce.

In discussing the question, whether this power is still in the States, in the case under consideration, we may dismiss from it the inquiry, whether it is surrendered by the mere grant to Congress, or is retained until Congress shall exercise the power. We may dismiss that inquiry, because it has been exercised, and the regulations which Congress deemed it proper to make, are now in full operation. The sole question is, can a State regulate commerce with foreign nations and among the States, while Congress is regulating it? . . .

But, the inspection laws are said to be regulations of commerce, and are certainly recognised in the constitution, as being passed in the exercise of a power remaining with the States.

That inspection laws may have a remote and considerable influence on commerce, will not be denied; but that a power to regulate commerce is the source from which the right to pass them is derived, cannot be admitted. The object of inspection laws, is to improve the quality of articles produced by the labour of a country; to fit them for exportation; or, it may be, for domestic use. They act upon the subject before it becomes an article of foreign commerce, or of commerce among the States, and prepare it for that purpose. They form a portion of that immense mass of legislation, which embraces every thing within the territory of a State, not surrendered to the general government: all which can be most advantageously exercised by the States themselves. Inspection laws, quarantine laws, health laws of every description, as well as laws for regulating the internal commerce of a State, and those which respect turnpike roads, ferries, &c., are component parts of this mass.

No direct general power over these objects is granted to Congress; and, consequently, they remain subject to State legislation. If the legislative power of the Union can reach them, it must be for national purposes; it must be where the power is expressly given for a special purpose, or is clearly incidental to some power which is expressly given. It is obvious, that the government of the Union, in the exercise of its express powers, that, for example, of regulating commerce with foreign nations and among the States, may use means that may also be employed by a State, in the exercise of its acknowledged powers; that, for example, of regulating commerce within the State. If Congress license vessels to sail from one port to another, in the same State, the act is supposed to be, necessarily, incidental to the power expressly granted to Congress, and implies no claim of a direct power to regulate the purely internal commerce of a State, or to act directly on its system of police. So, if a State, in passing laws on subjects acknowledged to be within its control, and with a view to those subjects, shall adopt a measure of the same character with one which Congress may adopt, it does not derive its authority from the particular power which has been granted, but from some other, which remains with the State, and may be executed by the same means. All experience shows, that the same measures, or measures scarcely distinguishable from each other, may flow from distinct powers; but this does not prove that the powers themselves are identical. Although the means used in their execution may sometimes approach each other so nearly as to be confounded, there are other situations in which they are sufficiently distinct to establish their individuality.

In our complex system, presenting the rare and difficult scheme of one general government, whose action extends over the whole, but which possesses only certain enumerated powers; and of numerous State governments, which retain and exercise all powers not delegated to the Union, contests respecting power must arise. Were it even otherwise, the measures taken by the respective governments to execute their acknowledged powers, would often be of the same description, and might, sometimes, interfere. This, however, does not prove that the one is exercising, or has a right to exercise, the powers of the other....

It has been contended by the counsel for the appellant, that, as the word "to regulate" implies in its nature, full power over the thing to be regulated, it excludes, necessarily, the action of all others that would perform the same operation on the same thing. That regulation is designed for the entire result, applying to those parts which remain as they were, as well as to those which are altered. It produces a uniform whole, which is as much disturbed and deranged by changing what the regulating power designs to leave untouched, as that on which it has operated.

There is great force in this argument, and the Court is not satisfied that it has been refuted.

Since, however, in exercising the power of regulating their own purely internal affairs, whether of trading or police, the States may sometimes enact laws, the validity of which depends on their interfering with, and being contrary to, an act of Congress passed in pursuance of the constitution, the Court will enter upon the inquiry, whether the laws of New York, as expounded by the highest tribunal of that State, have, in their application to this case, come into collision with an act of Congress, and deprived a citizen of a right to which that act entitles him. Should this collision exist, it will be immaterial whether those laws were passed in virtue of a concurrent power "to regulate commerce with foreign nations and among the several States," or, in virtue of a power to regulate their domestic trade and police. In one case and the other, the acts of New York must yield to the law of Congress; and the decision sustaining the privilege they confer, against a right given by a law of the Union, must be erroneous. . . .

It will at once occur, that, when a Legislature attaches certain privileges and exemptions to the exercise of a right over which its control is absolute, the law must imply a power to exercise the right. The privileges are gone, if the right itself be annihilated. It would be contrary to all reason, and to the course of human affairs, to say that a State is unable to strip a vessel of the particular privileges attendant on the exercise of a right, and yet may annul the right itself; that the State of New York cannot prevent an enrolled and licensed vessel, proceeding from Elizabethtown, in New Jersey, to New York, from enjoying, in her course, and on her entrance into port, all the privileges conferred by the act of Congress; but can shut her up in her own port, and prohibit altogether her entering the waters and ports of another State. To the Court it seems very clear, that the whole act on the subject of the coasting trade, according to those principles which govern the construction of statutes, implies, unequivocally, an authority to licensed vessels to carry on the coasting trade.

But we will proceed briefly to notice those sections which bear more directly on the subject.

The first section declares, that vessels enrolled by virtue of a previous law, and certain other vessels, enrolled as described in that act, and having a license in force, as is by the act required, "and no others, shall be deemed ships or vessels of the United States, entitled to the privileges of ships or vessels employed in the coasting trade."

This section seems to the Court to contain a positive enactment, the vessels it describes shall be entitled to the privileges of ships or vessels employed in the coasting trade. These privileges cannot be separated from the trade, and cannot be enjoyed, unless the trade may be prosecuted. The grant of the privilege is an idle, empty form, conveying nothing, unless it convey the right to which the privilege is attached, and in the exercise of which its whole value consists. To construe these words otherwise than as entitling the ships or vessels described, to carry on the coasting trade, would be, we think, to disregard the apparent intent of the act.

The fourth section directs the proper officer to grant to a vessel qualified to receive it, "a license for carrying on the coasting trade;" and prescribes its form. After reciting the compliance of the applicant with the previous requisites of the law, the operative words of the instrument are, "license is hereby granted for the said steam-boat, Bellona, to be employed in carrying on the coasting trade for one year from the date hereof, and no longer."

These are not the words of the officer; they are the words of the legislature; and convey as explicitly the authority the act intended to give, and operate as effectually, as if they had been inserted in any other part of the act, than in the license itself.

The word "license" means permission, or authority; and a license to do any particular thing, is a permission or authority to do that thing; and if granted by a person having power to grant it, transfers to the grantee the right to do whatever it purports to authorize. It certainly transfers to him all the right which the grantor can transfer, to do what is within the terms of the license.

Would the validity or effect of such an instrument be questioned by the respondent, if executed by persons claiming regularly under the laws of New York?

The license must be understood to be what it purports to be, a legislative authority to the steamboat Bellona, "to be employed in carrying on the coasting trade, for one year from this date." ...

But, if the license be a permit to carry on the coasting trade, the respondent denies that these boats were engaged in that trade, or that the decree under consideration has restrained them from prosecuting it. The boats of the appellant were, we are told, employed in the transportation of passengers; and this is no part of that commerce which Congress may regulate.

If, as our whole course of legislation on this subject shows, the power of Congress has been universally understood in America, to comprehend navigation, it is a very persuasive, if not a conclusive argument, to prove that the construction is correct; and, if it be correct, no clear distinction is perceived between the power to regulate vessels employed in transporting men for hire, and property for hire. The subject is transferred to Congress, and no exception to the grant can be admitted, which is not proved by the words or the nature of the thing. A coasting vessel employed in the transportation of passengers, is as much a portion of the American marine, as one employed in the transportation of a cargo; and no reason is perceived why such vessel should be withdrawn from the regulating power of that government, which has been thought best fitted for the purpose generally....

If we refer to the constitution, the inference to be drawn from it is rather against the distinction. The section which restrains Congress from prohibiting the migration or importation of such persons as any of the States may think proper to admit, until the year 1808, has always been considered as an exception from the power to regulate commerce, and certainly seems to class migration with importation. Migration applies as appropriately to voluntary, as importation does to involuntary, arrivals; and, so far as an exception from a power proves its existence, this section proves that the power to regulate commerce applies equally to the regulation of vessels employed in transporting men, who pass from place to place voluntarily, and to those who pass involuntarily.

If the power reside in Congress, as a portion of the general grant to regulate commerce, then acts applying that power to vessels generally, must be construed as comprehending all vessels. If none appear to be excluded by the language of the act, none can be excluded by construction. Vessels have always been employed to a greater or less extent in the transportation of passengers, and have never been supposed to be, on that account, withdrawn from the control or protection of Congress. Packets which ply along the coast, as well as those which make voyages between Europe and America, consider the transportation of passengers as an important part of their business. Yet it has never been suspected that the general laws of navigation did not apply to them....

The real and sole question seems to be, whether a steam machine, in actual use, deprives a vessel of the privileges conferred by a license....

In considering this question, the first idea which presents itself, is, that the laws of Congress for the regulation of commerce, do not look to the principle by which vessels are moved....

But all inquiry into this subject seems to the Court to be put completely at rest, by the act already mentioned, entitled, "An act for the enrolling and licensing of steam boats."

This act authorizes a steam boat employed, or intended to be employed, only in a river or bay of the United States, owned wholly or in part by an alien, resident within the United States, to be enrolled and licensed as if the same belonged to a citizen of the United States.

==This act demonstrates the opinion of Congress, that steam boats may be enrolled and licensed, in common with vessels using sails.== They are, of course, entitled to the same privileges, and can no more be restrained from navigating waters, and entering ports which are free to such vessels, than if they were wafted on their voyage by the winds, instead of being propelled by the agency of fire. The one element may be as legitimately used as the other....

The Court is aware that, in stating the train of reasoning by which we have been conducted to this result, much time has been consumed in the attempt to demonstrate propositions which may have been thought axioms. It is felt that the tediousness inseparable from the endeavour to prove that which is already clear, is imputable to a considerable part of this opinion. But it was unavoidable. The conclusion to which we have come, depends on a chain of principles which it was necessary to preserve unbroken; and, although some of them were thought nearly self evident, the magnitude of the question, the weight of character belonging to those from whose judgment we dissent, and the argument at the bar, demanded that we should assume nothing.

Powerful and ingenious minds, taking, as postulates, that the powers expressly granted to the government of the Union, are to be contracted by construction, into the narrowest possible compass, and that the original powers of the States are retained, if any possible construction will retain them, may, by a course of well digested, but refined and metaphysical reasoning, founded on these premises, explain away the constitution of our country, and leave it, a magnificent structure, indeed, to look at, but totally unfit for use. They may so entangle and perplex the understanding, as to obscure principles, which were before thought quite plain, and induce doubts where, if the mind were to pursue its own course, none would be perceived. In such a case, it is peculiarly necessary to recur to safe and fundamental principles to sustain those principles, and when sustained, to make them the tests of the arguments to be examined.

Mr. Justice Johnson.

The judgment entered by the Court in this cause, has my entire approbation; but having adopted my conclusions on views of the subject materially different from those of my brethren, I feel it incumbent on me to exhibit those views....

The words of the constitution are, "Congress shall have power to regulate commerce with foreign nations, and among the several States, and with the Indian tribes." ...

My opinion is founded on the application of the words of the grant to the subject of it.

The "power to regulate commerce," here meant to be granted, was that power to regulate commerce which previously existed in the States. But what was that power? The States were, unquestionably, supreme; and each possessed that power over commerce, which is acknowledged to reside in every sovereign State.... The power of a sovereign state over commerce ... amounts to nothing more than a power to limit and restrain it at pleasure. And since the power to prescribe the limits to its freedom, necessarily implies the power to determine what shall remain unrestrained, it follows, that the power must be exclusive; it can reside but in one potentate; and hence, the grant of this power carries with it the whole subject, leaving nothing for the State to act upon....

Commerce, in its simplest signification, means an exchange of goods; but in the advancement of society, labour, transportation, intelligence, care, and various mediums of exchange, become commodities, and enter into commerce; the subject, the vehicle, the agent, and their various operations, become the objects of commercial regulation. Ship building, the carrying trade, and propagation of seamen, are such vital agents of commercial prosperity, that the nation which could not legislate over these subjects, would not possess power to regulate commerce.

That such was the understanding of the framers of the constitution, is conspicuous from provisions contained in that instrument.

The first clause of the 9th section, not only considers the right of controlling personal ingress or migration, as implied in the powers previously vested in Congress over commerce, but acknowledges it as a legitimate subject of revenue. And, although the leading object of this section undoubtedly was the importation of slaves, yet the words are obviously calculated to comprise persons of all descriptions, and to recognise in Congress a power to prohibit, where the States permit, although they cannot permit when the States prohibit. The treaty making power undoubtedly goes further. So the fifth clause of the same section furnishes an exposition of the sense of the Convention as to the power of Congress over navigation: "nor shall vessels bound to or from one State, be obliged to enter, clear, or pay duties in another." ...

It is impossible, with the views which I entertain of the principle on which the commercial privileges of the people of United States, among themselves, rests, to concur in the view which this Court takes of the effect of the coasting license in this cause. I do not regard it as the foundation of the right set up in behalf of the appellant. If there was any one object riding over every other in the adoption of the constitution, it was to keep the commercial intercourse among the States free from all invidious and partial restraints. And I cannot overcome the conviction, that if the licensing act was repealed to-morrow, the rights of the appellant to a reversal of the decision complained of, would be as strong as it is under this license. One half the doubts in life arise from the defects of language, and if this instrument had been called an exemption instead of a license, it would have given a better idea of its character....

DECREE. [T]his Court is of the opinion, that the several licenses to [Gibbons'] steam boats ... to carry on the coasting trade ... were granted under an act of Congress, passed in pursuance of the constitution of the United States, [and] gave full authority to those vessels to navigate the waters of the United States, ... any law of the State of New York to the contrary notwithstanding....

Gibbons v. Ogden: Questions

1. What is the textual source of Congress' power to regulate commerce among the states?
2. What is the relation of the scope of congressional power over commerce and the scope of state power?
3. What types of interpretation does Marshall use (textual, structural, etc.)? Go through the rationale and identify arguments and classify them based on the type of interpretation used.
4. Must the power of Congress over commerce extend to regulation of at least some commercial activity that takes place within the borders of individual states? What are Marshall's arguments on this point?

5. What is the suggested rule of *Gibbons*? Is it a holding or dicta? What are the judicially enforceable limits, if any, on congressional power and what is the test for locating those limits? Does the test involve application of an abstract definition of "commerce," involve an empirical weighing of the economic consequences of the regulated activity, or both?

6. Does Marshall's opinion suggest that Congress lacks power to regulate purely intrastate commerce, or does it depend, and if so, on what? Is the opinion ambiguous on this point?

7. In the end, why does the steamboat monopoly fall? What law or privilege, if any, does it violate? Does it violate a constitutional federal statute and a privilege granted under the statute or does the monopoly simply and directly violate the Constitution?

8. Is congressional national regulation of wages or of child labor consistent or inconsistent with the power of Congress described in *Gibbons*?

9. Assume that after *Gibbons*, New York grants a steamboat monopoly to a company for operation exclusively within New York waters. Is this monopoly consistent or inconsistent with the rule of *Gibbons*? Would Congress have power to prohibit it under the rule of *Gibbons*?

10. Why might Southern slaveholders have been opposed to a broad interpretation of the power of Congress over commerce?

The Controversy over "Original Meaning"

In his controversial book, *Politics and the Constitution* (1953), Professor W.W. Crosskey argued that the Commerce Clause gave the Congress broad power to regulate all commercial activity in the United States. According to Crosskey, the Constitution should be interpreted in light of the common understanding of its words at the time of enactment. This method of analysis, now called "original meaning," is currently promoted by Justices Thomas and Scalia, among others. Crosskey insists that the Court wrongly assumed that "'among,' in the Commerce Clause, means 'between,' in the sense of 'from one to another of;' and, second, that the word 'States,' in the clause means 'the territorial divisions of the country.'" [I, 50](citation to volume and page).

According to Crosskey, in 18th-century usage the word "state" often meant the people of the state. Citing 18th-century sources, Crosskey gives many examples. One writer noted, "the state of New York are able to supply themselves with a sufficient quantity of that useful article NAILS." Another stated that "the state of Virginia are involved to an amount almost incredible in debts to the British merchants, which were not cancelled according to their hopes by the treaty of peace." In these cases, "state" referred to the people of the state. [I, 61.]

Crosskey suggests the phrase "among the states" in the 18th century meant "among, within, or intermingled with the people of the states" and included commercial activity within a state. Crosskey cites a proposed 1786 congressional ordinance that the superintendent of Indian affairs "place deputies among the several tribes" to prevent unrest. [I, 75] Crosskey also quotes Rufus King in the Constitutional Convention as saying to count slaves for purposes of representation "would excite great discontent among the states having no slaves." Since, Crosskey notes, "such discontents could hardly have been expected *between free state and free state*, the sensible view is that King meant ... they would arise *within the free states among their people*." [I, 70.]

Commerce, Crosskey insists, meant commercial activity in the 18th-century usage, and included manufacturing. He cites many examples. Daniel Defoe's 1728 pamphlet, *A Plan of the English Commerce* insisted that people should "distinguish between the Decay of the general commerce of a nation, and the Decay of any particular Branch of it; because some particular manufacture may decay, and even wear out, in a County, ... yet at the same Time the general Commerce may not at all be decayed or decreased." [I, 85, 86]. A "survey of American commerce" noted "the increase of shipbuilding, ... the new manufactories of articles necessary to the equipment of vessels, and ... the improvement in the art of shipbuilding...." [I, 89.] Crosskey concludes that commerce in 18th-century usage included "the buying and selling of movable goods, of houses and land, and manufacturing and shipbuilding." [I, 90.]

One critic of Crosskey pointed out prominent examples of contemporary usage that were consistent with the orthodox reading of the word "among" in the Commerce Clause. See Ernest J. Brown, *Book Review*, 67 Harv. L. Rev. 1439, 1447–55 (1954). Crosskey's work has been harshly criticized. See, e.g., Julius Goebel, *ex Parte Clio*, 54 Col. L. Rev. 450 (1954); Henry M. Hart, *Book Review, Politics and the Constitution*, 67 Harv. L. Rev. 1439 (1954). Crosskey's work, and that of his critics, show the difficulties of trying to discern *the* 18th-century meaning of certain words contained in constitutional text.

The possible approaches have been outlined in an article by Professor Randy Barnett, *The Original Meaning of the Commerce Clause*, 68 U. Chi. L. Rev. 101, 112 (2001):

> "Commerce" might be limited to *trade or exchange* of goods, which would exclude, for example, agriculture, manufacturing, and other methods of production, or it might expansively be interpreted to refer to *any gainful activity*. "To regulate" might be limited to "make regular," which would exclude, for example, any prohibition on trade as an end in itself, or it might expansively be interpreted to mean "to govern," which would include prohibitions as well as pure regulations. "[A]mong the several States" might be limited to commerce that takes place *between* (or between people of different states), as opposed to commerce that occurs between persons of the same state. Or "among the states" might expansively be interpreted to refer to commerce "among the people of the States" whether such commerce occurs between people in the same state or in different states.

Professor Barnett concludes that "there are good textual and contextual reasons to accept the narrower definition of each of these terms as their original meaning at the time of the founding." To the extent that such an original meaning interpretation is followed, most federal environmental, wage and hour, and worker safety regulations would seem to be unconstitutional. Do you agree? For a third approach to questions of original meaning, see Grant S. Nelson and Robert J. Pushaw, Jr., *Rethinking the Commerce Clause: Applying First Principles to Uphold Federal Commercial Regulations but Preserve State Control over Social Issues*, 85 Iowa L. Rev. 1 (1999).

Another critic of Crosskey, Paul Finkelman, argues that while "his lexicographic argument is interesting" it is ultimately "not persuasive." Finkelman notes that Crosskey's position "ignores by logic and fact. The logic is quite simple. Would the Southern States have adopted the Constitution in 1787 and 1788 if they had thought it would allow the Congress to regulate slavery or abolish the institution? Would they have endorsed a Commerce Clause that gave Congress power to regulate slavery in the states? It defies logic and reason to suppose this. It also defies the historical record." As Finkelman notes, from the first debates over the creation of national government in 1775, through the end of the Convention of 1787 and during the ratification debates, Southerners jealously protected slavery. They demanded the provision in Article I, §9, Paragraph 1 that prohibited

Congress from interfering with the African Slave Trade before 1808. Throughout these debates "[n]o one at the Convention" ever "suggested that the Commerce Clause would allow Congress to regulate the domestic slave trade or slavery within the states. Surely the ardent defenders of slavery at the Convention would have opposed the Commerce Clause if they had expected it to threaten what they constantly referred to as their vital domestic institution." Paul Finkelman, *The First American Constitutions: State and Federal*, 59 Tex. L. Rev. 1141, 1159, 1167, 1169–70 (1981). It is possible, of course, that slavery was seen as an institution that had special constitutional protection from what would otherwise be within the scope of federal power.

Slavery and Federal Power

The broad view of national power set out by the Court in *McCulloch* (1819) and *Gibbons* (1824) did not go unchallenged. A major motivation for criticism of broad claims of national power was a desire to protect the institution of slavery. In the years after the American Revolution, Northern states generally abolished slavery within their jurisdictions. As the nation expanded during the first half of the 19th century, the growth of population in free states began to outpace that of the slave states. Southern slaveholders began to fear that soon the North would have the votes in Congress to take actions that would threaten slavery in the Southern states. Major battles erupted in Congress over the "right" of Southerners to bring slaves into the territories and establish slavery there.

Consider the following speech by John Randolph of Virginia, delivered in Congress and reported in the press in the week before *Gibbons* was argued in the Supreme Court. Randolph spoke in opposition to a bill in Congress providing for construction of roads and canals.

> We are told that along with the regulation of foreign commerce, the States have yielded to the General Government, in as broad terms, *the regulation of domestic commerce*.... And it is argued that "to regulate commerce" is to prescribe the way in which it shall be carried on—which gives, by a *liberal* construction, the power to *construct* the way, that is, the roads and canals on which it is to be carried. [In addition Randolph noted claims that national power to build road and canals could be found in the war power and the power to provide for the general welfare.]
>
> If Congress possesses the power to do what is [now] proposed, they may ... emancipate every slave in the United States—and with stronger color of reason.... [For] was it not demonstrable ... that the existence of a large body of slaves [was] a source of danger [so that the common defense and general welfare could also justify emancipation]?

Quoted in Crosskey, *Politics and the Constitution*, I, 248–49 (1953).

C. The Preemptive Effect of the Commerce Clause Revisited

Note: *New York v. Miln*

In *Mayor of the City of New York v. Miln* (1837), the Court again considered the relationship between transportation and commerce. A New York act of 1824 required masters of vessels in New York to report the names, ages, and other information of all passengers brought into the state. The city brought suit against Miln to recover $15,000. Miln had an economic interest in the ship *The Emily* that made him liable if (as was the case) the master of the ship failed to comply with this law. Miln argued the law was an unconstitutional interference with interstate and international commerce. New York argued the statute was necessary to control the ingress of poor people. As a regulation of poor people, this law was consistent with English statutes that had allowed towns to prevent the settlement of paupers. However, the law also seemed to be an attempt to regulate international commerce, which was something the states could not do.

This was the first major Commerce Clause case for the Court under Chief Justice Taney. If the Court had followed the suggestion of (possibly) exclusive federal power in *Gibbons v. Ogden* (1824), this would have been a relatively simple decision. In *Gibbons*, which was among Chief Justice Marshall's most popular decisions, the Court had held that the transportation of people was a form of commerce that came under the jurisdiction of Congress. The New York statute seemed to clearly burden interstate commerce.

However, the Taney Court understood that the case was far more complicated. By this time, most of the slave states had prohibited the in-migration of free blacks. Starting in 1822, South Carolina and other Southern coastal states had adopted laws requiring the incarceration of free black sailors who entered their ports as crew members of visiting ships. In *Elkison v. Deliesseline* (1823), Justice William Johnson, while riding circuit, had declared, in dicta, that such laws were unconstitutional. But he had also asserted that he lacked jurisdiction in the case, and so did not intervene in South Carolina's enforcement of its Negro sailor law. If the Court found that New York could not regulate the in-migration of paupers, then it would be hard pressed not to apply the same rule, in some future Commerce Clause case, to Southern state laws regulating the in-migration or even the movement of free blacks. Only four years earlier, in 1832, South Carolina had adopted an ordinance purporting to nullify a federal tariff. A new tariff and a face-saving resolution by South Carolina had prevented a military conflict between South Carolina and the national government. But most observers understood that if the Supreme Court tried to interfere with the status of free blacks or slaves in the South, a conflict would quickly arise.

The Court avoided these difficult issues by deciding that New York's law was "not a regulation of commerce, but of police; and that being thus considered, it was passed in the exercise of a power which rightfully belonged to the states." The Court emphatically asserted that "a State has ... undeniable and unlimited jurisdiction over all persons and things within its territorial limits" and thus the state could regulate its own population "to advance the safety, happiness and prosperity of its people." The Court let the entire nation know that the states were free to pass "inspection laws, quarantine laws, health laws of every description, as well as laws for regulating the internal commerce of the State, etc."

This decision allowed the slave states, and some of the free states as well, to limit the in-migration of free blacks. It also allowed both the slave and the free states to ban the importation of slaves. Obviously, it allowed states to regulate immigration at a time when the national government did not do so. After the Civil War, the Supreme Court would interpret the 14th Amendment to prevent states from interfering with the internal migration of Americans, while eventually the national government would regulate foreign immigration. But, the police powers doctrine, articulated here, remains an integral part of American constitutional law and an important component of federalism.

Cooley v. Board of Wardens: Background

Gibbons avoided the question of whether congressional power over commerce (even without legislation) necessarily excluded state regulation of commerce. How does *Cooley v. Board of Wardens* deal with this problem?

As you saw in *Gibbons*, one aspect of the Commerce Clause is the power it gives to Congress. Another aspect is what limits the existence of the Commerce Clause places on state power. This question, in turn, divides into two questions. When, if ever, does the Commerce Clause prevent states from legislating on a subject even though Congress has not acted? This issue involves the negative effect of the Commerce Clause in its dormant state (i.e., in the absence of a congressional statute on the subject) on state laws—the *Dormant Commerce Clause*. You will see that the Court holds that in certain situations, even when Congress has not acted on a subject, the very existence of the Commerce Clause precludes state legislation. Congress can however, legislate to permit state regulation that the Court would otherwise strike down.

When Congress does legislate on a topic and when congressional legislation conflicts with a state statute, the state statute falls by virtue of the supremacy clause. The congressional statute displaces or *preempts* the state Law. *Gibbons* ultimately turned on preemption. The case that follows is a seminal case on the effect of the Commerce Clause in its dormant state. The decision in *Cooley* assumes that the federal act adopting state regulations of pilots was not effective as to the state statute passed for the port of Philadelphia because the state act was passed after the federal act. For that reason, *Cooley* basically treats the case as one where Congress has not legislated on the matter. Based on that assumption, the Court ruled on the issue of whether the state statute violated the negative effect of the Commerce Clause in its dormant state. We will consider the Dormant Commerce Clause in more detail in chapter 6.

Cooley v. Board of Wardens
53 U.S. 299 (1851)

[An act of the Pennsylvania legislature passed in 1803 required ships of a certain tonnage to employ a pilot before entering or leaving the port of Philadelphia. Cooley challenged the Pennsylvania act, claiming it violated the exclusive power of Congress to regulate commerce. By an act passed in 1789, the first Congress under the new Constitution declared that all pilots in the bays, inlets, rivers, harbors, and ports of the United States, shall continue to be regulated in conformity with the existing laws of the states. Counsel for Cooley agreed that Congress could adopt then-existing state laws. However, since the Pennsylvania statute was not in existence when Congress passed the act of 1789, he contended that Congress had not adopted it. Nor could Congress prospectively turn part of its exclusive power to regulate commerce over to the states. The decision of the Court in *Cooley* assumed that Congress could not authorize states to legislate prospectively in the area of its exclusive power. This aspect of the decision in *Cooley* has been changed by later decisions. Congress can now, in effect, prospectively authorize state legislation in what would otherwise be the domain of the exclusive power of Congress over commerce. It can do so by explicitly removing the prohibition on state legislation that the Court finds in the area of conditional exclusivity.

The Board of Wardens brought an action against Cooley for a pilotage fee. The fee was a penalty for sailing from the port of Philadelphia without a pilot, when one might have been had. The magistrate gave judgment for the Board of Wardens and Cooley appealed. The Pennsylvania Supreme Court affirmed, concluding that the Pennsylvania act did not violate any provision of the United States Constitution and Cooley appealed to the United States Supreme Court.

Cooley's attorney made the following argument:

> [W]e argue, that the power to regulate commerce is exclusive in Congress. [C]ongress may adopt state legislation when within constitutional limits, no doubt; yet it cannot be, that by general legislation of this kind, they can prospectively confer upon the states powers not given by the Constitution, or enable individual states to legislate on subjects clearly within the powers of Congress.... The Chief Justice, in speaking of this act in *The License Cases* (1847), says:
>
> "Undoubtedly Congress had the power, by assenting to the state laws then in force, to make them its own, and thus make the previous regulations of the states the regulations of the General Government. But it is equally clear, that as to all future laws by the states, if the Constitution deprives them of the power of making any regulations on the subject, an act of Congress could not restore it; for it will hardly be contended that an act of Congress can alter the Constitution, and confer upon a state a power which the Constitution declares it shall not possess.]"

Mr. Justice Curtis delivered the opinion of the court.

These cases are brought here by writs of error to the Supreme Court of the Commonwealth of Pennsylvania.

They are actions to recover half pilotage fees under the 29th section of the act of the Legislature of Pennsylvania, passed on the second day of March, 1803. The plaintiff in error alleges that the highest court of the state has decided against a right claimed by him under the Constitution of the United States. That right is to be exempted from the payment of the sums of money demanded, pursuant to the State law above referred to, because that law contravenes several provisions of the Constitution of the United States.

The particular section of the state law drawn in question is as follows:

> That every ship or vessel arriving from or bound to any foreign port or place, and every ship or vessel of the burden of seventy-five tons or more, sailing from or bound to any port not within the river Delaware, shall be obliged to receive a pilot....

We think this particular regulation concerning half-pilotage fees is an appropriate part of a general system of regulations of this subject. Testing it by the practice of commercial states and countries legislating on this subject, we find it has usually been deemed necessary to make similar provisions. Numerous laws of this kind are cited in the learned argument of the counsel for the defendant in error; and their fitness, as a part of the system of pilotage, in many places, may be inferred from their existence in so many different states and countries. Like other laws they are framed to meet the most usual cases; ... they rest upon the propriety of securing lives and property exposed to the perils of a dangerous navigation, by taking on board a person peculiarly skilled to encounter or avoid them; upon the policy of discouraging the commanders of vessels from refusing to receive such persons on board at the proper times and places....

It remains to consider the objection that [the Pennsylvania law] is repugnant to the third clause of the eighth section of the first article. "The Congress shall have power to regulate commerce with foreign nations and among the several states, and with the Indian tribes."

That the power to regulate commerce includes the regulation of navigation, we consider settled. And when we look to the nature of the service performed by pilots ... we are brought to the conclusion, that the regulation of the qualifications of pilots, of the modes and times of offering and rendering their services, of the responsibilities which shall rest upon them, of the powers they shall possess, of the compensation they may demand, and of the penalties by which their rights and duties may be enforced, do constitute regulations of navigation, and consequently of commerce, within the just meaning of this clause of the Constitution.

The power to regulate navigation is the power to prescribe rules in conformity with which navigation must be carried on. It extends to the persons who conduct it, as well as to the instruments used. Accordingly, the first Congress assembled under the Constitution passed laws, requiring the masters of ships and vessels of the United States to be citizens of the United States, and established many rules for the government and regulation of officers and seamen. These have been from time to time added to and changed, and we are not aware that their validity has been questioned....

It becomes necessary, therefore, to consider whether this law of Pennsylvania, being a regulation of commerce, is valid.

The act of Congress of the 7th of August, 1789, §4, is as follows:

> That all pilots in the bays, inlets, rivers, harbors, and ports of the United States shall continue to be regulated in conformity with the existing laws of the states, respectively, wherein such pilots may be, or with such laws as the states may respectively hereafter enact for the purpose, until further legislative provision shall be made by Congress.

If the law of Pennsylvania, now in question, had been in existence at the date of this act of Congress, we might hold it to have been adopted by Congress, and thus made a law of the United States, and so valid. Because this act does, in effect, give the force of an act of Congress, to the then existing state laws on this subject, so long as they should continue unrepealed by the state which enacted them.

But the law on which these actions are founded was not enacted till 1803. What effect then can be attributed to so much of the act of 1789, as declares, that pilots shall continue to be regulated in conformity, "with such laws as the states may respectively hereafter enact for the purpose, until further legislative provision shall be made by Congress?"

If the states were divested of the power to legislate on this subject by the grant of the commercial power to Congress, it is plain this act could not confer upon them power thus to legislate.... The grant of commercial power to Congress does not contain any terms which expressly exclude the states from exercising an authority over its subject-matter. If they are excluded it must be because the nature of the power, thus granted to Congress, requires that a similar authority should not exist in the states. If it were conceded on the one side, that the nature of this power, like that to legislate for the District of Columbia, is absolutely and totally repugnant to the existence of similar power in the states, probably no one would deny that the grant of the power to Congress, as effectually and perfectly excludes the states from all future legislation on the subject, as if express words had been used to exclude them. And on the other hand, if it were admitted that the existence of this power in Congress, like the power of taxation, is compatible with the existence of a similar power in the states, then it would be in conformity with the contemporary exposition of the Constitution (*Federalist*, No. 32), and with the judicial construction, given from time to time by this court, after the most deliberate consideration, to hold that the mere grant of such a power to Congress, did not imply a prohibition on the states to exercise the same power; that it is not the mere existence of such a power, but its exercise by Congress, which may be incompatible with the exercise of the same power by the states, and that the states may legislate in the absence of congressional regulations. *Wilson v. Blackbird Creek Co.* (1829).

The diversities of opinion, therefore, which have existed on this subject, have arisen from the different views taken of the nature of this power. But when the nature of a power like this is spoken of, when it is said that the nature of the power requires that it should be exercised exclusively by Congress, it must be intended to refer to the subjects of that power, and to say they are of such a nature as to require exclusive legislation by Congress. Now the power to regulate commerce, embraces a vast field, containing not only many, but exceedingly various subjects, quite unlike in their nature; some imperatively demanding a single uniform rule, operating equally on the commerce of the United States in every port; and some, like the subject now in question, as imperatively demanding that diversity, which alone can meet the local necessities of navigation.

Either absolutely to affirm, or deny that the nature of this power requires exclusive legislation by Congress, is to lose sight of the nature of the subjects of this power, and to assert concerning all of them, what is really applicable but to a part. Whatever subjects of this power are in their nature national, or admit only of one uniform system, or plan of regulation, may justly be said to be of such a nature as to require exclusive legislation by Congress. That this cannot be affirmed of laws for the regulation of pilots and pilotage is plain. The act of 1789 contains a clear and authoritative declaration by the first Congress, that the nature of this subject is such, that until Congress should find it necessary to exert its power, it should be left to the legislation of the states; that it is local and not national; that it is likely to be the best provided for, not by one system, or plan of regulations, but by as many as the legislative discretion of the several states should deem applicable to the local peculiarities of the ports within their limits.

Viewed in this light, so much of this act of 1789 as declares that pilots shall continue to be regulated "by such laws as the states may respectively hereafter enact for that purpose," instead of being held to be inoperative, as an attempt to confer on the states a power to legislate, of which the Constitution had deprived them, is allowed an appropriate and important signification. It manifests the understanding of Congress, at the outset of the government, that the nature of this subject is not such as to require its exclusive legislation. The practice of the states, and of the national government, has been in conformity with this declaration, from the origin of the national government to this time; and the nature of the subject when examined, is such as to leave no doubt of the superior fitness and propriety, not to say the absolute necessity, of different systems of regulation, drawn from local knowledge and experience, and conformed to local wants....

It is the opinion of a majority of the court that the mere grant to Congress of the power to regulate commerce, did not deprive the states of power to regulate pilots, and that although Congress has legislated on this subject, its legislation manifests an intention, with a single exception, not to regulate this subject, but to leave its regulation to the several states. To these precise questions, which are all we are called on to decide, this opinion must be understood to be confined....

[Daniel, J., concurred in the judgment. McLean and Wayne, JJ., dissented.]

Cooley v. Board of Wardens: Questions

1. According to *Cooley*, how do congressional and state power relate to each other?
2. What does the next case tell you about the extent to which Congress can consent to state regulation of what would otherwise be within exclusive federal power over interstate commerce?

In re Rahrer
140 U.S. 545 (1891)

... This was an application for a writ of habeas corpus made to the Circuit Court of the United States for the District of Kansas by Charles A. Rahrer, who alleged in his petition that he was illegally and wrongfully restrained of his liberty by [the] sheriff of Shawnee County, Kansas, in violation of the Constitution of the United States. [Rahrer, as agent for a Missouri company, had received and sold liquor shipped to him in its original package from Missouri to Kansas. Prior precedent suggested that interstate transportation of liquor in its original package could be regulated by Congress, but was not subject to state laws until the packages were broken open. Rahrer had apparently not broken open the original package. Kansas had a prohibition law, which Rahrer was accused of violating.] ...

The [1889] constitution of Kansas provides: "The manufacture and sale of intoxicating liquors shall be forever prohibited in this State, except for medical, scientific and mechanical purposes." [The Kansas statute Rahrer was accused of violating provided:

> Any person or persons who shall manufacture, sell, or barter any spirituous, malt, vinous, fermented, or other intoxicating liquors, shall be guilty of a misdemeanor, and punished as hereinafter provided: Provided, however, That such liquors may be sold for medical, scientific and mechanical purposes, as provided in this act....]

On August 8, 1890, an act of Congress was approved, entitled "An act to limit the effect of the regulations of commerce between the several States and with foreign countries in certain cases," which reads as follows: "That all fermented, distilled, or other intoxicating liquors or liquids transported into any State or Territory or remaining therein for use, consumption, sale or storage therein, shall upon arrival in such State or Territory be subject to the operation and effect of the laws of such State or Territory enacted in the exercise of its police powers, to the same extent and in the same manner as though such liquids or liquors had been produced in such State or Territory, and shall not be exempt therefrom by reason of being introduced therein in original packages or otherwise."

[The lower court dismissed the charges against Rahrer.]

Mr. Chief Justice Fuller, after stating the case, delivered the opinion of the court.

The power of the State to impose restraints and burdens upon persons and property in conservation and promotion of the public health, good order and prosperity, is a power originally and always belonging to the States, not surrendered by them to the general government nor directly restrained by the Constitution of the United States, and essentially exclusive....

The power of Congress to regulate commerce among the several States, when the subjects of that power are national in their nature, is also exclusive....

The laws of Iowa under consideration in *Bowman v. Railway Company* (1888) and *Leisy v. Hardin* (1890) were enacted in the exercise of the police power of the State, and not at all as regulations of commerce with foreign nations and among the States, but as they inhibited the receipt of an imported commodity, or its disposition before it had ceased to become an article of trade between one State and another, or another country and this, they amounted in effect to a regulation of such commerce. Hence, it was held that inasmuch as interstate commerce, consisting in the transportation, purchase, sale and exchange of commodities, is national in its character and must be governed by a uniform system, so long as Congress did not pass any law to regulate it specifically, or in such way as to allow the laws of the State to operate upon it, Congress thereby indicated its will that such commerce should be free and untrammeled, and therefore that the laws of Iowa, referred to, were inoperative, in so far as they amounted to regulations of foreign or interstate commerce, in inhibiting the reception of such articles within the State, or their sale upon arrival, in the form in which they were imported there from a foreign country or another State. It followed as a corollary, that when Congress acted at all, the result of its action must be to operate as a restraint upon that perfect freedom which its silence insured....

Congress has now spoken, and declared that imported liquors or liquids shall, upon arrival in a State, fall within the category of domestic articles of a similar nature. Is the law open to constitutional objection?

By the first clause of § 10 of Article I of the Constitution, certain powers are enumerated which the States are forbidden to exercise in any event; and by clauses two and three, certain others, which may be exercised with the consent of Congress. As to those in the first class, Congress cannot relieve from the positive restriction imposed. As to those in the second, their exercise may be authorized; and they include the collection of the revenue from imposts and duties on imports and exports, by state enactments, subject to the revision and control of Congress; and a tonnage duty, to the exaction of which only the consent of Congress is required. Beyond this, Congress is not empowered to enable the State to go in this direction. Nor can Congress transfer legislative powers to a State nor sanction a state law in violation of the Constitution; and if it can adopt a state law as its own, it must be one that it would be competent for it to enact itself, and not a law passed in the exercise of the police power. *Cooley v. Board of Wardens of Philadelphia* (1852).

It does not admit of argument that Congress can neither delegate its own powers nor enlarge those of a State. This being so, it is urged that the act of Congress cannot be sustained as a regulation of commerce, because the Constitution, in the matter of interstate commerce, operates ex proprio vigore as a restraint upon the power of Congress to so regulate it as to bring any of its subjects within the grasp of the police power of the State. In other words, it is earnestly contended that the Constitution guarantees freedom of commerce among the States in all things, and that not only may intoxicating liquors be imported from one State into another, without being subject to regulation under the laws of the latter, but that Congress is powerless to obviate that result.

Thus the grant to the general government of a power designed to prevent embarrassing restrictions upon interstate commerce by any State, would be made to forbid any restraint whatever. We do not concur in this view. In surrendering their own power over external commerce the States did not secure absolute freedom in such commerce, but only the protection from encroachment afforded by confiding its regulation exclusively to Congress.

By the adoption of the Constitution the ability of the several States to act upon the matter solely in accordance with their own will was extinguished, and the legislative will of the general government substituted. No affirmative guaranty was thereby given to any State of the right to demand as between it and the others what it could not have obtained before; while the object was undoubtedly sought to be attained of preventing commercial regulations partial in their character or contrary to the common interests. And the magnificent growth and prosperity of the country attest the success which has attended the accomplishment of that object. But this furnishes no support to the position that Congress could not, in the exercise of the discretion reposed in it, concluding that the common interests did not require entire freedom in the traffic in ardent spirits, enact the law in question. In so doing Congress has not attempted to delegate the power to regulate commerce, or to exercise any power reserved to the States, or to grant a power not possessed by the States, or to adopt state laws. It has taken its own course and made its own regulation, applying to these subjects of interstate commerce one common rule, whose uniformity is not affected by variations in state laws in dealing with such property....

No reason is perceived why, if Congress chooses to provide that certain designated subjects of interstate commerce shall be governed by a rule which divests them of that character at an earlier period of time than would otherwise be the case, it is not within its competency to do so.

The differences of opinion which have existed in this tribunal in many leading cases upon this subject, have arisen, not from a denial of the power of Congress, when exercised, but upon the question whether the inaction of Congress was in itself equivalent to the affirmative interposition of a bar to the operation of an undisputed power possessed by the States.

We recall no decision giving color to the idea that, when Congress acted, its action would be less potent than when it kept silent.

The framers of the Constitution never intended that the legislative power of the nation should find itself incapable of disposing of a subject matter specifically committed to its charge. The manner of that disposition brought into determination upon this record involves no ground for adjudging the act of Congress inoperative and void.

We inquire then whether fermented, distilled, or other intoxicating liquors or liquids transported into the State of Kansas, and there offered for sale and sold, after the passage of the act, became subject to the operation and effect of the existing laws of that State in reference to such articles....

Congress did not use terms of permission to the State to act, but simply removed an impediment to the enforcement of the state laws in respect to imported packages in their original condition, created by the absence of a specific utterance on its part. It imparted no power to the State not then possessed, but allowed imported property to fall at once upon arrival within the local jurisdiction....

Jurisdiction attached, not in virtue of the law of Congress, but because the effect of the latter was to place the property where jurisdiction could attach.

The decree is reversed, and the cause remanded for further proceedings in conformity with this opinion.

[Harlan, Gray and Brewer. JJ., concurred in the judgment.]

D. The Limited View of the Commerce Clause during the Late 19th and Early 20th Centuries

Chief Justice Marshall never resolved in *Gibbons* (1824) whether federal power over commerce was exclusive—that is whether commerce was beyond state regulation. His inclination that commerce might well be beyond state power led him to announce a theory to uphold much state legislation on the ground that it was not a regulation of commerce but an exercise of state police power. In this connection he sometimes emphasized that the matter was not yet a subject of commerce. In these cases, however, the Court suggested that congressional power to legislate and preempt remained, provided that the matter was within federal power over commerce or was "necessary and proper" for the regulation of commerce. By the later 19th and early 20th centuries, however, the Court embraced a theory of dual federalism in which there were subjects reserved to the states and, as a result, beyond congressional power over commerce. This view was not clearly distinct from the narrow view the Court took of federal power during this period.

The Court's constricted reading of federal power was significant because it occurred in a social context in which many Americans were demanding federal action to ameliorate some of the harsher effects of late 19th and early 20th century American industrial capitalism. The conditions and reactions to them are described by Howard Gillman in *The Constitution Besieged, The Rise and Demise of Lochner Era Police Powers Jurisprudence*, 76–77 (1993):

> Industrialization imposed brutalizing burdens on masses of people at the same time it showered unprecedented splendors on a select few. Speculative panics, business failures, and substantial unemployment occurred with unprecedented frequency, most notably from 1873 to 1878, 1882 to 1885, and 1893 to 1897. The hard, deflationary ("constitutional") currency fought for by conservatives after the war—represented in the passage of the Resumption Act of 1875, which authorized gold payments on greenbacks and other paper notes in 1879—gradually, and on occasion violently, pushed down wages and agricultural prices and ensured that investment capital would be available only to the select few who could extract new wealth most "efficiently." This resulted in intensified battles between wage earners seeking a greater share of the wealth being produced and owners seeking lower labor costs per unit of production. The latter achieved their goal not only through the innovations in production alluded to above but also through the importation of cheap immigrant labor, the use of convicts and child labor, and routine acts of violence against workers who tried to empower themselves through collective action. The success of financial and industrial elites is evident when one notes the enormous disparities in the distribution of wealth that arose during the Gilded Age. According to the 1890 census, 9 percent of the nation's families controlled 81 percent of the nation's wealth. The 1900 report of the U.S. Industrial Commission concluded that between 60 and 88 percent of the American people could be classified as poor or very poor. New forms of production and labor-saving technological innovations disenfranchised and impoverished traditionally autonomous producers; they also imposed a physical burden on the growing class of unskilled wage earners. It was not uncommon for the fiery furnaces of the steel mills to claim two hundred deaths a year in a single factory. By the 1890s, railroads alone were killing 6,000 to 7,000 and injuring 30,000 to 45,000 people a year; a third of those killed and three quarters of those injured were employees.

In the cases that follow you will see the Court struggling to define "commerce ... among the several states." Basically, the Court's approaches to the problem can be divided into two large categories. One tends to be a formal, definitional approach. For example, the Court distinguished manufacturing and agriculture from "commerce ... among the several states." This approach is typically justified as necessary to protect the role of the states in the federal system. It also tends to frustrate much federal economic regulation. Examples of federal economic regulation that are frustrated by this narrow reading of the Commerce Clause include national regulation of child labor, workplace safety, environmental protection, protection of the right to organize unions, minimum wage and maximum hour laws, and bans on discrimination based on sex, race, age, disability, or religion.

The second approach is empirical and economic. It asks, as an empirical, economic matter, whether economic activity (broadly defined) "affects" interstate commerce or commerce in other states. In the modern world, the answer is almost certainly "yes." This approach, which emerged most clearly during the New Deal, asks whether Congress could rationally believe that a class of activities, if aggregated, has a substantial effect on commerce. This approach defers to Congress and allows for substantial economic regulation if Congress chooses that path.

There are additional theories that appear in the cases. One allows Congress to regulate things that are within the "stream of commerce" or that obstruct its flow. Justices inclined to the formal, definitional, state-sovereignty approach, tend to limit the stream of commerce to transportation, thereby excluding manufacture, agriculture, and the final sale. From another perspective, most economic activity could be seen as part of the stream of commerce. For example, seeds and plows flow to the farmer, and corn flows out, eventually reaching the cereal manufacturer, whose corn flakes then flow to the supermarket. In this vision, the stream of commerce basically follows the empirical, economic approach.

Similarly, the Court has focused on whether the activities to be regulated "affect" interstate commerce. The narrower approach insists on a "direct" effect in order to exclude much economic activity. The broader empirical, economic approach rejects distinctions between "direct" and "indirect" effects. As you read Commerce Clause cases from the 19th Century to the present consider the following recurring themes:

1. Definitions of "commerce among the states."
2. How the power over commerce extends to intra-state activities (e.g, Houston, East & West Texas Ry. Co.) — including the concept of affecting commerce.
3. As to "affecting" commerce, whether the Court takes an economic and empirical approach — looking at the macro-economic effect in fact or whether instead it uses a more formal, verbal approach. To determine the effect, does the Court aggregate similar activities or focus on the individual activity under review in isolation?
4. Contrasting views of the 10th Amendment and views of federalism — the state/nation divide. Is the 10th Amendment an affirmative limit on federal power, similar to the 1st Amendment? Or does the 10th simply restate the rule that the federal government is one of delegated powers and what is not delegated (expressly or by implication) is reserved?
5. The significance of congressional motive. Can motive make an otherwise constitutional statute unconstitutional? Should this occur if Congress, in regulating something that economically affects commerce, does so for moral or other non-commercial purposes? Consider Article I, §9[1], limiting (presumably) the commerce power to ban the importation of slaves. This provision prevented the use of the commerce power to ban importation of slaves before 1808. In 1808 Congress did ban further importation of slaves. Was the ban primarily commercial or moral? If the motive was primarily moral, should the Court have struck down the ban?
6. Deference by the Court to the legislature compared to independent judicial review in which the Court makes independent decisions with little deference to Congress.

Background: The Tangled Lines of Commerce Clause Authority before the New Deal

During the 19th century, there was very little federal regulation of commerce. State regulations confronted the claim that they invaded the exclusive federal power to regulate commerce. In *Gibbons* (1824), Chief Justice Marshall suggested that certain state regulations—inspection laws for example—could be upheld because they acted on the subject before the items in question had entered commerce among the states. Marshall seems to have used this distinction to protect an area in which states had traditionally regulated, provided the regulation did not conflict with a supreme federal law. He implied that federal regulation of commercial subjects simply within the state—for example, licenses for ships operating between two points within the same state—could be upheld as incidental to the federal power over commerce. In the 19th century, the Court often upheld state regulations on the theory that they were not regulations of inter-state commerce.

As the federal government increased its commercial regulations during the late 19th and early 20th centuries, opponents of regulation began to attack the exercise of *federal* power as a violation of the Commerce Clause. The Court sometimes suggested that matters within a single state—manufacturing for example—were beyond federal power over commerce. Instead of protecting a concurrent state power to act so long as its regulations did not contravene supreme federal law, the Court began to assert that certain federal economic regulations affecting activities within a state were beyond the power of Congress because the Court did not consider them to be regulations of interstate commerce. Therefore, they exceeded federal power and invaded an area reserved to the states. At other times, the Court upheld federal regulations of activities within the state on the theory that they had a direct or substantial effect on interstate commerce or on the theory that they were simply a part of "the stream" or current of interstate commerce.

Before the change in the New Deal years, Commerce Clause decisions were not entirely consistent, to say the least. In *United States v. E.C. Knight Co.* (1895), the Court considered the application of the Sherman Anti-trust Act to a near total monopoly of the manufacture of sugar in the United States. The Sherman Act outlawed "every contract, combination ... or conspiracy in restraint of trade" or interstate commerce. It also declared void any attempt, combination, or conspiracy to monopolize. In *E.C. Knight*, the Court held that manufacturing was not commerce and decided that the Sherman Act could not reach the E.C. Knight Company's monopoly. In later cases, the Court found greater power under the Commerce Clause to reach monopoly practices. In *Addyston Pipe & Steel Co. v. United States* (1899), the Court held that the Sherman Act applied to a conspiracy among companies engaged in the manufacture and transportation of pipe.

In *Swift & Co. v. United States* (1905), the Court held the Sherman Act could be applied under the Commerce Clause to price fixing in the Chicago livestock yards. "Commerce among the states is not a technical legal conception, but a practical one, drawn from the course of business." The Court noted cattle were regularly sent from other states to Chicago and, after purchase, from there to other states. This amounted to "a current of commerce among the states, and the purchase of cattle is a part and incident of such commerce."

In *Southern R. Co. v. United States* (1911), the Court held that an act of Congress regulating train safety could apply to purely intrastate trains. The rationale was that both interstate and intrastate trains used the same tracks and that accidents involving intrastate trains would impede interstate commerce.

Houston, East and West Texas Rw. Co. v. United States (The Shreveport Rate Case) (1914) held Congress can authorize the Interstate Commerce Commission to require that intrastate rates be increased so as to be consistent with interstate rates.

Although the Court in *Hammer v. Dagenhart* (1918) invoked the rights of the states, the Court was not especially protective of the right of states to regulate economic matters either. For example, the Court sometimes found state minimum wage, maximum hour, and laws forbidding employers from banning labor union membership as a condition of employment to violate the Due Process Clause of the 14th Amendment. *Lochner v. New York* (1905) found a law that limited bakers to a sixty-hour work week to be a violation of the "liberty of contract" the majority found in the Due Process Clause. The Court found evidence of dangers to the health of bakers (which Justice Harlan in dissent found substantial) not to be sufficient to uphold the statute. In contrast, in *Holden v. Hardy* (1898), it had upheld an eight-hour day for miners because of the very substantial safety issues tied to tired or overworked miners.

The cases that follow in this section come from the era of the Court's interpretation of the Commerce Clause that runs from about 1890 until 1937. Even during this period, however, the Court was not entirely consistent. Sometimes it allowed a broader and sometimes a narrower scope to the power of Congress over commerce. During much of this period the narrower interpretation tended to predominate. What follows is an attempt to generalize about the Court's narrower interpretation.

First, the Court tended to limit commerce to the exchange of goods rather than reading the word as encompassing all gainful activity. Most importantly, the Court made a distinction throughout this period between commerce and what it called "manufacturing," which took place wholly within a state, and was therefore not part of "commerce." Second, it tended to interpret commerce "among the states" to mean commerce that crossed state lines rather than commerce in the midst of the states. Third, it interpreted the 10th Amendment to establish some affirmative limits on congressional power. Finally, the Court recognized that some activity that existed within one state had such a direct and substantial effect on commerce that crossed state lines so as to be within congressional power. Other substantial commerce within a state was treated as having only an indirect effect. The line between direct and indirect effects was often difficult to understand.

In its narrower interpretation of congressional power, the Court tended to embrace a formal analysis based on definitional tests for the purpose of determining whether the effect of an intrastate activity on commerce was substantial. The Court would speak of direct versus indirect effects, or manufacturing versus commerce — rather than engaging in an empirical, economic analysis of the actual effect of the activity in the real world. In determining whether an effect was direct and substantial, the Court would not aggregate all similar activity for purposes of judging the effect. There were probably several reasons for the Court's use of formal, definitional tests. During this era the Court was hostile to much — but by no means all — economic regulation. In addition, the Court insisted it was protecting federalism — the role of the states in a federal system.

At other times, however, the Court embraced a broader role for Congress. In these cases the Court took a broader view of what affected "interstate commerce." For example, the Interstate Commerce Commission could regulate intrastate railroad rates as part of a larger plan to regulate interstate rates. Congress could require safety devices on intrastate trains and regulate certain aspects of labor management relations because of the influence these would have on interstate rail traffic.

While the Court often adhered to a narrow understanding of federal (and often state) power over economic relations during the era from 1890 to 1937, the nation was experiencing profound economic change. Populists, Progressives, Labor, and others insisted that these changes made the Court's approach unrealistic.

In the second half of the 19th century, the nation was transformed from a land of more independent farmers and artisans to one increasingly characterized by giant corporations and workers. In this new economic environment, people began to challenge the presumption increasingly indulged in by the Court that state intervention in economic relations between employers and employees was illegitimate and could be justified only by showing some strong state interest other than protection of the weaker party to the bargain.

In his 1912 campaign, Theodore Roosevelt explained his objection to laissez faire economics and to the anti-regulatory effect of court decisions:

> The only way in which our people can increase their power over the big corporation that does wrong, the only way in which they can protect the working man in his conditions of work and life, the only way in which the people can prevent children working in industry or secure women an eight-hour day in industry, or secure compensation for men killed or crippled in industry, is by extending, instead of limiting, the powers of government.... There was once a time in history when the limitation of governmental power meant increasing liberty for the people. In the present day the limitation of governmental power, of governmental action, means the enslavement of the people by the great corporations who can only be held in check through the extension of governmental power.

Theodore Roosevelt, Address at San Francisco, Sept. 14, 1912 in W.H. Harbaugh, ed., *The Writings of Theodore Roosevelt*, 288, 290–91 (1967).

Roosevelt continued:

> [A] simple and poor society can exist as a democracy on a basis of sheer individualism. But a rich and complex industrial society cannot so exist; for some individuals, and especially those artificial individuals called corporations, become so very big that the ordinary individual is utterly dwarfed beside them, and cannot deal with them on terms of equality.

T. Roosevelt, *An Autobiography*, 257 (1975).

Champion v. Ames (The Lottery Case): Background

In *Champion v. Ames (The Lottery Case)* (1903), Congress had criminalized the transport of lottery tickets across state lines, even between states that allowed gambling. While all agreed that Congress could forbid the use of the mails to send lottery tickets pursuant to its authority over the postal service, Congress here relied on the Commerce Clause to justify a ban on *any* means of transportation. The case was seen as one directly raising the issue of whether or not the federal government could exercise generalized police powers, since the statute was openly directed at the immorality of gambling. After three oral arguments, the Court, in a 5–4 decision, held that the tickets were articles of commerce, that the power to regulate included the power to prohibit entirely, and that the 10th Amendment raised no problems with the federal government acting to accomplish a police power objective.

Champion v. Ames (The Lottery Case)
188 U.S. 321 (1903)

[Majority: Harlan, White, Holmes, Brown, McKenna. Dissenting: Fuller (C.J.), Brewer, Shiras, Peckham.]

Mr. Justice Harlan delivered the opinion of the court.

... It is to be remarked that the Constitution does not define what is to be deemed a legitimate regulation of interstate commerce. In *Gibbons v. Ogden* (1824) it was said that the power to regulate such commerce is the power to prescribe the rule by which it is to be governed. But this general observation leaves it to be determined, when the question comes before the court, whether Congress, in prescribing a particular rule, has exceeded its power under the Constitution. While our government must be acknowledged by all to be one of enumerated powers [*McCulloch v. Maryland* (1819)], the Constitution does not attempt to set forth all the means by which such powers may be carried into execution. It leaves to Congress a large discretion as to the means that may be employed in executing a given power. The sound construction of the Constitution, this court has said, "must allow to the national legislature that discretion, with respect to the means by which the powers it confers are to be carried into execution, which will enable that body to perform the high duties assigned to it, in the manner most beneficial to the people. Let the end be legitimate, let it be within the scope of the Constitution, and all means which are appropriate, which are plainly adapted to that end, which are not prohibited, but consist with the letter and spirit of the Constitution, are constitutional."

We have said that the carrying from state to state of lottery tickets constitutes interstate commerce, and that the regulation of such commerce is within the power of Congress under the Constitution. Are we prepared to say that a provision which is, in effect, a prohibition of the carriage of such articles from state to state is not a fit or appropriate mode for the regulation of that particular kind of commerce? If lottery traffic, carried on through interstate commerce, is a matter of which Congress may take cognizance and over which its power may be exerted, can it be possible that it must tolerate the traffic, and simply regulate the manner in which it may be carried on? Or may not Congress, for the protection of the people of all the states, and under the power to regulate interstate commerce, devise such means, within the scope of the Constitution, and not prohibited by it, as will drive that traffic out of commerce among the states?

In determining whether regulation may not under some circumstances properly take the form or have the effect of prohibition, the nature of the interstate traffic which it was sought by the act of May 2d, 1895, to suppress cannot be overlooked. When enacting that statute Congress no doubt shared the views upon the subject of lotteries heretofore expressed by this court. In *Phalen v. Virginia* (1850), after observing that the suppression of nuisances injurious to public health or morality is among the most important duties of government, this court said: "Experience has shown that the common forms of gambling are comparatively innocuous when placed in contrast with the widespread pestilence of lotteries. The former are confined to a few persons and places, but the latter infests the whole community; it enters every dwelling; it reaches every class; it preys upon the hard earnings of the poor; it plunders the ignorant and simple." In other cases we have adjudged that authority given by legislative enactment to carry on a lottery, although based upon a consideration in money, was not protected by the contract clause of the Constitution; this, for the reason that no state may bargain away its power to protect the public morals, nor excuse its failure to perform a public duty by saying that it had agreed, by legislative enactment, not to do so.

If a state, when considering legislation for the suppression of lotteries within its own limits, may properly take into view the evils that inhere in the raising of money, in that mode, why may not Congress, invested with the power to regulate commerce among the several states, provide that such commerce shall not be polluted by the carrying of lottery tickets from one state to another? In this connection it must not be forgotten that the power of Congress to regulate commerce among the states is plenary, is complete in itself, and is subject to no limitations except such as may be found in the Constitution. What provision in that instrument can be regarded as limiting the exercise of the power granted? What clause can be cited which, in any degree, countenances the suggestion that one may, of right, carry or cause to be carried from one state to another that which will harm the public morals? We cannot think of any clause of that instrument that could possibly be invoked by those who assert their right to send lottery tickets from state to state except the one providing that no person shall be deprived of his liberty without due process of law. We have said that the liberty protected by the Constitution embraces the right to be free in the enjoyment of one's faculties; "to be free to use them in all lawful ways; to live and work where he will; to earn his livelihood by any lawful calling; to pursue any livelihood or avocation, and for that purpose to enter into all contracts which may be proper." *Allgeyer v. Louisiana* (1897). But surely it will not be said to be a part of anyone's liberty, as recognized by the supreme law of the land, that he shall be allowed to introduce into commerce among the states an element that will be confessedly injurious to the public morals.

If it be said that the act of 1894 is inconsistent with the 10th Amendment, reserving to the states respectively, or to the people, the powers not delegated to the United States, the answer is that the power to regulate commerce among the states has been expressly delegated to Congress....

It is said, however, that if, in order to suppress lotteries carried on through interstate commerce, Congress may exclude lottery tickets from such commerce, that principle leads necessarily to the conclusion that Congress may arbitrarily exclude from commerce among the states any article, commodity, or thing, of whatever kind or nature, or however useful or valuable, which it may choose, no matter with what motive, to declare shall not be carried from one state to another. It will be time enough to consider the constitutionality of such legislation when we must do so. The present case does not require the court to declare the full extent of the power that Congress may exercise in the regulation of commerce among the states. We may, however, repeat, in this connection, what the court has heretofore said, that the power of Congress to regulate commerce among the states, although plenary, cannot be deemed arbitrary, since it is subject to such limitations or restrictions as are prescribed by the Constitution. This power, therefore, may not be exercised so as to infringe rights secured or protected by that instrument. It would not be difficult to imagine legislation that would be justly liable to such an objection as that stated, and be hostile to the objects for the accomplishment of which Congress was invested with the general power to regulate commerce among the several states. But, as often said, the possible abuse of a power is not an argument against its existence. There is probably no governmental power that may not be exerted to the injury of the public. If what is done by Congress is manifestly in excess of the powers granted to it, then upon the courts will rest the duty of adjudging that its action is neither legal nor binding upon the people. But if what Congress does is within the limits of its power, and is simply unwise or injurious, the remedy is that suggested by Chief Justice Marshall in *Gibbons v. Ogden*, when he said: "The wisdom and the discretion of Congress, their identity with the people, and the influence which their constituents possess at elections, are, in this, as in many other instances, as that, for example, of declaring war, the sole restraints on which they have relied, to secure them from its abuse. They are the restraints on which the people must often rely solely, in all representative governments." ...

Mr. Chief Justice Fuller, with whom concur Mr. Justice Brewer, Mr. Justice Shiras, and Mr. Justice Peckham, dissenting:

... The power of the state to impose restraints and burdens on persons and property in conservation and promotion of the public health, good order, and prosperity is a power originally and always belonging to the states, not surrendered by them to the general government, nor directly restrained by the Constitution of the United States, and essentially exclusive, and the suppression of lotteries as a harmful business falls within this power, commonly called, of police.

It is urged, however, that because Congress is empowered to regulate commerce between the several states, it, therefore, may suppress lotteries by prohibiting the carriage of lottery matter. Congress may, indeed, make all laws necessary and proper for carrying the powers granted to it into execution, and doubtless an act prohibiting the carriage of lottery matter would be necessary and proper to the execution of a power to suppress lotteries; but that power belongs to the states and not to Congress. To hold that Congress has general police power would be to hold that it may accomplish objects not entrusted to the general government, and to defeat the operation of the 10th Amendment, declaring that "the powers not delegated to the United States by the Constitution, nor prohibited by it to the states, are reserved to the states respectively, or to the people." ...

It will not do to say—a suggestion which has heretofore been made in this case—that state laws have been found to be ineffective for the suppression of lotteries, and therefore Congress should interfere. The scope of the Commerce Clause of the Constitution cannot be enlarged because of present views of public interest.

In countries whose fundamental law is flexible it may be that the homely maxim, "to ease the shoe where it pinches." may be applied, but under the Constitution of the United States it cannot be availed of to justify action by Congress or by the courts.

The Constitution gives no countenance to the theory that Congress is vested with the full powers of the British Parliament, and that, although subject to constitutional limitations, it is the sole judge of their extent and application; and the decisions of this court from the beginning have been to the contrary.

"To what purpose are powers limited, and to what purpose is that limitation committed to writing, if these limits may, at any time, be passed by those intended to be restrained?" asked Marshall, in *Marbury v. Madison* (1803).

"Should Congress," said the same great magistrate in *McCulloch v. Maryland*, "under the pretext of executing its powers, pass laws for the accomplishment of objects not entrusted to the government, it would become the painful duty of this tribunal, should a case requiring such a decision come before it, to say that such an act was not the law of the land."

And so Chief Justice Taney, referring to the extent and limits of the powers of Congress: "As the Constitution itself does not draw the line, the question is necessarily one for judicial decision, and depending altogether upon the words of the Constitution." *License Cases* (1847).

* * *

The Court later cited *Champion* as justification for upholding the federal Pure Food and Drug Act [*Hipolite Egg Co. v. U.S.* (1911)] and the Mann Act (making it a federal crime to transport women across state lines for immoral purposes) [*Hoke v. U.S.* (1913)].

Houston, East & West Texas Railway Company v. United States
234 U.S. 342 (1914)

[Majority: Hughes, White (C.J.), Van Devanter, Holmes, Lamar, Day, and McKenna. Dissenting: Lurton and Pitney.]

Mr. Justice Hughes delivered the opinion of the court:

These suits were brought in the commerce court by the Houston, East & West Texas Railway Company and the Houston & Shreveport Railroad Company, and by the Texas & Pacific Railway Company, respectively, to set aside an order of the Interstate Commerce Commission, dated March 11, 1912, upon the ground that it exceeded the Commission's authority.... [The order required raising intrastate rates set by the Texas Railroad Commission to match comparable interstate rates set by the Interstate Commerce Commission].

First. It is unnecessary to repeat what has frequently been said by this court with respect to the complete and paramount character of the power confided to Congress to regulate commerce among the several states. It is of the essence of this power that, where it exists, it dominates. Interstate trade was not left to be destroyed or impeded by the rivalries of local government. The purpose was to make impossible the recurrence of the evils which had overwhelmed the Confederation, and to provide the necessary basis of national unity by insuring "uniformity of regulation against conflicting and discriminating state legislation." By virtue of the comprehensive terms of the grant, the authority of Congress is at all times adequate to meet the varying exigencies that arise, and to protect the national interest by securing the freedom of interstate commercial intercourse from local control. *Gibbons v. Ogden* (1824).

Congress is empowered to regulate—that is, to provide the law for the government of interstate commerce; to enact "all appropriate legislation" for its "protection and advancement," to adopt measures "to promote its growth and insure its safety," "to foster, protect, control, and restrain." Its authority, extending to these interstate carriers as instruments of interstate commerce, necessarily embraces the right to control their operations in all matters having such a close and substantial relation to interstate traffic that the control is essential or appropriate to the security of that traffic, to the efficiency of the interstate service, and to the maintenance of conditions under which interstate commerce may be conducted upon fair terms and without molestation or hindrance.... Wherever the interstate and intrastate transactions of carriers are so related that the government of the one involves the control of the other, it is Congress, and not the state, that is entitled to prescribe the final and dominant rule, for otherwise Congress would be denied the exercise of its constitutional authority, and the state, and not the nation, would be supreme within the national field....

[I]n *Southern R. Co. v. United States* (1911), the question was presented whether the amendment to the safety appliance act [of 1903] was within the power of Congress in view of the fact that the statute was not confined to vehicles that were used in interstate traffic, but also embraced those used in intrastate traffic. The court answered affirmatively, because there was such a close relation between the two classes of traffic moving over the same railroad as to make it certain that the safety of the interstate traffic, and of those employed in its movement, would be promoted in a real and substantial sense by applying the requirements of the act to both classes of vehicles. So, in the *Second Employers' Liability Cases* (1912), it was insisted that while Congress had the authority to regulate the liability of a carrier for injuries sustained by one employee through the negligence of another, where all were engaged in interstate commerce, that power did not embrace instances where the negligent employee was engaged in intrastate commerce. The court said that this was a mistaken theory, as the causal negligence, when operating injuriously upon an employee engaged in interstate commerce, had the same effect with respect to that commerce as if the negligent employee were also engaged therein. The decision in *Employers' Liability Cases* (1908), is not opposed, for the statute there in question sought to regulate the liability of interstate carriers for injuries to any employee even though his employment had no connection whatever with interstate commerce.

While these decisions sustaining the Federal power relate to measures adopted in the interest of the safety of persons and property, they illustrate the principle that Congress, in the exercise of its paramount power, may prevent the common instrumentalities of interstate and intrastate commercial intercourse from being used in their intrastate operations to the injury of interstate commerce. This is not to say that Congress possesses the authority to regulate the internal commerce of a state, as such, but that it does possess the power to foster and protect interstate commerce, and to take all measures necessary or appropriate to that end, although intrastate transactions of interstate carriers may thereby be controlled.

This principle is applicable here. We find no reason to doubt that Congress is entitled to keep the highways of interstate communication open to interstate traffic upon fair and equal terms. That an unjust discrimination in the rates of a common carrier, by which one person or locality is unduly favored as against another under substantially similar conditions of traffic, constitutes an evil, is undeniable; and where this evil consists in the action of an interstate carrier in unreasonably discriminating against interstate traffic over its line, the authority of Congress to prevent it is equally clear. It is immaterial, so far as the protecting power of Congress is concerned, that the discrimination arises from intrastate rates as compared with interstate rates. The use of the instrument of interstate commerce in a discriminatory manner so as to inflict injury upon that commerce, or some part thereof, furnishes abundant ground for Federal intervention. Nor can the attempted exercise of state authority alter the matter, where Congress has acted, for a state may not authorize the carrier to do that which Congress is entitled to forbid and has forbidden.

It is to be noted—as the government has well said in its argument in support of the Commission's order—that the power to deal with the relation between the two kinds of rates, as a relation, lies exclusively with Congress. It is manifest that the state cannot fix the relation of the carrier's interstate and intrastate charges without directly interfering with the former, unless it simply follows the standard set by Federal authority.

The decree of the Commerce Court is affirmed in each case. Lurton and Pitney, JJ., dissent.

Hammer v. Dagenhart
247 U.S. 251 (1918)

[Majority: Day, White (C.J.), Van Devanter, McReynolds, Pitney. Dissenting: Holmes, McKenna, Brandeis, Clarke.]

Mr. Justice Day delivered the opinion of the Court.

A bill was filed in the United States District Court for the Western District of North Carolina by a father in his own behalf and as next friend of his two minor sons, one under the age of fourteen years and the other between the ages of fourteen and sixteen years, employees in a cotton mill at Charlotte, North Carolina, to enjoin the enforcement of the [September 1, 1916] act of Congress intended to prevent interstate commerce in the products of child labor.

The District Court held the act unconstitutional and entered a decree enjoining its enforcement. This appeal brings the case here....

The [plaintiff argues that the statute] is not a regulation of interstate and foreign commerce [and that it] contravenes the 10th Amendment to the Constitution....

The controlling question for decision is: Is it within the authority of Congress in regulating commerce among the states to prohibit the transportation in interstate commerce of manufactured goods, the product of a factory in which, within thirty days prior to their removal therefrom, children under the age of fourteen have been employed or permitted to work, or children between the ages of fourteen and sixteen years have been employed or permitted to work more than eight hours in any day, or more than six days in any week, or after the hour of 7 o'clock p.m., or before the hour of 6 o'clock a.m.?

The power essential to the passage of this act, the government contends, is found in the Commerce Clause of the Constitution which authorizes Congress to regulate commerce with foreign nations and among the states.

In *Gibbons v. Ogden* (1824), Chief Justice Marshall, speaking for this court, and defining the extent and nature of the commerce power, said, "It is the power to regulate; that is, to prescribe the rule by which commerce is to be governed." In other words, the power is one to control the means by which commerce is carried on, which is directly the contrary of the assumed right to forbid commerce from moving and thus destroying it as to particular commodities. But it is insisted that adjudged cases in this court establish the doctrine that the power to regulate given to Congress incidentally includes the authority to prohibit the movement of ordinary commodities and therefore that the subject is not open for discussion. The cases demonstrate the contrary. They rest upon the character of the particular subjects dealt with and the fact that the scope of governmental authority, state or national, possessed over them is such that the authority to prohibit is as to them but the exertion of the power to regulate.

The first of these cases is *Champion v. Ames* (1903), the so-called *Lottery Case*, in which it was held that Congress might pass a law having the effect to keep the channels of commerce free from use in the transportation of tickets used in the promotion of lottery schemes. In *Hipolite Egg Co. v. United States* (1911), this court sustained the power of Congress to pass the [June 30, 1906] Pure Food and Drug Act which prohibited the introduction into the states by means of interstate commerce of impure foods and drugs. In *Hoke v. United States* (1913), this court sustained the constitutionality of the so-called [June 25, 1910] "White Slave Traffic Act," whereby the transportation of a woman in interstate commerce for the purpose of prostitution was forbidden. In that case we said, having reference to the authority of Congress, under the regulatory power, to protect the channels of interstate commerce:

> If the facility of interstate transportation can be taken away from the demoralization of lotteries, the debasement of obscene literature, the contagion of diseased cattle or persons, the impurity of food and drugs, the like facility can be taken away from the systematic enticement to, and the enslavement in prostitution and debauchery of women, and, more insistently, of girls.

In *Caminetti v. United States* (1917), we held that Congress might prohibit the transportation of women in interstate commerce for the purposes of debauchery and kindred purposes. In *Clark Distilling Co. v. Western Maryland Railway Co.* (1917), the power of Congress over the transportation of intoxicating liquors was sustained. In the course of the opinion it was said:

> The power conferred is to regulate, and the very terms of the grant would seem to repel the contention that only prohibition of movement in interstate commerce was embraced. And the cogency of this is manifest, since if the doctrine were applied to those manifold and important subjects of interstate commerce as to which Congress from the beginning has regulated, not prohibited, the existence of government under the Constitution would be no longer possible.

And concluding the discussion which sustained the authority of the Government to prohibit the transportation of liquor in interstate commerce, the court said:

> ... The exceptional nature of the subject here regulated is the basis upon which the exceptional power exerted must rest and affords no ground for any fear that such power may be constitutionally extended to things which it may not, consistently with the guaranties of the Constitution embrace.

In each of these instances the use of interstate transportation was necessary to the accomplishment of harmful results. In other words, although the power over interstate transportation was to regulate, that could only be accomplished by prohibiting the use of the facilities of interstate commerce to effect the evil intended.

This element is wanting in the present case. The thing intended to be accomplished by this statute is the denial of the facilities of interstate commerce to those manufacturers in the states who employ children within the prohibited ages. The act in its effect does not regulate transportation among the states, but aims to standardize the ages at which children may be employed in mining and manufacturing within the states. The goods shipped are of themselves harmless. The act permits them to be freely shipped after thirty days from the time of their removal from the factory. When offered for shipment, and before transportation begins, the labor of their production is over, and the mere fact that they were intended for interstate commerce transportation does not make their production subject to federal control under the commerce power.

Commerce "consists of intercourse and traffic ... and includes the transportation of persons and property, as well as the purchase, sale and exchange of commodities." The making of goods and the mining of coal are not commerce, nor does the fact that these things are to be afterwards shipped, or used in interstate commerce, make their production a part thereof....

It is further contended that the authority of Congress may be exerted to control interstate commerce in the shipment of childmade goods because of the effect of the circulation of such goods in other states where the evil of this class of labor has been recognized by local legislation, and the right to thus employ child labor has been more rigorously re-

strained than in the state of production. In other words, that the unfair competition, thus engendered, may be controlled by closing the channels of interstate commerce to manufacturers in those states where the local laws do not meet what Congress deems to be the more just standard of other states.

There is no power vested in Congress to require the states to exercise their police power so as to prevent possible unfair competition. Many causes may co-operate to give one state, by reason of local laws or conditions, an economic advantage over others. The Commerce Clause was not intended to give to Congress a general authority to equalize such conditions....

The grant of power of Congress over the subject of interstate commerce was to enable it to regulate such commerce, and not to give it authority to control the states in their exercise of the police power over local trade and manufacture.

The grant of authority over a purely federal matter was not intended to destroy the local power always existing and carefully reserved to the states in the 10th Amendment to the Constitution....

In interpreting the Constitution it must never be forgotten that the nation is made up of states to which are entrusted the powers of local government. And to them and to the people the powers not expressly delegated to the national government are reserved. The power of the states to regulate their purely internal affairs by such laws as seem wise to the local authority is inherent and has never been surrendered to the general government. To sustain this statute would not be in our judgment a recognition of the lawful exertion of congressional authority over interstate commerce, but would sanction an invasion by the federal power of the control of a matter purely local in its character, and over which no authority has been delegated to Congress in conferring the power to regulate commerce among the states....

In our view the necessary effect of this act is, by means of a prohibition against the movement in interstate commerce of ordinary commercial commodities to regulate the hours of labor of children in factories and mines within the states, a purely state authority. Thus the act in a two-fold sense is repugnant to the Constitution. It not only transcends the authority delegated to Congress over commerce but also exerts a power as to a purely local matter to which the federal authority does not extend. The far reaching result of upholding the act cannot be more plainly indicated than by pointing out that if Congress can thus regulate matters entrusted to local authority by prohibition of the movement of commodities in interstate commerce, all freedom of commerce will be at an end, and the power of the states over local matters may be eliminated, and thus our system of government be practically destroyed.

For these reasons we hold that this law exceeds the constitutional authority of Congress. It follows that the decree of the District Court must be Affirmed.

Mr. Justice Holmes, dissenting.

The single question in this case is whether Congress has power to prohibit the shipment in interstate or foreign commerce of any product of a cotton mill situated in the United States, in which within thirty days before the removal of the product children under fourteen have been employed, or children between fourteen and sixteen have been employed more than eight hours in a day, or more than six days in any week, or between seven in the evening and six in the morning. The objection urged against the power is that the States have exclusive control over their methods of production and that Congress cannot meddle with them, and taking the proposition in the sense of direct intermeddling I agree to it and suppose that no one denies it. But if an act is within the powers specifically conferred upon Congress, it seems to me that it is not made any less constitutional because of the indirect effects that it may have, however obvious it may be that it will have those effects, and that we are not at liberty upon such grounds to hold it void.

The first step in my argument is to make plain what no one is likely to dispute—that the statute in question is within the power expressly given to Congress if considered only as to its immediate effects and that if invalid it is so only upon some collateral ground. The statute confines itself to prohibiting the carriage of certain goods in interstate or foreign commerce. Congress is given power to regulate such commerce in unqualified terms. It would not be argued today that the power to regulate does not include the power to prohibit. Regulation means the prohibition of something, and when interstate commerce is the matter to be regulated I cannot doubt that the regulation may prohibit any part of such commerce that Congress sees fit to forbid. At all events it is established by the *Lottery Case* and others that have followed it that a law is not beyond the regulative power of Congress merely because it prohibits certain transportation out and out. *Champion v. Ames* (1903). So I repeat that this statute in its immediate operation is clearly within the Congress's constitutional power.

The question then is narrowed to whether the exercise of its otherwise constitutional power by Congress can be pronounced unconstitutional because of its possible reaction upon the conduct of the States in a matter upon which I have admitted that they are free from direct control. I should have thought that that matter had been disposed of so fully as to leave no room for doubt. I should have thought that the most conspicuous decisions of this Court had made it clear that the power to regulate commerce and other constitutional powers could not be cut down or qualified by the fact that it might interfere with the carrying out of the domestic policy of any State.

The manufacture of oleomargarine is as much a matter of State regulation as the manufacture of cotton cloth. Congress levied a tax upon the compound when colored so as to resemble butter that was so great as obviously to prohibit the manufacture and sale. [We have] excluded any inquiry into the purpose of an act which apart from that purpose was within the power of Congress. Fifty years ago a tax on state banks, the obvious purpose and actual effect of which was to drive them, or at least their circulation, out of existence, was sustained, although the result was one that Congress had no constitutional power to require. The Court made short work of the argument as to the purpose of the Act. "The Judicial cannot prescribe to the Legislative Departments of the Government limitations upon the exercise of its acknowledged powers." *Veazie Bank v. Fenno* (1869). So it well might have been argued that the corporation tax was intended under the guise of a revenue measure to secure a control not otherwise belonging to Congress, but the tax was sustained....

The Pure Food and Drug Act which was sustained in *Hipolite Egg Co. v. United States* (1911), with the intimation that "no trade can be carried on between the States to which it [the power of Congress to regulate commerce] does not extend," applies not merely to articles that the changing opinions of the time condemn as intrinsically harmful but to others innocent in themselves, simply on the ground that the order for them was induced by a preliminary fraud. It does not matter whether the supposed evil precedes or follows the transportation. It is enough that in the opinion of Congress the transportation encourages the evil. I may add that in the cases on the so-called White Slave Act it was established that the means adopted by Congress as convenient to the exercise of its power might have the character of police regulations. *Hoke v. United States* (1913); *Caminetti v. United States* (1917).

The notion that prohibition is any less prohibition when applied to things now thought evil I do not understand. But if there is any matter upon which civilized countries have agreed—far more unanimously than they have with regard to intoxicants and some other matters over which this country is now emotionally aroused—it is the evil of premature and excessive child labor. I should have thought that if we were to introduce our own moral conceptions, where in my opinion they do not belong, this was preeminently a case for upholding the exercise of all its powers by the United States.

But I had thought that the propriety of the exercise of a power admitted to exist in some cases was for the consideration of Congress alone and that this Court always had disavowed the right to intrude its judgment upon questions of policy or morals. It is not for this Court to pronounce when prohibition is necessary to regulation if it ever may be necessary—to say that it is permissible as against strong drink but not as against the product of ruined lives.

The Act does not meddle with anything belonging to the States. They may regulate their internal affairs and their domestic commerce as they like. But when they seek to send their products across the State line they are no longer within their rights....

Mr. Justice McKenna, Mr. Justice Brandeis, and Mr. Justice Clarke concur in this opinion.

* * *

Why did the Court strike down congressional regulation in *Hammer v. Dagenhart*? Was the decision consistent with *Champion v. Ames*?

E. Populist and Progressive Discontent

The Income Tax of 1894: The *Pollock* Decisions and the Political Response

During the early 1890s, Populists urged a graduated income tax to meet the federal budget deficit. Congress imposed such an income tax in 1894. Although the tax provided for only a two percent tax rate on incomes above $4,000, it provoked a vituperous response from opponents, who dismissed it as "class legislation" and "war upon honest industry." U.S. Senator David Hill of New York described the tax as the work of "anarchists, communists, and socialists." John Forrest Dillon, a prominent Wall Street lawyer and former federal judge, characterized the tax as "class legislation of the most pronounced and vicious type" and argued that it was "violative of the constitutional rights of the property owner, subversive of the existing social policy, and essentially revolutionary." Elmer Ellis, *Public Opinion and the Income Tax, 1860–1900*, 27 Miss. Valley Hist. Rev. 225, 236–38 (1940); Arnold M. Paul, *Conservative Crisis and the Rule of Law: Attitudes of Bar and Bench, 1887–1895*, 164 (1960).

Efforts were immediately launched to challenge the constitutionality of the new income tax on the grounds that it was a "direct tax" required under Article I of the Constitution to be apportioned among the states based on population. Within months, a legal challenge to the tax supported by several of the nation's leading attorneys, made its way to the Supreme Court. Joseph Choate, one of the lawyers who brought the litigation challenging the tax, claimed in oral argument before the Court that the tax was "communistic in its purposes and tendencies, and is defended here upon principles as communistic, socialistic ... as ever have been addressed to any political assembly in the world."

The income tax appeared to be a constitutional exercise of congressional power. In fact, the Supreme Court had previously — and without dissent — sustained the use of an income tax promulgated during the Civil War against an argument that it was a direct tax. *Springer v. United States* (1881). But in the two *Pollock* decisions of the spring of 1895 — the first in which the Court considered, among other issues, the constitutionality of taxing income derived from real property and the second in which the Court considered the constitutionality of taxing income derived from personal property — the Court struck down the graduated income tax statute as an unconstitutional direct tax. *Pollock v. Farmers' Loan & Trust Co.* (1895) (holding unconstitutional tax on income from real estate); 158 U.S. 601 (1895) (holding unconstitutional tax on income from personal property). The conservative majority on the Court viewed the income tax as an attack on propertied interests. In his concurrence, Justice Stephen Field wrote ominously of the tax: "The present assault upon capital is but the beginning. It will be but the stepping-stone to others, larger and more sweeping, till our political contests become a war of the poor against the rich; a war constantly growing in intensity and bitterness."

The *Pollock* dissenters were vitriolic in their characterization of the majority's actions. Justice Howell Jackson labeled the Court's second *Pollock* decision "the most disastrous blow ever struck at the constitutional power of Congress." Justice Henry Brown characterized the decision as "nothing less than the surrender of the taxing power to the moneyed class," "fraught with immeasurable danger to the future of the country," and a decision that "approaches the proportions of a national calamity." Justice John Marshall Harlan, pounding the bench with his fist while delivering his dissent, called the decision "a disaster to the country," and predicted in a letter to his sons a few weeks later that the decision "will become as hateful with the American people as the *Dred Scott* case was when it was decided." David G. Farrelly, *Harlan's Dissent in the* Pollock *Case*, 24 So. Cal. L. Rev. 175, 180 (1951).

The *Pollock* decisions (along with *United States v. E.C. Knight Co.* (1895), in which the Court narrowly construed the Sherman Act to uphold the lawfulness of the Sugar Trust, and *In re Debs* (1895), in which the Court upheld the use of a federal injunction against labor leader Eugene Debs) were clearly among the most controversial decisions of the late 19th century, far more controversial than *Plessy v. Ferguson* (1896) the following term. The *Pollock* decisions provoked a strong "anti-Court" sentiment across the nation. As Alan Westin has noted, the *Pollock* decisions quickly became "a topic of heated conversation in every bank, barbershop, and barroom in the nation." Alan Furman Westin, *The Supreme Court, The Populist Movement and the Campaign of 1896* 15 J. Politics 3, 22 (1953). William Howard Taft later commented that "[n]othing has ever injured the prestige of the Supreme Court more" than the *Pollock* decisions. Quoted in Bruce Ackerman, *Taxation and the Constitution*, 99 Colum. L. Rev. 1, 4 (1999). For only the third time in the Court's history, popular reaction led to a constitutional amendment reversing a Court decision. As Michael Kammen has noted, after 1895 "the Court ceased to be sacred" in the minds of many Americans: "[o]nly in the wake of *Dred Scott* had politicization of the Court been more severe, and polarization over constitutional issues more sharp." Michael Kammen, *A Machine That Would Go of Itself: The Constitution in American Culture* 191–92 (1986).

During the election of 1896, both Democrats and Populists campaigned against the Court, evoking memories of the 1860 election in which the Court's *Dred Scott* decision had played an important role. The 1896 Democratic Party platform demanded a curb on the Court's power to review the constitutionality of congressional legislation. Sylvester Pennoyer, a former Democratic-Populist governor of Oregon, attacked the *Pollock* decisions in a series of articles in the *American Law Review* in 1896, calling for "the impeachment of the nullifying judges of the Supreme Court." Sylvester Pennoyer, *A Reply to The Foregoing*, 29 Amer. L. Rev. 856, 863 (1896). In fact, the *Pollock* decisions helped fuel a spirited debate among legal scholars, lawyers, and politicians concerning the merits of judicial review that would last well into the 20th century.

In response to the Court's decisions striking down the income tax, in 1913 the states ratified the 16th Amendment authorizing Congress to tax incomes.

Progressives Respond to "Judicial Activism"

During the late 19th and early 20th centuries, Congress passed laws regulating conditions of labor, claiming power to do so under the Commerce Clause. The Court struck down a number of these laws, emphasizing state sovereignty and lack of federal power. Yet, when states passed statutes regulating employment, the Court struck down a number of these as well—as violating a "liberty of contract" it discovered in the Due Process Clause of the 14th Amendment. For example, in *Lochner v. New York* (1905), the Court struck down a New York law that limited bakery employees to working ten hours a day and sixty hours a week. New York sought to justify the law as protecting the health of bakery workers. The state relied on medical texts that said bakers' working conditions— long hours standing in a hot, flour-dust-filled environment—produced occupational disease and a shortened life expectancy for bakers. The Court was unimpressed. The majority decided that the danger to health was not sufficient to justify the act. It warned that if such dangers to health could justify legislation regulating employment there would be no limit to government's "meddlesome" interference with liberty. The Court also rejected as illegitimate any justification based on inequality of bargaining power between employers and employees. Some state supreme courts reached similar results under state constitutions.

A number of governmental regulations of working conditions did survive constitutional scrutiny. In 1908, for example, the Court sustained a state regulation of hours worked by women because of the perceived danger to their health. *Muller v. Oregon* (1908). As a general matter, laws regulating the working conditions of men were more likely to be struck down. A state (but not federal) regulation of child labor survived a Supreme Court challenge. *Sturges & Burn Mfg. Co. v. Beauchamp* (1913). During the Progressive era the record of the Court was mixed, but protective labor regulation had a somewhat better chance of success. In the years from 1920 to 1933, the Court was more active in striking down protective labor regulations—for women as well as men. See generally, Melvin I. Urofsky, *Myth and Reality: The Supreme Court and Protective Legislation in the Progressive Era*, Yearbook 1983, Supreme Court Historical Society, 53–72; Melvin I. Urofsky, *State Courts and Protective Legislation during the Progressive Era: A Reevaluation*, 72 J. of American History, 63–91 (1985). Looking at a wide range of labor issues from 1885 to 1930, William E. Forbath describes a broad pattern of court decisions hostile both to unions and to protective labor laws for the average male worker. William E. Forbath, *Law and the Shaping of the American Labor Movement* (1991).

In *Adair v. United States* (1908), the Court's commerce and liberty of contract rationales coalesced. William Adair, a company supervisor, was prosecuted for discharging

O.B. Coppage from his job with the Louisville & Nashville Railroad Company because Coppage was a union member. In 1898, Congress had passed an act dealing with labor disputes involving interstate common carriers. The act required arbitration of labor disputes, and the act also made it a crime for a carrier in interstate commerce to discharge or threaten to discharge an employee because he was a member of a labor union.

Congress had enacted the statute after a bitter railroad strike had disrupted railroad service. The strike had been precipitated when the owner of the Pullman Sleeping Car Company had discharged workers who were presenting the workers' grievances to the owner. The congressional report accompanying the act said that discrimination against employees because of membership in labor unions tended to produce railway strikes that in turn interrupted the flow of interstate commerce.

The majority in *Adair* said that laws that interfered with liberty could be upheld—if required by the general good or the common welfare. But, in the absence of an employment contract limiting their rights, employees had the right, for whatever reason, to quit the services of their employer and employers had the right, for whatever reason, to dispense with the services of the employee. Both employer and employee had "an equality of right" and "any legislation that disturbs that equality is an arbitrary interference with the liberty of contract which no government can legally justify in a free land."

The federal government sought to justify the statute as a constitutional regulation of interstate commerce. The Court held "there is no such connection between interstate commerce and membership in a labor organization as to authorize Congress to make it a crime ... to discharge an employee because of such membership...."

The decisions in *Lochner* and *Adair* were not unique. Between 1880 and 1930, state and federal courts struck down labor and factory safety legislation in more than 100 cases. Laws that were struck down included prohibition on discrimination against union workers; requiring weighing of coal at the mine to insure miners were fully paid for coal they produced; laws prohibiting payment in scrip and regulating company stores; limitation of hours in private (and much more rarely public) employment; prohibition of manufacturing cigars in tenement houses; reforms dealing with injunctions against labor unions; a statute that prohibited firing or failing to renew contracts in order to intimidate workers so they would not vote; provision of attorneys' fees in successful suits to enforce mechanics' liens and claims for wages; and laws for inspection and regulation of workplaces. See, William Forbath, *Law and the Shaping of the American Labor Movement*, 177–92 (1991).

Social reformers, labor unions, Populists and Progressives who had worked for years for the passage of such laws were outraged. They responded with a number of proposals to limit the power of the courts to declare legislation unconstitutional. For example, in 1912, speaking to an Ohio convention called to revise the state's constitution, former president Theodore Roosevelt advocated a state constitutional provision that would allow the people, by popular vote, to "recall" any state court decision holding a state statute unconstitutional. In 1922, Senator Robert M. La Follette of Wisconsin proposed a constitutional amendment to permit Congress to reenact any federal statute that the Court had declared unconstitutional—a legislative override. (The modern constitution of Canada has a similar provision.) Still other proposals included recall of state judges and election of federal judges. Chief Justice Walter Clark of North Carolina, who thought federal judges were biased in favor of corporate interests, favored both election of federal judges and recall of judicial decisions. These and other proposals to deal with claimed abuse of judicial power were never successful at the federal level, but they show the intensity of critics' reaction to the course followed by the courts. For a fine discussion of the controversy over the judicial activism of the first third of the 20th century, see, William G. Ross, *A Muted Fury: Populists, Progressives, and Labor Unions Confront the Courts, 1890–1937*, 138–42, 194 (1994).

F. The New Deal: Political Realignment and the Commerce Clause

In 1929, the stock market, which had been at all time highs, collapsed. Over the next few years millions of people, perhaps 25% of the work force, were unemployed. National income fell from 85 billion in 1929 to 37 billion in 1933. Wages for those who were employed dropped to 40% of pre-Depression levels. Thousands of banks failed and depositors lost their savings. Homes and farms faced massive foreclosures, since owners were unable to make mortgage payments.

In 1932, Franklin Roosevelt won an overwhelming electoral victory and was re-elected by an even greater margin in 1936, carrying all but two states. Roosevelt advocated forceful government intervention in the economy in the interest both of economic recovery and social justice—government employment of the unemployed on public works (the Blue Ridge Parkway and the Riverwalk in San Antonio were New Deal employment projects), minimum wages, maximum hours, the right of labor to organize and bargain collectively, prohibition on child labor, environmental protection, etc. His political philosophy resembled that of his cousin, Theodore Roosevelt, the Progressive Republican. In his 1936 speech accepting the Democratic nomination, Roosevelt set out his political philosophy and his rejection of laissez faire economics:

> For too many of us the political equality we once had was meaningless in the face of economic inequality. A small group had concentrated into their own hands an almost complete control over other people's property, other people's money, other people's lives. For too many of us life was no longer free; liberty no longer real; men could no longer follow the pursuit of happiness.
>
> Against economic tyranny such as this, the American citizen could only appeal to the organized power of government....
>
> The royalists I have spoken of—the royalists of the economic order—have conceded that political freedom was the business of the government, but they have maintained that economic slavery was nobody's business.... [T]hey denied that the government could do anything to protect the citizen in his right to work and his right to live....

Basil Rauch, *The Roosevelt Reader,* 150–51 (1957).

A narrow reading of the Commerce Clause and a broad "liberty of contract" reading of the Due Process Clause of the 5th and 14th Amendments threatened to stifle New Deal initiatives. Because Roosevelt's program had overwhelming popular support, cases like *Carter Coal* (1936) and others striking down minimum wage and maximum hours involved a collision between judicial power and the democratic process. The Court's reading of the Due Process Clause raised similar problems. In *Adkins v. Children's Hospital* (1923), the Court had struck down, under the 5th Amendment Due Process Clause, a District of Columbia law prescribing minimum wages for women and children. The Court also struck down a state statute providing minimum wage for women under the 14th Amendment

Due Process Clause in *Morehead v. New York* (1936). That case, in turn, was overruled by *West Coast Hotel v. Parrish* (1937).

In *Schechter Poultry Co. v. United States* (1935), the Court, by a 9–0 vote, struck down a code, adopted under the National Industrial Recovery Act, that regulated wages, hours, and collective bargaining in the New York wholesale poultry slaughtering market. Schechter bought poultry locally in New York City and sold it only to local retailers. Ninety-six percent of the poultry sold in the New York City market came from out of state. The Court held Schechter's activities were not within the power of Congress to regulate commerce:

> Were these transactions "in" interstate commerce? Much is made of the fact that almost all the poultry coming to New York is sent there from other states. But the code provisions, as here applied, do not concern the transportation of the poultry from other states to New York, or the transactions of the commission men or others to whom it is consigned, or the sales made by such consignees to defendants. When defendants had made their purchases, whether at the West Washington Market in New York City or at the railroad terminals serving the city, or elsewhere, the poultry was trucked to their slaughterhouses in Brooklyn for local disposition. The interstate transactions in relation to that poultry then ended. Defendants held the poultry at their slaughterhouse markets for slaughter and local sale to retail dealers and butchers who in turn sold directly to consumers. Neither the slaughtering nor the sales by defendants were transactions in interstate commerce.

What interpretations of the Commerce Clause and methods of analysis support the result in the case? What type of interpretation would suggest a different result?

Carter v. Carter Coal Co. (1936) is set out below. What is the rationale for the decision? What tests are employed? What does the Court say about aggregating companies like Carter Coal for purposes of measuring the effect on interstate commerce?

The majority in *Carter* strikes down provisions of the Guffey Coal Act based on the Commerce Clause. Because the dissent found the Act to be consistent with the Commerce Clause, it is required to reach a second issue — whether or not the statute violates the 5th Amendment's Due Process Clause by interfering with "freedom of contract."

1. Shall the Court Defer to Congress?

Carter v. Carter Coal Co.
298 U.S. 238 (1936)

[Majority: Sutherland, Van Devanter, McReynolds, Butler, Roberts, and Hughes (in part). Concurring (in part): Cardozo, Brandeis, Stone. Dissenting (in part): Hughes (C.J.), Cardozo, Brandeis, Stone.]

[The 1935 Guffey Coal Act imposed an excise tax of 15% on the sale of bituminous coal by producers. The producers could get a 90% reduction in the tax if they complied with a Code formulated by the Bituminous Coal Commission which established minimum prices for coal; minimum wages and maximum hours, and the right of labor to bargain collectively. The Guffey Coal Act was promptly challenged as exceeding congressional power to regulate commerce.]

Mr. Justice Sutherland delivered the opinion of the Court: ...

By the terms of the act, every producer of bituminous coal within the United States is brought within its provisions.

Section 1 is a detailed assertion of circumstances thought to justify the act. It declares that the mining and distribution of bituminous coal throughout the United States by the producer are affected with a national public interest; and that the service of such coal in relation to industrial activities, transportation facilities, health and comfort of the people, conservation by controlled production and economical mining and marketing, maintenance of just and rational relations between the public, owners, producers, and employees, the right of the public to constant and adequate supplies of coal at reasonable prices, and the general welfare of the Nation, require that the bituminous coal industry should be regulated as the act provides.

[margin note: Reasons for Act]

Section 1, among other things, further declares that the production and distribution by producers of such coal bear upon and directly affect interstate commerce, and render regulation of production and distribution imperative for the protection of such commerce; that certain features connected with the production, distribution, and marketing have led to waste of the national coal resources, disorganization of interstate commerce in such coal, and burdening and obstructing interstate commerce therein; that practices prevailing in the production of such coal directly affect interstate commerce and require regulation for the protection of that commerce; and that the right of mine workers to organize and collectively bargain for wages, hours of labor, and conditions of employment should be guaranteed in order to prevent constant wage cutting and disparate labor costs detrimental to fair interstate competition, and in order to avoid obstructions to interstate commerce that recur in industrial disputes over labor relations at the mines. These declarations constitute not enactments of law, but legislative averments by way of inducement to the enactment which follows.

The substantive legislation begins with §2, which establishes in the Department of the Interior a National Bituminous Coal Commission, to be appointed and constituted as the section then specifically provides. Upon this commission is conferred the power to hear evidence and find facts upon which its orders and actions may be predicated....

Section 4 provides that the commission shall formulate the elaborate provisions contained therein into a working agreement to be known as the Bituminous Coal Code. These provisions require the organization of twenty-three coal districts, each with a district board the membership of which is to be determined in a manner pointed out by the act. Minimum prices for coal are to be established by each of these boards, which are authorized to make such classification of coals and price variation as to mines and consuming market areas as it may deem proper.... [The objectives cited in the act included stabilization of wages and working conditions, maximum hours of labor, and price stabilization.] The labor provisions of the code ... require that in order to effectuate the purposes of the act the district boards and code members shall accept specified conditions contained in the code, among which are the following:

Employees [are] given the right to organize and bargain collectively, through representatives of their own choosing, free from interference, restraint, or coercion of employers or their agents in respect of their concerted activities.

Such employees to have the right of peaceable assemblage for the discussion of the principles of collective bargaining and to select their own check-weighman to inspect the weighing or measuring of coal.

A labor board is created, consisting of three members, to be appointed by the President and assigned to the Department of Labor. Upon this board is conferred authority to adjudicate disputes arising under the provisions just stated, and to determine whether or not an organization of employees had been promoted, or is controlled or dominated by an employer in its organization, management, policy, or election of representatives. The board "may order a code member to meet the representatives of its employees for the purpose of collective bargaining." ...

Certain recitals contained in the act plainly suggest that its makers were of the opinion that its constitutionality could be sustained under some general federal power, thought to exist, apart from the specific grants of the Constitution. The fallacy of that view will be apparent when we recall fundamental principles which, although hitherto often expressed in varying forms of words, will bear repetition whenever their accuracy seems to be challenged. The recitals to which we refer are contained in § 1 (which is simply a preamble to the act), and, among others, are to the effect that the distribution of bituminous coal is of national interest, affecting the health and comfort of the people and the general welfare of the Nation; that this circumstance, together with the necessity of maintaining just and rational relations between the public, owners, producers, and employees, and the right of the public to constant and adequate supplies at reasonable prices, require regulation of the industry as the act provides. These affirmations—and the further ones that the production and distribution of such coal "directly affect interstate commerce," because of which and of the waste of the national coal resources and other circumstances, the regulation is necessary for the protection of such commerce—do not constitute an exertion of the will of Congress which is legislation, but a recital of considerations which in the opinion of that body existed and justified the expression of its will in the present act. Nevertheless, this preamble may not be disregarded. On the contrary it is important, because it makes clear, except for the pure assumption that the conditions described "directly" affect interstate commerce, that the powers which Congress undertook to exercise are not specific but of the most general character—namely, to protect the general public interest and the health and comfort of the people, to conserve privately-owned coal, maintain just relations between producers and employees and others, and promote the general welfare, by controlling nation-wide production and distribution of coal. These, it may be conceded, are objects of great worth; but are they ends, the attainment of which has been committed by the Constitution to the federal government? This is a vital question; for nothing is more certain than that beneficent aims, however great or well directed, can never serve in lieu of constitutional power.

The ruling and firmly established principle is that the powers which the general government may exercise are only those specifically enumerated in the Constitution, and such implied powers as are necessary and proper to carry into effect the enumerated powers. Whether the end sought to be attained by an act of Congress is legitimate is wholly a matter of constitutional power and not at all of legislative discretion. Legislative congressional discretion begins with the choice of means and ends with the adoption of methods and details to carry the delegated powers into effect. The distinction between these two things—power and discretion—is not only very plain but very important. For while the powers are rigidly limited to the enumerations of the Constitution, the means which may be employed to carry the powers into effect are not restricted, save that they must be appropriate, plainly adapted to the end, and not prohibited by, but consistent with, the letter and spirit of the Constitution. *McCulloch v. Maryland* (1819). Thus, it may be said that to a constitutional end many ways are open; but to an end not within the terms of the Constitution, all ways are closed.

The proposition, often advanced and as often discredited, that the power of the federal government inherently extends to purposes affecting the Nation as a whole with which the states severally cannot deal or cannot adequately deal, and the related notion that Congress, entirely apart from those powers delegated by the Constitution, may enact laws to promote the general welfare, have never been accepted but always definitely rejected by this court. Mr. Justice Story, as early as 1816, laid down the cardinal rule, which has ever since been followed—that the general government "can claim no powers which are not granted to it by the constitution, and the powers actually granted, must be such as are expressly given, or given by necessary implication." *Martin v. Hunter's Lessee* (1816). In the Framers Convention, the proposal to confer a general power akin to that just discussed was included in Mr. Randolph's resolutions, [which] declared that the National Legislature ought to enjoy the legislative rights vested in Congress by the Confederation, and "moreover to legislate in all cases to which the separate States are incompetent, or in which the harmony of the United States may be interrupted by the exercise of individual Legislation." The convention, however, declined to confer upon Congress power in such general terms; instead of which it carefully limited the powers which it thought wise to entrust to Congress by specifying them, thereby denying all others not granted expressly or by necessary implication. It made no grant of authority to Congress to legislate substantively for the general welfare, and no such authority exists, save as the general welfare may be promoted by the exercise of the powers which are granted.

The general rule with regard to the respective powers of the national and the state governments under the Constitution is not in doubt. The states were before the Constitution; and, consequently, their legislative powers antedated the Constitution. Those who framed and those who adopted that instrument meant to carve from the general mass of legislative powers, then possessed by the states, only such portions as it was thought wise to confer upon the federal government; and in order that there should be no uncertainty in respect of what was taken and what was left, the national powers of legislation were not aggregated but enumerated—with the result that what was not embraced by the enumeration remained vested in the states without change or impairment. Thus, "when it was found necessary to establish a national government for national purposes," this court said in *Munn v. Illinois* (1877), "a part of the powers of the States and of the people of the States was granted to the United States and the people of the United States. This grant operated as a further limitation upon the powers of the States, so that now the governments of the States possess all the powers of the Parliament of England, except such as have been delegated to the United States or reserved by the people." While the states are not sovereign in the true sense of that term, but only quasi sovereign, yet in respect of all powers reserved to them they are supreme—"as independent of the general government as that government within its sphere is independent of the States." *The Collector v. Day* (1870). And since every addition to the national legislative power to some extent detracts from or invades the power of the states, it is of vital moment that, in order to preserve the fixed balance intended by the Constitution, the powers of the general government be not so extended as to embrace any not within the express terms of the several grants or the implications necessarily to be drawn therefrom. It is no longer open to question that the general government, unlike the states, *Hammer v. Dagenhart* (1918), possesses no inherent power in respect of the internal affairs of the states; and emphatically not with regard to legislation. The question in respect of the inherent power of that government as to the external affairs of the Nation and in the field of international law is a wholly different matter which it is not necessary now to consider.

The determination of the Framers Convention and the ratifying conventions to preserve complete and unimpaired state self-government in all matters not committed to the general government is one of the plainest facts which emerges from the history of their deliberations. And adherence to that determination is incumbent equally upon the federal government and the states. State powers can neither be appropriated on the one hand nor abdicated on the other.... Every journey to a forbidden end begins with the first step; and the danger of such a step by the federal government in the direction of taking over the powers of the states is that the end of the journey may find the states so despoiled of their powers, or—what may amount to the same thing—so relieved of the responsibilities which possession of the powers necessarily enjoins, as to reduce them to little more than geographical subdivisions of the national domain. It is safe to say that if, when the Constitution was under consideration, it had been thought that any such danger lurked behind its plain words, it would never have been ratified....

"This Constitution, and the Laws of the United States which shall be made in Pursuance thereof ... shall be the supreme Law of the Land." (Const. art. 6, cl. 2.) The supremacy of the Constitution as law is thus declared without qualification. That supremacy is absolute; the supremacy of a statute enacted by Congress is not absolute but conditioned upon its being made in pursuance of the Constitution.... [The opinion of the Congress] or the court's opinion, that the statute will prove greatly or generally beneficial is wholly irrelevant to the inquiry....

Since the validity of the act depends upon whether it is a regulation of interstate commerce, the nature and extent of the power conferred upon Congress by the Commerce Clause becomes the determinative question in this branch of the case. The Commerce Clause (art. 1, §8, cl. 3) vests in Congress the power "To regulate Commerce with foreign Nations, and among the several States, and with the Indian Tribes." The function to be exercised is that of regulation. The thing to be regulated is the commerce described. In exercising the authority conferred by this clause of the Constitution, Congress is powerless to regulate anything which is not commerce, as it is powerless to do anything about commerce which is not regulation. We first inquire, then—What is commerce? The term, as this court many times has said, is one of extensive import. No all embracing definition has ever been formulated. The question is to be approached both affirmatively and negatively—that is to say, from the points of view as to what it includes and what it excludes.

In *Gibbons v. Ogden* (1824), Chief Justice Marshall said:

> Commerce, undoubtedly, is traffic, but it is something more—it is intercourse. It describes the commercial intercourse between nations, and parts of nations, in all its branches, and is regulated by prescribing rules for carrying on that intercourse.

As used in the Constitution, the word "commerce" is the equivalent of the phrase "intercourse for the purposes of trade," and includes transportation, purchase, sale, and exchange of commodities between the citizens of the different states. And the power to regulate commerce embraces the instruments by which commerce is carried on.

In *Adair v. United States* (1908), the phrase "Commerce among the several states" was defined as comprehending "traffic, intercourse, trade, navigation, communication, the transit of persons, and the transmission of messages by telegraph—indeed, every species on commercial intercourse among the several states." In *Veazie v. Moor* (1853), this court, after saying that the phrase could never be applied to transactions wholly internal, significantly added: "Nor can it be properly concluded, that, because the products of domestic enterprise in agriculture or manufactures, or in the arts, may ultimately become the subjects of foreign commerce, that the control of the means or the encouragements by which enterprise is fostered and protected, is legitimately within the import of the phrase foreign commerce, or fairly implied in any investiture of the power to regulate such commerce. A pretension as far reaching as this, would extend to contracts between citizen and citizen of the same State, would control the pursuits of the planter, the grazier, the manufacturer, the mechanic, the immense operations of the collieries and mines and furnaces of the country; for there is not one of these avocations, the results of which may not become the subjects of foreign commerce, and be borne either by turnpikes, canals, or railroads, from point to point within the several States, towards an ultimate destination, like the one above mentioned."

The distinction between manufacture and commerce was discussed in *Kidd v. Pearson* (1888), and it was said:

> No distinction is more popular to the common mind, or more clearly expressed in economic and political literature, than that between manufactures and commerce. Manufacture is transformation—the fashioning of raw materials into a change of form for use. The functions of commerce are different....

And then, as though foreseeing the present controversy, the opinion proceeds:

> Any movement towards the establishment of rules of production in this vast country, with its many different climates and opportunities, could only be at the sacrifice of the peculiar advantages of a large part of the localities in it, if not of every one of them....

Chief Justice Fuller, speaking for this court in *United States v. E. C. Knight Co.* (1895), [holding a monopoly over sugar manufacture was beyond the reach of the Sherman Act because it was not commerce] said:

> Doubtless the power to control the manufacture of a given thing involves, in a certain sense, the control of its disposition, but this is a secondary, and not the primary, sense; and, although the exercise of that power may result in bringing the operation of commerce into play, it does not control it, and affects it only incidentally and indirectly. Commerce succeeds to manufacture, and is not a part of it....
>
> It is vital that the independence of the commercial power and of the police power, and the delimitation between them, however sometimes perplexing, should always be recognized and observed, for, while the one furnishes the strongest bond of union, the other is essential to the preservation of the autonomy of the states as required by our dual form of government; and acknowledged evils, however grave and urgent they may appear to be, had better be borne, than the risk be run, in the effort to suppress them, of more serious consequences by resort to expedients of even doubtful constitutionality....
>
> The regulation of commerce applies to the subjects of commerce, and not to matters of internal police. Contracts to buy, sell, or exchange goods to be transported among the several states, the transportation and its instrumentalities, and articles bought, sold, or exchanged for the purposes of such transit among the states, or put in the way of transit, may be regulated; but this is because they form part of interstate trade or commerce. The fact that an article is manufactured for export to another state does not of itself make it an article of interstate commerce, and the intent of the manufacturer does not determine the time when the article or product passes from the control of the state and belongs to commerce.
>
> That commodities produced or manufactured within a state are intended to be sold or transported outside the state does not render their production or manufacture subject to federal regulation under the Commerce Clause....

Certain decisions of this court, superficially considered, seem to lend support to the defense of the act now under review. But upon examination, they will be seen to be inapposite. Thus, *Coronado Co. v. United Mine Workers* (1925), involved conspiracies to restrain interstate commerce in violation of the Anti-Trust Laws. The acts of the persons involved were local in character; but the intent was to restrain interstate commerce, and the means employed were calculated to carry that intent into effect. Interstate commerce was the direct object of attack; and the restraint of such commerce was the necessary consequence of the acts and the immediate end in view. The applicable law was concerned not with the character of the acts or of the means employed, which might be in and of themselves purely local, but with the intent and direct operation of those acts and means upon interstate commerce....

Another group of cases, of which *Swift & Company v. United States* (1905), is an example, rest upon the circumstance that the acts in question constituted direct interferences with the "flow" of commerce among the states. In the *Swift Case*, live stock was consigned and delivered to stockyards—not as a place of final destination, but, as the court said ... "a throat through which the current flows." The sales which ensued merely changed the private interest in the subject of the current without interfering with its continuity. It was nowhere suggested in these cases that the interstate commerce power extended to the growth or production of the things which, after production, entered the flow. If the court had held that the raising of the cattle, which were involved in the *Swift Case*, including the wages paid to and working conditions of the herders and others employed in the business, could be regulated by Congress, that decision and decisions holding similarly would be in point; for it is that situation, and not the one with which the court actually dealt, which here concerns us....

That the production of every commodity intended for interstate sale and transportation has some effect upon interstate commerce may be, if it has not already been, freely granted; and we are brought to the final and decisive inquiry, whether here that effect is direct, as the "Preamble" recites, or indirect. The distinction is not formal, but substantial in the highest degree, as we pointed out in the *Schechter* Case (1935). "If the Commerce Clause were construed," we there said, "to reach all enterprises and transactions which could be said to have an indirect effect upon interstate commerce, the federal authority would embrace practically all the activities of the people, and the authority of the state over its domestic concerns would exist only by sufferance of the federal government. Indeed, on such a theory, even the development of the state's commercial facilities would be subject to federal control." ...

Whether the effect of a given activity or condition is direct or indirect is not always easy to determine. The word "direct" implies that the activity or condition invoked or blamed shall operate proximately—not mediately, remotely, or collaterally—to produce the effect. It connotes the absence of an efficient intervening agency or condition. And the extent of the effect bears no logical relation to its character. The distinction between a direct and an indirect effect turns, not upon the magnitude of either the cause or the effect, but entirely upon the manner in which the effect has been brought about. If the production by one man of a single ton of coal intended for interstate sale and shipment, and actually so sold and shipped, affects interstate commerce indirectly, the effect does not become direct by multiplying the tonnage, or increasing the number of men employed, or adding to the expense or complexities of the business, or by all combined. It is quite true that rules of law are sometimes qualified by considerations of degree, as the government argues. But the matter of degree has no bearing upon the question here, since that question is not—What is the extent of the local activity or condition, or the extent of the effect produced upon interstate commerce? But—What is the relation between the activity or condition and the effect?

Much stress is put upon the evils which come from the struggle between employers and employees over the matter of wages, working conditions, the right of collective bargaining, etc., and the resulting strikes, curtailment, and irregularity of production and effect on prices; and it is insisted that interstate commerce is greatly affected thereby. But, in addition to what has just been said, the conclusive answer is that the evils are all local evils over which the federal government has no legislative control. The relation of employer and employee is a local relation. At common law, it is one of the domestic relations. The wages are paid for the doing of local work. Working conditions are obviously local conditions. The employees are not engaged in or about commerce, but exclusively in producing a commodity. And the controversies and evils, which it is the object of the act to regulate and minimize, are local controversies and evils affecting local work undertaken to accomplish that local result. Such effect as they may have upon commerce, however extensive it may be, is secondary and indirect. An increase in the greatness of the effect adds to its importance. It does not alter its character....

The only perceptible difference between that case and this is that in the *Schechter Case* the federal power was asserted with respect to commodities which had come to rest after their interstate transportation; while here, the case deals with commodities at rest before interstate commerce has begun. That difference is without significance....

Cardozo, J., joined by Brandeis and Stone, JJ., dissenting. [Omitted.]

* * *

What judicially enforceable constitutional tests do the post-*Gibbons*/pre-New Deal cases suggest to justify a limit on the power of Congress over commerce? Can congressional power be rationally limited by a *definitional*, a *stream of commerce*, or an *effect on commerce* test?

The Roosevelt Court Plan: The Court Changes Direction

The early New Deal legislative program suffered a series of serious defeats in the Supreme Court. The Court struck down the Railroad Retirement Act of 1934, the National Industrial Recovery Act of 1933 (probably a blessing in disguise), the Agricultural Adjustment Act of 1933, and the Bituminous Coal Conservation Act. As the decision in *Carter v. Carter Coal* (1936) suggests, the Court's reading of the Commerce Clause implied that essential parts of the New Deal program were unconstitutional—economic regulation, standards for workers in the form of minimum wage and maximum hours, laws protecting the right of labor to organize and bargain collectively, and many more.

On February 5, 1937, President Roosevelt sent to Congress a message proposing to allow the President to appoint an additional Supreme Court Justice for each Justice who had reached voluntary retirement age. Six members of the Court had passed the voluntary retirement age. Opponents dubbed the proposal a "court packing plan." Though Roosevelt had been re-elected by an overwhelming majority, resistance to the Court expansion plan was strong and came from many who otherwise supported the New Deal. Although there had been no changes for almost 70 years, Congress had changed the number of members on the Court several times before in American history. The Senate Judiciary Committee recommended rejection of the plan. Following the controversy, the Court seemed to change direction, a maneuver that a wit dubbed "the switch in time that saved nine." It first upheld state minimum wage legislation in *West Coast Hotel Co. v. Parrish* (1937) and later in the same year upheld the National Labor Relations Act (NLRA) in *NLRB v. Jones and Laughlin Steel* (1937).

The NLRA had been passed in 1935. The Act allowed employees to vote on whether or not they wanted to have a union. If the employees chose a union, the Act required the employer to bargain in good faith with the employees over terms and conditions of employment. The National Labor Relations Board, created by the NLRA, ordered Jones and Laughlin Steel to stop interfering with the rights of its employees to organize a union and bargain collectively. The company contended that the NLRA exceeded the power of Congress under the Commerce Clause. In a 5–4 decision, the Court upheld the Act, rejecting *Carter Coal*'s position that the employer-employee relationship and issues related to "production" were outside the scope of federal power. Chief Justice Hughes, writing for the Court, held in part:

> Respondent says that, whatever may be said of employees engaged in interstate commerce, the industrial relations and activities in the manufacturing department of respondent's enterprise are not subject to federal regulation. The argument rests upon the proposition that manufacturing in itself is not commerce. [Court cites eight cases, including *Carter Coal.*]
>
> The government distinguishes these cases. The various parts of respondent's enterprise are described as interdependent and as thus involving "a great movement of iron ore, coal and limestone along well-defined paths to the steel mills, thence through them, and thence in the form of steel products into the consuming centers of the country—a definite and well-understood course of business." It is urged that these activities constitute a "stream" or "flow" of commerce, of which the Aliquippa manufacturing plant is the focal point, and that industrial strife at that point would cripple the entire movement. Reference is made to our decision sustaining the Packers and Stockyards Act. *Stafford v. Wallace* (1922). The Court found that the stockyards were but a "throat" through which the current of commerce flowed and the transactions which there occurred could not be separated from that movement. Hence the sales at the stockyards were not regarded as merely local transactions, for, while they created "a local change of title," they did not "stop the flow," but merely changed the private interests in the subject of the current. Distinguishing the cases which upheld the power of the state to impose a nondiscriminatory tax upon property which the owner intended to transport to another state, but which was not in actual transit and was held within the state subject to the disposition of the owner, the Court remarked: "The question, it should be observed, is not with respect to the extent of the power of Congress to regulate interstate commerce, but whether a particular exercise of state power in view of its nature and operation must be deemed to be in conflict with this paramount authority." ...
>
> We do not find it necessary to determine whether these features of defendant's business dispose of the asserted analogy to the "stream of commerce" cases. The instances in which that metaphor has been used are but particular, and not exclusive, illustrations of the protective power which the government invokes in support of the present act. The congressional authority to protect interstate commerce from burdens and obstructions is not limited to transactions which can be deemed to be an essential part of a "flow" of interstate or foreign commerce. Burdens and obstructions may be due to injurious action springing from other sources. The fundamental principle is that the power to regulate commerce is the power to enact "all appropriate legislation" for its "protection or advancement"; to adopt measures "to promote its growth and insure its safety"; "to foster, protect, control, and restrain." That power is plenary and may be exerted to protect interstate commerce "no matter what the source of the dangers which threaten it." Although activities may be intrastate in character when separately con-

sidered, if they have such a close and substantial relation to interstate commerce that their control is essential or appropriate to protect that commerce from burdens and obstructions, Congress cannot be denied the power to exercise that control. Undoubtedly the scope of this power must be considered in the light of our dual system of government and may not be extended so as to embrace effects upon interstate commerce so indirect and remote that to embrace them, in view of our complex society, would effectually obliterate the distinction between what is national and what is local and create a completely centralized government. The question is necessarily one of degree...." Whatever amounts to more or less constant practice, and threatens to obstruct or unduly to burden the freedom of interstate commerce is within the regulatory power of Congress under the Commerce Clause, and it is primarily for Congress to consider and decide the fact of the danger and to meet it."

Shortly after the Court began to uphold New Deal measures, President Roosevelt gave the following speech.

"The Constitution of the United States Was a Layman's Document, Not a Lawyer's Contract"

[Address of Franklin Roosevelt on Constitution Day, September 17, 1937, given in Washington, D.C.]

My Fellow Americans:

One hundred fifty years ago tonight, thirty-eight weary delegates to a Convention in Philadelphia signed the constitution. Four handwritten sheets of parchment were enough to state the terms on which thirteen independent weak little republics agreed to try to survive together as one strong nation....

To hold to that [democratic] course our constitutional democratic form of government must meet the insistence of the great mass of our people that economic and social security and the standard of American living be raised from what they are to levels which the people know our resources justify....

The Constitution of the United States was a layman's document, not a lawyer's contract. *That* cannot be stressed too often. Madison, most responsible for it, was not a lawyer; nor was Washington or Franklin, whose sense of the give-and-take of life had kept the Convention together.

This great layman's document was a charter of general principles, completely different from the "whereases" and the "parties of the first part" and the fine print which lawyers put into leases and insurance policies and installment agreements.

When the Framers were dealing with what they rightly considered eternal verities, unchangeable by time and circumstance, they used specific language. In no uncertain terms, for instance, they forbade titles of nobility, the suspension of habeas corpus and the withdrawal of money from the Treasury except after appropriation by law. With almost equal definiteness they detailed the Bill of Rights.

But when they considered the fundamental powers of the new national government they used generality, implication and statement of mere objectives, as intentional phrases which flexible statesmanship of the future, within the Constitution, could adapt to time and circumstance. For instance, the framers used broad and general language capable of meeting evolution and change when they referred to commerce between the States, the taxing power and the general welfare. Even the Supreme Court was treated with that purposeful lack of specification. Contrary to the belief of many Americans, the Constitution says nothing about any power of the Court to declare legislation unconstitutional; nor does it mention the number of judges for the Court....

Again and again the Convention voted down proposals to give Justices of the Court a veto over legislation. Clearly a majority of the delegates believed that the relation of the Court to the Congress and the Executive, like the other subjects treated in general terms, would work itself out by evolution and change over the years.

But for one hundred and fifty years we have had an unending struggle between those who would preserve this original broad concept of the Constitution as a layman's instrument of government and those who would shrivel the Constitution into a lawyer's contract.

Those of us who really believe in the enduring wisdom of the Constitution hold no rancor against those who professionally or politically talk and think in purely legalistic phrases. We cannot seriously be alarmed when they cry "unconstitutional" at every effort to better the condition of our people.

Such cries have always been with us; and, ultimately, they have always been overruled.

Lawyers, distinguished in 1787, insisted that the Constitution itself was unconstitutional under the Articles of Confederation. But the ratifying conventions overruled them.

Lawyers, distinguished in their day, warned Washington and Hamilton that the protective tariff was unconstitutional, warned Jefferson that the Louisiana Purchase was unconstitutional, warned Monroe that to open up roads across the Alleghenies was unconstitutional. But the Executive and the Congress overruled them.

Lawyers, distinguished in their day, persuaded a divided Supreme Court that the Congress had no power to govern slavery in the territories, that the long-standing Missouri Compromise was unconstitutional. But a War Between the States overruled them.

That great Senatorial constitutional authority of his day, Senator Evarts, issued a solemn warning that the proposed Interstate Commerce Act and the Federal regulation of railway rates which the farmers demanded would be unconstitutional. But both the Senate and the Supreme Court overruled him.

Less than two years ago fifty-eight of the highest priced lawyers in the land gave the Nation (without cost to the Nation) a solemn and formal opinion that the Wagner Labor Relations Act was unconstitutional. And in a few months, first a national election and later the Supreme Court overruled them.

Lawyers, distinguished in their day, persuaded the Odd Man on the Supreme Court that the methods of financing the Civil War were unconstitutional. But a new Odd man overruled them.

For twenty years the Odd Man on the Supreme Court refused to admit that State minimum wage laws for women were constitutional. A few months ago, after my message to the Congress on the rejuvenation of the Judiciary, the Odd Man admitted that the Court had been wrong—for all those twenty years—and overruled himself.

In this constant struggle the lawyers of no political party, mine or any other, have had a consistent or unblemished record. But the lay rank and file of political parties has had a consistent record....

That lay rank and file can take cheer from the historic fact that every effort to construe the Constitution as a lawyer's contract rather than a layman's charter has ultimately failed. Whenever legalistic interpretation has clashed with contemporary sense on great questions of broad national policy, ultimately the people and the Congress have had their way.

But that word "ultimately" covers a terrible cost.

It cost a Civil War to gain recognition of the constitutional power of the Congress to legislate for the territories.

It cost twenty years of taxation on those least able to pay to recognize the constitutional power of the Congress to levy taxes on those most able to pay.

It cost twenty years of exploitation of women's labor to recognize the constitutional power of the States to pass minimum wage laws for their protection.

It has cost twenty years already—and no one knows how many more are to come—to obtain a constitutional interpretation that will let the Nation regulate the shipment in national commerce of goods sweated from the labor of little children.

We know it takes time to adjust government to the needs of society. But modern history proves that reforms too long delayed or denied have jeopardized peace, undermined democracy, and swept away civil and religious liberties.

Yes, time more than ever before is vital in statesmanship and in government, in all three branches of it.

We will no longer be permitted to sacrifice each generation in turn while the law catches up with life.

We can no longer afford the luxury of twenty-year lags.

You will find no justification in any of the language of the Constitution for delay in the reforms which the mass of the American people now demand.

Yet nearly every attempt to meet those demands for social and economic betterment has been jeopardized or actually forbidden by those who have sought to read into the Constitution language which the framers refused to write into the Constitution....

Nothing would so surely destroy the substance of what the Bill of Rights protects than its perversion to prevent social progress. The surest protection of the individual and of minorities is that fundamental tolerance and feeling for fair play which the Bill of Rights assumes. But tolerance and fair play would disappear here as it has in some other lands if the great mass of people were denied confidence in their justice, their security and their self-respect. Desperate people in other lands surrendered their liberties when freedom came merely to mean humiliation and starvation. The crisis of 1933 should make us understand that.

On this solemn anniversary I ask that the American people rejoice in the wisdom of their Constitution....

I ask that they guarantee the effectiveness of each of its parts by living by the Constitution as a whole. I ask that they have faith in its ultimate capacity to work out the problems of democracy, but that they justify that faith by making it work now rather than twenty years from now.

I ask that they give their fealty to the Constitution *itself* and not to its misinterpreters.

Samuel Rosenman, ed., *The Public Papers and Addresses of Franklin D. Roosevelt*, vol.6, pp. 359–66 (1938–1950).

A Theory Regarding Constitutional Change

The following excerpt is from a *Book Review* by Michael Kent Curtis of Bruce Ackerman's *We the People: Transformations* (1998) in 42 Am. J. Leg. Hist. 417 (1998).

For more than thirty years scholars of Constitutional Law have been obsessed with questions of legitimacy. They have engaged in an apparently endless debate between those who see original intent or original meaning of the constitutional text as *the* criteria of legitimacy and those who suggest other approaches. Although periodically people announce that the debate is spent or that all parties have become converts to some version of original meaning, the participants seem not to notice, and the debate goes on. Meanwhile, dramatic change continues to occur in American constitutional law, and the law pays limited attention to theory as to how it should behave. But a problem remains. If constitutional law is more than politics, how shall we account for major, widely accepted constitutional changes that do not fit comfortably into standard theories?

Bruce Ackerman has written a fresh, lively, splendid book about constitutional change and the role of "we the people" in effectuating it. Ackerman explores three major changes in American constitutional law: from the Articles of Confederation to the Constitution, from the pre-Civil War Constitution to the Reconstruction Amendments, and from a more laissez faire constitutionalism to the New Deal. He argues in illuminating detail that none of these changes fit what he calls a "hypertextualist" model—change that strictly follows the original meaning of the constitutional text—whether the provisions of Article V for amendment or (in the case of the ratification of the Constitution) the earlier provisions for amendment in the Articles of Confederation.

The Articles of Confederation provided they should be perpetual; no alteration was permitted unless agreed to by Congress and by all of the thirteen states. The body that became the Constitutional Convention was authorized to meet merely "for the sole and express purpose of revising the Articles." Only ten states were present throughout the convention. "We are presented, then," Ackerman notes, "with the spectacle of ten delegations urging nine states to bolt a solemn agreement ratified by all thirteen members of the Convention." The new Constitution was legitimated by appeal to the idea of popular sovereignty. Ackerman suggests that the theory of popular sovereignty can (in carefully limited circumstances) legitimate other changes that go beyond the text as well.

The problems with Reconstruction are as severe as those of the creation of the Constitution. The 13th Amendment abolishing slavery was proposed by a Congress from which the Southern states were absent. It was ratified by Southern state governments the Congress soon declared illegitimate. If the Southern state legislatures were illegitimate, how, Ackerman asks the "hypertextualist," can they validly ratify the Amendment? As to the 14th Amendment, Congress put the Southern states on notice that they would be denied all participation in the national government unless they ratified. As Ackerman sees it: "This is flat-out inconsistent with the limited Congressional role described in Article V. It follows that the process by which Congress procured ratification of the 14th Amendment simply cannot be squared with the text."

Ackerman rejects the conventional wisdom that followed the New Deal era: that *Lochner*'s (1905) "liberty of contract" and the old Court's limits on the power of the national government to regulate the economy were mistakes that the New Deal Court corrected by returning to the wisdom of John Marshall and the Framers. Though Ackerman has his share of scholarly allies, I am skeptical. The principles of the Framers or John Marshall had enfolded in them quite divergent possibilities. They should have been interpreted in light of the integrated national economy of the Depression era. I doubt that the limits the old Court put on national power to control the economy were the necessary or even the best legal reading. I also doubt that the best reading of due process, equal protection, privileges or immunities individual liberty principles of the 14th Amendment lead to *Lochner* when applied in the world of 1905. An amendment that sought to outlaw serfdom hardly seems to void maximum hour legislation or a requirement that workers be paid in cash rather than script.

At any rate, Ackerman's illuminating history shows that arguments about the illegitimacy and "non-textual" nature of these fundamental constitutional changes are not simply concocted by a law professor. The arguments were made powerfully and repeatedly by contemporaries in each of the events he considers. *We the People: Transformations* brings this largely forgotten history to life in a fresh and compelling way.

However you slice the history, Ackerman has shown that some of our most fundamental constitutional changes have occurred outside of the rules set out in Article V (and its predecessor) and in ways that cannot be defended on "hypertextualist" principles. An alternative explanation, of course, is the extreme "realist" one that grips many law students after the shock of studying constitutional law: Supreme Court justices enact their political policy preferences.

Ackerman believes in principled adjudication, and he rejects cynicism. He applies the lawyer's tools of legal analysis to constitutional history in an effort to discover rules for legitimate constitutional change outside Article V. Ackerman believes the change is legitimated by popular sovereignty. Legitimate fundamental changes follow a pattern. Essentially the process is one by which the proposed changes are clearly signaled to the electorate, approved by substantial majorities, and ratified in subsequent elections. At the end of the sequence, most of those who opposed the changes and challenged their legitimacy accept them. So, by this analysis, the Reconstruction Amendments and New Deal constitutionalism are legitimate after all—legitimated not by "hypertextualism" but by popular sovereignty. Of course, it follows that our most cherished constitutional provisions could also be changed outside of Article V—by a clear signal of intended changes, massive electoral success for the supporters of the change, and later elections that ratify the change.

Ackerman notes that presidents are tempted to effect fundamental constitutional change by judicial appointments even in the absence of the sort of popular mandate that he describes. At one level, *We The People: Transformations* is an effort to respond to this problem. And so, at the end of the book, Ackerman proposes safety devices and mechanisms for constitutional change in addition to Article V. Basically, his proposals for constitutional change would make it easier for "we the people" to effectuate constitutional change. The result would be to reduce the pressure for the less textually structured constitutional amendment process he describes.

* * *

The Constitution and the Minimum Wage

After holding in *Adkins v. Children's Hospital* (1923) that the Due Process Clause of the 5th Amendment prohibited a federal minimum wage for women, in 1936, in *Morehead v. New York ex rel Tipaldo*, the Court struck down a similar state law as a violation of the Due Process Clause of the 14th Amendment. The plaintiff, a laundry operator, had challenged the constitutionality of the New York state statute which, like the federal statute in *Adkins*, provided a minimum wage for women. The Court announced that "the State is without power by any form of legislation to prohibit, change or nullify contracts between employers and adult women workers as to the amount of wages to be paid." Justice Stone wrote an acid dissent: "the 14th Amendment has no more embedded in the Constitution our preference for some particular set of economic beliefs than it has adopted, in the name of liberty, the system of theology which we may happen to approve."

In *The Supreme Court Reborn: The Constitutional Revolution in the Age of Roosevelt* (1995) (to which this account is indebted), William E. Leuchtenburg reports that New Dealers were irate about the decision. He also quotes an upstate New York Republican newspaper: "The law that would jail any laundry-man for having an underfed horse should jail him for having an underfed girl employee." Leuchtenburg reports that following the decision "the wages of laundresses—mostly impoverished blacks and Puerto Rican and Italian immigrants—were slashed in half."

Though reaction to the 1936 *Morehead* decision was largely negative, it had supporters among newspapers in "cheap labor towns." In addition, Alice Paul of the National Women's Party hailed the decision because she believed that laws protecting only women suggested their inferiority. Historian Mary Beard protested that Alice Paul had "played into the hands of the rawest capitalists." Leuchtenburg, *supra* at 167–68.

Morehead was overturned in *West Coast Hotel v. Parrish* (1937), another case involving minimum wages for women. Four years later, the Court sustained a minimum wage law that applied to both men and women in *United States v. Darby* (1941).

2. The Emergence of a New (or Old?) View of the Commerce Clause

United States v. Darby
312 U.S. 100 (1941)

[Majority: Stone, Black, Frankfurter, McReynolds, Douglas, Murphy, Reed, Roberts, Hughes (C.J.).]

Mr. Justice Stone delivered the opinion of the Court.

The two principal questions raised by the record in this case are, first, whether Congress has constitutional power to prohibit the shipment in interstate commerce of lumber manufactured by employees whose wages are less than a prescribed minimum or whose weekly hours of labor at that wage are greater than a prescribed maximum, and, second, whether it has power to prohibit the employment of workmen in the production of goods "for interstate commerce" at other than prescribed wages and hours. A subsidiary question is whether in connection with such prohibitions Congress can require the employer subject to them to keep records showing the hours worked each day and week by each of his employees including those engaged "in the production and manufacture of goods to wit, lumber, for 'interstate commerce.'"

Appellee demurred to an indictment found in the district court for southern Georgia charging him with violation of §15(a)(1)(2) and (5) of the Fair Labor Standards Act of 1938, 29 U.S.C. §201, et seq. The district court sustained the demurrer and quashed the indictment....

The Fair Labor Standards Act set up a comprehensive legislative scheme for preventing the shipment in interstate commerce of certain products and commodities produced in the United States under labor conditions as respects wages and hours which fail to conform to standards set up by the Act. Its purpose, as we judicially know from the declaration of policy in § 2(a) of the Act, and the reports of Congressional committees proposing the legislation, is to exclude from interstate commerce goods produced for the commerce and to prevent their production for interstate commerce, under conditions detrimental to the maintenance of the minimum standards of living necessary for health and general well-being; and to prevent the use of interstate commerce as the means of competition in the distribution of goods so produced, and as the means of spreading and perpetuating such substandard labor conditions among the workers of the several states[1]....

The indictment charges that appellee is engaged, in the state of Georgia, in the business of acquiring raw materials, which he manufactures into finished lumber with the intent, when manufactured, to ship it in interstate commerce to customers outside the state, and that he does in fact so ship a large part of the lumber so produced. There are numerous counts charging appellee with the shipment in interstate commerce from Georgia to points outside the state of lumber in the production of which, for interstate commerce, appellee has employed workmen at less than the prescribed minimum wage or more than the prescribed maximum hours without payment to them of any wage for overtime. Other counts charge the employment by appellee of workmen in the production of lumber for interstate commerce at wages of less than 25 cents an hour or for more than the maximum hours per week without payment to them of the prescribed overtime wage.... [Darby's constitutional challenge was upheld by the lower court.]

The effect of the [lower] court's decision and judgment are thus to deny the power of Congress to prohibit shipment in interstate commerce of lumber produced for interstate commerce under the proscribed substandard labor conditions of wages and hours, its power to penalize the employer for his failure to conform to the wage and hour provisions in the case of employees engaged in the production of lumber which he intends thereafter to ship in interstate commerce in part or in whole according to the normal course of his business and its power to compel him to keep records of hours of employment as required by the statute and the regulations of the administrator.

The case comes here on assignments by the Government that the district court erred insofar as it held that Congress was without constitutional power to penalize the acts set forth in the indictment, [the shipment in interstate commerce, of goods produced for interstate commerce by employees whose wages and hours of employment do not conform to the requirements of the Act.] [T]he only question arising under the Commerce Clause with respect to such shipments is whether Congress has the constitutional power to prohibit them.

While manufacture is not of itself interstate commerce the shipment of manufactured goods interstate is such commerce and the prohibition of such shipment by Congress is indubitably a regulation of the commerce. The power to regulate commerce is the power "to prescribe the rule by which commerce is to be governed." *Gibbons v. Ogden* (1824). It extends not only to those regulations which aid, foster and protect the commerce, but

---

1. 'Sec. 2 (s 202). (a) The Congress hereby finds that the existence, in industries engaged in commerce or in the production of goods for commerce, of labor conditions detrimental to the maintenance of the minimum standard of living necessary for health, efficiency, and general well-being of workers (1) causes commerce and the channels and instrumentalities of commerce to be used to spread and perpetuate such labor conditions among the workers of the several States; (2) burdens commerce and the free flow of goods in commerce; (3) constitutes an unfair method of competition in commerce; (4) leads to labor disputes burdening and obstructing commerce and the free flow of goods in commerce; and (5) interferes with the orderly and fair marketing of goods in commerce.'

Section 3(b) defines 'commerce' as 'trade, commerce, transportation, transmission, or communication among the several States or from any State to any place outside thereof.'

embraces those which prohibit it. *Lottery Case (Champion v. Ames)* (1903). It is conceded that the power of Congress to prohibit transportation in interstate commerce includes noxious articles [*Lottery Case*; *Hipolite Egg Co. v. United States* (1911)*; Hoke v. United States* (1913)]*;* stolen articles, *Brooks v. United States* (1925); kidnapped persons, *Gooch v. United States* (1936)*;* and articles such as intoxicating liquor or convict made goods, traffic in which is forbidden or restricted by the laws of the state of destination. *Kentucky Whip & Collar Co. v. Illinois Central R. Co.* (1937).

But it is said that the present prohibition falls within the scope of none of these categories; that while the prohibition is nominally a regulation of the commerce its motive or purpose is regulation of wages and hours of persons engaged in manufacture, the control of which has been reserved to the states.... The power of Congress over interstate commerce "is complete in itself, may be exercised to its utmost extent, and acknowledges no limitations, other than are prescribed by the constitution." *Gibbons v. Ogden* (1824). That power can neither be enlarged nor diminished by the exercise or non-exercise of state power....

Such regulation is not a forbidden invasion of state power merely because either its motive or its consequence is to restrict the use of articles of commerce within the states of destination and is not prohibited unless by other Constitutional provisions. It is no objection to the assertion of the power to regulate interstate commerce that its exercise is attended by the same incidents which attend the exercise of the police power of the states....

The motive and purpose of the present regulation are plainly to make effective the Congressional conception of public policy that interstate commerce should not be made the instrument of competition in the distribution of goods produced under substandard labor conditions, which competition is injurious to the commerce and to the states from and to which the commerce flows. The motive and purpose of a regulation of interstate commerce are matters for the legislative judgment upon the exercise of which the Constitution places no restriction and over which the courts are given no control...." The judicial cannot prescribe to the legislative departments of the government limitations upon the exercise of its acknowledged power." *Veazie Bank v. Fenno* (1869).

Whatever their motive and purpose, regulations of commerce which do not infringe some constitutional prohibition are within the plenary power conferred on Congress by the Commerce Clause. Subject only to that limitation, presently to be considered, we conclude that the prohibition of the shipment interstate of goods produced under the forbidden substandard labor conditions is within the constitutional authority of Congress.

In the more than a century which has elapsed since the decision of *Gibbons v. Ogden* (1824), these principles of constitutional interpretation have been so long and repeatedly recognized by this Court as applicable to the Commerce Clause, that there would be little occasion for repeating them now were it not for the decision of this Court twenty-two years ago in *Hammer v. Dagenhart* (1918). In that case it was held by a bare majority of the Court over the powerful and now classic dissent of Mr. Justice Holmes setting forth the fundamental issues involved, that Congress was without power to exclude the products of child labor from interstate commerce. The reasoning and conclusion of the Court's opinion there cannot be reconciled with the conclusion which we have reached, that the power of Congress under the Commerce Clause is plenary to exclude any article from interstate commerce subject only to the specific prohibitions of the Constitution.

Hammer v. Dagenhart has not been followed. The distinction on which the decision was rested that Congressional power to prohibit interstate commerce is limited to articles which in themselves have some harmful or deleterious property—a distinction which was novel when made and unsupported by any provision of the Constitution—has long since been abandoned. *Brooks v. United States*; *Kentucky Whip & Collar Co.* The thesis of the opinion that the motive of the prohibition or its effect to control in some measure the use or production within the states of the article thus excluded from the commerce can operate to deprive the regulation of its constitutional authority has long since ceased to have force. *Lottery Case*; *Hipolite Egg Co. v. United States*. And finally we have declared "The authority of the Federal Government over interstate commerce does not differ in extent or character from that retained by the states over intrastate commerce." *United States v. Rock Royal Co-Operative, Inc.* (1939).

The conclusion is inescapable that *Hammer v. Dagenhart*, was a departure from the principles which have prevailed in the interpretation of the Commerce Clause both before and since the decision and that such vitality, as a precedent, as it then had has long since been exhausted. It should be and now is overruled.

Validity of the wage and hour requirements. Section 15(a)(2) and §§6 and 7 require employers to conform to the wage and hour provisions with respect to all employees engaged in the production of goods for interstate commerce. As appellee's employees are not alleged to be "engaged in interstate commerce" the validity of the prohibition turns on the question whether the employment, under other than the prescribed labor standards, of employees engaged in the production of goods for interstate commerce is so related to the commerce and so affects it as to be within the reach of the power of Congress to regulate it....

There remains the question whether such restriction on the production of goods for commerce is a permissible exercise of the commerce power. The power of Congress over interstate commerce is not confined to the regulation of commerce among the states. It extends to those activities intrastate which so affect interstate commerce or the exercise of the power of Congress over it as to make regulation of them appropriate means to the attainment of a legitimate end, the exercise of the granted power of Congress to regulate interstate commerce. See *McCulloch v. Maryland* (1819).

While this Court has many times found state regulation of interstate commerce, when uniformity of its regulation is of national concern, to be incompatible with the Commerce Clause even though Congress has not legislated on the subject, the Court has never implied such restraint on state control over matters intrastate not deemed to be regulations of interstate commerce or its instrumentalities even though they affect the commerce. *Minnesota Rate Cases* (1913). In the absence of Congressional legislation on the subject state laws which are not regulations of the commerce itself or its instrumentalities are not forbidden even though they affect interstate commerce.

But it does not follow that Congress may not by appropriate legislation regulate intrastate activities where they have a substantial effect on interstate commerce. A recent example is the National Labor Relations Act, for the regulation of employer and employee relations in industries in which strikes, induced by unfair labor practices named in the Act, tend to disturb or obstruct interstate commerce. See *NLRB v. Jones & Laughlin Steel Corp.* (1937). But long before the adoption of the National Labor Relations Act, this Court had many times held that the power of Congress to regulate interstate commerce extends to the regulation through legislative action of activities intrastate which have a substantial effect on the commerce or the exercise of the Congressional power over it....

Congress, having by the present Act adopted the policy of excluding from interstate commerce all goods produced for the commerce which do not conform to the specified labor standards, it may choose the means reasonably adapted to the attainment of the permitted end, even though they involve control of intrastate activities. Such legislation has often been sustained with respect to powers, other than the commerce power granted to the national government, when the means chosen, although not themselves within the granted power, were nevertheless deemed appropriate aids to the accomplishment of some purpose within an admitted power of the national government....

We think also that § 15(a)(2), now under consideration, is sustainable independently of § 15(a)(1), which prohibits shipment or transportation of the proscribed goods. As we have said the evils aimed at by the Act are the spread of substandard labor conditions through the use of the facilities of interstate commerce for competition by the goods so produced with those produced under the prescribed or better labor conditions; and the consequent dislocation of the commerce itself caused by the impairment or destruction of local businesses by competition made effective through interstate commerce. The Act is thus directed at the suppression of a method or kind of competition in interstate commerce which it has in effect condemned as "unfair", as the Clayton Act...has condemned other "unfair methods of competition" made effective through interstate commerce.

The Sherman Act and the National Labor Relations Act are familiar examples of the exertion of the commerce power to prohibit or control activities wholly intrastate because of their effect on interstate commerce. See as to the Sherman Act, *Northern Securities Company v. United States* (1904); *Swift & Co. v. United States* (1905). As to the National Labor Relations Act, see *National Labor Relations Board v. Fainblatt* (1939).

The means adopted by § 15(a)(2) for the protection of interstate commerce by the suppression of the production of the condemned goods for interstate commerce is so related to the commerce and so affects it as to be within the reach of the commerce power. Congress, to attain its objective in the suppression of nationwide competition in interstate commerce by goods produced under substandard labor conditions, has made no distinction as to the volume or amount of shipments in the commerce or of production for commerce by any particular shipper or producer. It recognized that in present day industry, competition by a small part may affect the whole and that the total effect of the competition of many small producers may be great. The legislation aimed at a whole embraces all its parts.

So far as *Carter v. Carter Coal Co.* (1936) is inconsistent with this conclusion, its doctrine is limited in principle by the decisions under the Sherman Act and the National Labor Relations Act, which we have cited and which we follow....

Our conclusion is unaffected by the 10th Amendment which provides: "The powers not delegated to the United States by the Constitution, nor prohibited by it to the States, are reserved to the States respectively, or to the people". The amendment states but a truism that all is retained which has not been surrendered. There is nothing in the history of its adoption to suggest that it was more than declaratory of the relationship between the national and state governments as it had been established by the Constitution before the amendment or that its purpose was other than to allay fears that the new national government might seek to exercise powers not granted, and that the states might not be able to exercise fully their reserved powers. See e.g., *Elliot's Debates, Annals of Congress*; Story, *Commentaries on the Constitution*....

Reversed.

United States v. Darby: Questions

1. Do *Darby* (and the following) post-New Deal cases on the Commerce Clause represent the abandonment of an attempt to restrain congressional power to regulate the economy?

2. What is the rule of the case? What is the significance of the Court's overruling *Hammer v. Dagenhart* (1918)?
3. How does the Court deal with the 10th Amendment? The Court cites *Gibbons v. Ogden* (1824). Is the citation appropriate? Why or why not?
4. After this decision, is there any classification of products that Congress could not exclude from interstate commerce?
5. What is the significance of congressional motive? If the Congress acts within its commerce power, does it matter that its motives are not primarily commercial?

Note: *Congress and Individual Rights*

Rebecca E. Zietlow

Congress has historically played an important role in defining and protecting individual rights. The Reconstruction Era was the genesis of this role. In 1833, the Supreme Court had held that the Bill of Rights did not apply to the states in Barron v. Baltimore. More importantly, neither the original Constitution nor the Bill of Rights empowered Congress to enact legislation protecting individual rights. During congressional debates over Reconstruction measures, Rep. John Bingham, the chief author of §1 of the 14th Amendment, argued that individual rights had "been unhappily disregarded by more than one state of this Union ... simply because of want of power in Congress to enforce that guarantee." *Cong. Globe*, 39th Cong., 1st Sess. 429 (Jan. 25, 1866). Bingham and his allies included congressional enforcement provisions in all three of the Reconstruction Amendments, the 13th, 14th, and 15th. All three amendments give Congress the power to enact "appropriate" legislation to enforce the measures—a reference to the broad test for congressional power that Justice Marshall had articulated in McCulloch v. Maryland. The Reconstruction Amendments thus represent a robust commitment to define and protect individual rights, a commitment that is also included in every constitutional amendment since Reconstruction which expands individual rights.

Beginning in Reconstruction, members of Congress have enacted numerous rights-protecting measures. Reconstruction Era statutes include the 1866 Civil Rights Act, which declares that "all persons" in the United States have "the same right ... to make and enforce contracts ... and to the full and equal benefit of the laws ... as is enjoyed by white citizens." Civil Rights Act of 1866, ch. 31, §1, 14 Stat. 27 (codified at 42 U.S.C. §§1981–1982 (2000)), and the 1871 Enforcement Act, which creates a private right of action for any individual who is deprived "of any rights, privileges or immunities secured by the Constitution and laws" by any person acting under color of state law, and prohibits conspiracies by state or private actors to prevent a person from "exercising any right or privilege of a citizen of the United States," including the right to vote, serve on juries, and "obtain equal protection of the law." Ku Klux Klan Act of 1871, ch. 22, §2(3), 17 Stat 13, codified in Rev. Stat. Of 1874, §1980, now 42 U.S.C. §1985(3). These Reconstruction Era statutes still play a central role in contemporary civil rights law.

After the end of Reconstruction, Congress did not enact any more civil rights legislation for almost a century. Jim Crow laws and state mandated segregation took over in the South, enforced by brutal violence, and private segregation reigned in the North. In the early Twentieth Century, individual rights were more often viewed in terms of economic rights, as members of the early labor movement demanded legal protections for the rights of workers. While the Court was enforcing the "right to contract" during the

Lochner Era, Congress responded to the labor movement and enacted statutes protecting the rights of workers. At first, the Court struck down those statutes on the grounds that they fell beyond congressional power or violated the right to contract. As a result of the Great Depression, and bowing to pressure from President Franklin Roosevelt, the Court backed down, enabling the New Deal Congress to enact the broadest legislative program establishing individual economic rights in our nation's history. Chief among those measures were the National Labor Relations Act, which established the worker's right to organize in a union, ch. 372, 49 Stat. 449 (1935) (codified as amended at 29 U.S.C. §§ 151–166 (2000)), the Fair Labor Standards Act, which established a federal minimum wage law, ch. 676, 52 Stat. 1060 (1938) (codified as amended at 29 U.S.C. §§ 201–219 (2000)), and the Social Security Act, which established a federal economic safety net, ch. 531, 49 Stat. 620 (1935). These measures represented a strong federal commitment to the economic welfare of people in the United States.

The expanded federal power over commerce achieved during the New Deal era eventually provided the constitutional basis for much civil rights legislation, including the Civil Rights Act of 1964. The 1964 Act banned discrimination in places of public accommodation (such as hotels, restaurants, movie theaters, etc.). It also banned discrimination in employment based on race, religion, national origin, or sex. Power under the Commerce Clause was crucial because the Court had held that Congress lacked power to reach private discrimination under the 14th Amendment. Later the Court did hold that racial discrimination in contracts and purchase of real estate could be banned under the 13th Amendment, but that later precedent still would not have provided a basis for banning sex discrimination, for example, or discrimination based on religion.

Unfortunately, racial equality was lacking from the New Deal economic measures because Roosevelt and his allies depended on the support of southern segregationist Democrats. Roosevelt by executive order did ban discrimination in defense plants. However, the economic and social pressures of the Depression and the Second World War led to the genesis of the modern civil rights movement. Hundreds of civil rights measures were introduced in Congress in the 1940s and 1950s, but they died in committees and filibusters led by segregationists. Still in July, 1948, President Truman, by executive order, decreed an end to segregation in the military. Earlier in 1947 Truman had appointed a Civil Rights Committee. It issued a landmark report calling for an end to racial discrimination. As the civil rights movement gained momentum, so did their supporters in Congress. At the 1963 March for Jobs and Freedom in Washington DC, where Martin Luther King gave his famous "I Have a Dream" speech, activists demanded legislation ending private segregation. Following the assassination of President John Kennedy and an 89 day filibuster, Congress enacted the 1964 Civil Rights Act, which prohibits race discrimination in employment, private accommodations, and by recipients of federal funds. Title VII of that act also prohibits employment discrimination based on gender, religion or ethnicity.

In 1965, Congress enacted a landmark Voting Rights Act over another prolonged filibuster, and the floodgates were open. The next three decades saw a explosion of activity as Congress enacted legislation to remedy discrimination on the basis of gender, disability and age, and establish a right to education for disabled children. During those years, Congress also expanded economic rights, establishing the Medicare and Medicaid programs, benefits for the disabled and funding for public housing. Congress continues to act regularly to expand individual rights. Recent measures include the 1996 Violence Against Women Act, the 2000 Trafficking Victims Protection Act, and the 2009 Lilly Ledbetter Pay Equity Act. These statutes are evidence that a significant number of members of Congress take seriously their duty to protect individual rights.

Like courts, Congress does not always act to expand rights. Judicial review plays a valuable role in protecting liberty interests and ensuring that legislatures do not violate the baseline of rights established by the Constitution. Moreover, Congress does not act unless it is pressured by political and social movements. Nevertheless, it is important to recognize that courts are not the only institution that protects individual rights, even the rights of minorities. Congress is mandated to do so by the Constitution, and throughout our history members of Congress have followed that mandate. The members of the Reconstruction Congress intended Congress to have broad power to do so, and courts should defer to that power.

* * *

See generally, Rebecca E. Zietlow, *Enforcing Equality: Congress, the Constitution, and the Protection of Individual Rights* (N.Y. Univ. Press 2006).

Wickard v. Filburn
317 U.S. 111 (1942)

[Majority: Jackson, Stone (C.J.), Black, Frankfurter, Byrnes, Douglas, Murphy, Reed, Roberts.]

Mr. Justice Jackson delivered the opinion of the Court.

The appellee filed his complaint against the Secretary of Agriculture of the United States, three members of the County Agricultural Conservation Committee for Montgomery County, Ohio, and a member of the State Agricultural Conservation Committee for Ohio. He sought to enjoin enforcement against himself of the marketing penalty imposed by the amendment of May 26, 1941, to the Agricultural Adjustment Act of 1938, upon that part of his 1941 wheat crop which was available for marketing in excess of the marketing quota established for his farm. He also sought a declaratory judgment that the wheat marketing quota provisions of the Act, as amended and applicable to him, were unconstitutional because not sustainable under the Commerce Clause or consistent with the Due Process Clause of the 5th Amendment....

The appellee for many years past has owned and operated a small farm in Montgomery County, Ohio, maintaining a herd of dairy cattle, selling milk, raising poultry, and selling poultry and eggs. It has been his practice to raise a small acreage of winter wheat, sown in the Fall and harvested in the following July; to sell a portion of the crop; to feed part to poultry and livestock on the farm, some of which is sold; to use some in making flour for home consumption, and to keep the rest for the following seeding. The intended disposition of the crop here involved has not been expressly stated.

In July of 1940, pursuant to the Agricultural Adjustment Act of 1938, as then amended, there were established for the appellee's 1941 crop a wheat acreage allotment of 11.1 acres and a normal yield of 20.1 bushels of wheat an acre. He was given notice of such allotment in July of 1940, before the Fall planting of his 1941 crop of wheat, and again in July of 1941, before it was harvested. He sowed, however, 23 acres, and harvested from his 11.9 acres of excess acreage 239 bushels, which, under the terms of the Act as amended on May 26, 1941, constituted farm marketing excess, subject to a penalty of 49 cents a bushel, or $117.11 in all. The appellee has not paid the penalty....

The general scheme of the Agricultural Adjustment Act of 1938 as related to wheat is to control the volume moving in interstate and foreign commerce in order to avoid surpluses and shortages and the consequent abnormally low or high wheat prices and obstructions to commerce....

II. It is urged that, under the Commerce Clause of the Constitution, Article I, § 8, clause 3, Congress does not possess the power it has in this instance sought to exercise. The question would merit little consideration, since our decision in *United States v. Darby* (1941), sustaining the federal power to regulate production of goods for commerce, except for the fact that this Act extends federal regulation to production not intended in any part for commerce, but wholly for consumption on the farm. The Act includes a definition of "market" and its derivatives, so that, as related to wheat, in addition to its conventional meaning, it also means to dispose of by feeding (in any form) to poultry or livestock which, or the products of which, are sold, bartered, or exchanged, or to be so disposed of.

Hence, marketing quotas not only embrace all that may be sold without penalty, but also what may be consumed on the premises. Wheat produced on excess acreage is designated as "available for marketing" as so defined, and the penalty is imposed thereon. Penalties do not depend upon whether any part of the wheat, either within or without the quota, is sold or intended to be sold. The sum of this is that the Federal Government fixes a quota including all that the farmer may harvest for sale or for his own farm needs, and declares that wheat produced on excess acreage may neither be disposed of nor used except upon payment of the penalty, or except it is stored as required by the Act or delivered to the Secretary of Agriculture.

Appellee says that this is a regulation of production and consumption of wheat. Such activities are, he urges, beyond the reach of Congressional power under the Commerce Clause, since they are local in character, and their effects upon interstate commerce are, at most, "indirect." In answer, the Government argues that the statute regulates neither production nor consumption, but only marketing, and, in the alternative, that, if the Act does go beyond the regulation of marketing, it is sustainable as a "necessary and proper" implementation of the power of Congress over interstate commerce.

The Government's concern lest the Act be held to be a regulation of production or consumption, rather than of marketing, is attributable to a few dicta and decisions of this Court which might be understood to lay it down that activities such as "production," "manufacturing," and "mining" are strictly "local" and, except in special circumstances which are not present here, cannot be regulated under the commerce power because their effects upon interstate commerce are, as matter of law, only "indirect." Even today, when this power has been held to have great latitude, there is no decision of this Court that such activities may be regulated where no part of the product is intended for interstate commerce or intermingled with the subjects thereof. We believe that a review of the course of decision under the Commerce Clause will make plain, however, that questions of the power of Congress are not to be decided by reference to any formula which would give controlling force to nomenclature such as "production" and "indirect" and foreclose consideration of the actual effects of the activity in question upon interstate commerce.

At the beginning, Chief Justice Marshall described the federal commerce power with a breadth never yet exceeded. *Gibbons v. Ogden* (1824). He made emphatic the embracing and penetrating nature of this power by warning that effective restraints on its exercise must proceed from political, rather than from judicial, processes.

For nearly a century, however, decisions of this Court under the Commerce Clause dealt rarely with questions of what Congress might do in the exercise of its granted power under the Clause, and almost entirely with the permissibility of state activity which it was claimed discriminated against or burdened interstate commerce. During this period, there was perhaps little occasion for the affirmative exercise of the commerce power, and the influence of the Clause on American life and law was a negative one, resulting almost wholly from its operation as a restraint upon the powers of the states. In discussion and decision, the point of reference, instead of being what was "necessary and proper" to the exercise by Congress of its granted power, was often some concept of sovereignty thought to be implicit in the status of statehood. Certain activities such as "production," "manufacturing," and "mining" were occasionally said to be within the province of state governments and beyond the power of Congress under the Commerce Clause.

It was not until 1887, with the enactment of the Interstate Commerce Act, that the interstate commerce power began to exert positive influence in American law and life. This first important federal resort to the commerce power was followed in 1890 by the Sherman Anti-Trust Act and, thereafter, mainly after 1903, by many others. These statutes ushered in new phases of adjudication, which required the Court to approach the interpretation of the Commerce Clause in the light of an actual exercise by Congress of its power thereunder.

When it first dealt with this new legislation, the Court adhered to its earlier pronouncements, and allowed but little scope to the power of Congress. *United States v. E. C. Knight Co.* (1895). These earlier pronouncements also played an important part in several of the five cases in which this Court later held that Acts of Congress under the Commerce Clause were in excess of its power.

Even while important opinions in this line of restrictive authority were being written, however, other cases called forth broader interpretations of the Commerce Clause destined to supersede the earlier ones, and to bring about a return to the principles first enunciated by Chief Justice Marshall in *Gibbons v. Ogden*.

Not long after the decision of *United States v. E. C. Knight Co.*, Mr. Justice Holmes, in sustaining the exercise of national power over intrastate activity, stated for the Court that "commerce among the States is not a technical legal conception, but a practical one, drawn from the course of business." *Swift & Co. v. United States* (1905). It was soon demonstrated that the effects of many kinds of intrastate activity upon interstate commerce were such as to make them a proper subject of federal regulation....

In the *Shreveport Rate Cases* (1914), the Court held that railroad rates of an admittedly intrastate character and fixed by authority of the state might, nevertheless, be revised by the Federal Government because of the economic effects which they had upon interstate commerce....

The Court's recognition of the relevance of the economic effects in the application of the Commerce Clause, exemplified by this statement, has made the mechanical application of legal formulas no longer feasible. Once an economic measure of the reach of the power granted to Congress in the Commerce Clause is accepted, questions of federal power cannot be decided simply by finding the activity in question to be "production," nor can consideration of its economic effects be foreclosed by calling them "indirect." The present Chief Justice has said in summary of the present state of the law:

> The commerce power is not confined in its exercise to the regulation of commerce among the states. It extends to those activities intrastate which so affect interstate commerce, or the exertion of the power of Congress over it, as to make regulation of them appropriate means to the attainment of a legitimate end, the effective execution of the granted power to regulate interstate commerce.... The power of Congress over interstate commerce is plenary and complete in itself, may

be exercised to its utmost extent, and acknowledges no limitations other than are prescribed in the Constitution....

Whether the subject of the regulation in question was "production," "consumption," or "marketing" is, therefore, not material for purposes of deciding the question of federal power before us. That an activity is of local character may help in a doubtful case to determine whether Congress intended to reach it. The same consideration might help in determining whether, in the absence of Congressional action, it would be permissible for the state to exert its power on the subject matter, even though, in so doing, it to some degree affected interstate commerce. But even if appellee's activity be local, and though it may not be regarded as commerce, it may still, whatever its nature, be reached by Congress if it exerts a substantial economic effect on interstate commerce, and this irrespective of whether such effect is what might at some earlier time have been defined as "direct" or "indirect."

The parties have stipulated a summary of the economics of the wheat industry....

The wheat industry has been a problem industry for some years....

The effect of consumption of home-grown wheat on interstate commerce is due to the fact that it constitutes the most variable factor in the disappearance of the wheat crop. Consumption on the farm where grown appears to vary in an amount greater than 20 percent of average production. The total amount of wheat consumed as food varies but relatively little, and use as seed is relatively constant.

The maintenance by government regulation of a price for wheat undoubtedly can be accomplished as effectively by sustaining or increasing the demand as by limiting the supply. The effect of the statute before us is to restrict the amount which may be produced for market and the extent, as well, to which one may forestall resort to the market by producing to meet his own needs. That appellee's own contribution to the demand for wheat may be trivial by itself is not enough to remove him from the scope of federal regulation where, as here, his contribution, taken together with that of many others similarly situated, is far from trivial. *Labor Board v. Fainblatt* (1939); *United States v. Darby* (1941).

It is well established by decisions of this Court that the power to regulate commerce includes the power to regulate the prices at which commodities in that commerce are dealt in and practices affecting such prices. One of the primary purposes of the Act in question was to increase the market price of wheat, and, to that end, to limit the volume thereof that could affect the market. It can hardly be denied that a factor of such volume and variability as home-consumed wheat would have a substantial influence on price and market conditions. This may arise because being in marketable condition such wheat overhangs the market, and, if induced by rising prices, tends to flow into the market and check price increases. But if we assume that it is never marketed, it supplies a need of the man who grew it which would otherwise be reflected by purchases in the open market. Home-grown wheat in this sense competes with wheat in commerce. The stimulation of commerce is a use of the regulatory function quite as definitely as prohibitions or restrictions thereon. This record leaves us in no doubt that Congress may properly have considered that wheat consumed on the farm where grown, if wholly outside the scheme of regulation, would have a substantial effect in defeating and obstructing its purpose to stimulate trade therein at increased prices....

III. The statute is also challenged as a deprivation of property without due process of law contrary to the 5th Amendment, both because of its regulatory effect on the appellee and because of its alleged retroactive effect. [The Court rejected the due process claim.]

Wickard v. Filburn: **Questions**

1. What test does the Court embrace for determining congressional power?
2. Is the test consistent with prior cases such as *Carter v. Carter Coal*? Why or why not?
3. How would you synthesize the results of *Wickard*, *Darby*, and *Jones & Laughlin Steel* into a rule? When is the Court likely to defer to legislative judgment?
4. Would the rule in *Gibbons* produce the result in *Wickard* if applied at the time of *Gibbons*? Would the rule in *Gibbons* produce the result in *Wickard* if applied in 1942? What had changed in the meantime? What is the significance of the great changes in our national economy for the power of Congress over commerce? If the framers intended to reserve a substantial sphere for the states and they also intended to give Congress power to regulate all commerce that has a significant effect on the national economy, can those two goals both still be achieved? If not, how should they be reconciled?

An Excerpt from Mark Twain's *Life on the Mississippi*: "Perplexing Lessons"

At the end of what seemed a tedious while, I had managed to pack my head full of islands, towns, bars, "points," and bends; and a curiously inanimate mass of lumber it was, too. However, inasmuch as I could shut my eyes and reel off a good long string of these names without leaving out more than ten miles of river in every fifty, I began to feel that I could take a boat down to New Orleans if I could make her skip those little gaps. But of course my complacency could hardly get started enough to lift my nose a trifle into the air, before Mr. Bixby would think of something to fetch it down again. One day he turned on me suddenly with this settler:—

"What is the shape of Walnut Bend?"

He might as well have asked me my grandmother's opinion of protoplasm. I reflected respectfully, and then said I didn't know it had any particular shape. My gunpowdery chief went off with a bang, of course, and then went on loading and firing until he was out of adjectives.

I had learned long ago that he only carried just so many rounds of ammunition, and was sure to subside into a very placable and even remorseful old smooth-bore as soon as they were all gone. That word "old" is merely affectionate; he was not more than thirty-four. I waited. By and by he said,—

"My boy, you've got to know the *shape* of the river perfectly. It is all there is left to steer by on a very dark night. Everything else is blotted out and gone. But mind you, it hasn't the same shape in the night that it has in the day-time."

"How on earth am I ever going to learn it, then?"

"How do you follow a hall at home in the dark? Because you know the shape of it. You can't see it."

"Do you mean to say that I've got to know all the million trifling variations of shape in the banks of this river as well as I know the shape of the front hall at home?"

"On my honor, you've got to know them *better* than any man ever did know the shapes of the halls in his own house...."

"Oh, don't say any more, please. Have I got to learn the shape of the river according to all these five hundred thousand different ways? If I tried to carry all that cargo in my head it would make me stoop-shouldered."

"*No.* You only learn *the* shape of the river; and you learn it with such absolute certainty that you can always steer by the shape that's *in your head*, and never mind the one that's before your eyes."

"Very well, I'll try it; but after I have learned it can I depend on it? Will it keep the same form and not go fooling around?"

Before Mr. Bixby could answer, Mr. W——— came in to take the watch, and he said,

"Bixby, you'll have to look out for President's Island and all that country clear away up above the Old Hen and Chickens. The banks are caving and the shape of the shores changing like everything. Why, you wouldn't know the point above 40. You can go up inside the old sycamore snag, now."[1]

So that question was answered. Here were leagues of shore changing shape. My spirits were down in the mud again. Two things seemed pretty apparent to me. One was, that in order to be a pilot a man had got to learn more than any one man ought to be allowed to know; and the other was, that he must learn it all over again in a different way every twenty-four hours....

G. The Commerce Clause and the Great Society

Heart of Atlanta: Background

The "sit-in" movement began in Greensboro, North Carolina in 1960. Students from North Carolina A&T State University sat down at the Woolworth Department Store lunch counter to request service. The management of the store refused to serve them and asked them to leave, but the students refused and were arrested for trespass. Soon, blacks and whites began protesting segregated lunch counters, theaters, hotels, and similar public facilities and the "sit-in" movement swept the South. Students were joined by white and black adults, including members of the clergy. As demonstrators were arrested, more and more took their place, often taxing the capacity of local jails.

In many locations, the "sit-ins" and marches to protest segregation were met by white violence, as well as police arrests. Angry whites beat protestors and so, on a number of occasions, did police, who sometimes turned clubs, high powered fire hoses, and police dogs on protestors—including fairly young children. Dr. Martin Luther King, Jr. taught that protestors should respond to attacks with non-violence.

In addition to the sit-in movement, protestors began organizing to demand that the right to vote be restored to black citizens. In much of the South, blacks had been effectively denied the right to vote since the beginning of the 20th century. Local officials responded to efforts to register blacks to vote in Mississippi, Alabama and elsewhere with arrests or simple refusals to register them. At the same time, in a number of Southern states, Klansmen and other angry whites bombed churches, homes, and offices belonging to those supporting civil rights and beat or killed movement supporters.

---

1. It may not be necessary, but still it can do no harm to explain that "inside" means between the snag and the shore.—M.T.

The proposed Civil Rights Act of 1964 was one response to the racial crisis that was wracking the nation. It banned racial discrimination in places of public accommodation and in employment. The Act was strongly supported by President Lyndon Johnson.

Most Republicans and Democrats in the Senate would vote for the Civil Rights Act. Almost all Southern Democrats and all of the few Southern Republicans in Congress voted against the Act. Still, Senator Barry Goldwater, soon to be the Republican nominee for president in 1964, opposed the Civil Rights Bill. Acting on the suggestion of his legal advisers William Rehnquist (later Chief Justice of the United States) and Robert Bork (later Solicitor General and an unsuccessful Reagan nominee to the Court), Goldwater stressed constitutional objections to the bill. It was he said, "a threat to the very essence of our system"—"a usurpation" of power "which 50 sovereign states have reserved for themselves." The bill passed, after the longest filibuster in Senate history up to that time. But Goldwater's opposition to it did not cease. Goldwater said that by attempting to legislate morality, the federal government had "incited hatred and violence" and that the Democratic Party had "protected the Supreme Court in a reign of judicial tyranny."

Many Southern Democrats began to see the Republican Party in a new and much more favorable light. Goldwater supporters took over the tiny Georgia Republican Party and evicted blacks from party positions. "The Negro has been read out of the Republican Party of Georgia here today," a Georgia Goldwater spokesman announced. Strom Thurmond of South Carolina switched parties. He said the switch was justified because the Democrats were engaged in a second Reconstruction. Thurmond joined Louisiana arch-segregationist Leander Perez to host a Louisiana Goldwater rally.

After the passage of the Civil Rights Act, Lyndon Johnson told his aide Bill Moyers that he had delivered the South to the Republicans "for your lifetime and mine." Goldwater carried five deep-South states and many leaders in the Goldwater movement became prominent officials in later Republican administrations. When Richard Nixon was elected President, many leaders of the Goldwater movement assumed high positions in the Department of Justice. William Rehnquist became an Assistant Attorney General and helped to vet prospective Supreme Court nominees, before Nixon nominated him to the Court.

See Taylor Branch, *Pillar of Fire: America in the King Years 1963–65* 301, 356–57, 404–05, 491–93 (1998).

Heart of Atlanta Motel v. United States
379 U.S. 241 (1964)

[Majority: Clark, Warren (C.J.), Goldberg, Brennan, White, Stewart, Harlan, Black, Douglas. Concurring: Black, Douglas, and Goldberg.]

Mr. Justice Clark delivered the opinion of the Court....

1. The Factual Background and Contentions of the Parties.

The case comes here on admissions and stipulated facts. Appellant owns and operates the Heart of Atlanta Motel which has 216 rooms available to transient guests. The motel is located on Courtland Street, two blocks from downtown Peachtree Street. It is readily accessible to interstate highways 75 and 85 and state highways 23 and 41. Appellant solicits patronage from outside the State of Georgia through various national advertising media, including magazines of national circulation; it maintains over 50 billboards and highway signs within the State, soliciting patronage for the motel; it accepts convention trade from outside Georgia and approximately 75% of its registered guests are from out of State.

Prior to passage of the Act the motel had followed a practice of refusing to rent rooms to Negroes, and it alleged that it intended to continue to do so. In an effort to perpetuate that policy this suit was filed.

The appellant contends that Congress in passing this Act exceeded its power to regulate commerce under Art. I, §8, cl. 3, of the Constitution of the United States; that the Act violates the 5th Amendment because appellant is deprived of the right to choose its customers and operate its business as it wishes resulting in a taking of its liberty and property without due process of law and a taking of its property without just compensation; and, finally, that by requiring appellant to rent available rooms to Negroes against its will, Congress is subjecting it to involuntary servitude in contravention of the 13th Amendment.

The appellees counter that the unavailability to Negroes of adequate accommodations interferes significantly with interstate travel, and that Congress, under the Commerce Clause, has power to remove such obstructions and restraints; that the 5th Amendment does not forbid reasonable regulation....

2. The History of the Act.

Congress first evidenced its interest in civil rights legislation in the Civil Rights or Enforcement Act of April 9, 1866. There followed four Acts, with a fifth, the Civil Rights Act of March 1, 1875, culminating the series. In 1883 this Court struck down the public accommodations sections of the 1875 Act in the *Civil Rights Cases* [as not authorized by the 13th or 14th Amendments]. No major legislation in this field had been enacted by Congress for 82 years when the Civil Rights Act of 1957 became law. It was followed by the Civil Rights Act of 1960. Three years later, on June 19, 1963, the late President Kennedy called for civil rights legislation in a message to Congress to which he attached a proposed bill. Its stated purpose was "to promote the general welfare by eliminating discrimination based on race, color, religion, or national origin in public accommodations through the exercise by Congress of the powers conferred upon it to enforce the provisions of the 14th and 15th Amendments, to regulate commerce among the several States, and to make laws necessary and proper to execute the powers conferred upon it by the Constitution."

Bills were introduced in each House of the Congress, embodying the President's suggestion. However, it was not until July 2, 1964, upon the recommendation of President Johnson, that the Civil Rights Act of 1964, here under attack, was finally passed....

3. Title II of the Act.

This Title is divided into seven sections beginning with §201(a) which provides that: "All persons shall be entitled to the full and equal enjoyment of the goods, services, facilities, privileges, advantages, and accommodations of any place of public accommodation, as defined in this section, without discrimination or segregation on the ground of race, color, religion, or national origin."

There are listed in §201(b) four classes of business establishments, each of which "serves the public" and "is a place of public accommodation" within the meaning of §201(a) "if its operations affect commerce, or if discrimination or segregation by it is supported by State action." The covered establishments are:

> "(1) any inn, hotel, motel, or other establishment which provides lodging to transient guests, other than an establishment located within a building which contains not more than five rooms for rent or hire and which is actually occupied by the proprietor of such establishment as his residence...."

Section 201(c) defines the phrase "affect commerce" as applied to the above establishments. It first declares that "any inn, hotel, motel, or other establishment which provides lodging to transient guests affects commerce per se."...

Section 201(d) declares that "discrimination or segregation" is supported by state action when carried on under color of any law, statute, ordinance, regulation or any custom or usage required or enforced by officials of the State or any of its subdivisions....

4. Application of Title II to Heart of Atlanta Motel.

It is admitted that the operation of the motel brings it within the provisions of §201(a) of the Act and that appellant refused to provide lodging for transient Negroes because of their race or color and that it intends to continue that policy unless restrained.

The sole question posed is, therefore, the constitutionality of the Civil Rights Act of 1964 as applied to these facts. The legislative history of the Act indicates that Congress based the Act on §5 and the Equal Protection Clause of the 14th Amendment as well as its power to regulate interstate commerce under Art. I, §8, cl. 3, of the Constitution.

The Senate Commerce Committee made it quite clear that the fundamental object of Title II was to vindicate "the deprivation of personal dignity that surely accompanies denials of equal access to public establishments." At the same time, however, it noted that such an objective has been and could be readily achieved "by congressional action based on the commerce power of the Constitution." Our study of the legislative record, made in the light of prior cases, has brought us to the conclusion that Congress possessed ample power in this regard, and we have therefore not considered the other grounds relied upon. This is not to say that the remaining authority upon which it acted was not adequate, a question upon which we do not pass, but merely that since the commerce power is sufficient for our decision here we have considered it alone. Nor is §201(d) or §202, having to do with state action, involved here and we do not pass upon either of those sections.

5. *The Civil Rights Cases*, and their Application.

In light of our ground for decision, it might be well at the outset to discuss the *Civil Rights Cases* (1883), which declared provisions of the Civil Rights Act of 1875 unconstitutional. We think that decision inapposite, and without precedential value in determining the constitutionality of the present Act. Unlike Title II of the present legislation, the 1875 Act broadly proscribed discrimination in "inns, public conveyances on land or water, theaters, and other places of public amusement," without limiting the categories of affected businesses to those impinging upon interstate commerce.... Although the principles which we apply today are those first formulated by Chief Justice Marshall in *Gibbons v. Ogden* (1824), the conditions of transportation and commerce have changed dramatically, and we must apply those principles to the present state of commerce. The sheer increase in volume of interstate traffic alone would give discriminatory practices which inhibit travel a far larger impact upon the Nation's commerce than such practices had on the economy of another day. Finally, there is language in the *Civil Rights Cases* which indicates that the Court did not fully consider whether the 1875 Act could be sustained as an exercise of the commerce power....

6. The Basis of Congressional Action.

While the Act as adopted carried no congressional findings the record of its passage through each house is replete with evidence of the burdens that discrimination by race or color places upon interstate commerce. This testimony included the fact that our people have become increasingly mobile with millions of people of all races traveling from State to State; that Negroes in particular have been the subject of discrimination in transient accommodations, having to travel great distances to secure the same; that often they have been unable to obtain accommodations and have had to call upon friends to put them up overnight; and that these conditions had become so acute as to require the listing of available lodging for Negroes in a special guidebook which was itself "dramatic testimony to the difficulties" Negroes encounter in travel. These exclusionary practices were found to be nationwide, the Under Secretary of Commerce testifying that there is "no question that this discrimination in the North still exists to a large degree" and in the West and Midwest as well. This testimony indicated a qualitative as well as quantitative effect on interstate travel by Negroes. The former was the obvious impairment of the Negro traveler's pleasure and convenience that resulted when he continually was uncertain of finding lodging. As for the latter, there was evidence that this uncertainty stemming from racial discrimination had the effect of discouraging travel on the part of a substantial portion of the Negro community. This was the conclusion not only of the Under Secretary of Commerce but also of the Administrator of the Federal Aviation Agency who wrote the Chairman of the Senate Commerce Committee that it was his "belief that air commerce is adversely affected by the denial to a substantial segment of the traveling public of adequate and desegregated public accommodations." We shall not burden this opinion with further details since the voluminous testimony presents overwhelming evidence that discrimination by hotels and motels impedes interstate travel.

7. The Power of Congress Over Interstate Travel.

The power of Congress to deal with these obstructions depends on the meaning of the Commerce Clause. Its meaning was first enunciated 140 years ago by the great Chief Justice John Marshall in *Gibbons v. Ogden* (1824), in these words:

> The subject to be regulated is commerce; and ... to ascertain the extent of the power, it becomes necessary to settle the meaning of the word. The counsel for the appellee would limit it to traffic, to buying and selling, or the interchange of commodities but it is something more: it is intercourse ... between nations, and parts of nations, in all its branches, and is regulated by prescribing rules for carrying on that intercourse.
>
> To what commerce does this power extend? The constitution informs us, to commerce "with foreign nations, and among the several States, and with the Indian tribes."
>
> It has, we believe, been universally admitted, that these words comprehend every species of commercial intercourse.... No sort of trade can be carried on ... to which this power does not extend.
>
> The subject to which the power is next applied, is to commerce "among the several States." The word "among" means intermingled....
>
> [I]t may very properly be restricted to that commerce which concerns more States than one.... The genius and character of the whole government seem to be, that its action is to be applied to all the ... internal concerns [of the Nation] which affect the States generally; but not to those which are completely within a particular State, which do not affect other States, and with which it is not necessary to interfere, for the purpose of executing some of the general powers of the government.
>
> We are now arrived at the inquiry—What is this power?" It is the power to regulate; that is, to prescribe the rule by which commerce is to be governed. This power, like all others vested in Congress, is complete in itself, may be exercised

to its utmost extent, and acknowledges no limitations, other than are prescribed in the constitution.... If, as has always been understood, the sovereignty of Congress ... is plenary as to those objects (specified in the Constitution), the power over commerce ... is vested in Congress as absolutely as it would be in a single government, having in its constitution the same restrictions on the exercise of the power as are found in the constitution of the United States. The wisdom and the discretion of Congress, their identity with the people, and the influence which their constituents possess at elections, are, in this, as in many other instances, as that, for example, of declaring war, the sole restraints on which they have relied, to secure them from its abuse. They are the restraints on which the people must often rely solely, in all representative governments.

In short, the determinative test of the exercise of power by the Congress under the Commerce Clause is simply whether the activity sought to be regulated is "commerce which concerns more States than one" and has a real and substantial relation to the national interest. Let us now turn to this facet of the problem.

That the "intercourse" of which the Chief Justice spoke included the movement of persons through more States than one was settled as early as 1849, in the *Passenger Cases* (*Smith v. Turner*), where Mr. Justice McLean stated: "That the transportation of passengers is a part of commerce is not now an open question."...

Nor does it make any difference whether the transportation is commercial in character....

The same interest in protecting interstate commerce which led Congress to deal with segregation in interstate carriers and the white-slave traffic has prompted it to extend the exercise of its power to gambling, *Lottery Case* (*Champion v Ames*) (1903); to criminal enterprises, *Brooks v. United States* (1925); to deceptive practices in the sale of products, *Federal Trade Comm. v. Mandel Bros., Inc.* (1959); to fraudulent security transactions, *Securities & Exchange Comm. v. Ralston Purina Co.* (1953); to misbranding of drugs, *Weeks v. United States* (1918); to wages and hours, *United States v. Darby* (1941); to members of labor unions, *NLRB v. Jones & Laughlin Steel Corp.* (1937); to crop control, *Wickard v. Filburn* (1942); to discrimination against shippers, *United States v. Baltimore & Ohio R. Co.* (1948); to the protection of small business from injurious price cutting, *Moore v. Mead's Fine Bread Co.* (1954); to resale price maintenance, *Hudson Distributors, Inc. v. Eli Lilly & Co.* (1964); to professional football, *Radovich v. National Football League* (1957); and to racial discrimination by owners and managers of terminal restaurants, *Boynton v. Com. of Virginia* (1960).

That Congress was legislating against moral wrongs in many of these areas rendered its enactments no less valid. In framing Title II of this Act Congress was also dealing with what it considered a moral problem. But that fact does not detract from the overwhelming evidence of the disruptive effect that racial discrimination has had on commercial intercourse. It was this burden which empowered Congress to enact appropriate legislation, and, given this basis for the exercise of its power, Congress was not restricted by the fact that the particular obstruction to interstate commerce with which it was dealing was also deemed a moral and social wrong.

It is said that the operation of the motel here is of a purely local character. But, assuming this to be true, "(i)f it is interstate commerce that feels the pinch, it does not matter how local the operation which applies the squeeze." *United States v. Women's Sportswear Mfg. Ass'n* (1949)....

Nor does the Act deprive appellant of liberty or property under the 5th Amendment. The commerce power invoked here by the Congress is a specific and plenary one authorized by the Constitution itself. The only questions are: (1) whether Congress had a rational basis for finding that racial discrimination by motels affected commerce, and (2) if it had such a basis, whether the means it selected to eliminate that evil are reasonable and appropriate. If they are, appellant has no "right" to select its guests as it sees fit, free from governmental regulation.

There is nothing novel about such legislation. Thirty-two States now have it on their books either by statute or executive order and many cities provide such regulation. Some of these Acts go back fourscore years....

It is doubtful if in the long run appellant will suffer economic loss as a result of the Act. Experience is to the contrary where discrimination is completely obliterated as to all public accommodations. But whether this be true or not is of no consequence since this Court has specifically held that the fact that a "member of the class which is regulated may suffer economic losses not shared by others ... has never been a barrier" to such legislation. *Bowles v. Willingham* (1944). Likewise in a long line of cases this Court has rejected the claim that the prohibition of racial discrimination in public accommodations interferes with personal liberty. See *District of Columbia v. John R. Thompson Co.* (1953), and cases there cited, where we concluded that Congress had delegated law-making power to the District of Columbia "as broad as the police power of a state" which included the power to adopt a "law prohibiting discriminations against Negroes by the owners and managers of restaurants in the District of Columbia." ...

We, therefore, conclude that the action of the Congress in the adoption of the Act as applied here to a motel which concededly serves interstate travelers is within the power granted it by the Commerce Clause of the Constitution, as interpreted by this Court for 140 years....

Affirmed.

[Justices Black, Douglas and Goldberg each wrote separate concurrences.]

Katzenbach v. McClung
379 U.S. 294 (1964)

[Majority: Clark, Warren (C.J.), Brennan, White, Stewart, Harlan, Black, Douglas, Goldberg. Concurring: Black, Douglas, and Goldberg.]

Mr. Justice Clark delivered the opinion of the Court.

... Ollie's Barbecue is a family-owned restaurant in Birmingham, Alabama, specializing in barbecued meats and homemade pies, with a seating capacity of 220 customers. It is located on a state highway 11 blocks from an interstate and a somewhat greater distance from railroad and bus stations. The restaurant caters to a family and white-collar trade with a take-out service for Negroes. It employs 36 persons, two-thirds of whom are Negroes. In the 12 months preceding the passage of the [1964 Civil Rights] Act, the restaurant purchased locally approximately $150,000 worth of food, $69,683 or 46% of which was meat that it bought from a local supplier who had procured it from outside the State. The District Court expressly found that a substantial portion of the food served in the restaurant had moved in interstate commerce. The restaurant has refused to serve Negroes in its dining accommodations since its original opening in 1927, and since July 2, 1964, it has been operating in violation of the Act. The court below concluded that if it were required to serve Negroes it would lose a substantial amount of business....

3. The Act As Applied.

Section 201(a) of Title II commands that all persons shall be entitled to the full and equal enjoyment of the goods and services of any place of public accommodation without discrimination or segregation on the ground of race, color, religion, or national origin....

Ollie's Barbecue admits that it is covered by these provisions of the Act. The Government makes no contention that the discrimination at the restaurant was supported by the State of Alabama. There is no claim that interstate travelers frequented the restaurant. The sole question, therefore, narrows down to whether Title II, as applied to a restaurant annually receiving about $70,000 worth of food which has moved in commerce, is a valid exercise of the power of Congress. The Government has contended that Congress had ample basis upon which to find that racial discrimination at restaurants which receive from out of state a substantial portion of the food served does, in fact, impose commercial burdens of national magnitude upon interstate commerce. The appellees' major argument is directed to this premise. They urge that no such basis existed. It is to that question that we now turn.

4. The Congressional Hearings....

The record is replete with testimony of the burdens placed on interstate commerce by racial discrimination in restaurants. A comparison of per capita spending by Negroes in restaurants, theaters, and like establishments indicated less spending, after discounting income differences, in areas where discrimination is widely practiced. This condition, which was especially aggravated in the South, was attributed in the testimony of the Under Secretary of Commerce to racial segregation....

Moreover there was an impressive array of testimony that discrimination in restaurants had a direct and highly restrictive effect upon interstate travel by Negroes. This resulted, it was said, because discriminatory practices prevent Negroes from buying prepared food served on the premises while on a trip, except in isolated and unkempt restaurants and under most unsatisfactory and often unpleasant conditions. This obviously discourages travel and obstructs interstate commerce for one can hardly travel without eating. Likewise, it was said, that discrimination deterred professional, as well as skilled, people from moving into areas where such practices occurred and thereby caused industry to be reluctant to establish there.

We believe that this testimony afforded ample basis for the conclusion that established restaurants in such areas sold less interstate goods because of the discrimination, that interstate travel was obstructed directly by it, that business in general suffered and that many new businesses refrained from establishing there as a result of it. Hence the District Court was in error in concluding that there was no connection between discrimination and the movement of interstate commerce. The court's conclusion that such a connection is outside "common experience" flies in the face of stubborn fact.

It goes without saying that, viewed in isolation, the volume of food purchased by Ollie's Barbecue from sources supplied from out of state was insignificant when compared with the total foodstuffs moving in commerce. But, as our late Brother Jackson said for the Court in *Wickard v. Filburn* (1942):

> That appellee's own contribution to the demand for wheat may be trivial by itself is not enough to remove him from the scope of federal regulation where, as here, his contribution, taken together with that of many others similarly situated, is far from trivial.

We noted in *Heart of Atlanta Motel* (1964) that a number of witnesses attested to the fact that racial discrimination was not merely a state or regional problem but was one of nationwide scope. Against this background, we must conclude that while the focus of the legislation was on the individual restaurant's relation to interstate commerce, Congress appropriately considered the importance of that connection with the knowledge that the discrimination was but "representative of many others throughout the country, the total incidence of which if left unchecked may well become far-reaching in its harm to commerce." *Polish National Alliance of U.S. v. NLRB* (1944).

With this situation spreading as the record shows, Congress was not required to await the total dislocation of commerce. As was said in *Consolidated Edison Co. of New York v. National Labor Relations Board* (1938):

> But it cannot be maintained that the exertion of federal power must await the disruption of that commerce. Congress was entitled to provide reasonable preventive measures and that was the object of the National Labor Relations Act.

5. The Power of Congress to Regulate Local Activities.

Article I, §8, cl. 3, confers upon Congress the power "(t)o regulate Commerce ... among the several States" and Clause 18 of the same Article grants it the power "(t)o make all Laws which shall be necessary and proper for carrying into Execution the foregoing Powers...." This grant, as we have pointed out in *Heart of Atlanta Motel* "extends to those activities intrastate which so affect interstate commerce, or the exertion of the power of Congress over it, as to make regulation of them appropriate means to the attainment of a legitimate end, the effective execution of the granted power to regulate interstate commerce." *United States v. Wrightwood Dairy Co.* (1942). Much is said about a restaurant business being local but "even if appellee's activity be local and though it may not be regarded as commerce, it may still, whatever its nature, be reached by Congress if it exerts a substantial economic effect on interstate commerce...." *Wickard v. Filburn*. The activities that are beyond the reach of Congress are "those which are completely within a particular State, which do not affect other States, and with which it is not necessary to interfere, for the purpose of executing some of the general powers of the government." *Gibbons v. Ogden* (1824). This rule is as good today as it was when Chief Justice Marshall laid it down almost a century and a half ago....

The appellees contend that Congress has arbitrarily created a conclusive presumption that all restaurants meeting the criteria set out in the Act "affect commerce." Stated another way, they object to the omission of a provision for a case-by-case determination—judicial or administrative—that racial discrimination in a particular restaurant affects commerce.

But Congress' action in framing this Act was not unprecedented. In *United States v. Darby* (1941), this Court held constitutional the Fair Labor Standards Act of 1938. There Congress determined that the payment of substandard wages to employees engaged in the production of goods for commerce, while not itself commerce, so inhibited it as to be subject to federal regulation. The appellees in that case argued, as do the appellees here, that the Act was invalid because it included no provision for an independent inquiry regarding the effect on commerce of substandard wages in a particular business. But the Court rejected the argument, observing that:

> [S]ometimes Congress itself has said that a particular activity affects the commerce, as it did in the present Act, the Safety Appliance Act, and the Railway Labor Act... In passing on the validity of legislation of the class last mentioned the only function of courts is to determine whether the particular activity regulated or prohibited is within the reach of the federal power.

Here, as there, Congress has determined for itself that refusals of service to Negroes have imposed burdens both upon the interstate flow of food and upon the movement of products generally. Of course, the mere fact that Congress has said when particular activity shall be deemed to affect commerce does not preclude further examination by this Court. But where we find that the legislators, in light of the facts and testimony before them, have a rational basis for finding a chosen regulatory scheme necessary to the protection of commerce, our investigation is at an end. The only remaining question—one answered in the affirmative by the court below—is whether the particular restaurant either serves or offers to serve interstate travelers or serves food a substantial portion of which has moved in interstate commerce....

Confronted as we are with the facts laid before Congress, we must conclude that it had a rational basis for finding that racial discrimination in restaurants had a direct and adverse effect on the free flow of interstate commerce. Insofar as the sections of the Act here relevant are concerned, §§ 201(b)(2) and (c), Congress prohibited discrimination only in those establishments having a close tie to interstate commerce, i.e., those, like the McClungs', serving food that has come from out of the State. We think in so doing that Congress acted well within its power to protect and foster commerce in extending the coverage of Title II only to those restaurants offering to serve interstate travelers or serving food, a substantial portion of which has moved in interstate commerce.

The absence of direct evidence connecting discriminatory restaurant service with the flow of interstate food, a factor on which the appellees place much reliance, is not, given the evidence as to the effect of such practices on other aspects of commerce, a crucial matter.

The power of Congress in this field is broad and sweeping; where it keeps within its sphere and violates no express constitutional limitation it has been the rule of this Court, going back almost to the founding days of the Republic, not to interfere. The Civil Rights Act of 1964, as here applied, we find to be plainly appropriate in the resolution of what the Congress found to be a national commercial problem of the first magnitude. We find it in no violation of any express limitations of the Constitution and we therefore declare it valid.

The judgment is therefore reversed.

[Concurring opinions by Black, Douglas and Goldberg, JJ., omitted.]

H. Dual Federalism and the Commerce Clause: The Rehnquist Revolution

Note: *Perez v. United States*

Following cases such as *Wickard* (1942), *Heart of Atlanta* (1964), and *Katzenbach v. McClung* 1964), many commentators believed that congressional power under the Commerce Clause was subject only to political—and not judicial—check.

Justice Stewart sounded a cautionary warning in his lone dissent in *Perez v. United States* (1971). The Court readily accepted Congress' decision to make *any* loan sharking a federal crime because loan sharking was often linked to organized crime and could be seen to have national effects. Justice Stewart stated:

> Congress surely has power under the Commerce Clause to enact criminal laws to protect the instrumentalities of interstate commerce, to prohibit the misuse

of the channels or facilities of interstate commerce, and to prohibit or regulate those intrastate activities that have a demonstrably substantial effect on interstate commerce. But under the statute before us a man can be convicted without any proof of interstate movement, of the use of the facilities of interstate commerce, or of facts showing that his conduct affected interstate commerce. I think the Framers of the Constitution never intended that the National Government might define as a crime and prosecute such wholly local activity through the enactment of federal criminal laws.

In order to sustain this law we would, in my view, have to be able at the least to say that Congress could rationally have concluded that loan sharking is an activity with interstate attributes that distinguish it in some substantial respect from other local crime. But it is not enough to say that loan sharking is a national problem, for all crime is a national problem. It is not enough to say that some loan sharking has interstate characteristics, for any crime may have an interstate setting. And the circumstance that loan sharking has an adverse impact on interstate business is not a distinguishing attribute, for interstate business suffers from almost all criminal activity, be it shoplifting or violence in the streets.

Because I am unable to discern any rational distinction between loan sharking and other local crime, I cannot escape the conclusion that this statute was beyond the power of Congress to enact. The definition and prosecution of local, intrastate crime are reserved to the States under the 9th and 10th Amendments.

This claim that there are *judicially* enforceable limits on congressional use of the Commerce Clause was prescient. In *United States v. Lopez* (1995) the Court held that the Gun-Free School Zones Act of 1990, which made it a federal crime to knowingly possess a firearm in a school zone, exceeded Congress' authority under the Commerce Clause. *Lopez*, a controversial 5–4 decision, marked the first time since *Carter Coal* in 1936 that the Court had overturned a statute based on the Commerce Clause. *Lopez* is discussed extensively in *United States v. Morrison* (2000), where the Court once again exercised heightened review.

Presidents Ronald Reagan (1981–1989) and George H.W. Bush (1989–1993) made reduction of the scope of the federal government and protection of the role of the states in the federal system campaign issues. President Reagan appointed three Justices to the Court, Justices O'Connor, Scalia, and Kennedy, and he elevated Justice Rehnquist to be Chief Justice. President Bush appointed Justices Souter and Thomas. Justices Rehnquist, O'Connor, Scalia, Kennedy, and Thomas have provided the five crucial votes in the Court's recent Commerce Clause and state sovereign immunity federalism decisions.

Excerpt from the Second Inaugural Address of President Ronald Reagan

January 21, 1985

... Four years ago, I spoke to you of a New Beginning, and we have accomplished that. But in another sense, our New Beginning is a continuation of that beginning created two centuries ago when, for the first time in history, government, the people said, was not our master, it is our servant; its only power is that which we the people allow it to have.

That system has never failed us, but for a time we failed the system. We asked things of government that government was not equipped to give. We yielded authority to the National Government that properly belonged to States or to local governments or to the people themselves. We allowed taxes and inflation to rob us of our earnings and savings and watched the great industrial machine that had made us the most productive people on Earth slow down and the number of unemployed increase.

By 1980 we knew it was time to renew our faith, to strive with all our strength toward the ultimate in individual freedom, consistent with an orderly society.

We believed then and now: There are no limits to growth and human progress when men and women are free to follow their dreams. And we were right to believe that. Tax rates have been reduced, inflation cut dramatically, and more people are employed than ever before in our history....

I will shortly submit a budget to the Congress aimed at freezing government program spending for the next year. Beyond this, we must take further steps to permanently control government's power to tax and spend. We must act now to protect future generations from government's desire to spend its citizens' money and tax them into servitude when the bills come due. Let us make it unconstitutional for the Federal Government to spend more than the Federal Government takes in.

We have already started returning to the people and to State and local governments responsibilities better handled by them. Now, there is a place for the Federal Government in matters of social compassion. But our fundamental goals must be to reduce dependency and upgrade the dignity of those who are infirm or disadvantaged. And here, a growing economy and support from family and community offer our best chance for a society where compassion is a way of life, where the old and infirm are cared for, the young and, yes, the unborn protected, and the unfortunate looked after and made self-sufficient....

United States v. Morrison
529 U.S. 598 (2000)

[Majority: Rehnquist (C.J.), O'Connor, Scalia, Kennedy, Thomas. Concurring: Thomas. Dissenting: Souter, Breyer, Stevens, and Ginsburg.]

Chief Justice Rehnquist delivered the opinion of the Court.

In these cases we consider the constitutionality of 42 U.S.C. § 13981, which provides a federal civil remedy for the victims of gender-motivated violence. The United States Court of Appeals for the Fourth Circuit, sitting en banc, struck down § 13981 because it concluded that Congress lacked constitutional authority to enact the section's civil remedy. Believing that these cases are controlled by our decisions in *United States v. Lopez* (1995), *United States v. Harris* (1883), and the *Civil Rights Cases* (1883), we affirm.

I. Petitioner Christy Brzonkala enrolled at Virginia Polytechnic Institute (Virginia Tech) in the fall of 1994. In September of that year, Brzonkala met respondents Antonio Morrison and James Crawford, who were both students at Virginia Tech and members of its varsity football team. Brzonkala alleges that, within 30 minutes of meeting Morrison and Crawford, they assaulted and repeatedly raped her. After the attack, Morrison allegedly told Brzonkala, "You better not have any ... diseases." In the months following the rape, Morrison also allegedly announced in the dormitory's dining room that he "like[d] to get girls drunk and...." ...

Brzonkala alleges that this attack caused her to become severely emotionally disturbed and depressed. She sought assistance from a university psychiatrist, who prescribed antidepressant medication. Shortly after the rape Brzonkala stopped attending classes and withdrew from the university.

In early 1995, Brzonkala filed a complaint against respondents under Virginia Tech's Sexual Assault Policy. During the school-conducted hearing on her complaint, Morrison admitted having sexual contact with her despite the fact that she had twice told him "no." After the hearing, Virginia Tech's Judicial Committee found insufficient evidence to punish Crawford, but found Morrison guilty of sexual assault and sentenced him to immediate suspension for two semesters.

Virginia Tech's dean of students upheld the judicial committee's sentence. However, in July 1995, Virginia Tech informed Brzonkala that Morrison intended to initiate a court challenge to his conviction under the Sexual Assault Policy. University officials told her that a second hearing would be necessary to remedy the school's error in prosecuting her complaint under that policy, which had not been widely circulated to students. The university therefore conducted a second hearing under its Abusive Conduct Policy, which was in force prior to the dissemination of the Sexual Assault Policy. Following this second hearing the Judicial Committee again found Morrison guilty and sentenced him to an identical 2-semester suspension. This time, however, the description of Morrison's offense was, without explanation, changed from "sexual assault" to "using abusive language."

Morrison appealed his second conviction through the university's administrative system. On August 21, 1995, Virginia Tech's senior vice president and provost set aside Morrison's punishment. She concluded that it was "'excessive when compared with other cases where there has been a finding of violation of the Abusive Conduct Policy.... '" Virginia Tech did not inform Brzonkala of this decision. After learning from a newspaper that Morrison would be returning to Virginia Tech for the fall 1995 semester, she dropped out of the university.

In December 1995, Brzonkala sued Morrison, Crawford, and Virginia Tech in the United States District Court for the Western District of Virginia. Her complaint alleged that Morrison's and Crawford's attack violated §13981 and that Virginia Tech's handling of her complaint violated Title IX of the Education Amendments of 1972....

[T]he court [of appeals] by a divided vote affirmed the District Court's conclusion that Congress lacked constitutional authority to enact §13981's civil remedy. Because the Court of Appeals invalidated a federal statute on constitutional grounds, we granted certiorari.

Section 13981 was part of the Violence Against Women Act of 1994. It states that "[a]ll persons within the United States shall have the right to be free from crimes of violence motivated by gender." 42 U.S.C. §13981(b). To enforce that right, subsection (c) declares:

> A person (including a person who acts under color of any statute, ordinance, regulation, custom, or usage of any State) who commits a crime of violence motivated by gender and thus deprives another of the right declared in subsection (b) of this section shall be liable to the party injured, in an action for the recovery of compensatory and punitive damages, injunctive and declaratory relief, and such other relief as a court may deem appropriate.

Section 13981 defines a "crim[e] of violence motivated by gender" as "a crime of violence committed because of gender or on the basis of gender, and due, at least in part, to an animus based on the victim's gender." §13981(d)(1). It also provides that the term "crime of violence" includes any

> (A) ... act or series of acts that would constitute a felony against the person or that would constitute a felony against property if the conduct presents a serious risk of physical injury to another, and that would come within the meaning of

State or Federal offenses described in § 16 of Title 18, whether or not those acts have actually resulted in criminal charges, prosecution, or conviction and whether or not those acts were committed in the special maritime, territorial, or prison jurisdiction of the United States; and

(B) includes an act or series of acts that would constitute a felony described in subparagraph (A) but for the relationship between the person who takes such action and the individual against whom such action is taken. § 13981(d)(2).

Further clarifying the broad scope of § 13981's civil remedy, subsection (e)(2) states that "[n]othing in this section requires a prior criminal complaint, prosecution, or conviction to establish the elements of a cause of action under subsection (c) of this section." And subsection (e)(3) provides a § 13981 litigant with a choice of forums: Federal and state courts "shall have concurrent jurisdiction" over complaints brought under the section.

Although the foregoing language of § 13981 covers a wide swath of criminal conduct, Congress placed some limitations on the section's federal civil remedy. Subsection (e)(1) states that "[n]othing in this section entitles a person to a cause of action under subsection (c) of this section for random acts of violence unrelated to gender or for acts that cannot be demonstrated, by a preponderance of the evidence, to be motivated by gender." Subsection (e)(4) further states that § 13981 shall not be construed "to confer on the courts of the United States jurisdiction over any State law claim seeking the establishment of a divorce, alimony, equitable distribution of marital property, or child custody decree."

Every law enacted by Congress must be based on one or more of its powers enumerated in the Constitution. "The powers of the legislature are defined and limited; and that those limits may not be mistaken or forgotten, the constitution is written." *Marbury v. Madison* (1803) (Marshall, C.J.). Congress explicitly identified the sources of federal authority on which it relied in enacting § 13981. It said that a "federal civil rights cause of action" is established "[p]ursuant to the affirmative power of Congress ... under § 5 of the 14th Amendment to the Constitution, as well as under § 8 of Article I of the Constitution." 42 U.S.C. § 13981(a). We address Congress' authority to enact this remedy under each of these constitutional provisions in turn.

II. Due respect for the decisions of a coordinate branch of Government demands that we invalidate a congressional enactment only upon a plain showing that Congress has exceeded its constitutional bounds. See *United States v. Lopez* (Kennedy, J., concurring); *United States v. Harris*. With this presumption of constitutionality in mind, we turn to the question whether § 13981 falls within Congress' power under Article I, § 8, of the Constitution. Brzonkala and the United States rely upon the third clause of the Article, which gives Congress power "[t]o regulate Commerce with foreign Nations, and among the several States, and with the Indian Tribes."

As we discussed at length in *Lopez*, our interpretation of the Commerce Clause has changed as our Nation has developed. We need not repeat that detailed review of the Commerce Clause's history here; it suffices to say that, in the years since *NLRB v. Jones & Laughlin Steel Corp.* (1937), Congress has had considerably greater latitude in regulating conduct and transactions under the Commerce Clause than our previous case law permitted.

Lopez emphasized, however, that even under our modern, expansive interpretation of the Commerce Clause, Congress' regulatory authority is not without effective bounds.

> [E]ven [our] modern-era precedents which have expanded congressional power under the Commerce Clause confirm that this power is subject to outer limits.

In *Jones & Laughlin Steel,* the Court warned that the scope of the interstate commerce power "must be considered in the light of our dual system of government and may not be extended so as to embrace effects upon interstate commerce so indirect and remote that to embrace them, in view of our complex society, would effectually obliterate the distinction between what is national and what is local and create a completely centralized government."

As we observed in *Lopez,* modern Commerce Clause jurisprudence has "identified three broad categories of activity that Congress may regulate under its commerce power" [citing *Hodel v. Virginia Surface Mining & Reclamation Assn., Inc.* (1981); *Perez v. United States* (1971)]. "First, Congress may regulate the use of the channels of interstate commerce" [citing *Heart of Atlanta Motel, Inc. v. United States* (1964); *United States v. Darby* (1941)]. "Second, Congress is empowered to regulate and protect the instrumentalities of interstate commerce, or persons or things in interstate commerce, even though the threat may come only from intrastate activities" (citing *Shreveport Rate Cases* (1914); *Perez*). "Finally, Congress' commerce authority includes the power to regulate those activities having a substantial relation to interstate commerce, ... i.e., those activities that substantially affect interstate commerce" (citing *Jones & Laughlin Steel*).

Petitioners do not contend that these cases fall within either of the first two of these categories of Commerce Clause regulation. They seek to sustain § 13981 as a regulation of activity that substantially affects interstate commerce. Given § 13981's focus on gender-motivated violence wherever it occurs (rather than violence directed at the instrumentalities of interstate commerce, interstate markets, or things or persons in interstate commerce), we agree that this is the proper inquiry.

Since *Lopez* most recently canvassed and clarified our case law governing this third category of Commerce Clause regulation, it provides the proper framework for conducting the required analysis of § 13981. In *Lopez,* we held that the Gun-Free School Zones Act of 1990, which made it a federal crime to knowingly possess a firearm in a school zone, exceeded Congress' authority under the Commerce Clause. Several significant considerations contributed to our decision.

First, we observed that 18 U.S.C. § 922(q) was "a criminal statute that by its terms has nothing to do with 'commerce' or any sort of economic enterprise, however broadly one might define those terms." Reviewing our case law, we noted that "we have upheld a wide variety of congressional Acts regulating intrastate economic activity where we have concluded that the activity substantially affected interstate commerce." Although we cited only a few examples, including *Wickard v. Filburn* (1942); *Hodel*; *Perez*; *Katzenbach v. McClung* (1964); and *Heart of Atlanta Motel,* we stated that the pattern of analysis is clear. *Lopez.* "Where economic activity substantially affects interstate commerce, legislation regulating that activity will be sustained."

Both petitioners and Justice Souter's dissent downplay the role that the economic nature of the regulated activity plays in our Commerce Clause analysis. But a fair reading of *Lopez* shows that the noneconomic, criminal nature of the conduct at issue was central to our decision in that case. ("The Act [does not] regulat[e] a commercial activity"), ("Even *Wickard,* which is perhaps the most far reaching example of Commerce Clause authority over intrastate activity, involved economic activity in a way that the possession of a gun in a school zone does not"), ("Section 922(q) is not an essential part of a larger regulation of economic activity"), ("Admittedly, a determination whether an intrastate activity is commercial or noncommercial may in some cases result in legal uncertainty. But, so long as Congress' authority is limited to those powers enumerated in the Constitution, and so long as those enumerated powers are interpreted as having judicially enforceable outer limits, congressional legislation under the Commerce Clause always will engender 'legal uncertainty'"), ("The possession of a gun in a local school zone is in no sense an economic activity that might, through repetition elsewhere, substantially affect any sort of interstate commerce"). [In his concurring opinion Justice Kennedy also stated that] *Lopez* did not alter our "practical conception of commercial regulation" and that Congress may "regulate in the commercial sphere on the assumption that we have a single market and a unified purpose to build a stable national economy." ("Were the Federal Government to take over the regulation of entire areas of traditional state concern, areas having nothing to do with the regulation of commercial activities, the boundaries between the spheres of federal and state authority would blur"), ("[U]nlike the earlier cases to come before the Court here neither the actors nor their conduct has a commercial character, and neither the purposes nor the design of the statute has an evident commercial nexus. The statute makes the simple possession of a gun within 1,000 feet of the grounds of the school a criminal offense. In a sense any conduct in this interdependent world of ours has an ultimate commercial origin or consequence, but we have not yet said the commerce power may reach so far"). *Lopez's* review of Commerce Clause case law demonstrates that in those cases where we have sustained federal regulation of intrastate activity based upon the activity's substantial effects on interstate commerce, the activity in question has been some sort of economic endeavor.

The second consideration that we found important in analyzing § 922(q) was that the statute contained "no express jurisdictional element which might limit its reach to a discrete set of firearm possessions that additionally have an explicit connection with or effect on interstate commerce." Such a jurisdictional element may establish that the enactment is in pursuance of Congress' regulation of interstate commerce.

Third, we noted that neither § 922(q) "'nor its legislative history contain[s] express congressional findings regarding the effects upon interstate commerce of gun possession in a school zone.'" While "Congress normally is not required to make formal findings as to the substantial burdens that an activity has on interstate commerce," the existence of such findings may "enable us to evaluate the legislative judgment that the activity in question substantially affect[s] interstate commerce, even though no such substantial effect [is] visible to the naked eye."

Finally, our decision in *Lopez* rested in part on the fact that the link between gun possession and a substantial effect on interstate commerce was attenuated. The United States argued that the possession of guns may lead to violent crime, and that violent crime "can be expected to affect the functioning of the national economy in two ways. First, the costs of violent crime are substantial, and, through the mechanism of insurance, those costs are spread throughout the population. Second, violent crime reduces the willingness of individuals to travel to areas within the country that are perceived to be unsafe." The Government also argued that the presence of guns at schools poses a threat to the educational process, which in turn threatens to produce a less efficient and productive workforce, which will negatively affect national productivity and thus interstate commerce.

We rejected these "costs of crime" and "national productivity" arguments because they would permit Congress to "regulate not only all violent crime, but all activities that might lead to violent crime, regardless of how tenuously they relate to interstate commerce." We noted that, under this but-for reasoning:

> Congress could regulate any activity that it found was related to the economic productivity of individual citizens: family law (including marriage, divorce, and

child custody), for example. Under the[se] theories..., it is difficult to perceive any limitation on federal power, even in areas such as criminal law enforcement or education where States historically have been sovereign. Thus, if we were to accept the Government's arguments, we are hard pressed to posit any activity by an individual that Congress is without power to regulate.

With these principles underlying our Commerce Clause jurisprudence as reference points, the proper resolution of the present cases is clear. Gender-motivated crimes of violence are not, in any sense of the phrase, economic activity. While we need not adopt a categorical rule against aggregating the effects of any noneconomic activity in order to decide these cases, thus far in our Nation's history our cases have upheld Commerce Clause regulation of intrastate activity only where that activity is economic in nature.

Like the Gun-Free School Zones Act at issue in *Lopez*, § 13981 contains no jurisdictional element establishing that the federal cause of action is in pursuance of Congress' power to regulate interstate commerce. Although *Lopez* makes clear that such a jurisdictional element would lend support to the argument that § 13981 is sufficiently tied to interstate commerce, Congress elected to cast § 13981's remedy over a wider, and more purely intrastate, body of violent crime.

In contrast with the lack of congressional findings that we faced in *Lopez*, § 13981 is supported by numerous findings regarding the serious impact that gender-motivated violence has on victims and their families. But the existence of congressional findings is not sufficient, by itself, to sustain the constitutionality of Commerce Clause legislation. As we stated in *Lopez*, "'[S]imply because Congress may conclude that a particular activity substantially affects interstate commerce does not necessarily make it so.'" Rather, "'[w]hether particular operations affect interstate commerce sufficiently to come under the constitutional power of Congress to regulate them is ultimately a judicial rather than a legislative question, and can be settled finally only by this Court.'"

In these cases, Congress' findings are substantially weakened by the fact that they rely so heavily on a method of reasoning that we have already rejected as unworkable if we are to maintain the Constitution's enumeration of powers. Congress found that gender-motivated violence affects interstate commerce

> by deterring potential victims from traveling interstate, from engaging in employment in interstate business, and from transacting with business, and in places involved in interstate commerce; ... [and] by diminishing national productivity, increasing medical and other costs, and decreasing the supply of and the demand for interstate products.

Given these findings and petitioners' arguments, the concern that we expressed in *Lopez* that Congress might use the Commerce Clause to completely obliterate the Constitution's distinction between national and local authority seems well founded. The reasoning that petitioners advance seeks to follow the but-for causal chain from the initial occurrence of violent crime (the suppression of which has always been the prime object of the States' police power) to every attenuated effect upon interstate commerce. If accepted, petitioners' reasoning would allow Congress to regulate any crime as long as the nationwide, aggregated impact of that crime has substantial effects on employment, production, transit, or consumption. Indeed, if Congress may regulate gender-motivated violence, it would be able to regulate murder or any other type of violence since gender-motivated violence, as a subset of all violent crime, is certain to have lesser economic impacts than the larger class of which it is a part.

Petitioners' reasoning, moreover, will not limit Congress to regulating violence but may, as we suggested in *Lopez*, be applied equally as well to family law and other areas of traditional state regulation since the aggregate effect of marriage, divorce, and child-rearing on the national economy is undoubtedly significant. Congress may have recognized this specter when it expressly precluded § 13981 from being used in the family law context. Under our written Constitution, however, the limitation of congressional authority is not solely a matter of legislative grace.

We accordingly reject the argument that Congress may regulate noneconomic, violent criminal conduct based solely on that conduct's aggregate effect on interstate commerce. The Constitution requires a distinction between what is truly national and what is truly local. *Lopez* (citing *Jones & Laughlin Steel*). In recognizing this fact we preserve one of the few principles that has been consistent since the Clause was adopted. The regulation and punishment of intrastate violence that is not directed at the instrumentalities, channels, or goods involved in interstate commerce has always been the province of the States. See, e.g., *Cohens v. Virginia* (1821) (stating that Congress "has no general right to punish murder committed within any of the States," and that it is "clear ... that congress cannot punish felonies generally"). Indeed, we can think of no better example of the police power, which the Founders denied the National Government and reposed in the States, than the suppression of violent crime and vindication of its victims. See, e.g., *Lopez* ("The Constitution ... withhold[s] from Congress a plenary police power"); (Thomas, J., concurring) ("[W]e always have rejected readings of the Commerce Clause and the scope of federal power that would permit Congress to exercise a police power") and (noting that the first Congresses did not enact nationwide punishments for criminal conduct under the Commerce Clause).

III. Because we conclude that the Commerce Clause does not provide Congress with authority to enact § 13981, we address petitioners' alternative argument that the section's civil remedy should be upheld as an exercise of Congress' remedial power under § 5 of the 14th Amendment. As noted above, Congress expressly invoked the 14th Amendment as a source of authority to enact § 13981....

[W]e conclude that Congress' power under § 5 does not extend to the enactment of § 13981.

IV. Petitioner Brzonkala's complaint alleges that she was the victim of a brutal assault.... [U]nder our federal system [her] remedy must be provided by the Commonwealth of Virginia, and not by the United States. The judgment of the Court of Appeals is Affirmed.

Justice Thomas, concurring.

The majority opinion correctly applies our decision in *United States v. Lopez* (1995), and I join it in full. I write separately only to express my view that the very notion of a "substantial effects" test under the Commerce Clause is inconsistent with the original understanding of Congress' powers and with this Court's early Commerce Clause cases. By continuing to apply this rootless and malleable standard, however circumscribed, the Court has encouraged the Federal Government to persist in its view that the Commerce Clause has virtually no limits. Until this Court replaces its existing Commerce Clause jurisprudence with a standard more consistent with the original understanding, we will continue to see Congress appropriating state police powers under the guise of regulating commerce.

Justice Souter, with whom Justice Stevens, Justice Ginsburg, and Justice Breyer join, dissenting.

The Court says both that it leaves Commerce Clause precedent undisturbed and that the Civil Rights Remedy of the Violence Against Women Act of 1994, 42 U.S.C. § 13981, exceeds Congress's power under that Clause. I find the claims irreconcilable and respectfully dissent.

Our cases, which remain at least nominally undisturbed, stand for the following propositions. Congress has the power to legislate with regard to activity that, in the aggregate, has a substantial effect on interstate commerce. See *Wickard v. Filburn* (1942); *Hodel v. Virginia Surface Mining & Reclamation Assn.* (1981). The fact of such a substantial effect is not an issue for the courts in the first instance, but for the Congress, whose institutional capacity for gathering evidence and taking testimony far exceeds ours. By passing legislation, Congress indicates its conclusion, whether explicitly or not, that facts support its exercise of the commerce power. The business of the courts is to review the congressional assessment, not for soundness but simply for the rationality of concluding that a jurisdictional basis exists in fact. Any explicit findings that Congress chooses to make, though not dispositive of the question of rationality, may advance judicial review by identifying factual authority on which Congress relied. Applying those propositions in these cases can lead to only one conclusion.

One obvious difference from *United States v. Lopez* (1995), is the mountain of data assembled by Congress, here showing the effects of violence against women on interstate commerce. Passage of the Act in 1994 was preceded by four years of hearings, which included testimony from physicians and law professors; from survivors of rape and domestic violence; and from representatives of state law enforcement and private business. The record includes reports on gender bias from task forces in 21 States, and we have the benefit of specific factual findings in the eight separate Reports issued by Congress and its committees over the long course leading to enactment. Compare *Hodel* (noting "extended hearings," "vast amounts of testimony and documentary evidence," and "years of the most thorough legislative consideration").

> With respect to domestic violence, Congress received evidence for the following findings:
>
>> Three out of four American women will be victims of violent crimes sometime during their life. Violence is the leading cause of injuries to women ages 15 to 44.... [A]s many as 50 percent of homeless women and children are fleeing domestic violence. Since 1974, the assault rate against women has outstripped the rate for men by at least twice for some age groups and far more for others. [B]attering "is the single largest cause of injury to women in the United States." An estimated 4 million American women are battered each year by their husbands or partners. Over 1 million women in the United States seek medical assistance each year for injuries sustained [from] their husbands or other partners. Between 2,000 and 4,000 women die every year from [domestic] abuse. [A]rrest rates may be as low as 1 for every 100 domestic assaults. Partial estimates show that violent crime against women costs this country at least 3 billion—not million, but billion—dollars a year. [E]stimates suggest that we spend $5 to $10 billion a year on health care, criminal justice, and other social costs of domestic violence. The evidence as to rape was similarly extensive, supporting these conclusions: [The incidence of] rape rose four times as fast as the total national crime rate over the past 10 years. According to one study, close to half a million girls now in high school will be raped before they graduate. [One hundred twenty-five thousand] college women can expect to be raped during this—or any—year. [T]hree-quarters of women never go to the movies alone after dark because of the fear of rape....
>
> Based on the data thus partially summarized, Congress found that
>
>> crimes of violence motivated by gender have a substantial adverse effect on interstate commerce, by deterring potential victims from traveling interstate, from

engaging in employment in interstate business, and from transacting with business, and in places involved, in interstate commerce ... by diminishing national productivity, increasing medical and other costs, and decreasing the supply of and the demand for interstate products....

Congress thereby explicitly stated the predicate for the exercise of its Commerce Clause power. Is its conclusion irrational in view of the data amassed? True, the methodology of particular studies may be challenged, and some of the figures arrived at may be disputed. But the sufficiency of the evidence before Congress to provide a rational basis for the finding cannot seriously be questioned. Cf. *Turner Broadcasting System, Inc. v. FCC* (1997) ("The Constitution gives to Congress the role of weighing conflicting evidence in the legislative process").

Indeed, the legislative record here is far more voluminous than the record compiled by Congress and found sufficient in two prior cases upholding Title II of the Civil Rights Act of 1964 against Commerce Clause challenges. In *Heart of Atlanta Motel, Inc. v. United States* (1964), and *Katzenbach v. McClung* (1964), the Court referred to evidence showing the consequences of racial discrimination by motels and restaurants on interstate commerce. Congress had relied on compelling anecdotal reports that individual instances of segregation cost thousands to millions of dollars. Congress also had evidence that the average black family spent substantially less than the average white family in the same income range on public accommodations, and that discrimination accounted for much of the difference.

While Congress did not, to my knowledge, calculate aggregate dollar values for the nationwide effects of racial discrimination in 1964, in 1994 it did rely on evidence of the harms caused by domestic violence and sexual assault, citing annual costs of $3 billion in 1990, and $5 to $10 billion in 1993. Equally important, though, gender-based violence in the 1990's was shown to operate in a manner similar to racial discrimination in the 1960's in reducing the mobility of employees and their production and consumption of goods shipped in interstate commerce. Like racial discrimination, "[g]ender-based violence bars its most likely targets — women — from full partic[ipation] in the national economy."

If the analogy to the Civil Rights Act of 1964 is not plain enough, one can always look back a bit further. In *Wickard*, we upheld the application of the Agricultural Adjustment Act to the planting and consumption of homegrown wheat. The effect on interstate commerce in that case followed from the possibility that wheat grown at home for personal consumption could either be drawn into the market by rising prices, or relieve its grower of any need to purchase wheat in the market. The Commerce Clause predicate was simply the effect of the production of wheat for home consumption on supply and demand in interstate commerce. Supply and demand for goods in interstate commerce will also be affected by the deaths of 2,000 to 4,000 women annually at the hands of domestic abusers, and by the reduction in the work force by the 100,000 or more rape victims who lose their jobs each year or are forced to quit. Violence against women may be found to affect interstate commerce and affect it substantially.

II. The Act would have passed muster at any time between *Wickard* in 1942 and *Lopez* in 1995, a period in which the law enjoyed a stable understanding that congressional power under the Commerce Clause, complemented by the authority of the Necessary and Proper Clause, Art. I. §8 cl. 18, extended to all activity that, when aggregated, has a substantial effect on interstate commerce. As already noted, this understanding was secure even against the turmoil at the passage of the Civil Rights Act of 1964, in the aftermath of which the Court not only reaffirmed the cumulative effects and rational basis features of the substantial effects test, see *Heart of Atlanta; McClung*, but declined to limit the commerce power through a formal distinction between legislation focused on "commerce" and statutes addressing "moral and social wrong[s]," *Heart of Atlanta*.

The fact that the Act does not pass muster before the Court today is therefore proof, to a degree that *Lopez* was not, that the Court's nominal adherence to the substantial effects test is merely that. Although a new jurisprudence has not emerged with any distinctness, it is clear that some congressional conclusions about obviously substantial, cumulative effects on commerce are being assigned lesser values than the once-stable doctrine would assign them. These devaluations are accomplished not by any express repudiation of the substantial effects test or its application through the aggregation of individual conduct, but by supplanting rational basis scrutiny with a new criterion of review.

Thus the elusive heart of the majority's analysis in these cases is its statement that Congress's findings of fact are "weakened" by the presence of a disfavored "method of reasoning." This seems to suggest that the "substantial effects" analysis is not a factual enquiry, for Congress in the first instance with subsequent judicial review looking only to the rationality of the congressional conclusion, but one of a rather different sort, dependent upon a uniquely judicial competence.

This new characterization of substantial effects has no support in our cases (the self-fulfilling prophecies of *Lopez* aside), least of all those the majority cites. Perhaps this explains why the majority is not content to rest on its cited precedent but claims a textual justification for moving toward its new system of congressional deference subject to selective discounts. Thus it purports to rely on the sensible and traditional understanding that the listing in the Constitution of some powers implies the exclusion of others unmentioned. See *Gibbons v. Ogden* (1824); *The Federalist* No. 45. The majority stresses that Art. I, §8, enumerates the powers of Congress, including the commerce power, an enumeration implying the exclusion of powers not enumerated. It follows, for the majority, not only that there must be some limits to "commerce," but that some particular subjects arguably within the commerce power can be identified in advance as excluded, on the basis of characteristics other than their commercial effects. Such exclusions come into sight when the activity regulated is not itself commercial or when the States have traditionally addressed it in the exercise of the general police power, conferred under the state constitutions but never extended to Congress under the Constitution of the Nation.

The premise that the enumeration of powers implies that other powers are withheld is sound; the conclusion that some particular categories of subject matter are therefore presumptively beyond the reach of the commerce power is, however, a non sequitur. From the fact that Art. I, §8, cl. 3 grants an authority limited to regulating commerce, it follows only that Congress may claim no authority under that section to address any subject that does not affect commerce. It does not at all follow that an activity affecting commerce nonetheless falls outside the commerce power, depending on the specific character of the activity, or the authority of a State to regulate it along with Congress. My disagreement with the majority is not, however, confined to logic, for history has shown that categorical exclusions have proven as unworkable in practice as they are unsupportable in theory.

II-A. Obviously, it would not be inconsistent with the text of the Commerce Clause itself to declare "noncommercial" primary activity beyond or presumptively beyond the scope of the commerce power. That variant of categorical approach is not, however, the sole textually permissible way of defining the scope of the Commerce Clause, and any such neat limitation would at least be suspect in the light of the final sentence of Article I, §8, authorizing Congress to make "all Laws ... necessary and proper" to give effect to its enumerated powers such as commerce. See *United States v. Darby* (1941) ("The power of Congress ... extends to those activities intrastate which so affect interstate commerce or the exercise of the power of Congress over it as to make regulation of them appropriate means to the attainment of a legitimate end, the exercise of the granted power of Congress to regulate interstate commerce"). ==Accordingly, for significant periods of our history, the Court has defined the commerce power as plenary, unsusceptible to categorical exclusions, and this was the view expressed throughout the latter part of the 20th century in the substantial effects test==. These two conceptions of the commerce power, plenary and categorically limited, are in fact old rivals, and today's revival of their competition summons up familiar history, a brief reprise of which may be helpful in posing what I take to be the key question going to the legitimacy of the majority's decision to breathe new life into the approach of categorical limitation.

Chief Justice Marshall's seminal opinion in *Gibbons v. Ogden*, construed the commerce power from the start with "a breadth never yet exceeded," *Wickard v. Filburn*. In particular, it is worth noting, the Court in *Wickard* did not regard its holding as exceeding the scope of Chief Justice Marshall's view of interstate commerce; *Wickard* applied an aggregate effects test to ostensibly domestic, noncommercial farming consistently with Chief Justice Marshall's indication that the commerce power may be understood by its exclusion of subjects, among others, "which do not affect other States," *Gibbons*.... And it was this understanding, free of categorical qualifications, that prevailed in the period after 1937 through *Lopez*, as summed up by Justice Harlan: "'Of course, the mere fact that Congress has said when particular activity shall be deemed to affect commerce does not preclude further examination by this Court. But where we find that the legislators ... have a rational basis for finding a chosen regulatory scheme necessary to the protection of commerce, our investigation is at an end.'" *Maryland v. Wirtz* (1968) (quoting *Katzenbach v. McClung* (1964))....

In the half century following the modern activation of the commerce power with passage of the Interstate Commerce Act in 1887, this Court from time to time created categorical enclaves beyond congressional reach by declaring such activities as "mining," "production," "manufacturing," and union membership to be outside the definition of "commerce" and by limiting application of the effects test to "direct" rather than "indirect" commercial consequences. See, e.g., *United States v. E.C. Knight Co.* (1895) (narrowly construing the Sherman Antitrust Act in light of the distinction between "commerce" and "manufacture"); *The Employers' Liability Cases* (1908) (invalidating law governing tort liability for common carriers operating in interstate commerce because the effects on commerce were indirect); *Adair v. United States* (1908) (holding that labor union membership fell outside "commerce"); *Hammer v. Dagenhart* (1918) (invalidating law prohibiting interstate shipment of goods manufactured with child labor as a regulation of "manufacture"); *A.L.A. Schechter Poultry Corp. v. United States* (1935) (invalidating regulation of activities that only "indirectly" affected commerce); *Railroad Retirement Bd. v. Alton R. Co.* (1935) (invalidating pension law for railroad workers on the grounds that conditions of employment were only indirectly linked to commerce); *Carter v. Carter Coal Co.* (1936) (holding that regulation of unfair labor practices in mining regulated "production," not "commerce").

Since adherence to these formalistically contrived confines of commerce power in large measure provoked the judicial crisis of 1937, one might reasonably have doubted that Members of this Court would ever again toy with a return to the days before *NLRB v.*

Jones & Laughlin Steel Corp. (1937), which brought the earlier and nearly disastrous experiment to an end. And yet today's decision can only be seen as a step toward recapturing the prior mistakes. Its revival of a distinction between commercial and noncommercial conduct is at odds with *Wickard*, which repudiated that analysis, and the enquiry into commercial purpose, first intimated by the *Lopez* concurrence, (opinion of Kennedy, J.), is cousin to the intent-based analysis employed in *Hammer*, but rejected for Commerce Clause purposes in *Heart of Atlanta*, and *Darby*.

Why is the majority tempted to reject the lesson so painfully learned in 1937? An answer emerges from contrasting *Wickard* with one of the predecessor cases it superseded. It was obvious in *Wickard* that growing wheat for consumption right on the farm was not "commerce" in the common vocabulary, but that did not matter constitutionally so long as the aggregated activity of domestic wheat growing affected commerce substantially. Just a few years before *Wickard*, however, it had certainly been no less obvious that "mining" practices could substantially affect commerce, even though *Carter Coal* had held mining regulation beyond the national commerce power. When we try to fathom the difference between the two cases, it is clear that they did not go in different directions because the *Carter Coal* Court could not understand a causal connection that the *Wickard* Court could grasp; the difference, rather, turned on the fact that the Court in *Carter Coal* had a reason for trying to maintain its categorical, formalistic distinction, while that reason had been abandoned by the time *Wickard* was decided. The reason was laissez-faire economics, the point of which was to keep government interference to a minimum. The Court in *Carter Coal* was still trying to create a laissez-faire world out of the 20th-century economy, and formalistic commercial distinctions were thought to be useful instruments in achieving that object. The Court in *Wickard* knew it could not do any such thing and in the aftermath of the New Deal had long since stopped attempting the impossible. Without the animating economic theory, there was no point in contriving formalisms in a war with Chief Justice Marshall's conception of the commerce power.

If we now ask why the formalistic economic/noneconomic distinction might matter today, after its rejection in *Wickard*, the answer is not that the majority fails to see causal connections in an integrated economic world. The answer is that in the minds of the majority there is a new animating theory that makes categorical formalism seem useful again. Just as the old formalism had value in the service of an economic conception, the new one is useful in serving a conception of federalism. It is the instrument by which assertions of national power are to be limited in favor of preserving a supposedly discernible, proper sphere of state autonomy to legislate or refrain from legislating as the individual States see fit. The legitimacy of the Court's current emphasis on the noncommercial nature of regulated activity, then, does not turn on any logic serving the text of the Commerce Clause or on the realism of the majority's view of the national economy. The essential issue is rather the strength of the majority's claim to have a constitutional warrant for its current conception of a federal relationship enforceable by this Court through limits on otherwise plenary commerce power. This conception is the subject of the majority's second categorical discount applied today to the facts bearing on the substantial effects test.

II-B. The Court finds it relevant that the statute addresses conduct traditionally subject to state prohibition under domestic criminal law, a fact said to have some heightened significance when the violent conduct in question is not itself aimed directly at interstate commerce or its instrumentalities. Again, history seems to be recycling, for the theory of traditional state concern as grounding a limiting principle has been rejected previously, and more than once. It was disapproved in *Darby* (1941), and held insufficient standing alone to limit the commerce power in *Hodel v. Virginia Surface Mining & Reclamation Assn., Inc.* (1981). In the particular context of the Fair Labor Standards Act it was rejected in *Maryland v. Wirtz* (1968), with the recognition that "[t]here is no general doctrine implied in the Federal Constitution that the two governments, national and state, are each to exercise its powers so as not to interfere with the free and full exercise of the powers of the other." The Court held it to be "clear that the Federal Government, when acting within delegated power, may override countervailing state interests, whether these be described as 'governmental' or 'proprietary' in character.'" While *Wirtz* was later overruled by *National League of Cities v. Usery* (1976), that case was itself repudiated in *Garcia v. San Antonio Metropolitan Transit Authority* (1985), which held that the concept of "traditional governmental function" (as an element of the immunity doctrine under *Hodel*) was incoherent, there being no explanation that would make sense of the multifarious decisions placing some functions on one side of the line, some on the other. The effort to carve out inviolable state spheres within the spectrum of activities substantially affecting commerce was, of course, just as irreconcilable with *Gibbons*'s explanation of the national commerce power as being as "absolut[e] as it would be in a single government."¹

The objection to reviving traditional state spheres of action as a consideration in commerce analysis, however, not only rests on the portent of incoherence, but is compounded by a further defect just as fundamental. The defect, in essence, is the majority's rejection of the Founders' considered judgment that politics, not judicial review, should mediate between state and national interests as the strength and legislative jurisdiction of the National Government inevitably increased through the expected growth of the national economy. Whereas today's majority takes a leaf from the book of the old judicial economists in saying that the Court should somehow draw the line to keep the federal relationship in a proper balance, Madison, Wilson, and Marshall understood the Constitution very differently.

Although Madison had emphasized the conception of a National Government of discrete powers (a conception that a number of the ratifying conventions thought was too indeterminate to protect civil liberties), Madison himself must have sensed the potential

---

1. The Constitution of 1787 did, in fact, forbid some exercises of the commerce power. Article I, §9, cl. 6, barred Congress from giving preference to the ports of one State over those of another. More strikingly, the Framers protected the slave trade from federal interference, see Art. I, §9, cl. 1, and confirmed the power of a State to guarantee the chattel status of slaves who fled to another State, see Art. IV, §2, cl. 3. These reservations demonstrate the plenary nature of the federal power; the exceptions prove the rule. Apart from them, proposals to carve islands of state authority out of the stream of commerce power were entirely unsuccessful. Roger Sherman's proposed definition of federal legislative power as excluding "matters of internal police" met Gouverneur Morris's response that "[t]he internal police ... ought to be infringed in many cases" and was voted down eight to two. 2 *Records of the Federal Convention of 1787*, pp. 25–26 (M. Farrand ed. 1911) (hereinafter Farrand). The Convention similarly rejected Sherman's attempt to include in Article V a proviso that "no state shall ... be affected in its internal police." 5 *Elliot's Debates* 551–52. Finally, Rufus King suggested an explicit bill of rights for the States, a device that might indeed have set aside the areas the Court now declares off-limits. 1 Farrand 493 ("As the fundamental rights of individuals are secured by express provisions in the State Constitutions; why may not a like security be provided for the Rights of States in the National Constitution"). That proposal, too, came to naught. In short, to suppose that enumerated powers must have limits is sensible; to maintain that there exist judicially identifiable areas of state regulation immune to the plenary congressional commerce power even though falling within the limits defined by the substantial effects test is to deny our constitutional history.

scope of some of the powers granted (such as the authority to regulate commerce), for he took care in *The Federalist* No. 46 to hedge his argument for limited power by explaining the importance of national politics in protecting the States' interests. The National Government "will partake sufficiently of the spirit [of the States], to be disinclined to invade the rights of the individual States, or the prerogatives of their governments." *The Federalist* No. 46. James Wilson likewise noted that "it was a favorite object in the Convention" to secure the sovereignty of the States, and that it had been achieved through the structure of the Federal Government. 2 *Elliot's Debates* 438–39. The Framers of the Bill of Rights, in turn, may well have sensed that Madison and Wilson were right about politics as the determinant of the federal balance within the broad limits of a power like commerce, for they formulated the 10th Amendment without any provision comparable to the specific guarantees proposed for individual liberties. In any case, this Court recognized the political component of federalism in the seminal *Gibbons* opinion. After declaring the plenary character of congressional power within the sphere of activity affecting commerce, the Chief Justice spoke for the Court in explaining that there was only one restraint on its valid exercise:

> The wisdom and the discretion of Congress, their identity with the people, and the influence which their constituents possess at elections, are, in this, as in many other instances, as that, for example, of declaring war, the sole restraints on which they have relied, to secure them from its abuse. They are the restraints on which the people must often rely solely, in all representative governments. *Gibbons* (1824).

Politics as the moderator of the congressional employment of the commerce power was the theme many years later in *Wickard*, for after the Court acknowledged the breadth of the *Gibbons* formulation it invoked Chief Justice Marshall yet again in adding that "[h]e made emphatic the embracing and penetrating nature of this power by warning that effective restraints on its exercise must proceed from political rather than judicial processes." Hence, "conflicts of economic interest ... are wisely left under our system to resolution by Congress under its more flexible and responsible legislative process. Such conflicts rarely lend themselves to judicial determination. And with the wisdom, workability, or fairness, of the plan of regulation we have nothing to do."

As with "conflicts of economic interest," so with supposed conflicts of sovereign political interests implicated by the Commerce Clause: the Constitution remits them to politics....

Today's majority ... finds no significance whatever in the state support for the Act based upon the States' acknowledged failure to deal adequately with gender-based violence in state courts, and the belief of their own law enforcement agencies that national action is essential.

The National Association of Attorneys General supported the Act unanimously ... and Attorneys General from 38 States urged Congress to enact the Civil Rights Remedy, representing that "the current system for dealing with violence against women is inadequate." It was against this record of failure at the state level that the Act was passed to provide the choice of a federal forum in place of the state-court systems found inadequate to stop gender-biased violence....

The collective opinion of state officials that the Act was needed continues virtually unchanged, and when the Civil Rights Remedy was challenged in court, the States came to its defense. Thirty-six of them and the Commonwealth of Puerto Rico have filed an amicus brief in support of petitioners in these cases, and only one State has taken respondents' side. It is, then, not the least irony of these cases that the States will be forced to enjoy the new federalism whether they want it or not....

III. All of this convinces me that today's ebb of the commerce power rests on error, and at the same time leads me to doubt that the majority's view will prove to be enduring law. There is yet one more reason for doubt. Although we sense the presence of *Carter Coal*, *Schechter*, and *Usery* once again, the majority embraces them only at arm's-length. Where such decisions once stood for rules, today's opinion points to considerations by which substantial effects are discounted. Cases standing for the sufficiency of substantial effects are not overruled; cases overruled since 1937 are not quite revived. The Court's thinking betokens less clearly a return to the conceptual straitjackets of *Schechter* and *Carter Coal* and *Usery* than to something like the unsteady state of obscenity law between *Redrup v. New York* (1967) and *Miller v. California* (1973), a period in which the failure to provide a workable definition left this Court to review each case ad hoc. As our predecessors learned then, the practice of such ad hoc review cannot preserve the distinction between the judicial and the legislative, and this Court, in any event, lacks the institutional capacity to maintain such a regime for very long. This one will end when the majority realizes that the conception of the commerce power for which it entertains hopes would inevitably fail the test expressed in Justice Holmes's statement that "[t]he first call of a theory of law is that it should fit the facts." O. Holmes, *The Common Law*. The facts that cannot be ignored today are the facts of integrated national commerce and a political relationship between States and Nation much affected by their respective treasuries and constitutional modifications adopted by the people. The federalism of some earlier time is no more adequate to account for those facts today than the theory of laissez-faire was able to govern the national economy 70 years ago.

Justice Breyer, with whom Justice Stevens joins, and with whom Justice Souter and Justice Ginsburg join as to Part I-A, dissenting.

No one denies the importance of the Constitution's federalist principles. Its state/federal division of authority protects liberty—both by restricting the burdens that government can impose from a distance and by facilitating citizen participation in government that is closer to home. The question is how the judiciary can best implement that original federalist understanding where the Commerce Clause is at issue....

I-A. Consider the problems. The "economic/noneconomic" distinction is not easy to apply. Does the local street corner mugger engage in "economic" activity or "noneconomic" activity when he mugs for money? See *Perez v. United States* (1971) (aggregating local "loan sharking" instances); *United States v. Lopez* (1995) (loan sharking is economic because it consists of "intrastate extortionate credit transactions"). Would evidence that desire for economic domination underlies many brutal crimes against women save the present statute? See United States General Accounting Office, Health, Education, and Human Services Division, *Domestic Violence: Prevalence and Implications for Employment Among Welfare Recipients* 7–8 (Nov.1998); *Brief for Equal Rights Advocates*, et al. as Amicus Curiae 10–12.

The line becomes yet harder to draw given the need for exceptions. The Court itself would permit Congress to aggregate, hence regulate, "noneconomic" activity taking place at economic establishments. See *Heart of Atlanta Motel, Inc. v. United States* (1964) (upholding civil rights laws forbidding discrimination at local motels); *Katzenbach v. McClung* (1964) (same for restaurants); *Lopez* (recognizing congressional power to aggregate, hence forbid, noneconomically motivated discrimination at public accommodations)....

More important, why should we give critical constitutional importance to the economic, or noneconomic, nature of an interstate-commerce-affecting cause? If chemical emanations through indirect environmental change cause identical, severe commercial harm outside a State, why should it matter whether local factories or home fireplaces release them? The Constitution itself refers only to Congress' power to "regulate Commerce ... among the several States," and to make laws "necessary and proper" to implement that power. Art. I, § 8, cls. 3, 18. The language says nothing about either the local nature, or the economic nature, of an interstate-commerce-affecting cause.

This Court has long held that only the interstate commercial effects, not the local nature of the cause, are constitutionally relevant. See *NLRB v. Jones & Laughlin Steel Corp.* (1937) (focusing upon interstate effects); *Wickard v. Filburn* (1942) (aggregating interstate effects of wheat grown for home consumption); *Heart of Atlanta Motel*, ("'[I]f it is interstate commerce that feels the pinch, it does not matter how local the operation which applies the squeeze'"). Nothing in the Constitution's language, or that of earlier cases prior to *Lopez*, explains why the Court should ignore one highly relevant characteristic of an interstate-commerce-affecting cause (how "local" it is), while placing critical constitutional weight upon a different, less obviously relevant, feature (how "economic" it is)....

[I]n a world where most everyday products or their component parts cross interstate boundaries, Congress will frequently find it possible to redraft a statute using language that ties the regulation to the interstate movement of some relevant object, thereby regulating local criminal activity or, for that matter, family affairs....

U.S. v. Morrison: Questions

1. Does *Morrison* depart from other pre-*Lopez* Commerce Clause cases? How? How much does it change the scope of federal power? How does it do so?
2. What are the three bases identified in *Lopez* and *Morrison* for congressional power over commerce? How does the Court in *Morrison* limit the commerce power — what tests does it suggest? How is rational basis analysis changed by *Morrison*? Is it completely eliminated or is its scope simply narrowed? If its scope is narrowed, how does the Court do so?
3. Review the abortion statute at the beginning of this chapter. Is the statute within the Commerce Clause power of Congress?
4. What do you think is the appropriate role of Congress in the regulation of commerce?

* * *

In *Morrison*, Justice Thomas referred to and reiterated his concurring opinion in *Lopez*, the gun-free school case. In his *Lopez* concurrence, which is excerpted below, Justice Thomas implicitly rejected most of the Court's Commerce Clause decisions rendered between 1937 and 2000.

Justice Thomas, concurring.

In an appropriate case, I believe that we must further reconsider our "substantial effects" test with an eye toward constructing a standard that reflects the text and history of the Commerce Clause without totally rejecting our more recent Commerce Clause jurisprudence.... I also want to point out the necessity of refashioning a coherent test that does not tend to "obliterate the distinction between what is national and what is local and create a completely centralized government." *NLRB v. Jones & Laughlin Steel Corp.* (1937).

I. At the time the original Constitution was ratified, "commerce" consisted of selling, buying, and bartering, as well as transporting for these purposes. See 1 S. Johnson, *A Dictionary of the English Language* 361 (4th ed. 1773) (defining commerce as "Intercour[s]e; exchange of one thing for another; interchange of any thing; trade; traffick");

N. Bailey, *An Universal Etymological English Dictionary* (26th ed. 1789) ("trade or traffic"); T. Sheridan, *A Complete Dictionary of the English Language* (6th ed. 1796) ("Exchange of one thing for another; trade, traffick").... In fact, when Federalists and Anti-Federalists discussed the Commerce Clause during the ratification period, they often used trade (in its selling/bartering sense) and commerce interchangeably. See *The Federalist* No. 4 (J. Jay) (asserting that countries will cultivate our friendship when our "trade" is prudently regulated by Federal Government); No. 7 (A. Hamilton) (discussing "competitions of commerce" between States resulting from state "regulations of trade"); No. 40 (J. Madison) (asserting that it was an "acknowledged object of the Convention ... that the regulation of trade should be submitted to the general government"); Lee, *Letters of a Federal Farmer No. 5,* in *Pamphlets on the Constitution of the United States* 319 (P. Ford ed. 1888); Smith, An Address to the People of the State of New York....

[T]he term "commerce" was used in contradistinction to productive activities such as manufacturing and agriculture. Alexander Hamilton, for example, repeatedly treated commerce, agriculture, and manufacturing as three separate endeavors. See, e.g., *The Federalist No. 36,* at 224 (referring to "agriculture, commerce, manufactures")....

Moreover, interjecting a modern sense of commerce into the Constitution generates significant textual and structural problems. For example, one cannot replace "commerce" with a different type of enterprise, such as manufacturing. When a manufacturer produces a car, assembly cannot take place "with a foreign nation" or "with the Indian Tribes." ...

The Constitution not only uses the word "commerce" in a narrower sense than our case law might suggest, it also does not support the proposition that Congress has authority over all activities that "substantially affect" interstate commerce. The Commerce Clause does not state that Congress may "regulate matters that substantially affect commerce with foreign Nations, and among the several States, and with the Indian Tribes." In contrast, the Constitution itself temporarily prohibited amendments that would "affect" Congress' lack of authority to prohibit or restrict the slave trade or to enact unproportioned direct taxation. Art. V. Clearly, the Framers could have drafted a Constitution that contained a "substantially affects interstate commerce" Clause had that been their objective.

In addition to its powers under the Commerce Clause, Congress has the authority to enact such laws as are "necessary and proper" to carry into execution its power to regulate commerce among the several States. U.S. Const., Art. I, §8, cl. 18. But on this Court's understanding of congressional power under these two Clauses, many of Congress' other enumerated powers under Art. I, §8, are wholly superfluous. After all, if Congress may regulate all matters that substantially affect commerce, there is no need for the Constitution to specify that Congress may enact bankruptcy laws, cl. 4, or coin money and fix the standard of weights and measures, cl. 5, or punish counterfeiters of United States coin and securities, cl. 6. Likewise, Congress would not need the separate authority to establish post offices and post roads, cl. 7, or to grant patents and copyrights, cl. 8, or to "punish Piracies and Felonies committed on the high Seas," cl. 10. It might not even need the power to raise and support an Army and Navy, cls. 12 and 13, for fewer people would engage in commercial shipping if they thought that a foreign power could expropriate their property with ease. Indeed, if Congress could regulate matters that substantially affect interstate commerce, there would have been no need to specify that Congress can regulate international trade and commerce with the Indians. As the Framers surely understood, these other branches of trade substantially affect interstate commerce.

Put simply, much if not all of Art. I, §8 (including portions of the Commerce Clause itself), would be surplusage if Congress had been given authority over matters that substantially affect interstate commerce. An interpretation of cl. 3 that makes the rest of § 8 superfluous simply cannot be correct. Yet this Court's Commerce Clause jurisprudence has endorsed just such an interpretation: The power we have accorded Congress has swallowed Art. I, § 8.... [T]hese fundamental textual problems should, at the very least, convince us that the "substantial effects" test should be reexamined.

II. The exchanges during the ratification campaign reveal the relatively limited reach of the Commerce Clause and of federal power generally. The Founding Fathers confirmed that most areas of life (even many matters that would have substantial effects on commerce) would remain outside the reach of the Federal Government. Such affairs would continue to be under the exclusive control of the States.... Yet, despite being well aware that agriculture, manufacturing, and other matters substantially affected commerce, the founding generation did not cede authority over all these activities to Congress.... The comments of Hamilton and others about federal power reflected the well-known truth that the new Government would have only the limited and enumerated powers found in the Constitution. See, e.g., 2 Debates 267–268 (A. Hamilton at New York Convention) (noting that there would be just cause for rejecting the Constitution if it would enable the Federal Government to "alter, or abrogate ... [a State's] civil and criminal institutions [or] penetrate the recesses of domestic life, and control, in all respects, the private conduct of individuals"); The *Federalist* No. 45, at 313 (J. Madison); 3 Debates 259 (J. Madison) (Virginia Convention); R. Sherman & O. Ellsworth, Letter to Governor Huntington, Sept. 26, 1787, in 3 Documentary History 352; J. Wilson, Speech in the State House Yard, Oct. 6, 1787, in 2 at 167–168. Agriculture and manufacture, since they were not surrendered to the Federal Government, were state concerns. See The *Federalist* No. 34 (A. Hamilton) (observing that the "internal encouragement of agriculture and manufactures" was an object of state expenditure). Even before the passage of the 10th Amendment, it was apparent that Congress would possess only those powers "herein granted" by the rest of the Constitution. Art. I, § 1.

Where the Constitution was meant to grant federal authority over an activity substantially affecting interstate commerce, the Constitution contains an enumerated power over that particular activity. Indeed, the Framers knew that many of the other enumerated powers in § 8 dealt with matters that substantially affected interstate commerce. Madison, for instance, spoke of the bankruptcy power as being "intimately connected with the regulation of commerce." The Federalist No. 42, at 287. Likewise, Hamilton urged that "[i]f we mean to be a commercial people or even to be secure on our Atlantic side, we must endeavour as soon as possible to have a navy."...

Even though the boundary between commerce and other matters may ignore "economic reality" and thus seem arbitrary or artificial to some, we must nevertheless respect a constitutional line that does not grant Congress power over all that substantially affects interstate commerce....

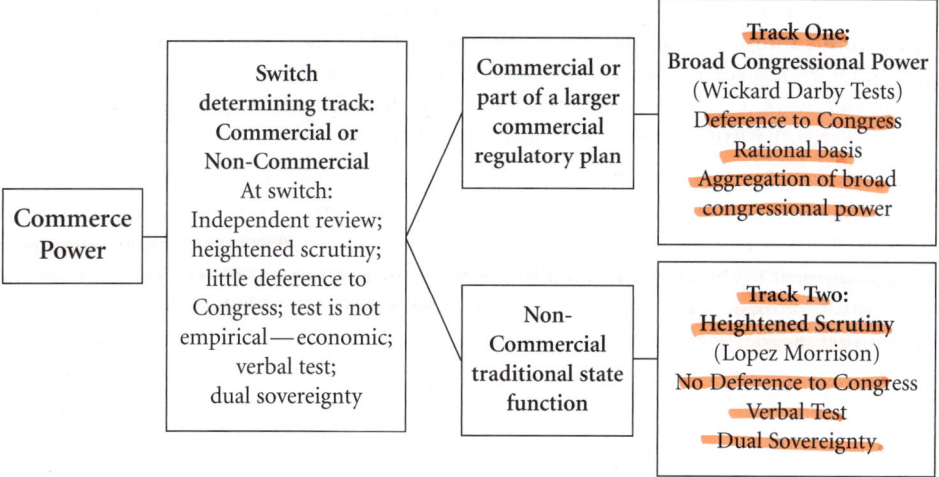

Gonzales v. Raich
545 U.S. 1 (2005)

[Majority: Stevens, Kennedy, Souter, Ginsburg, and Breyer. Concurring: Scalia. Dissenting: O'Connor, Rehnquist, C. J., and Thomas.]

Justice Stevens delivered the opinion of the Court.

California is one of at least nine States that authorize the use of marijuana for medicinal purposes. The question presented in this case is whether the power vested in Congress by Article I, § 8, of the Constitution "[t]o make all Laws which shall be necessary and proper for carrying into Execution" its authority to "regulate Commerce with foreign Nations, and among the several States" includes the power to prohibit the local cultivation and use of marijuana in compliance with California law.

I.... In 1996, California voters passed Proposition 215, now codified as the Compassionate Use Act of 1996. The proposition was designed to ensure that "seriously ill" residents of the State have access to marijuana for medical purposes, and to encourage Federal and State Governments to take steps towards ensuring the safe and affordable distribution of the drug to patients in need. The Act creates an exemption from criminal prosecution for physicians, as well as for patients and primary caregivers who possess or cultivate marijuana for medicinal purposes with the recommendation or approval of a physician. A "primary caregiver" is a person who has consistently assumed responsibility for the housing, health, or safety of the patient.

Respondents Angel Raich and Diane Monson are California residents who suffer from a variety of serious medical conditions and have sought to avail themselves of medical marijuana pursuant to the terms of the Compassionate Use Act. They are being treated by licensed, board-certified family practitioners, who have concluded, after prescribing a host of conventional medicines to treat respondents' conditions and to alleviate their associated symptoms, that marijuana is the only drug available that provides effective treatment. Both women have been using marijuana as a medication for several years pursuant to their doctors' recommendation, and both rely heavily on cannabis to function on a daily basis. Indeed, Raich's physician believes that forgoing cannabis treatments would certainly cause Raich excruciating pain and could very well prove fatal.

Respondent Monson cultivates her own marijuana, and ingests the drug in a variety of ways including smoking and using a vaporizer. Respondent Raich, by contrast, is unable to cultivate her own, and thus relies on two caregivers, litigating as "John Does," to provide her with locally grown marijuana at no charge. These caregivers also process the cannabis into hashish or keif, and Raich herself processes some of the marijuana into oils, balms, and foods for consumption.

On August 15, 2002, county deputy sheriffs and agents from the federal Drug Enforcement Administration (DEA) came to Monson's home. After a thorough investigation, the county officials concluded that her use of marijuana was entirely lawful as a matter of California law. Nevertheless, after a 3-hour standoff, the federal agents seized and destroyed all six of her cannabis plants.

Respondents thereafter brought this action against the Attorney General of the United States and the head of the DEA seeking injunctive and declaratory relief prohibiting the enforcement of the federal Controlled Substances Act (CSA), to the extent it prevents them from possessing, obtaining, or manufacturing cannabis for their personal medical use. In their complaint and supporting affidavits, Raich and Monson described the severity of their afflictions, their repeatedly futile attempts to obtain relief with conventional medications, and the opinions of their doctors concerning their need to use marijuana. Respondents claimed that enforcing the CSA against them would violate the Commerce Clause, the Due Process Clause of the 5th Amendment, the 9th and 10th Amendments of the Constitution, and the doctrine of medical necessity....

The obvious importance of the case prompted our grant of certiorari. The case is made difficult by respondents' strong arguments that they will suffer irreparable harm because, despite a congressional finding to the contrary, marijuana does have valid therapeutic purposes. The question before us, however, is not whether it is wise to enforce the statute in these circumstances; rather, it is whether Congress' power to regulate interstate markets for medicinal substances encompasses the portions of those markets that are supplied with drugs produced and consumed locally. Well-settled law controls our answer. The CSA is a valid exercise of federal power, even as applied to the troubling facts of this case. We accordingly vacate the judgment of the Court of Appeals [that enjoined application of the statute against the respondents].

II. Shortly after taking office in 1969, President Nixon declared a national "war on drugs." As the first campaign of that war, Congress set out to enact legislation that would consolidate various drug laws on the books into a comprehensive statute, provide meaningful regulation over legitimate sources of drugs to prevent diversion into illegal channels, and strengthen law enforcement tools against the traffic in illicit drugs....

Then in 1970, after declaration of the national "war on drugs," federal drug policy underwent a significant transformation.... [P]rompted by a perceived need to consolidate the growing number of piecemeal drug laws and to enhance federal drug enforcement powers, Congress enacted the Comprehensive Drug Abuse Prevention and Control Act.

Title II of that Act, the CSA, repealed most of the earlier antidrug laws in favor of a comprehensive regime to combat the international and interstate traffic in illicit drugs. The main objectives of the CSA were to conquer drug abuse and to control the legitimate and illegitimate traffic in controlled substances. Congress was particularly concerned with the need to prevent the diversion of drugs from legitimate to illicit channels.

To effectuate these goals, Congress devised a closed regulatory system making it unlawful to manufacture, distribute, dispense, or possess any controlled substance except in a manner authorized by the CSA. The CSA categorizes all controlled substances into five schedules. The drugs are grouped together based on their accepted medical uses, the potential for abuse, and their psychological and physical effects on the body. Each schedule is associated with a distinct set of controls regarding the manufacture, distribution, and use of the substances listed therein....

In enacting the CSA, Congress classified marijuana as a Schedule I drug.... Schedule I drugs are categorized as such because of their high potential for abuse, lack of any accepted medical use, and absence of any accepted safety for use in medically supervised treatment.... By classifying marijuana as a Schedule I drug, as opposed to listing it on a lesser schedule, the manufacture, distribution, or possession of marijuana became a criminal offense, with the sole exception being use of the drug as part of a Food and Drug Administration pre-approved research study.

The CSA provides for the periodic updating of schedules and delegates authority to the Attorney General, after consultation with the Secretary of Health and Human Services, to add, remove, or transfer substances to, from, or between schedules. Despite considerable efforts to reschedule marijuana, it remains a Schedule I drug.

III. Respondents in this case do not dispute that passage of the CSA, as part of the Comprehensive Drug Abuse Prevention and Control Act, was well within Congress' commerce power. Nor do they contend that any provision or section of the CSA amounts to an unconstitutional exercise of congressional authority. Rather, respondents' challenge is actually quite limited; they argue that the CSA's categorical prohibition of the manufacture and possession of marijuana as applied to the intrastate manufacture and possession of marijuana for medical purposes pursuant to California law exceeds Congress' authority under the Commerce Clause.

In assessing the validity of congressional regulation, none of our Commerce Clause cases can be viewed in isolation.... For the first century of our history, the primary use of the Clause was to preclude the kind of discriminatory state legislation that had once been permissible. Then, in response to rapid industrial development and an increasingly interdependent national economy, Congress "ushered in a new era of federal regulation under the commerce power," beginning with the enactment of the Interstate Commerce Act in 1887 [regulating railroads] and the Sherman Antitrust Act in 1890.

Cases decided during that "new era," which now spans more than a century, have identified three general categories of regulation in which Congress is authorized to engage under its commerce power. First, Congress can regulate the channels of interstate commerce. *Perez v. United States* (1971). Second, Congress has authority to regulate and protect the instrumentalities of interstate commerce, and persons or things in interstate commerce. Third, Congress has the power to regulate activities that substantially affect interstate commerce. *NLRB v. Jones & Laughlin Steel Corp.* (1937). Only the third category is implicated in the case at hand.

Our case law firmly establishes Congress' power to regulate purely local activities that are part of an economic "class of activities" that have a substantial effect on interstate commerce. See, *e.g., Perez; Wickard v. Filburn* (1942).... As we stated in *Wickard*, "even if appellee's activity be local and though it may not be regarded as commerce, it may still, whatever its nature, be reached by Congress if it exerts a substantial economic effect on interstate commerce." We have never required Congress to legislate with scientific exactitude. When Congress decides that the "total incidence" of a practice poses a threat to a national market, it may regulate the entire class....

Our decision in *Wickard* is of particular relevance. In *Wickard*, we upheld the application of regulations promulgated under the Agricultural Adjustment Act of 1938, which were designed to control the volume of wheat moving in interstate and foreign commerce in order to avoid surpluses and consequent abnormally low prices. The regulations established an allotment of 11.1 acres for Filburn's 1941 wheat crop, but he sowed 23 acres, intending to use the excess by consuming it on his own farm. Filburn argued that even though we had sustained Congress' power to regulate the production of goods for commerce, that power did not authorize "federal regulation [of] production not intended in any part for commerce but wholly for consumption on the farm. *Wickard*....

Justice Jackson's opinion for a unanimous Court rejected this submission. He wrote:

> The effect of the statute before us is to restrict the amount which may be produced for market and the extent as well to which one may forestall resort to the market by producing to meet his own needs. That appellee's own contribution to the demand for wheat may be trivial by itself is not enough to remove him from the scope of federal regulation where, as here, his contribution, taken together with that of many others similarly situated, is far from trivial.

Wickard thus establishes that Congress can regulate purely intrastate activity that is not itself "commercial," in that it is not produced for sale, if it concludes that failure to regulate that class of activity would undercut the regulation of the interstate market in that commodity.

The similarities between this case and *Wickard* are striking. Like the farmer in *Wickard*, respondents are cultivating, for home consumption, a fungible commodity for which there is an established, albeit illegal, interstate market. Just as the Agricultural Adjustment Act was designed "to control the volume [of wheat] moving in interstate and foreign commerce in order to avoid surpluses..." and consequently control the market price, a primary purpose of the CSA is to control the supply and demand of controlled substances in both lawful and unlawful drug markets.

In *Wickard*, we had no difficulty concluding that Congress had a rational basis for believing that, when viewed in the aggregate, leaving home-consumed wheat outside the regulatory scheme would have a substantial influence on price and market conditions. Here too, Congress had a rational basis for concluding that leaving home-consumed marijuana outside federal control would similarly affect price and market conditions.

More concretely, one concern prompting inclusion of wheat grown for home consumption in the 1938 Act was that rising market prices could draw such wheat into the interstate market, resulting in lower market prices. The parallel concern making it appropriate to include marijuana grown for home consumption in the CSA is the likelihood that the high demand in the interstate market will draw such marijuana into that market. While the diversion of homegrown wheat tended to frustrate the federal interest in stabilizing prices by regulating the volume of commercial transactions in the interstate market, the diversion of homegrown marijuana tends to frustrate the federal interest in eliminating commercial transactions in the interstate market in their entirety. In both cases, the regulation is squarely within Congress' commerce power because production of the commodity meant for home consumption, be it wheat or marijuana, has a substantial effect on supply and demand in the national market for that commodity.

Nonetheless, respondents suggest that *Wickard* differs from this case in three respects: (1) the Agricultural Adjustment Act, unlike the CSA, exempted small farming operations; (2) *Wickard* involved a "quintessential economic activity"—a commercial farm—whereas respondents do not sell marijuana; and (3) the *Wickard* record made it clear that the aggregate production of wheat for use on farms had a significant impact on market prices. Those differences, though factually accurate, do not diminish the precedential force of this Court's reasoning.

The fact that Filburn's own impact on the market was "trivial by itself" was not a sufficient reason for removing him from the scope of federal regulation. That the Secretary of Agriculture elected to exempt even smaller farms from regulation does not speak to his power to regulate all those whose aggregated production was significant, nor did that fact play any role in the Court's analysis. Moreover, even though Filburn was indeed a commercial farmer, the activity he was engaged in—the cultivation of wheat for home consumption—was not treated by the Court as part of his commercial farming operation. And while it is true that the record in the *Wickard* case itself established the causal connection between the production for local use and the national market, we have before us findings by Congress to the same effect.

Findings in the introductory sections of the CSA explain why Congress deemed it appropriate to encompass local activities within the scope of the CSA. The submissions of the parties and the numerous *amici* all seem to agree that the national, and international, market for marijuana has dimensions that are fully comparable to those defining the class of activities regulated by the Secretary pursuant to the 1938 statute. Respondents nonetheless insist that the CSA cannot be constitutionally applied to their activities because Congress did not make a specific finding that the intrastate cultivation and possession of marijuana for medical purposes based on the recommendation of a physician would substantially affect the larger interstate marijuana market. Be that as it may, we have never required Congress to make particularized findings in order to legislate, *see United States v. Lopez* (1995); *Perez*, absent a special concern such as the protection of free speech....

In assessing the scope of Congress' authority under the Commerce Clause, we stress that the task before us is a modest one. We need not determine whether respondents' activities, taken in the aggregate, substantially affect interstate commerce in fact, but only whether a "rational basis" exists for so concluding. *Lopez*; *Katzenbach v. McClung* (1964); *Heart of Atlanta Motel, Inc. v. United States* (1964). Given the enforcement difficulties that attend distinguishing between marijuana cultivated locally and marijuana grown elsewhere, 21 U. S. C. §801(5), and concerns about diversion into illicit channels, we have no difficulty concluding that Congress had a rational basis for believing that failure to regulate the intrastate manufacture and possession of marijuana would leave a gaping hole in the CSA. Thus, as in *Wickard*, when it enacted comprehensive legislation to regulate the interstate market in a fungible commodity, Congress was acting well within its authority to "make all Laws which shall be necessary and proper" to "regulate Commerce ... among the several States." U.S. Const., Art. I, §8. That the regulation ensnares some purely intrastate activity is of no moment....

IV. To support their contrary submission, respondents rely heavily on two of our more recent Commerce Clause cases. In their myopic focus, they overlook the larger context of modern-era Commerce Clause jurisprudence preserved by those cases. Moreover, even in the narrow prism of respondents' creation, they read those cases far too broadly. Those two cases, of course, are *Lopez* and *United States v. Morrison* (2000). As an initial matter, the statutory challenges at issue in those cases were markedly different from the challenge respondents pursue in the case at hand. Here, respondents ask us to excise individual applications of a concededly valid statutory scheme. In contrast, in both *Lopez* and *Morrison*, the parties asserted that a particular statute or provision fell outside Congress' commerce power in its entirety. This distinction is pivotal for we have often reiterated that "[w]here the class of activities is regulated and that class is within the reach of federal power, the courts have no power 'to excise, as trivial, individual instances' of the class." *Perez.*

At issue in *Lopez*, was the validity of the Gun-Free School Zones Act of 1990, which was a brief, single-subject statute making it a crime for an individual to possess a gun in a school zone. The Act did not regulate any economic activity and did not contain any requirement that the possession of a gun have any connection to past interstate activity or a predictable impact on future commercial activity. Distinguishing our earlier cases holding that comprehensive regulatory statutes may be validly applied to local conduct that does not, when viewed in isolation, have a significant impact on interstate commerce, we held the statute invalid. We explained:

> Section 922(q) is a criminal statute that by its terms has nothing to do with "commerce" or any sort of economic enterprise, however broadly one might define those terms. Section 922(q) is not an essential part of a larger regulation of economic activity, in which the regulatory scheme could be undercut unless the intrastate activity were regulated. It cannot, therefore, be sustained under our cases upholding regulations of activities that arise out of or are connected with a commercial transaction, which viewed in the aggregate, substantially affects interstate commerce.

The statutory scheme that the Government is defending in this litigation is at the opposite end of the regulatory spectrum. As explained above, the CSA, enacted in 1970 as part of the Comprehensive Drug Abuse Prevention and Control Act, was a lengthy and detailed statute creating a comprehensive framework for regulating the production, distribution, and possession of five classes of "controlled substances." ...

Nor does this Court's holding in *Morrison* [support Respondents]. The Violence Against Women Act of 1994 created a federal civil remedy for the victims of gender-motivated crimes of violence. The remedy was enforceable in both state and federal courts, and generally depended on proof of the violation of a state law. Despite congressional findings that such crimes had an adverse impact on interstate commerce, we held the statute unconstitutional because, like the statute in *Lopez*, it did not regulate economic activity. We concluded that "the noneconomic, criminal nature of the conduct at issue was central to our decision" in *Lopez*, and that our prior cases had identified a clear pattern of analysis: "'Where economic activity substantially affects interstate commerce, legislation regulating that activity will be sustained.'" *Morrison*.

Unlike those at issue in *Lopez* and *Morrison*, the activities regulated by the CSA are quintessentially economic. "Economics" refers to "the production, distribution, and consumption of commodities." *Webster's Third New International Dictionary* 720 (1966). The CSA is a statute that regulates the production, distribution, and consumption of commodities for which there is an established, and lucrative, interstate market. Prohibiting the intrastate possession or manufacture of an article of commerce is a rational (and commonly utilized) means of regulating commerce in that product. Such prohibitions include specific decisions requiring that a drug be withdrawn from the market as a result of the failure to comply with regulatory requirements as well as decisions excluding Schedule I drugs entirely from the market. Because the CSA is a statute that directly regulates economic, commercial activity, our opinion in *Morrison* casts no doubt on its constitutionality....

We have no difficulty concluding that Congress acted rationally in determining that none of the characteristics making up the purported class, whether viewed individually or in the aggregate, compelled an exemption from the CSA; rather, the subdivided class of activities defined by the Court of Appeals was an essential part of the larger regulatory scheme.

First, the fact that marijuana is used "for personal medical purposes on the advice of a physician" cannot itself serve as a distinguishing factor. The CSA designates marijuana as contraband for *any* purpose; in fact, by characterizing marijuana as a Schedule I drug, Congress expressly found that the drug has no acceptable medical uses. Moreover, the CSA is a comprehensive regulatory regime specifically designed to regulate which controlled substances can be utilized for medicinal purposes, and in what manner. Indeed, most of the substances classified in the CSA "have a useful and legitimate medical purpose." ...

Nor can it serve as an "objective marke[r]" or "objective facto[r]" to arbitrarily narrow the relevant class as the dissenters suggest. More fundamentally, if, as the principal dissent contends, the personal cultivation, possession, and use of marijuana for medicinal purposes is beyond the "'outer limits' of Congress' Commerce Clause authority," (Opinion of O'Connor, J.), it must also be true that such personal use of marijuana (or any other homegrown drug) for recreational purposes is also beyond those "'outer limits,'" whether or not a State elects to authorize or even regulate such use. Justice Thomas' separate dissent suffers from the same sweeping implications. That is, the dissenters' rationale logically extends to place *any* federal regulation (including quality, prescription, or quantity controls) of *any* locally cultivated and possessed controlled substance for *any* purpose beyond the "'outer limits'" of Congress' Commerce Clause authority. One need not have a degree in economics to understand why a nationwide exemption for the vast quantity of marijuana (or other drugs) locally cultivated for personal use (which presumably would include use by friends, neighbors, and family members) may have a substantial impact on the interstate market for this extraordinarily popular substance. The congressional judgment that an exemption for such a significant segment of the total market would undermine the orderly enforcement of the entire regulatory scheme is entitled to a strong presumption of validity. Indeed, that judgment is not only rational, but "visible to the naked eye," *Lopez*, under any commonsense appraisal of the probable consequences of such an open-ended exemption.

Second, limiting the activity to marijuana possession and cultivation "in accordance with state law" cannot serve to place respondents' activities beyond congressional reach. The Supremacy Clause unambiguously provides that if there is any conflict between federal and state law, federal law shall prevail. It is beyond peradventure that federal power over commerce is "'superior to that of the States to provide for the welfare or necessities of their inhabitants,'" however legitimate or dire those necessities may be....

Respondents acknowledge this proposition, but nonetheless contend that their activities were not "an essential part of a larger regulatory scheme" because they had been "isolated by the State of California, and [are] policed by the State of California," and thus remain "entirely separated from the market." The dissenters fall prey to similar reasoning. The notion that California law has surgically excised a discrete activity that is hermetically sealed off from the larger interstate marijuana market is a dubious proposition, and, more importantly, one that Congress could have rationally rejected....

The exemption for cultivation by patients and caregivers can only increase the supply of marijuana in the California market. The likelihood that all such production will promptly terminate when patients recover or will precisely match the patients' medical needs during their convalescence seems remote; whereas the danger that excesses will satisfy some of the admittedly enormous demand for recreational use seems obvious.[1] Moreover, that

---

1. For example, respondent Raich attests that she uses 2.5 ounces of cannabis a week. Yet as a resident of Oakland, she is entitled to possess up to 3 pounds of processed marijuana at any given time, nearly 20 times more than she uses on a weekly basis.

the national and international narcotics trade has thrived in the face of vigorous criminal enforcement efforts suggests that no small number of unscrupulous people will make use of the California exemptions to serve their commercial ends whenever it is feasible to do so.² Taking into account the fact that California is only one of at least nine States to have authorized the medical use of marijuana, a fact Justice O'Connor's dissent conveniently disregards in arguing that the demonstrated effect on commerce while admittedly "plausible" is ultimately "unsubstantiated," Congress could have rationally concluded that the aggregate impact on the national market of all the transactions exempted from federal supervision is unquestionably substantial.

So, from the "separate and distinct" class of activities identified by the Court of Appeals (and adopted by the dissenters), we are left with "the intrastate, noncommercial cultivation, possession and use of marijuana." Thus the case for the exemption comes down to the claim that a locally cultivated product that is used domestically rather than sold on the open market is not subject to federal regulation. Given the findings in the CSA and the undisputed magnitude of the commercial market for marijuana, our decisions in *Wickard* and the later cases endorsing its reasoning foreclose that claim.

V. Respondents also raise a substantive due process claim and seek to avail themselves of the medical necessity defense. These theories of relief were set forth in their complaint but were not reached by the Court of Appeals. We therefore do not address the question whether judicial relief is available to respondents on these alternative bases. We do note, however, the presence of another avenue of relief. As the Solicitor General confirmed during oral argument, the statute authorizes procedures for the reclassification of Schedule I drugs. But perhaps even more important than these legal avenues is the democratic process, in which the voices of voters allied with these respondents may one day be heard in the halls of Congress. Under the present state of the law, however, the judgment of the Court of Appeals must be vacated. The case is remanded for further proceedings consistent with this opinion....

Justice Scalia, concurring in the Judgment.

I agree with the Court's holding that the Controlled Substances Act (CSA) may validly be applied to respondents' cultivation, distribution, and possession of marijuana for personal, medicinal use. I write separately because my understanding of the doctrinal foundation on which that holding rests is, if not inconsistent with that of the Court, at least more nuanced.

Since *Perez v. United States* (1971), our cases have mechanically recited that the Commerce Clause permits congressional regulation of three categories: (1) the channels of interstate commerce; (2) the instrumentalities of interstate commerce, and persons or things in interstate commerce; and (3) activities that "substantially affect" interstate commerce.... The third category, however, is different in kind, and its recitation without explanation is misleading and incomplete.

It is *misleading* because, unlike the channels, instrumentalities, and agents of interstate commerce, activities that substantially affect interstate commerce are not themselves part of interstate commerce, and thus the power to regulate them cannot come from the

---

2. See, *e.g., People ex rel. Lungren* v. *Peron* (Cal. App. 1997) (recounting how a Cannabis Buyers' Club engaged in an "indiscriminate and uncontrolled pattern of sale to thousands of persons among the general public, including persons who had not demonstrated any recommendation or approval of a physician and, in fact, some of whom were not under the care of a physician, such as undercover officers," and noting that "some persons who had purchased marijuana on respondents' premises were reselling it unlawfully on the street.")

Commerce Clause alone. Rather, as this Court has acknowledged since at least *United States v. Coombs* (1838), Congress's regulatory authority over intrastate activities that are not themselves part of interstate commerce (including activities that have a substantial effect on interstate commerce) derives from the Necessary and Proper Clause. And the category of "activities that substantially affect interstate commerce," *United States v. Lopez* (1995), is *incomplete* because the authority to enact laws necessary and proper for the regulation of interstate commerce is not limited to laws governing intrastate activities that substantially affect interstate commerce. Where necessary to make a regulation of interstate commerce effective, Congress may regulate even those intrastate activities that do not themselves substantially affect interstate commerce.

I. Our cases show that the regulation of intrastate activities may be necessary to and proper for the regulation of interstate commerce in two general circumstances. Most directly, the commerce power permits Congress not only to devise rules for the governance of commerce between States but also to facilitate interstate commerce by eliminating potential obstructions, and to restrict it by eliminating potential stimulants. See *NLRB v. Jones & Laughlin Steel Corp.* (1937). That is why the Court has repeatedly sustained congressional legislation on the ground that the regulated activities had a substantial effect on interstate commerce. See, e.g., *Katzenbach v. McClung* (1964) (discrimination by restaurants); *Heart of Atlanta Motel, Inc. v. United States* (1964) (discrimination by hotels); *Mandeville Island Farms v. American Crystal Sugar Co.* (1948) (intrastate price-fixing); *Board of Trade of Chicago v. Olsen* (1923) (activities of a local grain exchange); *Stafford v. Wallace* (1922) (intrastate transactions at stockyard). *Lopez* and *United States v. Morrison* (2000) recognized the expansive scope of Congress's authority in this regard: "[T]he pattern is clear. Where economic activity substantially affects interstate commerce, legislation regulating that activity will be sustained."

This principle is not without limitation. In *Lopez* and *Morrison,* the Court—conscious of the potential of the "substantially affects" test to "'obliterate the distinction between what is national and what is local,'" rejected the argument that Congress may regulate *noneconomic* activity based solely on the effect that it may have on interstate commerce through a remote chain of inferences....

As we implicitly acknowledged in *Lopez*, however, Congress's authority to enact laws necessary and proper for the regulation of interstate commerce is not limited to laws directed against economic activities that have a substantial effect on interstate commerce. Though the conduct in *Lopez* was not economic, the Court nevertheless recognized that it could be regulated as "an essential part of a larger regulation of economic activity, in which the regulatory scheme could be undercut unless the intrastate activity were regulated." This statement referred to those cases permitting the regulation of intrastate activities "which in a substantial way interfere with or obstruct the exercise of the granted power." *United States v. Darby* (1941); *Shreveport Rate Cases* (1914). [W]here Congress has the authority to enact a regulation of interstate commerce, "it possesses every power needed to make that regulation effective."

Although this power "to make ... regulation effective" commonly overlaps with the authority to regulate economic activities that substantially affect interstate commerce, and may in some cases have been confused with that authority, the two are distinct. The regulation of an intrastate activity may be essential to a comprehensive regulation of interstate commerce even though the intrastate activity does not itself "substantially affect" interstate commerce. Moreover, as the passage from *Lopez* quoted above suggests, Congress may regulate even noneconomic local activity if that regulation is a necessary part of a more general regulation of interstate commerce. See *Lopez*. The relevant question is simply whether the means chosen are "reasonably adapted" to the attainment of a legitimate end under the commerce power. See *Darby*.

In *Darby*, for instance, the Court explained that "Congress, having ... adopted the policy of excluding from interstate commerce all goods produced for the commerce which do not conform to the specified labor standards," could not only require employers engaged in the production of goods for interstate commerce to conform to wage and hour standards, but could also require those employers to keep employment records in order to demonstrate compliance with the regulatory scheme. While the Court sustained the former regulation on the alternative ground that the activity it regulated could have a "great effect" on interstate commerce, it affirmed the latter on the sole ground that "[t]he requirement for records even of the intrastate transaction is an appropriate means to a legitimate end...."

III. The application of these principles to the case before us is straightforward. In the CSA, Congress has undertaken to extinguish the interstate market in Schedule I controlled substances, including marijuana. The Commerce Clause unquestionably permits this. The power to regulate interstate commerce "extends not only to those regulations which aid, foster and protect the commerce, but embraces those which prohibit it." *Darby*.... That simple possession is a noneconomic activity is immaterial to whether it can be prohibited as a necessary part of a larger regulation. Rather, Congress's authority to enact all of these prohibitions of intrastate controlled-substance activities depends only upon whether they are appropriate means of achieving the legitimate end of eradicating Schedule I substances from interstate commerce.

By this measure, I think the regulation must be sustained. Not only is it impossible to distinguish "controlled substances manufactured and distributed intrastate" from "controlled substances manufactured and distributed interstate," but it hardly makes sense to speak in such terms. Drugs like marijuana are fungible commodities. As the Court explains, marijuana that is grown at home and possessed for personal use is never more than an instant from the interstate market — and this is so whether or not the possession is for medicinal use or lawful use under the laws of a particular State. Congress need not accept on faith that state law will be effective in maintaining a strict division between a lawful market for "medical" marijuana and the more general marijuana market. "To impose on [Congress] the necessity of resorting to means which it cannot control, which another government may furnish or withhold, would render its course precarious, the result of its measures uncertain, and create a dependence on other governments, which might disappoint its most important designs, and is incompatible with the language of the constitution." *McCulloch v Maryland* (1819).

Finally, neither respondents nor the dissenters suggest any violation of state sovereignty of the sort that would render this regulation "inappropriate," except to argue that the CSA regulates an area typically left to state regulation....

I thus agree with the Court that, however the class of regulated activities is subdivided, Congress could reasonably conclude that its objective of prohibiting marijuana from the interstate market "could be undercut" if those activities were excepted from its general scheme of regulation. That is sufficient to authorize the application of the CSA to respondents.

Justice O'Connor, with whom the Chief Justice and Justice Thomas join as to all but Part III, dissenting.

We enforce the "outer limits" of Congress' Commerce Clause authority not for their own sake, but to protect historic spheres of state sovereignty from excessive federal encroachment and thereby to maintain the distribution of power fundamental to our federalist system of government. *United States v. Lopez* (1995); *NLRB v. Jones & Laughlin Steel Corp.* (1937). One of federalism's chief virtues, of course, is that it promotes innovation by allowing for the possibility that "a single courageous State may, if its citizens choose, serve as a laboratory; and try novel social and economic experiments without risk to the rest of the country." *New State Ice Co. v. Liebmann* (1932) (Brandeis, J., dissenting).

This case exemplifies the role of States as laboratories. The States' core police powers have always included authority to define criminal law and to protect the health, safety, and welfare of their citizens. Exercising those powers, California (by ballot initiative and then by legislative codification) has come to its own conclusion about the difficult and sensitive question of whether marijuana should be available to relieve severe pain and suffering. Today the Court sanctions an application of the federal Controlled Substances Act that extinguishes that experiment, without any proof that the personal cultivation, possession, and use of marijuana for medicinal purposes, if economic activity in the first place, has a substantial effect on interstate commerce and is therefore an appropriate subject of federal regulation. In so doing, the Court announces a rule that gives Congress a perverse incentive to legislate broadly pursuant to the Commerce Clause—nestling questionable assertions of its authority into comprehensive regulatory schemes—rather than with precision. That rule and the result it produces in this case are irreconcilable with our decisions in *Lopez* and *United States v. Morrison* (2000). Accordingly I dissent.

I. In *Lopez*, we considered the constitutionality of the Gun-Free School Zones Act of 1990, which made it a federal offense "for any individual knowingly to possess a firearm ... at a place the individual knows, or has reasonable cause to believe, is a school zone." We explained that "Congress' commerce authority includes the power to regulate those activities having a substantial relation to interstate commerce, *i.e.*, those activities that substantially affect interstate commerce." This power derives from the conjunction of the Commerce Clause and the Necessary and Proper Clause....

Our decision about whether gun possession in school zones substantially affected interstate commerce turned on four considerations. *Lopez*; see also *Morrison*. First, we observed that our "substantial effects" cases generally have upheld federal regulation of economic activity that affected interstate commerce, but that [the Gun Free Schools Act] was a criminal statute having "nothing to do with 'commerce' or any sort of economic enterprise." *Lopez*. In this regard, we also noted that "[the act] is not an essential part of a larger regulation of economic activity, in which the regulatory scheme could be undercut unless the intrastate activity were regulated. It cannot, therefore, be sustained under our cases upholding regulations of activities that arise out of or are connected with a commercial transaction, which viewed in the aggregate, substantially affects interstate commerce." Second, we noted that the statute contained no express jurisdictional requirement establishing its connection to interstate commerce.

Third, we found telling the absence of legislative findings about the regulated conduct's impact on interstate commerce. We explained that while express legislative findings are neither required nor, when provided, dispositive, findings "enable us to evaluate the legislative judgment that the activity in question substantially affect[s] interstate commerce, even though no such substantial effect [is] visible to the naked eye." Finally, we rejected as too attenuated the Government's argument that firearm possession in school zones could result in violent crime which in turn could adversely affect the national economy. The Constitution, we said, does not tolerate reasoning that would "convert congressional authority under the Commerce Clause to a general police power of the sort retained by the States." Later, in *Morrison*, we relied on the same four considerations to hold that §40302 of the Violence Against Women Act of 1994 exceeded Congress' authority under the Commerce Clause.

In my view, the case before us is materially indistinguishable from *Lopez* and *Morrison* when the same considerations are taken into account.

II-A. What is the relevant conduct subject to Commerce Clause analysis in this case? The Court takes its cues from Congress, applying the above considerations to the activity regulated by the Controlled Substances Act (CSA) in general. The Court's decision rests on two facts about the CSA: (1) Congress chose to enact a single statute providing a comprehensive prohibition on the production, distribution, and possession of all controlled substances, and (2) Congress did not distinguish between various forms of intrastate noncommercial cultivation, possession, and use of marijuana. Today's decision suggests that the federal regulation of local activity is immune to Commerce Clause challenge because Congress chose to act with an ambitious, all-encompassing statute, rather than piecemeal. In my view, allowing Congress to set the terms of the constitutional debate in this way, *i.e.*, by packaging regulation of local activity in broader schemes, is tantamount to removing meaningful limits on the Commerce Clause.

The Court's principal means of distinguishing *Lopez* from this case is to observe that the Gun-Free School Zones Act of 1990 was a "brief, single-subject statute," whereas the CSA is "a lengthy and detailed statute creating a comprehensive framework for regulating the production, distribution, and possession of five classes of 'controlled substances.'" Thus, according to the Court, it was possible in *Lopez* to evaluate in isolation the constitutionality of criminalizing local activity (there gun possession in school zones), whereas the local activity that the CSA targets (in this case cultivation and possession of marijuana for personal medicinal use) cannot be separated from the general drug control scheme of which it is a part.

Today's decision allows Congress to regulate intrastate activity without check, so long as there is some implication by legislative design that regulating intrastate activity is essential (and the Court appears to equate "essential" with "necessary") to the interstate regulatory scheme. Seizing upon our language in *Lopez* that the statute prohibiting gun possession in school zones was "not an essential part of a larger regulation of economic activity, in which the regulatory scheme could be undercut unless the intrastate activity were regulated," the Court appears to reason that the placement of local activity in a comprehensive scheme confirms that it is essential to that scheme. If the Court is right, then *Lopez* stands for nothing more than a drafting guide: Congress should have described the relevant crime as "transfer or possession of a firearm anywhere in the nation"—thus including commercial and noncommercial activity, and clearly encompassing some activity with assuredly substantial effect on interstate commerce. Had it done so, the majority hints, we would have sustained its authority to regulate possession of firearms in school zones. Furthermore, today's decision suggests we would readily sustain a congressional decision to attach the regulation of intrastate activity to a pre-existing comprehensive (or even not-so-comprehensive) scheme. If so, the Court invites increased federal regulation of local activity....

I cannot agree that our decision in *Lopez* contemplated such evasive or overbroad legislative strategies with approval.... If the Court always defers to Congress as it does today, little may be left to the notion of enumerated powers.

The hard work for courts, then, is to identify objective markers for confining the analysis in Commerce Clause cases. Here, respondents challenge the constitutionality of the CSA as applied to them and those similarly situated. I agree with the Court that we must look beyond respondents' own activities. Otherwise, individual litigants could always exempt themselves from Commerce Clause regulation merely by pointing to the obvious—that their personal activities do not have a substantial effect on interstate commerce.... The task is to identify a mode of analysis that allows Congress to regulate more than nothing (by declining to reduce each case to its litigants) and less than everything (by declining to let Congress set the terms of analysis). The analysis may not be the same in every case, for it depends on the regulatory scheme at issue and the federalism concerns implicated.

A number of objective markers are available to confine the scope of constitutional review here. Both federal and state legislation—including the CSA itself, the California Compassionate Use Act, and other state medical marijuana legislation—recognize that medical and nonmedical (*i.e.*, recreational) uses of drugs are realistically distinct and can be segregated, and regulate them differently.... Moreover, because fundamental structural concerns about dual sovereignty animate our Commerce Clause cases, it is relevant that this case involves the interplay of federal and state regulation in areas of criminal law and social policy, where "States lay claim by right of history and expertise." *Lopez* (Kennedy, J., concurring)...."[S]tate autonomy is a relevant factor in assessing the means by which Congress exercises its powers" under the Commerce Clause. *Garcia*, O'Connor, J., dissenting. California, like other States, has drawn on its reserved powers to distinguish the regulation of medicinal marijuana. To ascertain whether Congress' encroachment is constitutionally justified in this case, then, I would focus here on the personal cultivation, possession, and use of marijuana for medicinal purposes.

II-B. Having thus defined the relevant conduct, we must determine whether, under our precedents, the conduct is economic and, in the aggregate, substantially affects interstate commerce. Even if intrastate cultivation and possession of marijuana for one's own medicinal use can properly be characterized as economic, and I question whether it can, it has not been shown that such activity substantially affects interstate commerce. Similarly, it is neither self-evident nor demonstrated that regulating such activity is necessary to the interstate drug control scheme. The Court's definition of economic activity is breathtaking. It defines as economic any activity involving the production, distribution, and consumption of commodities. And it appears to reason that when an interstate market for a commodity exists, regulating the intrastate manufacture or possession of that commodity is constitutional either because that intrastate activity is itself economic, or because regulating it is a rational part of regulating its market. Putting to one side the problem endemic to the Court's opinion—the shift in focus from the activity at issue in this case to the entirety of what the CSA regulates, see *Lopez* ("depending on the level of generality, any activity can be looked upon as commercial")—the Court's definition of economic activity for purposes of Commerce Clause jurisprudence threatens to sweep all of productive human activity into federal regulatory reach. The Court uses a dictionary definition of economics to skirt the real problem of drawing a meaningful line between "what is national and what is local," *Jones & Laughlin Steel*. It will not do to say that Congress may regulate noncommercial activity simply because it may have an effect on the demand for commercial goods, or because the noncommercial endeavor can, in some sense, substitute for commercial activity. Most commercial goods or services have some sort of privately producible analogue. Home care substitutes for daycare. Charades games substitute for movie tickets.... We have already rejected the result that would follow—a federal police power. *Lopez*.

In *Lopez* and *Morrison*, we suggested that economic activity usually relates directly to commercial activity. See *Morrison* (intrastate activities that have been within Congress' power to regulate have been "of an apparent commercial character"); *Lopez* (distinguishing the

Gun-Free School Zones Act of 1990 from "activities that arise out of or are connected with a commercial transaction"). The homegrown cultivation and personal possession and use of marijuana for medicinal purposes has no apparent commercial character. Everyone agrees that the marijuana at issue in this case was never in the stream of commerce, and neither were the supplies for growing it. (Marijuana is highly unusual among the substances subject to the CSA in that it can be cultivated without any materials that have traveled in interstate commerce.) *Lopez* makes clear that possession is not itself commercial activity. And respondents have not come into possession by means of any commercial transaction; they have simply grown, in their own homes, marijuana for their own use, without acquiring, buying, selling, or bartering a thing of value....

The Court suggests that *Wickard v. Filburn* (1942), which we have identified as "perhaps the most far reaching example of Commerce Clause authority over intrastate activity," *Lopez*, established federal regulatory power over any home consumption of a commodity for which a national market exists. I disagree. *Wickard* involved a challenge to the Agricultural Adjustment Act of 1938 (AAA), which directed the Secretary of Agriculture to set national quotas on wheat production, and penalties for excess production. The AAA itself confirmed that Congress made an explicit choice not to reach — and thus the Court could not possibly have approved of federal control over — small-scale, non-commercial wheat farming. In contrast to the CSA's limitless assertion of power, Congress provided an exemption within the AAA for small producers. When Filburn planted the wheat at issue in *Wickard*, the statute exempted plantings less than 200 bushels (about six tons), and when he harvested his wheat it exempted plantings less than six acres. *Wickard*, then, did not extend Commerce Clause authority to something as modest as the home cook's herb garden. This is not to say that Congress may never regulate small quantities of commodities possessed or produced for personal use, or to deny that it sometimes needs to enact a zero tolerance regime for such commodities. It is merely to say that *Wickard* did not hold or imply that small-scale production of commodities is always economic, and automatically within Congress' reach.

Even assuming that economic activity is at issue in this case, the Government has made no showing in fact that the possession and use of homegrown marijuana for medical purposes, in California or elsewhere, has a substantial effect on interstate commerce. Similarly, the Government has not shown that regulating such activity is necessary to an interstate regulatory scheme. Whatever the specific theory of "substantial effects" at issue (*i.e.*, whether the activity substantially affects interstate commerce, whether its regulation is necessary to an interstate regulatory scheme, or both), a concern for dual sovereignty requires that Congress' excursion into the traditional domain of States be justified.

That is why characterizing this as a case about the Necessary and Proper Clause does not change the analysis significantly. Congress must exercise its authority under the Necessary and Proper Clause in a manner consistent with basic constitutional principles. *Garcia v. San Antonio Metropolitan Transit District* (1985) (O'Connor, J., dissenting) ("It is not enough that the 'end be legitimate'; the means to that end chosen by Congress must not contravene the spirit of the Constitution"). Congress cannot use its authority under the Clause to contravene the principle of state sovereignty embodied in the 10th Amendment. Likewise, that authority must be used in a manner consistent with the notion of enumerated powers — a structural principle that is as much part of the Constitution as the 10th Amendment's explicit textual command. Accordingly, something more than mere assertion is required when Congress purports to have power over local activity whose connection to an intrastate market is not self-evident. Otherwise, the Necessary and Proper Clause will always be a back door for unconstitutional federal regulation.... Indeed, if it were enough in "substantial effects" cases for the Court to supply conceivable justifications for intrastate regulation related to an interstate market, then we could have surmised in *Lopez* that guns in school zones are "never more than an instant from the interstate market" in guns already subject to extensive federal regulation, (Scalia, J., concurring in judgment), recast *Lopez* as a Necessary and Proper Clause case, and thereby upheld the Gun-Free School Zones Act of 1990. (According to the Court's and the concurrence's logic, for example, the *Lopez* court should have reasoned that the prohibition on gun possession in school zones could be an appropriate means of effectuating a related prohibition on "sell[ing]" or "deliver[ing]" firearms or ammunition to "any individual who the licensee knows or has reasonable cause to believe is less than eighteen years of age." 18 U. S. C. §922(b)(1).

There is simply no evidence that homegrown medicinal marijuana users constitute, in the aggregate, a sizable enough class to have a discernable, let alone substantial, impact on the national illicit drug market—or otherwise to threaten the CSA regime. Explicit evidence is helpful when substantial effect is not "visible to the naked eye." See *Lopez*. And here, in part because common sense suggests that medical marijuana users may be limited in number and that California's Compassionate Use Act and similar state legislation may well isolate activities relating to medicinal marijuana from the illicit market, the effect of those activities on interstate drug traffic is not self-evidently substantial.

In this regard, again, this case is readily distinguishable from *Wickard*. To decide whether the Secretary could regulate local wheat farming, the Court looked to "the actual effects of the activity in question upon interstate commerce." Critically, the Court was able to consider "actual effects" because the parties had "stipulated a summary of the economics of the wheat industry." After reviewing in detail the picture of the industry provided in that summary, the Court explained that consumption of homegrown wheat was the most variable factor in the size of the national wheat crop, and that on-site consumption could have the effect of varying the amount of wheat sent to market by as much as 20 percent. With real numbers at hand, the *Wickard* Court could easily conclude that "a factor of such volume and variability as home-consumed wheat would have a substantial influence on price and market conditions" nationwide. ("This record leaves us in no doubt" about substantial effects).

The Court recognizes that "the record in the *Wickard* case itself established the causal connection between the production for local use and the national market" and argues that "we have before us findings by Congress *to the same effect*." The Court refers to a series of declarations in the introduction to the CSA saying that (1) local distribution and possession of controlled substances causes "swelling" in interstate traffic; (2) local production and distribution cannot be distinguished from interstate production and distribution; (3) federal control over intrastate incidents "is essential to effective control" over interstate drug trafficking. 21 U. S. C. §§801(1)–(6). These bare declarations cannot be compared to the record before the Court in *Wickard*.

They amount to nothing more than a legislative insistence that the regulation of controlled substances must be absolute. They are asserted without any supporting evidence—descriptive, statistical, or otherwise.... Indeed, if declarations like these suffice to justify federal regulation, and if the Court today is right about what passes rationality review before us, then our decision in *Morrison* should have come out the other way....

The Government has not overcome empirical doubt that the number of Californians engaged in personal cultivation, possession, and use of medical marijuana, or the amount of marijuana they produce, is enough to threaten the federal regime. Nor has it shown that Compassionate Use Act marijuana users have been or are realistically likely to be responsible for the drug's seeping into the market in a significant way....

III. We would do well to recall how James Madison, the father of the Constitution, described our system of joint sovereignty to the people of New York: "The powers delegated by the proposed constitution to the federal government are few and defined. Those which are to remain in the State governments are numerous and indefinite.... The powers reserved to the several States will extend to all the objects which, in the ordinary course of affairs, concern the lives, liberties, and properties of the people, and the internal order, improvement, and prosperity of the State." *The Federalist* No. 45.

Relying on Congress' abstract assertions, the Court has endorsed making it a federal crime to grow small amounts of marijuana in one's own home for one's own medicinal use. This overreaching stifles an express choice by some States, concerned for the lives and liberties of their people, to regulate medical marijuana differently. If I were a California citizen, I would not have voted for the medical marijuana ballot initiative; if I were a California legislator I would not have supported the Compassionate Use Act. But whatever the wisdom of California's experiment with medical marijuana, the federalism principles that have driven our Commerce Clause cases require that room for experiment be protected in this case. For these reasons I dissent.

Justice Thomas, dissenting.

Respondents Diane Monson and Angel Raich use marijuana that has never been bought or sold, that has never crossed state lines, and that has had no demonstrable effect on the national market for marijuana. If Congress can regulate this under the Commerce Clause, then it can regulate virtually anything—and the Federal Government is no longer one of limited and enumerated powers.

I. Respondents' local cultivation and consumption of marijuana is not "Commerce ... among the several States." U. S. Const., Art. I, §8, cl. 3. By holding that Congress may regulate activity that is neither interstate nor commerce under the Interstate Commerce Clause, the Court abandons any attempt to enforce the Constitution's limits on federal power. The majority supports this conclusion by invoking, without explanation, the Necessary and Proper Clause. Regulating respondents' conduct, however, is not "necessary and proper for carrying into Execution" Congress' restrictions on the interstate drug trade. Art. I, §8, cl. 18. Thus, neither the Commerce Clause nor the Necessary and Proper Clause grants Congress the power to regulate respondents' conduct.

I-A. As I explained at length in *United States v. Lopez* (1995), the Commerce Clause empowers Congress to regulate the buying and selling of goods and services trafficked across state lines. (Concurring opinion). The Clause's text, structure, and history all indicate that, at the time of the founding, the term "'commerce' consisted of selling, buying, and bartering, as well as transporting for these purposes." (Thomas, J., concurring). Commerce, or trade, stood in contrast to productive activities like manufacturing and agriculture. Throughout founding-era dictionaries, Madison's notes from the Constitutional Convention, *The Federalist Papers*, and the ratification debates, the term "commerce" is consistently used to mean trade or exchange—not all economic or gainful activity that has some attenuated connection to trade or exchange. (Thomas, J., concurring). Barnett, *The Original Meaning of the Commerce Clause*, 68 U. Chi. L. Rev. 101, 112–25 (2001). The term "commerce" commonly meant trade or exchange (and shipping for these purposes) not simply to those involved in the drafting and ratification processes, but also to the general public. Barnett, *New Evidence of the Original Meaning of the Commerce Clause*, 55 Ark. L. Rev. 847, 857–62 (2003).

Even the majority does not argue that respondents' conduct is itself "Commerce among the several States." Art. I, §8, cl. 3. Monson and Raich neither buy nor sell the marijuana that they consume. They cultivate their cannabis entirely in the State of California—it never crosses state lines, much less as part of a commercial transaction. Certainly no evidence from the founding suggests that "commerce" included the mere possession of a good or some purely personal activity that did not involve trade or exchange for value. In the early days of the Republic, it would have been unthinkable that Congress could prohibit the local cultivation, possession, and consumption of marijuana.

On this traditional understanding of "commerce," the Controlled Substances Act (CSA), 21 U. S. C. §801 *et seq.*, regulates a great deal of marijuana trafficking that is interstate and commercial in character. The CSA does not, however, criminalize only the interstate buying and selling of marijuana. Instead, it bans the entire market—intrastate or interstate, noncommercial or commercial—for marijuana. Respondents are correct that the CSA exceeds Congress' commerce power as applied to their conduct, which is purely intrastate and noncommercial.

I-B. More difficult, however, is whether the CSA is a valid exercise of Congress' power to enact laws that are "necessary and proper for carrying into Execution" its power to regulate interstate commerce. Art. I, §8, cl. 18. The Necessary and Proper Clause is not a warrant to Congress to enact any law that bears some conceivable connection to the exercise of an enumerated power. Nor is it, however, a command to Congress to enact only laws that are absolutely indispensable to the exercise of an enumerated power. In *McCulloch v. Maryland* (1819), this Court, speaking through Chief Justice Marshall, set forth a test for determining when an Act of Congress is permissible under the Necessary and Proper Clause....

To act under the Necessary and Proper Clause ... Congress must select a means that is "appropriate" and "plainly adapted" to executing an enumerated power; the means cannot be otherwise "prohibited" by the Constitution; and the means cannot be inconsistent with "the letter and spirit of the [C]onstitution." D. Currie, *The Constitution in the Supreme Court: The First Hundred Years 1789–1888* (1985). The CSA, as applied to respondents' conduct, is not a valid exercise of Congress' power under the Necessary and Proper Clause.

II-B-1. Congress has exercised its power over interstate commerce to criminalize trafficking in marijuana across state lines. The Government contends that banning Monson and Raich's intrastate drug activity is "necessary and proper for carrying into Execution" its regulation of interstate drug trafficking. Art. I, §8, cl. 18. See 21 U. S. C. §801(6). However, in order to be "necessary," the intrastate ban must be more than "a reasonable means [of] effectuat[ing] the regulation of interstate commerce."(Majority opinion) (employing rational-basis review). It must be "plainly adapted" to regulating interstate marijuana trafficking—in other words, there must be an "obvious, simple, and direct relation" between the intrastate ban and the regulation of interstate commerce. *Sabri v. United States* (2004) (Thomas, J., concurring in judgment); see also *United States v. Dewitt* (1870) (finding ban on intrastate sale of lighting oils not "appropriate and plainly adapted means for carrying into execution" Congress' taxing power).

On its face, a ban on the intrastate cultivation, possession and distribution of marijuana may be plainly adapted to stopping the interstate flow of marijuana. Unregulated local growers and users could swell both the supply and the demand sides of the interstate marijuana market, making the market more difficult to regulate. (Majority opinion). But respondents do not challenge the CSA on its face. Instead, they challenge it as applied to their conduct. The question is thus whether the intrastate ban is "necessary and proper" as applied to medical marijuana users like respondents.

Respondents are not regulable simply because they belong to a large class (local growers and users of marijuana) that Congress might need to reach, if they also belong to a distinct and separable subclass (local growers and users of state-authorized, medical marijuana) that does not undermine the CSA's interstate ban. The Court of Appeals found that respondents' "limited use is distinct from the broader illicit drug market," because "th[eir] medicinal marijuana ... is not intended for, nor does it enter, the stream of commerce." If that is generally true of individuals who grow and use marijuana for medical purposes under state law, then even assuming Congress has "obvious" and "plain" reasons why regulating intrastate cultivation and possession is necessary to regulating the interstate drug trade, none of those reasons applies to medical marijuana patients like Monson and Raich.

California's Compassionate Use Act sets respondents' conduct apart from other intrastate producers and users of marijuana. The Act channels marijuana use to "seriously ill Californians," and prohibits "the diversion of marijuana for nonmedical purposes." California strictly controls the cultivation and possession of marijuana for medical purposes. To be eligible for its program, California requires that a patient have an illness that cannabis can relieve, such as cancer, AIDS, or arthritis, and that he obtain a physician's recommendation or approval. Qualified patients must provide personal and medical information to obtain medical identification cards, and there is a statewide registry of cardholders....

II. The majority advances three reasons why the CSA is a legitimate exercise of Congress' authority under the Commerce Clause: First, respondents' conduct, taken in the aggregate, may substantially affect interstate commerce; second, regulation of respondents' conduct is essential to regulating the interstate marijuana market; and, third, regulation of respondents' conduct is incidental to regulating the interstate marijuana market. Justice O'Connor explains why the majority's reasons cannot be reconciled with our recent Commerce Clause jurisprudence. The majority's justifications, however, suffer from even more fundamental flaws.

II-A. The majority holds that Congress may regulate intrastate cultivation and possession of medical marijuana under the Commerce Clause, because such conduct arguably has a substantial effect on interstate commerce. The majority's decision is further proof that the "substantial effects" test is a "rootless and malleable standard" at odds with the constitutional design.

The majority's treatment of the substantial effects test is rootless, because it is not tethered to either the Commerce Clause or the Necessary and Proper Clause. Under the Commerce Clause, Congress may regulate interstate commerce, not activities that substantially affect interstate commerce—any more than Congress may regulate activities that do not fall within, but that affect, the subjects of its other Article I powers. *Lopez* (Thomas, J., concurring). Whatever additional latitude the Necessary and Proper Clause affords, the question is whether Congress' legislation is essential to the regulation of interstate commerce itself—not whether the legislation extends only to economic activities that substantially affect interstate commerce.

The majority's treatment of the substantial effects test is malleable, because the majority expands the relevant conduct. By defining the class at a high level of generality (as the intrastate manufacture and possession of marijuana), the majority overlooks that individuals authorized by state law to manufacture and possess medical marijuana exert no demonstrable effect on the interstate drug market....

The substantial effects test is easily manipulated for another reason. This Court has never held that Congress can regulate noneconomic activity that substantially affects interstate commerce. *Morrison*.... If the majority is to be taken seriously, the Federal Government may now regulate quilting bees, clothes drives, and potluck suppers throughout the 50 States. This makes a mockery of Madison's assurance to the people of New York that the "powers delegated" to the Federal Government are "few and defined," while those of the States are "numerous and indefinite." *The Federalist* No. 45 (J. Madison).

Moreover, even a Court interested more in the modern than the original understanding of the Constitution ought to resolve cases based on the meaning of words that are actually in the document. Congress is authorized to regulate "Commerce," and respondents' conduct does not qualify under any definition of that term.[1] The majority's opinion only illustrates the steady drift away from the text of the Commerce Clause....

The majority's rewriting of the Commerce Clause seems to be rooted in the belief that, unless the Commerce Clause covers the entire web of human activity, Congress will be left powerless to regulate the national economy effectively. The interconnectedness of economic activity is not a modern phenomenon unfamiliar to the Framers....

One searches the Court's opinion in vain for any hint of what aspect of American life is reserved to the States. Yet this Court knows that "'[t]he Constitution created a Federal Government of limited powers.'" *New York v. United States* (1992). That is why today's decision will add no measure of stability to our Commerce Clause jurisprudence: This Court is willing neither to enforce limits on federal power, nor to declare the 10th Amendment a dead letter. If stability is possible, it is only by discarding the stand-alone substantial effects test and revisiting our definition of "Commerce among the several States." Congress may regulate interstate commerce—not things that affect it, even when summed together, unless truly "necessary and proper" to regulating interstate commerce.

II-B. The majority also inconsistently contends that regulating respondents' conduct is both incidental and essential to a comprehensive legislative scheme. I have already explained why the CSA's ban on local activity is not essential. However, the majority further claims that, because the CSA covers a great deal of interstate commerce, it "is of no moment" if it also "ensnares some purely intrastate activity." So long as Congress casts its net broadly over an interstate market, according to the majority, it is free to regulate interstate and intrastate activity alike. This cannot be justified under either the Commerce Clause or the Necessary and Proper Clause. If the activity is purely intrastate, then it may not be regulated under the Commerce Clause. And if the regulation of the intrastate activity is purely incidental, then it may not be regulated under the Necessary and Proper Clause....

Even in the absence of an express severability provision, it is implausible that this Court could set aside entire portions of the United States Code as outside Congress' power in *Lopez* and *Morrison*, but it cannot engage in the more restrained practice of invalidating particular applications of the CSA that are beyond Congress' power. This Court has regularly entertained as-applied challenges under constitutional provisions including the Commerce Clause, see *Katzenbach v. McClung* (1964); *Heart of Atlanta Motel, Inc. v. United States* (1964); *Wickard v. Filburn* (1942)....

---

1. See, ... *The Random House Dictionary of the English Language* 411 (2d ed. 1987) ("an interchange of goods or commodities, esp. on a large scale between different countries ... or between different parts of the same country"); Webster's 3d 456 ("the exchange or buying and selling of commodities esp. on a large scale and involving transportation from place to place").

The majority prevents States like California from devising drug policies that they have concluded provide much-needed respite to the seriously ill. It does so without any serious inquiry into the necessity for federal regulation or the propriety of "displac[ing] state regulation in areas of traditional state concern," *Lopez* (Kennedy, J., concurring).... Our federalist system, properly understood, allows California and a growing number of other States to decide for themselves how to safeguard the health and welfare of their citizens. I would affirm the judgment of the Court of Appeals. I respectfully dissent.

Gonzales v. Oregon: Note

In *Gonzales v. Oregon* (2006), the United States Supreme Court considered an interpretative rule promulgated by the Attorney General of the United States. The rule provided that physicians who assist in the suicide of terminally ill patients pursuant to the Oregon Death With Dignity Act would be violating the federal Controlled Substances Act (CSA). The State of Oregon sought an injunction enjoining enforcement of the Attorney General's interpretation of the CSA.

In a five-to-four decision, the Supreme Court, with Justice Kennedy writing for the majority (joined by Justices Breyer, Ginsburg, Souter, and Stevens), concluded that the Attorney General's interpretative rule exceeded his authority under the CSA. In resolving this case on statutory grounds, the Supreme Court avoided another constitutional battle between state and federal regulation similar to the one the Court resolved the year before in *Gonzales v. Raich* (2005).

III. Ducking the Issue: Statutory Construction as a Means of Avoiding Constitutional Interpretation

In Chapter 4's discussion of justiciability, *infra*, you will read a series of principles of judicial self-restraint suggested by Justice Brandeis. The last of these states:

> When the validity of an act of the Congress is drawn in question, and even if a serious doubt of constitutionality is raised, it is a cardinal principle that this Court will first ascertain whether a construction of the statute is fairly possible by which the question may be avoided.

The Court applied this principle in the following Commerce Clause cases.

Jones v. United States
529 U.S. 848 (2000)

[Majority: Ginsburg, Rehnquist (C.J.), Stevens, Thomas, Scalia, O'Connor, Kennedy, Souter, Breyer. Concurring: Stevens, Thomas, and Scalia.]

Justice Ginsburg delivered the opinion of the Court.

It is a federal crime under 18 U.S.C. §844(i) to damage or destroy, "by means of fire or an explosive, any ... property used in interstate or foreign commerce or in any activity affecting interstate or foreign commerce." This case presents the question whether arson of an owner-occupied private residence falls within §844(i)'s compass. Construing the statute's text, we hold that an owner-occupied residence not used for any commercial purpose does not qualify as property "used in" commerce or commerce-affecting activity; of such a dwelling, therefore, is not subject to federal prosecution under §844(i). Our construction of §844(i) is reinforced by the Court's opinion in *United States v. Lopez* (1995), and the interpretive rule that constitutionally doubtful constructions should be avoided where possible.

I. On February 23, 1998, petitioner Dewey Jones tossed a Molotov cocktail through a window into a home in Fort Wayne, Indiana, owned and occupied by his cousin. No one was injured in the ensuing fire, but the blaze severely damaged the home. A federal grand jury returned a three-count indictment charging Jones with arson, using a destructive device during and in relation to a crime of violence (the arson), and making an illegal destructive device. Jones was tried under that indictment in the Northern District of Indiana and convicted by a jury on all three counts. The District Court sentenced him, pursuant to the Sentencing Reform Act of 1984, to a total prison term of 35 years, to be followed by five years of supervised release. The court also ordered Jones to pay $77,396.87 to the insurer of the damaged home as restitution for its loss. Jones appealed....

II. Congress enacted 18 U.S.C. §844(i) as part of Title XI of the Organized Crime Control Act of 1970, "because of the need 'to curb the use, transportation, and possession of explosives.'" ... As now worded, §844(i) reads in relevant part:

> Whoever maliciously damages or destroys, or attempts to damage or destroy, by means of fire or an explosive, any building, vehicle, or other real or personal property used in interstate or foreign commerce or in any activity affecting interstate or foreign commerce shall be imprisoned for not less than 5 years and not more than 20 years, fined under this title, or both....

Were we to adopt the Government's expansive interpretation of §844(i), hardly a building in the land would fall outside the federal statute's domain. Practically every building in our cities, towns, and rural areas is constructed with supplies that have moved in interstate commerce, served by utilities that have an interstate connection, financed or insured by enterprises that do business across state lines, or bears some other trace of interstate commerce....

III. Our reading of §844(i) is in harmony with the guiding principle that "where a statute is susceptible of two constructions, by one of which grave and doubtful constitutional questions arise and by the other of which such questions are avoided, our duty is to adopt the latter." *Ashwander v. TVA* (1936) (Brandeis, J., concurring). In *Lopez,* this Court invalidated the Gun-Free School Zones Act, which made it a federal crime to possess a firearm within 1,000 feet of a school. The defendant in that case, a 12th-grade student, had been convicted for knowingly possessing a concealed handgun and bullets at his San Antonio, Texas, high school, in violation of the federal Act. Holding that the Act exceeded Congress' power to regulate commerce, the Court stressed that the area was one of traditional state concern, and that the legislation aimed at activity in which "neither the actors nor their conduct has a commercial character"(Kennedy, J., concurring).

Given the concerns brought to the fore in *Lopez,* it is appropriate to avoid the constitutional question that would arise were we to read §844(i) to render the "traditionally local criminal conduct" in which petitioner Jones engaged "a matter for federal enforcement." Our comprehension of §844(i) is additionally reinforced by other interpretive guides. We have instructed that "ambiguity concerning the ambit of criminal statutes should be resolved in favor of lenity," *Rewis v. United States* (1971), and that "when choice has to be made between two readings of what conduct Congress has made a crime, it is appropriate, before we choose the harsher alternative, to require that Congress should have spoken in language that is clear and definite," *United States v. Universal C.I.T. Credit Corp.* (1952). We have cautioned, as well, that "unless Congress conveys its purpose clearly, it will not be deemed to have significantly changed the federal-state balance" in the prosecution of crimes. To read §844(i) as encompassing the arson of an owner-occupied private home would effect such a change, for arson is a paradigmatic common-law state crime. See generally Poulos, *The Metamorphosis of the Law of Arson*, 51 Mo. L. Rev. 295 (1986).

IV. We conclude that §844(i) is not soundly read to make virtually every arson in the country a federal offense. We hold that the provision covers only property currently used in commerce or in an activity affecting commerce. The home owned and occupied by petitioner Jones's cousin was not so used—it was a dwelling place used for everyday family living. As we read §844(i), Congress left cases of this genre to the law enforcement authorities of the States. [The fact the residence used interstate natural gas, and had both a mortgage and an insurance policy from interstate institutions does not bring it within ambit of the statute.]

Our holding that §844(i) does not cover the arson of an owner-occupied dwelling means that Jones's §844(i) conviction must be vacated. Accordingly, the judgment of the Court of Appeals is reversed, and the case is remanded for further proceedings consistent with this opinion.

Solid Waste Agency of Northern Cook County v. United States Army Corps of Engineers
531 U.S. 159 (2001)

[Majority: Rehnquist (C.J.), O'Connor, Scalia, Kennedy, and Thomas. Dissenting: Stevens, Souter, Ginsburg, and Breyer.]

Chief Justice Rehnquist delivered the opinion of the Court.

Section 404(a) of the Clean Water Act (CWA or Act), regulates the discharge of dredged or fill material into "navigable waters." The United States Army Corps of Engineers (Corps) has interpreted §404(a) to confer federal authority over an abandoned sand and gravel pit in northern Illinois which provides habitat for migratory birds. We are asked to decide whether the provisions of §404(a) may be fairly extended to these waters, and, if so, whether Congress could exercise such authority consistent with the Commerce Clause, U.S. Const., Art. I, §8, cl. 3. We answer the first question in the negative and therefore do not reach the second....

Despite [the county's solid waste agency] SWANCC's securing the required water quality certification from the Illinois Environmental Protection Agency, the Corps refused to issue a §404(a) permit. The Corps found that SWANCC had not established that its proposal was the "least environmentally damaging, most practicable alternative" for disposal of nonhazardous solid waste; that SWANCC's failure to set aside sufficient funds to remediate leaks posed an "unacceptable risk to the public's drinking water supply"; and that the impact of the project upon area-sensitive species was "unmitigatable since a landfill surface cannot be redeveloped into a forested habitat."

Petitioner filed suit under the Administrative Procedure Act, in the Northern District of Illinois challenging both the Corps' jurisdiction over the site and the merits of its denial of the §404(a) permit. The District Court granted summary judgment to respondents on the jurisdictional issue, and petitioner abandoned its challenge to the Corps' permit decision. On appeal to the Court of Appeals for the Seventh Circuit, petitioner renewed its attack on respondents' use of the "Migratory Bird Rule" to assert jurisdiction over the site. Petitioner argued that respondents had exceeded their statutory authority in interpreting the CWA to cover nonnavigable, isolated, intrastate waters based upon the presence of migratory birds and, in the alternative, that Congress lacked the power under the Commerce Clause to grant such regulatory jurisdiction.

The Court of Appeals began its analysis with the constitutional question, holding that Congress has the authority to regulate such waters based upon "the cumulative impact doctrine, under which a single activity that itself has no discernible effect on interstate commerce may still be regulated if the aggregate effect of that class of activity has a substantial impact on interstate commerce." The aggregate effect of the "destruction of the natural habitat of migratory birds" on interstate commerce, the court held, was substantial because each year millions of Americans cross state lines and spend over a billion dollars to hunt and observe migratory birds. The Court of Appeals then turned to the regulatory question. The court held that the CWA reaches as many waters as the Commerce Clause allows and, given its earlier Commerce Clause ruling, it therefore followed that respondents' "Migratory Bird Rule" was a reasonable interpretation of the Act.

We granted certiorari, and now reverse....

We ... decline respondents' invitation to take what they see as the next ineluctable step after *Riverside Bayview Homes*' (1985) holding that isolated ponds, some only seasonal, wholly located within two Illinois counties, fall under § 404(a)'s definition of "navigable waters" because they serve as habitat for migratory birds....

Twice in the past six years we have reaffirmed the proposition that the grant of authority to Congress under the Commerce Clause, though broad, is not unlimited. See *United States v. Morrison* (2000); *United States v. Lopez* (1995). Respondents argue that the "Migratory Bird Rule" falls within Congress' power to regulate intrastate activities that "substantially affect" interstate commerce. They note that the protection of migratory birds is a "national interest of very nearly the first magnitude," *Missouri v. Holland* (1920), and that, as the Court of Appeals found, millions of people spend over a billion dollars annually on recreational pursuits relating to migratory birds. These arguments raise significant constitutional questions. For example, we would have to evaluate the precise object or activity that, in the aggregate, substantially affects interstate commerce. This is not clear, for although the Corps has claimed jurisdiction over petitioner's land because it contains water areas used as habitat by migratory birds, respondents now, *post litem motam*, focus upon the fact that the regulated activity is petitioner's municipal landfill, which is "plainly of a commercial nature." But this is a far cry, indeed, from the "navigable waters" and "waters of the United States" to which the statute by its terms extends.

These are significant constitutional questions raised by respondents' application of their regulations, and yet we find nothing approaching a clear statement from Congress that it intended § 404(a) to reach an abandoned sand and gravel pit such as we have here. Permitting respondents to claim federal jurisdiction over ponds and mudflats falling within the "Migratory Bird Rule" would result in a significant impingement of the States' traditional and primary power over land and water use. See, *e.g., Hess v. Port Authority Trans-Hudson Corporation* (1994). ("[R]egulation of land use [is] a function traditionally performed by local governments"). Rather than expressing a desire to readjust the federal-state balance in this manner, Congress chose to "recognize, preserve, and protect the primary responsibilities and rights of States ... to plan the development and use ... of land and water resources...." 33 U.S.C. § 1251(b). We thus read the statute as written to avoid the significant constitutional and federalism questions raised by respondents' interpretation, and therefore reject the request for administrative deference.

We hold that 33 CFR § 328.3(a)(3) (1999), as clarified and applied to petitioner's balefill site pursuant to the "Migratory Bird Rule," 51 Fed. Reg. 41217 (1986), exceeds the authority granted to respondents under § 404(a) of the CWA. The judgment of the Court of Appeals for the Seventh Circuit is therefore *Reversed.*

Justice Stevens, with whom Justice Souter, Justice Ginsburg, and Justice Breyer join, dissenting.

In 1969, the Cuyahoga River in Cleveland, Ohio, coated with a slick of industrial waste, caught fire. Congress responded to that dramatic event, and to others like it, by enacting the Federal Water Pollution Control Act (FWPCA) Amendments of 1972, as amended, 33 U.S.C. § 1251 *et seq.*, commonly known as the Clean Water Act (Clean Water Act, CWA, or Act). The Act proclaimed the ambitious goal of ending water pollution by 1985. The Court's past interpretations of the CWA have been fully consistent with that goal. Although Congress' vision of zero pollution remains unfulfilled, its pursuit has unquestionably retarded the destruction of the aquatic environment. Our Nation's waters no longer burn. Today, however, the Court takes an unfortunate step that needlessly weakens our principal safeguard against toxic water.

It is fair to characterize the Clean Water Act as "watershed" legislation. The statute endorsed fundamental changes in both the purpose and the scope of federal regulation of the Nation's waters. In § 13 of the Rivers and Harbors Appropriation Act of 1899 (RHA), Congress had assigned to the Army Corps of Engineers (Corps) the mission of regulating discharges into certain waters in order to protect their use as highways for the transportation of interstate and foreign commerce; the scope of the Corps' jurisdiction under the RHA accordingly extended only to waters that were "navigable." In the CWA, however, Congress broadened the Corps' mission to include the purpose of protecting the quality of our Nation's waters for esthetic, health, recreational, and environmental uses. The scope of its jurisdiction was therefore redefined to encompass all of "the waters of the United States, including the territorial seas." § 1362(7). That definition requires neither actual nor potential navigability.

The Court has previously held that the Corps' broadened jurisdiction under the CWA properly included an 80-acre parcel of low-lying marshy land that was not itself navigable, directly adjacent to navigable water, or even hydrologically connected to navigable water, but which was part of a larger area, characterized by poor drainage, that ultimately abutted a navigable creek. *United States v. Riverside Bayview Homes, Inc.* (1985). Our broad finding in *Riverside Bayview* that the 1977 Congress had acquiesced in the Corps' understanding of its jurisdiction applies equally to the 410-acre parcel at issue here. Moreover, once Congress crossed the legal watershed that separates navigable streams of commerce from marshes and inland lakes, there is no principled reason for limiting the statute's protection to those waters or wetlands that happen to lie near a navigable stream.

In its decision today, the Court draws a new jurisdictional line, one that invalidates the 1986 migratory bird regulation as well as the Corps' assertion of jurisdiction over all waters except for actually navigable waters, their tributaries, and wetlands adjacent to each. Its holding rests on two equally untenable premises: (1) that when Congress passed the 1972 CWA, it did not intend "to exert anything more than its commerce power over navigation," and (2) that in 1972 Congress drew the boundary defining the Corps' jurisdiction at the odd line on which the Court today settles.

As I shall explain, the text of the 1972 amendments affords no support for the Court's holding, and amendments Congress adopted in 1977 do support the Corps' present interpretation of its mission as extending to so-called "isolated" waters. Indeed, simple common sense cuts against the particular definition of the Corps' jurisdiction favored by the majority....

IV. Because I am convinced that the Court's miserly construction of the statute is incorrect, I shall comment briefly on petitioner's argument that Congress is without power to prohibit it from filling any part of the 31 acres of ponds on its property in Cook County, Illinois. The Corps' exercise of its § 404 permitting power over "isolated" waters that serve as habitat for migratory birds falls well within the boundaries set by this Court's Commerce Clause jurisprudence.

In *United States v. Lopez* (1995), this Court identified "three broad categories of activity that Congress may regulate under its commerce power": (1) channels of interstate commerce; (2) instrumentalities of interstate commerce, or persons and things in interstate commerce; and (3) activities that "substantially affect" interstate commerce. The migratory bird rule at issue here is properly analyzed under the third category. In order to constitute a proper exercise of Congress' power over intrastate activities that "substantially affect" interstate commerce, it is not necessary that each individual instance of the activity substantially affect commerce; it is enough that, taken in the aggregate, the *class of activities* in question has such an effect. *Perez v. United States* (1971) (noting that it is the "class" of regulated activities, not the individual instance, that is to be considered in the "affects" commerce analysis); see also *Hodel v. Virginia Surface Mining & Reclamation Assn., Inc.* (1981); *Wickard v. Filburn* (1942).

The activity being regulated in this case (and by the Corps' § 404 regulations in general) is the discharge of fill material into water. The Corps did not assert jurisdiction over petitioner's land simply because the waters were "used as habitat by migratory birds."

It asserted jurisdiction because petitioner planned to *discharge fill* into waters "used as habitat by migratory birds." Had petitioner intended to engage in some other activity besides discharging fill (*i.e.*, had there been no activity to regulate), or, conversely, had the waters not been habitat for migratory birds (*i.e.*, had there been no basis for federal jurisdiction), the Corps would never have become involved in petitioner's use of its land. There can be no doubt that, unlike the class of activities Congress was attempting to regulate in *United States v. Morrison*, (2000) ("[g]ender-motivated crimes"), and *Lopez* (possession of guns near school property), the discharge of fill material into the Nation's waters is almost always undertaken for economic reasons. See V. Albrecht & B. Goode, *Wetland Regulation in the Real World*, Exh. 3 (Feb.1994) (demonstrating that the overwhelming majority of acreage for which § 404 permits are sought is intended for commercial, industrial, or other economic use).

Moreover, no one disputes that the discharge of fill into "isolated" waters that serve as migratory bird habitat will, in the aggregate, adversely affect migratory bird populations. See, *e.g.*, 1 Secretary of the Interior, *Report to Congress, The Impact of Federal Programs on Wetlands: The Lower Mississippi Alluvial Plain and the Prairie Pothole Region* 79–80 (Oct.1988) ([a report of the Secretary of the Interior noted] that "isolated," phase 3 waters "are among the most important and also [the] most threatened ecosystems in the United States" because "[t]hey are prime nesting grounds for many species of North American waterfowl" and provide "[u]p to 50 percent of the [U.S.] production of migratory waterfowl"). Nor does petitioner dispute that the particular waters it seeks to fill are home to many important species of migratory birds, including the second-largest breeding colony of Great Blue Herons in northeastern Illinois and several species of waterfowl protected by international treaty and Illinois endangered species laws.

In addition to the intrinsic value of migratory birds, see *Missouri v. Holland* (1920) (noting the importance of migratory birds as "protectors of our forests and our crops" and as "a food supply"), it is undisputed that literally millions of people regularly participate in birdwatching and hunting and that those activities generate a host of commercial activities of great value. The causal connection between the filling of wetlands and the decline of commercial activities associated with migratory birds is not "attenuated," *Morrison*; it is direct and concrete. Cf. *Gibbs v. Babbitt* (4th Cir. 2000) ("The relationship between red wolf takings and interstate commerce is quite direct—with no red wolves, there will be no red wolf related tourism....").

Finally, the migratory bird rule does not blur the "distinction between what is truly national and what is truly local." *Morrison*. Justice Holmes cogently observed in *Missouri v. Holland* that the protection of migratory birds is a textbook example of a *national* problem. ("It is not sufficient to rely upon the States [to protect migratory birds]. The reliance is vain....") The destruction of aquatic migratory bird habitat, like so many other environmental problems, is an action in which the benefits (*e.g.,* a new landfill) are disproportionately local, while many of the costs (*e.g.,* fewer migratory birds) are widely dispersed and often borne by citizens living in other States. In such situations, described by economists as involving "externalities," federal regulation is both appropriate and necessary. Revesz, *Rehabilitating Interstate Competition: Rethinking the "Race-to-the-Bottom" Rationale for Federal Environmental Regulation*, 67 N.Y.U. L. Rev. 1210, 1222 (1992) ("The presence of interstate externalities is a powerful reason for intervention at the federal level"); cf. *Hodel*, (deferring to Congress' finding that nationwide standards were "essential" in order to avoid "destructive interstate competition" that might undermine environmental standards). Identifying the Corps' jurisdiction by reference to waters that serve as habitat for birds that migrate over state lines also satisfies this Court's expressed desire for some "jurisdictional element" that limits federal activity to its proper scope. *Morrison*.

The power to regulate commerce among the several States necessarily and properly includes the power to preserve the natural resources that generate such commerce. Cf. *Sporhase v. Nebraska ex rel. Douglas* (1982) (holding water to be an "article of commerce"). Migratory birds, and the waters on which they rely, are such resources. Moreover, the protection of migratory birds is a well-established federal responsibility. As Justice Holmes noted in *Missouri v. Holland,* the federal interest in protecting these birds is of "the first magnitude." Because of their transitory nature, they "can be protected only by national action."

Whether it is necessary or appropriate to refuse to allow petitioner to fill those ponds is a question on which we have no voice. Whether the Federal Government has the power to require such permission, however, is a question that is easily answered. If, as it does, the Commerce Clause empowers Congress to regulate particular "activities causing air or water pollution, or other environmental hazards that may have effects in more than one State," *Hodel,* it also empowers Congress to control individual actions that, in the aggregate, would have the same effect. *Perez* (1971); *Wickard* (1942). There is no merit in petitioner's constitutional argument....

* * *

In *Rapanos v.* United States (2006), the Court once again interpreted the Clean Water Act (CWA) narrowly to avoid reaching the question of its constitutionality under the Commerce Clause. Following the approach of *Solid Waste Agency of Northern Cook County,* the Court again suggested it would adopt a very narrow view of the scope of the Commerce Clause as a source for federal enforcement of environmental legislation. *Rapanos* involved challenges to the authority of the Army Corps of Engineers (Corps) to regulate the filling of wetlands by private developers. The Court rejected the government's argument that the CWA authorized the Corps to regulate wetlands that were directly connected to navigable waters only during certain periods of the year.

IV. Other Delegated Sources of National Power: The Power to Spend, the War Power, and the Treaty Power

A. The Taxing and Spending Power

Under the Articles of Confederation, the federal government had no power to tax individuals. Aware that the lack of taxing authority unduly limited the power of the federal government, the framers of the Constitution moved to provide Congress with the power to tax and spend. Article I, §8 provides that

> Congress shall have Power to lay and collect Taxes, Duties, Imposts and Excises, to pay the Debts and provide for the common Defence and general Welfare of the United States; but all Duties, Imposts and Excises shall be uniform throughout the United States.

One threshold question under Article I, §8 is whether Congress may tax and spend only for the purpose of carrying out one of the enumerated powers set forth in Article I, or whether Congress may also tax and spend for more general purposes, so long as those purposes can be considered for the "general Welfare of the United States." In *United States v. Butler* (1936), the Court embraced the latter, more expansive view of congressional taxing and spending power. In *Butler*, the Court considered the constitutionality of the Agricultural Adjustment Act of 1933, which, in part, offered subsidies to farmers to limit their crop production for the purpose of stabilizing farm prices. The Court in *Butler* declared the Agricultural Adjustment Act unconstitutional on grounds that it regulated "production" in violation of the 10th Amendment. This aspect of the *Butler* decision, as we have seen in our discussion above of the commerce power, has long been abandoned by the Court.

But the Court in *Butler* also considered the scope of the taxing and spending power and this aspect of the decision remains highly pertinent to considerations of the meaning of Article I, §8. The *Butler* Court observed that the debate over the scope of the taxing and spending power had its origins in a debate between James Madison and Alexander Hamilton. Madison took the view, in the Court's words, that the scope of the taxing and spending power was limited to "the other powers enumerated in [Article I]; that, as the United States is a government of limited and enumerated powers, the grant of the power to tax and spend for the general national welfare must be confined to the enumerated legislative fields committed to Congress." [Limited]

In contrast, Hamilton took the view that Congress could tax and spend for *any* purpose that Congress thought served "the general Welfare of the United States." As the *Butler* Court put it, Hamilton "maintained that the clause confers a power separate and [Broad] distinct from those later enumerated, is not restricted in meaning by the grant of them, and Congress consequently has a substantive power to tax and to appropriate, limited only by the requirement that it shall be exercised to provide for the general welfare of the United States." The *Butler* Court embraced the Hamiltonian view, leaving Congress with a broad power to tax and spend for the "general welfare" so long as Congress violates no other constitutional provisions. A spending program, for example, that favored only Episcopalians might be for the "general Welfare of the United States," but would nevertheless violate the 1st Amendment.

After *Butler*, the Court upheld a number of federal taxing and spending programs. For example, in *Steward Machine Co. v. Davis* (1937), the Court upheld the federal unemployment compensation system as a legitimate exercise of the taxing and spending power. Similarly, in *Helvering v. Davis* (1937), the Court upheld the old age pension program of the Social Security Act. The Court has continued to give Congress considerable latitude to tax and spend for the general welfare, subject to some constraints that we will consider in the cases that follow. In the wake of the Court's recent narrowing of Congress's power under the Commerce Clause, the taxing and spending power is likely to assume greater importance in congressional regulatory activities.

Buckley v. Valeo
424 U.S. 1 (1976)

[Per Curiam: Brennan, Stewart, Powell, Marshall, Blackmun, Stevens, White, Rehnquist, and Burger (C.J.). Dissenting (in part): Burger (C.J.), White, Marshall, Blackmun, and Rehnquist.]

[*Buckley* involved the constitutionality of a comprehensive campaign reform statute passed by Congress in the aftermath of the Watergate scandals. Most aspects of the case are discussed in the section on the 1st Amendment. Here we consider only the Court's discussion of public finance and the Spending Clause.]

III. PUBLIC FINANCING OF PRESIDENTIAL ELECTION CAMPAIGNS ...

III-A. Summary of Subtitle H

Section 9006 establishes a Presidential Election Campaign Fund (Fund), financed from general revenues in the aggregate amount designated by individual taxpayers, under §6096, who on their income tax returns may authorize payment to the Fund of one dollar of their tax liability in the case of an individual return or two dollars in the case of a joint return. The Fund consists of three separate accounts to finance (1) party nominating conventions, §9008(a), (2) general election campaigns, §9006(a), and (3) primary campaigns, §9037(a)....

For expenses in the general election campaign, §9004(a)(1) entitles each major-party candidate to $20,000,000. This amount is also adjusted for inflation. See §9004(a)(1). To be eligible for funds the candidate must pledge not to incur expenses in excess of the entitlement under §9004(a)(1) and not to accept private contributions except to the extent that the fund is insufficient to provide the full entitlement. §9003(b). Minor-party candidates are also entitled to funding, again based on the ratio of the vote received by the party's candidate in the preceding election to the average of the major-party candidates. §9004(a)(2)(A). Minor-party candidates must certify that they will not incur campaign expenses in excess of the major-party entitlement and that they will accept private contributions only to the extent needed to make up the difference between that amount and the public funding grant. §9003(c). New party candidates receive no money prior to the general election, but any candidate receiving 5% or more of the popular vote in the election is entitled to post-election payments according to the formula applicable to minor-party candidates. §9004(a)(3)....

III-B. Constitutionality of Subtitle H

Appellants argue that Subtitle H is invalid (1) as "contrary to the 'general welfare,'" Art. I, §8(2) because any scheme of public financing of election campaigns is inconsistent with the 1st Amendment, and (3) because Subtitle H invidiously discriminates against certain interests in violation of the Due Process Clause of the 5th Amendment. We find no merit in these contentions.

Appellants' "general welfare" contention erroneously treats the General Welfare Clause as a limitation upon congressional power. It is rather a grant of power, the scope of which is quite expansive, particularly in view of the enlargement of power by the Necessary and Proper Clause. *McCulloch v. Maryland* (1819). Congress has power to regulate Presidential elections and primaries, *United States v. Classic* (1941); and public financing of Presidential elections as a means to reform the electoral process was clearly a choice within the granted power. It is for Congress to decide which expenditures will promote the general welfare: "[T]he power of Congress to authorize expenditure of public moneys for public purposes is not limited by the direct grants of legislative power found in the Constitution." *United States v. Butler* (1936). Any limitations upon the exercise of that granted power must be found elsewhere in the Constitution. In this case, Congress was legislating for the "general welfare" to reduce the deleterious influence of large contributions on our political process, to facilitate communication by candidates with the electorate, and to free candidates from the rigors of fundraising. Whether the chosen means appear "bad," "unwise," or "unworkable" to us is irrelevant; Congress has concluded that the means are "necessary and proper" to promote the general welfare, and we thus decline to find this legislation without the grant of power in Art. I, §8.

Appellants' challenge to the dollar check-off provision (§6096) fails for the same reason. They maintain that Congress is required to permit taxpayers to designate particular candidates or parties as recipients of their money. But the appropriation to the Fund in §9006 is like any other appropriation from the general revenue except that its amount is determined by reference to the aggregate of the one- and two-dollar authorization on taxpayers' income tax returns. This detail does not constitute the appropriation any less an appropriation by Congress. The fallacy of appellants' argument is therefore apparent; every appropriation made by Congress uses public money in a manner to which some taxpayers object....

South Dakota v. Dole

483 U.S. 203 (1987)

[Majority: Rehnquist (C.J.), White, Marshall, Blackmun, Powell, Stevens, Scalia. Dissenting: Brennan and O'Connor.]

Chief Justice Rehnquist delivered the opinion of the Court.

Petitioner South Dakota permits persons 19 years of age or older to purchase beer containing up to 3.2% alcohol. In 1984 Congress enacted 23 U.S.C. §158, which directs the Secretary of Transportation to withhold a percentage of federal highway funds otherwise allocable from States "in which the purchase or public possession ... of any alcoholic beverage by a person who is less than twenty-one years of age is lawful." The State sued in United States District Court seeking a declaratory judgment that §158 violates the constitutional limitations on congressional exercise of the spending power and violates the 21st Amendment to the United States Constitution. The District Court rejected the State's claims, and the Court of Appeals for the Eighth Circuit affirmed.

In this Court, the parties direct most of their efforts to defining the proper scope of the 21st Amendment.... Relying on our statement in *California Retail Liquor Dealers Assn. v. Midcal Aluminum, Inc.* (1980), that the "21st Amendment grants the States virtually complete control over whether to permit importation or sale of liquor and how to structure the liquor distribution system," South Dakota asserts that the setting of minimum drinking ages is clearly within the "core powers" reserved to the States under §2 of the Amendment.[1] Section 158, petitioner claims, usurps that core power. The Secretary in response asserts that the 21st Amendment is simply not implicated by §158; the plain language of §2 confirms the States' broad power to impose restrictions on the sale and distribution of alcoholic beverages but does not confer on them any power to *permit* sales that Congress seeks to *prohibit*....

Despite the extended treatment of the question by the parties, however, we need not decide in this case whether that Amendment would prohibit an attempt by Congress to legislate directly a national minimum drinking age. Here, Congress has acted indirectly under its spending power to encourage uniformity in the States' drinking ages. As we explain below, we find this legislative effort within constitutional bounds even if Congress may not regulate drinking ages directly.

The Constitution empowers Congress to "lay and collect Taxes, Duties, Imposts, and Excises, to pay the Debts and provide for the common Defence and general Welfare of the United States." Art. I, §8, cl. 1. Incident to this power, Congress may attach conditions on the receipt of federal funds, and has repeatedly employed the power "to further broad policy objectives by conditioning receipt of federal moneys upon compliance by the recipient with federal statutory and administrative directives."... The breadth of this power was made clear in *United States v. Butler* (1936), where the Court, resolving a longstanding debate over the scope of the Spending Clause, determined that "the power of Congress to authorize expenditure of public moneys for public purposes is not limited by the direct grants of legislative power found in the Constitution." Thus, objectives not thought to be within Article I's "enumerated legislative fields," may nevertheless be attained through the use of the spending power and the conditional grant of federal funds.

The spending power is of course not unlimited, but is instead subject to several general restrictions articulated in our cases. The first of these limitations is derived from the language of the Constitution itself: the exercise of the spending power must be in pursuit of "the general welfare." See *Helvering v. Davis* (1937); *United States v. Butler*. In considering whether a particular expenditure is intended to serve general public purposes, courts should defer substantially to the judgment of Congress. *Helvering v. Davis*.[2] Second, we have required that if Congress desires to condition the States' receipt of federal funds, it "must do so unambiguously ... enabl[ing] the States to exercise their choice knowingly, cognizant of the consequences of their participation." *Pennhurst State School and Hospital v. Halderman* (1981). Third, our cases have suggested (without significant elabora-

---

1. Section 2 of the 21st Amendment provides: "The transportation or importation into any State, Territory, or possession of the United States for delivery or use therein of intoxicating liquors, in violation of the laws thereof, is hereby prohibited."

2. The level of deference to the congressional decision is such that the Court has more recently questioned whether "general welfare" is a judicially enforceable restriction at all. See *Buckley v. Valeo*, (per curiam).

tion) that conditions on federal grants might be illegitimate if they are unrelated "to the federal interest in particular national projects or programs." *Massachusetts v. United States* (1978) (plurality opinion). See also *Ivanhoe Irrigation Dist. v. McCracken* (1958), ("[T]he Federal Government may establish and impose reasonable conditions relevant to federal interest in the project and to the over-all objectives thereof"). Finally, we have noted that other constitutional provisions may provide an independent bar to the conditional grant of federal funds....

South Dakota does not seriously claim that § 158 is inconsistent with any of the first three restrictions mentioned above. We can readily conclude that the provision is designed to serve the general welfare, especially in light of the fact that "the concept of welfare or the opposite is shaped by Congress...." *Helvering v. Davis*. Congress found that the differing drinking ages in the States created particular incentives for young persons to combine their desire to drink with their ability to drive, and that this interstate problem required a national solution. The means it chose to address this dangerous situation were reasonably calculated to advance the general welfare. The conditions upon which States receive the funds, moreover, could not be more clearly stated by Congress. And the State itself, rather than challenging the germaneness of the condition to federal purposes, admits that it "has never contended that the congressional action was ... unrelated to a national concern in the absence of the 21st Amendment." Indeed, the condition imposed by Congress is directly related to one of the main purposes for which highway funds are expended—safe interstate travel. This goal of the interstate highway system had been frustrated by varying drinking ages among the States. A Presidential commission appointed to study alcohol-related accidents and fatalities on the Nation's highways concluded that the lack of uniformity in the States' drinking ages created "an incentive to drink and drive" because "young persons commut[e] to border States where the drinking age is lower." By enacting § 158, Congress conditioned the receipt of federal funds in a way reasonably calculated to address this particular impediment to a purpose for which the funds are expended.

The remaining question about the validity of § 158—and the basic point of disagreement between the parties—is whether the 21st Amendment constitutes an "independent constitutional bar" to the conditional grant of federal funds. *Lawrence County v. Lead-Deadwood School Dist.* (1985). Petitioner, relying on its view that the 21st Amendment prohibits direct regulation of drinking ages by Congress, asserts that "Congress may not use the spending power to regulate that which it is prohibited from regulating directly under the 21st Amendment." But our cases show that this "independent constitutional bar" limitation on the spending power is not of the kind petitioner suggests. *United States v. Butler*, for example, established that the constitutional limitations on Congress when exercising its spending power are less exacting than those on its authority to regulate directly.

We have also held that a perceived 10th Amendment limitation on congressional regulation of state affairs did not concomitantly limit the range of conditions legitimately placed on federal grants. In *Oklahoma v. Civil Service Comm'n* (1947), the Court considered the validity of the Hatch Act insofar as it was applied to political activities of state officials whose employment was financed in whole or in part with federal funds. The State contended that an order under this provision to withhold certain federal funds unless a state official was removed invaded its sovereignty in violation of the 10th Amendment. Though finding that "the United States is not concerned with, and has no power to regulate, local political activities as such of state officials," the Court nevertheless held that the Federal Government "does have power to fix the terms upon which its money allotments to states shall be disbursed." The Court found no violation of the State's sovereignty because the State could, and did, adopt "the 'simple expedient' of not yielding to what she urges is federal coercion. The offer of benefits to a state by the United States dependent upon cooperation by the state with federal plans, assumedly for the general welfare, is not unusual." See also *Steward Machine Co. v. Davis* (1937) ("There is only a condition which the state is free at pleasure to disregard or to fulfill").

These cases establish that the "independent constitutional bar" limitation on the spending power is not, as petitioner suggests, a prohibition on the indirect achievement of objectives which Congress is not empowered to achieve directly. Instead, we think that the language in our earlier opinions stands for the unexceptionable proposition that the power may not be used to induce the States to engage in activities that would themselves be unconstitutional. Thus, for example, a grant of federal funds conditioned on invidiously discriminatory state action or the infliction of cruel and unusual punishment would be an illegitimate exercise of the Congress' broad spending power. But no such claim can be or is made here. Were South Dakota to succumb to the blandishments offered by Congress and raise its drinking age to 21, the State's action in so doing would not violate the constitutional rights of anyone.

Our decisions have recognized that in some circumstances the financial inducement offered by Congress might be so coercive as to pass the point at which "pressure turns into compulsion." *Steward Machine Co. v. Davis*. Here, however, Congress has directed only that a State desiring to establish a minimum drinking age lower than 21 lose a relatively small percentage of certain federal highway funds. Petitioner contends that the coercive nature of this program is evident from the degree of success it has achieved. We cannot conclude, however, that a conditional grant of federal money of this sort is unconstitutional simply by reason of its success in achieving the congressional objective.

When we consider, for a moment, that all South Dakota would lose if she adheres to her chosen course as to a suitable minimum drinking age is 5% of the funds otherwise obtainable under specified highway grant programs, the argument as to coercion is shown to be more rhetoric than fact. As we said a half century ago in *Steward Machine Co. v. Davis*: "[E]very rebate from a tax when conditioned upon conduct is in some measure a temptation. But to hold that motive or temptation is equivalent to coercion is to plunge the law in endless difficulties. The outcome of such a doctrine is the acceptance of a philosophical determinism by which choice becomes impossible. Till now the law has been guided by a robust common sense which assumes the freedom of the will as a working hypothesis in the solution of its problems."

Here Congress has offered relatively mild encouragement to the States to enact higher minimum drinking ages than they would otherwise choose. But the enactment of such laws remains the prerogative of the States not merely in theory but in fact. Even if Congress might lack the power to impose a national minimum drinking age directly, we conclude that encouragement to state action found in §158 is a valid use of the spending power. Accordingly, the judgment of the Court of Appeals is

Affirmed.

Justice Brennan, dissenting.

I agree with Justice O'Connor that regulation of the minimum age of purchasers of liquor falls squarely within the ambit of those powers reserved to the States by the 21st Amendment. Since States possess this constitutional power, Congress cannot condition a federal grant in a manner that abridges this right. The Amendment, itself, strikes the proper balance between federal and state authority. I therefore dissent.

Justice O'Connor, dissenting.

The Court today upholds the National Minimum Drinking Age Amendment, [§ 158], as a valid exercise of the spending power conferred by Article I, § 8. But § 158 is not a condition on spending reasonably related to the expenditure of federal funds and cannot be justified on that ground. Rather, it is an attempt to regulate the sale of liquor, an attempt that lies outside Congress' power to regulate commerce because it falls within the ambit of § 2 of the 21st Amendment.

My disagreement with the Court is relatively narrow on the spending power issue: it is a disagreement about the application of a principle rather than a disagreement on the principle itself. I agree with the Court that Congress may attach conditions on the receipt of federal funds to further "the federal interest in particular national projects or programs." *Massachusetts v. United States* (1978); *Steward Machine Co. v. Davis* (1937). I also subscribe to the established proposition that the reach of the spending power "is not limited by the direct grants of legislative power found in the Constitution." *United States v. Butler* (1936). Finally, I agree that there are four separate types of limitations on the spending power: the expenditure must be for the general welfare, the conditions imposed must be unambiguous, they must be reasonably related to the purpose of the expenditure, and the legislation may not violate any independent constitutional prohibition. Insofar as two of those limitations are concerned, the Court is clearly correct that § 158 is wholly unobjectionable. Establishment of a national minimum drinking age certainly fits within the broad concept of the general welfare and the statute is entirely unambiguous. I am also willing to assume, arguendo, that the 21st Amendment does not constitute an "independent constitutional bar" to a spending condition.

But the Court's application of the requirement that the condition imposed be reasonably related to the purpose for which the funds are expended is cursory and unconvincing. We have repeatedly said that Congress may condition grants under the spending power only in ways reasonably related to the purpose of the federal program.... In my view, establishment of a minimum drinking age of 21 is not sufficiently related to interstate highway construction to justify so conditioning funds appropriated for that purpose....

Aside from these "concessions" by counsel, the Court asserts the reasonableness of the relationship between the supposed purpose of the expenditure—"safe interstate travel"—and the drinking age condition. The Court reasons that Congress wishes that the roads it builds may be used safely, that drunken drivers threaten highway safety, and that young people are more likely to drive while under the influence of alcohol under existing law than would be the case if there were a uniform national drinking age of 21. It hardly needs saying, however, that if the purpose of § 158 is to deter drunken driving, it is far too over and under-inclusive. It is over-inclusive because it stops teenagers from drinking even when they are not about to drive on interstate highways. It is under-inclusive because teenagers pose only a small part of the drunken driving problem in this Nation. [As Senator Hemphrey asserted] ("Eighty-four percent of all highway fatalities involving alcohol occur among those whose ages exceed 21"); [as Senator McClure said] ("Certainly, statistically, if you use that one set of statistics, then the mandatory drinking age ought to be raised at least to 30"); [Senator Symms remarked] ("[M]ost of the studies point out that the drivers of age 21–24 are the worst offenders").

When Congress appropriates money to build a highway, it is entitled to insist that the highway be a safe one. But it is not entitled to insist as a condition of the use of highway funds that the State impose or change regulations in other areas of the State's social and economic life because of an attenuated or tangential relationship to highway use or safety.

Indeed, if the rule were otherwise, the Congress could effectively regulate almost any area of a State's social, political, or economic life on the theory that use of the interstate transportation system is somehow enhanced. If, for example, the United States were to condition highway moneys upon moving the state capital, I suppose it might argue that interstate transportation is facilitated by locating local governments in places easily accessible to interstate highways—or, conversely, that highways might become overburdened if they had to carry traffic to and from the state capital. In my mind, such a relationship is hardly more attenuated than the one which the Court finds supports § 158....

The Spending Power: Questions

1. How does the Court treat the General Welfare Clause in *Buckley v. Valeo* and *South Dakota v. Dole*? What, if any, constitutional limits exist on the power to spend for the general welfare?

2. Does the power to spend for the general welfare in effect expand the delegated powers of Congress? Why or why not?

3. How closely will the Court scrutinize whether the expenditure is for the general welfare? What sort of scrutiny does it seem to use?

B. The War Power

Inherent National Power in Foreign Affairs. In *U.S. v. Curtiss-Wright Export Co.* (1936), Congress had authorized the President, in his discretion, to embargo arms sales to Bolivia and Paraguay, which were engaged in armed conflict. President Roosevelt imposed the embargo, which was challenged by Curtiss-Wright Export Co. as an unconstitutional delegation of power. The Court rejected the contention:

> The determination which we are called to make, therefore, is whether the Joint Resolution, as applied to that situation, is vulnerable to attack under the rule that forbids a delegation of the lawmaking power. In other words, assuming (but not deciding) that the challenged delegation, if it were confined to internal affairs, would be invalid, may it nevertheless be sustained on the ground that its exclusive aim is to afford a remedy for a hurtful condition within foreign territory?
>
> It will contribute to the elucidation of the question if we first consider the differences between the powers of the federal government in respect of foreign or external affairs and those in respect of domestic or internal affairs. That there are differences between them, and that these differences are fundamental, may not be doubted.
>
> The two classes of powers are different, both in respect of their origin and their nature. The broad statement that the federal government can exercise no powers except those specifically enumerated in the Constitution, and such implied powers as are necessary and proper to carry into effect the enumerated powers, is categorically true only in respect of our internal affairs. In that field, the primary purpose of the Constitution was to carve from the general mass of legislative powers then possessed by the states such portions as it was thought desirable to vest in the federal government, leaving those not included in the enumeration still in the states. *Carter v. Carter Coal Co.* (1936). That this doc-

trine applies only to powers which the states had is self-evident. And since the states severally never possessed international powers, such powers could not have been carved from the mass of state powers but obviously were transmitted to the United States from some other source. During the Colonial period, those powers were possessed exclusively by and were entirely under the control of the Crown. By the Declaration of Independence, "the Representatives of the United States of America" declared the United (not the several) Colonies to be free and independent states, and as such to have "full Power to levy War, conclude Peace, contract Alliances, establish Commerce and to do all other Acts and Things which Independent States may of right do."

As a result of the separation from Great Britain by the colonies, acting as a unit, the powers of external sovereignty passed from the Crown not to the colonies severally, but to the colonies in their collective and corporate capacity as the United States of America. Even before the Declaration, the colonies were a unit in foreign affairs, acting through a common agency—namely, the Continental Congress, composed of delegates from the thirteen colonies. That agency exercised the powers of war and peace, raised an army, created a navy, and finally adopted the Declaration of Independence. Rulers come and go; governments end and forms of government change; but sovereignty survives. A political society cannot endure without a supreme will somewhere. Sovereignty is never held in suspense. When, therefore, the external sovereignty of Great Britain in respect of the colonies ceased, it immediately passed to the Union. That fact was given practical application almost at once. The treaty of peace, made on September 3, 1783, was concluded between his Brittanic Majesty and the "United States of America."

The Union existed before the Constitution, which was ordained and established among other things to form "a more perfect Union." Prior to that event, it is clear that the Union, declared by the Articles of Confederation to be "perpetual," was the sole possessor of external sovereignty, and in the Union it remained without change save in so far as the Constitution in express terms qualified its exercise. The Framers' Convention was called and exerted its powers upon the irrefutable postulate that though the states were several their people in respect of foreign affairs were one. In that convention, the entire absence of state power to deal with those affairs was thus forcefully stated by Rufus King:

> The states were not "sovereigns" in the sense contended for by some. They did not possess the peculiar features of sovereignty—they could not make war, nor peace, nor alliances, nor treaties. Considering them as political beings, they were dumb, for they could not speak to any foreign sovereign whatever. They were deaf, for they could not hear any propositions from such sovereign. They had not even the organs or faculties of defence or offence, for they could not of themselves raise troops, or equip vessels, for war. 5 *Elliot's Debates*, 212.

It results that the investment of the federal government with the powers of external sovereignty did not depend upon the affirmative grants of the Constitution. The powers to declare and wage war, to conclude peace, to make treaties, to maintain diplomatic relations with other sovereignties, if they had never been mentioned in the Constitution, would have vested in the federal government as necessary concomitants of nationality.

Woods v. Miller Co.: Questions

1. What power is invoked to justify the congressional act imposing rent control?
2. What is the date of the decision? What is the relevance of the date to the asserted constitutional basis for rent control?
3. Are there potential dangers inherent in application of war powers in facts like *Woods*? What are they?
4. What are Justice Jackson's concerns?

Woods v. Miller Co.
333 U.S. 138 (1948)

[Majority: Douglas, Frankfurter, Vinson (C.J.), Black, Rutledge, Murphy, Reed, Burton, and Jackson. Concurring: Frankfurter and Jackson.]

Mr. Justice Douglas delivered the opinion of the Court.

The case is here on a direct appeal from a judgment of the District Court holding unconstitutional Title II of the Housing and Rent Act of 1947.

The Act became effective on July 1, 1947, and the following day the appellee demanded of its tenants increases of 40% and 60% for rental accommodations in the Cleveland Defense-Rental Area, and admitted violation of the Act and regulations adopted pursuant thereto. Appellant thereupon instituted this proceeding under §206(b) of the Act to enjoin the violations. A preliminary injunction issued. After a hearing it was dissolved and a permanent injunction denied.

The District Court was of the view that the authority of Congress to regulate rents by virtue of the war power ended with the Presidential Proclamation terminating hostilities on December 31, 1946, since that proclamation inaugurated "peace-in-fact" though it did not mark termination of the war. It also concluded that even if the war power continues, Congress did not act under it because it did not say so, and only if Congress says so, or enacts provisions so implying, can it be held that Congress intended to exercise such power....

We conclude, in the first place, that the war power sustains this legislation. The Court said in *Hamilton v. Kentucky Distilleries and Warehouse Co.* (1919) that the war power includes the power "to remedy the evils which have arisen from its rise and progress" and continues for the duration of that emergency. Whatever may be the consequences when war is officially terminated, the war power does not necessarily end with the cessation of hostilities. We recently held that it is adequate to support the preservation of rights created by wartime legislation. But it has a broader sweep. In *Hamilton* and *Ruppert v. Caffey* (1920), prohibition laws which were enacted after the Armistice in World War I were sustained as exercises of the war power because they conserved manpower and increased efficiency of production in the critical days during the period of demobilization, and helped to husband the supply of grains and cereals depleted by the war effort. Those cases followed the reasoning of *Stewart v. Kahn* (1870), which held that Congress had the power to toll the statute of limitations of the States during the period when the process of their courts was not available to litigants due to the conditions obtaining in the Civil War.

The constitutional validity of the present legislation follows a fortiori from those cases. The legislative history of the present Act makes abundantly clear that there has not yet been eliminated the deficit in housing which in considerable measure was caused by the heavy demobilization of veterans and by the cessation or reduction in residential construction during the period of hostilities due to the allocation of building materials to military projects. Since the war effort contributed heavily to that deficit, Congress has the power even after the cessation of hostilities to act to control the forces that a short supply of the needed article created. If that were not true, the Necessary and Proper Clause, Art. I, § 8, cl. 18, would be drastically limited in its application to the several war powers. The Court has declined to follow that course in the past. We decline to take it today. The result would be paralyzing. It would render Congress powerless to remedy conditions the creation of which necessarily followed from the mobilization of men and materials for successful prosecution of the war. So to read the Constitution would be to make it self-defeating.

We recognize the force of the argument that the effects of war under modern conditions may be felt in the economy for years and years, and that if the war power can be used in days of peace to treat all the wounds which war inflicts on our society, it may not only swallow up all other powers of Congress but largely obliterate the 9th and the 10th Amendments as well. There are no such implications in today's decision. We deal here with the consequences of a housing deficit greatly intensified during the period of hostilities by the war effort. Any power, of course, can be abused. But we cannot assume that Congress is not alert to its constitutional responsibilities. And the question whether the war power has been properly employed in cases such as this is open to judicial inquiry.

The question of the constitutionality of action taken by Congress does not depend on recitals of the power which it undertakes to exercise. Here it is plain from the legislative history that Congress was invoking its war power to cope with a current condition of which the war was a direct and immediate cause. Its judgment on that score is entitled to the respect granted like legislation enacted pursuant to the police power....

The fact that the property regulated suffers a decrease in value is no more fatal to the exercise of the war power than it is where the police power is invoked to the same end.

Mr. Justice Frankfurter concurring. [Omitted.]

Mr. Justice Jackson, concurring.

I agree with the result in this case, but the arguments that have been addressed to us lead me to utter more explicit misgivings about war powers than the Court has done. The Government asserts no constitutional basis for this legislation other than this vague, undefined and undefinable "war power."

No one will question that this power is the most dangerous one to free government in the whole catalogue of powers. It usually is invoked in haste and excitement when calm legislative consideration of constitutional limitation is difficult. It is executed in a time of patriotic fervor that makes moderation unpopular. And, worst of all, it is interpreted by the Judges under the influence of the same passions and pressures. Always, as in this case, the Government urges hasty decision to forestall some emergency or serve some purpose and pleads that paralysis will result if its claims to power are denied or their confirmation delayed.

Particularly when the war power is invoked to do things to the liberties of people, or to their property or economy that only indirectly affect conduct of the war and do not relate to the management of the war itself, the constitutional basis should be scrutinized with care.

I think we can hardly deny that the war power is as valid a ground for federal rent control now as it has been at any time. We still are technically in a state of war. I would not be willing to hold that war powers may be indefinitely prolonged merely by keeping legally alive a state of war that had in fact ended. I cannot accept the argument that war powers last as long as the effects and consequences of war for if so they are permanent—as permanent as the war debts. But I find no reason to conclude that we could find fairly that the present state of war is merely technical. We have armies abroad exercising our war power and have made no peace terms with our allies not to mention our principal enemies. I think the conclusion that the war power has been applicable during the lifetime of this legislation is unavoidable.

Hamdan v. Rumsfeld (2006): Note

In *Hamdan v. Rumsfeld* (2006), the Court invalidated the President's attempt to try alleged members of al Qaeda by military commission in part because his Executive Order conflicted with Congress' exercise of their war powers. Congress has the authority to "declare War ... and make Rules concerning Captures on Land and Water," Art. I, §8, cl. 11, to "raise and support Armies," *id.*, cl. 12, to "define and punish ... Offences against the Law of Nations," *id.*, cl. 10, and "To make Rules for the Government and Regulation of the land and naval Forces," *id.*, cl. 14. Pursuant to these powers, Congress passed the *Uniform Code of Military Justice* (UCMJ), 10 U.S.C. §801 *et seq.*, in 1950. The UCMJ replaced earlier congressional Articles of War. The UCMJ governs all aspects of the military justice system. Because Congress had legislated in this area, the Court ruled that the President was not free to bypass the established military justice system. *See Hamdan, infra.*

C. The Treaty Power

A treaty that shows that it is designed to become effective as domestic national law supersedes an earlier inconsistent law passed by Congress. However, later Congressional legislation will supersede provisions of a treaty with which it is inconsistent.

Missouri v. Holland: Questions

1. Lower courts had earlier held that Congress lacked power under the Commerce Clause to regulate migratory birds. How would this issue likely be resolved under modern Commerce Clause authority? Why is the statute upheld when Congress legislates to give effect to a treaty?

2. Why does the 10th Amendment attack on the statute passed pursuant to the treaty fail?

3. Under the authority of this case, would a treaty that violates specific guarantees of the Bill of Rights be upheld? What would you point to in the opinion bearing on that point? What kind of authority is it: a holding or dicta?

Missouri v. Holland
252 U.S. 416 (1920)

[Majority: Holmes, White (C.J.), McReynolds, Brandeis, Day, Clarke, and McKenna. Dissenting: Van Devanter and Pitney.]

Mr. Justice Holmes delivered the opinion of the Court.

This is a bill in equity brought by the State of Missouri to prevent a game warden of the United States from attempting to enforce the Migratory Bird Treaty Act of July 3,

1918, and the regulations made by the Secretary of Agriculture in pursuance of the same. The ground of the bill is that the statute is an unconstitutional interference with the rights reserved to the States by the 10th Amendment, and that the acts of the defendant done and threatened under that authority invade the sovereign right of the State and contravene its will manifested in statutes. The State also alleges a pecuniary interest, as owner of the wild birds within its borders and otherwise, admitted by the Government to be sufficient, but it is enough that the bill is a reasonable and proper means to assert the alleged quasi-sovereign rights of a State. A motion to dismiss was sustained by the District Court on the ground that the Act of Congress is constitutional. The State appeals.

On December 8, 1916, a treaty between the United States and Great Britain was proclaimed by the President. It recited that many species of birds in their annual migrations traversed many parts of the United States and of Canada, that they were of great value as a source of food and in destroying insects injurious to vegetation, but were in danger of extermination through lack of adequate protection. It therefore provided for specified closed seasons and protection in other forms, and agreed that the two powers would take or propose to their lawmaking bodies the necessary measures for carrying the treaty out. The above mentioned act of July 3, 1918, entitled an act to give effect to the convention, prohibited the killing, capturing or selling any of the migratory birds included in the terms of the treaty except as permitted by regulations compatible with those terms, to be made by the Secretary of Agriculture. Regulations were proclaimed on July 31, and October 25, 1918. It is unnecessary to go into any details, because, as we have said, the question raised is the general one whether the treaty and statute are void as an interference with the rights reserved to the States.

To answer this question it is not enough to refer to the 10th Amendment, reserving the powers not delegated to the United States, because by Article 2, §2, the power to make treaties is delegated expressly, and by Article 6 treaties made under the authority of the United States, along with the Constitution and laws of the United States made in pursuance thereof, are declared the supreme law of the land. If the treaty is valid there can be no dispute about the validity of the statute under Article 1, §8, as a necessary and proper means to execute the powers of the Government. The language of the Constitution as to the supremacy of treaties being general, the question before us is narrowed to an inquiry into the ground upon which the present supposed exception is placed.

It is said that a treaty cannot be valid if it infringes the Constitution, that there are limits, therefore, to the treaty-making power, and that one such limit is that what an act of Congress could not do unaided, in derogation of the powers reserved to the States, a treaty cannot do. An earlier act of Congress that attempted by itself and not in pursuance of a treaty to regulate the killing of migratory birds within the States had been held bad in the District Court. *United States v. Shauver* (E.D. Ark. 1914); *United States v. McCullagh* (D. Kan. 1915). Those decisions were supported by arguments that migratory birds were owned by the States in their sovereign capacity for the benefit of their people, and that under cases like *Geer v. Connecticut* (1896), this control was one that Congress had no power to displace. The same argument is supposed to apply now with equal force.

Whether the two cases cited were decided rightly or not they cannot be accepted as a test of the treaty power. Acts of Congress are the supreme law of the land only when made in pursuance of the Constitution, while treaties are declared to be so when made under the authority of the United States. It is open to question whether the authority of the United States means more than the formal acts prescribed to make the convention. We do not mean to imply that there are no qualifications to the treaty-making power; but they must be ascertained in a different way. It is obvious that there may be matters of the sharpest exigency for the national well being that an act of Congress could not deal with but that a treaty followed by such an act could, and it is not lightly to be assumed that, in matters requiring national action, "a power which must belong to and somewhere reside in every civilized government" is not to be found. What was said in that case with regard to the powers of the States applies with equal force to the powers of the nation in cases where the States individually are incompetent to act. We are not yet discussing the particular case before us but only are considering the validity of the test proposed. With regard to that we may add that when we are dealing with words that also are a constituent act, like the Constitution of the United States, we must realize that they have called into life a being the development of which could not have been foreseen completely by the most gifted of its begetters. It was enough for them to realize or to hope that they had created an organism; it has taken a century and has cost their successors much sweat and blood to prove that they created a nation. The case before us must be considered in the light of our whole experience and not merely in that of what was said a hundred years ago. The treaty in question does not contravene any prohibitory words to be found in the Constitution. The only question is whether it is forbidden by some invisible radiation from the general terms of the 10th Amendment. We must consider what this country has become in deciding what that amendment has reserved.

The State as we have intimated founds its claim of exclusive authority upon an assertion of title to migratory birds, an assertion that is embodied in statute. No doubt it is true that as between a State and its inhabitants the State may regulate the killing and sale of such birds, but it does not follow that its authority is exclusive of paramount powers. To put the claim of the State upon title is to lean upon a slender reed. Wild birds are not in the possession of anyone; and possession is the beginning of ownership. The whole foundation of the States' rights is the presence within their jurisdiction of birds that yesterday had not arrived, tomorrow may be in another State and in a week a thousand miles away. If we are to be accurate we cannot put the case of the State upon higher ground than that the treaty deals with creatures that for the moment are within the state borders, that it must be carried out by officers of the United States within the same territory, and that but for the treaty the State would be free to regulate this subject itself.

As most of the laws of the United States are carried out within the States and as many of them deal with matters which in the silence of such laws the State might regulate, such general grounds are not enough to support Missouri's claim. Valid treaties of course "are as binding within the territorial limits of the States as they are elsewhere throughout the dominion of the United States." No doubt the great body of private relations usually fall within the control of the State, but a treaty may override its power. We do not have to invoke the later developments of constitutional law for this proposition; it was recognized as early as *Hopkirk v. Bell* (1806), with regard to statutes of limitation, and even earlier, as to confiscation, in *Ware v. Hylton* (1796). It was assumed by Chief Justice Marshall with regard to the escheat of land to the State in *Chirac v. Chirac* (1817). So as to a limited jurisdiction of foreign consuls within a State. *Wildenhus' Case* (1887). Further illustration seems unnecessary, and it only remains to consider the application of established rules to the present case.

Here a national interest of very nearly the first magnitude is involved. It can be protected only by national action in concert with that of another power. The subject matter is only transitorily within the State and has no permanent habitat therein. But for the treaty and the statute there soon might be no birds for any powers to deal with. We see nothing in the Constitution that compels the Government to sit by while a food supply is cut off and the protectors of our forests and our crops are destroyed. It is not sufficient to rely upon the States. The reliance is vain, and were it otherwise, the question is whether the United States is forbidden to act. We are of opinion that the treaty and statute must be upheld.

Decree affirmed.

Mr. Justice Van Devanter and Mr. Justice Pitney dissent.

Reid v. Covert: Questions

1. What is the source of power relied on by the government to justify trying dependents of servicemen in military courts? What are the government's arguments and why do the government's arguments fail?
2. What use does Justice Black make of the debates from the drafting and ratification of the Constitution? What argument is he answering here and what type of argument is he making? What is the rationale for the Court's decision? What type of arguments are used to support it?

Reid v. Covert
354 U.S. 1 (1957)

[Plurality: Black, Warren (C.J.), Douglas, Brennan. Concurring: Frankfurter and Harlan. Dissenting: Clark and Burton.]

Mr. Justice Black announced the judgment of the Court and delivered an opinion, in which The Chief Justice, Mr. Justice Douglas, and Mr. Justice Brennan join.

These cases raise basic constitutional issues of the utmost concern. They call into question the role of the military under our system of government. They involve the power of Congress to expose civilians to trial by military tribunals, under military regulations and procedures, for offenses against the United States, thereby depriving them of trial in civilian courts, under civilian laws and procedures and with all the safeguards of the Bill of Rights. These cases are particularly significant because for the first time since the adoption of the Constitution wives of soldiers have been denied trial by jury in a court of law and forced to trial before courts-martial.

In No. 701 Mrs. Clarice Covert killed her husband, a sergeant in the United States Air Force, at an airbase in England. Mrs. Covert, who was not a member of the armed services, was residing on the base with her husband at the time. She was tried by a court-martial for murder under Article 118 of the Uniform Code of Military Justice (UCMJ). The trial was on charges preferred by Air Force personnel and the court-martial was composed of Air Force officers. The court-martial asserted jurisdiction over Mrs. Covert under Article 2(11) of the UCMJ, which provides:

The following persons are subject to this code:

(11) Subject to the provisions of any treaty or agreement to which the United States is or may be a party or to any accepted rule of international law, all persons serving with, employed by, or accompanying the armed forces without the continental limits of the United States....

Counsel for Mrs. Covert contended that she was insane at the time she killed her husband, but the military tribunal found her guilty of murder and sentenced her to life imprisonment. The judgment was affirmed by the Air Force Board of Review, but was reversed by the Court of Military Appeals, because of prejudicial errors concerning the defense of insanity. While Mrs. Covert was being held in this country pending a proposed retrial by court-martial in the District of Columbia, her counsel petitioned the District Court for a writ of habeas corpus to set her free on the ground that the Constitution forbade her trial by military authorities. [Stating] that "a civilian is entitled to a civilian trial," the District Court held that Mrs. Covert could not be tried by court martial and ordered her released from custody. The Government appealed directly to this Court.

In No. 713 Mrs. Dorothy Smith killed her husband, an Army officer, at a post in Japan where she was living with him. She was tried for murder by a court-martial and despite considerable evidence that she was insane was found guilty and sentenced to life imprisonment....

We hold that Mrs. Smith and Mrs. Covert could not constitutionally be tried by military authorities.

I. At the beginning we reject the idea that when the United States acts against citizens abroad it can do so free of the Bill of Rights. The United States is entirely a creature of the Constitution. Its power and authority have no other source. It can only act in accordance with all the limitations imposed by the Constitution. When the Government reaches out to punish a citizen who is abroad, the shield which the Bill of Rights and other parts of the Constitution provide to protect his life and liberty should not be stripped away just because he happens to be in another land. This is not a novel concept. To the contrary, it is as old as government. It was recognized long before Paul successfully invoked his right as a Roman citizen to be tried in strict accordance with Roman law. And many centuries later an English historian wrote:

> In a Settled Colony the inhabitants have all the rights of Englishmen. They take with them, in the first place, that which no Englishman can by expatriation put off, namely, allegiance to the Crown, the duty of obedience to the lawful commands of the Sovereign, and obedience to the Laws which Parliament may think proper to make with reference to such a Colony. But, on the other hand, they take with them all the rights and liberties of British Subjects; all the rights and liberties as against the Prerogative of the Crown, which they would enjoy in this country.

The rights and liberties which citizens of our country enjoy are not protected by custom and tradition alone, they have been jealously preserved from the encroachments of Government by express provisions of our written Constitution.

Among those provisions, Art. III, §2 and the 5th and 6th Amendments are directly relevant to these cases. Article III, §2 lays down the rule that:

> The Trial of all Crimes, except in Cases of Impeachment, shall be by Jury; and such Trial shall be held in the State where the said Crimes shall have been committed; but when not committed within any State, the Trial shall be at such Place or Places as the Congress may by Law have directed.

The 5th Amendment declares:

> No person shall be held to answer for a capital, or otherwise infamous crime, unless on a presentment or indictment of a Grand Jury, except in cases arising in the land or naval forces, or in the Militia, when in actual service in time of War or public danger....

And the 6th Amendment provides:

In all criminal prosecutions, the accused shall enjoy the right to a speedy and public trial, by an impartial jury of the State and district wherein the crime shall have been committed....

The language of Art. III, §2 manifests that constitutional protections for the individual were designed to restrict the United States Government when it acts outside of this country, as well as here at home. After declaring that all criminal trials must be by jury, the section states that when a crime is "not committed within any State, the Trial shall be at such Place or Places as the Congress may by Law have directed." If this language is permitted to have its obvious meaning, §2 is applicable to criminal trials outside of the States as a group without regard to where the offense is committed or the trial held. From the very first Congress, federal statutes have implemented the provisions of §2 by providing for trial of murder and other crimes committed outside the jurisdiction of any State "in the district where the offender is apprehended, or into which he may first be brought." The 5th and 6th Amendments, like Art. III, §2, are also all inclusive with their sweeping references to "no person" and to "all criminal prosecutions."

This Court and other federal courts have held or asserted that various constitutional limitations apply to the Government when it acts outside the continental United States. While it has been suggested that only those constitutional rights which are "fundamental" protect Americans abroad, we can find no warrant, in logic or otherwise, for picking and choosing among the remarkable collection of "Thou shalt nots" which were explicitly fastened on all departments and agencies of the Federal Government by the Constitution and its Amendments. Moreover, in view of our heritage and the history of the adoption of the Constitution and the Bill of Rights, it seems peculiarly anomalous to say that trial before a civilian judge and by an independent jury picked from the common citizenry is not a fundamental right.[1] As Blackstone wrote in his Commentaries:

> [T]he trial by jury ever has been, and I trust ever will be, looked upon as the glory of the English Law. And if it has so great an advantage over others in regulating civil property, how much must that advantage be heightened when it is applied to criminal cases. [I]t is the most transcendent privilege which any subject can enjoy, or wish for, that he cannot be affected either in his property, his liberty, or his person, but by the unanimous consent of twelve of his neighbors and equals. 3 *Blackstone's Commentaries* 379.

De Tocqueville observed:

> The institution of the jury ... places the real direction of society in the hands of the governed, or of a portion of the governed, and not in that of the government.... He who punishes the criminal is ... the real master of society.... All the sovereigns who have chosen to govern by their own authority, and to direct society instead of obeying its directions, have destroyed or enfeebled the institution of the jury. Alexis de Tocqueville, *Democracy in America* (Reeve trans. 1948 ed.), 282–83.

Trial by jury in a court of law and in accordance with traditional modes of procedure after an indictment by grand jury has served and remains one of our most vital barriers

---

1. The right to trial by jury in a criminal case is twice guaranteed by the Constitution. It is common knowledge that the fear that jury trial might be abolished was one of the principal sources of objection to the Federal Constitution and was an important reason for the adoption of the Bill of Rights. The 6th Amendment reaffirmed the right to trial by jury in criminal cases and the 7th Amendment insured such trial in civil controversies.

to governmental arbitrariness. These elemental procedural safeguards were embedded in our Constitution to secure their inviolateness and sanctity against the passing demands of expediency or convenience.

The keystone of supporting authorities mustered by the Court's opinion last June [in *Kinsella v. Krueger* (1956)] to justify its holding that Art. III, §2, and the 5th and 6th Amendments did not apply abroad was *In re Ross* (1891). The *Ross* case is one of those cases that cannot be understood except in its peculiar setting; even then, it seems highly unlikely that a similar result would be reached today. Ross was serving as a seaman on an American ship in Japanese waters. He killed a ship's officer, was seized and tried before a consular "court" in Japan. At that time, statutes authorized American consuls to try American citizens charged with committing crimes in Japan and certain other "non-Christian" countries. ...

The consular power approved in the *Ross* case was about as extreme and absolute as that of the potentates of the "non-Christian" countries to which the statutes applied. Under these statutes consuls could and did make the criminal laws, initiate charges, arrest alleged offenders, try them, and after conviction take away their liberty or their life—sometimes at the American consulate. Such a blending of executive, legislative, and judicial powers in one person or even in one branch of the Government is ordinarily regarded as the very acme of absolutism. Nevertheless, the Court sustained Ross' conviction by the consul. It stated that constitutional protections applied "only to citizens and others within the United States, or who are brought there for trial for alleged offenses committed elsewhere, and not to residents or temporary sojourners abroad." Despite the fact that it upheld Ross' conviction under United States laws passed pursuant to asserted constitutional authority, the Court went on to make a sweeping declaration that "(t)he Constitution can have no operation in another country."

The *Ross* approach that the Constitution has no applicability abroad has long since been directly repudiated by numerous cases. That approach is obviously erroneous if the United States Government, which has no power except that granted by the Constitution, can and does try citizens for crimes committed abroad. Thus the *Ross* case rested, at least in substantial part, on a fundamental misconception and the most that can be said in support of the result reached there is that the consular court jurisdiction had a long history antedating the adoption of the Constitution. The Congress has recently buried the consular system of trying Americans. We are not willing to jeopardize the lives and liberties of Americans by disinterring it. At best, the *Ross* case should be left as a relic from a different era.

The Court's opinion last Term also relied on the *"Insular Cases"* to support its conclusion that Article III and the 5th and 6th Amendments were not applicable to the trial of Mrs. Smith and Mrs. Covert. We believe that reliance was misplaced. The *"Insular Cases,"* which arose at the turn of the century, involved territories which had only recently been conquered or acquired by the United States. These territories, governed and regulated by Congress under Art. IV, §3, had entirely different cultures and customs from those of this country. This Court, although closely divided, ruled that certain constitutional safeguards were not applicable to these territories since they had not been "expressly or impliedly incorporated" into the Union by Congress. While conceding that "fundamental" constitutional rights applied everywhere, the majority found that it would disrupt long-established practices and would be inexpedient to require a jury trial after an indictment by a grand jury in the insular possessions.

The *"Insular Cases"* can be distinguished from the present cases in that they involved the power of Congress to provide rules and regulations to govern temporarily territories with wholly dissimilar traditions and institutions, whereas here the basis for governmental power is American citizenship. None of these cases had anything to do with military trials and they cannot properly be used as vehicles to support an extension of military jurisdiction to civilians. Moreover, it is our judgment that neither the cases nor their reasoning should be given any further expansion. The concept that the Bill of Rights and other constitutional protections against arbitrary government are inoperative when they become inconvenient or when expediency dictates otherwise is a very dangerous doctrine and if allowed to flourish would destroy the benefit of a written Constitution and undermine the basis of our government. If our foreign commitments become of such nature that the Government can no longer satisfactorily operate within the bounds laid down by the Constitution, that instrument can be amended by the method which it prescribes. But we have no authority, or inclination, to read exceptions into it which are not there.

II. At the time of Mrs. Covert's alleged offense, an executive agreement was in effect between the United States and Great Britain which permitted United States' military courts to exercise exclusive jurisdiction over offenses committed in Great Britain by American servicemen or their dependents. For its part, the United States agreed that these military courts would be willing and able to try and to punish all offenses against the laws of Great Britain by such persons. In all material respects, the same situation existed in Japan when Mrs. Smith killed her husband. Even though a court-martial does not give an accused trial by jury and other Bill of Rights protections, the Government contends that article 2(11) of UCMJ, insofar as it provides for the military trial of dependents accompanying the armed forces in Great Britain and Japan, can be sustained as legislation which is necessary and proper to carry out the United States' obligations under the international agreements made with those countries. The obvious and decisive answer to this, of course, is that no agreement with a foreign nation can confer power on the Congress, or on any other branch of Government, which is free from the restraints of the Constitution.

Article VI, the Supremacy Clause of the Constitution, declares:

> This Constitution, and the Laws of the United States which shall be made in Pursuance thereof; and all Treaties made, or which shall be made, under the Authority of the United States, shall be the supreme Law of the Land....

There is nothing in this language which intimates that treaties and laws enacted pursuant to them do not have to comply with the provisions of the Constitution. Nor is there anything in the debates which accompanied the drafting and ratification of the Constitution which even suggests such a result. These debates as well as the history that surrounds the adoption of the treaty provision in Article VI make it clear that the reason treaties were not limited to those made in "pursuance" of the Constitution was so that agreements made by the United States under the Articles of Confederation, including the important peace treaties which concluded the Revolutionary War, would remain in effect. It would be manifestly contrary to the objectives of those who created the Constitution, as well as those who were responsible for the Bill of Rights—let alone alien to our entire constitutional history and tradition—to construe Article VI as permitting the United States to exercise power under an international agreement without observing constitutional prohibitions. In effect, such construction would permit amendment of that document in a manner not sanctioned by Article V. The prohibitions of the Constitution were designed to apply to all branches of the National Government and they cannot be nullified by the Executive or by the Executive and the Senate combined.

There is nothing new or unique about what we say here. This Court has regularly and uniformly recognized the supremacy of the Constitution over a treaty. For example, in *Geofroy v. Riggs* (1890), it declared:

> The treaty power, as expressed in the constitution, is in terms unlimited except by those restraints which are found in that instrument against the action of the government or of its departments, and those arising from the nature of the government itself and of that of the States. It would not be contended that it extends so far as to authorize what the constitution forbids, or a change in the character of the government or in that of one of the States, or a session of any portion of the territory of the latter, without its consent.

This Court has also repeatedly taken the position that an Act of Congress, which must comply with the Constitution, is on a full parity with a treaty, and that when a statute which is subsequent in time is inconsistent with a treaty, the statute to the extent of conflict renders the treaty null. It would be completely anomalous to say that a treaty need not comply with the Constitution when such an agreement can be overridden by a statute that must conform to that instrument.

There is nothing in *State of Missouri v. Holland* (1920) [to the contrary]. There the Court carefully noted that the treaty involved was not inconsistent with any specific provision of the Constitution. The Court was concerned with the 10th Amendment which reserves to the States or the people all power not delegated to the National Government. To the extent that the United States can validly make treaties, the people and the States have delegated their power to the National Government and the 10th Amendment is no barrier.

In summary, we conclude that the Constitution in its entirety applied to the trials of Mrs. Smith and Mrs. Covert. Since their court-martial did not meet the requirements of Art. III, § 2, or the 5th and 6th Amendments we are compelled to determine if there is anything within the Constitution which authorizes the military trial of dependents accompanying the armed forces overseas.

III. Article I, § 8, cl. 14, empowers Congress "To make Rules for the Government and Regulation of the land and naval Forces." It has been held that this creates an exception to the normal method of trial in civilian courts as provided by the Constitution and permits Congress to authorize military trial of members of the armed services without all the safeguards given an accused by Article III and the Bill of Rights. But if the language of Clause 14 is given its natural meaning, the power granted does not extend to civilians—even though they may be dependents living with servicemen on a military base. The term "land and naval Forces" refers to persons who are members of the armed services and not to their civilian wives, children and other dependents. It seems inconceivable that Mrs. Covert or Mrs. Smith could have been tried by military authorities as members of the "land and naval Forces" had they been living on a military post in this country. Yet this constitutional term surely has the same meaning everywhere. The wives of servicemen are no more members of the "land and naval Forces" when living at a military post in England or Japan than when living at a base in this country or in Hawaii or Alaska.

The Government argues that the Necessary and Proper Clause ... when taken in conjunction with Art. I, § 8, cl. 14 [regarding control of the "land and naval Forces"] allows Congress to authorize the trial of Mrs. Smith and Mrs. Covert by military tribunals and under military law. The Government claims that the two clauses together constitute a broad grant of power "without limitation" authorizing Congress to subject all persons, civilians and soldiers alike, to military trial if "necessary and proper" to govern and regulate the land and naval forces. It was on a similar theory that Congress once went to the extreme of subjecting persons who made contracts with the military to court-martial jurisdiction with respect to frauds related to such contracts. In the only judicial test a Circuit Court held that the legislation was patently unconstitutional. *Ex parte Henderson* (1878).

It is true that the Constitution expressly grants Congress power to make all rules necessary and proper to govern and regulate those persons who are serving in the "land and naval Forces." But the Necessary and Proper Clause cannot operate to extend military jurisdiction to any group of persons beyond that class described in Clause 14—"the land and naval Forces." Under the grand design of the Constitution civilian courts are the normal repositories of power to try persons charged with crimes against the United States....

Further light is reflected on the scope of Art. I, §8, cl. 14 by the 5th Amendment. That Amendment which was adopted shortly after the Constitution reads:

> No person shall be held to answer for a capital, or otherwise infamous crime, unless on a presentment or indictment of a Grand Jury, *except in cases arising in the land or naval forces,* or in the Militia, when in actual service in time of War or public danger....

Since the exception in this Amendment for "cases arising in the land or naval forces" was undoubtedly designed to correlate with the power granted Congress to provide for the "Government and Regulation" of the armed services, it is a persuasive and reliable indication that the authority conferred by Clause 14 does not encompass persons who cannot fairly be said to be "in" the military service....

The tradition of keeping the military subordinate to civilian authority may not be so strong in the minds of this generation as it was in the minds of those who wrote the Constitution. The idea that the relatives of soldiers could be denied a jury trial in a court of law and instead be tried by court-martial under the guise of regulating the armed forces would have seemed incredible to those men, in whose lifetime the right of the military to try soldiers for any offenses in time of peace had only been grudgingly conceded. The Founders envisioned the army as a necessary institution, but one dangerous to liberty if not confined within its essential bounds. Their fears were rooted in history. They knew that ancient republics had been overthrown by their military leaders. They were familiar with the history of 17th century England, where Charles I tried to govern through the army and without Parliament. During this attempt, contrary to the Common Law, he used courts-martial to try soldiers for certain non-military offenses. This court-martialing of soldiers in peacetime evoked strong protests from Parliament. The reign of Charles I was followed by the rigorous military rule of Oliver Cromwell. Later, James II used the Army in his fight against Parliament and the People. He promulgated Articles of War (strangely enough relied on in the Government's brief) authorizing the trial of soldiers for non-military crimes by courts-martial. This action hastened the revolution that brought William and Mary to the throne upon their agreement to abide by a Bill of Rights which, among other things, protected the right of trial by jury. It was against this general background that two of the greatest English jurists, Lord Chief Justice Hale and Sir William Blackstone—men who exerted considerable influence on the Founders—expressed sharp hostility to any expansion of the jurisdiction of military courts....

Mr. Justice Frankfurter, concurring in the result.

These cases involve the constitutional power of Congress to provide for trial of civilian dependents accompanying members of the armed forces abroad by court-martial in capital cases. The normal method of trial of federal offenses under the Constitution is in a civilian tribunal. Trial of offenses by way of court-martial, with all the characteristics of its procedure so different from the forms and safeguards of procedure in the conventional courts, is an exercise of exceptional jurisdiction, arising from the power granted to Congress in Art. I, §8, cl. 14, of the Constitution of the United States "To make Rules for the Government and Regulation of the land and naval Forces." Article 2(11) of the Uniform Code of Military Justice and its predecessors were passed as an exercise of that power, and the agreements with England and Japan recognized that the jurisdiction to be exercised under those agreements was based on the relation of the persons involved to the military forces.

Trial by court-martial is constitutionally permissible only for persons who can, on a fair appraisal, be regarded as falling within the authority given to Congress under Article I to regulate the "land and naval Forces," and who therefore are not protected by specific provisions of Article III and the 5th and 6th Amendments....

Mr. Justice Harlan, concurring in the result. [Omitted.]

Mr. Justice Clark, with whom Mr. Justice Burton joins, dissenting.

The Court today releases two women from prosecution though the evidence shows that they brutally killed their husbands, both American soldiers, while stationed with them in quarters furnished by our armed forces on its military installations in foreign lands. In turning these women free, it declares unconstitutional an important section of an Act of Congress governing our armed forces. Furthermore, four of my brothers would specifically overrule and two would impair the long-recognized vitality of an old and respected precedent in our law, the case of *In re Ross* (1891), cited by this Court with approval in many opinions and as late as 1929 by a unanimous Court....

Chapter 3

Limits on Federal Power: The Federal Structure, the 10th Amendment, and State Sovereign Immunity

Contents

I.	National Power and State Power: The 10th Amendment	249
	State Intergovernmental Immunity and the 10th Amendment	252
	National League of Cities v. Usery	253
	Garcia v. San Antonio Metropolitan Transit Authority	263
	Printz v. United States	273
II.	National Power and State Power: State Sovereign Immunity	284
	Alden v. Maine	286
III.	The Rehnquist Court	304

Chapter 3

Limits on Federal Power: The Federal Structure, the 10th Amendment, and State Sovereign Immunity

Goals for your study of this material

1. To understand the various historical, textual, and structural arguments made in defense of the competing interpretations of the 10th Amendment.

2. To understand the test suggested by Chief Justice Marshall in *McCulloch v. Maryland* (1819) for determining whether an act of Congress exceeds the power of Congress under the Constitution. To understand how Justice Marshall deals with the 10th Amendment as a limit on congressional power.

3. To understand the meaning of the 10th Amendment as interpreted by various members of the Court since *National League of Cities v. Usery* (1976) and to understand how these positions might modify the post-New Deal 10th Amendment jurisprudence of the Court. To understand the extent to which the rule of *National League of Cities* affects the post-New Deal Commerce Clause jurisprudence of the Court.

4. To understand the rule of *Garcia v. San Antonio Metropolitan Transit Authority* (1985). To understand how the majority in *Garcia* expects the role of the states to be protected from the exercise of federal power. To understand how *Garcia*'s interpretation of the 10th Amendment differs from that in *National League of Cities*.

5. To understand the rule of *Printz v. United States* (1997). To understand how that case deals with the 10th Amendment as a limit on federal power.

I. National Power and State Power: The 10th Amendment

The 10th Amendment provides:

The powers not delegated to the United States by the Constitution, nor prohibited by it to the States, are reserved to the States respectively, or to the people.

The text of the 10th Amendment seems to make the question of whether a power is reserved to the states turn on an examination of the delegated powers. If the power is not delegated, it is reserved; but if it is delegated, it is not reserved. (Other modes of interpretation, that consider more than the text, might produce a different result, of course.)

Contrast the language of the 1st and 4th Amendments. The 1st Amendment provides:

> Congress shall make no law respecting an establishment of religion or prohibiting the free exercise thereof; or abridging the freedom of speech, or of the press....

The 4th Amendment provides:

> The right of the people to be secure in their person, houses, papers, and effects, against unreasonable searches and seizures, shall not be violated....

The 4th Amendment goes on to require that warrants specifically describe the person or place to be searched and the things to be seized. (A warrant that lacks this required specificity is called a general warrant and is invalid.) The 1st and 4th Amendments limit the *reach* of delegated powers. The question turns not on whether the action of Congress (banning the interstate shipment of certain types of books, for example) is generally the sort of thing Congress can do under the commerce power. Instead the question becomes whether an action that would otherwise be *within* the commerce power is nevertheless barred because of the specific prohibition contained in the 1st Amendment.

In proposing the Bill of Rights, James Madison noted that the function of the bills of rights as they existed in the states was "to limit and qualify the power of Government, by excepting out of the grant of power those cases in which the Government ought not to act, or to act only in a particular mode." 2 Bernard Schwartz, *The Bill of Rights, A Documentary History* at 1029. Madison also responded to the argument that many Federalists had made to prove a bill of rights was unnecessary under the Constitution. The Federalist argument had been that because the federal government was one of delegated powers, and because it had no delegated power to invade basic rights, the rights were secure without a bill of rights. Madison's response in the first Congress highlights the difference between the scope of a delegated power with and without an independent limit set out in a bill of rights. "The General Government," Madison noted, "has a right to pass all laws which shall be necessary to collect its revenue; the means for enforcing the collection are within the direction of the Legislature: May not general warrants be considered necessary for this purpose, [as well as for other purposes of the Constitution]?" *Id.* at 1030–31. The 4th Amendment would limit what otherwise could be within the reach of a delegated power.

Madison's description of the function of his proposed 10th Amendment was different. It was, he implied, simply a reminder that the federal government was one of delegated powers. "I find," Madison told the first Congress, "from looking into the amendments proposed by the State conventions, that several are particularly anxious that it should be declared in the constitution, that the powers not therein delegated should be reserved to the several States. Perhaps words which may define this more precisely than the whole of instrument now does, may be considered as superfluous. I admit they may deemed unnecessary: but there can be no harm in making such a declaration...." *Id.* at 1033.

Recall that in *McCulloch v. Maryland* (1819) Chief Justice Marshall noted that the 10th Amendment

> omits the word "expressly," and declares only that the powers not delegated to the United States, nor prohibited to the states, are reserved to the states or to the people, thus leaving the question, whether the particular power which may become the subject of contest has been delegated to the one government, or prohibited to the other, to depend on a fair construction of the whole instrument.

Marshall concluded with the following test for federal power:

> Let the end be legitimate, let it be within the scope of the constitution, and all means which are appropriate, which are plainly adapted to that end, which are not prohibited, but consist with the letter and spirit of the constitution, are constitutional.

The steamboat monopoly case of *Gibbons v. Ogden* (1824) also raised the issue of the line between state and national power. There Marshall suggested, but did not hold, that federal power to regulate commerce was exclusive. State police power to regulate certain commercial matters, he suggested, existed before items became the subject of commerce among the states. But Marshall seems to suggest that federal power often could also reach such subjects—and therefore potentially override state regulation. Immediately after noting that legal provisions such as inspection laws act on items before they become commerce among the states, Marshall says:

> No direct general power over these objects is granted to Congress, and consequently, they remain subject to State legislation. If the legislative power of the Union can reach them, it must be for national purposes; it must be where the power is expressly given for a special purpose, or is clearly incidental to some power which is expressly given.

In regulating commerce among the states, Marshall found it obvious that the national government could use means that could also be employed by a state. For example, Congress could license vessels to sail from one point to another within the same state as a power incidental to its power to regulate commerce among the states.

In later decisions, Marshall's seeming reservation of a concurrent state power over certain subjects (but one that Congress could override in the exercise of a delegated power) evolved into an area of independent state power that superseded the scope of congressional action. See, for example, *Hammer v. Dagenhart* (1918) (the child labor case). In *Hammer*, the Court said that the federal attempt to restrict child labor "not only transcends the authority delegated to Congress over commerce but also exerts a power as to a purely local matter to which the federal authority *does not extend*." (Emphasis added.)

From the time Democratic President Franklin Roosevelt had appointed several of the Justices (and eventually he appointed all of them) until around 1976, by which time Republican President Richard Nixon had appointed four of the Justices, it seemed that the delegated power of Congress over commerce (then broadly interpreted by the Court) was restricted only by independent limitations such as those in the 1st Amendment and by those imposed by the political process. The 10th Amendment was a truism, not an independent limit. The cases that follow show at least a limited resurgence of an earlier view. By that view, there are some independent affirmative limits—based either on the 10th Amendment or on the structure of the Constitution—on use of a delegated congressional power to invade what five of the Justices see as a sphere reserved to the states.

The effect of these affirmative limitations is to restrict the power of the elected Congress. In 2006 most of the Justices now on the Court were appointed by Presidents Reagan, Bush (I), and Bush (II). Each of these Presidents said they advocated "strict construction."

Nixon explained strict construction in terms of judicial restraint and deference to the Congress and the states when their actions were claimed to violate the Constitution. Later Presidents treated the term as signaling adherence to the "original intentions" of the framers of the Constitution or some other form of adherence to "original meaning." Of course, some of the Warren Court justices Nixon was criticizing thought they were the "true" strict interpreters of the Constitution.

Whether appointed by a self-avowed "strict constructionist" or not, all justices believe that the Constitution imposes some limits on the democratic process. They tend to disagree about what the limits should be. Decisions that critics have attacked as unsupported by original meaning include the decision upholding the right of married couples to use birth control devices, the abortion decision, school prayer decisions, decisions requiring states to obey more of the guarantees of the federal Bill of Rights, and the Warren Court's interpretation of some of the Bill of Rights protections for those accused of crime.

The justices appointed by Presidents who proclaim themselves strict constructionists have narrowed federal power under the Commerce Clause and expanded protection against (for example) uncompensated environmental regulation under the Takings Clause. Critics of these decisions insist they are not justified by the Constitution's text, history, or structure. As a result, both strict constructionists and their critics accuse each other of limiting the democratic process in ways that are not legitimate. You will read some of these controversial individual rights decisions in the individual rights portion of Constitutional Law and in Criminal Procedure. The decisions that follow illustrate some limits the current Court is imposing on congressional power and on its ability to apply federal protections against age discrimination, handicapped discrimination, and violations of wage and hour rules for state workers.

As you read these decisions, note the use of arguments based on text, constitutional structure, history, and precedent. In each case, who do you think gets the better of the argument? Does your view of this question coincide with which side you think should win?

State Intergovernmental Immunity and the 10th Amendment

National League of Cities: Background

1. Re-read the 10th Amendment and the first eight amendments. Is the 10th phrased like the other limits on power set out in the first eight amendments or is it significantly different?

2. How does the Court in *National League of Cities* read the 10th Amendment? Is it explicitly mentioned? Does this reading differ from the way the Court had interpreted it in post-New Deal cases? Did the Court suggest that the 10th Amendment provided a significant new limit on the general power of Congress over commerce or was the rule of the case limited to congressional regulation of the states as such? How does *National League of Cities* distinguish post-New Deal Commerce Clause cases?

3. What is the rule of *National League of Cities*? What is the rationale for the decision?
   a. What does the Court say about the constitutional status of the states in the federal system?
   b. What are the sovereign functions of the states?

c. Does the Fair Labor Standards Act interfere with a state's discharge of its sovereign functions? Why?

d. If so, should this preclude federal regulation?

4. Is the rule of the case workable?

5. What are Justice Brennan's main criticisms of the decision?

National League of Cities v. Usery
426 U.S. 833 (1976)

[Majority: Rehnquist, Blackmun, Burger (C.J.), Powell, and Stewart. Concurring: Blackmun. Dissenting: Brennan, Stevens, White, and Marshall]

Mr. Justice Rehnquist delivered the opinion of the Court.

Nearly 40 years ago Congress enacted the Fair Labor Standards Act, and required employers covered by the Act to pay their employees a minimum hourly wage and to pay them at one and one-half times their regular rate of pay for hours worked in excess of 40 during a work week. By this Act covered employers were required to keep certain records to aid in the enforcement of the Act, and to comply with specified child labor standards. This Court unanimously upheld the Act as a valid exercise of congressional authority under the commerce power in *United States v. Darby* (1941), observing:

> Whatever their motive and purpose, regulations of commerce which do not infringe some constitutional prohibition are within the plenary power conferred on Congress by the Commerce Clause.

The original Fair Labor Standards Act passed in 1938 specifically excluded the States and their political subdivisions from its coverage. In 1974, however, Congress enacted the most recent of a series of broadening amendments to the Act. By these amendments Congress has extended the minimum wage and maximum hour provisions to almost all public employees employed by the States and by their various political subdivisions. Appellants in these cases include individual cities and States, the National League of Cities, and the National Governors' Conference; they brought an action in the District Court for the District of Columbia which challenged the validity of the 1974 amendments. They asserted in effect that when Congress sought to apply the Fair Labor Standards Act provisions virtually across the board to employees of state and municipal governments it "infringed a constitutional prohibition" running in favor of the States as States. The gist of their complaint was not that the conditions of employment of such public employees were beyond the scope of the commerce power had those employees been employed in the private sector but that the established constitutional doctrine of intergovernmental immunity consistently recognized in a long series of our cases affirmatively prevented the exercise of this authority in the manner which Congress chose in the 1974 amendments.

I. In a series of amendments beginning in 1961 Congress began to extend the provisions of the Fair Labor Standards Act to some types of public employees. The 1961 amendments to the Act extended its coverage to persons who were employed in "enterprises" engaged in commerce or in the production of goods for commerce. And in 1966, with the amendment of the definition of employers under the Act, the exemption heretofore extended to the States and their political subdivisions was removed with respect to employees of state hospitals, institutions, and schools. We nevertheless sustained the validity of the combined effect of these two amendments in *Maryland v. Wirtz* (1968).... [W]e have decided that the "far-reaching implications" of *Wirtz* should be overruled, and that the judgment of the District Court must be reversed.

II. It is established beyond peradventure that the Commerce Clause of Art. I of the Constitution is a grant of plenary authority to Congress. That authority is, in the words of Mr. Chief Justice Marshall in *Gibbons v. Ogden* (1824), "the power to regulate; that is, to prescribe the rule by which commerce is to be governed."

When considering the validity of asserted applications of this power to wholly private activity, the Court has made it clear that "(e)ven activity that is purely intrastate in character may be regulated by Congress, where the activity, combined with like conduct by others similarly situated, affects commerce among the States or with foreign nations." *Fry v. United States* (1975). Congressional power over areas of private endeavor, even when its exercise may pre-empt express state-law determinations contrary to the result which has commended itself to the collective wisdom of Congress, has been held to be limited only by the requirement that "the means chosen by (Congress) must be reasonably adapted to the end permitted by the Constitution." *Heart of Atlanta Motel v. United States* (1964).

Appellants in no way challenge these decisions establishing the breadth of authority granted Congress under the commerce power. Their contention, on the contrary, is that when Congress seeks to regulate directly the activities of States as public employers, it transgresses an affirmative limitation on the exercise of its power akin to other commerce power affirmative limitations contained in the Constitution. Congressional enactments which may be fully within the grant of legislative authority contained in the Commerce Clause may nonetheless be invalid because found to offend against the right to trial by jury contained in the 6th Amendment, *United States v. Jackson* (1968), or the Due Process Clause of the 5th Amendment, *Leary v. United States* (1969). Appellants' essential contention is that the 1974 amendments to the Act, while undoubtedly within the scope of the Commerce Clause, encounter a similar constitutional barrier because they are to be applied directly to the States and subdivisions of States as employers.

This Court has never doubted that there are limits upon the power of Congress to override state sovereignty, even when exercising its otherwise plenary powers to tax or to regulate commerce which are conferred by Art. I of the Constitution. In *Wirtz*, for example, the Court took care to assure the appellants that it had "ample power to prevent ... 'the utter destruction of the State as a sovereign political entity,'" which they feared. Appellee Secretary in this case, both in his brief and upon oral argument, has agreed that our federal system of government imposes definite limits upon the authority of Congress to regulate the activities of the States as States by means of the commerce power. In *Fry*, the Court recognized that an express declaration of this limitation is found in the 10th Amendment:

> While the 10th Amendment has been characterized as a 'truism,' stating merely that 'all is retained which has not been surrendered,' *United States v. Darby*, it is not without significance. The Amendment expressly declares the constitutional policy that Congress may not exercise power in a fashion that impairs the States' integrity or their ability to function effectively in a federal system....

The expressions in these more recent cases trace back to earlier decisions of this Court recognizing the essential role of the States in our federal system of government. Mr. Chief Justice Chase, perhaps because of the particular time at which he occupied that office, had occasion more than once to speak for the Court on this point. In *Texas v. White* (1869), he declared that "(t)he Constitution, in all its provisions, looks to an indestructible Union, composed of indestructible States." In *Lane County v. Oregon* (1869), his opinion for the Court said: "Both the States and the United States existed before the Constitution. The people, through that instrument, established a more perfect union by substituting a national government, acting, with ample power, directly upon the citizens, instead of the Confederate government, which acted with powers, greatly restricted, only upon the States. But in many articles of the Constitution the necessary existence of the States, and, within their proper spheres, the independent authority of the States, is distinctly recognized." ...

Appellee Secretary argues that the cases in which this Court has upheld sweeping exercises of authority by Congress, even though those exercises pre-empted state regulation of the private sector, have already curtailed the sovereignty of the States quite as much as the 1974 amendments to the Fair Labor Standards Act. We do not agree. It is one thing to recognize the authority of Congress to enact laws regulating individual businesses necessarily subject to the dual sovereignty of the government of the Nation and of the State in which they reside. It is quite another to uphold a similar exercise of congressional authority directed, not to private citizens, but to the States as States. We have repeatedly recognized that there are attributes of sovereignty attaching to every state government which may not be impaired by Congress, not because Congress may lack an affirmative grant of legislative authority to reach the matter, but because the Constitution prohibits it from exercising the authority in that manner. In *Coyle v. Oklahoma* (1911), the Court gave this example of such an attribute: "The power to locate its own seat of government, and to determine when and how it shall be changed from one place to another, and to appropriate its own public funds for that purpose, are essentially and peculiarly state powers. That one of the original thirteen states could now be shorn of such powers by an act of Congress would not be for a moment entertained."

One undoubted attribute of state sovereignty is the States' power to determine the wages which shall be paid to those whom they employ in order to carry out their governmental functions, what hours those persons will work, and what compensation will be provided where these employees may be called upon to work overtime. The question we must resolve here, then, is whether these determinations are "'functions essential to separate and independent existence,'" so that Congress may not abrogate the States' otherwise plenary authority to make them. *Coyle.*

In their complaint appellants advanced estimates of substantial costs which will be imposed upon them by the 1974 amendments. Since the District Court dismissed their complaint, we take its well-pleaded allegations as true.... The State of California, which must devote significant portions of its budget to fire-suppression endeavors, estimated that application of the Act to its employment practices will necessitate an increase in its budget of between $8 million and $16 million....

Quite apart from the substantial costs imposed upon the States and their political subdivisions, the Act displaces state policies regarding the manner in which they will structure delivery of those governmental services which their citizens require. The Act, speaking directly to the States qua States, requires that they shall pay all but an extremely limited minority of their employees the minimum wage rates currently chosen by Congress. It may well be that as a matter of economic policy it would be desirable that States, just as private employers, comply with these minimum wage requirements. But it cannot be gainsaid that the federal requirement directly supplants the considered policy choices of the States' elected officials and administrators as to how they wish to structure pay scales in state employment. The State might wish to employ persons with little or no training, or those who wish to work on a casual basis, or those who for some other reason do not possess minimum employment requirements, and pay them less than the federally prescribed minimum wage....

This dilemma presented by the minimum wage restrictions may seem not immediately different from that faced by private employers, who have long been covered by the Act and who must find ways to increase their gross income if they are to pay higher wages while maintaining current earnings. The difference, however, is that a State is not merely a factor in the "shifting economic arrangements" of the private sector of the economy, *Kovacs v. Cooper* (1949) (Frankfurter, J., concurring), but is itself a coordinate element in the system established by the Framers for governing our Federal Union.

The degree to which the FLSA amendments would interfere with traditional aspects of state sovereignty can be seen even more clearly upon examining the overtime requirements of the Act. The general effect of these provisions is to require the States to pay their employees at premium rates whenever their work exceeds a specified number of hours in a given period....

This congressionally imposed displacement of state decisions may substantially restructure traditional ways in which the local governments have arranged their affairs. Although at this point many of the actual effects under the proposed amendments remain a matter of some dispute among the parties, enough can be satisfactorily anticipated for an outline discussion of their general import. The requirement imposing premium rates upon any employment in excess of what Congress has decided is appropriate for a governmental employee's workweek, for example, appears likely to have the effect of coercing the States to structure work periods in some employment areas, such as police and fire protection, in a manner substantially different from practices which have long been commonly accepted among local governments of this Nation. In addition, appellee represents that the Act will require that the premium compensation for overtime worked must be paid in cash, rather than with compensatory time off, unless such compensatory time is taken in the same pay period. This, too, appears likely to be highly disruptive of accepted employment practices....

Our examination of the effect of the 1974 amendments, as sought to be extended to the States and their political subdivisions, satisfies us that both the minimum wage and the maximum hour provisions will impermissibly interfere with the integral governmental functions of these bodies.... [E]ven if appellants may have overestimated the effect which the Act will have upon their current levels and patterns of governmental activity, the dispositive factor is that Congress has attempted to exercise its Commerce Clause authority to prescribe minimum wages and maximum hours to be paid by the States in their capacities as sovereign governments. In so doing, Congress has sought to wield its power in a fashion that would impair the States' "ability to function effectively in a federal system." *Fry*. The exercise of congressional authority does not comport with the federal system of government embodied in the Constitution. We hold that insofar as the challenged amendments operate to directly displace the States' freedom to structure integral operations in areas of traditional governmental functions, they are not within the authority granted Congress by Art. I, § 8, cl. 3.

III. One final matter requires our attention. Appellee has vigorously urged that we cannot, consistently with the Court's decisions in *Maryland v. Wirtz*, and *Fry*, rule against him here. It is important to examine this contention so that it will be clear what we hold today, and what we do not.

With regard to *Fry*, we disagree with appellee. There the Court held that the Economic Stabilization Act of 1970 was constitutional as applied to temporarily freeze the wages of state and local government employees. The Court expressly noted that the degree of intrusion upon the protected area of state sovereignty was in that case even less than that worked by the amendments to the FLSA which were before the Court in *Wirtz*. The Court recognized that the Economic Stabilization Act was "an emergency measure to counter severe inflation that threatened the national economy."

We think our holding today quite consistent with *Fry*....

With respect to the Court's decision in *Wirtz*, we reach a different conclusion....

Wirtz relied heavily on the Court's decision in *United States v. California* (1936). The opinion quotes the following language from that case:

> (We) look to the activities in which the states have traditionally engaged as marking the boundary of the restriction upon the federal taxing power. But there is no such limitation upon the plenary power to regulate commerce. The state can no more deny the power if its exercise has been authorized by Congress than can an individual.

But we have reaffirmed today that the States as States stand on a quite different footing from an individual or a corporation when challenging the exercise of Congress' power to regulate commerce. We think the dicta from *United States v. California* simply wrong. Congress may not exercise that power so as to force directly upon the States its choices as to how essential decisions regarding the conduct of integral governmental functions are to be made. We agree that such assertions of power if unchecked, would indeed, as Mr. Justice Douglas cautioned in his dissent in *Wirtz*, allow "the National Government (to) devour the essentials of state sovereignty," and would therefore transgress the bounds of the authority granted Congress under the Commerce Clause. While there are obvious differences between the schools and hospitals involved in *Wirtz*, and the fire and police departments affected here, each provides an integral portion of those governmental services which the States and their political subdivisions have traditionally afforded their citizens. We are therefore persuaded that *Wirtz* must be overruled.

The judgment of the District Court is accordingly reversed, and the cases are remanded for further proceedings consistent with this opinion.

So ordered.

[Note: The "rule" of *National League of Cities v. Usery* was subsequently set out by the Court as follows:

> In order to succeed, a claim that congressional commerce power legislation is invalid under the reasoning of *National League of Cities* must satisfy each of three requirements. First, there must be a showing that the challenged statute regulates the "States as States." Second, the federal regulation must address matters that are indisputably "attributes of state sovereignty." And third, it must be apparent that the states' compliance with the federal law would directly impair their ability "to structure integral operations in areas of traditional governmental functions."

Hodel v. Virginia Surface Min. and Reclamation Ass'n, Inc. (1981).]

Mr. Justice Blackmun, concurring.

The Court's opinion and the dissents indicate the importance and significance of this litigation as it bears upon the relationship between the Federal Government and our States. Although I am not untroubled by certain possible implications of the Court's opinion, some of them suggested by the dissents, I do not read the opinion so despairingly as does my Brother Brennan. In my view, the result with respect to the statute under challenge here is necessarily correct. I may misinterpret the Court's opinion, but it seems to me that it adopts a balancing approach, and does not outlaw federal power in areas such as environmental protection, where the federal interest is demonstrably greater and where state facility compliance with imposed federal standards would be essential. With this understanding on my part of the Court's opinion, I join it.

Mr. Justice Brennan, with whom Mr. Justice White and Mr. Justice Marshall join, dissenting.

The Court concedes, as of course it must, that Congress enacted the 1974 amendments pursuant to its exclusive power under Art. I, §8, cl. 3, of the Constitution "[t]o regulate Commerce ... among the several States." It must therefore be surprising that my Brethren should choose this bicentennial year of our independence to repudiate principles governing judicial interpretation of our Constitution settled since the time of Mr. Chief Justice John Marshall, discarding his postulate that the Constitution contemplates that restraints upon exercise by Congress of its plenary commerce power lie in the political process and not in the judicial process. For 152 years ago Mr. Chief Justice Marshall enunciated that principle to which, until today, his successors on this Court have been faithful.

> [T]he power over commerce ... is vested in Congress as absolutely as it would be in a single government, having in its constitution the same restrictions on the exercise of the power as are found in the constitution of the United States. The wisdom and the discretion of Congress, their identity with the people, and the influence which their constituents possess at elections, are ... the sole restraints on which they have relied, to secure them from its abuse. They are the restraints on which the people must often rely solely, in all representative governments. *Gibbons v. Ogden* (1824).

Only 34 years ago, *Wickard v. Filburn* (1942), reaffirmed that "[a]t the beginning Chief Justice Marshall ... made emphatic the embracing and penetrating nature of [Congress' commerce] power by warning that effective restraints on its exercise must proceed from political rather than from judicial processes."

My Brethren do not successfully obscure today's patent usurpation of the role reserved for the political process by their purported discovery in the Constitution of a restraint derived from sovereignty of the States on Congress' exercise of the commerce power. Mr. Chief Justice Marshall recognized that limitations "prescribed in the constitution," *Gibbons v. Ogden*, restrain Congress' exercise of the power. See *Katzenbach v. McClung* (1964); *United States v. Darby* (1941). Thus laws within the commerce power may not infringe individual liberties protected by the 1st Amendment, *Mabee v. White Plains Publishing Co.* (1946); the 5th Amendment, *Leary v. United States* (1969); or the 6th Amendment, *United States v. Jackson* (1968). But there is no restraint based on state sovereignty requiring or permitting judicial enforcement anywhere expressed in the Constitution; our decisions over the last century and a half have explicitly rejected the existence of any such restraint on the commerce power.

We said in *United States v. California* (1936), for example: "The sovereign power of the states is necessarily diminished to the extent of the grants of power to the federal government in the Constitution.... [T]he power of the state is subordinate to the constitutional exercise of the granted federal power." This but echoed another principle emphasized by Mr. Chief Justice Marshall: "If any one proposition could command the universal assent of mankind, we might expect it would be this: that the government of the Union, though limited in its powers, is supreme within its sphere of action. This would seem to result necessarily from its nature. It is the government of all; its powers are delegated by all; it represents all, and acts for all...." The government of the United States, then, though limited in its powers, is supreme; and its laws when made in pursuance of the constitution, form the supreme law of the land, 'any thing in the constitution or laws of any State to the contrary notwithstanding.'" *McCulloch v. Maryland* (1819). "[It] is not a controversy between equals" when the Federal Government "is asserting its sovereign power to regulate commerce.... [T]he interests of the nation are more important than those of any state." *Sanitary District v. United States* (1925). The commerce power "is an affirmative power commensurate with the national needs." *North American Co. v. SEC* (1946). The Constitution reserves to the States "only ... that authority which is consistent with, and not opposed to, the grant to Congress. There is no room in our scheme of government for the assertion of state power in hostility to the authorized exercise of Federal power." *The Minnesota Rate Cases* (1913). "The framers of the constitution never intended that the legislative power of the nation should find itself incapable of disposing of a subject-matter specifically committed to its charge." *In re Rahrer* (1891).

My Brethren thus have today manufactured an abstraction without substance, founded neither in the words of the Constitution nor on precedent. An abstraction having such profoundly pernicious consequences is not made less so by characterizing the 1974 amendments as legislation directed against the "States qua States." Of course, regulations that this Court can say are not regulations of "commerce" cannot stand, *Santa Cruz Fruit Packing Co. v. NLRB* (1938), and in this sense "[t]he Court has ample power to prevent ... 'the utter destruction of the State as a sovereign political entity.'" *Maryland v. Wirtz* (1968). But my Brethren make no claim that the 1974 amendments are not regulations of "commerce;" rather they overrule *Wirtz* in disagreement with historic principles that *United States v. California*, reaffirmed: "[W]hile the commerce power has limits, valid general regulations of commerce do not cease to be regulations of commerce because a State is involved. If a State is engaging in economic activities that are validly regulated by the Federal Government when engaged in by private persons, the State too may be forced to conform its activities to federal regulation." *Wirtz*. Clearly, therefore, my Brethren are also repudiating the long line of our precedents holding that a judicial finding that Congress has not unreasonably regulated a subject matter of "commerce" brings to an end the judicial role. "Let the end be legitimate, let it be within the scope of the constitution, and all means which are appropriate, which are plainly adapted to that end, which are not prohibited, but consist with the letter and spirit of the constitution, are constitutional." *McCulloch v. Maryland*.

The reliance of my Brethren upon the 10th Amendment as "an express declaration of [a state sovereignty] limitation," not only suggests that they overrule governing decisions of this Court that address this question but must astound scholars of the Constitution. [E]arly decisions, *Gibbons v. Ogden, McCulloch v. Maryland*, and *Martin v. Hunter's Lessee* (1816), hold that nothing in the 10th Amendment constitutes a limitation on congressional exercise of powers delegated by the Constitution to Congress. See F. Frankfurter, *The Commerce Clause Under Marshall, Taney and Waite* 39–40 (1937). Rather, as the 10th Amendment's significance was more recently summarized:

> The amendment states but a truism that all is retained which has not been surrendered. There is nothing in the history of its adoption to suggest that it was more than declaratory of the relationship between the national and state governments as it had been established by the Constitution before the amendment or that its purpose was other than to allay fears that the new national government might seek to exercise powers not granted, and that the states might not be able to exercise fully their reserved powers.... From the beginning and for many years the amendment has been construed as not depriving the national government of authority to resort to all means for the exercise of a granted power which are appropriate and plainly adapted to the permitted end.

United States v. Darby (1941).¹ ...

[T]he apposite decision ... to the question whether the Constitution implies a state-sovereignty restraint upon congressional exercise of the commerce power is *Case v. Bowles* (1946). The question there was whether the Emergency Price Control Act could apply to the sale by the State of Washington of timber growing on lands granted by Congress to the State for the support of common schools. The State contended that "there is a 'doctrine implied in the Federal Constitution that the two governments, national and state, are each to exercise its power so as not to interfere with the free and full exercise of the powers of the other'.... [and] that the Act cannot be applied to this sale because it was 'for the purpose of gaining revenue to carry out an essential governmental function, the education of its citizens.'" The Court emphatically rejected that argument, in an opinion joined by Mr. Chief Justice Stone, reasoning: "Since the Emergency Price Control Act has been sustained as a Congressional exercise of the war power, the [State's] argument is that the extent of that power as applied to state functions depends on whether these are 'essential' to the state government. The use of the same criterion in measuring the Constitutional power of Congress to tax has proved to be unworkable, and we reject it as a guide in the field here involved. Cf. *United States v. California* (1936)." ...

Today's repudiation of this unbroken line of precedents that firmly reject my Brethren's ill-conceived abstraction can only be regarded as a transparent cover for invalidating a congressional judgment with which they disagree. The only analysis even remotely resembling that adopted today is found in a line of opinions dealing with the Commerce Clause and the 10th Amendment that ultimately provoked a constitutional crisis for the Court in the 1930's. E.g., *Carter v. Carter Coal Co.* (1936); *United States v. Butler* (1936); *Hammer v. Dagenhart* (1918).... We tend to forget that the Court invalidated legislation during the Great Depression, not solely under the Due Process Clause, but also and primarily under the Commerce Clause and the 10th Amendment. It may have been the eventual abandonment of that overly restrictive construction of the commerce power that spelled defeat for the Court-packing plan, and preserved the integrity of this institution. See, e.g., *United States v. Darby* (1941); *Mulford v. Smith* (1939); *NLRB v. Jones & Laughlin Steel Corp.* (1937), but my Brethren today are transparently trying to cut back on that recognition of the scope of the commerce power. My Brethren's approach to this case is not far different from the dissenting opinions in the cases that averted the crisis. See, E.g., *Mulford v. Smith* (Butler, J., dissenting); *NLRB v. Jones & Laughlin Steel Corp* (McReynolds, J., dissenting)....

To argue, as do my Brethren, that the 1974 amendments are directed at the "States qua States," and "displac[e] state policies regarding the manner in which they will structure delivery of those governmental services which their citizens require," and therefore "directly penaliz[e] the States for choosing to hire governmental employees on terms different from those which Congress has sought to impose," is only to advance precisely the

---

1. In support of the first-quoted paragraph, *Darby* cited 2 J. Elliot, *Debates* 123, 131 (2d ed. 1787); 3 *Id.*, at 450, 464, 600; 4 *Id.*, at 140, 148; 1 *Annals of Congress*, 432, 761, 767–68 (1789); 2 J. Story, *Commentaries on the Constitution* §§ 1907–1908 (2d ed.1851) ("It is plain, therefore, that it could not have been the intention of the framers of this amendment to give it effect, as an abridgment of any of the powers granted under the constitution, whether they are express or implied, direct or incidental. Its sole design is to exclude any interpretation, by which other powers should be assumed beyond those which are granted"). Decisions expressly rejecting today's interpretation of the 10th Amendment also include *Sperry v. Florida ex rel. Florida Bar* (1963); *Oklahoma v. CSC* (1947); *Case v. Bowles* (1946); *Fernandez v. Wiener* (1945); *Oklahoma ex rel. Phillips v. Atkinson Co.* (1941); *United States v. Sprague* (1931).

unsuccessful arguments made by the State of Washington in *Case v. Bowles* (1946) and the State of California in *United States v. California*. The 1974 amendments are, however, an entirely legitimate exercise of the commerce power, not in the slightest restrained by any doctrine of state sovereignty cognizable in this Court, as *Case v. Bowles, United States v. California, Maryland v. Wirtz,* and our other pertinent precedents squarely and definitively establish. Moreover, since *Maryland v. Wirtz* is overruled, the Fair Labor Standards Act is invalidated in its application to all state employees "in [any areas] that the States have regarded as integral parts of their governmental activities." This standard is a meaningless limitation on the Court's state-sovereignty doctrine....

Also devoid of meaningful content is my Brethren's argument that the 1974 amendments "displac[e] State policies." The amendments neither impose policy objectives on the States nor deny the States complete freedom to fix their own objectives. My Brethren boldly assert that the decision as to wages and hours is an "undoubted attribute of state sovereignty," and then never say why. Indeed, they disclaim any reliance on the costs of compliance with the amendments in reaching today's result. This would enable my Brethren to conclude that, however insignificant the cost, any federal regulation under the commerce power "will nonetheless significantly alter or displace the States' abilities to structure employer-employee relationships." This then would mean that, whether or not state wages are paid for the performance of an "essential" state function [whatever that may mean], the newly discovered state-sovereignty constraint could operate as a flat and absolute prohibition against congressional regulation of the wages and hours of state employees under the Commerce Clause. The portent of such a sweeping holding is so ominous for our constitutional jurisprudence as to leave one incredulous....

Certainly the paradigm of sovereign action qua State is ... in the enactment and enforcement of state laws. Is it possible that my Brethren are signaling abandonment of the heretofore unchallenged principle that Congress "can, if it chooses, entirely displace the States to the full extent of the far-reaching Commerce Clause"?... It bears repeating "that effective restraints on ... exercise [of the commerce power] must proceed from political rather than from judicial processes." *Wickard v. Filburn* (1942).

It is unacceptable that the judicial process should be thought superior to the political process in this area. Under the Constitution the Judiciary has no role to play beyond finding that Congress has not made an unreasonable legislative judgment respecting what is "commerce." My Brother Blackmun suggests that controlling judicial supervision of the relationship between the States and our National Government by use of a balancing approach diminishes the ominous implications of today's decision. Such an approach, however, is a thinly veiled rationalization for judicial supervision of a policy judgment that our system of government reserves to Congress.

Judicial restraint in this area merely recognizes that the political branches of our Government are structured to protect the interests of the States, as well as the Nation as a whole, and that the States are fully able to protect their own interests in the premises. Congress is constituted of representatives in both the Senate and House Elected from the States. *The Federalist* No. 45 (J. Madison); *The Federalist* No. 46 (J. Madison). Decisions upon the extent of federal intervention under the Commerce Clause into the affairs of the States are in that sense decisions of the States themselves. Judicial redistribution of powers granted the National Government by the terms of the Constitution violates the fundamental tenet of our federalism that the extent of federal intervention into the States' affairs in the exercise of delegated powers shall be determined by the States' exercise of political power through their representatives in Congress. See Wechsler, *The Political Safeguards of Federalism: The Role of the States in the Composition and Selection of the National Gov-*

ernment, 54 Col. L. Rev. 543 (1954). There is no reason whatever to suppose that in enacting the 1974 amendments Congress, even if it might extensively obliterate state sovereignty by fully exercising its plenary power respecting commerce, had any purpose to do so. Surely the presumption must be to the contrary. Any realistic assessment of our federal political system, dominated as it is by representatives of the people elected from the States, yields the conclusion that it is highly unlikely that those representatives will ever be motivated to disregard totally the concerns of these States. *The Federalist* No. 46. Certainly this was the premise upon which the Constitution, as authoritatively explicated in *Gibbons v. Ogden*, was founded. Indeed, though the States are represented in the National Government, national interests are not similarly represented in the States' political processes. Perhaps my Brethren's concern with the Judiciary's role in preserving federalism might better focus on whether Congress, not the States, is in greater need of this Court's protection.

A sense of the enormous impact of States' political power is gained by brief reference to the federal budget. The largest estimate by any of the appellants of the cost impact of the 1974 amendments, $1 billion, pales in comparison with the financial assistance the States receive from the Federal Government. In fiscal 1977 the President's proposed budget recommends $60.5 billion in federal assistance to the States, exclusive of loans.... Appellants complain of the impact of the amended FLSA on police and fire departments, but the 1977 budget contemplates outlays for law enforcement assistance of $716 million....

No effort is made to distinguish the FLSA amendments sustained in *Wirtz* from the 1974 amendments. We are told at the outset that "the 'far-reaching implications' of *Wirtz*, should be overruled;" later it is said that the "reasoning in *Wirtz*" is no longer "authoritative." My Brethren then merely restate their essential function test and say that *Wirtz* must "therefore" be overruled. There is no analysis whether *Wirtz* reached the correct result, apart from any flaws in reasoning, even though we are told that "there are obvious differences" between this case and *Wirtz*. Are state and federal interests being silently balanced, as in the discussion of *Fry*? The best I can make of it is that the 1966 FLSA amendments are struck down and *Wirtz* is overruled on the basis of the conceptually unworkable essential-function test; and that the test is unworkable is demonstrated by my Brethren's inability to articulate any meaningful distinctions among state-operated railroads, state-operated schools and hospitals, and state-operated police and fire departments.

We are left then with a catastrophic judicial body blow at Congress' power under the Commerce Clause. Even if Congress may nevertheless accomplish its objectives for example, by conditioning grants of federal funds upon compliance with federal minimum wage and overtime standards, cf. *Oklahoma v. CSC* (1947), there is an ominous portent of disruption of our constitutional structure implicit in today's mischievous decision. I dissent.

Mr. Justice Stevens, dissenting. [Omitted.]

Garcia v. San Antonio Metropolitan Transit Authority: Background

1. What is the rule of *Garcia*?
2. What does the Court in *Garcia* envision as the mechanism for the protection of the role of the states in the federal system? How effective do you think this mechanism is? Does the change in the manner of election of United States Senators bear on this question?

3. How does the Court in *Garcia* read the 10th Amendment? Does it explicitly mention it? If not, does it implicitly take a position on it? How does this approach differ from that of *National League of Cities*?

4. How stable do you believe the precedent in *Garcia* will prove to be?

Garcia v. San Antonio Metropolitan Transit Authority
469 U.S. 528 (1985)

[Majority: Blackmun, Brennan, Stevens, Marshall, and White. Dissenting: Powell, Rehnquist, Burger (C.J.) and O'Connor.]

Justice Blackmun delivered the opinion of the Court.

We revisit in these cases an issue raised in *National League of Cities v. Usery* (1976). In that litigation, this Court, by a sharply divided vote, ruled that the Commerce Clause does not empower Congress to enforce the minimum-wage and overtime provisions of the Fair Labor Standards Act (FLSA) against the States "in areas of traditional governmental functions." Although *National League of Cities* supplied some examples of "traditional governmental functions," it did not offer a general explanation of how a "traditional" function is to be distinguished from a "nontraditional" one. Since then, federal and state courts have struggled with the task, thus imposed, of identifying a traditional function for purposes of state immunity under the Commerce Clause....

I.... The present controversy concerns the extent to which SAMTA [San Antonio Metropolitan Transit Authority] may be subjected to the minimum-wage and overtime requirements of the FLSA. When the FLSA was enacted in 1938, its wage and overtime provisions did not apply to local mass-transit employees or, indeed, to employees of state and local governments. In 1961, Congress extended minimum-wage coverage to employees of any private mass-transit carrier whose annual gross revenue was not less than $1 million. Five years later, Congress extended FLSA coverage to state and local-government employees for the first time by withdrawing the minimum-wage and overtime exemptions from public hospitals, schools, and mass-transit carriers whose rates and services were subject to state regulation. At the same time, Congress eliminated the overtime exemption for all mass-transit employees other than drivers, operators, and conductors. The application of the FLSA to public schools and hospitals was ruled to be within Congress' power under the Commerce Clause. *Maryland v. Wirtz* (1968).

The FLSA obligations of public mass-transit systems like SAMTA were expanded in 1974 when Congress provided for the progressive repeal of the surviving overtime exemption for mass-transit employees....

[On] September 17, 1979 ... the Wage and Hour Administration of the Department of Labor issued an opinion that SAMTA's operations "are not constitutionally immune from the application of the Fair Labor Standards Act" under *National League of Cities*.... On November 21 of that year, SAMTA filed this action against the Secretary of Labor in the United States District Court for the Western District of Texas. It sought a declaratory judgment that, contrary to the Wage and Hour Administration's determination, *National League of Cities* precluded the application of the FLSA's overtime requirements to SAMTA's operations....

II. Appellees have not argued that SAMTA is immune from regulation under the FLSA on the ground that it is a local transit system engaged in intrastate commercial activity. In a practical sense, SAMTA's operations might well be characterized as "local." Nonetheless, it long has been settled that Congress' authority under the Commerce Clause extends to intrastate economic activities that affect interstate commerce. See, e.g., *Hodel v. Virginia Surface Mining & Recl. Assn.* (1981); *Heart of Atlanta Motel, Inc. v. United States* (1964); *Wickard v. Filburn* (1942); *United States v. Darby* (1941). Were SAMTA a privately owned and operated enterprise, it could not credibly argue that Congress exceeded the bounds of its Commerce Clause powers in prescribing minimum wages and overtime rates for SAMTA's employees. Any constitutional exemption from the requirements of the FLSA therefore must rest on SAMTA's status as a governmental entity rather than on the "local" nature of its operations.

The prerequisites for governmental immunity under *National League of Cities* were summarized by this Court in *Hodel*. Under that summary, four conditions must be satisfied before a state activity may be deemed immune from a particular federal regulation under the Commerce Clause. First, it is said that the federal statute at issue must regulate "the 'States as States.'" Second, the statute must "address matters that are indisputably 'attribute[s] of state sovereignty.'" Third, state compliance with the federal obligation must "directly impair [the States'] ability 'to structure integral operations in areas of traditional governmental functions.'" Finally, the relation of state and federal interests must not be such that "the nature of the federal interest ... justifies state submission." (Quoting *National League of Cities*.)

The controversy in the present cases has focused on the third *Hodel* requirement—that the challenged federal statute trench on "traditional governmental functions." The District Court voiced a common concern: "Despite the abundance of adjectives, identifying which particular state functions are immune remains difficult." Just how troublesome the task has been is revealed by the results reached in other federal cases. Thus, courts have held that regulating ambulance services, licensing automobile drivers, operating a municipal airport, performing solid waste disposal, and operating a highway authority, are functions protected under *National League of Cities*. At the same time, courts have held that issuance of industrial development bonds, regulation of intrastate natural gas sales, regulation of traffic on public roads, regulation of air transportation, operation of a telephone system, leasing and sale of natural gas, operation of a mental health facility, and provision of in-house domestic services for the aged and handicapped, are not entitled to immunity. We find it difficult, if not impossible, to identify an organizing principle that places each of the cases in the first group on one side of a line and each of the cases in the second group on the other side. The constitutional distinction between licensing drivers and regulating traffic, for example, or between operating a highway authority and operating a mental health facility, is elusive at best.

Thus far, this Court itself has made little headway in defining the scope of the governmental functions deemed protected under *National League of Cities*. In that case the Court set forth examples of protected and unprotected functions, but provided no explanation of how those examples were identified. The only other case in which the Court has had occasion to address the problem is *Transportation Union v. Long Island R. Co.* (1982). We there observed: "The determination of whether a federal law impairs a state's authority with respect to 'areas of traditional [state] functions' may at times be a difficult one." (Quoting *National League of Cities*.) The accuracy of that statement is demonstrated by this Court's own difficulties in *Long Island* in developing a workable standard for "traditional governmental functions." We relied in large part there on "the historical reality that the operation of railroads is not among the functions traditionally performed by state and local governments," but we simultaneously disavowed "a static historical view of state functions generally immune from federal regulation." We held that the inquiry into a particular function's "traditional" nature was merely a means of determining whether the federal statute at issue unduly handicaps "basic state prerogatives," but we did not offer an explanation of what makes one state function a "basic prerogative" and another function not basic. Finally, having disclaimed a rigid reliance on the historical pedigree of state involvement in a particular area, we nonetheless found it appropriate to emphasize the extended historical record of federal involvement in the field of rail transportation.

Many constitutional standards involve "undoubte[d] ... gray areas," *Fry v. United States* (1975) (dissenting opinion), and, despite the difficulties that this Court and other courts have encountered so far, it normally might be fair to venture the assumption that case-by-case development would lead to a workable standard for determining whether a particular governmental function should be immune from federal regulation under the Commerce Clause. A further cautionary note is sounded, however, by the Court's experience in the related field of state immunity from federal taxation....

If these tax-immunity cases had any common thread, it was in the attempt to distinguish between "governmental" and "proprietary" functions....

The distinction the Court discarded as unworkable in the field of tax immunity has proved no more fruitful in the field of regulatory immunity under the Commerce Clause. Neither do any of the alternative standards that might be employed to distinguish between protected and unprotected governmental functions appear manageable. We rejected the possibility of making immunity turn on a purely historical standard of "tradition" in *Long Island*, and properly so. The most obvious defect of a historical approach to state immunity is that it prevents a court from accommodating changes in the historical functions of States, changes that have resulted in a number of once-private functions like education being assumed by the States and their subdivisions.[1] At the same time, the only apparent virtue of a rigorous historical standard, namely, its promise of a reasonably objective measure for state immunity, is illusory. Reliance on history as an organizing principle results in line-drawing of the most arbitrary sort; the genesis of state governmental functions stretches over a historical continuum from before the Revolution to the present, and courts would have to decide by fiat precisely how longstanding a pattern of state involvement had to be for federal regulatory authority to be defeated.

A nonhistorical standard for selecting immune governmental functions is likely to be just as unworkable as is a historical standard. The goal of identifying "uniquely" governmental functions, for example, has been rejected by the Court in the field of governmental tort liability in part because the notion of a "uniquely" governmental function is unmanageable. Another possibility would be to confine immunity to "necessary" governmental services, that is, services that would be provided inadequately or not at all unless the government provided them. The set of services that fits into this category, however, may well be negligible. The fact that an unregulated market produces less of some service than a State deems desirable does not mean that the State itself must provide the service; in most if not all cases, the State can "contract out" by hiring private firms to provide the service or simply by providing subsidies to existing suppliers. It also is open to question

---

1. Indeed, the "traditional" nature of a particular governmental function can be a matter of historical nearsightedness; today's self-evidently "traditional" function is often yesterday's suspect innovation. Thus, *National League of Cities* offered the provision of public parks and recreation as an example of a traditional governmental function. A scant 80 years earlier, however, in *Shoemaker v. United States* (1893), the Court pointed out that city commons originally had been provided not for recreation but for grazing domestic animals "in common," and that "[i]n the memory of men now living, a proposition to take private property [by eminent domain] for a public park ... would have been regarded as a novel exercise of legislative power."

how well equipped courts are to make this kind of determination about the workings of economic markets.

We believe, however, that there is a more fundamental problem at work here, a problem that explains why the Court was never able to provide a basis for the governmental/proprietary distinction in the intergovernmental tax-immunity cases and why an attempt to draw similar distinctions with respect to federal regulatory authority under *National League of Cities* is unlikely to succeed regardless of how the distinctions are phrased. The problem is that neither the governmental/proprietary distinction nor any other that purports to separate out important governmental functions can be faithful to the role of federalism in a democratic society. The essence of our federal system is that within the realm of authority left open to them under the Constitution, the States must be equally free to engage in any activity that their citizens choose for the common weal, no matter how unorthodox or unnecessary anyone else—including the judiciary—deems state involvement to be. Any rule of state immunity that looks to the "traditional," "integral," or "necessary" nature of governmental functions inevitably invites an unelected federal judiciary to make decisions about which state policies it favors and which ones it dislikes. "The science of government ... is the science of experiment," *Anderson v. Dunn* (1821), and the States cannot serve as laboratories for social and economic experiment, see *New State Ice Co. v. Liebmann* (1932) (Brandeis, J., dissenting), if they must pay an added price when they meet the changing needs of their citizenry by taking up functions that an earlier day and a different society left in private hands. In the words of Justice Black:

> There is not, and there cannot be, any unchanging line of demarcation between essential and non-essential governmental functions. Many governmental functions of today have at some time in the past been non-governmental. The genius of our government provides that, within the sphere of constitutional action, the people—acting not through the courts but through their elected legislative representatives—have the power to determine as conditions demand, what services and functions the public welfare requires. *Helvering v. Gerhardt* (1938) (concurring opinion).

We therefore now reject, as unsound in principle and unworkable in practice, a rule of state immunity from federal regulation that turns on a judicial appraisal of whether a particular governmental function is "integral" or "traditional." Any such rule leads to inconsistent results at the same time that it disserves principles of democratic self-governance, and it breeds inconsistency precisely because it is divorced from those principles. If there are to be limits on the Federal Government's power to interfere with state functions—as undoubtedly there are—we must look elsewhere to find them. We accordingly return to the underlying issue that confronted this Court in *National League of Cities*—the manner in which the Constitution insulates States from the reach of Congress' power under the Commerce Clause.

III. The central theme of *National League of Cities* was that the States occupy a special position in our constitutional system and that the scope of Congress' authority under the Commerce Clause must reflect that position. Of course, the Commerce Clause by its specific language does not provide any special limitation on Congress' actions with respect to the States. See *EEOC v. Wyoming* (1983) (concurring opinion). It is equally true, however, that the text of the Constitution provides the beginning rather than the final answer to every inquiry into questions of federalism, for "[b]ehind the words of the constitutional provisions are postulates which limit and control." *Principality of Monaco v. Mississippi* (1934). *National League of Cities* reflected the general conviction that the

Constitution precludes "the National Government [from] devour[ing] the essentials of state sovereignty." *Maryland v. Wirtz* (dissenting opinion). In order to be faithful to the underlying federal premises of the Constitution, courts must look for the "postulates which limit and control." ...

We doubt that courts ultimately can identify principled constitutional limitations on the scope of Congress' Commerce Clause powers over the States merely by relying on a priori definitions of state sovereignty. In part, this is because of the elusiveness of objective criteria for "fundamental" elements of state sovereignty, a problem we have witnessed in the search for "traditional governmental functions." There is, however, a more fundamental reason: the sovereignty of the States is limited by the Constitution itself. A variety of sovereign powers, for example, are withdrawn from the States by Article I, §10. Section 8 of the same Article works an equally sharp contraction of state sovereignty by authorizing Congress to exercise a wide range of legislative powers and (in conjunction with the Supremacy Clause of Article VI) to displace contrary state legislation. See *Hodel*. By providing for final review of questions of federal law in this Court, Article III curtails the sovereign power of the States' judiciaries to make authoritative determinations of law. See *Martin v. Hunter's Lessee* (1816). Finally, the developed application, through the 14th Amendment, of the greater part of the Bill of Rights to the States limits the sovereign authority that States otherwise would possess to legislate with respect to their citizens and to conduct their own affairs.

The States unquestionably do "retai[n] a significant measure of sovereign authority." *EEOC v. Wyoming* (Powell, J., dissenting). They do so, however, only to the extent that the Constitution has not divested them of their original powers and transferred those powers to the Federal Government. In the words of James Madison to the Members of the First Congress: "Interference with the power of the States was no constitutional criterion of the power of Congress. If the power was not given, Congress could not exercise it; if given, they might exercise it, although it should interfere with the laws, or even the Constitution of the States." 2 *Annals of Cong.* 1897 (1791). Justice Field made the same point in the course of his defense of state autonomy in his dissenting opinion in *Baltimore & Ohio R. Co. v. Baugh* (1893), a defense quoted with approval in *Erie R. Co. v. Tompkins* (1938):

> [T]he Constitution of the United States ... recognizes and preserves the autonomy and independence of the States—independence in their legislative and independence in their judicial departments. [Federal] [s]upervision over either the legislative or the judicial action of the States is in no case permissible except as to matters by the Constitution specifically authorized or delegated to the United States. Any interference with either, except as thus permitted, is an invasion of the authority of the State and, to that extent, a denial of its independence.

As a result, to say that the Constitution assumes the continued role of the States is to say little about the nature of that role. Only recently, this Court recognized that the purpose of the constitutional immunity recognized in *National League of Cities* is not to preserve "a sacred province of state autonomy." *EEOC v. Wyoming*. With rare exceptions, like the guarantee, in Article IV, §3, of state territorial integrity, the Constitution does not carve out express elements of state sovereignty that Congress may not employ its delegated powers to displace. James Wilson reminded the Pennsylvania ratifying convention in 1787: "It is true, indeed, sir, although it presupposes the existence of state governments, yet this Constitution does not suppose them to be the sole power to be respected." 2 *Debates in the Several State Conventions on the Adoption of the Federal Constitution* 439 (J. Elliot 2d ed. 1876) (Elliot). The power of the Federal Government is a "power to be respected" as well, and the fact that the States remain sovereign as to all powers not vested in Congress or denied them by the Constitution offers no guidance about where the frontier between state and federal power lies. In short, we have no license to employ freestanding conceptions of state sovereignty when measuring congressional authority under the Commerce Clause.

When we look for the States' "residuary and inviolable sovereignty," *The Federalist* No. 39 (J. Madison), in the shape of the constitutional scheme rather than in predetermined notions of sovereign power, a different measure of state sovereignty emerges. Apart from the limitation on federal authority inherent in the delegated nature of Congress' Article I powers, the principal means chosen by the Framers to ensure the role of the States in the federal system lies in the structure of the Federal Government itself. It is no novelty to observe that the composition of the Federal Government was designed in large part to protect the States from overreaching by Congress. The Framers thus gave the States a role in the selection both of the Executive and the Legislative Branches of the Federal Government. The States were vested with indirect influence over the House of Representatives and the Presidency by their control of electoral qualifications and their role in Presidential elections. U.S. Const., Art. I, §2, and Art. II, §1. They were given more direct influence in the Senate, where each State received equal representation and each Senator was to be selected by the legislature of his State. Art. I, §3. The significance attached to the States' equal representation in the Senate is underscored by the prohibition of any constitutional amendment divesting a State of equal representation without the State's consent. Art. V.

The extent to which the structure of the Federal Government itself was relied on to insulate the interests of the States is evident in the views of the Framers. James Madison explained that the Federal Government "will partake sufficiently of the spirit [of the States], to be disinclined to invade the rights of the individual States, or the prerogatives of their governments." *The Federalist* No. 46. Similarly, James Wilson observed that "it was a favorite object in the Convention" to provide for the security of the States against federal encroachment and that the structure of the Federal Government itself served that end. 2 Elliot, at 438–39. Madison placed particular reliance on the equal representation of the States in the Senate, which he saw as "at once a constitutional recognition of the portion of sovereignty remaining in the individual States, and an instrument for preserving that residuary sovereignty." *The Federalist* No. 62. He further noted that "the residuary sovereignty of the States [is] implied and secured by that principle of representation in one branch of the [federal] legislature." *The Federalist* No. 43. See also *McCulloch v. Maryland* (1819). In short, the Framers chose to rely on a federal system in which special restraints on federal power over the States inhered principally in the workings of the National Government itself, rather than in discrete limitations on the objects of federal authority. State sovereign interests, then, are more properly protected by procedural safeguards inherent in the structure of the federal system than by judicially created limitations on federal power.

The effectiveness of the federal political process in preserving the States' interests is apparent even today in the course of federal legislation. On the one hand, the States have been able to direct a substantial proportion of federal revenues into their own treasuries in the form of general and program-specific grants in aid. The federal role in assisting state and local governments is a longstanding one; Congress provided federal land grants to finance state governments from the beginning of the Republic, and direct cash grants were awarded as early as 1887 under the Hatch Act. In the past quarter-century alone, federal grants to States and localities have grown from $7 billion to $96 billion. As a result, federal grants now account for about one-fifth of state and local government expenditures. The States have obtained federal funding for such services as police and fire protection, education, public health and hospitals, parks and recreation, and sanitation. Moreover, at the same time that the States have exercised their influence to obtain federal support, they have been able to exempt themselves from a wide variety of obligations imposed by Congress under the Commerce Clause. For example, the Federal Power Act, the National Labor Relations Act, the Labor-Management Reporting and Disclosure Act, the Occupational Safety and Health Act, the Employee Retirement Income Security Act, and the Sherman Act all contain express or implied exemptions for States and their subdivisions. The fact that some federal statutes such as the FLSA extend general obligations to the States cannot obscure the extent to which the political position of the States in the federal system has served to minimize the burdens that the States bear under the Commerce Clause.

We realize that changes in the structure of the Federal Government have taken place since 1789, not the least of which has been the substitution of popular election of Senators by the adoption of the 17th Amendment in 1913, and that these changes may work to alter the influence of the States in the federal political process. Nonetheless, against this background, we are convinced that the fundamental limitation that the constitutional scheme imposes on the Commerce Clause to protect the "States as States" is one of process rather than one of result. Any substantive restraint on the exercise of Commerce Clause powers must find its justification in the procedural nature of this basic limitation, and it must be tailored to compensate for possible failings in the national political process rather than to dictate a "sacred province of state autonomy." See *EEOC v. Wyoming* (1983).

Insofar as the present cases are concerned, then, we need go no further than to state that we perceive nothing in the overtime and minimum-wage requirements of the FLSA, as applied to SAMTA, that is destructive of state sovereignty or violative of any constitutional provision. SAMTA faces nothing more than the same minimum-wage and overtime obligations that hundreds of thousands of other employers, public as well as private, have to meet....

IV. This analysis makes clear that Congress' action in affording SAMTA employees the protections of the wage and hour provisions of the FLSA contravened no affirmative limit on Congress' power under the Commerce Clause. The judgment of the District Court therefore must be reversed.

Of course, we continue to recognize that the States occupy a special and specific position in our constitutional system and that the scope of Congress' authority under the Commerce Clause must reflect that position. But the principal and basic limit on the federal commerce power is that inherent in all congressional action—the built-in restraints that our system provides through state participation in federal governmental action. The political process ensures that laws that unduly burden the States will not be promulgated. In the factual setting of these cases the internal safeguards of the political process have performed as intended....

Justice Powell, with whom The Chief Justice, Justice Rehnquist, and Justice O'Connor join, dissenting.

The Court today, in its 5–4 decision, overrules *National League of Cities v. Usery* (1976), a case in which we held that Congress lacked authority to impose the requirements of the Fair Labor Standards Act on state and local governments. Because I believe this decision substantially alters the federal system embodied in the Constitution, I dissent.

I. There are, of course, numerous examples over the history of this Court in which prior decisions have been reconsidered and overruled. There have been few cases, however, in which the principle of stare decisis and the rationale of recent decisions were ignored as abruptly as we now witness. The reasoning of the Court in *National League of Cities*, and the principle applied there, have been reiterated consistently over the past eight years. Since its decision in 1976, *National League of Cities* has been cited and quoted in opinions joined by every Member of the present Court.... Less than three years ago, in *Transportation Union v. Long Island R. Co.* (1982), a unanimous Court reaffirmed the principles of *National League of Cities* but found them inapplicable to the regulation of a railroad heavily engaged in interstate commerce. The Court stated:

> The key prong of the *National League of Cities* test applicable to this case is the third one (repeated and reformulated in *Hodel)*, which examines whether "the States' compliance with the federal law would directly impair their ability 'to structure integral operations in areas of traditional governmental functions.'"

The Court in that case recognized that the test "may at times be a difficult one," but it was considered in that unanimous decision as settled constitutional doctrine....

II. The Court finds that the test of state immunity approved in *National League of Cities* and its progeny is unworkable and unsound in principle. In finding the test to be unworkable, the Court begins by mischaracterizing *National League of Cities* and subsequent cases. In concluding that efforts to define state immunity are unsound in principle, the Court radically departs from long-settled constitutional values and ignores the role of judicial review in our system of government.

II-A. Much of the Court's opinion is devoted to arguing that it is difficult to define a priori "traditional governmental functions." *National League of Cities* neither engaged in, nor required, such a task. The Court discusses and condemns as standards "traditional governmental functions," "purely historical" functions, "'uniquely' governmental functions," and "'necessary' governmental services." But nowhere does it mention that *National League of Cities* adopted a familiar type of balancing test for determining whether Commerce Clause enactments transgress constitutional limitations imposed by the federal nature of our system of government. This omission is noteworthy, since the author of today's opinion joined *National League of Cities* and concurred separately to point out that the Court's opinion in that case "adopt[s] a balancing approach [that] does not outlaw federal power in areas ... where the federal interest is demonstrably greater and where state ... compliance with imposed federal standards would be essential." (Blackmun, J., concurring)....

II-B. Today's opinion does not explain how the States' role in the electoral process guarantees that particular exercises of the Commerce Clause power will not infringe on residual state sovereignty. Members of Congress are elected from the various States, but once in office they are Members of the Federal Government. Although the States participate in the Electoral College, this is hardly a reason to view the President as a representative of the States' interest against federal encroachment. We noted recently "[t]he hydraulic pressure inherent within each of the separate Branches to exceed the outer limits of its power...." *INS v. Chadha* (1983). The Court offers no reason to think that this pressure will not operate when Congress seeks to invoke its powers under the Commerce Clause, notwithstanding the electoral role of the States.

The Court apparently thinks that the State's success at obtaining federal funds for various projects and exemptions from the obligations of some federal statutes is indicative of the "effectiveness of the federal political process in preserving the States' interests...." But such political success is not relevant to the question whether the political processes are the proper means of enforcing constitutional limitations....

More troubling than the logical infirmities in the Court's reasoning is the result of its holding, i.e., that federal political officials, invoking the Commerce Clause, are the sole judges of the limits of their own power. This result is inconsistent with the fundamental principles of our constitutional system. See, e.g., *The Federalist* No. 78 (Hamilton). At least since *Marbury v. Madison* (1803), it has been the settled province of the federal judiciary "to say what the law is" with respect to the constitutionality of Acts of Congress. In rejecting the role of the judiciary in protecting the States from federal overreaching, the Court's opinion offers no explanation for ignoring the teaching of the most famous case in our history.

III-A. In our federal system, the States have a major role that cannot be pre-empted by the National Government. As contemporaneous writings and the debates at the ratifying conventions make clear, the States' ratification of the Constitution was predicated on this understanding of federalism. Indeed, the 10th Amendment was adopted specifically to ensure that the important role promised the States by the proponents of the Constitution was realized.

Much of the initial opposition to the Constitution was rooted in the fear that the National Government would be too powerful and eventually would eliminate the States as viable political entities. This concern was voiced repeatedly until proponents of the Constitution made assurances that a Bill of Rights, including a provision explicitly reserving powers in the States, would be among the first business of the new Congress. Samuel Adams argued, for example, that if the several States were to be joined in "one entire Nation, under one Legislature, the Powers of which shall extend to every Subject of Legislation, and its Laws be supreme & controul the whole, the Idea of Sovereignty in these States must be lost." Letter from Samuel Adams to Richard Henry Lee (Dec. 3, 1787), reprinted in *Anti-Federalists versus Federalists* 159 (J. Lewis ed. 1967). Likewise, George Mason feared that "the general government being paramount to, and in every respect more powerful than the state governments, the latter must give way to the former." Address in the Ratifying Convention of Virginia (June 4–12, 1788), reprinted in *Anti-Federalists versus Federalists*, at 208–09.

Anti-federalists raised these concerns in almost every state ratifying convention. See generally 1–4 *Debates in the Several State Conventions on the Adoption of the Federal Constitution*(J. Elliot 2d. ed. 1876). As a result, eight States voted for the Constitution only after proposing amendments to be adopted after ratification. All eight of these included among their recommendations some version of what later became the 10th Amendment. So strong was the concern that the proposed Constitution was seriously defective without a specific bill of rights, including a provision reserving powers to the States, that in order to secure the votes for ratification, the Federalists eventually conceded that such provisions were necessary. See 1 B. Schwartz, *The Bill of Rights: A Documentary History* 505 and passim (1971). It was thus generally agreed that consideration of a bill of rights would be among the first business of the new Congress. See generally 1 *Annals of Cong.* 432–37 (1789) (remarks of James Madison). Accordingly, the 10 Amendments that we know as the Bill of Rights were proposed and adopted early in the first session of the First Congress. 2 Schwartz, *The Bill of Rights*, at 983–1167.

This history, which the Court simply ignores, documents the integral role of the 10th Amendment in our constitutional theory. It exposes as well, I believe, the fundamental character of the Court's error today. Far from being "unsound in principle," judicial enforcement of the 10th Amendment is essential to maintaining the federal system so carefully designed by the Framers and adopted in the Constitution.

III-B. The Framers had definite ideas about the nature of the Constitution's division of authority between the Federal and State Governments. In *The Federalist* No. 39, for example, Madison explained this division by drawing a series of contrasts between the attributes of a "national" government and those of the government to be established by the Constitution. While a national form of government would possess an "indefinite supremacy over all persons and things," the form of government contemplated by the Constitution instead consisted of "local or municipal authorities [which] form distinct and independent portions of the supremacy, no more subject within their respective spheres to the general authority, than the general authority is subject to them, within its own sphere." *Id.* Under the Constitution, the sphere of the proposed government extended to jurisdiction of "certain enumerated objects only, ... leav[ing] to the several States a residuary and inviolable sovereignty over all other objects." ...

As I view the Court's decision today as rejecting the basic precepts of our federal system and limiting the constitutional role of judicial review, I dissent.

Justice Rehnquist, dissenting.

I join both Justice Powell's and Justice O'Connor's thoughtful dissents. Justice Powell's reference to the "balancing test" approved in *National League of Cities* is not identical with the language in that case, which recognized that Congress could not act under its commerce power to infringe on certain fundamental aspects of state sovereignty that are essential to "the States' separate and independent existence." Nor is either test, or Justice O'Connor's suggested approach, precisely congruent with Justice Blackmun's views in 1976, when he spoke of a balancing approach which did not outlaw federal power in areas "where the federal interest is demonstrably greater." But under any one of these approaches the judgment in these cases should be affirmed, and I do not think it incumbent on those of us in dissent to spell out further the fine points of a principle that will, I am confident, in time again command the support of a majority of this Court.

Justice O'Connor, with whom Justice Powell and Justice Rehnquist join, dissenting....

It has been difficult for this Court to craft bright lines defining the scope of the state autonomy protected by *National League of Cities*. Such difficulty is to be expected whenever constitutional concerns as important as federalism and the effectiveness of the commerce power come into conflict. Regardless of the difficulty, it is and will remain the duty of this Court to reconcile these concerns in the final instance. That the Court shuns the task today by appealing to the "essence of federalism" can provide scant comfort to those who believe our federal system requires something more than a unitary, centralized government. I would not shirk the duty acknowledged by *National League of Cities* and its progeny, and I share Justice Rehnquist's belief that this Court will in time again assume its constitutional responsibility.

Printz v. United States: Background

In 1992, the Court decided *New York v. United States*. The basic facts of the case are as follows. In the early 1980's, Congress confronted the fact that there were insufficient sites for the long-term storage of nuclear waste. In response, Congress enacted the Low-Level Radioactive Waste Policy Amendments of 1985. The statute required a state to enact a law consistent with federal guidelines for the disposal of nuclear waste. States that failed to do so would face consequences. The statute tried to encourage states to form compacts to safely store one another's waste. Creating an in-state site would guarantee states access to out-of-state sites. If a state failed to pass legislation creating an in-state disposal site by a certain deadline, the state was required to take title to and possession of all waste generated within its borders, and it became liable for any damages caused by the state's failure to take possession. The Court recognized that regulation of the interstate market in waste disposal is within Congress' commerce power, but struck the statute nonetheless.

Near the conclusion of the majority opinion Justice O'Connor commented:

> The take title provision appears to be unique. No other federal statute has been cited which offers a state government no option other than that of implementing legislation enacted by Congress. *Whether one views the take title provision as lying outside Congress' enumerated powers, or as infringing upon the core of state sovereignty reserved by the 10th Amendment, the provision is inconsistent with the federal structure of our Government established by the Constitution.*(Emphasis added.)

Was the "affirmative limitation" language of *National League of Cities* (1976) viable after *Garcia* (1985)? Is it viable after *New York*?

As you read *Printz* (1997), list and compare arguments by the dissent and the majority. With reference to historical arguments, start with the dissent and then look at the arguments by the majority. Do the same with other types of arguments, such as textual and structural ones and arguments from precedent. Most of the majority's arguments are attempts to respond to the dissent. You should use the same method for analyzing the decision in *Alden v. Maine* (1999).

Printz v. United States
521 U.S. 898 (1997)

[Majority: Scalia, Rehnquist (C.J.), O'Connor, Kennedy, and Thomas. Concurring: O'Connor and Thomas. Dissenting: Stevens, Souter, Ginsburg and Breyer.]

Justice Scalia delivered the opinion of the Court.

The question presented in these cases is whether certain interim provisions of the Brady Handgun Violence Prevention Act ... commanding state and local law enforcement officers to conduct background checks on prospective handgun purchasers and to perform certain related tasks, violate the Constitution.

[I. The Gun Control Act of 1968 (GCA) established a detailed federal scheme governing the distribution of firearms. In 1993, Congress amended the GCA by enacting the Brady Act, which required mandatory background checks of gun-buyers and the issuance of a permit before delivery of the weapon. While the Act called for the creation of a federal bureaucracy to conduct the checks, it required state law enforcement officers to conduct the checks during the interim period. Petitioners Jay Printz and Richard Mack were two state officers who challenged the statute, saying that forcing them to do the checks at the demand of the federal government violated constitutional principles of state sovereignty.] ...

II. [T]he Brady Act purports to direct state law enforcement officers to participate, albeit only temporarily, in the administration of a federally enacted regulatory scheme....

The petitioners here object to being pressed into federal service, and contend that congressional action compelling state officers to execute federal laws is unconstitutional. Because there is no constitutional text speaking to this precise question, the answer to the CLEOs' challenge must be sought in historical understanding and practice, in the structure of the Constitution, and in the jurisprudence of this Court. We treat those three sources, in that order, in this and the next two sections of this opinion.

Petitioners contend that compelled enlistment of state executive officers for the administration of federal programs is, until very recent years at least, unprecedented. The Government contends, to the contrary, that "the earliest Congresses enacted statutes that required the participation of state officials in the implementation of federal laws," *Brief for United States* 28....

The Government observes that statutes enacted by the first Congresses required state courts to record applications for citizenship, to transmit abstracts of citizenship applications and other naturalization records to the Secretary of State, and to register aliens seeking naturalization and issue certificates of registry. It may well be, however, that these requirements applied only in States that authorized their courts to conduct naturalization proceedings....

These early laws establish, at most, that the Constitution was originally understood to permit imposition of an obligation on state judges to enforce federal prescriptions, insofar as those prescriptions related to matters appropriate for the judicial power. That assumption was perhaps implicit in one of the provisions of the Constitution, and was explicit in another. In accord with the so-called Madisonian Compromise, Article III, § 1, established only a Supreme Court, and made the creation of lower federal courts optional with the Congress—even though it was obvious that the Supreme Court alone could not hear all federal cases throughout the United States. And the Supremacy Clause, Art. VI, cl. 2, announced that "the Laws of the United States ... shall be the supreme Law of the Land; and the Judges in every State shall be bound thereby." It is understandable why courts should have been viewed distinctively in this regard; unlike legislatures and executives, they applied the law of other sovereigns all the time....

To complete the historical record, we must note that there is not only an absence of executive-commandeering statutes in the early Congresses, but there is an absence of them in our later history as well, at least until very recent years. The Government points to the Act of August 3, 1882, ch. 376, which enlisted state officials "to take charge of the local affairs of immigration in the ports within such State, and to provide for the support and relief of such immigrants therein landing as may fall into distress or need of public aid"; to inspect arriving immigrants and exclude any person found to be a "convict, lunatic, idiot," or indigent; and to send convicts back to their country of origin "without compensation." The statute did not, however, *mandate* those duties, but merely empowered the Secretary of the Treasury "to *enter into contracts* with such State ... officers as *may be designated* for that purpose *by the governor* of any State" (emphasis added).

The Government cites the World War I selective draft law that authorized the President "to utilize the service of any or all departments and any or all officers or agents of the United States *and of the several States*, Territories, and the District of Columbia, and subdivisions thereof, in the execution of this Act," and made any person who refused to comply with the President's directions guilty of a misdemeanor (emphasis added). Act of May 18, 1917. However, it is far from clear that the authorization "to utilize the service" of state officers was an authorization to *compel* the service of state officers; and the misdemeanor provision surely applied only to refusal to comply with the President's *authorized* directions, which might not have included directions to officers of States whose governors had not volunteered their services. It is interesting that in implementing the Act President Wilson did not commandeer the services of state officers, but instead requested the assistance of the States' governors.... It is impressive that even with respect to a wartime measure the President should have been so solicitous of state independence.

The Government points to a number of federal statutes enacted within the past few decades that require the participation of state or local officials in implementing federal regulatory schemes. Some of these are connected to federal funding measures, and can perhaps be more accurately described as conditions upon the grant of federal funding than as mandates to the States; others, which require only the provision of information to the Federal Government, do not involve the precise issue before us here, which is the forced participation of the States' executive in the actual administration of a federal program....

III. The constitutional practice we have examined above tends to negate the existence of the congressional power asserted here, but is not conclusive. We turn next to consideration of the structure of the Constitution, to see if we can discern among its "essential postulate[s]," a principle that controls the present cases.

III-A. It is incontestable that the Constitution established a system of "dual sovereignty." *Gregory v. Ashcroft* (1991). Although the States surrendered many of their powers to the new Federal Government, they retained "a residuary and inviolable sovereignty," *The Federalist* No. 39 (J. Madison). This is reflected throughout the Constitution's text, including (to mention only a few examples) the prohibition on any involuntary reduction or combination of a State's territory, Art. IV, §3; the Judicial Power Clause, Art. III, §2, and the Privileges and Immunities Clause, Art. IV, §2, which speak of the "Citizens" of the States; the amendment provision, Article V, which requires the votes of three-fourths of the States to amend the Constitution; and the Guarantee Clause, Art. IV, §4, which "presupposes the continued existence of the states and ... those means and instrumentalities which are the creation of their sovereign and reserved rights," *Helvering v. Gerhardt* (1938). Residual state sovereignty was also implicit, of course, in the Constitution's conferral upon Congress of not all governmental powers, but only discrete, enumerated ones, Art. I, §8, which implication was rendered express by the 10th Amendment's assertion that "[t]he powers not delegated to the United States by the Constitution, nor prohibited by it to the States, are reserved to the States respectively, or to the people."

The Framers' experience under the Articles of Confederation had persuaded them that using the States as the instruments of federal governance was both ineffectual and provocative of federal-state conflict. See *The Federalist* No. 15. Preservation of the States as independent political entities being the price of union ... the Framers rejected the concept of a central government that would act upon and through the States, and instead designed a system in which the state and federal governments would exercise concurrent authority over the people — who were, in Hamilton's words, "the only proper objects of government," *The Federalist* No. 15...."The Framers explicitly chose a Constitution that confers upon Congress the power to regulate individuals, not States." [citing *New York v. United States* (1992)] The great innovation of this design was that "our citizens would have two political capacities, one state and one federal, each protected from incursion by the other"—"a legal system unprecedented in form and design, establishing two orders of government, each with its own direct relationship, its own privity, its own set of mutual rights and obligations to the people who sustain it and are governed by it." *U.S. Term Limits, Inc. v. Thornton* (1995) (Kennedy, J., concurring). The Constitution thus contemplates that a State's government will represent and remain accountable to its own citizens....

This separation of the two spheres is one of the Constitution's structural protections of liberty. "Just as the separation and independence of the coordinate branches of the Federal Government serve to prevent the accumulation of excessive power in any one branch, a healthy balance of power between the States and the Federal Government will reduce the risk of tyranny and abuse from either front." *Gregory*....

The power of the Federal Government would be augmented immeasurably if it were able to impress into its service—and at no cost to itself—the police officers of the 50 States.

III-B. We have thus far discussed the effect that federal control of state officers would have upon the first element of the "double security" alluded to by Madison: the division of power between State and Federal Governments. It would also have an effect upon the second element: the separation and equilibration of powers between the three branches of the Federal Government itself. The Constitution does not leave to speculation who is to administer the laws enacted by Congress; the President, it says, "shall take Care that the Laws be faithfully executed," Art. II, §3, personally and through officers whom he appoints (save for such inferior officers as Congress may authorize to be appointed by the "Courts of Law" or by "the Heads of Departments" who are themselves presidential appointees), Art. II, §2. The Brady Act effectively transfers this responsibility to thousands of CLEOs in the 50 States, who are left to implement the program without meaningful Presidential control (if indeed meaningful Presidential control is possible without the power to appoint and remove). The insistence of the Framers upon unity in the Federal Executive—to insure both vigor and accountability—is well known. That unity would be shattered, and the power of the President would be subject to reduction, if Congress could act as effectively without the President as with him, by simply requiring state officers to execute its laws.

III-C. The dissent of course resorts to the last, best hope of those who defend ultra vires congressional action, the Necessary and Proper Clause.... What destroys the dissent's Necessary and Proper Clause argument, however, is ... the Necessary and Proper Clause itself.... We in fact answered the dissent's Necessary and Proper Clause argument in *New York*: "[E]ven where Congress has the authority under the Constitution to pass laws requiring or prohibiting certain acts, it lacks the power directly to compel the States to require or prohibit those acts.... [T]he Commerce Clause, for example, authorizes Congress to regulate interstate commerce directly; it does not authorize Congress to regulate state governments' regulation of interstate commerce." *New York v. United States*....

IV. Finally, and most conclusively in the present litigation, we turn to the prior jurisprudence of this Court. Federal commandeering of state governments is such a novel phenomenon that this Court's first experience with it did not occur until the 1970's, when the Environmental Protection Agency promulgated regulations requiring States to prescribe auto emissions testing, monitoring and retrofit programs, and to designate preferential bus and carpool lanes....

[L]ater opinions of ours have made clear that the Federal Government may not compel the States to implement, by legislation or executive action, federal regulatory programs. In *Hodel v. Virginia Surface Mining & Reclamation Assn., Inc.* (1981) and *FERC v. Mississippi* (1982), we sustained statutes against constitutional challenge only after assuring ourselves that they did not require the States to enforce federal law. In *Hodel* we ... concluded that the Surface Mining Control and Reclamation Act ... merely made compliance with federal standards a precondition to continued state regulation in an otherwise pre-empted. *Hodel*. In *FERC*, we construed.... the Public Utility Regulatory Policies Act of 1978, to contain only the "command" that state agencies "consider" federal standards, and again only as a precondition to continued state regulation of an otherwise pre-empted field. We warned that "this Court never has sanctioned explicitly a federal command to the States to promulgate and enforce laws and regulations."

When we were at last confronted squarely with a federal statute that unambiguously required the States to enact or administer a federal regulatory program, our decision should have come as no surprise. At issue in *New York v. United States* (1992) were the so-called "take title" provisions of the Low-Level Radioactive Waste Policy Amendments Act of 1985, which required States either to enact legislation providing for the disposal of radioactive waste generated within their borders, or to take title to, and possession of the waste—effectively requiring the States either to legislate pursuant to Congress's directions, or to implement an administrative solution. We concluded that Congress could constitutionally require the States to do neither. "The Federal Government," we held, "may not compel the States to enact or administer a federal regulatory program."

The Government contends that *New York* is distinguishable on the following ground: unlike the "take title" provisions invalidated there, the background-check provision of the Brady Act does not require state legislative or executive officials to make policy, but instead issues a final directive to state CLEOs. It is permissible, the Government asserts, for Congress to command state or local officials to assist in the implementation of federal law so long as "Congress itself devises a clear legislative solution that regulates private conduct" and requires state or local officers to provide only "limited, non-policymaking help in enforcing that law." "[T]he constitutional line is crossed only when Congress compels the States to make law in their sovereign capacities." *Brief for United States* 16.

The Government's distinction between "making" law and merely "enforcing" it, between "policymaking" and mere "implementation," is an interesting one. It is perhaps not meant to be the same as, but it is surely reminiscent of, the line that separates proper congressional conferral of Executive power from unconstitutional delegation of legislative authority for federal separation-of-powers purposes. This Court has not been notably successful in describing the latter line; indeed, some think we have abandoned the effort to do so. We are doubtful that the new line the Government proposes would be any more distinct. Executive action that has utterly no policymaking component is rare, particularly at an executive level as high as a jurisdiction's chief law-enforcement officer. Is it really true that there is no policymaking involved in deciding, for example, what "reasonable efforts" shall be expended to conduct a background check? ... Is [a] decision whether to devote maximum "reasonable efforts" or minimum "reasonable efforts" not preeminently a matter of policy? It is quite impossible, in short, to draw the Government's proposed line at "no policymaking," and we would have to fall back upon a line of "not too much policymaking." How much is too much is not likely to be answered precisely; and an imprecise barrier against federal intrusion upon state authority is not likely to be an effective one.

Even assuming, moreover, that the Brady Act leaves no "policymaking" discretion with the States, we fail to see how that improves rather than worsens the intrusion upon state sovereignty. Preservation of the States as independent and autonomous political entities is arguably less undermined by requiring them to make policy in certain fields than ... by "reduc[ing] [them] to puppets of a ventriloquist Congress," *Brown v. EPA* (1975). It is an essential attribute of the States' retained sovereignty that they remain independent and autonomous within their proper sphere of authority. It is no more compatible with this independence and autonomy that their officers be "dragooned" (as Judge Fernandez put it in his dissent below) into administering federal law, than it would be compatible with the independence and autonomy of the United States that its officers be impressed into service for the execution of state laws....

The Government also maintains that requiring state officers to perform discrete, ministerial tasks specified by Congress does not violate the principle of *New York* because it does not diminish the accountability of state or federal officials. This argument fails even on its own terms. By forcing state governments to absorb the financial burden of implementing a federal regulatory program, Members of Congress can take credit for "solving" problems without having to ask their constituents to pay for the solutions with higher federal taxes. And even when the States are not forced to absorb the costs of implementing a federal program, they are still put in the position of taking the blame for its burdensomeness and for its defects. Under the present law, for example, it will be the CLEO and not some federal official who stands between the gun purchaser and immediate possession of his gun. And it will likely be the CLEO, not some federal official, who will be blamed for any error (even one in the designated federal database) that causes a purchaser to be mistakenly rejected....

Finally, the Government puts forward a cluster of arguments that can be grouped under the heading: "The Brady Act serves very important purposes, is most efficiently administered by CLEOs during the interim period, and places a minimal and only temporary burden upon state officers." ... Assuming all the mentioned factors were true, they might be relevant if we were evaluating whether the incidental application to the States of a federal law of general applicability excessively interfered with the functioning of state governments. But where, as here, it is the whole *object* of the law to direct the functioning of the state executive, and hence to compromise the structural framework of dual sovereignty, such a "balancing" analysis is inappropriate. It is the very *principle* of separate state sovereignty that such a law offends, and no comparative assessment of the various interests can overcome that fundamental defect....

V.... We held in *New York* that Congress cannot compel the States to enact or enforce a federal regulatory program. Today we hold that Congress cannot circumvent that prohibition by conscripting the State's officers directly. The Federal Government may neither issue directives requiring the States to address particular problems, nor command the States' officers, or those of their political subdivisions, to administer or enforce a federal regulatory program. It matters not whether policymaking is involved, and no case-by-case weighing of the burdens or benefits is necessary; such commands are fundamentally incompatible with our constitutional system of dual sovereignty. Accordingly, the judgment of the Court of Appeals for the Ninth Circuit is reversed.

It is so ordered.

Justice O'Connor, concurring.

Our precedent and our Nation's historical practices support the Court's holding today. The Brady Act violates the 10th Amendment to the extent it forces States and local law enforcement officers to perform background checks on prospective handgun owners and to accept Brady Forms from firearms dealers. Our holding, of course, does not spell the end of the objectives of the Brady Act.... Congress is ... free to amend the interim program to provide for its continuance on a contractual basis with the States if it wishes, as it does with a number of other federal programs.

In addition, the Court appropriately refrains from deciding whether other purely ministerial reporting requirements imposed by Congress on state and local authorities pursuant to its Commerce Clause powers are similarly invalid. See, e.g., 42 U.S.C. § 5779(a) (requiring state and local law enforcement agencies to report cases of missing children to the Department of Justice). The provisions invalidated here, however, which directly compel state officials to administer a federal regulatory program, utterly fail to adhere to the design and structure of our constitutional scheme.

Justice Thomas, concurring. [Omitted].

Justice Stevens, with whom Justice Souter, Justice Ginsburg, and Justice Breyer join, dissenting.

When Congress exercises the powers delegated to it by the Constitution, it may impose affirmative obligations on executive and judicial officers of state and local governments as well as ordinary citizens. This conclusion is firmly supported by the text of the Constitution, the early history of the Nation, decisions of this Court, and a correct understanding of the basic structure of the Federal Government.

These cases do not implicate the more difficult questions associated with congressional coercion of state legislatures addressed in *New York v. United States* (1992). Nor need we consider the wisdom of relying on local officials rather than federal agents to carry out aspects of a federal program ... The question is whether Congress, acting on behalf of the people of the entire Nation, may require local law enforcement officers to perform certain duties during the interim needed for the development of a federal gun control program. It is remarkably similar to the question, heavily debated by the Framers of the Constitution, whether the Congress could require state agents to collect federal taxes. Or the question whether Congress could impress state judges into federal service to entertain and decide cases that they would prefer to ignore.

Indeed, since the ultimate issue is one of power, we must consider its implications in times of national emergency. Matters such as the enlistment of air raid wardens, the administration of a military draft, the mass inoculation of children to forestall an epidemic, or perhaps the threat of an international terrorist, may require a national response before federal personnel can be made available to respond. If the Constitution empowers Congress and the President to make an appropriate response, is there anything in the 10th Amendment, "in historical understanding and practice, in the structure of the Constitution, [or] in the jurisprudence of this Court," that forbids the enlistment of state officers to make that response effective? More narrowly, what basis is there in any of those sources for concluding that it is the Members of this Court, rather than the elected representatives of the people, who should determine whether the Constitution contains the unwritten rule that the Court announces today?

Perhaps today's majority would suggest that no such emergency is presented by the facts of these cases. But such a suggestion is itself an expression of a policy judgment. And Congress' view of the matter is quite different from that implied by the Court today.

The Brady Act was passed in response to what Congress described as an "epidemic of gun violence." The Act's legislative history notes that 15,377 Americans were murdered with firearms in 1992, and that 12,489 of these deaths were caused by handguns. Congress expressed special concern that "[t]he level of firearm violence in this country is, by far, the highest among developed nations." The partial solution contained in the Brady Act, a mandatory background check before a handgun may be purchased, has met with remarkable success. Between 1994 and 1996, approximately 6,600 firearm sales each month to potentially dangerous persons were prevented by Brady Act checks; over 70% of the rejected purchasers were convicted or indicted felons. Whether or not the evaluation reflected in the enactment of the Brady Act is correct as to the extent of the danger and the efficacy of the legislation, the congressional decision surely warrants more respect than it is accorded in today's unprecedented decision.

I. The text of the Constitution provides a sufficient basis for a correct disposition of this case.

Article I, §8, grants the Congress the power to regulate commerce among the States. Putting to one side the revisionist views expressed by Justice Thomas in his concurring opinion in *United States v. Lopez* (1995), there can be no question that that provision adequately supports the regulation of commerce in handguns effected by the Brady Act. Moreover, the additional grant of authority in that section of the Constitution "[t]o make all Laws which shall be necessary and proper for carrying into Execution the foregoing Powers" is surely adequate to support the temporary enlistment of local police officers in the process of identifying persons who should not be entrusted with the possession of handguns.... Unlike the 1st Amendment, which prohibits the enactment of a category of laws that would otherwise be authorized by Article I, the 10th Amendment imposes no restriction on the exercise of delegated powers....

II. Under the Articles of Confederation the National Government had the power to issue commands to the several sovereign states, but it had no authority to govern individuals directly....

That method of governing proved to be unacceptable, not because it demeaned the sovereign character of the several States, but rather because it was cumbersome and inefficient.... The basic change in the character of the government that the Framers conceived was designed to enhance the power of the national government, not to provide some new, unmentioned immunity for state officers. Because indirect control over individual citizens ("the only proper objects of government") was ineffective under the Articles of Confederation, Alexander Hamilton explained that "we must *extend* the authority of the Union to the persons of the citizens." *The Federalist* No. 15 (emphasis added).

Indeed, the historical materials strongly suggest that the Founders intended to enhance the capacity of the federal government by empowering it—as a part of the new authority to make demands directly on individual citizens—to act through local officials....

More specifically, during the debates concerning the ratification of the Constitution, it was assumed that state agents would act as tax collectors for the federal government....

The Court's response to this powerful historical evidence is weak. The majority suggests that "none of these statements necessarily implies ... Congress could impose these responsibilities without the consent of the States." No fair reading of these materials can justify such an interpretation. As Hamilton explained, the power of the government to act on "individual citizens"—including "employ[ing] the ordinary magistracy" of the States—was an answer to the problems faced by a central government that could act only directly "upon the States in their political or collective capacities." *The Federalist* No. 27. The new Constitution would avoid this problem, resulting in "a regular and peaceable execution of the law of the Union."

This point is made especially clear in Hamilton's statement that "the legislatures, courts, and magistrates, of the respective members, will be incorporated into the operations of the national government *as far as its just and constitutional authority extends*; and *will be rendered auxiliary to the enforcement of its laws*" (second emphasis added)....

[The Court's] position, if correct, would undermine most of our post-New Deal Commerce Clause jurisprudence. As Justice O'Connor quite properly noted in *New York*, "[t]he Federal Government undertakes activities today that would have been unimaginable to the Framers."

More importantly, the fact that Congress did elect to rely on state judges and the clerks of state courts to perform a variety of executive functions, is surely evidence of a contemporary understanding that their status as state officials did not immunize them from federal service. The majority's description of these early statutes is both incomplete and at times misleading....

The Court's evaluation of the historical evidence, furthermore, fails to acknowledge the important difference between policy decisions that may have been influenced by respect for state sovereignty concerns, and decisions that are compelled by the Constitution. Thus, for example, the decision by Congress to give President Wilson the authority to utilize the services of state officers in implementing the World War I draft, see Act of May 18, 1917, surely indicates that the national legislature saw no constitutional impediment to the enlistment of state assistance during a federal emergency. The fact that the President was able to implement the program by respectfully "request[ing]" state action, rather than bluntly commanding it, is evidence that he was an effective statesman, but surely does not indicate that he doubted either his or Congress' power to use mandatory language if necessary....

III. The Court's "structural" arguments are not sufficient to rebut that presumption. The fact that the Framers intended to preserve the sovereignty of the several States simply does not speak to the question whether individual state employees may be required to perform federal obligations, such as registering young adults for the draft, creating state emergency response commissions designed to manage the release of hazardous substances, collecting and reporting data on underground storage tanks that may pose an environmental hazard, and reporting traffic fatalities, and missing children, to a federal agency....

Given the fact that the Members of Congress are elected by the people of the several States, with each State receiving an equivalent number of Senators in order to ensure that even the smallest States have a powerful voice in the legislature, it is quite unrealistic to assume that they will ignore the sovereignty concerns of their constituents. It is far more reasonable to presume that their decisions to impose modest burdens on state officials from time to time reflect a considered judgment that the people in each of the States will benefit therefrom.

Indeed, the presumption of validity that supports all congressional enactments has added force with respect to policy judgments concerning the impact of a federal statute upon the respective States....

Perversely, the majority's rule seems more likely to damage than to preserve the safeguards against tyranny provided by the existence of vital state governments. By limiting the ability of the Federal Government to enlist state officials in the implementation of its programs, the Court creates incentives for the National Government to aggrandize itself. In the name of State's rights, the majority would have the Federal Government create vast national bureaucracies to implement its policies....

Nor is there force to the assumption undergirding the Court's entire opinion that if this trivial burden on state sovereignty is permissible, the entire structure of federalism will soon collapse. These cases do not involve any mandate to state legislatures to enact new rules. When legislative action, or even administrative rule making, is at issue, it may be appropriate for Congress either to pre-empt the State's lawmaking power and fashion the federal rule itself, or to respect the State's power to fashion its own rules. But this case, unlike any precedent in which the Court has held that Congress exceeded its powers, merely involves the imposition of modest duties on individual officers....

Far more important than the concerns that the Court musters in support of its new rule is the fact that the Framers entrusted Congress with the task of creating a working structure of intergovernmental relationships around the framework that the Constitution authorized. Neither explicitly nor implicitly did the Framers issue any command that forbids Congress from imposing federal duties on private citizens or on local officials. As a general matter, Congress has followed the sound policy of authorizing federal agencies and federal agents to administer federal programs. That general practice, however, does not negate the existence of power to rely on state officials in occasional situations in which such reliance is in the national interest....

IV. Finally, the Court advises us that the "prior jurisprudence of this Court" is the most conclusive support for its position. That "prior jurisprudence" is *New York v. United States*. The case involved the validity of a federal statute that provided the States with three types of incentives to encourage them to dispose of radioactive wastes generated within their borders. The Court held that the first two sets of incentives were authorized by affirmative grants of power to Congress, and therefore "not inconsistent with the 10th Amendment." That holding, of course, sheds no doubt on the validity of the Brady Act.

The third so-called "incentive" gave the States the option either of adopting regulations dictated by Congress or of taking title to and possession of the low level radioactive waste. The Court concluded that, because Congress had no power to compel the state governments to take title to the waste, the "option" really amounted to a simple command to the States to enact and enforce a federal regulatory program....

Our statements, taken in context, clearly did not decide the question presented here, whether state executive officials—as opposed to state legislators—may in appropriate circumstances be enlisted to implement federal policy. The "take title" provision at issue in *New York* was beyond Congress' authority to enact because it was "in principle ... no different than a congressionally compelled subsidy from state governments to radioactive waste producers," almost certainly a legislative act....

Finally, the majority provides an incomplete explanation of our decision in *Testa v. Katt* (1947), and demeans its importance. In that case the Court unanimously held that state courts of appropriate jurisdiction must occupy themselves adjudicating claims brought by private litigants under the federal Emergency Price Control Act of 1942, regardless of how otherwise crowded their dockets might be with state law matters. That is a much greater imposition on state sovereignty than the Court's characterization of the case as merely holding that "state courts cannot refuse to apply federal law." That characterization describes only the narrower duty to apply federal law in cases that the state courts have consented to entertain.

The language drawn from the Supremacy Clause upon which the majority relies ("the Judges in every State shall be bound [by federal law], any Thing in the Constitution or Laws of any state to the Contrary notwithstanding"), expressly embraces that narrower conflict of laws principle. Art. VI, cl. 2. But the Supremacy Clause means far more. As *Testa* held, because the "Laws of the United States ... [are] the supreme Law of the Land," state courts of appropriate jurisdiction must hear federal claims whenever a federal statute, such as the Emergency Price Control Act, requires them to do so.

Hence, the Court's textual argument is quite misguided. The majority focuses on the Clause's specific attention to the point that "Judges in every State shall be bound." That language commands state judges to "apply federal law" in cases that they entertain, but it is not the source of their duty to accept jurisdiction of federal claims that they would prefer to ignore. Our opinions in *Testa*, and earlier the Second Employers' Liability Cases, rested generally on the language of the Supremacy Clause, without any specific focus on the reference to judges....

Even if the Court were correct in its suggestion that it was the reference to judges in the Supremacy Clause, rather than the central message of the entire Clause, that dictated the result in *Testa*, the Court's implied *expressio unius* argument that the Framers therefore did *not* intend to permit the enlistment of other state officials is implausible. Throughout our history judges, state as well as federal, have merited as much respect as executive agents. The notion that the Framers would have had no reluctance to "press state judges into federal service" against their will but would have regarded the imposition of a similar—indeed, far lesser—burden on town constables as an intolerable affront to principles of state sovereignty, can only be considered perverse. If such a distinction had been contemplated by the learned and articulate men who fashioned the basic structure of our government, surely some of them would have said so.

The provision of the Brady Act that crosses the Court's newly defined constitutional threshold is more comparable to a statute requiring local police officers to report the identity of missing children to the Crime Control Center of the Department of Justice than to an offensive federal command to a sovereign state. If Congress believes that such a statute will benefit the people of the Nation, and serve the interests of cooperative federalism better than an enlarged federal bureaucracy, we should respect both its policy judgment and its appraisal of its constitutional power.

Accordingly, I respectfully dissent.

Justice Souter, dissenting. [Omitted].

Justice Breyer, with whom Justice Stevens joins, dissenting. [Omitted].

* * *

Justice Thomas also included an interesting reference to the 2nd Amendment in his concurrence:

> Even if we construe Congress' authority to regulate interstate commerce to encompass those intrastate transactions that "substantially affect" interstate commerce, I question whether Congress can regulate the particular transactions at issue here. The Constitution, in addition to delegating certain enumerated powers to Congress, places whole areas outside the reach of Congress' regulatory authority. The 1st Amendment, for example, is fittingly celebrated for preventing Congress from "prohibiting the free exercise" of religion or "abridging the freedom of speech." The 2nd Amendment similarly appears to contain an express limitation on the government's authority. That Amendment provides: "[a] well regulated Militia, being necessary to the security of a free State, the right of the people to keep and bear arms, shall not be infringed." This Court has not had recent occasion to consider the nature of the substantive right safeguarded by the 2nd Amendment.[2] If, however, the 2nd Amendment is read to confer a personal right to "keep and bear arms," a colorable argument exists that the Federal Government's regulatory scheme, at least as it pertains to the purely intrastate sale or possession of firearms, runs afoul of that Amendment's protections.[3] As the

---

2. Our most recent treatment of the 2nd Amendment occurred in *United States v. Miller*, 307 U.S. 174 (1939), in which we reversed the District Court's invalidation of the National Firearms Act, enacted in 1934. In *Miller*, we determined that the 2nd Amendment did not guarantee a citizen's right to possess a sawed-off shotgun because that weapon had not been shown to be "ordinary military equipment" that could "contribute to the common defense." The Court did not, however, attempt to define, or otherwise construe, the substantive right protected by the 2nd Amendment.

3. Marshaling an impressive array of historical evidence, a growing body of scholarly commentary indicates that the "right to keep and bear arms" is, as the Amendment's text suggests, a personal

parties did not raise this argument, however, we need not consider it here. Perhaps, at some future date, this Court will have the opportunity to determine whether Justice Story was correct when he wrote that the right to bear arms "has justly been considered, as the palladium of the liberties of a republic." 3 J. Story, *Commentaries* § 1890, p. 746 (1833).

II. National Power and State Power: State Sovereign Immunity

Goals for your study of this material

1. To understand the meaning of the 11th Amendment and competing understandings of the current Supreme Court as to its scope and application.
2. To understand the interplay between the 10th and 11th Amendments.
3. To understand the rule of *Alden v. Maine* and how that case deals with the doctrine of sovereign immunity as a limit on federal power.

Alden v. Maine: Background

After the Revolution, the newly independent states incorporated English common law into their domestic law. Many also claimed the right of sovereign immunity that was enjoyed by the crown in England. This rule gave a state immunity from suits by private plaintiffs in state court. Article III of the Constitution extended federal court jurisdiction to cases "between a state and citizens of another state." The text did not address the question of whether federal jurisdiction over states as defendants existed only if the state had waived its sovereign immunity and thereby consented to the suit.

In *Chisholm v. Georgia* (1793), the Court allowed a citizen of South Carolina to make a claim against the state of Georgia for restitution of Tory lands that had been confiscated during the Revolution. The 11th Amendment was quickly passed in a direct attempt to supersede *Chisholm*. The 11th Amendment provides that:

> The judicial power of the United States shall not be construed to extend to any suit in law or equity, commenced or prosecuted against one of the United States by citizens of another state, or by citizens or subjects of any foreign state.

In *Hans v. Louisiana* (1890), the Court held that, despite the literal language of the Amendment that limited federal jurisdiction only to suits brought by "citizens of another state," citizens were also prohibited from suing their *own* state in federal court.

While the 11th Amendment operated to keep cases against states based on diversity jurisdiction out of federal court, it had not been a major impediment to the enforcement of federal rights against states. In large measure this had occurred due to a "fiction" that the Court adopted in *Ex parte Young* (1908). There, the Court made a distinction be-

---

right.... Other scholars, however, argue that the 2nd Amendment does not secure a personal right to keep or to bear arms.... Although somewhat overlooked in our jurisprudence, the Amendment has certainly engendered considerable academic, as well as public, debate.

tween a suit against the state itself and a suit against an official of a state. In *Ex parte Young*, the Court allowed a suit for declaratory and injunctive relief to be filed in federal court against a state attorney general who was attempting to enforce a statute that was alleged to be unconstitutional. It should be noted that the Court has subsequently permitted suits against state officials only for declaratory and injunctive relief and not for claims for money damages. But state officials sued in their individual capacity—as opposed to their official capacity—may be required to pay money damages for violation of federal rights. See, e.g., 42 U.S.C. § 1983.

Another limitation on the scope of the 11th Amendment is that it can be overridden by legislation Congress enacts pursuant to its enforcement powers under § 5 of the 14th Amendment if Congress clearly indicates its intent to do so. The Court has held that the 14th Amendment can override a state's 11th Amendment immunity from suit because the drafters and ratifiers of the 14th Amendment intended it to dramatically curtail state privileges.

In 1989, the Court ruled in a 4-1-4 plurality opinion that Congress could also abrogate a state's 11th Amendment immunity when exercising its power under the Commerce Clause. In *Pennsylvania v. Union Gas Co.* (1989), the Court held that Congress could use its commerce power to create a federal statutory cause of action for an individual against a state that could be tried in federal court. Justice Brennan made a structural argument that the power to regulate interstate commerce would be incomplete without the authority to render States liable in damages. Justice Brennan's opinion was joined by Justices Marshall, Blackmun, and Stevens. Justice White concurred in the judgment only. Justice Scalia's dissent was joined by Justices Rehnquist, O'Connor, and Kennedy.

By 1996, Justice Souter had replaced Justice Brennan, Justice Thomas had replaced Justice Marshall, Justice Ginsburg had replaced Justice White, and Justice Breyer had replaced Justice Blackmun. That year, the Court—in a 5–4 opinion—overruled *Union Gas*. In *Seminole Tribe of Florida v. Florida* (1996), the Court held that Congress, acting pursuant to its powers under the Commerce Clause, could *not* abrogate a state's 11th Amendment immunity against suit in federal court. Justice Thomas—as he did in *Lopez* and *Printz*—joined the *Union Gas* dissenters to provide the decisive fifth vote. This controversial opinion greatly expanded the scope of the 11th Amendment.

The Court's decision in *Seminole Tribe* did not disturb Congress' power to provide a cause of action against a state in federal court pursuant to its power under § 5 of the 14th Amendment. But, as we will see in Chapter 13, *infra*, in recent years, the Court has narrowed Congress's power to legislate pursuant to § 5 of the 14th Amendment, thereby expanding the protection to states from suit afforded by the 11th Amendment. In fact, on at least three occasions since 1999, the Court has struck down congressional legislation justified on § 5 grounds that allowed suits to proceed against state governments. *Florida Prepaid Postsecondary Education Expense Board v. College Savings Bank* (1999); *Kimel v. Florida Board of Regents* (2000); and *University of Alabama v. Garrett* (2001). In each of these cases, the Court found that Congress had exceeded its § 5 power; the statutes in question were still constitutional, but only pursuant to Congress's Commerce Clause power or, in the case of *College Savings Bank*, Congress's Commerce Clause and Patent Clause powers. Consequently, those portions of the statutes in question that applied to the states were barred by the 11th Amendment.

In 1999, the Court expanded on the *Seminole Tribe* rule and held that Congress could not rely on its Article I, § 8 powers to provide a federal statutory cause of action against a state even in *state* court. In *Alden v. Maine* (1999), the Court—with the same 5–4 split that occurred in *Seminole Tribe of Florida*—held that state sovereign immunity prohibited any Article I federal legislation providing an individual with a cause of action against a state. Statutes passed pursuant to the 14th Amendment are not covered by this rule. In so holding, the majority ruled that the states were protected, not by the force of the 11th Amendment, but by a historical commitment of the Framers to state sovereignty. The dissent contends that this argument represents judicial activism at its worst.

As you read the opinion, consider both the majority's and the dissent's arguments from text, structure, and history. Which opinion represents better constitutional law, as opposed to which opinion represents better public policy?

Alden v. Maine
527 U.S. 706 (1999)

[Majority: Kennedy, Rehnquist (C.J.), O'Conner, Scalia, and Thomas. Dissenting: Souter, Stevens, Ginsburg, and Breyer.]

Justice Kennedy delivered the opinion of the Court.

In 1992, petitioners, a group of probation officers, filed suit against their employer, the State of Maine, in the United States District Court for the District of Maine. The officers alleged the State had violated the overtime provisions of the Fair Labor Standards Act of 1938 (FLSA), 29 U.S.C. §201 et seq., and sought compensation and liquidated damages. While the suit was pending, this Court decided *Seminole Tribe of Fla. v. Florida* (1996), which made it clear that Congress lacks power under Article I to abrogate the States' sovereign immunity from suits commenced or prosecuted in the federal courts. Upon consideration of *Seminole Tribe*, the District Court dismissed petitioners' action, and the Court of Appeals affirmed. Petitioners then filed the same action in state court. The state trial court dismissed the suit on the basis of sovereign immunity, and the Maine Supreme Judicial Court affirmed....

We hold that the powers delegated to Congress under Article I of the United States Constitution do not include the power to subject nonconsenting States to private suits for damages in state courts ... we affirm the judgment sustaining dismissal of the suit.

I. The 11th Amendment makes explicit reference to the States' immunity from suits "commenced or prosecuted against one of the United States by Citizens of another State, or by Citizens or Subjects of any Foreign State." We have, as a result, sometimes referred to the States' immunity from suit as "11th Amendment immunity." The phrase is convenient shorthand but something of a misnomer, for the sovereign immunity of the States neither derives from nor is limited by the terms of the 11th Amendment. Rather, as the Constitution's structure, and its history, and the authoritative interpretations by this Court make clear, the States' immunity from suit is a fundamental aspect of the sovereignty which the States enjoyed before the ratification of the Constitution, and which they retain today (either literally or by virtue of their admission into the Union upon an equal footing with the other States) except as altered by the plan of the Convention or certain constitutional Amendments.

I-A. Although the Constitution establishes a National Government with broad, often plenary authority over matters within its recognized competence, the founding document "specifically recognizes the States as sovereign entities." *Seminole Tribe of Fla. v. Florida*. Various textual provisions of the Constitution assume the States' continued existence and active participation in the fundamental processes of governance. See *Printz v. United States* (1997) (citing Art. III, §2; Art. IV, §§2–4; Art. V). The limited and enumerated powers granted to the Legislative, Executive, and Judicial Branches of the National Government, moreover, underscore the vital role reserved to the States by the constitutional design, see, e.g., Art. I, §8; Art. II, §§2–3; Art. III, §2. Any doubt regarding the constitutional role of the States as sovereign entities is removed by the 10th Amendment, which, like the other provisions of the Bill of Rights, was enacted to allay lingering concerns about the extent of the national power....

I-B. The generation that designed and adopted our federal system considered immunity from private suits central to sovereign dignity. When the Constitution was ratified, it was well established in English law that the Crown could not be sued without consent in its own courts....

Although the American people had rejected other aspects of English political theory, the doctrine that a sovereign could not be sued without its consent was universal in the States when the Constitution was drafted and ratified....

The ratification debates, furthermore, underscored the importance of the States' sovereign immunity to the American people. Grave concerns were raised by the provisions of Article III which extended the federal judicial power to controversies between States and citizens of other States or foreign nations....

The leading advocates of the Constitution assured the people in no uncertain terms that the Constitution would not strip the States of sovereign immunity. One assurance was contained in *The Federalist* No. 81, written by Alexander Hamilton:

> It is inherent in the nature of sovereignty not to be amenable to the suit of an individual without its consent. This is the general sense, and the general practice of mankind; and the exemption, as one of the attributes of sovereignty, is now enjoyed by the government of every State in the Union. Unless therefore, there is a surrender of this immunity in the plan of the convention, it will remain with the States....

Despite the persuasive assurances of the Constitution's leading advocates and the expressed understanding of the only state conventions to address the issue in explicit terms [that immunity could survive], this Court held, just five years after the Constitution was adopted, that Article III authorized a private citizen of another State to sue the State of Georgia without its consent. *Chisholm v. Georgia* (1793)....

The text and history of the 11th Amendment also suggest that Congress acted not to change but to restore the original constitutional design. Although earlier drafts of the Amendment had been phrased as express limits on the judicial power granted in Article III, see, e.g., 3 *Annals of Congress* 651–52 (1793) ("The Judicial Power of the United States shall not extend to any suits in law or equity, commenced or prosecuted against one of the United States...."), the adopted text [of the 11th Amendment] addressed the proper interpretation of [Article III], see U.S. Const., Amdt. 11 ("The Judicial Power of the United States shall not be construed to extend to any suit in law or equity, commenced or prosecuted against one of the United States...."). By its terms, then, the 11th Amendment did not redefine the federal judicial power but instead overruled [*Chisholm*]....

[The] Constitution was understood, in light of its history and structure, to preserve the States' traditional immunity from private suits. As the Amendment clarified the only provisions of the Constitution that anyone had suggested might support a contrary understanding, there was no reason to draft with a broader brush.

Finally, the swiftness and near unanimity with which the 11th Amendment was adopted suggest "either that the Court had not captured the original understanding, or that the country had changed its collective mind most rapidly." D. Currie, *The Constitution in the Supreme Court: The First Century* 18, n. 101 (1985). The more reasonable interpretation, of course, is that regardless of the views of four Justices in *Chisholm*, the country as a whole—which had adopted the Constitution just five years earlier—had not understood the document to strip the States' of their immunity from private suits. Cf. Currie, *The Constitution in Congress*, at 196 ("It is plain that just about everybody in Congress agreed the Supreme Court had misread the Constitution").

Although the dissent attempts to rewrite history to reflect a different original understanding, its evidence is unpersuasive. The handful of state statutory and constitutional provisions authorizing suits or petitions of right against States only confirms the prevalence of the traditional understanding that a State could not be sued in the absence of an express waiver, for if the understanding were otherwise, the provisions would have been unnecessary....

The dissent's remaining evidence cannot bear the weight the dissent seeks to place on it. The views voiced during the ratification debates by Edmund Randolph and James Wilson, when reiterated by the same individuals in their respective capacities as advocate and Justice in *Chisholm*, were decisively rejected by the 11th Amendment....

In short, the scanty and equivocal evidence offered by the dissent establishes no more than what is evident from the decision in *Chisholm*—that some members of the founding generation disagreed with Hamilton, Madison, Marshall, Iredell, and the only state conventions formally to address the matter. The events leading to the adoption of the 11th Amendment, however, make clear that the individuals who believed the Constitution stripped the States of their immunity from suit were at most a small minority....

I-C. The Court has been consistent in interpreting the adoption of the 11th Amendment as conclusive evidence "that the decision in *Chisholm* was contrary to the well-understood meaning of the Constitution," *Seminole Tribe*, and that the views expressed by Hamilton, Madison, and Marshall during the ratification debates, and by Justice Iredell in his dissenting opinion in *Chisholm*, reflect the original understanding of the Constitution....

Following this approach, the Court has upheld States' assertions of sovereign immunity in various contexts falling outside the literal text of the 11th Amendment. In *Hans v. Louisiana*, the Court held that sovereign immunity barred a citizen from suing his own State under the federal-question head of jurisdiction. The Court was unmoved by the petitioner's argument that the 11th Amendment, by its terms, applied only to suits brought by citizens of other States.... Later decisions rejected similar requests to limit the principle of sovereign immunity to the strict language of the 11th Amendment. These cases held that nonconsenting States are immune from suits brought by federal corporations, *Smith v. Reeves* (1900), foreign nations, *Principality of Monaco* (1934), or Indian tribes, *Blatchford v. Native Village of Noatak* (1991), and concluded that sovereign immunity is a defense to suits in admiralty, though the text of the 11th Amendment addresses only suits "in law or equity," *Ex parte New York* (1921).

These holdings reflect a settled doctrinal understanding, consistent with the views of the leading advocates of the Constitution's ratification, that sovereign immunity derives not from the 11th Amendment but from the structure of the original Constitution itself....

II. In this case we must determine whether Congress has the power, under Article I, to subject non-consenting States to private suits in their own courts. As the foregoing discussion makes clear, the fact that the 11th Amendment by its terms limits only "[t]he

Judicial power of the United States" does not resolve the question. To rest on the words of the Amendment alone would be to engage in the type of ahistorical literalism we have rejected in interpreting the scope of the States' sovereign immunity since the discredited decision in *Chisholm*....

II-A. Petitioners contend the text of the Constitution and our recent sovereign immunity decisions establish that the States were required to relinquish this portion of their sovereignty. We turn first to these sources.

II-A-1. Article I, §8 grants Congress broad power to enact legislation in several enumerated areas of national concern. The Supremacy Clause, furthermore, provides:

> This Constitution, and the Laws of the United States which shall be made in Pursuance thereof ... shall be the supreme Law of the Land; and the Judges in every State shall be bound thereby, any Thing in the Constitution or Laws of any state to the Contrary notwithstanding. U.S. Const., Art. VI....

As is evident from its text, however, the Supremacy Clause enshrines as "the supreme Law of the Land" only those federal Acts that accord with the constitutional design. See *Printz*. Appeal to the Supremacy Clause alone merely raises the question whether a law is a valid exercise of the national power....

Nor can we conclude that the specific Article I powers delegated to Congress necessarily include, by virtue of the Necessary and Proper Clause or otherwise, the incidental authority to subject the States to private suits as a means of achieving objectives otherwise within the scope of the enumerated powers. Although some of our decisions had endorsed this contention ... they have since been overruled....

The cases we have cited, of course, came at last to the conclusion that neither the Supremacy Clause nor the enumerated powers of Congress confer authority to abrogate the States' immunity from suit in federal court. The logic of the decisions, however, does not turn on the forum in which the suits were prosecuted but extends to state-court suits as well.

The dissenting opinion seeks to reopen these precedents, contending that state sovereign immunity must derive either from the common law (in which case the dissent contends it is defeasible by statute) or from natural law (in which case the dissent believes it cannot bar a federal claim). As should be obvious to all, this is a false dichotomy. The text and the structure of the Constitution protect various rights and principles. Many of these, such as the right to trial by jury and the prohibition on unreasonable searches and seizures, derive from the common law. The common-law lineage of these rights does not mean they are defeasible by statute or remain mere common-law rights, however. They are, rather, constitutional rights, and form the fundamental law of the land.

Although the sovereign immunity of the States derives at least in part from the common-law tradition, the structure and history of the Constitution make clear that the immunity exists today by constitutional design....

Despite the dissent's assertion to the contrary, the fact that a right is not defeasible by statute means only that it is protected by the Constitution, not that it derives from natural law. Whether the dissent's attribution of our reasoning and conclusions to natural law results from analytical confusion or rhetorical device, it is simply inaccurate. We do not contend the founders could not have stripped the States of sovereign immunity and granted Congress power to subject them to private suit but only that they did not do so. By the same token, the contours of sovereign immunity are determined by the founders' understanding, not by the principles or limitations derived from natural law....

II-A-2. There are isolated statements in some of our cases suggesting that the 11th Amendment is inapplicable in state courts. [The Court contends all are distinguishable.] ...

II-B. Whether Congress has authority under Article I to abrogate a State's immunity from suit in its own courts is, then, a question of first impression. In determining whether there is "compelling evidence" that this derogation of the States' sovereignty is "inherent in the constitutional compact," *Blatchford v. Native Village of Noatak* (1991), we continue our discussion of history, practice, precedent, and the structure of the Constitution.

II-B-1. We look first to evidence of the original understanding of the Constitution. Petitioners contend that because the ratification debates and the events surrounding the adoption of the 11th Amendment focused on the States' immunity from suit in federal courts, the historical record gives no instruction as to the founding generation's intent to preserve the States' immunity from suit in their own courts.

We believe, however, that the founders' silence is best explained by the simple fact that no one, not even the Constitution's most ardent opponents, suggested the document might strip the States of the immunity. In light of the overriding concern regarding the States' war-time debts, together with the well known creativity, foresight, and vivid imagination of the Constitution's opponents, the silence is most instructive. It suggests the sovereign's right to assert immunity from suit in its own courts was a principle so well established that no one conceived it would be altered by the new Constitution....

In light of the language of the Constitution and the historical context, it is quite apparent why neither the ratification debates nor the language of the 11th Amendment addressed the States' immunity from suit in their own courts. The concerns voiced at the ratifying conventions, the furor raised by *Chisholm*, and the speed and unanimity with which the Amendment was adopted, moreover, underscore the jealous care with which the founding generation sought to preserve the sovereign immunity of the States. To read this history as permitting the inference that the Constitution stripped the States of immunity in their own courts and allowed Congress to subject them to suit there would turn on its head the concern of the founding generation—that Article III might be used to circumvent state-court immunity. In light of the historical record it is difficult to conceive that the Constitution would have been adopted if it had been understood to strip the States of immunity from suit in their own courts and cede to the Federal Government a power to subject nonconsenting States to private suits in these fora....

II-B-2. Our historical analysis is supported by early congressional practice, which provides "contemporaneous and weighty evidence of the Constitution's meaning." *Printz*. Although early Congresses enacted various statutes authorizing federal suits in state court ... we have discovered no instance in which they purported to authorize suits against nonconsenting States in these fora.

Even the recent statutes, moreover, do not provide evidence of an understanding that Congress has a greater power to subject States to suit in their own courts than in federal courts. On the contrary, the statutes purport to create causes of actions against the States which are enforceable in federal, as well as state, court. To the extent recent practice thus departs from longstanding tradition, it reflects not so much an understanding that the States have surrendered their immunity from suit in their own courts as the erroneous view, perhaps inspired by *Parden v. Terminal R. of Ala. Docks Dept.* (1964) and *Pennsylvania v. Union Gas* (1989), that Congress may subject non-consenting States to private suits in any forum.

II-B-3. The theory and reasoning of our earlier cases suggest the States do retain a constitutional immunity from suit in their own courts....

We have also relied on the States' immunity in their own courts as a premise in our 11th Amendment rulings. See *Hans*....

In particular, the exception to our sovereign immunity doctrine recognized in *Ex parte Young* (1908) is based in part on the premise that sovereign immunity bars relief against States and their officers in both state and federal courts, and that certain suits for declaratory or injunctive relief against state officers must therefore be permitted if the Constitution is to remain the supreme law of the land. As we explained in *General Oil Co. v. Crain* (1908), a case decided the same day as *Ex parte Young* and extending the rule of that case to state-court suits:

> It seems to be an obvious consequence that as a State can only perform its functions through its officers, a restraint upon them is a restraint upon its sovereignty from which it is exempt without its consent in the state tribunals, and exempt by the 11th Amendment of the Constitution of the United States, in the national tribunals. The error is in the universality of the conclusion, as we have seen. Necessarily to give adequate protection to constitutional rights a distinction must be made between valid and invalid state laws, as determining the character of the suit against state officers. And the suit at bar illustrates the necessity. If a suit against state officers is precluded in the national courts by the 11th Amendment to the Constitution, and may be forbidden by a State to its courts, as it is contended in the case at bar that it may be, without power of review by this court, it must be evident that an easy way is open to prevent the enforcement of many provisions of the Constitution.... See *Ex parte Young*, where this subject is fully discussed and the cases reviewed.

Had we not understood the States to retain a constitutional immunity from suit in their own courts, the need for the *Ex parte Young* rule would have been less pressing, and the rule would not have formed so essential a part of our sovereign immunity doctrine....

II-B-4. Our final consideration is whether a congressional power to subject nonconsenting States to private suits in their own courts is consistent with the structure of the Constitution. We look both to the essential principles of federalism and to the special role of the state courts in the constitutional design.

Although the Constitution grants broad powers to Congress, our federalism requires that Congress treat the States in a manner consistent with their status as residuary sovereigns and joint participants in the governance of the Nation....

Petitioners contend that immunity from suit in federal court suffices to preserve the dignity of the States. Private suits against nonconsenting States, however, present "the indignity of subjecting a State to the coercive process of judicial tribunals at the instance of private parties," *In re Ayers* (1887), regardless of the forum. Not only must a State defend or default but also it must face the prospect of being thrust, by federal fiat and against its will, into the disfavored status of a debtor, subject to the power of private citizens to levy on its treasury or perhaps even government buildings or property which the State administers on the public's behalf....

It is unquestioned that the Federal Government retains its own immunity from suit not only in state tribunals but also in its own courts. In light of our constitutional system recognizing the essential sovereignty of the States, we are reluctant to conclude that the States are not entitled to a reciprocal privilege.

Underlying constitutional form are considerations of great substance. Private suits against non-consenting States—especially suits for money damages—may threaten the financial integrity of the States. It is indisputable that, at the time of the founding, many of the States could have been forced into insolvency but for their immunity from private suits for money damages....

A congressional power to strip the States of their immunity from private suits in their own courts would pose more subtle risks as well. "The principle of immunity from litigation assures the states and the nation from unanticipated intervention in the processes of government."...

A general federal power to authorize private suits for money damages would place unwarranted strain on the States' ability to govern in accordance with the will of their citizens. Today, as at the time of the founding, the allocation of scarce resources among competing needs and interests lies at the heart of the political process. While the judgment creditor of the State may have a legitimate claim for compensation, other important needs and worthwhile ends compete for access to the public fisc. Since all cannot be satisfied in full, it is inevitable that difficult decisions involving the most sensitive and political of judgments must be made ... by the political process....

The asserted authority would blur not only the distinct responsibilities of the State and National Governments but also the separate duties of the judicial and political branches of the state governments, ... A State is entitled to ... assign[ ] to the political branches, rather than the courts, the responsibility for directing the payment of debts....

In light of history, practice, precedent, and the structure of the Constitution, we hold that the States retain immunity from private suit in their own courts, an immunity beyond the congressional power to abrogate by Article I legislation.

III. The constitutional privilege of a State to assert its sovereign immunity in its own courts does not confer upon the State a concomitant right to disregard the Constitution or valid federal law. The States and their officers are bound by obligations imposed by the Constitution and by federal statutes that comport with the constitutional design. We are unwilling to assume the States will refuse to honor the Constitution or obey the binding laws of the United States. The good faith of the States thus provides an important assurance that "[t]his Constitution, and the Laws of the United States which shall be made in Pursuance thereof ... shall be the supreme Law of the Land." U.S. Const., Art. VI.

Sovereign immunity, moreover, does not bar all judicial review of state compliance with the Constitution and valid federal law. Rather, certain limits are implicit in the constitutional principle of state sovereign immunity.

The first of these limits is that sovereign immunity bars suits only in the absence of consent. Many States, on their own initiative, have enacted statutes consenting to a wide variety of suits. The rigors of sovereign immunity are thus "mitigated by a sense of justice which has continually expanded by consent the suability of the sovereign." *Great Northern Life Ins. Co. v. Read* (1944). Nor, subject to constitutional limitations, does the Federal Government lack the authority or means to seek the States' voluntary consent to private suits. Cf. *South Dakota v. Dole* (1987).

The States have consented, moreover, to some suits pursuant to the plan of the Convention or to subsequent constitutional amendments. In ratifying the Constitution, the States consented to suits brought by other States or by the Federal Government. *Principality of Monaco* (1934) (collecting cases). A suit which is commenced and prosecuted against a State in the name of the United States by those who are entrusted with the constitutional duty to "take Care that the Laws be faithfully executed," U.S. Const., Art. II, §3, differs in kind from the suit of an individual: While the Constitution contemplates suits among the members of the federal system as an alternative to extralegal measures, the fear of private suits against non-consenting States was the central reason given by the founders who chose to preserve the States' sovereign immunity. Suits brought by the United States itself require the exercise of political responsibility for each suit prosecuted against a State, a control which is absent from a broad delegation to private persons to sue non-consenting States.

We have held also that in adopting the 14th Amendment, the people required the States to surrender a portion of the sovereignty that had been preserved to them by the original Constitution, so that Congress may authorize private suits against nonconsenting States pursuant to its §5 enforcement power. *Fitzpatrick v. Bitzer* (1976)....

The second important limit to the principle of sovereign immunity is that it bars suits against States but not lesser entities. The immunity does not extend to suits prosecuted against a municipal corporation or other governmental entity which is not an arm of the State.... Nor does sovereign immunity bar all suits against state officers.... [*Ex parte Young* (1908) allows suits which seek only] injunctive or declaratory relief.... Even a suit for money damages may be prosecuted against a state officer in his individual capacity for unconstitutional or wrongful conduct fairly attributable to the officer himself, so long as the relief is sought not from the state treasury but from the officer personally....

The principle of sovereign immunity as reflected in our jurisprudence strikes the proper balance between the supremacy of federal law and the separate sovereignty of the States. Established rules provide ample means to correct ongoing violations of law and to vindicate the interests which animate the Supremacy Clause. That we have, during the first 210 years of our constitutional history, found it unnecessary to decide the question presented here suggests a federal power to subject nonconsenting States to private suits in their own courts is unnecessary to uphold the Constitution and valid federal statutes as the supreme law.

IV. The sole remaining question is whether Maine has waived its immunity.... The State, we conclude, has not consented to suit.

V.... The judgment of the Supreme Judicial Court of Maine is Affirmed.

Justice Souter, with whom Justice Stevens, Justice Ginsburg, and Justice Breyer join, dissenting.

In *Seminole Tribe of Fla. v. Florida* (1996), a majority of this Court invoked the 11th Amendment to declare that the federal judicial power under Article III of the Constitution does not reach a private action against a State, even on a federal question. In the Court's conception, however, the 11th Amendment was understood as having been enhanced by a "background principle" of state sovereign immunity (understood as immunity to suit) that operated beyond its limited codification in the Amendment, dealing solely with federal citizen-state diversity jurisdiction. To the *Seminole Tribe* dissenters, of whom I was one, the Court's enhancement of the Amendment was at odds with constitutional history and at war with the conception of divided sovereignty that is the essence of American federalism.

Today's issue arises naturally in the aftermath of the decision in *Seminole Tribe*. The Court holds that the Constitution bars an individual suit against a State to enforce a federal statutory right under the Fair Labor Standards Act of 1938 (FLSA) when brought in the State's courts over its objection. In thus complementing its earlier decision, the Court of course confronts the fact that the state forum renders the 11th Amendment beside the point, and it has responded by discerning a simpler and more straightforward theory of state sovereign immunity than it found in *Seminole Tribe*: a State's sovereign immunity from all individual suits is a "fundamental aspect" of state sovereignty "confirm[ed]" by the 10th Amendment. As a consequence, *Seminole Tribe*'s contorted reliance on the 11th Amendment and its background was presumably unnecessary; the 10th would have done the work with an economy that the majority in *Seminole Tribe* would have welcomed. Indeed, if the Court's current reasoning is correct, the 11th Amendment itself was unnecessary. Whatever Article III may originally have said about the federal judicial power, the embarrassment to the State of Georgia occasioned by attempts in federal court to enforce the State's war debt could easily have been avoided if only the Court that decided *Chisholm v. Georgia* (1793) had understood a State's inherent, 10th Amendment right to be free of any judicial power, whether the court be state or federal, and whether the cause of action arise under state or federal law.

The sequence of the Court's positions prompts a suspicion of error, and skepticism is confirmed by scrutiny of the Court's efforts to justify its holding. There is no evidence that the 10th Amendment constitutionalized a concept of sovereign immunity as inherent in the notion of statehood, and no evidence that any concept of inherent sovereign immunity was understood historically to apply when the sovereign sued was not the font of the law. Nor does the Court fare any better with its subsidiary lines of reasoning, that the state-court action is barred by the scheme of American federalism, a result supposedly confirmed by a history largely devoid of precursors to the action considered here. The Court's federalism ignores the accepted authority of Congress to bind States under the FLSA and to provide for enforcement of federal rights in state court. The Court's history simply disparages the capacity of the Constitution to order relationships in a Republic that has changed since the founding.

On each point the Court has raised it is mistaken, and I respectfully dissent from its judgment.

I. The Court rests its decision principally on the claim that immunity from suit was "a fundamental aspect of the sovereignty which the States enjoyed before the ratification of the Constitution," an aspect which the Court understands to have survived the ratification of the Constitution in 1788 and to have been "confirm[ed]" and given constitutional status, by the adoption of the 10th Amendment in 1791. If the Court truly means by "sovereign immunity" what that term meant at common law, its argument would be insupportable. While sovereign immunity entered many new state legal systems as a part of the common law selectively received from England, it was not understood to be indefeasible or to have been given any such status by the new National Constitution, which did not mention it.... Had the question been posed, state sovereign immunity could not have been thought to shield a State from suit under federal law on a subject committed to national jurisdiction by Article I of the Constitution. Congress exercising its conceded Article I power may unquestionably abrogate such immunity. I set out this position at length in my dissent in *Seminole Tribe* and will not repeat it here.

The Court does not, however, offer today's holding as a mere corollary to its reasoning in *Seminole Tribe*, substituting the 10th Amendment for the 11th as the occasion demands, and it is fair to read its references to a "fundamental aspect" of state sovereignty as referring not to a prerogative inherited from the Crown, but to a conception necessarily implied by statehood itself. The conception is thus not one of common law so much as of natural law, a universally applicable proposition discoverable by reason. This, I take it, is the sense in which the Court so emphatically relies on Alexander Hamilton's reference in *The Federalist* No. 81 to the States' sovereign immunity from suit as an "inherent" right, a characterization that does not require, but is at least open to, a natural law reading.

I understand the Court to rely on the Hamiltonian formulation with the object of suggesting that its conception of sovereign immunity as a "fundamental aspect" of sovereignty was a substantially popular, if not the dominant, view in the periods of Revolution and Confederation. There is, after all, nothing else in the Court's opinion that would suggest a basis for saying that the ratification of the 10th Amendment gave this "fundamental aspect" its constitutional status and protection against any legislative tampering by Congress. The Court's principal rationale for today's result, then, turns on history: was the natural law conception of sovereign immunity as inherent in any notion of an independent State widely held in the United States in the period preceding the ratification of 1788 (or the adoption of the 10th Amendment in 1791)?

The answer is certainly no. There is almost no evidence that the generation of the Framers thought sovereign immunity was fundamental in the sense of being unalterable. Whether one looks at the period before the framing, to the ratification controversies, or to the early republican era, the evidence is the same. Some Framers thought sovereign immunity was an obsolete royal prerogative inapplicable in a republic; some thought sovereign immunity was a common-law power defeasible, like other common-law rights, by statute; and perhaps a few thought, in keeping with a natural law view distinct from the common-law conception, that immunity was inherent in a sovereign because the body that made a law could not logically be bound by it. Natural law thinking on the part of a doubtful few will not, however, support the Court's position.

I-A. The American Colonies did not enjoy sovereign immunity, that being a privilege understood in English law to be reserved for the Crown alone; "antecedent to the Declaration of Independence, none of the colonies were, or pretended to be, sovereign states," 1 J. Story, *Commentaries on the Constitution* § 207, p. 149 (5th ed. 1891). Several colonial charters, including those of Massachusetts, Connecticut, Rhode Island, and Georgia, expressly specified that the corporate body established thereunder could sue and be sued....

I-B. ... Around the time of the Constitutional Convention, then, there existed among the States some diversity of practice with respect to sovereign immunity; but despite a tendency among the state constitutions to announce and declare certain inalienable and natural rights of men and even of the collective people of a State, see, e.g., Pennsylvania Constitution, Art. III (1776), 8 *Sources and Documents of United States Constitutions*, at 278 ("That the people of this State have the sole, exclusive and inherent right of governing and regulating the internal police of the same"), no State declared that sovereign immunity was one of those rights. To the extent that States were thought to possess immunity, it was perceived as a prerogative of the sovereign under common law. And where sovereign immunity was recognized as barring suit, provisions for recovery from the State were in order, just as they had been at common law in England.

I-C. ... From a canvass of this spectrum of opinion expressed at the ratifying conventions, one thing is certain. No one was espousing an indefeasible, natural law view of sovereign immunity. The controversy over the enforceability of state debts subject to state law produced emphatic support for sovereign immunity from eminences as great as Madison and Marshall, but neither of them indicated adherence to any immunity conception outside the common law.

I-D. At the close of the ratification debates, the issue of the sovereign immunity of the States under Article III had not been definitively resolved, and in some instances the indeterminacy led the ratification conventions to respond in ways that point to the range of thinking about the doctrine. Several state ratifying conventions proposed amendments and issued declarations that would have exempted States from subjection to suit in federal court....

Unlike the Rhode Island proposal, which hinted at a clarification of Article III, the Virginia and North Carolina ratifying conventions proposed amendments that by their terms would have fundamentally altered the content of Article III. The Virginia Convention's proposal for a new Article III omitted entirely the language conferring federal jurisdiction over a controversy between a State and citizens of another State, and the North Carolina Convention proposed an identical amendment.... These proposals for omission suggest that the conventions of Virginia and North Carolina thought they had subjected themselves to citizen suits under Article III as enacted, and that they wished not to have done so.[1] There is, thus, no suggestion in their resolutions that Article III as drafted was fundamentally at odds with an indefeasible natural law sovereignty, or with a conception that went to the essence of what it meant to be a State. At all events, the state ratifying conventions' felt need for clarification on the question of state suability demonstrates that uncertainty surrounded the matter even at the moment of ratification. This uncertainty set the stage for the divergent views expressed in *Chisholm*.

I-E. If the natural law conception of sovereign immunity as an inherent characteristic of sovereignty enjoyed by the States had been broadly accepted at the time of the founding, one would expect to find it reflected somewhere in the five opinions delivered by the Court in *Chisholm v. Georgia* (1793). Yet that view did not appear in any of them. And since a bare two years before *Chisholm*, the Bill of Rights had been added to the original Constitution, if the 10th Amendment had been understood to give federal constitutional status to state sovereign immunity so as to endue it with the equivalent of the natural law conception, one would be certain to find such a development mentioned somewhere in the *Chisholm* writings. In fact, however, not one of the opinions espoused the natural law view, and not one of them so much as mentioned the 10th Amendment. Not even Justice Iredell, who alone among the Justices thought that a State could not be sued in federal court, echoed Hamilton or hinted at a constitutionally immutable immunity doctrine.

Chisholm presented the questions whether a State might be made a defendant in a suit brought by a citizen of another State, and if so, whether an action of assumpsit would lie against it. In representing *Chisholm*, Edmund Randolph, the Framer and then Attorney General, not only argued for the necessity of a federal forum to vindicate private rights against the States but rejected any traditional conception of sovereignty. He said that the sovereignty of the States, which he acknowledged, was no barrier to jurisdiction, because "the present Constitution produced a new order of things. It derives its origin immediately from the people.... The States are in fact assemblages of these individuals who are liable to process."

Justice Wilson took up the argument for the sovereignty of the people more vociferously. Building on a conception of sovereignty he had already expressed at the Pennsyl-

---

1. The Court says "there is no evidence that [the proposed amendments] were directed toward the question of sovereign immunity or that they reflect an understanding that the States would be subject to private suits without consent under Article III as drafted." No evidence, that is, except the proposed amendments themselves, which would have omitted the Citizen-State Diversity Clause. If the proposed omission is not evidence going to sovereign immunity to private suits, one wonders what would satisfy the Court.

vania ratifying convention, he began by noting what he took to be the pregnant silence of the Constitution regarding sovereignty:

> To the Constitution of the *United States* the term SOVEREIGN, is totally unknown. There is but one place where it could have been used with propriety. But, even in that place it would not, perhaps, have comported with the delicacy of those, who *ordained* and *established* the Constitution. They might have announced themselves 'SOVEREIGN' people of the *United States*: But serenely conscious of the *fact*, they avoided the *ostentatious declaration*.

As if to contrast his own directness with the Framers' delicacy, the Framer-turned-Justice explained in no uncertain terms that Georgia was not sovereign with respect to federal jurisdiction (even in a diversity case):

> As a Judge of this Court, I know, and can decide upon the knowledge, that the citizens of Georgia, when they acted upon the large scale of the Union, as a part of the 'People of the United States,' did not surrender the Supreme or Sovereign Power to that State; but, *as to the purposes of the Union*, retained it to themselves. *As to the purposes of the Union*, therefore, *Georgia is NOT a sovereign State*.

This was necessarily to reject any natural law conception of sovereign immunity as inherently attached to an American State, but this was not all. Justice Wilson went on to identify the origin of sovereign immunity in the feudal system that had, he said, been brought to England and to the common law by the Norman Conquest. After quoting Blackstone's formulation of the doctrine as it had developed in England, he discussed it in the most disapproving terms imaginable:

> This last position [that the King is sovereign and no court can have jurisdiction over him] is only a branch of a much more extensive principle, on which a plan of systematic despotism has been lately formed in *England*, and prosecuted with unwearied assiduity and care.... The principle is, that all human law must be prescribed by *a superior*. This principle I mean not now to examine. Suffice it, at present to say, that another principle, very different in its nature and operations, forms, in my judgment, the basis of sound and genuine jurisprudence; laws derived from the pure source of equality and justice must be founded on the CONSENT of those, whose obedience they require. The *sovereign*, when traced to his source, must be found in the *man*.

With this rousing conclusion of revolutionary ideology and rhetoric, Justice Wilson left no doubt that he thought the doctrine of sovereign immunity entirely anomalous in the American Republic. Although he did not speak specifically of a State's immunity in its own courts, his view necessarily requires that such immunity would not have been justifiable as a tenet of absolutist natural law.

Chief Justice Jay took a less vehement tone in his opinion, but he, too, denied the applicability of the doctrine of sovereign immunity to the States. He explained the doctrine as an incident of European feudalism and said that by contrast, "[n]o such ideas obtain here...."

Justice Iredell was the only Member of the Court to hold that the suit could not lie; but if his discussion was far-reaching, his reasoning was cautious. Its core was that the Court could not assume a waiver of the State's common-law sovereign immunity where Congress had not expressly passed such a waiver. Although Justice Iredell added, in what he clearly identified as dictum, that he was "strongly against" any construction of the Constitution "which will admit, under any circumstances, a compulsive suit against a State for the recovery of money," he made it equally clear that he understood sovereign immunity as a common-law doctrine passed to the States with independence....

In sum, then, in *Chisholm* two Justices (Jay and Wilson), both of whom had been present at the Constitutional Convention, took a position suggesting that States should not enjoy sovereign immunity (however conceived) even in their own courts; one (Cushing) was essentially silent on the issue of sovereign immunity in state court; one (Blair) took a cautious position affirming the pragmatic view that sovereign immunity was a continuing common law doctrine and that States would permit suit against themselves as of right; and one (Iredell) expressly thought that state sovereign immunity at common-law rightly belonged to the sovereign States. Not a single Justice suggested that sovereign immunity was an inherent and indefeasible right of statehood, and neither counsel for Georgia before the Circuit Court, nor Justice Iredell seems even to have conceived the possibility that the new 10th Amendment produced the equivalent of such a doctrine. This dearth of support makes it very implausible for today's Court to argue that a substantial (let alone a dominant) body of thought at the time of the framing understood sovereign immunity to be an inherent right of statehood, adopted or confirmed by the 10th Amendment....

The Court, citing *Hans v. Louisiana* (1890), says that the 11th Amendment "overruled" *Chisholm*, but the animadversion is beside the point. The significance of *Chisholm* is its indication that in 1788 and 1791 it was not generally assumed (indeed, hardly assumed at all) that a State's sovereign immunity from suit in its own courts was an inherent, and not merely a common-law, advantage. On the contrary, the testimony of five eminent legal minds of the day confirmed that virtually everyone who understood immunity to be legitimate saw it as a common-law prerogative (from which it follows that it was subject to abrogation by Congress as to a matter within Congress's Article I authority)....

Nor can the Court make good on its claim that the enactment of the 11th Amendment retrospectively reestablished the view that had already been established at the time of the framing (though eluding the perception of all but one Member of the Supreme Court), and hence "acted ... to restore the original constitutional design." There was nothing "established" about the position espoused by Georgia in the effort to repudiate its debts, and the Court's implausible suggestion to the contrary merely echoes the brio of its remark in *Seminole Tribe* that *Chisholm* was "contrary to the well-understood meaning of the Constitution." [Citing *Principality of Monaco v. Mississippi* (1934)]. The fact that *Chisholm* was no conceptual aberration is apparent from the ratification debates and the several state requests to rewrite Article III. There was no received view either of the role this sovereign immunity would play in the circumstances of the case or of a conceptual foundation for immunity doctrine at odds with *Chisholm's* reading of Article III. As an author on whom the Court relies, has it, "there was no unanimity among the Framers that immunity would exist," D. Currie, *The Constitution in the Supreme Court: The First Century* 19 (1985).

It should not be surprising, then, to realize that although much post-*Chisholm* discussion was disapproving (as the States saw their escape from debt cut off), the decision had champions "every bit as vigorous in defending their interpretation of the Constitution as were those partisans on the other side of the issue." Marcus & Wexler, *Suits Against States: Diversity of Opinion In The 1790s*, 1993 J. Sup.Ct. Hist. 73, 83; see, e.g., 5 *Documentary History of the Supreme Court*, at 251–52, 252–53, 262–64, 268–69 (newspaper articles supporting holding in *Chisholm*); 5 *Documentary History*, at 616 (statement of a Committee of Delaware Senate in support of holding in *Chisholm*). The federal citizen-state diversity jurisdiction was settled by the 11th Amendment; Article III was not "restored." ...

II. The Court's rationale for today's holding based on a conception of sovereign immunity as somehow fundamental to sovereignty or inherent in statehood fails for the lack of any substantial support for such a conception in the thinking of the founding era. The Court cannot be counted out yet, however, for it has a second line of argument looking not to a clause-based reception of the natural law conception or even to its recognition as a "background principle," see *Seminole Tribe*, but to a structural basis in the Constitution's creation of a federal system. Immunity, the Court says, "inheres in the system of federalism established by the Constitution," its "contours [being] determined by the founders' understanding, not by the principles or limitations derived from natural law." Again, "[w]e look both to the essential principles of federalism and to the special role of the state courts in the constitutional design." That is, the Court believes that the federal constitutional structure itself necessitates recognition of some degree of state autonomy broad enough to include sovereign immunity from suit in a State's own courts, regardless of the federal source of the claim asserted against the State. If one were to read the Court's federal structure rationale in isolation from the preceding portions of the opinion, it would appear that the Court's position on state sovereign immunity might have been rested entirely on federalism alone. If it had been, however, I would still be in dissent, for the Court's argument that state court sovereign immunity on federal questions is inherent in the very concept of federal structure is demonstrably mistaken.

II-A. ... "In America, the powers of sovereignty are divided between the government of the Union, and those of the States. They are each sovereign, with respect to the objects committed to it, and neither sovereign with respect to the objects committed to the other." *McCulloch v. Maryland* (1819).

Hence the flaw in the Court's appeal to federalism. The State of Maine is not sovereign with respect to the national objective of the FLSA.[2] It is not the authority that promulgated the FLSA, on which the right of action in this case depends. That authority is the United States acting through the Congress, whose legislative power under Article I of the Constitution to extend FLSA coverage to state employees has already been decided, see *Garcia v. San Antonio Metropolitan Transit Authority* (1985), and is not contested here....

III. If neither theory nor structure can supply the basis for the Court's conceptions of sovereign immunity and federalism, then perhaps history might. The Court apparently believes that because state courts have not historically entertained Commerce Clause-based federal-law claims against the States, such an innovation carries a presumption of unconstitutionality. At the outset, it has to be noted that this approach assumes a more cohesive record than history affords....

It was at one time, though perhaps not from the framing, believed that "Congress' authority to regulate the States under the Commerce Clause" was limited by "certain underlying elements of political sovereignty ... deemed essential to the States' 'separate and independent existence.'" See *Garcia* [quoting *Lane County v. Oregon* (1868)]. On this belief, the preordained balance between state and federal sovereignty was understood to trump the terms of Article I and preclude Congress from subjecting States to federal law

---

2. It is therefore sheer circularity for the Court to talk of the "anomaly," that would arise if a State could be sued on federal law in its own courts, when it may not be sued under federal law in federal court, *Seminole Tribe*. The short and sufficient answer is that the anomaly is the Court's own creation: the 11th Amendment was never intended to bar federal-question suits against the States in federal court. The anomaly is that *Seminole Tribe*, an opinion purportedly grounded in the 11th Amendment, should now be used as a lever to argue for state sovereign immunity in state courts, to which the 11th Amendment by its terms does not apply.

on certain subjects. (From time to time, wage and hour regulation has been counted among those subjects.) As a consequence it was rare, if not unknown, for state courts to confront the situation in which federal law enacted under the Commerce Clause provided the authority for a private right of action against a State in state court. The question of state immunity from a Commerce Clause-based federal-law suit in state court thus tended not to arise for the simple reason that acts of Congress authorizing such suits did not exist.

Today, however, in light of *Garcia* [overruling *National League of Cities v. Usery* (1976)], the law is settled that federal legislation enacted under the Commerce Clause may bind the States without having to satisfy a test of undue incursion into state sovereignty. "[T]he fundamental limitation that the constitutional scheme imposes on the Commerce Clause to protect the 'States as States' is one of process rather than one of result." *Garcia*. Because the commerce power is no longer thought to be circumscribed, the dearth of prior private federal claims entertained against the States in state courts does not tell us anything, and reflects nothing but an earlier and less expansive application of the commerce power.

Least of all is it to the point for the Court to suggest that because the Framers would be surprised to find States subjected to a federal-law suit in their own courts under the commerce power, the suit must be prohibited by the Constitution. The Framers' intentions and expectations count so far as they point to the meaning of the Constitution's text or the fair implications of its structure, but they do not hover over the instrument to veto any application of its principles to a world that the Framers could not have anticipated.

If the Framers would be surprised to see States subjected to suit in their own courts under the commerce power, they would be astonished by the reach of Congress under the Commerce Clause generally. The proliferation of Government, State and Federal, would amaze the Framers, and the administrative state with its reams of regulations would leave them rubbing their eyes. But the Framers' surprise at, say, the FLSA, or the Federal Communications Commission, or the Federal Reserve Board is no threat to the constitutionality of any one of them, for a very fundamental reason:

> [W]hen we are dealing with words that also are a constituent act, like the Constitution of the United States, we must realize that they have called into life a being the development of which could not have been foreseen completely by the most gifted of its begetters. It was enough for them to realize or to hope that they had created an organism; it has taken a century and has cost their successors much sweat and blood to prove that they created a nation. The case before us must be considered in the light of our whole experience and not merely in that of what was said a hundred years ago. *Missouri v. Holland* (1920) (Holmes, J.)...

IV-A. If today's decision occasions regret at its anomalous versions of history and federal theory, it is the more regrettable in being the second time the Court has suddenly changed the course of prior decision in order to limit the exercise of authority over a subject now concededly within the Article I jurisdiction of the Congress. The FLSA, which requires employers to pay a minimum wage, was first enacted in 1938, with an exemption for States acting as employers. See *Maryland v. Wirtz* (1968). In 1966, it was amended to remove the state employer exemption so far as it concerned workers in hospitals, institutions, and schools. In *Wirtz*, the Court upheld the amendment over the dissent's argument that extending the FLSA to these state employees was "such a serious invasion of state sovereignty protected by the 10th Amendment that it is ... not consistent with our constitutional federalism" (opinion of Douglas, J.).

In 1974, Congress again amended the FLSA, this time "extend[ing] the minimum wage and maximum hour provisions to almost all public employees employed by the States and by their various political subdivisions." *National League of Cities*. This time the Court went the other way: in *National League of Cities*, the Court held the extension of the Act to these employees an unconstitutional infringement of state sovereignty; for good measure, the Court overturned *Wirtz*, dismissing its reasoning as no longer authoritative.

But *National League of Cities* was not the last word. In *Garcia*, decided some nine years later, the Court addressed the question whether a municipally owned mass-transit system was exempt from the FLSA. In holding that it was not, the Court overruled *National League of Cities*, this time taking the position that Congress was not barred by the Constitution from binding the States as employers under the Commerce Clause. As already mentioned, the Court held that whatever protection the Constitution afforded to the States' sovereignty lay in the constitutional structure, not in some substantive guarantee. *Garcia* remains good law, its reasoning has not been repudiated, and it has not been challenged here.

The FLSA has not, however, fared as well in practice as it has in theory. The Court in *Seminole Tribe* created a significant impediment to the statute's practical application by rendering its damages provisions unenforceable against the States by private suit in federal court. Today's decision blocking private actions in state courts makes the barrier to individual enforcement a total one.

IV-B. The Court might respond to the charge that in practice it has vitiated *Garcia* by insisting, as counsel for Maine argued, that the United States may bring suit in federal court against a State for damages under the FLSA, on the authority of *United States v. Texas* (1892). See also *Seminole Tribe*. It is true, of course, that the FLSA does authorize the Secretary of Labor to file suit seeking damages, see 29 U.S.C. §216(c), but unless Congress plans a significant expansion of the National Government's litigating forces to provide a lawyer whenever private litigation is barred by today's decision and *Seminole Tribe*, the allusion to enforcement of private rights by the National Government is probably not much more than whimsy. Facing reality, Congress specifically found, as long ago as 1974, "that the enforcement capability of the Secretary of Labor is not alone sufficient to provide redress in all or even a substantial portion of the situations where compliance is not forthcoming voluntarily." S.Rep. No. 93-690, p. 27 (1974). One hopes that such voluntary compliance will prove more popular than it has in Maine, for there is no reason today to suspect that enforcement by the Secretary of Labor alone would likely prove adequate to assure compliance with this federal law in the multifarious circumstances of some 4.7 million employees of the 50 States of the Union....

So there is much irony in the Court's profession that it grounds its opinion on a deeply rooted historical tradition of sovereign immunity, when the Court abandons a principle nearly as inveterate, and much closer to the hearts of the Framers: that where there is a right, there must be a remedy....

Yet today the Court has no qualms about saying frankly that the federal right to damages afforded by Congress under the FLSA cannot create a concomitant private remedy. The right was "made for the benefit of" petitioners; they have been "hindered by another of that benefit"; but despite what has long been understood as the "necessary consequence of law," they have no action, cf. *Ashby v. White,* (Eng. QB 1702) 1702. It will not do for the Court to respond that a remedy was never available where the right in question was against the sovereign. A State is not the sovereign when a federal claim is pressed against it, and even the English sovereign opened itself to recovery and, unlike Maine, provided the remedy to complement the right. To the Americans of the founding generation it would have been clear (as it was to Chief Justice Marshall) that if the King would do right, the democratically chosen Government of the United States could do no less....

V. The Court has swung back and forth with regrettable disruption on the enforceability of the FLSA against the States, but if the present majority had a defensible position one could at least accept its decision with an expectation of stability ahead. As it is, any such expectation would be naive. The resemblance of today's state sovereign immunity to the *Lochner* era's industrial due process is striking. The Court began this century by imputing immutable constitutional status to a conception of economic self-reliance that was never true to industrial life and grew insistently fictional with the years, and the Court has chosen to close the century by conferring like status on a conception of state sovereign immunity that is true neither to history nor to the structure of the Constitution. I expect the Court's late essay into immunity doctrine will prove the equal of its earlier experiment in laissez-faire, the one being as unrealistic as the other, as indefensible, and probably as fleeting.

Alden v. Maine: Notes

1. The Court decided two other sovereign immunity cases the same day that it decided *Alden*. The votes were identical to the votes in *Alden*. *Florida Prepaid Postsecondary Education Expense Board v. College Savings Bank* (1999) involved a suit filed against Florida for patent infringement. The Court held that Congress could not abrogate state sovereign immunity under its patent powers and that there was insufficient evidence to allow Congress to base the statute on the 14th Amendment.

   A companion case, *College Savings Bank v. Florida Prepaid Postsecondary Education Expense Board* (1999), echoed the first case's holding, and also held that Congress cannot force a state to waive its sovereign immunity as a condition of engaging in conduct that has been regulated by Congress. The Trademark Remedy Clarification Act (TRCA), passed pursuant to the Commerce Clause, subjected states to suits brought under §43(a) of the Trademark Act of 1946 (Lanham Act) for false and misleading advertising. The Court overruled *Parden v. Terminal R. of Ala. Docks Dept.* (1964), which had recognized such an implied waiver.

2. *Kimel v. Florida Board of Regents* (2000) extended *Alden* immunity to claims brought in state court pursuant to the federal Age Discrimination in Employment Act (ADEA). The votes were identical to the votes in *Alden*. Similar to the *Florida Prepaid* cases, the Court held that the ADEA's attempt to overcome state sovereign immunity could not be based on the Commerce Clause. Furthermore, the Court held that the ADEA's attempt to overcome state sovereign immunity could not be based on the 14th Amendment, since the Equal Protection Clause provides only minimal protection to persons suffering discrimination on the basis of age.

3. The polarity of views on this issue has become marked. Justice O'Connor, writing for the majority in *Kimel*, stated:

   > In *Alden*, we explained that, "[a]lthough the sovereign immunity of the States derives at least in part from the common-law tradition, the structure and history of the Constitution make clear that the immunity exists today by constitutional design."... For purposes of today's decision, it is sufficient to note that we have

on more than one occasion explained the substantial reasons for adhering to that constitutional design.... Indeed, the present dissenters' refusal to accept the validity and natural import of decisions like *Hans*, rendered over a full century ago by this Court, makes it difficult to engage in additional meaningful debate on the place of state sovereign immunity in the Constitution.... Today we adhere to our holding in *Seminole Tribe*: Congress' powers under Article I of the Constitution do not include the power to subject States to suit at the hands of private individuals.

Justice Stevens, in an opinion joined by the other three dissenters, replied:

I remain convinced that *Union Gas* was correctly decided and that the decision of five Justices in *Seminole Tribe* to overrule that case was profoundly misguided. Despite my respect for stare decisis, I am unwilling to accept *Seminole Tribe* as controlling precedent.... [Federalism] is perverted when invoked to rely on sovereign immunity as a defense to deliberate violations of settled federal law. Further, *Seminole Tribe* is a case that will unquestionably have serious ramifications in future cases; indeed, it has already had such an effect, as in the Court's decision today and in the equally misguided opinion of *Alden v. Maine* (1999).... The kind of judicial activism manifested in [these] cases ... represents such a radical departure from the proper role of this Court that it should be opposed whenever the opportunity arises.

4. In *Board of Trustees of the University of Alabama v. Garrett* (2001), the Court considered a suit filed in federal court against a state claiming a violation of the Americans with Disabilities Act (ADA). The act prohibits discrimination in employment against a qualified person who has a disability. Patricia Garrett, a registered nurse, had been employed by the University of Alabama. She had been diagnosed with breast cancer, took substantial leave from work, was treated, and returned to work. On returning to work she was told she would have to give up her director's position, whereupon she took a lower paying job and sued under the ADA in federal court. A closely divided Supreme Court again held that the 11th Amendment barred suits in federal court against a state under any statute based upon the commerce power of Congress.

The Court recognized that Congress could abrogate a state's 11th Amendment immunity to suit in federal court under the 14th Amendment. The Court held, however, that its decisions established that the disabled received only rational basis protection under the 14th Amendment, a reading that limited the power of Congress. Congress could not expand the scope of the 14th Amendment as interpreted by the Court. It could remedy violations of standards the Court recognized, provided that its remedy was congruent and proportional to the problem. Here the Court found application of the ADA to the states did not meet this test. Congress had made extensive findings of state or local discrimination against the disabled, but the Court found these insufficient to support application of the act to state governments. (Local governments, the Court pointed out, do not enjoy 11th Amendment immunity, so the Court discounted the many instances of local violations cited by Congress.) The Justices continued to divide along the lines established in *Alden*.

5. In *Federal Maritime Commission v. South Carolina State Ports Authority* (2002), the *Alden* majority again extended the rationale of *Alden*. The Court held that the sovereign immunity of states reflected by the passage of the 11th Amendment precluded enforcement of federal statutes by individuals against states in administrative courts operated by Article II executive agencies.

6. In *Virginia Central Community College v. Katz* (2006), the Court held that a bankruptcy trustee's proceeding to set aside the debtor's preferential transfers to state agencies is not barred by sovereign immunity. In a 5–4 decision, the Court concluded that the reasons for the adoption of the Constitution's Bankruptcy Clause and legislation from the founding era suggested that this Article I power was intended to subordinate state sovereign immunity. In so holding, the Court distinguished congressional power over commerce and patents, which they had recently held must defer to state sovereignty. See *Florida Prepaid Postsecondary Education Expense Board v. College Savings Bank* (1999) (patent power) and *Kimel v. Florida Board of Regents* (2000) (Commerce Clause).

7. In *Northern Insurance Company of NY v. Chatham County, Ga.* (2006), an admiralty case, the Court held that sovereign immunity does not extend to counties and municipalities, even when they are exercising power delegated by the State, if they do not qualify as an "arm of the State" for 11th Amendment purposes. The Court determined that only the state's sovereign immunity survived the ratification of the Constitution.

III. The Rehnquist Court

The Rehnquist Court, which began with the elevation of William Rehnquist from Associate Justice to Chief Justice in 1986, has brought several fundamental changes to constitutional law. In particular, since 1986, the Court has articulated a new commitment to principles of federalism through its interpretation of the 10th, 11th, and 14th Amendments; limited Congress's power to regulate interstate commerce; and interpreted the Establishment Clause to permit religious organizations to receive governmental financial assistance, expressly overruling earlier Burger Court precedents.

Federalism. Perhaps the most significant doctrinal development of the Rehnquist Court has been in the area of federalism. In a series of decisions interpreting the 10th Amendment, the 11th Amendment, and §5 of the 14th Amendment, the Court has issued several opinions altering the jurisprudence of these amendments in order to protect the Court's conception of the fundamental principles of federalism.

In 1975, then-Justice Rehnquist wrote a lone dissent in *Fry v. United States* (1975), calling for a reinvigoration of the 10th Amendment as an affirmative limitation on the federal commerce power. (*Fry* upheld application of an across-the-board wage freeze statute to a state government.) His revisionist view commanded a 5–4 majority the next year in *National League of Cities v. Usery* (1976), holding that the 10th Amendment barred application of the Fair Labor Standards Act to state and local governments. In 1985, the Court, in another 5–4 decision, overruled *National League of Cities* and returned to a narrow construction of the 10th Amendment. In *Garcia v. San Antonio Metropolitan Transit Authority* (1985), the Court upheld the application of the Fair Labor Standards Act to a municipal employer. Then Justice Rehnquist predicted that, "in time," his interpretation of state sovereignty would "again command the support of a majority of this Court." Rehnquist's forecast came true during the 1990s. In *New York v. United States* (1992), the Court struck down a provision of the federal Low-Level Radioactive Waste Policy Amendments Act that required states to "take title" of radioactive wastes not disposed of by a certain date as violative of the role of the states in the federal system. The Court concluded that the "Federal Government may not compel the States to enact or administer a federal regulatory program" without violating state sovereignty. In *Printz v. United States* (1997), the Court considered the constitutionality of the Brady Handgun Violence Prevention Act that required states to conduct criminal background checks on handgun purchasers. The Court, in a 5–4 decision, held that the statute commandeered state officials to enforce a federal mandate in a manner violative of the 10th Amendment. The Court did subsequently reject a 10th Amendment challenge to the federal Driver's Privacy Protection Act that prohibited states from disclosing personal information gathered by state departments of motor vehicles. *Reno v. Condon* (2000). The Court in *Reno* emphasized that the statute did not require the states to engage in any regulatory activity, unlike *New York v. United States* and *Printz*.

The Rehnquist Court has also engaged in a significant reframing of 11th Amendment jurisprudence. In addition, the Court has restricted the enforcement power of Congress under §5 of the 14th Amendment. These developments have major implications for federalism. Since *Hans v. Louisiana* (1890), the Court has interpreted the 11th Amendment to bar suits against state governments without their consent by citizens of other states as well as the state's own citizens. In *Fitzpatrick v. Bitzer* (1976), the Court held that Congress *could* authorize suits against a state government without its consent pursuant to §5 of the 14th Amendment, since §5 constituted a limitation on the 11th Amendment. In *Pennsylvania v. Union Gas Co.* (1989), the Court in a 4-1-4 plurality decision went further and held that Congress could authorize suits against a state government pursuant to *any* of its constitutional powers without violating the 11th Amendment. But in *Seminole Tribe v. Florida* (1996), the Court overruled *Union Gas*, holding that Congress could only authorize suits against a state government pursuant to its §5 powers; the 11th Amendment barred authorization of such suits without the state's consent if based on its Article I, §8 powers.

In the meantime, the Court construed §5 of the 14th Amendment in a limited fashion. First, in *City of Boerne v. Flores* (1997), the Court held that Congress did not have authority under §5 to enact the Religious Freedom Restoration Act, a statute that imposed certain limitations on the ability of state and local governments (as well as Congress) to enact regulations that infringed on the exercise of religion. Following *Boerne*, the Court issued three more decisions in which the Court sharply narrowed Congress's authority to legislate under §5: *Florida Prepaid Postsecondary Education Expense Board v. College Savings Bank* (1999); *Kimel v. Florida Board of Regents* (2000); and *University of Alabama v. Garrett* (2001). In each of these decisions, the Court assessed the constitutionality of congressional statutes that permitted suits against state governments. In each instance, the Court held that Congress had exceeded its §5 power in enacting the statute and had therefore violated the 11th Amendment. In *Kimel* and *Garrett*, the Court's decisions limited two major pieces of civil rights legislation—the Age Discrimination in Employment Act and the Americans with Disabilities Act—by holding that state governments, consistent with the 11th Amendment, could not be sued for violations of these statutes. Had Congress properly enacted these statutes pursuant to its §5 power, the statutes would have survived 11th Amendment scrutiny; the Court's decision that Congress lacked §5 power to enact these civil rights statutes left them vulnerable to 11th Amendment attack.

Finally, in *Alden v. Maine* (1999), the Court considered the ability of Congress to provide state employees with a private cause of action in state court under the Fair Labor Standards Act. Since the case arose in state court, the 11th Amendment did not provide a clear textual basis for the Court's decision to reject the claim. Instead, the Court relied on state sovereign immunity to bar the suit, which the 5–4 majority discovered in the structure of the Constitution.

There is a stark exception to this trend towards federalism in the Rehnquist Court: the doctrine of preemption. The Rehnquist Court has issued a number of decisions in which it has interpreted very broadly federal statutes in a manner to preempt a variety of state regulation. *See, e.g., Geier v. American Honda Motor Co., Inc.* (2000) (preempting state product liability tort suit). Other exceptions include requiring states to obey the Family and Medical Leave Act for state employees and the decision on California's Medical Marijuana Act.

Commerce Clause. The Supreme Court held no federal laws unconstitutional on the grounds that they exceeded Congress's power to regulate interstate commerce between 1936 and 1995. Indeed, those years were characterized by great deference from the Court when construing statutes enacted by Congress pursuant to its commerce power. But in *United States v. Lopez* (1995), the Court in a 5–4 decision invalidated the Gun-Free School Zones Act of 1990 which made it a federal crime to possess a gun within 1,000 feet of a school.

In the process, the Court transformed Commerce Clause doctrine by scrutinizing closely the congressional decision whether a statute was substantially related to interstate commerce. The Court focused on the fact that possessing a gun at school is not commercial activity and that education was an area of traditional state concern. Five years later, in *United States v. Morrison* (2000), the Court struck down a civil damages provision of the federal Violence Against Women Act which had created a cause of action for victims of gender-motivated violence. The Court held that "[g]ender-motivated crimes of violence are not ... economic activity" and hence not sufficiently related to interstate commerce. *Morrison*, like *Lopez*, was a 5–4 decision with the identical breakdown of justices in the majority and the dissent.

In 2000–2001, the Court issued two decisions interpreting congressional statutes enacted pursuant to Congress's commerce power. Although the Court struck down neither statute, it did interpret both statutes very narrowly so as to avoid the constitutional issue under the Commerce Clause. In *Solid Waste Agency v. United States Corps of Engineers* (2001), the Court, in a 5–4 decision (with the same breakdown of justices as in *Lopez* and *Morrison*) held that the Army Corps of Engineers could not apply the federal Water Pollution Control Act to certain ponds and mudflats based on the presence of migratory birds. Writing for the majority, Chief Justice Rehnquist suggested that if the statute were interpreted in a manner so that it applied to the ponds and mudflats in question, it might well violate the Commerce Clause. Finally, in *Jones v. United States* (2000), the Court unanimously interpreted a federal arson statute not to apply to a private dwelling so as to avoid a consideration of the statute's constitutionality under the Commerce Clause. Each of these decisions, beginning with *Lopez*, have had federalism implications, restraining Congress's ability to regulate matters that are also traditionally regulated by state governments. However, the Court's decision in *Gonzales v. Raich* (2005) allowed federal pre-emption of California's medical marijuana statute.

Religion. Finally, the Rehnquist Court has also had a significant impact on one aspect of Establishment Clause jurisprudence. Since 1986, the Court has increasingly sustained the constitutionality of governmental programs that provide financial assistance to religious schools, decisions at odds with several Burger Court decisions. In fact, in two recent decisions, the Court has expressly overruled Burger Court precedents in this area. In *Agostini v. Felton* (1997), the Court in a 5–4 decision overruled *Aguilar v. Felton* (1985), in which the Court had held that public school teachers could not go onto the premises of private religious schools to provide remedial education without offending the Establishment Clause. In *Mitchell v. Helms* (2000), the Court in a 6–3 decision overruled *Wolman v. Walter* (1977), and *Meek v. Pittenger* (1975), both decisions in which the Court had prohibited the government from giving various types of educational assistance—state-funded field trips in *Wolman* and various instructional equipment in *Meek*—to private religious schools. In *Mitchell*, the Court sustained a governmental program that provided instructional equipment, including computers, to private religious schools. A plurality of four justices concluded that the constitutionality of aid to private religious schools should turn only on whether the aid provision applied equally to all schools—both religious and nonreligious—a conclusion squarely at odds with Burger Court precedents.

Chapter 4

Powers and Limits of the Federal Courts

Contents

I.	Federal Judicial Review	311
	A. The American Judicial System: A Graphic Portrayal	312
	B. Article III: Creating a Federal Court System	312
	C. *Marbury v. Madison*: Legal Analysis	313
	The Political Setting of *Marbury v. Madison*	313
	Analyzing Article III and § 13 of the Judiciary Act of 1789	315
	Marbury v. Madison	319
	D. The Scope of Federal Judicial Power over State Courts	330
	Martin v. Hunter's Lessee	332
	Cohens v. Virginia	336
	E. A Short History of the Marshall Court	339
	F. Judicial Review and the Political Process	343
	Abraham Lincoln's Speech on the *Dred Scott* Decision	343
	First Lincoln-Douglas Debate: Lincoln's Reply	346
	August 21, 1858	346
	From Abraham Lincoln's *First Inaugural Address*	347
	The "Southern Manifesto"	348
	Cooper v. Aaron	348
	G. The Scope of Federal Judicial Power over State Courts: The Adequate and Independent State Ground Doctrine	349
	Michigan v. Long	351
	Kentucky v. Wasson	355
	Oregon v. Henry	356
II.	Congressional Control over Federal Judicial Review	357
	Ex Parte McCardle	360
III.	Justiciability	364
	A. Advisory Opinions	366
	B. Political Questions	367
	Powell v. McCormack	369
	Nixon v. United States	376
	United States v. Stanley	381
	C. Standing	386
	1. Citizen and Taxpayer Standing: The Personal Injury Requirement	388
	Flast v. Cohen	390
	Hein v. Freedom from Religion Foundation, Inc.	399

   2. What Constitutes a Cognizable Injury?   405
City of Los Angeles v. Lyons   405
   3. Cause-in-Fact and Redressability   415
Warth v. Seldin   415
Craig v. Boren   425
   4. Citizen Suits: The Limits of Congressional Grants of Standing   428
   5. Ripeness and Mootness: When Did the Injury Occur?   430
DeFunis v. Odegaard   432

Chapter 4

Powers and Limits of the Federal Courts

In this chapter we consider the scope of the power of the federal judiciary and the limitations on the exercise of that power. The Supreme Court has established its right (and the right of the federal courts) to review for constitutionality the actions of the Congress and the Executive. It has established Supreme Court review over the branches of state governments to see if their actions comply with the Constitution, laws, and treaties of the United States. However, it has also developed doctrines to limit judicial power. The doctrines regarding advisory opinions, standing, mootness, ripeness, and political questions establish limits on the power of the federal courts. The Court has held that some of these limits on its powers are constitutionally mandated while some are a matter of judicial prudence.

I. Federal Judicial Review

Should the Supreme Court have the power to declare acts of Congress unconstitutional and render them null and void? Actions of the President? Acts of state legislatures? Why or why not? What force should a constitutional decision of the Court have? Should it simply bind the parties to the case? Should it also bind others who are similarly situated? Should it determine the constitutional interpretation to be followed by Congress, the President, and the state legislatures? Should it depend on the nature of the issue?

The current Canadian Constitution provides:

> The Constitution of Canada is the supreme law of Canada, and any law that is inconsistent with the provisions of the Constitution is, to the extent of the inconsistency, of no force or effect. § 52, Constitution Act, 1982.

In contrast, the French Constitution of 1791, provided:

> [Judicial] Tribunals cannot either interfere in the exercise of the Legislative Power, or suspend the execution of the laws.... Chapter V, § 4.

Read Article III closely. Does the text of Article III resolve the issue of whether federal courts can nullify unconstitutional legislation?

A. The American Judicial System: A Graphic Portrayal

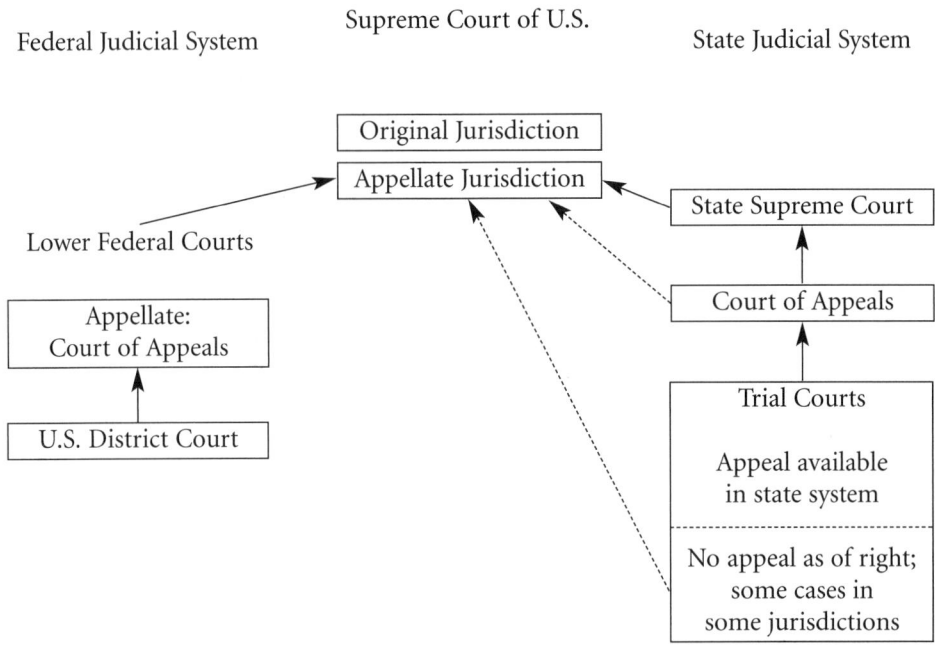

The broken lines (- - - -) represent the possibility of Supreme Court review from a court that is not the highest appellate court in the state. Such review is available when the petitioner has gone as far as possible in the state system. [See *Thompson v. Louisville* (1960).]

B. Article III: Creating a Federal Court System

In its first term, Congress drafted the Judiciary Act of 1789. This legislation created a new federal court system to supplement the existing state courts. Among its tasks, Congress had to determine what types of cases should be tried in district court and appealed to the Supreme Court and what types of cases could be tried in the original jurisdiction (trial) of the Supreme Court. *Marbury v. Madison* (1803) involved the interpretation of the portion of the Act that regulated the original (trial) jurisdiction of the Supreme Court.

Assume that you were staff counsel to the Senate Judiciary Committee in 1789. Read Article III closely and then draft a statute creating the federal court system. Think carefully about the relationship between a constitutional provision and its corresponding statute.

Your statute should regulate both the original and appellate jurisdiction of the Supreme Court of the United States. Give careful thought to what cases should be tried in the first instance in the Supreme Court and what cases should be tried first in the lower federal courts. Consider what can be tried in federal court in general and what can be tried in the Supreme Court in particular. Are the categories of original and appellate jurisdiction exclusive of each other? Why or why not? Assume that state court systems have been established and that appeals in the state system go to the state supreme court before encountering federal jurisdiction.

After you have drafted your statute, ask yourself the following questions about its operation:

1) May the Secretary of State be sued in federal court? Where? In district court? In the Supreme Court?

2) What may a federal court do if it determines that a federal statute is unconstitutional? May it render the statute void or must it enforce the statute and merely ask Congress to pass a new statute?

3) Consider how your statute would apply to the following situation: Assume that Congress, fearing that the President may order troops into battle without waiting for a declaration of war, passes a statute that requires congressional approval before American troops can be ordered to attack a foreign country. (The President vetoes the act, but the Congress overrides the veto.) Recognizing that this statute may raise constitutional questions and desiring a quick resolution of the matter, Congress specifies that any challenges to its constitutionality must be filed directly in the Supreme Court. Does your statute allow this? Does Article III allow this? If either your statute or Article III does not allow this, what happens to a legal challenge filed pursuant to the congressional statute?

C. *Marbury v. Madison*: Legal Analysis

Goals for the study of *Marbury v. Madison*

1. To better understand what is involved in the view that the Court can declare void an act of Congress that violates the Constitution. What are the steps involved in such a decision? What sorts of activities are required to make a decision? How carefully must one read the Act and the Constitution?
2. To understand the basic steps of analysis in the decision in *Marbury v. Madison*.
3. To suggest an alternative reading of both Article III and § 13 of the Judiciary Act to that chosen by the Court.
4. To reflect on the institution of judicial review, its legitimacy, and its limits.
5. To wonder if the power the Court has claimed needs to be limited in any way.

The Political Setting of *Marbury v. Madison*

By 1803, the federal judiciary had already been involved in a major political controversy. Federalist judges had presided over trials under the Sedition Act of 1798 and, as a result, had been embroiled in bitter partisan warfare between the Federalist Adams administration and the Jeffersonian Republicans. The Sedition Act of 1798 had been passed during an undeclared naval war between the United States and the French Republic. Before this conflict with France erupted, the Republicans had remained sympathetic to the French Revolution and French Republic after Federalists had turned against it. The French were inspiring revolutions against European monarchies, and Federalists feared American "Jacobeans" (including the Jeffersonians). The Sedition Act had made it a crime to make false and malicious criticisms of President Adams or the Congress. False and malicious criticisms of Vice President Jefferson (Adams' likely opponent in 1800) were not covered.

From the beginning, Republican congressmen charged that the act was a Federalist tool designed to crush all political opposition. They warned that it would be enforced against Republicans by politically-motivated Federalists—U.S. attorneys, marshals, and judges who had been appointed by Federalist presidents. Things turned out as the Republicans feared. The judges upheld the Act and jailed Jeffersonian critics of President John Adams. As applied, the Act reached "false" political *opinions* as well as false facts. Opinions that landed Jeffersonian Republicans in federal court and then in jail included statements that Adams was not up to the job, was given to ridiculous pomp, or was insufficiently republican. Jeffersonian newspaper editors and politicians were prosecuted, convicted, and imprisoned. According to some witnesses, "professed Democrats"—meaning Jeffersonian Republicans—were excluded from jury pools by Federalist judges or marshals.[1] To make things worse, troops commanded by Federalist officers in Pennsylvania cut down "liberty poles" that flew slogans critical of the Sedition Act and Adams and beat or horsewhipped newspaper editors who criticized their conduct.

By the standards of 1st Amendment law today, the Sedition Act was unconstitutional. Republicans argued that it violated the essential structure of elective republican government, exceeded the delegated power of Congress, and violated the 1st Amendment. Federalist judges justified their power to imprison critics of the government by citing Blackstone and English precedent. Following Blackstone, Federalist judges suggested that freedom of the press was merely a protection against prior restraint and that Jeffersonian Republicans were free to publish their newspapers without a license. However, Federalist courts and juries could then jail them for what they said. Republicans pointed out, to no avail, that this rule came from a nation with a king and a Parliament (one branch of which was hereditary) where sovereignty rested not with the people but with the King in Parliament.

Republican congressmen had no illusion about what was going on. Albert Gallatin commented on the Sedition Act conviction of fellow Republican congressman Matthew Lyon: "We may say what we please about the purity of our courts and juries ... decisions on political questions will always be influenced by party spirit."

Jefferson won the election of 1800. The Sedition Act had a sunset provision by which it (conveniently) expired at the end of Adams' term. It was not reenacted.

With Jefferson set to be inaugurated on March 4, 1801, the Federalist lame duck Congress that met in December promptly enacted the Judiciary Act of 1801, revamped the federal judiciary and created a number of new federal judgeships. In a separate act, Congress also created additional justices of the peace. Adams filled these new positions with Federalists. Some of the commissions for justices of the peace in the District of Columbia had been signed and sealed by Adams in the last hours of the Adams administration. But John Marshall, the newly appointed Chief Justice, who had still been serving as Secretary of State, failed to deliver them before Jefferson's inauguration.

In June of 1801, two of the new Federalist judges in the District of Columbia had instructed the new Republican District Attorney to begin a common law libel prosecution (the Sedition Act having expired with Adams' term) against the pro-Jefferson *National Intelligencer*. Its "crime" was publishing a letter harshly critical of the Federalist judiciary. The letter had accused the courts, among other things, of "destroying all freedom of opin-

---

1. See, e.g., Michael Kent Curtis, *Free Speech, "the People's Darling Privilege": Struggles for Freedom of Expression in American History* 66–79 (2000) [hereafter, Curtis, *Free Speech*]. For the classic account of the Sedition Act, see James Morton Smith, *Freedom's Fetters: The Alien and Sedition Laws and American Civil Liberties* (1956).

ion" and "of executing an unconstitutional Law."[2] The new Republican District Attorney refused to prosecute, the grand jury refused to indict, and the matter was dropped. Of course, Jefferson and the Republicans saw this event as simply another attack on Jeffersonians by a politically motivated Federalist judiciary. Jefferson was outraged. The *National Intelligencer* published a letter from a prominent Virginian: "It seems an absurdity," he wrote, "that the Courts of the United States should have any check or control, in the least degree, over the press or the opinions of citizens or others respecting the President, Congress, Judiciary, the Constitution, or, in short, respecting any subject whatever."[3]

The creation of the new federal judgeships in the Judiciary Act of 1801, which Adams had stuffed with partisan Federalists, filled Federalists with hope and Jeffersonian Republicans with alarm. As supporters of Jefferson saw it, Federalists were entrenching themselves in the judiciary to continue their war on Republicans. As one Republican congressman put it, Federalists had filled the "Judiciary with men who had manifested the most indecorous zeal in favor of the principles of the Federalist party."[4]

Marbury, one of the justices of the peace whose commission had not been delivered, sued James Madison, the new Secretary of State, for his commission. He filed his case not in a lower federal court, but in the Supreme Court. He sought a writ of mandamus to compel James Madison, the new Secretary of State, to deliver his commission. Jefferson's new administration ignored the Supreme Court's order to show cause and refused to appear to defend the suit. Meanwhile, the new Republican controlled Congress repealed the Judiciary Act of 1801 and postponed the next term of the Supreme Court until 1803.

The action in *Marbury v. Madison* seemed to be just another battle in the political war of the Federalists against the Republicans. Had Adams acted in a spirit of bipartisanship, and appointed a number of Republicans as well as Federalists as federal judges (or left many of the positions open for the new President to fill) perhaps the Republican reaction would have been different. Jeffersonian Republicans charged that if the overwhelmingly Federalist judiciary could issue writs of mandamus commanding Republican officials to engage in certain behavior, political control of the nation would lie in the hands of the Federalist bench and not the political branches.

As a practical matter, however, a major shift in political power had occurred. After the election of 1800, the Republicans controlled two of the three branches of the national government. They had repealed the Judiciary Act of 1801. Madison and the Attorney General refused to even appear in the *Marbury* case. So Marshall faced a harsh political reality that constrained his decision in Marbury's case.

The road out of this political thicket was far from clear and obvious.

Analyzing Article III and § 13 of the Judiciary Act of 1789

The Court could theoretically have dismissed Marbury's case for two separate reasons: 1) his case did not come within the terms of § 13 of the Judiciary Act of 1789 (that is, the Court lacked original jurisdiction under the statute); or 2) his case came within the terms of the statute, but the statute was unconstitutional. Does § 13 allow Marbury to file his action in the Supreme Court? If so, is the Act constitutional? To answer these questions,

---

2. 1 Charles Warren, *The Supreme Court in United States History (1789–1835)* 195 (1926).
3. *Id.* at 197, citing *National Intelligencer*, Nov. 18, 1801.
4. *Id.* at 193.

focus on the relevant portions of the Act and of Article III. Compare the Act with the corresponding constitutional provision.

As a general rule today, courts—when possible—avoid deciding constitutional questions. If a statute can reasonably be construed as constitutional, then the court should construe it that way to avoid having to resolve a constitutional question. What policies might explain such a rule? Perhaps the rule is related to the facts that the legislature is elected and judges are not, that it is easier to overturn mistaken judicial constructions of statutes than of the Constitution, and finally, to the fact that the rule postpones and sometimes avoids constitutional collisions between the Court and the elected branches of government.

Are there ways to construe § 13 of the Judiciary Act so that it is constitutional? Consider the following materials. A major goal here is for you to understand the method that underlies decisions as to whether statutes are unconstitutional. It is a question of comparison. You need to know what the statute says—in detail. If it contains words you don't understand, you need to find their meaning or possible meanings. Then you need to know exactly which constitutional provisions are relevant. You need to understand them in detail. If there are words you don't understand, you need to find their meaning or possible meanings. Then you need to compare the statute to the Constitution. Is § 13 consistent or inconsistent with the Constitution? Read Article III and § 13 closely.

ARTICLE III

SECTION 1. The judicial Power of the United States, shall be vested in one supreme Court, and in such inferior Courts as the Congress may from time to time ordain and establish. The Judges, both of the supreme and inferior Courts, shall hold their Offices during good Behaviour, and shall, at stated Times, receive for their Services, a Compensation, which shall not be diminished during their Continuance in Office.

SECTION 2.[1] The judicial Power shall extend to all Cases, in Law and Equity, arising under this Constitution, the Laws of the United States, and Treaties made, or which shall be made, under their Authority;—to all Cases affecting Ambassadors, other public Ministers and Consuls;—to all Cases of admiralty and maritime Jurisdiction;—to Controversies to which the United States shall be a Party;—to Controversies between two or more States;—between a State and Citizens of another State;[5]—between Citizens of different States,—between Citizens of the same State claiming Lands under Grants of different States, and between a State, or the Citizens thereof, and foreign States, Citizens or Subjects.

[2] In all Cases affecting Ambassadors, other public Ministers and Consuls, and those in which a State shall be Party, the supreme Court shall have original Jurisdiction. In all the other Cases before mentioned, the supreme Court shall have appellate Jurisdiction, both as to Law and Fact, with such Exceptions, and under such Regulations as the Congress shall make.

[3] The Trial of all Crimes, except in Cases of Impeachment, shall be by Jury; and such Trial shall be held in the State where the said Crimes shall have been committed; but when not committed within any State, the Trial shall be at such Place or Places as the Congress may by Law have directed.

---

5. This clause has been affected by the 11th Amendment.

SECTION 3.[1] Treason against the United States, shall consist only in levying War against them, or in adhering to their Enemies, giving them Aid and Comfort. No Person shall be convicted of Treason unless on the Testimony of two Witnesses to the same overt Act, or on Confession in open Court.

[2] The Congress shall have Power to declare the Punishment of Treason, but no Attainder of Treason shall work Corruption of Blood, or Forfeiture except during the Life of the Person attainted.

§ 13 of the Judiciary Act of 1789

And be it further enacted,

That the Supreme Court shall have exclusive jurisdiction of all controversies of a civil nature, where a state is a party, except between a state and its citizens;

and except also between a state and citizens of other states, or aliens, in which latter case it shall have original but not exclusive jurisdiction.

And shall have exclusively all such jurisdiction of suits or proceedings against ambassadors, or other public ministers, or their domestics, or domestic servants, as a court of law can have or exercise consistently with the law of nations;

and original, but not exclusive jurisdiction of all suits brought by ambassadors, or other public ministers, or in which a consul, or vice consul, shall be a party.

And the trial of issues of fact in the Supreme Court, in all actions at law against citizens of the United States, shall be by jury.

The Supreme Court shall also have appellate jurisdiction from the circuit courts and courts of the several states, in the cases herein after specially provided for;

and shall have power to issue writs of prohibition to the district courts, when proceeding as courts of admiralty and maritime jurisdiction, and writs of *mandamus*,

in cases warranted by the principles and usages of law,

to any courts appointed, or persons holding office, under the authority of the United States.

Judiciary Act of 1789, ch. 20, § 13, 1 Stat. 73, 80–81 (1789).

Article III and § 13 compared

Art. III, § 2, [2]: In all Cases affecting Ambassadors, **other public Ministers** and Consuls, and those in which a State shall be Party, the supreme Court shall have original Jurisdiction.

§ 13, 2nd sentence: [The Supreme Court] shall have **exclusively** all such jurisdiction of suits or proceedings against ambassadors, or other **public ministers**, or their domestics, or domestic servants, as a court of law can have or exercise consistently with the law of nations; and **original, but not exclusive** jurisdiction of all suits brought by ambassadors, or **other public ministers**, or in which a consul, or vice consul, shall be a party.

The case seems to be in the proper court if the Secretary of State is a "public minister." What does textual analysis of the statute's term "public minister" suggest? What does contextual analysis of this term's placement amidst the other categories mentioned in the 2nd sentence of § 13 suggest?

Art. III, § 2, [2]: In all the other Cases before mentioned, the supreme Court shall have appellate Jurisdiction, both as to Law and Fact, with such Exceptions, and under such Regulations as the Congress shall make.

§ 13, 4th sentence: The Supreme Court shall also have **appellate jurisdiction** from the circuit courts and courts of the several states, in the cases herein after specially provided for; and shall have power to issue **writs** of prohibition **to the district courts**, when proceeding as courts of admiralty and maritime jurisdiction, and **writs of *mandamus*, in cases warranted by the principles and usages of law**, to any courts appointed, or persons holding office, under the authority of the United States.

How does Chief Justice Marshall interpret the statute? In ¶¶ 66–67 he says:

The act to establish the judicial courts of the United States authorizes the supreme court "to issue writs of *mandamus*, in cases warranted by the principles and usages of law, to any courts appointed, or persons holding office, under the authority of the United States."

The secretary of state, being a person holding an office under the authority of the United States, *is precisely within the letter of the description*; and if this court is not authorized to issue a writ of mandamus to such an officer, *it must be because the law is unconstitutional.* . . .

In ¶¶ 68–74 Marshall concludes that the suit cannot be filed in the original jurisdiction of the Supreme Court and rejects the possibility that Congress could expand the original jurisdiction. In ¶ 77 he then says that a writ of mandamus against the Secretary of State would not be an appellate act:

It is the essential criterion of appellate jurisdiction, that it revises and corrects the proceedings in a cause already instituted, and does not create that case. Although, therefore, a mandamus may be directed to courts, yet to issue such a writ to an officer for the delivery of a paper, is in effect the same as to sustain an original action for that paper, and therefore seems not to belong to appellate, but to original jurisdiction.

Since a writ of mandamus against the Secretary of State can seemingly be justified by neither the original nor the appellate jurisdiction of the Supreme Court, Marshall concludes that the Congress' attempt to authorize such must be unconstitutional.

Is this conclusion necessarily correct? The statute states that the Supreme Court can issue writs of mandamus "in cases warranted by the principles and usages of law". If this is not a case "warranted by the principles and usages of law" then the Court would not be statutorily authorized to issue the writ and the case should be dismissed and re-filed in a district court. Justice Marshall never considers this argument in his opinion. What would be the significance of the case if it had been dismissed on statutory grounds?

Can the statute fairly be read as an attempt by Congress to enlarge the original jurisdiction of the Supreme Court? In which part of the statute is the reference to the mandamus power found? What rules of grammar are relevant to understanding the scope of the statute's grant of the mandamus power? Might the language address the possibility of the Supreme Court affirming a case in which a lower court had issued a mandamus?

Article III, § 2, cl. 2, clearly specifies that the original jurisdiction of the Supreme Court is available for cases involving ambassadors and states. The portion of § 13 of the Judiciary Act that *directly* addresses original jurisdiction mentions only ambassadors and states. How strong is Marshall's contention that the power to issue writs of mandamus against federal office holders, mentioned in the context of a description of appellate jurisdiction, implicitly shows congressional intent to increase the scope of the original jurisdiction of the Supreme Court? Might the limitation of the mandamus power to "cases warranted by the principles and usages of law" more likely reference the jurisdictional limitations that are contained in Article III, § 2?

Marbury v. Madison
5 U.S. 137 (1803)

Mr. Chief Justice Marshall delivered the opinion of the Court.

[1] At the last term, on the affidavits then read and filed with the clerk, a rule was granted in this case, requiring the secretary of state to show cause why a mandamus should not issue, directing him to deliver to William Marbury his commission as a justice of the peace for the county of Washington, in the district of Columbia.

[2] No cause has been shown, and the present motion is for a mandamus. The peculiar delicacy of this case, the novelty of some of its circumstances, and the real difficulty attending the points which occur in it, require a complete exposition of the principles on which the opinion to be given by the court is founded....

[3] In the order in which the court has viewed this subject, the following questions have been considered and decided.

[4] 1. Has the applicant a right to the commission he demands?

[5] 2. If he has a right, and that right has been violated, do the laws of his country afford him a remedy?

[6] 3. If they do afford him a remedy, is it a mandamus issuing from this court?

[7] The first object of inquiry is,

[8] 1. Has the applicant a right to the commission he demands?

[9] His right originates in an act of congress passed in February 1801, concerning the district of Columbia.

[10] After dividing the district into two counties, the eleventh section of this law enacts, "that there shall be appointed in and for each of the said counties, such number of discreet persons to be justices of the peace as the president of the United States shall, from time to time, think expedient, to continue in office for five years."

[11] It appears from the affidavits, that in compliance with this law, a commission for William Marbury as a justice of peace for the county of Washington was signed by John Adams, then president of the United States; after which the seal of the United States was affixed to it; but the commission has never reached the person for whom it was made out.

[12] In order to determine whether he is entitled to this commission, it becomes necessary to inquire whether he has been appointed to the office. For if he has been appointed, the law continues him in office for five years, and he is entitled to the possession of those evidences of office, which, being completed, became his property....

[13] This [case involves] an appointment made by the president, by and with the advice and consent of the senate, and is evidenced by no act but the commission itself. In such a case therefore the commission and the appointment seem inseparable; it being almost impossible to show an appointment otherwise than by proving the existence of a com-

mission: still the commission is not necessarily the appointment; though conclusive evidence of it.

[14] But at what stage does it amount to this conclusive evidence?

[15] The answer to this question seems an obvious one. The appointment being the sole act of the president, must be completely evidenced, when it is shown that he has done every thing to be performed by him....

[16] The last act to be done by the president, is the signature of the commission. He has then acted on the advice and consent of the senate to his own nomination. The time for deliberation has then passed. He has decided. His judgment, on the advice and consent of the senate concurring with his nomination, has been made, and the officer is appointed. This appointment is evidenced by an open, unequivocal act; and being the last act required from the person making it, necessarily excludes the idea of its being, so far as it respects the appointment, an inchoate and incomplete transaction.

[17] Some point of time must be taken when the power of the executive over an officer, not removable at his will, must cease. That point of time must be when the constitutional power of appointment has been exercised. And this power has been exercised when the last act, required from the person possessing the power, has been performed. This last act is the signature of the commission....

[18] The signature is a warrant for affixing the great seal to the commission; and the great seal is only to be affixed to an instrument which is complete. It attests, by an act supposed to be of public notoriety, the verity of the presidential signature.

[19] It is never to be affixed till the commission is signed, because the signature, which gives force and effect to the commission, is conclusive evidence that the appointment is made.

[20] The commission being signed, the subsequent duty of the secretary of state is prescribed by law, and not to be guided by the will of the president. He is to affix the seal of the United States to the commission, and is to record it.

[21] This is not a proceeding which may be varied, if the judgment of the executive shall suggest one more eligible, but is a precise course accurately marked out by law, and is to be strictly pursued. It is the duty of the secretary of state to conform to the law, and in this he is an officer of the United States, bound to obey the laws. He acts, in this respect, as has been very properly stated at the bar, under the authority of law, and not by the instructions of the president. It is a ministerial act which the law enjoins on a particular officer for a particular purpose....

[22] It is therefore decidedly the opinion of the court, that when a commission has been signed by the president, the appointment is made; and that the commission is complete when the seal of the United States has been affixed to it by the secretary of state.

[23] Where an officer is removable at the will of the executive, the circumstance which completes his appointment is of no concern; because the act is at any time revocable; and the commission may be arrested, if still in the office. But when the officer is not removable at the will of the executive, the appointment is not revocable and cannot be annulled. It has conferred legal rights which cannot be resumed.

[24] The discretion of the executive is to be exercised until the appointment has been made. But having once made the appointment, his power over the office is terminated in all cases, where by law the officer is not removable by him. The right to the office is then in the person appointed, and he has the absolute, unconditional power of accepting or rejecting it.

[25] Mr. Marbury, then, since his commission was signed by the president and sealed by the secretary of state, was appointed; and as the law creating the office gave the officer a right to hold for five years independent of the executive, the appointment was not revocable; but vested in the officer legal rights which are protected by the laws of his country.

[26] To withhold the commission, therefore, is an act deemed by the court not warranted by law, but violative of a vested legal right.

[27] This brings us to the second inquiry; which is,

[28] 2. If he has a right, and that right has been violated, do the laws of his country afford him a remedy?

[29] The very essence of civil liberty certainly consists in the right of every individual to claim the protection of the laws, whenever he receives an injury. One of the first duties of government is to afford that protection. In Great Britain the king himself is sued in the respectful form of a petition, and he never fails to comply with the judgment of his court....

[30] The government of the United States has been emphatically termed a government of laws, and not of men. It will certainly cease to deserve this high appellation, if the laws furnish no remedy for the violation of a vested legal right.

[31] If this obloquy is to be cast on the jurisprudence of our country, it must arise from the peculiar character of the case.

[32] It behoves us then to inquire whether there be in its composition any ingredient which shall exempt from legal investigation, or exclude the injured party from legal redress. In pursuing this inquiry the first question which presents itself, is, whether this can be arranged with that class of cases which come under the description of damnum absque injuria—a loss without an injury.

[33] This description of cases never has been considered, and it is believed never can be considered as comprehending offices of trust, of honour or of profit. The office of justice of peace in the district of Columbia is such an office; it is therefore worthy of the attention and guardianship of the laws. It has received that attention and guardianship. It has been created by special act of congress, and has been secured, so far as the laws can give security to the person appointed to fill it, for five years. It is not then on account of the worthlessness of the thing pursued, that the injured party can be alleged to be without remedy.

[34] Is it in the nature of the transaction? Is the act of delivering or withholding a commission to be considered as a mere political act belonging to the executive department alone, for the performance of which entire confidence is placed by our constitution in the supreme executive; and for any misconduct respecting which, the injured individual has no remedy?

[35] That there may be such cases is not to be questioned; but that every act of duty to be performed in any of the great departments of government constitutes such a case, is not to be admitted....

[36] It is not believed that any person whatever would attempt to maintain such a proposition.

[37] It follows then that the question, whether the legality of an act of the head of a department be examinable in a court of justice or not, must always depend on the nature of that act.

[38] If some acts be examinable, and others not, there must be some rule of law to guide the court in the exercise of its jurisdiction.

[39] In some instances there may be difficulty in applying the rule to particular cases; but there cannot, it is believed, be much difficulty in laying down the rule.

[40] By the constitution of the United States, the president is invested with certain important political powers, in the exercise of which he is to use his own discretion, and is accountable only to his country in his political character, and to his own conscience. To aid him in the performance of these duties, he is authorized to appoint certain officers, who act by his authority and in conformity with his orders.

[41] In such cases, their acts are his acts; and whatever opinion may be entertained of the manner in which executive discretion may be used, still there exists, and can exist, no power to control that discretion. The subjects are political. They respect the nation, not individual rights, and being entrusted to the executive, the decision of the executive is conclusive. The application of this remark will be perceived by adverting to the act of congress for establishing the department of foreign affairs. This officer, as his duties were prescribed by that act, is to conform precisely to the will of the president. He is the mere organ by whom that will is communicated. The acts of such an officer, as an officer, can never be examinable by the courts.

[42] But when the legislature proceeds to impose on that officer other duties; when he is directed peremptorily to perform certain acts; when the rights of individuals are dependent on the performance of those acts; he is so far the officer of the law; is amenable to the laws for his conduct; and cannot at his discretion sport away the vested rights of others.

[43] The conclusion from this reasoning is, that where the heads of departments are the political or confidential agents of the executive, merely to execute the will of the president, or rather to act in cases in which the executive possesses a constitutional or legal discretion, nothing can be more perfectly clear than that their acts are only politically examinable. But where a specific duty is assigned by law, and individual rights depend upon the performance of that duty, it seems equally clear that the individual who considers himself injured has a right to resort to the laws of his country for a remedy.

[44] If this be the rule, let us inquire how it applies to the case under the consideration of the court.

[45] The power of nominating to the senate, and the power of appointing the person nominated, are political powers, to be exercised by the president according to his own discretion. When he has made an appointment, he has exercised his whole power, and his discretion has been completely applied to the case. If, by law, the officer be removable at the will of the president, then a new appointment may be immediately made, and the rights of the officer are terminated. But as a fact which has existed cannot be made never to have existed, the appointment cannot be annihilated; and consequently if the officer is by law not removable at the will of the president, the rights he has acquired are protected by the law, and are not resumable by the president....

[46] It is then the opinion of the court,

[47] 1. That by signing the commission of Mr. Marbury, the president of the United States appointed him a justice of peace for the county of Washington in the district of Columbia; and that the seal of the United States, affixed thereto by the secretary of state, is conclusive testimony of the verity of the signature, and of the completion of the appointment; and that the appointment conferred on him a legal right to the office for the space of five years.

[48] 2. That, having this legal title to the office, he has a consequent right to the commission; a refusal to deliver which is a plain violation of that right, for which the laws of his country afford him a remedy.

[49] It remains to be inquired whether,

[50] 3. He is entitled to the remedy for which he applies. This depends on,

[51] 1. The nature of the writ applied for. And,

[52] 2. The power of this court.

[53] 1. The nature of the writ.

[54] Blackstone defines a mandamus to be, "a command issuing in the king's name from the court of king's bench, and directed to any person, corporation, or inferior court of judicature within the king's dominions, requiring them to do some particular thing therein specified which appertains to their office and duty, and which the court of king's bench has previously determined, or at least supposes, to be consonant to right and justice." ...

[55] This writ, if awarded, would be directed to an officer of government, and its mandate to him would be, to use the words of Blackstone, "to do a particular thing therein specified, which appertains to his office and duty, and which the court has previously determined or at least supposes to be consonant to right and justice." Or, in the words of Lord Mansfield, the applicant, in this case, has a right to execute an office of public concern, and is kept out of possession of that right.

[56] These circumstances certainly concur in this case.

[57] Still, to render the mandamus a proper remedy, the officer to whom it is to be directed, must be one to whom, on legal principles, such writ may be directed; and the person applying for it must be without any other specific and legal remedy.

[58] 1. With respect to the officer to whom it would be directed. The intimate political relation, subsisting between the president of the United States and the heads of departments, necessarily renders any legal investigation of the acts of one of those high officers peculiarly irksome, as well as delicate; and excites some hesitation with respect to the propriety of entering into such investigation. Impressions are often received without much reflection or examination; and it is not wonderful that in such a case as this, the assertion, by an individual, of his legal claims in a court of justice, to which claims it is the duty of that court to attend, should at first view be considered by some, as an attempt to intrude into the cabinet, and to intermeddle with the prerogatives of the executive.

[59] It is scarcely necessary for the court to disclaim all pretensions to such a jurisdiction. An extravagance, so absurd and excessive, could not have been entertained for a moment. The province of the court is, solely, to decide on the rights of individuals, not to inquire how the executive, or executive officers, perform duties in which they have a discretion. Questions, in their nature political, or which are, by the constitution and laws, submitted to the executive, can never be made in this court.

[60] But, if this be not such a question; if so far from being an intrusion into the secrets of the cabinet, it respects a paper, which, according to law, is upon record, and to a copy of which the law gives a right, on the payment of ten cents; if it be no intermeddling with a subject, over which the executive can be considered as having exercised any control; what is there in the exalted station of the officer, which shall bar a citizen from asserting, in a court of justice, his legal rights, or shall forbid a court to listen to the claim; or to issue a mandamus, directing the performance of a duty, not depending on executive discretion, but on particular acts of congress and the general principles of law?

[61] If one of the heads of departments commits any illegal act, under colour of his office, by which an individual sustains an injury, it cannot be pretended that his office alone exempts him from being sued in the ordinary mode of proceeding, and being compelled to obey the judgment of the law. How then can his office exempt him from this particular mode of deciding on the legality of his conduct, if the case be such a case as would, were any other individual the party complained of, authorize the process?

[62] It is not by the office of the person to whom the writ is directed, but the nature of the thing to be done, that the propriety or impropriety of issuing a mandamus is to be determined. Where the head of a department acts in a case in which executive discretion is to be exercised; in which he is the mere organ of executive will; it is again repeated, that any application to a court to control, in any respect, his conduct, would be rejected without hesitation.

[63] But where he is directed by law to do a certain act affecting the absolute rights of individuals, in the performance of which he is not placed under the particular direction of the president, and the performance of which the president cannot lawfully forbid, and therefore is never presumed to have forbidden; as for example, to record a commission, or a patent for land, which has received all the legal solemnities; or to give a copy of such record; in such cases, it is not perceived on what ground the courts of the country are further excused from the duty of giving judgment, that right to be done to an injured individual, than if the same services were to be performed by a person not the head of a department....

[64] This, then, is a plain case of a mandamus, either to deliver the commission, or a copy of it from the record; and it only remains to be inquired,

[65] Whether it can issue from this court.

[66] The act to establish the judicial courts of the United States authorizes the supreme court "to issue writs of mandamus, in cases warranted by the principles and usages of law, to any courts appointed, or persons holding office, under the authority of the United States."

[67] The secretary of state, being a person, holding an office under the authority of the United States, is precisely within the letter of the description; and if this court is not authorized to issue a writ of mandamus to such an officer, it must be because the law is unconstitutional, and therefore absolutely incapable of conferring the authority, and assigning the duties which its words purport to confer and assign.

[68] The constitution vests the whole judicial power of the United States in one supreme court, and such inferior courts as congress shall, from time to time, ordain and establish. This power is expressly extended to all cases arising under the laws of the United States; and consequently, in some form, may be exercised over the present case; because the right claimed is given by a law of the United States.

[69] In the distribution of this power it is declared that "the supreme court shall have original jurisdiction in all cases affecting ambassadors, other public ministers and consuls, and those in which a state shall be a party. In all other cases, the supreme court shall have appellate jurisdiction."

[70] It has been insisted at the bar, that as the original grant of jurisdiction to the supreme and inferior courts is general, and the clause, assigning original jurisdiction to the supreme court, contains no negative or restrictive words; the power remains to the legislature to assign original jurisdiction to that court in other cases than those specified in the article which has been recited; provided those cases belong to the judicial power of the United States.

[71] If it had been intended to leave it in the discretion of the legislature to apportion the judicial power between the supreme and inferior courts according to the will of that body, it would certainly have been useless to have proceeded further than to have defined the judicial power, and the tribunals in which it should be vested. The subsequent part of the section is mere surplusage, is entirely without meaning, if such is to be the construction. If congress remains at liberty to give this court appellate jurisdiction, where the constitution has declared their jurisdiction shall be original; and original jurisdiction where the constitution has declared it shall be appellate; the distribution of jurisdiction made in the constitution, is form without substance.

[72] Affirmative words are often, in their operation, negative of other objects than those affirmed; and in this case, a negative or exclusive sense must be given to them or they have no operation at all.

[73] It cannot be presumed that any clause in the constitution is intended to be without effect; and therefore such construction is inadmissible, unless the words require it....

[74] When an instrument organizing fundamentally a judicial system, divides it into one supreme, and so many inferior courts as the legislature may ordain and establish; then enumerates its powers, and proceeds so far to distribute them, as to define the jurisdiction of the supreme court by declaring the cases in which it shall take original jurisdiction, and that in others it shall take appellate jurisdiction, the plain import of the words seems to be, that in one class of cases its jurisdiction is original, and not appellate; in the other it is appellate, and not original. If any other construction would render the clause inoperative, that is an additional reason for rejecting such other construction, and for adhering to the obvious meaning.

[75] To enable this court then to issue a mandamus, it must be shown to be an exercise of appellate jurisdiction, or to be necessary to enable them to exercise appellate jurisdiction.

[76] It has been stated at the bar that the appellate jurisdiction may be exercised in a variety of forms, and that if it be the will of the legislature that a mandamus should be used for that purpose, that will must be obeyed. This is true; yet the jurisdiction must be appellate, not original.

[77] It is the essential criterion of appellate jurisdiction, that it revises and corrects the proceedings in a cause already instituted, and does not create that case. Although, therefore, a mandamus may be directed to courts, yet to issue such a writ to an officer for the delivery of a paper, is in effect the same as to sustain an original action for that paper, and therefore seems not to belong to appellate, but to original jurisdiction. Neither is it necessary in such a case as this, to enable the court to exercise its appellate jurisdiction.

[78] The authority, therefore, given to the supreme court, by the act establishing the judicial courts of the United States, to issue writs of mandamus to public officers, appears not to be warranted by the constitution; and it becomes necessary to inquire whether a jurisdiction, so conferred, can be exercised.

[79] The question, whether an act, repugnant to the constitution, can become the law of the land, is a question deeply interesting to the United States; but, happily, not of an intricacy proportioned to its interest. It seems only necessary to recognise certain principles, supposed to have been long and well established, to decide it.

[80] That the people have an original right to establish, for their future government, such principles as, in their opinion, shall most conduce to their own happiness, is the basis on which the whole American fabric has been erected. The exercise of this original

right is a very great exertion; nor can it nor ought it to be frequently repeated. The principles, therefore, so established are deemed fundamental. And as the authority, from which they proceed, is supreme, and can seldom act, they are designed to be permanent.

[81] This original and supreme will organizes the government, and assigns to different departments their respective powers. It may either stop here; or establish certain limits not to be transcended by those departments.

[82] The government of the United States is of the latter description. The powers of the legislature are defined and limited; and that those limits may not be mistaken or forgotten, the constitution is written. To what purpose are powers limited, and to what purpose is that limitation committed to writing; if these limits may, at any time, be passed by those intended to be restrained? The distinction between a government with limited and unlimited powers is abolished, if those limits do not confine the persons on whom they are imposed, and if acts prohibited and acts allowed are of equal obligation. It is a proposition too plain to be contested, that the constitution controls any legislative act repugnant to it; or, that the legislature may alter the constitution by an ordinary act.

[83] Between these alternatives there is no middle ground. The constitution is either a superior, paramount law, unchangeable by ordinary means, or it is on a level with ordinary legislative acts, and like other acts, is alterable when the legislature shall please to alter it.

[84] If the former part of the alternative be true, then a legislative act contrary to the constitution is not law: if the latter part be true, then written constitutions are absurd attempts, on the part of the people, to limit a power in its own nature illimitable.

[85] Certainly all those who have framed written constitutions contemplate them as forming the fundamental and paramount law of the nation, and consequently the theory of every such government must be, that an act of the legislature repugnant to the constitution is void.

[86] This theory is essentially attached to a written constitution, and is consequently to be considered by this court as one of the fundamental principles of our society. It is not therefore to be lost sight of in the further consideration of this subject.

[87] If an act of the legislature, repugnant to the constitution, is void, does it, notwithstanding its invalidity, bind the courts and oblige them to give it effect? Or, in other words, though it be not law, does it constitute a rule as operative as if it was a law? This would be to overthrow in fact what was established in theory; and would seem, at first view, an absurdity too gross to be insisted on. It shall, however, receive a more attentive consideration.

[88] It is emphatically the province and duty of the judicial department to say what the law is. Those who apply the rule to particular cases, must of necessity expound and interpret that rule. If two laws conflict with each other, the courts must decide on the operation of each.

[89] So if a law be in opposition to the constitution: if both the law and the constitution apply to a particular case, so that the court must either decide that case conformably to the law, disregarding the constitution; or conformably to the constitution, disregarding the law: the court must determine which of these conflicting rules governs the case. This is of the very essence of judicial duty.

[90] If then the courts are to regard the constitution; and the constitution is superior to any ordinary act of the legislature; the constitution, and not such ordinary act, must govern the case to which they both apply.

[91] Those then who controvert the principle that the constitution is to be considered, in court, as a paramount law, are reduced to the necessity of maintaining that courts must close their eyes on the constitution, and see only the law.

[92] This doctrine would subvert the very foundation of all written constitutions. It would declare that an act, which, according to the principles and theory of our government, is entirely void, is yet, in practice, completely obligatory. It would declare, that if the legislature shall do what is expressly forbidden, such act, notwithstanding the express prohibition, is in reality effectual. It would be giving to the legislature a practical and real omnipotence with the same breath which professes to restrict their powers within narrow limits. It is prescribing limits, and declaring that those limits may be passed at pleasure.

[93] That it thus reduces to nothing what we have deemed the greatest improvement on political institutions—a written constitution, would of itself be sufficient, in America where written constitutions have been viewed with so much reverence, for rejecting the construction. But the peculiar expressions of the constitution of the United States furnish additional arguments in favour of its rejection.

[94] The judicial power of the United States is extended to all cases arising under the constitution.

[95] Could it be the intention of those who gave this power, to say that, in using it, the constitution should not be looked into? That a case arising under the constitution should be decided without examining the instrument under which it arises?

[96] This is too extravagant to be maintained.

[97] In some cases then, the constitution must be looked into by the judges. And if they can open it at all, what part of it are they forbidden to read, or to obey?

[98] There are many other parts of the constitution which serve to illustrate this subject.

[99] It is declared that "no tax or duty shall be laid on articles exported from any state." Suppose a duty on the export of cotton, of tobacco, or of flour; and a suit instituted to recover it. Ought judgment to be rendered in such a case? Ought the judges to close their eyes on the constitution, and only see the Law?

[100] The constitution declares that "no bill of attainder or ex post facto law shall be passed."

[101] If, however, such a bill should be passed and a person should be prosecuted under it, must the court condemn to death those victims whom the constitution endeavours to preserve?

[102] "No person," says the constitution, "shall be convicted of treason unless on the testimony of two witnesses to the same overt act, or on confession in open court."

[103] Here the language of the constitution is addressed especially to the courts. It prescribes, directly for them, a rule of evidence not to be departed from. If the legislature should change that rule, and declare one witness, or a confession out of court, sufficient for conviction, must the constitutional principle yield to the legislative act?

[104] From these and many other selections which might be made, it is apparent, that the framers of the constitution contemplated that instrument as a rule for the government of courts, as well as of the legislature.

[105] Why otherwise does it direct the judges to take an oath to support it? This oath certainly applies, in an especial manner, to their conduct in their official character. How

immoral to impose it on them, if they were to be used as the instruments, and the knowing instruments, for violating what they swear to support....

[106] The oath of office, too, imposed by the legislature, is completely demonstrative of the legislative opinion on this subject. It is in these words: "I do solemnly swear that I will administer justice without respect to persons, and do equal right to the poor and to the rich; and that I will faithfully and impartially discharge all the duties incumbent on me as according to the best of my abilities and understanding, agreeably to the constitution and laws of the United States."

[107] Why does a judge swear to discharge his duties agreeably to the constitution of the United States, if that constitution forms no rule for his government? If it is closed upon him and cannot be inspected by him?

[108] If such be the real state of things, this is worse than solemn mockery. To prescribe, or to take this oath, becomes equally a crime.

[109] It is also not entirely unworthy of observation, that in declaring what shall be the supreme law of the land, the constitution itself is first mentioned; and not the laws of the United States generally, but those only which shall be made in pursuance of the constitution, have that rank.

[110] Thus, the particular phraseology of the constitution of the United States confirms and strengthens the principle, supposed to be essential to all written constitutions, that a law repugnant to the constitution is void, and that courts, as well as other departments, are bound by that instrument.

[111] The rule must be discharged.

Marbury v. Madison: Questions

1. What is Marbury claiming with reference to his commission? Does the Court say that his claim is valid? Why? What are the three questions the opinion seeks to answer? Does the Court hold it has jurisdiction to decide the case?
2. What statute does Marbury claim authorizes jurisdiction by the Supreme Court in his case? What constitutional provisions are involved?
3. What does the Court hold with reference to jurisdiction? Why?
4. Why exactly does the Court find § 13 of the Judiciary Act unconstitutional? What sentence of the Act does it interpret? How does the Court read that sentence? What does it claim the Act does that is forbidden by the Constitution?
5. What does "public minister" mean in Article III? What does "mandamus" mean in § 13?
6. If the Act is unconstitutional, what is the significance of that fact, according to the Court?
7. What are the steps in the argument by which the Court holds that acts of Congress that violate the Constitution are void?
8. Should John Marshall have participated in the decision of this case?
    a. Should Marshall have disqualified himself in this case? Recall that Marshall was President Adams' Secretary of State and had failed to deliver Marbury's commission. Moreover, this case was brought in the Supreme Court in the first instance—allegedly under the original jurisdiction of the Court; and, at the hearing before the Court, Marshall's brother was a witness.
    b. How can you explain Marshall's failure to disqualify himself?

9. Should the Court have organized the opinion differently?

    a. Should Marshall have decided the jurisdictional question first? If he had done so, how would the opinion be different? Would you be studying it today?

    b. If the Court lacked jurisdiction to decide the case, could Marshall justify his discussion of the merits, i.e., the first two of the three issues he identifies?

10. Do you think that Jefferson would have instructed Madison to obey if the Court had issued the writ of mandamus? Was Andrew Jackson wrong when he allegedly said of another case, "John Marshall has made his decision. Now let him enforce it."?

Marbury v. Madison: Notes

As may be apparent to you now, Chief Justice Marshall's solution to the *Marbury* dilemma is not as simple as it appears. You may conclude that the opinion in *Marbury* was written as it should have been or you may have a more critical view. Chief Justice Marshall's opinion is an argument justifying deciding the case as it was decided. Consider the following critical analysis.

First, it is quite dubious that §13 of the Judiciary Act of 1789 (passed by the first Congress, filled with a number of framers and ratifiers) attempted to expand the original jurisdiction of the Supreme Court. It provided:

> The Supreme Court shall also have ... power to issue ... writs of *mandamus, in cases warranted by the principles and usages of law* (emphasis added), to any courts appointed, or persons holding office, under the authority of the United States.

If the Supreme Court had no jurisdiction of the case, then, to put it mildly, it would not be "in accordance with the principles and usages of law" for it to have issued a mandamus or done anything at all, except to dismiss the case for lack of jurisdiction. Today, courts are expected to construe acts to avoid constitutional questions when they can reasonably do so. Here the Court construed the act in a peculiar way in order to have to reach a constitutional question and thus announce its authority to review an act of Congress.

However, even if the statute *did* attempt to expand the Court's original jurisdiction, it is not at all obvious that Article III prevents Congress from adding to the original jurisdiction of the Court—as opposed to subtracting from it.[1] Article III, §2, clause 2 provides:

> In all Cases affecting Ambassadors, or other public Ministers and Counsels, and those in which a State shall be Party, the supreme Court shall have original Jurisdiction. In all other Cases before mentioned, the supreme court shall have appellate Jurisdiction, both as to Law and Fact, with such Exceptions, and under such Regulations as the Congress shall make.

In any case, even assuming the Court was correct in concluding that Congress could not constitutionally expand its original jurisdiction, Marshall ignored the ordinary consequences of a finding of no jurisdiction. He proceeded to address the merits of Marbury's claim and to assert the Court's potential authority over President Jefferson. However, since there were no legal consequences to the Republicans flowing from the opinion—after all, the Federalist Marbury lost—there could be no *legal* confrontation between Marshall and the Republicans.

---

1. William Van Alystyne makes this point clear in his classic article on the case, *A Critical Guide to* Marbury v. Madison, 1969 Duke L.J. 1. This article is an excellent review of *Marbury*.

By addressing the merits before he held the Court without jurisdiction, Marshall was able to criticize President Jefferson. A less political and more conciliatory approach to the case (and the one with better legal support) would have been to reverse the order of the questions in the case, find no jurisdiction, dismiss the case, and avoid passing on the merits of Marbury's claim. With its exhaustive discussion of the merits, however, the Court provided grist for the Federalist newspaper mill. In reporting the decision, the *New England Palladum* wrote that "it has been solemnly decided in the Supreme Court, that Mr. Jefferson, the idol of democracy, the friend of the people, has trampled upon the charter of their liberties." The headline in the Federalist *New York Evening Post* read, "Constitution violated by the President." The *Post* suggested that the Court's decision had revealed "a subtle and smooth-faced hypocrisy concealing an ambition the most criminal, the most enormous, the most unprincipled." Jefferson's first act had been to "stretch his powers beyond their limits" in order to "commit an act of direct violence on the most sacred right of private property."[2]

There was hostile Republican newspaper comment on *Marbury*. But it was aimed, not at the Court's assertion of authority for judicial review, but at the Court's discussion of the merits of a case over which it had no jurisdiction.

For what proposition does *Marbury* stand?

1. Does it stand for the simple proposition that in litigation before the Court, the Court may refuse to give effect to an act of Congress pertaining to the *judicial power* if, in its judgment, the act contravenes the constitutional provisions which describe the judicial power?

2. Or does it stand for the proposition that in litigation before the Court, the Court may refuse to give effect to an act of Congress *pertaining to any topic* where, in the Court's judgment, that act is repugnant to the Constitution? Would Lincoln have conceded that much?

3. Does *Marbury* stand for the proposition that the Court has the ultimate responsibility for enforcing constitutional limitations upon all branches of the federal government, all branches of state government, and that these branches of government are bound by its decision?

D. The Scope of Federal Judicial Power over State Courts

Martin v. Hunter's Lessee: Background

Marbury dealt with a federal court striking down a federal statute. Should Supreme Court review extend to the nullification of judgments on matters of federal law rendered in state court? Section 25 of the Judiciary Act of 1789 addressed this issue:

> That a final judgment or decree in any suit, in the highest court of law or equity of a State in which a decision in the suit could be had, where is drawn in question the validity of a treaty or statute of, or an authority exercised under the

---

2. 1 Charles Warren, *The Supreme Court in United States History (1789–1835)* at 246–48 (citing *New England Palladium* (Boston), Apr. 12, 1803; and the *New York Evening Post*, Mar. 23, 1803) (1926).

United States, and the decision is against their validity; or where is drawn in question the validity of a statute of, or an authority exercised under, any State, on the ground of their being repugnant to the constitution, treaties or laws of the United States, and the decision is in favour of such their validity, or where is drawn in question the construction of any clause of the constitution, or of a treaty, or statute of, or commission held under the United States, and the decision is against the title, right, privilege or exemption specially set up or claimed by either party, under such clause of the said constitution, treaty, statute or commission, may be re-examined and reversed or affirmed in the Supreme Court of the United States upon a writ of error. [But] no other error shall be assigned or regarded as a ground of reversal in any such case as aforesaid, than such as appears on the face of the record, and immediately respects the before mentioned questions of validity or construction of the said constitution, treaties, statutes, commissions, or authorities in dispute.

Judiciary Act of 1789, ch. 20, §25, 1 Stat. 73, 85–87 (1789).

If §13 could be held unconstitutional, might §25 be unconstitutional as well?

Martin v. Hunter's Lessee involved the resolution of a property dispute. Virginia had passed legislation confiscating land owned by British aliens during the Revolution. One of the conditions in the 1783 Peace Treaty with Britain was that confiscated lands should be returned and there should be no more confiscations. In 1785, Virginia passed another confiscation law. *Martin v. Hunter's Lessee* involved a conflict between Hunter's lessee, claiming title under the 1785 Virginia statute, and Martin, relying on the protections of the 1783 Treaty. Hunter sued in Virginia state court and lost. He appealed and won in the Virginia Court of Appeals. Martin, relying on §25 of the Judiciary Act of 1789, then appealed to the United States Supreme Court. The Supreme Court reversed, and remanded the case to the Virginia Court of Appeals, directing them to enter judgment for Martin. They refused, and in the course of doing so, declared §25 unconstitutional.

The Virginia court did not challenge the authority of federal courts to reach federal questions. They agreed that the interpretation of the Treaty would have been a fit topic for *removal* into the federal system, but the case had not been removed. Their contention was that once a case is properly before the highest court of a state, the United States Supreme Court is required to defer to the opinion of another sovereign entity. One implication of this view would be to allow state courts to determine the scope of federal power—a position advocated by the anti-Federalists.

Questions

1. What constitutional provisions support the constitutionality of §25?
2. We have looked at different types of constitutional arguments—arguments from text, from structure, from policy, from precedent, and from history. Identify arguments from text, context, structure, history, precedent, etc., used in *Martin v. Hunter's Lessee*.
3. The Virginia court apparently did not think *Marbury v. Madison* was controlling, or perhaps it disagreed with that decision. At any rate, how many ways could you distinguish *Marbury* so as to argue that it did not apply to the facts in *Martin*?

Martin v. Hunter's Lessee
14 U.S. 304 (1816)

Story, J., delivered the opinion of the court.

This is a writ of error from the court of appeals of Virginia, founded upon the refusal of that court to obey the mandate of this court, requiring the judgment rendered in this very cause, at February term, 1813, to be carried into due execution. The following is the judgment of the court of appeals rendered on the mandate:

> The court is unanimously of opinion, that the appellate power of the supreme court of the United States does not extend to this court, under a sound construction of the constitution of the United States; that so much of the 25th section of the act of congress to establish the judicial courts of the United States, as extends the appellate jurisdiction of the supreme court to this court, is not in pursuance of the constitution of the United States; that the writ of error, in this cause, was improvidently allowed under the authority of that act; that the proceedings thereon in the supreme court were, *coram non judice*, in relation to this court, and that obedience to its mandate be declined by the court....

The constitution of the United States was ordained and established, not by the states in their sovereign capacities, but emphatically, as the preamble of the constitution declares, by "the people of the United States."...

The government ... of the United States, can claim no powers which are not granted to it by the constitution, and the powers actually granted, must be such as are expressly given, or given by necessary implication. On the other hand, this instrument, like every other grant, is to have a reasonable construction, according to the import of its terms; and where a power is expressly given in general terms, it is not to be restrained to particular cases, unless that construction grow out of the context expressly, or by necessary implication. The words are to be taken in their natural and obvious sense, and not in a sense unreasonably restricted or enlarged....

[We now consider] the great question as to the nature and extent of the appellate jurisdiction of the United States. We have already seen that appellate jurisdiction is given by the constitution to the supreme court in all cases where it has not original jurisdiction; subject, however, to such exceptions and regulations as congress may prescribe. It is, therefore, capable of embracing every case enumerated in the constitution, which is not exclusively to be decided by way of original jurisdiction. But the exercise of appellate jurisdiction is far from being limited by the terms of the constitution to the supreme court. There can be no doubt that congress may create a succession of inferior tribunals, in each of which it may vest appellate as well as original jurisdiction. The judicial power is delegated by the constitution in the most general terms, and may, therefore, be exercised by congress under every variety of form of appellate or original jurisdiction. And as there is nothing in the constitution which restrains or limits this power, it must, therefore, in all other cases, subsist in the utmost latitude of which, in its own nature, it is susceptible.

As, then, by the terms of the constitution, the appellate jurisdiction is not limited as to the supreme court, and as to this court it may be exercised in all other cases than those of which it has original cognizance, what is there to restrain its exercise over state tribunals in the enumerated cases? The appellate power is not limited by the terms of the third article to any particular courts. The words are, "the judicial power (which includes appellate power) shall extend to all cases," &c., and "in all other cases before mentioned the supreme court shall have appellate jurisdiction." It is the case, then, and not the court, that gives the jurisdiction. If the judicial power extends to the case, it will be in vain to search in the letter of the constitution for any qualification as to the tribunal where it depends. It is incumbent, then, upon those who assert such a qualification to show its existence by necessary implication....

[I]f, as has been contended, a discretion be vested in congress to establish, or not to establish, inferior courts at their own pleasure, and congress should not establish such courts, the appellate jurisdiction of the supreme Court would have nothing to act upon, unless it could act upon cases pending in the state courts. Under such circumstances it must be held that the appellate power would extend to state courts; for the constitution is peremptory that it shall extend to certain enumerated cases, which cases could exist in no other courts. Any other construction, upon this supposition, would involve this strange contradiction, that a discretionary power vested in congress, and which they might rightfully omit to exercise, would defeat the absolute injunctions of the constitution in relation to the whole appellate power....

It must, therefore, be conceded that the constitution not only contemplated, but meant to provide for cases within the scope of the judicial power of the United States, which might yet depend before state tribunals. It was foreseen that in the exercise of their ordinary jurisdiction, state courts would incidentally take cognizance of cases arising under the constitution, the laws, and treaties of the United States. Yet to all these cases the judicial power, by the very terms of the constitution, is to extend. It cannot extend by original jurisdiction if that was already rightfully and exclusively attached in the state courts, which (as has been already shown) may occur; it must, therefore, extend by appellate jurisdiction, or not at all. It would seem to follow that the appellate power of the United States must, in such cases, extend to state tribunals; and if in such cases, there is no reason why it should not equally attach upon all others within the purview of the constitution.

It has been argued [by Virginia] that such an appellate jurisdiction over state courts is inconsistent with the genius of our governments, and the spirit of the constitution. That the latter was never designed to act upon state sovereignties, but only upon the people, and that if the power exists, it will materially impair the sovereignty of the states, and the independence of their courts. We cannot yield to the force of this reasoning; it assumes principles which we cannot admit, and draws conclusions to which we do not yield our assent.

It is a mistake [for Virginia to contend] that the constitution was not designed to operate upon states, in their corporate capacities. It is crowded with provisions which restrain or annul the sovereignty of the states in some of the highest branches of their prerogatives. The 10th section of the first article contains a long list of disabilities and prohibitions imposed upon the states. Surely, when such essential portions of state sovereignty are taken away, or prohibited to be exercised, it cannot be correctly asserted that the constitution does not act upon the states. The language of the constitution is also imperative upon the states as to the performance of many duties. It is imperative upon the state legislatures to make laws prescribing the time, places, and manner of holding elections for senators and representatives, and for electors of president and vice-president. And in these, as well as some other cases, congress have a right to revise, amend, or supercede the laws which may be passed by state legislatures. When, therefore, the states are stripped of some of the highest attributes of sovereignty, and the same are given to the United States; when the legislatures of the states are, in some respects, under the control of congress, and in every case are, under the constitution, bound by the paramount authority of the United States; it is certainly difficult to support the argument that the appellate power over the decisions of state courts is contrary to the genius of our institutions. The courts of the United States can, without question, revise the proceedings of the executive and legislative authorities of the states, and if they are found to be contrary to the constitution, may declare them to be of no legal validity. Surely the exercise of the same right over judicial tribunals is not a higher or more dangerous act of sovereign power.

Nor can such a right be deemed to impair the independence of state judges. It is assuming the very ground in controversy to assert that they possess an absolute independence of the United States. In respect to the powers granted to the United States, they are not independent; they are expressly bound to obedience by the letter of the constitution; and if they should unintentionally transcend their authority, or misconstrue the constitution, there is no more reason for giving their judgments an absolute and irresistible force, than for giving it to the acts of the other co-ordinate departments of state sovereignty.

The argument urged [by Virginia of] the possibility of the abuse of the revising power, is equally unsatisfactory. It is always a doubtful course, to argue against the use or existence of a power, from the possibility of its abuse. It is still more difficult, by such an argument, to ingraft upon a general power a restriction which is not to be found in the terms in which it is given. From the very nature of things, the absolute right of decision, in the last resort, must rest somewhere—wherever it may be vested it is susceptible of abuse. In all questions of jurisdiction the inferior, or appellate court, must pronounce the final judgment; and common sense, as well as legal reasoning, has conferred it upon the latter....

It is further argued, that no great public mischief can result from a construction which shall limit the appellate power of the United States to cases in their own courts: first, because state judges are bound by an oath to support the constitution of the United States, and must be presumed to be men of learning and integrity; and, secondly, because congress must have an unquestionable right to remove all cases within the scope of the judicial power from the state courts to the courts of the United States, at any time before final judgment, though not after final judgment. As to the first reason—admitting that the judges of the state courts are, and always will be, of as much learning, integrity, and wisdom, as those of the courts of the United States, (which we very cheerfully admit,) it does not aid the argument. It is manifest that the constitution has proceeded upon a theory of its own, and given or withheld powers according to the judgment of the American people, by whom it was adopted. We can only construe its powers, and cannot inquire into the policy or principles which induced the grant of them. The constitution has presumed (whether rightly or wrongly we do not inquire) that state attachments, state prejudices, state jealousies, and state interests, might some times obstruct, or control, or be supposed to obstruct or control, the regular administration of justice. Hence, in controversies between states; between citizens of different states; between citizens claiming grants under different states; between a state and its citizens, or foreigners; and between citizens and foreigners, it enables the parties, under the authority of congress, to have the controversies heard, tried, and determined before the national tribunals. No other reason than that which has been stated can be assigned, why some, at least, of those cases should not have been left to the cognizance of the state courts. In respect to the other enumerated cases—the cases arising under the constitution, laws, and treaties of the United States, cases affecting ambassadors and other public ministers, and cases of admiralty and maritime jurisdiction—reasons of a higher and more extensive nature, touching the safety, peace, and sovereignty of the nation, might well justify a grant of exclusive jurisdiction.

This is not all. A motive of another kind, perfectly compatible with the most sincere respect for state tribunals, might induce the grant of appellate power over their decisions. That motive is the importance, and even necessity of uniformity of decisions throughout the whole United States, upon all subjects within the purview of the constitution. Judges of equal learning and integrity, in different states, might differently interpret a statute, or a treaty of the United States, or even the constitution itself: If there were no revising authority to control these jarring and discordant judgments, and harmonize them into uniformity, the laws, the treaties, and the constitution of the United States would be different in different states, and might, perhaps, never have precisely the same construction, obligation, or efficacy, in any two states. The public mischiefs that would attend such a state of things would be truly deplorable; and it cannot be believed that they could have escaped the enlightened convention which formed the constitution. What, indeed, might then have been only prophecy, has now become fact; and the appellate jurisdiction must continue to be the only adequate remedy for such evils....

On the whole, the court are of opinion, that the appellate power of the United States does extend to cases pending in the state courts; and that the 25th section of the judiciary act, which authorizes the exercise of this jurisdiction in the specified cases, by a writ of error, is supported by the letter and spirit of the constitution. We find no clause in that instrument which limits this power; and we dare not interpose a limitation where the people have not been disposed to create one.

Strong as this conclusion stands upon the general language of the constitution, it may still derive support from other sources. It is an historical fact, that this exposition of the constitution, extending its appellate power to state courts, was, previous to its adoption, uniformly and publicly avowed by its friends, and admitted by its enemies, as the basis of their respective reasonings, both in and out of the state conventions. It is an historical fact, that at the time when the judiciary act was submitted to the deliberations of the first congress, composed, as it was, not only of men of great learning and ability, but of men who had acted a principal part in framing, supporting, or opposing that constitution, the same exposition was explicitly declared and admitted by the friends and by the opponents of that system. It is an historical fact, that the supreme court of the United States have, from time to time, sustained this appellate jurisdiction in a great variety of cases, brought from the tribunals of many of the most important states in the union, and that no state tribunal has ever breathed a judicial doubt on the subject, or declined to obey the mandate of the supreme court, until the present occasion. This weight of contemporaneous exposition by all parties, this acquiescence of enlightened state courts, and these judicial decisions of the supreme court through so long a period, do, as we think, place the doctrine upon a foundation of authority which cannot be shaken, without delivering over the subject to perpetual and irremediable doubts....

It is the opinion of the whole court, that the judgment of the court of appeals of Virginia, rendered on the mandate in this cause, be reversed, and the judgment of the [trial court] be, and the same is hereby affirmed.

Cohens v. Virginia: Background

The controversy surrounding § 25 of the Judiciary Act of 1789 did not end with *Martin v. Hunter's Lessee*. In 1821, the Court addressed the issue of whether or not the federal Supreme Court could review judgments of state supreme courts in criminal cases. States' righters were in an uproar over both *Martin* (1816) and *McCulloch v. Maryland* (1819). Some scholars think that *Cohens v. Virginia* (1821) was contrived in order to give the Court a platform to reassert national authority over the states.

In 1812, Congress had passed a statute authorizing the government of Washington, D.C. to create a lottery in order to raise money for municipal purposes. Virginia law made selling lottery tickets illegal. The case involved the conviction of two brothers for selling the federal lottery tickets in Norfolk, Virginia.

By the time of the argument in *Cohens*, many Southerners had grown increasingly alarmed at what they considered an invasion of states' rights by the federal government. Thomas Jefferson, from his home at Monticello, wrote letters warning of what he saw as the consolidating tendency of the Court and the Congress. Jefferson was concerned that the Court was upholding acts of Congress that, as he saw it, threatened states' rights. In 1820, he described the "Judiciary of the United States" as a "subtle corps of sappers and miners constantly working underground to undermine the foundations of our confederated fabric. They are construing our Constitution from a co-ordination of a general and special government to a general and supreme one alone." 1 Charles Warren, *The Supreme Court in United States History* 546 (1935). When the Court prepared to hear *Cohens*, the Virginia legislature passed a resolution stating that the Court had no authority "to examine and correct" the decision of the Virginia Court. The Virginia legislature entered "their most solemn protest against the jurisdiction of that Court over the matter."

Questions

1. How could Virginia contend that *Martin v. Hunter's Lessee* was not directly controlling?
2. What effect, if any, should the 11th Amendment have had on this case?

Cohens v. Virginia
19 U.S. 264 (1821)

Mr. Chief Justice Marshall delivered the opinion of the Court....

The second section of the third article of the constitution defines the extent of the judicial power of the United States. Jurisdiction is given to the Courts of the Union in two classes of cases. In the first, their jurisdiction depends on the character of the cause, whoever may be the parties. This class comprehends "all cases in law and equity arising under this constitution, the laws of the United States, and treaties made, or which shall be made, under their authority." This clause extends the jurisdiction of the Court to all the cases described, without making in its terms any exception whatever, and without any regard to the condition of the party. If there be any exception, it is to be implied against the express words of the article.

In the second class, the jurisdiction depends entirely on the character of the parties. In this are comprehended "controversies between two or more States, between a State and citizens of another State," "and between a State and foreign States, citizens or subjects." If these be the parties, it is entirely unimportant what may be the subject of controversy. Be it what it may, these parties have a constitutional right to come into the Courts of the Union....

With the ample powers confided to this supreme government ... are connected many express and important limitations on the sovereignty of the States, which are made for the same purposes. The powers of the Union, on the great subjects of war, peace, and commerce, and on many others, are in themselves limitations of the sovereignty of the States; but in addition to these, the sovereignty of the States is surrendered in many instances where the surrender can only operate to the benefit of the people, and where, perhaps, no other power is conferred on Congress than a conservative power to maintain the principles established in the constitution. The maintenance of these principles in their purity is certainly among the great duties of the government. One of the instruments by which this duty may be peaceably performed, is the judicial department. It is authorized to decide all cases of every description, arising under the constitution or laws of the United States. From this general grant of jurisdiction, no exception is made of those cases in which a State may be a party. When we consider the situation of the government of the Union and of a State, in relation to each other; the nature of our constitution; the subordination of the State governments to that constitution; the great purpose for which jurisdiction over all cases arising under the constitution and laws of the United States, is confided to the judicial department; are we at liberty to insert in this general grant, an exception of those cases in which a State may be a party? Will the spirit of the constitution justify this attempt to control its words? We think it will not. We think a case arising under the constitution or laws of the United States, is cognizable in the Courts of the Union, whoever may be the parties to that case....

The mischievous consequences of the construction contended for on the part of Virginia, are also entitled to great consideration. It would prostrate, it has been said, the government and its laws at the feet of every State in the Union. And would not this be its effect? What power of the government could be executed by its own means, in any State disposed to resist its execution by a course of legislation? The laws must be executed by individuals acting within the several States. If these individuals may be exposed to penalties, and if the Courts of the Union cannot correct the judgments by which these penalties may be enforced, the course of the government may be, at any time, arrested by the will of one of its members. Each member will possess a veto on the will of the whole....

Let it be admitted, that the cases which have been put are extreme and improbable, yet there are gradations of opposition to the laws, far short to those cases, which might have a baneful influence on the affairs of the nation. Different States may entertain different opinions on the true construction of the constitutional powers of Congress. We know, that at one time, the assumption of the debts contracted by the several States, during the war of our revolution, was deemed unconstitutional by some of them. We know, too, that at other times, certain taxes, imposed by Congress, have been pronounced unconstitutional. Other laws have been questioned partially, while they were supported by the great majority of the American people. We have no assurance that we shall be less divided than we have been. States may legislate in conformity to their opinions, and may enforce those opinions by penalties. It would be hazarding too much to assert, that the judicatures of the States will be exempt from the prejudices by which the legislatures and people are influenced, and will constitute perfectly impartial tribunals. In many States the judges are dependent for office and for salary on the will of the legislature. The constitution of the United States furnishes no security against the universal adoption of this principle. When we observe the importance which that constitution attaches to the independence of judges, we are the less inclined to suppose that it can have intended to leave these constitutional questions to tribunals where this independence may not exist, in all cases where a State shall prosecute an individual who claims the protection of an act of Congress. These prosecutions may take place even without a legislative act. A person making a seizure under an act of Congress, may be indicted as a trespasser, if force has been employed, and of this a jury may judge. How extensive may be the mischief if the first decisions in such cases should be final.

These collisions may take place in times of no extraordinary commotion. But a constitution is framed for ages to come, and is designed to approach immortality as nearly as human institutions can approach it. Its course cannot always be tranquil. It is exposed to storms and tempests, and its framers must be unwise statesmen indeed, if they have not provided it, as far as its nature will permit, with the means of self-preservation from the perils it may be destined to encounter. No government ought to be so defective in its organization, as not to contain within itself the means of securing the execution of its own laws against other dangers than those which occur every day. Courts of justice are the means most usually employed; and it is reasonable to expect that a government should repose on its own Courts, rather than on others. There is certainly nothing in the circumstances under which our constitution was formed; nothing in the history of the times, which would justify the opinion that the confidence reposed in the States was so implicit as to leave in them and their tribunals the power of resisting or defeating, in the form of law, the legitimate measures of the Union. The requisitions of Congress, under the confederation, were as constitutionally obligatory as the laws enacted by the present Congress. That they were habitually disregarded, is a fact of universal notoriety. With the knowledge of this fact, and under its full pressure, a convention was assembled to change the system. Is it so improbable that they should confer on the judicial department the power of construing the constitution and laws of the Union in every case, in the last resort, and of preserving them from all violation from every quarter, so far as judicial decisions can preserve them, that this improbability should essentially affect the construction of the new system? We are told, and we are truly told, that the great change which is to give efficacy to the present system, is its ability to act on individuals directly, instead of acting through the instrumentality of State governments. But, ought not this ability, in reason and sound policy, to be applied directly to the protection of individuals employed in the execution of the laws, as well as to their coercion. Your laws reach the individual without the aid of any other power; why may they not protect him from punishment for performing his duty in executing them?

[Virginia contends that the operation of the 11th Amendment precludes appellate review of a judgment in a criminal case because the state is involved as a party.] It is, then, the opinion of the Court, that the defendant who removes a judgment rendered against him by a State Court into this Court, for the purpose of re-examining the question, whether that judgment be in violation of the constitution or laws of the United States, does not commence or prosecute a suit against the State, whatever may be its opinion where the effect of the writ may be to restore the party to the possession of a thing which he demands....

In opposition to it, the counsel [for Virginia] has presented in a great variety of forms, the idea already noticed, that the federal and State Courts must, of necessity, and from the nature of the constitution, be in all things totally distinct and independent of each other. If this Court can correct the errors of the Court of Virginia, he says it makes them Courts of the United States, or becomes itself a part of the judiciary of Virginia.

But, it has been already shown that neither of these consequences necessarily follows: The American people may certainly give to a national tribunal a supervising power over those judgments of the State Courts, which may conflict with the constitution, laws, or treaties, of the United States, without converting them into federal Courts, or converting the national into a State tribunal. The one Court still derives its authority from the State, the other still derives its authority from the nation.

If it shall be established, he says, that this Court has appellate jurisdiction over the State Courts in all cases enumerated in the 3d article of the constitution, a complete consolidation of the States, so far as respects judicial power is produced.

But, certainly, the mind of the gentleman who urged this argument is too accurate not to perceive that he has carried it too far; that the premises by no means justify the conclusion. "A complete consolidation of the States, so far as respects the judicial power," would authorize the legislature to confer on the federal Courts appellate jurisdiction from the State Courts in all cases whatsoever. The distinction between such a power, and that of giving appellate jurisdiction in a few specified cases in the decision of which the nation takes an interest, is too obvious not to be perceived by all....

After having bestowed upon this question the most deliberate consideration of which we are capable, the Court is unanimously of opinion, that the objections to its jurisdiction are not sustained....

[After finding it did have jurisdiction, the Court proceeded to consider the effect of the federal statute. The issue was whether a state could make criminal the sale of an item that had been authorized under federal law. On the merits, the Court ruled as a matter of statutory construction that Congress had not intended for the statute authorizing the lottery to preclude states from enforcing criminal laws prohibiting lotteries.]

* * *

Note the similarity between the outcomes in *Marbury* and *Cohens*. In both cases, the assertion of federal judicial power is potentially extremely controversial and, depending on how the case is decided, might result in a troubling confrontation. In both, Chief Justice Marshall establishes important and basic principles of federal judicial power. And in each case, he decides the case in favor of the party contesting the exercise of federal judicial power so that immediate confrontation is avoided.

Reaction to *Cohens*

Though the decision in *Cohens* had its supporters, advocates of states' rights were harshly critical of the decision. The *Richmond Enquirer* warned that "the Judiciary power, with a foot as noiseless as time and a spirit as greedy as the grave" was consigning to "destruction the rights of the states." It advocated repeal of §25 of the Judiciary Act—the section that provided for Supreme Court jurisdiction of certain cases coming from state courts and involving federal questions. Judge Spencer Roane of the Virginia Supreme Court wrote critical letters for the *Washington Gazette* and *Richmond Enquirer* (signed Hampden and Sidney). Roane called the decision a "monstrous" one produced by "love of power," and said that the Supreme Court was foisting "consolidation with all its terrors" on the nation. Roane demanded repeal of §25 as unwarranted by the Constitution. 1 Charles Warren, *The Supreme Court in United States History*, 552, 555–57 (1935).

E. A Short History of the Marshall Court

The Marshall Court is probably the most important in American constitutional history. It was the foundational court for much modern constitutional jurisprudence. When Marshall became Chief Justice, the Court had little stature within the government and no great presence in national politics. The Court's most significant decision of the previous decade, *Chisholm v. Georgia* (1793), had been effectively reversed by the 11th Amendment. But, by the time Marshall left the bench in 1835, the Court was a major factor in American law and politics. Presidents and legislators were concerned with Court opinions, even if they sometimes flouted them.

The controversy over the Second Bank of the United States illustrates the new significance of the Court. In 1832, President Andrew Jackson vetoed a bill to extend the charter of the bank. In doing so he went out of his way to explain why he had the power to do this, despite the Court's decision in *McCulloch v. Maryland* (1819) upholding the constitutionality of the Bank.

The Marshall Court was enormously successful in shaping the law, politics, and economic development of the nation in four areas: (1) instituting judicial review of both federal and state laws; (2) articulating the view that the powers set out in the Constitution were flexible and sufficient to meet changing needs; (3) establishing federal supremacy over the states; and (4) facilitating economic development, especially through expansive interpretations of the Commerce Clause. The Court had mixed success, however, in asserting its power as the final authority when dealing with the executive branch. Moreover, the Court completely failed to protect the rights of Native Americans, and set the nation on the road to a constitutional morass that led to more than a century of deprivation of Indian rights.

Chief Justice Marshall was a Federalist, appointed to office by the departing President John Adams, who considered the Chief Justice to be his "gift" to the American people. As Chief Justice, Marshall ended the practice of having the justices give their opinions seriatim, and instituted the policy of an "opinion of the Court," more often than not written by Marshall himself. His powerful, but genial, personality and his brilliant legal mind allowed him to dominate the Court, even as its membership gradually shifted from Federalist to Republican. Jefferson, for example, appointed William Johnson, in hopes that he would counteract Marshall's judicial nationalism. But Johnson, more often than not, supported Marshall. While he often wrote a concurring opinion in important cases, Johnson dissented from a Marshall-created majority in only a few important cases, and in none of the truly significant ones. Similarly, Justice Joseph Story, appointed by the Republican Madison, quickly came to follow Marshall's nationalist jurisprudence.

In *Marbury v. Madison* (1803), Chief Justice Marshall established the principle of judicial review of federal statutes. However, Marshall would never assert this power again. In fact, the Court would not strike down another congressional statute until Chief Justice Roger B. Taney struck down part of the Missouri Compromise in *Dred Scott v. Sandford* (1857).

While the Marshall Court never again struck down a federal law, Marshall and his brethren successfully asserted the supremacy of the Constitution over numerous state laws, particularly in five important decisions between 1810 and 1821.

In *Fletcher v. Peck* (1810), the Court struck down a popular Georgia statute that had been passed in the wake of the great Yazoo land fraud. In 1795, virtually all members of the Georgia legislature had been bribed to sell vast tracts of state-owed land for pennies an acre. The next year, all members of the legislature were defeated for re-election and a new legislature rescinded the sale. By this time, Peck had purchased some of the land in question either from original buyers or their successors. The Court ruled that as a holder in due course, Peck could receive a clear title to the land and that the Georgia law rescinding the sales violated the Contracts Clause of Article I, § 10 of the Constitution. The decision established an important precedent that secured land sales and stimulated Western settlement. The case also made clear that both the states and the national government had the power to "legitimately extinguish" what Marshall called "Indian title" to lands.

In *Martin v. Hunter's Lessee* (1816), Justice Story, writing for a unanimous Court, emphatically rejected the notion that a state could ignore a mandate of the Supreme Court. In this case involving a dispute over land ownership, Hunter claimed title to certain land based on a grant from the state of Virginia which had previously confiscated the land from Martin, a British subject. Martin claimed that the confiscation was ineffective because it violated the anti-confiscation clauses of two federal treaties between the United States and Britain. The Virginia Court of Appeals ruled in favor of Hunter; Martin appealed to the U.S. Supreme Court. The Court reversed and remanded the case to the Virginia Court of Appeals with instructions to enter judgment for Martin. But the Virginia court refused. Instead, it held that the section of the Judiciary Act of 1789 that granted the U.S. Supreme Court jurisdiction to hear appeals from state courts was unconstitutional. Justice Story, in a powerful opinion, affirmed that the Supreme Court had "the absolute right of decision, in the last resort" in cases involving federal questions. Story rejected the argument that "appellate jurisdiction over state courts is inconsistent with ... the spirit of the constitution."

The Court followed this with its decision in *McCulloch v. Maryland* (1819), striking down a Maryland law that was passed to prevent the Bank of the United States from operating in that state. Here, Chief Justice Marshall set out two important principles. First, he asserted that the states could not interfere with legitimate acts of Congress, thereby frustrating the intentions of the national legislature. Second, he held that the Bank of the United States was constitutional because both the structure of the Constitution and the "Necessary and Proper" Clause of Article I, §8, gave Congress vast and flexible powers to govern. Marshall declared: "Let the end be legitimate, let it be within the scope of the constitution, and all means which are appropriate, which are plainly adapted to that end, which are not prohibited, but consistent with the letter and spirit of the constitution, are constitutional." He reminded the nation that the Constitution was not a "legal code" but a plan for government that must be inherently flexible to meet the needs of a growing nation. "We must never forget," he wrote, "that it is a *constitution* we are expounding," and that this Constitution was "intended to endure for ages to come, and consequently, to be adapted to the various crises of human affairs."

In *Dartmouth College v. Woodward* (1819), the Court rejected an attempt by the state of New Hampshire to revoke the charter of Dartmouth College and to turn that private institution into a state university. As in *Fletcher v. Peck*, the Marshall Court used the Contracts Clause to void an action by a state legislature.

In *Cohens v. Virginia* (1821), Marshall upheld a Virginia law that prohibited the sale of tickets in Virginia for a Washington, D.C., lottery that had been authorized by Congress. The Cohen brothers appealed their Virginia conviction, arguing that the federal statute creating the lottery trumped the state law. Virginia objected to the Court hearing this appeal, arguing that the Supreme Court lacked jurisdiction to hear an appeal from a criminal conviction under state law. Marshall emphatically disagreed and asserted that if Virginia's view of the Constitution were correct, the Court would never be able to correct erroneous state decisions and that the government itself would be imperiled. Marshall argued that under Virginia's interpretation of the Constitution, "the nation does not possess a department capable of restraining peaceably, and by authority of law, any attempts which may be made, by a part, against the legitimate powers of the whole." Marshall argued that the United States is a "government for the whole" and that the Constitution and the laws passed under it are the "supreme law of the land." Marshall thus concluded that the Court had jurisdiction to hear the appeal from a state criminal court that raised federal questions. Although Marshall sustained the constitutionality of the Virginia law, the decision nevertheless infuriated states rights leaders in Virginia, like Judge Spencer Roane and John Taylor. Thomas Jefferson privately denounced both the decision and Marshall as "irresponsible."

Indeed, all five decisions angered states' rights advocates, but they set a standard that the federal Constitution and the acts of the Congress were the "supreme law of the land" and that the Court had the power to enforce this principle. Late in his tenure on the Court, however, Marshall did reject an attempt to apply the Bill of Rights to the states. In *Barron v. Baltimore* (1833), Marshall concluded that the Bill of Rights only limited the national government, and that the states were free to deny fundamental federal liberties and rights to their citizens.

Part of Marshall's nationalist jurisprudence emerged in his broad interpretation of the Commerce Clause. In one of his most popular decisions, *Gibbons v. Ogden* (1824), Marshall struck down New York's "steamboat monopoly," which prevented competition for water transportation in that state. He argued that Congress had pre-empted the New York statute so any vessel with a federal coasting license had a right to dock at any port in any state. New York could not prevent the ships of other states from doing business in New York. This case helped push the nation towards a system of unified and unrestricted commerce. While pushing for an open interstate commerce, Marshall and his colleagues recognized that some commerce might be regulated by the states. In *Brown v. Maryland* (1827), the Court struck down a state law that required wholesalers to purchase a license to sell "foreign articles, or commodities," but not to sell the same products produced in Maryland. However, Marshall explicitly noted that the states could tax any goods sold within the state if they were not in their "original package," because at that point they would be mixed up with all similar goods in the state. This rule allowed for regulation of internal commerce that taxed all goods equally, while prohibiting import taxes by states. Along the same lines, in *Willson v. Black Bird Marsh Creek Co.* (1829), Marshall upheld the right of a state to put a dam across a navigable creek, even though this dam interfered with interstate commerce. The Court ruled that Congress had the power to prevent such dams, but Congress had never chosen to exercise this right; in the absence of federal power, states could regulate and control the many small creeks and streams in the nation pursuant to their police power. This case showed that Marshall, the nationalist, was also capable of a flexible jurisprudence that accommodated the needs of local as well as national commerce.

The Marshall Court issued few important decisions involving slavery and, in most of them, the Court sided with slaveholders. The Court heard appeals from the District of Columbia in two cases in which blacks claimed to be free. In *Scott v. Negro Ben* (1810) and *Mima Queen and Child v. Hepburn* (1813), Marshall, speaking for the Court, rejected plausible freedom claims and showed no flexibility in applying legal rules that discriminated against blacks. In a rare dissent in *Mima Queen,* Justice Gabriel Duvall complained that Marshall should give greater consideration to what he called the "helpless condition" of blacks, whom Duvall believed were "entitled to all reasonable protection." In the more famous slave trading case, *The Antelope* (1825), Marshall concluded that the African slave trade, while a violation of the "law of nature," was not a violation of international law, and in the end condemned a number of the Africans to lifetime servitude. However, when Americans were involved in the illegal trade, the Marshall Court proved to be more assertive. In *The Emily and the Caroline* (1824), *The Merino* (1824), and *The St. Jago de Cuba* (1824), the Court upheld the convictions of slave traders who had sought to continue the African slave trade in violation of federal law. Significantly, Marshall did not write any of the opinions in these cases.

Perhaps the most tragic aspect of Marshall's jurisprudence concerned Native Americans. In *Fletcher v. Peck* (1810), the Court recognized the power of state governments to take lands from Indians with or without their consent. In *Johnson v. M'Intosh* (1823), Marshall held that under the "doctrine of discovery" Europeans had "an exclusive right to extinguish the Indian title of occupancy, either by purchase or conquest." Furthermore, Marshall found that Indians had no right to sell their land to anyone other than the government. They had no rights of ownership, but were merely "occupants." The Indians were "deemed incapable of transferring an absolute title" in the land they occupied. Moreover, in *Cherokee Nation v. Georgia* (1831), Marshall concluded that Indians were "domestic dependent nations" with no rights to sue in federal courts. They were, he argued, "in a state of pupilage" and their relationship to the United States was like "that of a ward to his guardian." Thus, while Georgia illegally trampled on the rights of the Cherokee — rights guaranteed by treaties — the Court would not interfere because the Cherokee had no right to take their case to the Court.

A year later, in *Worcester v. Georgia* (1832), the Court accepted an appeal from a white minister arrested for preaching to the Cherokees in violation of a Georgia law. Although the Court overturned the conviction on the basis of federal treaties, the Court's ruling went unenforced as Georgia flatly refused to release Worcester. (President Andrew Jackson allegedly said "Chief Justice Marshall had made his decision, now let *him* enforce it.") The Court had come a long way during the thirty-two years since Marshall had taken over the center chair, but it was not yet so powerful that it could compel a reluctant president to enforce its mandates.

When Marshall died he left a legacy of jurisprudence that by-and-large was accepted by the Congress and the executive branch. More importantly, he left an institution that had become an integral part of American life. During and after Marshall's tenure as Chief Justice, Americans turned to the Court to resolve interstate disputes and seemingly intractable political problems. Even when rejecting Marshall's policy results, as Jackson did in 1832 when he vetoed the recharter of the Bank of the United States, the executive branch felt compelled to confront the Court's position, and explain its own position. Without the power of either the purse or the sword, Marshall made the Court a force in American politics, as well as the court of last resort for many significant constitutional issues.

F. Judicial Review and the Political Process

What should be the effect of a Supreme Court decision on a constitutional question? Should it bind only the parties to the case? Should the political branches accept the decision as a rule for their political decisions on the issue decided? Does it depend? If so, on what? Consider the views of Abraham Lincoln.

In *Dred Scott v. Sandford* (1857) the Court held that African Americans who were the descendants of slaves could never be citizens of the United States or entitled to any of the protections of the Constitution (whether they were now free or not). It also held that Congress lacked the power to exclude slavery from any federal territory. The central plank in the 1856 Republican Party platform was that Congress should ban slavery from all federal territories. So, in effect, the *Dred Scott* decision said that the platform of the Republican Party was unconstitutional. Here are several of Lincoln's responses:

Abraham Lincoln's Speech on the *Dred Scott* Decision[*]
June 26, 1857

And now as to the *Dred Scott* decision. That decision declares two propositions — first, that a negro cannot sue in the U.S. Courts; and secondly, that Congress cannot prohibit

---

[*] Abraham Lincoln, *Speeches and Writings, 1832–1858: Speeches, Letters, and Miscellaneous Writings: The Lincoln-Douglas Debates* 392–95 (Don E. Fehrenbacher ed., 1989).

slavery in the Territories. It was made by a divided court—dividing differently on the different points. Judge [Stephen] Douglas does not discuss the merits of the decision; and, in that respect, I shall follow his example, believing I could no more improve on McLean and Curtis, than he could on Taney.

He denounces all who question the correctness of that decision, as offering violent resistance to it. But who resists it? Who has, in spite of the decision, declared Dred Scott free, and resisted the authority of his master over him?

Judicial decisions have two uses—first, to absolutely determine the case decided, and secondly, to indicate to the public how other similar cases will be decided when they arise. For the latter use, they are called "precedents" and "authorities."

We believe, as much as Judge Douglas, (perhaps more) in obedience to, and respect for the judicial department of government. We think its decisions on Constitutional questions, when fully settled, should control, not only the particular cases decided, but the general policy of the country, subject to be disturbed only by amendments of the Constitution as provided in that instrument itself. More than this would be revolution. But we think the *Dred Scott* decision is erroneous. We know the court that made it has often overruled its own decisions, and we shall do what we can to have it to overrule this. We offer no *resistance* to it.

Judicial decisions are of greater or less authority as precedents, according to circumstances. That this should be so accords both with common sense, and the customary understanding of the legal profession.

If this important decision had been made by the unanimous concurrence of the judges, and without any apparent partisan bias, and in accordance with legal public expectation, and with the steady practice of the departments throughout our history, and had been in no part based on assumed historical facts which are not really true; or, if wanting in some of these, it had been before the court more than once, and had there been affirmed and re-affirmed through a course of years, it then might be, perhaps would be, factious, nay, even revolutionary, to not acquiesce in it as a precedent.

But when, as it is true we find it wanting in all these claims to the public confidence, it is not resistance, it is not factious, it is not even disrespectful, to treat it as not having yet quite established a settled doctrine for the country—but Judge Douglas considers this view awful. Hear him:

> The courts are the tribunals prescribed by the Constitution and created by the authority of the people to determine, expound and enforce the law. Hence, whoever resists the final decision of the highest judicial tribunal, aims a deadly blow to our whole Republican system of government—a blow, which if successful would place all our rights and liberties at the mercy of passion, anarchy and violence. I repeat, therefore, that if resistance to the decisions of the Supreme Court of the United States, in a matter like the points decided in the *Dred Scott* case, clearly within their jurisdiction as defined by the Constitution, shall be forced upon the country as a political issue, it will become a distinct and naked issue between the friends and the enemies of the Constitution—the friends and the enemies of the supremacy of the laws.

Why this same Supreme Court once decided a national bank to be constitutional; but Gen. [Andrew] Jackson, as President of the United States, disregarded the decision, and vetoed a bill for a re-charter, partly on constitutional ground, declaring that each public functionary must support the Constitution, "*as he understands it.*" But hear the General's own words. Here they are, taken from his veto message:

> It is maintained by the advocates of the bank, that its constitutionality, in all its features, ought to be considered as settled by precedent, and by the decision of the Supreme Court. To this conclusion I cannot assent. Mere precedent is a dangerous source of authority, and should not be regarded as deciding questions of constitutional power, except where the acquiescence of the people and the States can be considered as well settled. So far from this being the case on this subject, an argument against the bank might be based on precedent. One Congress in 1791, decided in favor of a bank; another in 1811, decided against it. One Congress in 1815 decided against a bank; another in 1816 decided in its favor. Prior to the present Congress, therefore, the precedents drawn from that source were equal. If we resort to the States, the expressions of legislative, judicial, and executive opinions against the bank have been probably to those in its favor as four to one. There is nothing in precedent, therefore, which if its authority were admitted, ought to weigh in favor of the act before me.

I drop the quotations merely to remark that all there ever was, in the way of precedent up to the *Dred Scott* decision, on the points therein decided, had been against that decision. But hear Gen. Jackson further—

> If the opinion of the Supreme court covered the whole ground of this act, it ought not to control the co-ordinate authorities of this Government. The Congress, the executive and the court, must each for itself be guided by its own opinion of the Constitution. Each public officer, who takes an oath to support the Constitution, swears that he will support it as he understands it, and not as it is understood by others....

I have said, in substance, that the *Dred Scott* decision was, in part, based on assumed historical facts which were not really true; and I ought not to leave the subject without giving some reasons for saying this; I therefore give an instance or two, which I think fully sustain me. Chief Justice Taney, in delivering the opinion of the majority of the Court, insists at great length that negroes were no part of the people who made, or for whom was made, the Declaration of Independence, or the Constitution of the United States.

On the contrary, Judge Curtis, in his dissenting opinion, shows that in five of the then thirteen states, to wit, New Hampshire, Massachusetts, New York, New Jersey and North Carolina, free negroes were voters, and, in proportion to their numbers, had the same part in making the Constitution that the white people had. He shows this with so much particularity as to leave no doubt of its truth; and, as a sort of conclusion on that point, holds the following language:

> The Constitution was ordained and established by the people of the United States, through the action, in each State, of those persons who were qualified by its laws to act thereon in behalf of themselves and all other citizens of the State. In some of the States, as we have seen, colored persons were among those qualified by law to act on the subject. These colored persons were not only included in the body of "the people of the United States," by whom the Constitution was ordained and established; but in at least five of the States they had the power to act, and, doubtless, did act, by their suffrages, upon the question of its adoption.

First Lincoln-Douglas Debate: Lincoln's Reply*
August 21, 1858

Then what is necessary for the nationalization of slavery? It is simply the next *Dred Scott* decision. It is merely for the Supreme Court to decide that no *State* under the Constitution can exclude it, just as they have already decided that under the Constitution neither Congress nor the Territorial Legislature can do it. When that is decided and acquiesced in, the whole thing is done. This being true, and this being the way as I think that slavery is to be made national, let us consider what Judge Douglas is doing every day to that end. In the first place, let us see what influence he is exerting on public sentiment. In this and like communities, public sentiment is everything. With public sentiment, nothing can fail; without it, nothing can succeed. Consequently, he who moulds public sentiment goes deeper than he who enacts statutes or pronounces decisions. He makes statutes and decisions possible or impossible to be executed. This must be borne in mind, as also the additional fact that Judge Douglas is a man of vast influence, so great that it is enough for many men to profess to believe anything, when they once find out that Judge Douglas professes to believe it. Consider also the attitude he occupies at the head of a large party—a party which he claims has a majority of all the voters in the country. This man sticks to a decision which forbids the people of a Territory from excluding slavery, and he does so not because he says it is right in itself—he does not give any opinion on that—but because it has been *decided by the court*, and being decided by the court, he is, and you are bound to take it in your political action as *law*—not that he judges at all of its merits, but because a decision of the court is to him a "*Thus saith the Lord.*" [Applause.] He places it on that ground alone, and you will bear in mind that thus committing himself unreservedly to this decision, *commits him to the next one* just as firmly as to this. He did not commit himself on account of the merit or demerit of the decision, but it is a *Thus saith the Lord*. The next decision, as much as this, will be a *Thus saith the Lord*. There is nothing that can divert or turn him away from this decision. It is nothing that I point out to him that his great prototype, Gen. Jackson, did not believe in the binding force of decisions. It is nothing to him that Jefferson did not so believe. I have said that I have often heard him approve of Jackson's course in disregarding the decision of the Supreme Court pronouncing a National Bank constitutional. He says, I did not hear him say so. He denies the accuracy of my recollection. I say he ought to know better than I, but I will make no question about this thing, though it still seems to me that I heard him say it twenty times. [Applause and laughter.] I will tell him though, that he now claims to stand on the Cincinnati platform, which affirms that Congress *cannot* charter a National Bank, in the teeth of that old standing decision that Congress *can* charter a bank. [Loud applause.] And I remind him of another piece of history on the question of respect for judicial decisions, and it is a piece of Illinois history, belonging to a time when the large party to which Judge Douglas belonged, were displeased with a decision of the Supreme Court of Illinois, because they had decided that a Governor could not remove a Secretary of State. You will find the whole story in Ford's *History of Illinois*, and I know that Judge Douglas will not deny that he was then in favor of overslaughing that decision by the mode of adding five new Judges, so as to vote down the four old ones. Not only so, but it ended in *the Judge's sitting down on that very bench as one of the five new Judges to break down the four old ones*. [Cheers and laughter.] It was in this way precisely that he got his

---

* Abraham Lincoln, *Speeches and Writings, 1832–1858: Speeches, Letters, and Miscellaneous Writings: The Lincoln-Douglas Debates* 524–26 (Don E. Fehrenbacher ed., 1989).

title of Judge. Now, when the Judge tells me that men appointed conditionally to sit as members of a court, will have to be catechised beforehand upon some subject, I say "You know Judge; you have tried it." [Laughter.] When he says a court of this kind will lose the confidence of all men, will be prostituted and disgraced by such a proceeding, I say, "You know best, Judge; you have been through the mill." [Great laughter.] But I cannot shake Judge Douglas' teeth loose from the *Dred Scott* decision. Like some obstinate animal (I mean no disrespect,) that will hang on when he has once got his teeth fixed, you may cut off a leg, or you may tear away an arm, still he will not relax his hold. And so I may point out to the Judge, and say that he is bespattered all over, from the beginning of his political life to the present time, with attacks upon judicial decisions—I may cut off limb after limb of his public record, and strive to wrench him from a single dictum of the Court—yet I cannot divert him from it. He hangs to the last, to the *Dred Scott* decision. [Loud cheers.] These things show there is a purpose *strong as death and eternity* for which he adheres to this decision, and for which he will adhere to *all other decisions* of the same Court. [Vociferous applause.]

From Abraham Lincoln's *First Inaugural Address*

I do not forget the position assumed by some, that constitutional questions are to be decided by the Supreme Court; nor do I deny that such decisions must be binding in any case, upon the parties to a suit, as to the object of that suit, while they are also entitled to very high respect and consideration, in all parallel cases by other departments of the government. And while it is obviously possible that such decision may be erroneous in any given case, still the evil effect of following it, being limited to that particular case, with the chance that it may be overruled, and never become a precedent for other cases, can better be borne than could the evils of a different practice. At the same time the candid citizen must confess that if the policy of the government, upon vital questions, affecting the whole people, is to be irrevocably fixed by decisions of the Supreme Court, the instant they are made, in ordinary litigation between parties, in personal actions, the people will have ceased, to be their own rulers, having, to that extent, practically resigned their government, into the hands of that eminent tribunal. Nor is there, in this view, any assault upon the court, or the judges. It is a duty, from which they may not shrink, to decide cases properly brought before them; and it is no fault of theirs, if others seek to turn their decisions to political purposes.

4 *Collected Works of Abraham Lincoln*, 268 (Roy P. Basler, ed. 1953).

After the Civil War—and particularly after the end of Reconstruction, many Southern states passed legislation requiring segregation of schools, lunch counters, water fountains, etc. In *Plessy v. Ferguson* (1896), the Supreme Court upheld a Louisiana law that required segregated railroad cars against a challenge that the statute violated the Equal Protection Clause of the 14th Amendment—"no state shall ... deny to any person within its jurisdiction the equal protection of the laws." In *Brown v. Board of Education* (1954), the Court held state-imposed segregation violated the Equal Protection Clause of the 14th Amendment. The Court noted the importance of public education in modern times and that segregation could "affect the hearts and minds" of Negro children in a way "unlikely ever to be undone." It concluded that, in the field of public education, the doctrine of "separate but equal" has no place. Segregated schools were inherently unequal. Southern congressmen and senators signed a *Southern Manifesto* expressing their hostility against the decision. It was signed in March, 1956 by almost all the Representatives and Senators from the South.

The "Southern Manifesto"
102 Cong. Rec. 4515–16 (1956)

We regard the decision of the Supreme Court in the school cases as a clear abuse of judicial power. It climaxes a trend in the Federal judiciary undertaking to legislate, in derogation of the authority of Congress, and to encroach upon the reserved rights of the States and the people.

The original Constitution does not mention education. Neither does the 14th Amendment nor any other amendment. The debates preceding the submission of the 14th amendment clearly show that there was no intent that it should affect the systems of education maintained by the States.

The very Congress which proposed the amendment subsequently provided for segregated schools in the District of Columbia.

When the Amendment was adopted, in 1868, there were 37 States of the Union. Every one of the 26 States that had any substantial racial differences among its people either approved the operation of segregated schools already in existence or subsequently established such schools by action of the same lawmaking body which considered the 14th Amendment.

Though there has been no constitutional amendment or act of Congress changing this established legal principle almost a century old, the Supreme Court of the United States, with no legal basis for such action, undertook to exercise their naked judicial power and substituted their personal political and social ideas for the established law of the land.

This unwarranted exercise of power by the Court, contrary to the Constitution, is creating chaos and confusion in the States principally affected. It is destroying the amicable relations between the white and Negro races that have been created through 90 years of patient effort by the good people of both races. It has planted hatred and suspicion where there has been heretofore friendship and understanding.

With the gravest concern for the explosive and dangerous condition created by this decision and inflamed by outside meddlers:

We reaffirm our reliance on the Constitution as the fundamental law of the land.

We decry the Supreme Court's encroachments on rights reserved to the States and to the people, contrary to established law and to the Constitution.

We commend the motives of those States which have declared the intention to resist forced integration by any lawful means....

We pledge ourselves to use all lawful means to bring about a reversal of this decision which is contrary to the Constitution and to prevent the use of force in its implementation.

Cooper v. Aaron
358 U.S. 1 (1958)

[Majority: Warren (C.J.), Black, Frankfurter, Douglas, Burton, Clark, Harlan, Brennan, and Whittaker. The decision was issued in the name of the Court and signed individually by each justice.]

As this case reaches us it raises questions of the highest importance to the maintenance of our federal system of government. It necessarily involves a claim by the Governor and Legislature of a State that there is no duty on state officials to obey federal court orders resting on this Court's considered interpretation of the United States Constitution. Specifically it involves actions by the Governor and Legislature of Arkansas upon the premise that they are not bound by our holding in *Brown v. Board of Education* (1954).

... It is necessary only to recall some basic constitutional propositions which are settled doctrine.

Article VI of the Constitution makes the Constitution the "supreme Law of the Land." In 1803, Chief Justice Marshall, speaking for a unanimous Court, referring to the Constitution as "the fundamental and paramount law of the nation," declared in the notable case of *Marbury v. Madison* (1803) that "It is emphatically the province and duty of the judicial department to say what the law is." This decision declared the basic principle that the federal judiciary is supreme in the exposition of the law of the Constitution, and that principle has ever since been respected by this Court and the Country as a permanent and indispensable feature of our constitutional system. It follows that the interpretation of the 14th Amendment enunciated by this Court in the *Brown* case is the supreme law of the land, and Art. VI of the Constitution makes it of binding effect on the States "any Thing in the Constitution or Laws of any State to the Contrary notwithstanding." Every state legislator and executive and judicial officer is solemnly committed by oath taken pursuant to Art. VI, §3 "to support this Constitution." Chief Justice Taney, speaking for a unanimous Court in 1859, said that this requirement reflected the framers' "anxiety to preserve it [the Constitution] in full force, in all its powers, and to guard against resistance to or evasion of its authority, on the part of a State." *Ableman v. Booth* (1859).

No state legislator or executive or judicial officer can war against the Constitution without violating his undertaking to support it. Chief Justice Marshall spoke for a unanimous Court in saying that: "If the legislatures of the several states may, at will, annul the judgments of the courts of the United States, and destroy the rights acquired under those judgments, the constitution itself becomes a solemn mockery." *United States v. Peters* (1809).

* * *

Cooper v. Aaron set out that Court's understanding of *Marbury v. Madison*. We saw that fierce controversy followed *Marbury*, particularly with reference to assertions of appellate authority over state court judgments. How might a subsequent court, hostile to substantive judicial review, have limited the scope of *Marbury*?

G. The Scope of Federal Judicial Power over State Courts: The Adequate and Independent State Ground Doctrine

Federal courts (including the Supreme Court) are courts of limited jurisdiction. Subject matter jurisdiction of federal courts extends only to cases arising under the Constitution of the United States, laws of the United States, and treaties. While federal courts may also be called upon to decide a state law issue in cases of diversity of citizenship, in these cases federal courts are required to follow state law. If the state appellate court has clearly decided a point of state law, federal courts are required to follow the rule laid down by the state court.

If a state court has decided an issue based solely on state law, and if the state decision does not conflict with a federal constitutional provision, statute, or treaty, the United States Supreme Court has no jurisdiction to decide the case. For example, consider a

North Carolina case involving two automobiles that collide at an intersection. The plaintiff is speeding 50 miles per hour in a 25 mile per hour zone. The defendant runs a stop sign, and the two cars collide. North Carolina's rule is that contributory negligence which is a proximate cause of the collision is a total bar to the plaintiff's claim. Assume the plaintiff in the intersection collision case argues that North Carolina should replace contributory negligence with comparative negligence, but his case is dismissed at trial based on contributory negligence. The North Carolina Supreme Court affirms the decision. It rejects the plaintiff's argument for replacing contributory with comparative negligence. The plaintiff then appeals to the United States Supreme Court, arguing that the North Carolina state law rule should be comparative negligence. The Supreme Court should dismiss for lack of jurisdiction—assuming that the North Carolina contributory negligence rule does not conflict with a federal constitutional provision, statute, or treaty. In sum, if a state court decision is based on state law and the state law is "independent" of federal law in the sense that it does not conflict with federal law and is not said to be required by federal law, the Supreme Court lacks jurisdiction on appeal from the state court.

For example, in the case of *Oregon v. Henry* (Ore. 1987), the defendant—who was working in an adult bookstore—was convicted of violating an Oregon statute against selling obscene books, films, and magazines. The defendant claimed that the Oregon statute violated the freedom of speech and press guarantees of the Oregon Constitution. The Oregon Court agreed. Assume no federal law outlaws the sale of sex books entirely within the state of Oregon and under circumstances like those in this case. Since no federal constitutional provision, statute, or treaty provides a general right to be free from such material, the Oregon decision is "independent" of federal law. The United States Supreme Court would have no jurisdiction to review the case, provided that the state court made clear that it relied solely on the Oregon Constitution as opposed to the 1st Amendment of the federal Constitution.

Often, however, a litigant's claim may be based on both federal and state law. For example, assume a defendant in a criminal case has been charged with possessing marijuana in violation of a state statute. Before her trial, she files a motion to suppress evidence, contending that the search of her house where the marijuana was found violated both the 4th Amendment of the United States Constitution and a provision of the state constitution prohibiting unreasonable searches and seizures. Assume that she wins on both claims in the state supreme court. Assume further that the state court is wrong in its interpretation of the federal Constitution. The state court is the final judge of the meaning of the state constitutional provision for her case. So, of course, the state decision is correct as to the meaning of the state constitution. The federal Constitution sets minimum standards that the states must follow. States can, however, provide greater security for individual rights than the United States Supreme Court finds in the federal Constitution. States can do that provided that the state rule does not conflict with supreme federal law.

Does the United States Supreme Court have jurisdiction of the case? It depends. If the state court is quite clear that its decision of the state law claim is not based on the federal Constitution and is not influenced by federal law, then the United States Supreme Court has no jurisdiction. If it were to review the case, it could reverse only the incorrect interpretation of the federal Constitution. That would leave the decision based on the state constitutional provision standing. The defendant would still go free. The decision of the United States Supreme Court, on these assumed facts, cannot affect the outcome of the case. The Court sits to decide cases, not to issue advisory opinions. The Court should refuse to take the case because no decision it can make will affect the ultimate outcome of the case. What if the state court does not clearly distinguish between its decision based on the state and federal constitutions, leaving open at least a remote possibility that the state decision might have been influenced by its misreading of federal law? That issue is considered in the next case.

You might find yourself working as a law clerk to a state appellate judge. If your judge decides a case based both on federal grounds and on independent state grounds, how should your judge write his or her decision to protect the decision from reversal by the United States Supreme Court?

Litigants are required to raise federal constitutional issues and to preserve them in order to take advantage of them on appeal. This involves making the state court aware of the claim and reasserting it at each appropriate stage of the proceeding.

State law may have special requirements for raising and preserving federal constitutional issues. So long as the Supreme Court regards these requirements as reasonable and proper, they can be treated as an "adequate" basis for refusing to consider the federal constitutional claim.

Michigan v. Long: Background

The 4th Amendment to the United States Constitution protects "the people" against "unreasonable" searches and seizures. The Michigan state constitution has a similar provision. David Long was stopped for driving erratically. When the police arrived, Long met them at the back of his car. The police asked him for his registration, and Long walked back to the car to retrieve it. The officers said they observed a hunting knife in the car so they searched the car for weapons for their protection. Long was outside the car while they searched it. During the search, the officers found a leather pouch which they also searched for weapons. It contained marijuana. Long was then arrested. The officers decided to impound the car, and they immediately searched the trunk.

Long was charged with possession of a small bag of marijuana that police found underneath an armrest in his car and with possession of 75 pounds of marijuana that they found in his trunk. Long's conviction for possession of marijuana was reversed by the Michigan Supreme Court. The Court concluded that the search "was proscribed by the 4th Amendment of the United States Constitution and art. 1, §11 of the Michigan Constitution."

Michigan v. Long
463 U.S. 1032 (1983)

[Majority: O'Connor, Burger (C.J.), Powell, White, Rehnquist, and Blackmun. Concurring (in part): Blackmun. Dissenting: Brennan, Marshall, and Stevens.]

Justice O'Connor delivered the opinion of the Court....

We hold that the protective search of the passenger compartment was reasonable under the principles articulated in [the] decisions of this Court. [The Court remanded the issue of the search of the trunk to the state court.] We also examine Long's argument that the decision below rests upon an adequate and independent state ground, and we decide in favor of our jurisdiction....

II. Before reaching the merits, we must consider Long's argument that we are without jurisdiction to decide this case because the decision below rests on an adequate and independent state ground. The court below referred twice to the state constitution in its opinion, but otherwise relied exclusively on federal law. Long argues that the Michigan courts have provided greater protection from searches and seizures under the state constitution than is afforded under the 4th Amendment, and the references to the state constitution therefore establish an adequate and independent ground for the decision below.

It is, of course, "incumbent upon this Court ... to ascertain for itself ... whether the asserted non-federal ground independently and adequately supports the judgment." Although we have announced a number of principles in order to help us determine whether various forms of references to state law constitute adequate and independent state grounds,[1] we openly admit that we have thus far not developed a satisfying and consistent approach for resolving this vexing issue. In some instances, we have taken the strict view that if the ground of decision was at all unclear, we would dismiss the case.... In other instances, we have vacated or continued a case in order to obtain clarification about the nature of a state court decision. In more recent cases, we have ourselves examined state law to determine whether state courts have used federal law to guide their application of state law or to provide the actual basis for the decision that was reached.... In *Oregon v. Kennedy* (1982), we rejected an invitation to remand to the state court for clarification even when the decision rested in part on a case from the state court, because we determined that the state case itself rested upon federal grounds. We added that "[e]ven if the case admitted of more doubt as to whether federal and state grounds for decision were intermixed, the fact that the state court relied to the extent it did on federal grounds requires us to reach the merits."

This ad hoc method of dealing with cases that involve possible adequate and independent state grounds is antithetical to the doctrinal consistency that is required when sensitive issues of federal-state relations are involved. Moreover, none of the various methods of disposition that we have employed thus far recommends itself as the preferred method that we should apply to the exclusion of others, and we therefore determine that it is appropriate to reexamine our treatment of this jurisdictional issue in order to achieve the consistency that is necessary.

The process of examining state law is unsatisfactory because it requires us to interpret state laws with which we are generally unfamiliar, and which often, as in this case, have not been discussed at length by the parties. Vacation and continuance for clarification have also been unsatisfactory both because of the delay and decrease in efficiency of judicial administration, and, more important, because these methods of disposition place significant burdens on state courts to demonstrate the presence or absence of our jurisdiction.... Finally, outright dismissal of cases is clearly not a panacea because it cannot be doubted that there is an important need for uniformity in federal law, and that this need goes unsatisfied when we fail to review an opinion that rests primarily upon federal grounds and where the independence of an alleged state ground is not apparent from the four corners of the opinion....

---

1. For example, we have long recognized that "where the judgment of a state court rests upon two grounds, one of which is federal and the other non-federal in character, our jurisdiction fails if the non-federal ground is independent of the federal ground and adequate to support the judgment." ... We may review a state case decided on a federal ground even if it is clear that there was an available state ground for decision on which the state court could properly have relied.... Also, if, in our view, the state court "'felt compelled by what it understood to be federal constitutional considerations to construe ... its own law in the manner that it did,'" then we will not treat a normally adequate state ground as independent, and there will be no question about our jurisdiction.... Finally, "where the non-federal ground is so interwoven with the [federal ground] as not to be an independent matter, or is not of sufficient breadth to sustain the judgment without any decision of the other, our jurisdiction is plain." ...

Respect for the independence of state courts, as well as avoidance of rendering advisory opinions, have been the cornerstones of this Court's refusal to decide cases where there is an adequate and independent state ground. It is precisely because of this respect for state courts, and this desire to avoid advisory opinions, that we do not wish to continue to decide issues of state law that go beyond the opinion that we review, or to require state courts to reconsider cases to clarify the grounds of their decisions. Accordingly, when, as in this case, a state court decision fairly appears to rest primarily on federal law, or to be interwoven with the federal law, and when the adequacy and independence of any possible state law ground is not clear from the face of the opinion, we will accept as the most reasonable explanation that the state court decided the case the way it did because it believed that federal law required it to do so. If a state court chooses merely to rely on federal precedents as it would on the precedents of all other jurisdictions, then it need only make clear by a plain statement in its judgment or opinion that the federal cases are being used only for the purpose of guidance, and do not themselves compel the result that the court has reached. In this way, both justice and judicial administration will be greatly improved. If the state court decision indicates clearly and expressly that it is alternatively based on bona fide separate, adequate, and independent grounds, we, of course, will not undertake to review the decision.

This approach obviates in most instances the need to examine state law in order to decide the nature of the state court decision, and will at the same time avoid the danger of our rendering advisory opinions. It also avoids the unsatisfactory and intrusive practice of requiring state courts to clarify their decisions to the satisfaction of this Court. [This] approach will provide state judges with a clearer opportunity to develop state jurisprudence unimpeded by federal interference, and yet will preserve the integrity of federal law. "It is fundamental that state courts be left free and unfettered by us in interpreting their state constitutions. But it is equally important that ambiguous or obscure adjudications by state courts do not stand as barriers to a determination by this Court of the validity under the federal constitution of state action." *Minnesota v. National Tea Co.* (1940).

The principle that we will not review judgments of state courts that rest on adequate and independent state grounds is based, in part, on "the limitations of our own jurisdiction." *Herb v. Pitcairn* (1945). The jurisdictional concern is that we not "render an advisory opinion, and if the same judgment would be rendered by the state court after we corrected its views of federal laws, our review could amount to nothing more than an advisory opinion." Our requirement of a "plain statement" that a decision rests upon adequate and independent state grounds does not in any way authorize the rendering of advisory opinions. Rather, in determining, as we must, whether we have jurisdiction to review a case that is alleged to rest on adequate and independent state grounds, we merely assume that there are no such grounds when it is not clear from the opinion itself that the state court relied upon an adequate and independent state ground and when it fairly appears that the state court rested its decision primarily on federal law.

Our review of the decision below under this framework leaves us unconvinced that it rests upon an independent state ground. Apart from its two citations to the state constitution, the court below relied exclusively on its understanding of *Terry*[*v. Ohio* (1968)] and other federal cases. Not a single state case was cited to support the state court's holding that the search of the passenger compartment was unconstitutional. Indeed, the court declared that the search in this case was unconstitutional because "[t]he Court of Appeals erroneously applied the principles of *Terry v. Ohio* ... to the search of the interior of the vehicle in this case." The references to the state constitution in no way indicate that the decision below rested on grounds in any way independent from the state court's interpretation of federal law. Even if we accept that the Michigan constitution has been interpreted to provide independent protection for certain rights also secured under the 4th Amendment, it fairly appears in this case that the Michigan Supreme Court rested its decision primarily on federal law.

Rather than dismissing the case, or requiring that the state court reconsider its decision on our behalf solely because of a mere possibility that an adequate and independent ground supports the judgment, we find that we have jurisdiction in the absence of a plain statement that the decision below rested on an adequate and independent state ground....

V. The judgment of the Michigan Supreme Court is reversed, and the case is remanded for further proceedings not inconsistent with this opinion.

It is so ordered.

Justice Blackmun, concurring in part and concurring in the judgment.[Omitted.]

Justice Brennan, with whom Justice Marshall joins, dissenting.[Omitted.]

Justice Stevens, dissenting.

The jurisprudential questions presented in this case are far more important than the question whether the Michigan police officer's search of respondent's car violated the 4th Amendment. The case raises profoundly significant questions concerning the relationship between two sovereigns—the State of Michigan and the United States of America.

The Supreme Court of the State of Michigan expressly held "that the deputies' search of the vehicle was proscribed by the 4th Amendment of the United States Constitution and art. 1, §11 of the Michigan Constitution." The state law ground is clearly adequate to support the judgment, but the question whether it is independent of the Michigan Supreme Court's understanding of federal law is more difficult. Four possible ways of resolving that question present themselves: (1) asking the Michigan Supreme Court directly, (2) attempting to infer from all possible sources of state law what the Michigan Supreme Court meant, (3) presuming that adequate state grounds are independent unless it clearly appears otherwise, or (4) presuming that adequate state grounds are not independent unless it clearly appears otherwise. This Court has, on different occasions, employed each of the first three approaches; never until today has it even hinted at the 4th. In order to "achieve the consistency that is necessary," the Court today undertakes a reexamination of all the possibilities. It rejects the first approach as inefficient and unduly burdensome for state courts, and rejects the second approach as an inappropriate expenditure of our resources. Although I find both of those decisions defensible in themselves, I cannot accept the Court's decision to choose the fourth approach over the third—to presume that adequate state grounds are intended to be dependent on federal law unless the record plainly shows otherwise. I must therefore dissent....

The nature of the case before us hardly compels a departure from tradition. These are not cases in which an American citizen has been deprived of a right secured by the United States Constitution or a federal statute. Rather, they are cases in which a state court has upheld a citizen's assertion of a right, finding the citizen to be protected under both federal and state law. The complaining party is an officer of the state itself, who asks us to rule that the state court interpreted federal rights too broadly and "overprotected" the citizen.

Such cases should not be of inherent concern to this Court. The reason may be illuminated by assuming that the events underlying this case had arisen in another country, perhaps the Republic of Finland. If the Finnish police had arrested a Finnish citizen for possession of marijuana, and the Finnish courts had turned him loose, no American would have standing to object. If instead they had arrested an American citizen and acquitted him, we might have been concerned about the arrest but we surely could not have complained about the acquittal, even if the Finnish Court had based its decision on its understanding of the United States Constitution. That would be true even if we had a treaty with Finland requiring it to respect the rights of American citizens under the United States Constitution. We would only be motivated to intervene if an American citizen were unfairly arrested, tried, and convicted by the foreign tribunal.

In this case the State of Michigan has arrested one of its citizens and the Michigan Supreme Court has decided to turn him loose. The respondent is a United States citizen as well as a Michigan citizen, but since there is no claim that he has been mistreated by the State of Michigan, the final outcome of the state processes offended no federal interest whatever. Michigan simply provided greater protection to one of its citizens than some other State might provide or, indeed, than this Court might require throughout the country.

I believe that in reviewing the decisions of state courts, the primary role of this Court is to make sure that persons who seek to vindicate federal rights have been fairly heard....

I respectfully dissent.

Michigan v. Long: Notes

One way to understand the decision in *Michigan v. Long* is as a set of instructions to state courts that wish to decide cases based on state constitutions—not solely on the federal constitution. To protect decisions based (even as an alternate holding) on an independent state ground, the state court must make clear that, as to that ground, it is not relying on federal constitutional grounds. Here are two examples of state courts that have followed the *Michigan v. Long* principle. In both cases the states provided greater protection to individual liberties than are provided by the comparable federal standard. The courts were able to protect their decisions from Supreme Court review even though the decisions mentioned the federal constitution and diverged from the federal standard. In *Kentucky v. Wasson*, the Court found a right to engage in homosexual sodomy to be protected by the Kentucky constitution, even though it was not then protected by the federal Constitution. In *Oregon v. Henry*, the Court found a right to possess obscene material for sale to the public to be protected by the Oregon Constitution, even though it is not protected by the federal Constitution.

Kentucky v. Wasson
842 S.W.2d 487 (Ky. 1992)

Both courts below decided the issues solely on state constitutional law grounds, and our decision today, affirming the judgments of the lower courts, is likewise so limited. Federal constitutional protection under the Equal Protection Clause was not an issue reached in the lower courts and we need not address it. *Bowers v. Hardwick* (1986) held federal constitutional protection of the right of privacy was not implicated in laws penalizing homosexual sodomy. We discuss *Bowers* in particular, and federal cases in general, not in the process of construing the United States Constitution or federal law, but only where their reasoning is relevant to discussing questions of state law.

Oregon v. Henry
732 P.2d 9 (Ore. 1987)

Defendant concedes that the statute passes muster under the federal Court's current view of the 1st Amendment and therefore focuses his attack directly on the viability of the statute under Article I, §8, of the Oregon Constitution. We therefore address this issue as our own interpretation of the Oregon Constitution independent of any 1st Amendment analysis by the Supreme Court of the United States. *See State v. Kennedy* (Ore. 1983). We discuss the federal constitution and federal cases only when of assistance in the analysis of the Oregon Constitution....

Although the *Miller* test may pass federal constitutional muster and is recommended as a model for state legislatures by the *Attorney General's Commission on Pornography*, the test constitutes censorship forbidden by the Oregon Constitution. As Judge Tanzer aptly noted in *State v. Tidyman* (Ore. 1977), the problem with the United States Supreme Court's approach to obscene expression is that it permits government to decide what constitutes socially acceptable expression, which is precisely what Madison decried: "The difficulty [with the United States Supreme Court's approach] arises from the anomaly that the very purpose of the 1st Amendment is to protect expression which fails to conform to community standards."

We hold that characterizing expression as "obscenity" under any definition, be it *Roth*, *Miller* or otherwise, does not deprive it of protection under the Oregon Constitution. Obscene speech, writing or equivalent forms of communication are "speech" nonetheless. We emphasize that the prime reason that "obscene" expression cannot be restricted is that it is speech that does not fall within any historical exception to the plain wording of the Oregon Constitution that "no law shall be passed restraining the expression of [speech] freely on any subject whatsoever."

* * *

The following chart summarizes the criteria implicated by *Michigan v. Long*, *Kentucky v. Wasson*, and *Oregon v. Henry*.

Independent and Adequate State Ground:

Appeal or Petition for Certiorari from State Court to U.S. Supreme Court

Grounds for decision and appeal	Conflict	Result
1. State law only	No alleged conflict with U.S. Constitution or federal law. No federal claim.	U.S. Supreme Court has no jurisdiction.
2. State Constitutional provision only. *Kentucky v. Wasson*. *Oregon v. Henry*.	No alleged conflict with U.S. Constitution or federal law. No federal claim.	U.S. Supreme Court has no jurisdiction.
3. State criminal statute alleged to be unconstitutional based on federal + state constitutional grounds.	No alleged conflict of state *ground* with supreme federal law.	U.S. Supreme Court has no jurisdiction: adequate + independent state ground.

Clear statement of independence of state ground.		
4. Like 3 but state ground mentioned in passing without clear statement of independence.	No alleged conflict of state ground with supreme federal law.	U.S. Supreme Court will have jurisdiction. *Michigan v. Long.*
5. State criminal statute alleged to be unconstitutional based on federal + state constitutional grounds. Clear statement of independence of state ground.	State ground conflicts with federal constitution or law. State ground is therefore not independent.	U.S. Supreme Court has jurisdiction.

II. Congressional Control over Federal Judicial Review

In *Cooper v. Aaron* (1958), the Supreme Court claimed the authority to be the final interpreter of the meaning of the Constitution. However, Article III raises intriguing questions about congressional power to limit the Court's ability to assert this potent power. Since the lower federal courts are not created by the Constitution, in theory Congress could eliminate some (or all) of their jurisdiction. Note that the Constitution allows Congress to make exceptions to the appellate jurisdiction of the Supreme Court. If this power is interpreted to totally eliminate the appellate jurisdiction of the Court (and if the jurisdiction of the lower federal courts over federal questions was eliminated), then no federal court would have jurisdiction to decide most constitutional issues. In that case final authority would be in the state courts.

Three sections of Article III must be analyzed in order to determine the scope of congressional power to restrict the jurisdiction of the Supreme Court and the lower federal courts. First, Article III, §2, cl. 1, specifies how the federal court system is to be structured:

> The judicial Power of the United States, shall be vested in one supreme Court, and in such inferior Courts as the Congress may from time to time ordain and establish.

If Congress "*may* ... ordain and establish" inferior courts, must they? Art. III §1 states in part that

> The judicial Power *shall* extend to all Cases, in Law and Equity, arising under this Constitution, the Laws of the United States, and Treaties made, or which shall be made, under their Authority ...

Must Congress pass statutes insuring that the *federal* judicial power extends to *all* cases involving the Constitution, laws, or treaties of the United States?

Finally, Art. III, §2, cl. 2, establishes the original and appellate jurisdiction of the Supreme Court:

> In all Cases affecting Ambassadors, other public Ministers and Consuls, and those in which a State shall be Party, the supreme Court shall have original Jurisdiction. In all the other Cases before mentioned, the supreme Court shall have appellate Jurisdiction, both as to Law and Fact, *with such Exceptions, and under such Regulations as the Congress shall make.*

What, if any, limits are there to the types of exceptions can Congress make? Can Congress make exceptions to the appellate jurisdiction if it has also failed to establish the lower federal courts—or more likely, restricted access to the lower federal courts for a particular type of case?

Justice Story argued in *Martin v. Hunter's Lessee* (1816) that because "it is a duty of congress to vest the judicial power of the United States, it is a duty to vest the *whole* judicial power...." In 1850 the Court cast doubt on Story's position. In *Sheldon v. Sill* (1850), the Court considered a challenge to §11 of the Judiciary Act of 1789. The case arose when Sill (a resident of New York) filed suit against Sheldon (a resident of Michigan) to collect on a promissory note. Sill had purchased the note from Hastings (a resident of Michigan). Section 11 provides in part:

> [Federal courts shall not have] cognizance of any suit to recover the contents of any promissory note or other chose in action, in favor of an assignee, unless a suit might have been prosecuted in such court to recover the contents, if no assignment had been made.

Section 11 denied access to the diversity jurisdiction of federal court to Sill (of New York) in his suit against Sheldon (of Michigan) because Sill had been assigned the promissory note from Hastings (of Michigan), a party who would *not* be diverse to the defendant Sheldon. Sill claimed that because Article III provides for diversity jurisdiction and contains no exceptions for cases of assignments that the statute was unconstitutional. In broad language, the Court upheld §11:

> And it would seem to follow, also, that, having a right to prescribe, Congress may withhold from any court of its creation jurisdiction of any of the enumerated controversies. Courts created by statute can have no jurisdiction but such as the statute confers. No one of them can assert a just claim to jurisdiction exclusively conferred on another, or withheld from all. The Constitution has defined the limits of the judicial power of the United States, but has not prescribed how much of it shall be exercised by the Circuit Court; consequently, the statute which does prescribe the limits of their jurisdiction, cannot be in conflict with the Constitution, unless it confers powers not enumerated therein.

The rule in *Sheldon v. Sill* denies a party diversity jurisdiction in *all* federal courts—both the lower federal courts and the Supreme Court. This occurs because under *Sheldon v. Sill* the Supreme Court would not have appellate jurisdiction of a state court decision based solely on state law—even if the parties were diverse.

Congressional control of federal court jurisdiction is not very controversial in the diversity setting. Many find it more troubling when associated with congressional attacks on controversial Supreme Court precedent.

In the 1980s some conservatives attacked the doctrine by which the states were required to obey the guarantees of the federal Bill of Rights. For example, on July 21, 1982, George F. Will wrote that "[t]he court took a radically wrong turn when it 'incorporated' the 1st Amendment into the 14th Amendment, thereby imposing on states the restrictions that the author of that Amendment clearly intended to apply only to Congress."

(*Greensboro Record*, July 21, 1982, at A-12). (The rule requiring states to obey most, but not all of the guarantees of the federal Bill of Rights by virtue of §1 of the 14th Amendment is called the incorporation doctrine. It is discussed in Chapter 7, *infra*.)

In the text of a July 9, 1985, speech[1] to be delivered to the American Bar Association, Ronald Reagan's Attorney General, Edwin Meese, insisted that, to be legitimate, Supreme Court decisions must be based on "original intention." Mr. Meese, like George F. Will, did not explore the history of the framing of the 14th Amendment. Instead, he noted that the Supreme Court had not applied the Bill of Rights to the states until 1925. He said that the Court had expanded "the scope of the doctrine of incorporation" by applying more guarantees of the Bill of Rights to the states. "But," he wrote, "the most that can be done is to expand the scope; nothing can be done to shore up the intellectually shaky foundation upon which the doctrine rests. And nowhere else has the principle of federalism been dealt so politically violent and constitutionally suspect a blow as by the theory of incorporation." On July 31, 1985, *The Wall Street Journal* published an article by law professor Charles E. Rice. The headline described the incorporation doctrine as "Flimflam Under the 14th."

In the 2d session of the 97th Congress, Senator John East of North Carolina attempted to strip the federal judiciary of all jurisdiction over cases where parties attempted to enforce the Bill of Rights against the states. Senator East introduced S. 3018 to "reform the Federal judiciary...." The bill provided:

> The United States Supreme Court shall not have jurisdiction to review, by appeal, writ of certiorari, or otherwise, any case wherein any party claims the abridgment by a State, or by any political subdivision ... of any right secured by the first eight amendments to the Constitution of the United States.

The bill also provided that

> The district courts shall not have jurisdiction of any case or question which the Supreme Court does not have jurisdiction to review....

The effect of the bill was to withdraw from *all* federal courts all claims that states had violated guarantees of the Bill of Rights. Is either portion of Senator East's bill (which did not pass) constitutional standing alone? Can both portions together be constitutional? Is such a statute wise policy?

Ex Parte McCardle: Background

Analysis of contemporary attempts to craft jurisdiction-stripping statutes involves both the language of Article III and the meaning of *Ex Parte McCardle* (1868), the leading precedent in this area. For an excellent review of this case, see William Van Alstyne, *A Critical Guide to* Ex Parte McCardle, 15 Ariz. L. Rev. 229 (1973).

Section 14 of the Judiciary Act of 1789 had provided that petitions of habeas corpus filed in the Supreme Court could challenge the conditions of federal, but not state, imprisonment. While the petition was filed in the Supreme Court, it was technically considered to be in the Court's appellate jurisdiction because the petition was reviewing the conduct of a lower court. Following the Civil War, the Republican Congress passed the Habeas Corpus Act of 1867 to allow state prisoners to file habeas corpus petitions in fed-

---

1. In March, 2003, the speech was available online at http://www.politics.pomona.edu/dml/Lab Meese.htm.

eral court. The Congress believed that many state prisoners needed a federal forum to effectuate their rights. After all Southern states except Tennessee rejected the 14th Amendment, Congress also passed the Military Reconstruction Act of March 2, 1867. It provided for military rule of the South until the Southern states drafted new state constitutions acceptable to Congress providing for universal male suffrage, established new state governments, and ratified the proposed 14th Amendment. On fulfilling these conditions their representatives and senators would be seated in Congress, and the rebellious states would again be fully readmitted to the Union. The suspension of civilian government raised obvious questions of constitutional validity.

Mississippi was one of the states under military control. William McCardle was the editor of the *Vicksburg Times* and used his position to vilify the Northern troops and wage an inflammatory campaign against the creation of a new state constitution and the ratification of the 14th Amendment. Typical editorials called for the Northern troops and their sympathizers to be shot or made threats that he would publish the name of any white Mississippian who failed to boycott the election called to authorize a new state constitutional convention. The military commander had McCardle placed under arrest for disturbing the peace, inciting to insurrection and disorder, libel, and impeding Reconstruction. He was held in military custody and faced a military trial. In an act of extreme irony, McCardle then relied on the habeas provision of the 1868 Act—designed to protect Northern sympathizers from Southern state courts—to gain access to federal court to challenge the constitutionality of the Military Reconstruction Act. The lower court denied his claim, and he appealed to the Supreme Court.

The case was briefed and argued, but not decided. Congress, fearful that Reconstruction could be dealt a mortal blow, passed a statute revoking the appellate jurisdiction of the Supreme Court under the Habeas Corpus Act of 1867. The act was the only statute that McCardle had relied upon. Because he was being held in federal custody, McCardle might also have relied on the habeas jurisdiction of the Supreme Court provided by § 14 of the Judiciary Act of 1789. However, McCardle did not include that act as a basis for federal jurisdiction. The central question in the case was whether Congress was appropriately exercising its authority to make exceptions to the appellate jurisdiction of the Supreme Court.

Ex Parte McCardle
74 U.S. 506 (1868)

The Chief Justice delivered the opinion of the Court.

The first question necessarily is that of jurisdiction; for, if the act of March, 1868, takes away the jurisdiction defined by the act of February, 1867, it is useless, if not improper, to enter into any discussion of other questions.

It is quite true, as was argued by the counsel for the petitioner, that the appellate jurisdiction of this court is not derived from acts of Congress. It is, strictly speaking, conferred by the Constitution. But it is conferred "with such exceptions and under such regulations as Congress shall make."

It is unnecessary to consider whether, if Congress had made no exceptions and no regulations, this court might not have exercised general appellate jurisdiction under rules prescribed by itself. For among the earliest acts of the first Congress, at its first session, was the act of September 24th, 1789, to establish the judicial courts of the United States.

That act provided for the organization of this court, and prescribed regulations for the exercise of its jurisdiction.

The source of that jurisdiction, and the limitations of it by the Constitution and by statute, have been on several occasions subjects of consideration here. In the case of *Durousseau v. The United States* (1810) ... the court held, that while "the appellate powers of this court are not given by the judicial act, but are given by the Constitution," they are, nevertheless, "limited and regulated by that act, and by such other acts as have been passed on the subject." The court said, further, that the judicial act was an exercise of the power given by the Constitution to Congress "of making exceptions to the appellate jurisdiction of the Supreme Court." "They have described affirmatively," said the court, "its jurisdiction, and this affirmative description has been understood to imply a negation of the exercise of such appellate power as is not comprehended within it."

The principle that the affirmation of appellate jurisdiction implies the negation of all such jurisdiction not affirmed having been thus established, it was an almost necessary consequence that acts of Congress, providing for the exercise of jurisdiction, should come to be spoken of as acts granting jurisdiction, and not as acts making exceptions to the constitutional grant of it.

The exception to appellate jurisdiction in the case before us, however, is not an inference from the affirmation of other appellate jurisdiction. It is made in terms. The provision of the act of 1867, affirming the appellate jurisdiction of this court in cases of habeas corpus is expressly repealed. It is hardly possible to imagine a plainer instance of positive exception.

We are not at liberty to inquire into the motives of the legislature. We can only examine into its power under the Constitution; and the power to make exceptions to the appellate jurisdiction of this court is given by express words.

What, then, is the effect of the repealing act upon the case before us? We cannot doubt as to this. Without jurisdiction the court cannot proceed at all in any cause. Jurisdiction is power to declare the law, and when it ceases to exist, the only function remaining to the court is that of announcing the fact and dismissing the cause. And this is not less clear upon authority than upon principle.

Several cases were cited by the counsel for the petitioner in support of the position that jurisdiction of this case is not affected by the repealing act. But none of them, in our judgment, afford any support to it. They are all cases of the exercise of judicial power by the legislature, or of legislative interference with courts in the exercising of continuing jurisdiction.

On the other hand, the general rule, supported by the best elementary writers, is, that "when an act of the legislature is repealed, it must be considered, except as to transactions past and closed, as if it never existed." And the effect of repealing acts upon suits under acts repealed, has been determined by the adjudications of this court....

It is quite clear, therefore, that this court cannot proceed to pronounce judgment in this case, for it has no longer jurisdiction of the appeal; and judicial duty is not less fitly performed by declining ungranted jurisdiction than in exercising firmly that which the Constitution and the laws confer.

Counsel seem to have supposed, if effect be given to the repealing act in question, that the whole appellate power of the court, in cases of habeas corpus, is denied. But this is an error. The act of 1868 does not except from that jurisdiction any cases but appeals from Circuit Courts under the act of 1867. It does not affect the jurisdiction which was previously exercised.

The appeal of the petitioner in this case must be DISMISSED FOR WANT OF JURISDICTION.

Ex Parte McCardle: Notes

1. The fact that the revocation of the Habeas Corpus Act of 1867 did not preclude other methods of habeas review was illustrated the following year when another "unreconstructed" Mississippi editor successfully relied on §14 of the Judiciary Act of 1789 for jurisdiction to challenge his military arrest. *Ex Parte Yerger* (1869). The federal authorities, fearing the fate of the Military Reconstruction Act, transferred Yerger to state court, ending the case.

2. The *McCardle* opinion contains language making the holding of the case subject to divergent interpretations. First, the Court states:

    > We are not at liberty to inquire into the motives of the legislature. We can only examine into its power under the Constitution; and the power to make exceptions to the appellate jurisdiction of this court is given by express words.

    It then concludes the opinion with the following caveat:

    > Counsel seem to have supposed, if effect be given to the repealing act in question, that the whole appellate power of the court, in cases of habeas corpus, is denied. But this is an error. The act of 1868 does not except from that jurisdiction any cases but appeals from Circuit Courts under the act of 1867. It does not affect the jurisdiction which was previously exercised.

    Does *McCardle* resolve the question of how far Congress can go in restricting Supreme Court review?

    The power to "make exceptions" is a congressional power similar to any power found in Article I, §8. Like the Commerce Clause, it would be limited by any clear affirmative limitation found in the Constitution. Clearly, Congress could not deny Catholics, African Americans, or women access to the Supreme Court. A statute withdrawing the appellate jurisdiction of the Court over particular cases—such as those challenging school prayer as an establishment of religion—might also be held to be barred by the affirmative limitation of the 1st Amendment (as applied to the states by the 14th). Such a decision would raise difficult issues of whether the Court can and should decide Congress acted for the improper motive of facilitating the establishment of religion.

    The question is not simply academic as the bill proposed by Senator East shows. In addition, in 1979, Senator Helms of North Carolina introduced a proposal to eliminate Supreme Court jurisdiction and lower federal court jurisdiction over any case arising out of any state statute related to "voluntary prayers in public school and public buildings." On April 9, 1979, the Senate passed the provision as a rider to a bill on Supreme Court jurisdiction, but the proposal died in the House.

    The East and Helms bills would have eliminated Supreme Court appellate jurisdiction over certain subjects and would have also eliminated the jurisdiction of the lower federal courts over such subjects. The result would have been a withdrawal of federal judicial power from certain federal questions the Constitution suggests are within the judicial power of the United States. An argument in favor of the constitutionality of such action is that Congress has the power to eliminate the lower federal courts or to restrict their jurisdiction and has the power to make exceptions to the appellate jurisdiction of the Court. An argument against the constitutionality of such statutes is that they violate the provision of Article III, § 1 that provides that the federal judicial power extends to all cases arising under the Constitution of the United States, though this argument seems undermined by the decision in *Sheldon v. Sill* (1850) described above. Another argument is that a bill like that of Senator Helms is designed to circumvent the independent bar of the Establishment Clause as interpreted by the Court and is therefore unconstitutional. The question has not been definitively resolved.

Consider the following excerpt from the 2004 Republican Party Platform:

> The sound principle of judicial review has turned into an intolerable presumption of judicial supremacy. A Republican Congress, working with a Republican president, will restore the separation of powers and re-establish a government of law. There are different ways to achieve that goal, such as using Article III of the Constitution to limit federal court jurisdictions; for example, in instances where judges are abusing their power by banning the use of "under God" in the Pledge of Allegiance or prohibiting depictions of the Ten Commandments, and potential actions invalidating the Defense of Marriage Act (DOMA)....

One reason that jurisdiction-stripping statutes have failed to gain widespread Congressional support is respect for the institution of the Supreme Court. Ironically, if the state courts continued to follow Supreme Court precedent, the result of jurisdiction-stripping statutes would be to perpetuate the very legal standards that their proponents dispute. Under the Court's view of the Supremacy Clause, state supreme judges should follow the existing Supreme Court precedent. Without jurisdiction the Court could not change its precedent on an issue. Still, without Supreme Court supervision state courts might ignore or distinguish away precedent they chose not to follow.

There is an extensive body of scholarship on the issue of congressional control over federal jurisdiction. For a survey, see generally, Chemerinsky, *Constitutional Law: Principles and Policies*, 148–178 (2nd ed., 2002).

3. While the decision in *McCardle* did determine the result of the case in one sense, it can be seen as affecting only one basis for jurisdiction. This is so because McCardle, who was in federal captivity, could have asserted another basis for habeas jurisdiction. Contrast the situation where, instead of denying jurisdiction, Congress seeks to dictate the outcome of a case. The Court has ruled that when Congress attempts to dictate a binding result in a case such legislation invades the judicial role and violates the separation of powers.

United States v. Klein (1871) involved a congressional statute that regulated the return of property that had been seized from Confederates during the Civil War. According to statute, claimants could sue in the U.S. Court of Claims. Property could only be returned if the claimant could prove loyalty to the Union during the war. In *United States v. Padelford* (1870), the Court had ruled that Confederates who had received a presidential pardon could recover their property. In response to *Padelford*, Congress promptly passed a statute providing that receipt of a pardon that did not also include a finding that the person had in fact been loyal was proof of disloyalty. The statute required courts to dismiss any cases in which a pardon was used to justify recovery. The *Klein* Court invalidated the new statute, holding that Congress was not regulating jurisdiction but was seeking to dictate the result in cases that were properly before the Court.

III. Justiciability

Article III, §2, cl.1, says that the federal judicial power shall extend to "cases" and "controversies" arising under the Constitution and laws of the United States. What are "cases" and "controversies"? "Cases" and "controversies" must meet certain technical requirements. The Court will not issue an *advisory opinion*. The Court will not decide a case that meets its definition of a *political question*. A party who asserts a claim must have *standing*. Finally, the Court will require that the claim be *ripe* and not be *moot*. So, before deciding a case on the merits, the Court asks *what* the case involves, *who* is seeking the relief, and *when* the issue in question occurred—whether the controversy is sufficiently developed or has progressed to a point where a judicial decision would not affect the parties. If the Court finds that the case fails to meet these "case" and "controversy" requirements it will decline jurisdiction. Each of these questions involves issues of "justiciability."

The Supreme Court's attempt to answer this question relates to its view of the proper role of the judiciary in our system of government. These principles have been applied by the Court in very different ways at different times. The Court has established two types of limits. It has held that Article III imposes some limits on the judiciary when courts review legislative or executive action. In addition to these constitutional limits, the Court has also imposed voluntary or *prudential* limits on itself. In part, these are based on its attempt to avoid damaging collisions with the other branches of government.

In asking *what*, the Court inquires as to whether the litigants have an actual dispute that the court can resolve, or whether they are merely seeking an advisory opinion to shape their conduct. The Court will also examine whether the issue involves the application of legal standards, or, as a *political question*, raises policy issues that should be resolved by a representative organ of government.

In asking *who*, the Court inquires as to the *standing* of the plaintiff to prosecute the claims that he brings into court. In ordinary common law litigation there is congruence between an interested plaintiff and his personal claim, but the linkage can be tenuous in ideological challenges to governmental conduct. A plaintiff could theoretically obtain standing in a variety of ways to challenge governmental conduct: as a citizen, vindicating standards set out in the constitution; as a taxpayer, insuring that money is not spent in impermissible ways; or as an individual who has been individually harmed by the putative conduct. The individual could also form an organization that is concerned with the issues involved in the lawsuit and have the organization represent individuals. Finally, the Court occasionally allows individuals who are properly before the Court to represent the interests of third parties who are not themselves part of the litigation.

In asking *when*, the Court seeks to ensure that underlying facts are neither too new nor too old. They need to have developed to the point that the dispute can be seen to be *ripe*, meaning the claims are sufficiently concrete so that the Court is not speculating as to what may happen as the result of the governmental conduct. Similarly, if conditions have changed so the Court's decision will not affect the result, the case is *moot* and the Court will not intervene.

The concepts listed above can lead the Court to dismiss claims altogether. There are also rules of self-restraint that the Court follows with cases that are otherwise properly before the Court. Justice Brandeis, in a famous concurrence in *Ashwander v. Tennessee Valley Authority* (1936), summarized many of these:

> The Court developed, for its own governance in the cases confessedly within its jurisdiction, a series of rules under which it has avoided passing upon a large part of all the constitutional questions pressed upon it for decision. They are:
>
> 1. The Court will not pass upon the constitutionality of legislation in a friendly, nonadversary, proceeding, declining because to decide such questions "is legitimate only in the last resort, and as a necessity in the determination of real, earnest, and vital controversy between individuals. It never was the thought that, by means of a friendly suit, a party beaten in the legislature could transfer to the courts an inquiry as to the constitutionality of the legislative act." *Chicago & Grand Trunk Ry. Co. v. Wellman* (1892).
>
> 2. The Court will not "anticipate a question of constitutional law in advance of the necessity of deciding it." *Liverpool, N.Y. & Phila. Steamship Co. v. Emigration Commissioners* (1885)...." It is not the habit of the court to decide questions of a constitutional nature unless absolutely necessary to a decision of the case." *Burton v. United States* (1905).
>
> 3. The Court will not "formulate a rule of constitutional law broader than is required by the precise facts to which it is to be applied." *Liverpool, N.Y. & Phila. Steamship Co. v. Emigration Commissioners* (1885).
>
> 4. The Court will not pass upon a constitutional question although properly presented by the record, if there is also present some other ground upon which the case may be disposed of. This rule has found most varied application. Thus, if a case can be decided on either of two grounds, one involving a constitutional question, the other a question of statutory construction or general law, the Court will decide only the latter. *Siler v. Louisville & Nashville R. Co.* (1909).... Appeals from the highest court of a state challenging its decision of a question under the federal Constitution are frequently dismissed because the judgment can be sustained on an independent state ground. *Berea College v. Kentucky* (1908).
>
> 5. The Court will not pass upon the validity of a statute upon complaint of one who fails to show that he is injured by its operation. *Tyler v. Judges* (1900).... Among the many applications of this rule, none is more striking than the denial of the right of challenge to one who lacks a personal or property right. Thus, the challenge by a public official interested only in the performance of his official duty will not be entertained. *Columbus & Greenville Ry. Co. v. Miller* (1931).... In *Fairchild v. Hughes* (1922), the Court affirmed the dismissal of a suit brought by a citizen who sought to have the 19th Amendment declared unconstitutional. In *Massachusetts v. Mellon* (1923), the challenge of the federal Maternity Act was not entertained although made by the Commonwealth on behalf of all its citizens.
>
> 6. The Court will not pass upon the constitutionality of a statute at the instance of one who has availed himself of its benefits. *Great Falls Mfg. Co. v. Attorney General* (1888)....
>
> 7. "When the validity of an act of the Congress is drawn in question, and even if a serious doubt of constitutionality is raised, it is a cardinal principle that this

Court will first ascertain whether a construction of the statute is fairly possible by which the question may be avoided." *Crowell v. Benson* (1932).

A. Advisory Opinions

The Court insists that a case that a party presents for judicial resolution must involve an actual dispute. Some state constitutions specifically provide for advisory opinions. For example, when confronted with a bill requiring public school teachers to lead public school students in the Pledge of Allegiance, 1988 Democratic Presidential candidate Michael Dukakis, when governor of Massachusetts, requested and received an advisory opinion from the Massachusetts Supreme Court. In response to his questions on the constitutionality of the bill, five of the seven Massachusetts Supreme Court justices declared that compelling teachers who conscientiously object to leading the pledge was unconstitutional. *Opinions of the Justices to the Governor* (Mass. 1977). Dukakis then vetoed the bill, an act for which he was harshly criticized in his later presidential debate with then-Vice President George H.W. Bush. Some states and many foreign countries allow legislators to pose hypothetical questions to courts as an aid in drafting of statutes. These jurisdictions reason that it is foolish to expend resources to draft and pass a statute that will be found to be unconstitutional.

The Supreme Court has declined to issue advisory opinions from its beginnings. In 1793, England and France were at war. Thomas Jefferson, Secretary of State in George Washington's administration, had concerns about how to maintain American neutrality consistent with our obligations under various treaties. Jefferson asked the Supreme Court to advise the administration as to the Court's interpretation of several treaty provisions. The Court refused:

> [T]he three departments of government ... being in certain respects checks upon each other, and our being Judges of a Court in the last resort, are considerations which afford strong arguments against the propriety of our extra-judicially deciding the questions alluded to, especially as the power given by the Constitution to the President, of calling on the heads of departments for opinions, seems to have been *purposely* as well as expressly united to the *Executive* department.

3 Correspondence and Public Papers of John Jay 488–89 (Johnston ed. 1891). The President is free to accept or reject advice from his cabinet officers. In part, the Court seems to think that it would diminish the stature of the courts if it were to issue judicial opinions which could be accepted or ignored by the parties.

The Court will also find any case where the parties' interests are not truly adverse to be a request for an advisory opinion. The Court summarized its policies concerning advisory opinions in *Flast v. Cohen* (1968):

> [T]he power of English judges to deliver advisory opinions was well established at the time the Constitution was drafted.... And it is quite clear that "the oldest and most consistent thread in the federal law of justiciability is that the federal courts will not give advisory opinions." ... Thus, the implicit policies embodied in Article III, and not history alone, impose the rule against advisory opinions on federal courts. When the federal judicial power is invoked to pass upon the validity of actions by the Legislative and Executive Branches of the Government, the rule against advisory opinions implements the separation of powers prescribed by the Constitution and confines federal courts to the role assigned them

by Article III.... However, the rule against advisory opinions also recognizes that such suits often "are not pressed before the Court with that clear concreteness provided when a question emerges precisely framed and necessary for decision from a clash of adversary argument exploring every aspect of a multifaceted situation embracing conflicting and demanding interests." ... Consequently, the Article III prohibition against advisory opinions reflects the complementary constitutional considerations expressed by the justiciability doctrine: Federal judicial power is limited to those disputes which confine federal courts to a rule consistent with a system of separated powers and which are traditionally thought to be capable of resolution through the judicial process.

A viable case that requests a *declaratory judgment* is not a request for an advisory opinion. The declaratory judgment is merely the type of relief that the party has requested to resolve the actual conflict. At one time there was some confusion surrounding this issue; Congress passed the Declaratory Judgment Act of 1934, 28 U.S.C. §2201(a), to resolve this uncertainty. In practice, requests for declaratory judgment are typically joined with any request for injunctive relief.

B. Political Questions

The doctrines concerning *political questions* do not apply to *any* question about politics. For example, many questions about politics raise issues requiring consideration of the 1st Amendment or the Equal Protection Clause. Rather, the political question doctrine concerns those issues that the Court determines should be resolved by a political branch of government rather than the judiciary.

An early application of this doctrine arose in *Luther v. Borden* (1849). In 1842 Rhode Island was still governed by an only slightly updated version of its colonial charter. The charter government was characterized by disfranchisement and a malapportioned legislature. About 90% of adult males were unable to vote. Reform efforts made between 1820 and 1840 had failed. Reformers following the principles of the Declaration of Independence insisted that the people had a right to reform or replace their government, drafted a new "People's Constitution" and submitted it to a vote of all adult white male citizens. The People's Constitution was ratified and the reformers held elections and the elected officials attempted to set up a new state government. Rhode Island now had two governments. The Charter government with tacit support from President John Tyler declared martial law and suppressed the more democratic government. *Luther v. Borden* was a test case in which the reformers claimed that since the Charter government was not republican its officials lacked legal authority. They relied on the guarantee in Article IV, §4, that "The United States shall guarantee to every State in this Union a Republican Form of Government." The Supreme Court held that this case was not one for judicial resolution:

> Under this article of the Constitution it rests with Congress to decide what government is the established one in a State. For as the United States guarantee to each State a republican government, Congress must necessarily decide what government is established in the State before it can determine whether it is republican or not. And when the senators and representatives of a State are admitted into the councils of the Union, the authority of the government under which they are appointed, as well as its republican character, is recognized by the proper

constitutional authority. And its decision is binding on every other department of the government, and could not be questioned in a judicial tribunal.

The modern contours of the political question doctrine have been set out in *Baker v. Carr* (1962). *Baker* involved an equal protection challenge to the apportionment of seats in the Tennessee legislature, in which there were substantial variations in the population of legislative districts. Prior to *Baker*, in *Colegrove v. Green* (1946), the Court had dismissed a reapportionment claim concerning federal congressional districts as being a political question. The Court cited the command of Article I, §4, cl.1:

> The Times, Places and Manner of holding Elections for Senators and Representatives, shall be prescribed in each State by the Legislature thereof; but the Congress may at any time by Law make or alter such Regulations, except as to the Places of chusing Senators.

It held that "Courts ought not to enter this political thicket." However, in *Baker*, the Court rejected this view. It was quite unlikely that malapportioned legislatures would reform themselves through the political process — indeed they had failed to do so for many decades. Instead of avoiding the issue as a political question, the Court provided a judicial forum to allow disadvantaged voters to claim the benefit of the Equal Protection Clause. The Court later held that "one man, one vote" was a clear standard that could be derived from the Equal Protection Clause as to state elections. The Court also set out the classic statement of what constitutes a political question:

> It is apparent that several formulations which vary slightly according to the settings in which the questions arise may describe a political question, although each has one or more elements which identify it as essentially a function of the separation of powers. Prominent on the surface of any case held to involve a political question is found a textually demonstrable constitutional commitment of the issue to a coordinate political department; or a lack of judicially discoverable and manageable standards for resolving it; or the impossibility of deciding without an initial policy determination of a kind clearly for non-judicial discretion; or the impossibility of a court's undertaking independent resolution without expressing lack of the respect due coordinate branches of government; or an unusual need for unquestioning adherence to a political decision already made; or the potentiality of embarrassment from multifarious pronouncements by various departments on one question.

Questions

1. Where have we seen the issue of political questions discussed before? Reread the first section of *Marbury* at the beginning of this chapter.

2. Was the Court correct in *Baker v. Carr* in holding that manageable standards exist in connection with an Equal Protection challenge to a malapportioned state legislature? How manageable are the "tests" suggested for determining if a case raises a "political question"?

3. Assume that the United States is involved in a long and bloody land war with a nation in the Middle East. Congressman Long of Ohio makes a speech on the floor of the House. He says that the war is costing so many lives and so much treasure and is so difficult to win without resort to a nuclear holocaust that it should be abandoned. Congressman Garfield of Ohio moves to expel Long based on his speech. The House votes by a 2/3rds vote to expel Long. He seeks judicial review and the case reaches the

United States Supreme Court. Make arguments from text, history, policy, precedent, etc., bearing on the case. What arguments could be made for Long? What arguments against? What constitutional provisions are relevant? What cases are relevant? What aspects of the constitutional structure are relevant? How might you use the decision in *Powell v. McCormack*?

Consider the following sections of the Constitution, together with any others you believe are relevant: Article I, §2 [1], §5 [1] & [2], §6 [1] and Amendment I.

Powell v. McCormack
395 U.S. 486 (1969)

[Majority: Warren (C.J.), Douglas, Black, Fortas, Brennan, Marshall, White, and Harlan. Concurring: Douglas. Dissenting: Stewart.]

Mr. Chief Justice Warren delivered the opinion of the Court.

In November 1966, petitioner Adam Clayton Powell, Jr., was duly elected from the 18th Congressional District of New York to serve in the United States House of Representatives for the 90th Congress. However, pursuant to a House resolution, he was not permitted to take his seat. [A Special Subcommittee, investigating the incumbent Powell's conduct during the previous term, had issued a report concluding that Powell and certain staff employees had deceived the House authorities as to travel expenses. The report also indicated there was strong evidence that certain illegal salary payments had been made to Powell's wife at his direction.] Powell (and some of the voters of his district) then filed suit in Federal District Court, claiming that the House could exclude him only if it found he failed to meet the standing requirements of age, citizenship, and residence contained in Art. I, §2, of the Constitution—requirements the House specifically found Powell met—and thus had excluded him unconstitutionally. [John W. McCormack was named as defendant in his official capacity as Speaker of the House.] The District Court dismissed petitioners' complaint "for want of jurisdiction of the subject matter." A panel of the Court of Appeals affirmed the dismissal, although on somewhat different grounds, each judge filing a separate opinion. We have determined that it was error to dismiss the complaint and that petitioner Powell is entitled to a declaratory judgment that he was unlawfully excluded from the 90th Congress....

IV. EXCLUSION OR EXPULSION.

[House Resolution No. 278] excluding petitioner Powell was adopted by a vote in excess of two-thirds of the 434 Members of Congress—307 to 116. Article I, §5, grants the House authority to expel a member "with the Concurrence of two thirds."[1] ...

The Speaker ruled that House Resolution No. 278 contemplated an exclusion proceeding. We must reject respondents' suggestion that we overrule the Speaker and hold that, although the House manifested an intent to exclude Powell, its action should be tested by whatever standards may govern an expulsion....

---

1. Powell was "excluded" from the 90th Congress, i.e., he was not administered the oath of office and was prevented from taking his seat. If he had been allowed to take the oath and subsequently had been required to surrender his seat, the House's action would have constituted an "expulsion". Since we conclude that Powell was excluded from the 90th Congress, we express no view on what limitations may exist on Congress' power to expel or otherwise punish a member once he has been seated.

VI-B. Political Question Doctrine.

1. Textually Demonstrable Constitutional Commitment.

Respondents maintain that even if this case is otherwise justiciable, it presents only a political question. It is well established that the federal courts will not adjudicate political questions.... In *Baker v. Carr* (1962) we noted that political questions are not justiciable primarily because of the separation of powers within the Federal Government. After reviewing our decisions in this area, we concluded that on the surface of any case held to involve a political question was at least one of the following formulations:

> a textually demonstrable constitutional commitment of the issue to a co-ordinate political department; or a lack of judicially discoverable and manageable standards for resolving it; or the impossibility of deciding without an initial policy determination of a kind clearly for nonjudicial discretion; or the impossibility of a court's undertaking independent resolution without expressing lack of the respect due co-ordinate branches of government; or an unusual need for unquestioning adherence to a political decision already made; or the potentiality of embarrassment from multifarious pronouncements by various departments on one question.

Respondents' first contention is that this case presents a political question because under Art. I, §5, there has been a "textually demonstrable constitutional commitment" to the House of the "adjudicatory power" to determine Powell's qualifications. Thus it is argued that the House, and the House alone, has power to determine who is qualified to be a member.

In order to determine whether there has been a textual commitment to a coordinate department of the Government, we must interpret the Constitution. In other words, we must first determine what power the Constitution confers upon the House through Art. I, §5, before we can determine to what extent, if any, the exercise of that power is subject to judicial review. Respondents maintain that the House has broad power under §5, and, they argue, the House may determine which are the qualifications necessary for membership. On the other hand, petitioners allege that the Constitution provides that an elected representative may be denied his seat only if the House finds he does not meet one of the standing qualifications expressly prescribed by the Constitution.

If examination of §5 disclosed that the Constitution gives the House judicially unreviewable power to set qualifications for membership and to judge whether prospective members meet those qualifications, further review of the House determination might well be barred by the political question doctrine. On the other hand, if the Constitution gives the House power to judge only whether elected members possess the three standing qualifications set forth in the Constitution, further consideration would be necessary to determine whether any of the other formulations of the political question doctrine are "inextricable from the case at bar." *Baker v. Carr*....

In order to determine the scope of any "textual commitment" under Art. I, §5, we necessarily must determine the meaning of the phrase to "be the Judge of the Qualifications of its own Members."... Our examination of the relevant historical materials leads us to the conclusion that petitioners are correct and that the Constitution leaves the House without authority to exclude any person, duly elected by his constituents, who meets all the requirements for membership expressly prescribed in the Constitution.

VI-B-1-a. The Pre-Convention Precedents.

Since our rejection of respondents' interpretation of §5 results in significant measure from a disagreement with their historical analysis, we must consider the relevant historical antecedents in considerable detail. As do respondents, we begin with the English and colonial precedents.

[Early English precedents] seem to demonstrate that a member [of Parliament] could be excluded only if he had first been expelled....

Even if these cases could be construed to support respondents' contention, their precedential value was nullified prior to the Constitutional Convention. By 1782, after a long struggle, the arbitrary exercise of the power to exclude was unequivocally repudiated by a House of Commons resolution which ended the most notorious English election dispute of the 18th century—the John Wilkes case. While serving as a member of Parliament in 1763, Wilkes published an attack on a recent peace treaty with France, calling it a product of bribery and condemning the Crown's ministers as "the tools of despotism and corruption." R. Postgate, *That Devil Wilkes* 53 (1929). Wilkes and others who were involved with the publication in which the attack appeared were arrested. Prior to Wilkes' trial, the House of Commons expelled him for publishing "a false, scandalous, and seditious libel." 15 *Parl. Hist. Eng.* 1393 (1764). Wilkes then fled to France and was subsequently sentenced to exile. 9 L. Gipson, *The British Empire Before the American Revolution* 37 (1956).

Wilkes returned to England in 1768, the same year in which the Parliament from which he had been expelled was dissolved. He was elected to the next Parliament, and he then surrendered himself to the Court of King's Bench. Wilkes was convicted of seditious libel and sentenced to 22 months' imprisonment. The new Parliament declared him ineligible for membership and ordered that he be "expelled this House." 16 *Parl. Hist. Eng.* 545 (1769). Although Wilkes was re-elected to fill the vacant seat three times, each time the same Parliament declared him ineligible and refused to seat him. See 1 Gipson, *The British Empire Before the American Revolution* at 207–15 (1965).

Wilkes was released from prison in 1770 and was again elected to Parliament in 1774. For the next several years, he unsuccessfully campaigned to have the resolutions expelling him and declaring him incapable of re-election expunged from the record. Finally, in 1782, the House of Commons voted to expunge them, resolving that the prior House actions were "subversive of the rights of the whole body of electors of this kingdom." 22 *Parl. Hist. Eng.* 1411 (1782).

With the successful resolution of Wilkes' long and bitter struggle for the right of the British electorate to be represented by men of their own choice, it is evident that, on the eve of the Constitutional Convention, English precedent stood for the proposition that "the law of the land had regulated the qualifications of members to serve in parliament" and those qualifications were "not occasional but fixed." 16 *Parl. Hist. Eng.* 589, 590 (1769). Certainly English practice did not support, nor had it ever supported, respondents' assertion that the power to judge qualifications was generally understood to encompass the right to exclude members-elect for general misconduct not within standing qualifications. With the repudiation in 1782 of the only two precedents for excluding a member-elect who had been previously expelled, it appears that the House of Commons also repudiated any "control over the eligibility of candidates, except in the administration of the laws which define their (standing) qualifications." T. May's *Parliamentary Practice* 66 (1924)....

Wilkes' struggle and his ultimate victory had a significant impact in the American colonies. His advocacy of libertarian causes and his pursuit of the right to be seated in Parliament became a cause celebre for the colonists. "(T)he cry of 'Wilkes and Liberty' echoed loudly across the Atlantic Ocean as wide publicity was given to every step of Wilkes's public career in the colonial press.... The reaction in America took on significant proportions. Colonials tended to identify their cause with that of Wilkes. They saw him as a popular hero and a martyr to the struggle for liberty.... They named towns, counties, and even children in his honour." 11 Gipson, at 222. It is within this historical context that we must examine the Convention debates in 1787, just five years after Wilkes' final victory.

VI-B-1-b. Convention Debates.

Relying heavily on Charles Warren's analysis[2] of the Convention debates, petitioners argue that the proceedings manifest the Framers' unequivocal intention to deny either branch of Congress the authority to add to or otherwise vary the membership qualifications expressly set forth in the Constitution. We do not completely agree, for the debates are subject to other interpretations. However, we have concluded that the records of the debates, viewed in the context of the bitter struggle for the right to freely choose representatives which had recently concluded in England and in light of the distinction the Framers made between the power to expel and the power to exclude, indicate that petitioners' ultimate conclusion is correct.

The Convention opened in late May 1787. By the end of July, the delegates adopted, with a minimum of debate, age requirements for membership in both the Senate and the House. The Convention then appointed a Committee of Detail to draft a constitution incorporating these and other resolutions adopted during the preceding months. Two days after the Committee was appointed, George Mason, of Virginia, moved that the Committee consider a clause "requiring certain qualifications of landed property & citizenship" and disqualifying from membership in Congress persons who had unsettled accounts or who were indebted to the United States. 2 Farrand, *Records of the Federal Convention of 1787*, 121 (1966). A vigorous debate ensued. Charles Pinckney and General Charles C. Pinckney, both of South Carolina, moved to extend these incapacities to both the judicial and executive branches of the new government. But John Dickinson, of Delaware, opposed the inclusion of any statement of qualifications in the Constitution. He argued that it would be "impossible to make a compleat one, and a partial one would by implication tie up the hands of the Legislature from supplying the omissions." Dickinson's argument was rejected; and, after eliminating the disqualification of debtors and the limitation to "landed" property, the Convention adopted Mason's proposal to instruct the Committee of Detail to draft a property qualification.

The Committee reported in early August, proposing no change in the age requirement; however, it did recommend adding citizenship and residency requirements for membership. After first debating what the precise requirements should be, on August 8, 1787, the delegates unanimously adopted the three qualifications embodied in Art. I, § 2.

On August 10, the Convention considered the Committee of Detail's proposal that the "Legislature of the United States shall have authority to establish such uniform qualifications of the members of each House, with regard to property, as to the said Legislature shall seem expedient." The debate on this proposal discloses much about the views of the Framers on the issue of qualifications. For example, James Madison urged its rejection, stating that the proposal would vest

> an improper & dangerous power in the Legislature. The qualifications of electors and elected were fundamental articles in a Republican Govt. and ought to be fixed by the Constitution. If the Legislature could regulate those of either, it can by degrees subvert the Constitution. A Republic may be converted into an

---

2. See C. Warren, *The Making of the Constitution* at 399–426 (1928).

aristocracy or oligarchy as well by limiting the number capable of being elected, as the number authorised to elect.... It was a power also, which might be made subservient to the views of one faction against another. Qualifications founded on artificial distinctions may be devised, by the stronger in order to keep out partisans of [a weaker] faction.

Significantly, Madison's argument was not aimed at the imposition of a property qualification as such, but rather at the delegation to the Congress of the discretionary power to establish any qualifications. The parallel between Madison's arguments and those made in Wilkes' behalf is striking.

In view of what followed Madison's speech, it appears that on this critical day the Framers were facing and then rejecting the possibility that the legislature would have power to usurp the "indisputable right [of the people] to return whom they thought proper" to the legislature. Oliver Ellsworth, of Connecticut, noted that a legislative power to establish property qualifications was exceptional and "dangerous because it would be much more liable to abuse." Gouverneur Morris then moved to strike "with regard to property" from the Committee's proposal. His intention was "to leave the Legislature entirely at large." Hugh Williamson, of North Carolina, expressed concern that if a majority of the legislature should happen to be "composed of any particular description of men, of lawyers for example, ... the future elections might be secured to their own body." Madison then referred to the British Parliament's assumption of the power to regulate the qualifications of both electors and the elected and noted that "the abuse they had made of it was a lesson worthy of our attention. They had made the changes in both cases subservient to their own views, or to the views of political or Religious parties." Shortly thereafter, the Convention rejected both Gouverneur Morris' motion and the Committee's proposal. Later the same day, the Convention adopted without debate the provision authorizing each House to be "the judge of the ... qualifications of its own members."

One other decision made the same day is very important to determining the meaning of Art. I, § 5. When the delegates reached the Committee of Detail's proposal to empower each House to expel its members, Madison "observed that the right of expulsion ... was too important to be exercised by a bare majority of a quorum: and in emergencies (one) faction might be dangerously abused." He therefore moved that "with the concurrence of two-thirds" be inserted. With the exception of one State, whose delegation was divided, the motion was unanimously approved without debate, although Gouverneur Morris noted his opposition. The importance of this decision cannot be over-emphasized. None of the parties to this suit disputes that prior to 1787 the legislative powers to judge qualifications and to expel were exercised by a majority vote. Indeed, without exception, the English and colonial antecedents to Art. I, § 5, cls. 1 and 2, support this conclusion. Thus, the Convention's decision to increase the vote required to expel, because that power was "too important to be exercised by a bare majority," while at the same time not similarly restricting the power to judge qualifications, is compelling evidence that they considered the latter already limited by the standing qualifications previously adopted.

Respondents urge, however, that these events must be considered in light of what they regard as a very significant change made in Art. I, § 2, cl. 2, by the Committee of Style. When the Committee of Detail reported the provision to the Convention, it read:

> Every member of the House of Representatives shall be of the age of twenty five years at least; shall have been a citizen of (in) the United States for at least three

years before his election; and shall be, at the time of his election, a resident of the State in which he shall be chosen.

However, as finally drafted by the Committee of Style, these qualifications were stated in their present negative form. Respondents note that there are no records of the "deliberations" of the Committee of Style. Nevertheless, they speculate that this particular change was designed to make the provision correspond to the form used by Blackstone in listing the "standing incapacities" for membership in the House of Commons. See 1 W. *Blackstone's Commentaries***175–176. Blackstone, who was an apologist for the anti-Wilkes forces in Parliament, had added to his *Commentaries* after Wilkes' exclusion the assertion that individuals who were not ineligible for the Commons [could] be denied their seat if the Commons deemed them unfit for other reasons. Since *Blackstone's Commentaries* was widely circulated in the Colonies, respondents further speculate that the Committee of Style rephrased the qualifications provision in the negative to clarify the delegates' intention "only to prescribe the standing incapacities without imposing any other limit on the historic power of each house to judge qualifications on a case by case basis."

Respondents' argument is inherently weak, however, because it assumes that legislative bodies historically possessed the power to judge qualifications on a case-by-case basis. As noted above, the basis for that conclusion was the Walpole and Wilkes cases, which, by the time of the Convention, had been denounced by the House of Commons and repudiated by at least one State government. Moreover, respondents' argument misrepresents the function of the Committee of Style. It was appointed only "to revise the style of and arrange the articles which had been agreed to...." 2 Farrand 553. "[T]he Committee ... had no authority from the Convention to make alterations of substance in the Constitution as voted by the Convention, nor did it purport to do so; and certainly the Convention had no belief ... that any important change was, in fact, made in the provisions as to qualifications adopted by it on August 10." ...

The debates at the state conventions also demonstrate the Framers' understanding that the qualifications for members of Congress had been fixed in the Constitution. Before the New York convention, for example, Hamilton emphasized: "[T]he true principle of a republic is, that the people should choose whom they please to govern them. Representation is imperfect in proportion as the current of popular favor is checked. This great source of free government, popular election, should be perfectly pure, and the most unbounded liberty allowed." 2 *Debates on the Federal Constitution* 257 (J. Elliot ed. 1876) (hereinafter cited as *Elliot's Debates*). In Virginia, where the Federalists faced powerful opposition by advocates of popular democracy, Wilson Carey Nicholas, a future member of both the House and Senate and later Governor of the State, met the arguments that the new Constitution violated democratic principles with the following interpretation of Art. I, §2, cl. 2, as it respects the qualifications of the elected: "It has ever been considered a great security to liberty, that very few should be excluded from the right of being chosen to the legislature. This Constitution has amply attended to this idea. We find no qualifications required except those of age and residence, which create a certainty of their judgment being matured, and of being attached to their state." 3 *Elliot's Debates* 8.

VI-B-1-c. Post-Ratification.

As clear as these statements appear, respondents dismiss them as "general statements ... directed to other issues." They suggest that far more relevant is Congress' own understanding of its power to judge qualifications as manifested in post-ratification exclusion cases. Unquestionably, both the House and the Senate have excluded members-elect for reasons other than their failure to meet the Constitution's standing qualifications. For almost the first 100 years of its existence, however, Congress strictly limited its power to judge the qualifications of its members to those enumerated in the Constitution....

There was no significant challenge to these principles [until] the general upheaval produced in the [Civil] War's wake. In 1868, the House voted for the first time in its history to exclude a member-elect. It refused to seat two duly elected representatives for giving aid and comfort to the Confederacy...."This change was produced by the North's bitter enmity toward those who failed to support the Union cause during the war, and was effected by the Radical Republican domination of Congress. It was a shift brought about by the naked urgency of power and was given little doctrinal support." Comment, *Legislative Exclusion: Julian Bond and Adam Clayton Powell*, 35 U. Chi. L. Rev. 151, 157 (1967). From that time until the present, congressional practice has been erratic; and on the few occasions when a member-elect was excluded although he met all the qualifications set forth in the Constitution, there were frequently vigorous dissents. Even the annotations to the official manual of procedure for the 90th Congress manifest doubt as to the House's power to exclude a member-elect who has met the constitutionally prescribed qualifications. See *Rules of the House of Representatives*, H.R. Doc. No. 529, 89th Cong., 2d Sess., § 12, pp. 7–8 (1967).

Had these congressional exclusion precedents been more consistent, their precedential value still would be quite limited. That an unconstitutional action has been taken before surely does not render that same action any less unconstitutional at a later date. Particularly in view of the Congress' own doubts in those few cases where it did exclude members-elect, we are not inclined to give its precedents controlling weight. The relevancy of prior exclusion cases is limited largely to the insight they afford in correctly ascertaining the draftsmen's intent. Obviously, therefore, the precedential value of these cases tends to increase in proportion to their proximity to the Convention in 1787. And, what evidence we have of Congress' early understanding confirms our conclusion that the House is without power to exclude any member-elect who meets the Constitution's requirements for membership.

VI-B-1-d. Conclusion.

Had the intent of the Framers emerged from these materials with less clarity, we would nevertheless have been compelled to resolve any ambiguity in favor of a narrow construction of the scope of Congress' power to exclude members-elect. A fundamental principle of our representative democracy is, in Hamilton's words, "that the people should choose whom they please to govern them." 2 *Elliot's Debates* 257. As Madison pointed out at the Convention, this principle is undermined as much by limiting whom the people can select as by limiting the franchise itself. In apparent agreement with this basic philosophy, the Convention adopted his suggestion limiting the power to expel. To allow essentially that same power to be exercised under the guise of judging qualifications, would be to ignore Madison's warning, borne out in the Wilkes case and some of Congress' own post-Civil War exclusion cases, against "vesting an improper & dangerous power in the Legislature." 2 Farrand 249. Moreover, it would effectively nullify the Convention's decision to require a two-thirds vote for expulsion. Unquestionably, Congress has an interest in preserving its institutional integrity, but in most cases that interest can be sufficiently safeguarded by the exercise of its power to punish its members for disorderly behavior and, in extreme cases, to expel a member with the concurrence of two-thirds. In short, both the intention of the Framers, to the extent it can be determined, and an examination of the basic principles of our democratic system persuade us that the Constitution does not vest in the Congress a discretionary power to deny membership by a majority vote.

For these reasons, we have concluded that Art. I, § 5, is at most a "textually demonstrable commitment" to Congress to judge only the qualifications expressly set forth in the Constitution. Therefore, the "textual commitment" formulation of the political question doctrine does not bar federal courts from adjudicating petitioners' claims.

VI-B-2. Other Considerations.

Respondents' alternate contention is that the case presents a political question because judicial resolution of petitioners' claim would produce a "potentially embarrassing confrontation between coordinate branches" of the Federal Government. But, as our interpretation of Art. I, § 5, discloses, a determination of petitioner Powell's right to sit would require no more than an interpretation of the Constitution. Such a determination falls within the traditional role accorded courts to interpret the law, and does not involve a "lack of the respect due (a) coordinate (branch) of government," nor does it involve an "initial policy determination of a kind clearly for non-judicial discretion." *Baker v. Carr* (1962). Our system of government requires that federal courts on occasion interpret the Constitution in a manner at variance with the construction given the document by another branch. The alleged conflict that such an adjudication may cause cannot justify the courts' avoiding their constitutional responsibility....

Nor are any of the other formulations of a political question "inextricable from the case at bar." *Baker v. Carr*. Petitioners seek a determination that the House was without power to exclude Powell from the 90th Congress, which, we have seen, requires an interpretation of the Constitution—a determination for which clearly there are "judicially ... manageable standards." Finally, a judicial resolution of petitioners' claim will not result in "multifarious pronouncements by various departments on one question." For, as we noted in *Baker v. Carr*, it is the responsibility of this Court to act as the ultimate interpreter of the Constitution. *Marbury v. Madison* (1803). Thus, we conclude that petitioners' claim is not barred by the political question doctrine, and, having determined that the claim is otherwise generally justiciable, we hold that the case is justiciable.

VII. CONCLUSION....

Further, analysis of the "textual commitment" under Art. I, § 5 (see Part VI, B (1)), has demonstrated that in judging the qualifications of its members Congress is limited to the standing qualifications prescribed in the Constitution. Respondents concede that Powell met these. Thus, there is no need to remand this case to determine whether he was entitled to be seated in the 90th Congress. Therefore, we hold that, since Adam Clayton Powell, Jr., was duly elected by the voters of the 18th Congressional District of New York and was not ineligible to serve under any provision of the Constitution, the House was without power to exclude him from its membership....

It is so ordered.

Mr. Justice Douglas, concurring. [Omitted.]

Mr. Justice Stewart, dissenting.[Omitted.]

Nixon v. United States
506 U.S. 224 (1993)

[Majority: Rehnquist (C.J.), Stevens, O'Connor, Scalia, Kennedy, and Thomas. Concurring: Stevens, White, Blackmun, and Souter.]

Chief Justice Rehnquist delivered the opinion of the Court.

Petitioner Walter L. Nixon, Jr., asks this Court to decide whether Senate Rule XI, which allows a committee of Senators to hear evidence against an individual who has been impeached and to report that evidence to the full Senate, violates the Impeachment Trial Clause, Art. I, § 3, cl. 6. That Clause provides that the "Senate shall have the sole Power to try all Impeachments." But before we reach the merits of such a claim, we must decide whether it is "justiciable," that is, whether it is a claim that may be resolved by the courts. We conclude that it is not.

Nixon, a former Chief Judge of the United States District Court for the Southern District of Mississippi, was convicted by a jury of two counts of making false statements before a federal grand jury and sentenced to prison. The grand jury investigation stemmed from reports that Nixon had accepted a gratuity from a Mississippi businessman in exchange for asking a local district attorney to halt the prosecution of the businessman's son. Because Nixon refused to resign from his office as a United States District Judge, he continued to collect his judicial salary while serving out his prison sentence.

On May 10, 1989, the House of Representatives adopted three articles of impeachment for high crimes and misdemeanors. The first two articles charged Nixon with giving false testimony before the grand jury and the third article charged him with bringing disrepute on the Federal Judiciary.

After the House presented the articles to the Senate, the Senate voted to invoke its own Impeachment Rule XI, under which the presiding officer appoints a committee of Senators to "receive evidence and take testimony." Senate Impeachment Rule XI, reprinted in Senate Manual, S. Doc. No. 101-1, 186 (1989). The Senate committee held four days of hearings, during which 10 witnesses, including Nixon, testified. Pursuant to Rule XI, the committee presented the full Senate with a complete transcript of the proceeding and a Report stating the uncontested facts and summarizing the evidence on the contested facts. Nixon and the House impeachment managers submitted extensive final briefs to the full Senate and delivered arguments from the Senate floor during the three hours set aside for oral argument in front of that body. Nixon himself gave a personal appeal, and several Senators posed questions directly to both parties. The Senate voted by more than the constitutionally required two-thirds majority to convict Nixon on the first two articles. The presiding officer then entered judgment removing Nixon from his office as United States District Judge.

Nixon thereafter commenced the present suit, arguing that Senate Rule XI violates the constitutional grant of authority to the Senate to "try" all impeachments because it prohibits the whole Senate from taking part in the evidentiary hearings. See Art. I, § 3, cl. 6. Nixon [unsuccessfully] sought a declaratory judgment that his impeachment conviction was void and that his judicial salary and privileges should be reinstated. The District Court held that his claim was nonjusticiable ... and the Court of Appeals for the District of Columbia Circuit agreed. We granted certiorari....

A controversy is nonjusticiable—i.e., involves a political question—where there is "a textually demonstrable constitutional commitment of the issue to a coordinate political department; or a lack of judicially discoverable and manageable standards for resolving it...." *Baker v. Carr* (1962). But the courts must, in the first instance, interpret the text in question and determine whether and to what extent the issue is textually committed.... As the discussion that follows makes clear, the concept of a textual commitment to a coordinate political department is not completely separate from the concept of a lack of judicially discoverable and manageable standards for resolving it; the lack of judicially manageable standards may strengthen the conclusion that there is a textually demonstrable commitment to a coordinate branch.

In this case, we must examine Art. I, §3, cl. 6, to determine the scope of authority conferred upon the Senate by the Framers regarding impeachment. It provides:

> The Senate shall have the sole Power to try all Impeachments. When sitting for that Purpose, they shall be on Oath or Affirmation. When the President of the United States is tried, the Chief Justice shall preside: And no Person shall be convicted without the Concurrence of two thirds of the Members present.

The language and structure of this Clause are revealing. The first sentence is a grant of authority to the Senate, and the word "sole" indicates that this authority is reposed in the Senate and nowhere else. The next two sentences specify requirements to which the Senate proceedings shall conform: The Senate shall be on oath or affirmation, a two-thirds vote is required to convict, and when the President is tried the Chief Justice shall preside.

Petitioner argues that the word "try" in the first sentence imposes by implication an additional requirement on the Senate in that the proceedings must be in the nature of a judicial trial. From there petitioner goes on to argue that this limitation precludes the Senate from delegating to a select committee the task of hearing the testimony of witnesses, as was done pursuant to Senate Rule XI. "'[T]ry' means more than simply 'vote on' or 'review' or 'judge.' In 1787 and today, trying a case means hearing the evidence, not scanning a cold record." Petitioner concludes from this that courts may review whether or not the Senate "tried" him before convicting him.

There are several difficulties with this position which lead us ultimately to reject it. The word "try," both in 1787 and later, has considerably broader meanings than those to which petitioner would limit it. Older dictionaries define try as "[t]o examine" or "[t]o examine as a judge." See S. Johnson, *A Dictionary of the English Language* (1785). In more modern usage the term has various meanings. For example, try can mean "to examine or investigate judicially," "to conduct the trial of," or "to put to the test by experiment, investigation, or trial." *Webster's Third New International Dictionary* 2457 (1971). Petitioner submits that "try," as contained in T. Sheridan, *Dictionary of the English Language* (1796), means "to examine as a judge; to bring before a judicial tribunal." Based on the variety of definitions, however, we cannot say that the Framers used the word "try" as an implied limitation on the method by which the Senate might proceed in trying impeachments. "As a rule the Constitution speaks in general terms, leaving Congress to deal with subsidiary matters of detail as the public interests and changing conditions may require...."

The conclusion that the use of the word "try" in the first sentence of the Impeachment Trial Clause lacks sufficient precision to afford any judicially manageable standard of review of the Senate's actions is fortified by the existence of the three very specific requirements that the Constitution does impose on the Senate when trying impeachments: The Members must be under oath, a two-thirds vote is required to convict, and the Chief Justice presides when the President is tried. These limitations are quite precise, and their nature suggests that the Framers did not intend to impose additional limitations on the form of the Senate proceedings by the use of the word "try" in the first sentence.

Petitioner devotes only two pages in his brief to negating the significance of the word "sole" in the first sentence of Clause 6. As noted above, that sentence provides that "[t]he Senate shall have the sole Power to try all Impeachments." We think that the word "sole" is of considerable significance. Indeed, the word "sole" appears only one other time in the Constitution—with respect to the House of Representatives' "*sole* Power of Impeachment." Art. I, §2, cl. 5 (emphasis added). The commonsense meaning of the word "sole" is that the Senate alone shall have authority to determine whether an individual should be acquitted or convicted. The dictionary definition bears this out. "Sole" is defined as "having no companion," "solitary," "being the only one," and "functioning ... independently and without assistance or interference." ...

Petitioner also contends that the word "sole" should not bear on the question of justiciability because Art. II, §2, cl. 1, of the Constitution grants the President pardon authority "except in Cases of Impeachment." He argues that such a limitation on the President's pardon power would not have been necessary if the Framers thought that the Senate alone had authority to deal with such questions. But the granting of a pardon is in no sense an overturning of a judgment of conviction by some other tribunal; it is "[a]n executive action that mitigates or sets aside punishment for a crime." *Black's Law Dictionary* 1113 (6th ed. 1990)....

Petitioner finally argues that even if significance be attributed to the word "sole" in the first sentence of the Clause, the authority granted is to the Senate, and this means that "the Senate—not the courts, not a lay jury, not a Senate Committee—shall try impeachments." It would be possible to read the first sentence of the Clause this way, but it is not a natural reading. Petitioner's interpretation would bring into judicial purview not merely the sort of claim made by petitioner, but other similar claims based on the conclusion that the word "Senate" has imposed by implication limitations on procedures which the Senate might adopt. Such limitations would be inconsistent with the construction of the Clause as a whole, which, as we have noted, sets out three express limitations in separate sentences.

The history and contemporary understanding of the impeachment provisions support our reading of the constitutional language. The parties do not offer evidence of a single word in the history of the Constitutional Convention or in contemporary commentary that even alludes to the possibility of judicial review in the context of the impeachment powers. This silence is quite meaningful in light of the several explicit references to the availability of judicial review as a check on the Legislature's power with respect to bills of attainder, ex post facto laws, and statutes.

The Framers labored over the question of where the impeachment power should lie. Significantly, in at least two considered scenarios the power was placed with the Federal Judiciary. See 1 Farrand 21–22 (Virginia Plan); *id.*, at 244 (New Jersey Plan). Indeed, James Madison and the Committee of Detail proposed that the Supreme Court should have the power to determine impeachments. See 2 *id.*, at 551 (Madison); *id.*, at 178–79, 186 (Committee of Detail). Despite these proposals, the Convention ultimately decided that the Senate would have "the sole Power to try all Impeachments." Art. I, §3, cl. 6. According to Alexander Hamilton, the Senate was the "most fit depositary of this important trust" because its Members are representatives of the people. See *The Federalist* No. 65. The Supreme Court was not the proper body because the Framers "doubted whether the members of that tribunal would, at all times, be endowed with so eminent a portion of fortitude as would be called for in the execution of so difficult a task" or whether the Court "would possess the degree of credit and authority" to carry out its judgment if it conflicted with the accusation brought by the Legislature—the people's representative. In addition, the Framers believed the Court was too small in number: "The awful discretion, which a court of impeachments must necessarily have, to doom to honor or to infamy the most confidential and the most distinguished characters of the community, forbids the commitment of the trust to a small number of persons."

There are two additional reasons why the Judiciary, and the Supreme Court in particular, were not chosen to have any role in impeachments. First, the Framers recognized that most likely there would be two sets of proceedings for individuals who commit impeachable offenses—the impeachment trial and a separate criminal trial. In fact, the Constitution explicitly provides for two separate proceedings. See Art. I, §3, cl. 7. The Framers deliberately separated the two forums to avoid raising the specter of bias and to ensure independent judgments....

Certainly judicial review of the Senate's "trial" would introduce the same risk of bias as would participation in the trial itself.

Second, judicial review would be inconsistent with the Framers' insistence that our system be one of checks and balances. In our constitutional system, impeachment was designed to be the only check on the Judicial Branch by the Legislature....

Judicial involvement in impeachment proceedings, even if only for purposes of judicial review, is counterintuitive because it would eviscerate the "important constitutional check" placed on the Judiciary by the Framers. *The Federalist*, No. 81. Nixon's argument would place final reviewing authority with respect to impeachments in the hands of the same body that the impeachment process is meant to regulate....

In addition to the textual commitment argument, we are persuaded that the lack of finality and the difficulty of fashioning relief counsel against justiciability. See *Baker v. Carr*. We agree with the Court of Appeals that opening the door of judicial review to the procedures used by the Senate in trying impeachments would "expose the political life of the country to months, or perhaps years, of chaos." This lack of finality would manifest itself most dramatically if the President were impeached. The legitimacy of any successor, and hence his effectiveness, would be impaired severely, not merely while the judicial process was running its course, but during any retrial that a differently constituted Senate might conduct if its first judgment of conviction were invalidated. Equally uncertain is the question of what relief a court may give other than simply setting aside the judgment of conviction. Could it order the reinstatement of a convicted federal judge, or order Congress to create an additional judgeship if the seat had been filled in the interim?

Petitioner finally contends that a holding of nonjusticiability cannot be reconciled with our opinion in *Powell v. McCormack* (1969)....

Our conclusion in *Powell* was based on the fixed meaning of "[q]ualifications" set forth in Art. I, §2. The claim by the House that its power to "be the Judge of the Elections, Returns and Qualifications of its own Members" was a textual commitment of unreviewable authority was defeated by the existence of this separate provision specifying the only qualifications which might be imposed for House membership. The decision as to whether a Member satisfied these qualifications was placed with the House, but the decision as to what these qualifications consisted of was not.

In the case before us, there is no separate provision of the Constitution that could be defeated by allowing the Senate final authority to determine the meaning of the word "try" in the Impeachment Trial Clause.... [W]e conclude, after exercising that delicate responsibility, that the word "try" in the Impeachment Trial Clause does not provide an identifiable textual limit on the authority which is committed to the Senate.

For the foregoing reasons, the judgment of the Court of Appeals is

Affirmed.

Justice Stevens, concurring. [Omitted.]

Justice White, with whom Justice Blackmun joins, concurring in the judgment.[Omitted.]

Justice Souter, concurring in the judgment. [Omitted.]

United States v. Stanley
483 U.S. 669 (1987)

[Majority: Scalia, Rehnquist (C.J.), White, Blackmun, Powell. Concurring (in part) and dissenting (in part): Brennan, Marshall, Stevens, and O'Connor.]

Justice Scalia delivered the opinion of the Court.

In February 1958, James B. Stanley, a master sergeant in the Army stationed at Fort Knox, Kentucky, volunteered to participate in a program ostensibly designed to test the effectiveness of protective clothing and equipment as defenses against chemical warfare. He was released from his then-current duties and went to the Army's Chemical Warfare Laboratories at the Aberdeen Proving Grounds in Maryland. Four times that month, Stanley was secretly administered doses of lysergic acid diethylamide (LSD), pursuant to an Army plan to study the effects of the drug on human subjects. According to his 2nd Amended Complaint (the allegations of which we accept for purposes of this decision), as a result of the LSD exposure, Stanley has suffered from hallucinations and periods of incoherence and memory loss, was impaired in his military performance, and would on occasion "awake from sleep at night and, without reason, violently beat his wife and children, later being unable to recall the entire incident." He was discharged from the Army in 1969. One year later, his marriage dissolved because of the personality changes wrought by the LSD.

On December 10, 1975, the Army sent Stanley a letter soliciting his cooperation in a study of the long-term effects of LSD on "volunteers who participated" in the 1958 tests. This was the Government's first notification to Stanley that he had been given LSD during his time in Maryland. After an administrative claim for compensation was denied by the Army, Stanley filed suit under the Federal Tort Claims Act (FTCA), 28 U.S.C. § 2671 et seq., alleging negligence in the administration, supervision, and subsequent monitoring of the drug testing program.

The District Court granted the Government's motion for summary judgment, finding that Stanley "was at all times on active duty and participating in a bona fide Army program during the time the alleged negligence occurred," ... and that his FTCA suit was therefore barred by the doctrine of *Feres v. United States* (1950), which determined that "the Government is not liable under the Federal Tort Claims Act for injuries to servicemen where the injuries arise out of or are in the course of activity incident to service." The Court of Appeals for the Fifth Circuit agreed that the *Feres* doctrine barred Stanley's FTCA suit against the United States, but held that the District Court should have dismissed for lack of subject-matter jurisdiction rather than disposing of the case on the merits. The Government contended that a remand would be futile, because *Feres* would bar any claims that Stanley could raise either under the FTCA or directly under the Constitution against individual officers under *Bivens v. Six Unknown Fed. Narcotics Agents* (1971). The court concluded, however, that Stanley "has at least a colorable constitutional claim based on *Bivens*," and remanded "for the consideration of the trial court of any amendment which the appellant may offer, seeking to cure the jurisdictional defect."

Stanley then amended his complaint to add claims against unknown individual federal officers for violation of his constitutional rights. He also specifically alleged that the United States' failure to warn, monitor, or treat him after he was discharged constituted a separate tort which, because occurring subsequent to his discharge, was not "incident to service" within the *Feres* exception to the FTCA. The District Court dismissed the FTCA claim because the alleged negligence was not "separate and distinct from any acts occurring before discharge, so as to give rise to a separate actionable tort not barred by the

Feres doctrine." It refused, however, to dismiss the *Bivens* claims. The court rejected, inter alia, the Government's argument that the same considerations giving rise to the *Feres* exception to the FTCA should constitute "special factors" of the sort alluded to in *Bivens*, and other cases as bars to a *Bivens* action. It cited as sole authority for that rejection the Court of Appeals for the Ninth Circuit's decision in *Wallace v. Chappell* (9th Cir. 1981). Sua sponte, the court certified its order for interlocutory appeal under 28 U.S.C. § 1292(b)....

Motions to dismiss for lack of personal jurisdiction and improper venue were filed on behalf of some of the defendants (it was alleged that proper service had not been made on the others), but before those motions were ruled on, we issued our decision in *Chappell v. Wallace* (1983), holding that "enlisted military personnel may not maintain a suit to recover damages from a superior officer for alleged constitutional violations," and reversing the sole authority cited by the District Court in its prior order refusing to dismiss Stanley's *Bivens* claims....

I. Here, the "order appealed from" was an order refusing to dismiss Stanley's *Bivens* claims on the basis of our holding in *Chappell*. The Court of Appeals therefore had no jurisdiction to enter orders relating to Stanley's long-dismissed FTCA claims, whether or not, as Stanley argues, "the issues involved in the *Bivens* claim and the alleged immunity of the individual defendants closely parallels [sic] the government's immunity due to the *Feres* doctrine ... [and] that is what all parties were arguing about in the interlocutory appeal."...

II. That leaves the Court of Appeals' ruling that Stanley can proceed with his *Bivens* claims notwithstanding the decision in *Chappell*. In our view, the court took an unduly narrow view of the circumstances in which courts should decline to permit nonstatutory damages actions for injuries arising out of military service.

In *Bivens*, we held that a search and seizure that violates the 4th Amendment can give rise to an action for damages against the offending federal officials even in the absence of a statute authorizing such relief. We suggested in dictum that inferring such an action directly from the Constitution might not be appropriate when there are "special factors counselling hesitation in the absence of affirmative action by Congress," or where there is an "explicit congressional declaration that persons injured by a federal officer's violation of the 4th Amendment may not recover money damages from the agents, but must instead be remitted to another remedy, equally effective in the view of Congress." We subsequently held that actions for damages could be brought directly under the Due Process Clause of the 5th Amendment, *Davis v. Passman* (1979), and under the 8th Amendment's proscription against cruel and unusual punishment, *Carlson v. Green* (1980), repeating each time the dictum that "special factors counselling hesitation" or an "explicit congressional declaration" that another remedy is exclusive would bar such an action. In *Chappell* [and in *Bush v. Lucas* (1983), decided the same day], that dictum became holding. *Chappell* reversed a determination that no "special factors" barred a constitutional damages remedy on behalf of minority servicemen who alleged that because of their race their superior officers "failed to assign them desirable duties, threatened them, gave them low performance evaluations, and imposed penalties of unusual severity." We found "factors counselling hesitation" in "the need for special regulations in relation to military discipline, and the consequent need and justification for a special and exclusive system of military justice...." We observed that the Constitution explicitly conferred upon Congress the power, inter alia, "to make Rules for the Government and Regulation of the land and naval Forces," U.S. Const. Art. I, § 8, cl. 14, thus showing that "the Constitution contemplated that the Legislative Branch have plenary control over rights, duties, and responsibilities in the framework of the Military Establishment...."...

As we implicitly recognized in *Chappell*, there are varying levels of generality at which one may apply "special factors" analysis. Most narrowly, one might require reason to believe that in the particular case the disciplinary structure of the military would be affected—thus not even excluding all officer-subordinate suits, but allowing, for example, suits for officer conduct so egregious that no responsible officer would feel exposed to suit in the performance of his duties. Somewhat more broadly, one might disallow *Bivens* actions whenever an officer-subordinate relationship underlies the suit. More broadly still, one might disallow them in the officer-subordinate situation and also beyond that situation when it affirmatively appears that military discipline would be affected. (This seems to be the position urged by Stanley.) Fourth, as we think appropriate, one might disallow *Bivens* actions whenever the injury arises out of activity "incident to service."

We therefore reaffirm the reasoning of *Chappell* that the "special factors counseling hesitation"—"the unique disciplinary structure of the Military Establishment and Congress' activity in the field,"—extend beyond the situation in which an officer-subordinate relationship exists, and require abstention in the inferring of *Bivens* actions as extensive as the exception to the FTCA established by *Feres* and *United States v. Johnson*. We hold that no *Bivens* remedy is available for injuries that "arise out of or are in the course of activity incident to service."

For the foregoing reasons, we vacate the Court of Appeals' judgment that Stanley can assert an FTCA claim on remand to the District Court and reverse its judgment refusing to dismiss the *Bivens* claims against petitioners. The judgment of the Court of Appeals is reversed in part and vacated in part, and the case is remanded for further proceedings consistent with this opinion.

It is so ordered.

Justice Brennan, with whom Justice Marshall joins, and with whom Justice Stevens joins as to Part III, concurring in part and dissenting in part.

In experiments designed to test the effects of lysergic acid diethylamide (LSD), the Government of the United States treated thousands of its citizens as though they were laboratory animals, dosing them with this dangerous drug without their consent. One of the victims, James B. Stanley, seeks compensation from the Government officials who injured him. The Court holds that the Constitution provides him with no remedy, solely because his injuries were inflicted while he performed his duties in the Nation's Armed Forces. If our Constitution required this result, the Court's decision, though legally necessary, would expose a tragic flaw in that document. But in reality, the Court disregards the commands of our Constitution, and bows instead to the purported requirements of a different master, *military discipline,* declining to provide Stanley with a remedy because it finds "special factors counselling hesitation." *Bivens v. Six Unknown Fed. Narcotics Agents* (1971). This is abdication, not hesitation. I dissent.

I. Before addressing the legal questions presented, it is important to place the Government's conduct in historical context. The medical trials at Nuremberg in 1947 deeply impressed upon the world that experimentation with unknowing human subjects is morally and legally unacceptable. The United States Military Tribunal established the Nuremberg Code as a standard against which to judge German scientists who experimented with human subjects. Its first principle was:

"1. *The voluntary consent of the human subject is absolutely essential*....

"The duty and responsibility for ascertaining the quality of the consent rests upon each individual who initiates, directs or engages in the experiment. It is a personal duty and responsibility which may not be delegated to another with impunity." *United States v. Brandt (The Medical Case)*, 2 *Trials of War Criminals Before the Nuremberg Military Tribunals Under Control Council Law No. 10*, pp. 181–82 (1949).

The United States military developed the Code, which applies to all citizens—soldiers as well as civilians.

In the 1950's, in defiance of this principle, military intelligence agencies and the Central Intelligence Agency (CIA) began surreptitiously testing chemical and biological materials, including LSD. These programs, which were "designed to determine the potential effects of chemical or biological agents when used operationally against individuals unaware that they had received a drug," included drug testing on "unwitting, nonvolunteer" Americans. S. Rep. No. 94-755, Book I, p. 385 (1976) (S. Rep.). James B. Stanley, a master sergeant in the Army, alleges that he was one of 1,000 soldiers covertly administered LSD by Army Intelligence between 1955 and 1958.

The Army recognized the moral and legal implications of its conduct. In a 1959 Staff Study, the United States Army Intelligence Corps (USAINTC) discussed its covert administration of LSD to soldiers:

> It was always a tenet of Army Intelligence that the basic American principle of dignity and welfare of the individual will not be violated.... In intelligence, the stakes involved and the interests of national security may permit a more tolerant interpretation of moral-ethical values, but not legal limits, through necessity.... Any claim against the US Government for alleged injury due to EA 1729 [LSD] must be legally shown to have been due to the material. Proper security and appropriate operational techniques can protect the fact of employment of EA 1729.

(quoting *USAINTC Staff Study, Material Testing Program EA 1729*, p. 26 (Oct. 15, 1959)).

That is, legal liability could be avoided by covering up the LSD experiments.

When the experiments were uncovered, the Senate agreed with the Army's conclusion that its experiments were of questionable legality, and issued a strong condemnation:

> In the Army's tests, as with those of the CIA, individual rights were ... subordinated to national security considerations; informed consent and follow-up examinations of subjects were neglected in efforts to maintain the secrecy of the tests. Finally, the command and control problems which were apparent in the CIA's programs are paralleled by a lack of clear authorization and supervision in the Army's programs.

S. Rep., at 411.

Having invoked national security to conceal its actions, the Government now argues that the preservation of military discipline requires that Government officials remain free to violate the constitutional rights of soldiers without fear of money damages. What this case and others like it demonstrate, however, is that Government officials (military or civilian) must not be left with such freedom. See, e.g., *Jaffee v. United States* (3rd Cir. 1981) (en banc) (exposure of soldiers to nuclear radiation during atomic weapons testing); *Schnurman v. United States* (E.D. Va. 1980) (exposure of unknowing soldier to mustard gas); *Thornwell v. United States* (D.C. 1979) (soldiers used to test the effects of LSD without their knowledge); cf. *Barrett v. United States* (SDNY, May 5, 1987) (death of mental hospital patient used as the unconsenting subject of an Army experiment to test mescaline derivative).

II. Serious violations of the constitutional rights of soldiers must be exposed and punished. Of course, experimentation with unconsenting soldiers, like any constitutional violation, may be enjoined *if* and when discovered. An injunction, however, comes too late for those already injured; for these victims, "it is damages or nothing." *Bivens* (Harlan, J., concurring). The solution for Stanley and other soldiers, as for any citizen, lies in a *Bivens* action—an action for damages brought directly under the Constitution for the violation of constitutional rights by federal officials. But the Court today holds that no *Bivens* remedy is available for service-connected injuries, because "special factors counse[l] hesitation." The practical result of this decision is absolute immunity from liability for money damages for all federal officials who intentionally violate the constitutional rights of those serving in the military.

First, I will demonstrate that the Court has reached this result only by ignoring governing precedent. The Court confers absolute immunity from money damages on federal officials (military and civilian alike) without consideration of longstanding case law establishing the general rule that such officials *are* liable for damages caused by their intentional violations of well-established constitutional rights. If applied here, that rule would require a different result. Then I will show that the Court denies Stanley's *Bivens* action solely on the basis of an unwarranted extension of the narrow exception to this rule created in *Chappell v. Wallace* (1983). The Court's reading of *Chappell* tears it from its analytical moorings, ignores the considerations decisive in our immunity cases, and leads to an unjust and illogical result....

II. A. As the Court notes, I do not dispute that the question whether a *Bivens* action exists is "analytically distinct from the question of official immunity from *Bivens* liability." I contend only that the "special factors" analysis of *Bivens* and the functional analysis of immunity are based on identical judicial concerns which, when correctly applied, should not and do not (as either a logical or practical matter) produce different outcomes. Justice Stevens explained it well:

> The practical consequences of a holding that no remedy has been authorized against a public official are essentially the same as those flowing from a conclusion that the official has absolute immunity. Moreover, similar factors are evaluated in deciding whether to recognize an implied cause of action or a claim of immunity. In both situations, when Congress is silent, the Court makes an effort to ascertain its probable intent.

Mitchell v. Forsyth (1985) (concurring opinion).

Thus, the redundance which so troubles the Court in equation of the "special factors" analysis and the immunity analysis strikes me as evidence only that the analyses are being properly performed. And *Davis* cannot be characterized, as the Court asserts, as a *unique* case in which the "special factors" of *Bivens* were coextensive with the immunity granted....

II. B. Even when, as here, national security is invoked, federal officials bear the burden of demonstrating that the usual rule of qualified immunity should be abrogated. In *Mitchell v. Forsyth*, the Court found "no ... historical or common-law basis for an absolute immunity for officers carrying out tasks essential to national security." In language applicable here, the Court pointed out: "National security tasks ... are carried out in secret.... Under such circumstances, it is far more likely that actual abuses will go uncovered than that fancied abuses will give rise to unfounded and burdensome litigation." The Court highlighted the "danger that high federal officials will disregard constitutional rights in their zeal to protect the national security," and deemed it "sufficiently real to counsel against affording such officials an absolute immunity."

This analysis of official immunity in the national security context applies equally to officials giving orders to the military. In *Scheuer v. Rhodes* (1974), the Governor, the Adjutant General of the Ohio National Guard, and other National Guard officers were sued under 42 U.S.C. §1983 for damages arising from injuries suffered when the Guard was deployed and ordered to fire its guns during a civil disturbance. The Court awarded only qualified immunity to the highest military officer of the State—the Governor (who commanded the State National Guard)—and to executive and military officers involved in the decision to take military action. *Scheuer* demonstrates that executive officials may receive only qualified immunity even when the function they perform is military decision making....

IV. The subject of experimentation who has not volunteered is treated as an object, a sample. James Stanley will receive no compensation for this indignity. A test providing absolute immunity for intentional constitutional torts *only* when such immunity was essential to maintenance of military discipline would "take into account the special importance of defending our Nation without completely abandoning the freedoms that make it worth defending." *Goldman v. Weinberger* (1986) (O'Connor, J., dissenting). But absent a showing that military discipline is concretely (not abstractly) implicated by Stanley's action, its talismanic invocation does not counsel hesitation in the face of an intentional constitutional tort, such as the Government's experimentation on an unknowing human subject. Soldiers ought not be asked to defend a Constitution indifferent to their essential human dignity. I dissent.

Justice O'Connor, concurring in part and dissenting in part....

No judicially crafted rule should insulate from liability the involuntary and unknowing human experimentation alleged to have occurred in this case. Indeed, as Justice Brennan observes, the United States military played an instrumental role in the criminal prosecution of Nazi officials who experimented with human subjects during the Second World War, *ante*, and the standards that the Nuremberg Military Tribunals developed to judge the behavior of the defendants stated that the "voluntary consent of the human subject is absolutely essential ... to satisfy moral, ethical and legal concepts." *United States v. Brandt (The Medical Case)*, 2 *Trials of War Criminals Before the Nuremberg Military Tribunals Under Control Council Law No. 10*, p. 181 (1949). If this principle is violated the very least that society can do is to see that the victims are compensated, as best they can be, by the perpetrators. I am prepared to say that our Constitution's promise of due process of law guarantees this much. Accordingly, I would permit James Stanley's *Bivens* action to go forward, and I therefore dissent.

* * *

In *Vieth v. Jubelirer*, (2004), four members of the Court held that a challenge to political gerrymandering of congressional districts constituted a political question. The opinion is reported, *infra*, Volume 2, Chapter 12: Equal Protection, Section VIII-A-2. The Supreme Court and the Right to Vote.

C. Standing

Standing involves whether the individual bringing a cause of action is a proper party to invoke the court's jurisdiction as to some or all of his claims. The Court has summarized its current approach to standing in *Valley Forge Christian College v. Americans United for Separation of Church and State, Inc.* (1982):

> [A]t an irreducible minimum, Art. III requires the party who invokes the court's authority to "show that he personally has suffered some actual or threatened injury as a result of the putatively illegal conduct of the defendant" ... and that the injury "fairly can be traced to the challenged action" and "is likely to be redressed by a favorable decision"....

While standing is rarely a problem in traditional common law litigation, it can be a problem in actions against governmental actors. A party could fail to establish standing if the Court determines that her harm is not personal, if the alleged harm is too tenuous to be considered an injury, if the harm cannot be attributed to the government, or if the harm may not be remedied by a verdict against the government.

City Of Los Angeles v. Lyons (1983) illustrates both the conventional and problematic aspects of standing. Lyons filed suit against the City alleging that he was choked and injured by police following a routine traffic stop. He alleged that he was injured because the Police Department had improper policies regarding the use of force. He had standing to prosecute a damages claim because he alleged that he had suffered an individual harm, because he alleged that it was due to the government's policies and police conduct, and because a verdict would compensate him for his injury.

Lyons also sought an injunction that would prevent the police from continuing to use the chokeholds under the current policies. The Court dismissed this claim for lack of standing. The Court maintained that as to an injunction against future conduct that Lyons did not have a personal claim because he was no more likely than any other citizen of Los Angeles to be choked. He was thus left to the political process (or state court) to attempt to get the Police Department to change its policies.

Cases that raise standing difficulties are typically challenges to broad governmental policies or practices, often brought in the context of public interest litigation. Representative cases include challenges to policies of zoning boards and the practices of the IRS and the EPA. Justices who adopt a restrictive view of standing often share the policy position reflected by Justice Frankfurter's statement in *Colegrove v. Green* (1946):

> The Constitution has left the performance of many duties in our governmental scheme to depend on the fidelity of the executive and legislative action and, ultimately, on the vigilance of the people in exercising their political rights.

While *Colegrove* involved the political question doctrine, the underlying rationale also applies to standing.

An individual is free to assert multiple bases for standing in any given case. One could seek to vindicate one's rights as a *citizen*, as a *taxpayer*, or as an *individual*. Significant barriers exist for claims of both citizen and taxpayer standing. The Burger and Rehnquist Courts have said that the need for at least a somewhat unique personal injury precludes recognition of *any* citizen standing suit. The Court says that regardless of their merits, such cases must be left to the political process. Taxpayer suits also raise the issue of individual harm. So far, only taxpayer challenges to spending programs that violate the Establishment Clause have succeeded. Cases involving the issue of a personal injury are discussed in Part A, *infra*.

Even claims of individual standing have been subjected to heightened skepticism by the Burger and Rehnquist Courts. Individuals must first establish that they have suffered an injury that is recognized by the Court. For example, the Court is often reluctant to recognize harms as *injuries* if they have not already occurred. The fact that someone other than the plaintiff is likely to suffer the type of injury about which the plaintiff complains is typically not sufficient to establish standing for the plaintiff. The line between cases involving the doctrine of ripeness and between cases involving the issue of non-personal harm tend to blur. Cases involving the issue of what constitutes an injury are discussed in Part B, *infra*.

The second way in which it has become difficult to establish individual standing has been the adoption, by the Burger and Rehnquist Courts, of restrictive tests regarding the causation of the plaintiff's injury (once established) and whether or not a successful verdict will redress the plaintiff's injury. According to the Court, many harms to individuals are caused by third parties, and not the government that regulates the third parties. For example, if a district attorney does not prosecute the fathers of illegitimate children for failing to pay child support, is the injury to the child due to the lack of a threat of prosecution or due to the deadbeat father? Is the injury the lack of child support or the discrimination against the illegitimate children? Cases involving the issue of what constitutes the cause-in-fact of an injury and what serves to redress the injury are discussed in Part C, *infra*.

1. Citizen and Taxpayer Standing: The Personal Injury Requirement

A claimed legal injury is not enough for judicial redress unless the injury can be considered *personal*. Personal does not mean limited to one person. Class actions can potentially involve tens of thousands of people, but the people share a unique harm. The paradigm example of what the Court considers a non-personal injury is a violation by the government of a constitutional duty that affects all citizens equally. The Court says that such violations can only be remedied by the political process.

Two cases from the early years of the Burger Court illustrate this point. In *United States v. Richardson* (1974), a taxpayer brought an action in mandamus to compel the Secretary of the Treasury to publish an accounting of the receipts and expenditures of the Central Intelligence Agency (CIA). The taxpayer challenged the provisions of the Central Intelligence Agency Act of 1949, which provided that appropriations to and expenditures by the CIA shall not be made public, despite the requirement of Article I, §9, cl. 7 of the Constitution: "No Money shall be drawn from the Treasury, but in Consequence of Appropriations made by Law; and a regular Statement and Account of the Receipts and Expenditures of all public Money shall be published from time to time." The Court, in an opinion by Chief Justice Burger, distinguished Richardson's taxpayer claim from the recognized taxpayer claim involving spending in violation of the Establishment Clause. (See discussion of *Flast v. Cohen* (1968), *infra*.) In rejecting Richardson's claim, Burger commented:

> It can be argued that if respondent is not permitted to litigate this issue, no one can do so. In a very real sense, the absence of any particular individual or class to litigate these claims gives support to the argument that the subject matter is committed to the surveillance of Congress, and ultimately to the political process.

Justice Powell continued this line of analysis in his concurrence:

> Relaxation of standing requirements is directly related to the expansion of judicial power. It seems to me inescapable that allowing unrestricted taxpayer or citizen standing would significantly alter the allocation of power at the national level, with a shift away from a democratic form of government. I also believe that repeated and essentially head-on confrontations between the life-tenured branch and the representative branches of government will not, in the long run, be beneficial to either. The public confidence essential to the former and the vitality critical to the latter may well erode if we do not exercise self-restraint in the utilization of our power to negative the actions of the other branches. We should be ever mindful of the contradictions that would arise if a democracy were to permit general oversight of the elected branches of government by a non-representative, and in large measure insulated, judicial branch. Moreover, the argument that the Court should allow unrestricted taxpayer or citizen standing underestimates the ability of the representative branches of the Federal Government to respond to the citizen pressure that has been responsible in large measure for

the concurrent drift toward expanded standing. Indeed, taxpayer or citizen advocacy, given its potentially broad base, is precisely the type of leverage that in a democracy ought to be employed against the branches that were intended to be responsive to public attitudes about the appropriate operation of government. "We must as judges recall that, as Mr. Justice Holmes wisely observed, the other branches of the Government 'are ultimate guardians of the liberties and welfare of the people in quite as great a degree as the courts.'"

A companion case to *Richardson*, *Schlesinger v. Reservists Committee to Stop the War* (1974), reached a similar conclusion. Here plaintiffs challenged the military Reserve membership of a few members of Congress, alleging that it violated the Incompatibility Clause. Article I, § 6, cl.2 holds that "no Person holding any Office under the United States, shall be a Member of either House during his Continuance in Office." In rejecting plaintiffs' claim of citizen standing, Chief Justice Burger held:

> [S]tanding to sue may not be predicated upon an interest of the kind alleged here which is held in common by all members of the public, because of the necessarily abstract nature of the injury all citizens share. Concrete injury, whether actual or threatened, is that indispensable element of a dispute which serves in part to cast it in a form traditionally capable of judicial resolution....
>
> Respondents' motivation has indeed brought them sharply into conflict with petitioners, but as the Court has noted, motivation is not a substitute for the actual injury needed by the courts and adversaries to focus litigation efforts and judicial decision making....
>
> Our system of government leaves many crucial decisions to the political processes. The assumption that if respondents have no standing to sue, no one would have standing, is not a reason to find standing.

While a person never has standing as a citizen, there is currently a small exception for taxpayer challenges to spending programs. So far, the exception has been applied only to programs that are alleged to violate the Establishment Clause. The judicial philosophy of the Burger and Rehnquist Courts might seem to preclude expansion of taxpayer standing. So far, stare decisis continues to allow one narrow category.

The first taxpayer challenge arose in *Frothingham v. Mellon* (1923). *Frothingham* involved a challenge to the Maternity Act of 1921, a program providing grants to the states in an effort to reduce maternal and infant mortality. The plaintiff alleged that the federal program was "an attempted exercise of the power of local self-government reserved to the states by the 10th Amendment." Justice Sutherland dismissed the claim:

> [R]esident taxpayers may sue to enjoin an illegal use of the moneys of a municipal corporation.... The interest of a taxpayer of a municipality in the application of its moneys is direct and immediate and the remedy by injunction to prevent their misuse is not inappropriate. It is upheld by a large number of state cases and is the rule of this court.... The reasons which support the extension of the equitable remedy to a single taxpayer in such cases are based upon the peculiar relation of the corporate taxpayer to the corporation, which is not without some resemblance to that subsisting between stockholder and private corporation.... But the relation of a taxpayer of the United States to the federal government is very different. His interest in the moneys of the treasury—partly realized from taxation and partly from other sources—is shared with millions of others, is comparatively minute and indeterminable, and the effect upon future taxation, of any payment out of the funds, so remote, fluctuating and un-

certain, that no basis is afforded for an appeal to the preventive powers of a court of equity.

The administration of any statute, likely to produce additional taxation to be imposed upon a vast number of taxpayers, the extent of whose several liability is indefinite and constantly changing, is essentially a matter of public and not of individual concern. If one taxpayer may champion and litigate such a cause, then every other taxpayer may do the same, not only in respect of the statute here under review, but also in respect of every other appropriation act and statute whose administration requires the outlay of public money, and whose validity may be questioned. The bare suggestion of such a result, with its attendant inconveniences, goes far to sustain the conclusion which we have reached, that a suit of this character cannot be maintained....

The functions of government under our system are apportioned. To the legislative department has been committed the duty of making laws, to the executive the duty of executing them, and to the judiciary the duty of interpreting and applying them in cases properly brought before the courts. The general rule is that neither department may invade the province of the other and neither may control, direct, or restrain the action of the other.... We have no power per se to review and annul acts of Congress on the ground that they are unconstitutional. That question may be considered only when the justification for some direct injury suffered or threatened, presenting a justiciable issue, is made to rest upon such an act. Then the power exercised is that of ascertaining and declaring the law applicable to the controversy. It amounts to little more than the negative power to disregard an unconstitutional enactment, which otherwise would stand in the way of the enforcement of a legal right. The party who invokes the power must be able to show, not only that the statute is invalid, but that he has sustained or is immediately in danger of sustaining some direct injury as the result of its enforcement, and not merely that he suffers in some indefinite way in common with people generally. If a case for preventive relief be presented, the court enjoins, in effect, not the execution of the statute, but the acts of the official, the statute notwithstanding. Here the parties plaintiff have no such case. Looking through forms of words to the substance of their complaint, it is merely that officials of the executive department of the government are executing and will execute an act of Congress asserted to be unconstitutional; and this we are asked to prevent. To do so would be, not to decide a judicial controversy, but to assume a position of authority over the governmental acts of another and coequal department, an authority which plainly we do not possess.

* * *

In 1968, the Warren Court took a markedly different approach to the issue of taxpayer standing in *Flast v. Cohen*. What is the *Flast* test? Do you find the distinction of *Frothingham* convincing?

Flast v. Cohen

392 U.S. 83 (1968)

[Majority: Warren (C.J.), Black, Fortas, Brennan, Douglas, Marshall, White, and Stewart. Concurring: Douglas, Stewart, and Fortas. Dissenting: Harlan.]

[Federal taxpayers filed suit to enjoin the expenditure of federal funds for the purchase of textbooks and other instructional materials for use in parochial schools pursuant to the

Elementary and Secondary Education Act of 1965. A three-judge panel of the United States District Court for the Southern District of New York dismissed the complaint on the ground that plaintiffs lacked standing to maintain the action.]

Mr. Chief Justice Warren delivered the opinion of the Court.

In *Frothingham v. Mellon* (1923), this Court ruled that a federal taxpayer is without standing to challenge the constitutionality of a federal statute. That ruling has stood for 45 years as an impenetrable barrier to suits against Acts of Congress brought by individuals who can assert only the interest of federal taxpayers. In this case, we must decide whether the *Frothingham* barrier should be lowered when a taxpayer attacks a federal statute on the ground that it violates the Establishment and Free Exercise Clauses of the 1st Amendment....

For reasons explained at length below, we hold that appellants do have standing as federal taxpayers to maintain this action, and the judgment below must be reversed....

II. This Court first faced squarely the question whether a litigant asserting only his status as a taxpayer has standing to maintain a suit in a federal court in *Frothingham v. Mellon* and that decision must be the starting point for analysis in this case....

Although the barrier *Frothingham* erected against federal taxpayer suits has never been breached, the decision has been the source of some confusion and the object of considerable criticism. The confusion has developed as commentators have tried to determine whether *Frothingham* establishes a constitutional bar to taxpayer suits or whether the Court was simply imposing a rule of self-restraint which was not constitutionally compelled.[1] The conflicting viewpoints are reflected in the arguments made to this Court by the parties in this case. The Government has pressed upon us the view that *Frothingham* announced a constitutional rule, compelled by the Article III limitations on federal court jurisdiction and grounded in considerations of the doctrine of separation of powers. Appellants, however, insist that *Frothingham* expressed no more than a policy of judicial self-restraint which can be disregarded when compelling reasons for assuming jurisdiction over a taxpayer's suit exist. The opinion delivered in *Frothingham* can be read to support either position. The concluding sentence of the opinion states that, to take jurisdiction of the taxpayer's suit, "would be not to decide a judicial controversy, but to assume a position of authority over the governmental acts of another and co-equal department, an authority which plainly we do not possess." Yet the concrete reasons given for denying standing to a federal taxpayer suggest that the Court's holding rests on something less than a constitutional foundation. For example, the Court conceded that standing had previously been conferred on municipal taxpayers to sue in that capacity. However, the Court viewed the interest of a federal taxpayer in total federal tax revenues as "comparatively minute and indeterminable" when measured against a municipal taxpayer's interest in a smaller city treasury. This suggests that the petitioner in *Frothingham* was denied standing not because she was a taxpayer but because her tax bill was not large enough. In addition, the Court spoke of the "attendant inconveniences" of entertaining that taxpayer's suit because it might open the door of federal courts to countless such suits "in respect of every other appropriation act and statute whose administration requires the outlay of public money, and whose validity may be questioned." Such a statement suggests pure policy considerations.

To the extent that *Frothingham* has been viewed as resting on policy considerations, it has been criticized as depending on assumptions not consistent with modern con-

---

1. The prevailing view of the commentators is that *Frothingham* announced only a nonconstitutional rule of self-restraint....

ditions. For example, some commentators have pointed out that a number of corporate taxpayers today have a federal tax liability running into hundreds of millions of dollars, and such taxpayers have a far greater monetary stake in the Federal Treasury than they do in any municipal treasury. To some degree, the fear expressed in *Frothingham* that allowing one taxpayer to sue would inundate the federal courts with countless similar suits has been mitigated by the ready availability of the devices of class actions and joinder under the Federal Rules of Civil Procedure, adopted subsequent to the decision in *Frothingham*. Whatever the merits of the current debate over *Frothingham*, its very existence suggests that we should undertake a fresh examination of the limitations upon standing to sue in a federal court and the application of those limitations to taxpayer suits.

III. The jurisdiction of federal courts is defined and limited by Article III of the Constitution. In terms relevant to the question for decision in this case, the judicial power of federal courts is constitutionally restricted to "cases" and "controversies." ... Embodied in the words "cases" and "controversies" are two complementary but somewhat different limitations. In part those words limit the business of federal courts to questions presented in an adversary context and in a form historically viewed as capable of resolution through the judicial process. And in part those words define the role assigned to the judiciary in a tripartite allocation of power to assure that the federal courts will not intrude into areas committed to the other branches of government. Justiciability is the term of art employed to give expression to this dual limitation placed upon federal courts by the case-and-controversy doctrine....

[T]he Government's position is that the constitutional scheme of separation of powers, and the deference owed by the federal judiciary to the other two branches of government within that scheme, present an absolute bar to taxpayer suits challenging the validity of federal spending programs. The Government views such suits as involving no more than the mere disagreement by the taxpayer "with the uses to which tax money is put." ... Consequently, the Government contends that, under no circumstances, should standing be conferred on federal taxpayers to challenge a federal taxing or spending program. An analysis of the function served by standing limitations compels a rejection of the Government's position.

Standing is an aspect of justiciability and, as such, the problem of standing is surrounded by the same complexities and vagaries that inhere in justiciability. Standing has been called one of "the most amorphous (concepts) in the entire domain of public law." Some of the complexities peculiar to standing problems result because standing "serves, on occasion, as a shorthand expression for all the various elements of justiciability." In addition, there are at work in the standing doctrine the many subtle pressures which tend to cause policy considerations to blend into constitutional limitations.

Despite the complexities and uncertainties, some meaningful form can be given to the jurisdictional limitations placed on federal court power by the concept of standing. The fundamental aspect of standing is that it focuses on the party seeking to get his complaint before a federal court and not on the issues he wishes to have adjudicated. The "gist of the question of standing" is whether the party seeking relief has "alleged such a personal stake in the outcome of the controversy as to assure that concrete adverseness which sharpens the presentation of issues upon which the court so largely depends for illumination of difficult constitutional questions." *Baker v. Carr* (1962). In other words, when standing is placed in issue in a case, the question is whether the person whose standing is challenged is a proper party to request an adjudication of a particular issue and not whether the issue itself is justiciable....

When the emphasis in the standing problem is placed on whether the person invoking a federal court's jurisdiction is a proper party to maintain the action, the weakness of the Government's argument in this case becomes apparent. The question whether a particular person is a proper party to maintain the action does not, by its own force, raise separation of powers problems related to improper judicial interference in areas committed to other branches of the Federal Government. Such problems arise, if at all, only from the substantive issues the individual seeks to have adjudicated. Thus, in terms of Article III limitations on federal court jurisdiction, the question of standing is related only to whether the dispute sought to be adjudicated will be presented in an adversary context and in a form historically viewed as capable of judicial resolution. It is for that reason that the emphasis in standing problems is on whether the party invoking federal court jurisdiction has "a personal stake in the outcome of the controversy," *Baker v. Carr*, and whether the dispute touches upon "the legal relations of parties having adverse legal interests." A taxpayer may or may not have the requisite personal stake in the outcome, depending upon the circumstances of the particular case. Therefore, we find no absolute bar in Article III to suits by federal taxpayers challenging allegedly unconstitutional federal taxing and spending programs. There remains, however, the problem of determining the circumstances under which a federal taxpayer will be deemed to have the personal stake and interest that impart the necessary concrete adverseness to such litigation so that standing can be conferred on the taxpayer qua taxpayer consistent with the constitutional limitations of Article III....

IV. [O]ur decisions establish that, in ruling on standing, it is both appropriate and necessary to look to the substantive issues ... to determine whether there is a logical nexus between the status asserted and the claim sought to be adjudicated....

The nexus demanded of federal taxpayers has two aspects to it. First, the taxpayer must establish a logical link between that status and the type of legislative enactment attacked. Thus, a taxpayer will be a proper party to allege the unconstitutionality only of exercises of congressional power under the Taxing and Spending Clause of Art. I, § 8, of the Constitution. It will not be sufficient to allege an incidental expenditure of tax funds in the administration of an essentially regulatory statute. This requirement is consistent with the limitation imposed upon state-taxpayer standing in federal courts in *Doremus v. Board of Education* (1952). Secondly, the taxpayer must establish a nexus between that status and the precise nature of the constitutional infringement alleged. Under this requirement, the taxpayer must show that the challenged enactment exceeds specific constitutional limitations imposed upon the exercise of the congressional taxing and spending power and not simply that the enactment is generally beyond the powers delegated to Congress by Art. I, § 8. When both nexuses are established, the litigant will have shown a taxpayer's stake in the outcome of the controversy and will be a proper and appropriate party to invoke a federal court's jurisdiction.

The taxpayer-appellants in this case have satisfied both nexuses to support their claim of standing under the test we announce today. Their constitutional challenge is made to an exercise by Congress of its power under Art. I, § 8, to spend for the general welfare, and the challenged program involves a substantial expenditure of federal tax funds. In addition, appellants have alleged that the challenged expenditures violate the Establishment and Free Exercise Clauses of the 1st Amendment. Our history vividly illustrates that one of the specific evils feared by those who drafted the Establishment Clause and fought for its adoption was that the taxing and spending power would be used to favor one religion over another or to support religion in general....

The allegations of the taxpayer in *Frothingham v. Mellon* were quite different from those made in this case, and the result in *Frothingham* is consistent with the test of taxpayer standing announced today. The taxpayer in *Frothingham* attacked a federal spending program and she, therefore, established the first nexus required. However, she lacked standing because her constitutional attack was not based on an allegation that Congress, in enacting the Maternity Act of 1921, had breached a specific limitation upon its taxing and spending power. The taxpayer in *Frothingham* alleged essentially that Congress, by enacting the challenged statute, had exceeded the general powers delegated to it by Art. I, § 8, and that Congress had thereby invaded the legislative province reserved to the States by the 10th Amendment. To be sure, Mrs. Frothingham made the additional allegation that her tax liability would be increased as a result of the allegedly unconstitutional enactment, and she framed that allegation in terms of a deprivation of property without due process of law. However, the Due Process Clause of the 5th Amendment does not protect taxpayers against increases in tax liability, and the taxpayer in *Frothingham* failed to make any additional claim that the harm she alleged resulted from a breach by Congress of the specific constitutional limitations imposed upon an exercise of the taxing and spending power. In essence, Mrs. Frothingham was attempting to assert the States' interest in their legislative prerogatives and not a federal taxpayer's interest in being free of taxing and spending in contravention of specific constitutional limitations imposed upon Congress' taxing and spending power.

We have noted that the Establishment Clause of the 1st Amendment does specifically limit the taxing and spending power conferred by Art. I, § 8. Whether the Constitution contains other specific limitations can be determined only in the context of future cases. However, whenever such specific limitations are found, we believe a taxpayer will have a clear stake as a taxpayer in assuring that they are not breached by Congress. Consequently, we hold that a taxpayer will have standing consistent with Article III to invoke federal judicial power when he alleges that congressional action under the taxing and spending clause is in derogation of those constitutional provisions which operate to restrict the exercise of the taxing and spending power. The taxpayer's allegation in such cases would be that his tax money is being extracted and spent in violation of specific constitutional protections against such abuses of legislative power. Such an injury is appropriate for judicial redress, and the taxpayer has established the necessary nexus between his status and the nature of the allegedly unconstitutional action to support his claim of standing to secure judicial review. Under such circumstances, we feel confident that the questions will be framed with the necessary specificity, that the issues will be contested with the necessary adverseness and that the litigation will be pursued with the necessary vigor to assure that the constitutional challenge will be made in a form traditionally thought to be capable of judicial resolution. We lack that confidence in cases such as *Frothingham* where a taxpayer seeks to employ a federal court as a forum in which to air his generalized grievances about the conduct of government or the allocation of power in the Federal System....

Reversed.

Concurring opinions of Mr. Justice Douglas, Stewart, and Fortas omitted.

Mr. Justice Harlan, dissenting.

The problems presented by this case are narrow and relatively abstract, but the principles by which they must be resolved involve nothing less than the proper functioning of the federal courts, and so run to the roots of our constitutional system. The nub of my view is that the end result of *Frothingham v. Mellon* (1923) was correct, even though, like others, I do not subscribe to all of its reasoning and premises....

III. It seems to me clear that public actions [brought by individuals], whatever the constitutional provisions on which they are premised, may involve important hazards for the continued effectiveness of the federal judiciary. Although I believe such actions to be within the jurisdiction conferred upon the federal courts by Article III of the Constitution, there surely can be little doubt that they strain the judicial function and press to the limit judicial authority. There is every reason to fear that unrestricted public actions might well alter the allocation of authority among the three branches of the Federal Government. It is not, I submit, enough to say that the present members of the Court would not seize these opportunities for abuse, for such actions would, even without conscious abuse, go far toward the final transformation of this Court into the Council of Revision which, despite Madison's support, was rejected by the Constitutional Convention. I do not doubt that there must be "some effectual power in the government to restrain or correct the infractions" of the Constitution's several commands, but neither can I suppose that such power resides only in the federal courts. We must as judges recall that, as Mr. Justice Holmes wisely observed, the other branches of the Government "are ultimate guardians of the liberties and welfare of the people in quite as great a degree as the courts." The powers of the federal judiciary will be adequate for the great burdens placed upon them only if they are employed prudently, with recognition of the strengths as well as the hazards that go with our kind of representative government....

Accordingly, for the reasons contained in this opinion, I would affirm the judgment of the District Court.

The Burger Court revisited the issue of taxpayer standing in 1982. Do you find the Court's distinction of *Flast* to be convincing? Why do you think that the Court did not overrule *Flast*?

Hein v. Freedom from Religion Foundation, Inc.: Background

Schlesinger v. Reservists Committee to Stop the War (1974) held that taxpayers did not have standing to challenge the practice of allowing members of Congress also to be members of (and typically officers in) the reserve. This was alleged to violate Article I, §6 [2]: "No person holding any Office under the United States, shall be a Member of either House during his Continuance in Office." *United States v.* Richardson (1974) held taxpayers did not have standing to challenge appropriations for the Central Intelligence Agency. The appropriations were alleged to violate Article I, §9 [7] which provides that "a regular statement and Account of the Receipts and Expenditures of all public Money shall be published from time to time." These cases, which are referred to in *Hein*, did not involve the Establishment Clause.

In *Valley Forge Christian College v. Americans United for Separation of Church and State, Inc.* (1982), the Burger Court revisited *Flast* and *taxpayer* standing to make an Establishment Clause challenge. The Court distinguished *Flast* and denied the plaintiff taxpayer standing.

Article IV, §3, cl. 2, of the Constitution vests Congress with the "Power to dispose of and make all needful Rules and Regulations respecting the ... Property belonging to the United States." Following the Second World War, Congress enacted the Federal Property and Administrative Services Act of 1949, 40 U.S.C. §471 et seq. The Act was designed, in part, to provide "an economical and efficient system for ... the disposal of surplus property." 40 U.S.C. §471. Property that has outlived its usefulness to the Federal Government may be declared "surplus" and be transferred to private or other public entities.

Pursuant to the Act, the Secretary of Health, Education, and Welfare conveyed a 77-acre tract to the Valley Forge Christian College, a nonprofit educational institution operating under the supervision of a religious order known as the Assemblies of God. By its own description, petitioner's purpose was "to offer systematic training on the collegiate level to men and women for Christian service as either ministers or laymen." Americans United for Separation of Church and State, Inc. (Americans United) learned of the conveyance through a news release and brought suit. It claimed that the conveyance violated the Establishment Clause of the 1st Amendment.

Justice Rehnquist, writing for a 5–4 majority, limited *Flast* to direct exercises of the Article IV, §3, spending power. He found *Flast* inapplicable because 1) the actual decision to dispose of the property to the college had originated in the executive branch, even though it was pursuant to a general congressional authorization act, and 2) the disposal was not *spending*:

> Unlike the plaintiffs in *Flast*, respondents fail the first prong of the test for taxpayer standing. Their claim is deficient in two respects. First, the source of their complaint is not a congressional action, but a decision by HEW to transfer a parcel of federal property. *Flast* limited taxpayer standing to challenges directed "only [at] exercises of congressional power." ... See *Schlesinger v. Reservists Committee to Stop the War* (denying standing because the taxpayer plaintiffs "did not challenge an enactment under Art. I, §8, but rather the action of the Executive Branch").
>
> Second, and perhaps redundantly, the property transfer about which respondents complain was not an exercise of authority conferred by the Taxing and Spending Clause of Art. I, §8. The authorizing legislation, the Federal Property and Administrative Services Act of 1949, was an evident exercise of Congress' power under the Property Clause, Art. IV, §3, cl. 2. Respondents do not dispute this conclusion, and it is decisive of any claim of taxpayer standing under the *Flast* precedent.
>
> Any doubt that once might have existed concerning the rigor with which the *Flast* exception to the *Frothingham* principle ought to be applied should have been erased by this Court's recent decisions in *United States v. Richardson* (1974), and *Schlesinger v. Reservists Committee to Stop the War*....
>
> Implicit in the [Respondents' claim] foregoing is the philosophy that the business of the federal courts is correcting constitutional errors, and that "cases and controversies" are at best merely convenient vehicles for doing so and at worst nuisances that may be dispensed with when they become obstacles to that transcendent endeavor. This philosophy has no place in our constitutional scheme. It does not become more palatable when the underlying merits concern the Establishment Clause. Respondents' claim of standing implicitly rests on the presumption that violations of the Establishment Clause typically will not cause injury sufficient to confer standing under the "traditional" view of Art. III. But "[t]he assumption that if respondents have no standing to sue, no one would have standing, is not a reason to find standing." *Schlesinger v. Reservists Committee to Stop the War*.

Justice Brennan, joined by Justices Marshall and Blackmun dissented:

> The "case and controversy" limitation of Art. III overrides no other provision of the Constitution. To construe that Article to deny standing "'to the class for whose sake [a] constitutional protection is given,'" simply turns the Constitution on its head. Article III was designed to provide a hospitable forum in which persons en-

joying rights under the Constitution could assert those rights. How are we to discern whether a particular person is to be afforded a right of action in the courts? The Framers did not, of course, employ the modern vocabulary of standing. But this much is clear: The drafters of the Bill of Rights surely intended that the particular beneficiaries of their legacy should enjoy rights legally enforceable in courts of law....

In *Flast v. Cohen* (1968), federal taxpayers sought to challenge the Department of Health, Education, and Welfare's administration of the Elementary and Secondary Education Act of 1965.... The *Frothingham* [*v. Mellon*] rule stood as a seemingly absolute barrier to the maintenance of the claim. The Court held, however, that the *Frothingham* barrier could be overcome by any claim that met both requirements of a two-part "nexus" test....

It is at once apparent that the test of standing formulated by the Court in *Flast* sought to reconcile the developing doctrine of taxpayer "standing" with the Court's historical understanding that the Establishment Clause was intended to prohibit the Federal Government from using tax funds for the advancement of religion, and thus the constitutional imperative of taxpayer standing in certain cases brought pursuant to the Establishment Clause. The two-pronged "nexus" test offered by the Court, despite its general language, is best understood as "a determinant of standing of plaintiffs alleging only injury as taxpayers who challenge alleged violations of the Establishment and Free Exercise Clauses of the 1st Amendment," and not as a general statement of standing principles.... The test explains what forms of governmental action may be attacked by someone alleging only taxpayer status, and, without ruling out the possibility that history might reveal another similarly founded provision, explains why an Establishment Clause claim is treated differently from any other assertion that the Federal Government has exceeded the bounds of the law in allocating its largesse....

Blind to history, the Court attempts to distinguish this case from *Flast* by wrenching snippets of language from our opinions, and by perfunctorily applying that language under color of the first prong of *Flast*'s two-part nexus test. The tortuous distinctions thus produced are specious, at best: at worst, they are pernicious to our constitutional heritage.

First, the Court finds this case different from *Flast* because here the "source of [plaintiffs'] complaint is not a congressional action, but a decision by HEW to transfer a parcel of federal property." This attempt at distinction cannot withstand scrutiny....

More fundamentally, no clear division can be drawn in this context between actions of the Legislative Branch and those of the Executive Branch. The 1st Amendment binds the Government as a whole, regardless of which branch is at work in a particular instance.

Justice Stevens dissented separately.

In *Bowen v. Kendrick* (1988), the Court allowed taxpayer standing in a challenge to the Adolescent Family Life Act, 42 U.S.C. §300z et seq. The Secretary of the Department of Health and Human Services had funded many "pervasively" sectarian organizations to provide sexuality counseling pursuant to the Act. The Court found *Valley Forge* distinguishable. First, the challenge involved spending, not disposal of property. Second, while the selection of the grant recipients had been made within the executive branch, the statue had mentioned religious organizations as being within the purview of the statute ("such problems are best approached through a variety of integrated and essential services provided to adolescents and their families by other family members, *religious* and charitable organizations, voluntary associations, and other groups in the private sector as well as services provided by publicly sponsored initiatives). The Court noted:

> [In *Valley Forge* we] rejected the taxpayers' claim of standing for two reasons: first, because "the source of their complaint is not a congressional action, but a decision by HEW to transfer a parcel of federal property," and second, because "the property transfer about which [the taxpayers] complain was not an exercise of authority conferred by the Taxing and Spending Clause of Art. I, § 8." Appellants now contend that appellees' standing in this case is deficient for the former reason; they argue that a challenge to the AFLA "as applied" is really a challenge to executive action, not to an exercise of congressional authority under the Taxing and Spending Clause. We do not think, however, that appellees' claim that AFLA funds are being used improperly by individual grantees is any less a challenge to congressional taxing and spending power simply because the funding authorized by Congress has flowed through and been administered by the Secretary. Indeed, *Flast* itself was a suit against the Secretary of HEW, who had been given the authority under the challenged statute to administer the spending program that Congress had created.... The AFLA is at heart a program of disbursement of funds pursuant to Congress' taxing and spending powers, and appellees' claims call into question how the funds authorized by Congress are being disbursed pursuant to the AFLA's statutory mandate. In this litigation there is thus a sufficient nexus between the taxpayer's standing as a taxpayer and the congressional exercise of taxing and spending power, notwithstanding the role the Secretary plays in administering the statute.

In *Daimler Chrysler Corporation v. Cuno* (2006), the Court returned to the issue of taxpayer standing. The Court denied standing to taxpayers who complained that the use of tax revenues for industrial recruitment violated the constitutional limitations imposed by the operation of the Dormant Commerce Clause. The Court limited the scope of *Flast* to the Establishment Clause:

> Plaintiffs argue that an exception to the general prohibition on taxpayer standing should exist for *Commerce Clause* challenges to state tax or spending decisions, analogizing their *Commerce Clause* claim to the *Establishment Clause* challenge we permitted in *Flast v. Cohen* ... But as plaintiffs candidly concede, "only the *Establishment Clause*" has supported federal taxpayer suits since *Flast*....
>
> Whatever rights plaintiffs have under the *Commerce Clause*, they are fundamentally unlike the right not to "'contribute three pence ... for the support of any one [religious] establishment.'" *Flast* (quoting 2 *Writings of James Madison* 186 (G. Hunt ed. 1901)). Indeed, plaintiffs compare the *Establishment Clause* to the *Commerce Clause* at such a high level of generality that almost any constitutional constraint on government power would "specifically limit" a State's taxing and spending power for *Flast* purposes. [S]uch a broad application of *Flast*'s exception to the general prohibition on taxpayer standing would be quite at odds with its narrow application in our precedent and *Flast*'s own promise that it would not transform federal courts into forums for taxpayers'"generalized grievances."

In *Hein v. Freedom from Religion Foundation, Inc.* (2007), the Court denied taxpayer standing to make an Establishment Clause challenge to the operation of President Bush's White House Office of Faith-Based and Community Initiatives and the Executive Department Centers for Faith-Based and Community Initiatives. The programs were established within several federal agencies and departments. A plurality opinion by Justice Alito, joined by Chief Justice Roberts and Justice Kennedy, distinguished the program from the one upheld in *Bowen v. Kendrick* and continued the Court's approach of limiting *Flast* to its facts. Justice Scalia, joined by Justice Thomas, denied standing. However, he criticized the plurality's attempted distinction from *Flast* and called for it to be directly overruled. Justice Souter, joined by Justices Breyer, Ginsburg, and Stevens, dissented.

Hein v. Freedom from Religion Foundation, Inc.
551 U.S. 587 (2007)

Justice Alito announced the judgment of the Court and delivered an opinion in which the Chief Justice and Justice Kennedy join. Concurring, Kennedy and Scalia. Dissenting, Souter, Stevens, Ginsburg, and Breyer.

This is a lawsuit in which it was claimed that conferences held as part of the President's Faith-Based and Community Initiatives program violated the Establishment Clause of the 1st Amendment.... The plaintiffs contend that they meet the standing requirements of Article III of the Constitution because they pay federal taxes. It has long been established, however, that the payment of taxes is generally not enough to establish standing to challenge an action taken by the Federal Government. In light of the size of the federal budget, it is a complete fiction to argue that an unconstitutional federal expenditure causes an individual federal taxpayer any measurable economic harm....

In *Flast v. Cohen* (1968), we recognized a narrow exception to the general rule against federal tax-payer standing. Under *Flast*, a plaintiff asserting an Establishment Clause claim has standing to challenge a law authorizing the use of federal funds in a way that allegedly violates the Establishment Clause. In the present case, Congress did not specifically authorize the use of federal funds to pay for the conferences or speeches that the plaintiffs challenged. Instead, the conferences and speeches were paid for out of general Executive Branch appropriations.... The Court of Appeals, however, held that the plaintiffs have standing as taxpayers because the conferences were paid for with money appropriated by Congress. The question that is presented here is whether this broad reading of *Flast* is correct. We hold that it is not.... or citizens

I-A. In 2001, the President issued an executive order creating the White House Office of Faith-Based and Community Initiatives within the Executive Office of the President. Exec. Order No. 13199, 3 CFR 752 (2001 Comp.). The purpose of this new office was to ensure that "private and charitable community groups, including religious ones ... have the fullest opportunity permitted by law to compete on a level playing field, so long as they achieve valid public purposes" and adhere to "the bedrock principles of pluralism, nondiscrimination, evenhandedness, and neutrality." The office was specifically charged with the task of eliminating unnecessary bureaucratic, legislative, and regulatory barriers that could impede such organizations' effectiveness and ability to compete equally for federal assistance. By separate executive orders, the President also created Executive Department Centers for Faith-Based and Community Initiatives within several federal agencies and departments.... No congressional legislation specifically authorized the creation of the White House Office or the Executive Department Centers. Rather, they were "created entirely within the executive branch ... by Presidential executive order." Nor has Congress enacted any law specifically appropriating money for these entities' activities. Instead, their activities are funded through general Executive Branch appropriations. For example, the Department of Education's Center is funded from money appropriated for the Office of the Secretary of Education, while the Department of Housing and Urban Development's Center is funded through that Department's salaries and expenses account....

I. B. The respondents are Freedom From Religion Foundation, Inc., a nonstock corporation "opposed to government endorsement of religion".... The only asserted basis for standing was that the individual respondents are federal taxpayers who are "opposed to the use of Congressional taxpayer appropriations to advance and promote religion." In their capacity as federal taxpayers, respondents sought to challenge Executive Branch expenditures for these conferences, which, they contended, violated the Establishment Clause....

II-A. Article III of the Constitution limits the judicial power of the United States to the resolution of "Cases" and "Controversies," and "'Article III standing ... enforces the Constitution's case-or-controversy requirement.'" ... The constitutionally mandated standing inquiry is especially important in a case like this one, in which taxpayers seek "to challenge laws of general application where their own injury is not distinct from that suffered in general by other taxpayers or citizens." ... This is because "[t]he judicial power of the United States defined by Art. III is not an unconditioned authority to determine the constitutionality of legislative or executive acts." *Valley Forge Christian College v. Americans United for Separation of Church and State, Inc.* (1982)....

"We have no power *per se* to review and annul acts of Congress on the ground that they are unconstitutional. The question may be considered only when the justification for some direct injury suffered or threatened, presenting a justiciable issue, is made to rest upon such an act.... The party who invokes the power must be able to show not only that the statute is invalid but that he has sustained or is immediately in danger of sustaining some direct injury as the result of its enforcement, and not merely that he suffers in some indefinite way in common with people generally." *Frothingham v. Mellon*, decided with *Massachusetts v. Mellon* (1923)....

II-B. [The Freedom from Religion Plaintiff's] claim is that, having paid lawfully collected taxes into the Federal Treasury at some point, they have a continuing, legally cognizable interest in ensuring that those funds are not *used* by the Government in a way that violates the Constitution. We have consistently held that this type of interest is too generalized and attenuated to support Article III standing....

II-C. In *Flast*, the Court carved out a narrow exception to the general constitutional prohibition against taxpayer standing. The taxpayer-plaintiff in that case challenged the distribution of federal funds to religious schools under the Elementary and Secondary Education Act of 1965, alleging that such aid violated the Establishment Clause. The Court set out a two-part test for determining whether a federal taxpayer has standing to challenge an allegedly unconstitutional expenditure ... "by Congress of the taxing and spending power conferred by Art. I, § 8."

III-A. Respondents argue that this case falls within the *Flast* exception, which they read to cover any "expenditure of government funds in violation of the Establishment Clause." But this broad reading fails to observe "the rigor with which the *Flast* exception to the *Frothingham* principle ought to be applied." *Valley Forge.* The expenditures at issue in *Flast* were made pursuant to an express congressional mandate and a specific congressional appropriation....

The expenditures challenged in *Flast*, then, were funded by a specific congressional appropriation and were disbursed to private schools (including religiously affiliated schools) pursuant to a direct and unambiguous congressional mandate. Indeed, the *Flast* taxpayer-plaintiff's constitutional claim was premised on the contention that if the Government's actions were "'within the authority and intent of the Act, the Act is to that extent unconstitutional and void.'"... But as this Court later noted, *Flast* "limited taxpayer standing to challenges directed 'only [at] exercises of congressional power'" under the Taxing and Spending Clause. *Valley Forge*.

III-B. The link between congressional action and constitutional violation that supported taxpayer standing in *Flast* is missing here. [The Freedom from Religion Foundation] do[es] not challenge any specific congressional action or appropriation; nor do they ask the Court to invalidate any congressional enactment or legislatively created program as unconstitutional. That is because the expenditures at issue here were not made pursuant to any Act of Congress. Rather, Congress provided general appropriations to the Executive Branch to fund its day-to-day activities. These appropriations did not expressly authorize, direct, or even mention the expenditures of which respondents complain. Those expenditures resulted from executive discretion, not congressional action.

We have never found taxpayer standing under such circumstances.... In short, this case falls outside the "the narrow exception" that *Flast* "created to the general rule against tax-payer standing established in *Frothingham*." *Kendrick*. Because the expenditures that respondents challenge were not expressly authorized or mandated by any specific congressional enactment, respondents' lawsuit is not directed at an exercise of congressional power, see *Valley Forge*, and thus lacks the requisite "logical nexus" between taxpayer status "and the type of legislative enactment attacked." *Flast*.

IV-A. Respondents argue that it is "arbitrary" to distinguish between money spent pursuant to congressional mandate and expenditures made in the course of executive discretion, because "the injury to taxpayers in both situations is the very injury targeted by the Establishment Clause and *Flast*—the expenditure for the support of religion of funds exacted from taxpayers."... While respondents argue that Executive Branch expenditures in support of religion are no different from legislative extractions, *Flast* itself rejected this equivalence: "It will not be sufficient to allege an incidental expenditure of tax funds in the administration of an essentially regulatory statute."

Because almost all Executive Branch activity is ultimately funded by some congressional appropriation, extending the *Flast* exception to purely executive expenditures would effectively subject every federal action—be it a conference, proclamation or speech—to Establishment Clause challenge by any taxpayer in federal court....

IV-C. Over the years, *Flast* has been defended by some and criticized by others. But the present case does not require us to reconsider that precedent. [A] precedent is not always expanded to the limit of its logic. That was the approach that then-Justice Rehnquist took in his opinion for the Court in *Valley Forge*, and it is the approach we take here. We do not extend *Flast*, but we also do not overrule it. We leave *Flast* as we found it.... Relying on the provision of the Constitution that limits our role to resolving the "Cases" and "Controversies" before us, we decide only the case at hand.

The judgment of the Court of Appeals for the Seventh Circuit is reversed.

Justice Kennedy, concurring....

In my view the result reached in *Flast* is correct and should not be called into question. For the reasons set forth by Justice Alito, however, *Flast* should not be extended to permit taxpayer standing in the instant matter. And I join his opinion in full.... It must be remembered that, even where parties have no standing to sue, members of the Legislative and Executive Branches are not excused from making constitutional determinations in the regular course of their duties. Government officials must make a conscious decision to obey the Constitution whether or not their acts can be challenged in a court of law and then must conform their actions to these principled determinations.

Justice Scalia, with whom Justice Thomas joins, concurring in the judgment.

Today's opinion is, in one significant respect, entirely consistent with our previous cases addressing taxpayer standing to raise Establishment Clause challenges to government expenditures. Unfortunately, the consistency lies in the creation of utterly meaningless distinctions which separate the case at hand from the precedents that have come out differently, but which cannot possibly be (in any sane world) the reason it comes out differently. If this Court is to decide cases by rule of law rather than show of hands, we must surrender to logic and choose sides: Either *Flast v. Cohen* (1968), should be applied to (at a minimum) *all* challenges to the governmental expenditure of general tax revenues in a manner alleged to violate a constitutional provision specifically limiting the taxing and spending power, or *Flast* should be repudiated. For me, the choice is easy. *Flast* is wholly irreconcilable with the Article III restrictions on federal-court jurisdiction that this Court has repeatedly confirmed are embodied in the doctrine of standing.

I-A. There is a simple reason why our taxpayer-standing cases involving Establishment Clause challenges to government expenditures are notoriously inconsistent: We have inconsistently described the first element of the "irreducible constitutional minimum of standing," which minimum consists of (1) a "concrete and particularized" "'injury in fact'" that is (2) fairly traceable to the defendant's alleged unlawful conduct and (3) likely to be re-dressed by a favorable decision. See *Lujan v. Defenders of Wildlife* (1992). We have alternately relied on two entirely distinct conceptions of injury in fact, which for convenience I will call "Wallet Injury" and "Psychic Injury."

Wallet Injury is the type of concrete and particularized injury one would expect to be asserted in a *taxpayer* suit, namely, a claim that the plaintiff's tax liability is higher than it would be, but for the allegedly unlawful government action.... The stumbling block for suits challenging government expenditures based on this conventional type of injury is quite predictable. The plaintiff cannot satisfy the traceability and redressability prongs of standing. It is uncertain what the plaintiff's tax bill would have been had the allegedly forbidden expenditure not been made, and it is even more speculative whether the government will, in response to an adverse court decision, lower taxes rather than spend the funds in some other manner.

Psychic Injury, on the other hand, has nothing to do with the plaintiff's tax liability. Instead, the injury consists of the taxpayer's *mental displeasure* that money extracted from him is being spent in an unlawful manner....

I. B. We must initially decide whether Psychic Injury is consistent with Article III. If it is, we should apply *Flast* to *all* challenges to government expenditures in violation of constitutional provisions that specifically limit the taxing and spending power; if it is not, we should overturn *Flast*.

The plurality today avails itself of neither principled option....

II. A. Yet the plurality is also unwilling to acknowledge that the logic of *Flast* (its Psychic Injury rationale) is simply wrong, and *for that reason* should not be extended to other cases. Despite the lack of acknowledgment, however, that is the only plausible explanation for the plurality's indifference to whether the "distinguishing" fact is legally material, and for its determination to limit *Flast* to its "'*resul[t]*.'" Why, then, pick a distinguishing fact that may breathe life into *Flast* in future cases, preserving the disreputable disarray of our Establishment Clause standing jurisprudence? Why not hold that only taxpayers raising Establishment Clause challenges to expenditures pursuant to the Elementary and Secondary Education Act of 1965 have standing? That, I suppose, would be too obvious a repudiation of *Flast*, and thus an impediment to the plurality's pose of minimalism....

II. C. *Flast*'s adoption of Psychic Injury has to be addressed head-on. Minimalism is an admirable judicial trait, but not when it comes at the cost of meaningless and disingenuous distinctions that hold the sure promise of engendering further meaningless and disingenuous distinctions in the future. The rule of law is ill served by forcing lawyers and judges to make arguments that deaden the soul of the law, which is logic and reason. Either *Flast* was correct, and must be accorded the wide application that it logically dictates, or it was not, and must be abandoned in its entirety. I turn, finally, to that question.

III. Is a taxpayer's purely psychological displeasure that his funds are being spent in an allegedly unlawful manner ever sufficiently concrete and particularized to support Article III standing? The answer is plainly no....

Justice Souter, with whom Justice Stevens, Justice Ginsburg, and Justice Breyer join, dissenting.

Flast v. Cohen (1968), held that plaintiffs with an Establishment Clause claim could "demonstrate the necessary stake as taxpayers in the outcome of the litigation to satisfy Article III requirements." Here, the controlling, plurality opinion declares that *Flast* does not apply, but a search of that opinion for a suggestion that these taxpayers have any less stake in the outcome than the taxpayers in *Flast* will come up empty: the plurality makes no such finding, nor could it. Instead, the controlling opinion closes the door on these taxpayers because the Executive Branch, and not the Legislative Branch, caused their injury. I see no basis for this distinction in either logic or precedent, and respectfully dissent.

We held in *Flast*, and repeated just last Term, that the "'injury' alleged in Establishment Clause challenges to federal spending" is "the very 'extract[ion] and spen[ding]' of 'tax money' in aid of religion." *DaimlerChrysler Corp. v. Cuno* (2006). As the Court said in *Flast*, the importance of that type of injury has deep historical roots going back to the ideal of religious liberty in James Madison's *Memorial and Remonstrance Against Religious Assessments*, that the government in a free society may not "force a citizen to contribute three pence only of his property for the support of any one establishment" of religion. 2 *Writings of James Madison* 183, 186 (G. Hunt ed. 1901). Madison thus translated into practical terms the right of conscience described when he wrote that "[t]he Religion ... of every man must be left to the conviction and conscience of every man; and it is the right of every man to exercise it as these may dictate." Madison 184.... ("Since the founding of our country, there have been popular uprisings against procuring taxpayer funds to support church leaders, which was one of the hallmarks of an 'established' religion"); N. Feldman, *Divided By God: America's Church-State Problem—And What We Should Do About It* 48 (2005) ("The advocates of a constitutional ban on establishment were concerned about paying taxes to support religious purposes that their consciences told them not to support").

The right of conscience and the expenditure of an identifiable three pence raised by taxes for the support of a religious cause are therefore not to be split off from one another. The three pence implicates the conscience, and the injury from Government expenditures on religion is not accurately classified with the "Psychic Injury" that results whenever a congressional appropriation or executive expenditure raises hackles of disagreement with the policy supported, (Scalia, J., concurring in judgment)....

Here, there is no dispute that taxpayer money in identifiable amounts is funding conferences, and these are alleged to have the purpose of promoting religion.... When executive agencies spend identifiable sums of tax money for religious purposes, no less than when Congress authorizes the same thing, taxpayers suffer injury. And once we recognize the injury as sufficient for Article III, there can be no serious question about the other elements of the standing enquiry....

II. While *Flast* standing to assert the right of conscience is in a class by itself, it would be a mistake to think that case is unique in recognizing standing in a plaintiff without injury to flesh or purse. Cognizable harm takes account of the nature of the interest protected, which is the reason that "the constitutional component of standing doctrine incorporates concepts concededly not susceptible of precise definition," leaving it impossible "to make application of the constitutional standing requirement a mechanical exercise." *Allen v.* Wright (1984). The question, ultimately, has to be whether the injury alleged is "too abstract, or otherwise not appropriate, to be considered judicially cognizable." *Id.*

In the case of economic or physical harms, of course, the "injury in fact" question is straightforward. But once one strays from these obvious cases, the enquiry can turn subtle. Are esthetic harms sufficient for Article III standing? What about being forced to compete on an uneven playing field based on race (without showing that an economic loss resulted), or living in a racially gerrymandered electoral district? These injuries are no more concrete than seeing one's tax dollars spent on religion, but we have recognized each one as enough for standing. See *Friends of Earth, Inc. v. Laidlaw Environmental Services (TOC), Inc.* (2000) (esthetic injury); *Northeastern Fla. Chapter, Associated Gen. Contractors of America v. Jacksonville* (1993) ("The 'injury in fact' is the inability to compete on an equal footing in the bidding process, not the loss of a contract"); *United States v.* Hays (1995) (living in a racially gerrymandered electoral district). This is not to say that any sort of alleged injury will satisfy Article III, but only that intangible harms must be evaluated case by case.

Thus, *Flast* speaks for this Court's recognition (shared by a majority of the Court today) that when the Government spends money for religious purposes a taxpayer's injury is serious and concrete enough to be "judicially cognizable," *Allen*. The judgment of sufficient injury takes account of the Madisonian relationship of tax money and conscience, but it equally reflects the Founders' pragmatic "conviction that individual religious liberty could be achieved best under a government which was stripped of all power to tax, to support, or otherwise to assist any or all religions," *Everson v. Board of Ed. of Ewing* (1947), and the realization continuing to the modern day that favoritism for religion "'sends the ... message to ... nonadherents "that they are outsiders, not full members of the political community,"'" *McCreary County v. American Civil Liberties Union of Ky.* (2005).

Because the taxpayers in this case have alleged the type of injury this Court has seen as sufficient for standing, I would affirm.

Hein: Notes

1. Is the "mere" denial of constitutional right sufficient to provide standing? If not what else is needed? Compare *Richardson, Schlesinger, Flast, Valley Forge, DaimlerChrysler,* and *Hein*.
2. Assume that after a massive victory in the Presidential and Congressional elections, the victorious political party wishes to bestow Earldoms, an honorary title of nobility, on its largest contributors. Congress subsequently passes legislation authorizing the President to bestow the title upon those he deems fit. Corporations have volunteered to pay for the plaques and robes conferred on the earls, so no expense to the

taxpayers is involved. Is the act of Congress constitutional? May a taxpayer challenge it? May a citizen? Should a constitutional challenge be entertained by the Court?

3. Assume Congress passes the following Balanced Budget Amendment and it is ratified by the necessary number of states:

> "SECTION 1. Total outlays for any fiscal year shall not exceed total receipts for that fiscal year, unless three-fifths of the whole number of each House of Congress shall provide by law for a specific excess of outlays over receipts by a roll call vote.
>
> "SECTION 2. The limit on the debt of the United States held by the public shall not be increased, unless three-fifths of the whole number of each House shall provide by law for such an increase by a roll call vote.
>
> "SECTION 3. Prior to each fiscal year, the President shall transmit to the Congress a proposed budget for the United States Government for that fiscal year in which total outlays do not exceed total receipts.
>
> "SECTION 4. No bill to increase revenue shall become law unless approved by a majority of the whole number of each House by a roll call vote.
>
> "SECTION 5. The Congress may waive the provisions of this article for any fiscal year in which a declaration of war is in effect. The provisions of this article may be waived for any fiscal year in which the United States is engaged in military conflict which causes an imminent and serious military threat to national security and is so declared by a joint resolution, adopted by a majority of the whole number of each House, which becomes law.
>
> "SECTION 6. The Congress shall enforce and implement this article by appropriate legislation, which may rely on estimates of outlays and receipts.
>
> "SECTION 7. Total receipts shall include all receipts of the United States Government except those derived from borrowing. Total outlays shall include all outlays of the United States Government except for those for repayment of debt principal.
>
> "SECTION 8. This article shall take effect beginning with fiscal year 2006 or with the second fiscal year beginning after its ratification, whichever is later."

The President subsequently submits an unbalanced budget and the Congress passes an unbalanced budget by a simple majority in both houses. A citizen sues. What result? A taxpayer sues. What result?

2. What Constitutes a Cognizable Injury?

In some cases, where the Court recognizes that the plaintiff does have a more specific claim than citizens of the United States in general would have, the Court nonetheless rejects standing on the basis that the alleged harm is not sufficiently personal to constitute a cognizable injury or that the harm is too speculative.

City of Los Angeles v. Lyons
461 U.S. 95 (1983)

[Majority: White, Burger (C.J.), Powell, O'Connor, and Rehnquist. Dissenting: Marshall, Brennan, Blackmun, and Stevens.]

Justice White delivered the opinion of the Court.

The issue here is whether respondent Lyons satisfied the prerequisites for seeking injunctive relief in the federal district court.

I. This case began on February 7, 1977, when respondent, Adolph Lyons, filed a complaint for damages, injunction, and declaratory relief in the United States District Court for the Central District of California. The defendants were the City of Los Angeles and four of its police officers. The complaint alleged that on October 6, 1976, at 2 a.m., Lyons was stopped by the defendant officers for a traffic or vehicle code violation and that although Lyons offered no resistance or threat whatsoever, the officers, without provocation or justification, seized Lyons and applied a "chokehold"—either the "bar arm control" hold or the "carotid-artery control" hold or both—rendering him unconscious and causing damage to his larynx. Counts I through IV of the complaint sought damages against the officers and the City. Count V, with which we are principally concerned here, sought a preliminary and permanent injunction against the City barring the use of the control holds. That count alleged that the city's police officers, "pursuant to the authorization, instruction and encouragement of defendant City of Los Angeles, regularly and routinely apply these choke holds in innumerable situations where they are not threatened by the use of any deadly force whatsoever," that numerous persons have been injured as the result of the application of the chokeholds, that Lyons and others similarly situated are threatened with irreparable injury in the form of bodily injury and loss of life, and that Lyons "justifiably fears that any contact he has with Los Angeles police officers may result in his being choked and strangled to death without provocation, justification or other legal excuse." Lyons alleged the threatened impairment of rights protected by the 1st, 4th, 8th and 14th Amendments. Injunctive relief was sought against the use of the control holds "except in situations where the proposed victim of said control reasonably appears to be threatening the immediate use of deadly force." Count VI sought declaratory relief against the City, i.e., a judgment that use of the chokeholds absent the threat of immediate use of deadly force is a per se violation of various constitutional rights.

The District Court, by order, granted the City's motion for partial judgment on the pleadings and entered judgment for the City on Count V and VI. The Court of Appeals reversed the judgment for the City on Count V and VI, holding over the City's objection that despite our decisions in *O'Shea v. Littleton* (1974) and *Rizzo v. Goode* (1976), Lyons had standing to seek relief against the application of the chokeholds. The Court of Appeals held that there was a sufficient likelihood that Lyons would again be stopped and subjected to the unlawful use of force to constitute a case or controversy and to warrant the issuance of an injunction, if the injunction was otherwise authorized. We denied certiorari.

On remand ... [a] preliminary injunction was entered enjoining "the use of both the carotid-artery and bar arm holds under circumstances which do not threaten death or serious bodily injury." An improved training program and regular reporting and record keeping were also ordered. The Court of Appeals affirmed in a brief per curiam opinion stating that the District Court had not abused its discretion in entering a preliminary injunction. We granted certiorari ... and now reverse....

III. It goes without saying that those who seek to invoke the jurisdiction of the federal courts must satisfy the threshold requirement imposed by Article III of the Constitution by alleging an actual case or controversy.... Abstract injury is not enough. The plaintiff must show that he "has sustained or is immediately in danger of sustaining some direct injury" as the result of the challenged official conduct and the injury or threat of injury must be both "real and immediate," not "conjectural" or "hypothetical." ...

In *O'Shea v. Littleton*, we dealt with a case brought by a class of plaintiffs claiming that they had been subjected to discriminatory enforcement of the criminal law. Among other things, a county magistrate and judge were accused of discriminatory conduct in various respects, such as sentencing members of plaintiff's class more harshly than other defendants [and setting bail higher for African Americans than for whites]. The Court of Appeals reversed the dismissal of the suit by the District Court, ruling that if the allegations were proved, an appropriate injunction could be entered.

We reversed for failure of the complaint to allege a case or controversy. Although it was claimed in that case that particular members of the plaintiff class had actually suffered from the alleged unconstitutional practices, we observed that "[p]ast exposure to illegal conduct does not in itself show a present case or controversy regarding injunctive relief ... if unaccompanied by any continuing, present adverse effects." Past wrongs were evidence bearing on "whether there is a real and immediate threat of repeated injury." But the prospect of future injury rested "on the likelihood that [plaintiffs] will again be arrested for and charged with violations of the criminal law and will again be subjected to bond proceedings, trial, or sentencing before petitioners." The most that could be said for plaintiffs' standing was "that if [plaintiffs] proceed to violate an unchallenged law and if they are charged, held to answer, and tried in any proceedings before petitioners, they will be subjected to the discriminatory practices that petitioners are alleged to have followed." ... We could not find a case or controversy in those circumstances: the threat to the plaintiffs was not "sufficiently real and immediate to show an existing controversy simply because they anticipate violating lawful criminal statutes and being tried for their offenses." It was to be assumed "that [plaintiffs] will conduct their activities within the law and so avoid prosecution and conviction as well as exposure to the challenged course of conduct said to be followed by petitioners."

We ... went on to hold that even if the complaint presented an existing case or controversy, an adequate basis for equitable relief against petitioners had not been demonstrated:

> [Plaintiffs] have failed, moreover, to establish the basic requisites of the issuance of equitable relief in these circumstances—the likelihood of substantial and immediate irreparable injury, and the inadequacy of remedies at law. We have already canvassed the necessarily conjectural nature of the threatened injury to which [plaintiffs] are allegedly subjected. And if any of the [plaintiffs] are ever prosecuted and face trial, or if they are illegally sentenced, there are available state and federal procedures which could provide relief from the wrongful conduct alleged....

Another relevant decision for present purposes is *Rizzo v. Goode*, a case in which plaintiffs alleged widespread illegal and unconstitutional police conduct aimed at minority citizens and against City residents in general. The Court reiterated the holding in *O'Shea* that past wrongs do not in themselves amount to that real and immediate threat of injury necessary to make out a case or controversy. The claim of injury rested upon "what one or a small, unnamed minority of policemen might do to them in the future because of that unknown policeman's perception" of departmental procedures.... This hypothesis was "even more attenuated than those allegations of future injury found insufficient in *O'Shea* to warrant [the] invocation of federal jurisdiction." The Court also held that plaintiffs' showing at trial of a relatively few instances of violations by individual police officers, without any showing of a deliberate policy on behalf of the named defendants, did not provide a basis for equitable relief.

Golden v. Zwickler (1969), a case arising in an analogous situation, is directly apposite. Congressman Zwickler sought a declaratory judgment that a New York statute prohibiting anonymous handbills directly pertaining to election campaigns was unconstitutional. Although Zwickler had once been convicted under the statute, he was no longer a Congressman apt to run for reelection. A unanimous Court held that because it was "most unlikely" that Zwickler would again be subject to the statute, no case or controversy of "sufficient immediacy and reality" was present to allow a declaratory judgment....

IV. No extension of *O'Shea* and *Rizzo* is necessary to hold that respondent Lyons has failed to demonstrate a case or controversy with the City that would justify the equitable relief sought. Lyons' standing to seek the injunction requested depended on whether he was likely to suffer future injury from the use of the chokeholds by police officers. Count V of the complaint alleged the traffic stop and choking incident five months before. That Lyons may have been illegally choked by the police on October 6, 1976, while presumably affording Lyons standing to claim damages against the individual officers and perhaps against the City, does nothing to establish a real and immediate threat that he would again be stopped for a traffic violation, or for any other offense, by an officer or officers who would illegally choke him into unconsciousness without any provocation or resistance on his part. The additional allegation in the complaint that the police in Los Angeles routinely apply chokeholds in situations where they are not threatened by the use of deadly force falls far short of the allegations that would be necessary to establish a case or controversy between these parties.

In order to establish an actual controversy in this case, Lyons would have had not only to allege that he would have another encounter with the police but also to make the incredible assertion either, (1) that *all* police officers in Los Angeles *always* choke any citizen with whom they happen to have an encounter, whether for the purpose of arrest, issuing a citation or for questioning or, (2) that the City ordered or authorized police officers to act in such manner. Although Count V alleged that the City authorized the use of the control holds in situations where deadly force was not threatened, it did not indicate why Lyons might be realistically threatened by police officers who acted within the strictures of the City's policy. If, for example, chokeholds were authorized to be used only to counter resistance to an arrest by a suspect, or to thwart an effort to escape, any future threat to Lyons from the City's policy or from the conduct of police officers would be no more real than the possibility that he would again have an encounter with the police and that either he would illegally resist arrest or detention or the officers would disobey their instructions and again render him unconscious without any provocation.

Under *O'Shea* and *Rizzo*, these allegations were an insufficient basis to provide a federal court with jurisdiction to entertain Count V of the complaint.... For several reasons—each of them infirm, in our view—the Court of Appeals thought reliance on *O'Shea* and *Rizzo* was misplaced and reversed the District Court.

First, the Court of Appeals thought that Lyons was more immediately threatened than the plaintiffs in those cases since, according to the Court of Appeals, Lyons need only be stopped for a minor traffic violation to be subject to the strangleholds. But even assuming that Lyons would again be stopped for a traffic or other violation in the reasonably near future, it is untenable to assert, and the complaint made no such allegation, that strangleholds are applied by the Los Angeles police to every citizen who is stopped or arrested regardless of the conduct of the person stopped. We cannot agree that the "odds," that Lyons would not only again be stopped for a traffic violation but would also be subjected to a chokehold without any provocation whatsoever are sufficient to make out a federal case for equitable relief. We note that five months elapsed between October 6, 1976, and the filing of the complaint, yet there was no allegation of further unfortunate encounters between Lyons and the police.

[I]t is surely no more than speculation to assert either that Lyons himself will again be involved in one of those unfortunate instances, or that he will be arrested in the future and provoke the use of a chokehold by resisting arrest, attempting to escape, or threatening deadly force or serious bodily injury.

Second, the Court of Appeals viewed *O'Shea* and *Rizzo* as cases in which the plaintiffs sought "massive structural" relief against the local law enforcement systems and therefore that the holdings in those cases were inapposite to cases such as this where the plaintiff, according to the Court of Appeals, seeks to enjoin only an "established," "sanctioned" police practice assertedly violative of constitutional rights. *O'Shea* and *Rizzo*, however, cannot be so easily confined to their facts. If Lyons has made no showing that he is realistically threatened by a repetition of his experience of October, 1976, then he has not met the requirements for seeking an injunction in a federal court, whether the injunction contemplates intrusive structural relief or the cessation of a discrete practice.

The Court of Appeals also asserted that Lyons "had a live and active claim" against the City "if only for a period of a few seconds" while the stranglehold was being applied to him and that for two reasons the claim had not become moot so as to disentitle Lyons to injunctive relief: First, because under normal rules of equity, a case does not become moot merely because the complained of conduct has ceased; and second, because Lyons' claim is "capable of repetition but evading review" and therefore should be heard. We agree that Lyons had a live controversy with the City. Indeed, he still has a claim for damages against the City that appears to meet all Article III requirements. Nevertheless, the issue here is not whether that claim has become moot but whether Lyons meets the preconditions for asserting an injunctive claim in a federal forum. The equitable doctrine that cessation of the challenged conduct does not bar an injunction is of little help in this respect, for Lyons' lack of standing does not rest on the termination of the police practice but on the speculative nature of his claim that he will again experience injury as the result of that practice even if continued....

V. Lyons fares no better if it be assumed that his pending damages suit affords him Article III standing to seek an injunction as a remedy for the claim arising out of the October 1976 events....

Absent a sufficient likelihood that he will again be wronged in a similar way, Lyons is no more entitled to an injunction than any other citizen of Los Angeles; and a federal court may not entertain a claim by any or all citizens who no more than assert that certain practices of law enforcement officers are unconstitutional....

We decline the invitation to slight the preconditions for equitable relief; for as we have held, recognition of the need for a proper balance between state and federal authority counsels restraint in the issuance of injunctions against state officers engaged in the administration of the states' criminal laws in the absence of irreparable injury which is both great and immediate....

[S]tate courts need not impose the same standing or remedial requirements that govern federal court proceedings. The individual states may permit their courts to use injunctions to oversee the conduct of law enforcement authorities on a continuing basis. But this is not the role of a federal court absent far more justification than Lyons has proffered in this case.

The judgment of the Court of Appeals is accordingly

Reversed.

Justice Marshall, with whom Justice Brennan, Justice Blackmun and Justice Stevens join, dissenting.

The District Court found that the City of Los Angeles authorizes its police officers to apply life-threatening chokeholds to citizens who pose no threat of violence, and that respondent, Adolph Lyons, was subjected to such a chokehold. The Court today holds that a federal court is without power to enjoin the enforcement of the City's policy, no matter how flagrantly unconstitutional it may be. Since no one can show that he will be choked in the future, no one—not even a person who, like Lyons, has almost been choked to death—has standing to challenge the continuation of the policy. The City is free to continue the policy indefinitely as long as it is willing to pay damages for the injuries and deaths that result. I dissent from this unprecedented and unwarranted approach to standing....

I-B. Although the City instructs its officers that use of a chokehold does not constitute deadly force, since 1975 no less than 16 persons have died following the use of a chokehold by an LAPD police officer. Twelve have been Negro males.[1] The evidence submitted to the District Court established that for many years it has been the official policy of the City to permit police officers to employ chokeholds in a variety of situations where they face no threat of violence....

III. Since Lyons' claim for damages plainly gives him standing, and since the success of that claim depends upon a demonstration that the City's chokehold policy is unconstitutional, it is beyond dispute that Lyons has properly invoked the District Court's authority to adjudicate the constitutionality of the City's chokehold policy. The dispute concerning the constitutionality of that policy plainly presents a "case or controversy" under Article III. The Court nevertheless holds that a federal court has no power under Article III to adjudicate Lyons' request, in the same lawsuit, for injunctive relief with respect to that very policy....

III-A. It is simply disingenuous for the Court to assert that its decision requires "[n]o extension" of *O'Shea v. Littleton* (1974), and *Rizzo v. Goode* (1976). In contrast to this case *O'Shea* and *Rizzo* involved disputes focusing solely on the threat of future injury which the plaintiffs in those cases alleged they faced. In *O'Shea* the plaintiffs did not allege past injury and did not seek compensatory relief. In *Rizzo*, the plaintiffs sought only declaratory and injunctive relief and alleged past instances of police misconduct only in an attempt to establish the substantiality of the threat of future injury....

[T]he Court recognized in *O'Shea*, standing under Article III is established by an allegation of "threatened or actual injury."... Because the plaintiffs in *O'Shea* [and] *Rizzo* did not seek to redress past injury, their standing to sue depended entirely on the risk of future injury they faced. Apart from the desire to eliminate the possibility of future injury, the plaintiffs in those cases had no other personal stake in the outcome of the controversies.

By contrast, Lyons' request for prospective relief is coupled with his claim for damages based on past injury. In addition to the risk that he will be subjected to a chokehold in the future, Lyons has suffered past injury. Because he has a live claim for damages, he need not rely solely on the threat of future injury to establish his personal stake in the outcome of the controversy. In the cases relied on by the majority, the Court simply had no occasion to decide whether a plaintiff who has standing to litigate a dispute must clear a separate standing hurdle with respect to each form of relief sought....

III-C. By fragmenting the standing inquiry and imposing a separate standing hurdle with respect to each form of relief sought, the decision today departs significantly

---

1. Thus in a City where Negro males constitute 9% of the population, they have accounted for 75% of the deaths resulting from the use of chokeholds....

from this Court's traditional conception of the standing requirement and of the remedial powers of the federal courts. We have never required more than that a plaintiff have standing to litigate a claim. Whether he will be entitled to obtain particular forms of relief should he prevail has never been understood to be an issue of standing....

III-C-2. The Court's fragmentation of the standing inquiry is also inconsistent with the way the federal courts have treated remedial issues since the merger of law and equity. The federal practice has been to reserve consideration of the appropriate relief until after a determination of the merits, not to foreclose certain forms of relief by a ruling on the pleadings. The prayer for relief is no part of the plaintiff's cause of action....

IV. Apart from the question of standing, the only remaining question presented in the petition for certiorari is whether the preliminary injunction issued by the District Court must be set aside because it "constitute[s] a substantial interference in the operation of a municipal police department." *Petition for Certiorari* i. In my view it does not....

The principles of federalism simply do not preclude the limited preliminary injunction issued in this case. Unlike the permanent injunction at issue in *Rizzo*, the preliminary injunction involved here entails no federal supervision of the LAPD's activities. The preliminary injunction merely forbids the use of chokeholds absent the threat of deadly force, permitting their continued use where such a threat does exist. This limited ban takes the form of a preventive injunction, which has traditionally been regarded as the least intrusive form of equitable relief. Moreover, the City can remove the ban by obtaining approval of a training plan. Although the preliminary injunction also requires the City to provide records of the uses of chokeholds to respondent and to allow the court access to such records, this requirement is hardly onerous, since the LAPD already maintains records concerning the use of chokeholds....

V. Apparently because it is unwilling to rely solely on its unprecedented rule of standing, the Court goes on to conclude that, even if Lyons has standing, "[t]he equitable remedy is unavailable."...

The District Court concluded, on the basis of the facts before it, that Lyons was choked without provocation pursuant to an unconstitutional City policy. Given the necessarily preliminary nature of its inquiry, there was no way for the District Court to know the precise contours of the City's policy or to ascertain the risk that Lyons, who had alleged that the policy was being applied in a discriminatory manner, might again be subjected to a chokehold. But in view of the Court's conclusion that the unprovoked choking of Lyons was pursuant to a City policy, Lyons has satisfied "the usual basis for injunctive relief, 'that there exists some cognizable danger of recurrent violation.'" ... The risk of serious injuries and deaths to other citizens also supported the decision to grant a preliminary injunction. Courts of equity have much greater latitude in granting injunctive relief "in furtherance of the public interest ... than when only private interests are involved." ... In this case we know that the District Court would have been amply justified in considering the risk to the public, for after the preliminary injunction was stayed, five additional deaths occurred prior to the adoption of a moratorium.... Under these circumstances, I do not believe that the District Court abused its discretion....

VI. The Court's decision removes an entire class of constitutional violations from the equitable powers of a federal court. It immunizes from prospective equitable relief any policy that authorizes persistent deprivations of constitutional rights as long as no individual can establish with substantial certainty that he will be injured, or injured again, in the future. The Chief Justice asked in *Bivens v. Six Unknown Fed. Narcotics Agents* (1971) (dissenting opinion), "what would be the judicial response to a police order authorizing 'shoot to kill' with respect to every fugitive?" His answer was that it would be "easy to predict our collective wrath and outrage." We now learn that wrath and outrage cannot be translated into an order to cease the unconstitutional practice, but only an award of damages to those who are victimized by the practice and live to sue and to the survivors of those who are not so fortunate. Under the view expressed by the majority today, if the police adopt a policy of "shoot to kill," or a policy of shooting one out of ten suspects, the federal courts will be powerless to enjoin its continuation. The federal judicial power is now limited to levying a toll for such a systematic constitutional violation.

City of Los Angeles v. Lyons: Notes

1. It is often difficult to distinguish between a court's refusal to find standing because it finds no cognizable injury and the court's dismissal based on the independent issue of ripeness. In the ripeness situation, the court dismisses a case because the feared harm is so immature that it is not determinate. In the sense that Lyons sought relief based on fear of being choked in the future, one could say that the claim was not ripe. Since he had not been harmed by a future choking, one could also say he had no injury.

2. IRS regulations require that private schools that discriminate on the basis of race may not receive tax-exempt status. In *Allen v. Wright* (1984), parents of black children alleged that the IRS guidelines and procedures were inadequate to identify private schools that were in fact racially discriminatory, yet received tax-exempt status. The parents alleged that this practice drained white children from public schools, frustrating the attempt to desegregate the public schools and denying their children the opportunity to go to integrated public schools. The Court found there to be no cognizable injury and denied the parents standing:

    > Respondents' first claim of injury can be interpreted in two ways. It might be a claim simply to have the Government avoid the violation of law alleged in respondents' complaint. Alternatively, it might be a claim of stigmatic injury, or denigration, suffered by all members of a racial group when the Government discriminates on the basis of race.[1] Under neither interpretation is this claim of injury judicially cognizable.

    > This Court has repeatedly held that an asserted right to have the Government act in accordance with law is not sufficient, standing alone, to confer jurisdiction on a federal court. In *Schlesinger v. Reservists Committee to Stop the War* (1974), for example, the Court rejected a claim of citizen standing to challenge Armed Forces Reserve commissions held by Members of Congress as violating the Incompatibility Clause of Art. I, §6, of the Constitution. As citizens, the

---

1. We assume, arguendo, that the asserted stigmatic injury may be caused by the Government's grant of tax exemptions to racially discriminatory schools even if the Government is granting those exemptions without knowing or believing that the schools in fact discriminate. That is, we assume, without deciding, that the challenged Government tax exemptions are the equivalent of Government discrimination.

Court held, plaintiffs alleged nothing but "the abstract injury in nonobservance of the Constitution...." More recently, in *Valley Forge* (1982), we rejected a claim of standing to challenge a Government conveyance of property to a religious institution. Insofar as the plaintiffs relied simply on "'their shared individuated right'" to a Government that made no law respecting an establishment of religion, we held that plaintiffs had not alleged a judicially cognizable injury. [A]ssertion of a right to a particular kind of Government conduct, which the Government has violated by acting differently, cannot alone satisfy the requirements of Art. III without draining those requirements of meaning.... Respondents here have no standing to complain simply that their Government is violating the law.

Neither do they have standing to litigate their claims based on the stigmatizing injury often caused by racial discrimination. There can be no doubt that this sort of noneconomic injury is one of the most serious consequences of discriminatory government action and is sufficient in some circumstances to support standing. See *Heckler v. Mathews* (1984) [plaintiff alleged he was victim of sex discrimination in allocation of Social Security benefits]. Our cases make clear, however, that such injury accords a basis for standing only to "those persons who are personally denied equal treatment" by the challenged discriminatory conduct.

In *Moose Lodge No. 107 v. Irvis* (1972), the Court held that the plaintiff had no standing to challenge a club's racially discriminatory membership policies because he had never applied for membership. In *O'Shea v. Littleton* (1974), the Court held that the plaintiffs had no standing to challenge racial discrimination in the administration of their city's criminal justice system because they had not alleged that they had been or would likely be subject to the challenged practices. The Court denied standing on similar facts in *Rizzo v. Goode* (1976). In each of those cases, the plaintiffs alleged official racial discrimination comparable to that alleged by respondents here. Yet, standing was denied in each case because the plaintiffs were not personally subject to the challenged discrimination. Insofar as their first claim of injury is concerned, respondents are in exactly the same position: unlike the appellee in *Heckler v. Mathews*, they do not allege a stigmatic injury suffered as a direct result of having personally been denied equal treatment.

The consequences of recognizing respondents' standing on the basis of their first claim of injury illustrate why our cases plainly hold that such injury is not judicially cognizable. If the abstract stigmatic injury were cognizable, standing would extend nationwide to all members of the particular racial groups against which the Government was alleged to be discriminating by its grant of a tax exemption to a racially discriminatory school, regardless of the location of that school. All such persons could claim the same sort of abstract stigmatic injury respondents assert in their first claim of injury. A black person in Hawaii could challenge the grant of a tax exemption to a racially discriminatory school in Maine. Recognition of standing in such circumstances would transform the federal courts into "no more than a vehicle for the vindication of the value interests of concerned bystanders." *United States v. SCRAP* (1973). Constitutional limits on the role of the federal courts preclude such a transformation.[2]

---

2. Cf. *Valley Forge Christian College v. Americans United for Separation of Church and State, Inc.*: "Were we to recognize standing premised on an 'injury' consisting solely of an alleged violation of a '"personal constitutional right" to a government that does not establish religion,' a principled consistency

3. Environmental cases focus on whether the harm is generalized or specific. Environmental harm constitutes an injury if the party satisfies the Court that the activity complained of affects the complainant in a personal way. In *United States v. SCRAP* (1973), the Court granted standing to a group of law students to challenge the propriety of railroad rate hikes when they asserted that natural areas which they personally frequented would be degraded as a result of the increases. In contrast, in *Sierra Club v. Morton* (1972), the Court denied standing to the Sierra Club to stop a construction project in a national park because the complaint did not allege that any of its members had personally visited the park. (Upon remand, the Sierra Club amended its complaint and was granted standing.) In *Lujan v. Defenders of Wildlife* (1992), one group of plaintiffs was denied standing to assert the applicability of the Endangered Species Act outside the scope of the United States. These plaintiffs had alleged a desire to visit Egypt and Sri Lanka to see the allegedly endangered Nile crocodile and Asian elephant and leopard, respectively, as they had in their studies in the past. Because they did not allege a specific time for their projected visits, the Court found their plans to be too indefinite to constitute an injury. Lacking a concrete personal plan, the plaintiffs were considered to have only a generalized grievance.

4. A harm can also be too indefinite to constitute an injury. In *Laird v. Tatum* (1972), the Court, by a 5–4 vote, refused to grant standing to plaintiffs who alleged that the exercise of their 1st Amendment rights was being chilled by the mere existence, without more, of a governmental investigative and data-gathering activity that was alleged to be broader in scope than was reasonably necessary for the accomplishment of a valid governmental purpose. The Army was maintaining files on people who attended public anti-war protests. The Army justified the practice because of the possibility that troops might be called in to supplement local police in the event of major disturbances. The plaintiffs alleged that the Army was engaging in "surveillance of lawful civilian political activity" and that they were afraid to attend meetings for fear of being placed in a government file. The Court refused to recognize this fear as an injury:

> In recent years this Court has found in a number of cases that constitutional violations may arise from the deterrent, or "chilling," effect of governmental regulations that fall short of a direct prohibition against the exercise of 1st Amendment rights.... In none of these cases, however, did the chilling effect arise merely from the individual's knowledge that a governmental agency was engaged in certain activities or from the individual's concomitant fear that, armed with the fruits of those activities, the agency might in the future take some other and additional action detrimental to that individual. Rather, in each of these cases, the challenged exercise of governmental power was regulatory, proscriptive, or compulsory in nature, and the complainant was either presently or prospectively subject to the regulations, proscriptions, or compulsions that he was challenging.

---

would dictate recognition of respondents' standing to challenge execution of every capital sentence on the basis of a personal right to a government that does not impose cruel and unusual punishment, or standing to challenge every affirmative action program on the basis of a personal right to a government that does not deny equal protection of the laws, to choose but two among as many possible examples as there are commands in the Constitution."

3. Cause-in-Fact and Redressability

Warth v. Seldin: Questions

1. What type of injury must the plaintiff allege to establish personal standing? What does it mean to have a personal stake in the outcome of a case? Does the plaintiff need to show a distinct injury to him or herself?
2. How substantial must it be? Does it need to be economic?
3. Must the plaintiff prove that the defendant's conduct caused the injury?
   a. What facts are necessary to prove causation?
   b. Why is causation necessary?
   c. Why did some plaintiffs fail to establish it in *Warth*?
4. Are there limits on the ability of plaintiffs to assert the constitutional rights of third persons?
5. What types of plaintiffs were involved in *Warth*? Why did each type fail to assert standing?
6. Should the Court in *Warth* have decided the issue of standing before trial? Why or why not?

Warth v. Seldin
422 U.S. 490 (1975)

[Majority: Powell, Burger (C.J.), Blackmun, Stewart, and Rehnquist. Dissenting: Douglas, Brennan, White, and Marshall.]

Mr. Justice Powell delivered the opinion of the Court.

Petitioners, various organizations and individuals resident in the Rochester, N.Y., metropolitan area, brought this action in the District Court for the Western District of New York against the town of Penfield, an incorporated municipality adjacent to Rochester, and against members of Penfield's Zoning, Planning and Town Boards. Petitioners claimed that the town's zoning ordinance, by its terms and as enforced by the defendant board members, respondents here, effectively excluded persons of low and moderate income from living in the town, in contravention of petitioners' 1st, 9th, and 14th Amendment rights and in violation of 42 U.S.C. § 1981, § 1982, and § 1983. The District Court dismissed the complaint and denied a motion to add petitioner Housing Council in the Monroe County Area, Inc., as party-plaintiff and also a motion by petitioner Rochester Home Builders Association, Inc., for leave to intervene as party-plaintiff. The Court of Appeals for the Second Circuit affirmed, holding that none of the plaintiffs, and neither the Housing Council nor Home Builders Association, had standing to prosecute the action. We granted the petition for certiorari.... [W]e affirm.

II. We address first the principles of standing relevant to the claims asserted by the several categories of petitioners in this case. In essence the question of standing is whether the litigant is entitled to have the court decide the merits of the dispute or of particular issues. This inquiry involves both constitutional limitations on federal-court jurisdiction and prudential limitations on its exercise. In both dimensions it is founded in concern about the proper—and properly limited—role of the courts in a democratic society.

In its constitutional dimension, standing imports justiciability: whether the plaintiff has made out a "case or controversy" between himself and the defendant within the meaning of Art. III. This is the threshold question in every federal case, determining the power of the court to entertain the suit. As an aspect of justiciability, the standing question is whether the plaintiff has "alleged such a personal stake in the outcome of the controversy" as to warrant his invocation of federal-court jurisdiction and to justify exercise of the court's remedial powers on his behalf. The Art. III judicial power exists only to redress or otherwise to protect against injury to the complaining party, even though the court's judgment may benefit others collaterally. A federal court's jurisdiction therefore can be invoked only when the plaintiff himself has suffered "some threatened or actual injury resulting from the putatively illegal action." ...

Apart from this minimum constitutional mandate, this Court has recognized other limits on the class of persons who may invoke the courts' decisional and remedial powers. First, the Court has held that when the asserted harm is a "generalized grievance" shared in substantially equal measure by all or a large class of citizens, that harm alone normally does not warrant exercise of jurisdiction.... Second, even when the plaintiff has alleged injury sufficient to meet the "case or controversy" requirement, this Court has held that the plaintiff generally must assert his own legal rights and interests, and cannot rest his claim to relief on the legal rights or interests of third parties.... Without such limitations—closely related to Art. III concerns but essentially matters of judicial self-governance—the courts would be called upon to decide abstract questions of wide public significance even though other governmental institutions may be more competent to address the questions and even though judicial intervention may be unnecessary to protect individual rights.

Although standing in no way depends on the merits of the plaintiff's contention that particular conduct is illegal it often turns on the nature and source of the claim asserted. The actual or threatened injury required by Art. III may exist solely by virtue of "statutes creating legal rights, the invasion of which creates standing." ... Moreover, the source of the plaintiff's claim to relief assumes critical importance with respect to the prudential rules of standing that, apart from Art. III's minimum requirements, serve to limit the role of the courts in resolving public disputes. Essentially, the standing question in such cases is whether the constitutional or statutory provision on which the claim rests properly can be understood as granting persons in the plaintiff's position a right to judicial relief. In some circumstances, countervailing considerations may outweigh the concerns underlying the usual reluctance to exert judicial power when the plaintiff's claim to relief rests on the legal rights of third parties. In such instances, the Court has found, in effect, that the constitutional or statutory provision in question implies a right of action in the plaintiff. See generally Part IV, *infra*. Moreover, Congress may grant an express right of action to persons who otherwise would be barred by prudential standing rules. Of course, Art. III's requirement remains: the plaintiff still must allege a distinct and palpable injury to himself, even if it is an injury shared by a large class of other possible litigants....

III. With these general considerations in mind, we turn first to the claims of petitioners Ortiz, Reyes, Sinkler, and Broadnax, each of whom asserts standing as a person of low or moderate income and, coincidentally, as a member of a minority racial or ethnic group. We must assume, taking the allegations of the complaint as true, that Penfield's zoning ordinance and the pattern of enforcement by respondent officials have had the purpose and effect of excluding persons of low and moderate income, many of whom are members of racial or ethnic minority groups. We also assume, for purposes here, that such intentional exclusionary practices, if proved in a proper case, would be adjudged violative of the constitutional and statutory rights of the persons excluded.

But the fact that these petitioners share attributes common to persons who may have been excluded from residence in the town is an insufficient predicate for the conclusion that petitioners themselves have been excluded, or that the respondents' assertedly illegal actions have violated their rights. Petitioners must allege and show that they personally have been injured, not that injury has been suffered by other, unidentified members of the class to which they belong and which they purport to represent. Unless these petitioners can thus demonstrate the requisite case or controversy between themselves personally and respondents, "none may seek relief on behalf of himself or any other member of the class." ...

In their complaint, petitioners Ortiz, Reyes, Sinkler, and Broadnax alleged in conclusory terms that they are among the persons excluded by respondents' actions. None of them has ever resided in Penfield; each claims at least implicitly that he desires, or has desired, to do so. Each asserts, moreover, that he made some effort, at some time, to locate housing in Penfield that was at once within his means and adequate for his family's needs. Each claims that his efforts proved fruitless. We may assume, as petitioners allege, that respondents' actions have contributed, perhaps substantially, to the cost of housing in Penfield. But there remains the question whether petitioners' inability to locate suitable housing in Penfield reasonably can be said to have resulted, in any concretely demonstrable way, from respondents' alleged constitutional and statutory infractions. Petitioners must allege facts from which it reasonably could be inferred that, absent the respondents' restrictive zoning practices, there is a substantial probability that they would have been able to purchase or lease in Penfield and that, if the court affords the relief requested, the asserted inability of petitioners will be removed.

We find the record devoid of the necessary allegations. As the Court of Appeals noted, none of these petitioners has a present interest in any Penfield property; none is himself subject to the ordinance's strictures; and none has even been denied a variance or permit by respondent officials.... Instead, petitioners claim that respondents' enforcement of the ordinance against third parties—developers, builders, and the like—has had the consequence of precluding the construction of housing suitable to their needs at prices they might be able to afford. The fact that the harm to petitioners may have resulted indirectly does not in itself preclude standing. When a governmental prohibition or restriction imposed on one party causes specific harm to a third party, harm that a constitutional provision or statute was intended to prevent, the indirectness of the injury does not necessarily deprive the person harmed of standing to vindicate his rights. But it may make it substantially more difficult to meet the minimum requirement of Art. III: to establish that, in fact, the asserted injury was the consequence of the defendants' actions, or that prospective relief will remove the harm.

Here, by their own admission, realization of petitioners' desire to live in Penfield always has depended on the efforts and willingness of third parties to build low- and moderate-cost housing. The record specifically refers to only two such efforts: that of Penfield Better Homes Corp., in late 1969, to obtain the rezoning of certain land in Penfield to allow the construction of subsidized cooperative townhouses that could be purchased by persons of moderate income; and a similar effort by O'Brien Homes, Inc., in late 1971. But the record is devoid of any indication that these projects, or other like projects, would have satisfied petitioners' needs at prices they could afford, or that, were the court to remove the obstructions attributable to respondents, such relief would benefit petitioners. Indeed, petitioners' descriptions of their individual financial situations and housing needs suggest precisely the contrary—that their inability to reside in Penfield is the consequence of the economics of the area housing market, rather than of respondents' assertedly illegal acts. In short, the facts alleged fail to support an actionable causal relationship between Penfield's zoning practices and petitioners' asserted injury.

In support of their position, petitioners refer to several decisions in the District Courts and Courts of Appeals, acknowledging standing in low-income, minority-group plaintiffs to challenge exclusionary zoning practices. In those cases, however, the plaintiffs challenged zoning restrictions as applied to particular projects that would supply housing within their means, and of which they were intended residents. The plaintiffs thus were able to demonstrate that unless relief from assertedly illegal actions was forthcoming, their immediate and personal interests would be harmed. Petitioners here assert no like circumstances. Instead, they rely on little more than the remote possibility, unsubstantiated by allegations of fact, that their situation might have been better had respondents acted otherwise, and might improve were the court to afford relief.

We hold only that a plaintiff who seeks to challenge exclusionary zoning practices must allege specific, concrete facts demonstrating that the challenged practices harm him, and that he personally would benefit in a tangible way from the court's intervention.[3] ...

IV. The petitioners who assert standing on the basis of their status as taxpayers of the city of Rochester present a different set of problems. [The Court summarily rejects their claim.]

V. We turn next to the standing problems presented by the petitioner associations....

Even in the absence of injury to itself, an association may have standing solely as the representative of its members. The possibility of such representational standing, however, does not eliminate or attenuate the constitutional requirement of a case or controversy. The association must allege that its members, or any one of them, are suffering immediate or threatened injury as a result of the challenged action of the sort that would make out a justiciable case had the members themselves brought suit. So long as this can be established, and so long as the nature of the claim and of the relief sought does not make the individual participation of each injured party indispensable to proper resolution of the cause, the association may be an appropriate representative of its members, entitled to invoke the court's jurisdiction.

V-B. Petitioner Rochester Home Builders Association, in its intervenor-complaint, asserted standing to represent its member firms engaged in the development and construction of residential housing in the Rochester area, including Penfield. Home Builders alleged that the Penfield zoning restrictions, together with refusals by the town officials to grant variances and permits for the construction of low- and moderate-cost housing, had deprived some of its members of "substantial business opportunities and profits." App. 156. Home Builders claimed damages of $750,000 and also joined in the original plaintiffs' prayer for declaratory and injunctive relief.

---

3. This is not to say that the plaintiff who challenges a zoning ordinance or zoning practices must have a present contractual interest in a particular project. A particularized personal interest may be shown in various ways, which we need not undertake to identify in the abstract. But usually the initial focus should be on a particular project.... We also note that zoning laws and their provisions, long considered essential to effective urban planning, are peculiarly within the province of state and local legislative authorities. They are, of course, subject to judicial review in a proper case. But citizens dissatisfied with provisions of such laws need not overlook the availability of the normal democratic process.

As noted above, to justify any relief the association must show that it has suffered harm, or that one or more of its members are injured....

Home Builders alleges no monetary injury to itself, nor any assignment of the damages claims of its members. No award therefore can be made to the association as such. Moreover, in the circumstances of this case, the damages claims are not common to the entire membership, nor shared by all in equal degree. To the contrary, whatever injury may have been suffered is peculiar to the individual member concerned, and both the fact and extent of injury would require individualized proof. Thus, to obtain relief in damages, each member of Home Builders who claims injury as a result of respondents' practices must be a party to the suit, and Home Builders has no standing to claim damages on his behalf.

Home Builders' prayer for prospective relief fails for a different reason. It can have standing as the representative of its members only if it has alleged facts sufficient to make out a case or controversy had the members themselves brought suit. No such allegations were made. The complaint refers to no specific project of any of its members that is currently precluded either by the ordinance or by respondents' action in enforcing it. There is no averment that any member has applied to respondents for a building permit or a variance with respect to any current project. Indeed, there is no indication that respondents have delayed or thwarted any project currently proposed by Home Builders' members, or that any of its members has taken advantage of the remedial processes available under the ordinance. In short, insofar as the complaint seeks prospective relief, Home Builders has failed to show the existence of any injury to its members of sufficient immediacy and ripeness to warrant judicial intervention....

A like problem is presented with respect to petitioner Housing Council in the Monroe County Area, Inc. The affidavit accompanying the motion to join it as plaintiff states that the Council includes in its membership "at lease seventeen" groups that have been, are, or will be involved in the development of low- and moderate-cost housing. But with one exception, the complaint does not suggest that any of these groups has focused its efforts on Penfield or has any specific plan to do so. Again with the same exception, neither the complaint nor any materials of record indicate that any member of Housing Council has taken any step toward building housing in Penfield, or has had dealings of any nature with respondents. The exception is the Penfield Better Homes Corp. As we have observed above, it applied to respondents in late 1969 for a zoning variance to allow construction of a housing project designed for persons of moderate income.... It is therefore possible that in 1969, or within a reasonable time thereafter, Better Homes itself and possibly Housing Council as its representative would have had standing to seek review of respondents' action. The complaint, however, does not allege that the Penfield Better Homes project remained viable in 1972 when this complaint was filed, or that respondents' actions continued to block a then-current construction project. In short, neither the complaint nor the record supplies any basis from which to infer that the controversy between respondents and Better Homes, however vigorous it may once have been, remained a live, concrete dispute when this complaint was filed.

VI. The rules of standing, whether as aspects of the Art. III case-or-controversy requirement or as reflections of prudential considerations defining and limiting the role of the courts, are threshold determinants of the propriety of judicial intervention. It is the responsibility of the complainant clearly to allege facts demonstrating that he is a proper party to invoke judicial resolution of the dispute and the exercise of the court's remedial powers. We agree with the District Court and the Court of Appeals that none of the petitioners here has met this threshold requirement. Accordingly, the judgment of the Court of Appeals is

Affirmed.

Mr. Justice Douglas, dissenting....

Standing has become a barrier to access to the federal courts, much as "the political question" was in earlier decades. The mounting caseload of federal courts is well known. But cases such as this one reflect festering sores in our society; and the American dream teaches that if one reaches high enough and persists there is a forum where justice is dispensed. I would lower the technical barriers and let the courts serve that ancient need....

I would let the case go to trial and have all the facts brought out. Indeed, it would be better practice to decide the question of standing only when the merits have been developed.

I would reverse the Court of Appeals.

Mr. Justice Brennan, with whom Mr. Justice White and Mr. Justice Marshall join, dissenting.

In this case, a wide range of plaintiffs, alleging various kinds of injuries, claimed to have been affected by the Penfield zoning ordinance, on its face and as applied, and by other practices of the defendant officials of Penfield. Alleging that as a result of these laws and practices low- and moderate-income and minority people have been excluded from Penfield, and that this exclusion is unconstitutional, plaintiffs sought injunctive, declaratory, and monetary relief. The Court today, in an opinion that purports to be a "standing" opinion but that actually, I believe, has overtones of outmoded notions of pleading and of justiciability, refuses to find that any of the variously situated plaintiffs can clear numerous hurdles, some constructed here for the first time, necessary to establish "standing." While the Court gives lip service to the principle, oft repeated in recent years, that "standing in no way depends on the merits of the plaintiff's contention that particular conduct is illegal," in fact the opinion, which tosses out of court almost every conceivable kind of plaintiff who could be injured by the activity claimed to be unconstitutional, can be explained only by an indefensible hostility to the claim on the merits. I can appreciate the Court's reluctance to adjudicate the complex and difficult legal questions involved in determining the constitutionality of practices which assertedly limit residence in a particular municipality to those who are white and relatively well off, and I also understand that the merits of this case could involve grave sociological and political ramifications. But courts cannot refuse to hear a case on the merits merely because they would prefer not to, and it is quite clear, when the record is viewed with dispassion, that at least three of the groups of plaintiffs have made allegations, and supported them with affidavits and documentary evidence, sufficient to survive a motion to dismiss for lack of standing.

I. Before considering the three groups I believe clearly to have standing—the low-income, minority plaintiffs, Rochester Home Builders Association, Inc., and the Housing Council in the Monroe County Area, Inc.—it will be helpful to review the picture painted by the allegations as a whole, in order better to comprehend the interwoven interests of the various plaintiffs. Indeed, one glaring defect of the Court's opinion is that it views each set of plaintiffs as if it were prosecuting a separate lawsuit, refusing to recognize that the interests are intertwined, and that the standing of any one group must take into account its position vis-a-vis the others. For example, the Court says that the low-income minority plaintiffs have not alleged facts sufficient to show that but for the exclusionary practices claimed, they would be able to reside in Penfield. The Court then intimates that such a causal relationship could be shown only if "the initial focus (is) on a particular project." Later, the Court objects to the ability of the Housing Council to prosecute the suit on behalf of its member, Penfield Better Homes Corp., despite the fact that Better Homes had displayed an interest in a particular project, because that project was no longer live.

Thus, we must suppose that even if the low-income plaintiffs had alleged a desire to live in the Better Homes project, that allegation would be insufficient because it appears that that particular project might never be built. The rights of low-income minority plaintiffs who desire to live in a locality, then, seem to turn on the willingness of a third party to litigate the legality of preclusion of a particular project, despite the fact that the third party may have no economic incentive to incur the costs of litigation with regard to one project, and despite the fact that the low-income minority plaintiffs' interest is not to live in a particular project but to live somewhere in the town in a dwelling they can afford....

Thus, the portrait which emerges from the allegations and affidavits is one of total, purposeful, intransigent exclusion of certain classes of people from the town, pursuant to a conscious scheme never deviated from. Because of this scheme, those interested in building homes for the excluded groups were faced with insurmountable difficulties, and those of the excluded groups seeking homes in the locality quickly learned that their attempts were futile. Yet, the Court turns the very success of the allegedly unconstitutional scheme into a barrier to a lawsuit seeking its invalidation. In effect, the Court tells the low income minority and building company plaintiffs they will not be permitted to prove what they have alleged — that they could and would build and live in the town if changes were made in the zoning ordinance and its application — because they have not succeeded in breaching, before the suit was filed, the very barriers which are the subject of the suit.

II. Low-income and Minority Plaintiffs....

[T]he Court's real holding is not that these petitioners have not alleged an injury resulting from respondents' action, but that they are not to be allowed to prove one, because "realization of petitioners' desire to live in Penfield always has depended on the efforts and willingness of third parties to build low- and moderate-cost housing," and "the record is devoid of any indication that ... (any) projects, would have satisfied petitioners' needs at prices they could afford."

Certainly, this is not the sort of demonstration that can or should be required of petitioners at this preliminary stage....

Here, the very fact that, as the Court stresses, these petitioners' claim rests in part upon proving the intentions and capabilities of third parties to build in Penfield suitable housing which they can afford, coupled with the exclusionary character of the claim on the merits, makes it particularly inappropriate to assume that these petitioners' lack of specificity reflects a fatal weakness in their theory of causation. Obviously they cannot be expected, prior to discovery and trial, to know the future plans of building companies, the precise details of the housing market in Penfield, or everything which has transpired in 15 years of application of the Penfield zoning ordinance, including every housing plan suggested and refused. To require them to allege such facts is to require them to prove their case on paper in order to get into court at all, reverting to the form of fact pleading long abjured in the federal courts....

III. Associations Including Building Concerns....

[T]he Court ignores the thrust of the complaints and asks petitioners to allege the impossible. According to the allegations, the building concerns' experience in the past with Penfield officials has shown any plans for low- and moderate-income housing to be futile for, again according to the allegations, the respondents are engaged in a purposeful, conscious scheme to exclude such housing. Particularly with regard to a low- or moderate-income project, the cost of litigating, with respect to any particular project, the legality of a refusal to approve it may well be prohibitive. And the merits of the exclusion of this or that project is not at the heart of the complaint; the claim is that respondents will not approve any project which will provide residences for low- and moderate-income people.

When this sort of pattern-and-practice claim is at the heart of the controversy, allegations of past injury, which members of both of these organizations have clearly made, and of a future intent, if the barriers are cleared, again to develop suitable housing for Penfield, should be more than sufficient. The past experiences, if proved at trial, will give credibility and substance to the claim of interest in future building activity in Penfield. These parties, if their allegations are proved, certainly have the requisite personal stake in the outcome of this controversy, and the Court's conclusion otherwise is only a conclusion that this controversy may not be litigated in a federal court.

I would reverse the judgment of the Court of Appeals.

Warth v. Seldin: Notes

1. *Warth v. Seldin* is a watershed case of the Burger Court. It reflects the Burger Court's (1969–1986) much tougher judicial attitude toward standing. The rigorous cause-in-fact standard can be difficult for plaintiffs — even plaintiffs who might otherwise seem to have a personal stake in the controversy. The focus of the cause-in-fact standard is whether or not the governmental defendant can be seen to be creating the plaintiff's problem. When the Court believes that the plaintiff is in fact being injured by a third party, who may continue his behavior regardless of what the government does, the Court refuses to find causation. In *Warth*, the Court maintained that the individuals might not get affordable housing, regardless of changes in the zoning laws. Subsequent cases continued to focus on causation.

   The Court had applied the heightened causation standard in one case before *Warth*. In *Linda R.S. v. Richard D.* (1973), the Court denied standing to the mother of an illegitimate child who sought an injunction to force the district attorney to prosecute fathers of illegitimate children for nonsupport. The Court reasoned that, even if the fathers were prosecuted, there was no assurance that the mother would receive child support.

   In *Simon v. Eastern Kentucky Welfare Rights Organization* (1976), a low income advocacy group challenged an IRS regulation that allowed hospitals to gain tax-exempt status while providing fewer services for the indigent than formerly required. The Court denied the plaintiffs standing, reasoning that since the hospitals were free to choose not to provide any care to indigents, the government could not be considered to be the cause of their reduction in services. *Simon* is noteworthy because the Court announced that the cause-in-fact and redressability requirements were not just prudential considerations, but were in fact rooted in Article III. Justice Brennan noted in his concurrence:

   > [T]he most disturbing aspect of today's opinion is the Court's insistence on resting its decision regarding standing squarely on the irreducible Art. III minimum of injury in fact, thereby effectively placing its holding beyond congressional power to rectify. Thus, any time Congress chooses to legislate in favor of certain interests by setting up a scheme of incentives for third parties, judicial review of administrative action that allegedly frustrates the congressionally intended objective will be denied, because any complainant will be required to make an almost impossible showing. Clearly the Legislative Branch of the Government cannot supply injured individuals with the means to make the factual showing

in a specific context that the Court today requires. More specific indications of a congressional desire to confer standing upon such individuals would be germane, not to the Art. III injury-in-fact requirement, but only to the Court's "zone of interests" test for standing, that branch of standing lore which the Court assiduously avoids reaching.

In our modern-day society, dominated by complex legislative programs and large-scale governmental involvement in the everyday lives of all of us, judicial review of administrative action is essential both for protection of individuals illegally harmed by that action ... and to ensure that the attainment of congressionally mandated goals is not frustrated by illegal action....

As Justice Brennan points out, this holding is significant because it precludes Congress from granting statutory standing to this class of plaintiffs.

While the Court dismissed the plaintiffs in *Allen v. Wright* for a lack of injury, the court also addressed the cause-in-fact issue and held that the plaintiffs were suffering, if at all, from the decisions of the discriminatory schools, not the policies of the government. According to the Court, the schools could have chosen to forego the tax-exempt benefits and the plaintiffs would be no better off. *Allen* is also significant for clarifying that causation and redressability are two distinct factors:

The "fairly traceable" and "redressability" components of the constitutional standing inquiry were initially articulated by this Court as "two facets of a single causation requirement." C. Wright, *Law of Federal Courts*, p. 68, n. 43 (4th ed. 1983). To the extent there is a difference, it is that the former examines the causal connection between the assertedly unlawful conduct and the alleged injury, whereas the latter examines the causal connection between the alleged injury and the judicial relief requested. Cases such as this, in which the relief requested goes well beyond the violation of law alleged, illustrate why it is important to keep the inquiries separate if the 'redressability' component is to focus on the requested relief. Even if the relief respondents request might have a substantial effect on the desegregation of public schools, whatever deficiencies exist in the opportunities for desegregated education for respondents' children might not be traceable to IRS violations of law—grants of tax exemptions to racially discriminatory schools in respondents' communities.

Commentators have criticized the cause-in-fact test as one subject to judicial manipulation, because the rule is applied inconsistently depending on the Court's desire to reach the merits of the case. For a survey of the criticism of the Court's standing rules, see generally, Chemerinsky, *Constitutional Law: Principles and Policies*, pp. 78–82 (2d ed., 2002).

2. While the Court dismissed all of the putative plaintiffs in *Warth*, it recognized that *associations* can achieve standing in the proper case. Associations could have standing in their own right if they are being harmed, or can gain standing on behalf of their members. The Court clearly articulated the test for associational standing on behalf of members in *Hunt v. Washington State Apple Advertising Commission* (1977):

Thus we have recognized that an association has standing to bring suit on behalf of its members when: (a) its members would otherwise have standing to sue in their own right; (b) the interests it seeks to protect are germane to the organization's purpose; and (c) neither the claim asserted nor the relief requested requires the participation of individual members in the lawsuit.

3. The Court eventually accepted a challenge to restrictive zoning practices. In *Village of Arlington Heights v. Metropolitan Housing Development Corp.* (1977), the Court granted standing to a nonprofit developer who had contracted to purchase a tract of land within the boundaries of the village in order to build racially integrated low- and moderate-income housing. The contract was contingent upon securing rezoning as well as federal housing assistance. While the Court found this plaintiff to satisfy the *Warth* test for standing, it proceeded to rule against the plaintiff on the merits.

4. *Warth* also discussed the ability of a party with standing to raise claims of others not before the court. This concept is known as third party (or jus tertii) standing. While the Court generally refuses to allow third party claims for prudential reasons, there are four exceptions to this rule. First, the Court will allow a party who has standing to raise the rights of third parties if those parties have a difficulty raising their claim themselves. For example, in *NAACP v. Alabama* (1958), the NAACP was allowed assert its members' rights in a challenge to a state court order that would have required the association to disclose its membership list to the state. The NAACP "made an uncontroverted showing that on past occasions revelation of the identity of its rank-and-file members has exposed these members to economic reprisal, loss of employment, threat of physical coercion, and other manifestations of public hostility." Members therefore were unlikely to challenge the court order as individuals because the suit would reveal their membership—and subject them to the very retaliation they feared. Second, third party standing will be available if the party with standing has a close relationship to the third party, such as doctor-patient or seller-buyer. Next, third party standing will be available if the party with standing is raising the 1st Amendment rights of others in a challenge to a substantially overbroad statute. For example, a city could constitutionally pass a statute that states, "No one may camp in a park." A person camping in the park to illustrate the plight of homeless people could be convicted under such a statute. However, if the statute reads, "No 1st Amendment activity may occur in the park," it is substantially overbroad. The camping defendant can raise the rights of others, who may fear to engage in protected speech at the park, to avoid his conviction. The final category of third party standing involves the ability of associations to represent the interests of their members, as discussed above. How do the *Warth* tests fit into questions of third party standing?

Craig v. Boren: Background

1. *Craig v. Boren* involved a challenge to an Oklahoma statute that forbade 18–21 year old males from purchasing beer, while allowing purchases by 18–21 year old females. The complaint contained a cause of action for both an underage male and a vendor. Craig, the underage male, was not named as a class representative and his case became moot when he turned 21 during the course of the litigation. Whether or not the vendor had standing and whether the vendor could assert any of her customers' claims then became crucial.

To understand the issue, you need to understand something about the claim the vendor had on her own and the claim available to the 18–21 year old males who were denied the right to purchase beer. The vendor could claim that the statute that forbade her to sell beer to young men deprived her of the liberty to sell to them, thereby reducing her income. The problem with this claim is that, while it is enough of an injury to get the vendor personal standing, the vendor's economic liberty claim has a negligible chance of success on the merits under current law. Craig's claim was (and that of young men still in the 18–21 age group could be) that the gender discrimination inflicted by the statute violated the Equal Protection Clause. This claim had a much greater chance of success, but the vendor had not personally suffered sex discrimination. The third party standing issue was whether the vendor had standing in her own right under *Warth* and then could also assert the gender discrimination claim of the young men who were barred from the purchase of beer.

2. Consider this hypothetical as you read about third party standing in *Craig*.

The Right to Die Foundation supports the right of people to die if they choose. Most of its energy is devoted to problems of terminally ill patients. State laws typically make suicide criminal, punishing attempting or assisting suicide. The Foundation brings suit in federal court claiming that a state rule of law against assisting suicide (at least in cases of informed consent) violates the right to privacy of the person choosing suicide. The statute is alleged to violate the 14th Amendment. The plaintiffs in the suit include the society which alleges that it has among its members terminally ill patients who wish to commit suicide. A doctor also is a plaintiff, and she alleges that but for the rule she would assist terminally ill patients (acting on informed consent) in committing suicide.

   a. What is the issue in the case? Note carefully what claim is made.
   b. What authority governs how it should be resolved?
   c. How would you apply the authority to the facts?
   d. How do you resolve the case?

Craig v. Boren
429 U.S. 190 (1976)

[Majority: Brennan, Powell, Stevens, Marshall, Blackmun and White. Concurring: Powell, Stevens, and Stewart. Concurrence (in part): Blackmun. Dissenting: Burger (C.J.) and Rehnquist.]

Mr. Justice Brennan delivered the opinion of the Court.

The interaction of two sections of an Oklahoma statute, Okla. Stat., Tit. 37, §§ 241 and 245 prohibits the sale of "nonintoxicating" 3.2% beer to males under the age of 21 and to females under the age of 18. The question to be decided is whether such a gender-based differential constitutes a denial to males 18–20 years of age of the equal protection of the laws in violation of the 14th Amendment.

This action was brought in the District Court for the Western District of Oklahoma on December 20, 1972, by appellant Craig, a male then between 18 and 21 years of age, and by appellant Whitener, a licensed vendor of 3.2% beer. The complaint sought declaratory and injunctive relief against enforcement of the gender-based differential on the ground that it constituted invidious discrimination against males 18–20 years of age. A three-judge court convened under 28 U.S.C. § 2281 sustained the constitutionality of the statutory differential and dismissed the action.... We reverse.

I. We first address a preliminary question of standing. Appellant Craig attained the age of 21 after we noted probable jurisdiction. Therefore, since only declaratory and injunctive relief against enforcement of the gender-based differential is sought, the controversy has been rendered moot as to Craig. See, e.g., *DeFunis v. Odegaard* (1974).[1] The question thus arises whether appellant Whitener, the licensed vendor of 3.2% beer, who has a live controversy against enforcement of the statute, may rely upon the equal protection objections of males 18–20 years of age to establish her claim of unconstitutionality of the age-sex differential. We conclude that she may.

Initially, it should be noted that, despite having had the opportunity to do so, appellees never raised before the District Court any objection to Whitener's reliance upon the claimed unequal treatment of 18–20-year-old males as the premise of her equal protection challenge to Oklahoma's 3.2% beer law. Indeed, at oral argument Oklahoma acknowledged that appellees always "presumed" that the vendor, subject to sanctions and loss of license for violation of the statute, was a proper party in interest to object to the enforcement of the sex-based regulatory provision.... While such a concession certainly would not be controlling upon the reach of this Court's constitutional authority to exercise jurisdiction under Art. III, ... our decisions have settled that limitations on a litigant's assertion of jus tertii are not constitutionally mandated, but rather stem from a salutary "rule of self-restraint" designed to minimize unwarranted intervention into controversies where the applicable constitutional questions are ill-defined and speculative.... These prudential objectives, thought to be enhanced by restrictions on third-party standing, cannot be furthered here, where the lower court already has entertained the relevant constitutional challenge and the parties have sought or at least have never resisted an authoritative constitutional determination. In such circumstances, a decision by us to forgo consideration of the constitutional merits in order to await the initiation of a new challenge to the statute by injured third parties would be impermissibly to foster repetitive and time-consuming litigation under the guise of caution and prudence. Moreover, insofar as the applicable constitutional questions have been and continue to be presented vigorously and "cogently," ... the denial of jus tertii standing in deference to a direct class suit can serve no functional purpose. Our Brother Blackmun's comment is pertinent: "(I)t may be that a class could be assembled, whose fluid membership always included some (males) with live claims. But if the assertion of the right is to be 'representative' to such an extent anyway, there seems little loss in terms of effective advocacy from allowing its assertion by" the present jus tertii champion.

In any event, we conclude that appellant Whitener has established independently her claim to assert jus tertii standing. The operation of §§ 241 and 245 plainly has inflicted "injury in fact" upon appellant sufficient to guarantee her "concrete adverseness," and to satisfy the constitutionally based standing requirements imposed by Art. III. The legal duties created by the statutory sections under challenge are addressed directly to vendors such as appellant. She is obliged either to heed the statutory discrimination, thereby incurring a direct economic injury through the constriction of her buyers' market, or to disobey the statutory command and suffer, in the words of Oklahoma's Assistant Attorney General, "sanctions and perhaps loss of license." This Court repeatedly has recognized that such injuries establish the threshold requirements of a "case or controversy" mandated by Art. III. See, e.g., *Singleton v. Wulff* (1976) (doctors who receive payments for their abortion services are "classically adverse" to government as payer)....

---

1. Appellants did not seek class certification of Craig as representative of other similarly situated males 18–20 years of age....

As a vendor with standing to challenge the lawfulness of §§ 241 and 245, appellant Whitener is entitled to assert those concomitant rights of third parties that would be "diluted or adversely affected" should her constitutional challenge fail and the statutes remain in force. *Griswold v. Connecticut* (1965); see Note, *Standing to Assert Constitutional Jus Tertii*, 88 Harv. L. Rev. 423, 432 (1974). Otherwise, the threatened imposition of governmental sanctions might deter appellant Whitener and other similarly situated vendors from selling 3.2% beer to young males, thereby ensuring that "enforcement of the challenged restriction against the (vendor) would result indirectly in the violation of third parties' rights." *Warth v. Seldin* (1975). Accordingly, vendors and those in like positions have been uniformly permitted to resist efforts at restricting their operations by acting as advocates of the rights of third parties who seek access to their market or function....[2]

Indeed, the jus tertii question raised here is answered by our disposition of a like argument in *Eisenstadt v. Baird* (1972). There, as here, a state statute imposed legal duties and disabilities upon the claimant, who was convicted of distributing a package of contraceptive foam to a third party.[3] Since the statute was directed at Baird and penalized his conduct, the Court did not hesitate again as here to conclude that the "case or controversy" requirement of Art. III was satisfied. In considering Baird's constitutional objections, the Court fully recognized his standing to defend the privacy interests of third parties. Deemed crucial to the decision to permit jus tertii standing was the recognition of "the impact of the litigation on the third-party interests." Just as the defeat of Baird's suit and the "(e)nforcement of the Massachusetts statute will materially impair the ability of single persons to obtain contraceptives," so too the failure of Whitener to prevail in this suit and the continued enforcement of §§ 241 and 245 will "materially impair the ability of" males 18–20 years of age to purchase 3.2% beer despite their classification by an overt gender-based criterion. Similarly, just as the Massachusetts law in *Eisenstadt* "prohibit(ed), not use, but distribution," and consequently the least awkward challenger was one in Baird's position who was subject to that proscription, the law challenged here explicitly regulates the sale rather than use of 3.2% beer, thus leaving a vendor as the obvious claimant.

We therefore hold that Whitener has standing to raise relevant equal protection challenges to Oklahoma's gender-based law....

---

2. The standing question presented here is not answered by the principle stated in *United States v. Raines* (1960), that "one to whom application of a statute is constitutional will not be heard to attack the statute on the ground that impliedly it might also be taken as applying to other persons or other situations in which its application might be unconstitutional." In *Raines*, the Court refused to permit certain public officials of Georgia to defend against application of the Civil Rights Act to their official conduct on the ground that the statute also might be construed to encompass the "purely private actions" of others. The *Raines* rule remains germane in such a setting, where the interests of the litigant and the rights of the proposed third parties are in no way mutually interdependent. Thus, a successful suit against Raines did not threaten to impair or diminish the independent private rights of others, and consequently, consideration of those third-party rights properly was deferred until another day. Of course, the *Raines* principle has also been relaxed where legal action against the claimant threatens to "chill" the 1st Amendment rights of third parties....

3. The fact that Baird chose to disobey the legal duty imposed upon him by the Massachusetts, anticontraception statute, resulting in his criminal conviction, does not distinguish the standing inquiry from that pertaining to the anticipatory attack in this case. In both *Eisenstadt* and here, the challenged statutes compel jus tertii claimants either to cease their proscribed activities or to suffer appropriate sanctions. The existence of Art. III "injury in fact" and the structure of the claimant's relationship to the third parties are not altered by the litigative posture of the suit. And, certainly, no suggestion will be heard that Whitener's anticipatory challenge offends the normal requirements governing such actions....

Powell, J., concurring; Stevens, J., concurring; Blackmun, J., concurring in part; and Stewart, J., concurring in the judgment. [Omitted.]

Mr. Chief Justice Burger, dissenting....

At the outset I cannot agree that appellant Whitener has standing arising from her status as a saloonkeeper to assert the constitutional rights of her customers. In this Court "a litigant may only assert his own constitutional rights or immunities." *United States v. Raines* (1960). There are a few, but strictly limited exceptions to that rule; despite the most creative efforts, this case fits within none of them.

This is not *Sullivan v. Little Hunting Park* (1969), or *Barrows v. Jackson* (1953), for there is here no barrier whatever to Oklahoma males 18–20 years of age asserting, in an appropriate forum, any constitutional rights they may claim to purchase 3.2% beer. Craig's successful litigation of this very issue was prevented only by the advent of his 21st birthday. There is thus no danger of interminable dilution of those rights if appellant Whitener is not permitted to litigate them here. Cf. *Eisenstadt v. Baird* (1972).

Nor is this controlled by *Griswold v. Connecticut* (1965). It borders on the ludicrous to draw a parallel between a vendor of beer and the intimate professional physician-patient relationship which undergirded relaxation of standing rules in that case.

Even in *Eisenstadt*, the Court carefully limited its recognition of third-party standing to cases in which the relationship between the claimant and the relevant third party "was not simply the fortuitous connection between a vendor and potential vendees, but the relationship between one who acted to protect the rights of a minority and the minority itself." This is plainly not the case here....

In sum, permitting a vendor to assert the constitutional rights of vendees whenever those rights are arguably infringed introduces a new concept of constitutional standing to which I cannot subscribe....

Mr. Justice Rehnquist, dissenting. [Omitted.]

4. Citizen Suits: The Limits of Congressional Grants of Standing

Congress creates substantive rights of all kinds: the right not to suffer gender discrimination in employment, the right to a minimum wage, the right to be free from monopolistic conspiracies. When one suffers a clear personal invasion of such statutorily created rights, standing is readily available.

Congress has also passed many statutes, particularly in the environmental field, which authorize citizen suits against the government when an individual believes that duties imposed upon an executive agency by a particular statute are being violated. Such statutes seek to allow plaintiffs who might not otherwise have personal standing to sue for the enforcement of a statute. The plaintiff in effect becomes a private attorney general, vindicating the public interest. Congress routinely included such statutory authorizations for private lawsuits against the government as a way to insure accountability in executive agencies. *See, e.g.,* the Clean Water Act, 33 U.S.C. § 1365(e); the Clean Air Act, 42 U.S.C. § 7604; and the Safe Drinking Water Act of 1974, 42 U.S.C. § 300j-8. Are such suits properly considered individual suits, since the individual has a statutory basis for the suit, or should they be characterized as impermissible suits attempting to grant citizen standing?

In *Lujan v. Defenders of Wildlife* (1992), the Court addressed whether Congress could confer citizen standing for challenges to executive enforcement of the Endangered Species

Act (ESA). The Court ruled that Congress did not have the power to confer standing and declared the statute unconstitutional:

> The Court of Appeals found that respondents had standing for an additional reason: because they had suffered a "procedural injury." The so-called "citizen-suit" provision of the ESA provides, in pertinent part, that "any person may commence a civil suit on his own behalf (A) to enjoin any person, including the United States and any other governmental instrumentality or agency ... who is alleged to be in violation of any provision of this chapter." 16 U.S.C. § 1540(g).... To understand the remarkable nature of this holding one must be clear about what it does not rest upon: This is not a case where plaintiffs are seeking to enforce a procedural requirement the disregard of which could impair a separate concrete interest of theirs (e.g., the procedural requirement for a hearing prior to denial of their license application, or the procedural requirement for an environmental impact statement before a federal facility is constructed next door to them). Nor is it simply a case where concrete injury has been suffered by many persons, as in mass fraud or mass tort situations. Nor, finally, is it the unusual case in which Congress has created a concrete private interest in the outcome of a suit against a private party for the government's benefit, by providing a cash bounty for the victorious plaintiff. Rather, the court held that the injury-in-fact requirement had been satisfied by congressional conferral upon all persons of an abstract, self-contained, non-instrumental "right" to have the Executive observe the procedures required by law. We reject this view.
>
> We have consistently held that a plaintiff raising only a generally available grievance about government — claiming only harm to his and every citizen's interest in proper application of the Constitution and laws, and seeking relief that no more directly and tangibly benefits him than it does the public at large — does not state an Article III case or controversy....
>
> To permit Congress to convert the undifferentiated public interest in executive officers' compliance with the law into an "individual right" vindicable in the courts is to permit Congress to transfer from the President to the courts the Chief Executive's most important constitutional duty, to "take Care that the Laws be faithfully executed," Art. II, § 3. It would enable the courts, with the permission of Congress, "to assume a position of authority over the governmental acts of another and co-equal department," *Massachusetts v. Mellon* (1923), and to become "virtually continuing monitors of the wisdom and soundness of Executive action." *Laird v. Tatum* (1972). We have always rejected that vision of our role....

Even in those cases where the Court is willing to recognize that a statute confers personal — rather than citizen — standing, a plaintiff must show that he is within the zone of interests that the statute intends to protect. While this is ordinarily not difficult — a victim of discrimination is within the zone of interests intended to be protected by an anti-discrimination statute — it can present a difficulty in a more generalized setting. In *Association of Data Processing Service Organizations, Inc. v. Camp* (1970), the Court held that a group engaged in data processing could challenge a decision by the Comptroller of Currency that national banks could make data processing services available to other banks and to bank customers. While the Comptroller had issued the regulation pursuant to statutes that regulated banking — not data processing — the Court held that competitors of banks were within the zone of interests covered by the statutes and could challenge regulations that could hurt their business.

In contrast, the Court denied standing to a postal employee union in *Air Courier Conference of America v. American Postal Workers Union, AFL-CIO* (1991). The Postal Service's monopoly over mail delivery is codified in a group of statutes known as the Private Express Statutes (PES). The Postal Service decided to suspend part of the monopoly regarding international remailing. The employee union sued, fearing loss of jobs. The Court concluded that the language and legislative history of the PES showed that Congress was concerned with maintaining adequate revenues for the Postal Service—not with protecting employees' jobs or furthering job opportunities. Since the employees were not within the zone of interest of the statute, their association could not gain standing to challenge the decision.

5. Ripeness and Mootness: When Did the Injury Occur?

Ripeness and mootness are aspects of justiciability that focus on the timing of the alleged harm. If an alleged injury is not sufficiently imminent to pose a concrete case, the Court is typically unwilling to expend its resources to resolve a matter that possibly might not occur. In *Abbott Laboratories v. Gardner* (1967), a case involving a challenge to administrative action, the Court discussed the policies behind ripeness:

> Without undertaking to survey the intricacies of the ripeness doctrine it is fair to say that its basic rationale is to prevent the courts, through avoidance of premature adjudication, from entangling themselves in abstract disagreements over administrative policies, and also to protect the agencies from judicial interference until an administrative decision has been formalized and its effects felt in a concrete way by the challenging parties. The problem is best seen in a twofold aspect, requiring us to evaluate both the fitness of the issues for judicial decision and the hardship to the parties of withholding court consideration.

The Court denied the plaintiff standing for an injunctive claim in *City of Los Angeles v. Lyons* because of the uncertainty that he would be choked again. While Lyons' injunctive claim was framed as a standing issue, it involved ripeness. While ripeness concerns seem to be implicit in this aspect of standing, the Court talks about ripeness as an independent factor regarding justiciablity. There seems to be no clear pattern as to when the Court will say it is dismissing a case for lack of standing (indefinite injury) as opposed to dismissing a case for lack of ripeness.

In *Poe v. Ullman* (1961), the Court dismissed a challenge to a Connecticut statute that criminalized the use of contraceptive devices, even for married couples, and criminalized giving medical advice concerning such devices. Justice Frankfurter, writing for a plurality, found that the plaintiffs could not demonstrate a realistic threat of prosecution and refused to accept the case:

> The Connecticut law prohibiting the use of contraceptives has been on the State's books since 1879.... During the more than three-quarters of a century since its enactment, a prosecution for its violation seems never to have been initiated, save in *State v. Nelson* (1940). The circumstances of that case, decided in 1940, only prove the abstract character of what is before us. There, a test case was brought to determine the constitutionality of the Act as applied against two doctors and a nurse who had allegedly disseminated contraceptive information. After the Supreme Court of Errors sustained the legislation on appeal from a demurrer to the information, the State moved to dismiss the information. Neither counsel nor our own researchers have discovered any other attempt to enforce

the prohibition of distribution or use of contraceptive devices by criminal process. The unreality of these law suits is illumined by another circumstance. We were advised by counsel for appellants that contraceptives are commonly and notoriously sold in Connecticut drug stores....

The best teaching of this Court's experience admonishes us not to entertain constitutional questions in advance of the strictest necessity.... The various doctrines of "standing," "ripeness," and "mootness," which this Court has evolved ... are but several manifestations—each having its own "varied application"—of the primary conception that federal judicial power is to be exercised to strike down legislation, whether state or federal, only at the instance of one who is himself immediately harmed, or immediately threatened with harm, by the challenged action...."This court can have no right to pronounce an abstract opinion upon the constitutionality of a State law. Such law must be brought into actual or threatened operation upon rights properly falling under judicial cognizance, or a remedy is not to be had here." ... "The party who invokes the power (to annul legislation on grounds of its unconstitutionality) must be able to show not only that the statute is invalid, but that he has sustained or is immediately in danger of sustaining some direct injury as the result of its enforcement...." ...

[W]ith due regard to Dr. Buxton's standing as a physician and to his personal sensitiveness, we cannot accept, as the basis of constitutional adjudication, other than as chimerical the fear of enforcement of provisions that have during so many years gone uniformly and without exception unenforced.

Justiciability is of course not a legal concept with a fixed content or susceptible of scientific verification. Its utilization is the resultant of many subtle pressures, including the appropriateness of the issues for decision by this Court and the actual hardship to the litigants of denying them the relief sought. Both these factors justify withholding adjudication of the constitutional issue raised under the circumstances and in the manner in which they are now before the Court.

The Connecticut statute was eventually successfully challenged in *Griswold v. Connecticut* (1965) following a doctor's arrest.

One need not wait for an arrest. A claim will be considered ripe if there is evidence that an arrest is reasonably probable. In *Steffel v. Thompson* (1974), the Court found a challenge to a state trespass law to be justiciable even though the plaintiff had not been arrested. The Court held that

petitioner has alleged threats of prosecution that cannot be characterized as "imaginary or speculative." ... He has been twice warned to stop handbilling that he claims is constitutionally protected and has been told by the police that if he again handbills at the shopping center and disobeys a warning to stop he will likely be prosecuted. The prosecution of petitioner's handbilling companion is ample demonstration that petitioner's concern with arrest has not been "chimerical," *Poe v. Ullman* (1961). In these circumstances, it is not necessary that petitioner first expose himself to actual arrest or prosecution to be entitled to challenge a statute that he claims deters the exercise of his constitutional rights.

Plaintiffs who seek a federal forum to enjoin allegedly unconstitutional state statutes must walk a fine line. If the threat of arrest is not considered ripe, the case will be dismissed. However, if the individual is in fact arrested, the federal court will refuse to enjoin the state prosecution in order to consider the constitutionality of the state law at issue in the arrest. See *Younger v. Harris* (1971). The only way for a federal court to review the constitutionality of the state statute is on appeal to the United States Supreme Court (like in *Griswold v. Connecticut*) or on a subsequent petition for federal habeas corpus.

Consider the following hypothetical:

> A young man distributes leaflets criticizing a major corporation on the public sidewalk outside a shopping center that the corporation owns. A state statute provides that property owners may ban distribution of literature on public sidewalks immediately outside their premises. The young man is convicted, pays his fine, and then sues in federal court for a declaratory judgment, claiming that the statute violates his 1st and 14th Amendment rights. He also alleges that he wishes to distribute the literature, but has been told by the district attorney that he will be prosecuted if he does so. As a result, he alleges his right to free speech and press has been chilled.
>
> a. What case or controversy issue is raised?
> b. What authority bears on it?
> c. How would you apply the authority to the facts?
> d. How do you resolve the justiciability issue raised by the case?

Mootness represents the other end of the spectrum from ripeness. Courts will not expend their resources to decide a case if the case no longer needs to be resolved. Events often occur during the pendency of litigation that resolve the controversy. In *Craig v. Boren*, the consumer plaintiff turned 21 and could buy beer. In *Powell v. McCormack*, the 90th session of Congress concluded, ending the possibility of Adam Clayton Powell receiving injunctive relief. As with ripeness, mootness addresses the nature of the plaintiff's injury and could be the basis for a dismissal for lack of standing. However, as with ripeness, it is considered an independent issue regarding justiciability. Consider the impact of a pending graduation on the plaintiff's injury in the following case.

DeFunis v. Odegaard
416 U.S. 312 (1974)

Per Curiam: Burger (C.J.), Powell, Blackmun, Stewart, and Rehnquist. Dissenting: Brennan, Douglas, White, and Marshall.]

Per Curiam.

In 1971 the petitioner Marco DeFunis, Jr., applied for admission as a first-year student at the University of Washington Law School, a state-operated institution. The size of the incoming first-year class was to be limited to 150 persons, and the Law School received some 1,600 applications for these 150 places. DeFunis was eventually notified that he had been denied admission. He thereupon commenced this suit in a Washington trial court, contending that the procedures and criteria employed by the Law School Admissions Committee invidiously discriminated against him on account of his race in violation of the Equal Protection Clause of the 14th Amendment to the United States Constitution.

DeFunis brought the suit on behalf of himself alone, and not as the representative of any class, against the various respondents, who are officers, faculty members, and members of the Board of Regents of the University of Washington. He asked the trial court to issue a mandatory injunction commanding the respondents to admit him as a member of the first-year class entering in September 1971, on the ground that the Law School admissions policy had resulted in the unconstitutional denial of his application for admission. The trial court agreed with his claim and granted the requested relief. DeFunis was, accordingly, admitted to the Law School and began his legal studies there in the fall of 1971. On appeal, the Washington Supreme Court reversed the judgment of the trial court and held that the Law School admissions policy did not violate the Constitution. By this time DeFunis was in his second year at the Law School.

He then petitioned this Court for a writ of certiorari, and Mr. Justice Douglas, as Circuit Justice, stayed the judgment of the Washington Supreme Court pending the "final disposition of the case by this Court." By virtue of this stay, DeFunis has remained in law school, and was in the first term of his third and final year when this Court first considered his certiorari petition in the fall of 1973. Because of our concern that DeFunis' third-year standing in the Law School might have rendered this case moot, we requested the parties to brief the question of mootness before we acted on the petition. In response, both sides contended that the case was not moot. The respondents indicated that, if the decision of the Washington Supreme Court were permitted to stand, the petitioner could complete the term for which he was then enrolled but would have to apply to the faculty for permission to continue in the school before he could register for another term.

We granted the petition for certiorari on November 19, 1973. The case was in due course orally argued on February 26, 1974.

In response to questions raised from the bench during the oral argument, counsel for the petitioner has informed the Court that DeFunis has now registered "for his final quarter in law school." Counsel for the respondents have made clear that the Law School will not in any way seek to abrogate this registration. In light of DeFunis' recent registration for the last quarter of his final law school year, and the Law School's assurance that his registration is fully effective, the insistent question again arises whether this case is not moot, and to that question we now turn.

The starting point for analysis is the familiar proposition that "federal courts are without power to decide questions that cannot affect the rights of litigants in the case before them." The inability of the federal judiciary "to review moot cases derives from the requirement of Art. III of the Constitution under which the exercise of judicial power depends upon the existence of a case or controversy." ... Although as a matter of Washington state law it appears that this case would be saved from mootness by "the great public interest in the continuing issues raised by this appeal," the fact remains that under Art. III "(e)ven in cases arising in the state courts, the question of mootness is a federal one which a federal court must resolve before it assumes jurisdiction."

The respondents have represented that, without regard to the ultimate resolution of the issues in this case, DeFunis will remain a student in the Law School for the duration of any term in which he has already enrolled. Since he has now registered for his final term, it is evident that he will be given an opportunity to complete all academic and other requirements for graduation, and, if he does so, will receive his diploma regardless of any decision this Court might reach on the merits of this case. In short, all parties agree that DeFunis is now entitled to complete his legal studies at the University of Washington and to receive his degree from that institution. A determination by this Court of the legal issues tendered by the parties is no longer necessary to compel that result, and could not serve to prevent it. DeFunis did not cast his suit as a class action, and the only remedy he requested was an injunction commanding his admission to the Law School. He was not only accorded that remedy, but he now has also been irrevocably admitted to the final term of the final year of the Law School course. The controversy between the parties has thus clearly ceased to be "definite and concrete" and no longer "touch(es) the legal relations of parties having adverse legal interests."

It matters not that these circumstances partially stem from a policy decision on the part of the respondent Law School authorities. The respondents, through their counsel, the Attorney General of the State, have professionally represented that in no event will the status of DeFunis now be affected by any view this Court might express on the merits of this controversy. And it has been the settled practice of the Court, in contexts no less significant, fully to accept representations such as these as parameters for decision....

There is a line of decisions in this Court standing for the proposition that the "voluntary cessation of allegedly illegal conduct does not deprive the tribunal of power to hear and determine the case, i.e., does not make the case moot." *United States v. W.T. Grant Co.* (1953). These decisions and the doctrine they reflect would be quite relevant if the question of mootness here had arisen by reason of a unilateral change in the admissions procedures of the Law School. For it was the admissions procedures that were the target of this litigation, and a voluntary cessation of the admissions practices complained of could make this case moot only if it could be said with assurance that "there is no reasonable expectation that the wrong will be repeated." Otherwise, "(t)he defendant is free to return to his old ways" and this fact would be enough to prevent mootness because of the "public interest in having the legality of the practices settled." But mootness in the present case depends not at all upon a "voluntary cessation" of the admissions practices that were the subject of this litigation. It depends, instead, upon the simple fact that DeFunis is now in the final quarter of the final year of his course of study, and the settled and unchallenged policy of the Law School to permit him to complete the term for which he is now enrolled.

It might also be suggested that this case presents a question that is "capable of repetition, yet evading review," *Southern Pacific Terminal Co. v. ICC* (1911); *Roe v. Wade* (1973), and is thus amenable to federal adjudication even though it might otherwise be considered moot. But DeFunis will never again be required to run the gantlet of the Law School's admission process, and so the question is certainly not "capable of repetition" so far as he is concerned. Moreover, just because this particular case did not reach the Court until the eve of the petitioner's graduation from Law School, it hardly follows that the issue he raises will in the future evade review. If the admissions procedures of the Law School remain unchanged, there is no reason to suppose that a subsequent case attacking those procedures will not come with relative speed to this Court, now that the Supreme Court of Washington has spoken. This case, therefore, in no way presents the exceptional situation in which the *Southern Pacific Terminal* doctrine [of capable of repetition, yet evading review] might permit a departure from "(t)he usual rule in federal cases ... that an actual controversy must exist at stages of appellate or certiorari review, and not simply at the date the action is initiated." *Roe v. Wade.*

Because the petitioner will complete his law school studies at the end of the term for which he has now registered regardless of any decision this Court might reach on the merits of this litigation, we conclude that the Court cannot, consistently with the limitations of Art. III of the Constitution, consider the substantive constitutional issues tendered by the parties. Accordingly, the judgment of the Supreme Court of Washington is vacated, and the cause is remanded for such proceedings as by that court may be deemed appropriate.

It is so ordered.

Vacated and remanded.

Mr. Justice Douglas, dissenting. [Omitted.]

Mr. Justice Brennan, with whom Mr. Justice Douglas, Mr. Justice White, and Mr. Justice Marshall concur, dissenting.

I respectfully dissent. Many weeks of the school term remain, and petitioner may not receive his degree despite respondents' assurances that petitioner will be allowed to complete this term's schooling regardless of our decision. Any number of unexpected events—illness, economic necessity, even academic failure—might prevent his graduation at the end of the term. Were that misfortune to befall, and were petitioner required to register for yet another term, the prospect that he would again face the hurdle of the admissions policy is real, not fanciful; for respondents warn that "Mr. DeFunis would have to take some appropriate action to request continued admission for the remainder of his law school education, and some discretionary action by the University on such request would have to be taken." Respondents' Memorandum on the Question of Mootness 3–4. Thus, respondents' assurances have not dissipated the possibility that petitioner might once again have to run the gantlet of the University's allegedly unlawful admissions policy. The Court therefore proceeds on an erroneous premise in resting its mootness holding on a supposed inability to render any judgment that may affect one way or the other petitioner's completion of his law studies. For surely if we were to reverse the Washington Supreme Court, we could insure that, if for some reason petitioner did not graduate this spring, he would be entitled to re-enrollment at a later time on the same basis as others who have not faced the hurdle of the University's allegedly unlawful admissions policy.

In these circumstances, and because the University's position implies no concession that its admissions policy is unlawful, this controversy falls squarely within the Court's long line of decisions holding that the "(m)ere voluntary cessation of allegedly illegal conduct does not moot a case." *United States v. Concentrated Phosphate Export Assn.* (1968). Since respondents' voluntary representation to this Court is only that they will permit petitioner to complete this term's studies, respondents have not borne the "heavy burden" of demonstrating that there was not even a "mere possibility" that petitioner would once again be subject to the challenged admissions policy. On the contrary, respondents have positioned themselves so as to be "free to return to (their) old ways." ...

I can thus find no justification for the Court's straining to rid itself of this dispute. While we must be vigilant to require that litigants maintain a personal stake in the outcome of a controversy to assure that "the questions will be framed with the necessary specificity, that the issues will be contested with the necessity adverseness and that the litigation will be pursued with the necessary vigor to assure that the constitutional challenge will be made in a form traditionally thought to be capable of judicial resolution," *Flast v. Cohen* (1968), there is no want of an adversary contest in this case. Indeed, the Court concedes that, if petitioner has lost his stake in this controversy, he did so only when he registered for the spring term. But appellant took that action only after the case had been fully litigated in the state courts, briefs had been filed in this Court, and oral argument had been heard. The case is thus ripe for decision on a fully developed factual record with sharply defined and fully canvassed legal issues.

Moreover, in endeavoring to dispose of this case as moot, the Court clearly disserves the public interest. The constitutional issues which are avoided today concern vast numbers of people, organizations, and colleges and universities, as evidenced by the filing of twenty-six amicus curiae briefs. Few constitutional questions in recent history have stirred as much debate, and they will not disappear. They must inevitably return to the federal courts and ultimately again to this Court. Because avoidance of repetitious litigation serves the public interest, that inevitability counsels against mootness determinations, as here, not compelled by the record. Although the Court should, of course, avoid unnecessary decisions of constitutional questions, we should not transform principles of avoidance of constitutional decisions into devices for sidestepping resolution of difficult cases.

On what appears in this case, I would find that there is an extant controversy and decide the merits of the very important constitutional questions presented.

DeFunis: Notes

1. The Court eventually addressed the issue of affirmative action in higher education in *University of California Regents v. Bakke* (1978). The plaintiff in *Bakke* was denied admission to medical school twice before filing suit and, while he won in the lower court and obtained injunctive relief ordering his admission, the injunction had been stayed pending the University's appeal. Consequently, there were no issues regarding mootness.

2. While mootness would seem to be constitutionally based in the meaning of "case" or "controversy," the Court has created four prudential exceptions to the doctrine. First, a case will not be dismissed as moot if the circumstances of the case, for the individual plaintiff, are capable of repetition, yet the nature of the situation is so short-lived that one could never complete full judicial review. This exception is referred to as "capable of repetition, yet evading review." Examples include challenges to abortion statutes or challenges to court orders barring reporters from coverage of a trial.

   The second exception involves criminal cases where a defendant has completed his sentence, but his conviction continues to result in adverse collateral consequences. For example, in many states felons cannot vote or receive various types of licenses. Such a defendant would be able to continue to challenge his conviction.

   The third exception arises when a defendant voluntarily ceases the allegedly unlawful conduct, but is capable of resuming the conduct once the lawsuit is dismissed. An example would be a city dismissing a criminal charge against a defendant, but leaving the statute on the books.

   The final exception involves class actions. The Court will consider the claims of the class as a whole, rather than just the class representative. If the named plaintiff's claim becomes moot, the Court will continue to recognize the case as long as some class members' claims are not moot.

3. Consider the following hypothetical:

   > A state statute makes it a crime to distribute anonymous campaign literature. The plaintiff seeks a declaratory judgment that the statute is unconstitutional. He alleges that he intends to distribute anonymous handbills against his incumbent congressman. He further alleges that he will be prosecuted if he distributes the literature. The congressman dies before the election. Assume the plaintiff does not amend his complaint.

   a. What case or controversy issue is raised?

   b. What authority determines it? How do you apply the authority to the facts?

   c. What conclusion do you reach?

Chapter 5

The Role of the President

Contents

I.	The Scope of Executive Power	439
	Whitman v. American Trucking Associations, Inc.	440
	Youngstown Sheet & Tube Co. v. Sawyer	445
	Immigration and Naturalization Service v. Chadha	454
	Clinton v. City of New York	462
II.	The President as Commander-in-Chief	465
	The War Powers Resolution	471
III.	Appointments and the Separation of Powers	476
IV.	Executive Privilege: Judicial Immunities	479
	United States v. Nixon	479
	Nixon v. Fitzgerald	483
	Clinton v. Jones	497
	Note: The Aftermath of *Clinton v. Jones*	505

Chapter 5

The Role of the President

I. The Scope of Executive Power

The federal government is generally one of enumerated powers. Congress has those powers given it by Article I, and the judiciary has those powers given it by Article III. The President (and executive agencies) similarly has those powers bestowed by Article II. It is common wisdom that the legislature enacts statutes and that the executive branch implements and enforces them. However, the apparent simplicity of this description of the executive function dissolves into ambiguity when one tries to apply it to many real world situations.

The President can act pursuant to a direct grant of authority from Article II (e.g., appoint an ambassador) or act pursuant to a grant of authority from Congress. There is no controversy surrounding executive authority to enforce a law when Congress delegates a clear standard to the executive, by, for example, setting specific tax rates or criminalizing the interstate trafficking of specific drugs. However, often the congressional delegation to the executive branch is quite vague. In such a situation it is difficult to determine whether or not the executive branch is implementing the congressional standard or legislating its own. The *nondelegation doctrine* holds that Congress cannot delegate its authority to legislate to the executive. While modern courts agree that nondelegation is the proper rule in theory, there is disagreement over when it actually has occurred. Modern courts have been reluctant to find that impermissible delegation of legislative authority has occurred at all.

For example, many portions of the Clean Air Act dictate precisely what the Environmental Protection Agency (EPA) is supposed to do. 42 U.S.C. §7511(a)(1) sets out specific dates by which various areas must be in compliance with applicable ozone levels or face liability. 42 U.S.C. §7412(b)(1) lists over 150 different chemicals that Congress considers dangerous and orders the EPA to develop appropriate emission standards for each of them.

However, the criterion that is to be followed in developing the emission standards, 42 U.S.C. §7409(b)(1), is far from precise:

> National primary ambient air quality standards, prescribed under subsection (a) of this section shall be ambient air quality standards the attainment and maintenance of which in the judgment of the Administrator, based on such criteria and allowing an adequate margin of safety, are requisite to protect the public health....

Does such a standard impermissibly delegate legislative authority to the EPA?

Whitman v. American Trucking Associations, Inc. (2001) involved a challenge to standards set for ozone and particulate matter emissions by the EPA. The plaintiffs contended that the Clean Air Act required the EPA to consider implementation costs before it adopted an emission standard. They also argued that the statute impermissibly delegated legislative authority to the EPA. The portion of the opinion addressing the nondelegation doctrine is set out below.

Whitman v. American Trucking Associations, Inc.
531 U.S. 457 (2001)

[Majority: Scalia, Rehnquist (C.J.), Kennedy, Ginsburg, O'Connor, Thomas, Stevens, and Breyer. Concurring: Thomas. Concurring (in part): Stevens, Breyer, and Souter.

Justice Scalia delivered the opinion of the Court. . . .

I. Section 109(a) of the CAA [Clean Air Act], . . . requires the Administrator of the EPA to promulgate NAAQS [National Ambient Air Quality Standards] for each air pollutant for which "air quality criteria" have been issued. Once a NAAQS has been promulgated, the Administrator must review the standard (and the criteria on which it is based) "at five-year intervals" and make "such revisions . . . as may be appropriate." § 109(d)(1). These cases arose when, on July 18, 1997, the Administrator revised the NAAQS for particulate matter and ozone. . . . American Trucking Associations, Inc., . . . challenged the new standards in the Court of Appeals for the District of Columbia Circuit. . . .

The District of Columbia Circuit accepted some of the challenges and rejected others. It agreed . . . that § 109(b)(1) delegated legislative power to the Administrator in contravention of the United States Constitution, Art. I, § 1, because it found that the EPA had interpreted the statute to provide no "intelligible principle" to guide the agency's exercise of authority. The court thought, however, that the EPA could perhaps avoid the unconstitutional delegation by adopting a restrictive construction of § 109(b)(1), so instead of declaring the section unconstitutional the court remanded the NAAQS to the agency. (On this delegation point, Judge Tatel dissented, finding the statute constitutional as written.) On the second issue that the Court of Appeals addressed, it unanimously rejected respondents' argument that the court should depart from the rule of *Lead Industries Assn., Inc. v. EPA* (D.C. Cir. 1980), that the EPA may not consider the cost of implementing a NAAQS in setting the initial standard. . . .

The Administrator and the EPA petitioned this Court for review. . . . Respondents conditionally cross-petitioned for review. . . . We have now consolidated the cases for purposes of decision. . . .

III. Section 109(b)(1) of the CAA instructs the EPA to set "ambient air quality standards the attainment and maintenance of which in the judgment of the Administrator, based on [the] criteria [documents of § 108] and allowing an adequate margin of safety, are requisite to protect the public health." The Court of Appeals held that this section as interpreted by the Administrator did not provide an "intelligible principle" to guide the EPA's exercise of authority in setting NAAQS. "[The] EPA," it said, "lack[ed] any determinate criteria for drawing lines. It has failed to state intelligibly how much is too much." The court hence found that the EPA's interpretation (but not the statute itself) violated the nondelegation doctrine. We disagree.

In a delegation challenge, the constitutional question is whether the statute has delegated legislative power to the agency. Article I, § 1, of the Constitution vests "[a]ll legislative Powers herein granted . . . in a Congress of the United States." This text permits no delegation of those powers, *Loving v. United States* (1996) (Scalia, J., concurring in part and concurring in judgment), and so we repeatedly have said that when Congress confers decisionmaking authority upon agencies *Congress* must "lay down by legislative act an intelligible principle to which the person or body authorized to [act] is directed to conform." *J.W. Hampton, Jr., & Co. v. United States* (1928). We have never suggested that an agency can cure an unlawful delegation of legislative power by adopting in its discretion a limiting construction of the statute. Both *Fahey v. Mallonee* (1947), and *Lichter v. United States* (1948), mention agency regulations in the course of their nondelegation discussions, but *Lichter* did so because a subsequent Congress had incorporated the regulations into a revised version of the statute, and *Fahey* because the customary practices in the area, implicitly incorporated into the statute, were reflected in the regulations. The idea that an agency can cure an unconstitutionally standardless delegation of power by declining to exercise some of that power seems to us internally contradictory. The very choice of which portion of the power to exercise—that is to say, the prescription of the standard that Congress had omitted—would *itself* be an exercise of the forbidden legislative authority. Whether the statute delegates legislative power is a question for the courts, and an agency's voluntary self-denial has no bearing upon the answer.

We agree with the Solicitor General that the text of § 109(b)(1) of the CAA at a minimum requires that "[f]or a discrete set of pollutants and based on published air quality criteria that reflect the latest scientific knowledge, [the] EPA must establish uniform national standards at a level that is requisite to protect public health from the adverse effects of the pollutant in the ambient air." Requisite, in turn, "mean[s] sufficient, but not more than necessary." These limits on the EPA's discretion are strikingly similar to the ones we approved in *Touby v. United States* (1991), which permitted the Attorney General to designate a drug as a controlled substance for purposes of criminal drug enforcement if doing so was "'necessary to avoid an imminent hazard to the public safety.'" They also resemble the Occupational Safety and Health Act of 1970 provision requiring the agency to "'set the standard which most adequately assures, to the extent feasible, on the basis of the best available evidence, that no employee will suffer any impairment of health'"—which the Court upheld in *Industrial Union Dept., AFL-CIO v. American Petroleum Institute* (1980), and which even then-Justice Rehnquist, who alone in that case thought the statute violated the nondelegation doctrine (opinion concurring in judgment), would have upheld if, like the statute here, it did not permit economic costs to be considered.

The scope of discretion § 109(b)(1) allows is in fact well within the outer limits of our nondelegation precedents. In the history of the Court we have found the requisite "intelligible principle" lacking in only two statutes, one of which provided literally no guidance for the exercise of discretion, and the other of which conferred authority to regulate the entire economy on the basis of no more precise a standard than stimulating the economy by assuring "fair competition." See *Panama Refining Co. v. Ryan* (1935); *A.L.A. Schechter Poultry Corp. v. United States* (1935). We have, on the other hand, upheld the validity of § 11(b)(2) of the Public Utility Holding Company Act of 1935, 49 Stat. 821, which gave the Securities and Exchange Commission authority to modify the structure of holding company systems so as to ensure that they are not "unduly or unnecessarily complicate[d]" and do not "unfairly or inequitably distribute voting power among security holders." *American Power & Light Co. v. SEC* (1946). We have approved the wartime conferral of agency power to fix the prices of commodities at a level that "'will be generally fair and equitable and will effectuate the [in some respects conflicting] purposes of th[e] Act.'" *Yakus v. United States* (1944). And we have found an "intelligible principle" in various statutes authorizing regulation in the "public interest." See, *e.g., National Broadcasting Co. v. United States* (1943) (Federal Communications Commission's power to regulate airwaves); *New York Central Securities Corp. v. United States* (1932) (Interstate Commerce Commission's power to approve railroad consolidations). In short, we have "almost never felt qualified to second-guess Congress regarding the permissible degree of policy judgment that can be left to those executing or applying the law." *Mistretta v. United States* (1989) (Scalia, J., dissenting).

It is true enough that the degree of agency discretion that is acceptable varies according to the scope of the power congressionally conferred. See *Loving v. United States* (1967); *United States v. Mazurie* (1975). While Congress need not provide any direction to the EPA regarding the manner in which it is to define "country elevators," which are to be exempt from new-stationary-source regulations governing grain elevators, see 42 U.S.C. §7411(i), it must provide substantial guidance on setting air standards that affect the entire national economy. But even in sweeping regulatory schemes we have never demanded, as the Court of Appeals did here, that statutes provide a "determinate criterion" for saying "how much [of the regulated harm] is too much." In *Touby*, for example, we did not require the statute to decree how "imminent" was too imminent, or how "necessary" was necessary enough, or even—most relevant here—how "hazardous" was too hazardous. Similarly, the statute at issue in *Lichter* authorized agencies to recoup "excess profits" paid under wartime Government contracts, yet we did not insist that Congress specify how much profit was too much. It is therefore not conclusive for delegation purposes that, as respondents argue, ozone and particulate matter are "nonthreshold" pollutants that inflict a continuum of adverse health effects at any airborne concentration greater than zero, and hence require the EPA to make judgments of degree. "[A] certain degree of discretion, and thus of lawmaking, inheres in most executive or judicial action." *Mistretta v. United States* (Scalia, J., dissenting). Section 109(b)(1) of the CAA, which to repeat we interpret as requiring the EPA to set air quality standards at the level that is "requisite"—that is, not lower or higher than is necessary—to protect the public health with an adequate margin of safety, fits comfortably within the scope of discretion permitted by our precedent.

We therefore reverse the judgment of the Court of Appeals remanding for reinterpretation that would avoid a supposed delegation of legislative power. It will remain for the Court of Appeals—on the remand that we direct for other reasons—to dispose of any other preserved challenge to the NAAQS under the judicial-review provisions contained in 42 U.S.C. §7607(d)(9)....

IV.... To summarize our holdings in these unusually complex cases: (1) The EPA may not consider implementation costs in setting primary and secondary NAAQS under §109(b) of the CAA. 2) Section 109(b)(1) does not delegate legislative power to the EPA in contravention of Art. I, §1, of the Constitution. (3) The Court of Appeals had jurisdiction to review the EPA's interpretation of Part D of Title I of the CAA, relating to the implementation of the revised ozone NAAQS. (4) The EPA's interpretation of that Part is unreasonable.

The judgment of the Court of Appeals is affirmed in part and reversed in part, and the cases are remanded for proceedings consistent with this opinion.

It is so ordered.

Justice Thomas, concurring.

I agree with the majority that §109's directive to the agency is no less an "intelligible principle" than a host of other directives that we have approved. I also agree that the Court of Appeals' remand to the agency to make its own corrective interpretation does not accord with our understanding of the delegation issue. I write separately, however, to express my concern that there may nevertheless be a genuine constitutional problem with §109, a problem which the parties did not address.

The parties to these cases who briefed the constitutional issue wrangled over constitutional doctrine with barely a nod to the text of the Constitution. Although this Court since 1928 has treated the "intelligible principle" requirement as the only constitutional limit on congressional grants of power to administrative agencies, see *J.W. Hampton, Jr., & Co. v. United States* (1928), the Constitution does not speak of "intelligible principles." Rather, it speaks in much simpler terms: "*All* legislative Powers herein granted shall be vested in a Congress." U.S. Const., Art. 1, § 1 (emphasis added). I am not convinced that the intelligible principle doctrine serves to prevent all cessions of legislative power. I believe that there are cases in which the principle is intelligible and yet the significance of the delegated decision is simply too great for the decision to be called anything other than "legislative."

As it is, none of the parties to these cases has examined the text of the Constitution or asked us to reconsider our precedents on cessions of legislative power. On a future day, however, I would be willing to address the question whether our delegation jurisprudence has strayed too far from our Founders' understanding of separation of powers.

Justice Stevens, with whom Justice Souter joins, concurring in part and concurring in the judgment.

Section 109(b)(1) delegates to the Administrator of the Environmental Protection Agency (EPA) the authority to promulgate national ambient air quality standards (NAAQS). In Part III of its opinion, the Court convincingly explains why the Court of Appeals erred when it concluded that § 109 effected "an unconstitutional delegation of legislative power." *American Trucking Assns., Inc. v. EPA* (D.C. Cir. 1999) (*per curiam*). I wholeheartedly endorse the Court's result and endorse its explanation of its reasons, albeit with the following caveat.

The Court has two choices. We could choose to articulate our ultimate disposition of this issue by frankly acknowledging that the power delegated to the EPA is "legislative" but nevertheless conclude that the delegation is constitutional because adequately limited by the terms of the authorizing statute. Alternatively, we could pretend, as the Court does, that the authority delegated to the EPA is somehow not "legislative power." Despite the fact that there is language in our opinions that supports the Court's articulation of our holding, I am persuaded that it would be both wiser and more faithful to what we have actually done in delegation cases to admit that agency rulemaking authority is "legislative power."[1]

The proper characterization of governmental power should generally depend on the nature of the power, not on the identity of the person exercising it. See *Black's Law Dictionary* 899 (6th ed. 1990) (defining "legislation" as, *inter alia*, "[f]ormulation of rule[s] for the future"); 1 K. Davis & R. Pierce, *Administrative Law Treatise* § 2.3, p. 37 (3d ed. 1994) ("If legislative power means the power to make rules of conduct that bind everyone based on resolution of major policy issues, scores of agencies exercise legislative power routinely by promulgating what are candidly called 'legislative rules'"). If the NAAQS that the EPA promulgated had been prescribed by Congress, everyone would agree that those rules would be the product of an exercise of "legislative power." The same characterization is appropriate when an agency exercises rulemaking authority pursuant to a permissible delegation from Congress.

---

1. See *Mistretta v. United States* (1989) ("[O]ur jurisprudence has been driven by a practical understanding that in our increasingly complex society ... Congress simply cannot do its job absent an ability to delegate power ..."). See also *Loving v. United States* (1996) ("[The nondelegation] principle does not mean ... that only Congress can make a rule of prospective force"); 1 K. Davis & R. Pierce, *Administrative Law Treatise* § 2.6, p. 66 (3d ed. 1994) ("Except for two 1935 cases, the Court has never enforced its frequently announced prohibition on congressional delegation of legislative power").

My view is not only more faithful to normal English usage, but is also fully consistent with the text of the Constitution. In Article I, the Framers vested "All legislative Powers" in the Congress, Art. I, § 1, just as in Article II they vested the "executive Power" in the President, Art. II, § 1. Those provisions do not purport to limit the authority of either recipient of power to delegate authority to others. See *Bowsher v. Synar* (1986) (Stevens, J., concurring in judgment) ("Despite the statement in Article I of the Constitution that 'All legislative powers herein granted shall be vested in a Congress of the United States,' it is far from novel to acknowledge that independent agencies do indeed exercise legislative powers"); *INS v. Chadha* (1983) (White, J., dissenting) ("[L]egislative power can be exercised by independent agencies and Executive departments …"); 1 Davis & Pierce, *Administrative Law Treatise* § 2.6, 66 ("The Court was probably mistaken from the outset in interpreting Article I's grant of power to Congress as an implicit limit on Congress' authority to delegate legislative power"). Surely the authority granted to members of the Cabinet and federal law enforcement agents is properly characterized as "Executive" even though not exercised by the President. Cf. *Morrison v. Olson* (1988) (Scalia, J., dissenting) (arguing that the independent counsel exercised "executive power" unconstrained by the President).

It seems clear that an executive agency's exercise of rulemaking authority pursuant to a valid delegation from Congress is "legislative." As long as the delegation provides a sufficiently intelligible principle, there is nothing inherently unconstitutional about it. Accordingly, while I join Parts I, II, and IV of the Court's opinion, and agree with almost everything said in Part III, I would hold that when Congress enacted § 109, it effected a constitutional delegation of legislative power to the EPA.

Justice Breyer, concurring in part and concurring in the judgment. [Omitted.]

Youngstown Sheet & Tube Company v. Sawyer: Background and Questions

Article I, § 1 provides that: "all legislative Powers *herein granted* shall be vested in a Congress of the United States." [Emphasis added.] In contrast, Article II, § 1, cl.1, provides that: "the executive Power shall be vested in a President of the United States of America." Does this difference in language mean that there are executive powers not specified in the Constitution or may the President only execute powers specifically granted by Congress or by the Constitution? Article II later lists, in §§ 2 and 3, specific aspects of the executive power, including the power to serve as Commander-in-Chief, to negotiate treaties, to nominate judges and officers of the United States, etc. Does the listing of specific powers argue against the existence of implied executive powers, or should these be taken as the minimal powers available to the President? How does one resolve this question?

Whitman v. American Trucking Associations, Inc. (2001) involved executive conduct based on a vague delegation of legislative authority. *Youngstown Sheet & Tube Co. v. Sawyer* (1952) involved the President's assertion of executive power in a setting where there was no legislative delegation at all. The President also could not point to an enumerated executive power that explicitly authorized his action. He unsuccessfully relied on his power as Commander-in-Chief, his power to take care that the laws be faithfully executed, and the inherent authority provided by the vesting of the executive power in the President.

On April 8, 1952, Harry Truman ordered the federal government to seize control of American steel mills in an effort to avoid a strike that he believed would hinder the ability of the United States to prosecute the Korean War. Management and labor had failed to resolve the threatened strike after several months of negotiations over, among other issues, a proposed wage increase. On April 9, Truman sent a message to Congress inviting it to pass legislation that would either allow or prohibit the seizure. On April 21, he sent a letter to the President of the Senate, repeating his request. Congress never acted.

Management immediately filed suit to prevent the seizure because it feared that the government would give the workers the desired wage increase while in control, making it effectively impossible to rescind the increase when control returned to management. The seizure was declared illegal and the workers went on strike. The strike was settled through negotiations in July, 1952.

1. What does Truman contend are the possible sources of his power to seize the steel mills? Why are the Justices in the majority concerned about giving this power to the President?
2. What is Justice Black's position on the existence of implied executive powers? What do the other Justices say about the issue? Why does Vinson dissent?
3. Would it have made a difference if there had been a declaration of war regarding Korea?

Youngstown Sheet & Tube Co. v. Sawyer
343 U.S. 579 (1952)

[Majority: Black, Frankfurter, Douglas, Jackson, and Burton. Concurring: Frankfurter, Douglas, Jackson, Burton, and Clark. Dissenting: Vinson (C.J.), Reed, and Minton.]

Mr. Justice Black delivered the opinion of the Court.

We are asked to decide whether the President was acting within his constitutional power when he issued an order directing the Secretary of Commerce to take possession of and operate most of the Nation's steel mills. The mill owners argue that the President's order amounts to lawmaking, a legislative function which the Constitution has expressly confided to the Congress and not to the President. The Government's position is that the order was made on findings of the President that his action was necessary to avert a national catastrophe which would inevitably result from a stoppage of steel production, and that in meeting this grave emergency the President was acting within the aggregate of his constitutional powers as the Nation's Chief Executive and the Commander in Chief of the Armed Forces of the United States. The issue emerges here from the following series of events:

In the latter part of 1951, a dispute arose between the steel companies and their employees over terms and conditions that should be included in new collective bargaining agreements. Long-continued conferences failed to resolve the dispute. On December 18, 1951, the employees' representative, United Steelworkers of America, C.I.O., gave notice of an intention to strike when the existing bargaining agreements expired on December 31. The Federal Mediation and Conciliation Service then intervened in an effort to get labor and management to agree. This failing, the President on December 22, 1951, referred the dispute to the Federal Wage Stabilization Board to investigate and make recommendations for fair and equitable terms of settlement. This Board's report resulted in no settlement. On April 4, 1952, the Union gave notice of a nation-wide strike called to begin at 12:01 a.m. April 9. The indispensability of steel as a component of substantially all weapons and other war materials led the President to believe that the proposed work stoppage would immediately jeopardize our national defense and that governmental seizure of the steel mills was necessary in order to assure the continued availability of steel. Reciting these considerations for his action, the President, a few hours before the strike was to begin, issued Executive Order 10340.... The order directed the Secretary of Commerce to take possession of most of the steel mills and keep them running. The Secretary immediately issued his own possessory orders, calling upon the presidents of the various seized companies to serve as operating managers for the United States. They were directed to carry on their activities in accordance with regulations and directions of the Secretary. The next morning the President sent a message to Congress reporting his action. Twelve days later he sent a second message. Congress has taken no action.

Obeying the Secretary's orders under protest, the companies brought proceedings against him in the District Court. Their complaints charged that the seizure was not authorized by an act of Congress or by any constitutional provisions. The District Court was asked to declare the orders of the President and the Secretary invalid and to issue preliminary and permanent injunctions restraining their enforcement. [T]he United States asserted that a strike disrupting steel production for even a brief period would so endanger the well-being and safety of the Nation that the President had "inherent power" to do what he had done—power "supported by the Constitution, by historical precedent, and by court decisions." [T]he District Court on April 30 issued a preliminary injunction restraining the Secretary from "continuing the seizure and possession of the plant ... and from acting under the purported authority of Executive Order No. 10340." On the same day the Court of Appeals stayed the District Court's injunction. Deeming it best that the issues raised be promptly decided by this Court, we granted certiorari on May 3 and set the cause for argument on May 12....

II. The President's power, if any, to issue the order must stem either from an act of Congress or from the Constitution itself. There is no statute that expressly authorizes the President to take possession of property as he did here. Nor is there any act of Congress to which our attention has been directed from which such a power can fairly be implied....

Moreover, the use of the seizure technique to solve labor disputes in order to prevent work stoppages was not only unauthorized by any congressional enactment; prior to this controversy, Congress had refused to adopt that method of settling labor disputes. When the Taft-Hartley Act was under consideration in 1947, Congress rejected an amendment which would have authorized such governmental seizures in cases of emergency.... Instead, the plan sought to bring about settlements by use of the customary devices of mediation, conciliation, investigation by boards of inquiry, and public reports. In some instances temporary injunctions were authorized to provide cooling-off periods. All this failing, unions were left free to strike after a secret vote by employees as to whether they wished to accept their employers' final settlement offer.

It is clear that if the President had authority to issue the order he did, it must be found in some provision of the Constitution. And it is not claimed that express constitutional language grants this power to the President. The contention is that presidential power should be implied from the aggregate of his powers under the Constitution. Particular reliance is placed on provisions in Article II which say that "The executive Power shall be vested in a President ...;" that "he shall take Care that the Laws be faithfully executed;" and that he "shall be Commander in Chief of the Army and Navy of the United States."

The order cannot properly be sustained as an exercise of the President's military power as Commander in Chief of the Armed Forces. The Government attempts to do so by citing a number of cases upholding broad powers in military commanders engaged in day-to-day fighting in a theater of war. Such cases need not concern us here. Even though "theater of war" be an expanding concept, we cannot with faithfulness to our constitutional system hold that the Commander in Chief of the Armed Forces has the ultimate power as such to take possession of private property in order to keep labor disputes from stopping production. This is a job for the Nation's lawmakers, not for its military authorities.

Nor can the seizure order be sustained because of the several constitutional provisions that grant executive power to the President. In the framework of our Constitution, the President's power to see that the laws are faithfully executed refutes the idea that he is to be a lawmaker. The Constitution limits his functions in the lawmaking process to the recommending of laws he thinks wise and the vetoing of laws he thinks bad. And the Constitution is neither silent nor equivocal about who shall make laws which the President is to execute. The first section of the first article says that "All legislative Powers herein granted shall be vested in a Congress of the United States...." After granting many powers to the Congress, Article I goes on to provide that Congress may "make all Laws which shall be necessary and proper for carrying into Execution the foregoing Powers, and all other Powers vested by this Constitution in the Government of the United States, or in any Department or Officer thereof."

The President's order does not direct that a congressional policy be executed in a manner prescribed by Congress—it directs that a presidential policy be executed in a manner prescribed by the President. The preamble of the order itself, like that of many statutes, sets out reasons why the President believes certain policies should be adopted, proclaims these policies as rules of conduct to be followed, and again, like a statute, authorizes a government official to promulgate additional rules and regulations consistent with the policy proclaimed and needed to carry that policy into execution. The power of Congress to adopt such public policies as those proclaimed by the order is beyond question. It can authorize the taking of private property for public use. It can make laws regulating the relationships between employers and employees, prescribing rules designed to settle labor disputes, and fixing wages and working conditions in certain fields of our economy. The Constitution does not subject this lawmaking power of Congress to presidential or military supervision or control.

It is said that other Presidents without congressional authority have taken possession of private business enterprises in order to settle labor disputes. But even if this be true, Congress has not thereby lost its exclusive constitutional authority to make laws necessary and proper to carry out the powers vested by the Constitution "in the Government of the United States, or any Department or Officer thereof."

The Founders of this Nation entrusted the lawmaking power to the Congress alone in both good and bad times. It would do no good to recall the historical events, the fears of power and the hopes for freedom that lay behind their choice. Such a review would but confirm our holding that this seizure order cannot stand.

The judgment of the District Court is *Affirmed.*

Mr. Justice Frankfurter, concurring. [Omitted].

Mr. Justice Douglas, concurring.

There can be no doubt that the emergency which caused the President to seize these steel plants was one that bore heavily on the country. But the emergency did not create power; it merely marked an occasion when power should be exercised. And the fact that it was necessary that measures be taken to keep steel in production does not mean that the President, rather than the Congress, had the constitutional authority to act. The Congress, as well as the President, is trustee of the national welfare. The President can act more quickly than the Congress. The President with the armed services at his disposal can move with force as well as with speed. All executive power—from the reign of ancient kings to the rule of modern dictators—has the outward appearance of efficiency.

Legislative power, by contrast, is slower to exercise. There must be delay while the ponderous machinery of committees, hearings, and debates is put into motion. That takes time; and while the Congress slowly moves into action, the emergency may take its toll in wages, consumer goods, war production, the standard of living of the people, and perhaps even lives. Legislative action may indeed often be cumbersome, time-consuming, and apparently inefficient. But as Mr. Justice Brandeis stated in his dissent in *Myers v. United States* (1926):

> The doctrine of the separation of powers was adopted by the Convention of 1787, not to promote efficiency but to preclude the exercise of arbitrary power. The purpose was, not to avoid friction, but, by means of the inevitable friction incident to the distribution of the governmental powers among three departments, to save the people from autocracy....

The legislative nature of the action taken by the President seems to me to be clear. When the United States takes over an industrial plant to settle a labor controversy, it is condemning property. The seizure of the plant is a taking in the constitutional sense. *United States v. Pewee Coal Co.* (1951). A permanent taking would amount to the nationalization of the industry. A temporary taking falls short of that goal. But though the seizure is only for a week or a month, the condemnation is complete and the United States must pay compensation for the temporary possession. *United States v. General Motors Corp.* (1945); *United States v. Pewee Coal Co....*

The President has no power to raise revenues. That power is in the Congress by Article I, §8 of the Constitution. The President might seize and the Congress by subsequent action might ratify the seizure. But until and unless Congress acted, no condemnation would be lawful. The branch of government that has the power to pay compensation for a seizure is the only one able to authorize a seizure or make lawful one that the President has effected. That seems to me to be the necessary result of the condemnation provision in the 5th Amendment. It squares with the theory of checks and balances expounded by Mr. Justice Black in the opinion of the Court in which I join....

We pay a price for our system of checks and balances, for the distribution of power among the three branches of government. It is a price that today may seem exorbitant to many. Today a kindly President uses the seizure power to effect a wage increase and to keep the steel furnaces in production. Yet tomorrow another President might use the same power to prevent a wage increase, to curb trade-unionists, to regiment labor as oppressively as industry thinks it has been regimented by this seizure.

Mr. Justice Jackson, concurring in the judgment and opinion of the Court.

... The actual art of governing under our Constitution does not and cannot conform to judicial definitions of the power of any of its branches based on isolated clauses or even single Articles torn from context. While the Constitution diffuses power the better to secure liberty, it also contemplates that practice will integrate the dispersed powers into a workable government. It enjoins upon its branches separateness but interdependence, autonomy but reciprocity. Presidential powers are not fixed but fluctuate, depending upon their disjunction or conjunction with those of Congress. We may well begin by a somewhat over-simplified grouping of practical situations in which a President may doubt, or others may challenge, his powers, and by distinguishing roughly the legal consequences of this factor of relativity.

1. When the President acts pursuant to an express or implied authorization of Congress, his authority is at its maximum, for it includes all that he possesses in his own right plus all that Congress can delegate. In these circumstances, and in these only, may he be said (for what it may be worth) to personify the federal sovereignty. If his act is held unconstitutional under these circumstances, it usually means that the Federal Government as an undivided whole lacks power. A seizure executed by the President pursuant to an Act of Congress would be supported by the strongest of presumptions and the widest latitude of judicial interpretation, and the burden of persuasion would rest heavily upon any who might attack it.

2. When the President acts in absence of either a congressional grant or denial of authority, he can only rely upon his own independent powers, but there is a zone of twilight in which he and Congress may have concurrent authority, or in which its distribution is uncertain. Therefore, congressional inertia, indifference or quiescence may sometimes, at least as a practical matter, enable, if not invite, measures of independent presidential responsibility. In this area, any actual test of power is likely to depend on the imperatives of events and contemporary imponderables rather than on abstract theories of law.[1]

3. When the President takes measures incompatible with the expressed or implied will of Congress, his power is at its lowest ebb, for then he can rely only upon his own constitutional powers minus any constitutional powers of Congress over the matter. Courts can sustain exclusive presidential control in such a case only by disabling the Congress from acting upon the subject. Presidential claim to a power at once so conclusive and preclusive must be scrutinized with caution, for what is at stake is the equilibrium established by our constitutional system.

Into which of these classifications does this executive seizure of the steel industry fit? It is eliminated from the first by admission, for it is conceded that no congressional authorization exists for this seizure. That takes away also the support of the many precedents and declarations which were made in relation, and must be confined, to this category.

Can it then be defended under flexible tests available to the second category? It seems clearly eliminated from that class because Congress has not left seizure of private property an open field but has covered it by three statutory policies inconsistent with this seizure....

This leaves the current seizure to be justified only by the severe tests under the third grouping, where it can be supported only by any remainder of executive power after subtraction of such powers as Congress may have over the subject. In short, we can sustain the President only by holding that seizure of such strike-bound industries is within his domain and beyond control by Congress. Thus, this Court's first review of such seizures occurs under circumstances which leave presidential power most vulnerable to attack and in the least favorable of possible constitutional postures....

The Solicitor General seeks the power of seizure in three clauses of the Executive Article, the first reading, "The executive Power shall be vested in a President of the United States of America." Lest I be thought to exaggerate, I quote the interpretation which his brief puts upon it: "In our view, this clause constitutes a grant of all the executive pow-

---

1. Since the Constitution implies that the writ of habeas corpus may be suspended in certain circumstances but does not say by whom, President Lincoln asserted and maintained it as an executive function in the face of judicial challenge and doubt. *Ex parte Merryman* (C.C.D. Md. 1861); *Ex parte* (1866); see *Ex parte Bollman* (1807). Congress eventually ratified his action. Habeas Corpus Act of March 3, 1863, 12 Stat. 755....

ers of which the Government is capable." If that be true, it is difficult to see why the forefathers bothered to add several specific items, including some trifling ones....

The clause on which the Government next relies is that "The President shall be Commander in Chief of the Army and Navy of the United States...." These cryptic words have given rise to some of the most persistent controversies in our constitutional history. Of course, they imply something more than an empty title. But just what authority goes with the name has plagued presidential advisers who would not waive or narrow it by nonassertion yet cannot say where it begins or ends. It undoubtedly puts the Nation's armed forces under presidential command. Hence, this loose appellation is sometimes advanced as support for any presidential action, internal or external, involving use of force, the idea being that it vests power to do anything, anywhere, that can be done with an army or navy....

Assuming that we are in a war *de facto*, whether it is or is not a war *de jure*, does that empower the Commander in Chief to seize industries he thinks necessary to supply our army? The Constitution expressly places in Congress power "to raise and *support* Armies" and "to *provide* and *maintain* a Navy." (Emphasis supplied.) This certainly lays upon Congress primary responsibility for supplying the armed forces. Congress alone controls the raising of revenues and their appropriation and may determine in what manner and by what means they shall be spent for military and naval procurement. I suppose no one would doubt that Congress can take over war supply as a Government enterprise. On the other hand, if Congress sees fit to rely on free private enterprise collectively bargaining with free labor for support and maintenance of our armed forces, can the Executive, because of lawful disagreements incidental to that process, seize the facility for operation upon Government-imposed terms?...

What the power of command may include I do not try to envision, but I think it is not a military prerogative, without support of law, to seize persons or property because they are important or even essential for the military and naval establishment.

The third clause in which the Solicitor General finds seizure powers is that "he shall take Care that the Laws be faithfully executed...." That authority must be matched against words of the 5th Amendment that "No person shall be ... deprived of life, liberty or property, without due process of law...." One gives a governmental authority that reaches so far as there is law, the other gives a private right that authority shall go no farther. These signify about all there is of the principle that ours is a government of laws, not of men, and that we submit ourselves to rulers only if under rules.

The Solicitor General lastly grounds support of the seizure upon nebulous, inherent powers never expressly granted but said to have accrued to the office from the customs and claims of preceding administrations. The plea is for a resulting power to deal with a crisis or an emergency according to the necessities of the case, the unarticulated assumption being that necessity knows no law.

Loose and irresponsible use of adjectives colors all nonlegal and much legal discussion of presidential powers. "Inherent" powers, "implied" powers, "incidental" powers, "plenary" powers, "war" powers and "emergency" powers are used, often interchangeably and without fixed or ascertainable meanings.

The vagueness and generality of the clauses that set forth presidential powers afford a plausible basis for pressures within and without an administration for presidential action beyond that supported by those whose responsibility it is to defend his actions in court. The claim of inherent and unrestricted presidential powers has long been a persuasive dialectical weapon in political controversy. While it is not surprising that counsel should grasp support from such unadjudicated claims of power, a judge cannot accept self-serving press statements of the attorney for one of the interested parties as authority in answering a constitutional question, even if the advocate was himself. But prudence has counseled that actual reliance on such nebulous claims stop short of provoking a judicial test....

Germany, after the First World War, framed the Weimar Constitution, designed to secure her liberties in the Western tradition. However, the President of the Republic, without concurrence of the Reichstag, was empowered temporarily to suspend any or all individual rights if public safety and order were seriously disturbed or endangered. This proved a temptation to every government, whatever its shade of opinion, and in 13 years suspension of rights was invoked on more than 250 occasions. Finally, Hitler persuaded President Von Hindenberg to suspend all such rights, and they were never restored.

The French Republic provided for a very different kind of emergency government known as the "state of siege." It differed from the German emergency dictatorship, particularly in that emergency powers could not be assumed at will by the Executive but could only be granted as a parliamentary measure. And it did not, as in Germany, result in a suspension or abrogation of law but was a legal institution governed by special legal rules and terminable by parliamentary authority.

Great Britain also has fought both World Wars under a sort of temporary dictatorship created by legislation. As Parliament is not bound by written constitutional limitations, it established a crisis government simply by delegation to its Ministers of a larger measure than usual of its own unlimited power, which is exercised under its supervision by Ministers whom it may dismiss. This has been called the "high-water mark in the voluntary surrender of liberty," but, as Churchill put it, "Parliament stands custodian of these surrendered liberties, and its most sacred duty will be to restore them in their fullness when victory has crowned our exertions and our perseverance." Thus, parliamentary control made emergency powers compatible with freedom.

This contemporary foreign experience may be inconclusive as to the wisdom of lodging emergency powers somewhere in a modern government. But it suggests that emergency powers are consistent with free government only when their control is lodged elsewhere than in the Executive who exercises them. That is the safeguard that would be nullified by our adoption of the "'inherent powers' formula. Nothing in my experience convinces me that such risks are warranted by any real necessity, although such powers would, of course, be an executive convenience."...

Executive power has the advantage of concentration in a single head in whose choice the whole Nation has a part, making him the focus of public hopes and expectations. In drama, magnitude and finality his decisions so far overshadow any others that almost alone he fills the public eye and ear. No other personality in public life can begin to compete with him in access to the public mind through modern methods of communications. By his prestige as head of state and his influence upon public opinion he exerts a leverage upon those who are supposed to check and balance his power which often cancels their effectiveness....

The essence of our free Government is "leave to live by no man's leave, underneath the law"—to be governed by those impersonal forces which we call law. Our Government is fashioned to fulfill this concept so far as humanly possible. The Executive, except for recommendation and veto, has no legislative power. The executive action we have here originates in the individual will of the President and represents an exercise of authority without law. No one, perhaps not even the President, knows the limits of the power he may seek to exert in this instance and the parties affected cannot learn the limit of their rights. We do not know today what powers over labor or property would be claimed to flow from Government possession if we should legalize it, what rights to compensation would be claimed or recognized, or on what contingency it would end. With all its defects, delays and inconveniences, men have discovered no technique for long preserving free government except that the Executive be under the law, and that the law be made by parliamentary deliberations.

Such institutions may be destined to pass away. But it is the duty of the Court to be last, not first, to give them up.

Mr. Justice Burton, concurring in both the opinion and judgment of the Court. [Omitted.]

Mr. Justice Clark, concurring in the judgment of the Court.

... The limits of presidential power are obscure. However, Article II, no less than Article I, is part of "a constitution intended to endure for ages to come, and, consequently, to be adapted to the various *crises* of human affairs." Some of our Presidents, such as Lincoln, "felt that measures otherwise unconstitutional might become lawful by becoming indispensable to the preservation of the Constitution through the preservation of the nation."

Others, such as Theodore Roosevelt, thought the President to be capable, as a "steward" of the people, of exerting all power save that which is specifically prohibited by the Constitution or the Congress. In my view ... the Constitution does grant to the President extensive authority in times of grave and imperative national emergency. In fact, to my thinking, such a grant may well be necessary to the very existence of the Constitution itself. As Lincoln aptly said, "[is] it possible to lose the nation and yet preserve the Constitution?" In describing this authority I care not whether one calls it "residual," "inherent," "moral," "implied," "aggregate," "emergency," or otherwise. I am of the conviction that those who have had the gratifying experience of being the President's lawyer have used one or more of these adjectives only with the utmost of sincerity and the highest of purpose.

I conclude that where Congress has laid down specific procedures to deal with the type of crisis confronting the President, he must follow those procedures in meeting the crisis; but that in the absence of such action by Congress, the President's independent power to act depends upon the gravity of the situation confronting the nation. I cannot sustain the seizure in question because ... Congress had prescribed methods to be followed by the President in meeting the emergency at hand....

Mr. Chief Justice Vinson, with whom Mr. Justice Reed and Mr. Justice Minton join, dissenting.

The President of the United States directed the Secretary of Commerce to take temporary possession of the Nation's steel mills during the existing emergency because "a work stoppage would immediately jeopardize and imperil our national defense and the defense of those joined with us in resisting aggression, and would add to the continuing danger of our soldiers, sailors, and airmen engaged in combat in the field." The District Court ordered the mills returned to their private owners on the ground that the President's action was beyond his powers under the Constitution.

This Court affirms. Some members of the Court are of the view that the President is without power to act in time of crisis in the absence of express statutory authorization. Other members of the Court affirm on the basis of their reading of certain statutes. Because we cannot agree that affirmance is proper on any ground, and because of the transcending importance of the questions presented not only in this critical litigation but also to the powers of the President and of future Presidents to act in time of crisis, we are compelled to register this dissent.

I ... [Chief Justice Vinson argues that the President should have the power to seize the mills as an aspect of his authority to faithfully execute *other* statutes that regulate the economy.] The President has the duty to execute the foregoing legislative programs. Their successful execution depends upon continued production of steel and stabilized prices for steel....

[I]f the President has any power under the Constitution to meet a critical situation in the absence of express statutory authorization, there is no basis whatever for criticizing the exercise of such power in this case....

III. A review of executive action demonstrates that our Presidents have on many occasions exhibited the leadership contemplated by the Framers when they made the President Commander in Chief, and imposed upon him the trust to "take Care that the Laws be faithfully executed." With or without explicit statutory authorization, Presidents have at such times dealt with national emergencies by acting promptly and resolutely to enforce legislative programs, at least to save those programs until Congress could act. Congress and the courts have responded to such executive initiative with consistent approval....

[Chief Justice Vinson discusses instances of presidents asserting implied executive power throughout American history.] This ... cursory summary of executive leadership ... amply demonstrates that Presidents have taken prompt action to enforce the laws and protect the country whether or not Congress happened to provide in advance for the particular method of execution....

VI. The diversity of views expressed in the six opinions of the majority, the lack of reference to authoritative precedent, the repeated reliance upon prior dissenting opinions, the complete disregard of the uncontroverted facts showing the gravity of the emergency and the temporary nature of the taking all serve to demonstrate how far afield one must go to affirm the order of the District Court.

The broad executive power granted by Article II to an officer on duty 365 days a year cannot, it is said, be invoked to avert disaster. Instead, the President must confine himself to sending a message to Congress recommending action. Under this messenger-boy concept of the Office, the President cannot even act to preserve legislative programs from destruction so that Congress will have something left to act upon. There is no judicial finding that the executive action was unwarranted because there was in fact no basis for the President's finding of the existence of an emergency for, under this view, the gravity of the emergency and the immediacy of the threatened disaster are considered irrelevant as a matter of law.

Seizure of plaintiffs' property is not a pleasant undertaking. Similarly unpleasant to a free country are the draft which disrupts the home and military procurement which causes economic dislocation and compels adoption of price controls, wage stabilization and allocation of materials. The President informed Congress that even a temporary Government operation of plaintiffs' properties was "thoroughly distasteful" to him, but was necessary to prevent immediate paralysis of the mobilization program. Presidents have been in the past, and any man worthy of the Office should be in the future, free to take at least interim action necessary to execute legislative programs essential to survival of the Nation. A sturdy judiciary should not be swayed by the unpleasantness or unpopularity of necessary executive action, but must independently determine for itself whether the President was acting, as required by the Constitution, to "take Care that the Laws be faithfully executed."

As the District Judge stated, this is no time for "timorous" judicial action. But neither is this a time for timorous executive action. Faced with the duty of executing the defense programs which Congress had enacted and the disastrous effects that any stoppage in steel production would have on those programs, the President acted to preserve those programs by seizing the steel mills. There is no question that the possession was other than temporary in character and subject to congressional direction—either approving, disapproving or regulating the manner in which the mills were to be administered and returned to the owners. The President immediately informed Congress of his action and clearly stated his intention to abide by the legislative will. No basis for claims of arbitrary action, unlimited powers or dictatorial usurpation of congressional power appears from the facts of this case. On the contrary, judicial, legislative and executive precedents throughout our history demonstrate that in this case the President acted in full conformity with his duties under the Constitution. Accordingly, we would reverse the order of the District Court.

* * *

In *Youngstown Sheet & Tube Co. v. Sawyer* (1952), Justice Black emphasized the need for the executive to have an explicit constitutional or statutory basis to justify his conduct. The next two cases explore what Article II requires to create a valid statute. They also explore the question of whether or not there are limits on both Congress and the President should one branch attempt to modify rights granted by a valid statute. How are the issues involved in these cases related to the current non-enforcement of the nondelegation doctrine?

Immigration and Naturalization Service v. Chadha
462 U.S. 919 (1983)

[Majority: Burger (C.J.), Brennan, Marshall, Blackmun, Stevens, and O'Connor. Concurring: Powell. Dissenting: White and Rehnquist.]

Chief Justice Burger delivered the opinion of the Court.

[This case] presents a challenge to the constitutionality of the provision in §244(c)(2) of the Immigration and Nationality Act, authorizing one House of Congress, by resolution, to invalidate the decision of the Executive Branch, pursuant to authority delegated by Congress to the Attorney General of the United States, to allow a particular deportable alien to remain in the United States.

I. Chadha is an East Indian who was born in Kenya and holds a British passport. He was lawfully admitted to the United States in 1966 on a nonimmigrant student visa. His visa expired on June 30, 1972. On October 11, 1973, the District Director of the Immigration and Naturalization Service ordered Chadha to show cause why he should not be deported for having "remained in the United States for a longer time than permitted." Pursuant to §242(b) of the Immigration and Nationality Act (Act), a deportation hearing was held before an Immigration Judge on January 11, 1974. Chadha conceded that he was deportable for overstaying his visa and the hearing was adjourned to enable him to file an application for suspension of deportation under §244(a)(1) of the Act. Section 244(a)(1), at the time in question, provided:

As hereinafter prescribed in this section, the Attorney General may, in his discretion, suspend deportation and adjust the status to that of an alien lawfully admitted for permanent residence, in the case of an alien who applies to the Attorney General for suspension of deportation and—

Directive to Atty. General

(1) is deportable under any law of the United States except the provisions specified in paragraph (2) of this subsection; has been physically present in the United States for a continuous period of not less than seven years immediately preceding the date of such application, and proves that during all of such period he was and is a person of good moral character; and is a person whose deportation would, in the opinion of the Attorney General, result in extreme hardship to the alien or to his spouse, parent, or child, who is a citizen of the United States or an alien lawfully admitted for permanent residence.

After Chadha submitted his application for suspension of deportation, the deportation hearing was resumed on February 7, 1974. On the basis of evidence adduced at the hearing, affidavits submitted with the application, and the results of a character investigation conducted by the INS, the Immigration Judge, on June 25, 1974, ordered that Chadha's deportation be suspended. The Immigration Judge found that Chadha met the requirements of §244(a)(1): he had resided continuously in the United States for over seven years, was of good moral character, and would suffer "extreme hardship" if deported.

Pursuant to §244(c)(1) of the Act, the Immigration Judge suspended Chadha's deportation and a report of the suspension was transmitted to Congress. Section 244(c)(1) provides:

Upon application by any alien who is found by the Attorney General to meet the requirements of subsection (a) of this section the Attorney General may in his discretion suspend deportation of such alien. If the deportation of any alien is suspended under the provisions of this subsection, a complete and detailed statement of the facts and pertinent provisions of law in the case shall be reported to the Congress with the reasons for such suspension. Such reports shall be submitted on the first day of each calendar month in which Congress is in session.

Once the Attorney General's recommendation for suspension of Chadha's deportation was conveyed to Congress, Congress had the power under §244(c)(2) of the Act, to veto the Attorney General's determination that Chadha should not be deported. Section 244(c)(2) provides:

(2) In the case of an alien specified in paragraph (1) of subsection (a) of this subsection—

if during the session of the Congress at which a case is reported, or prior to the close of the session of the Congress next following the session at which a case is reported, either the Senate or the House of Representatives passes a resolution stating in substance that it does not favor the suspension of such deportation, the Attorney General shall thereupon deport such alien or authorize the alien's voluntary departure at his own expense under the order of deportation in the manner provided by law. If, within the time above specified, neither the Senate nor the House of Representatives shall pass such a resolution, the Attorney General shall cancel deportation proceedings.

The June 25, 1974, order of the Immigration Judge suspending Chadha's deportation remained outstanding as a valid order for a year and a half. For reasons not disclosed by the record, Congress did not exercise the veto authority reserved to it under §244(c)(2) until the first session of the 94th Congress. This was the final session in which Congress, pursuant to §244(c)(2), could act to veto the Attorney General's determination that Chadha should not be deported....

On December 12, 1975, Representative Eilberg, Chairman of the Judiciary Subcommittee on Immigration, Citizenship, and International Law, introduced a resolution opposing "the granting of permanent residence in the United States to [six] aliens," including Chadha. The resolution was referred to the House Committee on the Judiciary. On December 16, 1975, the resolution was discharged from further consideration by the House Committee on the Judiciary and submitted to the House of Representatives for a vote. The resolution had not been printed and was not made available to other Members of the House prior to or at the time it was voted on. So far as the record before us shows, the House consideration of the resolution was based on Representative Eilberg's statement from the floor that

> [i]t was the feeling of the committee, after reviewing 340 cases, that the aliens contained in the resolution [Chadha and five others] did not meet these statutory requirements, particularly as it relates to hardship; and it is the opinion of the committee that their deportation should not be suspended.

The resolution was passed without debate or recorded vote. Since the House action was pursuant to §244(c)(2), the resolution was not treated as an Art. I legislative act; it was not submitted to the Senate or presented to the President for his action.

After the House veto of the Attorney General's decision to allow Chadha to remain in the United States, the Immigration Judge reopened the deportation proceedings to implement the House order deporting Chadha. Chadha moved to terminate the proceedings on the ground that §244(c)(2) is unconstitutional. The Immigration Judge held that he had no authority to rule on the constitutional validity of §244(c)(2). On November 8, 1976, Chadha was ordered deported pursuant to the House action.

Chadha appealed the deportation order to the Board of Immigration Appeals, again contending that §244(c)(2) is unconstitutional. The Board held that it had "no power to declare unconstitutional an act of Congress" and Chadha's appeal was dismissed.

Pursuant to §106(a) of the Act, Chadha filed a petition for review of the deportation order in the United States Court of Appeals for the Ninth Circuit. The Immigration and Naturalization Service agreed with Chadha's position before the Court of Appeals and joined him in arguing that §244(c)(2) is unconstitutional. In light of the importance of the question, the Court of Appeals invited both the Senate and the House of Representatives to file briefs *amici curiae*.

[T]he Court of Appeals held that the House was without constitutional authority to order Chadha's deportation.... [W]e now affirm....

III-A. We turn now to the question whether action of one House of Congress under §244(c)(2) violates strictures of the Constitution. We begin, of course, with the presumption that the challenged statute is valid....

By the same token, the fact that a given law or procedure is efficient, convenient, and useful in facilitating functions of government, standing alone, will not save it if it is contrary to the Constitution. Convenience and efficiency are not the primary objectives—or the hallmarks—of democratic government and our inquiry is sharpened rather than blunted by the fact that congressional veto provisions are appearing with increasing frequency in statutes which delegate authority to executive and independent agencies:

> Since 1932, when the first veto provision was enacted into law, 295 congressional veto-type procedures have been inserted in 196 different statutes as follows: from 1932 to 1939, five statutes were affected; from 1940–49, nineteen statutes; between 1950–59, thirty-four statutes; and from 1960–69, forty-nine. From the year

1970 through 1975, at least one hundred sixty-three such provisions were included in eighty-nine laws. Abourezk, *The Congressional Veto: A Contemporary Response to Executive Encroachment on Legislative Prerogatives*, 52 Ind. L. Rev. 323, 324 (1977).

Justice White undertakes to make a case for the proposition that the one-House veto is a useful "political invention," and we need not challenge that assertion. We can even concede this utilitarian argument although the long-range political wisdom of this "invention" is arguable.... But policy arguments supporting even useful "political inventions" are subject to the demands of the Constitution which defines powers and, with respect to this subject, sets out just how those powers are to be exercised.

Explicit and unambiguous provisions of the Constitution prescribe and define the respective functions of the Congress and of the Executive in the legislative process. Since the precise terms of those familiar provisions are critical to the resolution of these cases, we set them out verbatim. Article I provides:

> All legislative Powers herein granted shall be vested in a Congress of the United States, which shall consist of a Senate *and* House of Representatives." Art. I, §1. (Emphasis added.)
>
> *Every* Bill which shall have passed the House of Representatives *and* the Senate, *shall,* before it becomes a law, be presented to the President of the United States...." Art. I, §7, cl. 2. (Emphasis added.)
>
> *Every* Order, Resolution, or Vote to which the Concurrence of the Senate and House of Representatives may be necessary (except on a question of Adjournment) *shall be* presented to the President of the United States; and before the Same shall take Effect, *shall be* approved by him, or being disapproved by him, *shall be* repassed by two thirds of the Senate and House of Representatives, according to the Rules and Limitations prescribed in the Case of a Bill. Art. I, §7, cl. 3. (Emphasis added.)

[T]he purposes underlying the Presentment Clauses, Art. I, §7, cls. 2, 3, and the bicameral requirement of Art. I, §1, and §7, cl. 2, guide our resolution of the important question presented in these cases. The very structure of the Articles delegating and separating powers under Arts. I, II, and III exemplify the concept of separation of powers, and we now turn to Art. I.

III-B. *The Presentment Clauses.* The records of the Constitutional Convention reveal that the requirement that all legislation be presented to the President before becoming law was uniformly accepted by the Framers. Presentment to the President and the Presidential veto were considered so imperative that the draftsmen took special pains to assure that these requirements could not be circumvented. During the final debate on Art. I, §7, cl. 2, James Madison expressed concern that it might easily be evaded by the simple expedient of calling a proposed law a "resolution" or "vote" rather than a "bill." 2 Farrand, *Records of the Federal Convention of 1787*, 301–02. As a consequence, Art. I, §7, cl. 3, was added. 2 Farrand 304–05.

The decision to provide the President with a limited and qualified power to nullify proposed legislation by veto was based on the profound conviction of the Framers that the powers conferred on Congress were the powers to be most carefully circumscribed. It is beyond doubt that lawmaking was a power to be shared by both Houses and the President....

The President's role in the lawmaking process also reflects the Framers' careful efforts to check whatever propensity a particular Congress might have to enact oppressive, improvident, or ill-considered measures.... [T]he Presentment Clauses serve the important purpose of assuring that a "national" perspective is grafted on the legislative process: ...

III-C. *Bicameralism.* The bicameral requirement of Art. I, §§ 1, 7, was of scarcely less concern to the Framers than was the Presidential veto and indeed the two concepts are interdependent. By providing that no law could take effect without the concurrence of the prescribed majority of the Members of both Houses, the Framers reemphasized their belief, already remarked upon in connection with the Presentment Clauses, that legislation should not be enacted unless it has been carefully and fully considered by the Nation's elected officials....

However familiar, it is useful to recall that apart from their fear that special interests could be favored at the expense of public needs, the Framers were also concerned, although not of one mind, over the apprehensions of the smaller states. Those states feared a commonality of interest among the larger states would work to their disadvantage; representatives of the larger states, on the other hand, were skeptical of a legislature that could pass laws favoring a minority of the people. It need hardly be repeated here that the Great Compromise, under which one House was viewed as representing the people and the other the states, allayed the fears of both the large and small states.

We see therefore that the Framers were acutely conscious that the bicameral requirement and the Presentment Clauses would serve essential constitutional functions. The President's participation in the legislative process was to protect the Executive Branch from Congress and to protect the whole people from improvident laws. The division of the Congress into two distinctive bodies assures that the legislative power would be exercised only after opportunity for full study and debate in separate settings. The President's unilateral veto power, in turn, was limited by the power of two-thirds of both Houses of Congress to overrule a veto thereby precluding final arbitrary action of one person. It emerges clearly that the prescription for legislative action in Art. I, §§ 1, 7, represents the Framers' decision that the legislative power of the Federal Government be exercised in accord with a single, finely wrought and exhaustively considered, procedure.

IV. The Constitution sought to divide the delegated powers of the new Federal Government into three defined categories, Legislative, Executive, and Judicial, to assure, as nearly as possible, that each branch of government would confine itself to its assigned responsibility. The hydraulic pressure inherent within each of the separate Branches to exceed the outer limits of its power, even to accomplish desirable objectives, must be resisted....

[One must first] establish that the challenged action under § 244(c)(2) is of the kind to which the procedural requirements of Art. I, § 7, apply. Not every action taken by either House is subject to the bicameralism and presentment requirements of Art. I. Whether actions taken by either House are, in law and fact, an exercise of legislative power depends not on their form but upon "whether they contain matter which is properly to be regarded as legislative in its character and effect." S. Rep. No. 1335, 54th Cong., 2d Sess., 8 (1897).

Examination of the action taken here by one House pursuant to § 244(c)(2) reveals that it was essentially legislative in purpose and effect. In purporting to exercise power defined in Art. I, § 8, cl. 4, to "establish an uniform Rule of Naturalization," the House took action that had the purpose and effect of altering the legal rights, duties, and relations of persons, including the Attorney General, Executive Branch officials and Chadha, all outside the Legislative Branch....

The legislative character of the one-House veto in these cases is confirmed by the character of the congressional action it supplants. Neither the House of Representatives nor the Senate contends that, absent the veto provision in § 244(c)(2), either of them, or both of them acting together, could effectively require the Attorney General to deport an alien once the Attorney General, in the exercise of legislatively delegated authority, had determined the alien should remain in the United States. Without the challenged provision in § 244(c)(2), this could have been achieved, if at all, only by legislation requiring deportation....

Finally, we see that when the Framers intended to authorize either House of Congress to act alone and outside of its prescribed bicameral legislative role, they narrowly and precisely defined the procedure for such action. There are four provisions in the Constitution, explicit and unambiguous, by which one House may act alone with the unreviewable force of law, not subject to the President's veto:

(a) The House of Representatives alone was given the power to initiate impeachments. Art. I, § 2, cl. 5;

(b) The Senate alone was given the power to conduct trials following impeachment on charges initiated by the House and to convict following trial. Art. I, § 3, cl. 6;

(c) The Senate alone was given final unreviewable power to approve or to disapprove Presidential appointments. Art. II, § 2, cl. 2;

(d) The Senate alone was given unreviewable power to ratify treaties negotiated by the President. Art. II, § 2, cl. 2.

Clearly, when the Draftsmen sought to confer special powers on one House, independent of the other House, or of the President, they did so in explicit, unambiguous terms. These carefully defined exceptions from presentment and bicameralism underscore the difference between the legislative functions of Congress and other unilateral but important and binding one-House acts provided for in the Constitution. These exceptions are narrow, explicit, and separately justified; none of them authorize the action challenged here. On the contrary, they provide further support for the conclusion that congressional authority is not to be implied and for the conclusion that the veto provided for in § 244(c)(2) is not authorized by the constitutional design of the powers of the Legislative Branch.

Since it is clear that the action by the House under § 244(c)(2) was not within any of the express constitutional exceptions authorizing one House to act alone, and equally clear that it was an exercise of legislative power, that action was subject to the standards prescribed in Art. I. The bicameral requirement, the Presentment Clauses, the President's veto, and Congress' power to override a veto were intended to erect enduring checks on each Branch and to protect the people from the improvident exercise of power by mandating certain prescribed steps....

The veto authorized by § 244(c)(2) doubtless has been in many respects a convenient shortcut; the "sharing" with the Executive by Congress of its authority over aliens in this manner is, on its face, an appealing compromise. In purely practical terms, it is obviously easier for action to be taken by one House without submission to the President; but it is crystal clear from the records of the Convention, contemporaneous writings and debates, that the Framers ranked other values higher than efficiency. The records of the Convention and debates in the States preceding ratification underscore the common desire to define and limit the exercise of the newly created federal powers affecting the states and the people. There is unmistakable expression of a determination that legislation by the national Congress be a step-by-step, deliberate and deliberative process....

V. We hold that the congressional veto provision in §244(c)(2) is severable from the Act and that it is unconstitutional. Accordingly, the judgment of the Court of Appeals is *Affirmed.*

Justice Powell, concurring in the judgment.

The Court's decision, based on the Presentment Clauses, Art. I, §7, cls. 2 and 3, apparently will invalidate every use of the legislative veto. The breadth of this holding gives one pause. Congress has included the veto in literally hundreds of statutes, dating back to the 1930's. Congress clearly views this procedure as essential to controlling the delegation of power to administrative agencies. One reasonably may disagree with Congress' assessment of the veto's utility, but the respect due its judgment as a coordinate branch of Government cautions that our holding should be no more extensive than necessary to decide these cases. In my view, the cases may be decided on a narrower ground. When Congress finds that a particular person does not satisfy the statutory criteria for permanent residence in this country it has assumed a judicial function in violation of the principle of separation of powers. Accordingly, I concur only in the judgment....

II. ... On its face, the House's action appears clearly adjudicatory. The House did not enact a general rule; rather it made its own determination that six specific persons did not comply with certain statutory criteria. It thus undertook the type of decision that traditionally has been left to other branches. Even if the House did not make a *de novo* determination, but simply reviewed the Immigration and Naturalization Service's findings, it still assumed a function ordinarily entrusted to the federal courts....

Justice White, dissenting.

Today the Court not only invalidates §244(c)(2) of the Immigration and Nationality Act, but also sounds the death knell for nearly 200 other statutory provisions in which Congress has reserved a "legislative veto."...

The prominence of the legislative veto mechanism in our contemporary political system and its importance to Congress can hardly be overstated. It has become a central means by which Congress secures the accountability of executive and independent agencies. Without the legislative veto, Congress is faced with a Hobson's choice: either to refrain from delegating the necessary authority, leaving itself with a hopeless task of writing laws with the requisite specificity to cover endless special circumstances across the entire policy landscape, or in the alternative, to abdicate its law-making function to the Executive Branch and independent agencies. To choose the former leaves major national problems unresolved; to opt for the latter risks unaccountable policymaking by those not elected to fill that role. Accordingly, over the past five decades, the legislative veto has been placed in nearly 200 statutes. The device is known in every field of governmental concern: reorganization, budgets, foreign affairs, war powers, and regulation of trade, safety, energy, the environment, and the economy.

I.... During the 1970's the legislative veto was important in resolving a series of major constitutional disputes between the President and Congress over claims of the President to broad impoundment, war, and national emergency powers. The key provision of the War Powers Resolution, 50 U.S.C. §1544(c), authorizes the termination by concurrent resolution of the use of armed forces in hostilities. A similar measure resolved the problem posed by Presidential claims of inherent power to impound appropriations. Congressional Budget and Impoundment Control Act of 1974, 31 U.S.C. §1403. In conference, a compromise was achieved under which permanent impoundments, termed "rescissions," would require approval through enactment of legislation. In contrast, temporary impoundments, or "deferrals," would become effective unless disapproved by one House. This compromise provided the President with flexibility, while preserving ultimate congressional control over the budget. Although the War Powers Resolution was enacted over President Nixon's veto, the Impoundment Control Act was enacted with the President's approval....

Even this brief review suffices to demonstrate that the legislative veto is more than "efficient, convenient, and useful." It is an important if not indispensable political invention that allows the President and Congress to resolve major constitutional and policy differences, assures the accountability of independent regulatory agencies, and preserves Congress' control over lawmaking. Perhaps there are other means of accommodation and accountability, but the increasing reliance of Congress upon the legislative veto suggests that the alternatives to which Congress must now turn are not entirely satisfactory.

The history of the legislative veto also makes clear that it has not been a sword with which Congress has struck out to aggrandize itself at the expense of the other branches— the concerns of Madison and Hamilton. Rather, the veto has been a means of defense, a reservation of ultimate authority necessary if Congress is to fulfill its designated role under Art. I as the Nation's lawmaker. While the President has often objected to particular legislative vetoes, generally those left in the hands of congressional Committees, the Executive has more often agreed to legislative review as the price for a broad delegation of authority. To be sure, the President may have preferred unrestricted power, but that could be precisely why Congress thought it essential to retain a check on the exercise of delegated authority....

III-B. ... The Court's holding today that all legislative-type action must be enacted through the lawmaking process ignores that legislative authority is routinely delegated to the Executive Branch, to the independent regulatory agencies, and to private individuals and groups.

"The rise of administrative bodies probably has been the most significant legal trend of the last century.... They have become a veritable fourth branch of the Government, which has deranged our three-branch legal theories...." *FTC v. Ruberoid Co.* (1952) (Jackson, J., dissenting).

This Court's decisions sanctioning such delegations make clear that Art. I does not require all action with the effect of legislation to be passed as a law....

If Congress may delegate lawmaking power to independent and Executive agencies, it is most difficult to understand Art. I as prohibiting Congress from also reserving a check on legislative power for itself. Absent the veto, the agencies receiving delegations of legislative or quasi-legislative power may issue regulations having the force of law without bicameral approval and without the President's signature. It is thus not apparent why the reservation of a veto over the exercise of that legislative power must be subject to a more exacting test. In both cases, it is enough that the initial statutory authorizations comply with the Art. I requirements....

If the effective functioning of a complex modern government requires the delegation of vast authority which, by virtue of its breadth, is legislative or "quasi-legislative" in character, I cannot accept that Art. I—which is, after all, the source of the nondelegation doctrine—should forbid Congress to qualify that grant with a legislative veto....

IV. ... I do not suggest that all legislative vetoes are necessarily consistent with separation-of-powers principles. A legislative check on an inherently executive function, for example, that of initiating prosecutions, poses an entirely different question. But the legislative veto device here—and in many other settings—is far from an instance of legislative tyranny over the Executive. It is a necessary check on the unavoidably expanding power of the agencies, both Executive and independent, as they engage in exercising authority delegated by Congress.

V. I regret that I am in disagreement with my colleagues on the fundamental questions that these cases present. But even more I regret the destructive scope of the Court's holding. It reflects a profoundly different conception of the Constitution than that held by the courts which sanctioned the modern administrative state. Today's decision strikes down in one fell swoop provisions in more laws enacted by Congress than the Court has cumulatively invalidated in its history. I fear it will now be more difficult "to insure that the fundamental policy decisions in our society will be made not by an appointed official but by the body immediately responsible to the people," *Arizona v. California* (1963) (Harlan, J., dissenting in part). I must dissent.

Justice Rehnquist, with whom Justice White joins, dissenting. [Omitted.]

Clinton v. City of New York: Background

In *Raines v. Byrd* (1997), the Court declined to consider the constitutionality of Congress' Line Item Veto Act, a statute that gave the president authority to "cancel in whole" certain provisions in an appropriation bill without vetoing the entire bill. The Court held that members of Congress did not have standing to challenge the constitutionality of the statute. Shortly thereafter, the President exercised his authority under the Act by canceling §4722(c) of the Balanced Budget Act of 1997, which provided New York with additional Medicaid funds and §968 of the Taxpayer Relief Act of 1997, which permitted the owners of certain food refiners and processors to defer recognition of capital gains if they sold their stock to eligible farmers' cooperatives. Various parties, including the City of New York, claiming they had been injured, filed separate actions against the President and other officials challenging the cancellations. The District Court determined that the plaintiffs had standing under Article III, and ruled that the Act's cancellation procedures violate the Presentment Clause, Art. I, §7, cl. 2. The Supreme Court expedited its review of the case.

Clinton v. City of New York
524 U.S. 417 (1998)

[Majority: Stevens, Rehnquist (C.J.), Kennedy, Souter, Thomas, and Ginsburg. Concurring: Kennedy. Concurring (in part) and dissenting (in part): Scalia and O'Connor. Dissenting: Breyer.]

Justice Stevens delivered the opinion of the Court....

We now hold that these appellees have standing to challenge the constitutionality of the Act and, reaching the merits, we agree that the cancellation procedures set forth in the Act violate the Presentment Clause, Art. I, §7, cl. 2, of the Constitution....

IV. The Line Item Veto Act gives the President the power to "cancel in whole" three types of provisions that have been signed into law: "(1) any dollar amount of discretionary budget authority; (2) any item of new direct spending; or (3) any limited tax benefit." 2 U.S.C. §691(a). It is undisputed that the New York case involves an "item of new direct spending" and that the Snake River case involves a "limited tax benefit" as those terms are defined in the Act. It is also undisputed that each of those provisions had been signed into law pursuant to Article I, §7, of the Constitution before it was canceled.

The Act requires the President to adhere to precise procedures whenever he exercises his cancellation authority. In identifying items for cancellation he must consider the legislative history, the purposes, and other relevant information about the items. See 2 U.S.C. §691(b). He must determine, with respect to each cancellation, that it will "(i) reduce the Federal budget deficit; (ii) not impair any essential Government functions; and (iii) not harm the national interest." §691(a)(A). Moreover, he must transmit a special message to Congress notifying it of each cancellation within five calendar days (excluding Sundays) after the enactment of the canceled provision. See §691(a)(B). It is undisputed that the President meticulously followed these procedures in these cases.

A cancellation takes effect upon receipt by Congress of the special message from the President. See §691b(a). If, however, a "disapproval bill" pertaining to a special message is enacted into law, the cancellations set forth in that message become "null and void." The Act sets forth a detailed expedited procedure for the consideration of a "disapproval bill," see §691d, but no such bill was passed for either of the cancellations involved in these cases. A majority vote of both Houses is sufficient to enact a disapproval bill. The Act does not grant the President the authority to cancel a disapproval bill, see §691(c), but he does, of course, retain his constitutional authority to veto such a bill.

The effect of a cancellation is plainly stated in §691e, which defines the principal terms used in the Act. With respect to both an item of new direct spending and a limited tax benefit, the cancellation prevents the item "from having legal force or effect." §§691e(4)(B)–(C). Thus, under the plain text of the statute, the two actions of the President that are challenged in these cases prevented one section of the Balanced Budget Act of 1997 and one section of the Taxpayer Relief Act of 1997 "from having legal force or effect." The remaining provisions of those statutes, with the exception of the second canceled item in the latter, continue to have the same force and effect as they had when signed into law.

In both legal and practical effect, the President has amended two Acts of Congress by repealing a portion of each. "[R]epeal of statutes, no less than enactment, must conform with Art. I." *INS v. Chadha* (1983)....

There are important differences between the President's "return" of a bill pursuant to Article I, §7, and the exercise of the President's cancellation authority pursuant to the Line Item Veto Act. The constitutional return takes place *before* the bill becomes law; the statutory cancellation occurs *after* the bill becomes law. The constitutional return is of the entire bill; the statutory cancellation is of only a part. Although the Constitution expressly authorizes the President to play a role in the process of enacting statutes, it is silent on the subject of unilateral Presidential action that either repeals or amends parts of duly enacted statutes.

There are powerful reasons for construing constitutional silence on this profoundly important issue as equivalent to an express prohibition. The procedures governing the enactment of statutes set forth in the text of Article I were the product of the great debates and compromises that produced the Constitution itself.... Our first President understood the text of the Presentment Clause as requiring that he either "approve all the parts of a Bill, or reject it in toto." What has emerged in these cases from the President's exercise of his statutory cancellation powers, however, are truncated versions of two bills that passed both Houses of Congress. They are not the product of the "finely wrought" procedure that the Framers designed....

[O]ur decision rests on the narrow ground that the procedures authorized by the Line Item Veto Act are not authorized by the Constitution. The Balanced Budget Act of 1997 is a 500-page document that became "Public Law 105-33" after three procedural steps were taken: (1) a bill containing its exact text was approved by a majority of the Members of the House of Representatives; (2) the Senate approved precisely the same text; and (3) that text was signed into law by the President. The Constitution explicitly requires that each of those three steps be taken before a bill may "become a Law." Art. I, §7. If one paragraph of that text had been omitted at any one of those three stages, Public Law 105-33 would not have been validly enacted. If the Line Item Veto Act were valid, it would authorize the President to create a different law—one whose text was not voted on by either House of Congress or presented to the President for signature. Something that might be known as "Public Law 105-33 as modified by the President" may or may not be desirable, but it is surely not a document that may "become a law" pursuant to the procedures designed by the Framers of Article I, §7, of the Constitution.

If there is to be a new procedure in which the President will play a different role in determining the final text of what may "become a law," such change must come not by legislation but through the amendment procedures set forth in Article V of the Constitution. Cf. *U.S. Term Limits, Inc. v. Thornton* (1995).

The judgment of the District Court is affirmed.

Justice Kennedy, concurring. [Omitted.]

Justice Scalia, with whom Justice O'Connor joins, and with whom Justice Breyer joins as to Part III, concurring in part and dissenting in part.

... [U]nlike the Court I find the President's cancellation of spending items to be entirely in accord with the Constitution....

III.... The Presentment Clause requires, in relevant part, that "[e]very Bill which shall have passed the House of Representatives and the Senate, shall, before it becomes a Law, be presented to the President of the United States; If he approve he shall sign it, but if not he shall return it" U.S. Const., Art. I, §7, cl. 2. There is no question that enactment of the Balanced Budget Act complied with these requirements: the House and Senate passed the bill, and the President signed it into law. It was only *after* the requirements of the Presentment Clause had been satisfied that the President exercised his authority under the Line Item Veto Act to cancel the spending item. Thus, the Court's problem with the Act is not that it authorizes the President to veto parts of a bill and sign others into law, but rather that it authorizes him to "cancel"—prevent from "having legal force or effect"—certain parts of duly enacted statutes.

Article I, §7 of the Constitution obviously prevents the President from canceling a law that Congress has not authorized him to cancel. Such action cannot possibly be considered part of his execution of the law, and if it is legislative action, as the Court observes, "'repeal of statutes, no less than enactment, must conform with Art. I.'" But that is not this case. It was certainly arguable, as an original matter, that Art. I, §7, also prevents the President from canceling a law which itself *authorizes* the President to cancel it. But as the Court acknowledges, that argument has long since been made and rejected. In 1809, Congress passed a law authorizing the President to cancel trade restrictions against Great Britain and France if either revoked edicts directed at the United States. Act of Mar. 1, 1809. Joseph Story regarded the conferral of that authority as entirely unremarkable in *The Orono* (C.C.D. Mass. 1812)....

Justice Breyer, with whom Justice O'Connor and Justice Scalia join as to Part III, dissenting.

I.... In my view the Line Item Veto Act does not violate any specific textual constitutional command, nor does it violate any implicit Separation of Powers principle. Consequently, I believe that the Act is constitutional....

III. The Court believes that the Act violates the literal text of the Constitution. A simple syllogism captures its basic reasoning:

> Major Premise: The Constitution sets forth an exclusive method for enacting, repealing, or amending laws.
>
> Minor Premise: The Act authorizes the President to "repea[l] or amen[d]" laws in a different way, namely by announcing a cancellation of a portion of a previously enacted law.
>
> Conclusion: The Act is inconsistent with the Constitution.

I find this syllogism unconvincing, however, because its Minor Premise is faulty. When the President "canceled" the two appropriation measures now before us, he did not *repeal* any law nor did he *amend* any law. He simply *followed* the law, leaving the statutes, as they are literally written, intact.

To understand why one cannot say, *literally speaking*, that the President has repealed or amended any law, imagine how the provisions of law before us might have been, but were not, written. Imagine that the canceled New York health care tax provision at issue here, had instead said the following:

> Section One. Taxes... that were collected by the State of New York from a health care provider before June 1, 1997, and for which a waiver of provisions [requiring payment] have been sought... are deemed to be permissible health care related taxes... *provided however that the President may prevent the just-mentioned provision from having legal force or effect if he determines x, y and z.* (Assume x, y and z to be the same determinations required by the Line Item Veto Act).

Whatever a person might say, or think, about the constitutionality of this imaginary law, there is one thing the English language would prevent one from saying. One could not say that a President who "prevent[s]" the deeming language from "having legal force or effect," see 2 U.S.C. §691e(4)(B), has either *repealed* or *amended* this particular hypothetical statute. Rather, the President has *followed* that law to the letter. He has exercised the power it explicitly delegates to him. He has executed the law, not repealed it.

It could make no significant difference to this linguistic point were the italicized proviso to appear, not as part of what I have called §1, but, instead, at the bottom of the statute page, say, referenced by an asterisk, with a statement that it applies to every spending provision in the Act next to which a similar asterisk appears. And that being so, it could make no difference if that proviso appeared, instead, in a different, earlier enacted law, along with legal language that makes it applicable to every future spending provision picked out according to a specified formula.

But, of course, this last mentioned possibility is this very case....

II. The President as Commander-in-Chief

In his first inaugural address Abraham Lincoln made an effort to reassure the South. He repeated a position he had taken many times before: "I have no purpose, directly or indirectly, to interfere with the institution of slavery in the States where it exists. I believe I have no lawful right to do so." He pointed out that the Republican Platform of 1860, while opposing the existence of slavery in the territories, had made a similar pledge. But the South seceded, and the war came. During the early part of the Civil War, Lincoln resisted calls to free the slaves.

Facing a Confederate invasion of Missouri, General John C. Fremont, issued a proclamation freeing slaves of persons who aided the rebellion. Lincoln countermanded the order, fearing that it would "alarm our Southern Union friends [and Unionist slaveholders and others in the border states like Kentucky], and turn them against us." In May of 1862, Lincoln revoked another general's order for emancipation, this one dealing with Georgia, Florida, and South Carolina. As the war dragged on, Lincoln reconsidered. Many Northerners had urged Lincoln to free the slaves at least in states in rebellion. Charles Sumner reminded him of the position taken by Congressman (and former President) John Quincy Adams. In response to Southern threats of secession over the slavery issue, Adams told Southern congressmen that the federal government lacked power to end slavery in the states. But, Adams said, if the South launched a civil war, a new power would come into existence—the war power—and that power would provide the legal basis to emancipate slaves of states in rebellion.

By early summer of 1862 Lincoln had drafted the Emancipation Proclamation and was only waiting for the appropriate moment—after a U.S. army victory—to announce it. Meanwhile, ever the politically astute leader, Lincoln famously said his goal was to save the Union and he would support any lawful means essential to that end—including freeing some, all, or none of the slaves. During this period, Lincoln also attempted, without much success to persuade border state politicians to support a plan for compensated emancipation.

In September of 1862, Lincoln issued his Preliminary Emancipation Proclamation. As of January 1, 1863 "all persons held as slaves within any state or designed part of a state, the people whereof shall then be in rebellion against the United States, shall be then, thenceforward, and forever free." On New Years day, 1863 Lincoln issued his Final Emancipation Proclamation, proclaiming freedom for slaves in accordance with his preliminary Proclamation. He acted as "President of the United States, by virtue of the power in me vested as Commander-in-Chief, of the Army and Navy of the United States in time of actual armed rebellion against authority and government of the United States, and as a fit and necessary war measure for suppressing said rebellion...." Even before this, Lincoln authorized and supported the use of black troops. He subsequently insisted that the blacks and former slaves who joined the Union army were essential to its success. He strongly supported and tirelessly lobbied for the adoption of the 13th Amendment, abolishing slavery throughout the nation, and became the first American president to receive a black man (Frederick Douglass) as a guest in the White House and to publicly share food with him at his summer residence, the soldier's home, near the outskirts of Washington, D.C.

During the Korean War, Chief Justice Vinson, dissenting, cited Lincoln to justify President Truman's attempt to seize the steel mills by relying on his powers as Commander-in-Chief. Presidents have relied on this power to justify a variety of conduct, even when there had not been a declaration of war. For example:

> Without declaration of war, President Lincoln took energetic action with the outbreak of the War Between the States. He summoned troops and paid them out of the Treasury without appropriation therefor. He proclaimed a naval block-

ade of the Confederacy and seized ships violating that blockade. Congress, far from denying the validity of these acts, gave them express approval. The most striking action of President Lincoln was the Emancipation Proclamation, issued in aid of the successful prosecution of the War Between the States, but wholly without statutory authority. *Youngstown Sheet & Tube Co. v. Sawyer* (1952) (Vinson, C.J., dissenting).

During the Civil War, Lincoln suspended habeas corpus. Franklin Roosevelt ordered the internment of Japanese-Americans living on the West coast following Pearl Harbor. However, in all of these instances, Congress quickly ratified the executive behavior, passing statutes which affirmed, at least in part, the executive conduct.

Should there be judicially-enforced limits on a president's use of the Article II war powers? Should questions about possible presidential overreaching be left to the political process for resolution? (Congress can arguably always limit funding for executive initiatives.) How significant should it be for a court whether or not Congress has declared war (which Congress has not done since 1941)?

In determining the proper authority of the executive and legislative branches regarding the use of armed force, consider the textual authority for each branch. Article 1, §8, states that Congress shall have Power:

> To declare War, grant Letters of Marque and Reprisal, and make Rules concerning Captures on Land and Water;
>
> To raise and support Armies, but no Appropriation of Money to that Use shall be for a longer Term than two Years;
>
> To provide and maintain a Navy;
>
> To make Rules for the Government and Regulation of the land and naval Forces;
>
> To provide for calling forth the Militia to execute the Laws of the Union, suppress Insurrections and repel Invasions; and
>
> To provide for organizing, arming, and disciplining, the Militia, and for governing such Part of them as may be employed in the Service of the United States, reserving to the States respectively, the Appointment of the Officers, and the Authority of training the Militia according to the discipline prescribed by Congress....
>
> Article II, §2, states that "The President shall be Commander in Chief of the Army and Navy of the United States, and of the Militia of the several States...."

The so-called "War On Terror" has brought the interplay among Congress, the President, and the Judiciary to the fore, as the George W. Bush administration consistently claimed authority as the "unitary executive" under the Constitution to implement military policies without congressional approval—or even in opposition to federal statutes or treaties—and argued that the courts should defer to such executive judgments. Proponents of a strong "unitary executive" theory contend that since national security is such a compelling interest and there is only *one* Commander-in-Chief, the President should be allowed to make decisions in this area independent of Article I or Article III input. The only check on presidential power in this area would be congressional power of the purse, impeachment, or constitutional amendment. *See, e.g., Symposium: Presidential Power in Historical Perspective: Reflections on Calabresi and Yoo's The Unitary Executive*, University of Pennsylvania Journal of Constitutional Law, February, 2010.

A controversial example of the implications of the unitary executive theory was the Bush administration's claim in the now famous "Bybee Memo" that it could define and then practice "torture" on terror suspects independently of congressional statutes or American treaty obligations. See, e.g., Jack Goldsmith, *The Terror Presidency: Law and Judgement Inside the Bush Administration* (2007).

As it related to detentions of alleged enemy combatants in this country or at the federal prison at Guantanamo Bay, Cuba, Bush administration claims of largely unreviewable power have been consistently rejected by the Supreme Court. In *Hamdi v. Rumsfeld* (2004), Justice O'Connor opined for a four person plurality (which would certainly have been joined by at least Justices Stevens and Ginsburg—who wrote separate opinions—on this point):

> We have long since made clear that a state of war is not a blank check for the President when it comes to the rights of the Nation's citizens. Whatever power the United States Constitution envisions for the Executive in its exchanges with other nations or with enemy organizations in times of conflict, it most assuredly envisions a role for all three branches when individual liberties are at stake. We have no reason to doubt that courts faced with these sensitive matters will pay proper heed both to the matters of national security that might arise in an individual case and to the constitutional limitations safeguarding essential liberties that remain vibrant even in times of security concerns.

In *Boumediene v. Bush* (2008), a majority of the Court again asserted the centrality of its institutional role in determining such controversial disputes:

> The Constitution grants Congress and the President the power to acquire, dispose of, and govern territory, not the power to decide when and where its terms apply. Even when the United States acts outside its borders, its powers are not "absolute and unlimited" but are subject "to such restrictions as are expressed in the Constitution." Abstaining from questions involving formal sovereignty and territorial governance is one thing. To hold the political branches have the power to switch the Constitution on or off at will is quite another.... [This contention] would permit a striking anomaly in our tripartite system of government, leading to a regime in which Congress and the President, not this Court, say "what the law is."

* * *

Little v. Barreme (1804) and *The Prize Cases* (1863)

Determining the scope of the President's war powers is not a problem of recent vintage. During the Revolutionary War, France and the United States signed a treaty of alliance. After the French Revolution, Great Britain and other European powers attacked France. The United States attempted to remain neutral and continued to trade with England, an act the Revolutionary French government saw as a breach of the 1778 Treaty of Alliance. France began to attack American ships trading with England and the United States retaliated by attacking French ships. By 1798, the two nations were involved in an undeclared naval war.

In response to this crisis, Congress passed the Non-Intercourse Act of February 1799, which prohibited American ships from sailing to French ports, and allowed for the confiscation of any cargo heading to a French port. The act did not authorize the confiscation of ships and cargoes *leaving* French ports. However, President John Adams issued an executive order directing the seizure of ships going either *to or from* France. *Little v. Barreme* arose when an American naval ship, acting pursuant to this presidential order, seized a ship coming *from* a French jurisdiction. The captain reasonably, but mistakenly, believed the ship to be American.

Under the prevailing law, a ship's captain was personally liable for damages resulting from an unlawful seizure of a vessel. The seized ship turned out to be a Danish ship. Still, the American captain would not have to pay the owner's damages if the seizure was based on probable cause and could be justified under American law. The contention of the owners of the Danish ship was that the American law passed by the Congress only provided for seizure of American ships sailing *to* France. The captain of the American ship that seized the Danish ship relied on Adams order directing the seizure of ships going either *to or from* France. If the presidential order was invalid, the seizure would be unlawful and could not be defended. This would be so because even an American ship could not be seized if the presidential order was invalid.

The case thus presents an early examination of the independent authority of the President, acting as Commander-in-Chief, to act in the context of seemingly inconsistent congressional legislation on the same topic. In *Little v. Barreme,* John Marshall invalidated the executive order of John Adams, the President who had appointed him to the bench. The Court held in relevant part:

> During the hostilities between the United States and France, an act for the suspension of all intercourse between the two nations was annually passed....
>
> The 5th section of this act authorizes the president of the United States, to instruct the commanders of armed vessels, "to stop and examine any ship or vessel of the United States on the high sea, which there may be reason to suspect to be engaged in any traffic or commerce contrary to the true tenor [of the act]; and if upon examination it should appear that such ship or vessel is *bound or sailing to* any port or place within the territory of the French republic or her dependencies" it is rendered lawful to seize such vessel, and send her into the United States for adjudication. (Emphasis added.)
>
> It is by no means clear that the president of the United States whose high duty it is to "take care that the laws be faithfully executed," and who is commander in chief of the armies and navies of the United States, might not, without any special authority for that purpose, in the then existing state of things, have empowered the officers commanding the armed vessels of the United States, to seize and send into port for adjudication, American vessels which were forfeited by being engaged in this illicit commerce. But when it is observed that ... the 5th section gives a special authority to seize on the high seas, and limits that authority to the seizure of vessels bound or sailing *to* a French port, the legislature seem to have prescribed that the manner in which this law shall be carried into execution ... [and to have] exclude[d] a seizure of any vessel not bound *to* a French port....
>
> [T]his act of congress appears to have received a different construction from the executive of the United States....
>
> A copy of this act was transmitted by the secretary of the navy, to the captains of the armed vessels, who were ordered to consider the 5th section as a part of their instructions. The same letter contained the following clause.
>
> "A proper discharge of the important duties enjoined on you, arising out of this act, will require the exercise of a sound and an impartial judgment. You are not only to do all that in you lies, *to prevent all intercourse, whether direct or circuitous, between the ports of the United States, and those of France or her depen-*

dencies, where the vessels are apparently as well as really American, and protected by American papers only, but you are to be vigilant that vessels or cargoes really American, but covered by Danish or other foreign papers, and bound *to or from* French ports, do not escape you." (Emphasis added.) ...

[However, in this situation] the instructions of the executive could not give a right [to the captain to seize a ship sailing *from* a French port]....

Employing reasoning that anticipates Justice Jackson's approach in *Youngstown,* Marshall held that the scope of the President's war powers as Commander-in-Chief is limited by a specific exercise of a proper congressional power. In contrast, a broad exercise of this power by Abraham Lincoln was upheld by the Court when Congress had subsequently ratified his conduct.

The Court revisited the scope of independent presidential authority as commander-in-chief in *The Prize Cases* (1863). This case involved four ships seized by the federal government at the very start of the Civil War. The case was the closest the Court came to reviewing the constitutionality of the Lincoln administration's prosecution of the War. On April 19, 1861, immediately after the attack on Fort Sumter, President Lincoln ordered a blockade of all Confederate ports. On April 27 he extended the blockage to Virginia and North Carolina when those states also joined the Confederacy. However, Congress did not enact a formal declaration of hostilities until July 13. On August 6, it passed another law retroactively confirming the President's power to institute the blockade. The four ships in this litigation were seized after Lincoln's proclamation of April 19, but before Congress acted on July 13.

The Court held in relevant part:

> Had the President a right to institute a blockade of ports in possession of persons in armed rebellion against the Government, on the principles of international law, as known and acknowledged among civilized States?...
>
> Whether the President in fulfilling his duties, as Commander-in-chief, in suppressing an insurrection, has met with such armed hostile resistance, and a civil war of such alarming proportions as will compel him to accord to them the character of belligerents, is a question to be decided by him, and this Court must be governed by the decisions and acts of the political department of the Government to which this power was entrusted. "He must determine what degree of force the crisis demands." The proclamation of blockade is itself official and conclusive evidence to the Court that a state of war existed which demanded and authorized a recourse to such a measure, under the circumstances peculiar to the case.
>
> If it were necessary to the technical existence of a war, that it should have a legislative sanction, we find it in almost every act passed at the extraordinary session of the Legislature of 1861, which was wholly employed in enacting laws to enable the Government to prosecute the war with vigor and efficiency. And finally, in 1861, we find Congress ... in anticipation of such astute objections, passing an act 'approving, legalizing, and making valid all the acts, proclamations, and orders of the President, &c., as if they had been issued and done under the previous express authority and direction of the Congress of the United States.' Without admitting that such an act was necessary under the circumstances, it is plain that if the President had in any manner assumed powers which it was necessary should have the authority or sanction of Congress ... this ratification has operated to perfectly cure the defect....

The objection made to this act of ratification, that it is ex post facto, and therefore unconstitutional and void, might possibly have some weight on the trial of an indictment in a criminal Court. But precedents from that source cannot be received as authoritative in a tribunal administering public and international law.

[W]e are of the opinion that the President had a right, jure belli, to institute a blockade of ports in possession of the States in rebellion, which neutrals are bound to regard.

* * *

The Vietnam "War" and the "War on Terror"

Congress and the President were in relative agreement regarding the prosecution of the First and Second World Wars. There was a formal declaration of war each time. The Vietnam era produced widespread debate about the wisdom and conduct of the war and the appropriate division of authority between the two branches. This debate has reemerged as a source of great public controversy since the invasion of Iraq. The George W. Bush administration's conduct of the "War on Terror" produced significant litigation as the federal courts struggled to define the proper roles of Congress and the President, as well as questions of individual liberty.

We first consider the War Powers Resolution. It was passed in 1973 as a result of congressional frustration over presidential conduct during the Vietnam War. The statute was passed over Richard Nixon's veto. Nixon considered it to be an unconstitutional intrusion into executive power.

As you read the Resolution, consider the following points:

1) What is the basis for Congress' assertion of power to pass § 1544(b)? What is the basis of President Nixon's argument that it is unconstitutional?

2) What significance, if any, does *INS v. Chadha* have to § 1544(c)?

3) Would a presidential challenge to the Resolution be justiciable? Would it present a political question?

The War Powers Resolution
50 U.S.C. §§ 1541–1548 (1973)

§ 1541. *Purpose and policy*

(a) *Congressional declaration*

It is the purpose of this chapter to fulfill the intent of the framers of the Constitution of the United States and insure that the collective judgment of both the Congress and the President will apply to the introduction of United States Armed Forces into hostilities, or into situations where imminent involvement in hostilities is clearly indicated by the circumstances, and to the continued use of such forces in hostilities or in such situations.

(b) *Congressional legislative power under necessary and proper clause*

Under article I, § 8, of the Constitution, it is specifically provided that the Congress shall have the power to make all laws necessary and proper for carrying into execution, not only its own powers but also all other powers vested by the Constitution in the Government of the United States, or in any department or officer thereof.

(c) *Presidential executive power as Commander-in-Chief; limitation*

The constitutional powers of the President as Commander in Chief to introduce United States Armed Forces into hostilities, or into situations where imminent involvement in hostilities is clearly indicated by the circumstances, are exercised only pursuant to (1) a declaration of war, (2) specific statutory authorization, or (3) a national emergency created by attack upon the United States, its territories or possessions, or its armed forces.

§ 1542. *Consultation; initial and regular consultations*

The President in every possible instance shall consult with Congress before introducing United States Armed Forces into hostilities or into situations where imminent involvement in hostilities is clearly indicated by the circumstances, and after every such introduction shall consult regularly with the Congress until United States Armed Forces are no longer engaged in hostilities or have been removed from such situations.

§ 1543. *Reporting requirement*

(a) *Written report; time of submission; circumstances necessitating submission; information reported*

In the absence of a declaration of war, in any case in which United States Armed Forces are introduced—

(1) into hostilities or into situations where imminent involvement in hostilities is clearly indicated by the circumstances;

(2) into the territory, airspace or waters of a foreign nation, while equipped for combat, except for deployments which relate solely to supply, replacement, repair, or training of such forces; or

(3) in numbers which substantially enlarge United States Armed Forces equipped for combat already located in a foreign nation;

the President shall submit within 48 hours to the Speaker of the House of Representatives and to the President pro tempore of the Senate a report, in writing, setting forth—

(A) the circumstances necessitating the introduction of United States Armed Forces;

(B) the constitutional and legislative authority under which such introduction took place; and

(C) the estimated scope and duration of the hostilities or involvement.

(b) *Other information reported*

The President shall provide such other information as the Congress may request in the fulfillment of its constitutional responsibilities with respect to committing the Nation to war and to the use of United States Armed Forces abroad.

(c) *Periodic reports; semiannual requirement*

[I]n no event shall he report to the Congress less often than once every six months.

§ 1544. *Congressional action* ...

(b) *Termination of use of United States Armed Forces; exceptions; extension period*

Within sixty calendar days after a report is submitted or is required to be submitted pursuant to § 1543(a)(1) of this title, whichever is earlier, the President shall terminate any use of United States Armed Forces with respect to which such report was submitted (or required to be submitted), unless the Congress (1) has declared war or has enacted a specific authorization for such use of United States Armed Forces, (2) has extended by law such sixty-day period, or (3) is physically unable to meet as a result of an armed attack upon the United States. Such sixty-day period shall be extended for not more than an additional thirty days if the President determines and certifies to the Congress in writing that unavoidable military necessity respecting the safety of United States Armed Forces requires the continued use of such armed forces in the course of bringing about a prompt removal of such forces.

(c) *Concurrent resolution for removal by President of United States Armed Forces*

Notwithstanding subsection (b) of this section, at any time that United States Armed Forces are engaged in hostilities outside the territory of the United States, its possessions and territories without a declaration of war or specific statutory authorization, such forces shall be removed by the President if the Congress so directs by concurrent resolution....

* * *

Prior to President Bush ordering an attack on Afghanistan following the attacks of September 11, 2001, Congress passed the following resolution, Public Law 107-40 (September 18, 2001):

Sec. 2. AUTHORIZATION FOR USE OF UNITED STATES ARMED FORCES.

(a) IN GENERAL—That the President is authorized to use all necessary and appropriate force against those nations, organizations, or persons he determines planned, authorized, committed, or aided the terrorist attacks that occurred on September 11, 2001, or harbored such organizations or persons, in order to prevent any future acts of international terrorism against the United States by such nations, organizations or persons.

(b) War Powers Resolution Requirements—

(1) SPECIFIC STATUTORY AUTHORIZATION—Consistent with §8(a)(1) of the War Powers Resolution, the Congress declares that this section is intended to constitute specific statutory authorization within the meaning of §5(b) of the War Powers Resolution.

(2) APPLICABILITY OF OTHER REQUIREMENTS—Nothing in this resolution supercedes any requirement of the War Powers Resolution.

Prior to President Bush ordering an attack on Iraq in 2002, Congress passed another resolution, Public Law 107-243 (October 16, 2002). It included, in part, the following:

Joint Resolution to Authorize the Use of United States Armed Forces Against Iraq

... Whereas after the liberation of Kuwait in 1991, Iraq entered into a United Nations sponsored cease-fire agreement pursuant to which Iraq unequivocally agreed, among other things, to eliminate its nuclear, biological, and chemical weapons programs and the means to deliver and develop them, and to end its support for international terrorism;

Whereas the efforts of international weapons inspectors, United States intelligence agencies, and Iraqi defectors led to the discovery that Iraq had large stockpiles of chemical weapons and a large scale biological weapons program, and that Iraq had an advanced nuclear weapons development program that was much closer to producing a nuclear weapon than intelligence reporting had previously indicated....

Whereas Iraq both poses a continuing threat to the national security of the United States and international peace and security in the Persian Gulf region and remains in material and unacceptable breach of its international obligations by, among other things, continuing to possess and develop a significant chemical and biological weapons capability, actively seeking a nuclear weapons capability, and supporting and harboring terrorist organizations....

Whereas members of al Qaida, an organization bearing responsibility for attacks on the United States, its citizens, and interests, including the attacks that occurred on September 11, 2001, are known to be in Iraq;

Whereas Iraq continues to aid and harbor other international terrorist organizations, including organizations that threaten the lives and safety of American citizens;

Whereas the attacks on the United States of September 11, 2001 underscored the gravity of the threat posed by the acquisition of weapons of mass destruction by international terrorist organizations;

Whereas Iraq's demonstrated capability and willingness to use weapons of mass destruction, the risk that the current Iraqi regime will either employ those weapons to launch a surprise attack against the United States or its Armed Forces or provide them to international terrorists who would do so, and the extreme magnitude of harm that would result to the United States and its citizens from such an attack, combine to justify action by the United States to defend itself....

Whereas the United States is determined to prosecute the war on terrorism and Iraq's ongoing support for international terrorist groups combined with its development of weapons of mass destruction in direct violation of its obligations under the 1991 cease-fire and other United Nations Security Council resolutions make clear that it is in the national security interests of the United States and in furtherance of the war on terrorism that all relevant United Nations Security Council resolutions be enforced, including through the use of force if necessary....

Whereas the President and Congress are determined to continue to take all appropriate actions against international terrorists and terrorist organizations, including those nations, organizations or persons who planned, authorized, committed or aided the terrorist attacks that occurred on September 11, 2001, or harbored such persons or organizations....

Now, therefore, be it resolved by the Senate and House of Representatives of the United States of America in Congress assembled,

SEC. 1. SHORT TITLE.

This joint resolution may be cited as the "Authorization for the Use of Military Force Against Iraq"....

SEC. 3. AUTHORIZATION FOR USE OF UNITED STATES ARMED FORCES.

(a) AUTHORIZATION. The President is authorized to use the Armed Forces of the United States as he determines to be necessary and appropriate in order to

(1) defend the national security of the United States against the continuing threat posed by Iraq; and

(2) enforce all relevant United Nations Security Council Resolutions regarding Iraq.

(b) PRESIDENTIAL DETERMINATION. In connection with the exercise of the authority granted in subsection (a) to use force the President shall, prior to such exercise or as soon there after as may be feasible, but no later than 48 hours after exercising such authority, make available to the Speaker of the House of Representatives and the President pro tempore of the Senate his determination that

> (1) reliance by the United States on further diplomatic or other peaceful means alone either (A) will not adequately protect the national security of the United States against the continuing threat posed by Iraq or (B) is not likely to lead to enforcement of all relevant United Nations Security Council resolutions regarding Iraq, and

> (2) acting pursuant to this resolution is consistent with the United States and other countries continuing to take the necessary actions against international terrorists and terrorist organizations, including those nations, organizations or persons who planned, authorized, committed or aided the terrorists attacks that occurred on September 11, 2001.

(c) WAR POWERS RESOLUTION REQUIREMENTS. [The Resolution included language similar to the Afghanistan AUMF regarding the continuing applicability of the War Powers Resolution.]

* * *

Following the invasion of Afghanistan, the George W. Bush administration sent captured enemy combatants that the military deemed particularly dangerous to a special prison at Guantanamo Bay, Cuba. The site was chosen because the location was on an American naval base that was under the de facto control of the United States but under the sovereign authority of Cuba.

A series of cases reached the Supreme Court as prisoners at Guantanamo filed habeas corpus petitions in federal court challenging the legitimacy of their arrests. These petitions were filed pursuant to the federal habeas statute, 18 U.S.C. §2241. A petition for habeas corpus does not ask a court for a full trial for the defendant, but requires the government to demonstrate to a neutral Article III fact-finder that there is reason to believe that the prisoner is in fact who the government contends he is and that there is evidence that indicates that the prisoner has committed the crimes for which he is charged. In *Johnson v. Eisentrager* (1950), the Court had rejected an attempt by noncitizens who were being held in Germany by United States forces after WWII to gain habeas corpus jurisdiction in federal court.

First, in *Rasul v. Bush* (2004), the Court held that the noncitizen petitioners had access to the jurisdiction of the federal courts pursuant to the terms of the habeas statute. Since Guantanamo was effectively under United States control, the Court held that *Johnson v. Eisentrager* did not control. The Court did not address the nature of the procedures that should be made available to the noncitizen petitioners.

Hamdi v. Rumsfeld (2004) was released the same day. *Hamdi* involved an American citizen who was being held indefinitely as an enemy combatant (and had neither been charged with violating any specific federal crimes or allowed access to counsel). Five members of the Court rejected Hamdi's argument that the Congressional Authorization for the Use of Military Force could not justify a program of indefinite detention and that the President acting alone had no such authority. However, a plurality of the Court held that Hamdi was entitled to minimal due process protections. Justices Scalia and Stevens held that he was entitled to constitutional protections provided by the Bill of Rights unless Congress acted to suspend the writ of habeas corpus, which it had not done. *See Chapter 9, section 3, infra.*

Following *Rasul*, a substantial number of habeas petitions were filed by or on behalf of Guantanamo detainees in the United States District Court for the District of Columbia. Congress responded by passing a statute to restrict the availability of habeas corpus. The *Detainee Treatment Act of 2005*, 28 U.S.C. §2241, purported to remove all existing federal court jurisdiction over claims brought by Guantanamo detainees, including habeas petitions.

This statute was passed while many cases were pending in the Supreme Court. In *Hamdan v. Rumsfeld* (2006), the Court ruled, as a matter of statutory interpretation, that the Act did not apply to such cases and proceeded to reach the merits of Hamdan's claim.

The President, citing the AUMF and his own Article II authority, had issued an order (*November 13 Order*) stating that those detainees who were to be prosecuted for war crimes (and not just detained for the duration of the war as enemy combatants) would be tried by military commission, as opposed to trial by court-martial or in the civilian criminal justice system. He subsequently issued *Military Commission Order No. 1*, which set out the procedures that would govern the trials. Among the procedures was the rule that defendants could be

> excluded from, and precluded from ever learning what evidence was presented during, any part of the proceeding that either the Appointing Authority or the presiding officer decides to "close." Grounds for such closure "include the protection of information classified or classifiable ...; information protected by law or rule from unauthorized disclosure; the physical safety of participants in Commission proceedings, including prospective witnesses; intelligence and law enforcement sources, methods, or activities; and other national security interests." § 6(B)(3).

The Bush administration did not seek any congressional legislation to ratify these policies.

In *Hamdan v. Rumsfeld* (2006), the Court invalidated the President's attempt to try alleged members of al Qaeda by military commission in part because his Executive Order conflicted with Congress' exercise of their war and treaty powers. Congress has the authority to "declare War ... and make Rules concerning Captures on Land and Water," Art. I, § 8, cl. 11, to "raise and support Armies," *id.*, cl. 12, to "define and punish ... Offences against the Law of Nations," *id.*, cl. 10, and "To make Rules for the Government and Regulation of the land and naval Forces," *id.*, cl. 14. Pursuant to these powers, Congress passed the *Uniform Code of Military Justice* (UCMJ), 10 U.S.C. § 801 et seq., in 1950. The UCMJ replaced earlier congressional Articles of War. The UCMJ governs all aspects of the military justice system. The Senate had also ratified various articles of the Geneva Conventions, binding the United States to certain standards of conduct when engaging in war. Because Congress had legislated in this area, the Court ruled that the President was not free to bypass the congressionally established military justice system.

Following *Hamdan*, the Bush administration finally sought legislation denying any statutory right to habeas corpus for the noncitizen detainees and implementing a framework for trial by Military Commission. In *Boumediene v. Bush* (2008), the Court confronted the question of whether the President and Congress, now acting in concert under the Military Commissions Act of 2006, 10 U.S.C s. 948a, could deny noncitizens, held under federal authority in territory under United States control, access to habeas corpus (or a functional equivalent). In a 5–4 decision, the Court struck down the statute. *See Chapter 9, section 3, infra*.

III. Appointments and the Separation of Powers

Article II, § 2, cl. 2 provides that the President

> shall nominate, and by and with the Advice and Consent of the Senate, shall appoint Ambassadors, other public Ministers and Consuls, Judges of the supreme

Court, and all other Officers of the United States, whose Appointments are not herein otherwise provided for, and which shall be established by Law: but the Congress may by Law vest the Appointment of such inferior Officers, as they think proper, in the President alone, in the Courts of Law, or in the Heads of Departments.

For the President to be able to set policy effectively, he needs to be able to appoint and dismiss the members of his Cabinet and the highest officials in the executive agencies. These "Officers of the United States" set and direct the implementation of the President's policy in the executive branch. However, in 1883 and continuing during the Progressive Era, reformers decided that total presidential control over employees of the executive branch had led to patronage abuses. The Congress established a civil service system for "inferior officers" to limit patronage politics.

Tension between the branches is inherent in the appointment of officials. A leading case in this area is *Morrison v. Olson* (1988). There the Court upheld the Ethics in Government Act of 1978. The Act had been passed in response to the Watergate scandal of the Nixon presidency. It required, for possible crimes involving the executive branch, the appointment of a special prosecutor beyond the control of the president or his attorney general.

The Watergate scandal took its name from a burglary of the offices of the Democratic National Committee, which, it turned out, had been committed by persons employed by the committee to re-elect President Nixon. The initial investigation of the Watergate burglary had been carried out as a routine matter by a federal prosecutor. Like all federal prosecutors, he was ultimately supervised by the Attorney General, who held office at the pleasure of the President.

The prosecutor periodically reported on his investigation directly to President Nixon who, as it turned out, was helping to orchestrate a coverup of the crime. In response to demands from Congress, Elliot Richardson, Nixon's Attorney General, promised to appoint a special prosecutor and to grant the prosecutor substantial independence. When the Special Prosecutor subpoenaed tape recordings of conversations engaged in between Nixon and his top aides after the burglary, Nixon ordered Attorney General Richardson to fire the Special Prosecutor, but Richardson refused. In the famous "Saturday Night Massacre" two Justice Department employees (Attorney General Elliot Richardson and his top assistant William Ruckelshaus) resigned rather than follow Nixon's order to fire Archibald Cox. Cox was then fired by the third ranking official in the Justice Department, Solicitor General Robert Bork.

In response to a firestorm of public criticism, Nixon was forced to appoint a new special prosecutor, Leon Jaworski. Like Cox, Jaworski subpoenaed the tapes and aggressively conducted the Watergate investigation. Ultimately Nixon resigned under threat of certain impeachment.

Congress decided that future investigations of misconduct in the executive branch should proceed with a substantially independent special prosecutor in order to prevent obvious political conflicts of interest. By the time of the *Morrison* decision, the Act called for a Special Prosecutor to be selected by and report to a 3 judge panel, rather than the Attorney General. He could be fired by the Attorney General, but only for "good cause." In *Morrison v. Olson*, the Act was challenged by Theodore Olson, a member of the executive branch who was being investigated by a Special Prosecutor.

Olson contended that the Act was unconstitutional because the Special Prosecutor should be considered an "Officer of the United States," to be nominated by the President and confirmed by the Senate. Olson further contended that prosecutorial discretion was a core executive function, so that granting it to someone outside the control of the President violated the separation of powers.

The Court of Appeals for the District of Columbia, in a 2–1 decision, ruled the statute unconstitutional. *In re Sealed Case* (D.C. Cir. 1988). The majority for the Court of Appeals ruled first that an independent counsel is not an "inferior Officer" of the United States for purposes of the Appointments Clause, Art. II, §2, cl. 2. Accordingly, the court found the Act invalid because it did not provide for the independent counsel to be nominated by the President and confirmed by the Senate, as the Clause requires for "principal" officers. In the majority's view, the Act also violated the Appointments Clause insofar as it empowered a court of law to appoint an "inferior" officer who performs core executive functions. The Circuit Court also held that the Act's delegation of various powers to the Special Division (the 3 judge panel supervising the Special Prosecutor) violated the judicial limitations of Article III. The Act's restrictions on the Attorney General's power to remove an independent counsel violated the separation of powers. Finally, the Act interfered with the Executive Branch's prerogative to "take care that the Laws be faithfully executed," Art. II § 3.

The Supreme Court reversed, ruling 7–1 that the Act was constitutional. The Court concluded:

> In sum ... it does not violate the Appointments Clause for Congress to vest the appointment of independent counsel in the Special Division [concluding he is an inferior officer]; ... the powers exercised by the Special Division under the Act do not violate Article III; and ... the Act does not violate the separation-of-powers principle by impermissibly interfering with the functions of the Executive Branch.

In rejecting the contention that Congress had exerted undue influence on the Executive Branch, the Court considered the Special Prosecutor in the context of these previous cases:

Myers v. United States (1926): The Court invalidated a statute providing that postmasters could only be removed by the president *with Senate consent,* holding statute infringes on "executive power" by prohibiting removal without concurrence of the legislative branch.

Humphrey's Executor v. United States (1935): The Court upheld a Statute creating 7-year terms for members of Federal Trade Commission (who are appointed by the President), but making them subject to removal only for "inefficiency, neglect of duty, or malfeasance in office." The Court distinguished *Myers* as involving officers performing *purely* executive functions, as opposed to the quasi-judicial functions of a FTC commissioner.

Buckley v. Valeo (1976): The Court invalidated a statute allowing Congress to appoint members of the Federal Election Commission, an administrative agency.

Bowsher v. Synar (1986): The Court invalidated a statute allowing Congress to remove the Comptroller General, the director of the General Accounting Office.

Central to the Court's conclusion that the Act did not interfere with the Executive branch was the fact that the Special Prosecutor could be dismissed by the Attorney General for dereliction of duty and therefore did not operate wholly outside the executive department.

The special prosecutor statute had a sunset provision. It lapsed on June 30, 1999, following several controversial investigations, the latest being Kenneth Starr's investigation of President Clinton. Starr's investigation initially concerned alleged improprieties surrounding the "Whitewater" land deal. Subsequently, Mr. Starr obtained permission to extend the investigation to allegations of obstruction of justice in connection with the Paula Jones lawsuit. This investigation ultimately led to the Monica Lewinsky affair and Clinton's false statements in connection with it.

IV. Executive Privilege: Judicial Immunities

A President could theoretically assert executive privilege or immunity in three scenarios: a) immunity from criminal prosecution; b) immunity from civil liability; and c) immunity from judicial process (e.g., responding to interrogatories, responding to a subpoena for documents, or being subpoenaed as a witness). Each of these categories can then be further broken down: a) criminal prosecution for crimes committed before entering office and criminal prosecution for crimes committed while in office; civil liability for conduct before entering office and civil liability for conduct while in office; and c) immunity from judicial process in criminal cases and immunity from judicial process in civil cases.

The cases that follow provide answers to some of these situations. *United States v. Nixon* (1974) holds that there is a presumptive privilege that presidential conversations are confidential; however, this privilege can be overcome in a criminal case, at least if the desired information does not involve military or diplomatic secrets. *Nixon v. Fitzgerald* (1982) holds that presidents have absolute immunity from civil liability for any act arguably within the scope of the office. *Clinton v. Jones* (1997) holds that presidents may be sued, while in office, for conduct that occurred prior to entering office.

Other situations remain subject to debate. The Court has not yet decided whether or not a sitting president can be compelled to be a witness in a civil case. *Clinton v. Jones* (a civil case holding a sitting president subject to civil suit) suggests that a sitting president *may* be required to provide testimony in a civil case.

Precedent is least helpful regarding the issue of criminal liability. Many argue that the unique role of the president, together with the provision for impeachment in Art. II, §4, suggests that presidents must be impeached and convicted before they can be subject to criminal liability. Historical practice supports this view. President Nixon was named as an unindicted co-conspirator regarding crimes committed by his agents during the Watergate scandal. He was subsequently pardoned, prior to a possible indictment, by President Ford. However, this asserted privilege against indictment apparently would apply only to the president because of his unique role. Spiro Agnew, Nixon's Vice President, was indicted while in office on charges of bribery and income tax evasion. The indictment forced his resignation, leading to the appointment of Gerald Ford.

United States v. Nixon
418 U.S. 683 (1974)

[Majority: Burger (C.J.), Powell, Blackmun, Brennan, Douglas, Marshall, White, and Stewart.]

Mr. Chief Justice Burger delivered the opinion of the Court.

This litigation presents for review the denial of a motion, filed in the District Court on behalf of the President of the United States, in the case of *United States* v. *Mitchell*, to quash a third-party subpoena *duces tecum* issued by the United States District Court for the District of Columbia, pursuant to Fed. Rule Crim. Proc. 17(c). The subpoena directed the President to produce certain tape recordings and documents relating to his conversations with aides and advisers. The court rejected the President's claims of absolute executive privilege, of lack of jurisdiction, and of failure to satisfy the requirements of Rule 17(c). The President appealed to the Court of Appeals. We granted both the United States' petition for certiorari before judgment, and also the President's cross-petition for certiorari before judgment, because of the public importance of the issues presented and the need for their prompt resolution.

On March 1, 1974, a grand jury of the United States District Court for the District of Columbia returned an indictment charging seven named individuals with various offenses, including conspiracy to defraud the United States and to obstruct justice. Although he was not designated as such in the indictment, the grand jury named the President, among others, as an unindicted co-conspirator. On April 18, 1974, upon motion of the Special Prosecutor a subpoena *duces tecum* was issued pursuant to Rule 17(c) to the President by the United States District Court and made returnable on May 2, 1974. This subpoena required the production, in advance of the September 9 trial date, of certain tapes, memoranda, papers, transcripts, or other writings relating to certain precisely identified meetings between the President and others. The Special Prosecutor was able to fix the time, place, and persons present at these discussions because the White House daily logs and appointment records had been delivered to him. On April 30, the President publicly released edited transcripts of 43 conversations; portions of 20 conversations subject to subpoena in the present case were included. On May 1, 1974, the President's counsel filed a "special appearance" and a motion to quash the subpoena....

On May 20, 1974, the District Court denied the motion to quash and the motions to expunge and for protective orders. It further ordered "the President or any subordinate officer, official, or employee with custody or control of the documents or objects subpoenaed," to deliver to the District Court, on or before May 31, 1974, the originals of all subpoenaed items, as well as an index and analysis of those items, together with tape copies of those portions of the subpoenaed recordings for which transcripts had been released to the public by the President on April 30....

IV. THE CLAIM OF PRIVILEGE

IV-A. [W]e turn to the claim that the subpoena should be quashed because it demands "confidential conversations between a President and his close advisors that it would be inconsistent with the public interest to produce." App. 48a. The first contention is a broad claim that the separation of powers doctrine precludes judicial review of a President's claim of privilege. The second contention is that if he does not prevail on the claim of absolute privilege, the court should hold as a matter of constitutional law that the privilege prevails over the subpoena *duces tecum*.

In the performance of assigned constitutional duties each branch of the Government must initially interpret the Constitution, and the interpretation of its powers by any branch is due great respect from the others. The President's counsel, as we have noted, reads the Constitution as providing an absolute privilege of confidentiality for all Presidential communications. Many decisions of this Court, however, have unequivocally reaffirmed the holding of *Marbury v. Madison* (1803), that "[i]t is emphatically the province and duty of the judicial department to say what the law is."

No holding of the Court has defined the scope of judicial power specifically relating to the enforcement of a subpoena for confidential Presidential communications for use in a criminal prosecution, but other exercises of power by the Executive Branch and the Legislative Branch have been found invalid as in conflict with the Constitution. *Powell v. McCormack* (1969); *Youngstown Sheet & Tube Co. v. Sawyer* (1952)....

Notwithstanding the deference each branch must accord the others, the "judicial Power of the United States" vested in the federal courts by Art. III, § 1, of the Constitution can no more be shared with the Executive Branch than the Chief Executive, for example, can share with the Judiciary the veto power, or the Congress share with the Judiciary the power to override a Presidential veto. Any other conclusion would be contrary to the basic concept of separation of powers and the checks and balances that flow from the scheme of a tripartite government. *The Federalist*, No. 47. We therefore reaffirm that it is the province and duty of this Court "to say what the law is" with respect to the claim of privilege presented in this case. *Marbury v. Madison*.

IV-B. In support of his claim of absolute privilege, the President's counsel urges two grounds, one of which is common to all governments and one of which is peculiar to our system of separation of powers. The first ground is the valid need for protection of communications between high Government officials and those who advise and assist them in the performance of their manifold duties; the importance of this confidentiality is too plain to require further discussion. Human experience teaches that those who expect public dissemination of their remarks may well temper candor with a concern for appearances and for their own interests to the detriment of the decisionmaking process. Whatever the nature of the privilege of confidentiality of Presidential communications in the exercise of Art. II powers, the privilege can be said to derive from the supremacy of each branch within its own assigned area of constitutional duties. Certain powers and privileges flow from the nature of enumerated powers; the protection of the confidentiality of Presidential communications has similar constitutional underpinnings.

The second ground asserted by the President's counsel in support of the claim of absolute privilege rests on the doctrine of separation of powers. Here it is argued that the independence of the Executive Branch within its own sphere insulates a President from a judicial subpoena in an ongoing criminal prosecution, and thereby protects confidential Presidential communications.

However, neither the doctrine of separation of powers, nor the need for confidentiality of high-level communications, without more, can sustain an absolute, unqualified Presidential privilege of immunity from judicial process under all circumstances. The President's need for complete candor and objectivity from advisers calls for great deference from the courts. However, when the privilege depends solely on the broad, undifferentiated claim of public interest in the confidentiality of such conversations, a confrontation with other values arises. Absent a claim of need to protect military, diplomatic, or sensitive national security secrets, we find it difficult to accept the argument that even the very important interest in confidentiality of Presidential communications is significantly diminished by production of such material for *in camera* inspection with all the protection that a district court will be obliged to provide.

The impediment that an absolute, unqualified privilege would place in the way of the primary constitutional duty of the Judicial Branch to do justice in criminal prosecutions would plainly conflict with the function of the courts under Art. III. In designing the structure of our Government and dividing and allocating the sovereign power among three co-equal branches, the Framers of the Constitution sought to provide a comprehensive system, but the separate powers were not intended to operate with absolute independence....

To read the Art. II powers of the President as providing an absolute privilege as against a subpoena essential to enforcement of criminal statutes on no more than a generalized claim of the public interest in confidentiality of nonmilitary and nondiplomatic discussions would upset the constitutional balance of "a workable government" and gravely impair the role of the courts under Art. III.

IV-C. Since we conclude that the legitimate needs of the judicial process may outweigh Presidential privilege, it is necessary to resolve those competing interests in a manner that preserves the essential functions of each branch. The right and indeed the duty to resolve that question does not free the Judiciary from according high respect to the representations made on behalf of the President.

The expectation of a President to the confidentiality of his conversations and correspondence, like the claim of confidentiality of judicial deliberations, for example, has all the values to which we accord deference for the privacy of all citizens and, added to those values, is the necessity for protection of the public interest in candid, objective, and even blunt or harsh opinions in Presidential decisionmaking. A President and those who assist him must be free to explore alternatives in the process of shaping policies and making decisions and to do so in a way many would be unwilling to express except privately. These are the considerations justifying a presumptive privilege for Presidential communications. The privilege is fundamental to the operation of Government and inextricably rooted in the separation of powers under the Constitution. In *Nixon v. Sirica* (D.C. Cir. 1973), the Court of Appeals held that such Presidential communications are "presumptively privileged," and this position is accepted by both parties in the present litigation. We agree with Mr. Chief Justice Marshall's observation, therefore, that "[i]n no case of this kind would a court be required to proceed against the president as against an ordinary individual." *United States v. Burr* (C.C.D. Va. 1807).

But this presumptive privilege must be considered in light of our historic commitment to the rule of law.... The very integrity of the judicial system and public confidence in the system depend on full disclosure of all the facts, within the framework of the rules of evidence. To ensure that justice is done, it is imperative to the function of courts that compulsory process be available for the production of evidence needed either by the prosecution or by the defense....

In this case the President ... does not place his claim of privilege on the ground they are military or diplomatic secrets. As to these areas of Art. II duties the courts have traditionally shown the utmost deference to Presidential responsibilities. In *Chicago & Southern Air Lines v. Waterman S. S. Corp.* (1948), dealing with Presidential authority involving foreign policy considerations, the Court said: "the President, both as Commander-in-Chief and as the Nation's organ for foreign affairs, has available intelligence services whose reports are not and ought not to be published to the world. It would be intolerable that courts, without the relevant information, should review and perhaps nullify actions of the Executive taken on information properly held secret." ...

No case of the Court, however, has extended this high degree of deference to a President's generalized interest in confidentiality. Nowhere in the Constitution, as we have noted earlier, is there any explicit reference to a privilege of confidentiality, yet to the extent this interest relates to the effective discharge of a President's powers, it is constitutionally based. ...

In this case we must weigh the importance of the general privilege of confidentiality of Presidential communications in performance of the President's responsibilities against the inroads of such a privilege on the fair administration of criminal justice. The interest in preserving confidentiality is weighty indeed and entitled to great respect. However, we cannot conclude that advisers will be moved to temper the candor of their remarks by the infrequent occasions of disclosure because of the possibility that such conversations will be called for in the context of a criminal prosecution....

We conclude that when the ground for asserting privilege as to subpoenaed materials sought for use in a criminal trial is based only on the generalized interest in confidentiality, it cannot prevail over the fundamental demands of due process of law in the fair administration of criminal justice. The generalized assertion of privilege must yield to the demonstrated, specific need for evidence in a pending criminal trial....

IV-E. ... It is elementary that *in camera* inspection of evidence is always a procedure calling for scrupulous protection against any release or publication of material not found by the court, at that stage, properly admissible in evidence and relevant to the issues of the trial for which it is sought. That being true of an ordinary situation, it is obvious that the District Court has a very heavy responsibility to see to it that Presidential conversations, which are either not relevant or not admissible, are accorded that high degree of respect due the President of the United States....

Since this matter came before the Court during the pendency of a criminal prosecution, and on representations that time is of the essence, the mandate shall issue forthwith.

Affirmed.

Mr. Justice Rehnquist took no part in the consideration or decision of these cases.

Nixon v. Fitzgerald
457 U.S. 731 (1982)

[Majority: Powell, Stevens, Burger (C.J.), Rehnquist and O'Connor. Concurring: Burger (C.J.). Dissenting: White, Brennan, Marshall, and Blackmun.]

Justice Powell delivered the opinion of the Court.

The plaintiff in this lawsuit seeks relief in civil damages from a former President of the United States. The claim rests on actions allegedly taken in the former President's official capacity during his tenure in office. The issue before us is the scope of the [civil] immunity possessed by the President of the United States.

I. [During the waning months of the Presidency of Lyndon B. Johnson in 1968, Fitzgerald, a management analyst with the Department of the Air Force, testified before a congressional Subcommittee about cost overruns and unexpected technical difficulties concerning the development of a particular airplane. In January 1970, during the Presidency of Richard M. Nixon, Fitzgerald was dismissed from his job during a departmental reorganization and reduction in force, in which his job was eliminated. At one point, Nixon told a press conference that he was responsible for the dismissal, although he later said he was not, but had confused Fitzgerald with someone else. Fitzgerald complained to the Civil Service Commission, alleging that his separation represented unlawful retaliation for his congressional testimony. The Commission rejected this claim, but concluded that Fitzgerald's dismissal offended applicable regulations because it was motivated by "reasons purely personal to" respondent. Fitzgerald thereafter filed suit. After earlier judicial rulings and extensive pretrial discovery, only three defendants were involved: Nixon and two White House aides (petitioners in *Harlow v. Fitzgerald* (1982)).] ...

III-A. ... In *Scheuer v. Rhodes* (1974), the Court considered the immunity available to state executive officials in a § 1983 suit alleging the violation of constitutional rights. In that case we rejected the officials' claim to absolute immunity under the doctrine of *Spalding v. Vilas* (1896), finding instead that state executive officials possessed a "good faith" immunity from § 1983 suits alleging constitutional violations. Balancing the purposes of § 1983 against the imperatives of public policy, the Court held that "in varying scope, a qualified immunity is available to officers of the executive branch of government, the variation being dependent upon the scope of discretion and responsibilities of the office and all the circumstances as they reasonably appeared at the time of the action on which liability is sought to be based."

As construed by subsequent cases, *Scheuer* established a two-tiered division of immunity defenses in § 1983 suits. To most executive officers *Scheuer* accorded qualified immunity. For them the scope of the defense varied in proportion to the nature of their official functions and the range of decisions that conceivably might be taken in "good faith." This "functional" approach also defined a second tier, however, at which the especially sensitive duties of certain officials—notably judges and prosecutors—required the continued recognition of absolute immunity....

This approach was reviewed in detail in *Butz v. Economou* (1978), when we considered for the first time the kind of immunity possessed by *federal* executive officials who are sued for constitutional violations. In *Butz* the Court rejected an argument, based on decisions involving federal officials charged with common-law torts, that all high federal officials have a right to absolute immunity from constitutional damages actions. Concluding that a blanket recognition of absolute immunity would be anomalous in light of the qualified immunity standard applied to state executive officials, we held that federal officials generally have the same qualified immunity possessed by state officials in cases under § 1983. In so doing we reaffirmed our holdings that some officials, notably judges and prosecutors, "because of the special nature of their responsibilities," "require a full exemption from liability." ...

III-B. Our decisions concerning the immunity of government officials from civil damages liability have been guided by the Constitution, federal statutes, and history. Additionally, at least in the absence of explicit constitutional or congressional guidance, our immunity decisions have been informed by the common law. This Court necessarily also has weighed concerns of public policy, especially as illuminated by our history and the structure of our government.[1]

This case now presents the claim that the President of the United States is shielded by absolute immunity from civil damages liability. In the case of the President the inquiries into history and policy, though mandated independently by our cases, tend to converge. Because the Presidency did not exist through most of the development of common law, any historical analysis must draw its evidence primarily from our constitutional heritage and structure. Historical inquiry thus merges almost at its inception with the kind of "public policy" analysis appropriately undertaken by a federal court. This inquiry involves policies and principles that may be considered implicit in the nature of the President's office in a system structured to achieve effective government under a constitutionally mandated separation of powers.

IV. Here a former President asserts his immunity from civil damages claims of two kinds. He stands named as a defendant in a direct action under the Constitution and in two statutory actions under federal laws of general applicability....

---

1. Although the Court in *Butz v. Economou* described the requisite inquiry as one of "public policy," the focus of inquiry more accurately may be viewed in terms of the "inherent" or "structural" assumptions of our scheme of government.

Applying the principles of our cases to claims of this kind, we hold that petitioner, as a former President of the United States, is entitled to absolute immunity from damages liability predicated on his official acts. We consider this immunity a functionally mandated incident of the President's unique office, rooted in the constitutional tradition of the separation of powers and supported by our history. Justice Story's analysis remains persuasive:

> There are ... incidental powers, belonging to the executive department, which are necessarily implied from the nature of the functions, which are confided to it. Among these, must necessarily be included the power to perform them.... The president cannot, therefore, be liable to arrest, imprisonment, or detention, while he is in the discharge of the duties of his office; and for this purpose his person must be deemed, in civil cases at least, to possess an official inviolability. 3 J. Story, *Commentaries on the Constitution of the United States* § 1563, pp. 418–19 (1st ed. 1833).

IV-A. The President occupies a unique position in the constitutional scheme. Article II, § 1, of the Constitution provides that "[t]he executive Power shall be vested in a President of the United States...." This grant of authority establishes the President as the chief constitutional officer of the Executive Branch, entrusted with supervisory and policy responsibilities of utmost discretion and sensitivity. These include the enforcement of federal law—it is the President who is charged constitutionally to "take Care that the Laws be faithfully executed," [Art. II, § 3]; the conduct of foreign affairs—a realm in which the Court has recognized that "[i]t would be intolerable that courts, without the relevant information, should review and perhaps nullify actions of the Executive taken on information properly held secret;" and management of the Executive Branch—a task for which "imperative reasons requir[e] an unrestricted power [in the President] to remove the most important of his subordinates in their most important duties."

In arguing that the President is entitled only to qualified immunity, the respondent relies on cases in which we have recognized immunity of this scope for governors and cabinet officers. We find these cases to be inapposite. The President's unique status under the Constitution distinguishes him from other executive officials.[2]

---

2. Noting that the Speech and Debate Clause provides a textual basis for congressional immunity, respondent argues that the Framers must be assumed to have rejected any similar grant of executive immunity. This argument is unpersuasive. First, a specific textual basis has not been considered a prerequisite to the recognition of immunity. No provision expressly confers judicial immunity. Yet the immunity of judges is well settled. Second, this Court already has established that absolute immunity may be extended to certain officials of the Executive Branch. [prosecutors.] Third, there is historical evidence from which it may be inferred that the Framers assumed the President's immunity from damages liability. At the Constitutional Convention several delegates expressed concern that subjecting the President even to impeachment would impair his capacity to perform his duties of office. The delegates of course did agree to an Impeachment Clause. But nothing in the debates suggests an expectation that the President would be subjected to the distraction of suits by disappointed private citizens. And Senator Maclay has recorded the views of Senator Ellsworth and Vice President John Adams—both delegates to the Convention—that "the President, personally, was not the subject to any process whatever.... For [that] would ... put it in the power of a common justice to exercise any authority over him and stop the whole machine of Government." *Journal of William Maclay* 167 (E. Maclay ed. 1890). Justice Story, writing in 1833, held it implicit in the separation of powers that the President must be permitted to discharge his duties undistracted by private lawsuits. 3 J. Story, *Commentaries on the Constitution of the United States* § 1563, pp. 418–19 (1st ed. 1833). Thomas Jefferson also argued that the President was not intended to be subject to judicial process. When Chief Justice Marshall held in *United States v. Burr* (C.C.D. Va. 1807) that a subpoena duces tecum can be issued to a President, Jefferson protested strongly, and stated his broader view of the proper relationship between the Judiciary and the President:

Because of the singular importance of the President's duties, diversion of his energies by concern with private lawsuits would raise unique risks to the effective functioning of government. As is the case with prosecutors and judges—for whom absolute immunity now is established—a President must concern himself with matters likely to "arouse the most intense feelings." Yet, as our decisions have recognized, it is in precisely such cases that there exists the greatest public interest in providing an official "the maximum ability to deal fearlessly and impartially with" the duties of his office. This concern is compelling where the officeholder must make the most sensitive and far-reaching decisions entrusted to any official under our constitutional system.[3] Nor can the sheer prominence of the President's office be ignored. In view of the visibility of his office and the effect of his actions on countless people, the President would be an easily identifiable target for suits for civil damages. Cognizance of this personal vulnerability frequently could distract a President from his public duties, to the detriment of not only the President and his office but also the Nation that the Presidency was designed to serve.

IV-B. Courts traditionally have recognized the President's constitutional responsibilities and status as factors counseling judicial deference and restraint. For example, while courts generally have looked to the common law to determine the scope of an official's evidentiary privilege, we have recognized that the Presidential privilege is "rooted in the separation of powers under the Constitution." *United States v. Nixon* (1974). It is settled law that the separation-of-powers doctrine does not bar every exercise of jurisdiction over the President of the United States. But our cases also have established that a court, before exercising jurisdiction, must balance the constitutional weight of the interest to be served against the dangers of intrusion on the authority and functions of the Executive Branch. When judicial action is needed to serve broad public interests—as when the Court acts, not in derogation of the separation of powers, but to maintain their proper balance, cf. *Youngstown Sheet & Tube Co. v. Sawyer* (1952), or to vindicate the public interest in an ongoing criminal prosecution, see *United States v. Nixon*—the exercise of ju-

---

The leading principle of our Constitution is the independence of the Legislature, executive and judiciary of each other, and none are more jealous of this than the judiciary. But would the executive be independent of the judiciary, if he were subject to the *commands* of the latter, & to imprisonment for disobedience; if the several courts could bandy him from pillar to post, keep him constantly trudging from north to south & east to west, and withdraw him entirely from his constitutional duties? The intention of the Constitution, that each branch should be independent of the others, is further manifested by the means it has furnished to each, to protect itself from enterprises of force attempted on them by the others, and to none has it given more effectual or diversified means than to the executive.

10 *The Works of Thomas Jefferson* 404 n. (P. Ford ed. 1905) (quoting a letter from President Jefferson to a prosecutor at the Burr trial).

In light of the fragmentary character of the most important materials reflecting the Framers' intent, we do think that the most compelling arguments arise from the Constitution's separation of powers and the Judiciary's historic understanding of that doctrine. But our primary reliance on constitutional structure and judicial precedent should not be misunderstood. The best historical evidence clearly supports the Presidential immunity we have upheld. Justice White's dissent cites some other materials, including ambiguous comments made at state ratifying conventions and the remarks of a single publicist. But historical evidence must be weighed as well as cited. When the weight of evidence is considered, we think we must place our reliance on the contemporary understanding of John Adams, Thomas Jefferson, and Oliver Ellsworth. Other powerful support derives from the actual history of private lawsuits against the President. Prior to the litigation explosion commencing with this Court's 1971 *Bivens* decision, fewer than a handful of damages actions ever were filed against the President. None appears to have proceeded to judgment on the merits.

3. Among the most persuasive reasons supporting official immunity is the prospect that damages liability may render an official unduly cautious in the discharge of his official duties....

risdiction has been held warranted. In the case of this merely private suit for damages based on a President's official acts, we hold it is not.

IV-C. In defining the scope of an official's absolute privilege, this Court has recognized that the sphere of protected action must be related closely to the immunity's justifying purposes. Frequently our decisions have held that an official's absolute immunity should extend only to acts in performance of particular functions of his office. But the Court also has refused to draw functional lines finer than history and reason would support.... In view of the special nature of the President's constitutional office and functions, we think it appropriate to recognize absolute Presidential immunity from damages liability for acts within the "outer perimeter" of his official responsibility.

Under the Constitution and laws of the United States the President has discretionary responsibilities in a broad variety of areas, many of them highly sensitive. In many cases it would be difficult to determine which of the President's innumerable "functions" encompassed a particular action....

This construction would subject the President to trial on virtually every allegation that an action was unlawful, or was taken for a forbidden purpose. Adoption of this construction thus would deprive absolute immunity of its intended effect. It clearly is within the President's constitutional and statutory authority to prescribe the manner in which the Secretary will conduct the business of the Air Force. Because this mandate of office must include the authority to prescribe reorganizations and reductions in force, we conclude that petitioner's alleged wrongful acts lay well within the outer perimeter of his authority.

V. A rule of absolute immunity for the President will not leave the Nation without sufficient protection against misconduct on the part of the Chief Executive. There remains the constitutional remedy of impeachment. In addition, there are formal and informal checks on Presidential action that do not apply with equal force to other executive officials. The President is subjected to constant scrutiny by the press. Vigilant oversight by Congress also may serve to deter Presidential abuses of office, as well as to make credible the threat of impeachment. Other incentives to avoid misconduct may include a desire to earn reelection, the need to maintain prestige as an element of Presidential influence, and a President's traditional concern for his historical stature.

The existence of alternative remedies and deterrents establishes that absolute immunity will not place the President "above the law." For the President, as for judges and prosecutors, absolute immunity merely precludes a particular private remedy for alleged misconduct in order to advance compelling public ends....

Chief Justice Burger, concurring. [Omitted.]

Justice White, with whom Justice Brennan, Justice Marshall, and Justice Blackmun join, dissenting.

The four dissenting Members of the Court in *Butz v. Economou* (1978), argued that all federal officials are entitled to absolute immunity from suit for any action they take in connection with their official duties. That immunity would extend even to actions taken with express knowledge that the conduct was clearly contrary to the controlling statute or clearly violative of the Constitution. Fortunately, the majority of the Court rejected that approach: We held that although public officials perform certain functions that entitle them to absolute immunity, the immunity attaches to particular functions—not to particular offices. Officials performing functions for which immunity is not absolute enjoy qualified immunity; they are liable in damages only if their conduct violated well-established law and if they should have realized that their conduct was illegal.

The Court now applies the dissenting view in *Butz* to the Office of the President: A President, acting within the outer boundaries of what Presidents normally do, may, without liability, deliberately cause serious injury to any number of citizens even though he knows his conduct violates a statute or tramples on the constitutional rights of those who are injured. Even if the President in this case ordered Fitzgerald fired by means of a trumped-up reduction in force, knowing that such a discharge was contrary to the civil service laws, he would be absolutely immune from suit. By the same token, if a President, without following the statutory procedures which he knows apply to himself as well as to other federal officials, orders his subordinates to wiretap or break into a home for the purpose of installing a listening device, and the officers comply with his request, the President would be absolutely immune from suit. He would be immune regardless of the damage he inflicts, regardless of how violative of the statute and of the Constitution he knew his conduct to be, and regardless of his purpose.

The Court intimates that its decision is grounded in the Constitution. If that is the case, Congress cannot provide a remedy against Presidential misconduct and the criminal laws of the United States are wholly inapplicable to the President. I find this approach completely unacceptable. I do not agree that if the Office of President is to operate effectively, the holder of that Office must be permitted, without fear of liability and regardless of the function he is performing, deliberately to inflict injury on others by conduct that he knows violates the law.

We have not taken such a scatter-gun approach in other cases. *Butz* held that absolute immunity did not attach to the office held by a member of the President's Cabinet but only to those specific functions performed by that officer for which absolute immunity is clearly essential. Members of Congress are absolutely immune under the Speech or Debate Clause of the Constitution, but the immunity extends only to their legislative acts. We have never held that in order for legislative work to be done, it is necessary to immunize all of the tasks that legislators must perform. Constitutional immunity does not extend to those many things that Senators and Representatives regularly and necessarily do that are not legislative acts. Members of Congress, for example, repeatedly importune the executive branch and administrative agencies outside hearing rooms and legislative halls, but they are not immune if in connection with such activity they deliberately violate the law. Neither is a Member of Congress or his aide immune from damages suits if in order to secure information deemed relevant to a legislative investigation, he breaks into a house and carries away records. Judges are absolutely immune from liability for damages, but only when performing a judicial function, and even then they are subject to criminal liability. The absolute immunity of prosecutors is likewise limited to the prosecutorial function. A prosecutor who directs that an investigation be carried out in a way that is patently illegal is not immune.

In *Marbury v. Madison* (1803), the Court, speaking through the Chief Justice, observed that while there were "important political powers" committed to the President for the performance of which neither he nor his appointees were accountable in court, "the question, whether the legality of an act of the head of a department be examinable in a court of justice or not, must always depend on the nature of that act." The Court nevertheless refuses to follow this course with respect to the President. It makes no effort to distinguish categories of Presidential conduct that should be absolutely immune from other categories of conduct that should not qualify for that level of immunity. The Court instead concludes that whatever the President does and however contrary to law he knows his conduct to be, he may, without fear of liability, injure federal employees or any other person within or without the Government.

Attaching absolute immunity to the Office of the President, rather than to particular activities that the President might perform, places the President above the law. It is a reversion to the old notion that the King can do no wrong. Until now, this concept had survived in this country only in the form of sovereign immunity. That doctrine forecloses suit against the Government itself and against Government officials, but only when the suit against the latter actually seeks relief against the sovereign. Suit against an officer, however, may be maintained where it seeks specific relief against him for conduct contrary to his statutory authority or to the Constitution. Now, however, the Court clothes the Office of the President with sovereign immunity, placing it beyond the law.[1]

In *Marbury v. Madison*, the Chief Justice, speaking for the Court, observed: "The government of the United States has been emphatically termed a government of laws, and not of men. It will certainly cease to deserve this high appellation, if the laws furnish no remedy for the violation of a vested legal right." Until now, the Court has consistently adhered to this proposition. In *Scheuer v. Rhodes* (1974), a unanimous Court held that the Governor of a State was entitled only to a qualified immunity. We reached this position, even though we recognized that

> [i]n the case of higher officers of the executive branch ... the inquiry is far more complex since the range of decisions and choices—whether the formulation of policy, of legislation, of budgets, or of day-to-day decisions—is virtually infinite.... In short, since the options which a chief executive and his principal subordinates must consider are far broader and far more subtle than those made by officials with less responsibility, the range of discretion must be comparably broad....

Unfortunately, the Court now abandons basic principles that have been powerful guides to decision. It is particularly unfortunate since the judgment in this case has few, if any, indicia of a judicial decision; it is almost wholly a policy choice, a choice that is without substantial support and that in all events is ambiguous in its reach and import....

The decisions dealing with the immunity of state officers involve the question of whether and to what extent Congress intended to abolish the common-law privileges by providing a remedy in the predecessor of 42 U.S.C. § 1983 for constitutional violations by state officials. Our decisions respecting immunity for federal officials—including absolute immunity for judges, prosecutors, and those officials doing similar work—also in large part reflect common-law views, as well as judicial conclusions as to what privileges are necessary if particular functions are to be performed in the public interest.

Unfortunately, there is little of this approach in the Court's decision today. The Court casually, but candidly, abandons the functional approach to immunity that has run through all of our decisions. Indeed, the majority turns this rule on its head by declaring that be-

---

1. It is ironic that this decision should come out at the time of the tenth anniversary of the Watergate affair. Even the popular press has drawn from that affair an insight into the character of the American constitutional system that is bound to be profoundly shaken by today's decision: "The important lesson that Watergate established is that no President is above the law. It is a banality, a cliche, but it is a point on which many Americans ... seem confused." 119 *Time*, No. 24, p. 28 (June 14, 1982). A majority of the Court shares this confusion.

The majority vigorously protests this characterization of its position, arguing that the President remains subject to law in the form of impeachment proceedings. But the abandonment of the rule of law here is not in the result reached, but in the manner of reaching it. The majority fails to apply to the President those principles which we have consistently used to determine the scope and credibility of an absolute immunity defense. It does this because of some preconceived notion of the inapplicability of general rules of law to the President....

cause the functions of the President's office are so varied and diverse and some of them so profoundly important, the office is unique and must be clothed with officewide, absolute immunity. This is policy, not law, and in my view, very poor policy.

I. In declaring the President to be absolutely immune from suit for any deliberate and knowing violation of the Constitution or of a federal statute, the Court asserts that the immunity is "rooted in the constitutional tradition of the separation of powers and supported by our history." The decision thus has all the earmarks of a constitutional pronouncement—absolute immunity for the President's office is mandated by the Constitution. Although the Court appears to disclaim this, it is difficult to read the opinion coherently as standing for any narrower proposition: Attempts to subject the President to liability either by Congress through a statutory action or by the courts through a *Bivens* (*Bivens v. Six Unknown Fed. Narcotics Agents* (1971)) proceeding would violate the separation of powers. Such a generalized absolute immunity cannot be sustained when examined in the traditional manner and in light of the traditional judicial sources.

The petitioner and the United States, as amicus, rely principally on two arguments to support the claim of absolute immunity for the President from civil liability: absolute immunity is an "incidental power" of the Presidency, historically recognized as implicit in the Constitution, and absolute immunity is required by the separation-of-powers doctrine. I will address each of these contentions.

I-A. The Speech or Debate Clause, Art. I, §6, guarantees absolute immunity to Members of Congress; nowhere, however, does the Constitution directly address the issue of Presidential immunity.[2] Petitioner nevertheless argues that the debates at the Constitutional Convention and the early history of constitutional interpretation demonstrate an implicit assumption of absolute Presidential immunity. In support of this position, petitioner relies primarily on three separate items: First, preratification remarks made during the discussion of Presidential impeachment at the Convention and in *The Federalist*; second, remarks made during the meeting of the first Senate; and third, the views of Justice Story.

The debate at the Convention on whether or not the President should be impeachable did touch on the potential dangers of subjecting the President to the control of another branch, the Legislature. Gouverneur Morris, for example, complained of the potential for dependency and argued that "[the President] can do no criminal act without Coadjutors who may be punished. In case he should be re-elected, that will be sufficient proof of his innocence." Colonel Mason responded to this by asking if "any man [shall] be above Justice" and argued that this was least appropriate for the man "who can commit the most extensive injustice." Madison agreed that "it [is] indispensable that some provision should be made for defending the Community against the incapacity, negligence or perfidy of the chief Magistrate." Pinckney responded on the other side, believing that if granted the power, the Legislature would hold impeachment "as a rod over the Executive and by that means effectually destroy his independence."

Petitioner concludes from this that the delegates meant impeachment to be the exclusive means of holding the President personally responsible for his misdeeds, outside of electoral politics. This conclusion, however, is hardly supported by the debate. Although some of the delegates expressed concern over limiting Presidential independence, the delegates voted 8 to 2 in favor of impeachment. Whatever the fear of subjecting the Presi-

---

2. In fact, insofar as the Constitution addresses the issue of Presidential liability, its approach is very different from that taken in the Speech or Debate Clause. The possibility of impeachment assures that the President can be held accountable to the other branches of Government for his actions; the Constitution further states that impeachment does not bar criminal prosecution.

dent to the power of another branch, it was not sufficient, or at least not sufficiently shared, to insulate the President from political liability in the impeachment process.

Moreover, the Convention debate did not focus on wrongs the President might commit against individuals, but rather on whether there should be a method of holding him accountable for what might be termed wrongs against the state. Thus, examples of the abuses that concerned delegates were betrayal, oppression, and bribery; the delegates feared that the alternative to an impeachment mechanism would be "tumults & insurrections" by the people in response to such abuses. 2 Farrand 67. The only conclusions that can be drawn from this debate are that the independence of the Executive was not understood to require a total lack of accountability to the other branches and that there was no general desire to insulate the President from the consequences of his improper acts.

Much the same can be said in response to petitioner's reliance on *The Federalist* No. 77. In that essay, Hamilton asked whether the Presidency combines "the requisites to safety in the republican sense—a due dependence on the people—a due responsibility." *The Federalist* No. 77. He answered that the constitutional plan met this test because it subjected the President to both the electoral process and the possibility of impeachment, including subsequent criminal prosecution. Petitioner concludes from this that these were intended to be the exclusive means of restraining Presidential abuses. This, by no means follows. Hamilton was concerned in *The Federalist* No. 77, as were the delegates at the Convention, with the larger political abuses—"wrongs against the state"—that a President might commit. He did not consider what legal means might be available for redress of individualized grievances.

That omission should not be taken to imply exclusion in these circumstances is well illustrated by comparing some of the remarks made in the state ratifying conventions with Hamilton's discussion in No. 77. In the North Carolina ratifying convention, for example, there was a discussion of the adequacy of the impeachment mechanism for holding executive officers accountable for their misdeeds. Governor Johnson defended the constitutional plan by distinguishing three legal mechanisms of accountability:

> If an officer commits an offence against an individual, he is amenable to the courts of law. If he commits crimes against the state, he may be indicted and punished. Impeachment only extends to high crimes and misdemeanors in a *public office*. It is a mode of trial pointed out for great misdemeanors against the public.

Governor Johnson surely did not contemplate that the availability of an impeachment mechanism necessarily implied the exclusion of other forms of legal accountability; rather, the method of accountability was to be a function of the character of the wrong. Mr. Maclaine, another delegate to the North Carolina Convention, clearly believed that the courts would remain open to individual citizens seeking redress from injuries caused by Presidential acts:

> The President is the superior officer, who is to see the laws put in execution. He is amenable for any maladministration in his office. Were it possible to suppose that the President should give wrong instructions to his deputies, whereby the citizens would be distressed, they would have redress in the ordinary courts of common law.

A similar distinction between different possible forms of Presidential accountability was drawn by Mr. Wilson at the Pennsylvania ratifying convention: "[The President] is placed high, and is possessed of power far from being contemptible; yet not a *single privilege* is annexed to his character; far from being above the laws, he is amenable to them in his private character as a citizen, and in his public character by *impeachment*."

There is no more reason to respect the views of Hamilton than those of Wilson: both were members of the Constitutional Convention; both were instrumental in securing the ratification of the Constitution. But more importantly, there is simply no express contradiction in their statements. Petitioner relies on an inference drawn from silence to create this contradiction. The surrounding history simply does not support this inference.

The second piece of historical evidence cited by petitioner is an exchange at the first meeting of the Senate, involving Vice President Adams and Senators Ellsworth and Maclay. The debate started over whether or not the words "the President" should be included at the beginning of federal writs, similar to the manner in which English writs ran in the King's name. Senator Maclay thought that this would improperly combine the executive and judicial branches. This, in turn, led to a discussion of the proper relation between the two. Senator Ellsworth and Vice President Adams defended the proposition that

> the President, personally, was not subject to any process whatever; could have no action, whatever, brought against him; was above the power of all judges, justices, &c. For [that] would ... put it in the power of a common justice to exercise any authority over him, and stop the whole machine of government.

In their view the impeachment process was the exclusive form of process available against the President. Senator Maclay ardently opposed this view and put the case of a President committing "murder in the street." In his view, in such a case neither impeachment nor resurrection were the exclusive means of holding the President to the law; rather, there was "loyal justice." Senator Maclay, who recorded the exchange, concludes his notes with the remark that none of this "is worth minuting, but it shows clearly how amazingly fond of the old leaven many people are." In his view, Senator Ellsworth and his supporters had not fully comprehended the difference in the political position of the American President and that of the British Monarch. Again, nothing more can be concluded from this than that the proper scope of Presidential accountability, including the question whether the President should be subject to judicial process, was no clearer then than it is now.

The final item cited by petitioner clearly supports his position, but is of such late date that it contributes little to understanding the original intent. In his Commentaries on the Constitution, published in 1833, Justice Story described the "incidental powers" of the President:

> Among these must necessarily be included the power to perform [his functions] without any obstruction or impediment whatsoever. The President cannot, therefore, be liable to arrest, imprisonment, or detention, while he is in the discharge of the duties of his office; and for this purpose his person must be deemed, in civil cases at least, to possess an official inviolability. In the exercise of his political powers he is to use his own discretion, and he is accountable only to his country and to his own conscience. His decision in relation to these powers is subject to no control, and his discretion, when exercised, is conclusive.

While Justice Story may have been firmly committed to this view in 1833, Senator Pinckney, a delegate to the Convention, was as firmly committed to the opposite view in 1800.

Senator Pinckney, arguing on the floor of the Senate, contrasted the privileges extended to Members of Congress by the Constitution with the lack of any such privileges extended to the President. He argued that this was a deliberate choice of the delegates to the Convention, who "well knew how oppressively the power of undefined privileges had been exercised in Great Britain, and were determined no such authority should ever be exercised here." 10 *Annals of Cong.* 72 (1800). Therefore, "[n]o privilege of this kind was intended for your Executive, nor any except that ... for your Legislature." *Id.*, at 74.

In previous immunity cases the Court has emphasized the importance of the immunity afforded the particular government official at common law. Clearly this sort of analysis is not possible when dealing with an office, the Presidency, that did not exist at common law. To the extent that historical inquiry is appropriate in this context, it is constitutional history, not common law, that is relevant. From the history discussed above, however, all that can be concluded is that absolute immunity from civil liability for the President finds no support in constitutional text or history, or in the explanations of the earliest commentators....

I. B.... We said in *Butz v. Economou* (1978), that "it is not unfair to hold liable the official who knows or should know he is acting outside the law, and ... insisting on an awareness of clearly established constitutional limits will not unduly interfere with the exercise of official judgment." Today's decision in *Harlow v. Fitzgerald* (1982) makes clear that the President, were he subject to civil liability, could be held liable only for an action that he knew, or as an objective matter should have known, was illegal and a clear abuse of his authority and power. In such circumstances, the question that must be answered is who should bear the cost of the resulting injury—the wrongdoer or the victim.

The principle that should guide the Court in deciding this question was stated long ago by Chief Justice Marshall: "The very essence of civil liberty certainly consists in the right of every individual to claim the protection of the laws, whenever he receives an injury." *Marbury v. Madison*. Much more recently, the Court considered the role of a damages remedy in the performance of the courts' traditional function of enforcing federally guaranteed rights: "Historically, damages have been regarded as the ordinary remedy for an invasion of personal interests in liberty." *Bivens v. Six Unknown Fed. Narcotics Agents*. To the extent that the Court denies an otherwise appropriate remedy, it denies the victim the right to be made whole and, therefore, denies him "the protection of the laws."

That the President should have the same remedial obligations toward those whom he injures as any other federal officer is not a surprising proposition. The fairness of the remedial principle the Court has so far followed—that the wrongdoer, not the victim, should ordinarily bear the costs of the injury—has been found to be outweighed only in instances where potential liability is "thought to injure the governmental decisionmaking process." The argument for immunity is that the possibility of a damages action will, or at least should, have an effect on the performance of official responsibilities. That effect should be to deter unconstitutional, or otherwise illegal, behavior. This may, however, lead officers to be more careful and "less vigorous" in the performance of their duties. Caution, of course, is not always a virtue and undue caution is to be avoided.

The possibility of liability may, in some circumstances, distract officials from the performance of their duties and influence the performance of those duties in ways adverse to the public interest. But when this "public policy" argument in favor of absolute immunity is cast in these broad terms, it applies to all officers, both state and federal: All officers should perform their responsibilities without regard to those personal interests threatened by the possibility of a lawsuit. Inevitably, this reduces the public policy argument to nothing more than an expression of judicial inclination as to which officers should be encouraged to perform their functions with "vigor," although with less care.

The Court's response, until today, to this problem has been to apply the argument to individual functions, not offices, and to evaluate the effect of liability on governmental decisionmaking within that function, in light of the substantive ends that are to be encouraged or discouraged. In this case, therefore, the Court should examine the functions implicated by the causes of action at issue here and the effect of potential liability on the performance of those functions.

II. The functional approach to the separation-of-powers doctrine and the Court's more recent immunity decisions converge on the following principle: The scope of immunity is determined by function, not office. The wholesale claim that the President is entitled to absolute immunity in all of his actions stands on no firmer ground than did the claim that all Presidential communications are entitled to an absolute privilege, which was rejected in favor of a functional analysis, by a unanimous Court in *United States v. Nixon* (1974). Therefore, whatever may be true of the necessity of such a broad immunity in certain areas of executive responsibility,[3] the only question that must be answered here is whether the dismissal of employees falls within a constitutionally assigned executive function, the performance of which would be substantially impaired by the possibility of a private action for damages. I believe it does not.

Respondent has so far proceeded in this action on the basis of three separate causes of action: two federal statutes—5 U.S.C. §7211 and 18 U.S.C. §1505—and the 1st Amendment. At this point in the litigation, the availability of these causes of action is not before us. Assuming the correctness of the lower court's determination that the two federal statutes create a private right of action, I find the suggestion that the President is immune from those causes of action to be unconvincing. The attempt to found such immunity upon a separation-of-powers argument is particularly unconvincing.

The first of these statutes, 5 U.S.C. §7211, states that "[t]he right of employees ... to ... furnish information to either House of Congress, or to a committee or Member thereof, may not be interfered with or denied." The second, 18 U.S.C. §1505, makes it a crime to obstruct congressional testimony. It does not take much insight to see that at least one purpose of these statutes is to assure congressional access to information in the possession of the Executive Branch, which Congress believes it requires in order to carry out its responsibilities. Insofar as these statutes implicate a separation-of-powers argument, I would think it to be just the opposite of that suggested by petitioner and accepted by the majority. In enacting these statutes, Congress sought to preserve its own constitutionally mandated functions in the face of a recalcitrant Executive....

The argument that Congress, by providing a damages action under these statutes (as is assumed in this case), has adopted an unconstitutional means of furthering its ends, must rest on the premise that Presidential control of executive employment decisions is a constitutionally assigned Presidential function with which Congress may not significantly interfere. This is a frivolous contention. In *United States v. Perkins* (1886), this Court held that "when Congress, by law, vests the appointment of inferior officers in the heads of Departments it may limit and restrict the power of removal as it deems best for the public interest." Whatever the rule may be with respect to high officers, see *Humphrey's Executor v. United States* (1935), with respect to those who fill traditional bureaucratic positions, restrictions on executive authority are the rule and not the exception. This case itself demonstrates the severe statutory restraints under which the President operates in this area....

Absolute immunity is appropriate when the threat of liability may bias the decisionmaker in ways that are adverse to the public interest. But as the various regulations and

---

3. I will not speculate on the Presidential functions which may require absolute immunity, but a clear example would be instances in which the President participates in prosecutorial decisions.

statutes protecting civil servants from arbitrary executive action illustrate, this is an area in which the public interest is demonstrably on the side of encouraging less "vigor" and more "caution" on the part of decisionmakers....

In *Bivens v. Six Unknown Fed. Narcotics Agents* we held that individuals who have suffered a compensable injury through a violation of the rights guaranteed them by the 4th Amendment may invoke the general federal-question jurisdiction of the federal courts in a suit for damages. That conclusion rested on two principles: First, "'[t]he very essence of civil liberty certainly consists in the right of every individual to claim the protection of the laws,'" quoting *Marbury v. Madison*; second, "[h]istorically, damages have been regarded as the ordinary remedy for an invasion of personal interests in liberty." In *Butz v. Economou*, we rejected the argument of the Federal Government that federal officers, including Cabinet officers, are absolutely immune from civil liability for such constitutional violations—a position that we recognized would substantially undercut our conclusion in *Bivens*. We held there that although the performance of certain limited functions will be protected by the shield of absolute immunity, the general rule is that federal officers, like state officers, have only a qualified immunity. Finally, in *Davis v. Passman* (1979), we held that a Congressman could be held liable for damages in a *Bivens*-type suit brought in federal court alleging a violation of individual rights guaranteed the plaintiff by the Due Process Clause. In my view, these cases have largely settled the issues raised by the *Bivens* problem here.

These cases established the following principles. First, it is not the exclusive prerogative of the Legislative Branch to create a federal cause of action for a constitutional violation. In the absence of adequate legislatively prescribed remedies, the general federal-question jurisdiction of the federal courts permits the courts to create remedies, both legal and equitable, appropriate to the character of the injury. Second, exercise of this "judicial" function does not create a separation-of-powers problem: We have held both executive and legislative officers subject to this judicially created cause of action and in each instance we have rejected separation-of-powers arguments. Holding federal officers liable for damages for constitutional injuries no more violates separation-of-powers principles than does imposing equitable remedies under the traditional function of judicial review. Third, federal officials will generally have a "qualified immunity" from such suits; absolute immunity will be extended to certain functions only on the basis of a showing that exposure to liability is inconsistent with the proper performance of the official's duties and responsibilities. Finally, Congress retains the power to restrict exposure to liability, and the policy judgments implicit in this decision should properly be made by Congress.

The majority fails to recognize the force of what the Court has already done in this area. Under the above principles, the President could not claim that there are no circumstances under which he would be subject to a *Bivens*-type action for violating respondent's constitutional rights. Rather, he must assert that the absence of absolute immunity will substantially impair his ability to carry out particular functions that are his constitutional responsibility. For the reasons I have presented above, I do not believe that this argument can be successfully made under the circumstances of this case.

It is, of course, theoretically possible that the President should be held to be absolutely immune because each of the functions for which he has constitutional responsibility would be substantially impaired by the possibility of civil liability. I do not think this argument is valid for the simple reason that the function involved here does not have this character. On which side of the line other Presidential functions would fall need not be decided in this case.

The majority opinion suggests a variant of this argument. It argues, not that every Presidential function has this character, but that distinguishing the particular functions involved in any given case would be "difficult." Even if this were true, it would not necessarily follow that the President is entitled to absolute immunity....

III. Because of the importance of this case, it is appropriate to examine the reasoning of the majority opinion....

Focusing on the actual arguments the majority offers for its holding of absolute immunity for the President, one finds surprisingly little. As I read the relevant section of the Court's opinion, I find just three contentions from which the majority draws this conclusion. Each of them is little more than a makeweight; together they hardly suffice to justify the wholesale disregard of our traditional approach to immunity questions.

First, the majority informs us that the President occupies a "unique position in the constitutional scheme," including responsibilities for the administration of justice, foreign affairs, and management of the Executive Branch. True as this may be, it says nothing about why a "unique" rule of immunity should apply to the President. The President's unique role may indeed encompass functions for which he is entitled to a claim of absolute immunity. It does not follow from that, however, that he is entitled to absolute immunity either in general or in this case in particular....

Second, the majority contends that because the President's "visibility" makes him particularly vulnerable to suits for civil damages, a rule of absolute immunity is required. The force of this argument is surely undercut by the majority's admission that "there is no historical record of numerous suits against the President." Even granting that a *Bivens* cause of action did not become available until 1971, in the 11 years since then there have been only a handful of suits....

Finally, the Court suggests that potential liability "frequently could distract a President from his public duties." Unless one assumes that the President himself makes the countless high-level executive decisions required in the administration of government, this rule will not do much to insulate such decisions from the threat of liability. The logic of the proposition cannot be limited to the President; its extension, however, has been uniformly rejected by this Court. See *Butz v. Economou*; *Harlow v. Fitzgerald*....

IV. The majority may be correct in its conclusion that "[a] rule of absolute immunity ... will not leave the Nation without sufficient protection against misconduct on the part of the Chief Executive." Such a rule will, however, leave Mr. Fitzgerald without an adequate remedy for the harms that he may have suffered. More importantly, it will leave future plaintiffs without a remedy, regardless of the substantiality of their claims. The remedies in which the Court finds comfort were never designed to afford relief for individual harms. Rather, they were designed as political safety valves. Politics and history, however, are not the domain of the courts; the courts exist to assure each individual that he, as an individual, has enforceable rights that he may pursue to achieve a peaceful redress of his legitimate grievances.

I find it ironic, as well as tragic, that the Court would so casually discard its own role of assuring "the right of every individual to claim the protection of the laws," *Marbury v. Madison*, in the name of protecting the principle of separation of powers. Accordingly, I dissent.

Justice Blackmun, with whom Justice Brennan and Justice Marshall join, dissenting. [Omitted.]

Clinton v. Jones: Questions

1. How does *Clinton v. Jones* interpret the decision in *Nixon v. Fitzgerald* with reference to the reasons for presidential immunity from civil actions for damages?
2. Compare the Court's use of history in footnote 2 of *Nixon v. Fitzgerald* with its evaluation of the same history in *Clinton v. Jones*.

Clinton v. Jones
520 U.S. 681 (1997)

[Majority: Stevens, Rehnquist (C.J.), O'Connor, Scalia, Kennedy, Souter, Thomas, and Ginsburg. Concurring: Breyer.]

Justice Stevens delivered the opinion of the Court.

This case raises a constitutional and a prudential question concerning the Office of the President of the United States. Respondent, a private citizen, seeks to recover damages from the current occupant of that office based on actions allegedly taken before his term began. The President submits that in all but the most exceptional cases the Constitution requires federal courts to defer such litigation until his term ends and that, in any event, respect for the office warrants such a stay. Despite the force of the arguments supporting the President's submissions, we conclude that they must be rejected.

Petitioner, William Jefferson Clinton, was elected to the Presidency in 1992, and reelected in 1996. His term of office expires on January 20, 2001. In 1991 he was the Governor of the State of Arkansas. Respondent, Paula Corbin Jones, is a resident of California. In 1991 she lived in Arkansas, and was an employee of the Arkansas Industrial Development Commission.

On May 6, 1994, she commenced this action in the United States District Court for the Eastern District of Arkansas by filing a complaint naming petitioner and Danny Ferguson, a former Arkansas State Police officer, as defendants. The complaint alleges two federal claims, and two state law claims over which the federal court has jurisdiction because of the diverse citizenship of the parties. As the case comes to us, we are required to assume the truth of the detailed—but as yet untested—factual allegations in the complaint.

Those allegations principally describe events that are said to have occurred on the afternoon of May 8, 1991, during an official conference held at the Excelsior Hotel in Little Rock, Arkansas. The Governor delivered a speech at the conference; respondent—working as a state employee—staffed the registration desk. She alleges that Ferguson persuaded her to leave her desk and to visit the Governor in a business suite at the hotel, where he made "abhorrent" sexual advances that she vehemently rejected. She further claims that her superiors at work subsequently dealt with her in a hostile and rude manner, and changed her duties to punish her for rejecting those advances. Finally, she alleges that after petitioner was elected President, Ferguson defamed her by making a statement to a reporter that implied she had accepted petitioner's alleged overtures, and that various persons authorized to speak for the President publicly branded her a liar by denying that the incident had occurred.

Respondent seeks actual damages of $75,000 and punitive damages of $100,000. Her complaint contains four counts. The first charges that petitioner, acting under color of state law, deprived her of rights protected by the Constitution, in violation of 42 U.S.C. § 1983. The second charges that petitioner and Ferguson engaged in a conspiracy to violate her federal rights, also actionable under federal law. See 42 U.S.C. § 1985. The third is a state common law claim for intentional infliction of emotional distress, grounded primarily on the incident at the hotel. The fourth count, also based on state law, is for defamation, embracing both the comments allegedly made to the press by Ferguson and the statements of petitioner's agents. Inasmuch as the legal sufficiency of the claims has not yet been challenged, we assume, without deciding, that each of the four counts states a cause of action as a matter of law. With the exception of the last charge, which arguably may involve conduct within the outer perimeter of the President's official responsibilities, it is perfectly clear that the alleged misconduct of petitioner was unrelated to any of his official duties as President of the United States and, indeed, occurred before he was elected to that office.

II. In response to the complaint, petitioner promptly advised the District Court that he intended to file a motion to dismiss on grounds of Presidential immunity, and requested the court to defer all other pleadings and motions until after the immunity issue was resolved. Relying on our cases holding that immunity questions should be decided at the earliest possible stage of the litigation, our recognition of the "'singular importance of the President's duties,'" and the fact that the question did not require any analysis of the allegations of the complaint, the court granted the request. Petitioner thereupon filed a motion "to dismiss ... without prejudice and to toll any statutes of limitation [that may be applicable] until he is no longer President, at which time the plaintiff may refile the instant suit." Extensive submissions were made to the District Court by the parties and the Department of Justice.

The District Judge denied the motion to dismiss on immunity grounds and ruled that discovery in the case could go forward, but ordered any trial stayed until the end of petitioner's Presidency. Although she recognized that a "thin majority" in *Nixon v. Fitzgerald* (1982), had held that "the President has absolute immunity from civil damage actions arising out of the execution of official duties of office," she was not convinced that "a President has absolute immunity from civil causes of action arising prior to assuming the office." She was, however, persuaded by some of the reasoning in our opinion in *Fitzgerald* that deferring the trial if one were required would be appropriate. Relying in part on the fact that respondent had failed to bring her complaint until two days before the 3-year period of limitations expired, she concluded that the public interest in avoiding litigation that might hamper the President in conducting the duties of his office outweighed any demonstrated need for an immediate trial.

Both parties appealed. A divided panel of the Court of Appeals affirmed the denial of the motion to dismiss, but because it regarded the order postponing the trial until the President leaves office as the "functional equivalent" of a grant of temporary immunity, it reversed that order. Writing for the majority, Judge Bowman explained that "the President, like all other government officials, is subject to the same laws that apply to all other members of our society," that he could find no "case in which any public official ever has been granted any immunity from suit for his unofficial acts," and that the rationale for official immunity "is inapposite where only personal, private conduct by a President is at issue." The majority specifically rejected the argument that, unless immunity is available, the threat of judicial interference with the Executive Branch through scheduling orders, potential contempt citations, and sanctions would violate separation-of-powers principles. Judge Bowman suggested that "judicial case management sensitive to the burdens of the presidency and the demands of the President's schedule" would avoid the perceived danger.

In dissent, Judge Ross submitted that even though the holding in *Fitzgerald* involved official acts, the logic of the opinion, which "placed primary reliance on the prospect that the President's discharge of his constitutional powers and duties would be impaired if he were subject to suits for damages," applies with equal force to this case. In his view, "unless exigent circumstances can be shown," all private actions for damages against a sitting President must be stayed until the completion of his term. In this case, Judge Ross saw no reason why the stay would prevent respondent from ultimately obtaining an adjudication of her claims....

III. The President, represented by private counsel, filed a petition for certiorari. The Acting Solicitor General, representing the United States, supported the petition, arguing that the decision of the Court of Appeals was "fundamentally mistaken" and created "serious risks for the institution of the Presidency." In her brief in opposition to certiorari, respondent argued that this "one-of-a-kind case is singularly inappropriate" for the exercise of our certiorari jurisdiction because it did not create any conflict among the Courts of Appeals, it "does not pose any conceivable threat to the functioning of the Executive Branch," and there is no precedent supporting the President's position.

While our decision to grant the petition expressed no judgment concerning the merits of the case, it does reflect our appraisal of its importance. The representations made on behalf of the Executive Branch as to the potential impact of the precedent established by the Court of Appeals merit our respectful and deliberate consideration....[1]

IV. Petitioner's principal submission — that "in all but the most exceptional cases," the Constitution affords the President temporary immunity from civil damages litigation arising out of events that occurred before he took office — cannot be sustained on the basis of precedent....

The principal rationale for affording certain public servants immunity from suits for money damages arising out of their official acts is inapplicable to unofficial conduct. In cases involving prosecutors, legislators, and judges we have repeatedly explained that the immunity serves the public interest in enabling such officials to perform their designated functions effectively without fear that a particular decision may give rise to personal liability. We explained in *Ferri v. Ackerman* (1979):

> As public servants, the prosecutor and the judge represent the interest of society as a whole. The conduct of their official duties may adversely affect a wide variety of different individuals, each of whom may be a potential source of future controversy. The societal interest in providing such public officials with the maximum ability to deal fearlessly and impartially with the public at large has long been recognized as an acceptable justification for official immunity. The point of immunity for such officials is to forestall an atmosphere of intimidation that would conflict with their resolve to perform their designated functions in a principled fashion.

That rationale provided the principal basis for our holding that a former President of the United States was "entitled to absolute immunity from damages liability predicated on his official acts," *Fitzgerald*. Our central concern was to avoid rendering the President "unduly cautious in the discharge of his official duties."[2]

---

1. The two questions presented in the certiorari petition are: "1. Whether the litigation of a private civil damages action against an incumbent President must in all but the most exceptional cases be deferred until the President leaves office"; and "2. Whether a district court, as a proper exercise of judicial discretion, may stay such litigation until the President leaves office." Our review is confined to these issues.

2. Petitioner draws our attention to dicta in *Fitzgerald*, which he suggests are helpful to his cause. We noted there that "[b]ecause of the singular importance of the President's duties, diversion of his

This reasoning provides no support for an immunity for *unofficial* conduct. As we explained in *Fitzgerald*, "the sphere of protected action must be related closely to the immunity's justifying purposes." Because of the President's broad responsibilities, we recognized in that case an immunity from damages claims arising out of official acts extending to the "outer perimeter of his authority." But we have never suggested that the President, or any other official, has an immunity that extends beyond the scope of any action taken in an official capacity. See *Fitzgerald* (Burger, C.J., concurring) (noting that "a President, like Members of Congress, judges, prosecutors, or congressional aides—all having absolute immunity—are not immune for acts outside official duties").

Moreover, when defining the scope of an immunity for acts clearly taken within an official capacity, we have applied a functional approach. "Frequently our decisions have held that an official's absolute immunity should extend only to acts in performance of particular functions of his office." Hence, for example, a judge's absolute immunity does not extend to actions performed in a purely administrative capacity. As our opinions have made clear, immunities are grounded in "the nature of the function performed, not the identity of the actor who performed it."

Petitioner's effort to construct an immunity from suit for unofficial acts grounded purely in the identity of his office is unsupported by precedent.

V. We are also unpersuaded by the evidence from the historical record to which petitioner has called our attention. He points to a comment by Thomas Jefferson protesting the subpoena duces tecum Chief Justice Marshall directed to him in the Burr trial, a statement in the diaries kept by Senator William Maclay of the first Senate debates, in which then Vice President John Adams and Senator Oliver Ellsworth are recorded as having said that "the President personally [is] not ... subject to any process whatever," lest it be "put ... in the power of a common Justice to exercise any Authority over him and Stop the Whole Machine of Government," and to a quotation from Justice Story's *Commentaries on the Constitution*. None of these sources sheds much light on the question at hand.[3]

---

energies by concern with private lawsuits would raise unique risks to the effective functioning of government," and suggested further that "[c]ognizance of ... personal vulnerability frequently could distract a President from his public duties." Petitioner argues that in this aspect the Court's concern was parallel to the issue he suggests is of great importance in this case, the possibility that a sitting President might be distracted by the need to participate in litigation during the pendency of his office. In context, however, it is clear that our dominant concern was with the diversion of the President's attention during the decisionmaking process caused by needless worry as to the possibility of damages actions stemming from any particular official decision. Moreover, *Fitzgerald* did not present the issue raised in this case because that decision involved claims against a *former* President.

3. Jefferson's argument provides little support for respondent's position. As we explain later, the prerogative Jefferson claimed was denied him by the Chief Justice in the very decision Jefferson was protesting, and this Court has subsequently reaffirmed that holding. See *United States v. Nixon* (1974). The statements supporting a similar proposition recorded in Senator Maclay's diary are inconclusive of the issue before us here for the same reason. In addition, this material is hardly proof of the unequivocal common understanding at the time of the founding. Immediately after mentioning the positions of Adams and Ellsworth, Maclay went on to point out in his diary that he virulently disagreed with them, concluding that his opponents' view "[s]hows clearly how amazingly fond of the old leven many People are." *Diary of Maclay* 168.

Finally, Justice Story's comments in his constitutional law treatise provide no substantial support for respondent's position. Story wrote that because the President's "incidental powers" must include "the power to perform [his duties], without any obstruction," he "cannot, therefore, be liable to arrest, imprisonment, or detention, while he is in the discharge of the duties of his office; and *for this* purpose his person must be deemed, in civil cases at least, to possess an official inviolability." 3 Story, § 1563, at 418–19 (emphasis added). Story said only that "*an* official inviolability," was necessary to preserve the President's ability to perform the functions of the office; he did not specify the dimen-

Respondent, in turn, has called our attention to conflicting historical evidence. Speaking in favor of the Constitution's adoption at the Pennsylvania Convention, James Wilson — who had participated in the Philadelphia Convention at which the document was drafted — explained that, although the President "is placed [on] high," "not a single privilege is annexed to his character; far from being above the laws, he is amenable to them in his private character as a citizen, and in his public character by impeachment." This description is consistent with both the doctrine of presidential immunity as set forth in *Fitzgerald*, and rejection of the immunity claim in this case. With respect to acts taken in his "public character" — that is, official acts — the President may be disciplined principally by impeachment, not by private lawsuits for damages. But he is otherwise subject to the laws for his purely private acts.

In the end, as applied to the particular question before us, we reach the same conclusion about these historical materials that Justice Jackson described when confronted with an issue concerning the dimensions of the President's power. "Just what our forefathers did envision, or would have envisioned had they foreseen modern conditions, must be divined from materials almost as enigmatic as the dreams Joseph was called upon to interpret for Pharoah. A century and a half of partisan debate and scholarly speculation yields no net result but only supplies more or less apt quotations from respected sources on each side.... They largely cancel each other." *Youngstown Sheet & Tube Co. v. Sawyer* (1952) (concurring opinion).

VI. Petitioner's strongest argument supporting his immunity claim is based on the text and structure of the Constitution. He does not contend that the occupant of the Office of the President is "above the law," in the sense that his conduct is entirely immune from judicial scrutiny. The President argues merely for a postponement of the judicial proceedings that will determine whether he violated any law. His argument is grounded in the character of the office that was created by Article II of the Constitution, and relies on separation-of-powers principles that have structured our constitutional arrangement since the founding.

As a starting premise, petitioner contends that he occupies a unique office with powers and responsibilities so vast and important that the public interest demands that he devote his undivided time and attention to his public duties. He submits that — given the nature of the office — the doctrine of separation of powers places limits on the authority of the Federal Judiciary to interfere with the Executive Branch that would be transgressed by allowing this action to proceed.

We have no dispute with the initial premise of the argument. [The Court cited examples of the extraordinary demands of the job.]

It does not follow, however, that separation of powers principles would be violated by allowing this action to proceed. The doctrine of separation of powers is concerned with the allocation of official power among the three co-equal branches of our Government. The Framers "built into the tripartite Federal Government ... a self-executing safeguard against the encroachment or aggrandizement of one branch at the expense of the other." *Buckley v. Valeo* (1976). Thus, for example, the Congress may not exercise the judicial power to revise final judgments, *Plaut v. Spendthrift Farm, Inc.* (1995), or the executive power to manage an airport, see *Metropolitan Washington Airports Authority v. Citizens*

---

sions of the necessary immunity. While we have held that an immunity from suits grounded on official acts is necessary to serve this purpose, see *Fitzgerald*, it does not follow that the broad immunity from *all* civil damages suits that petitioner seeks is also necessary.

for *Abatement of Aircraft Noise, Inc.* (1991) (holding that "[i]f the power is executive, the Constitution does not permit an agent of Congress to exercise it"). See *J. W. Hampton, Jr., & Co. v. United States* (1928) (Congress may not "invest itself or its members with either executive power or judicial power"). Similarly, the President may not exercise the legislative power to authorize the seizure of private property for public use. *Youngstown Sheet & Tube Co. v. Sawyer* (1952). And, the judicial power to decide cases and controversies does not include the provision of purely advisory opinions to the Executive, or permit the federal courts to resolve nonjusticiable questions.

Of course the lines between the powers of the three branches are not always neatly defined. But in this case there is no suggestion that the Federal Judiciary is being asked to perform any function that might in some way be described as "executive." Respondent is merely asking the courts to exercise their core Article III jurisdiction to decide cases and controversies. Whatever the outcome of this case, there is no possibility that the decision will curtail the scope of the official powers of the Executive Branch. The litigation of questions that relate entirely to the unofficial conduct of the individual who happens to be the President poses no perceptible risk of misallocation of either judicial power or executive power.

Rather than arguing that the decision of the case will produce either an aggrandizement of judicial power or a narrowing of executive power, petitioner contends that—as a by product of an otherwise traditional exercise of judicial power—burdens will be placed on the President that will hamper the performance of his official duties. We have recognized that "[e]ven when a branch does not arrogate power to itself ... the separation-of-powers doctrine requires that a branch not impair another in the performance of its constitutional duties." *Loving v. United States* (1996). As a factual matter, petitioner contends that this particular case—as well as the potential additional litigation that an affirmance of the Court of Appeals judgment might spawn—may impose an unacceptable burden on the President's time and energy, and thereby impair the effective performance of his office.

Petitioner's predictive judgment finds little support in either history or the relatively narrow compass of the issues raised in this particular case. As we have already noted, in the more than 200-year history of the Republic, only three sitting Presidents have been subjected to suits for their private actions. If the past is any indicator, it seems unlikely that a deluge of such litigation will ever engulf the Presidency. As for the case at hand, if properly managed by the District Court, it appears to us highly unlikely to occupy any substantial amount of petitioner's time.

Of greater significance, petitioner errs by presuming that interactions between the Judicial Branch and the Executive, even quite burdensome interactions, necessarily rise to the level of constitutionally forbidden impairment of the Executive's ability to perform its constitutionally mandated functions. "[O]ur ... system imposes upon the Branches a degree of overlapping responsibility, a duty of interdependence as well as independence the absence of which 'would preclude the establishment of a Nation capable of governing itself effectively.'" *Mistretta v. United States* (1989). As Madison explained, separation of powers does not mean that the branches "ought to have no *partial agency* in, or no *controul* over the acts of each other." The fact that a federal court's exercise of its traditional Article III jurisdiction may significantly burden the time and attention of the Chief Executive is not sufficient to establish a violation of the Constitution. Two long-settled propositions, first announced by Chief Justice Marshall, support that conclusion.

First, we have long held that when the President takes official action, the Court has the authority to determine whether he has acted within the law. Perhaps the most dramatic example of such a case is our holding that President Truman exceeded his constitutional authority when he issued an order directing the Secretary of Commerce to take possession of and operate most of the Nation's steel mills in order to avert a national catastrophe. *Youngstown Sheet & Tube Co. v. Sawyer.* Despite the serious impact of that decision on the ability of the Executive Branch to accomplish its assigned mission, and the substantial time that the President must necessarily have devoted to the matter as a result of judicial involvement, we exercised our Article III jurisdiction to decide whether his official conduct conformed to the law. Our holding was an application of the principle established in *Marbury v. Madison* (1803), that "[i]t is emphatically the province and duty of the judicial department to say what the law is."

Second, it is also settled that the President is subject to judicial process in appropriate circumstances. Although Thomas Jefferson apparently thought otherwise, Chief Justice Marshall, when presiding in the treason trial of Aaron Burr, ruled that a subpoena duces tecum could be directed to the President. *United States v. Burr* (C.C.D. Va. 1807). We unequivocally and emphatically endorsed Marshall's position when we held that President Nixon was obligated to comply with a subpoena commanding him to produce certain tape recordings of his conversations with his aides. *United States v. Nixon* (1974). As we explained, "neither the doctrine of separation of powers, nor the need for confidentiality of high-level communications, without more, can sustain an absolute, unqualified Presidential privilege of immunity from judicial process under all circumstances."

Sitting Presidents have responded to court orders to provide testimony and other information with sufficient frequency that such interactions between the Judicial and Executive Branches can scarcely be thought a novelty. President Monroe responded to written interrogatories. President Nixon—as noted above—produced tapes in response to a subpoena duces tecum, President Ford complied with an order to give a deposition in a criminal trial, and President Clinton has twice given videotaped testimony in criminal proceedings. Moreover, sitting Presidents have also voluntarily complied with judicial requests for testimony. President Grant gave a lengthy deposition in a criminal case under such circumstances, and President Carter similarly gave videotaped testimony for use at a criminal trial.

In sum, "[i]t is settled law that the separation-of-powers doctrine does not bar every exercise of jurisdiction over the President of the United States." *Fitzgerald.* If the Judiciary may severely burden the Executive Branch by reviewing the legality of the President's official conduct, and if it may direct appropriate process to the President himself, it must follow that the federal courts have power to determine the legality of his unofficial conduct. The burden on the President's time and energy that is a mere by product of such review surely cannot be considered as onerous as the direct burden imposed by judicial review and the occasional invalidation of his official actions. We therefore hold that the doctrine of separation of powers does not require federal courts to stay all private actions against the President until he leaves office.

The reasons for rejecting such a categorical rule apply as well to a rule that would require a stay "in all but the most exceptional cases." Indeed, if the Framers of the Constitution had thought it necessary to protect the President from the burdens of private litigation, we think it far more likely that they would have adopted a categorical rule than a rule that required the President to litigate the question whether a specific case belonged in the "exceptional case" subcategory. In all events, the question whether a specific case should receive exceptional treatment is more appropriately the subject of the exercise of judicial discretion than an interpretation of the Constitution. Accordingly, we turn to the question whether the District Court's decision to stay the trial until after petitioner leaves office was an abuse of discretion.

VII. The Court of Appeals described the District Court's discretionary decision to stay the trial as the "functional equivalent" of a grant of temporary immunity. Concluding that petitioner was not constitutionally entitled to such an immunity, the court held that it was error to grant the stay. Although we ultimately conclude that the stay should not have been granted, we think the issue is more difficult than the opinion of the Court of Appeals suggests.

Strictly speaking the stay was not the functional equivalent of the constitutional immunity that petitioner claimed, because the District Court ordered discovery to proceed. Moreover, a stay of either the trial or discovery might be justified by considerations that do not require the recognition of any constitutional immunity. The District Court has broad discretion to stay proceedings as an incident to its power to control its own docket. As we have explained, "[e]specially in cases of extraordinary public moment, [a plaintiff] may be required to submit to delay not immoderate in extent and not oppressive in its consequences if the public welfare or convenience will thereby be promoted." Although we have rejected the argument that the potential burdens on the President violate separation of powers principles, those burdens are appropriate matters for the District Court to evaluate in its management of the case. The high respect that is owed to the office of the Chief Executive, though not justifying a rule of categorical immunity, is a matter that should inform the conduct of the entire proceeding, including the timing and scope of discovery.

Nevertheless, we are persuaded that it was an abuse of discretion for the District Court to defer the trial until after the President leaves office. Such a lengthy and categorical stay takes no account whatever of the respondent's interest in bringing the case to trial. The complaint was filed within the statutory limitations period—albeit near the end of that period—and delaying trial would increase the danger of prejudice resulting from the loss of evidence, including the inability of witnesses to recall specific facts, or the possible death of a party.

The decision to postpone the trial was, furthermore, premature. The proponent of a stay bears the burden of establishing its need. In this case, at the stage at which the District Court made its ruling, there was no way to assess whether a stay of trial after the completion of discovery would be warranted. Other than the fact that a trial may consume some of the President's time and attention, there is nothing in the record to enable a judge to assess the potential harm that may ensue from scheduling the trial promptly after discovery is concluded. We think the District Court may have given undue weight to the concern that a trial might generate unrelated civil actions that could conceivably hamper the President in conducting the duties of his office. If and when that should occur, the court's discretion would permit it to manage those actions in such fashion (including deferral of trial) that interference with the President's duties would not occur. But no such impingement upon the President's conduct of his office was shown here.

VIII. We add a final comment on two matters that are discussed at length in the briefs: the risk that our decision will generate a large volume of politically motivated harassing and frivolous litigation, and the danger that national security concerns might prevent the President from explaining a legitimate need for a continuance.

We are not persuaded that either of these risks is serious. Most frivolous and vexatious litigation is terminated at the pleading stage or on summary judgment, with little if any personal involvement by the defendant. Moreover, the availability of sanctions provides a significant deterrent to litigation directed at the President in his unofficial capacity for purposes of political gain or harassment. History indicates that the likelihood that a significant number of such cases will be filed is remote. Although scheduling problems may arise, there is no reason to assume that the District Courts will be either unable to accommodate the President's needs or unfaithful to the tradition—especially in matters involving national security—of giving "the utmost deference to Presidential responsibilities." Several Presidents, including petitioner, have given testimony without jeopardizing the Nation's security. In short, we have confidence in the ability of our federal judges to deal with both of these concerns.

If Congress deems it appropriate to afford the President stronger protection, it may respond with appropriate legislation. As petitioner notes in his brief, Congress has enacted more than one statute providing for the deferral of civil litigation to accommodate important public interests. See, e.g., 11 U.S.C. §362 (litigation against debtor stayed upon filing of bankruptcy petition); Soldiers' and Sailors' Civil Relief Act of 1940, 50 U.S.C. App. §§501–525 (provisions governing, inter alia, tolling or stay of civil claims by or against military personnel during course of active duty). If the Constitution embodied the rule that the President advocates, Congress, of course, could not repeal it. But our holding today raises no barrier to a statutory response to these concerns.

The Federal District Court has jurisdiction to decide this case. Like every other citizen who properly invokes that jurisdiction, respondent has a right to an orderly disposition of her claims. Accordingly, the judgment of the Court of Appeals is affirmed.

Justice Breyer, concurring in the judgment. [Omitted.]

Note: The Aftermath of *Clinton v. Jones*

During the Clinton administration, Republicans in Congress demanded appointment of a special prosecutor to investigate alleged crimes by President and Mrs. Clinton, particularly with reference to an Arkansas land deal known as Whitewater. In accordance with the relevant federal statute, Chief Justice Rehnquist appointed a panel of three judges, who then appointed Kenneth Starr special prosecutor to investigate potential criminal behavior in connection with Whitewater.

The special prosecutor's investigation of the Whitewater land deal resulted in several convictions of people in Arkansas, but in the end, after several years and the expenditure of more than twenty million dollars, the prosecutor concluded that there was not sufficient evidence to justify prosecuting President Clinton or his wife in connection with Whitewater.

But in the meantime, an Arkansas state employee named Paula Jones had filed a lawsuit against President Clinton alleging that then Governor Clinton had made improper sexual advances to her. As far back as his campaign for the Democratic nomination in 1992, Clinton had been beset by charges of extra-marital affairs. On May 27, 1997, President Clinton's effort to delay discovery in the Jones case until he left office was, as you have seen, rejected by the Supreme Court.

In discovery, the lawyers for Jones sought evidence of all of Clinton's recent sexual encounters, not just those involving unwanted advances. In December 1997, Jones' lawyers subpoenaed Monica Lewinsky for a January deposition. In response, Lewinsky signed an affidavit denying sexual contact with President Clinton. That denial was false. In fact, in November 1995, President Clinton and Lewinsky had begun a sexual affair. Lewinsky discussed the affair with a friend named Linda Tripp in several phone conversations, some of which Tripp taped without Lewinsky's knowledge. On January 12, 1998, Linda Tripp provided special prosecutor Starr with information about Lewinsky's affair with President Clinton.

On January 16, 1998 Kenneth Starr received permission to expand his special prosecutor probe to include claims that Clinton encouraged Lewinsky to lie and otherwise obstructed justice. Lured to a Washington hotel for a meeting with Linda Tripp, Lewinsky was then accosted and interrogated by federal agents working for Special Prosecutor Kenneth Starr.

On January 17, 1998, Clinton gave his deposition in the Paula Jones case, and falsely denied having sexual relations with Lewinsky or even being alone with her. On January 28, 1998, during an encounter with the press, Clinton strongly and falsely denied an affair. The denial ("I never had sex with that woman, Ms. Lewinsky") was broadcast on television news shows. On January 29, 1998, the judge in the Paula Jones case excluded any evidence of Clinton's alleged consensual affair with Lewinsky from evidence in the Paula Jones trial. The judge reiterated the ruling on March 9, 1998.

Eventually, Special Prosecutor Starr granted Lewinsky and her parents full immunity from prosecution in return for her testimony against Clinton. A report which Starr provided to the House Judiciary Committee contained detailed descriptions of various sexual contacts between the President and Lewinsky and provided a picture of a semen-stained dress Lewinsky had saved as a memento.

In August, 1998, President Clinton appeared before a grand jury to testify about the Lewinsky affair and his alleged perjury and obstruction of justice connected with it. Starr forwarded the tape of the testimony to the Judiciary Committee which (on a party line vote) released it to the press. The Committee also released over 3000 pages of an appendix to Starr's report on the matter. The Lewinsky matter dominated the press for months; the news reports were quite critical of President Clinton's conduct and many predicted his impeachment and removal. Public opinion polls, however, showed a lack of support for removing the President in connection with the Lewinsky scandal.

In October, 1998 the House of Representatives authorized a full impeachment inquiry. The judge in the Paula Jones case dismissed her case. Pending appeal, President Clinton settled the case for $850,000. Ads highlighting Clinton's misdeeds in connection with the Lewinsky affair ran frequently during the 1998 congressional election campaign.

On December 19, 1998, the House of Representatives approved articles of impeachment against President Clinton, charging Clinton with lying under oath and obstruction of justice. After a trial in the Senate, with Chief Justice Rehnquist presiding, the Senate failed to convict. On the perjury charge, ten Republicans joined forty-five Democrats in voting not guilty. On the obstruction of justice charge, the Senate split 50–50.

Subsequently, Judge Susan Wright, who presided in the Paula Jones trial found President Clinton in contempt for his failure to testify truthfully. Clinton was suspended from the practice of law in Arkansas.

The Supreme Court assumed that proceeding with the trial of the Paula Jones case would not significantly interfere with the duties of the President. With the wisdom of hindsight, that assumption was grossly mistaken. Professor Michael Gerhardt, writes "[f]or many scholars, the fact that the lawsuit and its fallout paralyzed the national government for over a year flatly contradicts the Supreme Court's assumption in *Clinton v. Jones* that a civil lawsuit based on a President's activities before taking office could proceed without substantially interfering with a President's ability to do his job." Michael Gerhardt, *Clinton v. Jones, Encyclopedia of the American Constitution* (2000).

Others blame the President for the case's extensive fallout. They point out, correctly, that the President could have avoided both impeachment and contempt by being more candid or, for that matter, by not having engaged in the affair.

Chapter 6

Limits on State Power: Preemption, the Dormant Commerce Clause, and the Privileges and Immunities Clause

Contents

I.	Preemption	509
	Prigg v. Pennsylvania	511
	Geier v. American Honda Motor Company, Inc.	522
II.	The Dormant Commerce Clause	540
	A. The Dormant Commerce Clause: Introduction	541
	B. Discrimination or Even-Handed Treatment: Introductory Cases	543
	New Energy Company v. Limbach	545
	Southern Pacific Company v. Arizona	549
	Granholm v. Heald	557
	Kassel v. Consolidated Freightways Corporation	561
	C. Discrimination or Even-Handed Treatment: Complex Cases	573
	Dean Milk Company v. City of Madison	573
	Hunt v. Washington State Apple Advertising Commission	578
	City of Philadelphia v. New Jersey	583
	United Haulers Association, Inc. v. Oneida-Herkimer Solid Waste Management Authority	591
	Minnesota v. Clover Leaf Creamery Company	595
	D. Extra-Territorial Regulation	599
	E. The Market Participant Exception	600
	Reeves, Inc. v. Stake	600
	F. The Dormant Commerce Clause Reconsidered	606
III.	The Privileges and Immunities Clause of Article IV	610
	A. An Introduction to the Privileges and Immunities Clause of Article IV, §2	611
	B. The Current Approach to the Privileges and Immunities Clause of Article IV, §2	614
	Supreme Court of Virginia v. Friedman	615
IV.	Special Considerations: The World Trade Organization and the North American Free Trade Agreement	620

Chapter 6

Limits on State Power: Preemption, the Dormant Commerce Clause, and the Privileges and Immunities Clause

I. Preemption

Congress may use its Commerce Clause powers (or other powers) to prevent states from regulating activities that the states would otherwise be free to reach. When Congress explicitly bars state legislation on a subject and acts within a delegated power, the result is clear. The state statute is void. More difficult problems arise when Congress has not explicitly said how its legislation is to affect state laws. Because of the vast potential reach of congressional power, pre-emption is potentially a great threat to the role of the states. As Professor Ernest A. Young has noted, states enjoy the loyalty of their citizens and function as viable political units to the extent that they are able to legislate or provide common law protection on subjects of concern to their citizens. To the extent that federal statutes eliminate broad areas of state power, they tend to undermine the states as viable political units. Ernest A. Young, *State Sovereign Immunity and the Future of Federalism* 42–47, Supreme Court Review (1999); see also *Federalist* 46 (James Madison). The problem is exacerbated when the Court finds a state statute preempted though Congress has not spoken to the issue and both the state statute and the act of Congress could co-exist.

The Supreme Court has described the situations in which it will find preemption in various ways. The following description is from *Gade v. National Solid Waste Management Assn.* (1992):

> Preemption may be either expressed or implied, and is compelled whether Congress' command is [I.] explicitly stated in the statute's language or [II.] implicitly contained in its structure and purpose.... Absent explicit preemptive language, we have recognized at least two types of implied preemption: [II.A.] field preemption, where the scheme of federal regulation is so pervasive as to make reasonable the inference that Congress left no room for the States to supplement it, ... and [II.B.] conflict preemption, where [1.] compliance with both federal and state regulations is a physical impossibility, ... or where [2.] state law stands as an obstacle to the accomplishment and execution of the full purposes and objectives of Congress,....

Prigg v. Pennsylvania: **Background**

Article IV, § 2, cl. 2 provides:

> No Person held to Service or Labour in one State, under the Laws thereof, escaping into another State, shall in Consequence of any Law or Regulation therein, be discharged from such Service or Labour, but shall be delivered up on the Claim of the Party to whom such Service or Labour may be due.

After the American Revolution, most Northern states abolished slavery. In addition, of course, some slaves were freed by their masters. By 1842, there was a substantial free black population in Pennsylvania. As early as 1800, Congress considered, but did not act upon, a petition of free blacks from Philadelphia. They complained that free blacks were being kidnapped in free states and taken into slavery. At least one free black who had been kidnapped and sold into slavery escaped and wrote an account of his experience.

Had it not been for *Dred Scott v. Sandford* (1857), *Prigg v. Pennsylvania* (1842) would probably be the most famous slavery-related case to reach the Supreme Court. At the time it attracted a great deal of attention. It helped set the stage for the passage of the Fugitive Slave Act of 1850. Jurisprudentially, Justice Joseph Story's opinion asserted a number of important constitutional principles—some for the first time in U.S. history—that remain important today.

The facts of the case illustrate the complexity of returning fugitive slaves. Margaret Morgan was born in Maryland sometime around the War of 1812. Her parents, whose names are unknown, had been the slaves of a Harford County, Maryland, master named John Ashmore. Before Margaret's birth, Ashmore had told the slave couple they were free. Ashmore did not, however, legally emancipate them. Margaret grew up thinking she was free and married Jerry Morgan, a free black from nearby Pennsylvania. In 1830, the U.S. Census recorded Jerry Morgan, his wife, and two children as "free persons of color" living in Harford County. Meanwhile, John Ashmore died, and the probate of his estate did not indicate that Margaret or her parents were his property.

Sometime between 1830 and 1832, the Morgans moved to York, Pennsylvania. In 1837, John Ashmore's widow, also named Margaret, sought to recover Margaret Morgan as a fugitive slave. Her son-in-law, Nathan Beemis, and three neighbors, including Edward Prigg, went to Pennsylvania where they seized the entire Morgan family, and brought them before a local justice of the peace. By this time Margaret Morgan had at least one, and perhaps two, other children who had been born in Pennsylvania and were thus clearly free under Pennsylvania law.

An 1826 Pennsylvania statute, known as a "personal liberty law," made it a felony to remove a black from the state without first getting a certificate of removal from a Pennsylvania judge, justice of the peace, or other official. The York County justice of the peace would not give Beemis and Prigg this writ, probably because it was clear that Jerry Morgan was born in Pennsylvania, as were some of Margaret's children, and that Margaret herself had a strong claim to freedom. Beemis and Prigg then forcibly took Margaret and her children to Maryland, without the benefit of any legal authority.

Shortly after this, the York County grand jury indicted all four Marylanders for kidnapping. The Maryland governor refused to allow the extradition of the alleged kidnappers, although in private correspondence he agreed that they had indeed violated Pennsylvania law. Finally, in 1839, the two states reached an agreement. Only one of the kidnappers, Prigg, would be sent back for trial. If convicted he would not be jailed until after the case had gone to the Pennsylvania Supreme Court and, if necessary, to the U.S.

Supreme Court. Prigg was then returned to Pennsylvania where he was convicted of kidnapping. The Pennsylvania Supreme Court upheld the conviction without an opinion, and in 1842 the case reached the U.S. Supreme Court.

At issue for the Supreme Court was the constitutionality of the Fugitive Slave Act of 1793 and the Pennsylvania Personal Liberty Law of 1826. Prigg claimed a right to take a fugitive slave out of Pennsylvania under the 1793 law and the Fugitive Slave Clause of the U.S. Constitution. Pennsylvania argued that it had a right to protect its citizens and residents from being kidnapped.

Story's opinion was sweeping. He upheld the 1793 law and struck down the Pennsylvania law as interfering with the federal law. This appears to be an early use of the preemption doctrine in American Constitutional Law. He further asserted, in what is the most important early assertion of the "dormant" powers of Congress, that even if there were no federal law on fugitive slave rendition, the states did not have a right to legislate on the subject. Instead, he argued that in the absence of the federal law of 1793, Prigg had a common law right of recaption to take a fugitive slave where he found one. This dovetailed with Story's lifelong desire to create a federal common law. It also mirrored Story's other great opinion of the 1842 term, *Swift v. Tyson*, in which Story created a federal common law for commercial transactions.

The great losers in this case were the northern states, which could no longer effectively protect their black residents who were free under their state laws from kidnapping, and of course free blacks, like the Pennsylvania children of Margaret Morgan, who ended up as slaves for life. In an off-hand remark, Story asserted that the free states could not be forced to implement the Fugitive Slave Act of 1793, although he believed they had a patriotic duty to do so. Most northern states eventually used Story's logic here to withdraw from the process of returning fugitive slaves. Story's son argued that this was in fact his father's goal, and thus the decision was really pro-freedom. But there is no evidence to support this analysis. Indeed, Story's opinion and the withdrawal of northern enforcement led to southern demands for a new law, with federal enforcement. Story himself endorsed this idea in his private correspondence, and in 1850, Congress did exactly this with the adoption of the Fugitive Slave Act of 1850.

Prigg v. Pennsylvania
41 U.S. 539 (1842)

[The Pennsylvania legislature had emancipated all slaves in the state after the American Revolution. Pennsylvania then passed a series of statutes attempting to ensure that the emancipated slaves and other free persons of color within the state were not re-enslaved. The 1826 state statute set out below was the latest in a series of statutes to protect free blacks. Prigg and others were indicted for violation of a Pennsylvania statute that both provided for the return of fugitive slaves in accordance with a specified state judicial procedure and punished taking people out of the state for purposes of slavery unless state procedures were followed. Prigg had taken both Margaret Morgan and her children before a state judge who refused to proceed with the case. At that point, in violation of the state statute and without seeking any other judicial remedy, Prigg removed Margaret Morgan and her children. The indictment followed.

The Pennsylvania statute Prigg was accused of violating provided:

§ 1. If any person or persons shall, from and after the passing of this act, by force and violence, take and carry away, or cause to be taken or carried away, and shall, by fraud or false pretence, seduce, or cause to be seduced, or shall attempt so to take, carry away or seduce, any negro or mulatto, from any part or parts of this commonwealth, to any other place or places whatsoever, out of this commonwealth, with a design and intention of selling and disposing of, or of causing to be sold, or of keeping and detaining, or of causing to be kept and detained, such negro or mulatto, as a slave or servant for life, or for any term whatsoever, every such person or persons, his or their aiders or abettors, shall on conviction thereof, in any court of this commonwealth having competent jurisdiction, be deemed guilty of a felony....

§ 3. When a person held to labor or servitude in any of the United States, or in either of the territories thereof, under the laws thereof, shall escape into this commonwealth, the person to whom such labor or service is due, his or her duly authorized agent or attorney, constituted in writing, is hereby authorized to apply to any judge, justice of the peace or alderman, who, on such application, supported by the oath or affirmation of such claimant, or authorized agent or attorney as aforesaid, that the said fugitive hath escaped from his or her service, or from the service of the person for whom he is a duly constituted agent or attorney, shall issue his warrant, under his hand and seal, and directed to the sheriff, or any constable of the proper city or county, authorizing and empowering said sheriff or constable, to arrest and seize the said fugitive, who shall be named in said warrant, and to bring said fugitive before a judge of the proper county....

§ 6. The said fugitive from labor or service, when so arrested, shall be brought before a judge as aforesaid, and upon proof, to the satisfaction of such judge, that the person so seized or arrested doth [owe services as a slave], under the laws of the state or authority from which she or he fled from service or labor, to the person claiming him or her, it shall be the duty of such judge to give a certificate thereof to such claimant, or his or her duly authorized agent or attorney, which shall be sufficient warrant for removing the said fugitive to the state or territory from which she or he fled: Provided, that the oath of the owner or owners, or other person interested, shall in no case be received in evidence before the judge, on the hearing of the case. [In short, Pennsylvania seems to have required evidence from disinterested witnesses to prove the person was a slave.]

The jury in Prigg's case returned a special verdict in which it found Margaret Morgan was indeed a slave who

came into the state of Pennsylvania from the state of Maryland, some time in the year 1832; that at that time, and for a long period before that time, she was a slave for life, held to labor, and owing service or labor, under and according to the laws of the said state of Maryland, one of the United States, to a certain Margaret Ashmore, a citizen of the state of Maryland, residing in Harford county; and that the said negro woman, Margaret Morgan, escaped and fled from the state of Maryland, without the knowledge and consent of the said Margaret Ashmore; that in the month of February 1837, the within-named defendant, Edward Prigg, was duly and legally constituted and appointed by the said Margaret Ashmore, her agent or attorney, to seize and arrest the said negro woman, Margaret Morgan.

Based on the special verdict, the court found Prigg guilty, and his conviction was affirmed by the Supreme Court of Pennsylvania. Review by the United States Supreme Court followed.]

The case was argued, for the plaintiff in error, by Meredith and Nelson, under authority to appear in the case for the state of Maryland; and by Johnson, Attorney-General of Pennsylvania, and Hambly, for the commonwealth of Pennsylvania....

[Hambly, for Pennsylvania:]

The final decision of a great constitutional question should at all times be regarded as a subject for grave consideration and reflection; inasmuch as it may affect the happiness and prosperity, the lives and liberties of a whole nation. Among the people of this free country, there is nothing which should be guarded with more watchful jealousy, than the charter of their liberties; which being the fundamental law of the land, in its judicial construction, every one is immediately interested, from the highest dignitary to the meanest subject of the commonwealth. Any irreverential touch given to this ark of public safety should be rebuked, and every violence chastised; its sanctity should be no less than that of the domestic altar; its guardians should be Argus-eyed; and as the price of its purchase was blood, its privileges and immunities should be maintained, even if this price must be paid again....

The act of congress was passed 12th of February 1793; and authorizes the arrest of a fugitive from labor, and taking him before a judge of the circuit or district courts of the United States, or before any magistrate of a city or town corporate, and upon satisfactory proof, the judge or magistrate shall give a certificate which shall be sufficient warrant for the removal of the fugitive. The second section fixed a forfeiture of $500 on any person who shall obstruct, hinder, rescue or harbor such fugitive, &c. In the argument of this matter, it is asserted, that no legislation is needed; that the constitutional provision is ample; and that under the phrase "shall be surrendered, on claim," everything which legislation can give, is already secured; and that under this clause, a power is contained, in virtue of which, any one may step into a crowd and seize and carry off an alleged slave, "just as he would a stray horse," or any other article of personal property. If this conclusion be correct, it is surely a strange deduction from the language used in that clause, and in direct opposition to what would seem to be impliedly its meaning. If such be the true meaning of "claim," why does that clause say, that no state, by "any law or regulation therein," shall discharge from service? Why speak of "law or regulation," if none be allowed? Why allude to that which is forbidden and unlawful? Why speak of state laws or regulations, if the states dare not pass any? And why not at once use the language which obviously presented itself, and say, that "escaping into another state," shall not discharge from service or labor, without adding a word about "laws or regulations?" The conclusion is unsound, and altogether unwarranted. The language of the constitution not only pre-supposes legislation, but that this legislation not only is to be, or may be, but will be, by the states. It was just as much as saying to the states: You may pass laws upon the subject—you may make regulations—you may prescribe the time and manner of seizure, the authorities before whom the parties shall come for adjudication—but you shall not discharge a bona fide fugitive from labor from that service which he owes under the laws of the state from whence he fled. Your authorities shall say, whether, under the laws of that state, he owes service, and if he does, you shall hand him over....

Another most valid and substantial reason against this construction is, that it would be a violation of the very spirit of the instrument. If, under this term "claim," the stretch of power is so very great, that a man from a neighboring state can venture into Pennsylvania or Maryland, and upon his simple allegation, seize, and without reference to state authorities, carry off any one whom he may choose to single out as his fugitive from labor, it is a most unheard of violation of the true spirit and meaning of the whole of that instrument. The same power that can, upon simple allegation, seize and carry off a slave, can, on the allegation of service due, seize and carry off a freeman. There is no power, if neither congress nor the states can legislate, to dispute the question with the seizing party. In non-slave-holding states the presumption is, that every man is a freeman, until the contrary be proved. It is like every other legal presumption, in favor of the right. Every man is presumed to be innocent, until proved guilty. Every defendant against whom an action of debt is brought, is presumed not to owe, until the debt be proved. Now, in a slave-holding state, color always raises a presumption of slavery, which is directly contrary to the presumption in a free or non-slave-holding state; for in the latter, prima facie, every man is a freeman. If, then, under this most monstrous assumption of power, a freeman may be seized, where is our boasted freedom? What says the 4th article of the amendments to the constitution of the United States? "The right of the people to be secure in their persons, houses, papers and effects, against unreasonable searches and seizures, shall not be violated." [Or the 5th article:] "No person shall be deprived of life, liberty, or property, without due process of law."

But here we are met with the remark, that "slaves are no parties to the constitution;" that "we, the people," does not embrace them. This is admitted, but we are not arguing the want of power to "claim" and take a slave, but to claim and take a freeman! Admit the fact, that he is a slave, and you admit away the whole question. Pennsylvania says: Instead of preventing you from taking your slaves, we are anxious that you should have them; they are a population we do not covet, and all our legislation tends toward giving you every facility to get them; but we do claim the right of legislating upon this subject so as to bring you under legal restraint, which will prevent you from taking a freeman. If one can arrest and carry away a freeman, "without due process of law;" if their persons are not inviolate; your constitution is a waxen tablet, a writing in the sands; and instead of being, as is supposed, the freest country on earth, this is the vilest despotism which can be imagined! Is it possible, this clause can have such a meaning? Can it be, that a power so potent of mischief as this, could find no one of all those who had laid it in the indictment against the king of Great Britain, as one of the very chiefest of his crimes, "that he had transported our citizens beyond seas for trial," whose jealousy would not be aroused—whose fears would not be excited, at a grasp of power so mighty as is claimed for this clause? Think you not, that some one of those ardent, untiring, vigilant guardians of liberty, would have raised a warning voice against this danger? And that, too, when only eighteen months after the formation of this charter, although they had already in the body of the instrument carefully guarded the writ of habeas corpus, and provided for the trial of all crimes by jury, and in the state where committed, yet, as if their jealousy had been excited to fourfold vigilance, in their amendments provided for the personal security of the subject from "unreasonable seizure," and that no one should be "deprived of liberty, without due process of law." ...

[Johnson, Attorney General of Pennsylvania:]

The constitution does not aim at any abridgment of the state sovereignties on this subject, except in the single point of prohibiting them from setting fugitive slaves at liberty. In all other essential particulars, it wisely leaves them to the exercise of their own judgment. Different rules on this subject would naturally be established in different states. Less strictness of proof of the right of the master would be satisfactory in a slave state, than would be so in a free state....]

Justice Story delivered the opinion of the court.

This is a writ of error to the supreme court of Pennsylvania, brought under the 25th section of the judiciary act of 1789, ch. 20, for the purpose of revising the judgment of that court, in a case involving the construction of the constitution and laws of the United States. The facts are briefly these:

The plaintiff in error was indicted in the court of oyer and terminer for York county, for having, with force and violence, taken and carried away from that county, to the state of Maryland, a certain negro woman, named Margaret Morgan, with a design and intention of selling and disposing of, and keeping her, as a slave or servant for life, contrary to a statute of Pennsylvania, passed on the 26th of March 1826....

The plaintiff in error pleaded not guilty to the indictment; and at the trial, the jury found a special verdict, which, in substance, states, that the negro woman, Margaret Morgan, was a slave for life, and held to labor and service under and according to the laws of Maryland, to a certain Margaret Ashmore, a citizen of Maryland; that the slave escaped and fled from Maryland, into Pennsylvania, in 1832; that the plaintiff in error, being legally constituted the agent and attorney of the said Margaret Ashmore, in 1837, caused the said negro woman to be taken and apprehended as a fugitive from labor, by a state constable, under a warrant from a Pennsylvania magistrate; that the said negro woman was thereupon brought before the said magistrate, who refused to take further cognisance of the case; and thereupon, the plaintiff in error did remove, take and carry away the said negro woman and her children, out of Pennsylvania, into Maryland, and did deliver the said negro woman and her children into the custody and possession of the said Margaret Ashmore. The special verdict further finds, that one of the children was born in Pennsylvania, more than a year after the said negro woman had fled and escaped from Maryland. Upon this special verdict, the court of oyer and terminer of York county adjudged that the plaintiff in error was guilty of the offence charged in the indictment. A writ of error was brought from that judgment to the supreme court of Pennsylvania, where the judgment was, pro forma, affirmed. From this latter judgment, the present writ of error has been brought to this court....

The question arising in the case, as to the constitutionality of the statute of Pennsylvania, has been most elaborately argued at the bar. The counsel for the plaintiff in error have contended, that the statute of Pennsylvania is unconstitutional; first, because congress has the exclusive power of legislation upon the subject-matter, under the constitution of the United States, and under the act of the 12th of February 1793, ch. 51, which was passed in pursuance thereof; secondly, that if this power is not exclusive in congress, still the concurrent power of the state legislatures is suspended by the actual exercise of the power of congress; and thirdly, that if not suspended, still the statute of Pennsylvania, in all its provisions applicable to this case, is in direct collision with the act of congress, and therefore, is unconstitutional and void. The counsel for Pennsylvania maintain the negative of all these points.

Few questions which have ever come before this court involve more delicate and important considerations; and few upon which the public at large may be presumed to feel a more profound and pervading interest. We have accordingly given them our most deliberate examination; and it has become my duty to state the result to which we have arrived, and the reasoning by which it is supported.

Before, however, we proceed to the points more immediately before us, it may be well, in order to clear the case of difficulty, to say, that in the exposition of this part of the constitution, we shall limit ourselves to those considerations which appropriately and exclusively belong to it, without laying down any rules of interpretation of a more general nature. It will, indeed, probably, be found, when we look to the character of the constitution itself, the objects which it seeks to attain, the powers which it confers, the duties which it enjoins, and the rights which it secures, as well as the known historical fact, that many of its provisions were matters of compromise of opposing interests and opinions, that no uniform rule of interpretation can be applied to it, which may not allow, even if it does not positively demand, many modifications, in its actual application to particular clauses. And, perhaps, the safest rule of interpretation, after all, will be found to be to look to the nature and objects of the particular powers, duties and rights, with all the lights and aids of contemporary history; and to give to the words of each just such operation and force, consistent with their legitimate meaning, as may fairly secure and attain the ends proposed.

There are two clauses in the constitution upon the subject of fugitives, which stand in juxtaposition with each other, and have been thought mutually to illustrate each other.... [The second provides] "No person held to service or labor in one state, under the laws thereof, escaping into another, shall, in consequence of any law or regulation therein, be discharged from such service or labor; but shall be delivered up, on claim of the party to whom such service or labor may be due."

[This] clause is that, the true interpretation whereof is directly in judgment before us. Historically, it is well known, that the object of this clause was to secure to the citizens of the slave-holding states the complete right and title of ownership in their slaves, as property, in every state in the Union into which they might escape from the state where they were held in servitude. The full recognition of this right and title was indispensable to the security of this species of property in all the slave-holding states; and, indeed, was so vital to the preservation of their domestic interests and institutions, that it cannot be doubted, that it constituted a fundamental article, without the adoption of which the Union could not have been formed. Its true design was, to guard against the doctrines and principles prevalent in the non-slave-holding states, by preventing them from intermeddling with, or obstructing, or abolishing the rights of the owners of slaves.

By the general law of nations, no nation is bound to recognise the state of slavery, as to foreign slaves found within its territorial dominions, when it is in opposition to its own policy and institutions, in favor of the subjects of other nations where slavery is recognised. If it does it, it is as a matter of comity, and not as a matter of international right.... The state of slavery is deemed to be a mere municipal regulation, founded upon and limited to the range of the territorial laws. This was fully recognised in *Somerset's Case*, Lofft 1; s. c. 11 State Trials, by Harg. 340; which was decided before the American revolution. It is manifest, from this consideration, that if the constitution had not contained this clause, every non-slave-holding state in the Union would have been at liberty to have declared free all runaway slaves coming within its limits, and to have given them entire immunity and protection against the claims of their masters; a course which would have created the most bitter animosities, and engendered perpetual strife between the different states. The clause was, therefore, of the last importance to the safety and security of the southern states, and could not have been surrendered by them, without endangering their whole property in slaves. The clause was accordingly adopted into the constitution, by the unanimous consent of the framers of it; a proof at once of its intrinsic and practical necessity.

How, then, are we to interpret the language of the clause? The true answer is, in such a manner as, consistently with the words, shall fully and completely effectuate the whole objects of it. If, by one mode of interpretation, the right must become shadowy and unsubstantial, and without any remedial power adequate to the end, and by another mode, it will attain its just end and secure its manifest purpose, it would seem, upon principles of reasoning, absolutely irresistible, that the latter ought to prevail. No court of justice can be authorized so to construe any clause of the constitution as to defeat its obvious ends, when another construction, equally accordant with the words and sense thereof, will enforce and protect them.

The clause manifestly contemplates the existence of a positive, unqualified right on the part of the owner of the slave, which no state law or regulation can in any way qualify, regulate, control or restrain. The slave is not to be discharged from service or labor, in consequence of any state law or regulation. Now, certainly, without indulging in any nicety of criticism upon words, it may fairly and reasonably be said, that any state law or state regulation, which interrupts, limits, delays or postpones the right of the owner to the immediate possession of the slave, and the immediate command of his service and labor, operates, pro tanto, a discharge of the slave therefrom. The question can never be, how much the slave is discharged from; but whether he is discharged from any, by the natural or necessary operation of state laws or state regulations. The question is not one of quantity or degree, but of withholding or controlling the incidents of a positive and absolute right.

We have said, that the clause contains a positive and unqualified recognition of the right of the owner in the slave, unaffected by any state law or legislation whatsoever, because there is no qualification or restriction of it to be found therein; and we have no right to insert any, which is not expressed, and cannot be fairly implied. Especially, are we estopped from so doing, when the clause puts the right to the service or labor upon the same ground, and to the same extent, in every other state as in the state from which the slave escaped, and in which he was held to the service or labor. If this be so, then all the incidents to that right attach also. The owner must, therefore, have the right to seize and repossess the slave, which the local laws of his own state confer upon him, as property; and we all know that this right of seizure and recaption is universally acknowledged in all the slave-holding states. Indeed, this is no more than a mere affirmance of the principles of the common law applicable to this very subject. Mr. Justice Blackstone (3 *Bl. Com.* 4) lays it down as unquestionable doctrine. "Recaption or reprisal (says he) is another species of remedy by the mere act of the party injured. This happens, when any one hath deprived another of his property in goods or chattels personal, or wrongfully detains one's wife, child or servant; in which case, the owner of the goods, and the husband, parent or master, may lawfully claim and retake them, wherever he happens to find them, so it be not in a riotous manner, or attended with a breach of the peace." Upon this ground, we have not the slightest hesitation in holding, that under and in virtue of the constitution, the owner of a slave is clothed with entire authority, in every state in the Union, to seize and recapture his slave, whenever he can do it, without any breach of the peace or any illegal violence. In this sense, and to this extent, this clause of the constitution may properly be said to execute itself, and to require no aid from legislation, state or national.

But the clause of the constitution does not stop here; nor, indeed, consistently with its professed objects, could it do so. Many cases must arise, in which, if the remedy of the owner were confined to the mere right of seizure and recaption, he would be utterly without any adequate redress. He may not be able to lay his hands upon the slave. He may not be able to enforce his rights against persons, who either secrete or conceal, or withhold the slave. He may be restricted by local legislation, as to the mode of proofs of his ownership; as to the courts in which he shall sue, and as to the actions which he may bring; or the process he may use to compel the delivery of the slave. Nay! the local legislation may be utterly inadequate to furnish the appropriate redress, by authorizing no process in rem, or no specific mode of repossessing the slave, leaving the owner, at best, not that right which the constitution designed to secure, a specific delivery and repossession of the slave, but a mere remedy in damages; and that, perhaps, against persons utterly insolvent or worthless. The state legislation may be entirely silent on the whole subject, and its ordinary remedial process framed with different views and objects; and this may be innocently as well as designedly done, since every state is perfectly competent, and has the exclusive right, to prescribe the remedies in its own judicial tribunals, to limit the time as well as the mode of redress, and to deny jurisdiction over cases, which its own policy and its own institutions either prohibit or discountenance. If, therefore, the clause of the constitution had stopped at the mere recognition of the right, without providing or contemplating any means by which it might be established and enforced, in cases where it did not execute itself, it is plain, that it would have been, in a great variety of cases, a delusive and empty annunciation. If it did not contemplate any action, either through state or national legislation, as auxiliaries to its more perfect enforcement in the form of remedy, or of protection, then, as there would be no duty on either to aid the right, it would be left to the mere comity of the states, to act as they should please, and would depend for its security upon the changing course of public opinion, the mutations of public policy, and the general adaptations of remedies for purposes strictly according to the lex fori.

And this leads us to the consideration of the other part of the clause, which implies at once a guarantee and duty. It says, "but he (the slave) shall be delivered up, on claim of the party to whom such service or labor may be due." Now, we think it exceedingly difficult, if not impracticable, to read this language, and not to feel, that it contemplated some further remedial redress than that which might be administered at the hands of the owner himself. A claim is to be made! What is a claim? It is, in a just jurisdical sense, a demand of some matter, as of right, made by one person upon another, to do or to forbear to do some act or thing as a matter of duty. A more limited, but at the same time, an equally expressive, definition was given by Lord Dyer, as cited in *Stowel v. Zouch*, 1 Plowd. 359; and it is equally applicable to the present case: that "a claim is a challenge by a man of the propriety or ownership of a thing, which he has not in possession, but which is wrongfully detained from him." The slave is to be delivered up on the claim. By whom to be delivered up? In what mode to be delivered up? How, if a refusal takes place, is the right of delivery to be enforced? Upon what proofs? What shall be the evidence of a rightful recaption or delivery? When and under what circumstances shall the possession of the owner, after it is obtained, be conclusive of his right, so as to preclude any further inquiry or examination into it by local tribunals or otherwise, while the slave, in possession of the owner, is in transitu to the state from which he fled? These and many other questions will readily occur upon the slightest attention to the clause; and it is obvious, that they can receive but one satisfactory answer. They require the aid of legislation, to protect the right, to enforce the delivery, and to secure the subsequent possession of the slave. If, indeed, the constitution guaranties the right, and if it requires the delivery upon the claim of the owner (as cannot well be doubted), the natural inference certainly is, that the national government is clothed with the appropriate authority and functions to enforce it. The fundamental principle, applicable to all cases of this sort, would seem to be, that where the end is required, the means are given; and where the duty is enjoined, the ability to perform it is contemplated to exist, on the part of the functionaries to whom it is intrusted. The clause is found in the national constitution, and not in that of any state. It does not point out any state functionaries, or any state action, to carry its provisions into effect. The states cannot, therefore, be compelled to enforce them; and it might well be deemed an unconstitutional exercise of the power of interpretation, to insist, that the states are bound to provide means to carry into effect the duties of the national government, nowhere delegated or intrusted to them by the constitution. On the contrary, the natural, if not the necessary, conclusion is, that the national government, in the absence of all positive provisions to the contrary, is bound, through its own proper departments, legislative, judicial or executive, as the case may require, to carry into effect all the rights and duties imposed upon it by the constitution. The remark of Mr. Madison, in the *Federalist* (No. 43), would seem in such cases to apply with peculiar force. "A right (says he) implies a remedy; and where else would the remedy be deposited, than where it is deposited by the constitution?" meaning, as the context shows, in the government of the United States.

It is plain, then, that where a claim is made by the owner, out of possession, for the delivery of a slave, it must be made, if at all, against some other person; and inasmuch as the right is a right of property, capable of being recognised and asserted by proceedings before a court of justice, between parties adverse to each other, it constitutes, in the strictest sense, a controversy between the parties, and a case "arising under the constitution" of the United States, within the express delegation of judicial power given by that instrument. Congress, then, may call that power into activity, for the very purpose of giving effect to that right; and if so, then it may prescribe the mode and extent in which it shall be applied, and how, and under what circumstances, the proceedings shall afford a complete protection and guarantee to the right.

Congress has taken this very view of the power and duty of the national government. As early as the year 1791, the attention of congress was drawn to it (as we shall hereafter more fully see), in consequence of some practical difficulties arising under the other clause, respecting fugitives from justice escaping into other states. The result of their deliberations was the passage of the act of the 12th of February 1793, ch. 51, which, after having, in the first and second sections, provided by the case of fugitives from justice, by a demand to be made of the delivery, through the executive authority of the state where they are found, proceeds, in the third section, to provide, that when a person held to labor or service in any of the United States, shall escape into any other of the states or territories, the person to whom such labor or service may be due, his agent or attorney, is hereby empowered to seize or arrest such fugitive from labor, and take him or her before any judge of the circuit or district courts of the United States, residing or being within the state, or before any magistrate of a county, city or town corporate, wherein such seizure or arrest shall be made; and upon proof, to the satisfaction of such judge or magistrate, either by oral evidence or affidavit, that the person so seized or arrested, doth, under the laws of the state or territory from which he or she fled, owe service or labor to the person claiming him or her, it shall be the duty of such judge or magistrate, to give a certificate thereof to such claimant, his agent or attorney, which shall be sufficient warrant for removing the said fugitive from labor, to the state or territory from which he or she fled. The fourth section provides a penalty against any person, who shall knowingly and willingly obstruct or hinder such claimant, his agent or attorney, in so seizing or arresting such fugitive from labor, or rescue such fugitive from the claimant, or his agent or attorney, when so arrested, or who shall harbor or conceal such fugitive, after notice that he is such; and it also saves to the person claiming such labor or service, his right of action for or on account of such injuries.

In a general sense, this act may be truly said to cover the whole ground of the constitution, both as to fugitives from justice, and fugitive slaves; that is, it covers both the subjects, in its enactments; not because it exhausts the remedies which may be applied by congress to enforce the rights, if the provisions of the act shall in practice be found not to attain the object of the constitution; but because it points out fully all the modes of attaining those objects, which congress, in their discretion, have as yet deemed expedient or proper to meet the exigencies of the constitution. If this be so, then it would seem, upon just principles of construction, that the legislation of congress, if constitutional, must supersede all state legislation upon the same subject; and by necessary implication prohibit it. For, if congress have a constitutional power to regulate a particular subject, and they do actually regulate it in a given manner, and in a certain form, it cannot be, that the state legislatures have a right to interfere, and as it were, by way of compliment to the legislation of congress, to prescribe additional regulations, and what they may deem auxiliary provisions for the same purpose. In such a case, the legislation of congress, in what it does prescribe, manifestly indicates, that it does not intend that there shall be any further legislation to act upon the subject-matter. Its silence as to what it does not do, is as expressive of what its intention is, as the direct provisions made by it. This doctrine was fully recognised by this court, in the case of *Houston v. Moore* (1820); where it was expressly held, that where congress have exercised a power over a particular subject given them by the constitution, it is not competent for state legislation to add to the provisions of congress upon that subject; for that the will of congress upon the whole subject is as clearly established by what it has not declared, as by what it has expressed.

But it has been argued, that the act of congress is unconstitutional, because it does not fall within the scope of any of the enumerated powers of legislation confided to that body; and therefore, it is void. Stripped of its artificial and technical structure, the argument comes to this, that although rights are exclusively secured by, or duties are exclusively imposed upon, the national government, yet, unless the power to enforce these rights or to execute these duties, can be found among the express powers of legislation enumerated in the constitution, they remain without any means of giving them effect by any act of congress; and they must operate solely proprio vigore, however defective may be their operation; nay! even although, in a practical sense, they may become a nullity, from the want of a proper remedy to enforce them, or to provide against their violation. If this be the true interpretation of the constitution, it must, in a great measure, fail to attain many of its avowed and positive objects, as a security of rights, and a recognition of duties. Such a limited construction of the constitution has never yet been adopted as correct, either in theory or practice. No one has ever supposed, that congress could, constitutionally, by its legislation, exercise powers, or enact laws, beyond the powers delegated to it by the constitution. But it has, on various occasions, exercised powers which were necessary and proper as means to carry into effect rights expressly given, and duties expressly enjoined thereby. The end being required, it has been deemed a just and necessary implication, that the means to accomplish it are given also; or, in other words, that the power flows as a necessary means to accomplish the end....

The remaining question is, whether the power of legislation upon this subject is exclusive in the national government, or concurrent in the states, until it is exercised by congress. In our opinion, it is exclusive; and we shall now proceed briefly to state our reasons for that opinion. The doctrine stated by this court, in *Sturges v. Crowninshield* (1819), contains the true, although not the sole, rule or consideration, which is applicable to this particular subject. "Wherever," said Mr. Chief Justice Marshall, in delivering the opinion of the court, "the terms in which a power is granted to congress, or the nature of the power, require, that it should be exercised exclusively by congress, the subject is as completely taken from the state legislatures, as if they had been forbidden to act." The nature of the power, and the true objects to be attained by it, are then as important to be weighed, in considering the question of its exclusiveness, as the words in which it is granted....

It is scarcely conceivable, that the slave-holding states would have been satisfied with leaving to the legislation of the non-slave-holding states, a power of regulation, in the absence of that of congress, which would or might practically amount to a power to destroy the rights of the owner. If the argument, therefore, of a concurrent power in the states to act upon the subject-matter, in the absence of legislation by congress, be well founded; then, if congress had never acted at all, or if the act of congress should be repealed, without providing a substitute, there would be a resulting authority in each of the states to regulate the whole subject, at its pleasure, and to dole out its own remedial justice, or withhold it, at its pleasure, and according to its own views of policy and expediency. Surely, such a state of things never could have been intended, under such a solemn guarantee of right and duty. On the other hand, construe the right of legislation as exclusive in congress, and every evil and every danger vanishes. The right and the duty are then co-extensive and uniform in remedy and operation throughout the whole Union....

Upon these grounds, we are of opinion, that the act of Pennsylvania upon which this indictment is founded, is unconstitutional and void....

[Most concurring opinions omitted.]

Baldwin, Justice, concurred with the court in reversing the judgment of the Supreme Court of Pennsylvania, on the ground, that the act of the legislature was unconstitutional; inasmuch as the slavery of the person removed was admitted, the removal could not be kidnapping. But he dissented from the principles laid down by the court as the grounds of their opinion.

Geier v. American Honda Motor Company, Inc.: Background

In *Geier v. American Honda Motor Company, Inc.* (2000), the Court, in a 5–4 decision, ruled that the District of Columbia was preempted from recognizing a tort cause of action for negligence or defective design against a car manufacturer for failing to include a driver's side air bag on a 1987 automobile when there existed legislation and regulations providing a framework for automobile manufacturers to gradually implement airbags. The majority ruled that the statutes and regulations, read in light of a letter of comment by the Secretary of Transportation and the Government's Brief, presented a case of conflict preemption. The dissent vigorously disagreed.

Pursuant to its authority under the National Traffic and Motor Vehicle Safety Act of 1966 (NTMVSA), 15 U.S.C. § 1381 *et seq.*, the Department of Transportation promulgated Federal Motor Vehicle Safety Standard (FMVSS) 208, which required auto manufacturers to equip some, but not all, of their 1987 vehicles with passive restraints. A major aspect of the case involved resolving two seemingly inconsistent parts of the NTMVSA. The statute had an express preemption provision:

> Whenever a Federal motor vehicle safety standard established under this subchapter is in effect, no State or political subdivision of a State shall have any authority either to establish, or to continue in effect, with respect to any motor vehicle or item of motor vehicle equipment[,] any safety standard applicable to the same aspect of performance of such vehicle or item of equipment which is not identical to the Federal standard. 15 U.S.C. § 1392(d).

However, it also had a savings clause:

> Compliance with any Federal motor vehicle safety standard issued under this subchapter does not exempt any person from any liability under common law. 49 U.S.C. § 30103(e).

The majority concluded that the savings clause saved only lawsuits that did not conflict with agency behavior and did not create any type of burden on the Agency to declare that it intended to pre-empt state law.

The Court also had to determine the significance of Federal Motor Vehicle Safety Standard (FMVSS) 208. The crux of the issue was whether or not Standard 208:

1) represented only a minimum federal standard that manufacturers must meet, but one that would not insulate manufacturers from state tort liability should greater safety standards reasonably be required; or

2) represented part of a comprehensive regulatory plan that would be frustrated by allowing states to impose tort liability.

Interestingly, the Foreword to the National Highway Traffic Safety Administration collection of the regulations states that the regulations are minimum standards:

These Federal safety standards are regulations written in terms of minimum safety performance requirements for motor vehicles or items of motor vehicle equipment. These requirements are specified in such a manner "that the public is protected against unreasonable risk of crashes occurring as a result of the design, construction, or performance of motor vehicles and is also protected against unreasonable risk of death or injury in the event crashes do occur." (http://www.nhtsa.dot.gov/cars/rules/import/FMVSS/#SN208).

However, the majority, relying in large part on statements of the Secretary of Transportation at the time of the adoption of the standard and the position of the Solicitor General as *amicus curiae*, concluded that a comprehensive regulatory plan would be in conflict with independent state liability.

Geier v. American Honda Motor Company, Inc.
529 U.S. 861 (2000)

[Majority: Breyer, Rehnquist (C.J.), O'Connor, Scalia, and Kennedy. Dissent: Stevens, Souter, Thomas, and Ginsburg.]

Justice Breyer delivered the opinion of the Court.

This case focuses on the 1984 version of a Federal Motor Vehicle Safety Standard promulgated by the Department of Transportation under the authority of the National Traffic and Motor Vehicle Safety Act of 1966, 80 Stat. 718, 15 U.S.C. § 1381 *et seq.* The standard, FMVSS 208, required auto manufacturers to equip some, but not all, of their 1987 vehicles with passive restraints. We ask whether the Act pre-empts a state common-law tort action in which the plaintiff claims that the defendant auto manufacturer, who was in compliance with the standard, should nonetheless have equipped a 1987 automobile with airbags. We conclude that the Act, taken together with FMVSS 208, pre-empts the lawsuit.

I. In 1992, petitioner Alexis Geier, driving a 1987 Honda Accord, collided with a tree and was seriously injured. The car was equipped with manual shoulder and lap belts which Geier had buckled up at the time. The car was not equipped with airbags or other passive restraint devices.

Geier ... sued the car's manufacturer and its affiliates (hereinafter American Honda), under District of Columbia tort law. They claimed, among other things, that American Honda had designed its car negligently and defectively because it lacked a driver's side airbag. The District Court dismissed the lawsuit [finding the state tort action had been pre-empted. The Court of Appeals also found pre-emption.] ...

Several state courts have held to the contrary, namely, that neither the Act's express pre-emption nor FMVSS 208 pre-empts a "no airbag" tort suit.... All of the Federal Circuit Courts that have considered the question, however, have found pre-emption. One rested its conclusion on the Act's express pre-emption provision.... We granted certiorari to resolve these differences. We now hold that this kind of "no airbag" lawsuit conflicts with the objectives of FMVSS 208, a standard authorized by the Act, and is therefore pre-empted by the Act.

In reaching our conclusion, we consider three subsidiary questions. First, does the Act's express pre-emption provision pre-empt this lawsuit? We think not. Second, do ordinary pre-emption principles nonetheless apply? We hold that they do. Third, does this lawsuit actually conflict with FMVSS 208, hence with the Act itself? We hold that it does.

II. We first ask whether the Safety Act's express pre-emption provision pre-empts this tort action. The provision reads as follows:

> Whenever a Federal motor vehicle safety standard established under this subchapter is in effect, no State or political subdivision of a State shall have any authority either to establish, or to continue in effect, with respect to any motor vehicle or item of motor vehicle equipment[,] any safety standard applicable to the same aspect of performance of such vehicle or item of equipment which is not identical to the Federal standard. 15 U.S.C. § 1392(d)....

[T]he Act contains another provision which resolves [this issue]. That provision, a "saving" clause, says that "compliance with" a federal safety standard "does not exempt any person from any liability under common law." 15 U.S.C. § 1397(k). The saving clause assumes that there are some significant number of common-law liability cases to save. And a reading of the express pre-emption provision that excludes common-law tort actions gives actual meaning to the saving clause's literal language, while leaving adequate room for state tort law to operate—for example, where federal law creates only a floor, *i.e.*, a minimum safety standard.... We have found no convincing indication that Congress wanted to pre-empt, not only state statutes and regulations, but also common-law tort actions, in such circumstances. Hence the broad reading cannot be correct. The language of the pre-emption provision permits a narrow reading that excludes common-law actions. Given the presence of the saving clause, we conclude that the pre-emption clause must be so read.

III. We have just said that the saving clause *at least* removes tort actions from the scope of the express pre-emption clause. Does it do more? In particular, does it foreclose or limit the operation of ordinary pre-emption principles insofar as those principles instruct us to read statutes as pre-empting state laws (including common-law rules) that "actually conflict" with the statute or federal standards promulgated thereunder? Petitioners concede, as they must in light of *Freightliner Corp. v. Myrick* (1995), that the pre-emption provision, by itself, does not foreclose (through negative implication) "any possibility of implied [conflict] pre-emption," [discussing *Cipollone v. Liggett Group, Inc.* (1992)]. But they argue that the saving clause has that very effect.

We recognize that, when this Court previously considered the pre-emptive effect of the statute's language, it appeared to leave open the question of how, or the extent to which, the saving clause saves state-law tort actions that conflict with federal regulations promulgated under the Act.... We now conclude that the saving clause (like the express pre-emption provision) does not bar the ordinary working of conflict pre-emption principles.

[T]his Court has repeatedly "declined to give broad effect to saving clauses where doing so would upset the careful regulatory scheme established by federal law." ...

Neither do we believe that the pre-emption provision, the saving provision, or both together, create some kind of "special burden" beyond that inherent in ordinary pre-emption principles—which "special burden" would specially disfavor pre-emption here....

On the other hand, the saving clause reflects a congressional determination that occasional nonuniformity is a small price to pay for a system in which juries not only create, but also enforce, safety standards, while simultaneously providing necessary compensation to victims. That policy by itself disfavors pre-emption, at least some of the time. But we can find nothing in any natural reading of the two provisions that would favor one set of policies over the other where a jury-imposed safety standard actually conflicts with a federal safety standard.

The dissent, as we have said, contends nonetheless that the express pre-emption and saving provisions here, taken together, create a "special burden," which a court must impose "on a party" who claims conflict pre-emption under those principles. But nothing in the Safety Act's language refers to any "special burden." Nor can one find the basis for a "special burden" in this Court's precedents....

A "special burden" would also promise practical difficulty by further complicating well-established pre-emption principles that already are difficult to apply. The dissent does not contend that this "special burden" would apply in a case in which state law penalizes what federal law requires—*i.e.*, a case of impossibility. But if it would not apply in such a case, then how, or when, would it apply? This Court, when describing conflict pre-emption, has spoken of pre-empting state law that "under the circumstances of the particular case ... stands as an obstacle to the accomplishment and execution of the full purposes and objectives of Congress"—whether that "obstacle" goes by the name of "conflicting; contrary to; ... repugnance; difference; irreconcilability; inconsistency; violation; curtailment ... interference," or the like. *Hines v. Davidowitz* (1941).... The Court has not previously driven a legal wedge—only a terminological one—between "conflicts" that prevent or frustrate the accomplishment of a federal objective and "conflicts" that make it "impossible" for private parties to comply with both state and federal law. Rather, it has said that both forms of conflicting state law are "nullified" by the Supremacy Clause ... and it has assumed that Congress would not want either kind of conflict. The Court has thus refused to read general "saving" provisions to tolerate actual conflict both in cases involving impossibility ... and in "frustration-of-purpose" cases....

IV. The basic question, then, is whether a common-law "no airbag" action like the one before us actually conflicts with FMVSS 208. We hold that it does.

In petitioners' and the dissent's view, FMVSS 208 sets a minimum airbag standard. As far as FMVSS 208 is concerned, the more airbags, and the sooner, the better. But that was not the Secretary's view. DOT's comments, which accompanied the promulgation of FMVSS 208, make clear that the standard deliberately provided the manufacturer with a range of choices among different passive restraint devices. Those choices would bring about a mix of different devices introduced gradually over time; and FMVSS 208 would thereby lower costs, overcome technical safety problems, encourage technological development, and win widespread consumer acceptance—all of which would promote FMVSS 208's safety objectives. See generally 49 Fed. Reg. 28962 (1984).

IV-A. The history of FMVSS 208 helps explain why and how DOT sought these objectives.... In 1967, DOT, understanding that seatbelts would save many lives, required manufacturers to install manual seat belts in all automobiles. It became apparent, however, that most occupants simply would not buckle up their belts. DOT then began to investigate the feasibility of requiring "passive restraints," such as airbags and automatic seatbelts. In 1970, it amended FMVSS 208 to include some passive protection requirements while making clear that airbags were one of several "equally acceptable" devices and that it neither "'favored' nor expected the introduction of airbag systems." In 1971, it added an express provision permitting compliance through the use of nondetachable passive belts and in 1972, it mandated full passive protection for all front seat occupants for vehicles manufactured after August 15, 1975. Although the agency's focus was originally on airbags ... at no point did FMVSS 208 formally require the use of airbags. From the start, as in 1984, it permitted passive restraint options.

DOT gave manufacturers a further choice for new vehicles manufactured between 1972 and August 1975. Manufacturers could either install a passive restraint device such as automatic seatbelts or airbags or retain manual belts and add an "ignition interlock" device that in effect forced occupants to buckle up by preventing the ignition otherwise from turning on. The interlock soon became popular with manufacturers. And in 1974, when the agency approved the use of detachable automatic seatbelts, it conditioned that approval by providing that such systems must include an interlock system and a continuous warning buzzer to encourage reattachment of the belt. But the interlock and buzzer devices were most unpopular with the public. And Congress, responding to public pressure, passed a law that forbade DOT from requiring, or permitting compliance by means of, such devices.

IV-B. Read in light of this history, DOT's own contemporaneous explanation of FMVSS 208 makes clear that the 1984 version of FMVSS 208 reflected the following significant considerations. First, buckled up seatbelts are a vital ingredient of automobile safety.... Second, despite the enormous and unnecessary risks that a passenger runs by not buckling up manual lap and shoulder belts, more than 80% of front seat passengers would leave their manual seatbelts unbuckled. Third, airbags could make up for the dangers caused by unbuckled manual belts, but they could not make up for them entirely....

Fourth, passive restraint systems had their own disadvantages, for example, the dangers associated with, intrusiveness of, and corresponding public dislike for, nondetachable automatic belts. Fifth, airbags brought with them their own special risks to safety, such as the risk of danger to out-of-position occupants (usually children) in small cars....

Sixth, airbags were expected to be significantly more expensive than other passive restraint devices, raising the average cost of a vehicle price $320 for full frontal airbags over the cost of a car with manual lap and shoulder seatbelts (and potentially much more if production volumes were low). And the agency worried that the high replacement cost—estimated to be $800—could lead car owners to refuse to replace them after deployment.... Seventh, the public, for reasons of cost, fear, or physical intrusiveness, might resist installation or use of any of the then-available passive restraint devices....

FMVSS 208 reflected these considerations in several ways. Most importantly, that standard deliberately sought variety—a mix of several different passive restraint systems. It did so by setting a performance requirement for passive restraint devices and allowing manufacturers to choose among different passive restraint mechanisms, such as airbags, automatic belts, or other passive restraint technologies to satisfy that requirement.... And DOT explained why FMVSS 208 sought the mix of devices that it expected its performance standard to produce. DOT wrote that it had rejected a proposed FMVSS 208 "all airbag" standard because of safety concerns (perceived or real) associated with airbags, which concerns threatened a "backlash" more easily overcome "if airbags" were "not the only way of complying." It added that a mix of devices would help develop data on comparative effectiveness, would allow the industry time to overcome the safety problems and the high production costs associated with airbags, and would facilitate the development of alternative, cheaper, and safer passive restraint systems. And it would thereby build public confidence necessary to avoid another interlock-type fiasco.

The 1984 FMVSS 208 standard also deliberately sought a gradual phase-in of passive restraints. It required the manufacturers to equip only 10% of their car fleet manufactured after September 1, 1986, with passive restraints. It then increased the percentage in three annual stages, up to 100% of the new car fleet for cars manufactured after September 1, 1989. And it explained that the phased-in requirement would allow more time for manufacturers to develop airbags or other, better, safer passive restraint systems. It would help develop information about the comparative effectiveness of different systems, would lead to a mix in which airbags and other nonseatbelt passive restraint systems played a more prominent role than would otherwise result, and would promote public acceptance....

In sum, as DOT now tells us through the Solicitor General, the 1984 version of FMVSS 208 "embodies the Secretary's policy judgment that safety would best be promoted if manufacturers installed alternative protection systems in their fleets rather than one particular system in every car." Brief for United States as *Amicus Curiae*. Petitioners' tort suit claims that the manufacturers of the 1987 Honda Accord "had a duty to design, manufacture, distribute and sell a motor vehicle with an effective and safe passive restraint system, including, but not limited to, airbags."

In effect, petitioners' tort action depends upon its claim that manufacturers had a duty to install an airbag when they manufactured the 1987 Honda Accord. Such a state law—*i.e.*, a rule of state tort law imposing such a duty—by its terms would have required manufacturers of all similar cars to install airbags rather than other passive restraint systems, such as automatic belts or passive interiors. It thereby would have presented an obstacle to the variety and mix of devices that the federal regulation sought. It would have required all manufacturers to have installed airbags in respect to the entire District-of-Columbia-related portion of their 1987 new car fleet, even though FMVSS 208 at that time required only that 10% of a manufacturer's nationwide fleet be equipped with any passive restraint device at all. It thereby also would have stood as an obstacle to the gradual passive restraint phase-in that the federal regulation deliberately imposed. In addition, it could have made less likely the adoption of a state mandatory buckle-up law. Because the rule of law for which petitioners contend would have stood "as an obstacle to the accomplishment and execution of" the important means-related federal objectives that we have just discussed, it is pre-empted. *Hines;* see also *International Paper Company v. Ouellette* (1987); *Fidelity Federal Savings & Loan Ass'n v. de la Cuesta* (1982) (finding conflict and pre-emption where state law limited the availability of an option that the federal agency considered essential to ensure its ultimate objectives)....

One final point: We place some weight upon DOT's interpretation of FMVSS 208's objectives and its conclusion, as set forth in the Government's brief, that a tort suit such as this one would "'stand as an obstacle to the accomplishment and execution'" of those objectives.... Congress has delegated to DOT authority to implement the statute; the subject matter is technical; and the relevant history and background are complex and extensive. The agency is likely to have a thorough understanding of its own regulation and its objectives and is "uniquely qualified" to comprehend the likely impact on state requirements....

The judgment of the Court of Appeals is affirmed.

Justice Stevens, with whom Justice Souter, Justice Thomas, and Justice Ginsburg join, dissenting.

Airbag technology has been available to automobile manufacturers for over 30 years. There is now general agreement on the proposition "that, to be safe, a car must have an airbag." Indeed, current federal law imposes that requirement on all automobile manufacturers. See 49 U.S.C. § 30127; 49 C.F.R. § 571.208, S4.1.5.3 (1998). The question raised by petitioner's common-law tort action is whether that proposition was sufficiently obvious when Honda's 1987 Accord was manufactured to make the failure to install such a safety feature actionable under theories of negligence or defective design. The Court holds that an interim regulation motivated by the Secretary of Transportation's desire to foster gradual development of a variety of passive restraint devices deprives state courts of jurisdiction to answer that question. I respectfully dissent from that holding, and especially from the Court's unprecedented extension of the doctrine of pre-emption. As a preface to an explanation of my understanding of the statute and the regulation, these preliminary observations seem appropriate.

"This is a case about federalism," *Coleman v. Thompson* (1991), that is, about respect for "the constitutional role of the States as sovereign entities." *Alden v. Maine* (1999). It raises important questions concerning the way in which the Federal Government may exercise its undoubted power to oust state courts of their traditional jurisdiction over common-law tort actions. The rule the Court enforces today was not enacted by Congress and is not to be found in the text of any Executive Order or regulation. It has a unique origin: it is the product of the Court's interpretation of the final commentary accompanying an interim administrative regulation and the history of airbag regulation generally. Like many other judge-made rules, its contours are not precisely defined. I believe, however, that it is fair to state that if it had been expressly adopted by the Secretary of Transportation, it would have read as follows:

> No state court shall entertain a common-law tort action based on a claim that an automobile was negligently or defectively designed because it was not equipped with an airbag;

> Provided, however, that this rule shall not apply to cars manufactured before September 1, 1986, or after such time as the Secretary may require the installation of airbags in all new cars; and

> Provided further, that this rule shall not preclude a claim by a driver who was not wearing her seatbelt that an automobile was negligently or defectively designed because it was not equipped with any passive restraint whatsoever, or a claim that an automobile with particular design features was negligently or defectively designed because it was equipped with one type of passive restraint instead of another.

Perhaps such a rule would be a wise component of a legislative reform of our tort system. I express no opinion about that possibility. It is, however, quite clear to me that Congress neither enacted any such rule itself nor authorized the Secretary of Transportation to do so. It is equally clear to me that the objectives that the Secretary intended to achieve through the adoption of Federal Motor Vehicle Safety Standard 208 would not be frustrated one whit by allowing state courts to determine whether in 1987 the life-saving advantages of airbags had become sufficiently obvious that their omission might constitute a design defect in some new cars. Finally, I submit that the Court is quite wrong to characterize its rejection of the presumption against pre-emption, and its reliance on history and regulatory commentary rather than either statutory or regulatory text, as "ordinary experience-proved principles of conflict pre-emption."

I. The question presented is whether either the National Traffic and Motor Vehicle Safety Act of 1966 (Safety Act or Act), 80 Stat. 718, 15 U.S.C. § 1381 *et seq.*,[1] or the ver-

---

1. In 1994, the Safety Act was recodified at 49 U.S.C. § 30101 *et seq.*....

sion of Standard 208 promulgated by the Secretary of Transportation in 1984, 49 C.F.R. §§ 571.208, S4.1.3–S4.1.4 (1998), pre-empts common-law tort claims that an automobile manufactured in 1987 was negligently and defectively designed because it lacked "an effective and safe passive restraint system, including, but not limited to, airbags." In *Motor Vehicle Mfrs. Assn. of United States, Inc. v. State Farm Mut. Automobile Ins. Co.* (1983), we reviewed the first chapters of the "complex and convoluted history" of Standard 208. It was the "unacceptably high" rate of deaths and injuries caused by automobile accidents that led to the enactment of the Safety Act in 1966. The purpose of the Act, as stated by Congress, was "to reduce traffic accidents and deaths and injuries to persons resulting from traffic accidents." 15 U.S.C. § 1381. The Act directed the Secretary of Transportation or his delegate to issue motor vehicle safety standards that "shall be practicable, shall meet the need for motor vehicle safety, and shall be stated in objective terms." § 1392(a). The Act defines the term "safety standard" as a "minimum standard for motor vehicle performance, or motor vehicle equipment performance." § 1391(2).

Standard 208 covers "occupant crash protection." Its purpose "is to reduce the number of deaths of vehicle occupants, and the severity of injuries, by specifying vehicle crashworthiness requirements ... [and] equipment requirements for active and passive restraint systems." 49 C.F.R. § 571.208, S2 (1998). The first version of that standard, issued in 1967, simply required the installation of manual seatbelts in all automobiles. Two years later the Secretary formally proposed a revision that would require the installation of "passive occupant restraint systems," that is to say, devices that do not depend for their effectiveness on any action by the vehicle occupant. The airbag is one such system. The Secretary's proposal led to a series of amendments to Standard 208 that imposed various passive restraint requirements, culminating in a 1977 regulation that mandated such restraints in all cars by the model year 1984. The two commercially available restraints that could satisfy this mandate were airbags and automatic seatbelts; the regulation allowed each vehicle manufacturer to choose which restraint to install. In 1981, however, following a change of administration, the new Secretary first extended the deadline for compliance and then rescinded the passive restraint requirement altogether. In *Motor Vehicle Mfrs. Assn.* we affirmed a decision by the Court of Appeals holding that this rescission was arbitrary. On remand, Secretary Elizabeth Dole promulgated the version of Standard 208 that is at issue in this case.

The 1984 standard provided for a phase-in of passive restraint requirements beginning with the 1987 model year. In that year, vehicle manufacturers were required to equip a minimum of 10% of their new passenger cars with such restraints. While the 1987 Honda Accord driven by Ms. Geier was not so equipped, it is undisputed that Honda complied with the 10% minimum by installing passive restraints in certain other 1987 models. This minimum passive restraint requirement increased to 25% of 1988 models and 40% of 1989 models; the standard also mandated that "after September 1, 1989, all new cars must have automatic occupant crash protection." ... In response to a 1991 amendment to the Safety Act, the Secretary amended the standard to require that, beginning in the 1998 model year, all new cars have an airbag at both the driver's and right front passenger's positions.

Given that Secretary Dole promulgated the 1984 standard in response to our opinion invalidating her predecessor's rescission of the 1977 passive restraint requirement, she provided a full explanation for her decision not to require airbags in all cars and to phase in the new requirements. The initial 3-year delay was designed to give vehicle manufacturers adequate time for compliance. The decision to give manufacturers a choice between airbags and a different form of passive restraint, such as an automatic seatbelt, was motivated in part by safety concerns and in part by a desire not to retard the development of more effective systems. An important safety concern was the fear of a "public backlash" to an airbag mandate that consumers might not fully understand. The Secretary believed, however, that the use of airbags would avoid possible public objections to automatic seatbelts and that many of the public concerns regarding airbags were unfounded.

Although the standard did not require airbags in all cars, it is clear that the Secretary did intend to encourage wider use of airbags. One of her basic conclusions was that "automatic occupant protection systems that do not totally rely upon belts, such as airbags ... offer significant additional potential for preventing fatalities and injuries, at least in part because the American public is likely to find them less intrusive; their development and availability should be encouraged through appropriate incentives." The Secretary therefore included a phase-in period in order to encourage manufacturers to comply with the standard by installing airbags and other (perhaps more effective) nonbelt technologies that they might develop, rather than by installing less expensive automatic seatbelts. As a further incentive for the use of such technologies, the standard provided that a vehicle equipped with an airbag or other nonbelt system would count as 1.5 vehicles for the purpose of determining compliance with the required 10, 25, or 40% minimum passive restraint requirement during the phase-in period. 49 CFR § 571.208, S4.1.3.4(a)(1) (1998). With one oblique exception,[2] there is no mention, either in the text of the final standard or in the accompanying comments, of the possibility that the risk of potential tort liability would provide an incentive for manufacturers to install airbags. Nor is there any other specific evidence of an intent to preclude common-law tort actions.

II. Before discussing the pre-emption issue, it is appropriate to note that there is a vast difference between a rejection of Honda's threshold arguments in favor of federal pre-emption and a conclusion that petitioners ultimately would prevail on their common-law tort claims. I express no opinion on the possible merit, or lack of merit, of those claims....

Turning to the subject of pre-emption, Honda contends that the Safety Act's pre-emption provision, 15 U.S.C. § 1392(d), expressly pre-empts petitioners' common-law no-airbag claims. It also argues that the claims are in any event impliedly pre-empted because the imposition of liability in cases such as this would frustrate the purposes of Standard 208. I discuss these alternative arguments in turn.

III. When a state statute, administrative rule, or common-law cause of action conflicts with a federal statute, it is axiomatic that the state law is without effect. U.S. Const., Art. VI, cl. 2; *Cipollone v. Liggett Group, Inc.* (1992). On the other hand, it is equally clear that the Supremacy Clause does not give unelected federal judges carte blanche to use federal law as a means of imposing their own ideas of tort reform on the States. Because of the role of States as separate sovereigns in our federal system, we have long presumed that state laws—particularly those, such as the provision of tort remedies to compensate for personal injuries, that are within the scope of the States' historic police powers—are not to be pre-empted by a federal statute unless it is the clear and manifest purpose of Congress to do so....

When a federal statute contains an express pre-emption provision, "the task of statutory construction must in the first instance focus on the plain wording of [that provi-

---

2. In response to a comment that the manufacturers were likely to use the cheapest system to comply with the new standard, the Secretary stated that she believed "that competition, *potential liability for any deficient systems*[,] and pride in one's product would prevent this." [Emphasis added.]

sion], which necessarily contains the best evidence of Congress' pre-emptive intent." *CSX Transp., Inc. v. Easterwood* (1993). The Safety Act contains both an express pre-emption provision, 15 U.S.C. §1392(d), and a saving clause that expressly preserves common-law claims, §1397(k). The relevant part of the former provides:

> Whenever a Federal motor vehicle safety standard established under this subchapter is in effect, no State or political subdivision of a State shall have any authority either to establish, or to continue in effect, with respect to any motor vehicle or item of motor vehicle equipment[,] any safety standard applicable to the same aspect of performance of such vehicle or item of equipment which is not identical to the Federal standard.

The latter states:

> Compliance with any Federal motor vehicle safety standard issued under this subchapter does not exempt any person from any liability under common law.

Relying on §1392(d) and legislative history discussing Congress' desire for uniform national safety standards, Honda argues that petitioners' common-law no-airbag claims are expressly pre-empted because success on those claims would necessarily establish a state "safety standard" not identical to Standard 208. It is perfectly clear, however, that the term "safety standard" as used in these two sections refers to an objective rule prescribed by a legislature or an administrative agency and does not encompass case-specific decisions by judges and juries that resolve common-law claims. That term is used three times in these sections; presumably it is used consistently....

The Court does not disagree with this interpretation of the term "safety standard" in §1392(d). Because the meaning of that term as used by Congress in this statute is clear, the text of §1392(d) is itself sufficient to establish that the Safety Act does not expressly pre-empt common-law claims. In order to avoid the conclusion that the saving clause is superfluous, therefore, it must follow that it has a different purpose: to limit, or possibly to foreclose entirely, the possible pre-emptive effect of safety standards promulgated by the Secretary. The Court's approach to the case has the practical effect of reading the saving clause out of the statute altogether.

Given the cumulative force of the fact that §1392(d) does not expressly pre-empt common-law claims and the fact that §1397(k) was obviously intended to limit the pre-emptive effect of the Secretary's safety standards, it is quite wrong for the Court to assume that a possible implicit conflict with the purposes to be achieved by such a standard should have the same pre-emptive effect "'as an obstacle to the accomplishment and execution of the full purposes and objectives of Congress.'" Properly construed, the Safety Act imposes a special burden on a party relying on an arguable implicit conflict with a temporary regulatory policy—rather than a conflict with congressional policy or with the text of any regulation—to demonstrate that a common-law claim has been pre-empted.

IV. Even though the Safety Act does not expressly pre-empt common-law claims, Honda contends that Standard 208—of its own force—implicitly pre-empts the claims in this case.

"We have recognized that a federal statute implicitly overrides state law either when the scope of a statute indicates that Congress intended federal law to occupy a field exclusively, *English v. General Elec. Co.*, or when state law is in actual conflict with federal law. We have found implied conflict pre-emption where it is 'impossible for a private party to comply with both state and federal requirements,' or where state law 'stands as an obstacle to the accomplishment and execution of the full purposes and objectives of Congress.' *Hines v. Davidowitz* (1941)."

In addition, we have concluded that regulations "intended to pre-empt state law" that are promulgated by an agency acting non-arbitrarily and within its congressionally delegated authority may also have pre-emptive force.... In this case, Honda relies on the last of the implied pre-emption principles stated in *Freightliner Corp. v. Myrick* (1995), arguing that the imposition of common-law liability for failure to install an airbag would frustrate the purposes and objectives of Standard 208.

Both the text of the statute and the text of the standard provide persuasive reasons for rejecting this argument. The saving clause of the Safety Act arguably denies the Secretary the authority to promulgate standards that would pre-empt common-law remedies.[3] Moreover, the text of Standard 208 says nothing about pre-emption, and I am not persuaded that Honda has overcome our traditional presumption that it lacks any implicit pre-emptive effect.

Honda argues, and the Court now agrees, that the risk of liability presented by common-law claims that vehicles without airbags are negligently and defectively designed would frustrate the policy decision that the Secretary made in promulgating Standard 208. This decision, in their view, was that safety—including a desire to encourage "public acceptance of the airbag technology and experimentation with better passive restraint systems,"—would best be promoted through gradual implementation of a passive restraint requirement making airbags only one of a variety of systems that a manufacturer could install in order to comply, rather than through a requirement mandating the use of one particular system in every vehicle. In its brief supporting Honda, the United States agreed with this submission. It argued that if the manufacturers had known in 1984 that they might later be held liable for failure to install airbags, that risk "would likely have led them to install airbags in all cars," thereby frustrating the Secretary's safety goals and interfering with the methods designed to achieve them.

There are at least three flaws in this argument that provide sufficient grounds for rejecting it. First, the entire argument is based on an unrealistic factual predicate. Whatever the risk of liability on a no-airbag claim may have been prior to the promulgation of the 1984 version of Standard 208, that risk did not lead any manufacturer to install airbags in even a substantial portion of its cars. If there had been a realistic likelihood that the risk of tort liability would have that consequence, there would have been no need for Standard 208. The promulgation of that standard certainly did not increase the pre-existing risk of liability. Even if the standard did not create a previously unavailable pre-emption defense, it likely reduced the manufacturers' risk of liability by enabling them to point to the regulation and their compliance therewith as evidence tending to negate charges of negligent and defective design....

---

3. The Court contends, in essence, that a saving clause cannot foreclose implied conflict pre-emption. The cases it cites to support that point, however, merely interpreted the language of the particular saving clauses at issue and concluded that those clauses did not foreclose implied pre-emption; they do not establish that a saving clause in a given statute cannot foreclose implied pre-emption based on frustration of that statute's purposes, or even (more importantly for our present purposes) that a saving clause in a given statute cannot deprive a regulation issued pursuant to that statute of any implicit pre-emptive effect. See *United States v. Locke* (2000).... As stated in the text, I believe the language of this particular saving clause unquestionably limits, and possibly forecloses entirely, the pre-emptive effect that safety standards promulgated by the Secretary have on common-law remedies.... Under that interpretation, there is by definition no frustration of federal purposes—that is, no "tolerat[ion of] actual conflict,"—when tort suits are allowed to go forward. Thus, because there is a textual basis for concluding that Congress intended to preserve the state law at issue, I think it entirely appropriate for the party favoring pre-emption to bear a special burden in attempting to show that valid federal purposes would be frustrated if that state law were not pre-empted.

Second, even if the manufacturers' assessment of their risk of liability ultimately proved to be wrong, the purposes of Standard 208 would not be frustrated. In light of the inevitable time interval between the eventual filing of a tort action alleging that the failure to install an airbag is a design defect and the possible resolution of such a claim against a manufacturer, as well as the additional interval between such a resolution (if any) and manufacturers' "compliance with the state law duty in question," by modifying their designs to avoid such liability in the future, it is obvious that the phase-in period would have ended long before its purposes could have been frustrated by the specter of tort liability....

Third, despite its acknowledgement that the saving clause "preserves those actions that seek to establish greater safety than the minimum safety achieved by a federal regulation intended to provide a floor," the Court completely ignores the important fact that by definition all of the standards established under the Safety Act—like the British regulations that governed the number and capacity of lifeboats aboard the Titanic[4]—impose minimum, rather than fixed or maximum, requirements. 15 U.S.C. § 1391(2); see *Norfolk Southern R. Co. v. Shanklin* (2000) (Breyer, J., concurring) ("federal minimum safety standards should not pre-empt a state tort action"); *Hillsborough County v. Automated Medical Laboratories, Inc.* (1985). The phase-in program authorized by Standard 208 thus set minimum percentage requirements for the installation of passive restraints, increasing in annual stages of 10, 25, 40, and 100%. Those requirements were not ceilings, and it is obvious that the Secretary favored a more rapid increase. The possibility that exposure to potential tort liability might accelerate the rate of increase would actually further the only goal explicitly mentioned in the standard itself: reducing the number of deaths and severity of injuries of vehicle occupants. Had gradualism been independently important as a method of achieving the Secretary's safety goals, presumably the Secretary would have put a ceiling as well as a floor on each annual increase in the required percentage of new passive restraint installations....

V. For these reasons, it is evident that Honda has not crossed the high threshold established by our decisions regarding pre-emption of state laws that allegedly frustrate federal purposes: it has not demonstrated that allowing a common-law no-airbag claim to go forward would impose an obligation on manufacturers that directly and irreconcilably contradicts any primary objective that the Secretary set forth with clarity in Standard 208. *Gade v. National Solid Wastes Management Assn.* (1992) (Kennedy, J., concurring in part and concurring in judgment) ("A freewheeling judicial inquiry into whether [state law] is in tension with federal objectives would undercut the principle that it is Congress [and federal agencies,] rather than the courts[,] that pre-empt state law"). Furthermore, it is important to note that the text of Standard 208 (which the Court does not even bother to quote in its opinion), unlike the regulation we reviewed in *Fidelity Fed. Sav. & Loan Assn. v. De la Cuesta* (1982), does not contain any expression of an intent to displace state law. Given our repeated emphasis on the importance of the presumption against pre-emption, see, *e.g., CSX Transp., Inc. v. Easterwood; Rice v. Santa Fe Elevator Corp.* (1947), this silence lends additional support to the conclusion that the continuation of whatever common-law liability may exist in a case like this poses no danger of frustrating any of the Secretary's primary purposes in promulgating Standard 208. See *Hillsborough County v. Automated Medical Laboratories, Inc.; Silkwood v. Kerr-McGee Corp.* (1984) ("It

---

4. Statutory Rules and Orders 1018–1021, 1033 (1908). See Nader & Page, *Automobile-Design Liability and Compliance with Federal Standards*, 64 Geo. Wash. L. Rev. 415, 459 (1996) (noting that the Titanic "complied with British governmental regulations setting minimum requirements for lifeboats when it left port on its final, fateful voyage with boats capable of carrying only about [half] of the people on board"); W. Wade, *The Titanic: End of a Dream* 68 (1986).

is difficult to believe that [the Secretary] would, without comment, remove all means of judicial recourse for those injured by illegal conduct.")....

Our presumption against pre-emption is rooted in the concept of federalism. It recognizes that when Congress legislates "in a field which the States have traditionally occupied ... [,] we start with the assumption that the historic police powers of the States were not to be superseded by the Federal Act unless that was the clear and manifest purpose of Congress." *Rice v. Santa Fe Elevator Corp.;* see *Jones v. Rath Packing Co.* (1977). The signal virtues of this presumption are its placement of the power of pre-emption squarely in the hands of Congress, which is far more suited than the Judiciary to strike the appropriate state/federal balance (particularly in areas of traditional state regulation), and its requirement that Congress speak clearly when exercising that power. In this way, the structural safeguards inherent in the normal operation of the legislative process operate to defend state interests from undue infringement. *Garcia v. San Antonio Metropolitan Transit Authority* (1985).... In addition, the presumption serves as a limiting principle that prevents federal judges from running amok with our potentially boundless (and perhaps inadequately considered) doctrine of implied conflict pre-emption based on frustration of purposes—*i.e.*, that state law is pre-empted if it "stands as an obstacle to the accomplishment and execution of the full purposes and objectives of Congress." *Hines v. Davidowitz.*[5]

While the presumption is important in assessing the pre-emptive reach of federal statutes, it becomes crucial when the pre-emptive effect of an administrative regulation is at issue. Unlike Congress, administrative agencies are clearly not designed to represent the interests of States, yet with relative ease they can promulgate comprehensive and detailed regulations that have broad pre-emption ramifications for state law. We have addressed the heightened federalism and nondelegation concerns that agency pre-emption raises by using the presumption to build a procedural bridge across the political accountability gap between States and administrative agencies. Thus, even in cases where implied regulatory pre-emption is at issue, we generally "expect an administrative regulation to declare any intention to pre-empt state law with some specificity." *California Coastal Comm'n v. Granite Rock Co.* (1987); see *Hillsborough County v. Automated Medical Laboratories, Inc.* (1985) (noting that too easily implying pre-emption "would be inconsistent with the federal-state balance embodied in our Supremacy Clause jurisprudence," and stating that "because agencies normally address problems in a detailed manner and can speak through a variety of means, including regulations, preambles, interpretive statements, and responses to comments, we can expect that they will make their intentions clear if they intend for their regulations to be exclusive"); *Fidelity Fed. Sav. & Loan Assn. v. De la Cuesta* (noting that pre-emption inquiry is initiated "when the administrator promulgates regulations intended to pre-empt state law"). This expectation, which is shared by

---

5. Recently, one commentator has argued that our doctrine of frustration-of-purposes (or "obstacle") pre-emption is not supported by the text or history of the Supremacy Clause, and has suggested that we attempt to bring a measure of rationality to our pre-emption jurisprudence by eliminating it. Nelson, *Pre-emption*, 86 Va. L. Rev. 225, 231–32 ("Under the Supremacy Clause, pre-emption occurs if and only if state law contradicts a valid rule established by federal law, and the mere fact that the federal law serves certain purposes does not automatically mean that it contradicts everything that might get in the way of those purposes"). Obviously, if we were to do so, there would be much less need for the presumption against pre-emption (which the commentator also criticizes). As matters now stand, however, the presumption reduces the risk that federal judges will draw too deeply on malleable and politically unaccountable sources such as regulatory history in finding pre-emption based on frustration of purposes.

the Executive Branch,[6] serves to ensure that States will be able to have a dialog with agencies regarding pre-emption decisions *ex ante* through the normal notice-and-comment procedures of the Administrative Procedure Act (APA), 5 U.S.C. § 553.

When the presumption and its underpinnings are properly understood, it is plain that Honda has not overcome the presumption in this case. Neither Standard 208 nor its accompanying commentary includes the slightest specific indication of an intent to pre-empt common-law no-airbag suits. Indeed, the only mention of such suits in the commentary tends to suggest that they would not be pre-empted. In the Court's view, however, "the failure of the Federal Register to address pre-emption explicitly is ... not determinative," because the Secretary's consistent litigating position since 1989, the history of airbag regulation, and the commentary accompanying the final version of Standard 208 reveal purposes and objectives of the Secretary that would be frustrated by no-airbag suits. Pre-empting on these three bases blatantly contradicts the presumption against pre-emption....

Furthermore, the Court identifies no case in which we have upheld a regulatory claim of frustration-of-purposes implied conflict pre-emption based on nothing more than an ex post administrative litigating position and inferences from regulatory history and final commentary. The latter two sources are even more malleable than legislative history. Thus, when snippets from them are combined with the Court's broad conception of a doctrine of frustration-of-purposes pre-emption untempered by the presumption, a vast, undefined area of state law becomes vulnerable to pre-emption by any related federal law or regulation. In my view, however, "pre-emption analysis is, or at least should be, a matter of precise statutory [or regulatory] construction rather than an exercise in free-form judicial policymaking." 1 L. Tribe, *American Constitutional Law* § 6-28, p. 1177 (3d ed. 2000).

As to the Secretary's litigating position, it is clear that "an interpretation contained in a [legal brief], not one arrived at after, for example, a formal adjudication or notice-and-comment rulemaking[,] ... does not warrant *Chevron*-style deference." *Christensen v. Harris County* (2000) (referring to *Chevron U.S.A., Inc. v. Natural Resources Defense Council, Inc.* (1984). Moreover, our pre-emption precedents and the APA establish that even if the Secretary's litigating position were coherent, the lesser deference paid to it by the Court today would be inappropriate. Given the Secretary's contention that he has the authority to promulgate safety standards that pre-empt state law and the fact that he could promulgate a standard such as the one quoted supra, with relative ease, we should be quite reluctant to find pre-emption based only on the Secretary's informal effort to recast the 1984 version of Standard 208 into a pre-emptive mould.... Requiring the Secretary to put his pre-emptive position through formal notice-and-comment rulemaking—whether contemporaneously with the promulgation of the allegedly pre-emptive regulation or at any later time that the need for pre-emption becomes apparent—respects both the federalism and nondelegation principles that underlie the presumption against pre-emption in the regulatory context and the APA's requirement of new rulemaking when an agency substantially modifies its interpretation of a regulation. 5 U.S.C. § 551(5)....

Because neither the text of the statute nor the text of the regulation contains any indication of an intent to pre-empt petitioners' cause of action, and because I cannot agree with the Court's unprecedented use of inferences from regulatory history and commen-

---

6. See Exec. Order No. 12612, § 4(e), 3 C.F.R. 252, 255 (1988) ("When an Executive department or agency proposes to act through adjudication or rule-making to preempt State law, the department or agency shall provide all affected States notice and an opportunity for appropriate participation in the proceedings.")....

tary as a basis for implied pre-emption, I am convinced that Honda has not overcome the presumption against pre-emption in this case. I therefore respectfully dissent.

Geier v. American Honda Motor Company, Inc.: Note

The 2008 term of the Supreme Court saw a flurry of cases involving preemption. The number of cases accepted by the Court reflects the intensity of the recent political struggles over tort and consumer protection law. State law typically provides redress, for example, for those injured by defective products, injured by failure to warn, injured by fraud, or injured by violations of consumers' rights. The preemption issue received greater attention from 2000–2008 as advocates for injured persons and consumer groups grappled with industry groups and the George W. Bush administration. At its heart, preemption concerns both federalism or states' rights and the appropriate role of individual litigants or sometimes state attorneys general. Typically, cases involve efforts to redress claimed violations of consumer or other individual rights, and recovery by those injured by defective products, or defective performance. Many cases involve public safety. Those injured often use state courts to prosecute tort actions, while manufacturers have attempted to use pre-emption as a way to avoid or limit potential liability. Recent cases have involved the medical device industry, the pharmaceutical industry, the tobacco industry, and the banking industry.

In all pre-emption cases, the Court attempts to resolve whether or not state law (often common law tort law) is permissible since the topic is affected by federal legislation. Pre-emption is problematic because Congress could have resolved any of the litigated controversies if it made the applicable statute precise enough. However, given the political tradeoffs involved in passing controversial legislation, and the increasingly frequent approach of passing vague statutes that allow executive agencies to determine actual standards, statutory text is rarely conclusive. For example, litigated pre-emption cases do not involve attempts by states to alter the federally mandated size of warnings in tobacco advertisements; rather, they might involve the question of whether or not the existence of the federal statute regulating health warnings should preclude a state lawsuit for fraudulently withholding damaging medical evidence relevant to the safety of the product—a topic the legislation simply does not directly address.

While the Court talks of "express preemption" and "implied preemption" (with "field preemption" and "conflict preemption" as sub-categories of "implied"), the same balancing of interests occurs in virtually any preemption case where the federal standard cannot be seen mechanically to trump a parallel state rule, often a common law rule. Text and legislative history of the federal statute are the starting point for analysis. But the individual justice's views of several factors will often be decisive. These include the importance of the historic role of the states (for example in tort law), of compensation for injury, of state protection of public health and safety, of a uniform federal standard in the particular area, and the position, if any, of the relevant federal agency on state involvement. The last factor is a problematic means of determining the intent of a Congressional statute. This is so because agency behavior often varies radically from one presidential administration to the next. In view of these and other factors, seemingly quite similar statutory language can lead to different results.

The federal Employee Retirement Income Security Act of 1974 (ERISA) is an example of a statute with an express pre-emption clause. ERISA, 29 U.S.C. § 1132(a) *et seq.*, is a statute designed to regulate employee benefit plans. ERISA pre-empts all state laws "insofar as they may now or hereafter *relate to* any employee benefit plan," except that state "laws ... which *regulate* insurance, banking, or securities" are saved from pre-emption. 29 U.S.C. § 1144(a) and (b)(2)(A). These statutes have spawned over 3,000 ERISA pre-emption cases as courts have struggled to determine which state laws "relate to" an employee benefit plan, which state laws "regulate" insurance, banking, or securities, and what activities qualify as insurance, banking, or securities. While ostensibly involving "express" pre-emption, all of these cases involve the complex multi-factor analysis described above.

In *Aetna Health Care v. Davila* (2004), the Court found that a cause of action for failure to authorize appropriate treatment brought against a Health Maintenance Organization (HMO) pursuant to the Texas "Patient Bill of Rights" was pre-empted by ERISA. While the Court unanimously agreed that ERISA, as interpreted, occupied the field regarding employee benefits, Justices Ginsburg and Breyer, concurring, called on Congress to address and to correct the inequities that have arisen under the statute.

The federal Food, Drug and Cosmetic Act (FDCA), 21 U.S.C. § 301 *et seq.*, regulates drug safety. Following the mass tort litigation surrounding failed medical devices such as the Dalkon Shield, Congress passed the Medical Device Amendments of 1976 (MDA), 21 U.S.C. § 360c *et seq.*, which created a regime of detailed federal oversight. The MDA includes an express pre-emption provision that states:

> "Except as provided in subsection (b) of this section, no State or political subdivision of a State may establish or continue in effect with respect to a device intended for human use any *requirement*—
>
> (1) which is different from, or in addition to, any *requirement* applicable under this chapter to the device, and
>
> (2) which relates to the safety or effectiveness of the device or to any other matter included in a *requirement* applicable to the device under this chapter."

Unfortunately, the statute fails to define "requirement."

In *Medtronic, Inc. v. Lohr* (1996), the Court held by a vote of 5–4 that a medical negligence lawsuit was *not* pre-empted by this statute. Lohr sued after she was injured due to a flawed pacemaker wire. Medtronic argued that tort liability would impose a new "requirement" on the company, so her claims based on negligent manufacturing and failure to warn were preempted because Medtronic had received approval to market the device from the Food and Drug Administration. However, the Court considered it significant that the approval had come after a summary procedure. A new device does not have to go through full FDA review if it is found to be "substantially equivalent" to devices that had been on the market when the 1976 law took effect. Eighty to ninety percent of all medical devices now on the market, including a large majority of the new ones that come onto the market each year, fall within this category.

In contrast, in *Riegel v Medtronic, Inc.* (2008) the Court addressed the question of the meaning of the same MDA express preemption language for a device that had gone through a full FDA review. *Riegel* involved an injury due to an alleged defect in a balloon catheter used in heart surgery. Here the Court found pre-emption by a vote of 8–1. Justice Ginsburg's lone dissent, reproduced in part below, addresses the tensions implicit in this area and some relevant history.

Justice Ginsburg, dissenting.

The Medical Device Amendments of 1976 (MDA or Act), as construed by the Court, cut deeply into a domain historically occupied by state law. The MDA's pre-emption clause, the Court holds, spares medical device manufacturers from personal injury claims alleging flaws in a design or label once the application for the design or label has gained premarket approval from the Food and Drug Administration (FDA); a state damages remedy, the Court instructs, persists only for claims "premised on a violation of FDA regulations."[1] I dissent from today's constriction of state authority. Congress, in my view, did not intend § 360k(a) to effect a radical curtailment of state common-law suits seeking compensation for injuries caused by defectively designed or labeled medical devices....

I. Courts have "long presumed that Congress does not cavalierly pre-empt state-law causes of action." *Medtronic, Inc. v. Lohr* (1996). Pre-emption analysis starts with the assumption that "the historic police powers of the States [a]re not to be superseded ... unless that was the clear and manifest purpose of Congress." *Rice v. Santa Fe Elevator Corp.* (1947). "This assumption provides assurance that 'the federal-state balance' will not be disturbed unintentionally by Congress or unnecessarily by the courts."

The presumption against pre-emption is heightened "where federal law is said to bar state action in fields of traditional state regulation." Given the traditional "primacy of state regulation of matters of health and safety," courts assume "that state and local regulation related to [those] matters ... can normally coexist with federal regulations."

Federal laws containing a pre-emption clause do not automatically escape the presumption against pre-emption. See *Bates v. Dow Agrosciences LLC* (2005). A pre-emption clause tells us that Congress intended to supersede or modify state law to some extent. In the absence of legislative precision, however, courts may face the task of determining the substance and scope of Congress' displacement of state law. Where the text of a pre-emption clause is open to more than one plausible reading, courts ordinarily "accept the reading that disfavors pre-emption." *Bates*.

II. The MDA's pre-emption clause [21 USC § 360k(a)] states:

"[N]o State or political subdivision of a State may establish or continue in effect with respect to a device intended for human use any requirement—

(1) which is different from, or in addition to, any requirement applicable under this chapter to the device, and

(2) which relates to the safety or effectiveness of the device or to any other matter included in a requirement applicable to the device under this chapter."

"Absent other indication," the Court states, "reference to a State's 'requirements' includes its common-law duties." Regarding the MDA, however, "other indication" is not "[a]bsent." Contextual examination of the Act convinces me that § 360k(a)'s inclusion of the term "requirement" should not prompt a sweeping pre-emption of mine-run claims for relief under state tort law.

II-A. Congress enacted the MDA "to provide for the safety and effectiveness of medical devices intended for human use." A series of high-profile medical device failures that caused extensive injuries and loss of life propelled adoption of the MDA. Conspicuous among these failures was the Dalkon Shield intrauterine device, used by approximately 2.2 million women in the United States between 1970 and 1974. Aggressively promoted as a safe and effective form of birth control, the Dalkon Shield had been linked to 16 deaths and 25 miscarriages by the middle of 1975. By early 1976, "more than 500 lawsuits seeking compensatory and punitive damages totaling more than $400 million" had been filed. Given

---

1. The Court's holding does not reach an important issue outside the bounds of this case: the pre-emptive effect of § 360k(a) where evidence of a medical device's defect comes to light only *after* the device receives premarket approval.

the publicity attending the Dalkon Shield litigation and Congress' awareness of the suits at the time the MDA was under consideration, I find informative the absence of any sign of a legislative design to preempt state common-law tort actions.[2]

The Court recognizes that "§ 360k does not prevent a State from providing a damages remedy for claims premised on a violation of FDA regulations." That remedy, although important, does not help consumers injured by devices that receive FDA approval but nevertheless prove unsafe. The MDA's failure to create any federal compensatory remedy for such consumers further suggests that Congress did not intend broadly to pre-empt state common-law suits grounded on allegations independent of FDA requirements. It is "difficult to believe that Congress would, without comment, remove all means of judicial recourse" for large numbers of consumers injured by defective medical devices.

The former chief counsel to the FDA explained:

> Even the most thorough regulation of a product such as a critical medical device may fail to identify potential problems presented by the product. Regulation cannot protect against all possible injuries that might result from use of a device over time. Pre-emption of all such claims would result in the loss of a significant layer of consumer protection...."

The Court's construction of § 360k(a) has the "perverse effect" of granting broad immunity "to an entire industry that, in the judgment of Congress, needed more stringent regulation," not exemption from liability in tort litigation.

The MDA does grant the FDA authority to order certain remedial action if, *inter alia*, it concludes that a device "presents an unreasonable risk of substantial harm to the public health" and that notice of the defect "would not by itself be sufficient to eliminate the unreasonable risk." Thus the FDA may order the manufacturer to repair the device, replace it, refund the purchase price, cease distribution, or recall the device. The prospect of ameliorative action by the FDA, however, lends no support to the conclusion that Congress intended largely to preempt state common-law suits. Quite the opposite: Section 360h(d) states that "[c]ompliance with an order issued under this section shall not relieve any person from liability under Federal or State law." That provision anticipates "[court-awarded] damages for economic loss" from which the value of any FDA-ordered remedy would be subtracted.

II-B. Congress enacted the MDA after decades of regulating drugs and food and color additives under the Federal Food, Drug, and Cosmetic Act (FDCA). The FDCA contains no pre-emption clause....

Starting in 1938, the FDCA required that new drugs undergo preclearance by the FDA before they could be marketed. Nothing in the FDCA's text or legislative history suggested that FDA preclearance would immunize drug manufacturers from common-law tort suits.[3]

By the time Congress enacted the MDA in 1976, state common-law claims for drug labeling and design defects had continued unabated despite nearly four decades of FDA regulation. Congress' inclusion of a pre-emption clause in the MDA was not motivated by concern that similar state tort actions could be mounted regarding medical devices. Rather,

---

2. "[N]othing in the hearings, the Committee Reports, or the debates," the *Lohr* plurality noted, "suggest[ed] that any proponent of the legislation intended a sweeping pre-emption of traditional common-law remedies against manufacturers and distributors of defective devices. If Congress intended such a result, its failure even to hint at it is spectacularly odd, particularly since Members of both Houses were acutely aware of ongoing product liability litigation."

3. To the contrary, the bill did not need to create a federal claim for damages, witnesses testified, because "[a] common-law right of action exist[ed]."

Congress included § 360k(a) and (b) to empower the FDA to exercise control over state premarket approval systems installed at a time when there was no preclearance at the federal level....

In sum, state premarket regulation of medical devices, not any design to suppress tort suits, accounts for Congress' inclusion of a pre-emption clause in the MDA; no such clause figures in earlier federal laws regulating drugs and additives, for States had not installed comparable control regimes in those areas....

II. C. Section 360k(a) must preempt state common law suits, Medtronic contends, because Congress would not have wanted state juries to second guess the FDA's finding that a medical device is safe and effective when used as directed.

But the process for approving new drugs is at least as rigorous as the premarket approval process for medical devices....

For the reasons stated, I would hold that § 360k(a) does not preempt Riegel's suit. I would therefore reverse the judgment of the Court of Appeals in relevant part.

* * *

Justice Ginsburg mentions the regulatory system for drugs near the end of her *Riegel* opinion. The issue of pre-emption in the drug context was the central issue in *Wyeth v. Levine* (2009). Wyeth, a bass player, was injured when a drug which is safe when injected into muscle or via an IV-drip was injected directly into her vein or perhaps an artery, causing gangrene and the eventual amputation of part of her arm. The drug company's warning mentioned the risk of such injury by direct administration, but did not *prohibit* it. The FDA had approved the warning. The question involved whether or not the drug company on its own should have amended the warning in light of data it had received after the initial approval, pending FDA re-evaluation of the label. Justice Stevens, for five members of the Court, held that the common-law remedies were available. Justice Thomas concurred only in the judgment. Justice Alito, joined by Chief Justice Roberts and Justice Scalia, contended that such a result was inconsistent with the Court's ruling in *Geier v. American Honda Motor Company* (2000). A recurring issue in preemption cases is whether the federal standard is a minimum (floor) or the only standard (both a floor and a ceiling).

The Court's 2008 term also saw a significant case involving the longstanding controversies surrounding tobacco. In *Altria Group, Inc. v. Good* (2009), the Court in a 5–4 vote allowed a state consumer-fraud statute to be used to sue cigarette makers for fraudulently advertising that their light cigarettes delivered less tar and nicotine than regular brands. In doing so, a majority of the Court recognized that there is a distinction between lawsuits that relate only to the adequacy of health warnings and lawsuits that involve allegations of fraudulent concealment of safety risks. The dissent contended that any tobacco suit was about health and all should be pre-empted. While "light" cigarettes do in fact deliver less tar and nicotine per puff than ordinary cigarettes, plaintiffs alleged that defendants knew that, *as used by actual smokers*, the risk of "light" cigarettes was essentially identical to that of ordinary cigarettes.

The relevant statute is § 5(b) of the federal Cigarette Labeling Act. It provides that "[n]o requirement or prohibition based on smoking and health shall be imposed under State law with respect to the advertising or promotion of any cigarettes the packages of which are labeled in conformity with the provisions of this chapter." 15 U.S.C. § 1334(b).

Justice Stevens, writing for the Court, was able to garner a majority in support of a position he had previously articulated for a plurality in *Cipollone v. Liggett Group, Inc.* (1992).

The *Cipollone* plurality had concluded that the phrase "based on smoking and health," fairly but narrowly construed, did not preempt the common-law claims that cigarette manufacturers had fraudulently misrepresented and concealed a material fact, because the claim alleged a violation of the traditional common law duty not to deceive—a duty that is not "based on smoking and health."

In another 5–4 case, the Court held that the federal National Bank Act does not preempt states from filing suits to enforce state laws that regulate national banks. This case is seen as particularly significant given the regulatory failures at the federal level which contributed to the sub-prime mortgage crisis. The Office of the Comptroller of the Currency had issued regulations that attempted to limit regulation of national banks solely to the federal government. The National Bank Act itself does not do so. The National Banking Act provides that "No national bank shall be subject to any visitorial powers except as authorized by Federal law, vested in the courts…, or … directed by Congress." 12 U.S.C. §484(a). The Court held that "visitorial powers" meant administrative review but not the prosecution of law suits. The dissent contended that the Court should defer to the executive agency's interpretation of the statute

* * *

II. The Dormant Commerce Clause

Hypothetical Case

As you study the Dormant Commerce Clause and the Privileges and Immunities Clause, consider the following problem.

The legislature of the state of Colorado decides to convert all farming in the state to organic farming. Organic farmers grow crops without the use of pesticides or chemical fertilizers. The change is justified before the legislature by environmental and health concerns. Chemical fertilizers and pesticides used in Colorado contribute to pollution of the state's lakes and streams. In addition, the legislature acted because of evidence of a link between pesticide residues on food and health problems. Colorado has a large natural fertilizer industry. No manufacturers of chemical fertilizers are located in the state.

Organically grown crops are, in general, more expensive than those grown with pesticides and chemical fertilizers.

Three statutes are passed. The first prohibits non-organic farming in the state. In the second statute, Colorado prohibits the sale in the state of any produce grown by use of chemical fertilizer. A third prohibits the sale in the state of produce grown with the use of pesticides.

Jones is a Nevada grower of beets who uses both pesticides and chemical fertilizer. On a separate farm he grows some beets organically. Agri-Business, Inc., is a second Nevada beet grower. It also uses chemical fertilizers, but not pesticides. Both have sold their beets to supermarkets and public schools in Colorado in the past. Jones and Agri-Business sue the Colorado Commissioner of Agriculture, who oversees enforcement of the act, in Federal District Court. They seek an injunction against the Colorado statutes.

The particular pesticides used by the plaintiff Jones pose health hazards. In the case of beets treated with the pesticide, ten typical adult consumers in one million will develop cancer. For children, the figure is two hundred typical consumers in one million.

What claims are available to the plaintiffs in their attack on the *second* and *third* Colorado statutes? Consider each plaintiff separately. Assume that there is no federal statute bearing on the question. How should plaintiffs' claims be resolved?

A. The Dormant Commerce Clause: Introduction

Article I, §8, provides that Congress shall have the power to regulate commerce among the several states, with the Indian tribes and with foreign nations. If Congress acts pursuant to its delegated power to regulate commerce (and if the congressional statute does not violate a limit on congressional power), the congressional act will preempt a state statute that conflicts with it. A court faced with such a conflict is obligated by the Supremacy Clause to void the conflicting state statute. When Congress regulates commerce by statute, it actively uses its constitutional power.

The Commerce Clause cases we consider in this chapter are different. All involve challenges to state regulation based on the Commerce Clause. But none involve challenges based on a conflict with a law passed by Congress. Instead, they involve a claim that the Commerce Clause of its own force nullifies certain types of state laws, even though Congress has not spoken on the subject. They involve the negative effect of the Commerce Clause in its dormant state, or more briefly, the Dormant Commerce Clause. The doctrine is referred to as the Dormant Commerce Clause because Congress is passive or dormant (instead of actively legislating about the matter).

It has now long been established that the power of Congress to regulate commerce does not totally exclude state power. As a purely textual matter, it is therefore puzzling that the Commerce Clause is sometimes treated as an explicit prohibition on state legislation. The Dormant Commerce Clause doctrine has been justified in several ways. As a matter of history, a major impetus for establishing a new constitution was that the new states were erecting trade barriers against one another. The Constitution was a major step toward establishing a common market in the United States, and the Dormant Commerce Clause doctrine furthers that goal. The common market and the absence of trade barriers are justified as promoting economic efficiency.

The Dormant Commerce Clause protects people and commerce from outside the state from discrimination. A second justification is that out-of-staters are less able to protect themselves in the regulating state's political process. The doctrine is also sometimes justified by the legal fiction that congressional inaction reflects a congressional intent that certain subjects shall be free of state regulation.

Another curious aspect of the Dormant Commerce Clause doctrine is that the negative effect of the Dormant Commerce Clause is conditional. It is conditional because Congress can authorize state legislation that would otherwise violate the Dormant Commerce Clause—Congress can by ordinary legislation in effect reverse what appears to be a decision by the Court of a constitutional question. When Congress authorizes the state to do what the Court prohibited, state legislation that previously violated the Dormant Commerce Clause no longer does so. Other constitutional limits on the states—the Privileges and Immunities Clause of Article IV, §2, or the Equal Protection Clause, for example—are not limits Congress may authorize the states to violate. So state legislation that violates the Dormant Commerce Clause before Congress passes a law allowing such legislation, might still, in spite of the congressional statute, violate these or other constitutional limits on state power.

As formulated in *Gibbons v. Ogden* (1824) and certainly under modern doctrine established in cases such as *Wickard v. Filburn* (1942), the potential sweep of congressional power over commerce is vast. So a Dormant Commerce Clause doctrine that was as broad as congressional power over commerce would sweep away much, if not most, state legislation. In fact, the Dormant Commerce Clause doctrine is much more limited. The Dormant Commerce Clause (conditionally) voids only certain types of state legislation. Under current precedent, the clause will apply to state laws that discriminate against out-of-staters in favor of in-state residents or that discriminate against interstate commerce in favor of commerce within the state. (A law that prohibits out-of-staters from selling apples in North Carolina discriminates against those from out of state. A law that bars the importation of out-of-state apples into North Carolina discriminates against interstate commerce.) Such a discrimination raises a strong presumption against the validity of the state law. Still, such laws may be justified if they further a legitimate state objective that could not be pursued effectively by a non-discriminatory means or by a means that had a significantly less negative impact on out-of-staters or commerce from out of state. The Court sometimes refers to the scrutiny here as "strict" and in the charts we have provided we follow that terminology. Clearly, the Court uses some form of substantially heightened scrutiny in such discrimination cases. You should note, however, that the methodology may not be quite the same sort of strict scrutiny you will encounter, for example, in Equal Protection Clause cases.

How does one determine if a statute discriminates? In the easiest situation, one examines the language of the statute. If the statute on its face advantages those from within the state over out-of-staters, it discriminates. (Laws banning out-of-staters from selling apples in North Carolina and banning importation of out-of-state apples into the state are both examples of facial discrimination.) More difficult problems are presented when the statute is facially neutral but the facially neutral statute has an impact similar to one that discriminates on its face, or when the plaintiff claims that the statute is designed for the purpose of disadvantaging out-of-staters or commerce coming from outside the state. In such cases, the results are not entirely clear. The less plausible the state's justification for the arrangement that disadvantages those from out of state, the more likely the Court is to find the statute discriminatory. If the statute excludes all out-of-staters from a particular state market it is more likely to fall, while it is more likely to be sustained if some out-of-staters continue to have access to the market. For at least some justices, proof that the statute was designed to protect in-staters or in-state industry has justified striking down the statute. Others have been more skeptical of attempts to judge legislative purpose.

In examining statutes that discriminate against market participants from out of state, the Court focuses on the purpose or end pursued by the statute, on the means used to effectuate the end (for example, the discrimination against out-of-staters), and on the fit between the ends and the means. The purpose pursued by the statute must be constitutionally permissible and legitimate. For example, the purpose of a state statute might simply be to disadvantage those from out of state or, conversely, to protect industries within the state. Such a purpose would not be legitimate or constitutionally permissible. Or the purpose might be environmental protection, which *is* legitimate and permissible. The means used in the case of a statute that discriminates will always be a provision that discriminates either against out of state participants in the market or against interstate commerce. If the means are necessary to attain a legitimate end and if no alternative exists that would not burden or would impose substantially less of a burden on interstate commerce (or on those from out of state), then the fit between the ends and means will be tight and the statute is constitutional. In the typical situation, however, a legitimate end, such as conservation, can be achieved by means that do not simply disadvantage persons or commerce from out of state.

The other possibility is that state legislation treats in-staters and those from out of state the same and treats commerce within the state and commerce that comes from out of state the same. In this situation, the presumption favors constitutionality. Where the law does not discriminate, the Court has balanced the burden on interstate commerce against the benefit of the state legislation, striking down the legislation only when it concludes the burdens substantially outweigh the benefits. Some of the justices have rejected such balancing as illegitimate. They will strike down a state statute that burdens interstate commerce only if they conclude the benefit is so slight as to be illusory. Where the benefits are substantial, the Court typically upholds the statute.

Finally, you should note that the Dormant Commerce Clause typically limits the power of the state as a regulator. If the state is instead a participant in the market as a buyer or seller (of processed goods), then the strictures of the Dormant Commerce Clause typically do not apply.

The chart that follows (see next page) attempts to present these ideas visually, and to let you see one way to proceed through the steps of analysis. Each of the first divisions on the diagram represents a step or track of analysis. Go down the discrimination track if the state regulation discriminates against interstate commerce or prefers in-staters to out-of-staters. The second track of analysis is used if the regulation is even handed and does not discriminate against those from out of state or against interstate commerce in favor of intrastate commerce.

The chart is a model of the legal reality, and like all models, it oversimplifies in significant ways. For example, when will the Court find discrimination? Could a regulation that looks even handed be treated as discriminatory? In the typical practice of law, Dormant Commerce Clause problems and problems of preemption are constitutional problems you will be likely to encounter. In such a case, you will have an opportunity to study the complexities of the doctrine in greater depth.

B. Discrimination or Even-Handed Treatment: Introductory Cases

New Energy Company v. Limbach: Background

What is discrimination against interstate commerce? Could a statute that discriminates against interstate commerce still be upheld? What test is applied to discriminatory state statutes?

When is a state regulation of commerce even handed rather than discriminatory? What tests are applied when a state regulation is even handed?

Has Congress acted on the question before the Court in *New Energy*? Could Congress pass a statute making the Ohio statute constitutional?

What are the two aspects of the constitutional provision giving Congress power to regulate commerce revealed by *New Energy*?

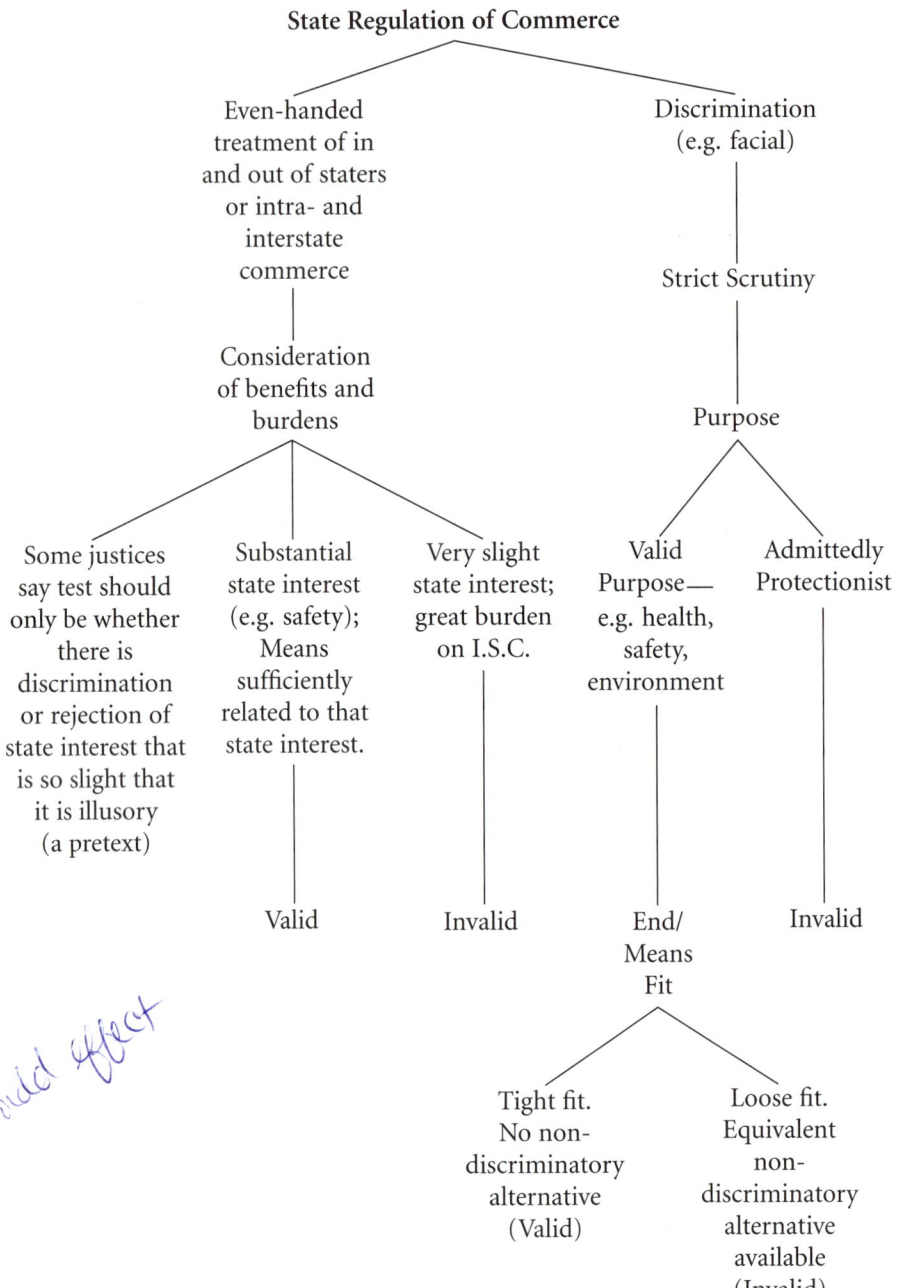

Policy Goals:
No state lines as a limit to commerce.
Dormant Commerce Clause protects interstate market, not particular participants.
See, Minnesota v. Cloverleaf Creamery, infra.

Problems

1. A Delaware statute requires that eggs imported to Delaware from another state must be marked with the postal zip code of the state and place of origin. Eggs produced in Delaware need not be marked. Assume that there are 131 zip codes in Delaware.

   Delaware asserts that imposing a labeling requirement on imported eggs will permit local authorities to isolate and remove from supermarkets' shelves those eggs produced in a geographic area known to be the source of an outbreak of salmonella poisoning. Still, no such limit is imposed on eggs from Delaware. There is no evidence in the record demonstrating that eggs imported to Delaware are more likely to be the source of salmonella than eggs produced locally. What challenge can be made to the Delaware statute? Is the statute constitutional?

2. State O provides that no person may ship out of state O any minnows seined in the waters of the state. The statute is justified as a conservation measure. Jones, a resident of Texas, sells minnows as bait fish and has traditionally bought them from a merchant in State O. The statute is enforced by the Fish and Game Commissioner of State O, who has impounded a shipment of minnows from state O destined for Jones in Texas. What sort of claim may Jones bring against the regulation of State O? What is the issue? What rules govern the resolution of the case? What purposes or policies are implicated by the state statute? How can you apply the rule to the facts? What is your conclusion? How can you construct a logical, step by step analysis of the problem? What cases might you cite to support the result you reach?

3. The state of M, by statute, prohibits importation of minnows for purposes of stocking the lakes of the state. Some out-of-state minnows carry diseases and parasites that would be a threat to the minnows of the state. There are no viable scientific tests for screening out-of-state fish for these diseases. The statute is challenged by Merton, an out-of-state minnow dealer, and Arthur, owner of several lakes in the state of M who wishes to stock them with out-of-state minnows. How should their challenge be analyzed and resolved? [After writing out this problem, if you wish, you may consult *Maine v. Taylor* (1986). You may conclude that looking at the answer before attempting the problem will rob the exercise of much of its use in helping understand the concepts.]

4. North Carolina prohibits the sale within the state of apples showing state grades. The state of Washington grades apples and "grade A" Washington apples are considered the nation's finest apples. A Washington "A" is superior to a USDA grade "A." The purpose of the statute, according to North Carolina, is to protect consumers. The state of Washington challenges the North Carolina statute in a suit brought against the official charged with enforcing the statute. How should the challenge to the North Carolina statute be analyzed and resolved?

New Energy Company v. Limbach
486 U.S. 269 (1988)

[Scalia, Rehnquist (C.J.), Kennedy, Blackmun, Brennan, Stevens, Marshall, White, and O'Connor.]

Justice Scalia delivered the opinion of the Court.

Appellant New Energy Company of Indiana has challenged the constitutionality of Ohio Rev. Code Ann. § 5735.145(B) (1986), a provision that awards a tax credit against the Ohio motor vehicle fuel sales tax for each gallon of ethanol sold (as a component of gasohol) by fuel dealers, but only if the ethanol is produced in Ohio or in a State that grants similar tax advantages to ethanol produced in Ohio. The question presented is whether §5735.145(B) discriminates against interstate commerce in violation of the Commerce Clause, U.S. Const., Art. I, §8, cl. 3.

I. Ethanol, or ethyl alcohol, is usually made from corn. In the last decade it has come into widespread use as an automotive fuel, mixed with gasoline in a ratio of 1 to 9 to produce what is called gasohol. The interest in ethanol emerged in reaction to the petroleum market dislocations of the early 1970's. The product was originally promoted as a means of achieving energy independence while providing a market for surplus corn; more recently, emphasis has shifted to its environmental advantages as a replacement for lead in enhancing fuel octane. Ethanol was, however (and continues to be), more expensive than gasoline, and the emergence of ethanol production on a commercial scale dates from enactment of the first federal subsidy, in the form of an exemption from federal motor fuel excise taxes, in 1978. Since then, many States, particularly those in the grain-producing areas of the country, have enacted their own ethanol subsidies. Ohio first passed such a measure in 1981, providing Ohio gasohol dealers a credit of so many cents per gallon of ethanol used in their product against the Ohio motor vehicle fuel sales tax payable on both ethanol and gasoline. This credit was originally available without regard to the source of the ethanol. In 1984, however, Ohio enacted §5735.145(B), which denies the credit to ethanol coming from States that do not grant a tax credit, exemption, or refund to ethanol from Ohio, or, if a State grants a smaller tax advantage than Ohio's, granting only an equivalent credit to ethanol from that State.

[New Energy] is an Indiana limited partnership that manufactures ethanol in South Bend, Indiana, for sale in several States, including Ohio. Indiana repealed its tax exemption for ethanol, effective July 1, 1985 at which time it also passed legislation providing a direct subsidy to Indiana ethanol producers (the sole one of which was [New Energy]). Thus, by reason of Ohio's reciprocity provision, appellant's ethanol sold in Ohio became ineligible for the Ohio tax credit. Appellant sought declaratory and injunctive relief in the Court of Common Pleas of Franklin County, Ohio, alleging that §5735.145(B) violated the Commerce Clause.... A divided Ohio Supreme Court [found] that the provision was not protectionist or unreasonably burdensome....

II. It has long been accepted that the Commerce Clause not only grants Congress the authority to regulate commerce among the States, but also directly limits the power of the States to discriminate against interstate commerce. See, e.g., *Hughes v. Oklahoma* (1979); *H.P. Hood & Sons, Inc. v. Du Mond* (1949); *Welton v. Missouri* (1876). This "negative" aspect of the Commerce Clause prohibits economic protectionism—that is, regulatory measures designed to benefit in-state economic interests by burdening out-of-state competitors. See, e.g., *Bacchus Imports, Ltd. v. Dias* (1984); *H.P. Hood & Sons*; *Guy v. Baltimore* (1880). Thus, state statutes that clearly discriminate against interstate commerce are routinely struck down, see, e.g., *Sporhase v. Nebraska ex rel. Douglas* (1982); *Lewis v. BT Investment Managers, Inc.* (1980); *Dean Milk Co. v. Madison* (1951), unless the discrimination is demonstrably justified by a valid factor unrelated to economic protectionism, see, e.g., *Maine v. Taylor* (1986).

The Ohio provision at issue here explicitly deprives certain products of generally available beneficial tax treatment because they are made in certain other States, and thus on its face appears to violate the cardinal requirement of nondiscrimination. [Ohio] argue[s], however, that the availability of the tax credit to some out-of-state manufacturers (those in states that give tax advantages to Ohio-produced ethanol) shows that the Ohio provision, far from discriminating against interstate commerce, is likely to promote it, by encouraging other States to enact similar tax advantages that will spur the interstate sale of ethanol. We rejected a similar contention in an earlier "reciprocity" case, *Great Atlantic & Pacific Tea Co. v. Cottrell* (1976). The regulation at issue there permitted milk from out of State to be sold in Mississippi only if the State of origin accepted Mississippi milk on a reciprocal basis. Mississippi put forward, among other arguments, the assertion that "the reciprocity requirement is in effect a free-trade provision, advancing the identical national interest that is served by the Commerce Clause." In response, we said that "Mississippi may not use the threat of economic isolation as a weapon to force sister States to enter into even a desirable reciprocity agreement." More recently, we characterized a Nebraska reciprocity requirement for the export of ground water from the State as "facially discriminatory legislation" which merited "'strictest scrutiny.'" *Sporhase v. Nebraska ex rel. Douglas,* quoting *Hughes v. Oklahoma.*

It is true that in *Cottrell* and *Sporhase* the effect of a State's refusal to accept the offered reciprocity was total elimination of all transport of the subject product into or out of the offering State; whereas in the present case the only effect of refusal is that the out-of-state product is placed at a substantial commercial disadvantage through discriminatory tax treatment. That makes no difference for purposes of Commerce Clause analysis. In the leading case of *Baldwin v. G.A.F. Seelig, Inc.* (1935), the New York law excluding out-of-state milk did not impose an absolute ban, but rather allowed importation and sale so long as the initial purchase from the dairy farmer was made at or above the New York State-mandated price. In other words, just as the appellant here, in order to sell its product in Ohio, only has to cut its profits by reducing its sales price below the market price sufficiently to compensate the Ohio purchaser-retailer for the forgone tax credit, so also the milk wholesaler-distributor in *Baldwin,* in order to sell its product in New York, only had to cut its profits by increasing its purchase price above the market price sufficiently to meet the New York-prescribed minimum. We viewed the New York law as "an economic barrier against competition" that was "equivalent to a rampart of customs duties." Similarly, in *Hunt v. Washington Apple Advertising Comm'n* (1977), we found invalid under the Commerce Clause a North Carolina statute that did not exclude apples from other States, but merely imposed additional costs upon Washington sellers and deprived them of the commercial advantage of their distinctive grading system. The present law likewise imposes an economic disadvantage upon out-of-state sellers; and the promise to remove that if reciprocity is accepted no more justifies disparity of treatment than it would justify categorical exclusion. We have indicated that reciprocity requirements are not per se unlawful. See *Cottrell.* But the case we cited for that proposition, *Kane v. New Jersey* (1916), discussed a context in which, if a State offered the reciprocity did not accept it, the consequence was, to be sure, *less favored* treatment for its citizens, but nonetheless treatment that complied with the minimum requirements of the Commerce Clause. Here, quite to the contrary, the threat used to induce Indiana's acceptance is, in effect, taxing a product made by its manufacturers at a rate higher than the same product made by Ohio manufacturers, without (as we shall see) justification for the disparity.

[Ohio] argue[s] that § 5735.145(B) should not be considered discrimination against interstate commerce because its practical scope is so limited. Apparently, only one Ohio ethanol manufacturer exists ... and only one out-of-state manufacturer ... is clearly disadvantaged by the provision. Our cases, however, indicate that where discrimination is patent, as it is here, neither a widespread advantage to in-state interests nor a widespread disadvantage to out-of-state competitors need be shown. For example, in *Bacchus Imports, Ltd. v. Dias,* we held unconstitutional under the Commerce Clause a special exemption from Hawaii's liquor tax for certain locally produced alcoholic beverages (okolehao and fruit wine), even though other locally produced alcoholic beverages were subject to the tax. And in *Lewis v. BT Investment Managers, Inc.*, we held unconstitutional a Florida statute that excluded from certain business activities in Florida not all out-of-state entities, but only out-of-state bank holding companies, banks, or trust companies. In neither of these cases did we consider the size or number of the in-state businesses favored or the out-of-state businesses disfavored relevant to our determination. Varying the strength of the bar against economic protectionism according to the size and number of in-state and out-of-state firms affected would serve no purpose except the creation of new uncertainties in an already complex field.

[Ohio] contends that even if § 5735.145(B) is discriminatory, the discrimination is not covered by the Commerce Clause because of the so-called market-participant doctrine. That doctrine differentiates between a State's acting in its distinctive governmental capacity, and a State's acting in the more general capacity of a market participant; only the former is subject to the limitations of the negative Commerce Clause. See *Hughes v. Alexandria Scrap Co.* (1976). Thus, for example, when a State chooses to manufacture and sell cement, its business methods, including those that favor its residents, are of no greater constitutional concern than those of a private business. See *Reeves, Inc. v. Stake* (1980).

The market-participant doctrine has no application here. The Ohio action ultimately at issue is neither its purchase nor its sale of ethanol, but its assessment and computation of taxes—a primeval governmental activity. To be sure, the tax credit scheme has the purpose and effect of subsidizing a particular industry, as do many dispositions of the tax laws. That does not transform it into a form of state participation in the free market. Our opinion in *Alexandria Scrap*, a case on which [Ohio] place[s] great reliance, does not remotely establish such a proposition. There we examined, and upheld against Commerce Clause attack on the basis of the market-participant doctrine, a Maryland cash subsidy program that discriminated in favor of in-state auto-hulk processors. The purpose of the program was to achieve the removal of unsightly abandoned autos from the State, and the Court characterized it as proprietary rather than regulatory activity, based on the analogy of the State to a private purchaser of the auto hulks. We have subsequently observed that subsidy programs unlike that of *Alexandria Scrap* might not be characterized as proprietary. See *Reeves, Inc.* We think it clear that Ohio's assessment and computation of its fuel sales tax, regardless of whether it produces a subsidy, cannot plausibly be analogized to the activity of a private purchaser.

It has not escaped our notice that the appellant here, which is eligible to receive a cash subsidy under Indiana's program for in-state ethanol producers, is the potential beneficiary of a scheme no less discriminatory than the one that it attacks, and no less effective in conferring a commercial advantage over out-of-state competitors. To believe the Indiana scheme is valid, however, is not to believe that the Ohio scheme must be valid as well. The Commerce Clause does not prohibit all state action designed to give its residents an advantage in the marketplace, but only action of that description in connection with the State's regulation of interstate commerce. Direct subsidization of domestic industry does not ordinarily run afoul of that prohibition; discriminatory taxation of out-of-state manufacturers does. Of course, even if the Indiana subsidy were invalid, retaliatory violation of the Commerce Clause by Ohio would not be acceptable. See *Cottrell*.

III. Our cases leave open the possibility that a State may validate a statute that discriminates against interstate commerce by showing that it advances a legitimate local purpose that cannot be adequately served by reasonable nondiscriminatory alternatives. See, e.g., *Maine v. Taylor*; *Sporhase v. Nebraska ex rel. Douglas*; *Hughes v. Oklahoma*; *Dean Milk Co. v. Madison*. This is perhaps just another way of saying that what may appear to be a "discriminatory" provision in the constitutionally prohibited sense—that is, a protectionist enactment—may on closer analysis not be so. However it be put, the standards for such justification are high. Cf. *Philadelphia v. New Jersey* (1978) ("[W]here simple economic protectionism is effected by state legislation, a virtually per se rule of invalidity has been erected"); *Hughes v. Oklahoma* ("[F]acial discrimination by itself may be a fatal defect" and "[a]t a minimum ... invokes the strictest scrutiny").

Appellees advance two justifications for the clear discrimination in the present case: health and commerce. As to the first, they argue that the provision encourages use of ethanol (in replacement of lead as a gasoline octane-enhancer) to reduce harmful exhaust emissions, both in Ohio itself and in surrounding States whose polluted atmosphere may reach Ohio. Certainly the protection of health is a legitimate state goal, and we assume for purposes of this argument that use of ethanol generally furthers it. But § 5735.145(B) obviously does not, except perhaps by accident. As far as ethanol use in Ohio itself is concerned, there is no reason to suppose that ethanol produced in a State that does not offer tax advantages to ethanol produced in Ohio is less healthy, and thus should have its importation into Ohio suppressed by denial of the otherwise standard tax credit. And as far as ethanol use outside Ohio is concerned, surely that is just as effectively fostered by other States' subsidizing ethanol production or sale in some fashion other than giving a tax credit to Ohio-produced ethanol; but these helpful expedients do not qualify for the tax credit. It could not be clearer that health is not the purpose of the provision, but is merely an occasional and accidental effect of achieving what is its purpose, favorable tax treatment for Ohio-produced ethanol.[1] Essentially the same reasoning also responds to appellees' second (and related) justification for the discrimination, that the reciprocity requirement is designed to increase commerce in ethanol by encouraging other States to enact ethanol subsidies. What is encouraged is not ethanol subsidies in general, but only favorable treatment for Ohio-produced ethanol. In sum, appellees' health and commerce justifications amount to no more than implausible speculation, which does not suffice to validate this plain discrimination against products of out-of-state manufacture.

For the reasons stated, the judgment of the Ohio Supreme Court is *Reversed*.

Southern Pacific Company v. Arizona
325 U.S. 761 (1945)

[Majority: Stone (C.J.), Frankfurter, Murphy, Reed, Roberts, and Jackson. Concurrence: Rutledge. Dissenting: Black and Douglas.]

Mr. Chief Justice Stone delivered the opinion of the Court.

The Arizona Train Limit Law of May 16, 1912, Arizona Code Ann., 1939, § 69-119, makes it unlawful for any person or corporation to operate within the state a railroad train of more than fourteen passenger or seventy freight cars, and authorizes the state to recover a money penalty for each violation of the Act. The questions for decision are whether Congress has, by legislative enactment, restricted the power of the states to reg-

---

1. We do not interpret the trial court's acceptance of appellees' proposed finding of fact of April 10, 1985, as a judicial finding that protecting health was in fact a purpose of the Ohio General Assembly, rather than merely one of several conceivable purposes for the enactment. In any event, a subjective purpose that has so little rational relationship to the provision in question is not merely implausible but, even if true, inadequate to validate patent discrimination against interstate commerce.

ulate the length of interstate trains as a safety measure and, if not, whether the statute contravenes the Commerce Clause of the Federal Constitution.

In 1940 the State of Arizona brought suit in the Arizona Superior Court against appellant, the Southern Pacific Company, to recover the statutory penalties for operating within the state two interstate trains, one a passenger train of more than fourteen cars, and one a freight train of more than seventy cars. Appellant answered, admitting the train operations, but defended on the ground that the statute offends against the Commerce Clause.... After an extended trial, without a jury, the court made detailed findings of fact on the basis of which it gave judgment for the railroad company. The Supreme Court of Arizona reversed and directed judgment for the state....

The [Arizona] Supreme Court left undisturbed the findings of the trial court and made no new findings. It held that the power of the state to regulate the length of interstate trains had not been restricted by Congressional action. It sustained the Act as a safety measure to reduce the number of accidents attributed to the operation of trains of more than the statutory maximum length, enacted by the state legislature in the exercise of its "police power." This power, the court held, extended to the regulation of the operations of interstate commerce in the interests of local health, safety and well-being. It thought that a state statute, enacted in the exercise of the police power, and bearing some reasonable relation to the health, safety and well-being of the people of the state, of which the state legislature is the judge, was not to be judicially overturned, notwithstanding its admittedly adverse effect on the operation of interstate trains....

Although the Commerce Clause conferred on the national government power to regulate commerce, its possession of the power does not exclude all state power of regulation. Ever since *Wilson v. Black Bird Creek Marsh Co.* (1829), and *Cooley v. Board of Wardens* (1852), it has been recognized that, in the absence of conflicting legislation by Congress, there is a residuum of power in the state to make laws governing matters of local concern which nevertheless in some measure affect interstate commerce or even, to some extent, regulate it. *Minnesota Rate Cases (Simpson v. Shepard)* (1913); *South Carolina State Highway Department v. Barnwell Bros.* (1938). Thus the states may regulate matters which, because of their number and diversity, may never be adequately dealt with by Congress. *Cooley v. Board of Wardens*; *South Carolina State Highway Department v. Barnwell Bros.*... When the regulation of matters of local concern is local in character and effect, and its impact on the national commerce does not seriously interfere with its operation, and the consequent incentive to deal with them nationally is slight, such regulation has been generally held to be within state authority. South Carolina State Highway Dept. v. Barnwell Bros.

But ever since *Gibbons v. Ogden* (1824), the states have not been deemed to have authority to impede substantially the free flow of commerce from state to state, or to regulate those phases of the national commerce which, because of the need of national uniformity, demand that their regulation, if any, be prescribed by a single authority.[1] *Cooley v. Board of Wardens*; *Leisy v. Hardin* (1890); *Minnesota Rate Cases*; *Edwards v. California* (1941). Whether or not this long recognized distribution of power between the national and the state governments is predicated upon the implications of the Commerce

---

1. In applying this rule the Court has often recognized that to the extent that the burden of state regulation falls on interests outside the state, it is unlikely to be alleviated by the operation of those political restraints normally exerted when interests within the state are affected. *Cooley v. Board of Wardens*....

Clause itself or upon the presumed intention of Congress, where Congress has not spoken, *In re Rahrer* (1891), the result is the same.

In the application of these principles some enactments may be found to be plainly within and others plainly without state power. But between these extremes lies the infinite variety of cases in which regulation of local matters may also operate as a regulation of commerce, in which reconciliation of the conflicting claims of state and national power is to be attained only by some appraisal and accommodation of the competing demands of the state and national interests involved....

For a hundred years it has been accepted constitutional doctrine that the Commerce Clause, without the aid of Congressional legislation, thus affords some protection from state legislation inimical to the national commerce, and that in such cases, where Congress has not acted, this Court, and not the state legislature, is under the Commerce Clause the final arbiter of the competing demands of state and national interests. *Cooley v. Board of Wardens*....

Congress has undoubted power to redefine the distribution of power over interstate commerce. It may either permit the states to regulate the commerce in a manner which would otherwise not be permissible, *In re Rahrer* ... or exclude state regulation even of matters of peculiarly local concern which nevertheless affect interstate commerce....

But in general Congress has left it to the courts to formulate the rules thus interpreting the Commerce Clause in its application, doubtless because it has appreciated the destructive consequences to the commerce of the nation if their protection were withdrawn and has been aware that in their application state laws will not be invalidated without the support of relevant factual material which will "afford a sure basis" for an informed judgment.... Meanwhile, Congress has accommodated its legislation, as have the states, to these rules as an established feature of our constitutional system. There has thus been left to the states wide scope for the regulation of matters of local state concern, even though it in some measure affects the commerce, provided it does not materially restrict the free flow of commerce across state lines, or interfere with it in matters with respect to which uniformity of regulation is of predominant national concern.

Hence the matters for ultimate determination here are the nature and extent of the burden which the state regulation of interstate trains, adopted as a safety measure, imposes on interstate commerce, and whether the relative weights of the state and national interests involved are such as to make inapplicable the rule, generally observed, that the free flow of interstate commerce and its freedom from local restraints in matters requiring uniformity of regulation are interests safeguarded by the Commerce Clause from state interference.

While this Court is not bound by the findings of the state court, and may determine for itself the facts of a case upon which an asserted federal right depends, the facts found by the state trial court showing the nature of the interstate commerce involved, and the effect upon it of the train limit law, are not seriously questioned. Its findings with respect to the need for and effect of the statute as a safety measure, although challenged in some particulars which we do not regard as material to our decision, are likewise supported by evidence. Taken together the findings supply an adequate basis for decision of the constitutional issue.

The findings show that the operation of long trains, that is trains of more than fourteen passenger and more than seventy freight cars, is standard practice over the main lines of the railroads of the United States, and that, if the length of trains is to be regulated at all, national uniformity in the regulation adopted, such as only Congress can prescribe, is practically indispensable to the operation of an efficient and economical national railway system....

The unchallenged findings leave no doubt that the Arizona Train Limit Law imposes a serious burden on the interstate commerce conducted by appellant. It materially impedes the movement of appellant's interstate trains through that state and interposes a substantial obstruction to the national policy proclaimed by Congress, to promote adequate, economical and efficient railway transportation service. Interstate Commerce Act, preceding § 1, 54 Stat. 899. Enforcement of the law in Arizona, while train lengths remain unregulated or are regulated by varying standards in other states, must inevitably result in an impairment of uniformity of efficient railroad operation because the railroads are subjected to regulation which is not uniform in its application. Compliance with a state statute limiting train lengths requires interstate trains of a length lawful in other states to be broken up and reconstituted as they enter each state according as it may impose varying limitations upon train lengths. The alternative is for the carrier to conform to the lowest train limit restriction of any of the states through which its trains pass, whose laws thus control the carriers' operations both within and without the regulating state....

If one state may regulate train lengths, so may all the others, and they need not prescribe the same maximum limitation. The practical effect of such regulation is to control train operations beyond the boundaries of the state exacting it because of the necessity of breaking up and reassembling long trains at the nearest terminal points before entering and after leaving the regulating state. The serious impediment to the free flow of commerce by the local regulation of train lengths and the practical necessity that such regulation, if any, must be prescribed by a single body having a nation-wide authority are apparent.

The trial court found that the Arizona law had no reasonable relation to safety, and made train operation more dangerous. Examination of the evidence and the detailed findings makes it clear that this conclusion was rested on facts found which indicate that such increased danger of accident and personal injury as may result from the greater length of trains is more than offset by the increase in the number of accidents resulting from the larger number of trains when train lengths are reduced. In considering the effect of the statute as a safety measure, therefore, the factor of controlling significance for present purposes is not whether there is basis for the conclusion of the Arizona Supreme Court that the increase in length of trains beyond the statutory maximum has an adverse effect upon safety of operation. The decisive question is whether in the circumstances the total effect of the law as a safety measure in reducing accidents and casualties is so slight or problematical as not to outweigh the national interest in keeping interstate commerce free from interferences which seriously impede it and subject it to local regulation which does not have a uniform effect on the interstate train journey which it interrupts.

The principal source of danger of accident from increased length of trains is the resulting increase of "slack action" of the train. Slack action is the amount of free movement of one car before it transmits its motion to an adjoining coupled car....

As the trial court found, reduction of the length of trains also tends to increase the number of accidents because of the increase in the number of trains. The application of the Arizona law compelled appellant to operate 30.08%, or 4,304, more freight trains in 1938 than would otherwise have been necessary. And the record amply supports the trial court's conclusion that the frequency of accidents is closely related to the number of trains run....

Upon an examination of the whole case, the trial court found that "if short-train operation may or should result in any decrease in the number or severity of the 'slack' or 'slack-surge' type of accidents or casualties, such decrease is substantially more than offset by the increased number of accidents and casualties from other causes that follow the arbitrary limitation of freight trains to 70 cars ... and passenger trains to 14 cars."

We think, as the trial court found, that the Arizona Train Limit Law, viewed as a safety measure, affords at most slight and dubious advantage, if any, over unregulated train lengths, because it results in an increase in the number of trains and train operations and the consequent increase in train accidents of a character generally more severe than those due to slack action. Its undoubted effect on the commerce is the regulation, without securing uniformity, of the length of trains operated in interstate commerce, which lack is itself a primary cause of preventing the free flow of commerce by delaying it and by substantially increasing its cost and impairing its efficiency. In these respects the case differs from those where a state, by regulatory measures affecting the commerce, has removed or reduced safety hazards without substantial interference with the interstate movement of trains....

Here we conclude that the state does go too far. Its regulation of train lengths, admittedly obstructive to interstate train operation, and having a seriously adverse effect on transportation efficiency and economy, passes beyond what is plainly essential for safety since it does not appear that it will lessen rather than increase the danger of accident. Its attempted regulation of the operation of interstate trains cannot establish nation-wide control such as is essential to the maintenance of an efficient transportation system, which Congress alone can prescribe. The state interest cannot be preserved at the expense of the national interest by an enactment which regulates interstate train lengths without securing such control, which is a matter of national concern. To this the interest of the state here asserted is subordinate....

Reversed.

Mr. Justice Rutledge concurs in the result.

Mr. Justice Black, dissenting.

In *Hennington v. Georgia* (1896), a case which involved the power of a state to regulate interstate traffic, this Court said, "The whole theory of our government, federal and state, is hostile to the idea that questions of legislative authority may depend ... upon opinions of judges as to the wisdom or want of wisdom in the enactment of laws under powers clearly conferred upon the legislature." What the Court decides today is that it is unwise governmental policy to regulate the length of trains. I am therefore constrained to note my dissent.

For more than a quarter of a century, railroads and their employees have engaged in controversies over the relative virtues and dangers of long trains. Railroads have argued that they could carry goods and passengers cheaper in long trains than in short trains. They have also argued that while the danger of personal injury to their employees might in some respects be greater on account of the operation of long trains, this danger was more than offset by an increased number of accidents from other causes brought about by the operation of a much larger number of short trains. These arguments have been, and are now, vigorously denied. While there are others, the chief causes assigned for the belief that long trains unnecessarily jeopardize the lives and limbs of railroad employees relate to "slack action." Cars coupled together retain a certain free play of movement, ranging between 11/2 inches and 1 foot, and this is called "slack action." Train brakes do not ordinarily apply or release simultaneously on all cars. This frequently results in a severe shock or jar to cars, particularly those in the rear of a train. It has always been the position of the employees that the dangers from "slack action" correspond to and are proportionate with the length of the train. The argument that "slack movements" are more dangerous in long trains than in short trains seems never to have been denied. The railroads have answered it by what is in effect a plea of confession and avoidance. They say that the added cost of running long trains places an unconstitutional burden on interstate commerce. Their second answer is that the operation of short trains requires the use of more separate train units; that a certain number of accidents resulting in injury are inherent in the operation of each unit, injuries which may be inflicted either on employees or on the public; consequently, they have asserted that it is not in the public interest to prohibit the operation of long trains.

In 1912, the year Arizona became a state, its legislature adopted and referred to the people several safety measures concerning the operation of railroads. One of these required railroads to install electric headlights, a power which the state had under this Court's opinion in *Atlantic Coast Line R. Co. v. Georgia* (1914). Another Arizona safety statute submitted at the same time required certain tests and service before a person could act as an engineer or train conductor, and thereby exercised a state power similar to that which this Court upheld in *Nashville, C. & St. L. R. Co. v. Alabama* (1888). The third safety statute which the Arizona legislature submitted to the electorate, and which was adopted by it, is the train limitation statute now under consideration. By its enactment the legislature and the people adopted the viewpoint that long trains were more dangerous than short trains, and limited the operation of train units to 14 cars for passenger and 70 cars for freight. This same question was considered in other states, and some of them, over the vigorous protests of railroads, adopted laws similar to the Arizona statute.

This controversy between the railroads and their employees, which was nation-wide, was carried to Congress. Extensive hearings took place. The employees' position was urged by members of the various Brotherhoods. The railroads' viewpoint was presented through representatives of their National Association. In 1937, the Senate Interstate Commerce Committee after its own exhaustive hearings unanimously recommended that trains be limited to 70 cars as a safety measure. The Committee in its Report reviewed the evidence and specifically referred to the large and increasing number of injuries and deaths suffered by railroad employees; it concluded that the admitted danger from slack movement was greatly intensified by the operation of long trains; that short trains reduce this danger; that the added cost of short trains to the railroad was no justification for jeopardizing the safety of railroad employees; and that the legislation would provide a greater degree of safety for persons and property, increase protection for railway employees and the public, and improve transportation services for shippers and consumers. The Senate passed the bill, but the House Committee failed to report it out.

During the hearings on that measure, frequent references were made to the Arizona statute. It is significant, however, that American railroads never once asked Congress to exercise its unquestioned power to enact uniform legislation on that subject, and thereby invalidate the Arizona Law. That which for some unexplained reason they did not ask Congress to do when it had the very subject of train length limitations under consideration, they shortly thereafter asked an Arizona state court to do.

In the state court a rather extraordinary "trial" took place. Charged with violating the law, the railroad admitted the charge. It alleged that the law was unconstitutional, however, and sought a trial of facts on that issue. The essence of its charge of unconstitutionality rested on one of these two grounds: (1) The legislature and people of Arizona erred in 1912 in determining that the running of long cars was dangerous; or (2) railroad conditions had so improved since 1912 that previous dangers did not exist to the same extent, and that the statute should be stricken down either because it cast an undue burden on interstate commerce by reason of the added cost, or because the changed conditions had rendered the Act "arbitrary and unreasonable." Thus, the issue which the court "tried" was not whether the railroad was guilty of violating the law, but whether the law was unconstitutional either because the legislature had been guilty of misjudging the facts concerning the degree of the danger of long trains, or because the 1912 conditions of danger no longer existed.

Before the state trial judge finally determined that the dangers found by the legislature in 1912 no longer existed, he heard evidence over a period of 5½ months which appears in about 3,000 pages of the printed record before us. It then adopted findings of fact submitted to it by the railroad, which cover 148 printed pages, and conclusions of law which cover 5 pages. We can best understand the nature of this "trial" by analogizing the same procedure to a defendant charged with violating a state or national safety appliance act, where the defendant comes into court and admits violation of the act. In such cases, the ordinary procedure would be for the court to pass upon the constitutionality of the act, and either discharge or convict the defendants. The procedure here, however, would justify quite a different trial method. Under it, a defendant is permitted to offer voluminous evidence to show that a legislative body has erroneously resolved disputed facts in finding a danger great enough to justify the passage of the law. This new pattern of trial procedure makes it necessary for a judge to hear all the evidence offered as to why a legislature passed a law and to make findings of fact as to the validity of those reasons. If under today's ruling a court does make findings, as to a danger contrary to the findings of the legislature, and the evidence heard "lends support" to those findings, a court can then invalidate the law. In this respect, the Arizona County Court acted, and this Court today is acting, as a "super-legislature."

Even if this method of invalidating legislative acts is a correct one, I still think that the "findings" of the state court do not authorize today's decision. That court did not find that there is no unusual danger from slack movements in long trains. It did decide on disputed evidence that the long train "slack movement" dangers were more than offset by prospective dangers as a result of running a larger number of short trains, since many people might be hurt at grade crossings. There was undoubtedly some evidence before the state court from which it could have reached such a conclusion. There was undoubtedly as much evidence before it which would have justified a different conclusion.

Under those circumstances, the determination of whether it is in the interest of society for the length of trains to be governmentally regulated is a matter of public policy. Someone must fix that policy—either the Congress, or the state, or the courts. A century and a half of constitutional history and government admonishes this Court to leave that choice to the elected legislative representatives of the people themselves, where it properly belongs both on democratic principles and the requirements of efficient government....

When we finally get down to the gist of what the Court today actually decides, it is this: Even though more railroad employees will be injured by "slack action" movements on long trains than on short trains, there must be no regulation of this danger in the absence of "uniform regulations." That means that no one can legislate against this danger except the Congress; and even though the Congress is perfectly content to leave the matter to the different state legislatures, this Court, on the ground of "lack of uniformity," will require it to make an express avowal of that fact before it will permit a state to guard against that admitted danger.

We are not left in doubt as to why, as against the potential peril of injuries to employees, the Court tips the scales on the side of "uniformity." For the evil it finds in a lack of uniformity is that it (1) delays interstate commerce, (2) increases its cost and (3) impairs its efficiency. All three of these boil down to the same thing, and that is that running shorter trains would increase the cost of railroad operations. The "burden" on commerce reduces itself to mere cost because there was no finding, and no evidence to support a finding, that by the expenditure of sufficient sums of money, the railroads could not enable themselves to carry goods and passengers just as quickly and efficiently with short trains as with long trains. Thus the conclusion that a requirement for long trains will "burden interstate commerce" is a mere euphemism for the statement that a requirement for long trains will increase the cost of railroad operations.

In the report of the Senate Committee, attention was called to the fact that in 1935, 6,351 railroad employees were injured while on duty, with a resulting loss of more than 200,000 working days, and that injuries to trainmen and enginemen increased more than 29% in 1936. Nevertheless, the Court's action in requiring that money costs outweigh human values is sought to be buttressed by a reference to the express policy of Congress to promote an "economical national railroad system." I cannot believe that if Congress had defined what it meant by "economical," it would have required money to be saved at the expense of the personal safety of railway employees. Its whole history for the past 25 years belies such an interpretation of its language. Judicial opinions rather than legislative enactments have tended to emphasize costs....

This record in its entirety leaves me with no doubt whatever that many employees have been seriously injured and killed in the past, and that many more are likely to be so in the future, because of "slack movement" in trains. Everyday knowledge as well as direct evidence presented at the various hearings, substantiates the report of the Senate Committee that the danger from slack movement is greater in long trains than in short trains. It may be that offsetting dangers are possible in the operation of short trains. The balancing of these probabilities, however, is not in my judgment a matter for judicial determination, but one which calls for legislative consideration. Representatives elected by the people to make their laws, rather than judges appointed to interpret those laws, can best determine the policies which govern the people. That at least is the basic principle on which our democratic society rests. I would affirm the judgment of the Supreme Court of Arizona.

Mr. Justice Douglas, dissenting.

I have expressed my doubts whether the courts should intervene in situations like the present and strike down state legislation on the grounds that it burdens interstate commerce. *McCarroll v. Dixie Greyhound Lines* (1940). My view has been that the courts should intervene only where the state legislation discriminated against interstate commerce or was out of harmony with laws which Congress had enacted. It seems to me particularly appropriate that that course be followed here. For Congress has given the Interstate Commerce Commission broad powers of regulation over interstate carriers. The Commission is the national agency which has been entrusted with the task of promoting a safe, adequate, efficient, and economical transportation service. It is the expert on this subject. It is in a position to police the field. And if its powers prove inadequate for the task, Congress, which has paramount authority in this field, can implement them.

But the Court has not taken that view. As a result, the question presented is whether the total effect of Arizona's train-limit as a safety measure is so slight as not to outweigh the national interest in keeping interstate commerce free from interferences which seriously impede or burden it.... Whether the question arises under the Commerce Clause or the 14th Amendment, I think the legislation is entitled to a presumption of validity.

If a State passed a law prohibiting the hauling of more than one freight car at a time, we would have a situation comparable in effect to a state law requiring all railroads within its borders to operate on narrow gauge tracks. The question is one of degree and calls for a close appraisal of the facts. I am not persuaded that the evidence adduced by the railroads overcomes the presumption of validity to which this train limit law is entitled. For the reasons stated by Mr. Justice Black, Arizona's train-limit law should stand as an allowable regulation enacted to protect the lives and limbs of the men who operate the trains.

Granholm v. Heald
544 U.S. 460 (2005)

[Majority: Kennedy, Scalia, Souter, Ginsburg, and Breyer. Dissenting: Stevens, O'-Connor, Thomas, and Rehnquist, (C.J.)]

Justice Kennedy delivered the opinion of the Court.

These consolidated cases present challenges to state laws regulating the sale of wine from out-of-state wineries to consumers in Michigan and New York. The details and mechanics of the two regulatory schemes differ, but the object and effect of the laws are the same: to allow in-state wineries to sell wine directly to consumers in that State but to prohibit out-of-state wineries from doing so, or, at the least, to make direct sales impractical from an economic standpoint. It is evident that the object and design of the Michigan and New York statutes is to grant in-state wineries a competitive advantage over wineries located beyond the States' borders.

We hold that the laws in both States discriminate against interstate commerce in violation of the Commerce Clause, Art. I, §8, cl. 3, and that the discrimination is neither authorized nor permitted by the 21st Amendment....

I. Like many other States, Michigan and New York regulate the sale and importation of alcoholic beverages, including wine, through a three-tier distribution system. Separate licenses are required for producers, wholesalers, and retailers. See FTC, *Possible Anticompetitive Barriers to E-Commerce: Wine* 5–7 (July 2003) (hereinafter *FTC Report*), available at http://www.ftc.gov/os/2003/07/winereport2.pdf (all Internet materials as visited May 11, 2005, and available in Clerk of Court's case file). The three-tier scheme is preserved by a complex set of overlapping state and federal regulations. For example, both state and federal laws limit vertical integration between tiers. *Id.*, at 5; 27 U. S. C. §205. We have held previously that States can mandate a three-tier distribution scheme in the exercise of their authority under the 21st Amendment. As relevant to today's cases, though, the three-tier system is, in broad terms and with refinements to be discussed, mandated by Michigan and New York only for sales from out-of-state wineries. In-state wineries, by contrast, can obtain a license for direct sales to consumers. The differential treatment between in-state and out-of-state wineries constitutes explicit discrimination against interstate commerce.

This discrimination substantially limits the direct sale of wine to consumers, an otherwise emerging and significant business. *FTC Report* 7. From 1994 to 1999, consumer spending on direct wine shipments doubled, reaching $500 million per year, or three percent of all wine sales. *Id.*, at 5. The expansion has been influenced by several related trends. First, the number of small wineries in the United States has significantly increased. By some estimates there are over 3,000 wineries in the country, more than three times the number 30 years ago, *FTC Report* 6. At the same time, the wholesale market has consolidated. Between 1984 and 2002, the number of licensed wholesalers dropped from 1,600 to 600. Riekhof & Sykuta, *Regulating Wine by Mail*, 27 Regulation, No. 3, pp. 30, 31 (Fall 2004), available at http://www.cato.org/pubs/regulation/regv27n3/v27n3-3.pdf. The increasing winery-to-wholesaler ratio means that many small wineries do not produce enough wine or have sufficient consumer demand for their wine to make it economical for wholesalers to carry their products. *FTC Report* 6. This has led many small wineries to rely on direct shipping to reach new markets. Technological improvements, in particular the ability of wineries to sell wine over the Internet, have helped make direct shipments an attractive sales channel....

The wine producers in the cases before us are small wineries that rely on direct consumer sales as an important part of their businesses. Domaine Alfred, one of the plaintiffs in the Michigan suit, is a small winery located in San Luis Obispo, California. It produces 3,000 cases of wine per year. Domaine Alfred has received requests for its wine from Michigan consumers but cannot fill the orders because of the State's direct-shipment ban. Even if the winery could find a Michigan wholesaler to distribute its wine, the wholesaler's markup would render shipment through the three-tier system economically infeasible.

Similarly, Juanita Swedenburg and David Lucas, two of the plaintiffs in the New York suit, operate small wineries in Virginia (the Swedenburg Estate Vineyard) and California (the Lucas Winery). Some of their customers are tourists, from other States, who purchase wine while visiting the wineries. If these customers wish to obtain Swedenburg or Lucas wines after they return home, they will be unable to do so if they reside in a State with restrictive direct-shipment laws. For example, Swedenburg and Lucas are unable to fill orders from New York, the Nation's second-largest wine market, because of the limits that State imposes on direct wine shipments....

II-A. Time and again this Court has held that, in all but the narrowest circumstances, state laws violate the Commerce Clause if they mandate "differential treatment of in-state and out-of-state economic interests that benefits the former and burdens the latter." *Oregon Waste Systems, Inc. v. Department of Environmental Quality of Ore.* (1994). See also *New Energy Co. of Ind. v. Limbach* (1988). This rule is essential to the foundations of the Union. The mere fact of nonresidence should not foreclose a producer in one State from access to markets in other States. States may not enact laws that burden out-of-state producers or shippers simply to give a competitive advantage to in-state businesses. This mandate "reflect[s] a central concern of the Framers that was an immediate reason for calling the Constitutional Convention: the conviction that in order to succeed, the new Union would have to avoid the tendencies toward economic Balkanization that had plagued relations among the Colonies and later among the States under the Articles of Confederation." *Hughes v. Oklahoma* (1979).

The rule prohibiting state discrimination against interstate commerce follows also from the principle that States should not be compelled to negotiate with each other regarding favored or disfavored status for their own citizens. States do not need, and may not attempt, to negotiate with other States regarding their mutual economic interests. Cf. U. S. Const., Art. I, §10, cl. 3. Rivalries among the States are thus kept to a minimum, and a proliferation of trade zones is prevented.

Laws of the type at issue in the instant cases contradict these principles. They deprive citizens of their right to have access to the markets of other States on equal terms. The perceived necessity for reciprocal sale privileges risks generating the trade rivalries and animosities, the alliances and exclusivity, that the Constitution and, in particular, the

Commerce Clause were designed to avoid. State laws that protect local wineries have led to the enactment of statutes under which some States condition the right of out-of-state wineries to make direct wine sales to in-state consumers on a reciprocal right in the shipping State. California, for example, passed a reciprocity law in 1986, retreating from the State's previous regime that allowed unfettered direct shipments from out-of-state wineries. Prior to 1986, all but three States prohibited direct-shipments of wine. The obvious aim of the California statute was to open the interstate direct-shipping market for the State's many wineries. The current patchwork of laws—with some States banning direct shipments altogether, others doing so only for out-of-state wines, and still others requiring reciprocity—is essentially the product of an ongoing, low-level trade war. Allowing States to discriminate against out-of-state wine "invite[s] a multiplication of preferential trade areas destructive of the very purpose of the Commerce Clause." *Dean Milk Co. v. Madison* (1951).

II-B. The discriminatory character of the Michigan system is obvious. Michigan allows in-state wineries to ship directly to consumers, subject only to a licensing requirement. Out-of-state wineries, whether licensed or not, face a complete ban on direct shipment. The differential treatment requires all out-of-state wine, but not all in-state wine, to pass through an in-state wholesaler and retailer before reaching consumers. These two extra layers of overhead increase the cost of out-of-state wines to Michigan consumers. The cost differential, and in some cases the inability to secure a wholesaler for small shipments, can effectively bar small wineries from the Michigan market.

The New York regulatory scheme differs from Michigan's in that it does not ban direct shipments altogether. Out-of-state wineries are instead required to establish a distribution operation in New York in order to gain the privilege of direct shipment. This, though, is just an indirect way of subjecting out-of-state wineries, but not local ones, to the three-tier system. New York and those allied with its interests defend the scheme by arguing that an out-of-state winery has the same access to the State's consumers as in-state wineries: All wine must be sold through a licensee fully accountable to New York; it just so happens that in order to become a licensee, a winery must have a physical presence in the State. There is some confusion over the precise steps out-of-state wineries must take to gain access to the New York market, in part because no winery has run the State's regulatory gauntlet. New York's argument, in any event, is unconvincing.

The New York scheme grants in-state wineries access to the State's consumers on preferential terms. The suggestion of a limited exception for direct shipment from out-of-state wineries does nothing to eliminate the discriminatory nature of New York's regulations. In-state producers, with the applicable licenses, can ship directly to consumers from their wineries. Out-of-state wineries must open a branch office and warehouse in New York, additional steps that drive up the cost of their wine....

In addition to its restrictive in-state presence requirement, New York discriminates against out-of-state wineries in other ways. Out-of-state wineries that establish the requisite branch office and warehouse in New York are still ineligible for a "farm winery" license, the license that provides the most direct means of shipping to New York consumers.... Out-of-state wineries may apply only for a commercial winery license. Unlike farm wineries, however, commercial wineries must obtain a separate certificate from the state liquor authority authorizing direct shipments to consumers; and, of course, for out-of-state wineries there is the additional requirement of maintaining a distribution operation in New York. New York law also allows in-state wineries without direct-shipping licenses to distribute their wine through other wineries that have the applicable licenses. This is another privilege not afforded out-of-state wineries.

We have no difficulty concluding that New York, like Michigan, discriminates against interstate commerce through its direct-shipping laws.

III. State laws that discriminate against interstate commerce face "a virtually *per se* rule of invalidity." *Philadelphia v. New Jersey* (1978). The Michigan and New York laws by their own terms violate this proscription. The two States, however, contend their statutes are saved by § 2 of the 21st Amendment, which provides: "The transportation or importation into any State, Territory, or possession of the United States for delivery or use therein of intoxicating liquors, in violation of the laws thereof, is hereby prohibited."

The States' position is inconsistent with our precedents and with the 21st Amendment's history. Section 2 does not allow States to regulate the direct shipment of wine on terms that discriminate in favor of in-state producers....

Justice Stevens, with whom Justice O'Connor joins, dissenting.

Congress' power to regulate commerce among the States includes the power to authorize the States to place burdens on interstate commerce. *Prudential Ins. Co. v. Benjamin* (1946). Absent such congressional approval, a state law may violate the unwritten rules described as the "Dormant Commerce Clause" either by imposing an undue burden on both out-of-state and local producers engaged in interstate activities or by treating out-of-state producers less favorably than their local competitors. See, *e.g., Pike v. Bruce Church, Inc.* (1970); *Philadelphia v. New Jersey* (1978). A state law totally prohibiting the sale of an ordinary article of commerce might impose an even more serious burden on interstate commerce. If Congress may nevertheless authorize the States to enact such laws, surely the people may do so through the process of amending our Constitution.

The New York and Michigan laws challenged in these cases would be patently invalid under well settled Dormant Commerce Clause principles if they regulated sales of an ordinary article of commerce rather than wine. But ever since the adoption of the 18th Amendment and the 21st Amendment, our Constitution has placed commerce in alcoholic beverages in a special category. Section 2 of the 21st Amendment expressly provides that "[t]he transportation or importation into any State, Territory, or possession of the United States for delivery or use therein of intoxicating liquors, in violation of the laws thereof, is hereby prohibited."

Today many Americans, particularly those members of the younger generations who make policy decisions, regard alcohol as an ordinary article of commerce, subject to substantially the same market and legal controls as other consumer products. That was definitely not the view of the generations that made policy in 1919 when the 18th Amendment was ratified or in 1933 when it was repealed by the 21st Amendment. On the contrary the moral condemnation of the use of alcohol as a beverage represented not merely the convictions of our religious leaders, but the views of a sufficiently large majority of the population to warrant the rare exercise of the power to amend the Constitution on two occasions. The 18th Amendment entirely prohibited commerce in "intoxicating liquors" for beverage purposes throughout the United States and the territories subject to its jurisdiction. While § 1 of the 21st Amendment repealed the nationwide prohibition, § 2 gave the States the option to maintain equally comprehensive prohibitions in their respective jurisdictions.

The views of judges who lived through the debates that led to the ratification of those Amendments are entitled to special deference. Foremost among them was Justice Brandeis, whose understanding of a State's right to discriminate in its regulation of out-of-state alcohol could not have been clearer:

"The plaintiffs ask us to limit [§ 2's] broad command. They request us to construe the Amendment as saying, in effect: The State may prohibit the importation of intoxicating liquors provided it prohibits the manufacture and sale within its borders; but if it permits such manufacture and sale, it must let imported liquors compete with the domestic on equal terms. To say that, would involve not a construction of the Amendment, but a rewriting of it.... Can it be doubted that a State might establish a state monopoly of the manufacture and sale of beer, and either prohibit all competing importations, or discourage importation by laying a heavy impost, or channelize desired importations by confining them to a single consignee?" *State Bd. Of Equalization of Cal. v. Young's Market Co.* (1936)....

My understanding (and recollection) of the historical context reinforces my conviction that the text of §2 should be "broadly and colloquially interpreted." *Carter v. Virginia* (1944) (Frankfurter, J., concurring). Indeed, the fact that the 21st Amendment was the only Amendment in our history to have been ratified by the people in state conventions, rather than by state legislatures, provides further reason to give its terms their ordinary meaning. Because the New York and Michigan laws regulate the "transportation or importation" of "intoxicating liquors" for "delivery or use therein," they are exempt from Dormant Commerce Clause scrutiny.

As Justice Thomas has demonstrated, the text of the 21st Amendment is a far more reliable guide to its meaning than the unwritten rules that the majority enforces today. I therefore join his persuasive and comprehensive dissenting opinion.

Justice Thomas, with whom The Chief Justice, Justice Stevens, and Justice O'Connor join, dissenting. [Omitted].

Kassel v. Consolidated Freightways Corporation: Background and Questions

1. *Kassell* involves a challenge to an Iowa statute that limited the length of "double" tractor trailers on Iowa highways. The case produced three opinions. Why did Justices Brennan and Marshall refuse to join Justice Powell's opinion? Why did Justice Rehnquist, Chief Justice Burger, and Justice Stewart dissent, rather than join Justice Brennan's opinion? What is the difference in approach in the three opinions?

2. How would each camp have voted in *New Energy*? Why? How would each camp have voted in *Southern Pacific*? Why?

Kassel v. Consolidated Freightways Corporation
450 U.S. 662 (1981)

[Plurality: Powell, White, Blackmun, and Stevens. Concurring: Brennan and Marshall. Dissenting: Rehnquist, Burger (C.J.), and Stewart.]

Justice Powell announced the judgment of the Court and delivered an opinion, in which Justice White, Justice Blackmun, and Justice Stevens joined.

The question is whether an Iowa statute that prohibits the use of certain large trucks within the State unconstitutionally burdens interstate commerce.

I. Appellee Consolidated Freightways Corporation of Delaware (Consolidated) is one of the largest common carriers in the country. It offers service in 48 States under a certificate of public convenience and necessity issued by the Interstate Commerce Commission. Among other routes, Consolidated carries commodities through Iowa on Interstate 80, the principal east-west route linking New York, Chicago, and the west coast, and on Interstate 35, a major north-south route.

Consolidated mainly uses two kinds of trucks. One consists of a three-axle tractor pulling a 40-foot two-axle trailer. This unit, commonly called a single, or "semi," is 55 feet in length overall. Such trucks have long been used on the Nation's highways. Consolidated also uses a two-axle tractor pulling a single-axle trailer which, in turn, pulls a single-axle dolly and a second single-axle trailer. This combination, known as a double, or twin, is 65 feet long overall. Many trucking companies, including Consolidated, increasingly prefer to use doubles to ship certain kinds of commodities. Doubles have larger capacities, and the trailers can be detached and routed separately if necessary. Consolidated would like to use 65-foot doubles on many of its trips through Iowa.

The State of Iowa, however, by statute restricts the length of vehicles that may use its highways. Unlike all other States in the West and Midwest, Iowa generally prohibits the use of 65-foot doubles within its borders. Instead, most truck combinations are restricted to 55 feet in length. Doubles, mobile homes, trucks carrying vehicles such as tractors and other farm equipment, and singles hauling livestock, are permitted to be as long as 60 feet. Notwithstanding these restrictions, Iowa's statute permits cities abutting the state line by local ordinance to adopt the length limitations of the adjoining State. Where a city has exercised this option, otherwise oversized trucks are permitted within the city limits and in nearby commercial zones.[1]

Iowa also provides for two other relevant exemptions. An Iowa truck manufacturer may obtain a permit to ship trucks that are as large as 70 feet. Permits also are available to move oversized mobile homes, provided that the unit is to be moved from a point within Iowa or delivered for an Iowa resident.[2]

Because of Iowa's statutory scheme, Consolidated cannot use its 65-foot doubles to move commodities through the State. Instead, the company must do one of four things: (i) use 55-foot singles; (ii) use 60-foot doubles; (iii) detach the trailers of a 65-foot double and shuttle each through the State separately; or (iv) divert 65-foot doubles around Iowa.

Dissatisfied with these options, Consolidated filed this suit in the District Court averring that Iowa's statutory scheme unconstitutionally burdens interstate commerce. Iowa defended the law as a reasonable safety measure enacted pursuant to its police power. The State asserted that 65-foot doubles are more dangerous than 55-foot singles and, in any event, that the law promotes safety and reduces road wear within the State by diverting much truck traffic to other States.

---

1. The Iowa Legislature in 1974 passed House Bill 671, which would have permitted 65-foot doubles. But Iowa Governor Ray vetoed the bill, noting that it "would benefit only a few Iowa-based companies while providing a great advantage for out-of-state trucking firms and competitors at the expense of our Iowa citizens." Governor's Veto Message of March 2, 1974, reprinted in App. 626. The "border-cities exemption" was passed by the General Assembly and signed by the Governor shortly thereafter....

2. The parochial restrictions in the mobile home provision were enacted after Governor Ray vetoed a bill that would have permitted the interstate shipment of all mobile homes through Iowa. Governor Ray commented, in his veto message:

"This bill ... would make Iowa a bridge state as these oversized units are moved into Iowa after being manufactured in another state and sold in a third. None of this activity would be of particular economic benefit to Iowa." Governor's Veto Message of March 16, 1972....

In a 14-day trial, both sides adduced evidence on safety, and on the burden on interstate commerce imposed by Iowa's law. On the question of safety, the District Court found that the "evidence clearly establishes that the twin is as safe as the semi." For that reason,

> there is no valid safety reason for barring twins from Iowa's highways because of their configuration.
>
> The evidence convincingly, if not overwhelmingly, establishes that the 65 foot twin is as safe as, if not safer than, the 60 foot twin and the 55 foot semi....
>
> Twins and semis have different characteristics. Twins are more maneuverable, are less sensitive to wind, and create less splash and spray. However, they are more likely than semis to jackknife or upset. They can be backed only for a short distance. The negative characteristics are not such that they render the twin less safe than semis overall. Semis are more stable but are more likely to "rear end" another vehicle....

In light of these findings, the District Court applied the standard we enunciated in *Raymond Motor Transportation, Inc. v. Rice* (1978), and concluded that the state law impermissibly burdened interstate commerce:

> [T]he balance here must be struck in favor of the federal interests. The *total effect* of the law as a safety measure in reducing accidents and casualties is so slight and problematical that it does not outweigh the national interest in keeping interstate commerce free from interferences that seriously impede it....

[T]he Eighth Circuit affirmed....

We now affirm....

II. [The Commerce] Clause permits Congress to legislate when it perceives that the national welfare is not furthered by the independent actions of the States. It is now well established, also, that the Clause itself is "a limitation upon state power even without congressional implementation." The Clause requires that some aspects of trade generally must remain free from interference by the States. When a State ventures excessively into the regulation of these aspects of commerce, it "trespasses upon national interests," and the courts will hold the state regulation invalid under the Clause alone.

The Commerce Clause does not, of course, invalidate all state restrictions on commerce. It has long been recognized that, "in the absence of conflicting legislation by Congress, there is a residuum of power in the state to make laws governing matters of local concern which nevertheless in some measure affect interstate commerce or even, to some extent, regulate it." ... [A] State's power to regulate commerce is never greater than in matters traditionally of local concern.... [R]egulations that touch upon safety—especially highway safety—are those that "the Court has been most reluctant to invalidate." *Raymond.* Indeed, "if safety justifications are not illusory, the Court will not second-guess legislative judgment about their importance in comparison with related burdens on interstate commerce." *Raymond* (Blackmun, J., concurring). Those who would challenge such bona fide safety regulations must overcome a "strong presumption of validity."

But the incantation of a purpose to promote the public health or safety does not insulate a state law from Commerce Clause attack. Regulations designed for that salutary purpose nevertheless may further the purpose so marginally, and interfere with commerce so substantially, as to be invalid under the Commerce Clause. In the Court's recent unanimous decision in *Raymond*, we declined to "accept the State's contention that the inquiry under the Commerce Clause is ended without a weighing of the asserted safety purpose against the degree of interference with interstate commerce." This "weighing" by a court requires—and indeed the constitutionality of the state regulation depends on—"a sensitive consideration of the weight and nature of the state regulatory concern in light of the extent of the burden imposed on the course of interstate commerce."

III. Applying these general principles, we conclude that the Iowa truck-length limitations unconstitutionally burden interstate commerce.

In *Raymond Motor Transportation, Inc. v. Rice*, the Court held that a Wisconsin statute that precluded the use of 65-foot doubles violated the Commerce Clause. This case is *Raymond* revisited. Here, as in *Raymond*, the State failed to present any persuasive evidence that 65-foot doubles are less safe than 55-foot singles. Moreover, Iowa's law is now out of step with the laws of all other Midwestern and Western States. Iowa thus substantially burdens the interstate flow of goods by truck. In the absence of congressional action to set uniform standards, some burdens associated with state safety regulations must be tolerated. But where, as here, the State's safety interest has been found to be illusory, and its regulations impair significantly the federal interest in efficient and safe interstate transportation, the state law cannot be harmonized with the Commerce Clause.[3]

III-A. Iowa made a more serious effort to support the safety rationale of its law than did Wisconsin in *Raymond*, but its effort was no more persuasive. As noted above, the District Court found that the "evidence clearly establishes that the twin is as safe as the semi." The record supports this finding.

The trial focused on a comparison of the performance of the two kinds of trucks in various safety categories. The evidence showed, and the District Court found, that the 65-foot double was at least the equal of the 55-foot single in the ability to brake, turn, and maneuver. The double, because of its axle placement, produces less splash and spray in wet weather. And, because of its articulation in the middle, the double is less susceptible to dangerous "off-tracking," and to wind.

None of these findings is seriously disputed by Iowa. Indeed, the State points to only three ways in which the 55-foot single is even arguably superior: singles take less time to be passed and to clear intersections; they may back up for longer distances; and they are somewhat less likely to jackknife.

The first two of these characteristics are of limited relevance on modern interstate highways. As the District Court found, the negligible difference in the time required to pass, and to cross intersections, is insignificant on 4-lane divided highways because passing does not require crossing into oncoming traffic lanes, *Raymond*, and interstates have few, if any, intersections. The concern over backing capability also is insignificant because it seldom is necessary to back up on an interstate. In any event, no evidence suggested any difference in backing capability between the 60-foot doubles that Iowa permits and the 65-foot doubles that it bans. Similarly, although doubles tend to jackknife somewhat more than singles, 65-foot doubles actually are less likely to jackknife than 60-foot doubles.

Statistical studies supported the view that 65-foot doubles are at least as safe overall as 55-foot singles and 60-foot doubles. One such study, which the District Court credited, reviewed Consolidated's comparative accident experience in 1978 with its own singles and doubles. Iowa's expert statistician admitted that this study provided "moderately strong evidence" that singles have a higher injury rate than doubles. Another study, pre-

---

3. It is highly relevant that here, as in *Raymond*, the state statute contains exemptions that weaken the deference traditionally accorded to a state safety regulation. See Part IV, *infra*.

pared by the Iowa Department of Transportation at the request of the state legislature, concluded that "[s]ixty-five foot twin trailer combinations have not been shown by experiences in other states to be less safe than 60 foot twin trailer combinations or conventional tractor-semitrailers". Numerous insurance company executives, and transportation officials from the Federal Government and various States, testified that 65-foot doubles were at least as safe as 55-foot singles. Iowa concedes that it can produce no study that establishes a statistically significant difference in safety between the 65-foot double and the kinds of vehicles the State permits. Nor ... did Iowa present a single witness who testified that 65-foot doubles were more dangerous overall than the vehicles permitted under Iowa law.... In sum, although Iowa introduced more evidence on the question of safety than did Wisconsin in *Raymond*, the record as a whole was not more favorable to the State.[4]

III-B. Consolidated, meanwhile, demonstrated that Iowa's law substantially burdens interstate commerce. Trucking companies that wish to continue to use 65-foot doubles must route them around Iowa or detach the trailers of the doubles and ship them through separately. Alternatively, trucking companies must use the smaller 55-foot singles or 60-foot doubles permitted under Iowa law. Each of these options engenders inefficiency and added expense. The record shows that Iowa's law added about $12.6 million each year to the costs of trucking companies. Consolidated alone incurred about $2 million per year in increased costs.

In addition to increasing the costs of the trucking companies (and, indirectly, of the service to consumers), Iowa's law may aggravate, rather than ameliorate, the problem of highway accidents. Fifty-five foot singles carry less freight than 65-foot doubles. Either more small trucks must be used to carry the same quantity of goods through Iowa, or the same number of larger trucks must drive longer distances to bypass Iowa. In either case, as the District Court noted, the restriction requires more highway miles to be driven to transport the same quantity of goods. Other things being equal, accidents are proportional to distance traveled. Thus, if 65-foot doubles are as safe as 55-foot singles, Iowa's law tends to *increase* the number of accidents, and to shift the incidence of them from Iowa to other States.

IV. Perhaps recognizing the weakness of the evidence supporting its safety argument, and the substantial burden on commerce that its regulations create, Iowa urges the Court simply to "defer" to the safety judgment of the State. It argues that the length of trucks is generally, although perhaps imprecisely, related to safety. The task of drawing a line is one that Iowa contends should be left to its legislature.

The Court normally does accord "special deference" to state highway safety regulations. This traditional deference "derives in part from the assumption that where such regulations do not discriminate on their face against interstate commerce, their burden usually falls on local economic interests as well as other States' economic interests, thus insuring that a State's own political processes will serve as a check against unduly burdensome regulations." Less deference to the legislative judgment is due, however, where the local regulation bears disproportionately on out-of-state residents and businesses. Such a disproportionate burden is apparent here. Iowa's scheme, although generally banning large doubles from the State, nev-

---

4. In suggesting that Iowa's law actually promotes safety, the dissenting opinion ignores the findings of the courts below and relies on largely discredited statistical evidence. The dissent implies that a statistical study identified doubles as more dangerous than singles.... At trial, however, the author of that study—Iowa's own statistician—conceded that his calculations were statistically biased, and therefore "not very meaningful." ...

ertheless has several exemptions that secure to Iowans many of the benefits of large trucks while shunting to neighboring States many of the costs associated with their use.

At the time of trial there were two particularly significant exemptions. First, singles hauling livestock or farm vehicles were permitted to be as long as 60 feet. As the Court of Appeals noted, this provision undoubtedly was helpful to local interests. Second, cities abutting other States were permitted to enact local ordinances adopting the larger length limitation of the neighboring State. This exemption offered the benefits of longer trucks to individuals and businesses in important border cities without burdening Iowa's highways with interstate through traffic.

The origin of the "border cities exemption" also suggests that Iowa's statute may not have been designed to ban dangerous trucks, but rather to discourage interstate truck traffic. In 1974, the legislature passed a bill that would have permitted 65-foot doubles in the State. Governor Ray vetoed the bill. He said:

> I find sympathy with those who are doing business in our state and whose enterprises could gain from increased cargo carrying ability by trucks. However, with this bill, the Legislature has pursued a course that would benefit only a few Iowa-based companies while providing a great advantage for out-of-state trucking firms and competitors at the expense of our Iowa citizens.

After the veto, the "border cities exemption" was immediately enacted and signed by the Governor.

It is thus far from clear that Iowa was motivated primarily by a judgment that 65-foot doubles are less safe than 55-foot singles. Rather, Iowa seems to have hoped to limit the use of its highways by deflecting some through traffic. In the District Court and Court of Appeals, the State explicitly attempted to justify the law by its claimed interest in keeping trucks out of Iowa. The Court of Appeals correctly concluded that a State cannot constitutionally promote its own parochial interests by requiring safe vehicles to detour around it.

V. In sum, the statutory exemptions, their history, and the arguments Iowa has advanced in support of its law in this litigation, all suggest that the deference traditionally accorded a State's safety judgment is not warranted. The controlling factors thus are the findings of the District Court, accepted by the Court of Appeals, with respect to the relative safety of the types of trucks at issue, and the substantiality of the burden on interstate commerce.

Because Iowa has imposed this burden without any significant countervailing safety interest, its statute violates the Commerce Clause. The judgment of the Court of Appeals is affirmed.

Justice Brennan, with whom Justice Marshall joins, concurring in the judgment.

Iowa's truck-length regulation challenged in this case is nearly identical to the Wisconsin regulation struck down in *Raymond Motor Transportation, Inc. v. Rice* (1978), as in violation of the Commerce Clause. In my view, the same Commerce Clause restrictions that dictated that holding also require invalidation of Iowa's regulation insofar as it prohibits 65-foot doubles.

The reasoning bringing me to that conclusion does not require, however, that I engage in the debate between my Brothers Powell and Rehnquist over what the District Court record shows on the question whether 65-foot doubles are more dangerous than shorter trucks. With all respect, my Brothers ask and answer the wrong question.

For me, analysis of Commerce Clause challenges to state regulations must take into account three principles: (1) The courts are not empowered to second-guess the empirical judgments of lawmakers concerning the utility of legislation. (2) The burdens imposed on commerce must be balanced against the local benefits actually sought to be achieved by the State's lawmakers, and not against those suggested after the fact by counsel. (3) Protectionist legislation is unconstitutional under the Commerce Clause, even if the burdens and benefits are related to safety rather than economics.

I. Both the opinion of my Brother Powell and the opinion of my Brother Rehnquist are predicated upon the supposition that the constitutionality of a state regulation is determined by the factual record created by the State's lawyers in trial court. But that supposition cannot be correct, for it would make the constitutionality of state laws and regulations depend on the vagaries of litigation rather than on the judgments made by the State's lawmakers.

In considering a Commerce Clause challenge to a state regulation, the judicial task is to balance the burden imposed on commerce against the local benefits sought to be achieved by the State's lawmakers. In determining those benefits, a court should focus ultimately on the regulatory purposes identified by the lawmakers and on the evidence before or available to them that might have supported their judgment. Since the court must confine its analysis to the purposes the lawmakers had for maintaining the regulation, the only relevant evidence concerns whether the lawmakers could rationally have believed that the challenged regulation would foster those purposes. It is not the function of the court to decide whether in fact the regulation promotes its intended purpose, so long as an examination of the evidence before or available to the lawmaker indicates that the regulation is not wholly irrational in light of its purposes.[1]

II. My Brothers Powell and Rehnquist make the mistake of disregarding the intention of Iowa's lawmakers and assuming that resolution of the case must hinge upon the argument offered by Iowa's attorneys: that 65-foot doubles are more dangerous than shorter trucks. They then canvass the factual record and findings of the courts below and reach opposite conclusions as to whether the evidence adequately supports that empirical judgment. I repeat: my Brothers Powell and Rehnquist have asked and answered the wrong question. For although Iowa's lawyers in this litigation have defended the truck-length regulation on the basis of the safety advantages of 55-foot singles and 60-foot doubles over 65-foot doubles, Iowa's actual rationale for maintaining the regulation had nothing to do with these purported differences. Rather, Iowa sought to discourage interstate truck traffic on Iowa's highways. Thus, the safety advantages and disadvantages of the types and lengths of trucks involved in this case are irrelevant to the decision.[2]

---

1. Moreover, I would emphasize that in the field of safety—and perhaps in other fields where the decisions of state lawmakers are deserving of a heightened degree of deference—the role of the courts is not to balance asserted burdens against intended benefits as it is in other fields. Compare *Raymond Motor Transportation, Inc. v. Rice* (Blackmun, J., concurring) (safety regulation), with *Pike v. Bruce Church, Inc.* (1970) (regulation intended "to protect and enhance the reputation of growers within the State"). In the field of safety, once the court has established that the intended safety benefit is not illusory, insubstantial, or nonexistent, it must defer to the State's lawmakers on the appropriate balance to be struck against other interests. I therefore disagree with my Brother Powell when he asserts that the degree of interference with interstate commerce may in the first instance be "weighed" against the State's safety interests:

> Regulations designed [to promote the public health or safety] nevertheless may further the purpose so marginally, and interfere with commerce so substantially, as to be invalid under the Commerce Clause....

2. My Brother Rehnquist claims that the "argument" that a court should defer to the actual purposes of the lawmakers rather than to the post hoc justifications of counsel "has been consistently rejected by the Court in other contexts."...

> If, as here, the only purpose ever articulated by the State's lawmakers for maintaining a regulation is illegitimate, I consider it contrary to precedent as well as to sound principles of

My Brother Powell concedes that "[i]t is ... far from clear that Iowa was motivated primarily by a judgment that 65-foot doubles are less safe than 55-foot singles. Rather, Iowa seems to have hoped to limit the use of its highways by deflecting some through traffic." This conclusion is more than amply supported by the record and the legislative history of the Iowa regulation. The Iowa Legislature has consistently taken the position that size, weight, and speed restrictions on interstate traffic should be set in accordance with uniform national standards. The stated purpose was not to further safety, but to achieve uniformity with other States. The Act setting the limitations challenged in this case, passed in 1947 and periodically amended since then, is entitled "An Act *to promote uniformity with other states* in the matter of limitations on the size, weight and speed of motor vehicles...." Following the proposals of the American Association of State Highway and Transportation Officials, the State has gradually increased the permissible length of trucks from 45 feet in 1947 to the present limit of 60 feet.

In 1974, the Iowa Legislature again voted to increase the permissible length of trucks to conform to uniform standards then in effect in most other States. This legislation, House Bill 671, would have increased the maximum length of twin trailer trucks operable in Iowa from 60 to 65 feet. But Governor Ray broke from prior state policy, and vetoed the legislation. The legislature did not override the veto, and the present regulation was thus maintained. In his veto, Governor Ray did not rest his decision on the conclusion that 55-foot singles and 60-foot doubles are any safer than 65-foot doubles, or on any other safety consideration inherent in the type or size of the trucks. Rather, his principal concern was that to allow 65-foot doubles would "basically ope[n] our state to literally thousands and thousands more trucks per year." This increase in interstate truck traffic would, in the Governor's estimation, greatly increase highway maintenance costs, which are borne by the citizens of the State, and increase the number of accidents and fatalities within the State. The legislative response was not to override the veto, but to accede to the Governor's action, and in accord with his basic premise, to enact a "border cities exemption." This permitted cities within border areas to allow 65-foot doubles while otherwise maintaining the 60-foot limit throughout the State to discourage interstate truck traffic.

Although the Court has stated that "[i]n no field has ... deference to state regulation been greater than that of highway safety," *Raymond Motor Transportation, Inc. v. Rice*, it has declined to go so far as to presume that size restrictions are inherently tied to public safety. The Court has emphasized that the "strong presumption of validity" of size restrictions "cannot justify a court in closing its eyes to uncontroverted evidence of record,"—here the obvious fact that the safety characteristics of 65-foot doubles did not provide the motivation for either legislators or Governor in maintaining the regulation.

III. Though my Brother Powell recognizes that the State's actual purpose in maintaining the truck-length regulation was "to limit the use of its highways by deflecting some through traffic," he fails to recognize that this purpose, being protectionist in na-

---

constitutional adjudication for the courts to base their analysis on purposes never conceived by the lawmakers. This is especially true where, as the dissent's strained analysis of the relative safety of 65-foot doubles to shorter trucks amply demonstrates, ... the post hoc justifications are implausible as well as imaginary. I would emphasize that, although my Brother Powell's plurality opinion does not give as much weight to the illegitimacy of Iowa's actual purpose as I do, see Part III, *infra*, both that opinion and this concurrence have found the actual motivation of the Iowa lawmakers in maintaining the truck-length regulation highly relevant to, if not dispositive of, the case.

ture, is impermissible under the Commerce Clause.[3] The Governor admitted that he blocked legislative efforts to raise the length of trucks because the change "would benefit only a few Iowa-based companies while providing a great advantage for out-of-state trucking firms and competitors at the expense of our Iowa citizens." ... Appellant Raymond Kassel, Director of the Iowa Department of Transportation, while admitting that the greater 65-foot length standard would be safer overall, defended the more restrictive regulations because of their benefits *within Iowa*:

> "Q: Overall, there would be fewer miles of operation, fewer accidents and fewer fatalities?
>
> A: Yes, on the national scene.
>
> Q: Does it not concern the Iowa Department of Transportation that banning 65-foot twins causes more accidents, more injuries and more fatalities?
>
> A: Do you mean outside of our state border?
>
> Q: Overall.
>
> A: Our primary concern is the citizens of Iowa and our own highway system we operate in this state." ...

The regulation has had its predicted effect. As the District Court found: "Iowa's length restriction causes the trucks affected by the ban to travel more miles over more dangerous roads in other states which means a greater overall exposure to accidents and fatalities. More miles of highway are subjected to wear. More fuel is consumed and greater transportation costs are incurred."

Iowa may not shunt off its fair share of the burden of maintaining interstate truck routes, nor may it create increased hazards on the highways of neighboring States in order to decrease the hazards on Iowa highways. Such an attempt has all the hallmarks of the "simple ... protectionism" this Court has condemned in the economic area. Just as a State's attempt to avoid interstate competition in economic goods may damage the prosperity of the Nation as a whole, so Iowa's attempt to deflect interstate truck traffic has been found to make the Nation's highways as a whole more hazardous. That attempt should therefore be subject to "a virtually per se rule of invalidity."

This Court's heightened deference to the judgments of state lawmakers in the field of safety, ... is largely attributable to a judicial disinclination to weigh the interests of safety against other societal interests, such as the economic interest in the free flow of commerce. Thus, "if safety justifications are not illusory, the Court will not second-guess legislative judgment about their importance *in comparison with related burdens on interstate commerce.*" *Raymond Motor Transportation, Inc. v. Rice* (Blackmun, J., concurring) (emphasis added). Here, the decision of Iowa's lawmakers to promote Iowa's safety and other interests at the direct expense of the safety and other interests of neighboring States merits no such deference. No special judicial acuity is demanded to perceive that this sort of parochial legislation violates the Commerce Clause. As Justice Cardozo has written, the Commerce Clause "was framed upon the theory that the peoples of the several states must sink or swim together, and that in the long run prosperity and salvation are in union and not division." *Baldwin v. G.A.F. Seelig, Inc.* (1935).

I therefore concur in the judgment.

---

3. It is not enough to conclude, as my Brother Powell does, that "the deference traditionally accorded a State's safety judgment is not warranted."

Justice Rehnquist, with whom The Chief Justice [Burger] and Justice Stewart join, dissenting.

The result in this case suggests, to paraphrase Justice Jackson, that the only state truck-length limit "that is valid is one which this Court has not been able to get its hands on." Although the plurality opinion and the opinion concurring in the judgment strike down Iowa's law by different routes, I believe the analysis in both opinions oversteps our "limited authority to review state legislation under the Commerce Clause," and seriously intrudes upon the fundamental right of the States to pass laws to secure the safety of their citizens. Accordingly, I dissent.

I. It is necessary to elaborate somewhat on the facts as presented in the plurality opinion to appreciate fully what the Court does today. Iowa's action in limiting the length of trucks which may travel on its highways is in no sense unusual. Every State in the Union regulates the length of vehicles permitted to use the public roads. Nor is Iowa a renegade in having length limits which operate to exclude the 65-foot doubles favored by Consolidated. These trucks are prohibited in other areas of the country as well, some 17 States and the District of Columbia, including all of New England and most of the Southeast.[1] While pointing out that Consolidated carries commodities through Iowa on Interstate 80, "the principal east-west route linking New York, Chicago, and the west coast," the plurality neglects to note that both Pennsylvania and New Jersey, through which Interstate 80 runs before reaching New York, also ban 65-foot doubles. In short, the persistent effort in the plurality opinion to paint Iowa as an oddity standing alone to block commerce carried in 65-foot doubles is simply not supported by the facts.

Nor does the plurality adequately convey the extent to which the lower courts permitted the 65-foot doubles to operate in Iowa. Consolidated sought to have the 60-foot length limit declared an unconstitutional burden on commerce when applied to the seven Interstate Highways in Iowa and "access routes to and from Plaintiff's terminals, and reasonable access from said Interstate Highways to facilities for food, fuel, repairs, or rest." The lower courts granted this relief, permitting the 65-foot doubles to travel *off the Interstates* as far as five miles for access to terminal and other facilities, or less if closer facilities were available. To the extent the plurality relies on characteristics of the Interstate Highways in rejecting Iowa's asserted safety justifications, it fails to recognize the scope of the District Court order it upholds.

With these additions to the relevant facts, we can now examine the appropriate analysis to be applied....

II. Although [the Commerce Clause] is phrased in terms of an affirmative grant of power to the National Legislature, we have read the Commerce Clause as imposing some limitations on the States as well, even in the absence of any action by Congress. The Court has hastened to emphasize, however, that the negative implication it has discerned in the Commerce Clause does not invalidate state legislation simply because the legislation burdens interstate commerce....

---

1. Doubles are prohibited in Maine, New Hampshire, Vermont, Massachusetts (except turnpike), Rhode Island, Connecticut, Pennsylvania, West Virginia, Virginia, Tennessee, North Carolina, South Carolina, Alabama, and the District of Columbia. Doubles are permitted to a maximum length of 55 feet in New York (on designated highways only, longer permitted on turnpike), New Jersey, Mississippi, and Georgia. Sixty-five foot doubles are restricted to designated highways in Oregon, North Dakota, Minnesota, Wisconsin, Michigan, Illinois, Missouri, Louisiana, Kentucky, Maryland, and Florida. See App. 605, 645.

Although the Court when it interprets the "dormant" aspect of the Commerce Clause will invalidate unwarranted state intrusion, such action is a far cry from simply undertaking to regulate when Congress has not because we believe such regulation would facilitate interstate commerce....

A determination that a state law is a rational safety measure does not end the Commerce Clause inquiry. A "sensitive consideration" of the safety purpose in relation to the burden on commerce is required. *Raymond Motor Transportation, Inc. v. Rice* (1978). When engaging in such a consideration the Court does not directly compare safety benefits to commerce costs and strike down the legislation if the latter can be said in some vague sense to "outweigh" the former. Such an approach would make an empty gesture of the strong presumption of validity accorded state safety measures, particularly those governing highways. It would also arrogate to this Court functions of forming public policy, functions which, in the absence of congressional action, were left by the Framers of the Constitution to state legislatures....

The purpose of the "sensitive consideration" referred to above is rather to determine if the asserted safety justification, although rational, is merely a pretext for discrimination against interstate commerce. We will conclude that it is if the safety benefits from the regulation are demonstrably trivial while the burden on commerce is great. Thus, the Court in *Bibb v. Navajo Freight Lines, Inc.* (1959) stated that the "strong presumption of validity" accorded highway safety measures could be overcome only when the safety benefits were "slight or problematical." ...

III. Iowa defends its statute as a highway safety regulation. There can be no doubt that the challenged statute is a valid highway safety regulation and thus entitled to the strongest presumption of validity against Commerce Clause challenges. As noted, all 50 States regulate the length of trucks which may use their highways.... There can also be no question that the particular limit chosen by Iowa—60 feet—is rationally related to Iowa's safety objective. Most truck limits are between 55 and 65 feet ... and Iowa's choice is thus well within the widely accepted range.

Iowa adduced evidence supporting the relation between vehicle length and highway safety....

[In] sum, there was sufficient evidence presented at trial to support the legislative determination that length is related to safety, and nothing in Consolidated's evidence undermines this conclusion.

The District Court approached the case as if the question were whether Consolidated's 65-foot trucks were as safe as others permitted on Iowa highways, and the Court of Appeals as if its task were to determine if the District Court's factual findings in this regard were "clearly erroneous." The question, however, is whether the Iowa Legislature has acted rationally in regulating vehicle lengths and whether the safety benefits from this regulation are more than slight or problematical...."Since the adoption of one weight or width regulation, rather than another, is a legislative and not a judicial choice, its constitutionality is not to be determined by weighing in the judicial scales the merits of the legislative choice and rejecting it if the weight of evidence presented in court appears to favor a different standard." *South Carolina State Highway Department v. Barnwell Brothers* (1938)....

It must be emphasized that there is nothing in the laws of nature which make 65-foot doubles an obvious norm. Consolidated operates 65-foot doubles on many of its routes simply because that is the largest size permitted in many States through which Consolidated travels. Doubles can and do come in smaller sizes; indeed, when Iowa adopted the present 60-foot limit in 1963, it was in accord with AASHTO recommendations. Striking down Iowa's law because Consolidated has made a voluntary business decision to employ 65-foot doubles, a decision based on the actions of other state legislatures, would essentially be compelling Iowa to yield to the policy choices of neighboring States. Under our constitutional scheme, however, there is only one legislative body which can preempt the rational policy determination of the Iowa Legislature and that is Congress. Forcing Iowa to yield to the policy choices of neighboring States perverts the primary purpose of the Commerce Clause, that of vesting power to regulate interstate commerce in Congress, where all the States are represented....

My Brother Brennan argues that the Court should consider only the purpose the Iowa legislators actually sought to achieve by the length limit, and not the purposes advanced by Iowa's lawyers in defense of the statute. This argument calls to mind what was said of the Roman Legions: that they may have lost battles, but they never lost a war, since they never let a war end until they had won it. The argument has been consistently rejected by the Court in other contexts ... and Justice Brennan can cite no authority for the proposition that possible legislative purposes suggested by a State's lawyers should not be considered in Commerce Clause cases. The problems with a view such as that advanced in the opinion concurring in the judgment are apparent. To name just a few, it assumes that individual legislators are motivated by one discernible "actual" purpose, and ignores the fact that different legislators may vote for a single piece of legislation for widely different reasons. How, for example, would a court adhering to the views expressed in the opinion concurring in the judgment approach a statute, the legislative history of which indicated that 10 votes were based on safety considerations, 10 votes were based on protectionism, and the statute passed by a vote of 40–20? What would the *actual* purpose of the *legislature* have been in that case? This Court has wisely "never insisted that a legislative body articulate its reasons for enacting a statute."

Both the plurality and the concurrence attach great significance to the Governor's veto of a bill passed by the Iowa Legislature permitting 65-foot doubles. Whatever views one may have about the significance of legislative motives, it must be emphasized that the law which the Court strikes down today was not passed to achieve the protectionist goals the plurality and the concurrence ascribe to the Governor. Iowa's 60-foot length limit was established in 1963, at a time when very few States permitted 65-foot doubles. Striking down legislation on the basis of asserted legislative motives is dubious enough, but the plurality and concurrence strike down the legislation involved in this case because of asserted impermissible motives for *not* enacting *other* legislation, motives which could not possibly have been present when the legislation under challenge here was considered and passed. Such action is, so far as I am aware, unprecedented in this Court's history.

Furthermore, the effort in both the plurality and the concurrence to portray the legislation involved here as protectionist is in error. Whenever a State enacts more stringent safety measures than its neighbors, in an area which affects commerce, the safety law will have the incidental effect of deflecting interstate commerce to the neighboring States. Indeed, the safety and protectionist motives cannot be separated: the whole purpose of safety regulation of vehicles is to *protect* the State from unsafe vehicles. If a neighboring State chooses *not* to protect its citizens from the danger discerned by the enacting State, that is its business, but the enacting State should not be penalized when the vehicles it considers unsafe travel through the neighboring State.

The other States with truck-length limits that exclude Consolidated's 65-foot doubles would not at all be paranoid in assuming that they might be next on Consolidated's "hit list." The true problem with today's decision is that it gives no guidance whatsoever to these States as to whether their laws are valid or how to defend them. For that matter, the decision gives no guidance to Consolidated or other trucking firms either. Perhaps, after all is said and done, the Court today neither says nor does very much at all. We know only that Iowa's law is invalid and that the jurisprudence of the "negative side" of the Commerce Clause remains hopelessly confused.

C. Discrimination or Even-Handed Treatment: Complex Cases

Dean Milk Company v. City of Madison
340 U.S. 349 (1951)

[Majority: Clark, Vinson (C.J.), Frankfurter, Reed, Burton, and Jackson. Dissenting: Black, Douglas, and Minton.]

Mr. Justice Clark delivered the opinion of the Court.

This appeal challenges the constitutional validity of two sections of an ordinance of the City of Madison, Wisconsin, regulating the sale of milk and milk products within the municipality's jurisdiction. One section in issue makes it unlawful to sell any milk as pasteurized unless it has been processed and bottled at an approved pasteurization plant within a radius of five miles from the central square of Madison.[1] Another section, which prohibits the sale of milk, or the importation, receipt or storage of milk for sale, in Madison unless from a source of supply possessing a permit issued after inspection by Madison officials, is attacked insofar as it expressly relieves municipal authorities from any duty to inspect farms located beyond twenty-five miles from the center of the city.[2]

Appellant is an Illinois corporation engaged in distributing milk and milk products in Illinois and Wisconsin. It contended below, as it does here, that both the five-mile limit on pasteurization plants and the twenty-five-mile limit on sources of milk violate the Commerce Clause and the 14th Amendment to the Federal Constitution. The Supreme Court of Wisconsin upheld the five-mile limit on pasteurization. As to the twenty-five-

---

1. General Ordinances of the City of Madison, 1949, §7.21 provides as follows:
   It shall be unlawful for any person, association or corporation to sell, offer for sale or have in his or its possession with intent to sell or deliver in the City of Madison, any milk, cream or milk products as pasteurized unless the same shall have been pasteurized and bottled in the manner herein provided within a radius of five miles from the central portion of the City of Madison otherwise known as the Capitol Square, at a plant housing the machinery, equipment and facilities, all of which shall have been approved by the Department of Public Health.

2. Id., §7.11, provides in pertinent part as follows:
   It shall be unlawful for any person to bring into or receive into the City of Madison, Wisconsin, or its police jurisdiction, for sale, or to sell, or offer for sale therein, or to have in storage where milk or milk products are sold or served, any milk or milk product as defined in this ordinance from a source not possessing a permit from the Health Commissioner of the City of Madison, Wisconsin.
   Only a person who complies with the requirements of this ordinance shall be entitled to receive and retain such a permit.
   On the filing of an application for a permit with the Health Commissioner, he shall cause the source of supply named therein to be inspected and shall cause all other necessary inspections and investigations to be made. The Department of Public Health shall not be obligated to inspect and issue permits to farms located beyond twenty-five (25) miles from the central portion of the City of Madison otherwise known as the Capitol Square.

mile limitation the court ordered the complaint dismissed for want of a justiciable controversy. This appeal, contest[s] both rulings....

The City of Madison is the county seat of Dane County. Within the county are some 5,600 dairy farms with total raw milk production in excess of 600,000,000 pounds annually and more than ten times the requirements of Madison. Aside from the milk supplied to Madison, fluid milk produced in the county moves in large quantities to Chicago and more distant consuming areas, and the remainder is used in making cheese, butter and other products. At the time of trial the Madison milkshed was not of "Grade A" quality by the standards recommended by the United States Public Health Service, and no milk labeled "Grade A" was distributed in Madison.

The area defined by the ordinance with respect to milk sources encompasses practically all of Dane County and includes some 500 farms which supply milk for Madison. Within the five-mile area for pasteurization are plants of five processors, only three of which are engaged in the general wholesale and retail trade in Madison. Inspection of these farms and plants is scheduled once every thirty days and is performed by two municipal inspectors, one of whom is full-time. The courts below found that the ordinance in question promotes convenient, economical and efficient plant inspection.

Appellant purchases and gathers milk from approximately 950 farms in northern Illinois and southern Wisconsin, none being within twenty-five miles of Madison. Its pasteurization plants are located at Chemung and Huntley, Illinois, about 65 and 85 miles respectively from Madison. Appellant was denied a license to sell its products within Madison solely because its pasteurization plants were more than five miles away.

It is conceded that the milk which appellant seeks to sell in Madison is supplied from farms and processed in plants licensed and inspected by public health authorities of Chicago, and is labeled "Grade A" under the Chicago ordinance which adopts the rating standards recommended by the United States Public Health Service. Both the Chicago and Madison ordinances, though not the sections of the latter here in issue, are largely patterned after the Model Milk Ordinance of the Public Health Service. However, Madison contends and we assume that in some particulars its ordinance is more rigorous than that of Chicago.

Upon these facts we find it necessary to determine only the issue raised under the Commerce Clause, for we agree with appellant that the ordinance imposes an undue burden on interstate commerce.

This is not an instance in which an enactment falls because of federal legislation which, as a proper exercise of paramount national power over commerce, excludes measures which might otherwise be within the police power of the states. See *Currin v. Wallace* (1939). There is no pertinent national regulation by the Congress....

Nor can there be objection to the avowed purpose of this enactment. We assume that difficulties in sanitary regulation of milk and milk products originating in remote areas may present a situation in which "upon a consideration of all the relevant facts and circumstances it appears that the matter is one which may appropriately be regulated in the interest of the safety, health and well-being of local communities...." *Parker v. Brown* (1943); see *H. P. Hood & Sons v. Du Mond* (1949). We also assume that since Congress has not spoken to the contrary, the subject matter of the ordinance lies within the sphere of state regulation even though interstate commerce may be affected.

But this regulation, ... in practical effect excludes from distribution in Madison wholesome milk produced and pasteurized in Illinois. "The importer ... may keep his milk or drink it, but sell it he may not." In thus erecting an economic barrier protecting a major local industry against competition from without the State, Madison plainly discriminates against interstate commerce.[3] This it cannot do, even in the exercise of its unquestioned power to protect the health and safety of its people, if reasonable nondiscriminatory alternatives, adequate to conserve legitimate local interests, are available. Cf. *Baldwin v. G.A.F. Seelig, Inc.* (1935); *Minnesota v. Barber* (1890). A different view, that the ordinance is valid simply because it professes to be a health measure, would mean that the Commerce Clause of itself imposes no limitations on state action other than those laid down by the Due Process Clause, save for the rare instance where a state artlessly discloses an avowed purpose to discriminate against interstate goods. Cf. *H. P. Hood & Sons v. Du Mond.* Our issue then is whether the discrimination inherent in the Madison ordinance can be justified in view of the character of the local interests and the available methods of protecting them.

It appears that reasonable and adequate alternatives are available. If the City of Madison prefers to rely upon its own officials for inspection of distant milk sources, such inspection is readily open to it without hardship for it could charge the actual and reasonable cost of such inspection to the importing producers and processors. Moreover, appellee Health Commissioner of Madison testified that as proponent of the local milk ordinance he had submitted the provisions here in controversy and an alternative proposal based on §11 of the Model Milk Ordinance recommended by the United States Public Health Service. The model provision imposes no geographical limitation on location of milk sources and processing plants, but excludes from the municipality milk not produced and pasteurized conformably to standards as high as those enforced by the receiving city.[4] In implementing such an ordinance, the importing city obtains milk ratings based on uniform standards and established by health authorities in the jurisdiction where production and processing occur. The receiving city may determine the extent of enforcement of sanitary standards in the exporting area by verifying the accuracy of safety ratings of specific plants or of the milkshed in the distant jurisdiction through the United States Public Health Service, which routinely and on request spot checks the local ratings. The Commissioner testified that Madison consumers "would be safeguarded adequately" under either proposal and that he had expressed no preference. The milk sanitarian of the Wisconsin State Board of Health testified that the State Health Department recommends the adoption of a provision based on the Model Ordinance. Both officials agreed that a local health officer would be justified in relying upon the evaluation by the Public Health Service of enforcement conditions in remote producing areas.

To permit Madison to adopt a regulation not essential for the protection of local health interests and placing a discriminatory burden on interstate commerce would invite a mul-

---

3. It is immaterial that Wisconsin milk from outside the Madison area is subjected to the same proscription as that moving in interstate commerce.

4. Section 11 of the United States Public Health Service Milk Ordinance as recommended in 1939 provides:
>Milk and milk products from points beyond the limits of routine inspection of the city of ... may not be sold in the city of..., or its police jurisdiction, unless produced and/or pasteurized under provisions equivalent to the requirements of this ordinance; provided that the health officer shall satisfy himself that the health officer having jurisdiction over the production and processing is properly enforcing such provisions.

The following comment on this section is contained in the Public Health Service Milk Code:
>It is suggested that the health officer approve milk or milk products from distant points without his inspection if they are produced and processed under regulations equivalent to those of this ordinance, and if the milk or milk products have been awarded by the State control agency a rating of 90 percent or more on the basis of the Public Health Service rating method. Federal Security Agency, Public Health Bulletin No. 220 (1939), 145.

tiplication of preferential trade areas destructive of the very purpose of the Commerce Clause. Under the circumstances here presented, the regulation must yield to the principle that "one state in its dealings with another may not place itself in a position of economic isolation." *Baldwin v. G.A.F. Seelig, Inc.*

For these reasons we conclude that the judgment below sustaining the five-mile provision as to pasteurization must be reversed.

The Supreme Court of Wisconsin thought it unnecessary to pass upon the validity of the twenty-five-mile limitation, apparently in part for the reason that this issue was made academic by its decision upholding the five-mile section. In view of our conclusion as to the latter provision, a determination of appellant's contention as to the other section is now necessary. As to this issue, therefore, we vacate the judgment below and remand for further proceedings not inconsistent with the principles announced in this opinion. It is so ordered.

Judgment vacated and cause remanded.

Mr. Justice Black, with whom Mr. Justice Douglas and Mr. Justice Minton concur, dissenting.

Today's holding invalidates §7.21 of the Madison, Wisconsin, ordinance on the following reasoning: (1) the section excludes wholesome milk coming from Illinois; (2) this imposes a discriminatory burden on interstate commerce; (3) such a burden cannot be imposed where, as here, there are reasonable, nondiscriminatory and adequate alternatives available. I disagree with the Court's premises, reasoning, and judgment.

(1) This ordinance does not exclude wholesome milk coming from Illinois or anywhere else. It does require that all milk sold in Madison must be pasteurized within five miles of the center of the city. But there was no finding in the state courts, nor evidence to justify a finding there or here, that appellant, Dean Milk Company, is unable to have its milk pasteurized within the defined geographical area. As a practical matter, so far as the record shows, Dean can easily comply with the ordinance whenever it wants to. Therefore, Dean's personal preference to pasteurize in Illinois, not the ordinance, keeps Dean's milk out of Madison.

(2) Characterization of §7.21 as a "discriminatory burden" on interstate commerce is merely a statement of the Court's result, which I think incorrect. The section does prohibit the sale of milk in Madison by interstate and intrastate producers who prefer to pasteurize over five miles distant from the city. But both state courts below found that §7.21 represents a good-faith attempt to safeguard public health by making adequate sanitation inspection possible. While we are not bound by these findings, I do not understand the Court to overturn them. Therefore, the fact that §7.21, like all health regulations, imposes some burden on trade, does not mean that it "discriminates" against interstate commerce.

(3) This health regulation should not be invalidated merely because the Court believes that alternative milk-inspection methods might insure the cleanliness and healthfulness of Dean's Illinois milk. I find it difficult to explain why the Court uses the "reasonable alternative" concept to protect trade when today it refuses to apply the same principle to protect freedom of speech. *Feiner v. New York* (1951). For while the "reasonable alternative" concept has been invoked to protect 1st Amendment rights, e.g., *Schneider v. New Jersey* (1939), it has not heretofore been considered an appropriate weapon for striking down local health laws. Since the days of Chief Justice Marshall, federal courts have left states and municipalities free to pass bona fide health regulations subject only "to the paramount authority of Congress if it decides to assume control...." *The Minnesota Rate Cases (Simpson v. Shepard)* (1913); *Gibbons v. Ogden* (1824); *Mintz v. Baldwin* (1933),

and see *Baldwin v. G.A.F. Seelig* (1935). This established judicial policy of refusing to invalidate genuine local health laws under the Commerce Clause has been approvingly noted even in our recent opinions measuring state regulation by stringent standards. See, e.g., *H. P. Hood & Sons v. Du Mond*. No case is cited, and I have found none, in which a bona fide health law was struck down on the ground that some other method of safeguarding health would be as good as, or better than, the one the Court was called on to review. In my view, to use this ground now elevates the right to traffic in commerce for profit above the power of the people to guard the purity of their daily diet of milk.

If, however, the principle announced today is to be followed, the Court should not strike down local health regulations unless satisfied beyond a reasonable doubt that the substitutes it proposes would not lower health standards. I do not think that the Court can so satisfy itself on the basis of its judicial knowledge. And the evidence in the record leads me to the conclusion that the substitute health measures suggested by the Court do not insure milk as safe as the Madison ordinance requires.

One of the Court's proposals is that Madison require milk processors to pay reasonable inspection fees at the milk supply "sources." Experience shows, however, that the fee method gives rise to prolonged litigation over the calculation and collection of the charges. To throw local milk regulation into such a quagmire of uncertainty jeopardizes the admirable milk-inspection systems in force in many municipalities. Moreover, nothing in the record before us indicates that the fee system might not be as costly to Dean as having its milk pasteurized in Madison. Surely the Court is not resolving this question by drawing on its "judicial knowledge" to supply information as to comparative costs, convenience, or effectiveness.

The Court's second proposal is that Madison adopt § 11 of the "Model Milk Ordinance." The state courts made no findings as to the relative merits of this inspection ordinance and the one chosen by Madison. The evidence indicates to me that enforcement of the Madison law would assure a more healthful quality of milk than that which is entitled to use the label of "Grade A" under the Model Ordinance. Indeed, the United States Board of Public Health, which drafted the Model Ordinance, suggests that the provisions are "minimum" standards only. The Model Ordinance does not provide for continuous investigation of all pasteurization plants as does § 7.21 of the Madison ordinance. Under § 11, moreover, Madison would be required to depend on the Chicago inspection system since Dean's plants, and the farms supplying them with raw milk, are located in the Chicago milkshed. But there is direct and positive evidence in the record that milk produced under Chicago standards did not meet the Madison requirements.

Furthermore, the Model Ordinance would force the Madison health authorities to rely on "spot checks" by the United States Public Health Service to determine whether Chicago enforced its milk regulations. The evidence shows that these "spot checks" are based on random inspection of farms and pasteurization plants: the United States Public Health Service rates the ten thousand or more dairy farms in the Chicago milkshed by a sampling of no more than two hundred farms. The same sampling technique is employed to inspect pasteurization plants. There was evidence that neither the farms supplying Dean with milk nor Dean's pasteurization plants were necessarily inspected in the last "spot check" of the Chicago milkshed made two years before the present case was tried.

From what this record shows, and from what it fails to show, I do not think that either of the alternatives suggested by the Court would assure the people of Madison as pure a supply of milk as they receive under their own ordinance. On this record I would uphold the Madison law. At the very least, however, I would not invalidate it without giving the parties a chance to present evidence and get findings on the ultimate issues the Court thinks crucial—namely, the relative merits of the Madison ordinance and the alternatives suggested by the Court today.

Hunt v. Washington State Apple Advertising Commission
432 U.S. 333 (1977)

[Majority: Burger (C.J.), Powell, Blackmun, Brennan, Stevens, Marshall, White, and Stewart.]

Mr. Chief Justice Burger delivered the opinion of the Court.

In 1973, North Carolina enacted a statute which required, *inter alia,* all closed containers of apples sold, offered for sale, or shipped into the State to bear "no grade other than the applicable U.S. grade or standard." N.C. Gen. Stat. §106-189.1 (1973). In an action brought by the Washington State Apple Advertising Commission, a three-judge Federal District Court invalidated the statute insofar as it prohibited the display of Washington State apple grades on the ground that it unconstitutionally discriminated against interstate commerce.

The specific questions presented on appeal are (a) whether the Commission had standing to bring this action; (b) if so, whether it satisfied the jurisdictional amount requirement of 28 U.S.C. §1331; and (c) whether the challenged North Carolina statute constitutes an unconstitutional burden on interstate commerce.

(1) Washington State is the Nation's largest producer of apples, its crops accounting for approximately 30% of all apples grown domestically and nearly half of all apples shipped in closed containers in interstate commerce. As might be expected, the production and sale of apples on this scale is a multimillion dollar enterprise which plays a significant role in Washington's economy. Because of the importance of the apple industry to the State, its legislature has undertaken to protect and enhance the reputation of Washington apples by establishing a stringent, mandatory inspection program, administered by the State's Department of Agriculture, which requires all apples shipped in interstate commerce to be tested under strict quality standards and graded accordingly. In all cases, the Washington State grades, which have gained substantial acceptance in the trade, are the equivalent of, or superior to, the comparable grades and standards adopted by the United States Department of Agriculture (USDA). Compliance with the Washington inspection scheme costs the State's growers approximately $1 million each year.

In addition to the inspection program, the state legislature has sought to enhance the market for Washington apples through the creation of a state agency, the Washington State Apple Advertising Commission, charged with the statutory duty of promoting and protecting the State's apple industry. The Commission itself is composed of 13 Washington apple growers and dealers who are nominated and elected within electoral districts by their fellow growers and dealers. Wash. Rev. Code §§15.24.020, 15.24.030 (1974). Among its activities are the promotion of Washington apples in both domestic and foreign markets through advertising, market research and analysis, and public education, as well as scientific research into the uses, development, and improvement of apples. Its activities are financed entirely by assessments levied upon the apple industry, §15.24.100; in the year during which this litigation began, these assessments totaled approximately $1.75 million. The assessments, while initially fixed by statute, can be increased only upon the majority vote of the apple growers themselves. §15.24.090.

In 1972, the North Carolina Board of Agriculture adopted an administrative regulation, unique in the 50 States, which in effect required all closed containers of apples shipped into or sold in the State to display either the applicable USDA grade or a notice indicating no classification. State grades were expressly prohibited. In addition to its obvious consequence—prohibiting the display of Washington State apple grades on containers of apples shipped into North Carolina, the regulation presented the Washington apple industry with a marketing problem of potentially nationwide significance. Washington apple growers annually ship in commerce approximately 40 million closed containers of apples, nearly 500,000 of which eventually find their way into North Carolina, stamped with the applicable Washington State variety and grade. It is the industry's practice to purchase these containers preprinted with the various apple varieties and grades, prior to harvest. After these containers are filled with apples of the appropriate type and grade, a substantial portion of them are placed in cold-storage warehouses where the grade labels identify the product and facilitate its handling. These apples are then shipped as needed throughout the year; after February 1 of each year, they constitute approximately two-thirds of all apples sold in fresh markets in this country. Since the ultimate destination of these apples is unknown at the time they are placed in storage, compliance with North Carolina's unique regulation would have required Washington growers to obliterate the printed labels on containers shipped to North Carolina, thus giving their product a damaged appearance. Alternatively, they could have changed their marketing practices to accommodate the needs of the North Carolina market, *i.e.*, repack apples to be shipped to North Carolina in containers bearing only the USDA grade, and/or store the estimated portion of the harvest destined for that market in such special containers. As a last resort, they could discontinue the use of the preprinted containers entirely. None of these costly and less efficient options was very attractive to the industry. Moreover, in the event a number of other States followed North Carolina's lead, the resultant inability to display the Washington grades could force the Washington growers to abandon the State's expensive inspection and grading system which their customers had come to know and rely on over the 60-odd years of its existence....

(2) In this Court, as before, the North Carolina officials vigorously contest the Washington Commission's standing to prosecute this action, either in its own right, or on behalf of that State's apple industry which it purports to represent. At the outset, appellants maintain that the Commission lacks the "personal stake" in the outcome of this litigation essential to its invocation of federal-court jurisdiction. *Baker v. Carr* (1962). The Commission, they point out, is a state agency, not itself engaged in the production and sale of Washington apples or their shipment into North Carolina. Rather, its North Carolina activities are limited to the promotion of Washington apples in that market through advertising. Appellants contend that the challenged statute has no impact on that activity since it prohibits only the display of state apple grades on closed containers of apples. Indeed, since the statute imposed no restrictions on the advertisement of Washington apples or grades other than the labeling ban, which affects only those parties actually engaged in the apple trade, the Commission is said to be free to carry on the same activities that it engaged in prior to the regulatory program. Appellants therefore argue that the Commission suffers no injury, economic or otherwise, from the statute's operation, and, as a result, cannot make out the "case or controversy" between itself and the appellants needed to establish standing in the constitutional sense. E.g., *Village of Arlington Heights v. Metropolitan Housing Development Corp.* (1977); *Warth v. Seldin* (1975).

Moreover, appellants assert, the Commission cannot rely on the injuries which the statute allegedly inflicts individually or collectively on Washington apple growers and dealers in order to confer standing on itself....

If the Commission were a voluntary membership organization—a typical trade association—its standing to bring this action as the representative of its constituents would be clear under prior decisions of this Court. In *Warth v. Seldin*, we stated:

Even in the absence of injury to itself, an association may have standing solely as the representative of its members.... The association must allege that its members, or any one of them, are suffering immediate or threatened injury as a result of the challenged action of the sort that would make out a justiciable case had the members themselves brought suit.... So long as this can be established, and so long as the nature of the claim and of the relief sought does not make the individual participation of each injured party indispensable to proper resolution of the cause, the association may be an appropriate representative of its members, entitled to invoke the court's jurisdiction....

We went on in *Warth* to elaborate on the type of relief that an association could properly pursue on behalf of its members:

[W]hether an association has standing to invoke the court's remedial powers on behalf of its members depends in substantial measure on the nature of the relief sought. If in a proper case the association seeks a declaration, injunction, or some other form of prospective relief, it can reasonably be supposed that the remedy, if granted, will inure to the benefit of those members of the association actually injured. Indeed, in all cases in which we have expressly recognized standing in associations to represent their members, the relief sought has been of this kind.

Thus we have recognized that an association has standing to bring suit on behalf of its members when: (a) its members would otherwise have standing to sue in their own right; (b) the interests it seeks to protect are germane to the organization's purpose; and c) neither the claim asserted nor the relief requested requires the participation of individual members in the lawsuit.

The prerequisites to "associational standing" described in *Warth* are clearly present here. The Commission's complaint alleged, and the District Court found as a fact, that the North Carolina statute had caused some Washington apple growers and dealers (a) to obliterate Washington State grades from the large volume of closed containers destined for the North Carolina market at a cost ranging from 5 to 15 cents per carton; (b) to abandon the use of preprinted containers, thus diminishing the efficiency of their marketing operations; or c) to lose accounts in North Carolina. Such injuries are direct and sufficient to establish the requisite "case or controversy" between Washington apple producers and appellants. Moreover, the Commission's attempt to remedy these injuries and to secure the industry's right to publicize its grading system is central to the Commission's purpose of protecting and enhancing the market for Washington apples. Finally, neither the interstate commerce claim nor the request for declaratory and injunctive relief requires individualized proof and both are thus properly resolved in a group context....

Under the circumstances presented here, it would exalt form over substance to differentiate between the Washington Commission and a traditional trade association representing the individual growers and dealers who collectively form its constituency. We therefore agree with the District Court that the Commission has standing to bring this action in a representational capacity....

(4). We turn finally to the appellants' claim that the District Court erred in holding that the North Carolina statute violated the Commerce Clause insofar as it prohibited the display of Washington State grades on closed containers of apples shipped into the State. Appellants do not really contest the District Court's determination that the challenged statute burdened the Washington apple industry by increasing its costs of doing business in the North Carolina market and causing it to lose accounts there. Rather, they maintain that any such burdens on the interstate sale of Washington apples were far outweighed by the local benefits flowing from what they contend was a valid exercise of North Carolina's inherent police powers designed to protect its citizenry from fraud and deception in the marketing of apples.

Prior to the statute's enactment, appellants point out, apples from 13 different States were shipped into North Carolina for sale. Seven of those States, including the State of Washington, had their own grading systems which, while differing in their standards, used similar descriptive labels (*e.g.*, fancy, extra fancy, etc.). This multiplicity of inconsistent state grades, as the District Court itself found, posed dangers of deception and confusion not only in the North Carolina market, but in the Nation as a whole. The North Carolina statute, appellants claim, was enacted to eliminate this source of deception and confusion by replacing the numerous state grades with a single uniform standard. Moreover, it is contended that North Carolina sought to accomplish this goal of uniformity in an evenhanded manner as evidenced by the fact that its statute applies to all apples sold in closed containers in the State without regard to their point of origin. Nonetheless, appellants argue that the District Court gave "scant attention" to the obvious benefits flowing from the challenged legislation and to the long line of decisions from this Court holding that the States possess "broad powers" to protect local purchasers from fraud and deception in the marketing of foodstuffs. *E.g., Florida Lime & Avocado Growers, Inc. v. Paul* (1963).

As the appellants properly point out, not every exercise of state authority imposing some burden on the free flow of commerce is invalid. *E.g., Great Atlantic & Pacific Tea Co. v. Cottrell* (1976). Although the Commerce Clause acts as a limitation upon state power even without congressional implementation, *e.g., Great Atlantic & Pacific Tea Co; Cooley v. Board of Wardens* (1852), our opinions have long recognized that, "in the absence of conflicting legislation by Congress, there is a residuum of power in the state to make laws governing matters of local concern which nevertheless in some measure affect interstate commerce or even, to some extent, regulate it." *Southern Pacific Co. v. Arizona* (1945).

Moreover, as appellants correctly note, that "residuum" is particularly strong when the State acts to protect its citizenry in matters pertaining to the sale of foodstuffs. *Florida Lime & Avocado Growers, Inc.* By the same token, however, a finding that state legislation furthers matters of legitimate local concern, even in the health and consumer protection areas, does not end the inquiry. Such a view, we have noted, "would mean that the Commerce Clause of itself imposes no limitations on state action ... save for the rare instance where a state artlessly discloses an avowed purpose to discriminate against interstate goods." *Dean Milk Co. v. Madison* (1951). Rather, when such state legislation comes into conflict with the Commerce Clause's overriding requirement of a national "common market," we are confronted with the task of effecting an accommodation of the competing national and local interests. *Pike v. Bruce Church, Inc.* (1970); *Great Atlantic & Pacific Tea Co.* We turn to that task.

As the District Court correctly found, the challenged statute has the practical effect of not only burdening interstate sales of Washington apples, but also discriminating against them. This discrimination takes various forms. The first, and most obvious, is the statute's consequence of raising the costs of doing business in the North Carolina market for Washington apple growers and dealers, while leaving those of their North Carolina counterparts unaffected. As previously noted, this disparate effect results from the fact that North Carolina apple producers, unlike their Washington competitors, were not forced to alter their marketing practices in order to comply with the statute. They were still free to market their wares under the USDA grade or none at all as they had done prior to the statute's enactment. Obviously, the increased costs imposed by the statute would tend to shield the local apple industry from the competition of Washington apple growers and dealers who are already at a competitive disadvantage because of their great distance from the North Carolina market.

Second, the statute has the effect of stripping away from the Washington apple industry the competitive and economic advantages it has earned for itself through its expensive inspection and grading system. The record demonstrates that the Washington apple-grading system has gained nationwide acceptance in the apple trade. Indeed, it contains numerous affidavits from apple brokers and dealers located both inside and outside of North Carolina who state their preference, and that of their customers, for apples graded under the Washington, as opposed to the USDA system, because of the former's greater consistency, its emphasis on color, and its supporting mandatory inspections. Once again, the statute had no similar impact on the North Carolina apple industry and thus operated to its benefit.

Third, by prohibiting Washington growers and dealers from marketing apples under their State's grades, the statute has a leveling effect which insidiously operates to the advantage of local apple producers. As noted earlier, the Washington State grades are equal or superior to the USDA grades in all corresponding categories. Hence, with free market forces at work, Washington sellers would normally enjoy a distinct market advantage vis-a-vis local producers in those categories where the Washington grade is superior. However, because of the statute's operation, Washington apples which would otherwise qualify for and be sold under the superior Washington grades will now have to be marketed under their inferior USDA counterparts. Such "downgrading" offers the North Carolina apple industry the very sort of protection against competing out-of-state products that the Commerce Clause was designed to prohibit. At worst, it will have the effect of an embargo against those Washington apples in the superior grades as Washington dealers withhold them from the North Carolina market. At best, it will deprive Washington sellers of the market premium that such apples would otherwise command.

Despite the statute's facial neutrality, the Commission suggests that its discriminatory impact on interstate commerce was not an unintended byproduct and there are some indications in the record to that effect. The most glaring is the response of the North Carolina Agriculture Commissioner to the Commission's request for an exemption following the statute's passage in which he indicated that before he could support such an exemption, he would "want to have the sentiment from our apple producers *since they were mainly responsible for this legislation being passed....*" (emphasis added). Moreover, we find it somewhat suspect that North Carolina singled out only closed containers of apples, the very means by which apples are transported in commerce, to effectuate the statute's ostensible consumer protection purpose when apples are not generally sold at retail in their shipping containers. However, we need not ascribe an economic protection motive to the North Carolina Legislature to resolve this case; we conclude that the challenged statute cannot stand insofar as it prohibits the display of Washington State grades even if enacted for the declared purpose of protecting consumers from deception and fraud in the marketplace.

When discrimination against commerce of the type we have found is demonstrated, the burden falls on the State to justify it both in terms of the local benefits flowing from the statute and the unavailability of nondiscriminatory alternatives adequate to preserve the local interests at stake. *Dean Milk Co. v. Madison....* North Carolina has failed to sustain that burden on both scores.

The several States unquestionably possess a substantial interest in protecting their citizens from confusion and deception in the marketing of foodstuffs, but the challenged statute does remarkably little to further that laudable goal at least with respect to Washington apples and grades. The statute, as already noted, permits the marketing of closed containers of apples under *no* grades at all. Such a result can hardly be thought to eliminate the problems of deception and confusion created by the multiplicity of differing state grades; indeed, it magnifies them by depriving purchasers of all information concerning the quality of the contents of closed apple containers. Moreover, although the statute is ostensibly a consumer protection measure, it directs its primary efforts, not at the consuming public at large, but at apple wholesalers and brokers who are the principal purchasers of closed containers of apples. And those individuals are presumably the most knowledgeable individuals in this area. Since the statute does nothing at all to purify the flow of information at the retail level, it does little to protect consumers against the problems it was designed to eliminate. Finally, we note that any potential for confusion and deception created by the Washington grades was not of the type that led to the statute's enactment. Since Washington grades are in all cases equal or superior to their USDA counterparts, they could only "deceive" or "confuse" a consumer to his benefit, hardly a harmful result.

In addition, it appears that nondiscriminatory alternatives to the outright ban of Washington State grades are readily available. For example, North Carolina could effectuate its goal by permitting out-of-state growers to utilize state grades only if they also marked their shipments with the applicable USDA label. In that case, the USDA grade would serve as a benchmark against which the consumer could evaluate the quality of the various state grades. If this alternative was for some reason inadequate to eradicate problems caused by state grades inferior to those adopted by the USDA, North Carolina might consider banning those state grades which, unlike Washington's, could not be demonstrated to be equal or superior to the corresponding USDA categories. Concededly, even in this latter instance, some potential for "confusion" might persist. However, it is the type of "confusion" that the national interest in the free flow of goods between the States demands be tolerated.

The judgment of the District Court is Affirmed.

City of Philadelphia v. New Jersey
437 U.S. 617 (1978)

[Majority: Stewart, Powell, Blackmun, Brennan, Stevens, Marshall, and White. Dissenting: Rehnquist and Burger (C.J.).]

Mr. Justice Stewart delivered the opinion of the Court.

A New Jersey law prohibits the importation of most "solid or liquid waste which originated or was collected outside the territorial limits of the State...." In this case we are required to decide whether this statutory prohibition violates the Commerce Clause of the United States Constitution.

I. The statutory provision in question is ch. 363 of 1973 N.J. Laws, which took effect in early 1974. In pertinent part it provides:

> No person shall bring into this State any solid or liquid waste which originated or was collected outside the territorial limits of the State, except garbage to be fed to swine in the State of New Jersey, until the commissioner [of the State Department of Environmental Protection] shall determine that such action can be permitted without endangering the public health, safety and welfare and has promulgated regulations permitting and regulating the treatment and disposal of such waste in this State. N.J. Stat. Ann. § 13:1I-10 (West Supp. 1978).

As authorized by ch. 363, the Commissioner promulgated regulations permitting four categories of waste to enter the State.[1] Apart from these narrow exceptions, however, New Jersey closed its borders to all waste from other States.

Immediately affected by these developments were the operators of private landfills in New Jersey, and several cities in other States that had agreements with these operators for waste disposal. They brought suit against New Jersey and its Department of Environmental Protection in state court, attacking the statute and regulations on a number of state and federal grounds. In an oral opinion granting the plaintiffs' motion for summary judgment, the trial court declared the law unconstitutional because it discriminated against interstate commerce. The New Jersey Supreme Court consolidated this case with another reaching the same conclusion, *Hackensack Meadowlands Development Comm'n v. Municipal Sanitary Landfill Auth.* (N.J. Super. Ct. Ch. Div. 1974). It found that ch. 363 advanced vital health and environmental objectives with no economic discrimination against, and with little burden upon, interstate commerce, and that the law was therefore permissible under the Commerce Clause of the Constitution. The court also found no congressional intent to pre-empt ch. 363 by enacting in 1965 the Solid Waste Disposal Act, 79 Stat. 997, 42 U.S.C. §3251 et seq., as amended by the Resource Recovery Act of 1970, 84 Stat. 1227.

The plaintiffs then appealed to this Court. After noting probable jurisdiction and hearing oral argument, we remanded for reconsideration of the appellants' pre-emption claim in light of the newly enacted Resource Conservation and Recovery Act of 1976, 90 Stat. 2795. Again the New Jersey Supreme Court found no federal pre-emption of the state law, and again we noted probable jurisdiction. We agree with the New Jersey court that the state law has not been pre-empted by federal legislation.[2] The dispositive question, therefore, is whether the law is constitutionally permissible in light of the Commerce Clause of the Constitution.[3]

---

1. Effective as of February 1974, these regulations provided as follows:
(a) No person shall bring into this State, or accept for disposal in this State, any solid or liquid waste which originated or was collected outside the territorial limits of this State. This Section shall not apply to:
1. Garbage to be fed to swine in the State of New Jersey;
2. Any separated waste material, including newsprint, paper, glass and metals, that is free from putrescible materials and not mixed with other solid or liquid waste that is intended for a recycling or reclamation facility;
3. Municipal solid waste to be separated or processed into usable secondary materials, including fuel and heat, at a resource recovery facility provided that not less than 70 per cent of the thru-put of any such facility is to be separated or processed into usable secondary materials; and
4. Pesticides, hazardous waste, chemical waste, bulk liquid, bulk semi-liquid, which is to be treated, processed or recovered in a solid waste disposal facility which is registered with the Department for such treatment, processing or recovery, other than by disposal on or in the lands of this State. N.J. Admin. Code 7:1-4.2 (Supp. 1977).

2. From our review of this federal legislation, we find no "clear and manifest purpose of Congress," *Rice v. Santa Fe Elevator Corp.* (1947), to pre-empt the entire field of interstate waste management or transportation, either by express statutory command, see *Jones v. Rath Packing Co.* (1977), or by implicit legislative design, see *City of Burbank v. Lockheed Air Terminal* (1973). To the contrary, Congress expressly has provided that "the collection and disposal of solid wastes should continue to be primarily the function of State, regional, and local agencies...." 42 U.S.C. §6901(a)(4) (1976 ed.). Similarly, ch. 363 is not pre-empted because of a square conflict with particular provisions of federal law or because of general incompatibility with basic federal objectives. See *Ray v. Atlantic Richfield Co.* (1978); *Jones v. Rath Packing Co.* In short, we agree with the New Jersey Supreme Court that ch. 363 can be enforced consistently with the program goals and the respective federal-state roles intended by Congress when it enacted the federal legislation.

3. U.S. Const., Art. I, §8, cl. 3.

II. Before it addressed the merits of the appellants' claim, the New Jersey Supreme Court questioned whether the interstate movement of those wastes banned by ch. 363 is "commerce" at all within the meaning of the Commerce Clause. Any doubts on that score should be laid to rest at the outset.

The state court expressed the view that there may be two definitions of "commerce" for constitutional purposes. When relied on "to support some exertion of federal control or regulation," the Commerce Clause permits "a very sweeping concept" of commerce. But when relied on "to strike down or restrict state legislation," that Clause and the term "commerce" have a "much more confined ... reach."

The state court reached this conclusion in an attempt to reconcile modern Commerce Clause concepts with several old cases of this Court holding that States can prohibit the importation of some objects because they "are not legitimate subjects of trade and commerce." ... These articles include items "which, on account of their existing condition, would bring in and spread disease, pestilence, and death, such as rags or other substances infected with the germs of yellow fever or the virus of small-pox, or cattle or meat or other provisions that are diseased or decayed, or otherwise, from their condition and quality, unfit for human use or consumption." *Bowman v. Chicago & Northwestern Ry. Co.* (1888). See also *Baldwin v. G.A.F. Seelig, Inc.* (1935) and cases cited therein. The state court found that ch. 363 as narrowed by the state regulations, banned only "those wastes which can[not] be put to effective use," and therefore those wastes were not commerce at all, unless "the mere transportation and disposal of valueless waste between states constitutes interstate commerce within the meaning of the constitutional provision."

We think the state court misread our cases, and thus erred in assuming that they require a two-tiered definition of commerce. In saying that innately harmful articles "are not legitimate subjects of trade and commerce," the *Bowman* Court was stating its conclusion, not the starting point of its reasoning. All objects of interstate trade merit Commerce Clause protection; none is excluded by definition at the outset. In *Bowman* and similar cases, the Court held simply that because the articles' worth in interstate commerce was far outweighed by the dangers inhering in their very movement, States could prohibit their transportation across state lines. Hence, we reject the state court's suggestion that the banning of "valueless" out-of-state wastes by ch. 363 implicates no constitutional protection. Just as Congress has power to regulate the interstate movement of these wastes, States are not free from constitutional scrutiny when they restrict that movement. Cf. *Hughes v. Alexandria Scrap Corp.* (1976)....

III-A. Although the Constitution gives Congress the power to regulate commerce among the States, many subjects of potential federal regulation under that power inevitably escape congressional attention "because of their local character and their number and diversity." *South Carolina State Highway Dept. v. Barnwell Bros., Inc.* (1938). In the absence of federal legislation, these subjects are open to control by the States so long as they act within the restraints imposed by the Commerce Clause itself. See *Raymond Motor Transportation, Inc. v. Rice* (1978). The bounds of these restraints appear nowhere in the words of the Commerce Clause, but have emerged gradually in the decisions of this Court giving effect to its basic purpose. That broad purpose was well expressed by Mr. Justice Jackson in his opinion for the Court in *H. P. Hood & Sons, Inc. v. Du Mond* (1949):

> This principle that our economic unit is the Nation, which alone has the gamut of powers necessary to control of the economy, including the vital power of erecting customs barriers against foreign competition, has as its corollary that the

states are not separable economic units. As the Court said in *Baldwin v. Seelig*, "what is ultimate is the principle that one state in its dealings with another may not place itself in a position of economic isolation."

The opinions of the Court through the years have reflected an alertness to the evils of "economic isolation" and protectionism, while at the same time recognizing that incidental burdens on interstate commerce may be unavoidable when a State legislates to safeguard the health and safety of its people. Thus, where simple economic protectionism is effected by state legislation, a virtually per se rule of invalidity has been erected. See, e.g., *H. P. Hood & Sons, Inc. v. Du Mond* (1949); *Toomer v. Witsell* (1948); *Baldwin v. G. A. F. Seelig, Inc.*; *Buck v. Kuykendall* (1925). The clearest example of such legislation is a law that overtly blocks the flow of interstate commerce at a State's borders. But where other legislative objectives are credibly advanced and there is no patent discrimination against interstate trade, the Court has adopted a much more flexible approach, the general contours of which were outlined in *Pike v. Bruce Church, Inc.* (1970):

> Where the statute regulates evenhandedly to effectuate a legitimate local public interest, and its effects on interstate commerce are only incidental, it will be upheld unless the burden imposed on such commerce is clearly excessive in relation to the putative local benefits.... If a legitimate local purpose is found, then the question becomes one of degree. And the extent of the burden that will be tolerated will of course depend on the nature of the local interest involved, and on whether it could be promoted as well with a lesser impact on interstate activities.

See also ... *Hunt v. Washington Apple Advertising Comm'n* (1977); *Great A & P Tea Co. v. Cottrell* (1976).

The crucial inquiry, therefore, must be directed to determining whether ch. 363 is basically a protectionist measure, or whether it can fairly be viewed as a law directed to legitimate local concerns, with effects upon interstate commerce that are only incidental.

III-B. The purpose of ch. 363 is set out in the statute itself as follows:

> The Legislature finds and determines that ... the volume of solid and liquid waste continues to rapidly increase, that the treatment and disposal of these wastes continues to pose an even greater threat to the quality of the environment of New Jersey, that the available and appropriate land fill sites within the State are being diminished, that the environment continues to be threatened by the treatment and disposal of waste which originated or was collected outside the State, and that the public health, safety and welfare require that the treatment and disposal within this State of all wastes generated outside of the State be prohibited.

The New Jersey Supreme Court accepted this statement of the state legislature's purpose. The state court additionally found that New Jersey's existing landfill sites will be exhausted within a few years; that to go on using these sites or to develop new ones will take a heavy environmental toll, both from pollution and from loss of scarce open lands; that new techniques to divert waste from landfills to other methods of disposal and resource recovery processes are under development, but that these changes will require time; and finally, that "the extension of the lifespan of existing landfills, resulting from the exclusion of out-of-state waste, may be of crucial importance in preventing further virgin wetlands or other undeveloped lands from being devoted to landfill purposes." Based on these findings, the court concluded that ch. 363 was designed to protect, not the State's economy, but its environment, and that its substantial benefits outweigh its "slight" burden on interstate commerce.

The appellants strenuously contend that ch. 363, "while outwardly cloaked 'in the currently fashionable garb of environmental protection,'... is actually no more than a legislative effort to suppress competition and stabilize the cost of solid waste disposal for New Jersey residents...." They cite passages of legislative history suggesting that the problem addressed by ch. 363 is primarily financial: Stemming the flow of out-of-state waste into certain landfill sites will extend their lives, thus delaying the day when New Jersey cities must transport their waste to more distant and expensive sites.

The appellees, on the other hand, deny that ch. 363 was motivated by financial concerns or economic protectionism. In the words of their brief, "[n]o New Jersey commercial interests stand to gain advantage over competitors from outside the state as a result of the ban on dumping out-of-state waste." Noting that New Jersey landfill operators are among the plaintiffs, the appellees' brief argues that "[t]he complaint is not that New Jersey has forged an economic preference for its own commercial interests, but rather that it has denied a small group of its entrepreneurs an economic opportunity to traffic in waste in order to protect the health, safety and welfare of the citizenry at large."

This dispute about ultimate legislative purpose need not be resolved, because its resolution would not be relevant to the constitutional issue to be decided in this case. Contrary to the evident assumption of the state court and the parties, the evil of protectionism can reside in legislative means as well as legislative ends. Thus, it does not matter whether the ultimate aim of ch. 363 is to reduce the waste disposal costs of New Jersey residents or to save remaining open lands from pollution, for we assume New Jersey has every right to protect its residents' pocketbooks as well as their environment. And it may be assumed as well that New Jersey may pursue those ends by slowing the flow of *all* waste into the State's remaining landfills, even though interstate commerce may incidentally be affected. But whatever New Jersey's ultimate purpose, it may not be accomplished by discriminating against articles of commerce coming from outside the State unless there is some reason, apart from their origin, to treat them differently. Both on its face and in its plain effect, ch. 363 violates this principle of nondiscrimination.

The Court has consistently found parochial legislation of this kind to be constitutionally invalid, whether the ultimate aim of the legislation was to assure a steady supply of milk by erecting barriers to allegedly ruinous outside competition, *Baldwin v. G. A. F. Seelig, Inc.*, or to create jobs by keeping industry within the State, *Foster-Fountain Packing Co. v. Haydel* (1928); *Johnson v. Haydel* (1928); *Toomer v. Witsell*; or to preserve the State's financial resources from depletion by fencing out indigent immigrants, *Edwards v. California* (1941). In each of these cases, a presumably legitimate goal was sought to be achieved by the illegitimate means of isolating the State from the national economy.

Also relevant here are the Court's decisions holding that a State may not accord its own inhabitants a preferred right of access over consumers in other States to natural resources located within its borders. *West v. Kansas Natural Gas Co.* (1911); *Pennsylvania v. West Virginia* (1923). These cases stand for the basic principle that a "State is without power to prevent privately owned articles of trade from being shipped and sold in interstate commerce on the ground that they are required to satisfy local demands or because they are needed by the people of the State." *Foster-Fountain Packing Co. v. Haydel.*

The New Jersey law at issue in this case falls squarely within the area that the Commerce Clause puts off limits to state regulation. On its face, it imposes on out-of-state commercial interests the full burden of conserving the State's remaining landfill space. It is true that in our previous cases the scarce natural resource was itself the article of commerce, whereas here the scarce resource and the article of commerce are distinct. But that difference is without consequence. In both instances, the State has overtly moved to slow or freeze the flow of commerce for protectionist reasons. It does not matter that the State has shut the article of commerce inside the State in one case and outside the State in the other. What is crucial is the attempt by one State to isolate itself from a problem common to many by erecting a barrier against the movement of interstate trade.

The appellees argue that not all laws which facially discriminate against out-of-state commerce are forbidden protectionist regulations. In particular, they point to quarantine laws, which this Court has repeatedly upheld even though they appear to single out interstate commerce for special treatment. See *Baldwin v. G.A.F. Seelig, Inc.*; *Bowman v. Chicago & Northwestern Ry. Co.* In the appellees' view, ch. 363 is analogous to such health-protective measures, since it reduces the exposure of New Jersey residents to the allegedly harmful effects of landfill sites.

It is true that certain quarantine laws have not been considered forbidden protectionist measures, even though they were directed against out-of-state commerce. See *Asbell v. Kansas* (1908); *Reid v. Colorado* (1902); *Bowman v. Chicago & Northwestern R. Co.* But those quarantine laws banned the importation of articles such as diseased livestock that required destruction as soon as possible because their very movement risked contagion and other evils. Those laws thus did not discriminate against interstate commerce as such, but simply prevented traffic in noxious articles, whatever their origin.

The New Jersey statute is not such a quarantine law. There has been no claim here that the very movement of waste into or through New Jersey endangers health, or that waste must be disposed of as soon and as close to its point of generation as possible. The harms caused by waste are said to arise after its disposal in landfill sites, and at that point, as New Jersey concedes, there is no basis to distinguish out-of-state waste from domestic waste. If one is inherently harmful, so is the other. Yet New Jersey has banned the former while leaving its landfill sites open to the latter. The New Jersey law blocks the importation of waste in an obvious effort to saddle those outside the State with the entire burden of slowing the flow of refuse into New Jersey's remaining landfill sites. That legislative effort is clearly impermissible under the Commerce Clause of the Constitution.

Today, cities in Pennsylvania and New York find it expedient or necessary to send their waste into New Jersey for disposal, and New Jersey claims the right to close its borders to such traffic. Tomorrow, cities in New Jersey may find it expedient or necessary to send their waste into Pennsylvania or New York for disposal, and those States might then claim the right to close their borders. The Commerce Clause will protect New Jersey in the future, just as it protects her neighbors now, from efforts by one State to isolate itself in the stream of interstate commerce from a problem shared by all. The judgment is

Reversed.

Mr. Justice Rehnquist, with whom The Chief Justice joins, dissenting.

A growing problem in our Nation is the sanitary treatment and disposal of solid waste.[1] For many years, solid waste was incinerated. Because of the significant environmental problems attendant on incineration, however, this method of solid waste disposal has declined in use in many localities, including New Jersey. "Sanitary" landfills have replaced inciner-

---

1. Congress specifically recognized the substantial dangers to the environment and public health that are posed by current methods of disposing of solid waste in the Resource Conservation and Recovery Act of 1976. As the Court recognizes, the laws under challenge here "can be enforced consistently with the program goals and the respective federal-state roles intended by Congress when it enacted" this and other legislation and are thus not pre-empted by any federal statutes.

ation as the principal method of disposing of solid waste. In ch. 363 of the 1973 N.J. Laws, the State of New Jersey legislatively recognized the unfortunate fact that landfills also present extremely serious health and safety problems. First, in New Jersey, "virtually all sanitary landfills can be expected to produce leachate, a noxious and highly polluted liquid which is seldom visible and frequently pollutes ... ground and surface waters." The natural decomposition process which occurs in landfills also produces large quantities of methane and thereby presents a significant explosion hazard. Landfills can also generate "health hazards caused by rodents, fires and scavenger birds" and, "needless to say, do not help New Jersey's aesthetic appearance nor New Jersey's noise or water or air pollution problems."

The health and safety hazards associated with landfills present appellees with a currently unsolvable dilemma. Other, hopefully safer, methods of disposing of solid wastes are still in the development stage and cannot presently be used. But appellees obviously cannot completely stop the tide of solid waste that its citizens will produce in the interim. For the moment, therefore, appellees must continue to use sanitary landfills to dispose of New Jersey's own solid waste despite the critical environmental problems thereby created.

The question presented in this case is whether New Jersey must also continue to receive and dispose of solid waste from neighboring States, even though these will inexorably increase the health problems discussed above.[2] The Court answers this question in the affirmative. New Jersey must either prohibit all landfill operations, leaving itself to cast about for a presently nonexistent solution to the serious problem of disposing of the waste generated within its own borders, or it must accept waste from every portion of the United States, thereby multiplying the health and safety problems which would result if it dealt only with such wastes generated within the State. Because past precedents establish that the Commerce Clause does not present appellees with such a Hobson's choice, I dissent.

The Court recognizes that States can prohibit the importation of items "'which, on account of their existing condition, would bring in and spread disease, pestilence, and death, such as rags or other substances infected with the germs of yellow fever or the virus of smallpox, or cattle or meat or other provisions that are diseased or decayed or otherwise, from their condition and quality, unfit for human use or consumption.'" *Bowman v. Chicago & Northwestern Ry. Co.* (1888). See *Baldwin v. G. A. F. Seelig, Inc.* (1935); *Sligh v. Kirkwood* (1915); *Asbell v. Kansas* (1908); *Railroad Co. v. Husen* (1878). As the Court points out, such "quarantine laws have not been considered forbidden protectionist measures, *even though they were directed against out-of-state commerce.*"

In my opinion, these cases are dispositive of the present one. Under them, New Jersey may require germ-infected rags or diseased meat to be disposed of as best as possible within the State, but at the same time prohibit the *importation* of such items for disposal at the facilities that are set up within New Jersey for disposal of such material generated *within* the State. The physical fact of life that New Jersey must somehow dispose of its own noxious items does not mean that it must serve as a depository for those of every other State. Similarly, New Jersey should be free under our past precedents to prohibit the importation of solid waste because of the health and safety problems that such waste poses to its citizens. The fact that New Jersey continues to, and indeed must continue to, dispose of its own solid waste does not mean that New Jersey may not prohibit the impor-

---

2. Regulations of the New Jersey Department of Environmental Protection "except from the ban on out-of-state refuse those types of solid waste which may have a value for recycling or for use as fuel." Thus, the ban under challenge would appear to be strictly limited to that waste which will be disposed of in sanitary landfills and thereby pose health and safety dangers to the citizens of New Jersey.

tation of even more solid waste into the State. I simply see no way to distinguish solid waste, on the record of this case, from germ-infected rags, diseased meat, and other noxious items.

The Court's effort to distinguish these prior cases is unconvincing. It first asserts that the quarantine laws which have previously been upheld "banned the importation of articles such as diseased livestock that required destruction as soon as possible because their very movement risked contagion and other evils." According to the Court, the New Jersey law is distinguishable from these other laws, and invalid, because the concern of New Jersey is not with the *movement* of solid waste but with the present inability to safely *dispose* of it once it reaches its destination. But I think it far from clear that the State's law has as limited a focus as the Court imputes to it: Solid waste which is a health hazard when it reaches its destination may in all likelihood be an equally great health hazard in transit.

Even if the Court is correct in its characterization of New Jersey's concerns, I do not see why a State may ban the importation of items whose movement risks contagion, but cannot ban the importation of items which, although they may be transported into the State without undue hazard, will then simply pile up in an ever increasing danger to the public's health and safety. The Commerce Clause was not drawn with a view to having the validity of state laws turn on such pointless distinctions.

Second, the Court implies that the challenged laws must be invalidated because New Jersey has left its landfills open to domestic waste. But, as the Court notes, this Court has repeatedly upheld quarantine laws "even though they appear to single out interstate commerce for special treatment." The fact that New Jersey has left its landfill sites open for domestic waste does not, of course, mean that solid waste is not innately harmful. Nor does it mean that New Jersey prohibits importation of solid waste for reasons other than the health and safety of its population. New Jersey must out of sheer necessity treat and dispose of its solid waste in some fashion, just as it must treat New Jersey cattle suffering from hoof-and-mouth disease. It does not follow that New Jersey must, under the Commerce Clause, accept solid waste or diseased cattle from outside its borders and thereby exacerbate its problems.

The Supreme Court of New Jersey expressly found that ch. 363 was passed "to preserve the health of New Jersey residents by keeping their exposure to solid waste and landfill areas to a minimum." The Court points to absolutely no evidence that would contradict this finding by the New Jersey Supreme Court. Because I find no basis for distinguishing the laws under challenge here from our past cases upholding state laws that prohibit the importation of items that could endanger the population of the State, I dissent.

United Haulers Ass'n, Inc. v. Oneida-Herkimer S.W.M.A.: Background

Disposal of solid waste continues to be a national problem. In 1989, as a way to finance the construction of a garbage processing plant, a town gave a private corporation a 5 year monopoly contract on solid waste from the town in exchange for building the plant. The contract also provided that all garbage from the area had to be processed by the corporation. The corporation agreed to sell the plant to the town for $1 after 5 years. The Court held this scheme violated the Dormant Commerce Clause. *C & A Carbone, Inc. v. Clarkstown* (1994). The vote was 6 to 3, with Justices Scalia and Thomas in the majority. Since *Carbone*, Justice Thomas has announced that the Dormant Commerce Clause doctrine should be rejected *in toto* and Justice Scalia has announced that it is unsound and should be applied only when stare decisis demands it.

In *United Haulers Assn., Inc. v. Oneida-Herkimer Solid Waste Management Authority* (2007), the court rejected a Dormant Commerce Clause challenge to a garbage scheme remarkably similar to the discredited *Clarkstown* program. A 6–3 majority (including Justices Thomas and Scalia) held *Carbone* did not control because the government ran the program from the start, rather than assuming control after 5 years. In concluding, Chief Justice Roberts invoked the specter of *Lochner v. New York* (1905), opining that the Court should be reluctant to interfere with strategies adopted by local governments to advance traditional police power concerns even if the policies have some incidental impact on interstate commerce.

United Haulers Association, Inc. v. Oneida-Herkimer Solid Waste Management Authority
550 U.S. 330 (2007)

[Plurality: Roberts (C.J.), Breyer, Souter, Ginsburg. Concurring in part: Scalia, Thomas. Dissenting: Alito, Stevens, Kennedy.]

Chief Justice Roberts delivered the opinion of the Court, except as to Part II-D.

"Flow control" ordinances require trash haulers to deliver solid waste to a particular waste processing facility. In *C & A Carbone, Inc. v.* Clarkstown (1994), this Court struck down under the Commerce Clause a flow control ordinance that forced haulers to deliver waste to a particular *private* processing facility. In this case, we face flow control ordinances quite similar to the one invalidated in *Carbone*. The only salient difference is that the laws at issue here require haulers to bring waste to facilities owned and operated by a state-created public benefit corporation. We find this difference constitutionally significant. Disposing of trash has been a traditional government activity for years, and laws that favor the government in such areas—but treat every private business, whether in-state or out-of-state, exactly the same—do not discriminate against interstate commerce for purposes of the Commerce Clause. Applying the Commerce Clause test reserved for regulations that do not discriminate against interstate commerce, we uphold these ordinances because any incidental burden they may have on interstate commerce does not outweigh the benefits they confer on the citizens of Oneida and Herkimer Counties.

I.... Traditionally, each city, town, or village within the Counties has been responsible for disposing of its own waste. Many had relied on local land-fills, some in a more environmentally responsible fashion than others. By the 1980's, the Counties confronted what they could credibly call a solid waste "'crisis.'" Many local landfills were operating without permits and in violation of state regulations....

The "crisis" extended beyond health and safety concerns. The Counties had an uneasy relationship with local waste management companies, enduring price fixing, pervasive overcharging, and the influence of organized crime. Dramatic price hikes were not uncommon.... In 1989, the Authority and the Counties entered into a Solid Waste Management Agreement, under which the Authority agreed to manage all solid waste within the Counties. Private haulers would remain free to pick up citizens' trash from the curb, but the Authority would take over the job of processing the trash, sorting it, and sending it off for disposal. To fulfill its part of the bargain, the Authority agreed to purchase and develop facilities for the processing and disposal of solid waste and recyclables generated in the Counties.

The Authority collected "tipping fees" to cover its operating and maintenance costs for these facilities.[1] The tipping fees significantly exceeded those charged for waste removal on the open market, but they allowed the Authority to do more than the average private waste disposer....

As described, the agreement had a flaw: Citizens might opt to have their waste hauled to facilities with lower tipping fees. To avoid being stuck with the bill for facilities that citizens voted for but then chose not to use, the Counties enacted "flow control" ordinances requiring that all solid waste generated within the Counties be delivered to the Authority's processing sites. Private haulers must obtain a permit from the Authority to collect waste in the Counties. Penalties for noncompliance with the ordinances include permit revocation, fines, and imprisonment....

The District Court read our decision in *Carbone* as categorically rejecting nearly all flow control laws. The court ruled in the haulers' favor, enjoining enforcement of the Counties' laws. The Second Circuit reversed, reasoning that *Carbone* and our other Dormant Commerce Clause precedents allow for a distinction between laws that benefit public as opposed to private facilities....

On remand and after protracted discovery, a Magistrate Judge and the District Court found that the haulers did not show that the ordinances imposed *any* cognizable burden on interstate commerce. The Second Circuit affirmed, assuming that the laws exacted some toll on interstate commerce, but finding any possible burden "modest" compared to the "clear and substantial" benefits of the ordinances....

II-A. ... Although the Constitution does not in terms limit the power of States to regulate commerce, we have long interpreted the Commerce Clause as an implicit restraint on state authority, even in the absence of a conflicting federal statute. See *Cooley v. Board of Wardens of Port of Philadelphia ex rel. Soc. for Relief of Distressed Pilots* (1852). To determine whether a law violates this so-called "dormant" aspect of the Commerce Clause, we first ask whether it discriminates on its face against interstate commerce. In this context, "'discrimination' simply means differential treatment of in-state and out-of-state economic interests that benefits the former and burdens the latter." Discriminatory laws motivated by "simple economic protectionism" are subject to a "virtually *per se* rule invalidity," *Philadelphia v. New Jersey* (1978), which can only be overcome by a showing that the State has no other means to advance a legitimate local purpose, *Maine v. Taylor* (1986).

II-B. ... In *Carbone*, the town of Clarkstown, New York, hired a private contractor to build a waste transfer station. According to the terms of the deal, the contractor would operate the facility for five years, charging an above-market tipping fee of $81 per ton; after five years, the town would buy the facility for one dollar. The town guaranteed that the facility would receive a certain volume of trash per year. To make good on its promise, Clarkstown passed a flow control ordinance requiring that all nonhazardous solid waste within the town be deposited at the transfer facility.

This Court struck down the ordinance, holding that it discriminated against interstate commerce by "hoard[ing] solid waste, and the demand to get rid of it, for the benefit of the preferred processing facility." According to the dissent, Clarkstown's ostensibly pri-

---

1. Tipping fees are disposal charges levied against collectors who drop off waste at a processing facility. They are called "tipping" fees because garbage trucks literally tip their back end to dump out the carried waste. As of 1995, haulers in the Counties had to pay tipping fees of at least $86 per ton, a price that ballooned to as much as $172 per ton if a particular load contained more than 25% recyclables.

vate transfer station was "essentially a municipal facility," and this distinction should have saved Clarkstown's ordinance because favoring local government is by its nature different from favoring a particular private company. The majority did not comment on the dissent's public-private distinction....

The *Carbone* majority stated that "[t]he *only conceivable distinction*" between the laws in the local processing cases and Clarkstown's flow control ordinance was that Clarkstown's ordinance favored a single local business, rather than a group of them.

If the Court thought Clarkstown's processing facility was public, that additional distinction was not merely "conceivable"—it was conceived, and discussed at length, by three Justices in dissent. *Carbone* cannot be regarded as having decided the public-private question.... Because the question is now squarely presented on the facts of the case before us, we decide that such flow control ordinances do not discriminate against interstate commerce for purposes of the Dormant Commerce Clause....

II-C. Compelling reasons justify treating these laws differently from laws favoring particular private businesses over their competitors. "Conceptually, of course, any notion of discrimination assumes a comparison of substantially similar entities." *General Motors Corp. v. Tracy* (1997). But States and municipalities are not private businesses—far from it.

Unlike private enterprise, government is vested with the responsibility of protecting the health, safety, and welfare of its citizens....

Given these differences, it does not make sense to regard laws favoring local government and laws favoring private industry with equal skepticism. As our local processing cases demonstrate, when a law favors in-state business over out-of-state competition, rigorous scrutiny is appropriate because the law is often the product of "simple economic protectionism." Laws favoring local government, by contrast, may be directed toward any number of legitimate goals unrelated to protectionism. Here the flow control ordinances enable the Counties to pursue particular policies with respect to the handling and treatment of waste generated in the Counties, while allocating the costs of those policies on citizens and businesses according to the volume of waste they generate.

The contrary approach of treating public and private entities the same under the Dormant Commerce Clause would lead to unprecedented and unbounded interference by the courts with state and local government. The Dormant Commerce Clause is not a roving license for federal courts to decide what activities are appropriate for state and local government to undertake, and what activities must be the province of private market competition. In this case, the citizens of Oneida and Herkimer Counties have chosen the government to provide waste management services, with a limited role for the private sector in arranging for transport of waste from the curb to the public facilities. The citizens could have left the entire matter for the private sector, in which case any regulation they undertook could not discriminate against interstate commerce. But it was also open to them to vest responsibility for the matter with their government, and to adopt flow control ordinances to support the government effort. It is not the office of the Commerce Clause to control the decision of the voters on whether government or the private sector should provide waste management services. "The Commerce Clause significantly limits the ability of States and localities to regulate or otherwise burden the flow of interstate commerce, but it does not elevate free trade above all other values." *Maine v. Taylor.* See *Exxon Corp. v. Governor of Maryland* (1978) (Commerce Clause does not protect "the particular structure or method of operation" of a market).

We should be particularly hesitant to interfere with the Counties' efforts under the guise of the Commerce Clause because "[w]aste disposal is both typically and traditionally a local government function." ...

Finally, it bears mentioning that the most palpable harm imposed by the ordinances—more expensive trash removal is likely to fall upon the very people who voted for the laws. Our Dormant Commerce Clause cases often find discrimination when a state shifts the costs of regulation to other states, because when "the burden of state regulation falls on interests outside the state, it is unlikely to be alleviated by the operation of those political restraints normally exerted when interests within the state *are affected*." *Southern Pacific Co. v.* Arizona (1945). Here, the citizens and businesses of the Counties bear the costs of the ordinances. There is no reason to step in and hand local businesses a victory they could not obtain through the political process.

We hold that the Counties' flow control ordinances, which treat in-state private business interests exactly the same as out-of-state ones, do not "discriminate against interstate commerce" for purposes of the Dormant Commerce Clause.

II-D. The Counties' flow control ordinances are properly analyzed under the test set forth in *Pike v. Bruce Church, Inc.* (1970), which is reserved for laws "directed to legitimate local concerns, with effects upon interstate commerce that are only incidental." *Philadelphia v. New Jersey*. Under the *Pike* test, we will uphold a nondiscriminatory statute like this one "unless the burden imposed on [interstate] commerce is clearly excessive in relation to the putative local benefits." ... We find it unnecessary to decide whether the ordinances impose any incidental burden on interstate commerce because any arguable burden does not exceed the public benefits of the ordinances. The ordinances give the Counties a convenient and effective way to finance their integrated package of waste disposal services. While "revenue generation is not a local interest that can justify *discrimination* against interstate commerce," we think it is a cognizable benefit for purposes of the *Pike* test.

At the same time, the ordinances are more than financing tools. They increase recycling in at least two ways, conferring significant health and environmental benefits upon the citizens of the Counties. First, they create enhanced incentives for recycling and proper disposal of other kinds of waste. Solid waste disposal is expensive in Oneida-Herkimer, but the Counties accept recyclables and many forms of hazardous waste for free, effectively encouraging their citizens to sort their own trash. Second, by requiring all waste to be deposited at Authority facilities, the Counties have markedly increased their ability to enforce recycling laws. If the haulers could take waste to any disposal site, achieving an equal level of enforcement would be much more costly, if not impossible. For these reasons, any arguable burden the ordinances impose on interstate commerce does not exceed their public benefits.

The Counties' ordinances are exercises of the police power in an effort to address waste disposal, a typical and traditional concern of local government. The haulers nevertheless ask us to hold that laws favoring public entities while treating all private businesses the same are subject to an almost *per se* rule of invalidity, because of asserted discrimination. In the alternative, they maintain that the Counties' laws cannot survive the more permissive *Pike* test, because of asserted burdens on commerce. There is a common thread to these arguments: They are invitations to rigorously scrutinize economic legislation passed under the auspices of the police power. There was a time when this Court presumed to make such binding judgments for society, under the guise of interpreting the Due Process Clause. See *Lochner v. New York* (1905). We should not seek to reclaim that ground for judicial supremacy under the banner of the Dormant Commerce Clause.

The judgments of the United States Court of Appeals for the Second Circuit are affirmed.

It is so ordered.

Justice Scalia, concurring in part. [Omitted.]

Justice Thomas, concurring in the judgment. [Omitted.]

Justice Alito, with whom Justice Stevens and Justice Kennedy join, dissenting. [Omitted.]

Minnesota v. Clover Leaf Creamery Company
449 U.S. 456 (1981)

[Majority: Brennan, Burger (C.J.), Blackmun, Marshall, White, and Stewart. Concurring (in part) and dissenting (in part): Powell. Dissenting: Stevens.]

Justice Brennan delivered the opinion of the Court:

In 1977, the Minnesota Legislature enacted a statute banning the retail sale of milk in plastic nonreturnable, nonrefillable containers, but permitting such sale in other nonreturnable, nonrefillable containers, such as paperboard milk cartons. 1977 Minn. Laws, ch. 268, Minn. Stat. § 116F.21 (1978). Respondents[1] contend that the statute violates the Equal Protection and Commerce Clauses of the Constitution.

I. The purpose of the Minnesota statute is set out as § 1:

> The legislature finds that the use of nonreturnable, nonrefillable containers for the packaging of milk and other milk products presents a solid waste management problem for the state, promotes energy waste, and depletes natural resources. The legislature therefore, in furtherance of the policies stated in Minnesota Statutes, § 116F.01,[2] determines that the use of nonreturnable, nonrefillable containers for packaging milk and other milk products should be discouraged and that the use of returnable and reusable packaging for these products is preferred and should be encouraged. 1977 Minn. Laws, ch. 268, § 1, codified as Minn. Stat. § 116F.21 (1978).

Section 2 of the Act forbids the retail sale of milk and fluid milk products, other than sour cream, cottage cheese, and yogurt, in nonreturnable, nonrefillable rigid or semi-rigid containers composed at least 50% of plastic.[3]

The Act was introduced with the support of the state Pollution Control Agency, Department of Natural Resources, Department of Agriculture, Consumer Services Division, and Energy Agency, and debated vigorously in both houses of the state legislature. Pro-

---

1. Respondents, plaintiffs below, are a Minnesota dairy that owns equipment for producing plastic nonreturnable milk jugs, a Minnesota dairy that leases such equipment, a non-Minnesota company that manufactures such equipment, a Minnesota company that produces plastic nonreturnable milk jugs, a non-Minnesota dairy that sells milk products in Minnesota in plastic nonreturnable milk jugs, a Minnesota milk retailer, a non-Minnesota manufacturer of polyethylene resin that sells such resin in many States, including Minnesota, and a plastics industry trade association.

2. Minnesota Stat. § 116F.01 (1978) provides in relevant part:
   Statement of policy. The legislature seeks to encourage both the reduction of the amount and type of material entering the solid waste stream and the reuse and recycling of materials. Solid waste represents discarded materials and energy resources, and it also represents an economic burden to the people of the state. The recycling of solid waste materials is one alternative for the conservation of material and energy resources, but it is also in the public interest to reduce the amount of materials requiring recycling or disposal.

3. Minnesota is apparently the first State so to regulate milk containers.

ponents of the legislation argued that it would promote resource conservation, ease solid waste disposal problems, and conserve energy. Relying on the results of studies and other information, they stressed the need to stop introduction of the plastic nonreturnable container before it became entrenched in the market. Opponents of the Act, also presenting empirical evidence, argued that the Act would not promote the goals asserted by the proponents, but would merely increase costs of retail milk products and prolong the use of ecologically undesirable paperboard milk cartons.

After the Act was passed, respondents filed suit in Minnesota District Court, seeking to enjoin its enforcement. The court conducted extensive evidentiary hearings into the Act's probable consequences, and found the evidence "in sharp conflict." Nevertheless, finding itself "as factfinder ... obliged to weigh and evaluate this evidence," the court resolved the evidentiary conflicts in favor of respondents, and concluded that the Act "will not succeed in effecting the Legislature's published policy goals...." The court further found that, contrary to the statement of purpose in §1, the "actual basis" for the Act "was to promote the economic interests of certain segments of the local dairy and pulpwood industries at the expense of the economic interests of other segments of the dairy industry and the plastics industry." The court therefore declared the Act "null, void, and unenforceable" and enjoined its enforcement, basing the judgment on substantive due process under the 14th Amendment to the United States Constitution and Art. 1, §7, of the Minnesota Constitution; equal protection under the 14th Amendment; and prohibition of unreasonable burdens on interstate commerce under Art. I, §8, of the United States Constitution.

The State appealed to the Supreme Court of Minnesota, which affirmed the District Court on the federal equal protection and due process grounds, without reaching the Commerce Clause or state-law issues. *Cloverleaf Creamery v. Minnesota* (Minn. 1979). Unlike the District Court, the State Supreme Court found that the purpose of the Act was "to promote the state interests of encouraging the reuse and recycling of materials and reducing the amount and type of material entering the solid waste stream," and acknowledged the legitimacy of this purpose. Nevertheless, ... the State Supreme Court held that "the evidence conclusively demonstrates that the discrimination against plastic nonrefillables is not rationally related to the Act's objectives." We now reverse.

II. The parties agree that the standard of review applicable to this case under the Equal Protection Clause is the familiar "rational basis" test. See *Vance v. Bradley* (1979); *New Orleans v. Dukes* (1976). Moreover, they agree that the purposes of the Act cited by the legislature—promoting resource conservation, easing solid waste disposal problems, and conserving energy—are legitimate state purposes. Thus, the controversy in this case centers on the narrow issue whether the legislative classification between plastic and nonplastic nonreturnable milk containers is rationally related to achievement of the statutory purposes.

[The Court finds that the classification is rational.]

III. The District Court also held that the Minnesota statute is unconstitutional under the Commerce Clause because it imposes an unreasonable burden on interstate commerce.[4] We cannot agree.

When legislating in areas of legitimate local concern, such as environmental protection and resource conservation, States are nonetheless limited by the Commerce Clause.

---

4. The Minnesota Supreme Court did not reach the Commerce Clause issue. The parties and amici have fully briefed and argued the question, and because of the obvious factual connection between the rationality analysis under the Equal Protection Clause and the balancing of interests under the Commerce Clause, we will reach and decide the question....

See ... *Hunt v. Washington Apple Advertising Comm'n* (1977); *Southern Pacific Co. v. Arizona* (1945). If a state law purporting to promote environmental purposes is in reality "simple economic protectionism," we have applied a "virtually per se rule of invalidity." *Philadelphia v. New Jersey* (1978).[5] Even if a statute regulates "evenhandedly," and imposes only "incidental" burdens on interstate commerce, the courts must nevertheless strike it down if "the burden imposed on such commerce is clearly excessive in relation to the putative local benefits." *Pike v. Bruce Church, Inc.* (1970). Moreover, "the extent of the burden that will be tolerated will of course depend on the nature of the local interest involved, and on whether it could be promoted as well with a lesser impact on interstate activities."

Minnesota's statute does not effect "simple protectionism," but "regulates evenhandedly" by prohibiting all milk retailers from selling their products in plastic, nonreturnable milk containers, without regard to whether the milk, the containers, or the sellers are from outside the State. This statute is therefore unlike statutes discriminating against interstate commerce, which we have consistently struck down. E.g., *Lewis v. BT Investment Managers, Inc.* (1980) (Florida statutory scheme prohibiting investment advisory services by bank holding companies with principal offices out of the State); *Hughes v. Oklahoma* (1979) (Oklahoma statute prohibiting the export of natural minnows from the State); *Philadelphia v. New Jersey* (New Jersey statute prohibiting importation of solid and liquid wastes into the State); *Hunt v. Washington Apple Advertising Comm'n* (North Carolina statute imposing additional costs on Washington, but not on North Carolina, apple shippers).

Since the statute does not discriminate between interstate and intrastate commerce, the controlling question is whether the incidental burden imposed on interstate commerce by the Minnesota Act is "clearly excessive in relation to the putative local benefits." *Pike v. Bruce Church, Inc.* We conclude that it is not.

The burden imposed on interstate commerce by the statute is relatively minor. Milk products may continue to move freely across the Minnesota border, and since most dairies package their products in more than one type of containers, the inconvenience of having to conform to different packaging requirements in Minnesota and the surrounding States should be slight.... Within Minnesota, business will presumably shift from manufacturers of plastic nonreturnable containers to producers of paperboard cartons, refillable bottles, and plastic pouches, but there is no reason to suspect that the gainers will be Minnesota firms, or the losers out-of-state firms. Indeed, two of the three dairies, the sole milk retailer, and the sole milk container producer challenging the statute in this litigation are Minnesota firms.[6]

Pulpwood producers are the only Minnesota industry likely to benefit significantly from the Act at the expense of out-of-state firms. Respondents point out that plastic resin, the raw material used for making plastic nonreturnable milk jugs, is produced entirely by

---

5. A court may find that a state law constitutes "economic protectionism" on proof either of discriminatory effect, see *Philadelphia v. New Jersey*, or of discriminatory purpose, see *Hunt v. Washington Apple Advertising Comm'n*. Respondents advance a "discriminatory purpose" argument, relying on a finding by the District Court that the Act's "actual basis was to promote the economic interests of certain segments of the local dairy and pulpwood industries at the expense of the economic interests of other segments of the dairy industry and the plastics industry." We have already considered and rejected this argument in the equal protection context, and do so in this context as well.

6. The existence of major in-state interests adversely affected by the Act is a powerful safeguard against legislative abuse. *South Carolina State Highway Dept. v. Barnwell Bros., Inc.* (1938).

non-Minnesota firms, while pulpwood, used for making paperboard, is a major Minnesota product. Nevertheless, it is clear that respondents exaggerate the degree of burden on out-of-state interests, both because plastics will continue to be used in the production of plastic pouches, plastic returnable bottles, and paperboard itself, and because out-of-state pulpwood producers will presumably absorb some of the business generated by the Act.

Even granting that the out-of-state plastics industry is burdened relatively more heavily than the Minnesota pulpwood industry, we find that this burden is not "clearly excessive" in light of the substantial state interest in promoting conservation of energy and other natural resources and easing solid waste disposal problems, which we have already reviewed in the context of equal protection analysis. We find these local benefits ample to support Minnesota's decision under the Commerce Clause. Moreover, we find that no approach with "a lesser impact on interstate activities," *Pike v. Bruce Church, Inc.*, is available. Respondents have suggested several alternative statutory schemes, but these alternatives are either more burdensome on commerce than the Act (as, for example, banning all nonreturnables) or less likely to be effective (as, for example, providing incentives for recycling).

In *Exxon Corp. v. Governor of Maryland*, we upheld a Maryland statute barring producers and refiners of petroleum products—all of which were out-of-state businesses—from retailing gasoline in the State. We stressed that the Commerce Clause "protects the interstate market, not particular interstate firms, from prohibitive or burdensome regulations." A nondiscriminatory regulation serving substantial state purposes is not invalid simply because it causes some business to shift from a predominantly out-of-state industry to a predominantly in-state industry. Only if the burden on interstate commerce clearly outweighs the State's legitimate purposes does such a regulation violate the Commerce Clause.

The judgment of the Minnesota Supreme Court is Reversed.

Justice Rehnquist took no part in the consideration or decision of this case.

Justice Powell, concurring in part and dissenting in part. [Omitted.]

Justice Stevens, dissenting. [Omitted.]

Review Questions

1. What is the Dormant Commerce Clause?
2. In these Dormant Commerce Clause cases, has Congress acted or are we concerned with the effect of the Commerce Clause on state regulation when there is no contradictory federal legislation?
3. Where have we seen this issue before?
4. If the Court finds that congressional power over commerce precludes the exercise of state power, does the Court have the final word on the subject? If not, what institution does?
5. As to subjects within the federal commerce power which are not "exclusively" reserved to federal regulation, may Congress displace state power if it chooses to do so?
6. Review the diagrams entitled: *The Commerce Power: The View of the Court*. Look at each of the diagrams. What situations do they represent? Which represents the negative effect of the Commerce Clause in the absence of federal legislation on the sub-

ject? Note how the situation changes when Congress legislates and asserts federal power over a subject or legislates and turns the subject over to the states.

7. From 1936 until quite recently, the Court uniformly used a rational basis test to evaluate challenges to congressional statutes based on the Commerce Clause. In Dormant Commerce Clause cases decided during the same time period, the Court often employed what it sometimes described as a strict scrutiny test. How can you explain the difference?

8. Consider the conflicting values.

    a. What are the virtues of federalism, of having a system of state and local as well as national government? Is there a relation between state power and democratic government? What is it?

    b. What is the great tension here? Is it between the values of federalism (particularly state regulatory power) and congressional power over commerce? Or is it between the values of federalism and state power on one side and a common market capitalism protected against much state regulation on the other? Is there a collision here between state power and relatively unregulated capitalism?

D. Extra-Territorial Regulation

In *Brown-Forman Distillers Corp. v. New York State Liquor Authority* (1986), the Court struck down a New York statute designed to see that New York liquor consumers enjoyed as low prices for their alcohol as those in other states. The following description of the case comes from *Healy v. The Beer Institute* (1989):

> The New York law at issue in *Brown-Forman* required every liquor distiller or producer selling to wholesalers within the State to affirm that the prices charged for every bottle or case of liquor were no higher than the lowest price at which the same product would be sold in any other State during the month covered by the particular affirmation. Brown-Forman was a liquor distiller that offered "promotional allowances" to wholesalers purchasing Brown-Forman products. The New York Liquor Authority, however, did not allow Brown-Forman to operate its rebate scheme in New York and, moreover, determined for the purposes of the affirmation law that the promotional allowances lowered the effective price charged to wholesalers outside New York. Because other States with affirmation laws similar to New York's did not deem the promotional allowances to lower the price charged to wholesalers, appellant argued that the New York law offered the company the Hobson's choice of lowering its New York prices, thereby violating the affirmation laws of other States, or of discontinuing the promotional allowances altogether. This, appellant alleged, amounted to extraterritorial regulation of interstate commerce in violation of the Commerce Clause.
>
> This Court agreed, reaffirming and elaborating on our established view that a state law that has the "practical effect" of regulating commerce occurring wholly outside that State's borders is invalid under the Commerce Clause. We began by reviewing past decisions, starting with *Baldwin v. G. A. F. Seelig, Inc.* (1935). The Court in *Seelig* struck down a New York statute that set minimum prices for milk purchased from producers in New York and other States and banned the resale within New York of milk that had been purchased for a lower price. Because Ver-

mont dairy farmers produced milk at a lower cost than New York dairy farmers, the effect of the statute was to eliminate the competitive economic advantage they enjoyed by equalizing the price of milk from all sources. Writing for the Court, Justice Cardozo pronounced that the Commerce Clause does not permit a State "to establish a wage scale or a scale of prices for use in other states, and to bar the sale of the products ... unless the scale has been observed." Relying on *Seelig*, the Court in *Brown-Forman* concluded: "While a State may seek lower prices for its consumers, it may not insist that producers or consumers in other States surrender whatever competitive advantages they may possess." ...

Applying these principles, we concluded that the New York statute had an impermissible extraterritorial effect: "Once a distiller has posted prices in New York, it is not free to change its prices elsewhere in the United States during the relevant month. Forcing a merchant to seek regulatory approval in one State before undertaking a transaction in another directly regulates interstate commerce." Although New York might regulate the sale of liquor within its borders, and might seek low prices for its residents, it was prohibited by the Commerce Clause from "'project[ing] its legislation into [other States] by regulating the price to be paid'" for liquor in those States. [T]he Court did not find the prospect of these extraterritorial effects to be speculative. The majority rejected as "Pollyannaish" the dissent's suggestion that flexible application by the relevant administrative bodies would obviate the problem and noted that the proliferation of affirmation laws after *Seagram & Sons, Inc. v. Hostetter* (1966) had greatly multiplied the likelihood that distillers would be subject to blatantly inconsistent obligations.

E. The Market Participant Exception

Reeves, Inc. v. Stake
447 U.S. 429 (1980)

[Majority: Blackmun, Burger (C.J.), Marshall, Stewart, and Rehnquist. Dissenting: Powell, Brennan, White, and Stevens.]

Mr. Justice Blackmun delivered the opinion of the Court.

The issue in this case is whether, consistent with the Commerce Clause, U. S. Const., Art. I, §8, cl. 3, the State of South Dakota, in a time of shortage, may confine the sale of the cement it produces solely to its residents.

I. In 1919, South Dakota undertook plans to build a cement plant. The project, a product of the State's then prevailing Progressive political movement, was initiated in response to recent regional cement shortages that "interfered with and delayed both public and private enterprises," and that were "threatening the people of this state." *Eakin v. South Dakota State Cement Comm'n* (S.D. 1921).[1] In 1920, the South Dakota Cement Commission an-

---

1. It was said that the plant was built because the only cement plant in the State "had been operating successfully for a number of years until it had been bought by the so-called trust and closed down." *Report of South Dakota State Cement Commission* 6 (1920). In its report advocating creation of a cement plant, the Commission noted both the substantial profits being made by private producers in the prevailing market, and the fact that producers outside the State were "now supplying all the cement used in" South Dakota. Under the circumstances, the Commission reasoned, it would not be to the "capitalists['] ... advantage to build a new plant within the state." This skepticism regarding private industry's ability to serve public needs was a hallmark of Progressivism. See, e.g., R. Hofs-

ticipated "[t]hat there would be a ready market for the entire output of the plant within the state." Report of State Cement Commission 9 (1920). The plant, however, located at Rapid City, soon produced more cement than South Dakotans could use. Over the years, buyers in no less than nine nearby States purchased cement from the State's plant. Between 1970 and 1977, some 40% of the plant's output went outside the State.

The plant's list of out-of-state cement buyers included petitioner Reeves, Inc. Reeves is a ready-mix concrete distributor organized under Wyoming law and with facilities in Buffalo, Gillette, and Sheridan, Wyo. From the beginning of its operations in 1958, and until 1978, Reeves purchased about 95% of its cement from the South Dakota plant. In 1977, its purchases were $1,172,000. In turn, Reeves has supplied three northwestern Wyoming counties with more than half their ready-mix concrete needs. For 20 years the relationship between Reeves and the South Dakota cement plant was amicable, uninterrupted, and mutually profitable.

As the 1978 construction season approached, difficulties at the plant slowed production. Meanwhile, a booming construction industry spurred demand for cement both regionally and nationally. The plant found itself unable to meet all orders. Faced with the same type of "serious cement shortage" that inspired the plant's construction, the Commission "reaffirmed its policy of supplying all South Dakota customers first and to honor all contract commitments, with the remaining volume allocated on a first come, first served basis."

Reeves, which had no pre-existing long-term supply contract, was hit hard and quickly by this development. On June 30, 1978, the plant informed Reeves that it could not continue to fill Reeves' orders, and on July 5, it turned away a Reeves truck. Unable to find another supplier, Reeves was forced to cut production by 76% in mid-July.

On July 19, Reeves brought this suit against the Commission, challenging the plant's policy of preferring South Dakota buyers, and seeking injunctive relief. After conducting a hearing and receiving briefs and affidavits, the District Court found no substantial issue of material fact and permanently enjoined the Commission's practice. The court reasoned that South Dakota's "hoarding" was inimical to the national free market envisioned by the Commerce Clause.

---

tadter, *The Age of Reform* 227 (1955) ("In the Progressive era the entire structure of business ... became the object of a widespread hostility"). South Dakota, earlier a bastion of Populism, *id.*, at 50, became a leading Progressivist State. See R. Nye, *Midwestern Progressive Politics* 217–18 (1959); G. Mowry, *Theodore Roosevelt and the Progressive Movement* 155, and n. 125 (1946). Roosevelt carried South Dakota in the election of 1912, *id.*, at 281, n. 69, and Robert La Follette—on a platform calling for public ownership of railroads and waterpower, see K. MacKay, *The Progressive Movement of 1924*, pp. 270–71 (app. 4) (1966)—ran strongly (36.9%) in the State in 1924. *Congressional Quarterly's Guide to U.S. Elections* 287 (1975).

The backdrop against which the South Dakota cement project was initiated is described in H. Schell, *History of South Dakota* 268–69 (3d ed. 1975):

> Although a majority of the voters [in 1918] had seemingly subscribed to a state-ownership philosophy, it was a question how far the Republican administration at Pierre would go in fulfilling campaign promises. As [Governor] Norbeck entered upon his second term, he again urged a state hail insurance law and advocated steps toward a state-owned coal mine, cement plant, and state-owned stockyards. He also recommended an appropriation for surveying dam sites for hydroelectric development. The lawmakers readily enacted these recommendations into law, except for the stockyards proposal....
>
> In retrospect, [Norbeck's] program must be viewed as a part of the Progressives' campaign against monopolistic prices. There was, moreover, the fervent desire to make the services of the state government available to agriculture.... These were basic tenets of the Progressive philosophy of government.

The United States Court of Appeals for the Eighth Circuit reversed.... We granted Reeves' petition for certiorari to consider once again the impact of the Commerce Clause on state proprietary activity.

II-A. [*Hughes v.*] *Alexandria Scrap* (1976) concerned a Maryland program designed to remove abandoned automobiles from the State's roadways and junkyards. To encourage recycling, a "bounty" was offered for every Maryland-titled junk car converted into scrap. Processors located both in and outside Maryland were eligible to collect these subsidies. The legislation, as initially enacted in 1969, required a processor seeking a bounty to present documentation evidencing ownership of the wrecked car. This requirement however, did not apply to "hulks," inoperable automobiles over eight years old. In 1974, the statute was amended to extend documentation requirements to hulks, which comprised a large majority of the junk cars being processed. Departing from prior practice, the new law imposed more exacting documentation requirements on out-of-state than in-state processors. By making it less remunerative for suppliers to transfer vehicles outside Maryland, the reform triggered a "precipitate decline in the number of bounty-eligible hulks supplied to appellee's [Virginia] plant from Maryland sources." Indeed, "[t]he practical effect was substantially the same as if Maryland had withdrawn altogether the availability of bounties on hulks delivered by unlicensed suppliers to licensed non-Maryland processors."

Invoking the Commerce Clause, a three-judge District Court struck down the legislation. It observed that the amendment imposed "substantial burdens upon the free flow of interstate commerce," and reasoned that the discriminatory program was not the least disruptive means of achieving the State's articulated objective. See generally *Pike v. Bruce Church, Inc.* (1970).

This Court reversed. It recognized the persuasiveness of the lower court's analysis if the inherent restrictions of the Commerce Clause were deemed applicable. In the Court's view, however, *Alexandria Scrap* did not involve "the kind of action with which the Commerce Clause is concerned." Unlike prior cases voiding state laws inhibiting interstate trade, "Maryland has not sought to prohibit the flow of hulks, or to regulate the conditions under which it may occur. Instead, it has entered into the market itself to bid up their price, as a purchaser, in effect, of a potential article of interstate commerce," and has restricted "its trade to its own citizens or businesses within the State."

Having characterized Maryland as a market participant, rather than as a market regulator, the Court found no reason to "believe the Commerce Clause was intended to require independent justification for [the State's] action." The Court couched its holding in unmistakably broad terms. "Nothing in the purposes animating the Commerce Clause prohibits a State, in the absence of congressional action, from participating in the market and exercising the right to favor its own citizens over others."

II-B. The basic distinction drawn in *Alexandria Scrap* between States as market participants and States as market regulators makes good sense and sound law. As that case explains, the Commerce Clause responds principally to state taxes and regulatory measures impeding free private trade in the national marketplace. *Hughes v. Alexandria Scrap*, citing *H.P. Hood & Sons v. DuMond* (1949) (referring to "home embargoes," "customs duties," and "regulations" excluding imports). There is no indication of a constitutional plan to limit the ability of the States themselves to operate freely in the free market. See L. Tribe, *American Constitutional Law* 336 (1978) ("the Commerce Clause was directed, as an historical matter, only at regulatory and taxing actions taken by states in their sovereign capacity"). The precedents comport with this distinction.

Restraint in this area is also counseled by considerations of state sovereignty,[2] the role of each State "'as guardian and trustee for its people,'" *Heim v. McCall* (1915), quoting *Atkin v. Kansas* (1903), and "the long recognized right of trader or manufacturer, engaged in an entirely private business, freely to exercise his own independent discretion as to parties with whom he will deal." *United States v. Colgate & Co.* (1919). Moreover, state proprietary activities may be, and often are, burdened with the same restrictions imposed on private market participants. Evenhandedness suggests that, when acting as proprietors, States should similarly share existing freedoms from federal constraints, including the inherent limits of the Commerce Clause.... Finally, as this case illustrates, the competing considerations in cases involving state proprietary action often will be subtle, complex, politically charged, and difficult to assess under traditional Commerce Clause analysis. Given these factors, *Alexandria Scrap* wisely recognizes that, as a rule, the adjustment of interests in this context is a task better suited for Congress than this Court.

III. South Dakota, as a seller of cement, unquestionably fits the "market participant" label more comfortably than a State acting to subsidize local scrap processors. Thus, the general rule of *Alexandria Scrap* plainly applies here. Petitioner argues, however, that the exemption for marketplace participation necessarily admits of exceptions. While conceding that possibility, we perceive in this case no sufficient reason to depart from the general rule.

III-A. In finding a Commerce Clause violation, the District Court emphasized "that the Commission ... made an election to become part of the interstate commerce system." The gist of this reasoning, repeated by petitioner here, is that one good turn deserves another. Having long exploited the interstate market, South Dakota should not be permitted to withdraw from it when a shortage arises. This argument is not persuasive. It is somewhat self-serving to say that South Dakota has "exploited" the interstate market. An equally fair characterization is that neighboring States long have benefited from South Dakota's foresight and industry. Viewed in this light, it is not surprising that *Alexandria Scrap* rejected an argument that the 1974 Maryland legislation challenged there was invalid because cars abandoned in Maryland had been processed in neighboring States for five years. As in *Alexandria Scrap*, we must conclude that "this chronology does not distinguish the case, for Commerce Clause purposes, from one in which a State offered [cement] only to domestic [buyers] from the start."

Our rejection of petitioner's market-exploitation theory fundamentally refocuses analysis. It means that to reverse we would have to void a South Dakota "residents only" policy even if it had been enforced from the plant's very first days. Such a holding, however, would interfere significantly with a State's ability to structure relations exclusively with its own citizens. It would also threaten the future fashioning of effective and creative programs for solving local problems and distributing government largesse. A healthy regard for federalism and good government renders us reluctant to risk these results.

---

2. See *American Yearbook Co. v. Askew* (M.D. Fla.1972) ("ad hoc" inquiry into burdening of interstate commerce "would unduly interfere with state proprietary functions if not bring them to a standstill"). Considerations of sovereignty independently dictate that marketplace actions involving "integral operations in areas of traditional governmental functions"—such as the employment of certain state workers—may not be subject even to congressional regulation pursuant to the commerce power. *National League of Cities v. Usery* (1976). It follows easily that the intrinsic limits of the Commerce Clause do not prohibit state marketplace conduct that falls within this sphere. Even where "integral operations" are not implicated, States may fairly claim some measure of a sovereign interest in retaining freedom to decide how, with whom, and for whose benefit to deal. *The Supreme Court, 1975 Term*, 90 Harv. L. Rev. 1, 56, 63 (1976).

To stay experimentation in things social and economic is a grave responsibility. Denial of the right to experiment may be fraught with serious consequences to the Nation. It is one of the happy incidents of the federal system that a single courageous State may, if its citizens choose, serve as a laboratory; and try novel social and economic experiments without risk to the rest of the country. *New State Ice Co. v. Liebmann* (1932) (Brandeis, J., dissenting).

III-B. Undaunted by these considerations, petitioner advances four more arguments for reversal:

First, petitioner protests that South Dakota's preference for its residents responds solely to the "non-governmental objectiv[e]" of protectionism. Therefore, petitioner argues, the policy is per se invalid. See *Philadelphia v. New Jersey* (1978).

We find the label "protectionism" of little help in this context. The State's refusal to sell to buyers other than South Dakotans is "protectionist" only in the sense that it limits benefits generated by a state program to those who fund the state treasury and whom the State was created to serve. Petitioner's argument apparently also would characterize as "protectionist" rules restricting to state residents the enjoyment of state educational institutions, energy generated by a state-run plant, police and fire protection, and agricultural improvement and business development programs. Such policies, while perhaps "protectionist" in a loose sense, reflect the essential and patently unobjectionable purpose of state government—to serve the citizens of the State.

Second, petitioner echoes the District Court's warning:

> If a state in this union, were allowed to hoard its commodities or resources for the use of their own residents only, a drastic situation might evolve. For example, Pennsylvania or Wyoming might keep their coal, the northwest its timber, and the mining states their minerals. The result being that embargo may be retaliated by embargo and commerce would be halted at state lines.

See, e.g., *Baldwin v. Montana Fish & Game Comm'n* (1978). This argument, although rooted in the core purpose of the Commerce Clause, does not fit the present facts. Cement is not a natural resource, like coal, timber, wild game, or minerals. Cf. *Hughes v. Oklahoma* (1979) (minnows); *Philadelphia v. New Jersey* (landfill sites); *Pennsylvania v. West Virginia* (1923) (natural gas).... It is the end product of a complex process whereby a costly physical plant and human labor act on raw materials. South Dakota has not sought to limit access to the State's limestone or other materials used to make cement. Nor has it restricted the ability of private firms or sister States to set up plants within its borders. Moreover, petitioner has not suggested that South Dakota possesses unique access to the materials needed to produce cement. Whatever limits might exist on a State's ability to invoke the *Alexandria Scrap* exemption to hoard resources which by happenstance are found there, those limits do not apply here.

③ Third, it is suggested that the South Dakota program is infirm because it places South Dakota suppliers of ready-mix concrete at a competitive advantage in the out-of-state market; Wyoming suppliers, such as petitioner, have little chance against South Dakota suppliers who can purchase cement from the State's plant and freely sell beyond South Dakota's borders.

The force of this argument is seriously diminished, if not eliminated by several considerations. The argument necessarily implies that the South Dakota scheme would be unobjectionable if sales in other States were totally barred. It therefore proves too much, for it would tolerate even a greater measure of protectionism and stifling of interstate commerce than the challenged system allows.... *Alexandria Scrap* approved a state program that "not only ... effectively protect[ed] scrap processors with existing plants in Maryland from the pressures of competitors with nearby out-of-state plants, but [that] implicitly offer[ed] to extend similar protection to any competitor ... willing to erect a scrap processing facility within Maryland's boundaries." Finally, the competitive plight of out-of-state ready-mix suppliers cannot be laid solely at the feet of South Dakota. It is attributable as well to their own States' not providing or attracting alternative sources of supply and to the suppliers' own failure to guard against shortages by executing long-term supply contracts with the South Dakota plant.

In its last argument, petitioner urges that, had South Dakota not acted, free market forces would have generated an appropriate level of supply at free market prices for all buyers in the region. Having replaced free market forces, South Dakota should be forced to replicate how the free market would have operated under prevailing conditions.

This argument appears to us to be simplistic and speculative. The very reason South Dakota built its plant was because the free market had failed adequately to supply the region with cement. See n. 1, *supra*. There is no indication, and no way to know, that private industry would have moved into petitioner's market area, and would have ensured a supply of cement to petitioner either prior to or during the 1978 construction season. Indeed, it is quite possible that petitioner would never have existed—far less operated successfully for 20 years—had it not been for South Dakota cement.

III-C. We conclude, then, that the arguments for invalidating South Dakota's resident-preference program are weak at best. Whatever residual force inheres in them is more than offset by countervailing considerations of policy and fairness. Reversal would discourage similar state projects, even though this project demonstrably has served the needs of state residents and has helped the entire region for more than a half century. Reversal also would rob South Dakota of the intended benefit of its foresight, risk, and industry.[3] Under these circumstances, there is no reason to depart from the general rule of *Alexandria Scrap*.

The judgment of the United States Court of Appeals is affirmed.

Mr. Justice Powell, with whom Mr. Justice Brennan, Mr. Justice White, and Mr. Justice Stevens join, dissenting.

The South Dakota Cement Commission has ordered that in times of shortage the state cement plant must turn away out-of-state customers until all orders from South Dakotans are filled. This policy represents precisely the kind of economic protectionism that the Commerce Clause was intended to prevent. The Court, however, finds no violation of the Commerce Clause, solely because the State produces the cement. I agree with the Court that the State of South Dakota may provide cement for its public needs without violating the Commerce Clause. But I cannot agree that South Dakota may withhold its cement from interstate commerce in order to benefit private citizens and businesses within the State....

---

3. The risk borne by South Dakota in establishing the cement plant is not to be underestimated. As explained in n. 1, the cement plant was one of several projects through which the Progressive state government sought to deal with local problems. The fate of other similar projects illustrates the risk borne by South Dakota taxpayers in setting up the cement plant at a cost of some $2 million. Thus, "[t]he coal mine was sold in early 1934 for $5,500 with an estimated loss of nearly $175,000 for its fourteen years of operation. The 1933 Legislature also liquidated the state bonding department and the state hail insurance project. The total loss to the taxpayers from the latter venture was approximately $265,000." H. Schell, *History of South Dakota*, 286 (3d ed. 1975).

By enforcing the Commerce Clause in this case, the Court would work no unfairness on the people of South Dakota. They still could reserve cement for public projects and share in whatever return the plant generated. They could not, however, use the power of the State to furnish themselves with cement forbidden to the people of neighboring States.

The creation of a free national economy was a major goal of the States when they resolved to unite under the Federal Constitution. The decision today cannot be reconciled with that purpose.

F. The Dormant Commerce Clause Reconsidered

In *Camps Newfound/Owatonna, Inc. v. Town of Harrison* (1997), a church camp brought an action challenging the constitutionality of Maine's property tax exemption statute for charitable institutions. The Court held 5–4 that the exemption statute, which singled out institutions that served mostly state residents for beneficial tax treatment and penalized those institutions that did principally interstate business, violated the Dormant Commerce Clause. The government argued that it was attempting to encourage charities that focused on local concerns.

In dissent, Justice Scalia, writing for Rehnquist, C.J., and Thomas, J., protested that:

> The Court's negative-commerce-clause jurisprudence has drifted far from its moorings. Originally designed to create a national market for commercial activity, it is today invoked to prevent a State from giving a tax break to charities that benefit the State's inhabitants. In my view, Maine's tax exemption, which excuses from taxation only that property used to relieve the State of its burden of caring for its residents, survives even our most demanding Commerce-Clause scrutiny....

Justice Thomas also launched a blistering attack, reproduced below, on the entire concept of the Dormant Commerce Clause.

> **Justice Thomas, ... dissenting.**
>
> The tax at issue here is a tax on real estate, the quintessential asset that does not move in interstate commerce. Maine exempts from its otherwise generally applicable property tax, and thereby subsidizes, certain charitable organizations that provide the bulk of their charity to Maine's own residents. By invalidating Maine's tax assessment on the real property of charitable organizations primarily serving non-Maine residents, because of the tax's alleged *indirect* effect on interstate commerce, the majority has essentially created a "dormant" Necessary and Proper Clause to supplement the "dormant" Commerce Clause. This move works a significant, unwarranted, and, in my view, improvident expansion in our "dormant," or "negative," Commerce Clause jurisprudence. For that reason, I join Justice Scalia's dissenting opinion.
>
> I write separately, however, because I believe that the improper expansion undertaken today is possible only because our negative Commerce Clause jurisprudence, developed primarily to invalidate discriminatory state taxation of interstate commerce, was already both overbroad and unnecessary. It was overbroad because, unmoored from any constitutional text, it brought within the supervisory authority of the federal courts state action far afield from the discriminatory taxes it was primarily designed to check. It was unnecessary because the Constitution would seem to provide an express check on the States' power to levy certain discriminatory taxes on the commerce of

other States—not in the judicially created negative Commerce Clause, but in the Article I, §10 Import-Export Clause, our decision in *Woodruff v. Parham* (1869), notwithstanding. That the expansion effected by today's decision finds some support in the morass of our negative Commerce Clause case law only serves to highlight the need to abandon that failed jurisprudence and to consider restoring the original Import-Export Clause check on discriminatory state taxation to what appears to be its proper role. [T]he tax (and tax exemption) at issue in this case seems easily to survive Import-Export Clause scrutiny; I would therefore, in all likelihood, sustain Maine's tax under that Clause as well, were we to apply it instead of the judicially created negative Commerce Clause.

I. The negative Commerce Clause has no basis in the text of the Constitution, makes little sense, and has proved virtually unworkable in application. In one fashion or another, every Member of the current Court and a goodly number of our predecessors have at least recognized these problems, if not been troubled by them. Because the expansion effected by today's holding further undermines the delicate balance in what we have termed "Our Federalism," *Younger v. Harris* (1971), I think it worth revisiting the underlying justifications for our involvement in the negative aspects of the Commerce Clause, and the compelling arguments demonstrating why those justifications are illusory.

To cover its exercise of judicial power in an area for which there is no textual basis, the Court has historically offered two different theories in support of its negative Commerce Clause jurisprudence. The first theory posited was that the Commerce Clause itself constituted an exclusive grant of power to Congress. The "exclusivity" rationale was likely wrong from the outset, however. See, e.g., *The Federalist* No. 32, (A. Hamilton) ("[N]otwithstanding the affirmative grants of general authorities, there has been the most pointed care in those cases where it was deemed improper that the like authorities should reside in the states, to insert negative clauses prohibiting the exercise of them by the states"). It was seriously questioned even in early cases. See *License Cases* (1847) (four, and arguably five, of the seven participating Justices contending that the Commerce Clause was not exclusive.) And, in any event, the Court has long since "repudiated" the notion that the Commerce Clause operates as an exclusive grant of power to Congress, and thereby forecloses state action respecting interstate commerce. *Southern Pacific Co. v. Arizona* (1945) ("Ever since *Willson v. Black-Bird Creek Marsh Co.* and *Cooley v. Board of Wardens* it has been recognized that, in the absence of conflicting legislation by Congress, there is a residuum of power in the state to make laws governing matters of local concern which nevertheless in some measure affect interstate commerce or even, to some extent, regulate it")....

The second theory offered to justify creation of a negative Commerce Clause is that Congress, by its silence, pre-empts state legislation. See *Robbins v. Shelby County Taxing Dist.* (1887) (asserting that congressional silence evidences congressional intent that there be no state regulation of commerce). In other words, we presumed that congressional "inaction" was "equivalent to a declaration that inter-State commerce shall be free and untrammelled." *Welton v. Missouri* (1876). To the extent that the "preemption-by-silence" rationale ever made sense, it too has long since been rejected by this Court in virtually every analogous area of the law.

For example, ever since the watershed case of *Erie R. Co. v. Tompkins* (1938), this Court has rejected the notion that it can create a federal common law to fill in great silences left by Congress, and thereby pre-empt state law. We have recognized that "a federal court could not generally apply a federal rule of decision, despite the existence of jurisdiction, in the absence of an applicable Act of Congress." *Milwaukee v. Illinois* (1981).

The limited areas in which we have created federal common law typically involve either uniquely federal issues or the rights and responsibilities of the United States or its agents. But where a federal rule is not essential, or where state law already operates within a particular field, we have applied state law rather than opting to create federal common law....

Similarly, even where Congress has legislated in an area subject to its authority, our pre-emption jurisprudence explicitly rejects the notion that mere congressional silence on a particular issue may be read as preempting state law:

As is always the case in our pre-emption jurisprudence, where "federal law is said to bar state action in fields of traditional state regulation ... we have worked on the 'assumption that the historic police powers of the States were not to be superseded by the Federal Act unless that was the clear and manifest purpose of Congress.'" *California Div. of Labor Standards Enforcement v. Dillingham Constr. N.A., Inc.* (1997).

To be sure, we have overcome our reluctance to preempt state law in two types of situations: (1) where a state law directly conflicts with a federal law; and (2) where Congress, through extensive legislation, can be said to have pre-empted the field. But those two forms of pre-emption provide little aid to defenders of the negative Commerce Clause. Conflict pre-emption only applies when there is a direct clash between an Act of Congress and a state statute, but the very premise of the negative Commerce Clause is the *absence* of congressional action.

Field pre-emption likewise is of little use in areas where Congress has failed to enter the field, and certainly does not support the general proposition of "preemption-by-silence" that is used to provide a veneer of legitimacy to our negative Commerce Clause forays. Furthermore, field pre-emption is itself suspect, at least as applied in the absence of a congressional command that a particular field be pre-empted. Perhaps recognizing this problem, our recent cases have frequently rejected field pre-emption in the absence of statutory language expressly requiring it.... Even when an express pre-emption provision has been enacted by Congress, we have narrowly defined the area to be pre-empted.

In the analogous context of statutory construction, we have similarly refused to rely on congressional inaction to alter the proper construction of a pre-existing statute. And, even more troubling, the "preemption-by-silence" rationale virtually amounts to legislation by default, in apparent violation of the constitutional requirements of bi-cameralism and presentment. Thus, even were we wrongly to assume that congressional silence evidenced a desire to pre-empt some undefined category of state laws, and an intent to delegate such policy-laden categorization to the courts, treating unenacted congressional intent as if it were law would be constitutionally dubious.

In sum, neither of the Court's proffered theoretical justifications—exclusivity or pre-emption-by-silence—currently supports our negative Commerce Clause jurisprudence, if either ever did. Despite the collapse of its theoretical foundation, I suspect we have nonetheless adhered to the negative Commerce Clause because we believed it necessary to check state measures contrary to the perceived *spirit*, if not the actual letter, of the Constitution. Thus, in one of our early uses of the negative Commerce Clause, we invalidated a state tax on the privilege of selling goods "which are not the growth, produce, or manufacture of the State." *Welton v. Missouri* (1876). And in *Cook v. Pennsylvania* (1878), we struck down a state tax on out-of-state goods sold at auction. To this day, we find discriminatory state taxes on out-of-state goods to be "virtually per se invalid" under our negative Commerce Clause. See, e.g., *West Lynn Creamery, Inc. v. Healy* (1994). Though each of these cases reached what intuitively seemed to be a desirable result—and in some cases arguably was the constitutionally *correct* result, as I describe below—

the negative Commerce Clause rationale upon which they rested remains unsettling because of that rationale's lack of a textual basis.

Moreover, our negative Commerce Clause jurisprudence has taken us well beyond the invalidation of obviously discriminatory taxes on interstate commerce. We have used the Clause to make policy-laden judgments that we are ill-equipped and arguably unauthorized to make....

Any test that requires us to assess (1) whether a particular statute serves a "legitimate" local public interest; (2) whether the effects of the statute on interstate commerce are merely "incidental" or "clearly excessive in relation to the putative benefits"; (3) the "nature" of the local interest; and (4) whether there are alternative means of furthering the local interest that have a "lesser impact" on interstate commerce, and even then makes the question "one of degree," surely invites us, if not compels us, to function more as legislators than as judges....

Moreover, our open-ended balancing tests in this area have allowed us to reach different results based merely "on differing assessments of the force of competing analogies." *Oklahoma Tax Comm'n v. Jefferson Lines, Inc.* (1995). The examples are almost too numerous to count, but there is perhaps none that more clearly makes the point than a comparison of our decisions in *Philadelphia v. New Jersey* (1978), and its progeny, on the one hand, and *Bowman v. Chicago & Northwestern R. Co.* (1888), and its progeny, on the other. In *Bowman*, we recognized that States can prohibit the importation of "cattle or meat or other provisions that are diseased or decayed, or otherwise, from their condition and quality, unfit for human use or consumption," a view to which we have adhered for more than a century, see, e.g., *Maine v. Taylor* (1986). In *Philadelphia*, however, we held that New Jersey could not prohibit the importation of "solid or liquid waste which originated or was collected outside the territorial limits of the State." The cases were arguably distinguishable, but only on policy grounds and not on any distinction derived from the text of the Constitution itself.

Similarly, we have in some cases rejected attempts by a State to limit use of the State's own natural resources to that State's residents. See, e.g., *Hughes v. Oklahoma* (1979). But in other cases, we have upheld just such preferential access. Cf. *Baldwin v. Fish and Game Comm'n of Mont.* (1978). Again, the distinctions turned on often subtle policy judgments, not the text of the Constitution.

In my view, none of this policy-laden decision making is proper. Rather, the Court should confine itself to interpreting the text of the Constitution, which itself seems to prohibit in plain terms certain of the more egregious state taxes on interstate commerce described above, and leaves to Congress the policy choices necessary for any further regulation of interstate commerce....

* * *

In *Department of Revenue of Kentucky v. Davis* (2008), the Court followed the rationale of *United Haulers, supra,* rejecting a Dormant Commerce Clause challenge when a state taxed income derived from out-of-state municipal bonds while exempting the income from similar Kentucky bonds.

Concurring, Justice Scalia announced that

> I will apply our negative Commerce Clause doctrine only when *stare decisis* compels me to do so. In my view it is "an unjustified judicial invention, not to be expanded beyond its existing domain." ... *Stare decisis* does not compel invalidation of Kentucky's statute....

Also concurring, Justice Thomas continued his attack on the Dormant Commerce Clause that he began in the Maine camp case:

> I agree with the Court that Kentucky's differential tax scheme is constitutional. But rather than apply a body of doctrine that "has no basis in the Constitution and has proved unworkable in practice," I would entirely "discard the Court's negative Commerce Clause jurisprudence." "[T]he negative Commerce Clause has no basis in the text of the Constitution, makes little sense, and has proved virtually unworkable in application." Because Congress' authority to regulate commerce "among the several States," U. S. Const., Art. I, §8, cl. 3, necessarily includes the power "to prevent state regulation of interstate commerce," the text of the Constitution makes clear that the Legislature—not the Judiciary—bears the responsibility of curbing what it perceives as state regulatory burdens on interstate commerce.
>
> As the Court acknowledges, Kentucky's differential tax scheme is far from unique. For nearly a century, some States have treated income derived from out-of-state bonds differently than that derived from their in-state counterparts. At present, the vast majority of the States do so. The practice is thus both longstanding and widespread, yet Congress has refrained from preempting it. In the "face of [this] congressional silence," we have no authority to invalidate Kentucky's differential tax scheme.

III. The Privileges and Immunities Clause of Article IV

Questions to Consider

1. Review the language of the Article IV Privileges and Immunities Clause. What does the interstate Privileges and Immunities Clause prohibit? What other provisions are contained in Article IV? Do they shed any light on the purposes of the Article IV Privileges and Immunities Clause?

2. What are the steps of analysis the Court appears to follow? What are the elements one must establish to show a violation of the Article IV Privileges and Immunities Clause?

3. Are corporations protected by the clause? Are aliens?

4. What types of interests are protected by the clause? What types of interests are not protected?

5. Could a state statute violate both the Privileges and Immunities Clause of Article IV and also violate the Dormant Commerce Clause?

6. How would you summarize the rules that govern the application of the Privileges and Immunities Clause of Article IV?

Problems to Consider

1. To shrimp in the waters of the state, South Carolina charges a $25.00 license fee for in-state shrimp boats and a $2500.00 license fee for out-of-state shrimp boats. Emer-

ald Point Shrimping, a North Carolina corporation, and James Taylor, an individual North Carolina proprietor who owns and operates his own shrimp boat, have both been criminally prosecuted for failing to acquire the license required for out-of-state shrimpers. (Both tendered the $25.00 fee, but their offers were rejected because they were an out-of-state corporation and individual, respectively.) What defenses are available to Emerald Point and Taylor? How should they be analyzed and resolved?

2. The City of Camden, New Jersey, is engaged in building a number of new municipal buildings and is engaged in hiring workers for the projects. The projects are partly funded by federal funds. The city has a set-aside program by which 50% of the jobs in the city building program must be awarded to Camden residents. The set-aside program is specifically authorized by federal regulations enacted in connection with the federal funding program. James Jobs lives in Trenton, New Jersey, and he would otherwise be qualified to work on the project. Indeed, but for the set-aside program, Jobs alleges that he would have been hired. What legal theories are available to Jobs? Which have the best chance of success? How should the problem be analyzed? Is *Dean Milk* relevant? Why or why not?

A. An Introduction to the Privileges and Immunities Clause of Article IV, §2

Article IV, §2, clause 1 provides that "[t]he citizens of each State shall be entitled to all Privileges and Immunities of Citizens in the several States." The text of the clause might be read in different ways. It might be read to protect a body of national constitutional privileges and immunities of American citizens from, for example, being abridged by the states. Most of these rights would not depend on state law and, in that sense, would be absolute—that is to say, changes in state law would not reduce their scope. The clause has not typically been read in this way. Instead, the clause is typically interpreted simply to prevent discrimination against out-of-state interests under state law. Early descriptions of the function of the clause were not entirely clear or consistent.

In *Corfield v. Coryell* (Cir. Ct. E.D. Pa. 1823), Justice Bushrod Washington said the clause protects rights or interests "which are fundamental; which belong, of right to the citizens of all free governments." He said these "may be comprehended under the following general heads: Protection by the government, the enjoyment of life and liberty, with the right to acquire and possess property of every kind, and to pursue and obtain happiness and safety, subject nevertheless to such restraints as the government may prescribe for the general good of the whole." But in *Corfield*, Justice Washington held that New Jersey *could* prohibit out-of-staters from gathering clams from New Jersey waters on the grounds that the clams were common property of state residents. To the extent that *Corfield* suggested that the clause, at least in part, protected a body of national privileges that did not depend on state law, the case has been largely repudiated. The Dormant Commerce Clause now protects the right of access of out-of-state businesses to natural resources (including clams) in other states. And the Privileges and Immunities Clause of Article IV is not now typically read to protect a body of national privileges whose dimensions are set by federal law.

In *Paul v. Virginia* (1869), the Court said that the Privileges and Immunities Clause was designed "to place the citizens of each State upon the same footing with citizens of other States.... It relieves them from the disabilities of alienage in other States; it inhibits discriminating legislation against them by other States; it gives them the right of free ingress into other states, and egress from them; it insures to them in other States the same freedom possessed by the citizens of those States in the acquisition and enjoyment of property and in the pursuit of happiness."

The reading of the clause currently embraced by the Supreme Court is that it is primarily, if not exclusively, an anti-discrimination provision. The clause provides out-of-staters a limited right of equality of treatment when they temporarily visit other states. The discrimination prohibited is a particular type of discrimination between a state's own citizens and citizens from other states. The clause has generally been read as if it said "the citizens of each state shall be entitled to the privileges and immunities of citizens of the state they temporarily visit."

As currently interpreted by the Supreme Court, the limited right of equality applies to fundamental interests. These include equal access to the courts of the state, an equal right to purchase real property, an equal right to pursue basic economic occupations, and to obtain medical treatment at least in private hospitals, as well as equality in state constitutional rights. But as to rights under Article IV, state law, not federal law, typically sets the dimensions of the right. For example, if citizens of South Carolina are allowed to engage in the business of shining shoes or harvesting and selling venus fly traps, then South Carolina must accord citizens of North Carolina the same rights while in South Carolina. But, as far as the Privileges and Immunities Clause of Article IV is concerned, South Carolina could outlaw either of these occupations, provided it did so for its citizens and citizens of other states alike. But fundamental interests do not, so far, require equality in pursuit of sport as well as livelihood. States *can* charge out-of-staters higher fees for hunting licenses.

A state might attempt to limit the right to exercise federal constitutional rights within the state to its citizens — providing, for example, that only state citizens could criticize state leaders within the borders of the state. States rarely do this sort of thing. If one did, the legislation would, of course, violate the guarantees of free speech and press, applied to the states by the 14th Amendment. To the extent that it discriminated against out-of-state citizens, it might also violate the Privileges and Immunities Clause.

Georgia allowed state residents to obtain an abortion if a doctor determined that continuation of the pregnancy would endanger a woman's heath. Citizens from outside the state could not obtain abortions on the same terms. In *Doe v. Bolton* (1973), the Court held that attempting to limit access to abortion in this way violated Article IV. *Doe* was a companion case to *Roe v. Wade* (1973), the case that established that women had a fundamental, but limited, right to obtain an abortion. After the decision in *Roe*, of course, a state could not violate the limited right to abortion regardless of whether it discriminated against those from out of state.

The Privileges and Immunities Clause of Article IV overlaps to a considerable extent with the Dormant Commerce Clause. A state law limiting economic activity to in-state residents could violate both provisions. Unlike the Dormant Commerce Clause, however, the Court has so far limited the Privileges and Immunities Clause to natural citizens. Neither aliens nor corporations may take advantage of the clause.

Finally you should note that there is a second clause in the Constitution that uses the words "privileges" and "immunities." The 14th Amendment provides, "No state shall make or enforce any law which shall abridge the privileges or immunities *of citizens of the United States.*" [Emphasis added.] For many years the Supreme Court seemed to deprive the 14th Amendment clause of any significant meaning, but recently the clause has shown signs of life. What the 14th Amendment clause was intended to mean and how it should be interpreted are subjects of much academic controversy. The question is explored in Chapter 7 on the application of the Bill of Rights to the states.

Two charts appear below. The first illustrates the steps of analysis involved in a claim brought pursuant to the Article IV Privileges and Immunities Clause. The second contrasts the elements of a claim brought pursuant to the Article IV Privileges and Immunities Clause with a claim brought pursuant to the Dormant Commerce Clause.

Analysis of Article IV, §2 Privileges and Immunities Claim:

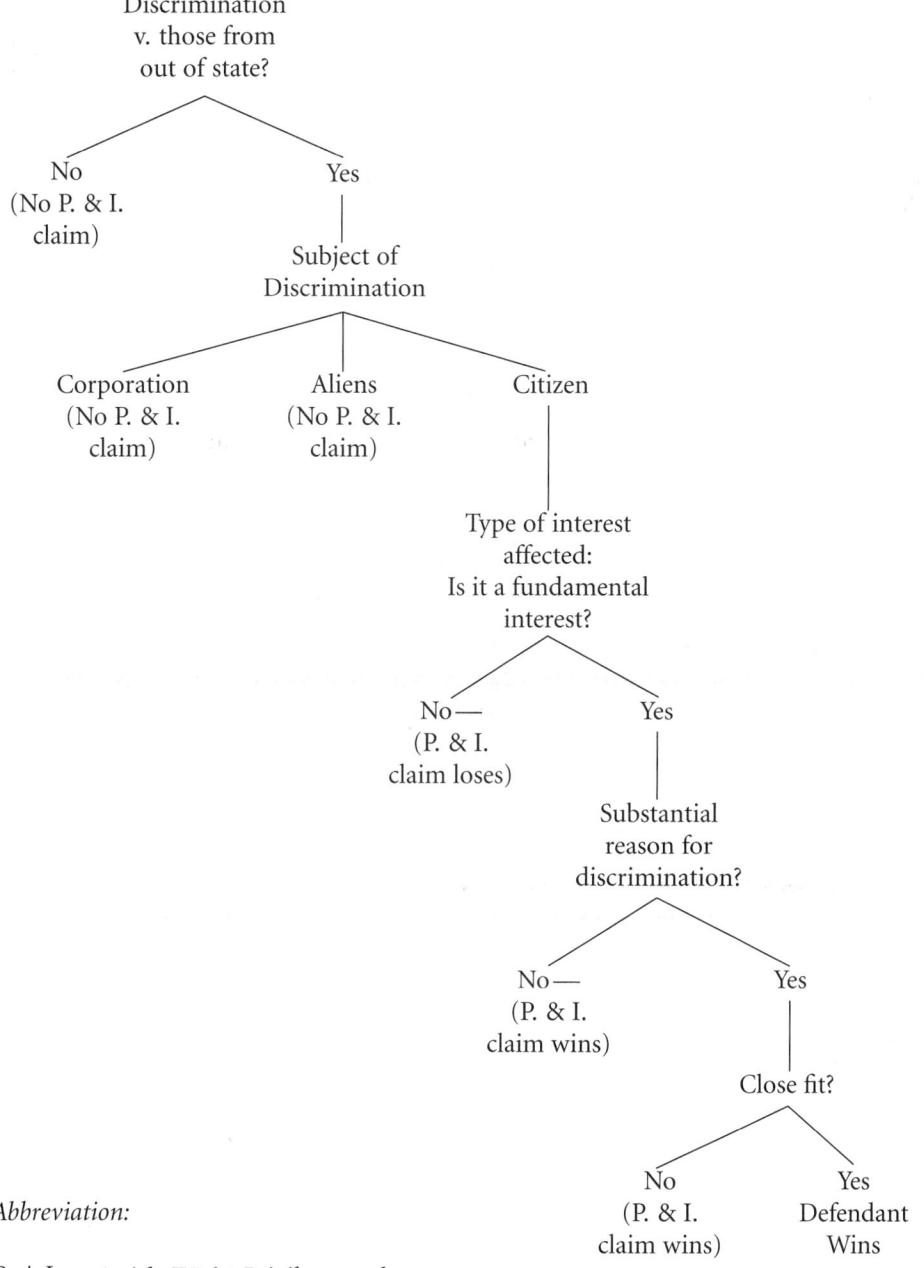

Abbreviation:

P. & I. —*Article IV, §2 Privileges and Immunities Clause*

Dormant Commerce Clause

Party	May be a Plaintiff?	Must the challenge involve a fundamental interest?	Is there a market participant exception?
Individual citizen:	Yes	No	Yes
Individual Alien:	Yes	No	Yes
Corporation:	Yes	No	Yes

Article IV Privileges and Immunities Clause

Party	May be a Plaintiff?	Must the challenge involve a fundamental interest?	Is there a market participant exception?
Individual citizen:	Yes	Yes	No
Individual Alien:	No	Not Applicable	N/A
Corporation:	No	N/A	N/A

B. The Current Approach to the Privileges and Immunities Clause of Article IV, §2

In *Baldwin v. Fish and Game Commission of Montana* (1978), plaintiffs attacked higher fees charged by Montana to out-of-state hunters: "For the 1976 season, the Montana resident could purchase a [hunting] license solely for elk for $9. The nonresident, in order to hunt elk, was required to purchase a combination license at a cost of $225; this entitled him to take one elk, one deer, one black bear, and game birds, and to fish with hook and line. A resident was not required to buy any combination of licenses, but if he did, the cost to him of all the privileges granted by the nonresident combination license was $30. The nonresident thus paid seven and one half times as much as the resident, and if the nonresident wished to hunt only elk, he paid 25 times as much as the resident." Plaintiffs challenged the higher fees charged to out-of-staters as compared to citizens of Montana as a violation of the Privileges and Immunities Clause of Article IV.

The Court rejected the claim. It noted:

> When the Privileges and Immunities Clause has been applied to specific cases, it has been interpreted to prevent a State from imposing unreasonable burdens on citizens of other States in their pursuit of common callings within the State, *Ward v. Maryland* (1871); in the ownership and disposition of privately held property within the State, *Blake v. McClung* (1898); and in access to the courts of the State, *Canadian Northern R. Co. v. Eggen* (1920).
>
> It has not been suggested, however, that state citizenship or residency may never be used by a State to distinguish among persons. Suffrage, for example, always has been understood to be tied to an individual's identification with a particular State. See, e.g., *Dunn v. Blumstein* (1972). No one would suggest that the Privileges and Immunities Clause requires a State to open its polls to a person who declines to assert that the State is the only one where he claims a right to vote. The same is true as to qualification for an elective office of the State.... Nor must a State always apply all its laws or all its services equally to anyone, resident or nonresident, who may request it so to do. *Canadian Northern R.*

Co. v. Eggen; cf. *Sosna v. Iowa* (1975); *Shapiro v. Thompson* (1969). Some distinctions between residents and nonresidents merely reflect the fact that this is a Nation composed of individual States, and are permitted; other distinctions are prohibited because they hinder the formation, the purpose, or the development of a single Union of those States. Only with respect to those "privileges" and "immunities" bearing upon the vitality of the Nation as a single entity must the State treat all citizens, resident and nonresident, equally. Here we must decide into which category falls a distinction with respect to access to recreational big-game hunting.

The Court proceeded to reject the claim that big game hunting was one of the protected privileges and immunities.

Does the distinction made by Montana between residents and nonresidents in establishing access to elk hunting threaten a basic right in a way that offends the Privileges and Immunities Clause? Merely to ask the question seems to provide the answer. We repeat much of what already has been said above: Elk hunting by nonresidents in Montana is a recreation and a sport. In itself—wholly apart from license fees—it is costly and obviously available only to the wealthy nonresident or to the one so taken with the sport that he sacrifices other values in order to indulge in it and to enjoy what it offers. It is not a means to the nonresident's livelihood. The mastery of the animal and the trophy are the ends that are sought; appellants are not totally excluded from these. The elk supply, which has been entrusted to the care of the State by the people of Montana, is finite and must be carefully tended in order to be preserved.

Appellants' interest in sharing this limited resource on more equal terms with Montana residents simply does not fall within the purview of the Privileges and Immunities Clause. Equality in access to Montana elk is not basic to the maintenance or well-being of the Union....

Supreme Court of Virginia v. Friedman
487 U.S. 59 (1988)

[Majority: Kennedy, Blackmun, Brennan, Stevens, Marshall, White, and O'Connor. Dissenting: Rehnquist (C.J.) and Scalia.]

Justice Kennedy delivered the opinion of the Court.

Qualified lawyers admitted to practice in other States may be admitted to the Virginia Bar "on motion," that is, without taking the bar examination which Virginia otherwise requires. The State conditions such admission on a showing, among other matters, that the applicant is a permanent resident of Virginia. The question for decision is whether this residency requirement violates the Privileges and Immunities Clause of the United States Constitution, Art. IV, §2, cl. 1. We hold that it does.

I. Myrna E. Friedman was admitted to the Illinois Bar by examination in 1977 and to the District of Columbia Bar by reciprocity in 1980. From 1977 to 1981, she was employed by the Department of the Navy in Arlington, Virginia, as a civilian attorney, and from 1982 until 1986, she was an attorney in private practice in Washington, D.C. In January 1986, she became associate general counsel for ERC International, Inc., a Delaware corporation. Friedman practices and maintains her offices at the company's principal place of business in Vienna, Virginia. Her duties at ERC International include drafting contracts and advising her employer and its subsidiaries on matters of Virginia law.

From 1977 to early 1986, Friedman lived in Virginia. In February 1986, however, she married and moved to her husband's home in Cheverly, Maryland. In June 1986, Friedman applied for admission to the Virginia Bar on motion.

The applicable rule, promulgated by the Supreme Court of Virginia pursuant to statute, is Rule 1A:1. The Rule permits admission on motion of attorneys who are licensed to practice in another jurisdiction, provided the other jurisdiction admits Virginia attorneys without examination. The applicant must have been licensed for at least five years and the Virginia Supreme Court must determine that the applicant:

(a) Is a proper person to practice law.

(b) Has made such progress in the practice of law that it would be unreasonable to require him to take an examination.

(c) Has become a permanent resident of the Commonwealth.

(d) Intends to practice full time as a member of the Virginia bar.

In a letter accompanying her application, Friedman alerted the Clerk of the Virginia Supreme Court to her change of residence, but argued that her application should nevertheless be granted. Friedman gave assurance that she would be engaged full-time in the practice of law in Virginia, that she would be available for service of process and court appearances, and that she would keep informed of local rules. She also asserted that "there appears to be no reason to discriminate against my petition as a nonresident for admission to the Bar on motion," that her circumstances fit within the purview of this Court's decision in *Supreme Court of New Hampshire v. Piper* (1985), and that accordingly she was entitled to admission under the Privileges and Immunities Clause of the Constitution, Art. IV, §2, cl. 1.

The Clerk wrote Friedman that her request had been denied. He explained that because Friedman was no longer a permanent resident of the Commonwealth of Virginia, she was not eligible for admission to the Virginia Bar pursuant to Rule 1A:1. He added that the court had concluded that our decision in *Piper*, which invalidated a residency requirement imposed on lawyers who had passed a State's bar examination, was "not applicable" to the "discretionary requirement in Rule 1A:1 of residence as a condition of admission by reciprocity."

Friedman then commenced this action, against the Supreme Court of Virginia and its Clerk, in the United States District Court for the Eastern District of Virginia. She alleged that the residency requirement of Rule 1A:1 violated the Privileges and Immunities Clause. The District Court entered summary judgment in Friedman's favor, holding that the requirement of residency for admission without examination violates the Clause.[1]

The Court of Appeals for the Fourth Circuit unanimously affirmed....

The Supreme Court of Virginia and its Clerk filed a timely notice of appeal. We noted probable jurisdiction, and we now affirm.

II. Article IV, §2, cl. 1, of the Constitution provides that the "Citizens of each State shall be entitled to all Privileges and Immunities of Citizens in the several States." The provision was designed "to place the citizens of each State upon the same footing with citizens

---

1. The District Court did not address Friedman's claims that the residency requirement of Rule 1A:1 also violates the Commerce Clause and the Equal Protection Clause of the 14th Amendment. The Court of Appeals did not pass on these contentions either, and our resolution of Friedman's claim that the residency requirement violates the Privileges and Immunities Clause makes it unnecessary for us to reach them.

of other States, so far as the advantages resulting from citizenship in those States are concerned." *Paul v. Virginia* (1869). See also *Toomer v. Witsell* (1948) (the Privileges and Immunities Clause "was designed to insure to a citizen of State A who ventures into State B the same privileges which the citizens of State B enjoy"). The Clause "thus establishes a norm of comity without specifying the particular subjects as to which citizens of one State coming within the jurisdiction of another are guaranteed equality of treatment." *Austin v. New Hampshire* (1975).

While the Privileges and Immunities Clause cites the term "Citizens," for analytic purposes citizenship and residency are essentially interchangeable. See *United Building & Construction Trades Council v. Mayor and Council of Camden* (1984). When examining claims that a citizenship or residency classification offends privileges and immunities protections, we undertake a two-step inquiry. First, the activity in question must be "'sufficiently basic to the livelihood of the Nation... as to fall within the purview of the Privileges and Immunities Clause....'" *Id.*, quoting *Baldwin v. Montana Fish & Game Comm'n* (1978). For it is "'[o]nly with respect to those "privileges" and "immunities" bearing on the vitality of the Nation as a single entity' that a State must accord residents and nonresidents equal treatment." *Supreme Court of New Hampshire v. Piper*, quoting *Baldwin*. Second, if the challenged restriction deprives nonresidents of a protected privilege, we will invalidate it only if we conclude that the restriction is not closely related to the advancement of a substantial state interest. *Piper*. Appellants assert that the residency requirement offends neither part of this test. We disagree.

II-A. Appellants concede, as they must, that our decision in *Piper* establishes that a nonresident who takes and passes an examination prescribed by the State, and who otherwise is qualified for the practice of law, has an interest in practicing law that is protected by the Privileges and Immunities Clause. Appellants contend, however, that the discretionary admission provided for by Rule 1A:1 is not a privilege protected by the Clause for two reasons. First, appellants argue that the bar examination "serves as an adequate, alternative means of gaining admission to the bar." In appellants' view, "[s]o long as any applicant may gain admission to a State's bar, without regard to residence, by passing the bar examination," the State cannot be said to have discriminated against nonresidents "as a matter of fundamental concern." Second, appellants argue that the right to admission on motion is not within the purview of the Clause because, without offense to the Constitution, the State could require all bar applicants to pass an examination. Neither argument is persuasive.

We cannot accept appellants' first theory because it is quite inconsistent with our precedents. We reaffirmed in *Piper* the well-settled principle that "'one of the privileges which the Clause guarantees to citizens of State A is that of doing business in State B on terms of substantial equality with the citizens of that State.'" *Piper*, quoting *Toomer v. Witsell*. See also *United Building & Construction Trades Council* ("Certainly, the pursuit of a common calling is one of the most fundamental of those privileges protected by the Clause"). After reviewing our precedents, we explicitly held that the practice of law, like other occupations considered in those cases, is sufficiently basic to the national economy to be deemed a privilege protected by the Clause. See *Piper*. The clear import of *Piper* is that the Clause is implicated whenever, as is the case here, a State does not permit qualified nonresidents to practice law within its borders on terms of substantial equality with its own residents.

Nothing in our precedents, moreover, supports the contention that the Privileges and Immunities Clause does not reach a State's discrimination against nonresidents when such discrimination does not result in their total exclusion from the State. In *Ward v.*

Maryland (1871), for example, the Court invalidated a statute under which residents paid an annual fee of $12 to $150 for a license to trade foreign goods, while nonresidents were required to pay $300. Similarly, in *Toomer*, the Court held that nonresident fishermen could not be required to pay a license fee 100 times the fee charged to residents. In *Hicklin v. Orbeck* (1978), the Court invalidated a statute requiring that residents be hired in preference to nonresidents for all positions related to the development of the State's oil and gas resources. Indeed, as the Court of Appeals correctly noted, the New Hampshire rule struck down in *Piper* did not result in the total exclusion of nonresidents from the practice of law in that State.

Further, we find appellants' second theory—that Virginia could constitutionally require that all applicants to its bar take and pass an examination—quite irrelevant to the question whether the Clause is applicable in the circumstances of this case. A State's abstract authority to require from resident and nonresident alike that which it has chosen to demand from the nonresident alone has never been held to shield the discriminatory distinction from the reach of the Privileges and Immunities Clause. Thus, the applicability of the Clause to the present case no more turns on the legality *vel non* of an examination requirement than it turned on the inherent reasonableness of the fees charged to nonresidents in *Toomer* and *Ward*. The issue instead is whether the State has burdened the right to practice law, a privilege protected by the Privileges and Immunities Clause, by discriminating among otherwise equally qualified applicants solely on the basis of citizenship or residency. We conclude it has.

II-B. Our conclusion that the residence requirement burdens a privilege protected by the Privileges and Immunities Clause does not conclude the matter, of course; for we repeatedly have recognized that the Clause, like other constitutional provisions, is not an absolute. See, *e.g., Piper*; *United Building & Construction Trades Council*; *Toomer*. The Clause does not preclude disparity in treatment where substantial reasons exist for the discrimination and the degree of discrimination bears a close relation to such reasons. See *United Building & Construction Trades Council*. In deciding whether the degree of discrimination bears a sufficiently close relation to the reasons proffered by the State, the Court has considered whether, within the full panoply of legislative choices otherwise available to the State, there exist alternative means of furthering the State's purpose without implicating constitutional concerns. See *Piper*.

Appellants offer two principal justifications for the Rule's requirement that applicants seeking admission on motion reside within the Commonwealth of Virginia. First, they contend that the residence requirement assures, in tandem with the full-time practice requirement, that attorneys admitted on motion will have the same commitment to service and familiarity with Virginia law that is possessed by applicants securing admission upon examination. Attorneys admitted on motion, appellants argue, have "no personal investment" in the jurisdiction; consequently, they "are entitled to no presumption that they will willingly and actively participate in bar activities and obligations, or fulfill their public service responsibilities to the State's client community." Second, appellants argue that the residency requirement facilitates enforcement of the full-time practice requirement of Rule 1A:1. We find each of these justifications insufficient to meet the State's burden of showing that the discrimination is warranted by a substantial state objective and closely drawn to its achievement.

We acknowledge that a bar examination is one method of assuring that the admitted attorney has a stake in his or her professional licensure and a concomitant interest in the integrity and standards of the bar. A bar examination, as we know judicially and from our own experience, is not a casual or lighthearted exercise. The question, however, is whether lawyers who are admitted in other States and seek admission in Virginia are less likely to respect the bar and further its interests solely because they are nonresidents. We cannot say this is the case. While *Piper* relied on an examination requirement as an indicium of the nonresident's commitment to the bar and to the State's legal profession, see *Piper*, it does not follow that when the State waives the examination it may make a distinction between residents and nonresidents.

Friedman's case proves the point. She earns her living working as an attorney in Virginia, and it is of scant relevance that her residence is located in the neighboring State of Maryland. It is indisputable that she has a substantial stake in the practice of law in Virginia. Indeed, despite appellants' suggestion at oral argument that Friedman's case is "atypical," the same will likely be true of all nonresident attorneys who are admitted on motion to the Virginia Bar, in light of the State's requirement that attorneys so admitted show their intention to maintain an office and a regular practice in the State. This requirement goes a long way toward ensuring that such attorneys will have an interest in the practice of law in Virginia that is at least comparable to the interest we ascribed in *Piper* to applicants admitted upon examination. Accordingly, we see no reason to assume that nonresident attorneys who, like Friedman, seek admission to the Virginia bar on motion will lack adequate incentives to remain abreast of changes in the law or to fulfill their civic duties.

Further, to the extent that the State is justifiably concerned with ensuring that its attorneys keep abreast of legal developments, it can protect these interests through other equally or more effective means that do not themselves infringe constitutional protections. While this Court is not well positioned to dictate specific legislative choices to the State, it is sufficient to note that such alternatives exist and that the State, in the exercise of its legislative prerogatives, is free to implement them. The Supreme Court of Virginia could, for example, require mandatory attendance at periodic continuing legal education courses. See *Piper*. The same is true with respect to the State's interest that the nonresident bar member does his or her share of volunteer and *pro bono* work. A "nonresident bar member, like the resident member, could be required to represent indigents and perhaps to participate in formal legal-aid work." *Piper*.

We also reject appellants' attempt to justify the residency restriction as a necessary aid to the enforcement of the full-time practice requirement of Rule 1A:1. Virginia already requires, pursuant to the full-time practice restriction of Rule 1A:1, that attorneys admitted on motion maintain an office for the practice of law in Virginia. As the Court of Appeals noted, the requirement that applicants maintain an office in Virginia facilitates compliance with the full-time practice requirement in nearly the identical manner that the residency restriction does, rendering the latter restriction largely redundant. The office requirement furnishes an alternative to the residency requirement that is not only less restrictive, but also is fully adequate to protect whatever interest the State might have in the full-time practice restriction.

III. We hold that Virginia's residency requirement for admission to the State's bar without examination violates the Privileges and Immunities Clause. The nonresident's interest in practicing law on terms of substantial equality with those enjoyed by residents is a privilege protected by the Clause. A State may not discriminate against nonresidents unless it shows that such discrimination bears a close relation to the achievement of substantial state objectives. Virginia has failed to make this showing. Accordingly, the judgment of the Court of Appeals is affirmed.

Chief Justice Rehnquist, with whom Justice Scalia joins, dissenting.

Three Terms ago the Court invalidated a New Hampshire Bar rule which denied admission to an applicant who had passed the state bar examination because she was not, and would not become, a resident of the State. *Supreme Court of New Hampshire v. Piper* (1985). In the present case the Court extends the reasoning of *Piper* to invalidate a Virginia Bar rule allowing admission on motion without examination to qualified applicants, but restricting the privilege to those applicants who have become residents of the State.

For the reasons stated in my dissent in *Piper*, I also disagree with the Court's decision in this case. I continue to believe that the Privileges and Immunities Clause of Article IV, §2, does not require States to ignore residency when admitting lawyers to practice in the way that they must ignore residency when licensing traders in foreign goods, *Ward v. Maryland* (1871), or when licensing commercial shrimp fishermen, *Toomer v. Witsell* (1948).

I think the effect of today's decision is unfortunate even apart from what I believe is its mistaken view of the Privileges and Immunities Clause. Virginia's rule allowing admission on motion is an ameliorative provision, recognizing the fact that previous practice in another State may qualify a new resident of Virginia to practice there without the necessity of taking another bar examination. The Court's ruling penalizes Virginia, which has at least gone part way towards accommodating the present mobility of our population, but of course leaves untouched the rules of those States which allow no reciprocal admission on motion. Virginia may of course retain the privilege of admission on motion without enforcing a residency requirement even after today's decision, but it might also decide to eliminate admission on motion altogether.

IV. Special Considerations: The World Trade Organization and the North American Free Trade Agreement[1]

by Richard Schneider

Is it strange that a casebook on U.S. constitutional law contains a squib on the World Trade Organization ("WTO") and the North American Free Trade Agreement ("NAFTA")? No. Would it be strange for a treatise on German constitutional law or on French constitutional law to contain salient observations on the role of the European Court of Justice and the Treaty Establishing the European Community? No. Would it be unaccountable for a discussion of U.S. state environmental laws to contain references to possible interactions with federal environmental laws? In each case the answer is no. Why? In each case one body of law contains designs of supremacy over another body of law. One cannot study a body of law and ignore such designs. "We are writing the constitution of a single global economy." So spoke Renato Ruggiero, the former WTO Director General. It would be irresponsible now for a casebook on American constitutional law to ignore the influence of the WTO and NAFTA on the U.S. constitutional system.

You exist, for the most part, in a world with known legal boundaries. Your actions and the actions of the public bodies that govern your actions are answerable to a closed set of legal determinants: statutory laws, case laws, and, in our case, the U.S. Constitution and the cases decided by the U.S. Supreme Court, all of which have made the text

---

1. © Richard Schneider, November 1, 2010.

of the Constitution meaningful. This casebook develops the interactions of those legal determinants in the world of constitutional reasoning. Now, suddenly comes the realization — perhaps through a federal or state statute that cannot be applied, although it is not unconstitutional, or through a court decision that cannot be enforced — that there is perhaps another authority that can alter drastically the legal boundaries that you thought you understood. You wake up in an entirely different world that somehow seems much less predictable and perhaps much more rapacious.

What is this force that has such power? Call it NAFTA. Call it the WTO. NAFTA became the law of the United States on January 1, 1994. It links Canada, Mexico, and the United States. Thought was given to expanding it in the early 2000s to embrace other Latin American countries in an arrangement to be called the Free Trade Agreement of the Americas ("FTAA"). The World Trade Organization became a part of U.S. law on January 1, 1995, after it also received the support of both houses of Congress and the signature of President Clinton. The WTO, as of July 23, 2008, has 153 member countries and numerous observer countries from all over the world. Both NAFTA and the WTO required implementing legislation passed by Congress. What kinds of laws and court decisions could be affected by the WTO or NAFTA?

NAFTA and the WTO establish free trade regimes in goods and numerous services. Countries in each organization agree to accord national treatment and most-favored nation status to such goods and services coming into their territory from other member countries. NAFTA and the WTO are administered by separate institutions and subject to different methods of dispute settlement and adjudication. In each case, however, the integrity of the free trade system is the principal priority of the organizations. Very complicated dispute resolution procedures can be summarized in part as follows. The NAFTA Secretariat administers the dispute settlement provisions that have been agreed upon by Canada, Mexico, and the United States. While consultation is required, final dispute settlement occurs in an arbitration proceeding. Procedures under the WTO also require consultation, but can trigger appointment of a panel of independent experts who make a determination, which can then be appealed to an Appellate Body for a final and binding resolution. Only member countries can bring complaints to the dispute settlement process. In the case of both NAFTA and the WTO, final decisions of their constituent bodies cannot be appealed to member country courts. Finally and importantly, NAFTA contains a separate provision for actions by private investors against a member country.

How could these dispute resolution procedures affect the administration and enforcement of otherwise constitutionally adopted U.S. laws and regulations? The following examples, some actual and some hypothetical, illustrate paradigm cases:

1. Acting pursuant to the Clean Air Act of 1990, the Environmental Protection Agency promulgated regulations in 1994 intended to reduce air pollution by strictly limiting certain contents of reformulated and conventional gasoline made in and imported into the United States.[2] Consecutive decisions of a panel and the Appellate Body affirmed that the EPA had violated the WTO and that the United States should bring its gas content regulations "into conformity with its obligations under the *General Agreement*" or, in other words, the WTO.[3]

---

2. 40 CFR 80, 59 Fed. Reg. 7716, February 16, 1994.

3. "United States — Standards for Reformulated and Conventional Gasoline," AB-1996-1, Report of the Appellate Body, April 29, 1996, adopted by the Dispute Settlement Body, May 20, 1996, 35 I.L.M. 603, 633 (1996).

2. Congress (hypothetically) decides to protect certain U.S. fish and wildlife by banning or placing restrictions on the importation of certain food products into the United States that carry exotic disease agents. Countries that export such food products to the United States complain to the WTO that the U.S. ban or restrictions violate relevant portions of the WTO and of the Agreement on the Application of Sanitary and Phytosanitary Measures. A WTO dispute panel is empowered to scrutinize the U.S. ban or restrictions for their compliance with the WTO, thereby creating the risk that the legislation will have to be rescinded or changed even though it is fully constitutional.

3. The United States decides to act to conserve sea turtles, an endangered species, from death or harm that occurs during shrimp harvesting. Congress amends the Endangered Species Act in 1989 to require that foreign nations, as a condition to selling their shrimp in U.S. markets, certify that their fishermen have caught the shrimp in a manner that does not kill or threaten sea turtles. A number of countries bring WTO actions against the United States, arguing that the amendment to the Endangered Species Act constitutes a violation of the WTO agreements. The U.S. legislation is scrutinized by the Dispute Settlement Body through panel reports and Appellate Body decisions. The United States is required to amend its legislation.[4]

4. After much debate, Congress (hypothetically) enacts legislation to ban the sale in the U.S. of goods made abroad by workers who do not benefit from certain minimal standards in work conditions and pay. Actions are brought in the WTO by numerous developing countries, many run by despotic governments, who argue that lower than minimal standards and cheap labor comprise their greatest comparative advantage. The WTO, after completion of the entire dispute settlement process, orders the U.S. to lift its prohibitions.

5. The State of California enacts standards into its environmental law that prohibit the use, marketing, and sale, in California, of a gas additive called MTBE because the additive has been discovered to be harmful to human health. An investor in Canada who makes methanol (a component of MTBE) and sells it in California stands to lose its entire California-based business. The investor brings a private action before an arbitral tribunal under Chapter 11 of NAFTA to argue that the California legislation is tantamount to expropriation and should therefore trigger a $900 million reimbursement to the Canadian investor.

6. A Mississippi trial court finds a Canadian company and its U.S. subsidiary in violation of certain provisions of U.S. law and Mississippi state law with respect to the conduct of their funeral business in Mississippi. After the verdict in the trial court requires the Canadian company to pay compensatory and punitive damages to the Mississippi claimant, the Canadian company files a claim before the International Centre for Settlement of Investment Disputes under Chapter 11 of NAFTA to allege that the U.S. subsidiary has been the victim of treatment in the state court that is tantamount to expropriation. The Canadian company seeks $600 million in damages under NAFTA.

In each of the above examples, results reached constitutionally through federal or state democratic deliberative processes, or through the judicial branch in the case of the last

---

4. See WTO ruling in favor of compliance of the U.S. amendments to the underlying legislation with the *General Agreement*. June 15, 2001.

example, are threatened with virtual reversal as a result of actions contemplated or brought under WTO or NAFTA dispute settlement processes, none of whose adjudicators are democratically-elected. Either Congress or the state government concerned must revoke or substantially amend its offending legislation or else suffer retaliatory trade actions or be required to pay large judgments. In any case, the overall effect is to chill the willingness of Congress or state governments to enact legislation to protect health and the environment or to redress injustices created by unfair employment conditions abroad.

Thinking about the validity of federal and state statutes, and even of court decisions, can no longer be limited to the usual inquiries. In many cases, deliberations must now be devoted to the various international trade arrangements to which the United States has agreed.

Chapter 7

The Incorporation of the Bill of Rights

Contents

I.	Introduction	627
	A. The Constitution and Individual Rights	627
	Goals for Chapter 7	629
	Review and Overview of American Constitutional History	630
	A Brief History of the Adoption of the Constitution and Its Most Significant Amendments	631
	Chronological Overview of Key Events Related to Incorporation	633
	Interpreting the 14th Amendment: Types of Constitutional Argument	635
	B. A Hypothetical Case	636
	Hypothetical Question	636
II.	Application of the Bill of Rights to the States: 1791–1833	637
	Barron v. Mayor and City Council of Baltimore	637
III.	From *Barron* to the Adoption of the 14th Amendment: The Pre-Civil War Background	640
	A. The Privileges and Immunities Clause of Article IV	640
	B. Subsequent Decisions: The Response to *Barron*	641
	C. The Bill of Rights: 1833–57	643
	D. *Dred Scott v. Sandford*: Rights of Free Blacks and Slavery in the Territories	643
	Dred Scott v. Sandford	645
	From St. George Tucker, *A Dissertation on Slavery*	655
	Criticisms of *Dred Scott* by John A. Bingham and Abraham Lincoln	655
	E. Historical Linguistics: Common Use of the Words "Privileges and Immunities" before the Adoption of the 14th Amendment	658
IV.	The Drafting of the 14th Amendment	661
	A "Black Code": Regulating Freedmen in Louisiana	662
	A. The Congressional Response to the Black Codes and the Legacy of Slavery	663
	B. The Congressional Debates on the 14th Amendment	665
	Speeches by Congressmen after the 39th Congress Adjourns	681
	The 14th Amendment: The Final Version	681
	Bingham speaking in 1871, after Ratification of the 14th Amendment	682
V.	Applying Methods of Interpretation to the 14th Amendment's First Section	684
	A Brief Note on "State Action" and Cities and Counties	685
	Hypothetical Concerning the Incorporation of the 2nd Amendment	685
VI.	Reconstruction and the Initial Judicial Response	686
	A. A Post-Ratification Case on the Article IV, §2, Privileges and Immunities Clause	686

		B. Reconstruction	686
		Reconstruction Era Civil Rights Legislation	688
		C. Early Interpretation of the 14th Amendment	690
		Slaughter-House Cases	691
VII.	The Bill of Rights and Incorporation after *Slaughter-House*		709
		A. 1873–1905	709
		B. 1905–1947: *Twining*, *Palko*, and *Adamson*	710
		Palko v. Connecticut	714
		1. Incorporation: From *Palko* to *Adamson*	716
		Adamson v. California	716
		2. Incorporation after *Adamson*	720
		The Historical Debate	720
		C. The Warren Court Approach—Incorporation: From *Mapp* to *Duncan*	721
		Duncan v. Louisiana	722
		1. Incorporation: Due Process and Procedures Not Forbidden by the Bill of Rights	729
		2. Incorporation after *Duncan*	729
VIII.	Incorporation: Approaches, Effects, and Further Thoughts	730
		A Typology of Positions on Application of the Bill of Rights to the States	730
		Approaches to Application of the Bill of Rights to the States: A Graphic Portrayal	730
		The Resurrection of a Reconstruction Statute	731
		Attorney General Meese Critiques Incorporation	731
IX.	The Warren Court	732
X.	A Short Note on Political Transformation: 1948–2008	737
XI.	The Roberts Court and Incorporation	742
		A. The Right to Bear Arms: A Personal Right Limiting the Federal Government	742
		District of Columbia v. Heller	742
		B. The Right to Bear Arms: An Incorporated Right	753
		McDonald v. City of Chicago	753

Chapter 7

The Incorporation of the Bill of Rights

I. Introduction

A. The Constitution and Individual Rights

The Constitution contains provisions that confer powers on the federal government, and provisions that limit the powers of both the federal and state governments. Guarantees of individual rights, of course, limit governmental power. This part of the book will focus on some of the limitations on governmental power found in the Bill of Rights and the 13th and 14th Amendments. A detailed examination of guarantees for those accused of crimes must await a separate course in criminal procedure.

The Constitution provided for powers of the judiciary, of Congress, and of the President, and regulated the relations among the three branches. It treated states as pre-existing governments with pre-existing powers. Particularly in connection with the powers of Congress, the Court's decisions have focused on the relation of the states to the national government in our federal system—the concept known as federalism. The original Constitution set several explicit limits on the power of the states, and the Court found additional implicit limits:

- The Supremacy Clause allows the federal government to simply override state laws, if Congress acts within its powers and is clear about its purpose to do so.
- Article I, §10, forbids states from passing bills of attainder, ex post facto laws, or laws impairing the obligation of contracts.
- The Dormant Commerce Clause protects interstate commerce from protectionist state conduct.
- The interstate Privileges and Immunities Clause of Article IV, §2, protects those from out of state against many forms of discrimination, particularly with respect to economic matters. As to these matters, the Court holds that the Constitution envisions that we shall be one nation with citizens enjoying some minimum measure of freedom to travel and trade in all the states.

The level of scrutiny applied by the Court separates those subjects left largely up to the political process from those in which the Court takes a much more active role. From 1936 until at least 1995 the Court allowed Congress broad discretion in enforcing the Commerce Clause and left federal, and much state, economic regulation largely up to the political process. It upheld regulations that were "rational" in relation to a conceivable state interest. In contrast, in the case of the Dormant Commerce Clause and the Privileges and Immunities Clause of Article IV, §2, the Court often subjected state legislation to a much higher level of scrutiny.

Before and during the early years of the New Deal, the Court sometimes held federal economic regulation unconstitutional as beyond the delegated power of Congress. It used a much more robust scrutiny than the low level rational basis the later New Deal Court embraced in deciding economic challenges. For example, the Court struck down federal laws prohibiting child labor and regulating working conditions. At the same time that the Court was limiting the power of Congress to regulate the national economy by its limited reading of the scope of *federal* power under the Commerce Clause, it also limited *state* regulation of economic matters. It did so by its broad reading of the word "liberty" in the Due Process Clause of the 14th Amendment. This use of the Due Process Clause became known as substantive due process. (We will explore these developments in detail in the next chapter.)

Though it was slower to do so, the Court, during this era of economic substantive due process (very roughly 1896–1936), also imposed substantive due process limits on state power to regulate non-economic liberties. These liberties included the right to teach and study a foreign language before the eighth grade in school, the right of parents to send their children to parochial schools, and, by the 1930s, the right to freedom of speech. As to these matters, the Court often used a higher level of scrutiny and gave less deference to the decisions of Congress and the state legislatures.

The higher degree of judicial scrutiny of *most* social and economic legislation ended during the New Deal. Most judges, and especially those appointed by Franklin Roosevelt, viewed the use of the Due Process Clause to strike down economic legislation as an abuse of judicial power. By 1937, the Court was giving greater deference to legislatures on most issues of economic regulation. But, a question remained during this transitional period (roughly 1936 to 1948): what role would the Court assume with reference to non-economic individual rights? Free speech and the right to send one's child to a non-public school had also been protected from state action by the Court's now disfavored expansive substantive reading of the Due Process Clause.

The materials that follow begin to focus on the rights of the individual and how those rights limit governmental power. The first subject we consider is the "incorporation" (really the application) of the national Bill of Rights as a limit on the powers of states and localities. Application of the Bill of Rights to the states involves use of *federal* judicial power to enforce individual rights. To the extent that states are required to obey Bill of Rights guarantees, state governmental power is limited and the role of the Court in interpreting appropriate limits is expanded. Application of the Bill of Rights to the states implicates both federalism and individual rights.

The Court confronted the issue of whether the rights in the Bill of Rights should apply to the states, under the 14th Amendment, in the latter part of the 19th century and during the 20th century. Before the ratification of the 14th Amendment in 1868, the Court had considered the issue of application settled by its decision in *Barron v. Baltimore* (1833). There the Court had held that none of the guarantees of the federal Bill of Rights limited state or local governments. The 14th Amendment, ratified shortly after the end of the Civil War, provided that:

> No State shall make or enforce any law which shall abridge the privileges or immunities of citizens of the United States; nor shall any State deprive any person

of life, liberty, or property, without due process of law; nor deny to any person within its jurisdiction the equal protection of the laws.

The meaning of these majestic phrases has been a subject of controversy ever since.

The question raised by "incorporation" is this: does the 14th Amendment require that we be one nation with respect to issues such as free speech, freedom of religion, the right to jury trial, and protection against unreasonable searches? That is, should we have *minimum* national standards on these issues? States can always provide higher protection to individual rights, provided the protection does not conflict with federal law or the federal Constitution. Increasingly, in recent years, some state courts have found higher protection for individual rights under their state constitutions. See, e.g., Hans A. Linde, *First Things First: Rediscovering the States Bills of Rights*, 9 U. Balt. L. Rev. 379 (1980).

How should the question of application of the Bill of Rights to the states be analyzed? Should it depend on the current ethical aspirations of the American people, as understood by the Court? Should analysis instead be based on something else? On evolving precedent? Upon the "original intent" of the people who framed or ratified the 14th Amendment? On the common understanding of the words "privileges or immunities" or "deprivation of life, liberty or property without due process" in the years 1866–68? On the history that gave rise to the Amendment? On the Constitution's structure? On what the Court sees as "implicit in the concept of ordered liberty"? Should the decision instead be based on some combination of these factors? Should it be based on something else?

While, in one sense, the following material is new, in another it raises familiar issues: federalism, individual rights, and how we should interpret the Constitution. We will look again at methods of interpretation—text, context, history, structure, policy, and precedent. We will look especially at issues of original intent and original meaning in this section. These ideas have often been used by the Court. Justices Scalia and Thomas suggest we should treat original meaning as a primary method of constitutional interpretation. To what extent do original intent or original meaning provide clear answers? To what extent should we rely on them in determining constitutional meaning? As you have learned, perhaps to your dismay, the black letter "rules" the Court establishes in constitutional decisions change over time. (This is also true in every other area of the law.) So, the rules you learn today may not be the rules in ten years. But, to a much greater degree, methods of interpretation endure and can last you a legal lifetime.

A major purpose of this section is to help you learn more about methods of constitutional interpretation by applying them to the problem of the application of the national Bill of Rights to the states. What should the words of the 14th Amendment mean on this issue? How can you frame an analysis using various methods of interpretation? You should keep these questions in mind as you follow the long and circuitous path that leads to the current rule on the application of Bill of Rights liberties to the states.

Goals for Chapter 7

1. Know what is meant by the *incorporation doctrine*: how the doctrine developed and the range of approaches taken by different Justices—e.g., no incorporation, selective incorporation, selective incorporation plus application of other less textual rights, total incorporation, and total incorporation plus.

2. Understand the difference between a *substantive* protection of liberty and a *procedural* protection.

3. Know what is meant by arguments based on text, context, structure, history, precedent, and policy, and be able to identify such arguments in judicial opinions. Understand when arguments based on text, context, history, policy, precedent, and structure are most crucial.
4. Be able to make such arguments for and against incorporation of the Bill of Rights against the states.
5. Know the *Palko v. Connecticut* (1937) and the *Duncan v. Louisiana* (1968) tests for incorporation, how they are different, and how to apply the *Duncan* test.
6. Know how one might use *Murray's Lessee* (1856) on the issue of incorporation.
7. Understand the effect of the incorporation doctrine on civil suits against state and local officials based on 42 U.S.C. § 1983 — i.e., how the meaning of that statute would have been different without incorporation.
8. Think about when arguments that have failed are likely to be resurrected, whether it is appropriate to make arguments that have failed in the past, and if so, how to do it.

Review and Overview of American Constitutional History

In theory, the federal government is one of limited, enumerated power. To see if the federal government has power to act on a subject, one can look at the Constitution (and its judicial interpretation) to find if the power is delegated or implied. Article I, § 8, establishes most of the powers of Congress. The federal government is supreme in its sphere of operation. If a law passed by Congress and within federal power conflicts with a state law, the state law falls because of the Supremacy Clause.

In contrast to the federal Constitution, state constitutions created governments of general powers. They have "broad police powers" to protect the health, safety, welfare, etc., of people within the states. The states existed before the Constitution, and their powers are limited by the Constitution, but, by one widely-held view, are not derived from it.

Limitations on both state and national power typically can be enforced by courts.

As to the federal government, a citizen's rights might be protected because federal powers to invade them were not delegated or implied. For example, when Anti-Federalists complained about the lack of a Bill of Rights in the proposed federal Constitution (including a lack of protection for free press), the Federalist answer was that Congress had no power over the press.

A citizen's rights might also be protected because invasion of them was specifically forbidden even as to delegated powers. *See* Article I, § 9; the Bill of Rights; Article III, §§ 2 and 3. In addition, rights might be protected, though less explicitly in the text, such as the right to travel. Finally, a structural analysis (for example, how a government founded on popular sovereignty must operate) might provide additional limitations.

State governments were typically governments of general (that is, not enumerated) power. Before the Civil War, state governments regulated most aspects of a citizen's life and could establish, regulate, or abrogate rights such as free speech, free press, and free exercise of religion. States could permit or forbid slavery. The powers of the states were limited by supreme federal law; state laws that conflicted with federal law were preempted. State powers were also limited by specific prohibitions in the federal Constitution. Article IV, § 2, prevented states from discriminating against out-of-staters. Article I, § 10, among other things, prevented states from entering treaties or passing bills of attainder, ex post facto laws, or laws impairing the obligation of contracts. Federal constitutional limits on the states did not include the Bill of Rights, as the Court held in *Barron v. Baltimore* (1833). But, at times, the Court seemed to suggest limits that were not explicit in the text, such as the Dormant Commerce Clause. In addition, state constitutions could limit state power. States typically had their own bill of rights and other limits on state power.

The states and the federal government have historically differed in their legislative power to protect individual rights from *private* invasion—that is, by other citizens rather than the government. As governments of general power, states could typically provide such protection. With a few remarkable exceptions (e.g., protection for rights of owners of fugitive slaves and later the rights secured by the 13th Amendment), the Court has often denied that the federal government has power to protect individual rights from private action.

Usually, federal constitutional guarantees are interpreted to protect against governmental, not private, action. Congressional legislative power to enforce the guarantees of the 14th Amendment (for example) has been interpreted in the same way. But the Court also has suggested Congress has a right to protect the operations of the federal government and the rights of citizens in their dealings with the federal government. For example, even before the Civil War, Congress probably had the power to protect the right to petition the federal government against individual or state interference. The federal government also had the right to protect people coming to Washington to transact business with it. These are essentially structural limitations. Powers are implied from the nature of the government.

The Civil War Amendments raised the possibility of a substantial increase in federal protection of citizens' rights against state governments and perhaps against private action. Today, the 13th, 14th, 15th, and later Amendments have substantially increased federal power. In addition, especially after 1936, exercise of federal power under the Commerce Clause and Spending Clauses substantially increased. States continue to operate as governments of general jurisdiction. The scope of state power is actually or potentially limited by the vast growth of federal power.

From 1868 through the 1880s, none of the guarantees of the federal Bill of Rights were applied to the states. During the next 50 years, the Justices debated which guarantees of individual rights, beyond those that limited the states in the original Constitution, should be applied to the states. Much of the debate centered on provisions of the Bill of Rights and whether they should be incorporated by reference, either through the "liberty" of the Due Process Clause or as constitutional "privileges or immunities" protected by the Privileges or Immunities Clause.

A Brief History of the Adoption of the Constitution and Its Most Significant Amendments

The Constitutional Convention met in Philadelphia in 1787. Many leaders believed the Articles of Confederation were too feeble and needed revision. Under the Articles, the governing body was a Congress in which each state had one vote. Nine affirmative votes were required for most important actions. Congress lacked power to tax individuals and was forced to resort to requisitions on the states—much like the procedure used by the United Nations today. The Articles lacked a significant national judiciary or executive. Although the Constitutional Convention had been called merely to revise the Articles, it scrapped them and replaced them with an entirely new document. Only nine of the thirteen states were required for ratification, not all thirteen as the Articles required. The Constitution was ratified in 1788. It allowed the national government to act directly on individuals: to tax individuals, to prosecute them for crimes against the national government, etc.

The original Constitution lacked a Bill of Rights. Proposals for a Bill of Rights surfaced late in the Constitutional Convention and failed. The lack of a Bill of Rights was a source of strong objection to the new Constitution. Supporters of the Constitution (Federalists) made three main arguments that a Bill of Rights was unnecessary. First, they said that bills of rights were securities for the people against kings and in America the people were sovereign and did not need to be protected against themselves. Second, the Constitution already contained guarantees of individual rights, such as the Treason Clause, the Habeas Corpus Clause, and the provision against ex post facto laws—so more was not needed. Finally, they said listing rights was dangerous because it would imply governmental power over the subject—for example, the provision that the government cannot take private property for public use without compensation meant the government could do so with compensation. Many explicitly argued that the new federal government had no power over speech or press, so no protection was needed on that score.

The original Bill of Rights was largely drafted and presented by James Madison of Virginia during the first session of the new federal Congress. Madison insisted that the Bill of Rights would protect liberty by producing public support for the guarantees and that it would arm the judiciary with a check on the legislature and executive. His original plan was to insert the Amendments into the body of the Constitution rather than append them as a separate entity. In addition to the provisions that passed and became the first ten Amendments, Madison had proposed inserting the following in Article I, § 10: "*No State shall violate the equal rights of conscience, or the freedom of the press, or trial by jury in criminal cases.*" In support of this provision, Madison said, "State Governments are as liable to attack the invaluable privileges as the General Government is, and therefore ought to be as cautiously guarded against."* The proposal passed the House with free speech added to the list, but was rejected by the Senate.

In 1866, immediately following the Civil War, Congress proposed the 14th Amendment to the Constitution. The Amendment provides in part:

> All persons born or naturalized in the United States ... are citizens of the United States and of the State wherein they reside. No state shall make or enforce any law which shall abridge the privileges or immunities of citizens of the United States; nor shall any State deprive any person of life, liberty, or property without due process of law....

In the thirty years before the framing of the 14th Amendment, the words "privileges and immunities" had often been used to describe rights of American citizens such as those in the Bill of Rights. Michael Kent Curtis, *No State Shall Abridge, The Fourteenth Amendment and the Bill of Rights*, 64–65, 75–76 (1986) [hereafter, *No State Shall Abridge*]. The words "privileges and immunities" were also used in the Article IV, § 2, Privileges and Immunities Clause which secured to the citizens of each state the privileges and immunities of citizens in the several states. According to the orthodox reading today, that Clause guarantees out-of-staters equality with residents of a state in certain basic interests, such as the right to own property, to contract, and to the protection of basic rights accorded

---

* B. Schwartz, Vol. 2, *The Bill of Rights, A Documentary History* at 1027, 1033.

by the state. If understood in this way, such rights could be reduced by a state provided it treated in-state and out-of-state citizens equally.

Chronological Overview of Key Events Related to Incorporation

1787: The Constitutional Convention in Philadelphia draws up the Constitution. It was ratified in 1788 after heated Federalist/Anti-Federalist debate. James Madison, Alexander Hamilton and John Jay write a series of pro-ratification editorials, now known as The Federalist Papers. A major source of controversy is the lack of a bill of rights.

1789: George Washington is inaugurated as first President of the United States. First Congress; Bill of Rights proposed; Judiciary Act of 1789 creates federal courts.

1791: Bill of Rights ratified.

1803: *Marbury v. Madison* (6–0): Chief Justice John Marshall articulates the principle of judicial review. Under this doctrine, the Supreme Court now passes on the constitutionality of acts of Congress and of state legislatures and nullifies unconstitutional legislation.

1820: The Missouri Compromise: Congress admits Missouri as a slave state and Maine as a free state to maintain the balance between slave and free states in the Senate. Congress agrees that in the future, states admitted below 36 degrees 30 minutes latitude may be slave, above will be free.

1831: William Lloyd Garrison begins publication of the abolitionist periodical, the *Liberator*. The Nat Turner slave revolt in Virginia leads to harsher regulation of slavery in the South. In the years that follow, Southern states search interstate travelers and others for anti-slavery books; abolitionists and critics of slavery caught in the South are whipped (or worse). By 1856, Southern postmasters seize and remove pro-Republican newspapers from the mails. The increasing conflict over slavery ultimately brings on the Civil War.

1833: *Barron v. Baltimore* (7–0): Guarantees of the Bill of Rights limit only the federal government, not the states.

1850: Compromise of 1850: Congress admits California as a free state but passes a much stricter Fugitive Slave Act.

1854: Kansas-Nebraska Act: Congress repeals the Missouri Compromise, allowing voters in each territory to decide whether to be a slave or free state. A war breaks out in the Kansas territory between the pro and anti-slavery forces.

1857: *Dred Scott v. Sandford*: The Court rules that Congress lacks the power to outlaw slavery in federal territory and that even *free* blacks cannot be citizens of the United States and are thus unprotected by the Constitution's guarantees of individual rights. Hinton Helper publishes the *Impending Crisis*, an indictment of slavery. Lincoln's Republican party uses it as a campaign document. Southern states treat circulation of the book as a crime. Southern officials search out-of-state travelers for "incendiary literature."

1860: *State v. Worth* (N.C. 1860): North Carolina Supreme Court affirms the conviction of minister Daniel Worth for circulating an anti-slavery book, the *Impending Crisis*, which was used as a Republican campaign document. The statute provided for both imprisonment and whipping for convicted offenders. Abraham Lincoln is elected as a Republican President. As a result, South Carolina secedes, followed by most (but not all) of the other slave states.

1865: Lincoln is assassinated five days after Lee's surrender to Grant at Appomattox. Andrew Johnson becomes President upon Lincoln's assassination. The 13th Amendment is ratified. The 13th Amendment, by its implied repeal of the Clause by which slaves counted as 3/5ths of a person for purposes of representation in the federal House and the electoral college, meant that the South, having lost the war, might return to political power on the backs of disenfranchised Americans of African descent.

1866: The 14th Amendment is proposed. Section 1 limited the states from abridging certain individual rights. Section 2 dealt with the problems raised by the 13th Amendment and the 3/5ths Clause.

1866–76: Reconstruction. White and Black Republican coalitions rule the post-war South, but are ultimately driven from power by political terrorism. The "Jim Crow" era is later secured by racist statutes.

1868: The 14th Amendment is ratified. Susan B. Anthony and Elizabeth Cady Stanton bitterly oppose the Amendment because §2 reduces a state's congressional representation *only* if it restricts the voting rights of *males*. Victoria Woodhull addresses the Judiciary Committee of the House of Representatives arguing that women should have the right to vote under the 14th Amendment. The Committee, with several congressmen dissenting, issues a negative report.

1872: The federal Amnesty Act restores full political privileges to Confederate oath-breakers.

1872–76: Attack upon and eventual overthrow of Reconstruction in the South.

1873: *Slaughter-House Cases* (5–4): The Court begins the liquidation of the Privileges or Immunities Clause of the 14th Amendment. Following the decision, the Court holds one after another of the guarantees of the Bill of Rights do not limit the states.

Bradwell v. State: Following the approach of *Slaughter-House* on the limited scope of the Privileges or Immunities Clause of the 14th Amendment, the Court upholds Illinois' ban on women practicing law, ruling it is not a privilege of national citizenship. No equal protection claim was made.

1875: *Minor v. Happersett* (9–0): The Court rules that citizenship does not give women the right to vote under the Privileges or Immunities Clause of the 14th Amendment; therefore, women's political rights are under the jurisdiction of each individual state. Mrs. Minor's husband had to sue on her behalf since married women, like children, could not file suit on their own.

1877: Under the Compromise of 1877, which is regarded as the formal end of Reconstruction, Republicans get the presidency in a contested election, and federal troops are withdrawn from the South.

1883: *Civil Rights Cases* (8–1): Court holds that Congress lacks power under either the 13th or 14th Amendment to pass a statute that prohibits racial discrimination in public accommodations by individuals or corporations. The Court also holds that the 14th Amendment's protections are limited to "state action."

1900: *Maxwell v. Dow* (8–1): The Supreme Court, in an opinion written by Justice Peckham, soon to be the author of *Lochner v. New York*, rules that the criminal jury trial guarantee of the 6th Amendment does not limit the states. The Court warns that application of Bill of Rights as a limit on the states would threaten state sovereignty.

1925: *Gitlow v. New York* (7–2): The Court assumes that rights to free speech and free press limit the states. By the 1930s, the Court begins to refer to the absorption of the 1st Amendment into the 14th as a limit on the states under the Due Process Clause of the 14th Amendment.

1937: *Palko v. Connecticut* (8–1): By this time the Court has required states to obey the free speech and press guarantees and to some degree the right to counsel as aspects of "liberty" under the Due Process Clause of the 14th Amendment. In *Palko*, this selective incorporation of guarantees of the Bill of Rights into the 14th Amendment is rationalized on the theory that the absorbed rights are implicit in the concept of ordered liberty.

1947: *Adamson v. California* (5–4): The Court refuses to apply the privilege against self-incrimination to the states. In dissent, Justice Black—joined by three other justices—advocates total incorporation and cites his reading of the historical record.

1953–69: Warren Court: The Court embraces expanded national protection for free speech, the rights of those accused of crimes, and freedom from state-imposed racial discrimination. Most of the still-unincorporated Bill of Rights guarantees are applied to the states. The Court also upholds the Civil Rights Act of 1964, which banned discrimination in public accommodations and employment. It also upholds the Voting Rights Act of 1965, which provided strong and effective remedies against state racial discrimination in voting.

1967: *Duncan v. Louisiana* (7–2): The Court holds the right to jury trial fundamental to the American scheme of justice and so incorporated into the 14th Amendment's Due Process Clause as a limit on the states.

1999: *Saenz v. Roe* (7–2): Court invokes the Privileges or Immunities Clause of the 14th Amendment to strike down California's refusal to pay new residents a higher rate of welfare than they had received in their previous state. The limit applied until they had resided in California for one year.

2010: *McDonald v. Chicago* (5–4): The court holds that an individual right to bear arms is incorporated as a limit on the states. Justice Thomas concurs basing incorporation on the Privileges or Immunities Clause.

Interpreting the 14th Amendment: Types of Constitutional Argument

The first problem we will explore is whether the 14th Amendment requires states to respect the liberties set out in the Bill of Rights. The Civil War and the ratification of the 13th and 14th Amendments have been called "the Second American revolution." The federal Constitution led to a more powerful central government than had existed under the Articles of Confederation. The original Constitution provided a few limits on the federal government and the states in the interest of individual rights. The subsequent adoption of the Bill of Rights provided guarantees of many basic individual liberties, at least against the new national government.

In the revolutionary era, states had drafted their own constitutions with *state* bills of rights. The Civil War and Recnstruction (the second American Revolution) eventually produced an additional *federal* source of freedom for citizens against violations of basic liberties by *their own state governments.* Reconstruction era statutes provided a forum in *federal court* for claims of denial of rights and privileges of citizens of the United States. The contempt powers of federal judges provided a potentially potent weapon against recalcitrant state officials.

As you consider the effect of the 14th Amendment, recall the types of constitutional arguments that can be made. To see the type of argument being made (textual, contextual, structural, from precedent, historical, or policy) ask yourself where the argument starts; what are its premises. Please re-read the discussion of types of constitutional arguments in Chapter 1.

B. A Hypothetical Case

1. Does either the 14th Amendment "Due Process" or "Privileges or Immunities" Clause *incorporate* by reference, as a limit on the states, *liberties,* rights, *privileges, or immunities* set out in the Bill of Rights? Would it be reasonable to describe free speech or free exercise of religion, for example, as a "privilege" or as an "immunity"? Why or why not? What sorts of arguments can you construct?

2. Read the 13th, 14th, 15th, and 19th Amendments. Pay particular attention to § 1 of the 14th Amendment.

3. Consider the following hypothetical case in connection with your study of incorporation. It is included here in hopes that you will think about the problem as you read the material that follows.

Hypothetical Question

In 1870 Benjamin F. La Tourgee, a U.S. citizen, was arrested in Louisiana. He was charged with "advocacy of integration of the races." For purposes of this hypothetical, you should assume that after the Civil War the Louisiana legislature had made it a crime to advocate integration of the races. La Tourgee was prosecuted under that law. You should also assume that, as of 1870, state segregation of railway cars was constitutionally permissible and did not violate the Equal Protection Clause of the 14th Amendment.

La Tourgee had delivered a speech advocating the integration of railroad cars which were segregated by Louisiana law at the time. LaTourgee said, among other things, that the state law should be repealed. Before the Civil War, Southern states had, in effect, made it a crime to advocate the abolition of slavery. This was possible because of *Barron v. Baltimore* (1833). Consider this case as one of first impression, arising after the ratification of the 14th Amendment and before the *Slaughter-House Cases* (1873). Then consider it again after you have read *Slaughter-House.* As counsel for La Tourgee, make an argument that the state statute under which he was convicted violates a right of free speech that is protected by § 1 of the 14th Amendment. What arguments are available that advocating changing the law should be a federally protected right, especially under § 1 of the 14th Amendment? Consider how you would use text, context, history, policy, precedent, and structure to make your arguments.

Consider the holding and rationale of *Barron,* as well as the following information.

Webster's New Collegiate Dictionary (1974) defines the following words:

- a "citizen," in part, is "one entitled to the rights and privileges of a freeman; a native or naturalized citizen who owes allegiance to a government and is entitled to reciprocal protection from it."
- "due process" is "a course of legal proceedings carried out regularly and in accordance with established rules and principles—called also due process of law."
- "privilege" is "a right or immunity granted as a particular benefit...." *The Random House Webster's* defines "privilege" as "1. a right, immunity, or benefit, enjoyed by a particular person or a restricted group of persons ... 5. any of the rights common to all citizens under modern constitutional government." [A total of nine usages are listed.]
- "immunity" is an "exemption from normal legal duties, penalties, or liabilities, granted to a special group of people."
- "liberty" is "freedom from unjust or undue governmental control."

The Constitution includes the following provisions:

- The Preamble provides: "We the People of the United States, in Order to form a more perfect Union, establish Justice, insure domestic Tranquility, provide for the common defence, promote the general Welfare, and secure the Blessings of Liberty to ourselves and our Posterity, do ordain and establish this Constitution for the United States of America."
- Article IV, §4, provides: "The United States shall guarantee to every State in this Union a Republican Form of Government...."
- The 1st Amendment provides, in part: "Congress shall make no law ... abridging the freedom of speech, or of the press, or the right of the people peaceably to assemble, and petition the Government for a redress of grievances."

(If you believe other Sections of the Constitution bear on the issue, you should of course consider them, even though they are not specifically set out here.)

Use as many of the types of arguments we have identified as you appropriately can. Are there places in the constitutional text that suggest the type of government to be established? How are these Sections relevant to a structural argument?

Consider this problem now and as you read *all* of the material on incorporation.

II. Application of the Bill of Rights to the States: 1791–1833

Should the states have been required to obey the guarantees of the federal Bill of Rights *before* the passage of the 14th Amendment? Why or why not? What sorts of arguments can you construct? Consider the following case.

Barron v. Mayor and City Council of Baltimore
32 U.S. 243 (1833)

[The plaintiff, who owned a wharf in the eastern section of Baltimore, instituted this action against the city of Baltimore to recover damages for injuries to the wharf property arising from street work by the city, work that deposited sand and gravel in the area of his wharf, making the wharf useless. Barron claimed that the city, in causing damage to his waterfront, had taken his property for public use and that compensation was therefore due in accordance with the 5th Amendment to the Constitution. On this point Barron contended that this Amendment "declares principles which regulate the legislation of the states, for the protection of the people in each and all of the States, regarded as citizens of the United States, or as inhabitants subject to the laws of the Union." (The paragraphs below are numbered in order to facilitate discussion.)]

Mr. Chief Justice Marshall delivered the opinion of the court.

[1] The judgment brought up by this writ of error having been rendered by the court of a state, this tribunal can exercise no jurisdiction over it, unless it be shown to come within the provisions of the twenty-fifth section of the judicial act [of 1789, which requires the existence of a federal question].

[2] The plaintiff in error contends that it comes within that clause in the 5th Amendment to the Constitution, which inhibits the taking of private property for public use without just compensation. He insists that this amendment, being in favor of the liberty of the citizen, ought to be so construed as to restrain the legislative power of a state, as well as that of the United States. If this proposition be untrue, the court can take no jurisdiction of the cause.

[3] The question thus presented is, we think, of great importance, but not of much difficulty.

[4] The Constitution was ordained and established by the people of the United States for themselves, for their own government, and not for the government of the individual States. Each State established a constitution for itself, and in that constitution, provided such limitations and restrictions on the powers of its particular government, as its judgment dictated. The people of the United States framed such a government for the United States as they supposed best adapted to their situation and best calculated to promote their interests. The powers they conferred on this government were to be exercised by itself; and the limitations on power, if expressed in general terms, are naturally, and, we think, necessarily applicable to the government created by the instrument. They are limitations of power granted in the instrument itself; not of distinct governments, framed by different persons and for different purposes.

[5] If these propositions be correct, the 5th Amendment must be understood as restraining the power of the general government, not as applicable to the States. In their several constitutions, they have imposed such restrictions on their respective governments, as their own wisdom suggested; such as they deemed most proper for themselves. It is a subject on which they judge exclusively, and with which others interfere no further than they are supposed to have a common interest.

[6] The counsel for the plaintiff in error insists that the Constitution was intended to secure the people of the several States against the undue exercise of power by their respective State governments; as well as against that which might be attempted by their general government. In support of this argument, he relies on the inhibitions contained in the tenth section of the first article.

[7] We think that section affords a strong, if not a conclusive, argument in support of the opinion already indicated by the court.

[8] The preceding section contains restrictions which are obviously intended for the exclusive purpose of restraining the exercise of power by the departments of the general

government. Some of them use language applicable only to congress; others are expressed in general terms. The third clause, for example, declares that "no bill of attainder or ex post facto law shall be passed." No language can be more general; yet the demonstration is complete, that it applies solely to the government of the United States. In addition to the general arguments furnished by the instrument itself, some of which have been already suggested, the succeeding section, the avowed purpose of which is to restrain State legislation, contains in terms the very prohibition. It declares, that "no State shall pass any bill of attainder or ex post facto law." This provision, then, of the ninth section, however comprehensive its language, contains no restrictions on State legislation.

[9] The ninth section having enumerated, in the nature of a bill of rights, the limitations intended to be imposed on the powers of the general government, the tenth proceeds to enumerate those which were to operate on the state legislatures. These restrictions are brought together in the same section, and are by express words applied to the States. "No State shall enter into any treaty," &c. Perceiving, that in a constitution framed by the people of the United States, for the government of all, no limitation of the action of government on the people would apply to the state government, unless expressed in terms, the restrictions contained in the tenth section are in direct words so applied to the states.

[10] It is worthy of remark, too, that these inhibitions generally restrain state legislation on subjects entrusted to the general government, or in which the people of all the states feel an interest.

[11] A state is forbidden to enter into any treaty, alliance or confederation. If these compacts are with foreign nations, they interfere with the treaty-making power, which is conferred entirely on the general government; if with each other, for political purposes, they can scarcely fail to interfere with the general purpose and intent of the Constitution. To grant letters of marque and reprisal, would lead directly to war; the power of declaring which is expressly given to Congress. To coin money is also the exercise of a power conferred on Congress. It would be tedious to recapitulate the several limitations on the powers of the states which are contained in this section. They will be found, generally, to restrain state legislation on subjects entrusted to the government of the Union, in which the citizens of all the states are interested. In these alone, were the whole people concerned. The question of their application to states is not left to construction. It is averred in positive words.

[12] If the original Constitution, in the ninth and tenth sections of the first article, draws this plain and marked line of discrimination between the limitations it imposes on the powers of the general government, and on those of the state; if, in every inhibition intended to act on state power, words are employed, which directly express that intent; some strong reason must be assigned for departing from this safe and judicious course in framing the amendments, before that departure can be assumed.

[13] We search in vain for that reason.

[14] Had the people of the several states, or any of them, required changes in their constitutions; had they required additional safeguards to liberty from the apprehended encroachments of their particular governments: the remedy was in their own hands, and would have been applied by themselves. A convention would have been assembled by the discontented state, and the required improvements would have been made by itself. The unwieldy and cumbrous machinery of procuring a recommendation from two-thirds of Congress, and the assent of three-fourths of their sister states, could never have occurred to any human being, as a mode of doing that which might be effected by the state itself. Had the framers of these amendments intended them to be limitations on the powers of

the state governments they would have imitated the framers of the original Constitution, and have expressed that intention. Had Congress engaged in the extraordinary occupation of improving the constitutions of the several states, by affording the people additional protection from the exercise of power by their own governments, in matters which concerned themselves alone, they would have declared this purpose in plain and intelligible language.

[15] But it is universally understood, it is a part of the history of the day, that the great revolution which established the Constitution of the United States, was not effected without immense opposition. Serious fears were extensively entertained, that those powers which the patriot statesmen, who then watched over the interests of our country, deemed essential to union, and to the attainment of those invaluable objects for which union was sought, might be exercised in a manner dangerous to liberty. In almost every convention by which the Constitution was adopted, amendments to guard against the abuse of power were recommended. These amendments demanded security against the apprehended encroachments of the general government not against those of the local governments.

[16] In compliance with a sentiment thus generally expressed, to quiet fears thus extensively entertained, amendments were proposed by the required majority in Congress, and adopted by the States. These amendments contain no expression indicating an intention to apply them to the State governments. This court cannot so apply them.

[17] We are of the opinion, that the provision in the 5th Amendment to the Constitution, declaring that private property shall not be taken for public use, without just compensation, is intended solely as a limitation on the exercise of power by the government of the United States, and is not applicable to the legislation of the States. We are, therefore, of opinion, that there is no repugnancy between the several acts of the general assembly of Maryland, given in evidence by the defendants at the trial of this cause in the court of that State, and the Constitution of the United States.

[18] This court, therefore, has no jurisdiction of the cause, and it is dismissed....

III. From *Barron* to the Adoption of the 14th Amendment: The Pre-Civil War Background

A. The Privileges and Immunities Clause of Article IV

The Privileges and Immunities Clause in the original Constitution, Article IV, §2, provides: "The Citizens of each State shall be entitled to all Privileges and Immunities of Citizens in the several States." An early decision on Article IV, §2, was *Corfield v. Coryell* (C.C.E.D. Pa. 1823).

In *Corfield*, a Pennsylvania citizen challenged a New Jersey statute that limited gathering oysters in New Jersey waters to New Jersey residents. Justice Bushrod Washington, a Supreme Court Justice "riding circuit," decided the case. Justice Washington held that the oysters were common property of citizens of New Jersey and that the state could exclude those from out of state from the property. (This common property doctrine as a limit on the privileges and immunities guaranteed by Article IV is no longer the law.)

In dicta, Justice Washington defined "Privileges and Immunities of Citizens in the several States" as follows:

We feel no hesitation in confining these expressions to those privileges and immunities which are, in their nature, fundamental; which belong, of right, to the citizens of all free governments; and which have, at all times, been enjoyed by the citizens of the several States which compose this Union, from the time of their becoming free, independent, and sovereign. What these fundamental principles are, it would perhaps be more tedious than difficult to enumerate. They may, however, be all comprehended under the following general heads: Protection by the government; the enjoyment of life and liberty, with the right to acquire and possess property of every kind, and to pursue and obtain happiness and safety; subject nevertheless to such restraints as the government may justly prescribe for the general good of the whole. The right of a citizen of one state to pass through, or to reside in any other state, for purposes of trade, agriculture, professional pursuits, or otherwise; to claim the benefit of the writ of habeas corpus; to institute and maintain actions of any kind in the courts of the state; to take, hold, and dispose of property, either real or personal; and an exemption from higher taxes or impositions than are paid by the other citizens of the state; may be mentioned as some of the particular privileges and immunities of citizens, which are clearly embraced by the general description of privileges deemed to be fundamental: to which may be added, the elective franchise, as regulated and established by the laws or constitution of the state in which it is to be exercised. These, and many others which might be mentioned, are, strictly speaking, privileges and immunities....

A number of cases held that Article IV, §2, privileges or immunities only protected temporary visitors from out of state and allowed them to enjoy certain privileges allowed under state law. In short, these courts read the provision as modern courts do—to prohibit laws that discriminate against out-of-staters, but not laws that limit rights of in-staters and out-of-staters alike.

B. Subsequent Decisions: The Response to *Barron*

In *Livingston v. Moore* (1833), the Court said that the 7th Amendment requirement of a civil jury trial did not apply to the states: "As to the amendments of the constitution of the United States, they must be put out of the case; since it is now settled, that those amendments do not extend to the states; and this observation disposes of the next exception, which relies on the seventh article of those amendments." In *Permoli v. New Orleans* (1845), the Court rejected a 1st Amendment religious liberty claim raised in an attack on a New Orleans city ordinance. It explained that the Constitution did not protect religious liberty against the states.

A minority of state courts refused to follow the Supreme Court's rule that the guarantees of the federal Bill of Rights did not limit the states. Perhaps the most emphatic was the Supreme Court of Georgia. For example, in *Nunn v. State* (Ga. 1846), and *Campbell v. State* (Ga. 1852), Chief Justice Lumpkin of the Georgia Supreme Court described various rights in the federal Bill of Rights as "privileges," including the rights claimed by the defendant in those cases—the "privilege" of bearing arms and the "privilege" to confront witnesses. In *Nunn*, Lumpkin said that "We do not believe that, because the people withheld this arbitrary power of disfranchisement from Congress, they ever intended to confer it on the local legislatures. This right is too dear to be confided to a republican legislature." He continued:

> The right of the people peaceably to assemble and petition the government for a redress of grievances; to be secure in their persons, houses, papers, and effects, against unreasonable searches and seizures; in all criminal prosecutions, to be confronted with the witness against them; to be publicly tried by an impartial jury; and to have the assistance of counsel for their defence, *is as perfect under the States as the national legislature, and cannot be violated by either.*

In *Campbell*, Lumpkin insisted that the 6th Amendment privilege of the accused to confront witnesses also limited the states. He believed the same rule applied to other Amendments as well. Lumpkin insisted that the doctrine "that Congress may not exercise this power, but that each State Legislature may do so for itself" falsely implied, for example, that "a National press and State press, were quite separate and distinct." In fact, however, it should "constantly be borne in mind, that notwithstanding we may have different governments ... we have but one people; ... and that it is in vain to shield them from a blow aimed by the Federal arm, if they are liable to be prostrated by one dealt with equal fatality by their own."

Like Justice Black almost one hundred years later, Lumpkin exhibited an almost religious reverence when he wrote of "the ten amendments — but for the apparent irreverence, I would say *commandments* — which were added to the Constitution." He summarily rejected any state's rights claim to violate the rights in the Bill of Rights. "From such *State rights*," Lumpkin exclaimed, "good Lord deliver us!" He continued:

> While this Court yields to none in its devotion to State *rights*, and would be the first to *resist* all attempts at Federal usurpation, it feels itself called on by the blood of the many martyrs, who nobly died to maintain the great principles of civil liberty contained in these amendments — *our American Magna Charta* — to stand by, support and defend the rights which they guarantee, against all encroachments, whether proceeding from the National or State governments.

Some Specific Questions about *Barron*

1. What values are promoted by the decision in *Barron*? What values are subordinated by the decision?

2. Look at the chronology for 1828–1840 at the beginning of the casebook. Does it give you further perspective on *Barron*?

3. Identify the types of arguments made (text, structure, etc.) in the numbered paragraphs. For example, look at the restrictions on state power in Article I, § 10, mentioned by *Barron*. Look at the form chosen for the final version of § 1 of the 14th Amendment. Can you make arguments from precedent and context about the significance of using the "no state shall" form in § 1?

4. In answering the following questions, what parts of the constitutional text do you invoke?

    a. Today, if your client was arrested in Washington, D.C., for violating a *congressional* statute that made it a crime to distribute socialist literature in the District of Columbia, to what Amendment would you appeal?

    b. What if Congress had passed a statute in 1857 making it a crime to distribute anti-slavery publications in the Kansas territory? On what Amendment would you rely?

c. What if the state of North Carolina had enacted a statute banning anti-slavery publications and your client was prosecuted under that statute in 1860? On what Amendment would you rely? Would you succeed? Where else might you look for protection?

d. What if your client was prosecuted in 1949 under a Mississippi statute that makes it a crime to advocate integration of public schools? On what Amendment(s) would you rely? Are your chances of success different than they would be in 1860? Why?

C. The Bill of Rights: 1833–57

Barron v. Baltimore (1833), is the seminal case on the issue of application of the Bill of Rights to state and local governments prior to the 14th Amendment.

In *Murray's Lessee* (1856), a customs collector whose account was more than a million dollars short, challenged a summary procedure the United States government used to attach a lien to his property. The Court discussed the meaning of the Due Process Clause of the 5th Amendment. It noted "It ... was not left to the legislative power to enact *any* process which might be devised. The article is a restraint on the legislative as well as on the executive and judicial powers...." The Court nonetheless rejected the challenge. The Court said:

> That the warrant now in question is legal process, is not denied. It was issued in conformity with an act of Congress. But is it "due process of law?" The constitution contains no description [in the Due Process Clause] of those processes which it was intended to allow or forbid.... To what principles, then, are we to resort to ascertain whether this process, enacted by Congress, is due process? To this the answer must be twofold. [First,] we must examine the constitution itself, to see whether this process be in conflict with any of its provisions.

The Court went on to say that processes sanctioned by long historic usage at the time of the adoption of the Constitution were also processes that Congress was permitted to use (if they did not contravene the text). It was because of the historic use of the summary writ at issue that the Court approved its usage.

1. According to *Murray's Lessee*, how could you find out if legislation passed the test of due process?

2. What amendment is the Court construing in *Murray's Lessee*? Why is this pre-14th Amendment case pertinent to the 14th Amendment? What type of analysis is involved in claiming that the meaning of due process in the 5th Amendment is relevant to due process in the 14th, i.e., is it an argument from text, context, etc.?

3. Are there any procedural guarantees in the Constitution, and especially the Bill of Rights? What are they? How might you argue from the passage in *Murray's Lessee* that at least some of the guarantees of the Bill of Rights limit the states under the 14th Amendment? Which ones would apply under this argument?

D. *Dred Scott v. Sandford*: Rights of Free Blacks and Slavery in the Territories

1. *Dred Scott v. Sandford* (1857) is a case in which a slave sought his freedom because of his residence in a free state. For our purposes, *Dred Scott* is important for several reasons:

- The holding that free blacks could not be American citizens, denying them any constitutional protections, is relevant to the Citizenship Clause of the 14th Amendment.
- *Dred Scott* describes rights under the federal Constitution as "rights, privileges, or immunities." It holds that these "rights, privileges, or immunities" belong only to citizens of the United States. *Dred Scott*'s use of these words is therefore relevant to the meaning of the phrase "privileges or immunities of citizens of the United States" in the 14th Amendment.
- As we study equal protection we will be looking at the law and race relations. *Dred Scott* is a milestone in American race relations.

2. *Dred Scott* is one event in a chain of conflicts that led to the Civil War. Slavery had been a source of controversy from the beginning of the Republic.

In 1787, the Continental Congress passed the Northwest Ordinance, prohibiting the existence of slavery in the Northwest Territories. The Louisiana Purchase practically doubled the size of the nation. Much of the new land was suitable for slave-based agriculture. When Missouri, part of the Louisiana Territory, wanted to enter the Union, there were eleven free and eleven slave states. A proposal to require the slave state of Missouri to abolish slavery as a condition of entry produced intense sectional conflict. Under the Missouri Compromise of 1820, Maine was admitted as a free state and Missouri as a slave state. The Compromise also prohibited slavery in the Louisiana Territory north of the 36th parallel and allowed it below that line.

Victory in the war with Mexico in 1848 brought substantial new territory to the nation and renewed controversy over slavery in the new territories. The Compromise of 1850 allowed California to enter as a free state, while the Southern states got passage of a harsh federal fugitive slave law.

The Kansas-Nebraska Act in 1854 repealed the Missouri Compromise and allowed voters in each territory to decide on slavery. Pro and anti-slavery advocates streamed into Kansas and war erupted between the two factions. *Dred Scott,* issued in 1857, just two days after the inauguration of President James Buchanan, was decided in this politically charged atmosphere. The decision in *Dred Scott* made it quite doubtful that the voters of the territories could exclude slavery prior to statehood. The election of Abraham Lincoln in 1860, on a platform of excluding slavery from the territories, was followed by secession.

3. While *Dred Scott* held that the 5th Amendment prevented Congress from banning slavery in the federal territories, the Republican party contended that it required exactly the opposite. Republicans argued that no one could be deprived of their liberty without due process by the federal government. Therefore slaves held on federal territory without benefit of trial were deprived of liberty without due process. The Republican party platform in 1856 provided:

> Resolved: That, with our Republican fathers, we hold it to be a self-evident truth, that all men are endowed with the inalienable right to life, liberty and the pursuit of happiness, and that the primary object and ulterior design of our Federal Government were to secure these rights to all persons under its exclusive jurisdiction; that, as our Republican fathers, when they had abolished Slavery in all our National Territory* ordained that no person shall be de-

---

* This statement refers to the banning of slavery in the Northwest Territory by the Northwest Ordinance of 1787. The Louisiana Purchase and westward expansion resurrected the issue of slavery outside the original thirteen states.

prived of life, liberty, or property, without due process of law, it becomes our duty to maintain this provision of the Constitution against all attempts to violate it for the purpose of establishing Slavery in the Territories of the United States by positive legislation, prohibiting its existence or extension therein.

That we deny the authority of Congress, of a Territorial Legislat[ure], of any individual, or association of individuals, to give legal existence to Slavery in any Territory of the United States, while the present Constitution shall be maintained.

4. Note the language of Article III, § 2: "The judicial Power shall extend to all Cases, in Law and Equity ... between Citizens of different States." Note that the *Dred Scott* decision construes this language to mean: "The judicial Power shall extend to all Cases, in Law and Equity ... between Citizens of different States *who are also citizens of the United States*."

5. The facts in *Dred Scott* are somewhat complicated. The following simple version will be sufficient for our purposes. Dred Scott was a slave. His master took him to the northern or free part of the Missouri territory. Congress had banned slavery in this area as part of the Missouri Compromise. By a common law rule, followed by many states, a slave taken by his master to live or establish a domicile in free territory became free. If the visit was merely a temporary one, by the majority approach, the slave was not emancipated. Emancipation by establishing a domicile in free territory continued even if the former slave returned to live in his slave state. Both Northern and Southern courts had followed this rule. But, by 1857, some Northern courts were freeing slaves who came as temporary visitors and some Southern courts were refusing to recognize the emancipation of slaves who returned to slave states after establishing domicile in a free state. Dred Scott sued for his freedom in federal court in Missouri (a slave state). He claimed that his master had established a domicile in a free territory—the part of the Missouri territory in which slavery was forbidden by the Missouri Compromise. As a result, he claimed that he was entitled to his freedom. The defense denied that Dred Scott could sue in federal court based on diversity since Dred Scott as a black (free or slave) could not be a *citizen* for diversity purposes. It also claimed that the Missouri Compromise violated the 5th Amendment. Chief Justice Taney's decision agreed with the defense and denied United States citizenship to all who were descended from slaves, whether they were now free or not, and whether their states recognized them as state citizens or not.

Dred Scott v. Sandford
60 U.S. 393 (1857)

[Taney, (C.J.), delivered the opinion of the Court. McLean and Curtis dissenting.]

Mr. Chief Justice Taney delivered the opinion of the Court.

[Dred Scott], who was also the plaintiff in the court below, was, with his wife and children, held as slaves by the defendant, in the State of Missouri; and he brought this action in the Circuit Court of the United States for that district, to assert the title of himself and his family to freedom....

The question is simply this: Can a negro, whose ancestors were imported into this country, and sold as slaves, become a member of the political community formed and brought into existence by the Constitution of the United States, and as such become entitled to all the rights, and privileges, and immunities, guaranteed by that instrument to the citizen? One of which rights is the privilege of suing in a court of the United States in the cases specified in the Constitution.

It will be observed, that the plea [that as a negro Dred Scott could not sue in federal court] applies to that class of persons only whose ancestors were negroes of the African race, and imported into this country, and sold and held as slaves. The only matter in issue before the court, therefore, is, whether the descendants of such slaves, when they shall be emancipated, or who are born of parents who had become free before their birth, are citizens of a State, in the sense in which the word citizen is used in the Constitution of the United States. And this being the only matter in dispute on the pleadings, the court must be understood as speaking in this opinion of that class only, that is, of those persons who are the descendants of Africans who were imported into this country, and sold as slaves....

The words "people of the United States" and "citizens" are synonymous terms, and mean the same thing. They both describe the political body who, according to our republican institutions, form the sovereignty, and who hold the power and conduct the Government through their representatives. They are what we familiarly call the "sovereign people," and every citizen is one of this people, and a constituent member of this sovereignty. The question before us is, whether the class of persons described in the plea in abatement compose a portion of this people, and are constituent members of this sovereignty? We think they are not, and that they are not included, and were not intended to be included, under the word "citizens" in the Constitution, and can therefore claim none of the rights and privileges which that instrument provides for and secures to citizens of the United States. On the contrary, they were at that time considered as a subordinate and inferior class of beings, who had been subjugated by the dominant race, and, whether emancipated or not, yet remained subject to their authority, and had no rights or privileges but such as those who held the power and the Government might choose to grant them.

It is not the province of the court to decide upon the justice or injustice, the policy or impolicy, of these laws. The decision of that question belonged to the political or lawmaking power; to those who formed the sovereignty and framed the Constitution. The duty of the court is, to interpret the instrument they have framed, with the best lights we can obtain on the subject, and to administer it as we find it, according to its true intent and meaning when it was adopted.

In discussing this question, we must not confound the rights of citizenship which a State may confer within its own limits, and the rights of citizenship as a member of the Union. It does not by any means follow, because he has all the rights and privileges of a citizen of a State, that he must be a citizen of the United States. He may have all of the rights and privileges of the citizen of a State, and yet not be entitled to the rights and privileges of a citizen in any other State. For, previous to the adoption of the Constitution of the United States, every State had the undoubted right to confer on whomsoever it pleased the character of citizen, and to endow him with all its rights. But this character of course was confined to the boundaries of the State, and gave him no rights or privileges in other States beyond those secured to him by the laws of nations and the comity of States. Nor have the several States surrendered the power of conferring these rights and privileges by adopting the Constitution of the United States. Each State may still confer them upon an alien, or any one it thinks proper, or upon any class or description of persons; yet he would not be a citizen in the sense in which that word is used in the Constitution of the United States, nor entitled to sue as such in one of its courts, nor to the privileges and immunities of a citizen in the other States. The rights which he would acquire would be restricted to the State which gave them. The Constitution has conferred on Congress the right to establish an uniform rule of naturalization, and this right is evidently exclusive, and has always been held by this court to be so. Consequently, no State, since the adoption of the Constitution, can by naturalizing an alien invest him with the rights and privileges secured to a citizen of a State under the Federal Government, although, so far as the State alone was concerned, he would undoubtedly be entitled to the rights of a citizen, and clothed with all the rights and immunities which the Constitution and laws of the State attached to that character....

The question then arises, whether the provisions of the Constitution, in relation to the personal rights and privileges to which the citizen of a State should be entitled, embraced the negro African race, at that time in this country, or who might afterwards be imported, who had then or should afterwards be made free in any State; and to put it in the power of a single State to make him a citizen of the United States, and endue him with the full rights of citizenship in every other State without their consent? Does the Constitution of the United States act upon him whenever he shall be made free under the laws of a State, and raised there to the rank of a citizen, and immediately clothe him with all the privileges of a citizen in every other State, and in its own courts?

The court thinks the affirmative of these propositions cannot be maintained. And if it cannot, the plaintiff in error could not be a citizen of the State of Missouri, within the meaning of the Constitution of the United States, and, consequently, was not entitled to sue in its courts.

It is true, every person, and every class and description of persons, who were at the time of the adoption of the Constitution recognized as citizens in the several States, became also citizens of this new political body; but none other; it was formed by them, and for them and their posterity, but for no one else. And the personal rights and privileges guarantied to citizens of this new sovereignty were intended to embrace those only who were then members of the several State communities, or who should afterwards by birthright or otherwise become members, according to the provisions of the Constitution and the principles on which it was founded. It was the union of those who were at that time members of distinct and separate political communities into one political family, whose power, for certain specified purposes, was to extend over the whole territory of the United States. And it gave to each citizen rights and privileges outside of his State which he did not before possess, and placed him in every other State upon a perfect equality with its own citizens as to rights of person and rights of property; it made him a citizen of the United States.

It becomes necessary, therefore, to determine who were citizens of the several States when the Constitution was adopted. And in order to do this, we must recur to the Governments and institutions of the thirteen colonies, when they separated from Great Britain and formed new sovereignties, and took their places in the family of independent nations. We must inquire who, at that time, were recognized as the people or citizens of a State, whose rights and liberties had been outraged by the English Government; and who declared their independence, and assumed the powers of Government to defend their rights by force of arms.

In the opinion of the court, the legislation and histories of the times, and the language used in the Declaration of Independence, show, that neither the class of persons who had been imported as slaves, nor their descendants, whether they had become free or not, were then acknowledged as a part of the people, nor intended to be included in the general words used in that memorable instrument.

It is difficult at this day to realize the state of public opinion in relation to that unfortunate race, which prevailed in the civilized and enlightened portions of the world at the time of the Declaration of Independence, and when the Constitution of the United States was framed and adopted. But the public history of every European nation displays it in a manner too plain to be mistaken.

They had for more than a century before been regarded as beings of an inferior order, and altogether unfit to associate with the white race, either in social or political relations; and so far inferior, that they had no rights which the white man was bound to respect; and that the negro might justly and lawfully be reduced to slavery for his benefit. He was bought and sold, and treated as an ordinary article of merchandise and traffic, whenever a profit could be made by it. This opinion was at that time fixed and universal in the civilized portion of the white race. It was regarded as an axiom in morals as well as in politics, which no one thought of disputing, or supposed to be open to dispute; and men in every grade and position in society daily and habitually acted upon it in their private pursuits, as well as in matters of public concern, without doubting for a moment the correctness of this opinion....

We refer to these historical facts for the purpose of showing the fixed opinions concerning that race, upon which the statesmen of that day spoke and acted. It is necessary to do this, in order to determine whether the general terms used in the Constitution of the United States, as to the rights of man and the rights of the people, was intended to include them, or to give to them or their posterity the benefit of any of its provisions.

The language of the Declaration of Independence is equally conclusive:

It begins by declaring that, "when in the course of human events it becomes necessary for one people to dissolve the political bands which have connected them with another, and to assume among the powers of the earth the separate and equal station to which the laws of nature and nature's God entitle them, a decent respect for the opinions of mankind requires that they should declare the causes which impel them to the separation."

It then proceeds to say: "We hold these truths to be self-evident: that all men are created equal; that they are endowed by their Creator with certain unalienable rights; that among them is life, liberty, and the pursuit of happiness; that to secure these rights, Governments are instituted, deriving their just powers from the consent of the governed."

The general words above quoted would seem to embrace the whole human family, and if they were used in a similar instrument at this day would be so understood. But it is too clear for dispute, that the enslaved African race were not intended to be included, and formed no part of the people who framed and adopted this declaration; for if the language, as understood in that day, would embrace them, the conduct of the distinguished men who framed the Declaration of Independence would have been utterly and flagrantly inconsistent with the principles they asserted; and instead of the sympathy of mankind, to which they so confidently appealed, they would have deserved and received universal rebuke and reprobation....

This state of public opinion had undergone no change when the Constitution was adopted, as is equally evident from its provisions and language.

The brief preamble sets forth by whom it was formed, for what purposes, and for whose benefit and protection. It declares that it is formed by the *people* of the United States; that is to say, by those who were members of the different political communities in the several States; and its great object is declared to be to secure the blessings of liberty to themselves and their posterity. It speaks in general terms of the *people* of the United States, and of *citizens* of the several States, when it is providing for the exercise of the powers granted or the privileges secured to the citizen. It does not define what description of persons are intended to be included under these terms, or who shall be regarded as a citizen and one of the people. It uses them as terms so well understood, that no further description or definition was necessary.

But there are two clauses in the Constitution which point directly and specifically to the negro race as a separate class of persons, and show clearly that they were not regarded as a portion of the people or citizens of the Government then formed.

One of these clauses reserves to each of the thirteen States the right to import slaves until the year 1808, if it thinks proper. And the importation which it thus sanctions was unquestionably of persons of the race of which we are speaking, as the traffic in slaves in the United States had always been confined to them. And by the other provision the States pledge themselves to each other to maintain the right of property of the master, by delivering up to him any slave who may have escaped from his service, and be found within their respective territories. By the first above-mentioned clause, therefore, the right to purchase and hold this property is directly sanctioned and authorized for twenty years by the people who framed the Constitution. And by the second, they pledge themselves to maintain and uphold the right of the master in the manner specified, as long as the Government they then formed should endure....

[The Court recites laws of Northern states from the period after the revolution up to 1833 forbidding racial intermarriage; bastardizing the children of such unions; and a Connecticut law outlawing a school for young black women. It also recited state and federal laws prohibiting blacks from joining the militia.]

No one, we presume, supposes that any change in public opinion or feeling, in relation to this unfortunate race, in the civilized nations of Europe or in this country, should induce the court to give to the words of the Constitution a more liberal construction in their favor than they were intended to bear when the instrument was framed and adopted. Such an argument would be altogether inadmissible in any tribunal called on to interpret it. If any of its provisions are deemed unjust, there is a mode prescribed in the instrument itself by which it may be amended; but while it remains unaltered, it must be construed now as it was understood at the time of its adoption. It is not only the same in words, but the same in meaning, and delegates the same powers to the Government, and reserves and secures the same rights and privileges to the citizen; and as long as it continues to exist in its present form, it speaks not only in the same words, but with the same meaning and intent with which it spoke when it came from the hands of its framers, and was voted on and adopted by the people of the United States. Any other rule of construction would abrogate the judicial character of this court, and make it the mere reflex of the popular opinion or passion of the day. This court was not created by the Constitution for such purposes. Higher and graver trusts have been confided to it, and it must not falter in the path of duty....

And upon a full and careful consideration of the subject, the court is of the opinion, that, upon the facts stated in the plea in abatement, Dred Scott was not a citizen of Missouri within the meaning of the Constitution of the United States, and not entitled as such to sue in its courts; and, consequently, that the Circuit Court had no jurisdiction of the case, and that the judgment on the plea in abatement is erroneous.

We are aware that doubts are entertained by some of the members of the court, whether the plea in abatement is legally before the court upon this writ of error; but if that plea is regarded as waived, or out of the case upon any other ground, yet the question as to the jurisdiction of the Circuit Court is presented on the face of the bill of exception itself, taken by the plaintiff at the trial; for he admits that he and his wife were born slaves, but endeavors to make out his title to freedom and citizenship by showing that they were taken by their owner to certain places, hereinafter mentioned, where slavery could not by law exist, and that they thereby became free, and upon their return to Missouri became citizens of that State.

Now, if the removal of which he speaks did not give them their freedom, then by his own admission he is still a slave; and whatever opinions may be entertained in favor of the citizenship of a free person of the African race, no one supposes that a slave is a citizen of the State or of the United States. If, therefore, the acts done by his owner did not make them free persons, he is still a slave, and certainly incapable of suing in the character of a citizen....

In considering this part of the controversy, two questions arise: 1. Was he, together with his family, free in Missouri by reason of the stay in the territory of the United States hereinbefore mentioned? And 2. If they were not, is Scott himself free by reason of his removal to Rock Island, in the State of Illinois, as stated in the above admissions?

We proceed to examine the first question.

The act of Congress, upon which the plaintiff relies, declares that slavery and involuntary servitude, except as a punishment for crime, shall be forever prohibited in all that part of the territory ceded by France, under the name of Louisiana, which lies north of thirty-six degrees thirty minutes north latitude, and not included within the limits of Missouri. And the difficulty which meets us at the threshold of this part of the inquiry is, whether Congress was authorized to pass this law under any of the powers granted to it by the Constitution; for if the authority is not given by that instrument, it is the duty of this court to declare it void and inoperative, and incapable of conferring freedom upon any one who is held as a slave under the laws of any one of the States....

But the power of Congress over the person or property of a citizen can never be a mere discretionary power under our Constitution and form of Government. The powers of the Government and the rights and privileges of the citizen are regulated and plainly defined by the Constitution itself. And when the Territory becomes a part of the United States, the Federal Government enters into possession in the character impressed upon it by those who created it. It enters upon it with its powers over the citizen strictly defined, and limited by the Constitution, from which it derives its own existence, and by virtue of which alone it continues to exist and act as a Government and sovereignty. It has no power of any kind beyond it; and it cannot, when it enters a Territory of the United States, put off its character, and assume discretionary or despotic powers which the Constitution has denied to it. It cannot create for itself a new character separated from the citizens of the United States, and the duties it owes them under the provisions of the Constitution. The Territory being a part of the United States, the Government and the citizen both enter it under the authority of the Constitution, with their respective rights defined and marked out; and the Federal Government can exercise no power over his person or property, beyond what that instrument confers, nor lawfully deny any right which it has reserved.

A reference to a few of the provisions of the Constitution will illustrate this proposition.

For example, no one, we presume, will contend that Congress can make any law in a Territory respecting the establishment of religion, or the free exercise thereof, or abridging the freedom of speech or of the press, or the right of the people of the Territory peaceably to assemble, and to petition the Government for the redress of grievances.

Nor can Congress deny to the people the right to keep and bear arms, nor the right to trial by jury, nor compel any one to be a witness against himself in a criminal proceeding.

These powers, and others, in relation to rights of person, which it is not necessary here to enumerate, are, in express and positive terms, denied to the General Government;

and the rights of private property have been guarded with equal care. Thus the rights of property are united with the rights of person, and placed on the same ground by the 5th Amendment to the Constitution, which provides that no person shall be deprived of life, liberty, and property, without due process of law. And an act of Congress which deprives a citizen of the United States of his liberty or property, merely because he came himself or brought his property into a particular Territory of the United States, and who had committed no offense against the laws, could hardly be dignified with the name of due process of law....

Upon these considerations, it is the opinion of the court that the act of Congress which prohibited a citizen from holding and owning property of this kind in the territory of the United States north of the line therein mentioned, is not warranted by the Constitution, and is therefore void; and that neither Dred Scott himself, nor any of his family, were made free by being carried into this territory; even if they had been carried there by the owner, with the intention of becoming a permanent resident....

[**Justices Wayne, Nelson, Grier, Daniel, Campbell, and Catron concurring. Omitted**].

[**Justice McLean dissenting. Omitted**].

Mr. Justice Curtis, dissenting.

... [U]nder the allegations contained in this plea, and admitted by the demurrer, the question is, whether any person of African descent, whose ancestors were sold as slaves in the United States, can be a citizen of the United States. If any such person can be a citizen, this plaintiff has the right to the judgment of the court that he is so; for no cause is shown by the plea why he is not so, except his descent and the slavery of his ancestors.

The first section of the second article of the Constitution uses the language, "a citizen of the United States at the time of the adoption of the Constitution." One mode of approaching this question is, to inquire who were citizens of the United States at the time of the adoption of the Constitution.

Citizens of the United States at the time of the adoption of the Constitution can have been no other than citizens of the United States under the Confederation. By the Articles of Confederation, a Government was organized, the style whereof was, "The United States of America." This Government was in existence when the Constitution was framed and proposed for adoption, and was to be superseded by the new Government of the United States of America, organized under the Constitution. When, therefore, the Constitution speaks of citizenship of the United States, existing at the time of the adoption of the Constitution, it must necessarily refer to citizenship under the Government which existed prior to and at the time of such adoption....

[I]t may safely be said that the citizens of the several States were citizens of the United States under the Confederation.

That Government was simply a confederacy of the several States, possessing a few defined powers over subjects of general concern, each State retaining every power, jurisdiction, and right, not expressly delegated to the United States in Congress assembled. And no power was thus delegated to the Government of the Confederation, to act on any question of citizenship, or to make any rules in respect thereto. The whole matter was left to stand upon the action of the several States, and to the natural consequence of such action, that the citizens of each State should be citizens of that Confederacy into which that State had entered, the style whereof was, "The United States of America."

To determine whether any free persons, descended from Africans held in slavery, were citizens of the United States under the Confederation, and consequently at the time of the adoption of the Constitution of the United States, it is only necessary to know whether any such persons were citizens of either of the States under the Confederation, at the time of the adoption of the Constitution.

Of this there can be no doubt. At the time of the ratification of the Articles of Confederation, all free native-born inhabitants of the States of New Hampshire, Massachusetts, New York, New Jersey, and North Carolina, though descended from African slaves, were not only citizens of those States, but such of them as had the other necessary qualifications possessed the franchise of electors, on equal terms with other citizens.

The Supreme Court of North Carolina, in the case of the *State v. Manuel* (N.C. 1838), has declared the law of that State on this subject, in terms which I believe to be as sound law in the other States I have enumerated, as it was in North Carolina.

"According to the laws of this State," says Judge Gaston, in delivering the opinion of the court,

> all human beings within it, who are not slaves, fall within one of two classes. Whatever distinctions may have existed in the Roman laws between citizens and free inhabitants, they are unknown to our institutions. Before our Revolution, all free persons born within the dominions of the King of Great Britain, whatever their color or complexion, were native-born British subjects—those born out of his allegiance were aliens. Slavery did not exist in England, but it did in the British colonies. Slaves were not in legal parlance persons, but property. The moment the incapacity, the disqualification of slavery, was removed, they became persons, and were then either British subjects, or not British subjects, according as they were or were not born within the allegiance of the British King. Upon the Revolution, no other change took place in the laws of North Carolina than was consequent on the transition from a colony dependent on a European King, to a free and sovereign State. Slaves remained slaves. British subjects in North Carolina became North Carolina freemen. Foreigners, until made members of the State, remained aliens. Slaves, manumitted here, became freemen, and therefore, if born within North Carolina, are citizens of North Carolina, and all free persons born within the State are born citizens of the State. The Constitution extended the elective franchise to every freeman who had arrived at the age of twenty-one, and paid a public tax; and it is a matter of universal notoriety, that, under it, free persons, without regard to color, claimed and exercised the franchise, until it was taken from free men of color a few years since by our amended Constitution.

In the *State v. Newsom* (N.C. 1844), the same court referred to [the] case of *State v. Manuel*, and said: "That case underwent a very laborious investigation, both by the bar and the bench. The case was brought here by appeal, and was felt to be one of great importance in principle. It was considered with an anxiety and care worthy of the principle involved, and which give it a controlling influence and authority on all questions of a similar character."

An argument from speculative premises, however well chosen, that the then state of opinion in the Commonwealth of Massachusetts was not consistent with the natural rights of people of color who were born on that soil, and that they were not, by the Constitution of 1780 of that State, admitted to the condition of citizens, would be received with surprise by the people of that State, who know their own political history. It is true, beyond all controversy, that persons of color, descended from African slaves, were by that Constitution made citizens of the State; and such of them as have had the necessary qualifications, have held and exercised the elective franchise, as citizens, from that time to the present. (See *Commonwealth v. Aves* (Ma. 1836)).

The Constitution of New Hampshire conferred the elective franchise upon "every inhabitant of the State having the necessary qualifications," of which color or descent was not one.

The Constitution of New York gave the right to vote to "every male inhabitant, who shall have resided," &c.; making no discrimination between free colored persons and others. That of New Jersey, [gave the vote] to "all inhabitants of this colony, of full age, who are worth 50 Pounds Sterling proclamation money, clear estate."

New York, by its Constitution of 1820, required colored persons to have some qualifications as prerequisites for voting, which white persons need not possess. And New Jersey, by its present Constitution, restricts the right to vote to white male citizens. But these changes can have no other effect upon the present inquiry, except to show, that before they were made, no such restrictions existed; and colored in common with white persons, were not only citizens of those States, but entitled to the elective franchise on the same qualifications as white persons, as they now are in New Hampshire and Massachusetts. I shall not enter into an examination of the existing opinions of that period respecting the African race, nor into any discussion concerning the meaning of those who asserted, in the Declaration of Independence, that all men are created equal; that they are endowed by their Creator with certain inalienable rights; that among these are life, liberty, and the pursuit of happiness. My own opinion is, that a calm comparison of these assertions of universal abstract truths, and of their own individual opinions and acts, would not leave these men under any reproach of inconsistency; that the great truths they asserted on that solemn occasion, they were ready and anxious to make effectual, wherever a necessary regard to circumstances, which no statesman can disregard without producing more evil than good, would allow; and that it would not be just to them, nor true in itself, to allege that they intended to say that the Creator of all men had endowed the white race, exclusively, with the great natural rights which the Declaration of Independence asserts. But this is not the place to vindicate their memory. As I conceive, we should deal here, not with such disputes, if there can be a dispute concerning this subject, but with those substantial facts evinced by the written Constitutions of States, and by the notorious practice under them. And they show, in a manner which no argument can obscure, that in some of the original thirteen States, free colored persons, before and at the time of the formation of the Constitution, were citizens of those States.

The fourth of the fundamental articles of the Confederation was as follows: "The free inhabitants of each of these States, paupers, vagabonds, and fugitives from justice, excepted, shall be entitled to all the privileges and immunities of free citizens in the several States."

The fact that free persons of color were citizens of some of the several States, and the consequence, that this fourth article of the Confederation would have the effect to confer on such persons the privileges and immunities of general citizenship, were not only known to those who framed and adopted those articles, but the evidence is decisive, that the fourth article was intended to have that effect, and that more restricted language, which would have excluded such persons, was deliberately and purposely rejected.

On the 25th of June, 1778, the Articles of Confederation being under consideration by the Congress, the delegates from South Carolina moved to amend this fourth article, by inserting after the word "free," and before the word "inhabitants," the word "white," so that the privileges and immunities of general citizenship would be secured only to white persons. Two States voted for the amendment, eight States against it, and the vote of one State was divided. The language of the article stood unchanged, and both by its terms of inclusion, "free inhabitants," and the strong implication from its terms of exclusion, "paupers, vagabonds, and fugitives from justice," who alone were excepted, it is clear, that under the Confederation, and at the time of the adoption of the Constitution, free colored persons of African descent might be, and, by reason of their citizenship in certain States, were entitled to the privileges and immunities of general citizenship of the United States.

Did the Constitution of the United States deprive them or their descendants of citizenship?

That Constitution was ordained and established by the people of the United States, through the action, in each State, of those persons who were qualified by its laws to act thereon, in behalf of themselves and all other citizens of that State. In some of the States, as we have seen, colored persons were among those qualified by law to act on this subject. These colored persons were not only included in the body of "the people of the United States," by whom the Constitution was ordained and established, but in at least five of the States they had the power to act, and doubtless did act, by their suffrages, upon the question of its adoption. It would be strange, if we were to find in that instrument anything which deprived of their citizenship any part of the people of the United States who were among those by whom it was established.

I can find nothing in the Constitution which, *proprio vigore*, deprives of their citizenship any class of persons who were citizens of the United States at the time of its adoption, or who should be native-born citizens of any State after its adoption; nor any power enabling Congress to disfranchise persons born on the soil of any State, and entitled to citizenship of such State by its Constitution and laws. And my opinion is, that, under the Constitution of the United States, every free person born on the soil of a State, who is a citizen of that State by force of its Constitution or laws, is also a citizen of the United States.

I will proceed to state the grounds of that opinion.

The first section of the second article of the Constitution uses the language, "a natural-born citizen." It thus assumes that citizenship may be acquired by birth. Undoubtedly, this language of the Constitution was used in reference to that principle of public law, well understood in this country at the time of the adoption of the Constitution, which referred citizenship to the place of birth. At the Declaration of Independence, and ever since, the received general doctrine has been, in conformity with the common law, that free persons born within either of the colonies were subjects of the King; that by the Declaration of Independence, and the consequent acquisition of sovereignty by the several States, all such persons ceased to be subjects, and became citizens of the several States, except so far as some of them were disfranchised by the legislative power of the States, or availed themselves, seasonably, of the right to adhere to the British Crown in the civil contest....

Questions about *Dred Scott*

1. Does *Dred Scott* explain the addition of the Citizenship Clause to the 14th Amendment?
2. According to *Dred Scott*, the rights and privileges of the Constitution and Bill of Rights are whose rights? That is to say, to what group do they exclusively belong?

3. Suppose a federal territory bans anti-slavery speech or press in 1859. A free black person is convicted of violating the statute. To what Amendment might she appeal? What effect would *Dred Scott* have on her constitutional claim?

4. What does the decision in *Dred Scott* say about whether Courts should read the Constitution to promote justice or liberty? Do you agree or disagree?

From St. George Tucker, *A Dissertation on Slavery*

Consider the following from St. George Tucker, a Virginia Republican, law teacher, judge and author of a version of *Blackstone's Commentaries*, revised to make it suitable for republican America. In 1796, Tucker published *A Dissertation on Slavery*:

> Whilst we were offering up vows at the shrine of Liberty ... whilst we swore irreconcilable hostility to her enemies, and hurled defiance in the faces; whilst we adjured the God of Hosts to witness our resolution to live free, or die ... we were imposing upon our fellow men, who differ in complexion from us, a slavery, ten thousand times more cruel than the utmost extremity of those grievances and oppressions of which we complained. Such are the inconsistencies of human nature; such the blindness of those who pluck not the beam out of their own eyes, whilst they can espy a moat, in the eyes of their brother; such that partial system of morality which confines rights and injuries, to particular complexions; such the effect of that self-love which justifies, or condemns, not according to principle, but to the agent. Had we turned our eyes inwardly when we supplicated the Father of Mercies to aid the injured and oppressed ... should we not have stood more self convicted than the contrite publican!... Should we not have loosed their chains, and broken their fetters? [I]s it not our duty to embrace the first moment of constitutional health and vigor, to effectuate so desirable an object ...? To form a just estimate of this obligation, to demonstrate the incompatibility of a state of slavery with the principles of our government, and of that revolution upon which it is found, to elucidate the practicability of its total, though gradual, abolition, it will be proper to consider the nature of slavery....

St. George Tucker, *A Dissertation on Slavery* 7–9.

Criticisms of *Dred Scott* by John A. Bingham and Abraham Lincoln

Some historians have been very critical of the "history" presented by the Chief Justice in *Dred Scott*. *See*, e.g., Don Fehrenbacher, *The Dred Scott Case* (1978). *But see,* Mark A. Graber, *Desperately Ducking Slavery: Dred Scott and Contemporary Constitutional Theory,* 14 Const. Comment. 271 (1997). Consider the following criticism by John A. Bingham, a Republican anti-slavery congressman from Ohio and later the chief drafter of §1 of the 14th Amendment.

Congressman John Bingham of Ohio, on Citizenship. From *The Congressional Globe,* 35th Cong. 2d Sess., 1859, pp. 983–84:

> Who are citizens of the United States? Sir, they are those, and those only, who owe allegiance to the Government for the United States; not the base allegiance imposed upon the Saxon by the Conqueror, which required him to meditate in solitude and darkness at the sound of the curfew; but the allegiance which requires the citizen not only to obey, but to support and defend, if need be with his life, the Constitution of his country. All

free persons born and domiciled within the jurisdiction of the United States, are citizens of the United States from birth; all aliens become citizens of the United States only by act of naturalization, under the laws of the United States. What I have said on this question of United States citizenship, and the words "the people," as used in the Constitution of the United States, is sustained by jurists and the decisions of the courts, Federal and State.

Rawle writes as follows:

> The citizens of each State constituted the citizens of the United States when the Constitution was adopted. The rights which appertain to them as citizens of those respective Commonwealths accompanied them in the formation of the great compound Commonwealth which ensued. They became citizens of the latter, without ceasing to be citizens of the former; and he who was subsequently born a citizen of a State, became, at the moment of his birth, a citizen of the United States.—*Rawle on the Constitution,* p. 86.

Chancellor Kent says:

> If a slave, born in the United States, be manumitted, or otherwise lawfully discharged from bondage, or if a black man be born within the United States, and born free, he becomes thenceforward a citizen.—*2 Kent's Com.,* 4th ed., p. 257—Note.

For the benefit of the other side of the House, who profess a more than Eastern devotion to the Supreme Court of the United States, and its decision in the *Dred Scott* case, I quote from the opinion of the Chief Justice in that case the following:

> The words "people of the United States," and "citizens," are synonymous terms, and mean the same thing. They both describe the political body who, according to our republican institutions, form the sovereignty, and who hold the power and conduct the Government through their representatives.—*19 Howard, S.C. R.,* p. 404.

Who, sir, are citizens of the United States? First, all free persons born and domiciled within the United States—not all free white persons, but all free persons. You will search in vain, in the Constitution of the United States, for that word *white*; it is not there. You will look in vain for it in that first form of national Government—the Articles of Confederation; it is not there. The omission of this word—this phrase of caste—from our national charter, was not accidental, but intentional. I beg leave to refer gentlemen to the Journal of the Continental Congress, volume 2, p. 606. By this reference it will be seen that in that Congress, on the 25th June, 1778, the Articles of Confederation being under consideration, it was moved by delegates of South Carolina to amend the fourth article, by inserting after the word "free" and before the word "inhabitants," the word "white," so that "the privileges and immunities of citizens in the several States should be limited exclusively to white inhabitants." The vote on this amendment was taken by States, and stood two States for, and eight against it, and one equally divided. This action of the Congress of 1778 was a clear and direct avowal that all free inhabitants, white and black, except "paupers, vagabonds, and fugitives from justice," (which were expressly excepted,) were entitled to all the privileges and immunities of free citizens in the several States."

At the time of the adoption of the Constitution, only some States, South Carolina, Virginia, and Delaware, made *color* a qualification or basis of suffrage. In five of the others the elective franchise was exercised by free inhabitants, black and white; and therefore, in five of the States, black men cooperated with white men in the elections, and in the formation of the Constitution of the United States. Inasmuch as black men helped to make the Constitution, as well as to achieve the independence of the country by the terrible trial by battle, it is not surprising that the Constitution of the United States does not exclude them from the body politic, and the privileges and immunities of citizens of the United States. That great instrument included in the new body politic, by the name of "the people of the United States," all the then free inhabitants or citizens of the United States, whether white or black, not even excepting, as did the Articles of Confederation, paupers, vagabonds, or fugitives from justice. Thenceforward all these classes, being free inhabitants, irrespective of age, or sex, or complexion, and their descendants, were citizens of the United States. No distinctions were made against the poor and in favor of the rich, or against the free-born blacks and in favor of the whites. This Government rests upon the absolute equality of natural rights amongst men. There is not, and cannot be, any equality in the enjoyment of political or conventional rights, because that is impossible....

* * *

Here is Abraham Lincoln's response to *Dred Scott* and arguments that the Declaration of Independence did not include Americans of African descent. From the *Lincoln-Douglas Debates*:

There is a natural disgust in the minds of nearly all white people, to the idea of an indiscriminate amalgamation of the white and black races; and Judge [Stephen] Douglas evidently is basing his chief hope, upon the chances of being able to appropriate the benefit of this disgust to himself. If he can, by much drumming and repeating, fasten the odium of that idea upon his adversaries, he thinks he can struggle through the storm. He therefore clings to this hope, as a drowning man to the last plank. He makes an occasion for lugging it in from the opposition to the *Dred Scott* decision. He finds the Republicans insisting that the Declaration of Independence includes ALL men, black as well as white; and forthwith he boldly denies that it includes negroes at all, and proceeds to argue gravely that all who contend it does, do so only because they want to vote, and eat, and sleep, and marry with negroes! He will have it that they cannot be consistent else. Now I protest against that counterfeit logic which concludes that, because I do not want a black woman for a *slave* I must necessarily want her for a *wife*. I need not have her for either, I can just leave her alone. In some respects she certainly is not my equal; but in her natural right to eat the bread she earns with her own hands without asking leave of any one else, she is my equal, and the equal of all others.

Chief Justice Taney, in his opinion in the *Dred Scott* case, admits that the language of the Declaration is broad enough to include the whole human family, but he and Judge Douglas argue that the authors of that instrument did not intend to include negroes, by the fact that they did not at once, actually place them on an equality with the whites. Now this grave argument comes to just nothing at all, by the other fact, that they did not at once, *or ever afterwards*, actually place all white people on an equality with one or another. And this is the staple argument of both the Chief Justice and the Senator, for doing this obvious violence to the plain unmistakable language of the Declaration. I think the authors of that notable instrument intended to include *all* men, but they did not intend to declare all men equal *in all respects*. They did not mean to say all were equal in color, size, intellect, moral developments, or social capacity. They defined with tolerable distinctness, in what respects they did consider all men created equal—equal in "certain inalienable rights, among which are life, liberty, and the pursuit of happiness." This they said, and this they meant. They did not mean to assert the obvious untruth, that all were then actually enjoying that equality, nor yet, that they were about to confer it immediately upon them. In fact they had no power to confer such a boon. They meant simply to declare the *right*, so that the *enforcement* of it might follow as fast as circumstances should permit. They meant to set up a standard maxim for free society, which should be familiar to all, and revered by all; constantly looked to, constantly labored for, and even though never perfectly attained, constantly approximated, and thereby constantly spreading and deepening its influence, and augmenting the happiness and value of life to all people of all colors everywhere. The assertion that "all men are created equal" was of no practical use in effecting our separation from Great Britain; and it was placed in the Declaration, not for that, but for future use. Its authors meant it to be, thank God, it is now proving itself, a stumbling block to those who in after times might seek to turn a free people back into the hateful paths of despotism. They knew the proneness of prosperity to breed tyrants, and they meant when such should re-appear in this fair land and commence their vocation they should find left for them at least one hard nut to crack.

I have now briefly expressed my view of the *meaning* and *objects* of that part of the Declaration of Independence which declares that "all men are created equal."

Now let us hear Judge Douglas' view of the same subject, as I find it in the printed report of his late speech. Here it is:

> No man can vindicate the character, motives and conduct of the signers of the Declaration of Independence except upon the hypothesis that they referred to the white race alone, and not to the African, when they declared all men to have been created equal — that they were speaking of British subjects on this continent being equal to British subjects born and residing in Great Britain — that they were entitled to the same inalienable rights, and among them were enumerated life, liberty and the pursuit of happiness. The Declaration was adopted for the purpose of justifying the colonists in the eyes of the civilized world in withdrawing their allegiance from the British crown, and dissolving their connection with the mother country.

My good friends, read that carefully over some leisure hour, and ponder well upon it — see what a mere wreck — mangled ruin — it makes of our once glorious Declaration.

E. Historical Linguistics: Common Use of the Words "Privileges and Immunities" before the Adoption of the 14th Amendment

The 14th Amendment provided in part that "No State shall make or enforce any law which shall abridge the privileges or immunities of citizens of the United States." An original meaning approach to interpretation would focus on the common understanding of the words "privileges or immunities of citizens of the United States" in the years 1866–68. How would you go about constructing such an analysis from the representative materials set out below? Consider the following examples:

From the 1830s

From the 1830s to 1860, mobs in the North had periodically disrupted abolitionist meetings, demanded that their newspapers stop publishing, and demolished the presses of those that refused. In 1837, a mob was determined to silence Elijah Lovejoy, who was a minister and an anti-slavery editor in Illinois. Mobs destroyed three of his presses and, in a confrontation over the mob attempt to destroy the fourth, Lovejoy was killed. Most of the following comments are from a tidal wave of protests that followed the killing:

> The *Newark Advertiser* described "the right of free discussion" as an "inalienable privilege of freedom."
>
> "Liberty of speech," insisted the *Berkshire Courier*, "must not be surrendered. It was one of the *privileges* left us by our fathers."
>
> Free speech was "a 'home-bred right,' a *'fireside privilege,'*" according to a Concord, New Hampshire public meeting.
>
> A public meeting in Susquehanna County, Pennsylvania resolved that "*freedom of the press is a right* too sacred to be in the least invaded—*a privilege* too dear to be shackled or impaired by public enactments or lawless violence."

In addition to describing rights such as free speech, free press and free exercise of religion as "privileges" or "immunities," the critics commonly described them as belonging to American citizens or citizens of the United States.

On the Eve of the Civil War

In 1860, Congress was in an uproar over Republican endorsement of *Impending Crisis*, a book by Hinton Helper that called on non-slaveholding Southerners to unite for political action against slavery. The book had a passage urging violent resistance if the slaveholding elite attempted to suppress democratic action against slavery. A number of Republicans had endorsed a project to reprint a "compendium" of the book as a campaign document.

Southern congressmen and senators saw the book as a call for slave revolts and viewed Republican endorsers as criminals. North Carolina, for example, prosecuted and convicted a Republican minister who circulated the book. *State v. Worth* (N.C.1860). In contrast, during the controversy over the book Republicans in the United States Senate voted for a resolution that proclaimed that "free discussion of the morality and expediency of slavery should never be interfered with by the laws of any State, or of the United States; and the freedom of speech and of the press, on this and every other subject of domestic and national policy, should be maintained inviolate in all the States." Consider the following exchange between Owen Lovejoy, brother of Elijah, now a Republican Congressman from Illinois, and Representative Elbert Martin of Virginia:

> Lovejoy: "[I insist on] the right of discussing this question of slavery anywhere, on any square foot of American soil ... to which the privileges and immunities of the Constitution extend." "[T]hat Constitution guarantees to me free speech...."
>
> Martin: "And if you come among us we will ... hang you...."
>
> Lovejoy: "I have no doubt of it."*

During the Civil War

Reference to basic liberties, such as free speech, as "privileges" or "immunities" of American citizens continued during the Civil War. The words were used in this way by people on all sides of the debate. As in earlier examples, the word "rights" and the words "privileges" and "immunities" were often used interchangeably.

---

* *Globe* 36 (1) app. 202, 205 (1860).

The prosecution of Clement Vallandigham

A major controversy swirled around Union General Ambrose Burnside's military arrest and military trial of Democratic politician Clement Vallandigham for making an anti-war speech. Resolutions protesting the Vallandigham arrest were widely reprinted in the press. A typical resolution quoted Daniel Webster: "It is the ancient and undoubted prerogative of this people to canvass public measures and the merits of public men. It is a 'home-bred right'—a fireside *privilege*. It has been enjoyed in every house, cottage and cabin in the nation." The resolution continued, "This high *constitutional privilege* we shall defend and exercise in all places; in time of war, in time of peace, and at all times." In an article critical of the arrest, the *National Intelligencer* wrote: "We believe that the Government might better afford to let Mr. Vallandigham and [abolitionist] Mr. Phillips enjoy the *privilege* of 'free speech' according to their respective notions of propriety, than to proceed against either of them for words spoken in public discussion."

In their widely reprinted rejoinder to President Lincoln on the Vallandigham case, Democrats from Albany, New York referred to federal constitutional guarantees of free speech, search and seizure, grand jury indictment, and jury trial. They noted that these "sacred rights and *immunities* which were designed to be protected by these constitutional guarantees have not been preserved to the people during your administration." There are a great many other examples.

Though a number of Republicans and opponents of slavery were critical of the Vallandigham arrest, others defended the administration and castigated those Republicans and abolitionists who joined the Democrats in criticism. The *Chicago Tribune* was one of the strongest defenders of tough measures against anti-war speech. "Since the arrest of the treason-shrieker, Vallandigham," the *Chicago Tribune* noted, "his disciples fill the air with cries about the Constitutional right of 'free speech.' We wish to ask those Copperhead defenders of free speech how much of this *Constitutional and sacred privilege* did their party allow to be exercised in the South before the war broke out?" General Burnside suggested, in a communication widely reprinted, that since soldiers had given up their *privilege* of free speech (that "freedom of discussion and criticism"), civilians should likewise curtail their exercise of that privilege.

After the Vallandigham arrest, and the massive criticism it produced, General Burnside struck again. This time he seized the *Chicago Times* newspaper, impounded copies of the paper, and banned further publication. Again, massive protests erupted, joined even by a number of Republicans and abolitionists. President Lincoln countermanded the order. Celebrating one mass protest meeting, the recently liberated *Chicago Times* wrote:

> Wednesday was a day for Chicago to be proud of. By the voice of her citizens she proclaimed to the world that the right of free speech has not yet passed away; that *immunity* of thought and discussion are yet among the inalienable *privileges* of men born to freedom.... Twenty thousand bold men with one acclaim decreed that speech and press shall be untrammeled, and that despotism shall not usurp the *inborn rights of the American citizen*.

The Congressional Debate on the Abolition of Slavery (1864)

Representative James Wilson, who would be the Chair of the Judiciary Committee in the 39th Congress, said, "Freedom of religious opinion, freedom of speech and of press, and the right of assemblage for the purpose of petition belong to every American citizen, high or low, rich or poor, wherever he may be within the jurisdiction of the United

States. With these rights no State may interfere without breach of the bond that holds the Union together." Slavery had practically destroyed these rights. Wilson continued:

> [Slavery had] persecuted religionists, denied *the privilege of free discussion,* prevented free elections, [and] trampled upon *all the constitutional guarantees* belonging to the citizen.... Throughout all the dominions of slavery republican government, constitutional liberty, the blessings of our free institutions were mere fables. An aristocracy enjoyed unlimited power, while the people were pressed to the earth and *denied the inestimable privileges which by right they should have enjoyed ... by the Constitution.**

* * *

For further discussion of the original meaning of the Privileges or Immunities Clause of the 14th Amendment and of problems with the idea of original meaning, *see* Michael Kent Curtis, *Historical Linguistics, Inkblots, and Life After Death: The Privileges or Immunities of Citizens of the United States,* 78 N.C. L. Rev. 1071 (2000).

IV. The Drafting of the 14th Amendment

As conventionally understood today, the Article IV equality guarantee is limited to those fundamental interests that a state chooses to provide for its own citizens—such as pursuit of the common occupations of life. South Carolina cannot limit the business of selling cigarettes to its own residents, though as a matter of federal constitutional law it could prohibit both in-staters and out-of-staters from selling cigarettes in the state. Since the guarantee is simply one of equality, states can deny state law privileges to in-staters and out-of-staters alike. Before the 1866 drafting of the 14th Amendment, this was also a common reading of Article IV, §2. But not all read the provision in that way.

Before the Civil War, some leading Republicans read the Privileges and Immunities Clause of Article IV, §2, to protect a body of "absolute" national rights from state violation. They read the Clause to provide "The Citizens of each State shall be entitled to all Privileges and Immunities of Citizens [*of the United States*] in the several States" and read those privileges *to include those in the Bill of Rights.* For those who held this view, such "absolute" rights would be *in addition to* guaranteeing out-of-staters equality with in-state citizens as to certain state law fundamental interests. These people believed that, *Barron v. Baltimore* (1833) notwithstanding, the guarantees of the Bill of Rights did or should limit state and local governments (which are merely creatures of states). Michael Kent Curtis, *No State Shall Abridge,* 37–38, 60–61 (1986). Others also believed that the guarantees in the Bill of Rights limited the states but relied on other theories—such as the Republican Government Clause of Article IV.

In the years leading up to the Civil War, Republican presidential candidates had been unable to campaign in the South. In 1859, leading Republicans (including John Bingham—future author of §1 of the 14th Amendment), had endorsed a project to publish an abridgement of an anti-slavery book, Hinton Helper's *Impending Crisis.* In 1860, Rev. Daniel Worth, an anti-slavery activist and Wesleyan minister, was prosecuted in North Carolina for distributing copies of the book. He was convicted of violating a statute that

---

* *Globe* 38 (1) 1202 (1864).

made it a crime to disseminate matter that had a tendency to cause slaves or free negroes to be discontent, even though Worth had given the book only to whites. *See State v. Worth* (NC. 1860). *See also* Michael K. Curtis, *The 1859 Crisis Over Hinton Helper's Book*, 68 Chi.-Kent L. Rev. 1113, 1141–76 (1993).

With the advent of the Civil War, Southern congressmen and senators withdrew from Congress, leaving the South unrepresented. After the Confederacy surrendered in 1865, with congressmen from the former Confederate states still absent, President Andrew Johnson, Lincoln's successor, accepted temporary governments established by the Southern states. The 13th Amendment was ratified in 1865, though the former Confederate ratifying states were still not represented in Congress.

Andrew Johnson insisted on prompt re-admission to Congress of congressmen and senators from the former rebel states. His only preconditions were that they must at once ratify the 13th Amendment and repeal their ordinances of secession, conditions with which the former Confederate states complied. However, congressional Republicans insisted on further conditions, many of which were later set out in the 14th Amendment.

Republicans complained that ex-rebels were exercising too much power in these provisional governments. Before the adoption of the 14th Amendment, Southern provisional governments adopted regulations for the newly freed slaves called the Black Codes. These Codes limited the rights of newly freed slaves to own property, to move about freely, to testify against whites, to bear arms, to speak or preach or assemble, etc. The Black Codes appalled most Republicans. An excerpt from a representative local code follows.*

A "Black Code": Regulating Freedmen in Louisiana

WHEREAS it was formerly made the duty of the police jury to make suitable regulations for the police of slaves within the limits of the parish; and whereas slaves have become emancipated by the action of the ruling powers; and whereas it is necessary for public order, as well as for the comfort and correct deportment of said freedmen, that suitable regulations should be established for their government in their changed condition, the following ordinances are adopted with the approval of the United States military authorities commanding in said parish, viz:

Sec. 1 ... *Be it ordained by the police jury of the parish of St. Landry,* that no negro shall be allowed to pass within the limits of said parish without special permit in writing from his employer. Whoever shall violate this provision shall pay a fine of two dollars and fifty cents, or in default thereof shall be forced to work four days on the public road, or suffer corporeal punishment as provided hereinafter.

Sec. 2 ... Every negro who shall be found absent from the residence of his employer after ten o'clock at night, without a written permit from his employer, shall pay a fine of five dollars, or in default thereof, shall be compelled to work five days on the public road, or suffer corporeal punishment as hereinafter provided.

Sec. 3 ... No negro shall be permitted to rent or keep a house within said parish. Any negro violating this provision shall be immediately ejected and compelled to find an employer; and any person who shall rent, or give the use of any house to any negro, in violation of this section, shall pay a fine of five dollars for each offence.

---

* Walter L. Fleming, 1 *Documentary History of Reconstruction*, 279–81.

Sec. 4 ... Every negro is required to be in the regular service of some white person, or former owner, who shall be held responsible for the conduct of said negro. But said employer or former owner may permit said negro to hire his own time by special permission in writing, which permission shall not extend over seven days at any one time. Any negro violating the provisions of this section shall be fined five dollars for each offence, or in default of the payment thereof shall be forced to work five days on the public road, or suffer corporeal punishment as hereinafter provided.

Sec. 5 ... No public meetings or congregations of negroes shall be allowed within said parish after sunset; but such public meetings and congregations may be held between the hours of sunrise and sunset, by the special permission in writing of the captain of patrol, within whose beat such meetings shall take place. This prohibition, however, is not to prevent negroes from attending the usual church services, conducted by white ministers and priests. Every negro violating the provisions of this section shall pay a fine of five dollars, or in default thereof shall be compelled to work five days on the public road, or suffer corporeal punishment as hereinafter provided.

Sec. 6 ... No negro shall be permitted to preach, exhort, or otherwise declaim to congregations of colored people, without a special permission in writing from the president of the police jury. Any negro violating the provisions of this section shall pay a fine of ten dollars, or in default shall be forced to work ten days on the public road, or suffer corporeal punishment as hereinafter provided.

Sec. 7 ... No negro who is not in the military service shall be allowed to carry firearms, or any kind of weapons, within the parish, without the special written permission of his employers, approved and indorsed by the nearest and most convenient chief of patrol. Any one violating the provisions of this section shall forfeit his weapons and pay a fine of five dollars, or in default of the payment of said fine, shall be forced to work five days on the public road, or suffer corporeal punishment as hereinafter provided.

Sec. 8 ... No negro shall sell, barter, or exchange any articles of merchandise or traffic within said parish without the special written permission of his employer, specifying the article of sale, barter or traffic. Any one thus offending shall pay a fine of one dollar for each offense, and suffer the forfeiture of said articles, or in default of the payment of said fine shall work one day on the public road, or suffer corporeal punishment as hereinafter provided....

Sec. 14 ... The corporeal punishment provided for in the foregoing sections shall consist in confining the body of the offender within a barrel placed over his or her shoulders, in the manner practiced in the army, such confinement not to continue longer than twelve hours, and for such time within the aforesaid limit as shall be fixed by the captain or chief of patrol who inflicts the penalty.

A. The Congressional Response to the Black Codes and the Legacy of Slavery

In response to the Black Codes, such as the one set out above, Congress passed the Civil Rights Bill of 1866. The Civil Rights Bill made all persons born in the United States and not subject to any foreign power, excluding Indians not taxed, "citizens of the United States." It further provided:

[S]uch citizens, of every race and color, without regard to any previous condition of slavery ... shall have the same right, in every State and Territory in the

United States, to make and enforce contracts, to sue, be parties, and give evidence, to inherit, purchase, lease, sell, hold and convey real and personal property, and *to full and equal benefit of all laws and proceedings for the security of person and property, as is enjoyed by white citizens....*

One obvious purpose of the Civil Rights Bill was to void the Black Codes. Did Congress have the power to do so, under the 13th Amendment, even before the 14th Amendment was ratified? That subject was disputed. Congressman John Bingham insisted that a constitutional amendment was needed. The Civil Rights Bill of 1866 was vetoed by President Andrew Johnson, who denied that Congress had the power to pass it. Congress overrode the veto.

At the same time the Civil Rights Bill was being debated, Congress considered the prototype of the 14th Amendment, set out below. The prototype gave Congress power to pass laws, but it did not by its terms limit the states.

Several congressmen suggested that the 14th Amendment incorporated the substantial protections of the Civil Rights Act of 1866. Does that fact argue against reading the 14th Amendment to apply the Bill of Rights to the states? Should the intent of the drafters and those who proposed the 14th Amendment be a factor in deciding its meaning? How large a factor should original intent be? Should we be concerned with the intent of the framers, of the ratifiers, or of both? Should we instead focus on the historic common understanding of the words used in a constitutional provision—the "original meaning"? How clear must the historical record be?

Congressional debate over a proposed 14th Amendment occurred in 1866, after the defeat of the South in the Civil War. With secession, Southern congressmen and senators had departed, so that Southern states were without representation during the Civil War and the early post-war period. With the end of the Civil War, Congress passed the 13th Amendment. Southern states quickly ratified the Amendment and then insisted on re-admission to Congress, *with increased representation*—because with the 13th Amendment former slaves became whole persons for purposes of calculating representation in the House. (Article I, §3, had treated slaves as 3/5 of a person for this purpose.) Republicans in Congress thought that something needed to be done to prevent Southern states from enjoying increased representation based on counting *disfranchised* Americans of African descent for purposes of representation in the House and the Electoral College. They also thought additional guarantees of civil liberty needed to be incorporated into the Constitution and that both of these things should occur *before* Southern states were re-admitted.

Consider the following excerpts from the 14th Amendment debates in Congress. Be prepared to discuss each excerpt in some detail. This sort of legislative history is different from much of your law school reading so far. Why read this sort of material? What conclusions do you reach after reading it? Note, for example, the views of Bingham, Howard, and Hale.

There are several possible barriers to understanding some of the excerpts from the debates that follow. Many of the Republican congressmen had unorthodox legal ideas. For example, Republicans generally thought blacks were citizens and *Dred Scott* was wrong. A number understood the Bill of Rights and the states in ways not consistent with *Barron v. Baltimore* (1833). For example, Farnsworth seems to think states are already required to obey the Bill of Rights; in his view §1 adds nothing but equal protection. Of course, this assumes that it is already the case—contrary to *Barron*—that no state can deprive any person of life, liberty, or property without due process. Some read the original Privileges and Immunities Clause of Article IV or some other provision to obligate states to obey the Bill of Rights—even before the 14th amendment. Congressman Bingham thought there was a constitutional obligation to obey the Bill of Rights, but not one that could be enforced. His statement that every word of the prototype is in the Constitution, while not literally accurate, is close; but of course he put the words together to reach a new legal result (congressional power to enforce guarantees of liberty) that he fully recognized did not accord with Supreme Court precedent. Note that the final version of the Privileges or Immunities Clause changes. It now protects the privileges or immunities of citizens of the United States (language different from the Article IV Privileges and Immunities Clause).

Because a number of Republicans held unorthodox constitutional views, our current legal assumptions—e.g., that *Barron* was a correct statement of the law at least until the passage of the 14th Amendment or that the Privileges and Immunities Clause of Article IV was merely an equality provision—may not be an accurate way to understand their views. So when Senator Luke Poland of Maine says that the Privileges or Immunities Clause of the 14th Amendment probably does no more than the Article IV provision was intended to do, the unanswered problem is what he thought Article IV was intended to do. Poland may or may not have thought it was merely a provision protecting out-of-staters from discrimination under state law. Still one can (and some do) cite his remarks to counter the claim that the 14th Amendment was designed to apply the Bill of Rights to the states.

A person who clearly held unorthodox views (by modern standards) is John A. Bingham, the main author of § 1 of the 14th Amendment. When Bingham says the first (and abandoned) version of his amendment makes no changes to the Constitution except for enforcement, he assumes an unenforceable obligation of state officials to obey the Bill of Rights. In this portion of the debate, Bingham emphasizes the need to enforce the Bill of Rights, and he highlights the problem posed by *Barron*.

As always, chronology is crucial. There are two versions of the 14th Amendment under discussion. The first provides that Congress shall have the power to make "all laws which shall be necessary and proper to secure to the citizens of each State all privileges and immunities of citizens in the several States, and all persons in the several states equal protection in the right of life, liberty, and property." It is replaced with the second, current version that provides that "No State shall make or enforce any law which shall abridge the privileges or immunities of citizens of the United States" or deprive any person of life, liberty, or property without due process of law or deny any person within its jurisdiction the equal protection of the laws.

B. The Congressional Debates on the 14th Amendment

The following selections from the debates are from the *Congressional Globe,* 39th Cong., 1st sess. (1866). What inferences can you draw from this material with reference to the 14th Amendment and application of the Bill of Rights to the states? What are the positions of Congressman Bingham, Congressman Hale, and Senator Howard on this issue? Do you find statements from others that contradict what Bingham and Howard have to say on the relation of the 14th Amendment and the Bill of Rights? What type of argument is involved? For fuller excerpts from the debates, *see* Alfred Avins, *The Reconstruction Amendment Debates* (1967).

The first excerpt is from Congressman John Bingham of Ohio, a moderate Republican, a member of the Joint Committee that produced the final version of the 14th Amendment, and the principal drafter of § 1. In 1866, moderate Republicans were likely to favor immediate readmission of the Southern states once they had complied with conditions such as those in the 14th Amendment. Radical Republicans were more likely to insist that black suffrage should be part of the settlement prior to the readmission of the Southern states, and they were more critical of prompt readmission.

Bingham was a lawyer and a strongly anti-slavery Republican. He emphasized the denials of civil liberty that had accompanied slavery. Here Bingham discusses the prototype of § 1 on February 26, 1866. Note that this prototype is different from the Amendment as it passed. How is it different? What is the significance of the difference?

[*Globe*, 39(1) 1033–34 (1866)]:

RIGHTS OF CITIZENS

Mr. BINGHAM, from the select joint committee on reconstruction, reported back a joint resolution (H.R. No. 68) proposing an amendment to the Constitution of the United States.

The joint resolution was read, as follows:

> *Resolved by the Senate and House of Representatives of the United States of America in Congress assembled, (two thirds of both Houses concurring.) That the following article be proposed to the Legislatures of the several States as an amendment to the Constitution of the United States, which, when ratified by three fourths of the said Legislatures, shall be valid as part of said Constitution, namely:*
>
> ARTICLE—*The Congress shall have power to make all laws which shall be necessary and proper to secure to the citizens of each State all privileges and immunities of citizens in the several States, and to all persons in the several States equal protection in the rights of life, liberty, and property.*

Mr. BINGHAM. Mr. Speaker, this resolution, as the House is aware, has received its first and second readings. It comes back from the committee in the precise form in which it was originally reported. I do not propose at present to detain the House with any very extended remarks in support of it. I ask, however, the attention of the House to the fact that the amendment proposed stands in the very words of the Constitution of the United States as it came to us from the hands of its illustrious framers. Every word of the proposed amendment is today in the Constitution of our country, save the words conferring the express grant of power upon the Congress of the United States. The residue of the resolution, as the House will see by a reference to the Constitution, is the language of the second section of the fourth article, and of a portion of the 5th Amendment adopted by the First Congress in 1789, and made part of the Constitution of the country. The language of the second section of the fourth article is—

> *The citizens of each State shall be entitled to all privileges and immunities of citizens in the several States.*

The fifth article of the amendment provides that—

> *No person shall be deprived of life, liberty, or property, without due process of law.*

Sir, it has been the want of the Republic that there was not an express grant of power in the Constitution to enable the whole people of every State, by congressional enactment, to enforce obedience to these requirements of the Constitution. Nothing can be plainer to thoughtful men than that if the grant of power had been originally conferred upon the Congress of the nation, and legislation had been upon your statute-books to enforce these requirements of the Constitution in every State, that rebellion, which has scarred and blasted the land, would have been an impossibility.

I ask the attention of the House to the further consideration that the proposed amendment does not impose upon any State of the Union, or any citizen of any State of the Union, any obligation which is not now enjoined upon them by the very letter of the Constitution. I need not remind gentlemen here that the Constitution, as originally framed, and as adopted by the whole people of this country, provides that—

> *This Constitution, and the laws of the United States which shall be made in pursuance thereof, and all treaties made, or which shall be made, under the authority of the United States, shall be the supreme law of the land; and the judges in every State shall be bound thereby, anything in the constitution or laws of any State to the contrary notwithstanding.*

Could words be stronger, could words be more forceful, to enjoin upon every officer of every State the obligation to obey these great provisions of the Constitution, in their letter and their spirit? I submit to the judgment of the House, that it is impossible for mortal man to frame a formula of words more obligatory than those already in that instrument, enjoining this great duty upon the several States and the several officers of every State in the Union.

And, sir, it is equally clear by every construction of the Constitution, its contemporaneous construction, its continued construction, legislative, executive, and judicial, that these great provisions of the Constitution, this immortal bill of rights embodied in the Constitution, rested for its execution and enforcement hitherto upon the fidelity of the States. The House knows, sir, the country knows, the civilized world knows, that the legislative, executive, and judicial officers of eleven States within this Union within the last five years, in utter disregard of these injunctions of your Constitution, in utter disregard of that official oath, which the Constitution required they should severally take and faithfully keep when they entered upon the discharge of their respective duties, have violated in every sense of the word these provisions of the Constitution of the United States, the enforcement of which are absolutely essential to American nationality.

By order, then, of the committee, sir, and for the purpose of giving to the whole people the care in future of the unity of the Government which constitutes us one people, and without which American nationality would cease to be, I propose the adoption of this amendment to the House, and through the House I press it upon the consideration of the loyal people of the whole country.

* * *

The next excerpt is from Congressman Robert Hale, a conservative Republican from New York. Which clause of the prototype does Hale primarily address and object to? Do his remarks bear on whether states should be required to obey the Bill of Rights? What does Hale think about the obligation of states to obey the Bill of Rights? Does he object to Bingham's proposal because he thinks it would be improper to require states to obey the federal Bill of Rights?

Note the discussion of women's rights. What clause of the proposed amendment does Hale find particularly troublesome with reference to the role of the states? Also in this excerpt are comments by Congressmen Bingham, Thaddeus Stevens of Pennsylvania, and Charles Eldridge of Wisconsin. Stevens was a lawyer, a radical Republican, a member of the Joint Committee on Reconstruction, and a leader of Republicans in Congress. Eldridge was a Democratic lawyer.

[*Globe*, 39(1) 1063–64 (1866)]:

Mr. HALE. Mr. Speaker, it is with great hesitation I rise to address the House today, for the reason especially that in the brief time allotted for the purpose, I feel that I have been entirely unable to prepare myself as one should be prepared to discuss a subject so important....

But it does seem to me, with the little knowledge that I possess of constitutional law, and with the very brief and hasty examination that I have been enabled to give to this matter, that no weight or authority of members of this House today ought to bring us to pass this amendment without at least a most careful and scrutinizing examination. It does seem to me that the tenor and effect of the amendment proposed here by this committee is to bring about a more radical change in the system of this Government, to institute a wider departure from the theory upon which our fathers formed it than ever before was proposed in any legislative or constitutional assembly. Listening to the remarks of the distinguished member of the committee [Mr. BINGHAM] who reported this joint resolution to the House, one would be led to think that this amendment was a subject of the most trivial consequence. He tells us, and tells us with an air of gravity that I could not but admire, that the words of the resolution are all in the Constitution as it stands, with the single exception of the power given to Congress to legislate. A very important exception, it strikes me, but one to which the gentleman seems to attach very little weight....

Now, Mr. Speaker, what is the theory of our Constitution? I will not undertake to elaborate this matter too far; but briefly, imperfectly, and within very scanty limits, let me attempt an answer to this question. In general terms, is it not that all powers relating to the existence and sovereignty of the nation, powers relating to our foreign relations, powers relating to peace and war, to the enforcement of the law of nations and international law, are the powers given to Congress and to the Federal Government by the Constitution, while all powers having reference to the relation of the individual to the municipal government, the powers of local jurisdiction and legislation, are in general reserved to the States?

What is the effect of the amendment which the committee on reconstruction propose for the sanction of this House and the States of the Union? I submit that it is in effect a provision under which all State legislation, in its codes of civil and criminal jurisprudence and procedure, affecting the individual citizen, may be overridden, may be repealed or abolished, and the law of Congress established instead. I maintain that in this respect it is an utter departure from every principle ever dreamed of by the men who framed our Constitution.

Mr. STEVENS. Does the gentleman mean to say that, under this provision, Congress could interfere in any case where the legislation of a State was equal, impartial to all? Or is it not simply to provide that, where any State makes a distinction in the same law between different classes of individuals, Congress shall have power to correct such discrimination and inequality? Does this proposition mean anything more than that?

Mr. HALE. I will answer the gentleman. In my judgment it does go much further than the remarks of the gentleman would imply; but even if it goes no further than that—and I will discuss this point more fully before I conclude—it is still open to the same objection, that it proposes an entire departure from the theory of the Federal Government in meddling with these matters of State jurisdiction at all.

I now come directly, as I was coming in due order when the gentleman's very pertinent inquiry arrested my attention, to the consideration whether this is as has been maintained by the gentleman who reported the resolution, and by others, simply a provision for the equality of individual citizens before the laws of the several States. I submit, Mr. Speaker, that it means much more than that. Let me read the language of the resolution, striking out, for the purpose of making it more clear, that part which is simply irrelevant to the matter which I here discuss:

> *The Congress shall have power to make all laws which shall be necessary and proper to secure to all persons in the several States equal protection in the rights of life, liberty, and property.*

Now, I say to the gentleman from Pennsylvania [Mr. Stevens] that reading the language in its grammatical and legal construction it is a grant of the fullest and most ample power to Congress to make all laws "necessary and proper to secure to all persons in the several States protection in the rights of life, liberty, and property," with the simple provision that such protection shall be equal. It is not a mere provision that when the States undertake to give protection which is unequal Congress may equalize it; it is a grant of power in general terms—a grant of the right to legislate for the protection of life, liberty, and property, simply qualified with the condition that it shall be equal legislation. That is my construction of the proposition as it stands here. It may differ from that of other gentlemen....

Take a single case by way of illustration, and I take it simply to illustrate the point, without expressing any opinion whatever on the desirability or undesirability of a change in regard to it. [In many states at this time, married women could not contract, own personal property in their own name, bring legal actions on their own, etc. Their legal status was somewhat similar to the status of children today.] Take the case of the rights of married women; did any one ever assume that Congress was to be invested with the power to legislate on that subject, and to say that married women, in regard to their rights or property, should stand on the same footing with men and unmarried women? There is not a State in the Union where disability of married women in relation to the rights of property does not to a greater or lesser extent still exist. Many of the States have taken steps for the partial abolition of that distinction in years past, some to a greater extent and others to a lesser extent. But I apprehend there is not today a State in the Union where there is not a distinction between the rights of married women, as to property, and the rights of *femmes sole* and men.

Mr. STEVENS. If I do not interrupt the gentleman I will say a word. When a distinction is made between two married people or two *femmes sole*, then it is unequal legislation; but where all of the same class are dealt with in the same way then there is no pretense of inequality.

Mr. HALE. The gentleman will pardon me; his argument seems to me to be more specious than sound. The language of the section under consideration gives to *all persons* equal protection. Now, if that means you shall extend to one married woman the same protection you extend to another, and not the same you extend to unmarried women or men, then by parity of reasoning it will be sufficient if you extend to one negro the same rights you do to another, but not those you extend to a white man. I think, if the gentleman from Pennsylvania claims that the resolution only intends that all of a certain class shall have equal protection, such class legislation may certainly as well satisfy the requirements of this resolution in the case of the negro as in the case of the married woman. The line of distinction is, I take it, quite as broadly marked between negroes and white men as between married and unmarried women.

It was not within the purview of the original Constitution to grant the power of legislation to Congress on subjects of this character. Mr. Speaker, the powers conferred on Congress are all contained in the eighth section of the first article of the Constitution. I ask the House to look at these provisions, their nature, their general scope, the accuracy, precision, and care with which they are defined, and compare them with what I cannot but characterize, with all my respect and deference for the committee on reconstruction, as the extremely vague, loose, and indefinite provisions of the proposed amendment....

Again, the gentleman from Ohio [Mr. Bingham] refers us to the fifth article of the amendments to the Constitution as the basis of the present resolution, and as the source from which he has taken substantially the language of that clause of the proposed amendment I am considering. Now, what are these amendments to the Constitution, numbered from one to ten, one of which is the fifth article in question? What is the nature and object of these articles? They do not contain, from beginning to end, a grant of power anywhere. On the contrary, they are all restrictions of power. They constitute the bill of rights, a bill of rights for the protection of the citizen, and defining and limiting the power of Federal and State legislation. They are not matters upon which legislation can be based. They begin with the proposition that "Congress shall make *no law*," &c.; and if I were to follow the example of my friend from California [Mr. Higby], I might perhaps claim that here was a sufficient prohibition against the legislation sought to be provided for by this amendment. Throughout they are prohibitions against legislation....

Mr. BINGHAM. The gentleman will allow me to ask him to point to a single decision. The gentleman says that the sufficiency of the Constitution has been tested and found in the past. I ask him now if he knows of a single decision in which the sufficiency of the Constitution to secure to a party aggrieved in his person within a State the right to protection by the prosecution of a suit, which by the organic law of the State was denied to him, has ever been affirmed, either by Federal statute or Federal decision, or whether the nation has not been dumb in the presence of the organic act of a State which declares that eight hundred thousand natural-born citizens of the United States shall be denied the right to prosecute a suit in their courts, either for the vindication of a right or the redress of a wrong? Where is the decision? I want an answer.

Mr. HALE. The gentleman will always get an answer when he asks me a question. It is never necessary for him to accompany his questions with a warning.

I have not been able to prepare a brief for this argument, and therefore I cannot refer the gentleman to any case. As I never claim to be a very learned constitutional lawyer I have no hesitation in making the admission that I do not know of a case where it has ever been decided that the United States Constitution is sufficient for the protection of the liberties of the citizen. But still I have, somehow or other, gone along with the impression that there is that sort of protection thrown over us in some way, whether with or without the sanction of a judicial decision that we are so protected. Of course, I may be entirely mistaken in all this, but I have certainly somehow had that impression.

Mr. ELDRIDGE. I wish to know if the gentleman from Ohio [Mr. Bingham] has found or heard of a case in which the Constitution of the United States has been pronounced to be insufficient?...

Mr. BINGHAM. I beg leave to say that I am ready to answer the gentleman now, and to produce such a decision, whether the gentleman from New York is or is not....

[In a subsequent speech, Bingham returned to the question of the sufficiency of the Constitution to protect civil liberties.]

[*Globe*, 39(1) 1089–90 (1866)]:

Mr. BINGHAM. A gentleman on the other side interrupted me and wanted to know if I could cite a decision showing that the power of the Federal Government to enforce in the United States courts the bill of rights under the articles of amendment to the Constitution had been denied. I answered that I was prepared to introduce such decisions; and that is exactly what makes plain the necessity of adopting this amendment.

Mr. Speaker, on this subject I refer the House and the country to ... *Barron vs. Baltimore*, involving the question whether the provisions of the fifth article of the amendments to the Constitution are binding upon the State of Maryland and to be enforced in the Federal courts. The Chief Justice says: [Bingham quotes *Barron* to the effect that the Bill of Rights does not limit the states and then resumes.] ...

Why, I ask, should not the "injunctions and prohibitions," addressed by the people in the Constitution to the States and the Legislatures of States, be enforced by the people through the proposed amendment? By the decisions read the people are without remedy. It is admitted in the argument of Mr. Webster ... that the State Legislatures may by direct violations of their duty and oaths avoid the requirements of the Constitution, and thereby do an act which would break up any government.

Those oaths have been disregarded; those requirements of our Constitution have been broken; they are disregarded today in Oregon; they are disregarded today, and have been disregarded for the last five, ten, or twenty years in every one of the eleven States, recently in insurrection.

The question is, simply, whether you will give by this amendment to the people of the United States the power, by legislative enactment, to punish officials of States for violation of the oaths enjoined upon them by their Constitution? That is the question, and the whole question. The adoption of the proposed amendment will take from the States no rights that belong to the States. They elect their Legislatures; they enact their laws for punishment of crimes against life, liberty, or property; but in the event of the adoption of this amendment, if they conspire together to enact laws refusing equal protection to life, liberty, or property, the Congress is thereby vested with power to hold them to answer before the bar of the national courts for the violation of their oaths and of the rights of their fellow-men. Why should it not be so? That is the question....

What more could have been added to that instrument to secure the enforcement of these provisions of the bill of rights in every State, other than the additional grant of power which we ask this day? Nothing at all. And I am perfectly confident that that grant of power would have been there but for the fact that its insertion in the Constitution would have been utterly incompatible with the existence of slavery in any State; for although slaves might not have been admitted to be citizens they must have been admitted to be persons. That is the only reason why it was not there. There was a fetter upon the conscience of the nation; the people could not put it there and permit slavery in any State thereafter. Thank God, that fetter has been broken; it has turned to dust before the breath of the people, speaking as the voice of God and solemnly ordaining that slavery is forever prohibited everywhere within the Republic except as punishment for crime on due conviction. Even now for crimes men may be enslaved in States, notwithstanding the new amendment.

As slaves were not protected by the Constitution, there might be some color of excuse for the slave States in their disregard for the requirement of the bill of rights as to slaves and refusing them protection in life or property; though, in my judgment, there could be no possible apology for reducing men made like themselves, in the image of God, to level with the brutes of the field, and condemning them to toil without reward, to live without knowledge, and die without hope.

But, sir, there never was even colorable excuse, much less apology, for any man North or South claiming that any State Legislature or State court, or State Executive, has any right to deny protection to any free citizen of the United States within their limits in the rights of life, liberty, and property. Gentlemen who oppose this amendment oppose the grant of power to enforce the bill of rights.

* * *

After these arguments, a motion was made to postpone consideration of the prototype of the 14th Amendment. Immediately before the February 28, 1866 vote to postpone consideration of the prototype, Congressman Giles Hotchkiss of New York, a lawyer, observed:

> His [Bingham's] amendment is not as strong as the Constitution now is. The Constitution now gives equal rights to a certain extent to all citizens. This amendment provides that Congress may pass laws to enforce these rights. Why not provide by an amendment to the Constitution that no State shall discriminate against any class of its citizens; and let that amendment stand as a part of the organic law of the land subject only to be defeated by another constitutional amendment? We may pass laws here to-day, and the next Congress may wipe them out. Where is your guarantee then? *Globe* 39(1) 1095 (1866).

The vote to postpone carried. In effect it sent the issue back to the Joint Committee on Reconstruction for further work. What finally emerged was the final version of § 1 minus the Citizenship Clause, which was added later as an amendment in the Senate.

[The next excerpt is from Congressman Roswell Hart of New York speaking in late March 1866 after the passage of the Civil Rights Bill but before the final passage of the 14th Amendment. Hart was a lawyer and a radical Republican. Here he is not directly discussing the 14th Amendment or its prototype, but the closely related subject of Reconstruction. The 14th Amendment became the centerpiece of the Reconstruction program of the 39th Congress. The excerpt is important because it illustrates that many Republicans did not accept the rule in *Barron* as a correct statement of what the law was or should be. For another example, *see* Senator Nye, *Globe* 39(1) 1072 (1866).]

[*Globe*, 39(1) 1629 (1866)]:

Mr. HART. The Constitution clearly describes that to be a republican form of government for which it was expressly framed. A government which shall "establish justice, insure domestic tranquility, provide for the common defense, promote the general welfare, and secure the blessings of liberty;" a government whose "citizens shall be entitled to all privileges and immunities of other citizens;" where "no law shall be made prohibiting the free exercise of religion;" where "the right of the people to keep and bear arms shall not be infringed;" where "the right to the people to be secure in their persons, houses, papers, and effects, against unreasonable searches and seizures, shall not be violated," and where "no person shall be deprived of life, liberty, or property without due process of law."

Have these rebellious States such a form of government? If they have not, it is the duty of the United States to guaranty that they have it speedily.

* * *

The first version of the Bingham amendment had been sent back to the Joint Committee on Reconstruction. What emerged was an amendment much like the present 14th Amendment. The Citizenship Clause, however, was added after the initial Senate debate. Here is the amendment with § 1 as it existed during the first House discussion of the new version. This is also the new version of the 14th Amendment the House will send to the Senate after the debate that follows.

ARTICLES

Sec. 1. No State shall make or enforce any law which shall abridge the privileges or immunities of citizens of the United States; nor shall any State deprive any person of life, liberty, or property, without due process of law; nor deny to any person within its jurisdiction the equal protection of the laws.

Sec. 2. Representatives shall be apportioned among the several States which may be included within the Union, according to their respective numbers, counting the whole number of persons in each State, excluding Indians not taxed. But whenever, in any State, the elective franchise shall be denied to any portion of its male citizens not less than twenty-one years of age, or in any way abridged, except for participation in rebellion, or other crimes, the basis or representation in such State shall be reduced in the proportion which the number of such male citizens shall bear to the whole number of male citizens not less than twenty-one years of age.

Sec. 3. Until the 4th day of July, in the year 1870, all persons who voluntarily adhered to the late insurrection, giving it aid and comfort, shall be excluded from the right to vote for Representatives in Congress and for electors for President and Vice President of the United States.

Sec. 4. Neither the United States nor any State shall assume or pay any debt or obligation already incurred, or which may hereafter be incurred, in aid of insurrection or of war against the United States, or any claim for compensation for loss of involuntary service or labor.

Sec. 5. The Congress shall have power to enforce by appropriate legislation the provisions of this article.

[The following excerpt is from a speech by Thaddeus Stevens, a leader of House Republicans and Member of the Joint Committee that proposed the 14th Amendment:]

[*Globe,* 39(1) 2459 (1866)]:

Mr. STEVENS. I can hardly believe that any person can be found who will not admit that every one of these provisions is just. They are all asserted, in some form or other, in our Declaration or organic law. But the Constitution limits only the action of Congress, and is not a limitation on the States. The amendment supplies that defect, and allows Congress to correct the unjust legislation of the States, so far that the law which operates upon one man shall operate *equally* upon all.... Whatever law protects the white man shall afford "equal" protection to the black man. Whatever means of redress is afforded to one shall be afforded to all. Whatever law allows a white man to testify in court shall allow the man of color to do the same. These are great advantages over their present codes. Now different degrees of punishment are inflicted ... according to the color of the skin. Now color disqualifies a man from testifying in courts, or being tried in the same way as white men. I need not enumerate these partial and oppressive laws. Unless the Constitution should restrain them those States will all, I fear, keep up this discrimination, and crush to death the hated freedmen. Some answer, "Your civil rights bill secures the same things." That is partly true, but a law is repealable by a majority. And I need hardly say that the first time that the South with their copperhead allies obtain the command of Congress it will be repealed....

[The next excerpt is from radical Republican Congressman Thomas Elliot of Massachusetts, a lawyer, speaking about the 14th Amendment on May 9, 1866. Radicals like Elliot favored black suffrage. Some were extremely radical—even favoring suffrage for women. What does Elliot understand § 1 to be about?]

[*Globe*, 39(1) 2511 (1866)]:

Mr. ELLIOT. This amendment is not, as I believe, all that ought to be offered by that committee and passed by this House and made by the loyal Legislatures of the United States a part of our organic law; but it is right as far as it goes, and upon careful examination I find contained in it no compromise of principle.... The time will come, I do not doubt, when in this Union of ours all men stand equal before the law in their political and civil rights....

I support the first section because the doctrine it declares is right, and if, under the Constitution as it now stands, Congress has not the power to prohibit State legislation discriminating against classes of citizens or depriving any persons of life, liberty, or property without due process of law, or denying to any persons within the State the equal protection of the laws, then, in my judgment, such power should be distinctly conferred. I voted for the civil rights bill, and I did so under a conviction that we have ample power to enact into law the provisions of that bill. But I shall gladly do what I may to incorporate into the Constitution provisions which will settle the doubt which some gentlemen entertain upon that question.

The second section, Mr. Speaker, is, in my judgment, as nearly correct as it can be without being fully, in full measure, right. But one thing is right, and that is secured by the amendment. Manifestly no State should have its basis of national representation enlarged by reason of a portion of citizens within its borders to which the elective franchise is denied. If political power shall be lost because of such denial, not imposed because of participation in rebellion or other crime, it is to be hoped that political interests may work in the line of justice, and that the end will be the impartial enfranchisement of all citizens not disqualified by crime. Whether that end shall be attained or not, this will be secured: that the measure of political power of any State shall be determined by that portion of its citizens which can speak and act at the polls, and shall not be enlarged because of the residence within the State of portions of its citizens denied the right of franchise. So much for the second section of the amendment. It is not all that I wish and would demand; but odious inequalities are removed by it and representation will be equalized and the political rights of all citizens will under its operation be, as we believe, ultimately recognized and admitted....

[The next excerpt is from radical Republican Congressman John Farnsworth of Illinois, a lawyer, speaking on May 10, 1866. What is the significance of his views for application of the Bill of Rights to the States? How can he believe that requiring states to obey the Due Process Clause is surplusage?]

[*Globe*, 39(1) 2539–40 (1866)]:

Mr. FARNSWORTH. I intend to vote for this amendment in the form reported, with the exception of the third section. It is not all I could wish; it is not all I hope may yet be adopted and ratified; for I am not without hope that Congress and the people of the several States may yet rise above a mean prejudice and do equal and exact justice to all men, by putting in practice that "self-evident truth" of the Declaration of Independence, that Governments "derive their just powers from the consent of the governed," and giving to every citizen, white or black, who has not forfeited the right by his crimes, the ballot. But I do not think it is becoming in a legislator to oppose some good because the measure is not all he wants.

The first section of the amendment proposed is as follows:

> *Sec. 1. No State shall make or enforce any law which shall abridge the privileges or immunities of citizens of the United States; nor shall any State deprive any person*

of life, liberty, or property, without due process of law; nor deny to any person within its jurisdiction the equal protection of its laws.

So far as this section is concerned, there is but one clause in it which is not already in the Constitution, and it might as well in my opinion read, "No State shall deny to any person within its jurisdiction the equal protection of the laws." But a reaffirmation of a good principle will do no harm, and I shall not therefore oppose it on account of what I may regard as surplusage.

"Equal protection of the laws;" can there be any well-founded objection to this? Is not this the very foundation of a republican government? Is it not the undeniable right to every subject of the Government to receive "equal protection of the laws" with every other subject? How can he have and enjoy equal rights of "life, liberty, and the pursuit of happiness" without "equal protection of the laws?" This is so self-evident and just that no man whose soul is not too cramped and dwarfed to hold the smallest germ of justice can fail to see and appreciate it....

If the freedmen are so degraded and ignorant as to be unworthy of enfranchisement; if they are not capable of governing themselves, but must be held in subjection to and governed by their late masters, then they are not fit to govern the country through the votes of others. They shall not by any such prestidigitation, be dead at the ballot-box, but alive here, dumb, without a voice for their own government, and with thirty-two voices on this floor, and thirty-two votes for President and Vice President. They shall not be used to swell their rebel masters into giants and dwarf the loyal and patriotic men of the free States into Tom Thumbs! If you deny to any portion of the loyal citizens of your State the right to vote for Representatives you shall not assume to represent them, and, as you have done for so long a time, misrepresent and oppress them. This is a step in the right direction; and although I should prefer to see incorporated into the Constitution a guarantee of universal suffrage, as we cannot get the required two thirds for that, I cordially support this proposition as the next best.

This amendment, too, I fully believe, will in a reasonably short period bring universal suffrage.

[The next excerpt is from Rep. John H. Bromall, a Republican Congressman from Pennsylvania speaking on the Civil Rights Bill, in March of 1866. Bromall was a lawyer.]

[*Globe,* 39(1) 1263 (1866)]:

Mr. BROMALL. But it is said by the minority in this body that we have no right under the Constitution to pass the [Civil Rights] law; that the General Government was never intended to be intrusted with the power to protect individual persons; that that was to be left to the States. What, then, does the preamble mean? An ordinary reader would look there for the object and intent of the document. [After quoting the preamble, Bromall continued]:

This certainly has the appearance of being designed to protect the rights of individuals within ... the jurisdiction of the Government. Yet, strange as it may seem while the Government has been always held competent to protect its meanest citizen within the domain of any European potentate, it has been considered powerless to guard the citizen of Pennsylvania against the illegal arrest, under the color of State law, of the most obscure municipality in Virginia. [I]t had no power to protect the personal liberty of the agent of the State of Massachusetts in the city of Charleston, or to enable him to sue in the State courts. [Bromall cites the General Welfare Clause and Article IV, § 2 to argue for federal power to protect the liberty of individuals within the states.]

But throwing aside the letter of the Constitution, there are characteristics of Governments that belong to them as such, without which they would cease to be Governments. The rights and duties of allegiance and protection are corresponding rights and duties....

Will [opponents of the Civil Rights Bill of 1866] say that the rights of citizens of the United States can be safely intrusted to the governments of the several States? If this were true it might afford some excuse for neglecting to provide the appropriate legislation, but none for refusing it. But it is not true. For thirty years prior to 1860 everybody knows that the rights and immunities of citizens were habitually and systematically denied in certain States to citizens of other States: the right of speech, the right of transit, the right of domicile, the right to sue, the writ of habeas corpus, and the right of petition. [W]ill it be said with the disappearance of the peculiar institution this state of things also disappeared?

[In the next excerpt, we hear again from Bromall, this time on the 14th Amendment. Do his earlier remarks affect your interpretation of those set out now?]

[*Globe,* 39(1) 2498 (1866)]:

Mr. BROMALL. We propose first, to give power to the government of the United States to protect its own citizens within the States, within its own jurisdiction. Who will deny the necessity of this? No one. The fact that all who will vote for the pending measure, or whose votes are asked for it, voted for this proposition in another shape, in the civil rights bill, shows that it will meet favor in the House. It may be asked, why should we put a provision in the Constitution which is already contained in an act of Congress. [He responds that the provision removes any doubt about the power to pass the Civil Rights Act.]

[The next portion of a speech is from Senator Luke Poland, Republican of Maine who is also discussing the 14th Amendment. Poland was a lawyer and former Chief Justice of the Maine Supreme Court.]

[*Globe,* 39(1) 2961 (1866)]:

Mr. POLAND. The clause of the first proposed amendment that "no State shall make or enforce any law which shall abridge the privileges or immunities of citizens of the United States," secures nothing beyond what was intended by the original provision in the Constitution, that "the citizens of each State shall be entitled to all privileges and immunities of citizens in the several States."

But the radical difference in the social systems of the several States, and the great extent to which the doctrine of State rights or State sovereignty was carried, induced mainly, as I believe, by and for the protection of the peculiar system of the South, led to a practical repudiation of the existing provision on this subject, and it was disregarded in many of the States. State legislation was allowed to override it....

[The next excerpt is from Congressman Bingham, the principal drafter of § 1, speaking about the 14th Amendment on May 10, 1866.]

[*Globe,* 39(1) 2542 (1866)]:

Mr. BINGHAM. The necessity for the first section of this amendment to the Constitution, Mr. Speaker, is one of the lessons that have been taught to your committee and taught to all the people of this country by the history of the past four years of terrific conflict—that history in which God is, and in which He teaches the profoundest lessons to men and nations. There was a want hitherto, and there remains a want now, in the Constitution of our country, which the proposed amendment will supply. What is that?

It is the power in the people, the whole people of the United States, by express authority of the Constitution to do that by congressional enactment which hitherto they have not had the power to do, and have never even attempted to do; that is, to protect by national law the privileges and immunities of all the citizens of the Republic and the inborn rights of every person within its jurisdiction whenever the same shall be abridged or denied by the unconstitutional acts of any State.

Allow me, Mr. Speaker, in passing, to say that this amendment takes from no State any right that ever pertained to it. No State ever had the right, under the forms of law or otherwise, to deny to any freeman the equal protection of the laws or to abridge the privileges or immunities of any citizen of the Republic, although many of them have assumed and exercised the power, and that without remedy. The amendment does not give, as the second section shows, the power to Congress of regulating suffrage in the several States.

The second section excludes the conclusion that by the first section suffrage is subjected to congressional law; save, indeed, with this exception, that as the right in the people of each State to a republican government and to choose their Representatives in Congress is of the guarantees of the Constitution, by this amendment a remedy might be given directly for a case supposed by Madison, where treason might change a State government from a republican to a despotic government, and thereby deny suffrage to the people. Why should any American citizen object to that? But, sir, it has been suggested, not here, but elsewhere, if this section does not confer suffrage the need of it is not perceived. To all such I beg leave again to say, that many instances of State injustice and oppression have already occurred in the State legislation of this Union, of flagrant violations of the guaranteed privileges of citizens of the United States, for which the national Government furnished and could furnish by law no remedy whatever. Contrary to the express letter of your Constitution, "cruel and unusual punishments" have been inflicted under State laws within this Union upon citizens, not only for crimes committed, but for sacred duty done, for which and against which the Government of the United States had provided no remedy and could provide none.

Sir, the words of the Constitution that "the citizens of each State shall be entitled to all privileges and immunities of citizens in the several States" include, among other privileges, the right to bear true allegiance to the Constitution and laws of the United States, and to be protected in life, liberty, and property.

[The next excerpt is from George Latham, Republican Congressman from West Virginia, speaking in late May 1866.]

[*Globe,* 39(1) 2883 (1866)]:

Mr. LATHAM. The first provides that no State shall make any discrimination in civil rights of citizens of the United States on account of race, color, or previous condition of slavery. If the term "civil rights" be construed not to include what is properly understood as "political rights," I think this provision just within itself, and that it probably includes nothing more than the Constitution originally intended to include.... Besides, sir, the "civil rights bill," which is now a law ... covers exactly the same ground as this amendment....

* * *

Senator Jacob Howard was a radical Republican from Michigan who favored black suffrage and was disappointed that it was not included in the 14th Amendment. He was a member of the Joint Committee and was chosen to explain the Amendment to the Senate. Note that the Amendment is still not in its final form. In the excerpt below, what does Howard say is included in the words "privileges or immunities"? What part of § 1 is still missing at this point?

The title given in the *Globe* is "Reconstruction" because the 14th Amendment was a major effort to deal with the need to "reconstruct" the nation after the ordeal of the Civil War. Furthermore, Congress had to deal with the problem that had resulted from Southern senators and congressmen withdrawing from Congress at the start of the Civil War. The 39th Congress (in power following the War) had refused to seat representatives of the rebellious states without further conditions. The 14th Amendment was a prime condition. Congress provided that Southern states would not be readmitted to representation in Congress unless the rebellious state seeking readmission had first ratified it.

[*Globe*, 39(1) 2764–65 (1866)]: The 14th Amendment, Not in Final Form.

RECONSTRUCTION.

The Senate, as in Committee of the Whole, proceeded to consider the joint resolution (H.R. No. 127) proposing an amendment to the Constitution of the United States, which was read as follows:

Resolved by the Senate and House of Representatives of the United States of America in Congress assembled, (two thirds of both Houses concurring.) That the following article be proposed to the Legislatures of the several States as an amendment to the Constitution of the United States, which, when ratified by three fourths of said Legislatures, shall be valid as part of the Constitution, namely:

ARTICLE

Sec. 1. No State shall make or enforce any law which shall abridge the privileges or immunities of citizens of the United States; nor shall any State deprive any person of life, liberty, or property, without due process of law; nor deny to any person within its jurisdiction the equal protection of the laws.

Sec. 2. Representatives shall be apportioned among the several States which may be included within the Union, according to their respective numbers, counting the whole number of persons in each State, excluding Indians not taxed. But whenever, in any State, the elective franchise shall be denied to any portion of its male citizens not less than twenty-one years of age, or in any way abridged, except for participation in rebellion, or other crimes, the basis of representation in such State shall be reduced in the proportion which the number of such male citizens shall bear to the whole number of male citizens not less than twenty-one years of age.

Sec. 3. Until the 4th day of July, in the year 1870, all persons who voluntarily adhered to the late insurrection, giving it aid and comfort, shall be excluded from the right to vote for Representatives in Congress and for electors for President and Vice President of the United States.

Sec. 4. Neither the United States nor any State shall assume or pay any debt or obligation already incurred, or which may hereafter be incurred, in aid of insurrection or of war against the United States, or any claim for compensation for loss of involuntary service or labor.

Sec. 5. The Congress shall have power to enforce by appropriate legislation the provisions of this article.

Mr. HOWARD. Mr. President ... I can only promise to present to the Senate, in a very succinct way, the views and the motives which influenced that committee, so far as I understand those views and motives, in presenting the report which is now before us for consideration, and the ends it aims to accomplish....

> *No State shall make or enforce any law which shall abridge the privileges or immunities of citizens of the United States; nor shall any State deprive any person of life, liberty, or property without due process of law; nor deny to any person within its jurisdiction the equal protection of the laws.*

It will be observed that this is a general prohibition upon all the States, as such, from abridging the privileges and immunities of the citizens of the United States. That is its first clause, and I regard it as very important. It also prohibits each one of the States from depriving any person of life, liberty, or property without due process of law, or denying to any person within the jurisdiction of the State the equal protection of its laws.

The first clause of this section relates to the privileges and immunities of citizens of the United States as such, and as distinguished from all other persons not citizens of the United States. It is not, perhaps, very easy to define with accuracy what is meant by the expression, "citizen of the United States," although that expression occurs twice in the Constitution, once in reference to the President of the United States, in which instance it is declared that none but a citizen of the United States shall be President and again in reference to Senators, who are likewise to be citizens of the United States. Undoubtedly the expression is used in both those instances in the same sense in which it is employed in the amendment now before us. A citizen of the United States is held by the courts to be a person who was born within the limits of the United States and the subject to their laws. Before the adoption of the Constitution of the United States, the citizens of each State were, in a qualified sense at least, aliens to one another, for the reason that the several States before that event were regarded by each other as independent Governments, each one possessing a sufficiency of sovereign power to enable it to claim the right of naturalization; and, undoubtedly, each one of them possessed for itself the right of naturalizing foreigners, and each one, also, if it had seen fit so to exercise its sovereign power, might have declared the citizens of every other State to be aliens in reference to itself. With a view to prevent such confusion and disorder, and to put the citizens of the several States on an equality with each other as to all fundamental rights, a clause was introduced in the Constitution declaring that "the citizens of each State shall be entitled to all privileges and immunities of citizens in the several States."

The effect of this clause was to constitute *ipso facto* the citizens of each one of the original States citizens of the United States. And how did they antecedently become citizens of the several States? By birth or by naturalization. They became such in virtue of national law, or rather of natural law which recognizes persons born within the jurisdiction of every country as being subjects or citizens of that country. Such persons were, therefore, citizens of the United States as were born in the country or were made such by naturalization; and the Constitution declares that they are entitled, as citizens, to all the privileges and immunities of citizens in the several States. They are, by constitutional right, entitled to these privileges and immunities, and may assert this right and these privileges and immunities, and ask for their enforcement whenever they go within the limits of the several States of the Union.

It would be a curious question to solve what are the privileges and immunities of citizens of each of the States in the several States. I do not propose to go at any length into that question at this time. It would be a somewhat barren discussion. But it is certain the clause was inserted in the Constitution for some good purpose. It has in view some results beneficial to the citizens of the several States, or it would not be found there; yet I am not aware that the Supreme Court have ever undertaken to define either the nature or extent of the privileges and immunities thus guaranteed. Indeed, if my recollection serves me, that court, on a certain occasion not many years since, when this question seemed to present itself to them, very modestly declined to go into a definition of them, leaving questions arising under the clause to be discussed and adjudicated when they should happen practically to arise. But we may gather some intimation of what probably will be the opinion of the judiciary by referring to a case adjudged many years ago in one of the circuit courts of the United States by Judge Washington; and I will trouble the Senate but for a moment by reading what that very learned and excellent judge says about these privileges and immunities of the citizens of each State in the several States. It is the case of *Corfield v. Coryell* (C.C.E.D. Pa. 1823)....

Such is the character of the privileges and immunities spoken of in the second section of the fourth article of the Constitution. To these privileges and immunities, whatever they may be—for they are not and cannot be fully defined in their entire extent and precise nature—to these should be added the personal rights guaranteed and secured by the first eight amendments of the Constitution; such as the freedom of speech and of the press; the right of the people peaceably to assemble and petition the Government for a redress of grievances, a right appertaining to each and all the people; the right to keep and to bear arms; the right to be exempted from the quartering of soldiers in a house without the consent of the owner; the right to be exempt from unreasonable searches and seizures, and from any search or seizure except by virtue of a warrant issued upon a formal oath or affidavit; the right of an accused person to be informed of the nature of the accusation against him, and his right to be tried by an impartial jury of the vicinage; and also the right to be secure against excessive bail and against cruel and unusual punishments.

Now sir, here is a mass of privileges, immunities, and rights, some of them secured by the second section of the fourth article of the Constitution, which I have recited, some by the first eight amendments of the Constitution; and it is a fact well worthy of attention that the course of decision of our courts and the present settled doctrine is, that all these immunities, privileges, rights, thus guaranteed by the Constitution or recognized by it, are secured to the citizen solely as a citizen of the United States and as a party in their courts. They do not operate in the slightest degree as a restraint or prohibition upon State legislation. States are not affected by them, and it has been repeatedly held that the restriction contained in the Constitution against the taking of private property for public use without just compensation is not a restriction upon State legislation, but applies only to the legislation of Congress.

Now, sir, there is no power given in the Constitution to enforce and to carry out any of these guarantees. They are not powers granted by the Constitution to Congress, and of course do not come within the sweeping clause of the Constitution authorizing Congress to pass all laws necessary and proper for carrying out the foregoing or granted powers, but they stand simply as a bill of rights in the Constitution, without power on the part of Congress to give them full effect; while at the same time the States are not restrained from violating the principles embraced in them except by their own local constitutions, which may be altered from year to year. The great object of the first section of this amendment is, therefore, to restrain the power of the States and compel them at all times to respect these great fundamental guarantees. How will it be done under the present amendment? As I have remarked, they are not powers granted to Congress, and therefore it is necessary, if they are to be effectuated and enforced, as they assuredly ought to be, that additional power should be given to Congress to that end. This is done by the fifth section of this amendment, which declares that "the Congress shall have power to enforce by appropriate legislation the provisions of this article." Here is a direct affirmative delegation of power to Congress to carry out all the principles of all these guarantees, a power not found in the Constitution.

The last two clauses of the first section of the amendment disable a State from depriving not merely a citizen of the United States, but any person, whoever he may be, of life, liberty, or property without due process of law, or from denying to him the equal protection of the laws of the State. This abolishes all class legislation in the States and does away with the injustice of subjecting one caste of persons to a code not applicable to another. It prohibits the hanging of a black man for a crime for which the white man is not to be hanged. It protects the black man in his fundamental rights as a citizen with the same shield which it throws over the white man. Is it not time, Mr. President, that we extend to the black man, I had almost called it the poor privilege of the equal protection of the law? Ought not the time to be now passed when one measure of justice is to be meted out to a member of one caste while another and a different measure is meted out to the member of another caste, both castes being alike citizens of the United States, both bound to obey the same laws, to sustain the burdens of the same Government, and both equally responsible to justice and to God for the deeds done in the body?

But, sir, the first section of the proposed amendment does not give to either of these classes the right of voting. The right of suffrage is not, in law, one of the privileges or immunities thus secured by the Constitution. It is merely the creature of law. It has always been regarded in this country as the result of positive local law, not regarded as one of those fundamental rights lying at the basis of all society and without which a people cannot exist except as slaves, subject to a despotism.

Speeches by Congressmen after the 39th Congress Adjourns

Some of the congressmen who spoke about the 14th amendment in 1866 after Congress had adjourned mentioned freedom of speech; others made general references to protecting the constitutional rights of American citizens. Some described § 1 by referring to the Civil Rights Bill of 1866. Republican Senator John Sherman is an example. He was quoted in the *Cincinnati Commercial*, Sept. 29, 1866 at p. 1:

> The first section was an embodiment of the Civil Rights Bill, namely: that every body—man, woman, and child—without regard to color, should have equal rights before the law; that is all there is to it; that every body born in this country or naturalized by our laws should stand equal before the laws—should have the right to go from county to county, and from State to State, to make contracts, to sue and be sued, to contract and be contracted with; that is the sum and substance of the first clause.... We are bound by every obligation, by [the service of black soldiers] on the battlefield, by their heroes who are buried in our cause, by their patriotism in the hour that tried our country, we are bound to protect them in all their natural rights.

The 14th Amendment: The Final Version

Sec. 1. All persons born or naturalized in the United States, and subject to the jurisdiction thereof, are citizens of the United States and of the State wherein they reside. No State shall make or enforce any law which shall abridge the privileges or immunities of citizens of the United States; nor shall any State deprive any person of life, liberty, or property, without due process of law; nor deny to any person within its jurisdiction the equal protection of the laws.

[Sec. 2 reduced representation of states that denied the right to vote to any part of their male population who were 21 years of age or older.]

[Sec. 3 prohibited office holding by those who had taken an oath to support the Constitution and then had "engaged in insurrection or rebellion" until Congress should remove the disability.]

[Sec. 4 guaranteed the validity of the Union debt and prohibited payment of the Confederate debt or payment for emancipated slaves.]

Sec. 5. The Congress shall have the power to enforce, by appropriate legislation, the provisions of this article.

The 14th Amendment was proposed by Congress on June 16, 1866; Congress declared it ratified on July 21, 1868.

* * *

Bingham speaking in 1871, after Ratification of the 14th Amendment

[*Globe,* 42(1) House Appendix 84 (1871)]:

Mr. BINGHAM. I answer the gentleman, how I came to change the form of February to the words now in the first section of the fourteenth article of amendment, as they stand, and I trust will forever stand, in the Constitution of my country. I had read — and that is what induced me to attempt to impose by constitutional amendments new limitations upon the power of the States — the great decision of Marshall in *Barron vs. Baltimore* (1833), wherein the Chief Justice said, in obedience to his official oath and the Constitution as it then was:

> *The amendments [to the Constitution] contain no expression indicating an intention to apply them to the State governments. This court cannot so apply them. — 7 Peters,* p. 250.

In this case the city had taken private property for public use, without compensation as alleged, and there was no redress for the wrong in the Supreme Court of the United States; and only for this reason, the first eight amendments were not limitations on the power of the States.

And so afterward, in the case of the *Livingston vs. Moore* (1833), the court ruled, "it is now settled that the amendments [to the Constitution] do not extend to the States." They were but limitations upon Congress. Jefferson well said of the first eight articles of amendments to the Constitution of the United States, they constitute the American Bill of Rights. Those amendments secured the citizens against any deprivation of any essential rights of person by any act of Congress, and among other things thereby they were secured in their persons, houses, papers, and effects against unreasonable searches and seizures, in the inviolability of their homes in times of peace, by declaring that no soldier shall in time of peace be quartered in any house without the consent of the owner. They secured trial by jury; they secured the right to be informed of the nature and cause of accusations which might in any case be made against them; they secured compulsory process for witnesses, and to be heard in defense by counsel. They secured, in short, all the rights dear to the American citizen. And yet it was decided, and rightfully, that these amendments, defining and protecting the rights of men and citizens, were only limitations on the power of Congress, not on the power of the States.

In reexamining that case of *Barron*, Mr. Speaker, after my struggle in the House in February, 1866, to which the gentleman has alluded, I noted and apprehended as I never did before, certain words in that opinion of Marshall. Referring to the first eight articles of amendments to the Constitution of the United States, the Chief Justice said: "Had the framers of these amendments intended them to be limitations on the powers of the State governments they would have imitated the framers of the original Constitution, and have expressed that intention." *Barron v. Baltimore.*

Acting upon this suggestion I did imitate the framers of the original Constitution. As they had said "no State shall emit bills of credit, pass any bill of attainder, *ex post facto* law, or law impairing the obligations of contracts"; imitating their example and imitating it to the letter, I prepared the provision of the first section of the 14th Amendment as it stands in the Constitution, as follows:

> *No State shall make or enforce any law which shall abridge the privileges or immunities of the citizens of the United States, nor shall any State deprive any person of life, liberty, or property without due process of law, nor deny to any person within its jurisdiction the equal protection of the laws.*

I hope the gentleman now knows why I changed the form of the amendment of February, 1866.

Mr. Speaker, that the scope and meaning of the limitations imposed by the first section, of the 14th Amendment of the Constitution may be more fully understood, permit me to say that the privileges and immunities of citizens of the United States, as contradistinguished from citizens of a State, are chiefly defined in the first eight amendments to the Constitution of the United States. Those eight amendments are as follows: [He proceeded to read them verbatim.]

These eight articles I have shown never were limitations upon the power of the States, until made so by the 14th Amendment. The words of that amendment, "no State shall make or enforce any law which shall abridge the privileges or immunities of citizens of the United States," are an express prohibition upon every State of the Union, which may be enforced under existing laws of Congress, and such other laws for their better enforcement as Congress may make.

Mr. Speaker, [*Corfield v. Coryell* (C.C.E.D. Pa. 1823)] is only a construction of the second section, fourth article of the original Constitution, to wit, "The citizens of each State shall be entitled to all privileges and immunities of citizens in the several States." In that case the court only held that in civil rights the State could not refuse to extend to citizens of other States the same general rights secured to its own.

In the case of *Bank of Augusta v. Earle* (1839) Mr. Webster said that—

> *For the purposes of trade, it is evidently not in the power of any State to impose any hindrance or embarrassment, [etc.], upon citizens of other States, or to place them, on coming there, upon a different footing from her own citizens.* — Webster's Works 112.

The learned Justice Story declared that—

> *The intention of the clause ("the citizens of each State shall be entitled to all privileges and immunities of citizens in the several States,") was to confer on the citizens*

of each State a general citizenship, and communicated all the privileges and immunities which a citizen of the same State would be entitled to under the same circumstances. — Story on the Constitution, vol. 2, page 605.

Is it not clear that other and different privileges and immunities than those to which a citizen of a State was entitled are secured by the provision of the fourteenth article, that no State shall abridge the privileges and immunities of citizens of the United States, which are defined in the eight articles of amendment, and which were not limitations on the power of the States before the 14th Amendment made them limitations?

Sir, before the ratification of the 14th Amendment, the State could deny to any citizen the right of trial by jury, and it was done. Before that the State could abridge the freedom of the press, and it was so done in half of the States of the Union. Before that a State as in the case of the State of Illinois, could make it a crime punishable by fine and imprisonment for any citizen within her limits, in obedience to the injunction of our divine Master, to help a slave who was ready to perish; to give him shelter, or break with him his crust of bread. The validity of that State restriction upon the rights of conscience and the duty of life was affirmed, to the shame and disgrace of America, in the Supreme Court of the United States; but nevertheless affirmed in obedience to the requirements of the Constitution. *Moore v. Illinois* (1852).

Under the Constitution as it is, not as it was, and by force of the 14th Amendment, no State hereafter can imitate the bad example of Illinois, to which I have referred, nor can any State ever repeat the example of Georgia and send men to the penitentiary, as did that State, for teaching the Indian to read the lessons of the New Testament, to know that new evangel, "The pure in heart shall see God."

Mr. Speaker, this House may safely follow the example of the makers of the Constitution and the builders of the Republic, by passing laws for enforcing all the privileges and immunities of citizens of the United States, as guaranteed by the amended Constitution and expressly enumerated in the Constitution. Do gentlemen say that by so legislating we would strike down the rights of the State? God forbid. I believe our dual system of government essential to our national existence. That Constitution which Washington so aptly said made us one people, is essential to our nationality and essential to the protection of the rights of all the people at home and abroad. The State governments are also essential to the local administration of the law, which makes it omnipresent, visible to every man within the vast extent of the Republic, in every place, whether by the wayside or by the fireside, restraining him by its terrors from the wrong, and protecting him by its power, in the right.

Who is there here to say that any State ever had the right to defeat the very object for which all government is made?

V. Applying Methods of Interpretation to the 14th Amendment's First Section

1. What effect should § 1 of the 14th Amendment (ratified in 1868) have on the duty of the states to obey the guarantees of liberty set out in the original Bill of Rights? Read § 1. What do the words mean to you in their common (i.e. non-technical) meaning? What is "due process"? What are "privileges" or "immunities"? What does the dic-

tionary say "privilege" means, for example? What is meant by "abridge?" What does the word "liberty" mean in the Due Process Clause? What does "due" mean? What does "process" mean? Look up the meaning of these words in the dictionary.

2. Make a textual argument as to why guarantees of the Bill of Rights should limit the states under the 14th Amendment's first section. Try to break the argument down into steps. What is the significance of the phrase "citizens of the United States"? Do citizens of the United States have any rights? Make an argument based on context, on precedent, on structure, and on history. As to each of these, what authority or evidence could you point to?

3. Now make the same argument *against* application of the Bill of Rights to the states. Can you make a contextual argument against application or an argument based on context plus precedent against application? Do the words "privileges" and "immunities" appear elsewhere in the Constitution? Which argument is stronger? Why?

A Brief Note on "State Action" and Cities and Counties

The 14th Amendment provides that "no state shall" abridge privileges or immunities of citizens or deny any person due process or equal protection. Cities, counties, school boards, prisons, and other governmental bodies are all creations of state law and thus are simply subdivisions of the state. Action by any of these entities is treated as state action for 14th Amendment purposes.

Hypothetical Concerning the Incorporation of the 2nd Amendment

Assume this hypothetical case comes before the Supreme Court:

The town of Richland, Indiana, after a rash of shootings, has barred possession of any guns — rifles, shotguns, handguns, machine guns, etc. — within the limits of the town. The Court has held that the 2nd Amendment confers an individual right to bear arms that cannot be denied by the federal government. (Before that decision, on several occasions, the Court had held that the 2nd Amendment does not limit the states under the 14th Amendment.)

James Marksman has been arrested for possession of a handgun, a rifle, and a shotgun within Richland's town limits. What constitutional argument can Marksman make? How can you craft an argument on his behalf using text, context, history, precedent, structure, and policy?

1. What arguments might you make from text? What resources are available to help determine the meaning of the words? What arguments might you make from context? From precedent? From history? From structure?

2. Recall the congressional background of the 14th Amendment: framing the 14th Amendment. How can you use this material? How can you use the Black Codes?

3. Argument from structure: how could this type of argument bear on the incorporation issue?

* * *

Optional reading: For one effort to apply methods of interpretation to the 14th Amendment-Bill of Rights issue, *see* Michael Kent Curtis, *Resurrecting the Privileges or Immuni-*

ties Clause and Revising the Slaughter-House Cases Without Exhuming Lochner: *Individual Rights and the Fourteenth Amendment*, 38 B.C. L. Rev. 1–67 (1996); Akhil Reed Amar, *The Bill of Rights: Creation and Reconstruction* (1998). *See also No State Shall Abridge*, 26–56. For a short article on the 14th Amendment and the Bill of Rights, *see* Michael Kent Curtis, *Conceived in Liberty*, 65 N.C. L. Rev. 889–99 (1987). For an opposing view, *see* Raoul Berger, *Government By Judiciary*, chapter on Incorporation of the Bill of Rights; *see also* William E. Nelson, *The Fourteenth Amendment* (1988), James Bond, *No Easy Walk to Freedom* (1997), and Michael Perry, *We the People: The Fourteenth Amendment and the Supreme Court* (1999).

VI. Reconstruction and the Initial Judicial Response

A. A Post-Ratification Case on the Article IV, § 2, Privileges and Immunities Clause

Paul v. Virginia (1868) rejected an Article IV, § 2, privileges and immunities challenge to a statute that imposed higher burdens on insurance companies incorporated in other states than on those incorporated in Virginia. The Court held a corporation was not a citizen for Article IV, § 2, purposes. The Court said:

> [Article IV, § 2, relieves citizens from other states] from the disabilities of alienage in other States; it inhibits discriminating legislation against them by other States.... But the privileges and immunities secured to citizens of each State in the several States, by the provision in question, are those privileges and immunities which are common to the citizens in the latter States under their [own] Constitution and laws by virtue of their being citizens [of their own state].

What is the effect of this case on the theory that Article IV, § 2, protects against state denial of privileges of citizens of the United States that the state must accord to its citizens and to citizen visitors from other states as well?

B. Reconstruction

Historical context: When the 14th Amendment was initially presented to them for ratification, Southern states (except for Tennessee) refused to ratify it. Congress then divided the Southern states into military districts. Congress provided that the Southern states could only be re-admitted if they ratified the 14th Amendment and, in addition, created new state constitutions approved by Congress. Congress also set requirements for electing representatives to the state constitutional conventions. It required election by manhood suffrage, but it excluded those Southerners who had taken an oath to support the United States Constitution and then joined the Confederacy. (As a result of the exclusion of members of the military and political office-holders, much of the Southern political elite were not allowed to vote for delegates to the state conventions.)

Congress required the new state constitutions to enfranchise males 21 years of age or older, including the newly freed slaves. The Confederates who had taken the oath to support the United States and then joined the Confederacy were generally also enfranchised by the Southern state constitutional conventions or by state legislatures in the next few years. The new state constitutions were approved by an electorate that included the newly freed slaves. Southern governments were established, the required number of states ratified the 14th Amendment, and Southern congressmen and senators were re-admitted to Congress.

For a time, a Republican bi-racial coalition ruled the South. State services were expanded—including the provision of public education. In 1870, the 15th Amendment was ratified, prohibiting denial of the right to vote based on race.

Allowing the newly freed slaves to vote, hold office, serve on juries, testify in court, own property, etc., on the same basis as white citizens struck many in the South as intolerable despotism. The most extreme determined that Republicans must abandon office voluntarily, or be forced out of office by violence. The KKK and similar organizations were organized to effect this end. Congress enacted federal civil rights legislation to respond, first to the Black Codes and then to address Klan violence.

There was substantial and violent resistance to Reconstruction in the South, much of it spearheaded by terrorist groups such as the Ku Klux Klan. The Klan had considerable support from members of the old Southern elite. At first, Congress and President Grant moved vigorously to protect the political rights of Republicans and Americans of African descent. Their efforts included use of federal troops and President Grant's suspension of the writ of habeas corpus in certain parts of the South. As the conflict dragged on, however, the nation lost the will to combat private violence. Enforcement was made much more difficult by a series of Supreme Court decisions that crippled enforcement efforts.

For one example of what was going on throughout the South, consider the following excerpts from Vernon Wharton, *The Negro in Mississippi (1865–1890)* (1965). The following excerpts describe events in 1874. Violence was also widespread in 1873, the time of the *Slaughter-House* decision, and it is alluded to in Justice Bradley's dissenting opinion.

The following excerpts describe the end of Reconstruction in Mississippi:

- Once the general policy had been adopted [by self-styled Redeemers] that Negro and Republican control of state government was to be broken at any cost, a number of methods were followed for its accomplishment. One of these involved the intimidation of those whites who still worked with the Republican party.... As early as December 1874 the Hinds County Gazette declared that death should be meted out to those who continued their opposition. "All other means having been exhausted to abate the horrible condition of things [Republican rule effected by a white Republican coalition with newly freed African-Americans] the thieves and robbers, and scoundrels, white and black, deserve death and ought to be killed.... The thieves kept in office by [Republican] Governor Ames ... ought to be compelled to leave the State or abide the consequences. [p. 185]

- Against the Negroes themselves one of the most powerful forces used was economic pressure. All over the state, Democratic clubs announced that no Negro who voted Republican could hope for any form of employment the following year.... [T]he Democratic leaders of the state, while they often denied the existence of violence, or tried to shift the blame for it to the Negroes, never actually repudiated its use.... [T]he Democratic press adopted the slogan, "Carry the election peaceably if we can, forcibly if we must." ... Democratic clubs provided themselves with the latest style of repeating rifles. [p. 187]

- A few nights later, the Republicans endeavored to hold a meeting in Yazoo City. Their hall was invaded by a number of Democrats, led by their "rope bearer," H.M. Dixon. In the confusion which followed a native white Republican was killed, and several Negroes were wounded. The white sheriff escaped with his life by fleeing to Jackson. White militia then took charge of the county, and systematically lynched the Negro leaders in each superior's district. [p. 191]

* * *

Professor J. G. de Roulhac Hamilton had a very different view. In 1914, Professor Hamilton contended that Reconstruction was an era when "selfish politicians, backed by the federal government, for party purposes attempted to Africanize the State and deprive the people through misrule and oppression of most that life held dear." J. G. de Roulhac Hamilton, *Reconstruction in North Carolina* (Vol. LVIII of *Studies in History, Economics and Public Law* edited by the faculty of Political Science of Columbia University) (1964 reprint of 1914 edition).

Reconstruction Era Civil Rights Legislation

To address the deprivations of civil rights and civil liberties in the post-Civil War South, Congress passed a series of civil statutes designed to give the victims a *federal* cause of action in *federal* court. Congress enacted *federal criminal* statutes as well. The Civil Rights Act of 1866, passed prior to the adoption of the 14th Amendment, was based in part on the 13th Amendment. (Some Republicans also justified the Civil Rights Act of 1866 based on an independent Congressional power to enforce the guarantees of the federal Bill of Rights or Article IV, §4's guarantee of privileges or immunities or republican government.) Statutes passed after 1868 could be based on either the 13th or 14th Amendments. After 1870, the 15th Amendment was used to attempt to justify statutes designed to protect the right to vote. We will discuss the differing scope of the three Amendments in later chapters. The following statutes originated during this era. The current form of the statute is given, if amended.

- **Criminal Provisions:**

18 U.S.C. §241 (1870). *Conspiracy against rights.*

If two or more persons conspire to injure, oppress, threaten, or intimidate any person in any State, Territory, Commonwealth, Possession, or District in the free exercise or enjoyment of any right or privilege secured to him by the Constitution or laws of the United States, or because of his having so exercised the same; or

If two or more persons go in disguise on the highway, or on the premises of another, with intent to prevent or hinder his free exercise or enjoyment of any right or privilege so secured—

They shall be fined under this title or imprisoned not more than ten years, or both; and if death results from the acts committed in violation of this section or if such acts include kidnapping or an attempt to kidnap, aggravated sexual abuse or an attempt to commit aggravated sexual abuse, or an attempt to kill, they shall be fined under this title or imprisoned for any term of years or for life, or both, or may be sentenced to death.

18 U.S.C. §242 (1866, amended in 1870). *Deprivation of rights under color of law.* Whoever, under color of any law, statute, ordinance, regulation, or custom, willfully subjects any person in any State, Territory, Commonwealth, Possession, or District to the deprivation of any rights, privileges, or immunities secured or protected by the Consti-

tution or laws of the United States, or to different punishments, pains, or penalties, on account of such person being an alien, or by reason of his color, or race, than are prescribed for the punishment of citizens, shall be fined under this title or imprisoned not more than one year, or both; and if bodily injury results from the acts committed in violation of this section or if such acts include the use, attempted use, or threatened use of a dangerous weapon, explosives, or fire, shall be fined under this title or imprisoned not more than ten years, or both; and if death results from the acts committed in violation of this section or if such acts include kidnapping or an attempt to kidnap, aggravated sexual abuse, or an attempt to commit aggravated sexual abuse, or an attempt to kill, shall be fined under this title, or imprisoned for any term of years or for life, or both, or may be sentenced to death.

- Civil Provisions:

42 U.S.C. § 1981 (1866 and 1870). *Equal rights under the law*

(a) *Statement of equal rights.* All persons within the jurisdiction of the United States shall have the same right in every State and Territory to make and enforce contracts, to sue, be parties, give evidence, and to the full and equal benefit of all laws and proceedings for the security of persons and property as is enjoyed by white citizens, and shall be subject to like punishment, pains, penalties, taxes, licenses, and exactions of every kind, and to no other.

(b) *"Make and enforce contracts" defined.* For purposes of this section, the term "make and enforce contracts" includes the making, performance, modification, and termination of contracts, and the enjoyment of all benefits, privileges, terms, and conditions of the contractual relationship.

(c) *Protection against impairment.* The rights protected by this section are protected against impairment by nongovernmental discrimination and impairment under color of State law.

42 U.S.C. § 1982 (1866). *Property rights of citizens.* All citizens of the United States shall have the same right, in every State and Territory, as is enjoyed by white citizens thereof to inherit, purchase, lease, sell, hold, and convey real and personal property.

42 U.S.C. § 1983 (1871). *Civil action for deprivation of rights.* Every person who, under color of any statute, ordinance, regulation, custom, or usage, of any State or Territory or the District of Columbia, subjects, or causes to be subjected, any citizen of the United States or other person within the jurisdiction thereof to the deprivation of any rights, privileges, or immunities secured by the Constitution and laws, shall be liable to the party injured in an action at law, suit in equity, or other proper proceeding for redress....

42 U.S.C. § 1985 (1871). *Conspiracy to interfere with civil rights.*

(1) [Conspiracies to prevent federal officers from performing duties]....

(2) [Obstructing justice]....

(3) *Depriving persons of rights or privileges.* If two or more persons in any State or Territory conspire, or go in disguise on the highway or on the premises of another, for the purpose of depriving ... any person or class of persons of the equal protection of the laws, or of equal privileges and immunities under the laws; or for the purpose of preventing or hindering the constituted authorities of any State or Territory from giving or securing to all persons within such State or Territory the equal protection of the laws ... the party so injured or deprived may have an action for the recovery of damages occasioned by such injury or deprivation, against any one or more of the conspirators.

In 1976 Congress passed the following statute. It provides for attorney's fees and various costs for victorious plaintiffs in constitutional violation cases.

42 U.S.C. § 1988 (1976). *Proceedings in vindication of civil rights.*

(a) *Applicability of statutory and common law.*...

(b) *Attorney's fees.* In any action or proceeding to enforce a provision of sections 1981, 1981a, 1982, 1983, 1985, and 1986 of this title, title IX of Public Law 92-318 [20 U.S.C. § 1681 et seq.], the Religious Freedom Restoration Act of 1993 [42 U.S.C. § 2000bb et seq.], title VI of the Civil Rights Act of 1964 [42 U.S.C. § 2000d et seq.], or section 13981 of this title, the court, in its discretion, may allow the prevailing party, other than the United States, a reasonable attorney's fee as part of the costs....

(c) *Expert fees.* In awarding an attorney's fee under subsection (b) of this section in any action or proceeding to enforce a provision of section 1981 or 1981a of this title, the court, in its discretion, may include expert fees as part of the attorney's fee.

C. Early Interpretation of the 14th Amendment

Slaughter-House Cases: Background and Questions

As historian Michael A. Ross has written, "of all the noxious nuisances in a city famous for its filth, the [New Orleans] slaughterhouses and bone-boiling establishments were by far the worst." They were scattered throughout the city—located beside hospitals, schools, businesses, and tenement houses. The animals—300,000 per year—were driven to slaughter in these bloody, filthy slaughterhouses. Entrails, liver, blood, urine, dung, and other refuse from slaughtering were thrown into the streets or into the Mississippi river where some of it was sucked up into the pipes that provided the city with drinking water.

The Republican-dominated Louisiana legislature, following an approach used by New York City, passed a statute requiring the city's butchers to use a new, centralized, state-of-the-art slaughterhouse located well away from the downtown neighborhoods. The city's butchers, whose substantial market power had allowed them to charge high prices, could no longer use their private slaughterhouses. The new facility was open to all butchers on payment of a fee. Indeed, in significant respects, it increased competition. Blacks, who typically lacked sufficient capital to build their own slaughterhouses, could now use the new facility. They needed only enough capital to buy animals for slaughter.

Many Louisiana whites bitterly resented the biracial Republican state government, which had passed laws requiring integrated schools, hotels, railroads, and steamboats. The whites had resisted paying taxes, so the state government was strapped for funds; its effort to fund improvements by bonds had not been successful. So the Louisiana legislature resorted to a common 19th century device—granting a franchise to private capitalists willing to make the necessary investment. While there was now only one slaughterhouse, there were many more potential butchers. Indeed, critics of the law seemed to admit that before the new slaughterhouse, the city's butchers had enjoyed monopoly power. But, they argued, "you do not destroy a monopoly by setting up another...." A full discussion can be found in Michael A. Ross, *Justice Miller's Reconstruction*: The Slaughter-House Cases, *Health Codes, and Civil Rights in New Orleans, 1861–1873*, 64 The Journal of Southern History, 648–76 (1998).

1. Do these facts make you sympathetic to the result reached by Justice Miller upholding the Louisiana statute? What is the issue in the case? Is the opinion broader than it needs to be to protect the state's regulatory power?

2. According to the Court, what was the motivating purpose behind § 1 of the 14th Amendment? How does the Court's statement compare with what you know about the history of the Amendment?
3. If the Court is right about the overriding purpose of § 1, what did the Court's construction of the 14th Amendment's Privileges or Immunities Clause do to advance that purpose?
4. What is the specter raised by the Court in *Slaughter-House*? What are the dangers the Court fears from a broad interpretation of the 14th Amendment? What do you think of these fears?
5. What does *Slaughter-House* say are "the privileges or immunities of citizens of the United States" protected by the 14th Amendment? What are the "privileges and immunities" that attach to state citizenship? How does the Court use *Corfield* (C.C.E.D. Pa. 1823) to argue for its limited list of privileges of national citizenship?
6. Does the opinion present problems for using the 14th Amendment to provide national protection against the states for the liberties found in the Bill of Rights?
7. What is the relevance of Justice Bradley's dissent to the issue of incorporation of the Bill of Rights?
8. After *Slaughter-House* and later cases, the application of the Bill of Rights to the states through the 14th Amendment appeared to have been eliminated, along with any use of the Privileges or Immunities Clause. What is the likelihood of resurrection? Should we dismiss constitutional arguments because they seem foreclosed by precedent? We will read *Saenz v. Roe* (1999), to conclude our study of the Equal Protection Clause. In *Saenz*, the Court invoked the Privileges or Immunities Clause of the 14th Amendment to strike down California's refusal to pay new residents a higher rate of welfare than they had received in their previous state until they had resided in California for one year.
9. Was *Slaughter-House* a positive or negative decision for Americans of African descent in the Southern states?

Slaughter-House Cases
83 U.S. 36 (1873)

[Majority: Miller, Clifford, Davis, Strong, Hunt. Dissenting: Field, Chase (C.J.), Bradley, Swayne.]

Mr. Justice Miller ... delivered the opinion of the Court.

... The records show that the plaintiffs in error relied upon, and asserted throughout the entire course of the litigation in the State courts, that the grant of privileges in the charter of defendant, which they were contesting, was a violation of the most important provisions of the 13th and 14th articles of amendment of the Constitution of the United States. The jurisdiction and the duty of this court to review the judgment of the State court on those questions is clear and is imperative.

The statute thus assailed as unconstitutional was passed March 8th, 1869, and is entitled "An act to protect the health of the city of New Orleans, to locate the stock-landings and slaughter-houses, and to incorporate the Crescent City Live-Stock Landing and Slaughter-House Company."

The first section forbids the landing or slaughtering of animals whose flesh is intended for food, within the city of New Orleans and other parishes and boundaries named and defined, or the keeping or establishing any slaughter-houses or abattoirs within those limits except by the corporation thereby created, which is also limited to certain places afterwards mentioned. Suitable penalties are enacted for violations of this prohibition.

The second section designates the corporators, gives the name to the corporation, and confers on it the usual corporate powers.

The third and fourth sections authorize the company to establish and erect within certain territorial limits, therein defined, one or more stock-yards, stock-landings, and slaughter-houses, and imposes upon it the duty of erecting, on or before the first day of June, 1869, one grand slaughter-house of sufficient capacity for slaughtering five hundred animals per day.

It declares that the company, after it shall have prepared all the necessary buildings, yards, and other conveniences for that purpose, shall have the sole and exclusive privilege of conducting and carrying on the live-stock landing and slaughter-house business within the limits and privilege granted by the act, and that all such animals shall be landed at the stock-landings and slaughtered at the slaughter-houses of the company, and *nowhere else*. Penalties are enacted for infractions of this provision, and prices fixed for the maximum charges of the company for each steamboat and for each animal landed....

These are the principal features of the statute, and are all that have any bearing upon the questions to be decided by us.

This statute is denounced not only as creating a monopoly and conferring odious and exclusive privileges upon a small number of persons at the expense of the great body of the community of New Orleans, but it is asserted that it deprives a large and meritorious class of citizens—the whole of the butchers of the city—of the right to exercise their trade, the business to which they have been trained and on which they depend for the support of themselves and their families, and that the unrestricted exercise of the business of butchering is necessary to the daily subsistence of the population of the city.

But a critical examination of the act hardly justifies these assertions....

It is, however, the slaughter-house privilege, which is mainly relied on to justify the charges of gross injustice to the public, and invasion of private right.

It is not, and cannot be successfully controverted, that it is both the right and the duty of the legislative body—the supreme power of the State or municipality—to prescribe and determine the localities where the business of slaughtering for a great city may be conducted. To do this effectively it is indispensable that all persons who slaughter animals for food shall do it in those places *and nowhere else*.

The statute under consideration defines these localities and forbids slaughtering in any other. It does not, as has been asserted, prevent the butcher from doing his own slaughtering. On the contrary, the Slaughter-House Company is required, under a heavy penalty, to permit any person who wishes to do so, to slaughter in their houses; and they are bound to make ample provision for the convenience of all the slaughtering for the entire city. The butcher then is still permitted to slaughter, to prepare, and to sell his own meats; but he is required to slaughter at a specified place and to pay a reasonable compensation for the use of the accommodations furnished him at that place....

The power here exercised by the legislature of Louisiana is, in its essential nature, one which has been, up to the present period in the constitutional history of this country, always conceded to belong to the States, however it may *now* be questioned in some of its details.

"Unwholesome trades, slaughter-houses, operations offensive to the senses, the deposit of powder, the application of steam power to propel cars, the building with combustible materials, and the burial of the dead, may all," says Chancellor Kent, "be interdicted by law, in the midst of dense masses of population, on the general and rational principle, that every person ought so to use his property as not to injure his neighbors; and that private interests must be made subservient to the general interests of the community." This is called the police power; and it is declared by Chief Justice Shaw that it is much easier to perceive and realize the existence and sources of it than to mark its boundaries, or prescribe limits to its exercise.

This power is, and must be from its very nature, incapable of any very exact definition or limitation. Upon it depends the security of social order, the life and health of the citizen, the comfort of an existence in a thickly populated community, the enjoyment of private and social life, and the beneficial use of property....

It may, therefore, be considered as established, that the authority of the legislature of Louisiana to pass the present statute is ample, unless some restraint in the exercise of that power be found in the constitution of that State or in the amendments to the Constitution of the United States, adopted since the date of the decisions [which the Court had] cited....

The plaintiffs in error accepting this issue, allege that the statute is a violation of the Constitution of the United States in these several particulars:

- That it creates an involuntary servitude forbidden by the 13th article of amendment;
- That it abridges the privileges and immunities of citizens of the United States;
- That it denies to the plaintiffs the equal protection of the laws; and,
- That it deprives them of their property without due process of law; contrary to the provisions of the first section of the 14th article of amendment.

This court is thus called upon for the first time to give construction to these articles.

We do not conceal from ourselves the great responsibility which this duty devolves upon us. No questions so far-reaching and pervading in their consequences, so profoundly interesting to the people of this country, and so important in their bearing upon the relations of the United States, and of the several States to each other and to the citizens of the States and of the United States, have been before this court during the official life of any of its present members....

Twelve articles of amendment were added to the Federal Constitution soon after the original organization of the government under it in 1789. Of these all but the last were adopted so soon afterwards as to justify the statement that they were practically contemporaneous with the adoption of the original; and the 12th, adopted in eighteen hundred and three, was so nearly so as to have become, like all the others, historical and of another age. But within the last eight years three other articles of amendment of vast importance have been added by the voice of the people to that now venerable instrument.

The most cursory glance at these articles discloses a unity of purpose, when taken in connection with the history of the times, which cannot fail to have an important bearing on any question of doubt concerning their true meaning. Nor can such doubts, when any reasonably exist, be safely and rationally solved without a reference to that history; for in it is found the occasion and the necessity for recurring again to the great source of power in this country, the people of the States, for additional guarantees of human rights; additional powers to the Federal government; additional restraints upon those of the States. Fortunately that history is fresh within the memory of us all, and its leading features, as they bear upon the matter before us, free from doubt.

The institution of African slavery, as it existed in about half the States of the Union, and the contests pervading the public mind for many years, between those who desired its curtailment and ultimate extinction and those who desired additional safeguards for its security and perpetuation, culminated in the effort, on the part of most of the States in which slavery existed, to separate from the Federal government, and to resist its authority. This constituted the war of the rebellion, and whatever auxiliary causes may have contributed to bring about this war, undoubtedly the overshadowing and efficient cause was African slavery.

In that struggle slavery, as a legalized social relation, perished. It perished as a necessity of the bitterness and force of the conflict. When the armies of freedom found themselves upon the soil of slavery they could do nothing less than free the poor victims whose enforced servitude was the foundation of the quarrel. And when hard pressed in the contest these men (for they proved themselves men in that terrible crisis) offered their services and were accepted by thousands to aid in suppressing the unlawful rebellion, slavery was at an end wherever the Federal government succeeded in that purpose. The proclamation of President Lincoln expressed an accomplished fact as to a large portion of the insurrectionary districts, when he declared slavery abolished in them all. But the war being over, those who had succeeded in re-establishing the authority of the Federal government were not content to permit this great act of emancipation to rest on the actual results of the contest or the proclamation of the Executive, both of which might have been questioned in after times, and they determined to place this main and most valuable result in the Constitution of the restored Union as one of its fundamental articles. Hence the 13th article of amendment of that instrument. Its two short sections seem hardly to admit of construction, so vigorous is their expression and so appropriate to the purpose we have indicated....

To withdraw the mind from the contemplation of this grand yet simple declaration of the personal freedom of all the human race within the jurisdiction of this government—a declaration designed to establish the freedom of four millions of slaves—and with a microscopic search endeavor to find in it a reference to servitudes, which may have been attached to property in certain localities, requires an effort, to say the least of it.

That a personal servitude was meant is proved by the use of the word "involuntary," which can only apply to human beings. The exception of servitude as a punishment for crime gives an idea of the class of servitude that is meant. The word servitude is of larger meaning than slavery, as the latter is popularly understood in this country, and the obvious purpose was to forbid all shades and conditions of African slavery. It was very well understood that in the form of apprenticeship for long terms, as it had been practiced in the West India Islands, on the abolition of slavery by the English government, or by reducing the slaves to the condition of serfs attached to the plantation, the purpose of the article might have been evaded, if only the word slavery had been used. The case of the apprentice slave, held under a law of Maryland, liberated by Chief Justice Chase, on a writ of habeas corpus under this article, illustrates this course of observation. [*In re Turner* (D. Md. 1867).] And it is all that we deem necessary to say on the application of that article to the statute of Louisiana, now under consideration.

The process of restoring to their proper relations with the Federal government and with the other States ... before the assembling of Congress, developed the fact that, notwithstanding the formal recognition by those States of the abolition of slavery, the condition of the slave race would, without further protection of the Federal government, be almost as bad as it was before. Among the first acts of legislation adopted by several of the States in the legislative bodies which claimed to be in their normal relations with the Federal government, were laws which imposed upon the colored race onerous disabilities and burdens, and curtailed their rights in the pursuit of life, liberty, and property to such an extent that their freedom was of little value, while they had lost the protection which they had received from their former owners from motives both of interest and humanity.

They were in some States forbidden to appear in the towns in any other character than menial servants. They were required to reside on and cultivate the soil without the right to purchase or own it. They were excluded from many occupations of gain, and were not permitted to give testimony in the courts in any case where a white man was a party. It was said that their lives were at the mercy of bad men, either because the laws for their protection were insufficient or were not enforced.

These circumstances, whatever of falsehood or misconception may have been mingled with their presentation, forced upon the statesmen who had conducted the Federal government in safety through the crisis of the rebellion, and who supposed that by the 13th article of amendment they had secured the result of their labors, the conviction that something more was necessary in the way of constitutional protection to the unfortunate race who had suffered so much. They accordingly passed through Congress the proposition for the 14th Amendment, and they declined to treat as restored to their full participation in the government of the Union the States which had been in insurrection, until they ratified that article by a formal vote of their legislative bodies.

Before we proceed to examine more critically the provisions of this amendment, on which the plaintiffs in error rely, let us complete and dismiss the history of the recent amendments, as that history relates to the general purpose which pervades them all. A few years' experience satisfied the thoughtful men who had been the authors of the other two amendments that, notwithstanding the restraints of those articles on the States, and the laws passed under the additional powers granted to Congress, these were inadequate for the protection of life, liberty, and property, without which freedom to the slave was no boon. They were in all those States denied the right of suffrage. The laws were administered by the white man alone. It was urged that a race of men distinctively marked as was the negro, living in the midst of another and dominant race, could never be fully secured in their person and their property without the right of suffrage.

Hence the 15th Amendment.... The negro having, by the 14th Amendment, been declared to be a citizen of the United States, is thus made a voter in every State of the Union.

We repeat, then, in the light of this recapitulation of events, almost too recent to be called history, but which are familiar to us all; and on the most casual examination of the language of these amendments, no one can fail to be impressed with the one pervading purpose found in them all, lying at the foundation of each, and without which none of them would have been even suggested; we mean the freedom of the slave race, the security and firm establishment of that freedom, and the protection of the newly-made freeman and citizen from the oppressions of those who had formerly exercised unlimited dominion over him. It is true that only the 15th Amendment, in terms, mentions the negro by speaking of his color and his slavery. But it is just as true that each of the other articles was addressed to the grievances of that race, and designed to remedy them as the 15th.

We do not say that no one else but the negro can share in this protection. Both the language and spirit of these articles are to have their fair and just weight in any question of construction. Undoubtedly while negro slavery alone was in the mind of the Congress which proposed the 13th article, it forbids any other kind of slavery, now or hereafter. If Mexican peonage or the Chinese coolie labor system shall develop slavery of the Mexican or Chinese race within our territory, this amendment may safely be trusted to make it void. And so if other rights are assailed by the States which properly and necessarily fall within the protection of these articles, that protection will apply, though the party interested may not be of African descent. But what we do say, and what we wish to be understood is, that in any fair and just construction of any section or phrase of these amendments, it is necessary to look to the purpose which we have said was the pervading spirit of them all, the evil which they were designed to remedy, and the process of continued addition to the Constitution, until that purpose was supposed to be accomplished, as far as constitutional law can accomplish it.

The first section of the 14th article, to which our attention is more specially invited, opens with a definition of citizenship—not only citizenship of the United States, but citizenship of the States. No such definition was previously found in the Constitution, nor had any attempt been made to define it by act of Congress. It had been the occasion of much discussion in the courts, by the executive departments, and in the public journals.... [I]t had been held by this court, in the celebrated *Dred Scott v. Sandford* (1857) case, only a few years before the outbreak of the civil war, that a man of African descent, whether a slave or not, was not and could not be a citizen of a State or of the United States. This decision, while it met the condemnation of some of the ablest statesmen and constitutional lawyers of the country, had never been overruled; and if it was to be accepted as a constitutional limitation of the right of citizenship, then all the negro race who had recently been made freemen, were still, not only not citizens, but were incapable of becoming so by anything short of an amendment to the Constitution.

To remove this difficulty primarily, and to establish a clear and comprehensive definition of citizenship which should declare what should constitute citizenship of the United States, and also citizenship of a State, the first clause of the first section was framed.

> All persons born or naturalized in the United States, and subject to the jurisdiction thereof, are citizens of the United States and of the State wherein they reside.

The first observation we have to make on this clause is, that it puts at rest both the questions which we stated to have been the subject of differences of opinion. It declares that persons may be citizens of the United States without regard to their citizenship of a particular State, and it overturns the *Dred Scott* decision by making *all persons* born within the United States and subject to its jurisdiction citizens of the United States. That its main purpose was to establish the citizenship of the negro can admit of no doubt....

The next observation is more important in view of the arguments of counsel in the present case. It is, that the distinction between citizenship of the United States and citizenship of a State is clearly recognized and established. Not only may a man be a citizen of the United States without being a citizen of a State, but an important element is necessary to convert the former into the latter. He must reside within the State to make him a citizen of it, but it is only necessary that he should be born or naturalized in the United States to be a citizen of the Union.

It is quite clear, then, that there is a citizenship of the United States, and a citizenship of a State, which are distinct from each other, and which depend upon different characteristics or circumstances in the individual.

We think this distinction and its explicit recognition in this amendment of great weight in this argument, because the next paragraph of this same section, which is the one mainly relied on by the plaintiffs in error, speaks only of privileges and immunities of citizens of the United States, and does not speak of those of citizens of the several States. The argument, however, in favor of the plaintiffs rests wholly on the assumption that the citizenship is the same, and the privileges and immunities guaranteed by the clause are the same.

The language is, "No State shall make or enforce any law which shall abridge the privileges or immunities of citizens *of the United States*." It is a little remarkable, if this clause was intended as a protection to the citizen of a State against the legislative power of his own State, that the word citizen of the State should be left out when it is so carefully used, and used in contradistinction to citizens of the United States, in the very sentence which precedes it. It is too clear for argument that the change in phraseology was adopted understandingly and with a purpose.

Of the privileges and immunities of the citizen of the United States, and of the privileges and immunities of the citizen of the State, and what they respectively are, we will presently consider; but we wish to state here that it is only the former which are placed by this clause under the protection of the Federal Constitution, and that the latter, whatever they may be, are not intended to have any additional protection by this paragraph of the amendment.

If, then, there is a difference between the privileges and immunities belonging to a citizen of the United States as such, and those belonging to the citizen of the State as such, the latter must rest for their security and protection where they have heretofore rested; for they are not embraced by this paragraph of the amendment.

The first occurrence of the words "privileges and immunities" in our constitutional history, is to be found in the fourth of the articles of the old Confederation. It declares

> that the better to secure and perpetuate mutual friendship and intercourse among the people of the different States in this Union, the free inhabitants of each of these States, paupers, vagabonds, and fugitives from justice excepted, shall be entitled to all the privileges and immunities of free citizens in the several States; and the people of each State shall have free ingress and regress to and from any other State, and shall enjoy therein all the privileges of trade and commerce, subject to the same duties, impositions, and restrictions as the inhabitants thereof respectively.

In the Constitution of the United States, which superseded the Articles of Confederation, the corresponding provision is found in § 2 of the fourth article, in the following words: "The citizens of each State shall be entitled to all the privileges and immunities of citizens of the several States."

There can be but little question that the purpose of both these provisions is the same, and that the privileges and immunities intended are the same in each. In the article of the Confederation we have some of these specifically mentioned, and enough perhaps to give some general idea of the class of civil rights meant by the phrase.

Fortunately we are not without judicial construction of this clause of the Constitution. The first and the leading case on the subject is that of *Corfield v. Coryell*, decided by Mr. Justice Washington in the Circuit Court for the District of Pennsylvania in 1823.

"The inquiry," he says,

> is, what are the privileges and immunities of citizens of the several States? We feel no hesitation in confining these expressions to those privileges and immunities which are *fundamental*; which belong of right to the citizens of all free governments, and which have at all times been enjoyed by citizens of the several States which compose this Union, from the time of their becoming free, independent, and sovereign. What these fundamental principles are, it would be more tedious than difficult to enumerate. They may all, however, be comprehended under the following general heads: protection by the government, with the right to acquire and possess property of every kind, and to pursue and obtain happiness and safety, subject, nevertheless, to such restraints as the government may prescribe for the general good of the whole....

The description, when taken to include others not named, but which are of the same general character, embraces nearly every civil right for the establishment and protection of which organized government is instituted. They are, in the language of Judge Washington, those rights which are fundamental. Throughout his opinion, they are spoken of as rights belonging to the individual as a citizen of a State. They are so spoken of in the constitutional provision which he was construing. And they have always been held to be the class of rights which the State governments were created to establish and secure....

The constitutional provision there alluded to did not create those rights, which it called privileges and immunities of citizens of the States. It threw around them in that clause no security for the citizen of the State in which they were claimed or exercised. Nor did it profess to control the power of the State governments over the rights of its own citizens.

Its sole purpose was to declare to the several States, that whatever those rights, as you grant or establish them to your own citizens, or as you limit or qualify, or impose restrictions on their exercise, the same, neither more nor less, shall be the measure of the rights of citizens of other States within your jurisdiction.

It would be the vainest show of learning to attempt to prove by citations of authority, that up to the adoption of the recent amendments, no claim or pretence was set up that those rights depended on the Federal government for their existence or protection, beyond the very few express limitations which the Federal Constitution imposed upon the States—such, for instance, as the prohibition against ex post facto laws, bills of attainder, and laws impairing the obligation of contracts. But with the exception of these and a few other restrictions, the entire domain of the privileges and immunities of citizens of the States, as above defined, lay within the constitutional and legislative power of the States, and without that of the Federal government. Was it the purpose of the 14th Amendment, by the simple declaration that no State should make or enforce any law which shall abridge the privileges and immunities of *citizens of the United States*, to transfer the security and protection of all the civil rights which we have mentioned, from the States to the Federal government? And where it is declared that Congress shall have the power to enforce that article, was it intended to bring within the power of Congress the entire domain of civil rights heretofore belonging exclusively to the States?

All this and more must follow, if the proposition of the plaintiffs in error be sound. For not only are these rights subject to the control of Congress whenever in its discretion any of them are supposed to be abridged by State legislation, but that body may also pass laws in advance, limiting and restricting the exercise of legislative power by the States, in their most ordinary and usual functions, as in its judgment it may think proper on all such subjects. And still further, such a construction followed by the reversal of the judgments of the Supreme Court of Louisiana in these cases, would constitute this court a perpetual censor upon all legislation of the States, on the civil rights of their own citizens, with authority to nullify such as it did not approve as consistent with those rights, as they existed at the time of the adoption of this amendment. The argument we admit is not always the most conclusive which is drawn from the consequences urged against the adoption of a particular construction of an instrument. But when, as in the case before us, these consequences are so serious, so far-reaching and pervading, so great a departure from the structure and spirit of our institutions; when the effect is to fetter and degrade the State governments by subjecting them to the control of Congress, in the exercise of powers heretofore universally conceded to them of the most ordinary and fundamental character; when in fact it radically changes the whole theory of the relations of the State and Federal governments to each other and of both these governments to the people; the argument has a force that is irresistible, in the absence of language which expresses such a purpose too clearly to admit of doubt.

We are convinced that no such results were intended by the Congress which proposed these amendments, nor by the legislatures of the States which ratified them.

Having shown that the privileges and immunities relied on in the argument are those which belong to citizens of the States as such, and that they are left to the State governments for security and protection, and not by this article placed under the special care of the Federal government, we may hold ourselves excused from defining the privileges and immunities of citizens of the United States which no State can abridge, until some case involving those privileges may make it necessary to do so.

But lest it should be said that no such privileges and immunities are to be found if those we have been considering are excluded, we venture to suggest some which owe their existence to the Federal government, its National character, its Constitution, or its laws.

One of these is well described in the case of *Crandall v. Nevada* (1867). It is said to be the right of the citizen of this great country, protected by implied guarantees of its Constitution, "to come to the seat of government to assert any claim he may have upon that government, to transact any business he may have with it, to seek its protection, to share its offices, to engage in administering its functions. He has the right of free access to its seaports, through which all operations of foreign commerce are conducted, to the sub-treasuries, land offices, and courts of justice in the several States." And quoting from the language of Chief Justice Taney in another case, it is said "that *for all the great purposes for which the Federal government* was established, we are one people, with one common country, *we are all citizens of the United States;*" and it is, as such citizens, that their rights are supported in this court in *Crandall v. Nevada*.

Another privilege of a citizen of the United States is to demand the care and protection of the Federal government over his life, liberty, and property when on the high seas or within the jurisdiction of a foreign government. Of this there can be no doubt, nor that the right depends upon his character as a citizen of the United States. The right to peaceably assemble and petition for redress of grievances, the privilege of the writ of habeas corpus, are rights of the citizen guaranteed by the Federal Constitution. The right to use the navigable waters of the United States, however they may penetrate the territory of the several States, all rights secured to our citizens by treaties with foreign nations, are dependent upon citizenship of the United States, and not citizenship of a State. One of these privileges is conferred by the very article under consideration. It is that a citizen of the United States can, of his own volition, become a citizen of any State of the Union by a bona fide residence therein, with the same rights as other citizens of that State. To these may be added the rights secured by the 13th and 15th articles of amendment, and by the other clause of the 14th, next to be considered.

But it is useless to pursue this branch of the inquiry, since we are of opinion that the rights claimed by these plaintiffs in error, if they have any existence, are not privileges and immunities of citizens of the United States within the meaning of the clause of the 14th Amendment under consideration....

The argument has not been much pressed in these cases that the defendant's charter deprives the plaintiffs of their property without due process of law, or that it denies to them the equal protection of the law. The first of these paragraphs has been in the Constitution since the adoption of the 5th Amendment, as a restraint upon the Federal power. It is also to be found in some form of expression in the constitutions of nearly all the States, as a restraint upon the power of the States. This law then, has practically been the same as it now is during the existence of the government, except so far as the present amendment may place the restraining power over the States in this matter in the hands of the Federal government.

We are not without judicial interpretation, therefore, both State and National, of the meaning of this clause. And it is sufficient to say that under no construction of that provision that we have ever seen, or any that we deem admissible, can the restraint imposed by the State of Louisiana upon the exercise of their trade by the butchers of New Orleans be held to be a deprivation of property within the meaning of that provision.

"Nor shall any State deny to any person within its jurisdiction the equal protection of the laws."

In the light of the history of these amendments, and the pervading purpose of them, which we have already discussed, it is not difficult to give a meaning to this clause. The existence of laws in the States where the newly emancipated negroes resided, which discriminated with gross injustice and hardship against them as a class, was the evil to be remedied by this clause, and by it such laws are forbidden.

If, however, the States did not conform their laws to its requirements, then by the fifth section of the article of amendment Congress was authorized to enforce it by suitable legislation. We doubt very much whether any action of a State not directed by way of discrimination against the negroes as a class, or on account of their race, will ever be held to come within the purview of this provision. It is so clearly a provision for that race and that emergency, that a strong case would be necessary for its application to any other....

In the early history of the organization of the government, its statesmen seem to have divided on the line which should separate the powers of the National government from those of the State governments, and though this line has never been very well defined in public opinion, such a division has continued from that day to this.

The adoption of the first eleven amendments to the Constitution so soon after the original instrument was accepted, shows a prevailing sense of danger at that time from the Federal power. And it cannot be denied that such a jealousy continued to exist with many patriotic men until the breaking out of the late civil war. It was then discovered that the true danger to the perpetuity of the Union was in the capacity of the State organizations to combine and concentrate all the powers of the State, and of contiguous States, for a determined resistance to the General Government.

Unquestionably this has given great force to the argument, and added largely to the number of those who believe in the necessity of a strong National government.

But, however pervading this sentiment, and however it may have contributed to the adoption of the amendments we have been considering, we do not see in those amendments any purpose to destroy the main features of the general system. Under the pressure of all the excited feeling growing out of the war, our statesmen have still believed that the existence of the State with powers for domestic and local government, including the regulation of civil rights—the rights of person and of property—was essential to the perfect working of our complex form of government, though they have thought proper to impose additional limitations on the States, and to confer additional power on that of the Nation.

But whatever fluctuations may be seen in the history of public opinion on this subject during the period of our national existence, we think it will be found that this court, so far as its functions required, has always held with a steady and an even hand the balance between State and Federal power, and we trust that such may continue to be the history of its relation to that subject so long as it shall have duties to perform which demand of it a construction of the Constitution, or of any of its parts.

The judgments of the Supreme Court of Louisiana in these cases are affirmed.

Mr. Justice Field, dissenting.

… It is also sought to justify the act in question on the same principle that exclusive grants for ferries, bridges, and turnpikes are sanctioned. But it can find no support there. Those grants are of franchises of a public character appertaining to the government. Their use usually requires the exercise of the sovereign right of eminent domain.…

Nor is there any analogy between this act of Louisiana and the legislation which confers upon the inventor of a new and useful improvement an exclusive right to make and sell to others his invention. The government in this way only secures to the inventor the temporary enjoyment of that which, without him, would not have existed. It thus only recognizes in the inventor a temporary property in the product of his own brain.

The act of Louisiana presents the naked case, unaccompanied by any public considerations, where a right to pursue a lawful and necessary calling, previously enjoyed by every citizen, and in connection with which a thousand persons were daily employed, is taken away and vested exclusively for twenty-five years, for an extensive district and a large population, in a single corporation, or its exercise is for that period restricted to the establishments of the corporation, and there allowed only upon onerous conditions.

If exclusive privileges of this character can be granted to a corporation of seventeen persons, they may, in the discretion of the legislature, be equally granted to a single individual. If they may be granted for twenty-five years they may be equally granted for a century, and in perpetuity.…

The question presented is, therefore, one of the gravest importance, not merely to the parties here, but to the whole country. It is nothing less than the question whether the recent amendments to the Federal Constitution protect the citizens of the United States against the deprivation of their common rights by State legislation. In my judgment the 14th Amendment does afford such protection, and was so intended by the Congress which framed and the States which adopted it.…

The amendment does not attempt to confer any new privileges or immunities upon citizens, or to enumerate or define those already existing. It assumes that there are such privileges and immunities which belong of right to citizens as such, and ordains that they shall not be abridged by State legislation. If this inhibition has no reference to privileges and immunities of this character, but only refers, as held by the majority of the court in their opinion, to such privileges and immunities as were before its adoption specially designated in the Constitution or necessarily implied as belonging to citizens of the United States, it was a vain and idle enactment, which accomplished nothing, and most unnecessarily excited Congress and the people on its passage. With privileges and immunities thus designated or implied no State could ever have interfered by its laws, and no new constitutional provision was required to inhibit such interference. The supremacy of the Constitution and the laws of the United States always controlled any State legislation of that character. But if the amendment refers to the natural and inalienable rights which belong to all citizens, the inhibition has a profound significance and consequence.

What, then, are the privileges and immunities which are secured against abridgment by State legislation?

In the first section of the Civil Rights Act Congress has given its interpretation to these terms, or at least has stated some of the rights which, in its judgment, these terms include; it has there declared that they include the right "to make and enforce contracts, to sue, be parties and give evidence, to inherit, purchase, lease, sell, hold, and convey real and personal property, and to full and equal benefit of all laws and proceedings for the security of person and property." ...

The terms, privileges and immunities, are not new in the amendment; they were in the Constitution before the amendment was adopted. They are found in the second section of the 4th article.... In *Corfield v. Coryell* (C.C.E.P. Pa. 1823), Mr. Justice Washington said he had "no hesitation in confining these expressions to those privileges and immunities which were, in their nature, fundamental; which belong of right to citizens of all free governments...." In the discussions in Congress upon the passage of the Civil Rights Act repeated reference was made to this language of Mr. Justice Washington. It was cited by Senator Trumbull with the observation that it enumerated the very rights belonging to a citizen of the United States set forth in the first section of the act, and with the statement that all persons born in the United States, being declared by the act citizens of the United States, would thenceforth be entitled to the rights of citizens, and that these were the great fundamental rights set forth in the act; and that they were set forth "as appertaining to every freeman."

The privileges and immunities designated in the second section of the 4th article of the Constitution are, then, according to the decision cited, those which of right belong to the citizens of all free governments, and they can be enjoyed under that clause by the citizens of each State in the several States upon the same terms and conditions as they are enjoyed by the citizens of the latter States. No discrimination can be made by one State against the citizens of other States in their enjoyment, nor can any greater imposition be levied than such as is laid upon its own citizens. It is a clause which insures equality in the enjoyment of these rights between citizens of the several States whilst in the same State....

What the clause in question did for the protection of the citizens of one State against hostile and discriminating legislation of other States, the 14th Amendment does for the protection of every citizen of the United States against hostile and discriminating legislation against him in favor of others, whether they reside in the same or in different States. If under the fourth article of the Constitution equality of privileges and immunities is secured between citizens of different States, under the 14th Amendment the same equality is secured between citizens of the United States....

The common law of England, as is thus seen, condemned all monopolies in any known trade or manufacture, and declared void all grants of special privileges whereby others could be deprived of any liberty which they previously had, or be hindered in their lawful trade....

The common law of England is the basis of the jurisprudence of the United States. It was brought to this country by the colonists, together with the English statutes, and was established here so far as it was applicable to their condition.... And when the Colonies separated from the mother country no privilege was more fully recognized or more completely incorporated into the fundamental law of the country than that every free subject in the British empire was entitled to pursue his happiness by following any of the known established trades and occupations of the country, subject only to such restraints as equally affected all others. The immortal document which proclaimed the independence of the country declared as self-evident truths that the Creator had endowed all men "with certain inalienable rights, and that among these are life, liberty, and the pursuit of happiness; and that to secure these rights governments are instituted among men."...

This equality of right, with exemption from all disparaging and partial enactments, in the lawful pursuits of life, throughout the whole country, is the distinguishing privilege of citizens of the United States. To them, everywhere, all pursuits, all professions, all avocations are open without other restrictions than such as are imposed equally upon all others of the same age, sex, and condition. The State may prescribe such regulations for every pursuit and calling of life as will promote the public health, secure the good order and advance the general prosperity of society, but when once prescribed, the pursuit or calling must be free to be followed by every citizen who is within the conditions designated, and will conform to the regulations. This is the fundamental idea upon which our institutions rest, and unless adhered to in the legislation of the country our government will be a republic only in name. The 14th Amendment, in my judgment, makes it essential to the validity of the legislation of every State that this equality of right should be respected. How widely this equality has been departed from, how entirely rejected and trampled upon by the act of Louisiana, I have already shown. And it is to me a matter of profound regret that its validity is recognized by a majority of this court, for by it the right of free labor, one of the most sacred and imprescriptible rights of man, is violated. As stated by the Supreme Court of Connecticut, in *Norwich Gas Light Co. v. Norwich City Gas Co.* (Ct. 1856), grants of exclusive privileges, such as is made by the act in question, are opposed to the whole theory of free government, and it requires no aid from any bill of rights to render them void. That only is a free government, in the American sense of the term, under which the inalienable right of every citizen to pursue his happiness is unrestrained, except by just, equal, and impartial laws....

I am authorized by the Chief Justice, Mr. Justice Swayne, and Mr. Justice Bradley, to state that they concur with me in this dissenting opinion.

Mr. Justice Bradley, also dissenting.

I concur in the opinion which has just been read by Mr. Justice Field; but desire to add a few observations for the purpose of more fully illustrating my views on the important question decided in these cases, and the special grounds on which they rest.

The 14th Amendment to the Constitution of the United States, § 1, declares that no State shall make or enforce any law which shall abridge the privileges and immunities of citizens of the United States.

The legislature of Louisiana, under pretense of making a police regulation for the promotion of the public health, passed an act conferring upon a corporation, created by the act, the exclusive right, for twenty-five years, to have and maintain slaughter-houses, landings for cattle, and yards for confining cattle intended for slaughter, within the parishes of Orleans, Jefferson, and St. Bernard, a territory containing nearly twelve hundred square miles, including the city of New Orleans; and prohibiting all other persons from building, keeping, or having slaughter-houses, landings for cattle, and yards for confining cattle intended for slaughter within the said limits; and requiring that all cattle and other animals to be slaughtered for food in that district should be brought to the slaughter-houses and works of the favored company to be slaughtered, and a payment of a fee to the company for such act....

First. Is it one of the rights and privileges of a citizen of the United States to pursue such civil employment as he may choose to adopt, subject to such reasonable regulations as may be prescribed by law?

Secondly. Is a monopoly, or exclusive right, given to one person to the exclusion of all others, to keep slaughter-houses, in a district of nearly twelve hundred square miles, for the supply of meat for a large city, a reasonable regulation of that employment which the legislature has a right to impose?

The first of these questions is one of vast importance, and lies at the very foundations of our government. The question is now settled by the 14th Amendment itself, that citizenship of the United States is the primary citizenship in this country; and that State citizenship is secondary and derivative, depending upon citizenship of the United States and the citizen's place of residence. The States have not now, if they ever had, any power to restrict their citizenship to any classes or persons. A citizen of the United States has a perfect constitutional right to go to and reside in any State he chooses, and to claim citizenship therein, and an equality of rights with every other citizen; and the whole power of the nation is pledged to sustain him in that right. He is not bound to cringe to any superior, or to pray for any act of grace, as a means of enjoying all the rights and privileges enjoyed by other citizens. And when the spirit of lawlessness, mob violence, and sectional hate can be so completely repressed as to give full practical effect to this right, we shall be a happier nation, and a more prosperous one than we now are. Citizenship of the United States ought to be, and according to the Constitution, is, a sure and undoubted title to equal rights in any and every State in this Union, subject to such regulations as the legislature may rightfully prescribe. If a man be denied full equality before the law, he is denied one of the essential rights of citizenship as a citizen of the United States.

Every citizen, then, being primarily a citizen of the United States, and, secondarily, a citizen of the State where he resides, what, in general, are the privileges and immunities of a citizen of the United States? Is the right, liberty, or privilege of choosing any lawful employment one of them?

If a State legislature should pass a law prohibiting the inhabitants of a particular township, county, or city, from tanning leather or making shoes, would such a law violate any privileges or immunities of those inhabitants as citizens of the United States, or only their privileges and immunities as citizens of that particular State? Or if a State legislature should pass a law of caste, making all trades and professions, or certain enumerated trades and professions, hereditary, so that no one could follow any such trades or professions except that which was pursued by his father, would such a law violate the privileges and immunities of the people of that State as citizens of the United States, or only as citizens of the State? Would they have no redress but to appeal to the courts of that particular State?

This seems to me to be the essential question before us for consideration. And, in my judgment, the right of any citizen to follow whatever lawful employment he chooses to adopt (submitting himself to all lawful regulations) is one of his most valuable rights, and one which the legislature of a State cannot invade, whether restrained by its own constitution or not....

The people of this country brought with them to its shores the rights of Englishmen; the rights which had been wrested from English sovereigns at various periods of the nation's history. One of these fundamental rights was expressed in these words, found in Magna Charta: "No freeman shall be taken or imprisoned, or be disseized of his freehold or liberties or free customs, or be outlawed or exiled, or any otherwise destroyed; nor will we pass upon him or condemn him but by lawful judgment of his peers or by the law of the land." English constitutional writers expound this article as rendering life, liberty, and property inviolable, except by due process of law....

I think sufficient has been said to show that citizenship is not an empty name, but that, in this country at least, it has connected with it certain incidental rights, privileges, and immunities of the greatest importance. And to say that these rights and immunities attach only to State citizenship, and not to citizenship of the United States, appears to me to evince a very narrow and insufficient estimate of constitutional history and the rights of men, not to say the rights of the American people.

On this point the often-quoted language of Mr. Justice Washington, in *Corfield v. Coryell* (C.C.E.D. Pa. 1823), is very instructive. Being called upon to expound that clause in the fourth article of the Constitution, which declares that "the citizens of each State shall be entitled to all the privileges and immunities of citizens in the several States," he says: "The inquiry is, what are the privileges and immunities of citizens in the several States? We feel no hesitation in confining these expressions to those privileges and immunities which are, in their nature, *fundamental*; which belong, of right, to the citizens of all free governments, and which have at all times been enjoyed by the citizens of the several States which compose this Union from the time of their becoming free, independent, and sovereign. What these fundamental privileges are it would perhaps be more tedious than difficult to enumerate. They may, however, be all comprehended under the following general heads: Protection by the government; the enjoyment of life and liberty, with the right to acquire and possess property of every kind, and to pursue and obtain happiness and safety, subject, nevertheless, to such restraints as the government may justly prescribe for the general good of the whole; the right of a citizen of one State to pass through, or to reside in, any other State for purposes of trade, agriculture, professional pursuits, or otherwise; to claim the benefit of the writ of *habeas corpus;* to institute and maintain actions of any kind in the courts of the State; to take, hold, and dispose of property, either real or personal; and an exemption from higher taxes or impositions than are paid by the other citizens of the State, may be mentioned as some of the particular privileges and immunities of citizens which are clearly embraced by the general description of privileges deemed to be fundamental."

It is pertinent to observe that both the clause of the Constitution referred to, and Justice Washington in his comment on it, speak of the privileges and immunities of citizens *in* a State; not of citizens *of* a State. It is the privileges and immunities of citizens, that is, of citizens as such, that are to be accorded to citizens of other States when they are found in any State; or, as Justice Washington says, "privileges and immunities which are, in their nature, fundamental; which belong, of right, to the citizens of all free governments."

It is true the courts have usually regarded the clause referred to as securing only an equality of privileges with the citizens of the State in which the parties are found. Equality before the law is undoubtedly one of the privileges and immunities of every citizen. I am not aware that any case has arisen in which it became necessary to vindicate any other fundamental privilege of citizenship; although rights have been claimed which were not deemed fundamental, and have been rejected as not within the protection of this clause. Be this, however, as it may, the language of the clause is as I have stated it, and seems fairly susceptible of a broader interpretation than that which makes it a guarantee of mere equality of privileges with other citizens.

But we are not bound to resort to implication, or to the constitutional history of England, to find an authoritative declaration of some of the most important privileges and immunities of citizens of the United States. It is in the Constitution itself. The Constitution, it is true, as it stood prior to the recent amendments, specifies, in terms, only a few of the personal privileges and immunities of citizens, but they are very comprehensive in their character. The States were merely prohibited from passing bills of attainder, *ex post facto* laws, laws impairing the obligation of contracts, and perhaps one or two more. But others of the greatest consequence were enumerated, although they were only secured, in express terms, from invasion by the Federal government; such as the right of *habeas corpus,* the right of trial by jury, of free exercise of religious worship, the right of free speech and a free press, the right peaceably to assemble for the discussion of public measures, the right to be secure against unreasonable searches and seizures, and above all, and including almost all the rest, the right of *not being deprived of life, liberty, or property, without due process of law.* These, and still others are specified in the original Constitution, or in the early amendments of it, as among the privileges and immunities of citizens of the United States, or, what is still stronger for the force of the argument, the rights of all persons, whether citizens or not....

[Justice Swayne, dissenting. Omitted].

A Note on *Slaughter-House*

For articles on the *Slaughter-House Cases, see* Richard L. Aynes, *Constricting the Law of Freedom: Justice Miller, The Fourteenth Amendment, and the Slaughter-House Cases* 70 Chi.-Kent L. Rev. 627 (1994) and the articles it cites. *See also* Bryan H. Wildenthal, *The Lost Compromise: Reassessing the Early Understanding in Court and Congress on Incorporation of the Bill of Rights in the Fourteenth Amendment,* 61 Ohio St. L.J. 1051 (2000). For a description of the early attempts to protect civil liberty, Republicans in the South, and Americans of African descent, *see* Robert J. Kaczorowski, *The Politics of Judicial Interpretation: The Federal Courts, The Department of Justice and Civil Rights, 1866–1876* (1985).

On the significance of *Slaughter-House* consider Kaczorowski, *The Politics of Judicial Interpretation,* at 143:

> The Supreme Court's selection of a case involving the civil rights of Southern white butchers as the occasion for its initial determination of the national government's authority to secure civil rights is more than ironic. The decision appears to have been a masterful political stratagem of the Court enabling it to decide politically explosive legal questions in a seemingly nonpolitical way. The Court thereby resolved many of the legal issues inherent in the national protection of civil rights outside the political content that made their resolution so urgent and controversial.

Note the effect of the *Slaughter-House* decision and subsequent cases on the civil rights legislation passed by Congress during Reconstruction and designed to protect the basic constitutional rights of American citizens—especially the rights of Americans of African descent and Republicans that were under attack in the South. Since *Slaughter-House* seems to suggest, and later cases held, that the rights and privileges of citizens of the United States were quite limited and did not include most basic constitutional rights, Reconstruction legislation that protected the rights, privileges, and immunities of citizens of the United States now became largely toothless. These implications were made explicit in 1876 in *United States v. Cruikshank* (1876). Some scholars, in contrast, read *Slaughter-House* as consistent with incorporation of Bill of Rights liberties into the 14th Amendment and suggest that the change occurred in later cases. Do you see why some revisionist scholars have suggested that *Slaughter-House* is actually fully consistent with application of the guarantees in the Bill of Rights to the states?

Racial violence in the South was not limited to random acts of vigilantism, but often occurred as part of a virtual civil war as self-styled "Conservatives" attempted to restore white supremacy. Until well into the 20th century, those determined to eliminate blacks from Southern politics often (though not always) became the dominant force in Southern states' Democratic parties. *Cruikshank* followed a disputed Louisiana gubernatorial election. White and black Republicans claimed victory and Republicans sought to retain possession of a county courthouse in Colfax, Louisiana. They armed themselves against an expected assault by conservative Democrats.

The Democrats arrived, armed with rifles and a cannon. In the ensuing siege, the courthouse caught fire and the Republicans surrendered. They came out of the courthouse, waving a white flag, only to be killed. Their bodies were mutilated and left in the sun. Reports of the number of dead ranged from 50 to 280. News of the "Colfax Massacre" shocked the nation. When state officials did nothing, the federal government was forced to act. The defendants were indicted under the 1870 federal Enforcement Act (entitled "An Act to enforce the right[s] of citizens of the United States").

The Court held the indictment failed to state an offense for two reasons. First, since basic Bill of Rights liberties were protected only against the action of the national government, they could not be protected by the national government from threats from other quarters. Second, since the 14th Amendment limited only the states, power under it could not reach private violence in any case. This is a "state action limitation," and we will return to state action later. The state action argument is essentially a syllogism: The 14th Amendment limits only action by states. Private individuals are not states. Therefore, the 14th Amendment does not reach private individuals who invade the rights it protects.

The *Cruikshank* Court explained each basis for its decision:

> The first and ninth counts state the intent of the defendants to have been to hinder and prevent the citizens named in the free exercise and enjoyment of their "lawful right and privilege to peaceably assemble together with each other and with other citizens of the United States for a peaceful and lawful purpose." The right of the people peaceably to assemble for lawful purposes existed long before the adoption of the Constitution of the United States. In fact, it is, and always has been, one of the attributes of citizenship under a free government.... It was not, therefore, a right granted to the people by the Constitution. The government of the United States when established found it in existence, with the obligation on the part of the States to afford it protection. As no direct power over it was granted to Congress, it remains ... subject to State jurisdiction. Only such existing rights were committed by the people to the protection of Congress as came within the general scope of the authority granted to the national government.
>
> The 1st Amendment to the Constitution prohibits Congress from abridging "the right of the people to assemble and to petition the government for a redress of

grievances." This, like the other amendments proposed and adopted at the same time, was not intended to limit the powers of the State governments in respect to their own citizens, but to operate upon the National government alone. *Barron v. Baltimore* (1833). It is now too late to question the correctness of this construction....

The particular amendment now under consideration assumes the existence of the right of the people to assemble for lawful purposes, and protects it against encroachment by Congress. The right was not created by the amendment; neither was its continuance guaranteed, except as against congressional interference. For their protection in its enjoyment, therefore, the people must look to the States. The power for that purpose was originally placed there, and it has never been surrendered to the United States.

The right of the people peaceably to assemble for the purpose of petitioning Congress for a redress of grievances, or for any thing else connected with the powers or the duties of the national government, is an attribute of national citizenship, and, as such, under the protection of, and guaranteed by, the United States.... If it had been alleged in these counts that the object of the defendants was to prevent a meeting for such a purpose, the case would have been within the statute, and within the scope of the sovereignty of the United States. Such, however, is not the case. The offence, as stated in the indictment, will be made out, if it be shown that the object of the conspiracy was to prevent a meeting for any lawful purpose whatever.

The second and tenth counts are equally defective. The right there specified is that of "bearing arms for a lawful purpose." This is not a right granted by the Constitution. Neither is it in any manner dependent upon that instrument for its existence. The 2nd Amendment declares that it shall not be infringed; but this, as has been seen, means no more than that it shall not be infringed by Congress. This is one of the amendments that has no other effect than to restrict the powers of the national government, leaving the people to look for their protection against any violation by their fellow-citizens of the rights it recognizes, to [the states]....

The Court also cited a second reason to dismiss the indictment: "The 14th Amendment prohibits a State from depriving any person of life, liberty, or property, without due process of law; but this adds nothing to the rights of one citizen as against another. It simply furnishes an additional guaranty against any encroachment by the States." ...

* * *

The disputed presidential election of 1876 was settled in the Compromise of 1877. During Reconstruction, federal troops had been used because feeble Republican state governments were unable to control Klan violence. With the compromise, the Federal government withdrew the troops from the South. Eventually, Americans of African descent were excluded from the political process in the South, first by violence and then by state statutes. The "redemption" of the South did not occur all at once, however. A number of Americans of African descent continued to be able to vote until the late 1890s, when the ruling Democratic elite grew fearful of losing power.

Political violence was used against Populists as well as Republicans. By the 1890s, plummeting agricultural prices, high railroad freight and grain elevator rates, the rise of consolidated corporate power, and the laissez faire approach of Democrats in the South, led many Southern farmers and others to defect to the Populist party. In 1894, for example, an inter-racial Populist-Republican fusion ticket won control of both houses of the North Carolina legislature. Though the picture varies from state to state, Populists were powerful elsewhere in the South as well. (The 1896 Populist party platform advocated government ownership of railroads, a progressive income tax, government employment for the unemployed in times of depression, etc.) In North Carolina, the Fusionists threatened to facilitate black participation in the political process and to create a powerful coalition based on appeal to economic class. The Democratic response was to appeal to race instead of class, calling for white solidarity. A renewed wave of violence and electoral fraud helped to quell the revolt. *See, e.g.,* H. Leon Prather, Sr., *We Have Taken A City, in Democracy Betrayed: The Wilmington Race Riot of 1898 and Its Legacy* (David S. Cecelski and Timothy Tyson, eds. 1998); and C. Vann Woodward, *Tom Watson, Agrarian Rebel* (1938).

Conservative Southern leaders soon sought a way to manipulate the law to effectuate the goals that violence had first accomplished. Southern states subsequently passed literacy tests—requiring that voters be able to read and understand the Constitution in order to qualify to vote—and poll taxes. These barriers were designed to eliminate not only black voters, but also poorer whites.

According to one scholar, there was also a second response to threats like those of the Populists. A political faction that often called itself "Conservative," and that became a powerful force in the Southern Democratic party, waged a largely successful battle to present a revisionist history of the Civil War favorable to the South and to purge textbooks and teachers who questioned the wisdom of the Civil War and of the ante-bellum slaveholding elite. The approved books depicted the Civil War as a struggle not to protect slavery, but for states rights. They depicted Reconstruction as a time when ignorant blacks and selfish Yankees and scalawags subjected the South to gross misrule. *See, e.g.,* Fred Arthur Bailey, *Free Speech and the Lost Cause in the Old Dominion*, 103 Va. Mag. Hist. and Bio. 237 (1995); *see also The Myth of the Lost Cause* (Gary W. Gallagher and Alan T. Nollan, eds., 2000), Charles B. Dew, *Apostles of Disunion: Southern Secession Commissioners and the Causes of the Civil War* (2001).

The roles of the Democratic and Republican parties during this era may seem confusing to modern readers. In its early years before the Civil War and during the war, the Republican party was the more radical party, the Democratic party the more conservative party. Americans of African descent supported the Republican party heavily until the New Deal. But as Democratic Presidents Truman, Kennedy, and Johnson supported civil rights legislation (and the 1964 Republican presidential nominee, Barry Goldwater, opposed civil rights legislation) most Americans of African descent began to support the Democratic Party.

VII. The Bill of Rights and Incorporation after *Slaughter-House*

A. 1873–1905

The initial cases construing the 14th Amendment rejected claims that Bill of Rights guarantees limited the states under either the Due Process or Privileges or Immunities Clauses. The one exception was a case holding that states were required to pay just compensation for property taken for public use, *Chicago, Burlington & Quincy Railroad v. Chicago* (1897). Meanwhile, the Court read the Due Process Clause broadly to protect economic interests in *Lochner v. New York* (1905). The cases listed below followed the *Slaughter-House Cases* (1873):

1. *United States v. Cruikshank* (1876). As mentioned above, a group of armed whites in Louisiana killed over sixty blacks as part of a struggle for political control. The whites were indicted under a Reconstruction statute that punished conspiracies to deprive persons of rights, privileges, or immunities of citizens of the United States. The rights that the defendants allegedly violated were the right to assemble and to bear arms. The Court held these rights were merely limits on the federal government.

2. *Walker v. Sauvinet* (1876). The federal right to a civil jury trial held not to limit the states.

3. *Hurtado v. California* (1884). The federal right to a grand jury indictment held not to limit the states.

4. *Presser v. Illinois* (1886). The federal right to bear arms held not to limit the states.

5. *Chicago, Burlington, & Quincy Railroad v. Chicago* (1897). 14th Amendment Due Process Clause held to prohibit states taking private property for public use without compensation.

6. *Maxwell v. Dow* (1900). The federal right to a criminal jury trial held not to limit the states; therefore, Maxwell's Utah conviction by a jury of eight instead of twelve did not violate the 14th Amendment Due Process Clause.

7. *Lochner v. New York* (1905). A New York law limiting hours of work for bakers was held to violate the Due Process Clause of the 14th Amendment.

B. 1905–1947: *Twining, Palko,* and *Adamson*

1. *Twining v. New Jersey* (1908), involved state court prosecutions for giving bank inspectors false information. The defendants did not testify and the prosecutor commented on this fact to prove their guilt. The defendants claimed this action violated their privileges as American citizens under the Privileges or Immunities Clause and also violated the Due Process Clause. Justice Moody, a Theodore Roosevelt appointee, wrote for the Court and rejected both claims. In part he said:

> The general question, therefore, is, whether such a law violates the 14th Amendment, either by abridging the privileges or immunities of citizens of the United States, or by depriving persons of their life, liberty or property without due process of law. In order to bring themselves within the protection of the Constitution it is incumbent on the defendants to prove two propositions: first, that the exemption from compulsory self-incrimination is guaranteed by the Federal Constitution against impairment by the States; and, second, if it be so guaranteed, that the exemption was in fact impaired in the case at bar. The first proposition naturally presents itself for earlier consideration....

> [W]henever a new limitation or restriction is declared it is a matter of grave import, since, to that extent, it diminishes the authority of the State, so necessary to the perpetuity of our dual form of government, and changes its relation to its people and to the Union....

[T]he contention which must now be examined [is] that the safeguards of personal rights which are enumerated in the first eight Articles of amendment to the Federal Constitution, sometimes called the Federal Bill of Rights, though they were by those Amendments originally secured only against National action, are among the privileges and immunities of citizens of the United States, which this clause of the 14th Amendment protects against state action. This view has been, at different times, expressed by justices of this court (Mr. Justice Field in *O'Neil v. Vermont* (1892); Mr. Justice Harlan in the same case, and in *Maxwell v. Dow* (1900)), and was undoubtedly that entertained by some of those who framed the Amendment. It is, however, not profitable to examine the weighty arguments in its favor, for the question is no longer open in this court. The right of trial by jury in civil cases, guaranteed by the 7th Amendment, *Walker v. Sauvinet* (1876), and the right to bear arms guaranteed by the 2nd Amendment, *Presser v. Illinois* (1885), have been distinctly held not to be privileges and immunities of citizens of the United States guaranteed by the 14th Amendment against abridgment by the States, and in effect the same decision was made in respect of the guarantee against prosecution, except by indictment of a grand jury, contained in the 5th Amendment....

The *Twining* Court proceeded to consider and reject the due process claim. In the process of doing so, however, it raised the possibility that some Bill of Rights liberties would be incorporated as a limit on the states after all.

[The due process] contention requires separate consideration, for it is possible that some of the personal rights safeguarded by the first eight Amendments against national action may also be safeguarded against state action, because a denial of them would be a denial of due process of law. *Chicago, Burlington & Quincy Railroad v. Chicago* (1897). If this is so, it is not because those rights are enumerated in the first eight Amendments, but because they are of such a nature that they are included in the conception of due process of law. Few phrases of the law are so elusive of exact apprehension as this....

First. What is due process of law may be ascertained by an examination of those settled usages and modes of proceedings existing in the common and statute law of England before the emigration of our ancestors, and shown not to have been unsuited to their civil and political condition by having been acted on by them after the settlement of this country. This test was adopted by the court, speaking through Mr. Justice Curtis, in *Murray's Lessee v. Hoboken Land & Improvement Co.* (1856)....

Second. It does not follow, however, that a procedure settled in English law at the time of the emigration, and brought to this country and practiced by our ancestors, is an essential element of due process of law. If that were so the procedure of the first half of the seventeenth century would be fastened upon the American jurisprudence like a straight jacket, only to be unloosed by constitutional amendment. That, said Mr. Justice Matthews, "would be to deny every quality of the law but its age, and to render it incapable of progress or improvement."

Third. But, consistently with the requirements of due process, no change in ancient procedure can be made which disregards those fundamental principles, to be ascertained from time to time by judicial action, which have relation to process of law and protect the citizen in his private right, and guard him against the arbitrary action of government. This idea has been many times expressed in differing words by this court, and it seems well to cite some expressions of it. The words "due process of law" "were intended to secure the individual from the arbitrary exercise of the powers of government, unrestrained by the established principles of private rights and distributive justice." *Bank of Columbia v. Okely* (1819) (approved in *Hurtado v. California* (1884))....

The question under consideration may first be tested by the application of these settled doctrines of this court. If the statement of Mr. Justice Curtis, as elucidated in *Hurtado v. California*, is to be taken literally, that alone might almost be decisive. For nothing is more certain, in point of historical fact, than that the practice of compulsory self-incrimination in the courts and elsewhere existed for four hundred years after the granting of Magna Carta, continued throughout the reign of Charles I (though then beginning to be seriously questioned), gained at least some foothold among the early colonists of this country, and was not entirely omitted at trials in England until the 18th century. *Wigmore on Evidence*, §2250; *Hallam's Constitutional History of England*, ch. VIII, 2 Widdleton's American ed., 37 (describing the criminal jurisdiction of the Court of Star Chamber); *Bentham's Rationale of Judicial Evidence*, book IX, ch. III, §IV....

This description of the questioning of the accused and the meeting of contending arguments finds curious confirmation in the report of the trial, in 1637, of Ann Hutchinson (which resulted in banishment), for holding and encouraging certain theological views which were not approved by the majority of the early Massachusetts rulers. 1 *Hart's American History Told by Contemporaries*, 382. The trial was presided over and the examination very largely conducted by Governor Winthrop, who had been for some years before his emigration an active lawyer and admitted to the Inner Temple [one of the Inns of Court that supplied English barristers]. An examination of the report of this trial will show that he was not aware of any privilege against self-incrimination or conscious of any duty to respect it. Stephen says of the trials between 1640 and 1660: "In some cases the prisoner was questioned, but never to any greater extent than that which it is practically impossible to avoid when a man has to defend himself without counsel. When so questioned the prisoners usually refused to answer." He further says: "Soon after the Revolution of 1688 the practice of questioning the prisoner died out." But committing magistrates were authorized to take the examination of persons suspected, which if not under oath, was admissible against him on his trial, until by [statute] the prisoner was given the option whether he would speak, and warned that what he said might be used against him....

But ... we prefer to rest our decision on broader grounds, and inquire whether the exemption from self-incrimination is of such a nature that it must be included in the conception of due process. Is it a fundamental principle of liberty and justice which inheres in the very idea of free government and is the inalienable right of a citizen of such a government? If it is, and if it is of a nature that pertains to process of law, this court has declared it to be essential to due process of law.

In approaching such a question it must not be forgotten that in a free representative government nothing is more fundamental than the right of the people through their appointed servants to govern themselves in accordance with their own will, except so far as they have restrained themselves by constitutional limits specifically established, and that in our peculiar dual form of government nothing is more fundamental than the full power of the State to order its own affairs and govern its own people, except so far as the Federal Constitution expressly or by fair implication has withdrawn that power. The power of the people of the States to make and alter their laws at pleasure is the greatest security for liberty and justice, this court has said in *Hurtado v. California*. We are not invested with the jurisdiction to pass upon the expediency, wisdom or justice of the laws of the States as declared by their courts, but only to determine their conformity with the Federal Constitution and the paramount laws enacted pursuant to it....

Justice John Marshall Harlan* dissented:

I am of the opinion that as immunity from self-incrimination was recognized in the 5th Amendment of the Constitution and placed beyond violation by any Federal agency, it should be deemed one of the immunities of citizens of the United States which the 14th Amendment in express terms forbids any State from abridging—as much so, for instance, as the right of free speech (1st Amend.), or the exemption from cruel or unusual punishments (8th Amend.), or the exemption from being put twice in jeopardy of life or limb for the same offense (5th Amend.), or the exemption from unreasonable searches and seizures of one's person, house, papers or effects (4th Amend.). Even if I were anxious or willing to cripple the operation of the 14th Amendment by strained or narrow interpretations, I should feel obliged to hold that when that Amendment was adopted all these last-mentioned exemptions were among the immunities belonging to citizens of the United States, which, after the adoption of the 14th Amendment, no State could impair or destroy. But, as I read the opinion of the court, it will follow from the general principles underlying it, or from the reasoning pursued therein, that the 14th Amendment would be no obstacle whatever in the way of a state law or practice under which, for instance, cruel or unusual punishments (such as the thumb screw, or the rack or burning at the stake) might be inflicted. So of a state law which infringed the right of free speech, or authorized unreasonable searches or seizures of persons, their houses, papers or effects, or a state law under which one accused of crime could be put in jeopardy twice or oftener, at the pleasure of the prosecution, for the same offense....

Is there any way you could rely on *Twining* to argue for application of at least some specific rights in the Bill of Rights to the States? On what language in the opinion would you rely?

2. *Meyer v. Nebraska* (1923). The Court held that the Due Process Clause voided the conviction of a teacher convicted under a state statute that prohibited teaching a foreign language to a child below the eighth grade. The Court did not explicitly mention free speech but said that due process "denotes ... the right of the individual to contract, to engage in any of the common occupations of life, to acquire useful knowledge, to marry, establish a home, and bring up children, to worship God according to the dictates of his own conscience, and, generally, to enjoy those privileges long recognized at common law as essential to the orderly pursuit of happiness by free men."

---

* The first Justice John Marshall Harlan (appointed by Hayes, served 1877–1911), grandfather of the later one (appointed by Eisenhower, served 1955–1971).

3. *Gitlow v. New York* (1925). The Court assumed that free speech and press limit the states under the Due Process Clause of the 14th Amendment.

4. *Near v. Minnesota* (1931) and *Stromberg v. California* (1931). The Court squarely held that free speech and press limit the states under the Due Process Clause of the 14th Amendment.

5. *Powell v. Alabama* (1932). Right to counsel in capital cases must be provided by the states.

6. *Palko v. Connecticut* (1937). Federal double jeopardy standard held not to limit the states.

Palko v. Connecticut: Background

It violates the double jeopardy guarantee of the 5th Amendment to retry a person for a crime if the person has previously been acquitted of that same offense. This rule applies even if errors were made in the defendant's favor during the course of the trial. When a person is tried for first degree murder, it is common practice to instruct the jury on the lesser included offenses of second degree murder and manslaughter. A conviction of a lesser included offense constitutes an implied acquittal of all higher offenses. In the case that follows, Palko was deprived of the benefit of this federal constitutional rule. Why?

Questions

1. What is *Palko*'s test for determining whether particular guarantees of the Bill of Rights limit the states?
2. Under this test, are most guarantees of the Bill of Rights applicable to the states? Why?
3. Would broad recognition by many states, in their own constitutional law, of a protection also found in the Bill of Rights justify its application to all of the states under *Palko*? Why or why not?
4. How does Justice Cardozo use the words "privileges and immunities" in *Palko*? Does he treat the words as meaning the same thing as "the guarantees of the Bill of Rights"? What would be the effect of substituting this definition of "privileges or immunities" for those words in § 1 of the 14th Amendment? Does the way *Palko* uses the words "privileges or immunities" provide a textual argument for a different result from that reached by the Court?

Palko v. Connecticut
302 U.S. 319 (1937)

[Majority: Cardozo, Hughes (C.J.), McReynolds, Brandeis, Sutherland, Stone, Roberts, and Black. Dissenting: Butler.]

[Palko was initially charged with first degree murder. He was convicted of second degree murder and sentenced to life imprisonment. The State, as allowed by statute, successfully appealed an alleged error in the trial and had the case remanded for a new trial. Palko was convicted again, but this time was sentenced to death. The second trial would have constituted double jeopardy under the 5th Amendment if it had been in federal court. He appealed his conviction, asserting that subjecting him to double jeopardy violated the 14th Amendment as well.]

Mr. Justice Cardozo delivered the opinion of the Court.

... We have said that in appellant's view the 14th Amendment is to be taken as embodying the prohibitions of the 5th. His thesis is even broader. Whatever would be a violation of the original bill of rights (Amendments 1 to 8) if done by the federal government is now equally unlawful by force of the 14th Amendment if done by a state. There is no such general rule. [The Court here listed cases refusing to apply guarantees of the Bill of Rights such as jury trial and the privilege against self incrimination to the states.] ...

On the other hand, the due process clause of the 14th Amendment may make it unlawful for a state to abridge by its statutes the freedom of speech which the 1st Amendment safeguards against encroachment by the Congress, *De Jonge v. Oregon* (1937), or the like freedom of the press, *Near v. Minnesota* (1931), or the free exercise of religion, cf., *Pierce v. Society of Sisters* (1925), or the right of peaceable assembly, without which speech would be unduly trammeled, *De Jonge v. Oregon*, *Herndon v. Lowry* (1937), or the right of one accused of crime to the benefit of counsel, *Powell v. Alabama* (1932). In these and other situations immunities that are valid as against the federal government by force of the specific pledges of particular amendments have been found to be implicit in the concept of ordered liberty, and thus, through the 14th Amendment, become valid as against the states.

The line of division may seem to be wavering and broken if there is a hasty catalogue of the cases on the one side and the other. Reflection and analysis will induce a different view. There emerges the perception of a rationalizing principle which gives to discrete instances a proper order and coherence. The right to trial by jury and the immunity from prosecution except as the result of an indictment may have value and importance. Even so, they are not of the very essence of a scheme of ordered liberty. To abolish them is not to violate a "principle of justice so rooted in the traditions and conscience of our people as to be ranked as fundamental." *Snyder v. Massachusetts* (1934); *Brown v. Mississippi* (1936). Few would be so narrow or provincial as to maintain that a fair and enlightened system of justice would be impossible without them. What is true of jury trials and indictments is true also, as the cases show, of the immunity from compulsory self-incrimination. *Twining v. New Jersey* (1908). This too might be lost, and justice still be done. Indeed, today as in the past there are students of our penal system who look upon the immunity as a mischief rather than a benefit, and who would limit its scope, or destroy it altogether. No doubt there would remain the need to give protection against torture, physical or mental. Justice, however, would not perish if the accused were subject to a duty to respond to orderly inquiry. The exclusion of these immunities and privileges from the privileges and immunities protected against the action of the States has not been arbitrary or casual. It has been dictated by a study and appreciation of the meaning, the essential implications, of liberty itself.

We reach a different plane of social and moral values when we pass to the privileges and immunities that have been taken over from the earlier articles of the Federal Bill of Rights and brought within the 14th Amendment by a process of absorption. These in their origin were effective against the federal government alone. If the 14th Amendment has absorbed them, the process of absorption has had its source in the belief that neither liberty nor justice would exist if they were sacrificed. *Twining v. New Jersey*. This is true, for illustration, of freedom of thought and speech. Of that freedom one may say that it is the matrix, the indispensable condition, of nearly every other form of freedom.... Cf. *Near v. Minnesota*; *De Jonge v. Oregon*....

The state is not attempting to wear the accused out by a multitude of cases with accumulated trials. It asks no more than this, that the case against him shall go on until there shall be a trial free from the corrosion of substantial legal error. This is not cruelty at all, nor even vexation in any immoderate degree. If the trial had been infected with error adverse to the accused, there might have been review at his instance.... The edifice of justice stands, its symmetry, to many, greater than before.

The conviction of appellant is not in derogation of any privileges or immunities that belong to him as a citizen of the United States.

There is argument in his behalf that the privileges and immunities clause of the 14th Amendment as well as the due process clause has been flouted by the judgment.

Maxwell v. Dow (1900) [holding the right to trial by jury in criminal cases does not limit the states] gives all the answer that is necessary.

The judgment is affirmed.

Mr. Justice Butler dissents.

1. Incorporation: From Palko to Adamson

1. *Cantwell v. Connecticut* (1940). Right to free exercise of religion held to limit the states under the 14th Amendment.
2. *Everson v. Board of Education* (1947). The rule against government establishment of religion held to limit the states under the Due Process Clause of the 14th Amendment.
3. *Adamson v. California* (1947). Federal privilege against self-incrimination held not to limit the states.

Adamson v. California: Questions

1. What is Justice Black's position on application of the Bill of Rights to the states? What is Justice Frankfurter's? Do you agree with Black or Frankfurter? Why? Do Justice Black and those Justices who agree with him treat the Privileges or Immunities Clause as dead and beyond hope of revival?
2. How is the position taken by Justices Rutledge and Murphy different from that taken by Justice Black? How is it similar?
3. Make arguments for and against incorporation of the privilege against self-incrimination using text, context, structure, history, precedent, and policy. Evaluate the arguments. Which do you find the most persuasive? Why?

Adamson v. California
332 U.S. 46 (1947)

[Majority: Reed, Frankfurter, Vinson (C.J.), Burton, and Jackson. Concurrence: Frankfurter. Dissenting: Black, Douglas, Murphy, and Rutledge.]

[Adamson was convicted in state court of first degree murder and sentenced to death. He appealed on the grounds that allowing the prosecution to comment on his failure to take the stand violated the Privileges or Immunities and Due Process Clauses of the 14th Amendment.]

Mr. Justice Reed delivered the opinion of the Court.

... We shall assume, but without any intention thereby of ruling upon the issue, that state permission by law to the court, counsel and jury to comment upon and consider the failure of defendant "to explain or to deny by his testimony any evidence or facts in the case against him" would infringe defendant's privilege against self-incrimination under the 5th Amendment if this were a trial in a court of the United States under a similar law. Such an assumption does not determine appellant's rights under the 14th Amendment. It is settled law that the clause of the 5th Amendment, protecting a person against being compelled to be a witness against himself, is not made effective by the 14th Amendment as a protection against state action on the ground that freedom from testimonial compulsion is a right of national citizenship, or because it is a personal privilege or immunity secured by the Federal Constitution as one of the rights of man that are listed in the Bill of Rights....

The Slaughter-House Cases (1873) decided ... that these rights, as privileges and immunities of state citizenship, remained under the sole protection of the state governments.... The power to free defendants in state trials from self-incrimination was specifically determined to be beyond the scope of the privileges and immunities clause of the 14th Amendment in *Twining v. New Jersey* (1908). "The privilege against self-incrimination may be withdrawn and the accused put upon the stand as a witness for the state." ... This construction has become embedded in our federal system as a functioning element in preserving the balance between national and state power. We reaffirm the conclusion of the *Twining* and *Palko v. Connecticut* (1937) cases that protection against self-incrimination is not a privilege or immunity of national citizenship....

Mr. Justice Frankfurter, concurring.

... To suggest that it is inconsistent with a truly free society to begin prosecutions without an indictment, to try petty civil cases without the paraphernalia of a common law jury, to take into consideration that one who has full opportunity to make a defense remains silent is, in de Tocqueville's phrase, to confound the familiar with the necessary.

The short answer to the suggestion that the provision of the 14th Amendment, which ordains "nor shall any State deprive any person of life, liberty, or property, without due process of law," was a way of saying that every State must thereafter initiate prosecutions through indictment by a grand jury, must have a trial by a jury of 12 in criminal cases, and must have trial by such a jury in common law suits where the amount in controversy exceeds $20, is that it is a strange way of saying it. It would be extraordinarily strange for a Constitution to convey such specific commands in such a roundabout and inexplicit way. After all, an amendment to the Constitution should be read in a "'sense most obvious to the common understanding at the time of its adoption.'... For it was for public adoption that it was proposed." See Mr. Justice Holmes in *Eisner v. Macomber* (1920). Those reading the English language with the meaning which it ordinarily conveys, those conversant with the political and legal history of the concept of due process, those sensitive to the relations of the States to the central government as well as the relation of some of the provisions of the Bill of Rights to the process of justice, would hardly recognize the 14th Amendment as a cover for the various explicit provisions of the first eight Amendments. Some of these are enduring reflections of experience with human nature, while some express the restricted views of Eighteenth-Century England regarding the best methods for the ascertainment of facts. The notion that the 14th Amendment was a covert way of imposing upon the States all the rules which it seemed important to Eighteenth Century statesmen to write into the Federal Amendments, was rejected by judges who were themselves witnesses of the process by which the 14th Amendment became part of the Constitution.... Remarks of a particular proponent of the Amendment, no matter how influential, are not to be deemed part of the Amendment. What was submitted for ratification was his proposal, not his speech. Thus, at the time of the ratification of the 14th Amendment the constitutions of nearly half of the ratifying States did not have the rigorous requirements of the 5th Amendment for instituting criminal proceedings through a grand jury. It could hardly have occurred to these States that by ratifying the Amendment they uprooted their established methods for prosecuting crime and fastened upon themselves a new prosecutorial system....

Mr. Justice Black, [with whom Mr. Justice Douglas joins,] dissenting.

[The Court's] decision reasserts a constitutional theory spelled out in *Twining v. New Jersey* (1908), that this Court is endowed by the Constitution with boundless power under "natural law" periodically to expand and contract constitutional standards to conform to the Court's conception of what at a particular time constitutes "civilized decency" and "fundamental principles of liberty and justice." Invoking this *Twining* rule, the Court concludes that although comment upon testimony in a federal court would violate the 5th Amendment, identical comment in a state court does not violate today's fashion in civilized decency and fundamentals and is therefore not prohibited by the Federal Constitution as amended....

I agree that if *Twining* be reaffirmed, the result reached might appropriately follow. But I would not reaffirm the *Twining* decision. I think that decision and the "natural law" theory of the Constitution upon which it relies, degrade the constitutional safeguards of the Bill of Rights and simultaneously appropriate for this Court a broad power which we are not authorized by the Constitution to exercise. Furthermore, the *Twining* decision rested on previous cases and broad hypotheses which have been undercut by intervening decisions of this Court....

Past history provided strong reasons for the apprehensions which brought these procedural amendments into being and attest the wisdom of their adoption. For the fears of arbitrary court action sprang largely from the past use of courts in the imposition of criminal punishments to suppress speech, press, and religion. Hence the constitutional limitations of courts' powers were, in the view of the Founders, essential supplements to the 1st Amendment, which was itself designed to protect the widest scope for all people to believe and to express the most divergent political, religious, and other views....

My study of the historical events that culminated in the 14th Amendment, and the expressions of those who sponsored and favored, as well as those who opposed its submission and passage, persuades me that one of the chief objects that the provisions of the Amendment's first section, separately, and as a whole, were intended to accomplish was to make the Bill of Rights applicable to the states. With full knowledge of the import of the *Barron v. Baltimore* (1833) decision, the framers and backers of the 14th Amendment proclaimed its purpose to be to overturn the constitutional rule that case had announced. This historical purpose has never received full consideration or exposition in any opinion of this Court interpreting the Amendment....

The Court's opinion in *Twining*, and the dissent in that case, made it clear that the Court intended to leave the states wholly free to compel confessions, so far as the Federal Constitution is concerned. Yet in a series of cases since *Twining* this Court has held that the 14th Amendment does bar all American courts, state or federal, from convicting people of crime on coerced confessions. *Chambers v. Florida* (1940); *Ashcraft v. Tennessee* (1944) and cases cited....

The Court in *Twining* evidently was forced to resort for its degradation of the privilege to the fact that Governor Winthrop in trying Mrs. Ann Hutchison in 1627 was evidently "not aware of any privilege against self-incrimination or conscious of any duty to respect it." Of course not. Mrs. Hutchison was tried, if trial it can be called, for holding unorthodox religious views. People with a consuming belief that their religious convictions must be forced on others rarely ever believe that the unorthodox have any rights which should or can be rightfully respected. As a result of her trial and compelled admissions, Mrs. Hutchison was found guilty of unorthodoxy and banished from Massachusetts. The lamentable experience of Mrs. Hutchison and others, contributed to the overwhelming sentiment that demanded adoption of a Constitutional Bill of Rights. The founders of this Government wanted no more such "trials" and punishments as Mrs. Hutchison had to undergo. They wanted to erect barriers that would bar legislators from passing laws that encroached on the domain of belief, and that would, among other things, strip courts and all public officers of a power to compel people to testify against themselves.

I cannot consider the Bill of Rights to be an outworn 18th Century "strait jacket" as the *Twining* opinion did. Its provisions may be thought outdated abstractions by some. And it is true that they were designed to meet ancient evils. But they are the same kind of human evils that have emerged from century to century wherever excessive power is sought by the few at the expense of the many. In my judgment the people of no nation can lose their liberty so long as a Bill of Rights like ours survives and its basic purposes are conscientiously interpreted, enforced and respected so as to afford continuous protection against old, as well as new, devices and practices which might thwart those purposes. I fear to see the consequences of the Court's practice of substituting its own concepts of decency and fundamental justice for the language of the Bill of Rights as its point of departure in interpreting and enforcing that Bill of Rights. If the choice must be between the selective process of the *Palko v. Connecticut* (1937) decision applying some of the Bill of Rights to the States, or the *Twining* rule applying none of them, I would choose the *Palko* selective process. But rather than accept either of these choices, I would follow what I believe was the original purpose of the 14th Amendment—to extend to all the people of the nation the complete protection of the Bill of Rights. To hold that this Court can determine what, if any, provisions of the Bill of Rights will be enforced, and if so to what degree, is to frustrate the great design of a written Constitution....

Mr. Justice Murphy, with whom Mr. Justice Rutledge joins, dissenting.

While in substantial agreement with the views of Mr. Justice Black, I have one reservation and one addition to make.

I agree that the specific guarantees of the Bill of Rights should be carried over intact into the first section of the 14th Amendment. But I am not prepared to say that the latter is entirely and necessarily limited by the Bill of Rights. Occasions may arise where a proceeding falls so far short of conforming to fundamental standards of procedure as to warrant constitutional condemnation in terms of a lack of due process despite the absence of a specific provision in the Bill of Rights....

* * *

For a recent biography of Justice Black, see Roger Newman, *Hugo Black: A Biography* (1994).

2. Incorporation after Adamson

1. *In re Oliver* (1948). Public trial required by 14th Amendment Due Process Clause.
2. *Cole v. Arkansas* (1948). Notice of charges required by 14th Amendment Due Process Clause in a criminal prosecution.

The Historical Debate

There are two types of critics of the incorporation doctrine. Some reject application of any of the guarantees of the Bill of Rights (except due process) to the states. Others object to *total* incorporation but follow some version of selective incorporation. Critics of incorporation have made several assertions. They have pointed out that a number of states did not provide grand jury indictment and did not change their laws or constitutions after they ratified the 14th Amendment. They have also asserted that, except for Bingham and Howard, none of the speakers who discussed § 1 during the 1866 debates on ratification of the 14th Amendment suggested that its protections encompassed all of the Bill of Rights. In addition, they say some speakers suggested that the 14th Amendment was equivalent to the Civil Rights Act of 1866 and they claim that the language of the Act could not be read to include the Bill of Rights as a limit on the states. Most critics of incorporation have only looked at the 1866 debates on the 14th Amendment and the Civil Rights Act.

Those who say that the historical record supports application of the Bill of Rights to the states insist that the debates must be understood in a larger context. They say that the 14th Amendment needs to be understood in light of more than thirty years of state suppression of civil liberties in the interest of protecting slavery. For example, states, or mobs tolerated by the states, banned or burned anti-slavery publications, suppressed ministers who preached against slavery, searched to find and suppress anti-slavery literature, and drove people who supported the Republican candidate for president out of the state.

Those who believe that the historical record supports incorporation have also noted that many Republicans believed that states were required to obey the guarantees of the Bill of Rights even before ratification of the 14th Amendment. As a result, they read statements by Republicans that the 14th Amendment will protect all constitutional rights of citizens as supporting application of the Bill of Rights to the states. They also point to the long historical practice of describing rights in the Bill of Rights as "privileges" or "immunities" that belong to citizens of the United States.

As to the claim that the 14th Amendment merely incorporated the equality protections of the Civil Rights Act of 1866, first they note that the 14th Amendment prohibited the states from denying any person life, liberty, or property without due process of law. Second, they point out that some supporters of the Civil Rights Act read its language to encompass Bill of Rights liberties such as freedom of speech and the right to bear arms. They note that the Black Codes often included provisions that both denied equality to black citizens and deprived them of basic rights in the Bill of Rights. Finally, framers of the 14th Amendment and those who ratified it were aware of episodes of intimidation and mob violence similar to that which had occurred prior to the Civil War.

In *Adamson v. California* (1947), Justice Black cited an early scholarly work by Horace Flack, *The Adoption of the Fourteenth Amendment* (1908), which supported total application of the privileges in the Bill of Rights to the states. Justice Black's dissenting opinion in *Adamson* and his historical argument provoked a scholarly counter attack by Professor Charles Fairman. Charles Fairman, *Does the Fourteenth Amendment Incorporate the Bill of Rights?*, 2 Stan. L. Rev. 5 (1949). Fairman's analysis was in turn criticized by W.W. Crosskey, in *Legislative History and the Constitutional Limits on State Authority*, 22 U. Chi. L. Rev. 1 (1954). In *Duncan v. Louisiana* (1968), Justice Harlan cites Fairman to justify his position and Justice Black responds. Although Black lost the battle in *Adamson*, he came close to winning the incorporation war, as the cases which follow show. The incorporation doctrine came under renewed attack in Raoul Berger's widely discussed book, *Government by Judiciary* (1977). Berger's historical conclusions were in turn challenged, *see e.g.*, Michael Kent Curtis, *The Bill of Rights as a Limitation on State Authority: A Reply to Professor Berger*, 16 Wake Forest L. Rev. 45 (1980). Berger defended himself, *Incorporation of the Bill of Rights in The Fourteenth Amendment: A Nine-Lived Cat*, 42 Ohio St. L.J. 435 (1981). This defense was in turn challenged, Curtis, *Further Adventures of the Nine Lived Cat: A Response to Mr. Berger on Incorporation of the Bill of Rights*, 43 Ohio St. L.J. 89 (1982).

A history of the incorporation doctrine is set out in Michael Kent Curtis, *No State Shall Abridge*. See also Akhil Reed Amar, *The Bill of Rights: Creation and Reconstruction* (1998) and *The Bill of Rights and the Fourteenth Amendment*, 101 Yale. L.J. 1193 (1992); Bryan H. Wildenthal, *The Road to Twining: Reassessing the Disincorporation of the Bill of Rights*, 61 Ohio St. L.J. 1457 (2000); and Richard Aynes, *On Misreading John Bingham and the Fourteenth Amendment*, 103 Yale L.J. 57 (1993). On the connection between the crusade against slavery and the 14th Amendment, *see e.g.*, Jacobus Ten Broek, *Equal Under Law* (1965); Howard Jay Graham, *Everyman's Constitution* (1968), and William M. Wiecek, *The Sources of Antislavery Constitutionalism in America, 1760–1848* (1977). For a symposium discussion of incorporation, *see The Fourteenth Amendment and the Bill of Rights*, 18 J. Contemp. Legal Issues 1–533 (2009). The forgoing lists only a small part of the literature; there are numerous other important studies.

C. The Warren Court Approach — Incorporation: From *Mapp* to *Duncan*

1. *Mapp v. Ohio* (1961). The Court held that the 4th Amendment applies to the states with the same coverage as it has with respect to the federal government, including the exclusionary rule—the rule providing that illegally obtained evidence should be excluded from trial.

2. *Gideon v. Wainwright* (1963). 6th Amendment right to counsel held to apply to the states under the 14th Amendment's Due Process Clause.

3. *Malloy v. Hogan* (1964). Privilege against compelled self-incrimination held to apply to the states under the 14th Amendment's Due Process Clause.

4. *Pointer v. Texas* (1965). Confrontation Clause of the 6th Amendment (cross examination) held to apply to the states under the 14th Amendment's Due Process Clause.

5. *Griswold v. Connecticut* (1965). Right of married couples to use birth control devices found in the penumbras of the Bill of Rights.

6. *Klopfer v. North Carolina* (1967). 6th Amendment right to speedy trial applied to the states under the 14th Amendment.

7. *Washington v. Texas* (1967). Compulsory process for obtaining witnesses applied to the states through the 14th Amendment.

8. *Duncan v. Louisiana* (1968). Right to jury trial held fundamental to the American scheme of justice and so incorporated in the 14th Amendment's Due Process Clause as a limit on the States.

Duncan v. Louisiana: Questions

1. What is the test for application of Bill of Rights guarantees to the states announced in *Duncan*? How does it differ from the *Palko* test?
2. Which test is more likely to promote application of Bill of Rights guarantees to the states? Why?
3. Which approach allows greater latitude for judicial choice—*Palko*, *Duncan*, or Justice Black's approach in *Adamson*?
4. How does Justice Black treat the 14th Amendment's Privileges or Immunities Clause in *Duncan*?

Duncan v. Louisiana
391 U.S. 145 (1968)

[Majority: White, Black, Douglas, Warren (C.J.), Brennan, Fortas, and Marshall. Concurring: Black, Douglas and Fortas. Dissenting: Harlan and Stewart.]

Mr. Justice White delivered the opinion of the Court.

Appellant, Gary Duncan, was convicted of simple battery in the Twenty-fifth Judicial District Court of Louisiana. Under Louisiana law simple battery is a misdemeanor, punishable by a maximum of two years' imprisonment and a $300 fine. Appellant sought trial by jury, but because the Louisiana Constitution grants jury trials only in cases in which capital punishment or imprisonment at hard labor may be imposed, the trial judge denied the request. Appellant was convicted and sentenced to serve 60 days in the parish prison and pay a fine of $150. Appellant sought review in the Supreme Court of Louisiana, asserting that the denial of jury trial violated rights guaranteed to him by the United States Constitution. The Supreme Court, finding "[n]o error of law in the ruling complained of," denied appellant a writ of certiorari. Pursuant to 28 U.S.C. § 1257(2) appellant sought review in this Court, alleging that the 6th and 14th Amendments to the United States Constitution secure the right to jury trial in state criminal prosecutions where a sentence as long as two years may be imposed....

Appellant was 19 years of age when tried. While driving on Highway 23 in Plaquemines Parish on October 18, 1966, he saw two younger cousins engaged in a conversation by the side of the road with four white boys. Knowing his cousins, Negroes who had recently transferred to a formerly all-white high school, had reported the occurrence of racial incidents at the school, Duncan stopped the car, got out, and approached the six boys. At trial the white boys and a white onlooker testified, as did appellant and his cousins. The testimony was in dispute on many points, but the witnesses agreed that appellant and the white boys spoke to each other, that appellant encouraged his cousins to break off the encounter and enter his car, and that appellant was about to enter the car himself for the purpose of driving away with his cousins. The whites testified that just before getting in the car appellant slapped Herman Landry, one of the white boys, on the elbow. The Negroes testified that appellant had not slapped Landry, but had merely touched him. The trial judge concluded that the State had proved beyond a reasonable doubt that Duncan had committed simple battery, and found him guilty.

I. The 14th Amendment denies the States the power to "deprive any person of life, liberty, or property, without due process of law." In resolving conflicting claims concerning the meaning of this spacious language, the Court has looked increasingly to the Bill of Rights for guidance; many of the rights guaranteed by the first eight Amendments to the Constitution have been held to be protected against state action by the Due Process Clause of the 14th Amendment. That clause now protects the right to compensation for property taken by the State [*Chicago, Burlington, & Quincy Railroad v. Chicago* (1897)]; the rights of speech, press, and religion covered by the 1st Amendment [*See, e.g., Fiske v. Kansas* (1927)]; the 4th Amendment rights to be free from unreasonable searches and seizures and to have excluded from criminal trials any evidence illegally seized [*Mapp v. Ohio* (1961)]; the right guaranteed by the 5th Amendment to be free of compelled self-incrimination [*Malloy v. Hogan* (1964)]; and the 6th Amendment rights to counsel [*Gideon v. Wainwright* (1963)], to a speedy [*Klopfer v. North Carolina* (1967)] and public [*In re Oliver* (1948)] trial, to confrontation of opposing witnesses [*Pointer v. Texas* (1965)], and to compulsory process for obtaining witnesses [*Washington v. Texas* (1967)].

The test for determining whether a right extended by the 5th and 6th Amendments with respect to federal criminal proceedings is also protected against state action by the 14th Amendment has been phrased in a variety of ways in the opinions of this Court. The question has been asked whether a right is among those "fundamental principles of liberty and justice which lie at the base of all our civil and political institutions," *Powell v. Alabama* (1932).... Because we believe that trial by jury in criminal cases is fundamental to the American scheme of justice, we hold that the 14th Amendment guarantees a right of jury trial in all criminal cases which—were they to be tried in a federal court—would come within the 6th Amendment's guarantee.[1] ... Since we consider the appeal

---

1. In one sense recent cases applying provisions of the first eight Amendments to the States represent a new approach to the "incorporation" debate. Earlier the Court can be seen as having asked, when inquiring into whether some particular procedural safeguard was required of a State, if a civilized system could be imagined that would not accord the particular protection. For example, *Palko v. Connecticut* (1937), stated: "The right to trial by jury and the immunity from prosecution except as the result of an indictment may have value and importance. Even so, they are not of the very essence of a scheme of ordered liberty.... Few would be so narrow or provincial as to maintain that a fair and enlightened system of justice would be impossible without them." The recent cases, on the other hand, have proceeded upon the valid assumption that state criminal processes are not imaginary and theoretical schemes but actual systems bearing virtually every characteristic of the common-law system that has been developing contemporaneously in England and in this country. The question thus is whether given this kind of system a particular procedure is fundamental—whether, that is, a procedure is necessary to an Anglo-American regime of ordered liberty. It is this sort of inquiry that can justify the conclusions that state courts must exclude evidence seized in violation of the 4th Amendment, *Mapp v. Ohio*; that state prosecutors may not comment on a defendant's failure to testify, *Griffin v. California* (1965); and that criminal punishment may not be imposed for the status of narcotics addiction, *Robinson v. California* (1962). Of immediate relevance for this case are the Court's holdings that the States must comply with certain provisions of the 6th Amendment, specifically that the States may not refuse a speedy trial, confrontation of witnesses, and the assistance, at state expense if necessary, of counsel. Of each of these determinations that a constitutional provision originally written to bind the Federal Government should bind the States as well it might be said that the limitation in question is not necessarily fundamental to fairness in every criminal system that might be imagined but is fundamental in the context of the criminal processes maintained by the American States.

When the inquiry is approached in this way the question whether the States can impose criminal punishment without granting a jury trial appears quite different from the way it appeared in the older cases opining that States might abolish jury trial. *See, e.g., Maxwell v. Dow* (1900). A criminal process which was fair and equitable but used no juries is easy to imagine. It would make use of alternative guarantees and protections which would serve the purposes that the jury serves in the English and Amer-

before us to be such a case, we hold that the Constitution was violated when appellant's demand for jury trial was refused.

The history of trial by jury in criminal cases has been frequently told....

Even such skeletal history is impressive support for considering the right to jury trial in criminal cases to be fundamental to our system of justice, an importance frequently recognized in the opinions of this Court....

Jury trial continues to receive strong support. The laws of every State guarantee a right to jury trial in serious criminal cases; no State has dispensed with it; nor are there significant movements underway to do so....

We are aware of prior cases in this Court in which the prevailing opinion contains statements contrary to our holding today that the right to jury trial in serious criminal cases is a fundamental right and hence must be recognized by the States as part of their obligation to extend due process of law to all persons within their jurisdiction.... None of these cases, however, dealt with a State which had purported to dispense entirely with a jury trial in serious criminal cases. *Maxwell v. Dow* (1900) held that no provision of the Bill of Rights applied to the States—a position long since repudiated—and that the Due Process Clause of the 14th Amendment did not prevent a State from trying a defendant for a noncapital offense with fewer than 12 men on the jury. It did not deal with a case in which no jury at all had been provided. In neither *Palko v. Connecticut* (1937) nor *Snyder v. Massachusetts* (1934) was jury trial actually at issue, although both cases contain important dicta asserting that the right to jury trial is not essential to ordered liberty and may be dispensed with by the States regardless of the 6th and 14th Amendments. These observations, though weighty and respectable, are nevertheless dicta, unsupported by holdings in this Court that a State may refuse a defendant's demand for a jury trial when he is charged with a serious crime.... Respectfully, we reject the prior dicta regarding jury trial in criminal cases.

The guarantees of jury trial in the Federal and State Constitutions reflect a profound judgment about the way in which law should be enforced and justice administered. A right to jury trial is granted to criminal defendants in order to prevent oppression by the Government.[2] Those who wrote our constitutions knew from history and experience that it was necessary to protect against unfounded criminal charges brought to eliminate enemies and against judges too responsive to the voice of higher authority. The framers of the constitutions strove to create an independent judiciary but insisted upon further protection against arbitrary action. Providing an accused with the right to be tried by a jury of his peers gave him an inestimable safeguard against the corrupt or overzealous prosecutor and against the compliant, biased, or eccentric judge.... Beyond this, the jury trial provisions in the Federal and State Constitutions reflect a fundamental decision about

---

ican systems. Yet no American State has undertaken to construct such a system. Instead, every American State, including Louisiana, uses the jury extensively, and imposes very serious punishments only after a trial at which the defendant has a right to a jury's verdict. In every State, including Louisiana, the structure and style of the criminal process—the supporting framework and the subsidiary procedures—are of the sort that naturally complement jury trial, and have developed in connection with and in reliance upon jury trial.

2. "The [jury trial] clause was clearly intended to protect the accused from oppression by the Government...." *Singer v. United States* (1965). "The first object of any tyrant in Whitehall would be to make Parliament utterly subservient to his will; and the next to overthrow or diminish trial by jury, for no tyrant could afford to leave a subject's freedom in the hands of twelve of his countrymen. So that trial by jury is more than an instrument of justice and more than one wheel of the constitution: it is the lamp that shows that freedom lives." P. Devlin, *Trial by Jury* 164 (1956).

the exercise of official power—a reluctance to entrust plenary powers over the life and liberty of the citizen to one judge or to a group of judges. Fear of unchecked power, so typical of our State and Federal Governments in other respects, found expression in the criminal law in this insistence upon community participation in the determination of guilt or innocence. The deep commitment of the Nation to the right of jury trial in serious criminal cases as a defense against arbitrary law enforcement qualifies for protection under the Due Process Clause of the 14th Amendment, and must therefore be respected by the States....

Even where defendants are satisfied with bench trials, the right to a jury trial very likely serves its intended purpose of making judicial or prosecutorial unfairness less likely.[3]

II. Louisiana's final contention is that even if it must grant jury trials in serious criminal cases, the conviction before us is valid and constitutional because here the petitioner was tried for simple battery and was sentenced to only 60 days in the parish prison. We are not persuaded. It is doubtless true that there is a category of petty crimes or offenses which is not subject to the 6th Amendment jury trial provision and should not be subject to the 14th Amendment jury trial requirement here applied to the States. Crimes carrying possible penalties up to six months do not require a jury trial if they otherwise qualify as petty offenses, *Cheff v. Schnackenberg* (1966). But the penalty authorized for a particular crime is of major relevance in determining whether it is serious or not and may in itself, if severe enough, subject the trial to the mandates of the 6th Amendment. *District of Columbia v. Clawans* (1937)....

The judgment below is reversed and the case is remanded for proceedings not inconsistent with this opinion.

Mr. Justice Black, with whom Mr. Justice Douglas joins, concurring.

The Court today holds that the right to trial by jury guaranteed defendants in criminal cases in federal courts by Art. III of the United States Constitution and by the 6th Amendment is also guaranteed by the 14th Amendment to defendants tried in state courts. With this holding I agree for reasons given by the Court. I also agree because of reasons given in my dissent in *Adamson v. California* (1947)....

All of these holdings making Bill of Rights' provisions applicable as such to the States mark, of course, a departure from the *Twining v. New Jersey* (1908) doctrine holding that none of those provisions were enforceable as such against the States.... What I wrote [in

---

3. Louisiana also asserts that if due process is deemed to include the right to jury trial, States will be obligated to comply with all past interpretations of the 6th Amendment, an amendment which in its inception was designed to control only the federal courts and which throughout its history has operated in this limited environment where uniformity is a more obvious and immediate consideration. In particular, Louisiana objects to application of the decisions of this Court interpreting the 6th Amendment as guaranteeing a 12-man jury in serious criminal cases, *Thompson v. Utah* (1898); as requiring a unanimous verdict before guilt can be found, *Maxwell v. Dow*; and as barring procedures by which crimes subject to the 6th Amendment jury trial provision are tried in the first instance without a jury but at the first appellate stage by de novo trial with a jury, *Callan v. Wilson* (1888). It seems very unlikely to us that our decision today will require widespread changes in state criminal processes. First, our decisions interpreting the 6th Amendment are always subject to reconsideration, a fact amply demonstrated by the instant decision. In addition, most of the States have provisions for jury trials equal in breadth to the 6th Amendment, if that amendment is construed, as it has been, to permit the trial of petty crimes and offenses without a jury. Indeed, there appear to be only four States in which juries of fewer than 12 can be used without the defendant's consent for offenses carrying a maximum penalty of greater than one year. Only in Oregon and Louisiana can a less-than-unanimous jury convict for an offense with a maximum penalty greater than one year....

Adamson] in 1947 was the product of years of study and research. My appraisal of the legislative history followed 10 years of legislative experience as a Senator of the United States, not a bad way, I suspect, to learn the value of what is said in legislative debates, committee discussions, committee reports, and various other steps taken in the course of passage of bills, resolutions, and proposed constitutional amendments. My Brother Harlan's objections to my *Adamson* dissent history, like that of most of the objectors, relies most heavily on a criticism written by Professor Charles Fairman and published in the Stanford Law Review. 2 Stan. L. Rev. 5 (1949). I have read and studied this article extensively, including the historical references, but am compelled to add that in my view it has completely failed to refute the inferences and arguments that I suggested in my *Adamson* dissent. Professor Fairman's "history" relies very heavily on what was *not* said in the state legislatures that passed on the 14th Amendment. Instead of relying on this kind of negative pregnant, my legislative experience has convinced me that it is far wiser to rely on what *was* said.... The historical appendix to my *Adamson* dissent leaves no doubt in my mind that both its sponsors and those who opposed it believed the 14th Amendment made the first eight Amendments of the Constitution (the Bill of Rights) applicable to the States.

In addition to the adoption of Professor Fairman's "history," the dissent [in this case] states that "the great words of the four clauses of the first section of the 14th Amendment would have been an exceedingly peculiar way to say that 'The rights heretofore guaranteed against federal intrusion by the first eight Amendments are henceforth guaranteed against state intrusion as well.'" In response to this I can say only that the words "No State shall make or enforce any law which shall abridge the privileges or immunities of citizens of the United States" seem to me an eminently reasonable way of expressing the idea that henceforth the Bill of Rights shall apply to the States.[1] What more precious "privilege" of American citizenship could there be than that privilege to claim the protections of our great Bill of Rights? I suggest that any reading of "privileges or immunities of citizens of the United States" which excludes the Bill of Rights' safeguards renders the words of this section of the 14th Amendment meaningless....

[Under the approach advocated by Justice Harlan] the Due Process Clause is treated as prescribing no specific and clearly ascertainable constitutional command that judges must obey in interpreting the Constitution, but rather as leaving judges free to decide at any particular time whether a particular rule or judicial formulation embodies an "immutable principl(e) of free government" or is "implicit in the concept of ordered liberty," or whether certain conduct "shocks the judge's conscience" or runs counter to some other similar, undefined and undefinable standard....

[T]he "fundamental fairness" test is one on a par with that of shocking the conscience of the Court. Each of such tests depends entirely on the particular judge's idea of ethics and morals instead of requiring him to depend on the boundaries fixed by the written words of the Constitution. Nothing in the history of the phrase "due process of law" suggests that constitutional controls are to depend on any particular judge's sense of values....

Finally I want to add that I am not bothered by the argument that applying the Bill of Rights to the States "according to the same standards that protect those personal rights against federal encroachment," interferes with our concept of federalism in that it may prevent States from trying novel social and economic experiments. I have never believed

---

1. My view has been and is that the 14th Amendment, *as a whole*, makes the Bill of Rights applicable to the States. This would certainly include the language of the Privileges and Immunities Clause, as well as the Due Process Clause.

that under the guise of federalism the States should be able to experiment with the protections afforded our citizens through the Bill of Rights....

It seems to me totally inconsistent to advocate on the one hand, the power of this Court to strike down any state law or practice which it finds "unreasonable" or "unfair" and, on the other hand, urge that the States be given maximum power to develop their own laws and procedures....

I believe as strongly as ever that the 14th Amendment was intended to make the Bill of Rights applicable to the States. I have been willing to support the selective incorporation doctrine, however, as an alternative, although perhaps less historically supportable than complete incorporation. The selective incorporation process, if used properly, does limit the Supreme Court in the 14th Amendment field to specific Bill of Rights' protections only and keeps judges from roaming at will in their own notions of what policies outside the Bill of Rights are desirable and what are not. And, most importantly for me, the selective incorporation process has the virtue of having already worked to make most of the Bill of Rights' protections applicable to the States....

Mr. Justice Harlan, whom Mr. Justice Stewart joins, dissenting.

... The States have always borne primary responsibility for operating the machinery of criminal justice within their borders, and adapting it to their particular circumstances. In exercising this responsibility, each State is compelled to conform its procedures to the requirements of the Federal Constitution. The Due Process Clause of the 14th Amendment requires that those procedures be fundamentally fair in all respects. It does not, in my view, impose or encourage nationwide uniformity for its own sake; it does not command adherence to forms that happen to be old; and it does not impose on the States the rules that may be in force in the federal courts except where such rules are also found to be essential to basic fairness.

The Court's approach to this case is an uneasy and illogical compromise among the views of various Justices on how the Due Process Clause should be interpreted. The Court does not say that those who framed the 14th Amendment intended to make the 6th Amendment applicable to the States. And the Court concedes that it finds nothing unfair about the procedure by which the present appellant was tried. Nevertheless, the Court reverses his conviction: it holds, for some reason not apparent to me, that the Due Process Clause incorporates the particular clause of the 6th Amendment that requires trial by jury in federal criminal cases—including, as I read its opinion, the sometimes trivial accompanying baggage of judicial interpretation in federal contexts....

I. I believe I am correct in saying that every member of the Court for at least the last 135 years has agreed that our Founders did not consider the requirements of the Bill of Rights so fundamental that they should operate directly against the States.[1] They were wont to believe rather that the security of liberty in America rested primarily upon the dispersion of governmental power across a federal system.[2] ...

A few members of the Court have taken the position that the intention of those who drafted the first section of the 14th Amendment was simply, and exclusively, to make the provisions of the first eight Amendments applicable to state action.[3] This view has never

---

1. *Barron v. Baltimore* (1833), held that the first eight Amendments restricted only federal action.
2. The locus classicus for this viewpoint is *The Federalist* No. 51 (Madison).
3. *See Adamson v. California* (1947) (dissenting opinion of Black, J.); *O'Neil v. Vermont* (1892) (dissenting opinion of Harlan, J.); H. Black, "Due Process of Law," in *A Constitutional Faith* 23 (1968).

been accepted by this Court. In my view, often expressed elsewhere,[4] the first section of the 14th Amendment was meant neither to incorporate, nor to be limited to, the specific guarantees of the first eight Amendments. The overwhelming historical evidence marshaled by Professor Fairman demonstrates, to me conclusively, that the Congressmen and state legislators who wrote, debated, and ratified the 14th Amendment did not think they were "incorporating" the Bill of Rights and the very breadth and generality of the Amendment's provisions suggest that its authors did not suppose that the Nation would always be limited to mid-19th century conceptions of "liberty" and "due process of law".... [N]either history, nor sense, supports using the 14th Amendment to put the States in a constitutional straitjacket with respect to their own development in the administration of criminal or civil law....

Apart from the approach taken by the absolute incorporationists, I can see only one method of analysis that has any internal logic. That is to start with the words "liberty" and "due process of law" and attempt to define them in a way that accords with American traditions and our system of government. This approach, involving a much more discriminating process of adjudication than does "incorporation," is, albeit difficult, the one that was followed throughout the 19th and most of the present century. It entails a "gradual process of judicial inclusion and exclusion," [*Davidson v. City of New Orleans* (1878)], seeking, with due recognition of constitutional tolerance for state experimentation and disparity, to ascertain those "immutable principles ... of justice which inhere in the very idea of free government which no member of the Union may disregard." [*Holden v. Hardy* (1898)]....

II.... When a criminal defendant contends that his state conviction lacked "due process of law," the question before this Court, in my view, is whether he was denied any element of fundamental procedural fairness. Believing, as I do, that due process is an evolving concept and that old principles are subject to re-evaluation in light of later experience, I think it appropriate to deal on its merits with the question whether Louisiana denied appellant due process of law when it tried him for simple assault without a jury....

In sum, there is a wide range of views on the desirability of trial by jury, and on the ways to make it most effective when it is used; there is also considerable variation from State to State in local conditions such as the size of the criminal caseload, the ease or difficulty of summoning jurors, and other trial conditions bearing on fairness. We have before us, therefore, an almost perfect example of a situation in which the celebrated dictum of Mr. Justice Brandeis should be invoked. It is, he said,

> one of the happy incidents of the federal system that a single courageous state may, if its citizens choose, serve as a laboratory....

New State Ice Co. v. Liebmann (1932) (dissenting opinion).

This Court, other courts, and the political process are available to correct any experiments in criminal procedure that prove fundamentally unfair to defendants. That is not what is being done today: instead, and quite without reason, the Court has chosen to impose upon every State one means of trying criminal cases; it is a good means, but it is not the only fair means, and it is not demonstrably better than the alternatives States might devise.

I would affirm the judgment of the Supreme Court of Louisiana.

* * *

---

4. [S]ee, e.g., my opinions in *Poe v. Ullman*, (1961) (dissenting), and *Griswold v. Connecticut* (1965) (concurring).

In *Democracy in America*, De Tocqueville emphasized the democratic character of the American civil and criminal jury. "The institution of the jury ... places the real direction of society in the hands of the governed, ... and not in that of the government.... [It] invests the people, or that class of citizens, with the direction of society.... The jury system as it is understood in America appears to me to be as direct and as extreme a consequence of the sovereignty of the people as universal suffrage. They are two instruments of equal power, which contribute to the supremacy of the majority. All the sovereigns who have chosen to ... direct society instead of obeying its directions, have destroyed or enfeebled the institution of the jury." 2 Alexis de Tocqueville, *Democracy in America* 294 (Henry Reeve Text, revised by Francis Bowen, Vintage Books, 1945). *See* Akhil Reed Amar, *The Bill of Rights: Creation and Reconstruction* 88 (1998). English historian, E. P. Thompson expressed a similar view: "Time and again, when judges and law officers, mounted on high horses, have been riding at breakneck speed toward some convenient despotism, those shadowy figures—not particularly good nor especially true—have risen from the bushes beside the highway and flung a gate across their path. They are known to historians as the Gang of Twelve." E. P. Thompson, *The State Versus Its Enemies*, in *Writing by Candlelight* 103 (1980).

1. Incorporation: Due Process and Procedures Not Forbidden by the Bill of Rights

The Court has held some criminal procedures not explicitly listed in the Bill of Rights are nonetheless required by due process. *In re Winship* (1970), held proof beyond a reasonable doubt was required by the Due Process Clause because it "plays a vital role in the American scheme of criminal procedure." Justice Black dissented: "I realize that it is far easier to substitute individual judges' ideas of 'fairness' for the fairness prescribed by the Constitution, but I shall not at any time surrender my belief that the document itself should be our guide...."

2. Incorporation after Duncan

1. *Benton v. Maryland* (1969). 14th Amendment Due Process Clause claims of double jeopardy in state proceedings "must be judged not by the watered-down standard enunciated in *Palko*, but under this Court's interpretations of the 5th Amendment."

2. *Williams v. Florida* (1970). The Court held a conviction by a unanimous jury of six is consistent with the 14th Amendment. Justice Harlan concurred, but said the Court was diluting the federal protection to reconcile the "'jot for jot and case for case' application of the federal right to the States with the reality of federalism." Justice Marshall dissented and warned that the Court seemed headed toward stripping the jury trial of its historic requirements.

3. *Schilb v. Kuebel* (1971). The Court, in dicta, said the 8th Amendment's guarantee against excessive bail had been assumed to apply to the states.

4. *Alexander v. Louisiana* (1972). The Court, in dicta, said the federal grand jury indictment requirement still did not apply to the states.

5. *Apodaca v. Oregon* (1972). The Court upheld an Oregon conviction under a statute allowing conviction by a jury vote of 10–2.

6. *Burch v. Louisiana* (1979). The Court invalidated a state statute allowing conviction by 5 of 6 jurors. The Court said, "having already departed from the strictly historical re-

quirements of jury trial, it is inevitable that lines must be drawn somewhere if the substance of the right to jury trial is to be preserved."

7. *Browning-Ferris Industries v. Kelco Disposal, Inc.* (1989). The Court refused to decide if the 8th Amendment's ban on excessive fines applies to the states through the 14th Amendment.

8. *McDonald* v. *Chicago* (2010). In a 5–4 decision, the Court holds that an individual right to bear arms is incorporated as a limit on the states. Justice Thomas concurs basing incorporation on the Privileges or Immunities Clause.

9. The Supreme Court has so far not held that *all* rights in the Bill of Rights limit state power. Those the Court has not yet applied to the states include the right to grand jury indictment and the protection against quartering troops.

VIII. Incorporation: Approaches, Effects, and Further Thoughts

A Typology of Positions on Application of the Bill of Rights to the States

What are the logical and actual possibilities for application of the federal Bill of Rights and less textually explicit liberties (such as the right to use birth control devices) to the states through the 14th Amendment? Possibilities range from no application to applying all Bill of Rights liberties plus some other less textually explicit ones.

Where would the cases studied in this unit on incorporation of the Bill of Rights fit on a typology of possible positions? Where would the views of Justice Black, of the second Justice Harlan, and of Justice White in *Duncan* fit? After thinking about this question, consider the following chart.

Approaches to Application of the Bill of Rights to the States: A Graphic Portrayal

No incorporation		*Barron*
Weak selective	Fundamental principles of liberty and justice. Selective absorption.	*Palko*
Strong selective	Fundamental to American system of justice. Bill of Rights as a guide. Guarantees applied with gloss of federal precedent.	*Duncan*
Strong selective plus	Other fundamental principles of liberty and justice included, though less explicit in the text.	*Griswold*
Total incorporation	Liberties limited to those quite explicit in the text of the Constitution. Guarantees applied with federal gloss.	Black in *Adamson*
Total incorporation plus	All liberties in the Bill of Rights plus less textually explicit liberties.	Murphy and Rutledge in *Adamson*

The Resurrection of a Reconstruction Statute

Once the Court began to incorporate guarantees like those in the 4th Amendment against the states, it also breathed new life into Reconstruction era statutes like 42 U.S.C. § 1983. Section 1983 provides a civil action for those who suffer deprivation, under color of law, of rights, privileges, or immunities secured by the Constitution. After incorporation, as we have seen, the Court held that many liberties in the Bill of Rights were secured against state action. In *Monroe v. Pape* (1961), the Court held that the plaintiffs had a cause of action against Chicago police officers who, allegedly without any warrant, broke into their home. The incident occurred in the early morning. The police allegedly rousted them from bed, made them stand naked in the living room, and ransacked every room, emptying drawers and ripping mattress covers. They then took the father to the police station, where he was detained on "open" charges for ten hours while he was interrogated about a two-day-old murder. The plaintiffs further alleged that he was not taken before a magistrate, though one was accessible; that he was not permitted to call his family or attorney; and that he was subsequently released without criminal charges being brought against him.

The Court held that Congress, by enacting § 1983, intended to give a remedy to parties deprived of constitutional rights, privileges and immunities by a state or local official's abuse of his position. Section 1983 then emerged from nearly a century of dormancy and became the primary vehicle for constitutional tort actions against state government officials.

Attorney General Meese Critiques Incorporation

The incorporation debate was enlivened on July 9, 1985, by a speech given by Edwin Meese to the American Bar Association. Mr. Meese was Attorney General of the United States, appointed by President Ronald Reagan. Mr. Meese's speech contained the following passage:

> [B]oth Federalists and anti-Federalists agreed that the [Bill of Rights] were a curb on national power. When this view was questioned before the Supreme Court in *Barron v. Baltimore* (1833), Chief Justice Marshall wholeheartedly agreed. The Constitution said what it meant and meant what it said. Neither political expediency nor judicial desire was sufficient to change the clear import of the language of the Constitution. The Bill of Rights did not apply to the states—and, he said, that was that.
>
> Until 1925, that is.
>
> Since then a good portion of constitutional adjudication has been aimed at extending the scope of the doctrine of incorporation; nothing can be done to shore up the intellectually shaky foundation upon which the doctrine rests. And nowhere has the principle of federalism been dealt so politically violent and constitutionally suspect a blow as by the theory of incorporation.

* * *

1. What values are furthered by requiring states to follow the commands of the federal Bill of Rights? What constitutional values are subordinated by such a rule?
2. We have seen the Court move from *no* application of *any* federal Bill of Rights liberties to the states, to a doctrine that applies *most* of them. What does this evolution tell you about the benefits and limits of simply learning the current rule? What does it suggest about the importance of understanding methods of making constitutional arguments? Is one type of understanding (either of doctrine or of method) adequate without the other?

IX. The Warren Court

The Warren Court decided a number of cases requiring states to obey the guarantees of the Bill of Rights. It is useful here to look at the Court in the broader context of the overall pattern of its decisions. Constitutional law, like all law, is a product of the eras in which the Court functions. Recent eras include the New Deal Court (appointed by President Franklin Roosevelt), the Warren Court, the Burger Court (transformed by President Richard Nixon's appointments), the Rehnquist Court—in which seven Justices were appointed by Republican Presidents—and now the Roberts Court.

In a brief account, it is possible to give only a very general and incomplete sketch of the activities of the Warren Court. For a recent book on the subject, *see* Lucas A. Powe, Jr., *The Warren Court and American Politics* (2000). For a shorter treatment, see the entry on the Warren Court in the *Encyclopedia of the American Constitution* (2000), and the biography of Earl Warren in the *Oxford Companion to the Supreme Court* (1997).

Two members of the Warren Court had been appointed by Franklin Roosevelt and served even after Earl Warren retired—Hugo Black (1937) and William O. Douglas (1939). Earl Warren (1953), John Marshall Harlan (1955), William Brennan (1956), and Potter Stewart (1958) were appointed by President Eisenhower. President Kennedy appointed Arthur Goldberg (1962) and Byron White (1962). President Johnson appointed Abe Fortas (1965), who replaced Arthur Goldberg, and Thurgood Marshall (1967). In contrast to the Rehnquist Court, several of the Justices on the Warren Court had substantial political experience. Warren had been a district attorney and Attorney General and Governor of California. Hugo Black had served in the United States Senate.

As you have seen, the Warren Court substantially increased the number of Bill of Rights liberties that were applied to the states. In addition, the Court held these guarantees had the same effect whether applied against the federal government or the states. For example, evidence seized in violation of the 4th Amendment had long been excluded in federal trials. As part of its practice of applying federal precedent to set the meaning of incorporated rights, the Warren Court applied the federal exclusionary rule to the states in *Mapp v. Ohio* (1961). These and other decisions dealing with habeas corpus meant the Court could review many criminal law convictions coming from the South in the turbulent civil rights era of the 1960s, the nation's second Reconstruction. Incorporation of the Bill of Rights into the 14th Amendment was an issue in the first Reconstruction as well, though in that case the Court rejected incorporation.

The Warren Court made other far-reaching decisions as well. Its decisions reflected a concern with greater equity and social justice for groups that had often been left out. For example, the Court expanded access of the poor to more nearly equal criminal justice and it protected political participation uninhibited by the poll tax. It attempted to dismantle the legal racial caste system, which had plagued blacks in much of the country. It embraced a generous interpretation of many individual rights set out in the Bill of Rights, such as freedom of speech. Finally, its decisions supported a broader democracy characterized by greater equality in the right to vote.

In 1954, the Court ruled that public school segregation violated the Equal Protection Clause. However, the Court next decided that its ruling must be implemented with "all deliberate speed," and the pace of actual school desegregation in the South was slow. The Court soon applied its decision to all aspects of state mandated segregation. In *Loving v. Virginia* (1967), it held a ban on racial intermarriage violated equal protection.

In *Torcaso v. Watkins* (1961), the Court struck down a Maryland constitutional provision that required all public officers to affirm a belief in God. The Court noted that Buddhism, Taoism, Ethical Culture and Secular Humanism were religions that did not teach "what would generally be considered a belief in the existence of God." It held the Maryland provision violated the Establishment Clause.

The Court's most controversial religion decision banned state mandated school prayer. In *Engel v. Vitale* (1962), the Court, speaking through Justice Black, held that the Establishment Clause meant that in the United States "it is no part of the business of government to compose official prayers for any group of the American people to recite as part of a religious program carried on by government." Religion was instead a matter for "the people themselves and those they choose to look to for religious guidance."

While many Jewish and Protestant denominations praised the *Engel* decision, many Southern Protestant and Catholic leaders were harshly critical. The Reverend Billy Graham was "shocked." The Jesuit weekly *America* said the decision was "asinine" and "stupid." There was hostile reaction in Congress as well. Congressman Mendel Rivers of South Carolina denounced the Court for giving "aid and comfort to Moscow" with its "malicious, atheistic decision," and Congressman George Andrews of Alabama said the Court had "put Negroes in the school and now they've driven God out."

The Court decided 1st Amendment cases that struck some commentators as yet another threat to morality. In *Kingsley's Pictures v. Regents* (1959), a New York statute required censors to ban "immoral" films, as well as those that met the constitutional definition of obscenity. The Court struck down New York's decision censoring a film version of the D. H. Lawrence novel, *Lady Chatterley's Lover*. The censors found the film immoral because it suggested that adultery could, at least in some circumstances, be acceptable and desirable. The Court held that a motion picture could not be suppressed because it advocated an idea. "It is contended that the State's action was justified because the motion picture attractively portrays a relationship which is contrary to the moral standards, the religious precepts, and the legal code of its citizenry. This argument misconceives what it is that the Constitution protects." 1st Amendment protection was not "confined to the expression of ideas that are conventional or shared by a majority. It protects advocacy of the opinion that adultery may sometimes be proper, no less than advocacy of socialism or the single tax."

In *Roth v. United States* (1957), the Court had held that obscenity was not protected by the 1st Amendment guarantee. Still, the Court noted that sex and obscenity were not synonymous, and nine years later it dramatically limited the scope of the constitutional definition of obscenity. In *Memoirs v. Massachusetts* (1966), the Court found a sexually explicit 18th century English novel that depicted the heroine's adventures in a whorehouse to be constitutionally protected. A plurality found the book not obscene because it was not entirely worthless—not "utterly without redeeming social value." Justices Black and Douglas concurred, holding that obscenity laws violated the 1st Amendment's prohibition on laws abridging freedom of speech.

The Warren Court issued other decisions that were broadly protective of freedom of speech. In *New York Times v. Sullivan* (1964), it considered an Alabama libel verdict against the New York Times and a number of ministers who had published an advertisement protesting a jailing of Dr. Martin Luther King Jr. The ad was harshly critical of local law enforcement officials, and it contained factual errors. An Alabama jury found the ad had libeled the Montgomery police commissioner. In finding the ad protected by freedom of the press, the Court noted "a profound national commitment to the principle that debate on public issues should be uninhibited, robust, and wide-open, and that it may well include vehement, caustic and sometimes unpleasantly sharp attacks on government and public officials." The ad was a "protest on one of the major public issues of our time." Unless it was intentionally or recklessly false (which the Court independently found it was not) it was constitutionally protected.

Those protected by the Court's free speech decisions spanned the ideological spectrum. In *Brandenburg v. Ohio* (1969), the Court considered the case of an Ohio Klansman convicted of advocating violence as a means of political change. Brandenburg had made a racist speech that called for returning blacks to Africa and Jews to Israel. He suggested violence might be necessary if the Congress, President, and Supreme Court continued to oppress the white race. The Court held only speech directed to inciting or producing imminent lawless action and plainly likely to produce such action could be proscribed. In *Bond v. Floyd* (1966), the Court's decision involved both free speech and the right of voters to choose their representatives. It held the Georgia state legislature could not exclude an elected state representative because he had endorsed both harsh criticisms of the Vietnam War and expressions of sympathy for young men who refused to serve. *New York Times v. Sullivan* and *Bond v. Floyd* were decisions that gave very broad protection to discussion of public affairs as crucial to the democratic process.

The Court's free expression decisions were not uniformly protective. In *United States v. O'Brien* (1968), the Court upheld the conviction of a man who burned his draft card to protest the war in Vietnam. In *Walker v. Birmingham* (1967), it also upheld the conviction of a minister held in contempt for violating a court order that itself violated the 1st Amendment. The Court held the minister should have appealed instead of violating the order. And it upheld the conviction of protestors against segregation for continuing to protest in the jailhouse yard after being ordered to leave.

The Court's vision of constitutional democracy produced some of its most significant decisions. *Baker v. Carr* (1962), involved a challenge to apportionment of the Tennessee legislature. If legislators should represent voters, not geographical areas, the Tennessee legislature was grossly mal-apportioned. The Court held the case justiciable. It soon held that the Equal Protection Clause of the 14th Amendment requires state legislatures to craft legislative districts in a manner that provided equal representation.

In January, 1964, the states ratified the 24th Amendment, providing that the right to vote in federal elections could not be abridged based on failure to pay any poll tax or other tax. In 1965, in *Harper v. Board of Elections* (1966), the Court held the few remaining state poll taxes requirements violated the Equal Protection Clause of the 14th Amendment. The Court characterized the right to vote as fundamental, and it subjected barriers that disadvantaged the poor to substantially heightened scrutiny. It concluded that wealth, "like race, creed, or color" was not "germane" to the ability to vote. Justice Harlan dissented and insisted that the final burial of the poll tax (by then limited to four states) should be left to the political process. Harlan noted correctly the existence of property qualifications early in American history (before the 14th Amendment) and the fact that the framers of the 14th Amendment did not regard it as conferring the right to vote on blacks or anyone else.

In addition to the poll tax case, the Warren Court decided a number of cases that dealt with problems of poverty and access to justice. In federal court since 1938, the Court had required indigents to be provided with counsel. In *Gideon v. Wainwright* (1963), the Court held that the 6th Amendment right to counsel applied to the states and required them to provide lawyers for indigent defendants at trial.

As early as 1956, in *Griffin v. Illinois* (1956), the Court had interpreted the Equal Protection Clause to require transcripts to be provided without charge to indigent criminal defendants so they could appeal their cases. In *Douglas v. California* (1963), the Court extended *Griffin*'s rationale to include the right to counsel for the first criminal appeal. The evil to be remedied was "discrimination against the indigent. For there can be no equal justice where the kind of appeal a man enjoys 'depends on the amount of money he has.'" (Recently, Justices Scalia and Thomas have suggested that *Griffin* should be re-examined and probably overruled.)

Other Warren Court decisions also involved statutes that fell most harshly on the poor. In *Levy v. Louisiana* (1968), the Court held that children born outside of marriage could not be denied the right to pursue a wrongful death action based on the death of their mother. The discrimination against illegitimate children violated equal protection.

The New Deal Court had been critical of its predecessor's habit of finding economic liberties in the Due Process Clause. Critics had emphasized the lack of a clear textual basis for the decisions. The Warren Court continued to follow the approach of the New Deal Court and applied low level rational basis review to most business regulations. But in *Griswold v. Connecticut* (1965), it struck down Connecticut's law that made it a crime to use or provide birth control devices, even to married couples. But the Court, consistently with its rejection of *Lochner v. New York* (1905) era substantive due process, did not find the right to use birth control devices simply in the liberty of the Due Process Clause. Instead, it found the right in the penumbras of liberties in the Bill of Rights—including some that had not yet been held to limit the states.

Some of the most controversial decisions of the Warren Court dealt with criminal procedure. In *Miranda v. Arizona* (1966), for example, the Court ruled that persons accused of crimes must be informed of their right to remain silent and to a lawyer. If they requested a lawyer, the Court said questioning must then cease. As noted above, the exclusionary rule was applied to state prosecutions both in confession and search and seizure cases. In the long run, most scholars believe that the decision, which imposed a rule the FBI had used for years, has not been shown to have seriously hampered law enforcement. But in the short run, as a result of its criminal procedure decisions, some accused of crimes got new trials and some people who were factually guilty were freed. The Court soon made many of its criminal procedure decisions prospective only, but the operative date was the date of the trial, not the date of the police conduct. As a result, it faced headlines reading "confessed murderer freed." The Court refused to make decisions retroactive unless, like the right to counsel, they bore directly on the accuracy of the fact finding process. It upheld police power to stop and frisk people with less than probable cause and rejected exclusion of blood tests and other physical tests on the claim that they were compelled self-incrimination. Earl Warren, who had been a prosecutor and Attorney General of California, had a more nuanced view of constitutional criminal procedure than some of his critics suggested.

George Wallace was a Segregationist and governor of Alabama who stood in the school house door at the University of Alabama to resist integration of the school by a black student. In 1968, he ran for President, first in Democratic primaries. Wallace did remarkably well among Northern blue collar workers. He then went on to run for President as the candidate of the American Independent party. George Wallace's standard 1968 campaign speech said: "If you walk out of this hotel tonight and someone knocks you on the head, he'll be out of jail before you're out of the hospital, and on Monday morning they will try the policeman instead of the criminal." After Wallace's success with the crime issue, Richard Nixon injected it into his campaign. In his 1968 campaign speech, Richard

Nixon said, "some of our courts have gone too far in weakening the peace forces against the criminal forces." Wallace and Nixon enjoyed public support on the crime issue. The Gallup Poll reported that 63% of Americans thought that the Court was too protective of those accused of crime.

In many of its decisions, the Warren Court was not a lone innovator, nor was its movement in the direction of racial equality unique. President Franklin Roosevelt had issued a Fair Employment executive order banning racial discrimination in federal and defense projects. President Harry Truman had integrated the armed forces. The Eisenhower administration had favored legislation to protect the right of blacks to vote. The Kennedy and Johnson Administrations had supported a public accommodations act and a voting rights act.

Major gains in civil rights occurred during the presidency of Lyndon Johnson. Johnson's leadership secured the passage of the Civil Rights Act of 1964, which outlawed discrimination in public accommodations and employment, and of the Voting Rights Act of 1965, which provided strong protection against racial discrimination in the right to vote. The Act led to a massive increase in blacks voting in the South and largely ended overt racial discrimination in voting. The Court held both acts constitutional. Johnson also initiated a War on Poverty. The Court's decisions on race and poverty occurred in a larger political context.

The end of the Warren Court was marked by the election of Richard Nixon and the decline in the fortunes of the national Democratic party. Storm clouds had been gathering for some time. Johnson's escalation of the war in Vietnam had produced a deep split in the Democratic party. With Johnson's support for strong civil rights enforcement, Southern states had begun to defect to the Republican party. While most of the nation at first supported the Vietnam War, Congress (no doubt reflecting public sentiment) was unwilling to raise taxes to pay for it. Inflation began to undermine a long period of prosperity. Many Americans were distressed by fear of crime and appalled by the counter-culture of the 1960s. Urban rioting increased their concern. Although Johnson acted firmly against urban rioting, it further undermined his administration. As civil rights questions moved from the South to the North and some courts began to order busing to end segregated schools, Northern support of integration eroded.

When Johnson nominated Associate Justice Abe Fortas to replace Chief Justice Earl Warren, the reaction against the Warren Court became quite clear. Fortas faced angry and hostile questions about his judicial philosophy from many members of the Senate Judiciary Committee. Senators particularly questioned his votes in criminal procedure cases and his votes in obscenity cases. One witness provided the committee with an Abe Fortas film festival, studded with scenes from movies Fortas had held not to be obscene. Serious ethical questions contributed to Fortas' defeat and forced his eventual resignation from the Court. Still, his judicial philosophy was a major issue raised by those who opposed elevating him to Chief Justice.

In 1968, Nixon barely defeated Hubert Humphrey for the presidency. But George Wallace and Richard Nixon together polled 57% of the vote, to Humphrey's 43%. Humphrey's showing was particularly dismal in Southern states.

For many in the Nixon administration, the Warren Court was an example of what a Supreme Court should not be. Nixon promised to put people on the Court who would be "strict constructionists" and subsequent Republican presidential candidates (except Gerald Ford) have echoed the pledge.

The reaction against various controversial decisions of the Warren Court and the Burger Court's abortion decision in *Roe v. Wade* (1973) (written by one Nixon Justice and joined by two others) has helped to spark recent debate over the proper role of the Court in the American constitutional system. Should the Court's constitutional decisions be limited to either the original intent of those who framed the Constitution and its amendments or to how the words were originally understood by citizens at the time of ratification? If we use an historical approach, do we follow our current understanding of the broader values they proclaimed or their understanding of the application of those values in their time? If we follow a narrow understanding of either original intent or original meaning as the sole guide, then how can innovative constitutional decisions be justified? Can later constitutional amendments taken together justify a revised understanding that goes beyond the narrow letter of the amendments? For example, consider the expansion of the right to vote to blacks, women, and those eighteen years of age or older; and consider the abolition of the poll tax in federal elections; and state repudiation of property qualifications. Do these changes support the idea of a federal right to vote that may not be abridged or should the right to vote be left where the framers of the original Constitution placed it—in the discretion of each state?

There is no doubt that the Warren Court was quite different from many of its predecessors—at least before the New Deal Court. While some earlier Courts had narrowed or struck down civil rights legislation and legislation against child labor or enforcing limits on hours of work, the Warren Court upheld sweeping civil rights laws and gave no encouragement to those who sought to void simple economic regulation. Its voting rights decisions reflected an implicit view that the Constitution had become more democratic over time and with various Amendments that expanded and protected the right to vote—the 15th, the 19th, and the poll tax Amendment. Its free speech decisions were among the most protective of expression and political dissent that the Court had uttered up to that time. It overruled a number of cases. *Plessy v. Ferguson* (1896), which upheld state imposed segregation, was only one of many. In contrast to the Rehnquist and Roberts Courts, it virtually never held acts of Congress unconstitutional. In many areas its decisions provided a national minimum standard for civil liberty. G. Edward White, writing in the *Encyclopedia of the American Constitution* says that the Warren Court was different, but not because its reasoning was more flawed or its exercise of power more presumptuous. Instead, he says, previous activist Courts had benefited entrenched elites, for example slave owners and businesses that sought to avoid government regulation. The Warren Court benefited blacks, the poor, those accused of crimes, those purveying sexually-oriented books and films, urban and suburban voters, and those who objected to government sponsored religious exercises.

The Court was part of an era in American history when many believed government could help to transform the nation into a more just, caring, and humane society and that the Court had an important role in this process. Today, many see this vision as arrogant and misguided. Others hope to see it re-emerge. At any rate, one way to understand the Warren Court is as a high water mark of an era of American history that ran from Franklin Roosevelt's New Deal to Lyndon Johnson's Great Society.

X. A Short Note on Political Transformation: 1948–2008

For about ten years after the Civil War and after the Reconstruction of the Southern states that enfranchised black male voters, the Republican party was dominant in the

Southern states. The national Republican party was strongly committed to the rights of Americans of African descent during this period. But white and black Republicans in the South faced political terrorism designed to remove them from political power. Self styled Southern "Conservatives" or Democrats began a campaign of violence that (together with other factors) helped to shift political control in many parts of the South. By 1878, much of the South had been "redeemed" from Republican rule. Though initially, in the early 1870s, the Congress passed laws to deal with the violence, crucial provisions dealing with private violence were gutted by the Supreme Court.

The election of 1876 was quite close and the outcome hinged on results in a few disputed Southern states. Republicans and Democrats reached what is known as the "Compromise of 1877." As David W. Blight explains in his book, *Race and Reunion, the Civil War in American Memory* (2001), many in both political parties, North and South, longed for reunion and peace and saw federal protection of Americans of African descent in the South as an impediment. This thinking helped to produce the 1877 compromise. As Blight explains,

> At the heart of the Compromise of 1877 was the understanding that [President] Hayes [the Republican victor under the compromise] would institute a "new Southern policy," one that would leave the South alone to deal with all questions of governance and race relations. As for black voting rights, even Grant himself had told his cabinet that he had come to see the 15th Amendment as a mistake, a law that "had done the Negro no good." By April, *The Nation* [a leading national magazine that had been pro-Republican] had rejoiced in the compromise and announced that the "negro will disappear from the field of national politics. Henceforth, the nation as a nation, will have nothing more to do with him." A reconciliationist vision mixed with racism stood triumphant ushering the emancipationist vision of the Civil war into an increasingly blurred past. (Blight, p. 138).

But, in spite of political terrorism and the results of the Compromise, Americans of African descent continued to vote in large numbers in many parts of the South until the turn of the century, when they were disfranchised by legislation and state constitutional amendments. However, the Democratic party, supported by much of the pre-Civil War Southern elite, remained mostly dominant.

In the 1890s, a Populist revolt (and in some states a Republican-Populist coalition) threatened Democratic control in the South. Political terrorists swung into action again. For example, in 1898 a racial massacre and coup ejected the duly elected city government in Wilmington, North Carolina. The event was the capstone of the white supremacy campaign in North Carolina. *See,* H. Leon Prater, Sr., *We have Taken A City,* in *Democracy Betrayed: The Wilimington Race Riot of 1898 and Its Legacy* (David S. Celelski & Timothy B. Tyson, eds. 1998).

Around 1900, many Southern states amended their post-Civil War constitutions and disfranchised black voters. By this point many Northern Republicans had given up on strong action to protect black rights in the South. Still, the Republican party remained the party historically most committed to the rights of Americans of African descent.

During and after the New Deal of the 1930s, the position of the Democratic party toward racial equality began to evolve. The national Democratic party gradually began to embrace equality for Americans of African descent. Under pressure from black leaders, Democratic President Franklin Roosevelt banned racial discrimination in defense plants. His successor, Democrat Harry Truman, created a President's Committee on Civil Rights.

Its 1947 Report, *To Secure These Rights*, condemned segregation—including segregation of the armed forces. In a February 1948 message to Congress, Truman announced his plan to de-segregate the armed forces by Executive Order. Truman's political adviser, Clark Clifford, had encouraged him to pursue black support in the North as a means to success in the 1948 presidential election.

In 1948, the Democratic party platform committed the party to eliminate "all racial, religious, and economic discrimination," and called for protection of racial and religious minorities in "the right to live, the right to work, the right to vote, the full and equal protection of the laws, on a basis of equality with all citizens, as guaranteed by the Constitution." Specifically, the platform demanded full and equal political participation and equal opportunity in employment and in the military. Delegates from several deep-South states walked out of the 1948 Democratic convention in protest.

The Democrats were not alone in support of civil rights. The 1948 Republican party platform advocated a constitutional amendment providing equal rights for women, denounced lynching, and announced that "equal opportunity to work and to advance in life" should never be denied "to any individual because of race, religion, color, or country of origin." The Republican platform also favored necessary federal legislation to protect the right to equality.

Faced with two major political party platforms committed to civil rights, disaffected Southern politicians launched a States Rights party and nominated Strom Thurmond of South Carolina for President. On civil rights, the States Rights party platform was clear: "We stand for segregation of the races and the racial integrity of each race...." The platform condemned the Democratic convention for its "civil rights program calling for the elimination of segregation," for calling for equal employment opportunity, and for calling for protection of voting rights.

Truman won the election, but Thurmond, the States' Rights candidate, carried South Carolina, Louisiana, Alabama, and Mississippi. The historically "Solid South" was beginning to break away from the Democrats.

Most Republicans and Democrats in the Senate would vote for the Civil Rights Act of 1964. Almost all Democrats outside of the South supported the Act as did a strong majority of Republicans. However, almost all Southern Democrats and all of the few Southern Republicans in Congress voted against the Act. In addition, Senator Barry Goldwater, soon to be the Republican nominee for President in 1964, opposed the Civil Rights Bill. Acting on the suggestion of his legal advisers, William Rehnquist (later Chief Justice of the United States) and Robert Bork (later Solicitor General and an unsuccessful Reagan nominee to the Court), Goldwater stressed constitutional objections to the Bill. It was he said, "a threat to the very essence of our system" and "a usurpation" of power "which 50 sovereign states have reserved for themselves."

The Bill eventually passed, though it was held up by Southern senators for 87 days—the longest filibuster in Senate history to that time. But Goldwater's opposition to it did not cease. Goldwater said that by attempting to legislate morality, the federal government had "incited hatred and violence" and that the Democratic party had "protected the Supreme Court in a reign of judicial tyranny."

Objectors did not just cite states' rights. They also objected to what they saw as interference with the rights of private property. Goldwater's adviser, William Rehnquist had written an opinion piece for an Arizona newspaper opposing a Phoenix civil rights ordinance, and Ronald Reagan, another Goldwater supporter, was active in the referendum campaign to repeal California's ban on racial discrimination in the sale of housing. (California voters agreed with Reagan.) By the time of his confirmation hearings for a post on the Court, Rehnquist testified that he had changed his view on public accommodation acts, as did many others.

Goldwater also opposed the 1965 Voting Rights Act as unnecessary. Goldwater's eloquent supporter, actor Ronald Reagan, agreed with him in opposing the Voting Rights Act.

The Voting Rights Act of 1965 greatly accelerated the restoration of the right to vote to Americans of African descent in the South. In Mississippi, for example, black registration rose from less than 10% of potential black voters in 1964 to almost 60% in 1968. In Alabama, it went from 24% to 57%. In the South as a whole, registration of Americans of African descent rose to a record 62%.

After the 1964 and 1965 Acts, many Southern Democrats began to see the Republican party in a new and much more favorable light. Goldwater supporters took over the tiny Georgia Republican party and evicted blacks from party positions. "The Negro has been read out of the Republican party of Georgia here today," a Georgia Goldwater spokesman announced. Strom Thurmond of South Carolina, the States Rights-segregationist candidate, switched parties. He said the switch was justified because the Democrats were engaged in a second Reconstruction. Thurmond joined Louisiana arch-Segregationist Leander Perez to host a Louisiana Goldwater rally.

After the passage of the Civil Rights Act of 1964, Lyndon Johnson told his aide Bill Moyers that he had delivered the South to the Republicans "for your lifetime and mine." In 1964, Goldwater carried five deep-South states and many former Democratic leaders in the Goldwater movement became Republicans.

In 1968 and 1972, seeing a political opening, Republican Richard Nixon pursued a "Southern Strategy," appealing to formerly Democratic Southern voters. In 1968, the Democratic presidential nominee was Johnson's Vice President, Hubert Humphrey, who had spearheaded the 1948 platform plank on Civil Rights. Humphrey carried only one Southern state, Texas. The rest were divided between Richard Nixon and the segregationist governor of Alabama, George Wallace, who had run a third party campaign. Wallace carried South Carolina, Alabama, Georgia, Mississippi, Louisiana, and Arkansas. Nixon carried the others.

Civil rights was not the only issue. Others included the Warren Court's criminal procedure and school prayer decisions, "law and order" generally, and the war in Vietnam. Nixon continued Goldwater's criticism of many Supreme Court decisions, including the rights of the accused and obscenity. Nixon called for Justices who would be "strict constructionists." After Richard Nixon's election as President in 1968, leaders of the Goldwater movement, including Robert Bork, assumed high positions in the Department of Justice. William Rehnquist became an Assistant Attorney General, helping to vet prospective Supreme Court nominees until Nixon nominated him to the Court.

The presidential campaign of 1968 paved the way for long term Republican electoral success in the South. In the 2000 presidential election, George W. Bush won the popular vote in every Southern state, with the possible exception of Florida. In 2004, the result was the same. In 2008, the deep-South remained Republican, though Barack Obama carried three Southern states: Virginia, North Carolina, and Florida.

Of course, over time, many changed their views on the 1964 and 1965 Civil Rights Acts. These included Democrats such as Robert Byrd and almost all leading Republicans. After an amendment to the Voting Rights Act, the Republican National Committee and the NAACP brought suits to create minority-majority districts in the South and elsewhere. An effect was to insure that more Americans of African descent were elected to Congress from the South. Another effect was to elect far more Republicans from the remaining heavily white districts.

Critiques of allegedly activist judges have been a Republican staple at least since the Goldwater campaign. Before that, Democratic President Franklin Roosevelt complained about judges injecting personal views into their decisions. He proposed expanding the Court as a remedy. Now in 2010, with a solidly "conservative" Court, "liberals" have begun to complain of "conservative" activism—striking down many federal and state laws—and some "conservative" intellectuals have begun to justify a much more active judicial role in returning to what they see as the original understanding of the Constitution.

As we have seen, political leaders who characterized themselves as "conservative" were often highly critical of "judicial activism"—the alleged lack of judicial deference to the decisions of the democratic process. Many "conservatives" treated the incorporation doctrine decisions of the Warren Court as an example of an unjustified judicial activism that undermined federalism. The statement of Ronald Reagan's Attorney General Ed Meese, *supra*, is one example, but Mr. Meese was not alone in his critique. An op-ed piece in the *Wall Street Journal* by Charles Rice attacked the incorporation doctrine under the headline "Flimflam Under the 14th." The sub-headline proclaimed "Doctrine is a fraud." George Will, the nationally syndicated columnist, wrote that the Supreme Court took a "radically wrong turn when it incorporated the 1st Amendment into the 14th." Senator John East of North Carolina, another critic of the doctrine, introduced a bill to cut off federal court jurisdiction of Bill of Rights questions. On the historical question of the purposes of the 14th Amendment, some progressive scholars agreed with conservative critics, though most did not agree that incorporation should be rolled back.

On the Warren Court, Justice Harlan was a critic of a number of incorporation decisions (applying jury trial to the states, for example), believing the "liberty" of the Due Process Clause protected both more and less than the Bill of Rights. He focused on "due process," not on the enumerated Bill of Rights guarantees. In *McDonald v. City of Chicago* (2010), a decision that incorporated of the 2nd Amendment as a limit on the states, Justice Stevens, in dissent, adopted a position similar to that of Justice Harlan—due process protected both more and less than the rights in the Bill of Rights. Still, Stevens believed that more Bill of Rights protections were included in due process than Justice Harlan had. Like the position that had been taken by Harlan, Stevens found the incorporation decision in *McDonald* insufficiently protective of the values of federalism and insufficiently deferential to the legislature. Justice Breyer, in a separate dissent, raised similar concerns.

Four of the Justices, those appointed by Ronald Reagan and George W. Bush, supported incorporation of almost all the Bill of Rights guarantees, cited the Warren Court approach with approval, and extended incorporation to the Right to Bear Arms. Following Warren Court decisions, they rejected the idea that a right need not be incorporated if a civilized society could exist without it. Quoting a decision by Justice Brennan, they held that the meaning of the guarantees must be the same in both federal and state cases.

Justice Thomas concurred, but he based incorporation on the Privileges or Immunities Clause, not on the Due Process Clause. Both he and Justice Scalia continued to criticize, for example, the use of the Due Process Clause to protect less textually explicit rights, such as the private sexual practices of consenting adults. They favored a test that would limit protected liberties to those with a long historical pedigree and, sometimes it seems, consistent with existing practices at the time of framing and ratification—at least, when those practices continued long after ratification.

XI. The Roberts Court and Incorporation

A. The Right to Bear Arms: A Personal Right Limiting the Federal Government

District of Columbia v. Heller
554 U.S. ___, 128 S.Ct. 2783 (2008)

[Majority: Scalia, Roberts (C.J.), Kennedy, Thomas, and Alito. Dissenting: Stevens, Breyer, Souter, and Ginsburg.]

Justice Scalia delivered the opinion of the Court.

We consider whether a District of Columbia prohibition on the possession of usable handguns in the home violates the 2nd Amendment to the Constitution.

I. The District of Columbia generally prohibits the possession of handguns. It is a crime to carry an unregistered firearm, and the registration of handguns is prohibited. Wholly apart from that prohibition, no person may carry a handgun without a license....

Respondent Dick Heller is a D.C. special police officer authorized to carry a handgun while on duty at the Federal Judicial Center. He applied for a registration certificate for a handgun that he wished to keep at home, but the District refused. He thereafter filed a lawsuit in the Federal District Court for the District of Columbia seeking, on 2nd Amendment grounds, to enjoin the city from enforcing the bar on the registration of handguns, the licensing requirement insofar as it prohibits the carrying of a firearm in the home without a license, and the trigger-lock requirement insofar as it prohibits the use of "functional firearms within the home."...

II-A. The 2nd Amendment provides: "A well regulated Militia, being necessary to the security of a free State, the right of the people to keep and bear Arms, shall not be infringed." In interpreting this text, we are guided by the principle that "[t]he Constitution was written to be understood by the voters; its words and phrases were used in their normal and ordinary as distinguished from technical meaning." *United States v. Sprague* (1931); see also *Gibbons v. Ogden* (1824)....

The 2nd Amendment is naturally divided into two parts: its prefatory clause and its operative clause. The former does not limit the latter grammatically, but rather announces a purpose.... Although this structure of the 2nd Amendment is unique in our Constitution, other legal documents of the founding era, particularly individual-rights provisions of state constitutions, commonly included a prefatory statement of purpose....

Logic demands that there be a link between the stated purpose and the command....

1. Operative Clause.

a. "Right of the People." The first salient feature of the operative clause is that it codifies a "right of the people." The unamended Constitution and the Bill of Rights use the phrase "right of the people" two other times, in the 1st Amendment's Assembly-and-Petition Clause and in the 4th Amendment's Search-and-Seizure Clause....

Three provisions of the Constitution refer to "the people" in a context other than "rights"—the famous preamble ("We the people"), § 2 of Article I (providing that "the people" will choose members of the House), and the 10th Amendment (providing that those powers not given the Federal Government remain with "the States" or "the people"). Those provisions arguably refer to "the people" acting collectively — but they deal with the exercise or reservation of powers, not rights. Nowhere else in the Constitution does a "right" attributed to "the people" refer to anything other than an individual right....

What is more, in all six other provisions of the Constitution that mention "the people," the term unambiguously refers to all members of the political community, not an unspecified subset....

As we will describe below, the "militia" in colonial America consisted of a subset of "the people"—those who were male, able bodied, and within a certain age range. Reading the 2nd Amendment as protecting only the right to "keep and bear Arms" in an organized militia therefore fits poorly with the operative clause's description of the holder of that right as "the people."

We start therefore with a strong presumption that the 2nd Amendment right is exercised individually and belongs to all Americans.

b. "Keep and bear Arms." We move now from the holder of the right—"the people"—to the substance of the right: "to keep and bear Arms."...

The phrase "keep arms" was not prevalent in the written documents of the founding period that we have found, but there are a few examples, all of which favor viewing the right to "keep Arms" as an individual right unconnected with militia service. William Blackstone, for example, wrote that Catholics convicted of not attending service in the Church of England suffered certain penalties, one of which was that they were not permitted to "keep arms in their houses."...

In *Muscarello v. United States* (1998), in the course of analyzing the meaning of "carries a firearm" in a federal criminal statute, Justice Ginsburg wrote that "[s]urely a most familiar meaning is, as the Constitution's 2nd Amendment ... indicate[s]: 'wear, bear, or carry ... upon the person or in the clothing or in a pocket, for the purpose ... of being armed and ready for offensive or defensive action in a case of conflict with another person.'"... Although the phrase implies that the carrying of the weapon is for the purpose of "offensive or defensive action," it in no way connotes participation in a structured military organization.

From our review of founding-era sources, we conclude that this natural meaning was also the meaning that "bear arms" had in the 18th century.... Nine state constitutional provisions written in the 18th century or the first two decades of the 19th, which enshrined a right of citizens to "bear arms in defense of themselves and the state" or "bear arms in defense of himself and the state."...

c. Meaning of the Operative Clause. Putting all of these textual elements together, we find that they guarantee the individual right to possess and carry weapons in case of confrontation.... We look to this because it has always been widely understood that the 2nd Amendment, like the 1st and 4th Amendments, codified a *pre-existing* right.... As we said in *United States v. Cruikshank* (1876), "[t]his is not a right granted by the Constitution. Neither is it in any manner dependent upon that instrument for its existence."...

By the time of the founding, the right to have arms had become fundamental for English subjects. Blackstone, whose works, we have said, "constituted the preeminent authority on English law for the founding generation," *Alden v. Maine* (1999), cited the arms provision of the Bill of Rights as one of the fundamental rights of Englishmen.... It was, he said, "the natural right of resistance and self-preservation," and "the right of having and using arms for self-preservation and defence[.]"...

In the tumultuous decades of the 1760's and 1770's, the Crown began to disarm the inhabitants of the most rebellious areas.... A New York article of April 1769 said that "[i]t is a natural right which the people have reserved to themselves, confirmed by the Bill of Rights, to keep arms for their own defence."...

There seems to us no doubt, on the basis of both text and history, that the 2nd Amendment conferred an individual right to keep and bear arms. Of course the right was not unlimited, just as the 1st Amendment's right of free speech was not. Thus, we do not read the 2nd Amendment to protect the right of citizens to carry arms for *any sort* of confrontation, just as we do not read the 1st Amendment to protect the right of citizens to speak for *any purpose*....

2. Prefatory Clause....

a. "Well-Regulated Militia." In *United States v. Miller* (1939), we explained that "the Militia comprised all males physically capable of acting in concert for the common defense." That definition comports with founding-era sources....

Unlike armies and navies, which Congress is given the power to create ("to raise ... Armies"; "to provide ... a Navy," Art. I, §8, cls. 12–13), the militia is assumed by Article I already to be *in existence*. Congress is given the power to "provide for calling forth the militia," §8, cl. 15; and the power not to create, but to "organiz[e]" it[.] ... This is fully consistent with the ordinary definition of the militia as all able-bodied men. From that pool, Congress has plenary power to organize the units that will make up an effective fighting force....

b. "Security of a Free State." ... There are many reasons why the militia was thought to be "necessary to the security of a free state." First, of course, it is useful in repelling invasions and suppressing insurrections. Second, it renders large standing armies unnecessary[.] ... Third, when the able-bodied men of a nation are trained in arms and organized, they are better able to resist tyranny.

3. Relationship between Prefatory Clause and Operative Clause....

Does the preface fit with an operative clause that creates an individual right to keep and bear arms? It fits perfectly, once one knows the history that the founding generation knew[.] ... That history showed that the way tyrants had eliminated a militia consisting of all the able-bodied men was not by banning the militia but simply by taking away the people's arms[.] ...

It is therefore entirely sensible that the 2nd Amendment's prefatory clause announces the purpose for which the right was codified: to prevent elimination of the militia.... [M]ost [Americans] undoubtedly thought it even more important for self-defense and hunting. But the threat that the new Federal Government would destroy the citizens' militia by taking away their arms was the reason that right ... was codified in a written Constitution....

II-B. Our interpretation is confirmed by analogous arms-bearing rights in state constitutions that preceded and immediately followed adoption of the 2nd Amendment. Four States adopted analogues to the Federal 2nd Amendment in the period between independence and the ratification of the Bill of Rights.... Between 1789 and 1820, nine States adopted 2nd Amendment analogues. Four of them ... referred to the right of the people to "bear arms in defence of themselves and the State." ... That of the nine state constitutional protections for the right to bear arms enacted immediately after 1789 at least seven unequivocally protected an individual citizen's right to self-defense is strong evidence that that is how the founding generation conceived of the right....

II-D. We now address how the 2nd Amendment was interpreted from immediately after its ratification through the end of the 19th Century.... As we will show, virtually all interpreters of the 2nd Amendment in the century after its enactment interpreted the amendment as we do.

1. Post-ratification Commentary....

In 1825, William Rawle, a prominent lawyer who had been a member of the Pennsylvania Assembly that ratified the Bill of Rights, published an influential treatise, which analyzed the 2nd Amendment as follows:

> ... The prohibition is general. No clause in the constitution could by any rule of construction be conceived to give to congress a power to disarm the people....

Antislavery advocates routinely invoked the right to bear arms for self-defense. Joel Tiffany, for example, ... wrote that "the right to keep and bear arms, also implies the right to use them if necessary in self defence[.]" ... A Treatise on the Unconstitutionality of American Slavery (1849). In his famous Senate speech about the 1856 "Bleeding Kansas" conflict, Charles Sumner proclaimed:

> ... Never was this efficient weapon more needed in just self-defence, than now in Kansas, and at least one article in our National Constitution must be blotted out, before the complete right to it can in any way be impeached....

2. Pre-Civil War Case Law

The 19th-century cases that interpreted the 2nd Amendment universally support an individual right unconnected to militia service. In *Houston v. Moore* (1820), this Court held that States have concurrent power over the militia, at least where not preempted by Congress. [Both] the Court and [Justice] Story [dissenting] derived the States' power over the militia from the nonexclusive nature of federal power, not from the 2nd Amendment, whose preamble merely "confirms and illustrates" the importance of the militia.... In the famous fugitive-slave case of *Johnson v. Tompkins* (CC Pa. 1833), [Justice] Baldwin, sitting as a circuit judge, cited both the 2nd Amendment and the Pennsylvania analogue for his conclusion that a citizen has "a right to carry arms in defence of his property or person, and to use them, if either were assailed[.] ..."

In *Nunn v. State* (Ga. 1846), the Georgia Supreme Court construed the 2nd Amendment as protecting the "*natural* right of self-defence" ...:

> The right of the whole people, ... and not militia only, to keep and bear *arms* ... shall not be *infringed*, curtailed, or broken in upon, in the smallest degree; and all this for the important end to be attained: the rearing up and qualifying a well-regulated militia, so vitally necessary to the security of a free State....

3. Post-Civil War Legislation....

Blacks were routinely disarmed by Southern States after the Civil War. Those who opposed these injustices frequently stated that they infringed blacks' constitutional right to keep and bear arms.... A joint congressional Report decried:

> [I]n some parts of [South Carolina], armed parties are, without proper authority, engaged in seizing all firearms found in the hands of the freemen. Such conduct is in clear and direct violation of their personal rights as guaranteed by the Constitution....

4. Post-Civil War Commentators.

Every late-19th-century legal scholar that we have read interpreted the 2nd Amendment to secure an individual right unconnected with militia service. The most famous was the judge and professor Thomas Cooley ...:

> The alternative to a standing army is "a well-regulated militia," but this cannot exist unless the people are trained to bearing arms....

III. Like most rights, the right secured by the 2nd Amendment is not unlimited.... [N]othing in our opinion should be taken to cast doubt on longstanding prohibitions on the possession of firearms by felons and the mentally ill, or laws forbidding the carrying of firearms in sensitive places such as schools and government buildings, or laws imposing conditions and qualifications on the commercial sale of arms....

IV. ... As we have said, the law totally bans handgun possession in the home. It also requires that any lawful firearm in the home be disassembled or bound by a trigger lock, at all times, rendering it inoperable.

As the quotations earlier in this opinion demonstrate, the inherent right of self-defense has been central to the 2nd Amendment right.... Under any of the standards of scrutiny that we have applied to enumerated constitutional rights, banning from the home "the most preferred firearm in the nation to 'keep' and use for protection of one's home and family," would fail constitutional muster....

We are aware of the problem of handgun violence in this country.... The Constitution leaves the District of Columbia a variety of tools for combating that problem, including some measures regulating handguns. But the enshrinement of constitutional rights necessarily takes certain policy choices off the table. These include the absolute prohibition of handguns held and used for self-defense in the home. Undoubtedly, some think that the 2nd Amendment is outmoded in a society where our standing army is the pride of our Nation, where well-trained police forces provide personal security, and where gun violence is a serious problem. That is perhaps debatable, but what is not debatable is that it is not the role of this Court to pronounce the 2nd Amendment extinct.

We affirm the judgment of the Court of Appeals. *It is so ordered.*

Justice Stevens, with whom Justice Souter, Justice Ginsburg, and Justice Breyer join, dissenting.

The question presented by this case is not whether the 2nd Amendment protects a "collective right" or an "individual right." Surely it protects a right that can be enforced by individuals. But a conclusion that the 2nd Amendment protects an individual right does not tell us anything about the scope of that right....

Whether it also protects the right to possess and use guns for nonmilitary purposes like hunting and personal self-defense is the question presented by this case. The text of the Amendment, its history, and our decision in *United States v. Miller* (1939), provide a clear answer to that question.

The 2nd Amendment was adopted to protect the right of the people of each of the several States to maintain a well-regulated militia. It was a response to concerns raised during the ratification of the Constitution that the power of Congress to disarm the state militias and create a national standing army posed an intolerable threat to the sovereignty of the several States. Neither the text of the Amendment nor the arguments advanced by its proponents evidenced the slightest interest in limiting any legislature's authority to regulate private civilian uses of firearms....

The view of the Amendment we took in *Miller*—that it protects the right to keep and bear arms for certain military purposes, but that it does not curtail the Legislature's power to regulate the nonmilitary use and ownership of weapons—is both the most natural reading of the Amendment's text and the interpretation most faithful to the history of its adoption.

Since our decision in *Miller*, hundreds of judges have relied on the view of the Amendment we endorsed there; we ourselves affirmed it in 1980. See *Lewis v. United States* (1980).

I. ... *"A well regulated Militia, being necessary to the security of a free State"*

The preamble to the 2nd Amendment makes three important points. It identifies the preservation of the militia as the Amendment's purpose; it explains that the militia is necessary to the security of a free State; and it recognizes that the militia must be "well regulated." In all three respects it is comparable to provisions in several State Declarations of Rights that were adopted roughly contemporaneously with the Declaration of Independence. Those state provisions highlight the importance members of the founding generation attached to the maintenance of state militias; they also underscore the profound fear shared by many in that era of the dangers posed by standing armies....

The preamble thus both sets forth the object of the Amendment and informs the meaning of the remainder of its text. Such text should not be treated as mere surplusage, for "[i]t cannot be presumed that any clause in the constitution is intended to be without effect." *Marbury v. Madison* (1803)....

"The right of the people"

The centerpiece of the Court's textual argument is its insistence that the words "the people" as used in the 2nd Amendment must have the same meaning, and protect the same class of individuals, as when they are used in the 1st and 4th Amendments.... But the Court *itself* reads the 2nd Amendment to protect a "subset" significantly narrower than the class of persons protected by the 1st and 4th Amendments; when it finally drills down on the substantive meaning of the 2nd Amendment, the Court limits the protected class to "law-abiding, responsible citizens." ... The Court offers no way to harmonize its conflicting pronouncements.

The Court ... overlooks the significance of the way the Framers used the phrase "the people" in these constitutional provisions. In the 1st Amendment, no words define the class of individuals entitled to speak, to publish, or to worship; in that Amendment it is only the right peaceably to assemble, and to petition the Government for a redress of grievances, that is described as a right of "the people." These rights contemplate collective action. While the right peaceably to assemble protects the individual rights of those persons participating in the assembly, its concern is with action engaged in by members of a group, rather than any single individual....

Similarly, the words "the people" in the 2nd Amendment refer back to the object announced in the Amendment's preamble. They remind us that it is the collective action of individuals having a duty to serve in the militia that the text directly protects....

"To keep and bear Arms"

... The Amendment's use of the term "keep" in no way contradicts the military meaning conveyed by the phrase "bear arms" and the Amendment's preamble. To the contrary, a number of state militia laws in effect at the time of the 2nd Amendment's drafting used the term "keep" to describe the requirement that militia members store their arms at their homes, ready to be used for service when necessary....

This reading is confirmed by the fact that the clause protects only one right, rather than two. It does not describe a right "to keep arms" and a separate right "to bear arms." Rather, the single right that it does describe is both a duty and a right to have arms available and ready for military service, and to use them for military purposes when necessary....

II. ... Two themes relevant to our current interpretive task ran through the debates on the original Constitution. "On the one hand, there was a widespread fear that a national standing Army posed an intolerable threat to individual liberty and to the sovereignty of the separate States." *Perpich v. Department of Defense* (1990).... On the other hand, the Framers recognized the dangers inherent in relying on inadequately trained militia members "as the primary means of providing for the common defense[.]"... In order to respond to those twin concerns, a compromise was reached: Congress would be authorized to raise and support a national Army, and Navy, and also to organize, arm, discipline, and provide for the calling forth of "the Militia."... [T]he States respectively would retain the right to appoint the officers and to train the militia in accordance with the discipline prescribed by Congress.

But the original Constitution's retention of the militia and its creation of divided authority over that body did not prove sufficient to allay fears about the dangers posed by a standing army.... As George Mason argued during the debates in Virginia on the ratification of the original Constitution:

> The militia may be here destroyed by that method which has been practiced in other parts of the world before; that is, by rendering them useless—by disarming them....

This sentiment was echoed at a number of state ratification conventions ...; The proposed amendments sent by the States of Virginia, North Carolina, and New York focused on the importance of preserving the state militias and reiterated the dangers posed by standing armies. New Hampshire sent a proposal that differed significantly from the others; while also invoking the dangers of a standing army, it suggested that the Constitution should more broadly protect the use and possession of weapons, without tying such a guarantee expressly to the maintenance of the militia. The States of Maryland, Pennsylvania, and Massachusetts sent no relevant proposed amendments to Congress, but in each of those States a minority of the delegates advocated related amendments. While the Maryland minority proposals were exclusively concerned with standing armies and conscientious objectors, the unsuccessful proposals in both Massachusetts and Pennsylvania would have protected a more broadly worded right, less clearly tied to service in a state militia. Faced with all of these options, it is telling that James Madison chose to craft the 2nd Amendment as he did.

Madison, charged with the task of assembling the proposals for amendments sent by the ratifying States, was the principal draftsman of the 2nd Amendment. He had before him, or at the very least would have been aware of, all of these proposed formulations....

With all of these sources upon which to draw, it is strikingly significant that Madison's first draft omitted any mention of nonmilitary use or possession of weapons. Rather, his original draft repeated the essence of the two proposed amendments sent by Virginia ... "The right of the people to keep and bear arms shall not be infringed; a well armed, and well regulated militia being the best security of a free country....

[I]t is reasonable to assume that all participants in the drafting process were fully aware of the other formulations that would have protected civilian use and possession of weapons and that their choice to craft the Amendment as they did represented a rejection of those alternative formulations....

III. Although it gives short shrift to the drafting history of the 2nd Amendment, the Court dwells at length on four other sources....

The Court's reliance on Article VII of the 1689 English Bill of Rights—which, like most of the evidence offered by the Court today, was considered in *Miller*—is misguided both because Article VII was enacted in response to different concerns from those that motivated the Framers of the 2nd Amendment, and because the guarantees of the two provisions were by no means coextensive....

The Court's reliance on Blackstone's Commentaries on the Laws of England is unpersuasive for the same reason as its reliance on the English Bill of Rights. Blackstone's invocation of "'the natural right of resistance and self-preservation,'" and "'the right of having and using arms for self-preservation and defence'" referred specifically to Article VII in the English Bill of Rights....

The Court also excerpts ... commentary by a number of additional scholars, some near in time to the framing and others post-dating it by close to a century.... Their views are not altogether clear, they tended to collapse the 2nd Amendment with Article VII of the English Bill of Rights, and they appear to have been unfamiliar with the drafting history of the 2nd Amendment....

The Court suggests that by the post-Civil War period, the 2nd Amendment was understood to secure a right to firearm use and ownership for purely private purposes like personal self-defense.... All of the statements the Court cites were made long after the framing of the Amendment and cannot possibly supply any insight into the intent of the Framers; and all were made during pitched political debates, so that they are better characterized as advocacy than good-faith attempts at constitutional interpretation....

IV. ... In 1792, the year after the Amendment was ratified, Congress passed a statute that purported to establish "an Uniform Militia throughout the United States." The statute commanded every able-bodied white male citizen between the ages of 18 and 45 to be enrolled therein and to "provide himself with a good musket or firelock[.]" ... The statute ... confirmed the way those in the founding generation viewed firearm ownership: as a duty linked to military service....

[T]he dominant understanding of the 2nd Amendment's inapplicability to private gun ownership continued well into the 20th century. The first two federal laws directly restricting civilian use and possession of firearms—the 1927 Act prohibiting mail delivery of ... firearms capable of being concealed on the person," and the 1934 Act prohibiting the possession of sawed-off [firearms] and machine guns—were enacted over minor 2nd Amendment objections dismissed by the vast majority of the legislators who participated in the debates....

Indeed, the 2nd Amendment was not even mentioned ... during the legislative proceedings that led to the passage of the 1934 Act.... [T]he *Miller* Court unanimously concluded that the 2nd Amendment did not apply to the possession of a firearm that did not have "some reasonable relationship to the preservation or efficiency of a well regulated militia."...

V. The Court concludes its opinion by declaring that it is not the proper role of this Court to change the meaning of rights "enshrine[d]" in the Constitution. But the right the Court announces was not "enshrined" in the 2nd Amendment by the Framers; it is the product of today's law-changing decision....

Until today, it has been understood that legislatures may regulate the civilian use and misuse of firearms so long as they do not interfere with the preservation of a well-regulated militia.... For these reasons, I respectfully dissent.

Justice Breyer, with whom Justice Stevens, Justice Souter, and Justice Ginsburg join, dissenting.

I. ... The majority's conclusion is wrong for two independent reasons. The first reason is that set forth by Justice Stevens—namely, that the 2nd Amendment protects militia-related, not self-defense-related, interests....

The second independent reason is that the protection the Amendment provides is not absolute.... I shall show that the District's law is consistent with the 2nd Amendment even if that Amendment is interpreted as protecting a wholly separate interest in individual self-defense....

The law is tailored to the urban crime problem in that it is local in scope ...; the law concerns handguns, which are specially linked to urban gun deaths and injuries ...; and at the same time, the law imposes a burden upon gun owners that seems proportionately no greater than restrictions in existence at the time the 2nd Amendment was adopted. In these circumstances, the District's law falls within the zone that the 2nd Amendment leaves open to regulation by legislatures....

III.... The majority is wrong when it says that the District's law is unconstitutional "[u]nder any of the standards of scrutiny that we have applied to enumerated constitutional rights." ... It certainly would not be unconstitutional under, for example, a "rational basis" standard, ... *Heller v. Doe* (1993). The law at issue here, which in part seeks to prevent gun-related accidents, at least bears a "rational relationship" to that "legitimate" life-saving objective....

[Heller] proposes that the Court adopt a "strict scrutiny" test.... But the majority implicitly, and appropriately, rejects that suggestion by broadly approving a set of laws—prohibitions on concealed weapons, forfeiture by criminals of the 2nd Amendment right, prohibitions on firearms in certain locales, and governmental regulation of commercial firearm sales....

[A]lmost every gun-control regulation will seek to advance ... a "primary concern of every government—a concern for the safety and indeed the lives of its citizens." *United States v. Salerno* (1987). The Court has deemed that interest, as well as "the Government's general interest in preventing crime," to be "compelling,".... Thus, any attempt *in theory* to apply strict scrutiny to gun regulations will *in practice* turn into an interest-balancing inquiry, with the interests protected by the 2nd Amendment on one side and the governmental public-safety concerns on the other....

I would simply adopt such an interest-balancing inquiry explicitly. The fact that important interests lie on both sides of the constitutional equation suggests that review of gun-control regulation is not a context in which a court should effectively presume either constitutionality (as in rational-basis review) or unconstitutionality (as in strict scrutiny). Rather ... the Court generally asks whether the statute burdens a protected interest in a way or to an extent that is out of proportion to the statute's salutary effects upon other important governmental interests....

In applying this kind of standard the Court normally defers to a legislature's empirical judgment in matters where a legislature is likely to have greater expertise and greater institutional fact-finding capacity....

IV. ... In determining whether this regulation violates the 2nd Amendment, I shall ask how the statute seeks to further the governmental interests that it serves, how the statute burdens the interests that the 2nd Amendment seeks to protect, and whether there are practical less burdensome ways of furthering those interests....

IV-A-1. First, consider the facts as the legislature saw them when it adopted the District statute. [T]he major substantive goal of the District's handgun restriction is "to reduce the potentiality for gun-related crimes and gun-related deaths from occurring within the District of Columbia." The committee concluded, ... that "[t]he easy availability of firearms in the United States has been a major factor contributing to the drastic increase in gun-related violence and crime over the past 40 years." It reported to the Council "startling statistics," regarding gun-related crime, accidents, and deaths....

The committee informed the Council that guns were "responsible for 69 deaths in this country each day," for a total of "[a]pproximately 25,000 gun-deaths ... each year," along with an additional 200,000 gun-related injuries.... And according to the committee, "[f]or every intruder stopped by a homeowner with a firearm, there are 4 gun-related accidents within the home."

In respect to local crime, the committee observed that there were 285 murders in the District during 1974—a record number.... Citing an article from the American Journal of Psychiatry, the committee reported that "[m]ost murders are committed by previously law-abiding citizens, in situations where spontaneous violence is generated by anger, passion or intoxication, and where the killer and victim are acquainted." ...

The committee report furthermore presented statistics strongly correlating handguns with crime. Of the 285 murders in the District in 1974, 155 were committed with handguns.... Nor were handguns only linked to murders, as statistics showed that they were used in roughly 60% of robberies and 26% of assaults....

IV-A-2. [The District of Columbia], and their *amici*, have presented us with more recent statistics that tell much the same story that the committee report told 30 years ago....

From 1993 to 1997, there were 180,533 firearm-related deaths in the United States, an average of over 36,000 per year.... More male teenagers die from firearms than from all natural causes combined....

Statistics further suggest that urban areas, such as the District, have different experiences with gun-related death, injury, and crime, than do less densely populated rural areas. A disproportionate amount of violent and property crimes occur in urban areas, and urban criminals are more likely than other offenders to use a firearm during the commission of a violent crime....

IV-A-3. [Heller] and his many *amici* for the most part do not disagree about the *figures* set forth in the preceding subsection, but they do disagree strongly with the District's *predictive judgment* that a ban on handguns will help solve the crime and accident problems that those figures disclose....

[T]his Court, in 1st Amendment cases applying intermediate scrutiny, has said that our "sole obligation" in reviewing a legislature's "predictive judgments" is "to assure that ..." the legislature "has drawn reasonable inferences based on substantial evidence." *Turner Broadcasting System, Inc. v. FCC* (1997). [T]he District's judgment, while open to question, is nevertheless supported by "substantial evidence."

There is no cause here to depart from the standard set forth in *Turner*, for the District's decision represents the kind of empirically based judgment that legislatures, not courts, are best suited to make. See *Nixon v. Shrink Missouri Government PAC* (2000) (Breyer, J., concurring)....

IV-B. I next assess the extent to which the District's law burdens the interests that the 2nd Amendment seeks to protect....

IV-B-3. The District's law does prevent a resident from keeping a loaded handgun in his home. And it consequently makes it more difficult for the householder to use the handgun for self-defense in the home against intruders, such as burglars. As the Court of Appeals noted, statistics suggest that handguns are the most popular weapon for self defense.... To that extent the law burdens to some degree an interest in self-defense that for present purposes I have assumed the Amendment seeks to further.

IV-C. In weighing needs and burdens, we must take account of the possibility that there are reasonable, but less restrictive alternatives.... See *Nixon* (Breyer, J., concurring).... Here I see none....

[T]he ban's very objective is to reduce significantly the number of handguns in the District, say, for example, by allowing a law enforcement officer immediately to assume that *any* handgun he sees is an *illegal* handgun. And there is no plausible way to achieve that objective other than to ban the guns....

[T]he very attributes that make handguns particularly useful for self-defense are also what make them particularly dangerous. That they are easy to hold and control means that they are easier for children to use. That they are maneuverable and permit a free hand likely contributes to the fact that they are by far the firearm of choice for crimes such as rape and robbery. That they are small and light makes them easy to steal, and concealable....

If it is indeed the case, as the District believes, that the number of guns contributes to the number of gun-related crimes, accidents, and deaths, then, although there may be less restrictive, *less effective* substitutes for an outright ban, there is no less restrictive *equivalent* of an outright ban.

Licensing restrictions would not similarly reduce the handgun population, and the District may reasonably fear that even if guns are initially restricted to law-abiding citizens, they might be stolen and thereby placed in the hands of criminals....

IV-D. The upshot is that the District's objectives are compelling; its predictive judgments as to its law's tendency to achieve those objectives are adequately supported; the law does impose a burden upon any self-defense interest that the Amendment seeks to secure; and there is no clear less restrictive alternative.... Does the District's law *disproportionately* burden Amendment-protected interests? Several considerations, taken together, convince me that it does not.

First, the District law is tailored to the life-threatening problems it attempts to address....

Second, the self-defense interest in maintaining loaded handguns in the home to shoot intruders is not the *primary* interest, but at most a subsidiary interest, that the 2nd Amendment seeks to serve....

Further, any self-defense interest at the time of the Framing could not have focused exclusively upon urban-crime related dangers....

Third, irrespective of what the Framers *could have thought*, we know what they *did think*. Samuel Adams, who lived in Boston, advocated a constitutional amendment that would have precluded the Constitution from ever being "construed" to "prevent the people of the United States, who are peaceable citizens, from keeping their own arms." Samuel Adams doubtless knew that the Massachusetts Constitution contained somewhat similar protection. And he doubtless knew that Massachusetts law prohibited Bostonians from keeping loaded guns in the house. So how could Samuel Adams have advocated such protection *unless* he thought that the protection was *consistent* with local regulation that seriously impeded urban residents from using their arms against intruders?...

Of course the District's law and the colonial Boston law are not identical. But the Boston law disabled an even wider class of weapons (indeed, all firearms). And its existence shows at the least that local legislatures could impose (as here) serious restrictions on the right to use firearms....

Fourth, a contrary view, as embodied in today's decision, will have unfortunate consequences....

[T]he majority's decision threatens severely to limit the ability of more knowledgeable, democratically elected officials to deal with gun-related problems.... I cannot understand how one can take from the elected branches of government the right to decide whether to insist upon a handgun-free urban populace in a city now facing a serious crime problem....

VI. For these reasons, I conclude that the District's measure is a proportionate, not a disproportionate, response to the compelling concerns that led the District to adopt it....

B. The Right to Bear Arms: An Incorporated Right

McDonald v. City of Chicago
561 U. S. ___, 130 S.Ct. 3020 (2010)

Justice Alito announced the judgment of the Court and delivered the opinion of the Court with respect to Parts I, II-A, II-B, II-D, III-A, and III-B, in which the Chief Justice, Justice Scalia, Justice Kennedy, and Justice Thomas join, and an opinion with respect to Parts II-C, IV, and V, in which the Chief Justice, Justice Scalia, and Justice Kennedy join. [Justices Stevens, Breyer, Ginsburg, and Sotomayor dissented.]

Two years ago, in *District of Columbia v. Heller* (2008), we held that the 2nd Amendment protects the right to keep and bear arms for the purpose of self-defense, and we struck down a District of Columbia law that banned the possession of handguns in the home. The city of Chicago (City) and the village of Oak Park, a Chicago suburb, have laws that are similar to the District of Columbia's, but Chicago and Oak Park argue that their laws are constitutional because the 2nd Amendment has no application to the States. We have previously held that most of the provisions of the Bill of Rights apply with full force to both the Federal Government and the States. Applying the standard that is well established in our case law, we hold that the 2nd Amendment right is fully applicable to the States.

I. Otis McDonald, Adam Orlov, Colleen Lawson, and David Lawson (Chicago petitioners) are Chicago residents who would like to keep handguns in their homes for self defense but are prohibited from doing so by Chicago's firearms laws....

Chicago enacted its handgun ban to protect its residents "from the loss of property and injury or death from firearms." The Chicago petitioners and their *amici*, however, argue that the handgun ban has left them vulnerable to criminals. Chicago Police Department statistics, we are told, reveal that the City's handgun murder rate has actually increased since the ban was enacted and that Chicago residents now face one of the highest murder rates in the country and rates of other violent crimes that exceed the average in comparable cities.

Several of the Chicago petitioners have been the targets of threats and violence. For instance, Otis McDonald, who is in his late seventies, lives in a high-crime neighborhood. He is a community activist involved with alternative policing strategies, and his efforts to improve his neighborhood have subjected him to violent threats from drug dealers....

After our decision in *Heller*, the Chicago petitioners and two groups filed suit against the City in the United States District Court for the Northern District of Illinois....

II. A. Petitioners argue that the Chicago and Oak Park laws violate the right to keep and bear arms for two reasons. Petitioners' primary submission is that this right is among the "privileges or immunities of citizens of the United States" and that the narrow interpretation of the Privileges or Immunities Clause adopted in the *Slaughter-House Cases* (1873) should now be rejected. As a secondary argument, petitioners contend that the 14th Amendment's Due Process Clause "incorporates" the 2nd Amendment right.

Chicago and Oak Park (municipal respondents) maintain that a right set out in the Bill of Rights applies to the States only if that right is an indispensable attribute of *any* "'civilized'" legal system. If it is possible to imagine a civilized country that does not recognize the right, the municipal respondents tell us, then that right is not protected by due process. And since there are civilized countries that ban or strictly regulate the private possession of handguns, the municipal respondents maintain that due process does not preclude such measures. [W]e begin by recounting this Court's analysis over the years of the relationship between the provisions of the Bill of Rights and the States.

II. B. The Bill of Rights, including the 2nd Amendment, originally applied only to the Federal Government.... The constitutional Amendments adopted in the aftermath of the Civil War fundamentally altered our country's federal system. The provision at issue in this case, §1 of the 14th Amendment, provides, among other things, that a State may not abridge "the privileges or immunities of citizens of the United States" or deprive "any person of life, liberty, or property, without due process of law."

Four years after the adoption of the 14th Amendment, this Court was asked to interpret the Amendment's reference to "the privileges or immunities of citizens of the United States."... Justice Samuel Miller's opinion for the Court *Slaughter-House Cases* concluded that the Privileges or Immunities Clause protects only those rights "which owe their existence to the Federal government, its National character, its Constitution, or its laws." The Court held that other fundamental rights—rights that predated the creation of the Federal Government and that "the State governments were created to establish and secure"—were not protected by the Clause.

In drawing a sharp distinction between the rights of federal and state citizenship, the Court relied on two principal arguments. First, the Court emphasized that the 14th Amendment's Privileges or Immunities Clause spoke of "the privileges or immunities of *citizens of the United States*," and the Court contrasted this phrasing with the wording in the first sentence of the 14th Amendment and in the Privileges and Immunities Clause of Article IV, both of which refer to *state* citizenship. Second, the Court stated that a contrary reading would "radically chang[e] the whole theory of the relations of the State and Federal governments to each other and of both these governments to the people," and the Court refused to conclude that such a change had been made "in the absence of language which expresses such a purpose too clearly to admit of doubt."...

Finding no constitutional protection against state intrusion of the kind envisioned by the Louisiana statute [one state authorized slaughterhouse open to all butchers], the Court upheld the statute. Four Justices dissented.... Justice Bradley's dissent observed that "we are not bound to resort to implication ... to find an authoritative declaration of some of the most important privileges and immunities of citizens of the United States. It is in the Constitution itself." Justice Bradley would have construed the Privileges or Immunities Clause to include those rights enumerated in the Constitution as well as some unenumerated rights. Justice Swayne described the majority's narrow reading of the Privileges or Immunities Clause as "turn[ing] ... what was meant for bread into a stone."

Today, many legal scholars dispute the correctness of the narrow *Slaughter-House* interpretation. See, *e.g.*, *Saenz v. Roe* (1999) (Thomas, J., dissenting) (scholars of the 14th Amendment agree "that the Clause does not mean what the Court said it meant in 1873")....

Three years after the decision in the *Slaughter-House Cases*, the Court decided *United States v. Cruikshank* (1876), the first of the three 19th-century cases on which the Seventh Circuit relied [in rejecting the right to bear arms claim.] In that case, the Court reviewed convictions stemming from the infamous Colfax Massacre in Louisiana on Easter Sunday 1873. Dozens of blacks, many unarmed, were slaughtered by a rival band of armed white men. Cruikshank himself allegedly marched unarmed African-American prisoners through the streets and then had them summarily executed. Ninety-seven men were indicted for participating in the massacre, but only nine went to trial. Six of the nine were acquitted of all charges; the remaining three were acquitted of murder but convicted under the Enforcement Act of 1870, for banding and conspiring together to deprive their victims of various constitutional rights, including the right to bear arms.

The Court reversed all of the convictions, including those relating to the deprivation of the victims' right to bear arms. *Cruikshank*. The Court wrote that the right of bearing arms for a lawful purpose "is not a right granted by the Constitution" and is not "in any manner dependent upon that instrument for its existence." "The 2nd Amendment," the Court continued, "declares that it shall not be infringed; but this ... means no more than that it shall not be infringed by Congress. Our later decisions in *Presser v. Illinois* (1886), and *Miller v. Texas* (1894), reaffirmed that the 2nd Amendment applies only to the Federal Government." *Heller*....

II. C. [T]he Seventh Circuit concluded that *Cruikshank*, *Presser*, and *Miller* doomed petitioners' claims at the Court of Appeals level....

We see no need to reconsider [the narrow reading of the Privileges or Immunities Clause] here. For many decades, the question of the rights protected by the 14th Amendment against state infringement has been analyzed under the Due Process Clause of that Amendment and not under the Privileges or Immunities Clause. We therefore decline to disturb the *Slaughter-House* holding.

At the same time, however, this Court's decisions in *Cruikshank*, *Presser*, and *Miller* do not preclude us from considering whether the Due Process Clause of the 14th Amendment makes the 2nd Amendment right binding on the States ... As explained more fully below, *Cruikshank*, *Presser*, and *Miller* all preceded the era in which the Court began the process of "selective incorporation" under the Due Process Clause....

Indeed, *Cruikshank* has not prevented us from holding that other rights that were at issue in that case are binding on the States through the Due Process Clause. In *Cruikshank*, the Court held that the general "right of the people peaceably to assemble for lawful purposes," which is protected by the 1st Amendment, applied only against the Federal Government and not against the States. Nonetheless, over 60 years later the Court held that the right of peaceful assembly was a "fundamental righ[t] ... safeguarded by the due process clause of the 14th Amendment." *De Jonge v. Oregon* (1937). We follow the same path here and thus consider whether the right to keep and bear arms applies to the States under the Due Process Clause.

II. D. 1. In the late 19th century, the Court began to consider whether the Due Process Clause prohibits the States from infringing rights set out in the Bill of Rights. See *Hur-*

tado v. California (1884) (due process does not require grand jury indictment); *Chicago, B. & Q. R. Co. v. Chicago* (1897) (due process prohibits States from taking of private property for public use without just compensation). Five features of the approach taken during the ensuing era should be noted.

First, the Court viewed the due process question as entirely separate from the question whether a right was privilege or immunity of national citizenship. See *Twining v. New Jersey* (1908).

Second, the Court explained that the only rights protected against state infringement by the Due Process Clause were those rights "of such a nature that they are included in the conception of due process of law." While it was "possible that some of the personal rights safeguarded by the first eight Amendments against National action [might] also be safeguarded against state action," the Court stated, this was "not because those rights are enumerated in the first eight Amendments." *Twining*.

The Court used different formulations in describing the boundaries of due process. For example, in *Twining*, the Court referred to "immutable principles of justice which inhere in the very idea of free government which no member of the Union may disregard." In *Snyder v. Massachusetts* (1934), the Court spoke of rights that are "so rooted in the traditions and conscience of our people as to be ranked as fundamental." And in *Palko v. Connecticut* (1937), the Court famously said that due process protects those rights that are "the very essence of a scheme of ordered liberty" and essential to "a fair and enlightened system of justice."

Third, in some cases decided during this era the Court "can be seen as having asked, when inquiring into whether some particular procedural safeguard was required of a State, if a civilized system could be imagined that would not accord the particular protection." *Duncan v. Louisiana* (1968)....

Fourth, the Court during this era was not hesitant to hold that a right set out in the Bill of Rights failed to meet the test for inclusion within the protection of the Due Process Clause....

Finally, even when a right set out in the Bill of Rights was held to fall within the conception of due process, the protection or remedies afforded against state infringement sometimes differed from the protection or remedies provided against abridgment by the Federal Government. To give one example, in *Betts v. Brady* (1942) the Court held that, although the 6th Amendment required the appointment of counsel in all federal criminal cases in which the defendant was unable to retain an attorney, the Due Process Clause required appointment of counsel in state criminal proceedings only where "want of counsel in [the] particular case ... result[ed] in a conviction lacking in ... fundamental fairness."...

II. D. 2. An alternative theory regarding the relationship between the Bill of Rights and §1 of the 14th Amendment was championed by Justice Black. This theory held that §1 of the 14th Amendment totally incorporated all of the provisions of the Bill of Rights. See, *e.g., Adamson v. California* (1947) (Black, J., dissenting); *Duncan* (Black, J., concurring). As Justice Black noted, the chief congressional proponents of the 14th Amendment espoused the view that the Amendment made the Bill of Rights applicable to the States and, in so doing, overruled this Court's decision in *Barron v. Baltimore* (1833).[1] *Adam-*

---

1. Senator Jacob Howard, who spoke on behalf of the Joint Committee on Reconstruction and sponsored the Amendment in the Senate, stated that the Amendment protected all of "the personal rights guaranteed and secured by the first eight amendments of the Constitution." *Cong. Globe*, 39th Cong., 1st Sess. 2765 (1866) (hereinafter 39th *Cong. Globe*). Representative John Bingham, the principal author of the text of §1, said that the Amendment would "arm the Congress ... with the power to enforce the bill of rights as it stands in the Constitution today." A. Amar, *The Bill of Rights: Creation and*

son (dissenting opinion).² Nonetheless, the Court never has embraced Justice Black's "total incorporation" theory.

II. D. 3. While Justice Black's theory was never adopted, the Court eventually moved in that direction by initiating what has been called a process of "selective incorporation," *i.e.*, the Court began to hold that the Due Process Clause fully incorporates particular rights contained in the first eight Amendments. See, *e.g., Gideon v. Wainright* (1963); *Duncan; Benton v. Maryland* (1969).

The decisions during this time abandoned three of the previously noted characteristics of the earlier period. The Court made it clear that the governing standard is not whether *any* "civilized system [can] be imagined that would not accord the particular protection." *Duncan*. Instead, the Court inquired whether a particular Bill of Rights guarantee is fundamental to *our* scheme of ordered liberty and system of justice; (referring to those "fundamental principles of liberty and justice which lie at the base of all *our* civil and political institutions.")

The Court also shed any reluctance to hold that rights guaranteed by the Bill of Rights met the requirements for protection under the Due Process Clause. The Court eventually incorporated almost all of the provisions of the Bill of Rights. Only a handful of the Bill of Rights protections remain unincorporated.

Finally, the Court abandoned "the notion that the 14th Amendment applies to the States only a watered-down, subjective version of the individual guarantees of the Bill of

---

Reconstruction 183 (1998) (hereinafter Amar, *Bill of Rights*). After ratification of the Amendment, Bingham maintained the view that the rights guaranteed by §1 of the 14th Amendment "are chiefly defined in the first eight amendments to the Constitution of the United States." *Cong. Globe*, 42d Cong., 1st Sess., App. 84 (1871). Finally, Representative Thaddeus Stevens, the political leader of the House and acting chairman of the Joint Committee on Reconstruction, stated during the debates on the Amendment that "the Constitution limits only the action of Congress, and is not a limitation on the States. This amendment supplies that defect, and allows Congress to correct the unjust legislation of the States." 39th *Cong. Globe* 2459; see also M. Curtis, *No State Shall Abridge: The Fourteenth Amendment and the Bill of Rights* 112 (1986) (counting at least 30 statements during the debates in Congress interpreting §1 to incorporate the Bill of Rights); Brief for Constitutional Law Professors as *Amici Curiae* 20 (collecting authorities and stating that "[n]ot a single senator or representative disputed [the incorporationist] understanding" of the 14th Amendment).

2. The municipal respondents and some of their *amici* dispute the significance of these statements. They contend that the phrase "privileges or immunities" is not naturally read to mean the rights set out in the first eight Amendments, and that "there is 'support in the legislative history for no fewer than four interpretations of the ... Privileges or Immunities Clause.'" Brief for Municipal Respondents 69 (quoting Currie, *The Reconstruction Congress*, 75 U. Chi. L. Rev. 383, 406 (2008)). They question whether there is sound evidence of "'any strong public awareness of nationalizing the *entire* Bill of Rights.'" Brief for Municipal Respondents 69 (quoting Wildenthal, *Nationalizing the Bill of Rights: Revisiting the Original Understanding of the Fourteenth Amendment in 1866–67*, 68 Ohio St. L. J. 1509, 1600 (2007)). Scholars have also disputed the total incorporation theory. See, *e.g.*, Fairman, *Does the Fourteenth Amendment Incorporate the Bill of Rights?* 2 Stan. L. Rev. 5 (1949); Berger, *Incorporation of the Bill of Rights in the Fourteenth Amendment: A Nine-Lived Cat*, 42 Ohio St. L. J. 435 (1981).

Proponents of the view that §1 of the 14th Amendment makes all of the provisions of the Bill of Rights applicable to the States respond that the terms privileges, immunities, and rights were used interchangeably at the time, see, *e.g.*, Curtis, *supra*, at 64–65, and that the position taken by the leading congressional proponents of the Amendment was widely publicized and understood, see, *e.g.*, Wildenthal; Hardy, *Original Popular Understanding of the Fourteenth Amendment as Reflected in the Print Media of 1866–1868* (2009). A number of scholars have found support for the total incorporation of the Bill of Rights. See Curtis, *supra*, at 57–130; Aynes, *On Misreading John Bingham and the Fourteenth Amendment*, 103 Yale L. J. 57, 61 (1993); see also Amar, *Bill of Rights* 181–230. We take no position with respect to this academic debate.

Rights," stating that it would be "incongruous" to apply different standards "depending on whether the claim was asserted in a state or federal court." *Malloy v. Hogan* (1964). Instead, the Court decisively held that incorporated Bill of Rights protections "are all to be enforced against the States under the 14th Amendment according to the same standards that protect those personal rights against federal encroachment."

Employing this approach, the Court overruled earlier decisions in which it had held that particular Bill of Rights guarantees or remedies did not apply to the States. See, *e.g.*, *Mapp v. Ohio* (1961) (overruling in part *Wolf v. Colorado* (1949)); *Gideon*, (overruling *Betts*); *Malloy*,(overruling *Adamson* and *Twining*); *Benton* (overruling *Palko*).

III. With this framework in mind, we now turn directly to the question whether the 2nd Amendment right to keep and bear arms is incorporated in the concept of due process. In answering that question, as just explained, we must decide whether the right to keep and bear arms is fundamental to *our* scheme of ordered liberty, *Duncan*, or as we have said in a related context, whether this right is "deeply rooted in this Nation's history and tradition," *Washington v. Glucksberg* (1997).

III. A. Our decision in *Heller* points unmistakably to the answer. Self-defense is a basic right, recognized by many legal systems from ancient times to the present day, and in *Heller,* we held that individual self-defense is "the *central component*" of the 2nd Amendment right. Explaining that "the need for defense of self, family, and property is most acute" in the home, we found that this right applies to handguns because they are "the most preferred firearm in the nation to 'keep' and use for protection of one's home and family"....

Heller makes it clear that this right is "deeply rooted in this Nation's history and tradition." *Glucksberg. Heller* explored the right's origins, noting that the 1689 English Bill of Rights explicitly protected a right to keep arms for self defense, and that by 1765, Blackstone was able to assert that the right to keep and bear arms was "one of the fundamental rights of Englishmen."

Blackstone's assessment was shared by the American colonists. As we noted in *Heller*, King George III's attempt to disarm the colonists in the 1760's and 1770's "provoked polemical reactions by Americans invoking their rights as Englishmen to keep arms."

The right to keep and bear arms was considered no less fundamental by those who drafted and ratified the Bill of Rights. "During the 1788 ratification debates, the fear that the federal government would disarm the people in order to impose rule through a standing army or select militia was pervasive in Anti-federalist rhetoric." ...

This understanding persisted in the years immediately following the ratification of the Bill of Rights. In addition to the four States that had adopted 2nd Amendment analogues before ratification, nine more States adopted state constitutional provisions protecting an individual right to keep and bear arms between 1789 and 1820....

III. B. 1. By the 1850's, the perceived threat that had prompted the inclusion of the 2nd Amendment in the Bill of Rights—the fear that the National Government would disarm the universal militia—had largely faded as a popular concern, but the right to keep and bear arms was highly valued for purposes of self-defense ... Abolitionist authors wrote in support of the right ... And when attempts were made to disarm "Free-Soilers" in "Bloody Kansas," Senator Charles Sumner ... proclaimed that "[n]ever was [the rifle] more needed in just self-defense than now in Kansas." ...

After the Civil War, many of the over 180,000 African Americans who served in the Union Army returned to the States of the old Confederacy, where systematic efforts were made to disarm them and other blacks. The laws of some States formally prohibited African Americans from possessing firearms ... Throughout the South, armed parties, often consisting of ex-Confederate soldiers serving in the state militias, forcibly took firearms from newly freed slaves.... The Report of the Joint Committee on Reconstruction—which was widely reprinted in the press and distributed by Members of the 39th Congress to their constituents shortly after Congress approved the 14th Amendment—contained numerous examples of such abuses. See, *e.g.*, Joint Committee on Reconstruction (1866)....

The most explicit evidence of Congress' aim appears in § 14 of the Freedmen's Bureau Act of 1866, which provided that "the right ... to have full and equal benefit of all laws and proceedings concerning personal liberty, personal security, and the acquisition, enjoyment, and disposition of estate, real and personal, *including the constitutional right to bear arms*, shall be secured to and enjoyed by all the citizens ... without respect to race or color, or previous condition of slavery." Section 14 thus explicitly guaranteed that "all the citizens," black and white, would have "the constitutional right to bear arms." ...

Congress, however, ultimately deemed these legislative remedies insufficient. Southern resistance, Presidential vetoes, and this Court's pre-Civil-War precedent persuaded Congress that a constitutional amendment was necessary to provide full protection for the rights of blacks. Today, it is generally accepted that the 14th Amendment was understood to provide a constitutional basis for protecting the rights set out in the Civil Rights Act of 1866.

In debating the 14th Amendment, the 39th Congress referred to the right to keep and bear arms as a fundamental right deserving of protection. Senator Samuel Pomeroy described three "indispensable safeguards of liberty under our form of Government." One of these, he said, was the right to keep and bear arms:

"Every man ... should have the right to bear arms for the defense of himself and family and his homestead. And if the cabin door of the freedman is broken open and the intruder enters for purposes as vile as were known to slavery, then should a well-loaded musket be in the hand of the occupant to send the polluted wretch to another world, where his wretchedness will forever remain complete." ...

Evidence from the period immediately following the ratification of the 14th Amendment only confirms that the right to keep and bear arms was considered fundamental. In an 1868 speech addressing the disarmament of freedmen, Representative Stevens emphasized the necessity of the right: "Disarm a community and you rob them of the means of defending life. Take away their weapons of defense and you take away the inalienable right of defending liberty." "The 14th amendment, now so happily adopted, settles the whole question."And in debating the Civil Rights Act of 1871, Congress routinely referred to the right to keep and bear arms and decried the continued disarmament of blacks in the South. Finally, legal commentators from the period emphasized the fundamental nature of the right ...

The right to keep and bear arms was also widely protected by state constitutions at the time when the 14th Amendment was ratified. In 1868, 22 of the 37 States in the Union had state constitutional provisions explicitly protecting the right to keep and bear arms....

III. B. 2. Despite all this evidence, municipal respondents contend that Congress, in the years immediately following the Civil War, merely sought to outlaw "discriminatory measures taken against freedmen, which it addressed by adopting a non-discrimination principle" and that even an outright ban on the possession of firearms was regarded as acceptable, "so long as it was not done in a discriminatory manner." ...

First, while § 1 of the 14th Amendment contains "an antidiscrimination rule," namely, the Equal Protection Clause, municipal respondents can hardly mean that § 1 does no more than prohibit discrimination. If that were so, then the 1st Amendment, as applied to the States, would not prohibit nondiscriminatory abridgments of the rights to freedom of speech or freedom of religion; the 4th Amendment, as applied to the States, would not prohibit all unreasonable searches and seizures but only discriminatory searches and seizures—and so on. We assume that this is not municipal respondents' view, so what they must mean is that the 2nd Amendment should be singled out for special—and specially unfavorable—treatment. We reject that suggestion.

Second, municipal respondents' argument ignores the clear terms of the Freedmen's Bureau Act of 1866, which acknowledged the existence of the right to bear arms. If that law had used language such as "the equal benefit of laws concerning the bearing of arms," it would be possible to interpret it as simply a prohibition of racial discrimination. But § 14 speaks of and protects "the constitutional right to bear arms," an unmistakable reference to the right protected by the 2nd Amendment. And it protects the "full and equal benefit" of this right in the States ...

Third, if the 39th Congress had outlawed only those laws that discriminate on the basis of race or previous condition of servitude, African Americans in the South would likely have remained vulnerable to attack by many of their worst abusers: the state militia and state peace officers....

Fourth, municipal respondents' purely antidiscrimination theory of the 14th Amendment disregards the plight of whites in the South who opposed the Black Codes. If the 39th Congress and the ratifying public had simply prohibited racial discrimination with respect to the bearing of arms, opponents of the Black Codes would have been left without the means of self-defense—as had abolitionists in Kansas in the 1850's.

Fifth, the 39th Congress' response to proposals to disband and disarm the Southern militias is instructive. Despite recognizing and deploring the abuses of these militias, the 39th Congress balked at a proposal to disarm them. Disarmament, it was argued, would violate the members' right to bear arms, and it was ultimately decided to disband the militias but not to disarm their members....

IV. Municipal respondents' remaining arguments are at war with our central holding in *Heller*: that the 2nd Amendment protects a personal right to keep and bear arms for lawful purposes, most notably for self-defense within the home. Municipal respondents, in effect, ask us to treat the right recognized in *Heller* as a second-class right, subject to an entirely different body of rules than the other Bill of Rights guarantees that we have held to be incorporated into the Due Process Clause.... [They urge the adoption of a test that would not incorporate the right to bear arms since it is denied by many advanced and civilized societies.]

This line of argument is, of course, inconsistent with the long-established standard we apply in incorporation cases. See *Duncan*. And the present-day implications of municipal respondents' argument are stunning. For example, many of the rights that our Bill of Rights provides for persons accused of criminal offenses are virtually unique to this country. If *our* understanding of the right to a jury trial, the right against self-incrimination, and the right to counsel were necessary attributes of *any* civilized country, it would follow that the United States is the only civilized Nation in the world.

Municipal respondents attempt to salvage their position by suggesting that their argument applies only to substantive as opposed to procedural rights. But even in this trimmed form, municipal respondents' argument flies in the face of more than a half-century of precedent. For example, in *Everson v. Board of Ed.* (1947), the Court held that the 14th Amendment incorporates the Establishment Clause of the 1st Amendment. Yet several of the countries that municipal respondents recognize as civilized have established state churches....

The right to keep and bear arms ... is not the only constitutional right that has controversial public safety implications. All of the constitutional provisions that impose restrictions on law enforcement and on the prosecution of crimes fall into the same category....

We likewise reject municipal respondents' argument that we should depart from our established incorporation methodology on the ground that making the 2nd Amendment binding on the States and their subdivisions is inconsistent with principles of federalism and will stifle experimentation. Municipal respondents point out—quite correctly—that conditions and problems differ from locality to locality and that citizens in different jurisdictions have divergent views on the issue of gun control....

There is nothing new in the argument that, in order to respect federalism and allow useful state experimentation, a federal constitutional right should not be fully binding on the States. This argument was made repeatedly and eloquently by Members of this Court who rejected the concept of incorporation and urged retention of the two track approach to incorporation. Throughout the era of "selective incorporation," Justice Harlan in particular, invoking the values of federalism and state experimentation, fought a determined rearguard action to preserve the two-track approach.

Time and again, however, those pleas failed. Unless we turn back the clock or adopt a special incorporation test applicable only to the 2nd Amendment, municipal respondents' argument must be rejected. Under our precedents, if a Bill of Rights guarantee is fundamental from an American perspective, then, unless *stare decisis* counsels otherwise, that guarantee is fully binding on the States and thus *limits* (but by no means eliminates) their ability to devise solutions to social problems that suit local needs and values. As noted by the 38 States that have appeared in this case as *amici* supporting petitioners, "[s]tate and local experimentation with reasonable firearms regulations will continue under the 2nd Amendment." ...

V. A. We turn, finally, to the two dissenting opinions. Justice Stevens' eloquent opinion covers ground already addressed, and therefore little need be added in response. Justice Stevens would "'ground the prohibitions against state action squarely on due process, without intermediate reliance on any of the first eight Amendments.'" (quoting *Malloy* (Harlan, J., dissenting)).The question presented in this case, in his view, "is whether the particular right asserted by petitioners applies to the States because of the 14th Amendment itself, standing on its own bottom." He would hold that "[t]he rights protected against state infringement by the 14th Amendment's Due Process Clause need not be identical in shape or scope to the rights protected against Federal Government infringement by the various provisions of the Bill of Rights."

As we have explained, the Court, for the past half century, has moved away from the two-track approach. If we were now to accept Justice Stevens' theory across the board, decades of decisions would be undermined. We assume that this is not what is proposed. What is urged instead, it appears, is that this theory be revived solely for the individual right that *Heller* recognized, over vigorous dissents.

The relationship between the Bill of Rights' guarantees and the States must be governed by a single, neutral principle. It is far too late to exhume what Justice Brennan, writing for the Court 46 years ago, derided as "the notion that the 14th Amendment applies to the States only a watered-down, subjective version of the individual guarantees of the Bill of Rights." *Malloy*.

V. B. Justice Breyer's dissent makes several points to which we briefly respond. To begin, while there is certainly room for disagreement about *Heller*'s analysis of the history of the right to keep and bear arms, nothing written since *Heller* persuades us to reopen the question there decided. Few other questions of original meaning have been as thoroughly explored.

Justice Breyer's conclusion that the 14th Amendment does not incorporate the right to keep and bear arms appears to rest primarily on four factors: First, "there is no popular consensus" that the right is fundamental, second, the right does not protect minorities or persons neglected by those holding political power; third, incorporation of the 2nd Amendment right would "amount to a significant incursion on a traditional and important area of state concern, altering the constitutional relationship between the States and the Federal Government" and preventing local variations; and fourth, determining the scope of the 2nd Amendment right in cases involving state and local laws will force judges to answer difficult empirical questions regarding matters that are outside their area of expertise. Even if we believed that these factors were relevant to the incorporation inquiry, none of these factors undermines the case for incorporation of the right to keep and bear arms for self-defense.

First, we have never held that a provision of the Bill of Rights applies to the States only if there is a "popular consensus" that the right is fundamental, and we see no basis for such a rule. But in this case, as it turns out, there is evidence of such a consensus. An *amicus* brief submitted by 58 Members of the Senate and 251 Members of the House of Representatives urges us to hold that the right to keep and bear arms is fundamental. Another brief submitted by 38 States takes the same position.

Second, petitioners and many others who live in high-crime areas dispute the proposition that the 2nd Amendment right does not protect minorities and those lacking political clout....

Third, Justice Breyer is correct that incorporation of the 2nd Amendment right will to some extent limit the legislative freedom of the States, but this is always true when a Bill of Rights provision is incorporated. Incorporation always restricts experimentation and local variations, but that has not stopped the Court from incorporating virtually every other provision of the Bill of Rights....

Finally, Justice Breyer is incorrect that incorporation will require judges to assess the costs and benefits of firearms restrictions and thus to make difficult empirical judgments in an area in which they lack expertise. As we have noted, while his opinion in *Heller* recommended an interest-balancing test, the Court specifically rejected that suggestion....

* * *

In *Heller*, we held that the 2nd Amendment protects the right to possess a handgun in the home for the purpose of self-defense. Unless considerations of *stare decisis* counsel otherwise, a provision of the Bill of Rights that protects a right that is fundamental from an American perspective applies equally to the Federal Government and the States. We therefore hold that the Due Process Clause of the 14th Amendment incorporates the 2nd Amendment right recognized in *Heller*. The judgment of the Court of Appeals is reversed, and the case is remanded for further proceedings.

Justice Scalia, concurring.

I join the Court's opinion. Despite my misgivings about Substantive Due Process as an original matter, I have acquiesced in the Court's incorporation of certain guarantees in the Bill of Rights "because it is both long established and narrowly limited." This case does not require me to reconsider that view, since straightforward application of settled doctrine suffices to decide it.

I write separately only to respond to some aspects of Justice Stevens' dissent.... [M]uch of what Justice Stevens writes is a broad condemnation of the theory of interpretation which underlies the Court's opinion, a theory that makes the traditions of our people paramount. He proposes a different theory, which he claims is more "cautiou[s]" and respectful of proper limits on the judicial role. It is that claim I wish to address.

I. A. After stressing the substantive dimension of what he has renamed the "liberty clause," Justice Stevens proceeds to urge readoption of the theory of incorporation articulated in *Palko v. Connecticut* (1937). But in fact he does not favor application of that theory at all. For whether *Palko* requires only that "a fair and enlightened system of justice would be impossible without" the right sought to be incorporated, or requires in addition that the right be rooted in the "traditions and conscience of our people," many of the rights Justice Stevens thinks are incorporated could not pass muster under either test: abortion (*Planned Parenthood of Southeastern Pa. v. Casey*) (1992); homosexual sodomy, (*Lawrence v. Texas* (2003)); the right to have excluded from criminal trials evidence obtained in violation of the 4th Amendment, (*Mapp v. Ohio* (1961)); and the right to teach one's children foreign languages (*Meyer v. Nebraska* (1923)), among others....

Not *all* such rights are in, however, since only "*some* fundamental aspects of personhood, dignity, and the like" are protected. Exactly what is covered is not clear. But whatever else is in, he *knows* that the right to keep and bear arms is out, despite its being as "deeply rooted in this Nation's history and tradition," *Washington v. Glucksberg*, (1997).... I can find no other explanation for such certitude except that Justice Stevens, despite his forswearing of "personal and private notions,"deeply believes it should be out.

The subjective nature of Justice Stevens' standard is also apparent from his claim that it is the courts' prerogative—indeed their *duty*—to update the Due Process Clause so that it encompasses new freedoms the Framers were too narrow-minded to imagine. Courts, he proclaims, must "do justice to [the Clause's] urgent call and its open texture" by exercising the "interpretive discretion the latter embodies." (Why the *people* are not up to the task of deciding what new rights to protect, even though it is *they* who are authorized to make changes, see U.S. Const., Art. V, is never explained.) ...

Justice Thomas, concurring in part and concurring in the judgment.

I agree with the Court that the 14th Amendment makes the right to keep and bear arms set forth in the 2nd Amendment "fully applicable to the States." I write separately because I believe there is a more straightforward path to this conclusion, one that is more faithful to the 14th Amendment's text and history.

Applying what is now a well-settled test, the plurality opinion concludes that the right to keep and bear arms applies to the States through the 14th Amendment's Due Process Clause because it is "fundamental" to the American "scheme of ordered liberty," (citing *Duncan v. Louisiana* (1968)), and "'deeply rooted in this Nation's history and tradition,'" (quoting *Washington v. Glucksberg* (1997)). I agree with that description of the right. But I cannot agree that it is enforceable against the States through a clause that speaks only to "process." Instead, the right to keep and bear arms is a privilege of American citizenship that applies to the States through the 14th Amendment's Privileges or Immunities Clause ...

[I]f this case were litigated before the 14th Amendment's adoption in 1868, the answer to that question would be simple. [*Barron v. Baltimore* (1833)] ...

The provision at issue here, § 1 of the 14th Amendment, significantly altered our system of government. The first sentence of that section provides that "[a]ll persons born or naturalized in the United States and subject to the jurisdiction thereof, are citizens of the United States and of the State wherein they reside." This unambiguously overruled this Court's contrary holding in *Dred Scott v. Sandford* (1857), that the Constitution did not recognize black Americans as citizens of the United States or their own State.

The meaning of § 1's next sentence has divided this Court for many years. That sentence begins with the command that "[n]o State shall make or enforce any law which shall abridge the privileges or immunities of citizens of the United States." On its face, this appears to grant the persons just made United States citizens a certain collection of rights — *i.e.*, privileges or immunities — attributable to that status.

This Court's precedents accept that point, but define the relevant collection of rights quite narrowly.... *Slaughter-House Cases* (1873) [and a clearly narrow approach was followed in subsequent cases.] ...

While this Court has at times concluded that a right gains "fundamental" status only if it is essential to the American "scheme of ordered liberty" or "'deeply rooted in this Nation's history and tradition,'" (quoting *Glucksberg*), the Court has just as often held that a right warrants Due Process Clause protection if it satisfies a far less measurable range of criteria, see *Lawrence v. Texas* (2003) (concluding that the Due Process Clause protects "liberty of the person both in its spatial and in its more transcendent dimensions"). Using the latter approach, the Court has determined that the Due Process Clause applies rights against the States that are not mentioned in the Constitution at all, even without seriously arguing that the Clause was originally understood to protect such rights.

All of this is a legal fiction. The notion that a constitutional provision that guarantees only "process" before a person is deprived of life, liberty, or property could define the substance of those rights strains credulity for even the most casual user of words. Moreover, this fiction is a particularly dangerous one. The one theme that links the Court's substantive due process precedents together is their lack of a guiding principle to distinguish "fundamental" rights that warrant protection from nonfundamental rights that do not....

I cannot accept a theory of constitutional interpretation that rests on such tenuous footing. This Court's substantive due process framework fails to account for both the text of the 14th Amendment and the history that led to its adoption, filling that gap with a jurisprudence devoid of a guiding principle. I believe the original meaning of the 14th Amendment offers a superior alternative, and that a return to that meaning would allow this Court to enforce the rights the 14th Amendment is designed to protect with greater clarity and predictability than the substantive due process framework has so far managed....

II. "It cannot be presumed that any clause in the constitution is intended to be without effect." *Marbury v. Madison* (1803) (Marshall, C. J.). Because the Court's Privileges or Immunities Clause precedents have presumed just that, I set them aside for the moment and begin with the text ...

II. A. 1. At the time of Reconstruction, the terms "privileges" and "immunities" had an established meaning as synonyms for "rights." The two words, standing alone or paired together, were used interchangeably with the words "rights," "liberties," and "freedoms," and had been since the time of Blackstone....

II. A. 2. The group of rights-bearers to whom the Privileges or Immunities Clause applies is, of course, "citizens." By the time of Reconstruction, it had long been established that both the States and the Federal Government existed to preserve their citizens' inalienable rights, and that these rights were considered "privileges" or "immunities" of citizenship ...

II. A. 3. ... Article IV, § 2 was derived from a similar clause in the Articles of Confederation, and reflects the dual citizenship the Constitution provided to all Americans after replacing that "league" of separate sovereign States....

The text examined so far demonstrates three points about the meaning of the Privileges or Immunities Clause in § 1. First, "privileges" and "immunities" were synonyms for "rights." Second, both the States and the Federal Government had long recognized the inalienable rights of their citizens. Third, Article IV, § 2 of the Constitution protected traveling citizens against state discrimination with respect to the fundamental rights of state citizenship.

Two questions still remain, both provoked by the textual similarity between § 1's Privileges or Immunities Clause and Article IV, § 2. The first involves the nature of the rights at stake: Are the privileges or immunities of "citizens of the United States" recognized by § 1 the same as the privileges and immunities of "citizens in the several States" to which Article IV, § 2 refers? The second involves the restriction imposed on the States: Does § 1, like Article IV, § 2, prohibit only discrimination with respect to certain rights *if* the State chooses to recognize them, or does it require States to recognize those rights? I address each question in turn.

II. B. I start with the nature of the rights that § 1's Privileges or Immunities Clause protects.... Section 1 protects the rights of citizens "of the United States" specifically. The evidence overwhelmingly demonstrates that the privileges and immunities of such citizens included individual rights enumerated in the Constitution, including the right to keep and bear arms.

II. B. 1. Nineteenth-century treaties through which the United States acquired territory from other sovereigns routinely promised inhabitants of the newly acquired territories that they would enjoy all of the "rights," "privileges," and "immunities" of United States citizens....

Commentators of the time explained that the rights and immunities of "citizens of the United States" recognized in these treaties "undoubtedly mean[t] those privileges that are common to all citizens of this republic." ...

II. B. 2. Evidence from the political branches in the years leading to the 14th Amendment's adoption demonstrates broad public understanding that the privileges and immunities of United States citizenship included rights set forth in the Constitution, just as Webster and his allies had argued.... Records from the 39th Congress further support this understanding.

II. B. 2. a. After the Civil War, Congress established the Joint Committee on Reconstruction to investigate circumstances in the Southern States and to determine whether, and on what conditions, those States should be readmitted to the Union. See *Cong. Globe*, 39th Cong., 1st Sess., 6, 30 (1865) (M. Curtis, *No State Shall Abridge: The Fourteenth Amendment and the Bill of Rights* 57 (1986) (hereinafter Curtis). That Committee would ultimately recommend the adoption of the 14th Amendment, justifying its recommendation by submitting a report to Congress that extensively catalogued the abuses of civil rights in the former slave States and argued that "adequate security for future peace and safety ... can only be found in such changes of the organic law as shall determine the civil rights and privileges of all citizens in all parts of the republic." ...

II. B. 2. b. (1) By the time the debates on the 14th Amendment resumed, [Representative John A.] Bingham had amended his draft of § 1 to include the text of the Privileges or Immunities Clause that was ultimately adopted. Senator Jacob Howard introduced the new draft on the floor of the Senate in the third speech relevant here. Howard explained that the Constitution recognized "a mass of privileges, immunities, and rights, some of them secured by the second section of the fourth article of the Constitution, ... some by the first eight amendments of the Constitution," and that "there is no power given in the Constitution to enforce and to carry out any of these guarantees" against the States. Howard then stated that "the great object" of §1 was to "restrain the power of the States and compel them at all times to respect these great fundamental guarantees." Section 1, he indicated, imposed "a general prohibition upon all the States, as such, from abridging the privileges and immunities of the citizens of the United States."

In describing these rights, Howard explained that they included "the privileges and immunities spoken of" in Article IV, § 2. Although he did not catalogue the precise "nature" or "extent" of those rights, he thought "*Corfield v. Coryell*" provided a useful description. Howard then submitted that

> [t]o these privileges and immunities, whatever they may be—... should be added *the personal rights guarantied and secured by the first eight amendments of the Constitution*; such as the freedom of speech and of the press; the right of the people peaceably to assemble and petition the Government for a redress of grievances, [and] ... *the right to keep and to bear arms*....

II. B. 2. b. (2) When read against this backdrop, the civil rights legislation adopted by the 39th Congress in 1866 further supports this view. Between passing the 13th Amendment—which outlawed slavery alone—and the 14th Amendment, Congress passed two significant pieces of legislation. The first was the Civil Rights Act of 1866, which provided that "all persons born in the United States" were "citizens of the United States" and that "such citizens, of every race and color, ... shall have the same right" to, among other things, "full and equal benefit of all laws and proceedings for the security of person and property, as is enjoyed by white citizens."

Both proponents and opponents of this Act described it as providing the "privileges" of citizenship to freedmen, and defined those privileges to include constitutional rights, such as the right to keep and bear arms....

Three months later, Congress passed the Freedmen's Bureau Act, which also entitled all citizens to the "full and equal benefit of all laws and proceedings concerning personal liberty" and "personal security." The Act stated expressly that the rights of personal liberty and security protected by the Act "includ[ed] the constitutional right to bear arms."

II. B. 2. b. (3) There is much else in the legislative record. Many statements by Members of Congress corroborate the view that the Privileges or Immunities Clause enforced constitutionally enumerated rights against the States. See Curtis 112 (collecting examples). I am not aware of any statement that directly refutes that proposition. That said, the record of the debates—like most legislative history—is less than crystal clear. In particular, much ambiguity derives from the fact that at least several Members described §1 as protecting the privileges and immunities of citizens "in the several States," harkening back to Article IV, §2. These statements can be read to support the view that the Privileges or Immunities Clause protects some or all the fundamental rights of "citizens" described in *Corfield*. They can also be read to support the view that the Privileges or

Immunities Clause, like Article IV, §2, prohibits only state discrimination with respect to those rights it covers, but does not deprive States of the power to deny those rights to all citizens equally.

I examine the rest of the historical record with this understanding. But for purposes of discerning what the public most likely thought the Privileges or Immunities Clause to mean, it is significant that the most widely publicized statements by the legislators who voted on §1—Bingham, Howard, and even Hale—point unambiguously toward the conclusion that the Privileges or Immunities Clause enforces at least those fundamental rights enumerated in the Constitution against the States, including the 2nd Amendment right to keep and bear arms.

II. B. 3. Interpretations of the 14th Amendment in the period immediately following its ratification help to establish the public understanding of the text at the time of its adoption.

Some of these interpretations come from Members of Congress. During an 1871 debate on a bill to enforce the 14th Amendment, Representative Henry Dawes listed the Constitution's first eight Amendments, including "the right to keep and bear arms," before explaining that after the Civil War, the country "gave the most grand of all these rights, privileges, and immunities, by one single amendment to the Constitution, to four millions of American citizens" who formerly were slaves. "It is all these," Dawes explained, "which are comprehended in the words 'American citizen.'" ...

Legislation passed in furtherance of the 14th Amendment demonstrates even more clearly this understanding. For example, Congress enacted the Civil Rights Act of 1871, which was titled in pertinent part "An Act to enforce the Provisions of the 14th Amendment to the Constitution of the United States," and which is codified in the still-existing 42 U. S. C. §1983 ...

This evidence plainly shows that the ratifying public understood the Privileges or Immunities Clause to protect constitutionally enumerated rights, including the right to keep and bear arms. As the Court demonstrates, there can be no doubt that §1 was understood to enforce the 2nd Amendment against the States. In my view, this is because the right to keep and bear arms was understood to be a privilege of American citizenship guaranteed by the Privileges or Immunities Clause.

II. C. The next question is whether the Privileges or Immunities Clause merely prohibits States from discriminating among citizens if they recognize the 2nd Amendment's right to keep and bear arms [no], or whether the Clause requires States to recognize the right [yes]....

II. C. 1. I begin, again, with the text. The Privileges or Immunities Clause opens with the command that "*No State shall*" abridge the privileges or immunities of citizens of the United States. Amdt. 14, §1. The very same phrase opens Article I, §10 of the Constitution, which prohibits the States from "pass[ing] any Bill of Attainder" or "ex post facto Law, among other things. Article I, §10 is one of the few constitutional provisions that limits state authority. In *Barron*, when Chief Justice Marshall interpreted the Bill of Rights as lacking "plain and intelligible language" restricting state power to infringe upon individual liberties, he pointed to Article I, §10 as an example of text that would have accomplished that task....

This interpretation is strengthened when one considers that the Privileges or Immunities Clause uses the verb "abridge," rather than "discriminate," to describe the limit it imposes on state authority. The Webster's dictionary in use at the time of Reconstruction defines the word "abridge" to mean "[t]o deprive; to cut off; ... as, to *abridge* one of his rights."

Webster, *An American Dictionary of the English Language*. The Clause is thus best understood to impose a limitation on state power to infringe upon pre-existing substantive rights. It raises no indication that the Framers of the Clause used the word "abridge" to prohibit only discrimination....

II. C. 2. a. I turn first to public debate at the time of ratification. It is true that the congressional debates over § 1 were relatively brief. It is also true that there is little evidence of extensive debate in the States. Many state legislatures did not keep records of their debates, and the few records that do exist reveal only modest discussion. See Curtis 145. These facts are not surprising.

First, however consequential we consider the question today, the nationalization of constitutional rights was not the most controversial aspect of the 14th Amendment at the time of its ratification. The Nation had just endured a tumultuous civil war, and §§ 2, 3, and 4 — which reduced the representation of States that denied voting rights to blacks, deprived most former Confederate officers of the power to hold elective office, and required States to disavow Confederate war debts — were far more polarizing and consumed far more political attention ...

Second, the congressional debates on the 14th Amendment reveal that many representatives, and probably many citizens, believed that the 13th Amendment, the 1866 Civil Rights legislation, or some combination of the two, had already enforced constitutional rights against the States. Justice Black's dissent in *Adamson* chronicles this point in detail. Regardless of whether that understanding was accurate as a matter of constitutional law, it helps to explain why Congressmen had little to say during the debates about § 1.

Third, while *Barron* made plain that the Bill of Rights was not legally enforceable against the States, the significance of that holding should not be overstated. Like the Framers, many 19th-century Americans understood the Bill of Rights to declare inalienable rights that pre-existed all government. Thus, even though the Bill of Rights technically applied only to the Federal Government, many believed that it declared rights that no legitimate government could abridge....

II. C. 2. b. In the contentious years leading up to the Civil War, those who sought to retain the institution of slavery found that to do so, it was necessary to eliminate more and more of the basic liberties of slaves, free blacks, and white abolitionists ...

Southern blacks were not alone in facing threats to their personal liberty and security during the antebellum era. Mob violence in many Northern cities presented dangers as well ...

II. C. 2. c. After the Civil War, Southern anxiety about an uprising among the newly freed slaves peaked. As Representative Thaddeus Stevens is reported to have said, "[w]hen it was first proposed to free the slaves, and arm the blacks, did not half the nation tremble? The prim conservatives, the snobs, and the male waiting-maids in Congress, were in hysterics." K. Stampp, *The Era of Reconstruction, 1865–1877*, p. 104 (1965) (hereinafter *Era of Reconstruction*)....

[Justice Thomas recounts the controversy and defense of the right of the newly freed slaves to have arms.]

These statements are consistent with the arguments of abolitionists during the antebellum era that slavery, and the slave States' efforts to retain it, violated the constitutional rights of individuals — rights the abolitionists described as among the privileges and immunities of citizenship ...

Section 1 guaranteed the rights of citizenship in the United States and in the several States without regard to race. But it was understood that liberty would be assured little protection if § 1 left each State to decide which privileges or immunities of United States citizenship it would protect. As Frederick Douglass explained before § 1's adoption, "the Legislatures of the South can take from him the right to keep and bear arms, as they can — they would not allow a negro to walk with a cane where I came from, they would not allow five of them to assemble together." ... This history confirms what the text of the Privileges or Immunities Clause most naturally suggests: Consistent with its command that "[n]o State shall ... abridge" the rights of United States citizens, the Clause establishes a minimum baseline of federal rights, and the constitutional right to keep and bear arms plainly was among them....

III. B...I agree with the Court that the 2nd Amendment is fully applicable to the States. I do so because the right to keep and bear arms is guaranteed by the 14th Amendment as a privilege of American citizenship.

Justice Stevens, dissenting.

In *District of Columbia v. Heller* (2008), the Court answered the question whether a federal enclave's "prohibition on the possession of usable handguns in the home violates the 2nd Amendment to the Constitution." The question we should be answering in this case is whether the Constitution "guarantees individuals a fundamental right," enforceable against the States, "to possess a functional, personal firearm, including a handgun, within the home." That is a different — and more difficult — inquiry than asking if the 14th Amendment "incorporates" the 2nd Amendment....

In support of their claim that the city of Chicago's handgun ban violates the Constitution, they now rely primarily on the Privileges or Immunities Clause of the 14th Amendment. They rely secondarily on the Due Process Clause of that Amendment. Neither submission requires the Court to express an opinion on whether the 14th Amendment places any limit on the power of States to regulate possession, use, or carriage of firearms outside the home.

I agree with the plurality's refusal to accept petitioners' primary submission. Their briefs marshal an impressive amount of historical evidence for their argument that the Court interpreted the Privileges or Immunities Clause too narrowly in the *Slaughter-House Cases* (1873). But the original meaning of the [Privileges or Immunities] Clause is not as clear as they suggest[1] — and not nearly as clear as it would need to be to dislodge 137 years of precedent.... Moreover, the suggestion that invigorating the Privileges or Immunities Clause will reduce judicial discretion strikes me as implausible, if not exactly backwards....

I further agree with the plurality that there are weighty arguments supporting petitioners' second submission, insofar as it concerns the possession of firearms for lawful self-defense in the home. But these arguments are less compelling than the plurality suggests; they are much less compelling when applied outside the home; and their validity

---

1. Cf., *e.g.*, Currie, *The Reconstruction Congress*, 75 U. Chi. L. Rev. 383, 406 (2008) (finding "some support in the legislative history for no fewer than four interpretations" of the Privileges or Immunities Clause, two of which contradict petitioners' submission) ...; Rosenthal, *The New Originalism Meets the 14th Amendment: Original Public Meaning and the Problem of Incorporation*, 18 J. Contemporary Legal Issues 361 (2009) (detailing reasons to doubt that the Clause was originally understood to apply the Bill of Rights to the States); Hamburger, *Privileges or Immunities*, 105 Nw. U. L. Rev. (forthcoming 2011), online at http://ssrn.com/abstract=1557870 (as visited June 25, 2010, and available in Clerk of Court's case file) (arguing that the Clause was meant to ensure freed slaves were afforded "the Privileges and Immunities" specified in Article IV, § 2, cl. 1 of the Constitution)....

does not depend on the Court's holding in *Heller*. For that holding sheds no light on the meaning of the Due Process Clause of the 14th Amendment. Our decisions construing [the Due Process] Clause to render various procedural guarantees in the Bill of Rights enforceable against the States likewise tell us little about the meaning of the word "liberty" in the Clause or about the scope of its protection of nonprocedural rights.

This is a substantive due process case....

I. Substantive Content

The first, and most basic, principle established by our cases is that the rights protected by the Due Process Clause are not merely procedural in nature. [S]ubstance and procedure are often deeply entwined. Upon closer inspection, the text can be read to "impos[e] nothing less than an obligation to give substantive content to the words 'liberty' and 'due process of law,'" *Washington v. Glucksberg* (1997) (Souter, J., concurring in judgment), lest superficially fair procedures be permitted to "destroy the enjoyment" of life, liberty, and property, *Poe v. Ullman* (1961) (Harlan, J., dissenting).... Procedural guarantees are hollow unless linked to substantive interests; and no amount of process can legitimize some deprivations.

I have yet to see a persuasive argument that the Framers of the 14th Amendment thought otherwise. To the contrary, the historical evidence suggests that, at least by the time of the Civil War if not much earlier, the phrase "due process of law" had acquired substantive content as a term of art within the legal community ... This understanding is consonant with the venerable "notion that governmental authority has implied limits which preserve private autonomy," a notion which predates the founding and which finds reinforcement in the Constitution's 9th Amendment, see *Griswold v. Connecticut* (1965) (Goldberg, J., concurring). The Due Process Clause cannot claim to be the source of our basic freedoms—no legal document ever could—but it stands as one of their foundational guarantors in our law.

If text and history are inconclusive on this point, our precedent leaves no doubt: It has been "settled" for well over a century that the Due Process Clause "applies to matters of substantive law as well as to matters of procedure." *Whitney v. California* (1927) (Brandeis, J., concurring). Time and again, we have recognized that in the 14th Amendment as well as the 5th, the "Due Process Clause guarantees more than fair process, and the 'liberty' it protects includes more than the absence of physical restraint." *Glucksberg*.... Some of our most enduring precedents, accepted today by virtually everyone, were substantive due process decisions. See, *e.g., Loving v. Virginia* (1967) (recognizing due-process as well as equal-protection-based right to marry person of another race); *Bolling v. Sharpe* (1954) (outlawing racial segregation in District of Columbia public schools); *Pierce v. Society of Sisters* (1925) (vindicating right of parents to direct upbringing and education of their children); *Meyer v. Nebraska* (1923) (striking down prohibition on teaching of foreign languages).

Liberty

The second principle woven through our cases is that substantive due process is fundamentally a matter of personal liberty.... It is the liberty clause that reflects and renews "the origins of the American heritage of freedom [and] the abiding interest in individual liberty that makes certain state intrusions on the citizen's right to decide how he will live his own life intolerable." *Fitzgerald v. Porter Memorial Hospital*, (7th Cir. 1975) (Stevens, J.) ...

[T]he term "incorporation," like the term "unenumerated rights," is something of a misnomer. Whether an asserted substantive due process interest is explicitly named in one of the first eight Amendments to the Constitution or is not mentioned, the underlying inquiry is the same: We must ask whether the interest is "comprised within the term liberty." *Whitney* (Brandeis, J., concurring). As the second Justice Harlan has shown, ever since the Court began considering the applicability of the Bill of Rights to the States, "the Court's usual approach has been to ground the prohibitions against state action squarely on due process, without intermediate reliance on any of the first eight Amendments." *Malloy v. Hogan* (1964) (dissenting opinion); see also Frankfurter, *Memorandum on "Incorporation" of the Bill of Rights into the Due Process Clause of the 14th Amendment*, 78 Harv. L. Rev. 746, 747–50 (1965)....

In his own classic opinion in *Griswold* (concurring in judgment), Justice Harlan memorably distilled these precedents' lesson: "While the relevant inquiry may be aided by resort to one or more of the provisions of the Bill of Rights, it is not dependent on them or any of their radiations. The Due Process Clause of the 14th Amendment stands ... on its own bottom." Inclusion in the Bill of Rights is neither necessary nor sufficient for an interest to be judicially enforceable under the 14th Amendment....

Federal/State Divergence

The third precept to emerge from our case law flows from the second: The rights protected against state infringement by the 14th Amendment's Due Process Clause need not be identical in shape or scope to the rights protected against Federal Government infringement by the various provisions of the Bill of Rights.... Although the enactment of the 14th Amendment profoundly altered our legal order, it "did not unstitch the basic federalist pattern woven into our constitutional fabric." ... The Constitution still envisions a system of divided sovereignty, still "establishes a federal republic where local differences are to be cherished as elements of liberty" in the vast run of cases ... [and] still allocates a general "police power ... to the States and the States alone." Elementary considerations of constitutional text and structure suggest there may be legitimate reasons to hold state governments to different standards than the Federal Government in certain areas.

It is true, as the Court emphasizes, that we have made numerous provisions of the Bill of Rights fully applicable to the States.... But we have never accepted a "total incorporation" theory of the 14th Amendment, whereby the Amendment is deemed to subsume the provisions of the Bill of Rights en masse. And we have declined to apply several provisions to the States in any measure. See, *e.g., Minneapolis & St. Louis R. Co. v. Bombolis* (1916) (7th Amendment); *Hurtado v. California*, (1884) (Grand Jury Clause). We have, moreover, resisted a uniform approach to the 6th Amendment's criminal jury guarantee, demanding 12-member panels and unanimous verdicts in federal trials, yet not in state trials. See *Apodaca v. Oregon* (1972) (plurality opinion); *Williams v. Florida* (1970)....

It is true, as well, that during the 1960's the Court decided a number of cases involving procedural rights in which it treated the Due Process Clause as if it transplanted language from the Bill of Rights into the 14th Amendment. See, *e.g., Benton v. Maryland* (1969) (Double Jeopardy Clause); *Pointer v. Texas* (1965) (Confrontation Clause). "Jot-for-jot" incorporation was the norm in this expansionary era. Yet at least one subsequent opinion suggests that these precedents require perfect state/federal congruence only on matters "'at the core'" of the relevant constitutional guarantee. *Crist v. Bretz* (1978). In my judgment, this line of cases is best understood as having concluded that, to ensure a criminal trial satisfies essential standards of fairness, some procedures should be the same in state and federal courts: the need for certainty and uniformity is more pressing, and the margin for error slimmer, when criminal justice is at issue. That principle has little relevance to ... a *non* procedural rule set forth in the Bill of Rights....

Notwithstanding ... dicta in *Malloy*, it is therefore an overstatement to say that the Court has "abandoned," a "two-track approach to incorporation." The Court moved away from that approach in the area of criminal procedure. But the 2nd Amendment differs in fundamental respects from its neighboring provisions in the Bill of Rights.... [I]f some 1960's opinions purported to establish a general method of incorporation, that hardly binds us in this case. The Court has not hesitated to cut back on perceived Warren Court excesses in more areas than I can count.

I do not mean to deny that there can be significant practical, as well as aesthetic, benefits from treating rights symmetrically with regard to the State and Federal Governments.... In a federalist system such as ours, however, [jot for jot incorporation] can carry substantial costs. When a federal court insists that state and local authorities follow its dictates on a matter not critical to personal liberty or procedural justice, the latter may be prevented from engaging in the kind of beneficent "experimentation in things social and economic" that ultimately redounds to the benefit of all Americans. *New State Ice Co. v. Liebmann* (1932) (Brandeis, J., dissenting). The costs of federal courts imposing a uniform national standard may be especially high when the relevant regulatory interests vary significantly across localities, and when the ruling implicates the States' core police powers.

Furthermore, there is a real risk that, by demanding the provisions of the Bill of Rights apply identically to the States, federal courts will cause those provisions to "be watered down in the needless pursuit of uniformity." *Duncan v. Louisiana* (1968) (Harlan, J., dissenting)....

II. So far, I have explained that substantive due process analysis generally requires us to consider the term "liberty" in the 14th Amendment, and that this inquiry may be informed by but does not depend upon the content of the Bill of Rights.... When confronted with a substantive due process claim, we must ask whether the allegedly unlawful practice violates values "implicit in the concept of ordered liberty." *Palko v. Connecticut* (1937). If the practice in question lacks any "oppressive and arbitrary" character, if judicial enforcement of the asserted right would not materially contribute to "a fair and enlightened system of justice," then the claim is unsuitable for substantive due process protection. Implicit in Justice Cardozo's test is a recognition that the postulates of liberty have a universal character....

Justice Cardozo's test undeniably requires judges to apply their own reasoned judgment, but that does not mean it involves an exercise in abstract philosophy. In addition to other constraints ... historical and empirical data of various kinds ground the analysis. Textual commitments laid down elsewhere in the Constitution, judicial precedents, English common law, legislative and social facts, scientific and professional developments, practices of other civilized societies, and, above all else, the "'traditions and conscience of our people,'" *Palko*, are critical variables....

Duncan did not jettison the *Palko* test so much as refine it: The judge is still tasked with evaluating whether a practice "is fundamental ... to ordered liberty," within the context of the "Anglo-American" system. Several of our most important recent decisions confirm the proposition that substantive due process analysis—from which, once again, "incorporation" analysis derives—must not be wholly backward looking. See, *e.g., Lawrence v. Texas* (2003) ("[H]istory and tradition are the starting point but not in all cases the ending point of the substantive due process inquiry"); *Michael H. v. Gerald D.* (1989) (garnering only two votes for history-driven methodology that "consult[s] the most specific tradition available"); see also (Breyer, J., dissenting) (explaining that post-*Duncan* "incorporation" cases continued to rely on more than history)....

The Court hinges its entire decision on one mode of intellectual history, culling selected pronouncements and enactments from the 18th and 19th centuries to ascertain what Americans thought about firearms. Relying on *Duncan* and *Glucksberg*, the plurality suggests that only interests that have proved "fundamental from an American perspective," or "'deeply rooted in this Nation's history and tradition,'" to the Court's satisfaction, may qualify for incorporation into the 14th Amendment. To the extent the Court's opinion could be read to imply that the historical pedigree of a right is the exclusive or dispositive determinant of its status under the Due Process Clause, the opinion is seriously mistaken.

A rigid historical test is inappropriate in this case, most basically, because our substantive due process doctrine has never evaluated substantive rights in purely, or even predominantly, historical terms....

[W]hen the Court has used the Due Process Clause to recognize rights distinct from the trial context — rights relating to the primary conduct of free individuals — Justice Cardozo's test has been our guide. The right to free speech, for instance, has been safeguarded from state infringement not because the States have always honored it, but because it is "essential to free government" and "to the maintenance of democratic institutions" — that is, because the right to free speech is implicit in the concept of ordered liberty. *Thornhill v. Alabama* (1940); see also, *e.g., Loving* (discussing right to marry person of another race). While the verbal formula has varied, the Court has largely been consistent in its liberty-based approach to substantive interests outside of the adjudicatory system. As the question before us indisputably concerns such an interest, the answer cannot be found in a granular inspection of state constitutions or congressional debates.

More fundamentally, a rigid historical methodology is unfaithful to the Constitution's command. For if it were really the case that the 14th Amendment's guarantee of liberty embraces only those rights "so rooted in our history, tradition, and practice as to require special protection," *Glucksberg*, then the guarantee would serve little function, save to ratify those rights that state actors have *already* been according the most extensive protection ... That approach is unfaithful to the expansive principle Americans laid down when they ratified the 14th Amendment and to the level of generality they chose when they crafted its language; it promises an objectivity it cannot deliver and masks the value judgments that pervade any analysis of what customs, defined in what manner, are sufficiently "'rooted'"; it countenances the most revolting injustices in the name of continuity,[2] for we must never forget that not only slavery but also the subjugation of women and other rank forms of discrimination are part of our history; and it effaces this Court's distinctive role in saying what the law is, leaving the development and safekeeping of liberty to majoritarian political processes. It is judicial abdication in the guise of judicial modesty.

No, the liberty safeguarded by the 14th Amendment is not merely preservative in nature but rather is a "dynamic concept." Stevens, *The Bill of Rights: A Century of Progress* (1972). Its dynamism provides a central means through which the Framers enabled the Constitution to "endure for ages to come," *McCulloch v. Maryland* (1819).... "The task of giving concrete meaning to the term 'liberty,'" I have elsewhere explained at some length, "was a part of the work assigned to future generations." The judge who would outsource the interpretation of "liberty" to historical sentiment has turned his back on a task the Constitution assigned to him and drained the document of its intended vitality.

---

2. See *Bowers v. Hardwick*, (1986) (Blackmun, J., dissenting) ("Like Justice Holmes, I believe that '[i]t is revolting to have no better reason for a rule of law than that so it was laid down in the time of Henry IV. It is still more revolting if the grounds upon which it was laid down have vanished long since, and the rule simply persists from blind imitation of the past'" (quoting Holmes, *The Path of the Law*, 10 Harv. L. Rev. 457, 469 (1897))).

III. At this point a difficult question arises. In considering such a majestic term as "liberty" and applying it to present circumstances, how are we to do justice to its urgent call and its open texture—and to the grant of interpretive discretion the latter embodies—without injecting excessive subjectivity or unduly restricting the States' "broad latitude in experimenting with possible solutions to problems of vital local concern"? One part of the answer, already discussed, is that we must ground the analysis in historical experience and reasoned judgment, and never on "merely personal and private notions." *Rochin v. California* (1952). Our precedents place a number of additional constraints on the decisional process. Although "guideposts for responsible decision making in this unchartered area are scarce and open-ended," significant guideposts do exist....

[W]e have eschewed attempts to provide any all-purpose, top-down, totalizing theory of "liberty."... The Framers did not express a clear understanding of the term to guide us, and the now-repudiated *Lochner v. New York* (1905) line of cases attests to the dangers of judicial overconfidence in using substantive due process to advance a broad theory of the right or the good. In its most durable precedents, the Court "has not attempted to define with exactness the liberty ... guaranteed" by the 14th Amendment. *Meyer*; see also, *e.g., Bolling*. By its very nature, the meaning of liberty cannot be "reduced to any formula; its content cannot be determined by reference to any code." *Poe* (Harlan, J., dissenting).

Yet while "the 'liberty' specially protected by the 14th Amendment" is "perhaps not capable of being fully clarified," it is capable of being refined and delimited.... Ever since "the deviant economic due process cases [were] repudiated," our doctrine has steered away from "laws that touch economic problems, business affairs, or social conditions," *Griswold* and has instead centered on "matters relating to marriage, procreation, contraception, family relationships, and child rearing and education," *Paul v. Davis* (1976). Government action that shocks the conscience, pointlessly infringes settled expectations, trespasses into sensitive private realms or life choices without adequate justification, perpetrates gross injustice, or simply lacks a rational basis will always be vulnerable to judicial invalidation. Nor does the fact that an asserted right falls within one of these categories end the inquiry. More fundamental rights may receive more robust judicial protection, but the strength of the individual's liberty interests and the State's regulatory interests must always be assessed and compared. No right is absolute.

Rather than seek a categorical understanding of the liberty clause, our precedents have thus elucidated a conceptual core. The clause safeguards, most basically, "the ability independently to define one's identity," *Roberts v. United States Jaycees* (1984), "the individual's right to make certain unusually important decisions that will affect his own, or his family's, destiny," and the right to be respected as a human being. Self-determination, bodily integrity, freedom of conscience, intimate relationships, political equality, dignity and respect—these are the central values we have found implicit in the concept of ordered liberty.

Another key constraint on substantive due process analysis is respect for the democratic process. If a particular liberty interest is already being given careful consideration in, and subjected to ongoing calibration by, the States, judicial enforcement may not be appropriate....

Recognizing a new liberty right is a momentous step. It takes that right, to a considerable extent, "outside the arena of public debate and legislative action." Sometimes that momentous step must be taken; some fundamental aspects of personhood, dignity, and the like do not vary from State to State, and demand a baseline level of protection. But sensitivity to the interaction between the intrinsic aspects of liberty and the practical realities of contemporary society provides an important tool for guiding judicial discretion....

Several rules of the judicial process help enforce ... restraint. [T]he Court has applied both the doctrine of *stare decisis*—adhering to precedents, respecting reliance interests, prizing stability ... and the common-law method—taking cases and controversies as they present themselves, proceeding slowly and incrementally, building on what came before. This restrained methodology was evident even in the heyday of "incorporation" during the 1960's ...

IV. The question in this case, then, is not whether the 2nd Amendment right to keep and bear arms (whatever that right's precise contours) applies to the States because the Amendment has been incorporated into the 14th Amendment. It has not been. The question, rather, is whether the particular right asserted by petitioners applies to the States because of the 14th Amendment itself, standing on its own bottom. And to answer that question, we need to determine, first, the nature of the right that has been asserted and, second, whether that right is an aspect of 14th Amendment "liberty." Even accepting the Court's holding in *Heller*, it remains entirely possible that the right to keep and bear arms identified in that opinion is not judicially enforceable against the States, or that only part of the right is so enforceable. It is likewise possible for the Court to find in this case that some part of the *Heller* right applies to the States, and then to find in later cases that other parts of the right also apply, or apply on different terms.

As noted at the outset, the liberty interest petitioners have asserted is the "right to possess a functional, personal firearm, including a handgun, within the home." The city of Chicago allows residents to keep functional firearms, so long as they are registered, but it generally prohibits the possession of handguns, sawed-off shotguns, machine guns, and short barreled rifles. See Chicago, Ill., Municipal Code § 8-20-050 (2009). Petitioners' complaint centered on their desire to keep a handgun at their domicile....

Understood as a plea to keep their preferred type of firearm in the home, petitioners' argument has real force....

The State generally has a lesser basis for regulating private as compared to public acts, and firearms kept inside the home generally pose a lesser threat to public welfare as compared to firearms taken outside. The historical case for regulation is likewise stronger outside the home, as many States have for many years imposed stricter, and less controversial, restrictions on the carriage of arms than on their domestic possession....

[A] rule limiting the federal constitutional right to keep and bear arms to the home would be less intrusive on state prerogatives and easier to administer. Having unleashed in *Heller* a tsunami of legal uncertainty, and thus litigation, and now on the cusp of imposing a national rule on the States in this area for the first time in United States history, the Court could at least moderate the confusion, upheaval, and burden on the States by adopting a rule that is clearly and tightly bounded in scope....

In short, while the utility of firearms, and handguns in particular, to the defense of hearth and home is certainly relevant to an assessment of petitioners' asserted right, there is no freestanding self-defense claim in this case. The question we must decide is whether the interest in keeping in the home a firearm of one's choosing—a handgun, for petitioners—is one that is "comprised within the term liberty" in the 14th Amendment. *Whitney* (Brandeis, J., concurring).

V.... I am ultimately persuaded that a better reading of our case law supports the city of Chicago. I would not foreclose the possibility that a particular plaintiff—say, an elderly widow who lives in a dangerous neighborhood and does not have the strength to operate a long gun—may have a cognizable liberty interest in possessing a handgun. But I cannot accept petitioners' broader submission. A number of factors, taken together, lead me to this conclusion.

First, firearms have a fundamentally ambivalent relationship to liberty. Just as they can help homeowners defend their families and property from intruders, they can help thugs and insurrectionists murder innocent victims. The threat that firearms will be misused is far from hypothetical, for gun crime has devastated many of our communities. *Amici* calculate that approximately one million Americans have been wounded or killed by gunfire in the last decade. Urban areas such as Chicago suffer disproportionately from this epidemic of violence.... Just as some homeowners may prefer handguns because of their small size, light weight, and ease of operation, some criminals will value them for the same reasons. In recent years, handguns were reportedly used in more than four-fifths of firearm murders and more than half of all murders nationwide.

Hence, in evaluating an asserted right to be free from particular gun-control regulations, liberty is on both sides of the equation. Guns may be useful for self-defense, as well as for hunting and sport, but they also have a unique potential to facilitate death and destruction.... *Your* interest in keeping and bearing a certain firearm may diminish *my* interest in being and feeling safe from armed violence. And while granting you the right to own a handgun might make you safer on any given day—assuming the handgun's marginal contribution to self-defense outweighs its marginal contribution to the risk of accident, suicide, and criminal mischief—it may make you and the community you live in less safe overall, owing to the increased number of handguns in circulation. It is at least reasonable for a democratically elected legislature to take such concerns into account....

The idea that deadly weapons pose a distinctive threat to the social order—and that reasonable restrictions on their usage therefore impose an acceptable burden on one's personal liberty—is as old as the Republic.... The power a man has in the state of nature "of doing whatsoever he thought fit for the preservation of himself and the rest of mankind, he gives up," to a significant extent, "to be regulated by laws made by the society." J. Locke, *Second Treatise of Civil Government* § 129, p. 64 (J. Gough ed. 1947)....

[G]uns that start out in the home may not stay in the home. Even if the government has a weaker basis for restricting domestic possession of firearms as compared to public carriage—and even if a blanket, statewide prohibition on domestic possession might therefore be unconstitutional—the line between the two is a porous one. A state or local legislature may determine that a prophylactic ban on an especially portable weapon is necessary to police that line.

Second, the right to possess a firearm of one's choosing is different in kind from the liberty interests we have recognized under the Due Process Clause. Despite the plethora of substantive due process cases that have been decided in the post-*Lochner* century, I have found none that holds, states, or even suggests that the term "liberty" encompasses either the common-law right of self-defense or a right to keep and bear arms....

Third, the experience of other advanced democracies, including those that share our British heritage, undercuts the notion that an expansive right to keep and bear arms is intrinsic to ordered liberty. Many of these countries place restrictions on the possession, use, and carriage of firearms far more onerous than the restrictions found in this Nation.

See Municipal Respondents' Brief 21–23(discussing laws of England, Canada, Australia, Japan, Denmark, Finland, Luxembourg, and New Zealand). That the United States is an international outlier in the permissiveness of its approach to guns does not suggest that our laws are bad laws. It does suggest that this Court may not need to assume responsibility for making our laws still more permissive....

Fourth, the 2nd Amendment differs in kind from the Amendments that surround it.... Generally, the inclusion of a liberty interest in the Bill of Rights points toward the conclusion that it is of fundamental significance and ought to be enforceable against the States. But the 2nd Amendment plays a peculiar role within the Bill, as announced by its peculiar opening clause. Even accepting the *Heller* Court's view that the Amendment protects an individual right to keep and bear arms disconnected from militia service, it remains undeniable that "the purpose for which the right was codified" was "to prevent elimination of the militia." *Heller*; see also *United States v. Miller* (1939) (2nd Amendment was enacted "[w]ith obvious purpose to assure the continuation and render possible the effectiveness of [militia] forces")....

The 2nd Amendment, in other words, "is a federalism provision," *Elk Grove Unified School Dist. v. Newdow* (2004) (Thomas, J., concurring in judgment). It is directed at preserving the autonomy of the sovereign States, and its logic therefore "resists" incorporation by a federal court *against* the States....

I accept that the evolution in Americans' understanding of the 2nd Amendment may help shed light on the question whether a right to keep and bear arms is comprised within 14th Amendment "liberty." But the reasons that motivated the Framers to protect the ability of militiamen to keep muskets available for military use when our Nation was in its infancy, or that motivated the Reconstruction Congress to extend full citizenship to the freed men in the wake of the Civil War, have only a limited bearing on the question that confronts the homeowner in a crime-infested metropolis today. The many episodes of brutal violence against African-Americans that blight our Nation's history do not suggest that every American must be allowed to own whatever type of firearm he or she desires—just that no group of Americans should be systematically and discriminatorily disarmed and left to the mercy of racial terrorists. And the fact that some Americans may have thought or hoped that the 14th Amendment would nationalize the 2nd Amendment hardly suffices to justify the conclusion that it did.

Fifth, although it may be true that Americans' interest in firearm possession and state-law recognition of that interest are "deeply rooted" in some important senses, it is equally true that the States have a long and unbroken history of regulating firearms....

This history of intrusive regulation is not surprising given that the very text of the 2nd Amendment calls out for regulation, and the ability to respond to the social ills associated with dangerous weapons goes to the very core of the States' police powers.... Our precedent is crystal clear on this ... point. See, *e.g., Gonzales v. Oregon* (2006) ("[T]he structure and limitations of federalism ... allow the States great latitude under their police powers to legislate as to the protection of the lives, limbs, health, comfort, and quiet of all persons"); *United States v. Morrison* (2000) ("[W]e can think of no better example of the police power, which the Founders denied the National Government and reposed in the States, than the suppression of violent crime and vindication of its victims"). Compared with today's ruling, most if not all of this Court's decisions requiring the States to comply with other provisions in the Bill of Rights did not exact nearly so heavy a toll in terms of state sovereignty....

VII. The fact that the right to keep and bear arms appears in the Constitution should not obscure the novelty of the Court's decision to enforce that right against the States.

By its terms, the 2nd Amendment does not apply to the States; read properly, it does not even apply to individuals outside of the militia context. The 2nd Amendment was adopted to protect the *States* from federal encroachment. And the 14th Amendment has never been understood by the Court to have "incorporated" the entire Bill of Rights. There was nothing foreordained about today's outcome....

Justice Breyer, with whom Justice Ginsburg and Justice Sotomayor join, dissenting.

In my view, Justice Stevens has demonstrated that the 14th Amendment's guarantee of "substantive due process" does not include a general right to keep and bear firearms for purposes of private self-defense ...

The Court, however, does not expressly rest its opinion upon "substantive due process" concerns. Rather, it directs its attention to this Court's "incorporation" precedents and asks whether the 2nd Amendment right to private self-defense is "fundamental" so that it applies to the States through the 14th Amendment.

I shall therefore separately consider the question of "incorporation." I can find nothing in the 2nd Amendment's text, history, or underlying rationale that could warrant characterizing it as "fundamental" insofar as it seeks to protect the keeping and bearing of arms for private self-defense purposes. Nor can I find any justification for interpreting the Constitution as transferring ultimate regulatory authority over the private uses of firearms from democratically elected legislatures to courts or from the States to the Federal Government. I therefore conclude that the 14th Amendment does not "incorporate" the 2nd Amendment's right "to keep and bear Arms." And I consequently dissent.

I. The 2nd Amendment says: "A well regulated Militia, being necessary to the security of a free State, the right of the people to keep and bear Arms, shall not be infringed." Two years ago, in *District of Columbia v. Heller* (2008), the Court rejected the pre-existing judicial consensus that the 2nd Amendment was primarily concerned with the need to maintain a "well regulated Militia." Although the Court acknowledged that "the threat that the new Federal Government would destroy the citizens' militia by taking away their arms *was the reason* that right ... was codified in a written Constitution," the Court asserted that "individual self defense ... was the *central component* of the right itself." *Heller*. The Court went on to hold that the 2nd Amendment restricted Congress' power to regulate handguns used for self-defense, and the Court found unconstitutional the District of Columbia's ban on the possession of handguns in the home.

The Court based its conclusions almost exclusively upon its reading of history....

Since *Heller*, historians, scholars, and judges have continued to express the view that the Court's historical account was flawed. [Citing, *e.g.*, Konig, *Why the 2nd Amendment Has a Preamble: Original Public Meaning and the Political Culture of Written Constitutions in Revolutionary America*, 56 UCLA L. Rev. 1295 (2009); Finkelman, *It Really Was About a Well Regulated Militia*, 59 Syracuse L. Rev. 267 (2008) and about eight other articles.]

Consider as an example of these critiques an *amici* brief filed in this case by historians who specialize in the study of the English Civil Wars. They tell us that *Heller* misunderstood a key historical point ... *Heller*'s conclusion that "individual self-defense" was "the *central component*" of the 2nd Amendment's right "to keep and bear Arms" rested upon its view that the Amendment "codified a *pre-existing* right" that had "nothing whatever to do with service in a militia." That view in turn rested in significant part upon Blackstone having described the right as "'the right of having and using arms for self-preservation and defence,'" which reflected the provision in the English Declaration of Right of 1689 that gave the King's Protestant "'subjects'" the right to "'have Arms for their defence suitable to their Conditions, and as allowed by law.'" The Framers, said the majority, understood that right "as permitting a citizen to 'repe[l] force by force' when 'the intervention of society in his behalf, may be too late to prevent an injury.'"

The historians now tell us, however, that the right to which Blackstone referred had ... *everything*, to do with the militia. As properly understood at the time of the English Civil Wars, the historians claim, the right to bear arms "ensured that *Parliament* had the power" to arm the citizenry: "to defend the realm" in the case of a foreign enemy, and to "secure the right of 'self preservation,'" or "self-defense," should "*the sovereign* usurp the English Constitution." English Historians' Brief. Thus, the Declaration of Right says that private persons can possess guns only "as allowed by law." Moreover, when Blackstone referred to "'the right of having and using arms for self-preservation and defence,'" he was referring to the right of the people "*to take part in the militia* to defend their political liberties," and *to the right of Parliament* (which represented the people) to *raise a militia* even when the King sought to deny it that power. (quoting 1 Blackstone 140). Nor can the historians find any convincing reason to believe that the Framers had something different in mind than what Blackstone himself meant....

If history, and history alone, is what matters, why would the Court not now reconsider *Heller* in light of these more recently published historical views? At the least, where *Heller*'s historical foundations are so uncertain, why extend its applicability?...

In my own view, the Court should not look to history alone but to other factors as well—above all, in cases where the history is so unclear that the experts themselves strongly disagree. It should, for example, consider the basic values that underlie a constitutional provision and their contemporary significance. And it should examine as well the relevant consequences and practical justifications that might, or might not, warrant removing an important question from the democratic decision-making process.

II. A. In my view, taking *Heller* as a given, the 14th Amendment does not incorporate the 2nd Amendment right to keep and bear arms for purposes of private self defense. Under this Court's precedents, to incorporate the private self-defense right the majority must show that the right is, *e.g.*, "fundamental to the American scheme of justice," *Duncan v. Louisiana* (1968); see also (plurality opinion) (finding that the right is "fundamental" and therefore incorporated. And this it fails to do....

[T]he Court has either explicitly or implicitly made clear in its opinions that the right in question has remained fundamental over time.... I thus think it proper, above all where history provides no clear answer, to look to other factors in considering whether a right is sufficiently "fundamental" to remove it from the political process in every State. I would include among those factors the nature of the right; any contemporary disagreement about whether the right is fundamental; the extent to which incorporation will further other, perhaps more basic, constitutional aims; and the extent to which incorporation will advance or hinder the Constitution's structural aims, including its division of powers among different governmental institutions (and the people as well). Is incorporation needed, for example, to further the Constitution's effort to ensure that the government treats each individual with equal respect? Will it help maintain the democratic form of government that the Constitution foresees?...

II. B. How do these considerations apply here? For one thing, I would apply them only to the private self-defense right directly at issue. After all, the Amendment's militia-related purpose is primarily to protect *States* from *federal* regulation, not to protect individuals from militia-related regulation.... It is difficult to see how a right that, as the majority concedes, has "largely faded as a popular concern" could possibly be so fundamental that it would warrant incorporation through the 14th Amendment. Hence, the incorporation of the 2nd Amendment cannot be based on the militia-related aspect of what *Heller* found to be more extensive 2nd Amendment rights....

[A]s *Heller* concedes, the private self-defense right that the Court would incorporate has nothing to do with "the *reason*" the Framers "codified" the right to keep and bear arms "in a written Constitution." *Heller* immediately adds that the self-defense right was nonetheless "the *central component* of the right." In my view, this is the historical equivalent of a claim that water runs uphill. See Part I, *supra*. But, taking it as valid, the Framers' basic *reasons* for including language in the Constitution would nonetheless seem more pertinent (in deciding about the contemporary *importance* of a right) than the particular *scope* 17th- or 18th-century listeners would have then assigned to the words they used. And examination of the Framers' motivation tells us they did not think the private armed self-defense right was of paramount importance...

Moreover, every State regulates firearms extensively, and public opinion is sharply divided on the appropriate level of regulation.... One side believes the right essential to protect the lives of those attacked in the home; the other side believes it essential to regulate the right in order to protect the lives of others attacked with guns.... [T]he appropriate level of firearm regulation has thus long been, and continues to be, a hotly contested matter of political debate ...

Moreover, there is no reason here to believe that incorporation of the private self-defense right will further any other or broader constitutional objective. We are aware of no argument that gun-control regulations target or are passed with the purpose of targeting "discrete and insular minorities." Nor will incorporation help to assure equal respect for individuals. Unlike the 1st Amendment's rights of free speech, free press, assembly, and petition, the private self-defense right does not comprise a necessary part of the democratic process that the Constitution seeks to establish. See, *e.g., Whitney v. California*, (1927) (Brandeis, J., concurring). [T]he private self-defense right does not significantly seek to protect individuals who might otherwise suffer unfair or inhumane treatment at the hands of a majority. [I]t does not involve matters as to which judges possess a comparative expertise, by virtue of their close familiarity with the justice system and its operation. And, unlike the 5th Amendment's insistence on just compensation, it does not involve a matter where a majority might unfairly seize for itself property belonging to a minority.

Finally, incorporation of the right *will* work a significant disruption in the constitutional allocation of decision making authority, thereby interfering with the Constitution's ability to further its objectives.

First, on any reasonable accounting, the incorporation of the right recognized in *Heller* would amount to a significant incursion on a traditional and important area of state concern, altering the constitutional relationship between the States and the Federal Government. Private gun regulation is the quintessential exercise of a State's "police power"—*i.e.*, the power to "protec[t] ... the lives, limbs, health, comfort, and quiet of all persons, and the protection of all property within the State," by enacting "all kinds of restraints and burdens" on both "persons and property." *Slaughter-House Cases* (1873).... A decade ago, we wrote that there is "no better example of the police power" than "the suppression of violent crime." *United States v. Morrison* (2000). And examples in which the Court has deferred to state legislative judgments in respect to the exercise of the police power are legion....

Second, determining the constitutionality of a particular state gun law requires finding answers to complex empirically based questions of a kind that legislatures are better able than courts to make. See, *e.g., Los Angeles v. Alameda Books, Inc.* (2002) (plurality opinion)....

Suppose, for example, that after a gun regulation's adoption the murder rate went up. Without the gun regulation would the murder rate have risen even faster? How is this conclusion affected by the local recession which has left numerous people unemployed? What about budget cuts that led to a downsizing of the police force? How effective was that police force to begin with? And did the regulation simply take guns from those who use them for lawful purposes without affecting their possession by criminals?

Consider too that countless gun regulations of many shapes and sizes are in place in every State and in many local communities. Does the right to possess weapons for self-defense extend outside the home? ... What sort of guns are necessary for self-defense? Handguns? ... Semiautomatic weapons? When is a gun semi-automatic? ... Does time-of-day matter? Does the presence of a child in the house matter? Does the presence of a convicted felon in the house matter? Do police need special rules permitting pat downs designed to find guns? When do registration requirements become severe to the point that they amount to an unconstitutional ban? Who can possess guns and of what kind? Aliens? Prior drug offenders? Prior alcohol abusers? How would the right interact with a state or local government's ability to take special measures during, say, national security emergencies? As the questions suggest, state and local gun regulation can become highly complex, and these "are only a few uncertainties that quickly come to mind."

The difficulty of finding answers to these questions is exceeded only by the importance of doing so. Firearms cause well over 60,000 deaths and injuries in the United States each year. Those who live in urban areas, police officers, women, and children, all may be particularly at risk.... Some experts have calculated, for example, that Chicago's handgun ban has saved several hundred lives, perhaps close to 1,000, since it was enacted in 1983. Other experts argue that stringent gun regulations "can help protect police officers operating on the front lines against gun violence," have reduced homicide rates in Washington, D. C., and Baltimore, and have helped to lower New York's crime and homicide rates.

At the same time, the opponents of regulation cast doubt on these studies. And who is right? ...

In answering such questions judges cannot simply refer to judicial homilies, such as Blackstone's 18th-century perception that a man's home is his castle. Nor can the plurality so simply reject, by mere assertion, the fact that "incorporation will require judges to assess the costs and benefits of firearms restrictions." How can the Court assess the strength of the government's regulatory interests without addressing issues of empirical fact? How can the Court determine if a regulation is appropriately tailored without considering its impact? And how can the Court determine if there are less restrictive alternatives without considering what will happen if those alternatives are implemented? ...

The fact is that judges do not know the answers to the kinds of empirically based questions that will often determine the need for particular forms of gun regulation. Nor do they have readily available "tools" for finding and evaluating the technical material submitted by others....

At the same time, there is no institutional need to send judges off on this "mission-almost-impossible." Legislators are able to "amass the stuff of actual experience and cull conclusions from it." ...

In *New State Ice Co. v. Liebmann* (1932), Justice Brandeis stated in dissent:

> ... There must be power in the States and the Nation to remold, through experimentation, our economic practices and institutions to meet changing social and economic needs. I cannot believe that the framers of the 14th Amendment, or the States which ratified it, intended to deprive us of the power to correct [the social problems we face]....

Third, the ability of States to reflect local preferences and conditions—both key virtues of federalism—here has particular importance. The incidence of gun ownership varies substantially as between crowded cities and uncongested rural communities ... Thus, approximately 60% of adults who live in the relatively sparsely populated Western States of Alaska, Montana, and Wyoming report that their household keeps a gun, while fewer than 15% of adults in the densely populated Eastern States of Rhode Island, New Jersey, and Massachusetts say the same.

The nature of gun violence also varies as between rural communities and cities. Urban centers face significantly greater levels of firearm crime and homicide, while rural communities have proportionately greater problems with non homicide gun deaths, such as suicides and accidents....

It is thus unsurprising that States and local communities have historically differed about the need for gun regulation as well as about its proper level. Nor is it surprising that "primarily, and historically," the law has treated the exercise of police powers, including gun control, as "matter[s] of local concern."

Fourth, although incorporation of any right removes decisions from the democratic process, the incorporation of this particular right does so without strong offsetting justification—as the example of Oak Park's handgun ban helps to show. Oak Park decided to ban handguns in 1983, after a local attorney was shot to death with a handgun that his assailant had smuggled into a courtroom in a blanket.... The public decided to keep the ban by a vote of 8,031 to 6,368. And since that time, Oak Park now tells us, crime has decreased and the community has seen no accidental handgun deaths.

Given the empirical and local value-laden nature of the questions that lie at the heart of the issue, why, in a Nation whose Constitution foresees democratic decisionmaking, is it so *fundamental* a matter as to require taking that power from the people?...

In sum, the police power, the superiority of legislative decision-making, the need for local decisionmaking, the comparative desirability of democratic decisionmaking, the lack of a manageable judicial standard, and the life threatening harm that may flow from striking down regulations all argue against incorporation.... At the same time, the important factors that favor incorporation in other instances—*e.g.*, the protection of broader constitutional objectives—are not present here....

III.... The plurality, in seeking to justify incorporation, asks whether the interests the 2nd Amendment protects are "'deeply rooted in this Nation's history and tradition.'" It looks to selected portions of the Nation's history for the answer. And it finds an affirmative reply.

As I have made clear, I do not believe history is the only pertinent consideration....

* * *

In sum, the Framers did not write the 2nd Amendment in order to protect a private right of armed self defense. There has been, and is, no consensus that the right is, or was, "fundamental." No broader constitutional interest or principle supports legal treatment of that right as fundamental. To the contrary, broader constitutional concerns of an institutional nature argue strongly against that treatment.

Moreover, nothing in 18th-, 19th-, 20th-, or 21st-century history shows a consensus that the right to private armed self-defense, as described in *Heller*, is "deeply rooted in this Nation's history or tradition" or is otherwise "fundamental." Indeed, incorporating the right recognized in *Heller* may change the law in many of the 50 States. Read in the majority's favor, the historical evidence is at most ambiguous. And, in the absence of any other support for its conclusion, ambiguous history cannot show that the 14th Amendment incorporates a private right of self-defense against the States.

With respect, I dissent.

Chapter 8

Substantive Due Process

Contents

I.	Introduction	787
	Chronological Overview of Key Events Related to Substantive Due Process	787
	Goals for Chapter 8	790
	What Is Substantive Due Process?	791
II.	A Model of Substantive Due Process Analysis	796
III.	Liberty and Economic Rights	799
	A. The History of Economic Substantive Due Process, Part I	799
	Lochner v. New York	809
	Lochner-Era Economic Legislation Hypothetical	817
	The Brandeis Brief	817
	B. The History of Economic Substantive Due Process, Part II	818
	Fireside Chat on the "Court Packing" Bill	822
	Forces that Shape Constitutional Law	824
	The Demise of Economic Rights as "Liberty" Subject to Heightened Scrutiny	826
	United States v. Carolene Products Co.	827
	Carolene Products' Footnote Four	828
	Williamson v. Lee Optical of Oklahoma, Inc.	829
	FCC v. Beach Communications, Inc.	831
	Modern Economic Legislation Hypothetical	833
IV.	The Origins of Substantive Protection for Non-Economic Rights	834
	Meyer v. Nebraska	836
	Buck v. Bell	838
	Buck Revisited	839
	Skinner v. Oklahoma ex rel. Williamson	841
	Robinson v. California	843
	Rochin v. California	843
V.	Liberty and Sexual Privacy	844
	Poe v. Ullman	844
	Griswold v. Connecticut	848
	Eisenstadt v. Baird	856
	Roe v. Wade	858
	A. The Evolution of Privacy Holdings from *Griswold* to *Casey*	868
	Planned Parenthood of Southeastern Pennsylvania v. Casey	870
	B. The Language of "Fundamental Rights" versus "Liberty Interests"	890
	"Partial Birth" Abortion	892
	Gonzales v. Carhart	897

		C. Abortion Politics	910
		D. Substantive Due Process after *Roe*	911
VI.	Liberty and the Family		912
		Moore v. City of East Cleveland	912
		Michael H. v. Gerald D.	921
		Substantive Due Process and Less Textually Explicit Rights	926
VII.	Liberty and Sexual Autonomy: Restrictions on Private Sexual Behavior		926
	A.	Liberty and Sodomy: *Bowers*	927
		Bowers v. Hardwick	929
		Justice Powell's Reconsideration	936
	B.	Liberty and Sodomy: *Bowers* Repudiated	937
		Kentucky v. Wasson	937
		Lawrence v. Texas	944
	C.	Homosexuality and Politics	959
	D.	The Constitutional Status of Gay Marriage	960
		Varnum v. Brien	964
VIII.	Liberty and the "Right" to Die		967
		Washington v. Glucksberg	970
		Justice Souter's History of Substantive Due Process	982
IX.	The Takings Clause		986
		Miller v. Schoene	989
		Lucas v. South Carolina Coastal Council	990

Chapter 8

Substantive Due Process

I. Introduction

The 14th Amendment provides, in part, that "No State shall make or enforce any law which shall abridge the privileges or immunities of citizens of the United States; nor shall any State deprive any person of life, liberty, or property, without due process of law." The *Slaughter-House Cases* (1873), and those that followed it held that the Privileges or Immunities Clause did not provide persons much *federal* protection against their own state governments. Could a litigant find such protection in the Due Process Clause? What kind of liberties would be protected? Would it only provide procedural safeguards for these liberties?

Chronological Overview of Key Events Related to Substantive Due Process

1761: *Writs of Assistance Case.* James Otis, in the Massachusetts colony, challenges writs of assistance (general search warrants that allowed searches without specifying in advance the person or place to be searched). Otis argues: even if authorized by Parliament, the writs are illegal because "An Act Against the Constitution is void."

1776: The *Declaration of Independence* refers to the natural law tradition familiar to the era: "We hold these truths to be self-evident: that all men are created equal; that they are endowed, by their Creator, with certain unalienable rights; that among these are life, liberty, and the pursuit of happiness."

1798: *Calder v. Bull.* Justice Chase and Justice Iredell debate the propriety of the Supreme Court enforcing natural law principles.

1823: In *Corfield v. Coryell*, Justice Bushrod Washington discusses "fundamental" rights as he interprets the Privileges and Immunities Clause of Article IV, § 2.

1856: *Wyndehamer v. The People.* New York's highest court uses substantive due process analysis to overturn a state law allowing for the confiscation of liquor. Court declares "all property is equally sacred in the view of the constitution" and that a mere statute cannot deprive a citizen of rights, including the right to property.

1857: *Dred Scott v. Sanford.* The U.S. Supreme Court uses substantive due process analysis to assert that Congress cannot deprive a person of lawfully held property (slaves) merely by a statute banning slavery in a federal territory. Such a statute abridged the substantive due process rights of the slaveowner. Chief Justice Taney wrote that "the right of property in a slave is distinctly and expressly affirmed in the Constitution" and Congress had "the duty of guarding and protecting the owner [of slave property] in his rights," just like Congress had the duty to protect every other form of property.

1873: *Slaughter-House Cases* (5–4). The Court eviscerates the Privileges or Immunities Clause of the 14th Amendment in this and later cases. Consequently, later challenges to state legislation alleged to invade individual rights would have to look to the Due Process Clause or the Equal Protection Clause.

1877: Compromise of 1877, regarded as formal end of Reconstruction. Republicans get the Presidency in a contested election. Federal troops withdrawn from the South.

Munn v. Illinois (7–2). The Court upholds a state regulation of grain elevators against claims that it violated due process and rights to private property.

Railroad strikes across the nation. Industrial warfare continues to flare up in the late 19th and early 20th centuries.

1884: *Hurtado v. California*. The Court asserts that "Law is something more than mere will exerted as an act of power.... [I]t exclud[es], as not due process of law ... special, partial and arbitrary exertions of power under the forms of legislation."

1886: *Wabash, St. Louis & Pacific Rw. Co. v. Illinois* (6–3). The Court limits state power to regulate railroads.

Santa Clara County v. Southern Pacific Rw. Co. (9–0). The Court holds the 14th Amendment's protection of "persons" includes corporations.

1892: People's Party (Populists). The People's Party brings the farmer's protest movement into national politics. The party nominates General James B. Weaver for president in 1892. Its 1896 platform favors direct election of Senators; a progressive income tax; provisions for initiatives and referenda; government ownership of railroads, on the theory that either "the government must own the railroads or the railroads will own the government"; employment of labor on public works in times of depression; and other "radical" measures.

1894: Workers at the Pullman manufacturing plant strike, leading to a sympathy strike by railroad workers; federal troops sent to Chicago to break strike; strike is broken; federal courts issue injunctions vs. railroad union, its leaders, and locals; communication between locals is forbidden. (The broad decision upholding federal authority to punish unions under the commerce and postal powers in *In re Debs* (1895) contrasts with the Court's restrictive holdings with reference to the power of the federal government under the 13th and 14th Amendments to punish Klansmen for violations of the rights of Republicans and blacks in the South during Reconstruction.)

1895: In *United States v. E.C. Knight Co.* (8–1), the Court articulates a narrow definition of commerce. In *Pollock v. Farmers' Loan and Trust Co.* the Court holds the federal income tax unconstitutional.

1897: *Allgeyer v. Louisiana* (9–0). The Court holds there is a right to make contracts protected by the Due Process Clause of the 14th Amendment.

1905: *Lochner v. New York* (5–4). Court holds a state law limiting hours of work for bakers violates liberty of contract said to be secured by the Due Process Clause of the 14th Amendment. "Freedom of contract" and "substantive due process" will mark the "*Lochner* Era," circa 1900–1936.

1918: *Hammer v. Dagenhart* (5–4). The Court holds that Congress may not prohibit movement in commerce of articles made by child labor, ruling that manufacturing is not commerce.

1923: *Meyer v. Nebraska* (7–2). The Court invalidates a state statute prohibiting the teaching of foreign languages in schools as a violation of the "liberty" of the Due

Process Clause; shows *Lochner* Court's recognition of personal as well as economic rights as "liberty."

1929: Wall Street's crash brings the far-from-uniform prosperity of the Harding-Coolidge-Hoover era to an end and triggers the Great Depression. Widespread unemployment, bank failures, business and personal bankruptcy, and foreclosure of mortgages on homes and farms.

1932: Franklin Roosevelt elected President. Legislation proposed and enacted after his inauguration in 1933 marks the start of the New Deal. Roosevelt serves until 1945.

1935: *Schechter Poultry Corp. v. United States.* The Court invalidates a key New Deal measure (setting minimum wages, maximum hours, and codes of fair competition—including setting minimum prices). The Court holds the act is an unconstitutional delegation of power to the President and exceeds the power of Congress to regulate commerce.

1936: FDR re-elected in a landslide. Carries 46 of 48 states.

1937: *West Coast Hotel v. Parrish* (5–4). The Court allows a *state* minimum wage law for women to stand.

1941: *United States v. Darby* (9–0). The Court overrules *Hammer v. Dagenhart*, allowing Congress to ban interstate transportation of items made in violation of the Fair Labor Standards Act.

1942: *Wickard v. Filburn* (9–0). The Court adopts an extremely deferential aggregate impact test for determining scope of federal commerce power.

Skinner v. Oklahoma (7–2–0). The Court invalidates criminal eugenics law (mandatory sterilization for larceny but not embezzlement) as violating Equal Protection Clause. Heightened scrutiny of statute that involved fundamental right of procreation.

1955: *Williamson v. Lee Optical* (8–0). Burial of substantive due process and of heightened equal protection scrutiny for most purely economic regulation.

1963: Lyndon Johnson (LBJ) assumes presidency following assassination of JFK.

1964: Congress passes Civil Rights Act of 1964 following 75-day filibuster by Southern Senators. The Act prohibits racial discrimination in most public accommodations and prohibits employment discrimination based on race, national origin, religion, or sex.

Johnson re-elected in 1964, defeating "new conservative" Barry Goldwater, who criticizes civil rights legislation and carries several states in the South. Further erosion of once solidly Democratic South. Johnson launches War on Poverty at home. After the 1964 election he begins a gradual but eventually massive escalation of war in Vietnam. Widespread protests against the war begin after escalation.

Heart of Atlanta Motel v. United States (6–3). The Court upholds public accommodation part of Civil Rights Act of 1964 based on the Commerce Clause.

1965: *Griswold v. Connecticut.* Court upholds right of married couples to use birth control devices under 14th Amendment "right to privacy."

Voting Rights Act of 1965. Six days of rioting in Watts. In 1967 a "Long Hot Summer" of northern rioting begins.

1968: LBJ declines to run for re-election in face of anti-war protests. Dr. Martin Luther King, Jr. and Robert Kennedy assassinated. Students seize control of administrative buildings at several universities. Richard Nixon elected President. Governor George Wallace of Alabama runs as candidate of American Independent Party and receives 46 electoral votes. Nixon calls for appointment of strict constructionists to Court and greater comparative role for states in the federal system.

1973: President Nixon fires special prosecutor Archibald Cox.

Frontiero v. Richardson (4–4–1). View that gender discrimination should receive strict scrutiny receives 4 votes; three Justices say to wait for the ratification of the Equal Rights Amendment to resolve the issue.

Roe v. Wade (7–2). Limited right to abortion protected under the 14th Amendment Due Process Clause.

1980: Ronald Reagan elected President.

1985: *Bowers v. Hardwick* (5–4). The Court rejects substantive due process challenge by a homosexual to state sodomy law. Law upheld as applied to private, homosexual, consensual, sexual acts taking place in the home.

1992: Bill Clinton elected President.

Planned Parenthood v. Casey (plurality decision). The Court rejects calls for reversal of *Roe v. Wade*, but allows much regulation of abortion under "undue burden" standard.

1997: *Washington v. Glucksberg* (5–4). The Court holds a Washington state statute's ban on physician-assisted suicide for terminally ill patients does not violate the Due Process Clause of the 14th Amendment. The Court emphasizes the Nation's history, legal traditions, and practices which it said demonstrate that the Anglo-American common law has disapproved of assisting suicide for 700 years.

2003: *Lawrence v. Texas* (6–3). The Court overrules *Bowers*.

2007: *Gonzales v. Carhardt* (5–4). The Court upholds a congressional statute banning "partial birth abortion" in the absence of a health exception.

2010: *McDonald v. City of Chicago* (5–4). The Court finds that a substantive right to possess a handgun in the home is protected by the guarantee of liberty in the Due Process Clause.

Goals for Chapter 8

1. To understand the difference between procedural and substantive protection of liberty.

2. To understand the types of scrutiny the Court uses when examining legislation challenged as a violation of substantive due process. What is the purpose of having different levels of scrutiny?

3. To understand the methods the Court uses for deciding that an interest is entitled to heightened protection under the Due Process Clause. What is the significance of the constitutional text, of history and tradition, of precedent, of reason, of ideas of inherent rights, and of analogical reasoning?

4. To understand the rise and fall of economic substantive due process and the technique the Court used to eliminate it.

5. To understand how the Court's analysis differs if it finds challenged legislation interferes with a fundamental right, a liberty interest, or simply an economic interest. Which type of analysis allows more latitude for judges to implement their values? Which does more to constrain judicial choice?

6. To understand the effect of the type of interest on the level of scrutiny. A related goal is to understand how the type of interest and the level of scrutiny affect the likelihood that the legislation will survive judicial challenge.

7. To understand the significance of Footnote 4 in *Carolene Products* (1938) as a theoretical basis for the Court to apply strict or minimal scrutiny.

What Is Substantive Due Process?

"[N]or shall any state deprive any person of life, liberty, or property, without due process of law." One reading of the Due Process Clause of the 14th Amendment claims that the government need only provide *procedural* due process and regularity in its conduct. By this view the government could deprive people of life, liberty, or property so long as appropriate procedures were used. However, the Court has long held that there are some aspects of "liberty" that the government cannot regulate no matter how much process is provided. For historical support for finding substantive protections of liberty in the Due Process Clauses, *see* Frederick Mark Gedicks, *An Originalist Defense of Substantive Due Process: Magna Carta, Higher-Law Constitutionalism, and the Fifth Amendment*, 58 Emory L. J. 585, 594 (2009) (arguing "that one widely shared understanding of the Due Process Clause of the 5th Amendment in the late 18th century encompassed judicial recognition and enforcement of unenumerated substantive rights"). These rights (of persons and corporations) are determined by the "substantive" content that the Court finds in the 14th Amendment's protection of *liberty* in the Due Process Clause. In substantive due process cases the Court determines the scope of protections individuals enjoy against government intrusion. For citizens, these protections might have been found in the language and history of the 14th Amendment's Privileges or Immunities Clause. However, in the *Slaughter-House Cases* (1873) and later cases, the Court interpreted the Privileges or Immunities Clause very narrowly. As corporations and individuals pressed for protection against governmental action that they claimed deprive them of their "rights," litigants turned to the grant of "liberty" found in the 14th Amendment's Due Process Clause.

The issues raised by substantive due process cases are not unique. The controversy over substantive due process is basically a controversy over the proper scope of judicial review in the American political system. By what right do judges decide that acts passed by legislatures and approved by the executive are unconstitutional and void?

In 1803, in *Marbury v. Madison,* the Court announced that judges could hold laws unconstitutional. In *Democracy in America* (1835), Alexis de Tocqueville observed that American judges were more powerful than those of other nations. "The cause of this difference lies in the simple fact that the Americans have acknowledged the right to judges to found their decisions on the Constitution rather than on the laws. [T]hey have permitted them not to apply such laws as may appear to them to be unconstitutional."

In *Marbury*, Chief Justice Marshall justified judicial review. He noted that the Constitution is an act of the sovereign people that explicitly limits the power of the legislature and requires courts to apply the Constitution in deciding cases. But some skeptics ask whether the Court is vindicating the will of the people and the states that ratified the Constitution and its amendments. Is the Court instead *imposing its own will?* Others ask why the decisions of a minority of "we the people" long dead should continue to be binding unless a modern-day super-majority changes them by amendment.

The popular sovereignty justification for judicial review requires an aggrieved party to point to a constitutional right or to a lack of constitutional power in order to overturn legislation. The court may not strike down legislation merely because it believes it represents bad public policy. Sometimes the issue is simple and the answer seems clear. The 26th Amendment guarantees that eighteen-year-olds can vote. Judicial enforcement of this Amendment is not very controversial because of the specificity of the text. In theory and often in practice, when a statute violates a clear constitutional command, the Court will simply strike the statute down. For example, the government could not attempt to prevent eighteen-year-olds from voting in presidential elections. However, the textual and historical basis of many of the rights claimed under other clauses is less clear. When is a search unreasonable; a punishment cruel or unusual; a law a violation of the freedom of speech, equal protection, or due process?

Questions of the proper application of judicial review have been controversial throughout American history. There was, for example, a great uproar over *Dred Scott v. Sandford* (1857) and later over decisions limiting the power of legislatures to prohibit child labor and set minimum wages and maximum hours.

The Court has struck down statutes as violating *liberty*—either the "liberty" mentioned in the Due Process Clause or the "liberty" the Court finds in the penumbras of the Bill of Rights. The issue of enforcing less textually explicit rights is intensely controversial. Do or should people have either inherent or traditional rights beyond those explicitly set out in the Constitutional text? If so, should the Court enforce those rights, or leave the matter to the legislature? If it should enforce the rights, how should it determine their content? The materials that follow suggest various answers. A few Justices seem to be willing to find inherent rights. Most look to history, tradition, and analogy to previously decided cases. Some Justices insist on a long historic recognition of the *precise* right claimed. Others have a more dynamic view of our historic traditions. Few, however, are entirely consistent in their view of the proper judicial role.

Natural Law theory asserts that by nature all people have certain inherent rights which can be found through human reason. *Positive Law* theory asserts that people's rights are *only* those set by established governmental methods for making laws. The conflict between natural law and positive law goes back to the beginnings of the Court—and before. In the 13th-century, Thomas Aquinas maintained that duly enacted positive human law was inferior to natural law: an unjust law should not be considered a law at all. It was, instead, an act of violence.

The Levellers were a group of 17th-century English democrats. They appealed to natural law to support their claims to individual rights and the right of all men to vote for representatives to Parliament. Another group of 17th-century English radicals were the Diggers. They also appealed to natural law to justify occupation and cultivation of tracts of unused land by the poor.

Thomas Hobbes was a 17th-century English political theorist. He feared that natural law would unsettle the established law and government. In his *Leviathan* (1651), he emphasized that "[i]t is not wisdom, but authority that makes a law." Hobbes said that courts should be concerned only with that which was consistent with or contrary to officially promulgated rules; they should not examine the underlying justice of a governmental act. Hobbes also feared the common law and its legal reasoning because he felt that it gave unconstrained power to judges.

Great Britain had no written constitution. William Blackstone, in his famous *Commentaries on the Laws of England*, suggested that the power of Parliament was essentially unlimited. The other view, of course, was that even without a written constitution limiting the power of Parliament, certain basic principles of law limited government power. A famous case leading up to the American Revolution was *Paxton's Case* (1761), better known as the *Writs of Assistance Case*. In an effort to combat smuggling, which escaped taxation, colonial officials in Massachusetts were issuing "writs of assistance." These were *general* search warrants. They allowed sheriffs and other officials to search *any* house or other place. The object of the search was to find goods imported without paying customs duties.

The writ of assistance or general warrant was issued in advance and gave blanket power to search. It was not limited to specific persons, places or times. James Otis challenged the legality of the writ in *Paxton's Case* (1761). He appealed to unwritten constitutional principles. Otis argued: "All precedents are under the controul of the principles of the law.... No Acts of Parliament can establish such a writ.... it would be void. An act against the Constitution is void." Sixty years later, John Adams said of the case, "Then and there the child of Independence was born."

The Declaration of Independence is an appeal to natural law. It declares the "self-evident" truths that all persons

> are created equal, that they are endowed by their Creator with certain unalienable Rights, that among these are Life, Liberty, and the pursuit of happiness. That to secure these Rights Governments are instituted among Men, deriving their just Powers from the Consent of the Governed....

A classic early exchange on the proper role of natural law in constitutional lawmaking came in the Court's decision in *Calder v. Bull* (1798). Justice Chase opined that higher law principles constrained the legislature's power to enact positive law:

> I cannot subscribe to the omnipotence of a State Legislature, or that it is absolute and without control; although its authority should not be expressly restrained by the Constitution, or fundamental law, of the State. The people of the United States erected their Constitutions, or forms of government, to establish justice, to promote the general welfare, to secure the blessings of liberty; and to protect their persons and property from violence. The purposes for which men enter into society will determine the nature and terms of the social compact; and as they are the foundation of the legislative power, they will decide what are the proper objects of it: The nature, and ends of legislative power will limit the exercise of it. This fundamental principle flows from the very nature of our free Republican governments, that no man should be compelled to do what the laws do not require; nor to refrain from acts which the laws permit. There are acts which the Federal, or State, Legislature cannot do, without exceeding their authority. There are certain vital principles in our free Republican governments, which will determine and over-rule an apparent and flagrant abuse of legislative power; as to authorize manifest injustice by positive law; or to take away that security for personal liberty, or private property, for the protection whereof the government was established. An ACT of the Legislature (for I cannot call it a law) contrary to the great first principles of the social compact, cannot be considered a rightful exercise of legislative authority. The obligation of a law in governments established on express compact, and on republican principles, must be determined by the nature of the power, on which it is founded. A few instances will suffice to explain what I mean. A law that punished a citizen for an innocent action, or, in other words, for an act, which, when done, was in violation of no existing law; a law that destroys, or impairs, the lawful private contracts of citizens; a law that makes a man a Judge in his own cause; or a law that takes property from A. and gives it to B: It is against all reason and justice, for a people to entrust a

Legislature with SUCH powers; and, therefore, it cannot be presumed that they have done it. The genius, the nature, and the spirit, of our State Governments, amount to a prohibition of such acts of legislation; and the general principles of law and reason forbid them.... To maintain that our Federal, or State, Legislature possesses such powers, if they had not been expressly restrained; would, in my opinion, be a political heresy, altogether inadmissible in our free republican governments.

Justice Iredell offered the positivist reply:

If, then, a government, composed of Legislative, Executive and Judicial departments, were established, by a Constitution, which imposed no limits on the legislative power, the consequence would inevitably be, that whatever the legislative power chose to enact, would be lawfully enacted, and the judicial power could never interpose to pronounce it void. It is true, that some speculative jurists have held, that a legislative act against natural justice must, in itself, be void; but I cannot think that, under such a government, any Court of Justice would possess a power to declare it so. Sir William Blackstone, having put the strong case of an act of Parliament, which should authorize a man to try his own cause, explicitly adds, that even in that case, "there is no court that has power to defeat the intent of the Legislature, when couched in such evident and express words, as leave no doubt whether it was the intent of the Legislature, or no." (1 Blackstone's *Commentaries* 91.) ...

[I]t has been the policy of all the American states, which have, individually, framed their state constitutions since the revolution, and of the people of the United States, when they framed the Federal Constitution, to define with precision the objects of the legislative power, and to restrain its exercise within marked and settled boundaries. If any act of Congress, or of the Legislature of a state, violates those constitutional provisions, it is unquestionably void.... If, on the other hand, the Legislature of the Union, or the Legislature of any member of the Union, shall pass a law, within the general scope of their constitutional power, the Court cannot pronounce it to be void, merely because it is, in their judgment, contrary to the principles of natural justice. The ideas of natural justice are regulated by no fixed standard: the ablest and the purest men have differed upon the subject; and all that the Court could properly say, in such an event, would be, that the Legislature (possessed of an equal right of opinion) had passed an act which, in the opinion of the judges, was inconsistent with the abstract principles of natural justice....

The controversy over inherent rights continues. Consider for example the following statement by Chief Justice William Rehnquist:

The [difficulty with the] notion of the living Constitution is that it seems to ignore totally the nature of political value judgments in a democratic society. If such a society adopts a constitution and incorporates in that constitution safeguards for individual liberty, these safeguards indeed do take on a generalized moral rightness or goodness. They assume a general social acceptance neither because of any intrinsic worth nor because of any unique origins in someone's idea of natural justice but instead simply because they have been incorporated in a constitution by the people. Within the limits of our Constitution, the representatives of the people in the executive branches of the state and national governments enact laws. The laws that emerge after a typical political struggle in which various individual value judgments are debated likewise take on a form of moral goodness because they have been enacted into positive law. It is the fact of their enactment that gives them whatever moral claim they have upon us as a society, however, and not any independent virtue they may have in any particular citizen's own scale of values.

Beyond the Constitution and the laws in our society, there simply is no basis other than the individual conscience of the citizen that may serve as a platform for the launching of moral judgments. There is no conceivable way in which I can logically demonstrate to you that the judgments of my conscience are superior to the judgments of your conscience, and vice versa. Many of us necessarily feel strongly and deeply about our own moral judgments, but they remain only personal moral judgments until in some way given the sanction of law.

William H. Rehnquist, *Observation: The Notion of a Living Constitution* 54 Tex. L. Rev. 693, 704 (1976).

In the chapter on incorporation, we looked at whether a Bill of Rights guarantee, which applied to the *federal* government, should also be applied to the *states*. We only incidentally considered the *scope* of that right and the existence of additional *implicit* rights. In substantive due process cases, the existence and scope of the right is our primary focus. Assuming that the 5th and 14th Amendments guarantee a right to "liberty" against governmental action, what are the dimensions of that liberty? Does it include the right to sell unpasteurized milk, to work in a factory for more than sixty hours a week, to use birth control devices, or to engage in either heterosexual or homosexual sodomy? How should the Court go about answering these questions?

Many substantive due process arguments will be familiar. Justices will argue over the weight that should be given to text, tradition, and reason. In the incorporation debate, Justice Black argued that the Due Process and Privileges or Immunities Clauses should be interpreted only to include rights explicit in the constitutional text. Justices Rutledge and Murphy thought that these clauses included both the liberties in the Bill of Rights and other fundamental rights. The second Justice Harlan thought that the fundamental rights protected by the 14th Amendment were both more and less extensive than those protected by the Bill of Rights. One of the charms of the incorporation theory for Justice Black was his belief that the text of the Constitution could substantially constrain the judicial role. Incorporation by reference cannot work for rights not explicitly set out in the text. Opponents of incorporation, such as the second Justice Harlan, insisted that the guarantees of the Bill of Rights such as freedom of speech were hardly self-defining.

Substantive due process analysis goes beyond incorporation. It involves two steps. First, the Court will assert its authorization to act—that it is vindicating a constitutional norm, and not merely advancing its own policy goals. Second, if the Court finds a violation of a constitutional command, then it will make the legislature justify both its goal and chosen method for addressing that goal. Regulations that do not violate a constitutionally protected liberty (or exceed a delegated federal power) are presumed to be constitutional. Those that do threaten a constitutionally protected liberty will be subject to some level of scrutiny. The problem, of course, is to identify which liberties will receive heightened protection and to determine what level of scrutiny will be applied.

At different times, the Court has used different approaches. The present Court often proceeds as follows when no precedent is on point or when it seeks to change existing law. First, the Court will look to the Constitution's text for the source of the asserted right. If the text is inconclusive, the Court may consider the historical traditions of the United States or it may employ analogical reasoning, comparing the present case to existing legal precedent.

The Court will then require the government to attempt to justify the regulation. In doing so, it will employ a sliding scale. The degree of scrutiny will depend on the nature of the right or interest on which the legislation impinges. The Court will scrutinize why the legislature acted (the *end* it was seeking to accomplish) and it will examine the method the legislature used to reach its goal (the *means*). The government's justification must be compelling and its means necessary (or narrowly tailored) when the Court finds that the legislation will impact a *fundamental* constitutional right. The rigor of scrutiny is correspondingly reduced when lesser interests are affected.

The relationship between the ends and means can be illustrated graphically.* The legislature's *end* is often to suppress a harm. For example, lead-poisoning of children who eat paint chips is a harm. The *means* is the regulatory method the legislature selects to address the harm. When it regulates, the legislature selects a trait that it believes characterizes that which creates the harm. Here, lead in paint would be the relevant trait. Requiring the elimination of lead in paint would be the means to address the harm of lead-poisoning. Thus, end is associated with harm and means is associated with trait. A statute is perfectly rational if all those who have the trait contribute to the harm, and if no one contributes to the harm who lacks the trait. In contrast, a statute is perfectly irrational if no one who has the regulated trait contributes to the harm.

Most statutes do not fall into these categories. Most statutes are either under-inclusive, over-inclusive, or both. A statute is under-inclusive if there are more people who create the harm than the legislature has selected to regulate. For example, if a legislature is concerned about air pollution and begins to regulate factory emissions, but leaves automobiles alone, the statute is under-inclusive. Under-inclusiveness ordinarily is not a serious failing in most economic and social legislation, because courts will allow legislatures to go "one step at a time."

A statute is over-inclusive if many of the people who have the regulated trait do not in fact contribute to the harm. For example, during World War II, the government thought that some Japanese-Americans were disloyal. Even if this were so, most were not. When the government sent *all* Americans of Japanese ancestry living on the west coast to internment camps, the action was grossly over-inclusive. Ordinarily, over-inclusiveness is a much greater failing than under-inclusiveness because innocent people are being adversely affected.

The degree of rationality of under-inclusive or over-inclusive statutes depends on the fit between the harm and the trait and the number of cases involved. As the number of over-inclusive or under-inclusive cases increases, the rationality of the statute declines. The diagrams on the following page illustrate these concepts.

II. A Model of Substantive Due Process Analysis

Here we consider the method of analysis used in substantive due process cases. As you read these cases, you will see four levels of scrutiny that the Court has used in evaluating the ends/means fit: *strict scrutiny, rational basis with bite, rational basis,* and *no scrutiny*. The clearest categories are strict scrutiny and rational basis. If the Court finds a *funda-*

---

* This analysis was pioneered by Joseph Tussman & Jacobus Ten Broek, *The Equal Protection of the Laws*, 37 Cal. L. Rev. 341 (1949).

mental right is implicated, it will (at least in theory) employ strict scrutiny. The Court often says that the state must have a "compelling" end and the means selected to effectuate it must be "narrowly tailored." Cases also use language such as "necessary" or "least restrictive" to describe the means. The idea is that the means chosen must have the least possible

---

Diagrams

Recall that in these diagrams, the *end* pursued by the legislature is the elimination of a *harm*. The *means* is legislative regulation of a *trait* in a way claimed to address the *harm*.

1.

   COMPLETELY IRRATIONAL

   Nothing contributing to the Harm is caused by persons with the selected Trait. This statute is COMPLETELY IRRATIONAL. (The means selected completely fail to accomplish the end.)

2. UNDER-INCLUSIVE

   All those with the Trait cause the Harm, but some causing the Harm do not possess the Trait. This statute is UNDER-INCLUSIVE. (Regulating the selected trait will partially accomplish the end (address the harm), but there are many who cause the harm who are not reached by the selected means.)

3. OVER-INCLUSIVE

   All those causing the Harm possess the selected Trait, but some with the Trait do not cause the Harm. This statute is OVER-INCLUSIVE. (Regulating the selected trait will address the harm, but there are many who have the selected trait who do not contribute to the harm.)

4. UNDER- and OVER-inclusive

   Some with the Trait cause the Harm; some with the Trait do not cause the Harm; and some cause the Harm who do not have the Trait. This statute is both UNDER- and OVER-INCLUSIVE. (Regulating the selected trait will partially address the harm, but there are many who have the trait who do not contribute to the harm and many who contribute to the harm that do not have the trait.)

5. PERFECTLY RATIONAL

   Regulating the Trait addresses the Harm and only those with the Trait cause the Harm. This statute is PERFECTLY RATIONAL.

impact on the fundamental right while still allowing the state substantially to reach its desired (and compelling) goal. This burden on the state is very great. Challengers are typically successful if the court recognizes that a fundamental right has been impinged. An example of a right that the Court has said is fundamental is the right of a married couple to have access to contraception.

Rational basis review has been used to examine ordinary social and economic legislation that impacts a citizen in his pursuit of lawful activities. The state need only have a "legitimate" (*i.e.*, lawful) end and the means need only be rational or reasonable. In practice, this standard is very easily met; challengers almost never prevail. Of course, if the economic regulation is characterized as a "taking" or as a violation of the interstate Privileges and Immunities Clause, scrutiny is substantially heightened.

Strict scrutiny had been criticized for being "strict in theory but fatal in fact." However, the claim is inaccurate. Strict scrutiny is not *always* fatal.

The Burger and Rehnquist Courts began to withdraw from aggressive judicial supervision of legislation on controversial social topics. So they began to resist the recognition of new fundamental rights. For example, the Court has refused to find a fundamental right, and thus apply strict scrutiny, in the case of the so-called "right to die." In addition, in some cases where rights had been characterized as fundamental, the Court has dropped the use of that term and has avoided the words "strict scrutiny." Indeed, the shift from *fundamental rights* analysis to *liberty interest* analysis and the corresponding shift from strict scrutiny to a less exacting standard of review has characterized substantive due process analysis since *Roe v. Wade* (1973). The Court has typically categorized the right asserted in connection with these controversial topics as a "liberty interest," and used a heightened form of rational basis review, often referred to by scholars as "rational basis with bite." The language used to evaluate the ends/means fit is the same as for rational basis, but the Court will actually *examine* the fit, rather than passively accept the legislature's classification.

The chart that follows sets out a summary of the Court's substantive due process analysis in cases since the 1960's. The last category, "Decisional Method," includes two types of decision making: categorical analysis and ad hoc balancing. In categorical analysis, the Court constructs categories in advance and applies specified methods for each category. This is true for Equal Protection as well as for Substantive Due Process. For example, the Court will apply strict scrutiny if it finds that a statute fits in the category of intentional racial discrimination. In ad hoc balancing, the Court considers and weighs all the factors it finds relevant to the individual case and reaches results based on the totality of the particular circumstances.

Categorical analysis is used for three of the four types of rights or interests that appear on the chart on page 800. Once an asserted right is put into one of these categories, the outcome is highly predictable. In the "personal liberty interest" category (employing rational basis with bite) the outcome of any given challenge is most problematic. Here the Court will engage in ad hoc balancing as it examines the rationality of the ends/means fit. In the case of rational basis with bite, the Court's use of under-inclusive and over-inclusive analysis is more rigorous than at traditional rational basis review, but less consistently rigorous than in the case of strict scrutiny.

The Court also sometimes strikes down legislation as a violation of due process or equal protection because the end pursued is not constitutionally legitimate. For example, bans on racial intermarriage were justified as a means of preserving the "purity" of the white race. While the fit between ends and means may be tight, the Court does not recognize the end as constitutionally legitimate. The problem here is to decide why ends are not constitutionally legitimate.

In viewing the chart on page 800, note that the 1st vertical column concerns the factors one might consider in determining the nature of the alleged right, which subsequently dictates which of the 4 levels of scrutiny will apply (2nd vertical column). Once one determines the appropriate level of scrutiny, the last 4 columns then describe the methods of analysis. Consider the categories and standards a kind of model or template that one might use as a basis of analysis when confronting a new factual situation. Of course, the law is always evolving, and new situations may produce new approaches. Any chart is, at best, an imperfect picture of reality.

III. Liberty and Economic Rights

A. The History of Economic Substantive Due Process, Part I

The substantive due process material that follows is divided into two large groups of cases. The first considers the use of the Due Process Clause to void what are basically economic regulations. The second deals with use of the Due Process Clause to challenge regulation in other areas of personal rights or interests, such as birth control, sexual choices, abortion, and the right to assistance in ending life. Judicial approaches to these issues have varied with major political shifts in American society.

The Evolution of the American Economy

The industrial revolution of the late 19th and early 20th centuries gradually transformed America from a land with many small farmers and independent artisans to a land with many larger corporate enterprises. The independent artisan or the small farmer was his or her own boss with apprentices or laborers who hoped in turn to become their own bosses. As corporations grew larger, some consolidated into "trusts," employing large numbers of workers.

The new economic arrangements were more efficient, with efficiency defined as producing more goods more cheaply. These goods, in turn, were selected by consumers over the more expensive products produced by individual artisans. For example, consumers soon selected cheaper manufactured shoes over more expensive ones made individually to order. Small shopkeepers also found themselves threatened by chain stores—a trend that continues to this day. As a percentage of all persons working, the proportion of self-employed has fallen from about 30% in 1900 to around 9% today.

As the frontier—with its promise of cheap or free land—closed, another source of independence also disappeared. The economic conditions in these early years of industrialization have been sketched by Howard Gilman:

> Industrialization imposed brutalizing burdens on masses of people at the same time it showered unprecedented splendors on a select few. Speculative panics, business failures, and substantial unemployment occurred with unprecedented frequency, most notably from 1873 to 1878, 1882 to 1885, and 1893 to 1897. The hard, deflationary ("constitutional") currency fought for by conservatives after the war—represented in the passage of the Resumption Act of 1875, which authorized gold payments on greenbacks and other paper notes in 1879—gradually, and on occasion violently, pushed down wages and agricultural prices and ensured that investment capital would be available only to the select few who could extract new wealth most "efficiently." This resulted in intensified battles

A Model of Substantive Due Process Analysis: Chart

PL'S CLAIM: NATURE OF RIGHT OR INTEREST	HIERARCHY OF RIGHTS/ INTERESTS	SCRUTINY	APPLIED SCRUTINY	DIAGNOSIS	DECISIONAL METHOD
Possible factors affecting recognition: Text; Penumbra; precedent + analogy; history + tradition; (reasoned judgment). Social consensus vs. natural or inherent rights	"Fundamental right" (the highest form of a liberty interest)	Strict	E: Constitutional + compelling objective M: Constitutional + narrowly tailored F: Tight	PR: Very Tight UI: Looser OI: Looser Still OI + UI: Very Loose PI: Worst Possible	Categorical analysis (also called categorical balancing)
	Personal liberty interests (but not a fundamental right)	Heightened, but not "strict"; rational basis "with bite"?	E: Constitutional Objective M: Constitutional + not an undue burden? F: rational evaluation	PR: Very Tight UI: Looser OI: Looser Still OI + UI: Very Loose PI: Worst Possible	Ad hoc balancing
	Ordinary liberty interests (e.g., mere economic interests, without more)	Low level rational basis	E&M: Constitutional + deference to legislature Fit: very permissive rational evaluation	PR: Very Tight UI: Looser OI: Looser Still OI + UI: Very Loose PI: Worst Possible	Categorical analysis
	No protected interests? (See FN 6[3] in *Michael H.*)	No scrutiny	No right to judicial weighing	PR: Very Tight UI: Looser OI: Looser Still OI + UI: Very Loose PI: Worst Possible	Categorical analysis

Key: PL: Plaintiff; E=end; M=means; F=fit; Legit.=legitimate; Const.=constitutional; PR=perfectly rational; UI=underinclusive; OI=overinclusive; PI=perfectly irrational

between wage earners seeking a greater share of the wealth being produced and owners seeking lower labor costs per unit of production. The latter achieved their goal not only through the innovations in production alluded to above but also through the importation of cheap immigrant labor, the use of convicts and child labor, and routine acts of violence against workers who tried to empower themselves through collective action. The success of financial and industrial elites is evident when one notes the enormous disparities in the distribution of wealth that arose during the Gilded Age. According to the 1890 census, 9 percent of the nation's families controlled 81 percent of the nation's wealth. The 1900 report of the U.S. Industrial Commission concluded that between 60 and 88 percent of the American people could be classified as poor or very poor. New forms of production and labor-saving technological innovations disenfranchised and impoverished traditionally autonomous producers; they also imposed a physical burden on the growing class of unskilled wage earners. It was not uncommon for the fiery furnaces of the steel mills to claim two hundred deaths a year in a single factory. By the 1890s, railroads alone were killing 6,000 to 7,000 and injuring 30,000 to 45,000 people a year; a third of those killed and three quarters of those injured were employees.

Howard Gillman, *The Constitution Besieged, The Rise and Demise of Lochner Era Police Powers Jurisprudence* 76–77 (1993).

These conditions produced substantial political protest. Populists, Progressives, union members, and other reformers demanded government action to deal with what they saw as the injustices of economic life. Many saw the problem as a reincarnation of the struggle against the "slave power." "The unholy and lawless determination to acquire wealth and personal comfort at the expense of a weaker and less fortunate race, was the underlying spirit of slavery," wrote Populist James B. Weaver. But, "in the very midst of the struggle for overthrow of the slave oligarchy, our institutions were assailed by another foe mightier than the former, equally cruel, wider in its field of operation, infinitely greater in wealth, and immeasurably more difficult to control." Weaver said, "[i]t will be readily understood that we allude to the sudden growth of corporate power...." James Weaver, *A Call to Action* (1892).

The Role of the Court

Shortly after ratification of the 14th Amendment in 1868, the Supreme Court resisted demands that it strike down state economic legislation under the Due Process or Equal Protection Clauses. (State courts could always invalidate state legislation under their own state constitutions.) The *Slaughter-House Cases* (1873) rejected an invitation to become a "perpetual censor on state legislation." But soon the Court found itself slipping into just such a role. In *Munn v. Illinois* (1877), the Court rejected a due process challenge to a statute that limited the amount that owners of private grain elevators could charge farmers, holding that the rates were related to the public interest: "For protection against abuses by the Legislatures the people must resort to the polls, not the courts." But even *Munn* seemed to require exceptional circumstances to justify regulation—a business "affected with a public interest." Soon, however, the Court assumed a much more active role, carefully scrutinizing economic legislation against what it now read as the requirements of the Due Process and Equal Protection Clauses. Basically, the Court read these clauses to require government "neutrality" in conflicts between labor and capital. Both labor and capital must be free to contract unless some overriding public concern such as health or safety justified state intervention. Certain legislative justifications were considered illegitimate. For example, several *Lochner*-era cases said redressing the disparity in bargaining power between the rich and the poor or capital and labor was not an adequate justification for legislation.

The judicial presumption ran in favor of "freedom to contract" and the burden of justification rested on the state. When legislation was insufficiently comprehensive—when it failed to address all the evils advanced to justify the statute—courts often concluded that the statute was improperly aimed at helping special groups. In theory, that defect could be cured by making the statute more comprehensive. As a practical matter, the more comprehensive any reform, the more opposition it will likely encounter in the legislature. For example, it might be considerably easier to pass a law regulating the manufacturing of cigars in tenement houses, than it would be to regulate all manufacturing.

The reformers' demands for government action collided with a judicial ideology that substantially limited, but did not altogether forbid, reform. Two doctrines advanced this ideology. The first limited federal power over commerce among the several states, making national regulation of matters such as child labor, wages, and working conditions more difficult. (In theory, the problem could be attacked at the state level. But a state-by-state approach posed special problems. If New York banned child labor and North Carolina did not, New York manufacturers argued that they would suffer a competitive disadvantage—because children could be paid less. Indeed, furniture factories might move to North Carolina.)

The second doctrine required that the government be "neutral" in economic struggles. By this view, state governments could use their police powers to protect public health, safety, and morals, but not to equalize the relation between employers and employees. When workers went to the legislature for protection, the courts too often (in the view of progressives, populists, and labor unions) found the legislation invalid. Populist and Progressive critics denied that the government was actually neutral during the *Lochner* era. After all, they noted corporations had consolidated capital and acquired immense power in good part because of existing legal rules. In contrast, they charged that courts were less friendly to efforts by workers to combine into labor unions.

For example, in *Coppage v. Kansas* (1915), Kansas had made it a crime for an employer to exact a promise not to join or retain membership in a labor union as a condition of securing or retaining employment. The Court held the statute violated the 14th Amendment's Due Process Clause:

> Included in the right of personal liberty and the right of private property—partaking of the nature of each—is the right to make contracts for the acquisition of property. Chief among such contracts is that of personal employment, by which labor and other services are exchanged for money or other forms of property. If this right be struck down or arbitrarily interfered with, there is a substantial impairment of liberty in the long-established constitutional sense. The right is as essential to the laborer as to the capitalist, to the poor as to the rich; for the vast majority of persons have no other honest way to begin to acquire property, save by working for money.
>
> An interference with this liberty so serious as that now under consideration, and so disturbing of equality of right, must be deemed to be arbitrary, unless it be supportable as a reasonable exercise of the police power of the state. But, notwithstanding the strong general presumption in favor of the validity of state laws, we do not think the statute in question, as construed and applied in this case, can be sustained as a legitimate exercise of that power.... But, in this case,

the Kansas court of last resort has held that Coppage, the plaintiff in error, is a criminal, punishable with fine or imprisonment under this statute simply and merely because, while acting as the representative of the railroad company and dealing with Hedges, an employee at will and a man of full age and understanding, subject to no restraint or disability, Coppage insisted that Hedges should freely choose whether he would leave the employ of the Company or would agree to refrain from association with the union while so employed.... Nor can a State, by designating as 'coercion' conduct which is not such in truth, render criminal any normal and essentially innocent exercise of personal liberty or of property rights; for to permit this would deprive the 14th Amendment of its effective force in this regard....

[W]hat possible relation has the ... the Act to the public health, safety, morals, or general welfare? None is suggested, and we are unable to conceive of any. The Act, as the construction given to it by the state court shows, is intended to deprive employers of a part of their liberty of contract, to the corresponding advantage of the employed and the upbuilding of the labor organizations. But no attempt is made, or could reasonably be made, to sustain the purpose to strengthen these voluntary organizations, any more than other voluntary associations of persons, as a legitimate object for the exercise of the police power....

As to the interest of the employed, it is said by the Kansas Supreme Court to be a matter of common knowledge that "employees, as a rule, are not financially able to be as independent in making contracts for the sale of their labor as are employers in making contracts of purchase thereof." No doubt, wherever the right of private property exists, there must and will be inequalities of fortune; and thus it naturally happens that parties negotiating about a contract are not equally unhampered by circumstances. This applies to all contracts, and not merely to that between employer and employee. Indeed, a little reflection will show that wherever the right of private property and the right of free contract co-exist, each party when contracting is inevitably more or less influenced by the question whether he has much property, or little, or none; for the contract is made to the very end that each may gain something that he needs or desires more urgently than that which he proposes to give in exchange. And, since it is self-evident that, unless all things are held in common, some persons must have more property than others, it is from the nature of things impossible to uphold freedom of contract and the right of private property without at the same time recognizing as legitimate those inequalities of fortune that are the necessary result of the exercise of those rights. But the 14th Amendment ... recognizes "liberty" and "property" as co-existent human rights, and debars the states from any unwarranted interference with either.

[A] state may not ... declar[e] in effect that the public good requires the removal of those inequalities that are but the normal and inevitable result of their exercise, and then invok[e] the police power in order to remove the inequalities.... The police power is broad, and not easily defined, but it cannot be given the wide scope that is here asserted for it, without in effect nullifying the constitutional guaranty.

We need not refer to the numerous and familiar cases in which this court has held that the power may properly be exercised for preserving the public health, safety, morals, or general welfare, and that such police regulations may reasonably limit the enjoyment of personal liberty, including the right of making contracts. They are reviewed in *Holden v. Hardy* (1898). An evident and controlling distinction is this: that in those cases it has been held permissible for the states to adopt regulations fairly deemed necessary to secure some object directly affecting the public welfare, even though the enjoyment of private rights of liberty and property be thereby incidentally hampered; while in that portion of the Kansas statute which is now under consideration—that is to say, aside from coercion, etc.—there is no object or purpose, expressed or implied, that is claimed to have reference to health, safety, morals, or public welfare, beyond the supposed desirability of leveling inequalities of fortune by depriving one who has property of some part of what is characterized as his "financial independence." In short, an interference with the normal exercise of personal liberty and property rights is the primary object of the statute, and not an incident to the advancement of the general welfare. But, in our opinion, the 14th Amendment debars the states from striking down personal liberty or property rights, or materially restricting their normal exercise, excepting so far as may be incidentally necessary for the accomplishment of some other and paramount object, and one that concerns the public welfare. The mere restriction of liberty or of property rights cannot of itself be denominated "public welfare," and treated as a legitimate object of the police power; for such restriction is the very thing that is inhibited by the Amendment.

* * *

Contrast *Coppage* to one modern progressive view of the need for governmental regulation of the marketplace. This analysis is typified by philosopher of science Karl Popper in *The Open Society and Its Enemies,* vol. 2, 124–25 (1966):

> Freedom ... defeats itself, if it is unlimited. Unlimited freedom means that a strong man is free to bully one who is weak and to rob him of his freedom. This is why we demand that the state should limit freedom to a certain extent, so that everyone's freedom is protected by law. Nobody should be at the *mercy* of others, but all should have a *right* to be protected by the state.
>
> Now ... these considerations, originally meant to apply to the realm of brute-force, of physical intimidation, must be applied to the economic realm also. Even if the state protects its citizens from being bullied by physical violence ... it may defeat our ends by its failure to protect them from the misuse of economic power. In such a state, the economically strong is still free to bully one who is economically weak, and to rob him of his freedom. [U]nlimited economic freedom can be just as self-defeating as unlimited physical freedom, and economic power may be nearly as dangerous as physical violence; for those who possess a surplus of food can force those who are starving into a "freely" accepted servitude, without using violence.... [A] minority which is economically strong may in this way exploit the majority of those who are economically weak.

The result of the Court's early 20th century decisions was that state efforts to assist employees in their conflicts with employers were often ruled illegitimate. But the state could still act to protect public health and welfare when the Court was convinced by justifications advanced for the statutes. Since mining was dangerous to health, the state could limit the hours miners worked underground. Since a sleepy engineer might endanger the public, the state could limit his hours of work. In *Muller v. Oregon* (1908), faced with a massive brief on the impact of long hours of work for women on health and family life, the Court upheld an eight-hour workday for women. On the other hand, states were not allowed to protect employees from being fired because of union membership or to protect their health and safety if the Court did not find the justification convincing.

Such cases were often decided under the Due Process Clause, but similar reasoning applied to equal protection claims. For example, in *Gulf, Colorado & Santa Fe Ry. Co. v. Ellis* (1897), the Court invalidated a statute that attempted to provide attorney's fees to individuals who successfully sued railroads. The traditional American rule is that each party bears its own costs. Railroads were the only type of defendant singled out by the statute. The Texas legislature passed the statute to allow attorneys' fees not to exceed $10.00 to successful plaintiffs in the following types of lawsuits: claims of $50.00 or less for personal services rendered or labor done, for damages, for overcharges on freight, or for claims for stock killed or injured. The Court struck down the statute:

> No individuals are thus punished, and no other corporations. The act singles out a certain class of debtors, and punishes them when, for like delinquencies, it punishes no others. They are not treated as other debtors, or equally with other debtors. They cannot appeal to the courts, as other litigants, under like conditions, and with like protection. If litigation terminates adversely to them, they are mulcted in the attorney's fees of the successful plaintiff; if it terminates in their favor, they recover no attorney's fees. It is no sufficient answer to say that they are punished only when adjudged to be in the wrong. They do not enter the courts upon equal terms.

As this case shows, rationales for such laws were often treated as inadequate because they were under-inclusive—the law failed to reach all those causing the harm. As the Court noted in the *Gulf, Colorado, and Santa Fe* case:

> If it be said that this penalty is cast only upon corporations, that to them special privileges are granted, and therefore upon them special burdens may be imposed, it is a sufficient answer to say that the penalty is not imposed upon all corporations. The burden does not go with the privilege. Only railroads, of all corporations, are selected to bear this penalty. The rule of equality is ignored.

For the Court, interference with a person's economic liberty required special justification. This liberty was then extended to corporations, which were treated as simply another "person" within the meaning of the 14th Amendment. Such interferences were presumptively invalid and the Court tended to be suspicious of justifications based on unequal bargaining power. The *Gulf, Colorado & Santa Fe* dissent saw things differently and reversed the presumption:

> The legislature of a state must be presumed to have acted from lawful motives, unless the contrary appears upon the face of the statute. If, for instance, the legislature of Texas was satisfied, from observation and experience, that railroad corporations within the state were accustomed, beyond other corporations or persons, to unconscionably resist the payment of such petty claims, with the object of exhausting the patience and the means of the claimants, by prolonged litigation, and perhaps repeated appeals, railroad corporations alone might well be required, when ultimately defeated in a suit upon such a claim, to pay a moderate attorney's fee, as a just, though often inadequate, contribution to the expenses to which they had put the plaintiff in establishing a rightful demand. Whether such a state of things as above supposed did in fact exist, and whether,

for that or other reasons, sound policy required the allowance of such a fee to either party, or to the plaintiff only, were questions to be determined by the legislature.

The dissenters also focused, however indirectly, on the economic realities of the situation:

> It is to be regretted that so important a precedent as this case may afford for interference by the national judiciary with the legislation of the several states on little questions of costs should be established upon argument ex parte in behalf of the railroad corporation, without any argument for the original plaintiff. But it is hardly surprising that the owner of a claim for $50 only, having been compelled to follow up, through all the courts of the state, the contest over this $10 fee, should at last have become discouraged, and unwilling to undergo the expense of employing counsel to maintain his rights before this court.

* * *

During this period many industrial employers paid their employees with scrip rather than legal tender. Scrip was a piece of paper giving the employee credit for his wages, but it was redeemable only in the company store or as payment for rent in company housing. Progressive reformers successfully lobbied many state legislatures to require payment in legal tender. Some state courts invalidated such legislation, holding that the Due Process Clause of their state constitutions prevented such limitations on freedom of contract. The Supreme Court of Pennsylvania, in *Godcharles v. Wigeman* (Pa. 1886), struck down a statute requiring that employees be paid in cash or by check:

> The first, second, third, and fourth sections of the Act of June 29, 1881, are utterly unconstitutional and void, inasmuch as by them an attempt has been made by the legislature to do what, in this country, cannot be done; that is, prevent persons who are sui juris from making their own contracts. The Act is an infringement alike of the rights of the employer and the employee. More than this, it is an insulting attempt to put the laborer under a legislative tutelage, which is not only degrading to his manhood, but subversive of his rights as a citizen of the United States. He may sell his labor for what he thinks best, whether money or goods, just as his employer may sell his iron or coal; and any and every law that proposes to prevent him from so doing is an infringement of his constitutional privileges, and consequently vicious and void.

But other courts (and a majority by 1915), upheld such laws. For example, the Supreme Court of Colorado, in *In re House Bill No. 147* (Colo. 1897), held: "the legislature may, in the exercise of the police power, enact laws of this character [banning scrip], when necessary to prevent oppression and fraud, and for the protection of classes of individuals against unconscionable dealings." The Supreme Court of the United States gave several justifications for upholding a similar law in *Knoxville Iron Co. v. Harbison* (1901):

> [This statute is] tending towards equality between employer and employee in the matter of wages; intended and well calculated to promote peace and good order, and to prevent strife, violence, and bloodshed. Such being the character, purpose, and tendency of the act, we have no hesitation in holding that it is valid, both as general legislation, without reference to the state's reserved police power, and also as a wholesome regulation adopted in the proper exercise of that power.

As this case shows, *Lochner*-era jurisprudence was not monolithic and the line between permissible and impermissible state regulation was vague indeed.

If the legislature could protect public health, might not maximum hours, minimum wages, and a host of other economic regulations be justified based on quite general conceptions of health? In *Lochner v. New York* (1905), as we will see, the Court required a specific and unique justification and decided that the public health rationale in that case was insufficient.

Law professors and historians are divided in their evaluation of the *Lochner* era. Of course, to this day, people remain divided on the appropriate role of the government in regulating the market and providing social insurance.

History, Judges, and Politics

In the post-Civil War Gilded Age, from 1876 to 1901, all presidents (except Cleveland, a conservative Democrat) were Republican and generally conservative. For many, laissez-faire economics and limited government were the dominant ideologies. Great corporations were organized, businesses merged and consolidated into larger units, and trusts were organized. The Civil War income tax was ended and revenue was raised by the tariff. Individual and corporate debt increased. The Panic of 1893 was followed by an economic depression. There were, however, many cross currents. Congress passed the Sherman Antitrust Act and some labor-protective legislation, though the Court eventually struck the latter down. At the state level, Populists and other reformers were sometimes successful in procuring legislative reforms.

In this environment, more people began to challenge the world view that shaped the Court's approach to economic regulation. As Howard Gilman notes:

> The foundation upon which the vision of the neutral state was originally erected and subsequently reproduced was the argument that the market could provide for and protect personal autonomy and social independence. It was because of that claim that the founders could insist on removing state power from the struggles that shaped the relationships between groups or classes in the market, be they debtors and creditors, employees and employers, or producers and consumers. The assumption underlying the constitutional structure and its supporting ideology was that the most serious threat to liberty and the most serious violation of the principle of equality was the injustice of factional politics, as represented by the allegedly unsavory behavior of state legislatures in the 1780s. The market freedom repeatedly and forcefully celebrated in party platforms and court opinions was not freedom from all restraint; it was freedom from the corrupt use of public power by competing social groups. Market freedom, or "liberty of contract," was linked inextricably with the commitment to faction-free legislation....

> But by the final decade of the 19th century, in light of the obvious failure of the industrialized economy to order social relations harmoniously and without coercion and to guarantee opportunity and self-sufficiency for all, the position began to be advanced by some commentators in legal scholarship that the long-standing aversion to special burdens and benefits had become anachronistic, and that consequently the judiciary's conception of the scope of the police powers had to adjust to a new social order, one that was unknown to both Jefferson and Hamilton....

> The assumptions about social dependency underlying this conception were elaborated by [Seymour D. Thompson, the editor of the American Law Review] in

an address before the Kansas Bar Association in 1892. Most of his remarks focused on the enormous powers that corporations had attained over the previous few years, how the "barons of corporate power, outrivaling in wealth and splendor the merchant kings of Venice," [had] "purchased, by bribery and corruption, exclusive privileges from the temporary tenants of legislative power" and how they had "found means to combine all the corporations engaged in producing particular commodities so as to engross those commodities, suppress all competition therein, crush out and destroy all rival producers; and, aided by the Chinese Wall of a protective tariff excluding the world's competition." But toward the end of his discussion Thompson addressed the topic of the state judiciary's approach to labor legislation, which led him to exclaim: "What mockery to talk about the freedom of contract where only *one* of the contracting parties is free!" He observed that economists proceed on the assumption that "labor, like any other commodity, is subject merely to the law of supply and demand. I grant that such is the general and often the inexorable law; but I protest that it is within the power of human institutions to mitigate its rigor." He argued that this public responsibility was especially important when dealing with the condition of wage earners in capitalist forms of production. "The owner of a horse has an interest that it shall be well fed, warmly housed and kept in good condition. The late slave-owner had the same motive in respect of his human chattel, and this motive operated as a protection to his chattel. But the corporate manager has no such motive.... [T]he worn out wage-worker of the corporation [who] falls by the wayside finds his place immediately filled in by the 'hungry pauper that crowds forward from some human breeding ground.'" Thompson cited a recent encyclical from the Pope insisting that the remuneration offered a workman by an employer "must be enough to support the wage earner in reasonable and frugal comfort." Thompson added: "Surely the State can find some way, without too much repressing human liberty, to see to it that every man who is able and willing to work shall get enough to support a family and a home in frugal economy."

Howard Gilman, *The Constitution Besieged, The Rise and Fall of Lochner Era Jurisprudence* (1993).

Lochner v. New York: **Background and Questions**

In *Lochner v. New York* (1905), the Court invalidated reform legislation that limited the number of hours per week that a baker could work. The Court held that the statute interfered with the employer's and bakers' 14th Amendment "liberty" of contract.

1. What "liberty" is the Court protecting in *Lochner*? Where in the Constitution does the Court locate this liberty interest? What is the status of incorporation of the Bill of Rights as a limit on the states in 1905?

2. What test (and level of scrutiny) does the Court apply in *Lochner* to assess the constitutionality of the challenged legislation? Is there a difference between the test as stated and as applied by the Court?

3. What level of scrutiny does Justice Holmes apply in his dissent? What level of scrutiny does Justice Harlan apply in his dissent? How does the analysis in Justice Harlan's opinion differ from that of Peckham and Holmes?

4. Assess the persuasiveness of each of the *Lochner* opinions.

5. "To Lochnerize" has become a verb, and for some it is a pejorative one. What does it mean?

Lochner v. New York
198 U.S. 45 (1905)

[Majority: Peckham, Fuller, Brewer, Brown, and McKenna. Dissenting: Harlan, White, Day, and Holmes.]

Mr. Justice Peckham delivered the opinion of the court.

The indictment, it will be seen, charges that the plaintiff in error violated the labor law of the state of New York, in that he wrongfully and unlawfully required and permitted an employee working for him to work more than sixty hours in one week....

It is not an act merely fixing the number of hours which shall constitute a legal day's work, but an absolute prohibition upon the employer permitting, under any circumstances, more than ten hours' work to be done in his establishment. The employee may desire to earn the extra money which would arise from his working more than the prescribed time, but this statute forbids the employer from permitting the employee to earn it.

The statute necessarily interferes with the right of contract between the employer and employees, concerning the number of hours in which the latter may labor in the bakery of the employer. The general right to make a contract in relation to his business is part of the liberty of the individual protected by the 14th Amendment of the Federal Constitution. *Allgeyer v. Louisiana* (1897). Under that provision no state can deprive any person of life, liberty, or property without due process of law. The right to purchase or to sell labor is part of the liberty protected by this amendment, unless there are circumstances which exclude the right. There are, however, certain powers, existing in the sovereignty of each state in the Union, somewhat vaguely termed police powers, the exact description and limitation of which have not been attempted by the courts. Those powers, broadly stated and without, at present, any attempt at a more specific limitation, relate to the safety, health, morals and general welfare of the public. Both property and liberty are held on such reasonable conditions as may be imposed by the governing power of the state in the exercise of those powers, and with such conditions the 14th Amendment was not designed to interfere. *Mugler v. Kansas* (1887)....

Therefore, when the state, by its legislature, in the assumed exercise of its police powers, has passed an act which seriously limits the right to labor or the right of contract in regard to their means of livelihood between persons who are sui juris (both employer and employee), it becomes of great importance to determine which shall prevail—the right of the individual to labor for such time as he may choose, or the right of the state to prevent the individual from laboring, or from entering into any contract to labor, beyond a certain time prescribed by the state.

This Court has recognized the existence and upheld the exercise of the police powers of the states in many cases which might fairly be considered as border ones, and it has, in the course of its determination of questions regarding the asserted invalidity of such statutes, on the ground of their violation of the rights secured by the Federal Constitution, been guided by rules of a very liberal nature, the application of which has resulted, in numerous instances, in upholding the validity of state statutes thus assailed. Among the later cases where the state law has been upheld by this Court is that of *Holden v. Hardy* (1898). A provision in the act of the legislature of Utah was there under consideration, the act limiting the employment of workmen in all underground mines or workings, to eight hours per day, "except in cases of emergency, where life or property is in imminent danger." It also limited the hours of labor in smelting and other institutions for the reduction or refining of ores or metals to eight hours per day, except in like cases of emergency. The act was held to be a valid exercise of the police powers of the state....

There is nothing in *Holden v. Hardy* which covers the case now before us.... *Knoxville Iron Co. v. Harbison* (1901), is equally far from an authority for this legislation. The employees in that case were held to be at a disadvantage with the employer in matters of wages, they being miners and coal workers, and the act simply provided for the cashing of coal orders when presented by the miner to the employer....

Petit v. Minnesota (1900), was upheld as a proper exercise of the police power relating to the observance of Sunday, and the case held that the legislature had the right to declare that, as matter of law, keeping barber shops open on Sunday was not a work of necessity or charity.

It must, of course, be conceded that there is a limit to the valid exercise of the police power by the state.... Otherwise the 14th Amendment would have no efficacy and the legislatures of the states would have unbounded power.... In every case that comes before this Court, therefore, where legislation of this character is concerned, and where the protection of the Federal Constitution is sought, the question necessarily arises: Is this a fair, reasonable, and appropriate exercise of the police power of the state, or is it an unreasonable, unnecessary, and arbitrary interference with the right of the individual to his personal liberty, or to enter into those contracts in relation to labor which may seem to him appropriate or necessary for the support of himself and his family? Of course the liberty of contract relating to labor includes both parties to it. The one has as much right to purchase as the other to sell labor.

This is not a question of substituting the judgment of the Court for that of the legislature. If the act be within the power of the state it is valid, although the judgment of the court might be totally opposed to the enactment of such a law. But the question would still remain: Is it within the police power of the state? And that question must be answered by the court.

The question whether this act is valid as a labor law, pure and simple, may be dismissed in a few words. There is no reasonable ground for interfering with the liberty of person or the right of free contract, by determining the hours of labor, in the occupation of a baker. There is no contention that bakers as a class are not equal in intelligence and capacity to men in other trades or manual occupations, or that they are not able to assert their rights and care for themselves without the protecting arm of the state.... They are in no sense wards of the state. Viewed in the light of a purely labor law, with no reference whatever to the question of health, we think that a law like the one before us involves neither the safety, the morals, nor the welfare, of the public, and that the interest of the public is not in the slightest degree affected by such an act. The law must be upheld, if at all, as a law pertaining to the health of the individual engaged in the occupation of a baker. It does not affect any other portion of the public than those who are engaged in that occupation. Clean and wholesome bread does not depend upon whether the baker works but ten hours per day or only sixty hours a week....

It is a question of which of two powers or rights shall prevail—the power of the state to legislate or the right of the individual to liberty of person and freedom of contract. The mere assertion that the subject relates though but in a remote degree to the public health does not necessarily render the enactment valid. The act must have a more direct relation, as a means to an end, and the end itself must be appropriate and legitimate, before an act can be held to be valid which interferes with the general right of an individual to be free in his person and in his power to contract in relation to his own labor....

We think the limit of the police power has been reached and passed in this case. There is, in our judgment, no reasonable foundation for holding this to be necessary or appropriate as a health law to safeguard the public health or the health of the individuals who are following the trade of a baker....

We think that there can be no fair doubt that the trade of a baker, in and of itself, is not an unhealthy one to that degree which would authorize the legislature to interfere with the right to labor, and with the right of free contract on the part of the individual, either as employer or employee. In looking through statistics regarding all trades and occupations, it may be true that the trade of a baker does not appear to be as healthy as some other trades, and is also vastly more healthy than still others. To the common understanding the trade of a baker has never been regarded as an unhealthy one.... Some occupations are more healthy than others, but we think there are none which might not come under the power of the legislature to supervise and control the hours of working therein, if the mere fact that the occupation is not absolutely and perfectly healthy is to confer that right upon the legislative department of the Government.... It is unfortunately true that labor, even in any department, may possibly carry with it the seeds of unhealthiness. But are we all, on that account, at the mercy of legislative majorities? A printer, a tinsmith, a locksmith, a carpenter, a cabinetmaker, a dry goods clerk, a bank's, a lawyer's, or a physician's clerk, or a clerk in almost any kind of business, would all come under the power of the legislature, on this assumption. No trade, no occupation, no mode of earning one's living, could escape this all-pervading power, and the acts of the legislature in limiting the hours of labor in all employments would be valid, although such limitation might seriously cripple the ability of the laborer to support himself and his family. In our large cities there are many buildings into which the sun penetrates for but a short time in each day, and these buildings are occupied by people carrying on the business of bankers, brokers, lawyers, real estate, and many other kinds of business, aided by many clerks, messengers, and other employees. Upon the assumption of the validity of this act under review, it is not possible to say that an act, prohibiting lawyers or bank clerks, or others, from contracting to labor for their employers more than eight hours a day would be invalid....

It is also urged, pursuing the same line of argument, that it is to the interest of the state that its population should be strong and robust, and therefore any legislation which may be said to tend to make people healthy must be valid as health laws, enacted under the police power. If this be a valid argument and a justification for this kind of legislation, it follows that the protection of the Federal Constitution from undue interference with liberty of person and freedom of contract is visionary, wherever the law is sought to be justified as a valid exercise of the police power. Scarcely any law but might find shelter under such assumptions, and conduct, properly so called, as well as contract, would come under the restrictive sway of the legislature. Not only the hours of employees, but the hours of employers, could be regulated, and doctors, lawyers, scientists, all professional men, as well as athletes and artisans, could be forbidden to fatigue their brains and bodies by prolonged hours of exercise, lest the fighting strength of the state be impaired. We mention these extreme cases because the contention is extreme. We do not believe in the soundness of the views which uphold this law.... The act is not, within any fair meaning of the term, a health law, but is an illegal interference with the rights of individuals, both employers and employees, to make contracts regarding labor upon such terms as they may think best, or which they may agree upon with the other parties to such contracts. Statutes of the nature of that under review, limiting the hours in which grown and intelligent men may labor to earn their living, are mere meddlesome interferences with the rights of the individual, and they are not saved from condemnation by the claim that they are passed in the exercise of the police power and upon the subject of the health of the individual whose rights are interfered with, unless there be some fair ground, reasonable in and of itself, to say that there is material danger to the public health, or to the health of the employees, if the hours of labor are not curtailed....

This interference on the part of the legislatures of the several states with the ordinary trades and occupations of the people seems to be on the increase.... [A list of examples follows].

The Supreme Court of Illinois, in *Bessette v. People* (1901), held that a law ... providing for the regulation and licensing of horseshoers, was unconstitutional as an illegal interference with the liberty of the individual in adopting and pursuing such calling as he may choose, subject only to the restraint necessary to secure the common welfare. See also *Godcharles v. Wigeman* (Pa. 1886), *Low v. Rees Printing Co.* (Neb. 1894). In these cases the courts upheld the right of free contract and the right to purchase and sell labor upon such terms as the parties may agree to.

It is impossible for us to shut our eyes to the fact that many of the laws of this character, while passed under what is claimed to be the police power for the purpose of protecting the public health or welfare, are, in reality, passed from other motives. We are justified in saying so when, from the character of the law and the subject upon which it legislates, it is apparent that the public health or welfare bears but the most remote relation to the law. The purpose of a statute must be determined from the natural and legal effect of the language employed; and whether it is or is not repugnant to the Constitution of the United States must be determined from the natural effect of such statutes when put into operation, and not from their proclaimed purpose....

It is manifest to us that the limitation of the hours of labor as provided for in this section of the statute under which the indictment was found, and the plaintiff in error convicted, has no such direct relation to and no such substantial effect upon the health of the employee, as to justify us in regarding the section as really a health law. It seems to us that the real object and purpose were simply to regulate the hours of labor between the master and his employees (all being men, sui juris), in a private business, not dangerous in any degree to morals, or in any real and substantial degree, to the health of the employees. Under such circumstances the freedom of master and employee to contract with each other in relation to their employment, and in defining the same, cannot be prohibited or interfered with, without violating the Federal Constitution.

The judgment of the Court of Appeals of New York as well as that of the Supreme Court and of the County Court of Oneida County must be reversed and the case remanded to the County Court for further proceedings not inconsistent with this opinion.

Mr. Justice Holmes, dissenting.

I regret sincerely that I am unable to agree with the judgment in this case, and that I think it my duty to express my dissent.

This case is decided upon an economic theory which a large part of the country does not entertain. If it were a question whether I agreed with that theory, I should desire to study it further and long before making up my mind. But I do not conceive that to be my duty, because I strongly believe that my agreement or disagreement has nothing to do with the right of a majority to embody their opinions in law. It is settled by various decisions of this court that state constitutions and state laws may regulate life in many ways which we as legislators might think as injudicious or if you like as tyrannical as this, and which equally with this interfere with the liberty to contract. Sunday laws and usury laws are ancient examples. A more modern one is the prohibition of lotteries. The liberty of the citizen to do as he likes so long as he does not interfere with the liberty of others to do the same, which has been a shibboleth for some well-known writers, is interfered with by school laws, by the Post Office, by every state or municipal institution which takes his money for purposes thought desirable, whether he likes it or not. The 14th Amendment does not enact Mr. Herbert Spencer's *Social Statics*. The other day we sustained the Massachusetts vaccination law. *Jacobson v. Massachusetts* (1905). United States and state statutes and decisions cutting down the liberty to contract by way of combination are familiar to this court. *Northern Securities Co. v. United States* (1904). Two years ago we upheld the prohibition of sales of stock on margins or for future delivery in the Constitution of California. *Otis v. Parker* (1903). The decision sustaining an eight-hour law for miners is still recent. *Holden v. Hardy* (1898). Some of these laws embody convictions or prejudices which judges are likely to share. Some may not. But a constitution is not intended to embody a particular economic theory, whether of paternalism and the organic relation of the citizen to the state or of laissez-faire. It is made for people of fundamentally differing views, and the accident of our finding certain opinions natural and familiar or novel and even shocking ought not to conclude our judgment upon the question whether statutes embodying them conflict with the Constitution of the United States.

General propositions do not decide concrete cases. The decision will depend on a judgment or intuition more subtle than any articulate major premise. But I think that the proposition just stated, if it is accepted, will carry us far toward the end. Every opinion tends to become a law. I think that the word liberty in the 14th Amendment, is perverted when it is held to prevent the natural outcome of a dominant opinion, unless it can be said that a rational and fair man necessarily would admit that the statute proposed would infringe fundamental principles as they have been understood by the traditions of our people and our law. It does not need research to show that no such sweeping condemnation can be passed upon the statute before us. A reasonable man might think it a proper measure on the score of health. Men whom I certainly could not pronounce unreasonable would uphold it as a first installment of a general regulation of the hours of work. Whether in the latter aspect it would be open to the charge of inequality I think it unnecessary to discuss.

Mr. Justice Harlan (with whom Mr. Justice White and Mr. Justice Day concurred), dissenting: ...

I take it to be firmly established that what is called the liberty of contract may, within certain limits, be subjected to regulations designed and calculated to promote the general welfare or to guard the public health, the public morals or the public safety. "The liberty secured by the Constitution of the United States to every person within its jurisdiction does not import," this court has recently said, "an absolute right in each person to be, at all times and in all circumstances, wholly freed from restraint. There are manifold restraints to which every person is necessarily subject for the common good." *Jacobson v. Massachusetts* (1905).

Granting then that there is a liberty of contract which cannot be violated even under the sanction of direct legislative enactment, but assuming, as according to settled law we may assume, that such liberty of contract is subject to such regulations as the state may reasonably prescribe for the common good and the well-being of society, what are the conditions under which the judiciary may declare such regulations to be in excess of legislative authority and void? Upon this point there is no room for dispute; for the rule is universal that a legislative enactment, Federal or state, is never to be disregarded or held invalid unless it be, beyond question, plainly and palpably in excess of legislative power.... If there be doubt as to the validity of the statute, that doubt must therefore be resolved in favor of its validity, and the courts must keep their hands off, leaving the legislature to meet the responsibility for unwise legislation. If the end which the legislature seeks to accomplish be one to which its power extends, and if the means employed to that end, although not the wisest or best, are yet not plainly and palpably unauthorized by law, then the court cannot interfere. In other words, when the validity of a statute is questioned, the burden of proof, so to speak, is upon those who assert it to be unconstitutional. *McCulloch v. Maryland* (1819).

Let these principles be applied to the present case. By the statute in question it is provided that "[n]o employee shall be required, or permitted, to work in a biscuit, bread or cake bakery or confectionery establishment more than sixty hours in any one week, or more than ten hours in any one day, unless for the purpose of making a shorter work day on the last day of the week; nor more hours in any one week than will make an average of ten hours per day for the number of days during such week in which such employee shall work."

It is plain that this statute was enacted in order to protect the physical well-being of those who work in bakery and confectionery establishments. It may be that the statute had its origin, in part, in the belief that employers and employees in such establishments were not upon an equal footing, and that the necessities of the latter often compelled them to submit to such exactions as unduly taxed their strength. Be this as it may, the statute must be taken as expressing the belief of the people of New York that, as a general rule, and in the case of the average man, labor in excess of sixty hours during a week in such establishments may endanger the health of those who thus labor. Whether or not this be wise legislation it is not the province of the court to inquire. Under our systems of government the courts are not concerned with the wisdom or policy of legislation. So that in determining the question of power to interfere with liberty of contract, the court may inquire whether the means devised by the state are germane to an end which may be lawfully accomplished and have a real or substantial relation to the protection of health, as involved in the daily work of the persons, male and female, engaged in bakery and confectionery establishments. But when this inquiry is entered upon I find it impossible, in view of common experience, to say that there is here no real or substantial relation between the means employed by the state and the end sought to be accomplished by its legislation. *Mugler v. Kansas* (1887). Nor can I say that the statute has no appropriate or direct connection with that protection to health which each state owes to her citizens, *Patterson v. Kentucky* (1878); or that it is not promotive of the health of the employees in question, *Holden v. Hardy* (1898); or that the regulation prescribed by the state is utterly unreasonable and extravagant or wholly arbitrary, *Gundling v. Chicago* (1900). Still less can I say that the statute is, beyond question, a plain, palpable invasion of rights secured by the fundamental law. *Jacobson v. Massachusetts*. Therefore I submit that this court will transcend its functions if it assumes to annul the statute of New York. It must be remembered that this statute does not apply to all kinds of business. It applies only to work in bakery and confectionery establishments, in which, as all know, the air constantly breathed by workmen is not as pure and healthful as that to be found in some other establishments or out of doors.

Professor Hirt in his treatise on the "Diseases of the Workers" has said: "The labor of the bakers is among the hardest and most laborious imaginable, because it has to be performed under conditions injurious to the health of those engaged in it. It is hard, very hard work, not only because it requires a great deal of physical exertion in an overheated workshop and during unreasonably long hours, but more so because of the erratic demands of the public, compelling the baker to perform the greater part of his work at night, thus depriving him of an opportunity to enjoy the necessary rest and sleep—a fact which is highly injurious to his health." Another writer says: "The constant inhaling of flour dust causes inflammation of the lungs and of the bronchial tubes. The eyes also suffer through this dust, which is responsible for the many cases of running eyes among the bakers. The long hours of toil to which all bakers are subjected produce rheumatism, cramps, and swollen legs. The intense heat in the workshops induces the workers to resort to cooling drinks, which together with their habit of exposing the greater part of their bodies to the change in the atmosphere, is another source of a number of diseases of various organs. Nearly all bakers are palefaced and of more delicate health than the workers of other crafts, which is chiefly due to their hard work and their irregular and unnatural mode of living, whereby the power of resistance against disease is greatly diminished. The average age of a baker is below that of other workmen; they seldom live over their fiftieth year, most of them dying between the ages of forty and fifty. During periods of epidemic diseases the bakers are generally the first to succumb to the disease, and the number swept away during such periods far exceeds the number of other crafts in comparison to the men employed in the respective industries. When, in 1720, the plague visited the city of Marseilles, France, every baker in the city succumbed to the epidemic, which caused considerable excitement in the neighboring cities and resulted in measures for the sanitary protection of the bakers."

In the Eighteenth Annual Report by the New York Bureau of Statistics of Labor it is stated that among the occupations involving exposure to conditions that interfere with nutrition is that of a baker. In that Report it is also stated that, "from a social point of view, production will be increased by any change in industrial organization which diminishes the number of idlers, paupers, and criminals. Shorter hours of work, by allowing higher standards of comfort and purer family life, promise to enhance the industrial efficiency of the wage-working class—improved health, longer life, more content and greater intelligence and inventiveness."...

We judicially know that the question of the number of hours during which a workman should continuously labor has been, for a long period, and is yet, a subject of serious consideration among civilized peoples, and by those having special knowledge of the laws of health....

We also judicially know that the number of hours that should constitute a day's labor in particular occupations involving the physical strength and safety of workmen has been the subject of enactments by Congress and by nearly all of the states. Many, if not most, of those enactments fix eight hours as the proper basis of a day's labor.

I do not stop to consider whether any particular view of this economic question presents the sounder theory.... It is enough for the determination of this case, and it is enough for this court to know, that the question is one about which there is room for debate and for an honest difference of opinion. There are many reasons of a weighty, substantial character, based upon the experience of mankind, in support of the theory that, all things considered, more than ten hours' steady work each day, from week to week, in a bakery or confectionery establishment, may endanger the health and shorten the lives of the workmen, thereby diminishing their physical and mental capacity to serve the state, and to provide for those dependent upon them.

If such reasons exist that ought to be the end of this case, for the state is not amenable to the judiciary, in respect of its legislative enactments, unless such enactments are plainly, palpably, beyond all question, inconsistent with the Constitution of the United States. We are not to presume that the state of New York has acted in bad faith. Nor can we assume that its legislature acted without due deliberation, or that it did not determine this question upon the fullest attainable information, and for the common good. We cannot say that the state has acted without reason nor ought we to proceed upon the theory that its action is a mere sham. Our duty, I submit, is to sustain the statute as not being in conflict with the Federal Constitution, for the reason—and such is an all-sufficient reason—it is not shown to be plainly and palpably inconsistent with that instrument. Let the state alone in the management of its purely domestic affairs, so long as it does not appear beyond all question that it has violated the Federal Constitution. This view necessarily results from the principle that the health and safety of the people of a state are primarily for the state to guard and protect.

I take leave to say that the New York statute, in the particulars here involved, cannot be held to be in conflict with the 14th Amendment, without enlarging the scope of the Amendment far beyond its original purpose, and without bringing under the supervision of this court matters which have been supposed to belong exclusively to the legislative departments of the several states when exerting their conceded power to guard the health and safety of their citizens by such regulations as they in their wisdom deem best. Health laws of every description constitute, said Chief Justice Marshall, a part of that mass of legislation which "embraces everything within the territory of a state, not surrendered to the general government; all which can be most advantageously exercised by the states themselves." *Gibbons v. Ogden* (1824). A decision that the New York statute is void under the 14th Amendment will, in my opinion, involve consequences of a far-reaching and mischievous character; for such a decision would seriously cripple the inherent power of the states to care for the lives, health and well-being of their citizens. Those are matters which can be best controlled by the states. The preservation of the just powers of the states is quite as vital as the preservation of the powers of the General Government.

When this court had before it the question of the constitutionality of a statute of Kansas making it a criminal offense for a contractor for public work to permit or require his employees to perform labor upon such work in excess of eight hours each day, it was contended that the statute was in derogation of the liberty both of employees and employer. It was further contended that the Kansas statute was mischievous in its tendencies. This court, while disposing of the question only as it affected public work, held that the Kansas statute was not void under the 14th Amendment. But it took occasion to say what may well be here repeated: "The responsibility therefore rests upon legislators, not upon the courts. No evils arising from such legislation could be more far reaching than those that might come to our system of government if the judiciary, abandoning the sphere assigned to it by the fundamental law, should enter the domain of legislation, and upon grounds merely of justice or reason or wisdom annul statutes that had received the sanction of the people's representatives. We are reminded by counsel that it is the solemn duty of the courts in cases before them to guard the constitutional rights of the citizen against merely arbitrary power. That is unquestionably true. But it is equally true—indeed, the public interests imperatively demand—that legislative enactments should be recognized and enforced by the courts as embodying the will of the people, unless they are plainly and palpably beyond all question in violation of the fundamental law of the Constitution." *Atkin v. Kansas* (1903).

The judgment in my opinion should be affirmed.

Lochner-Era Economic Legislation Hypothetical

A state statute bans the use of used fabric to stuff mattresses. The state claims its objectives are public health (the used cloth could carry disease) and protection of consumers from deceit. Assume that this statute is passed in the heyday of *Lochner* jurisprudence. Is there a framework of analysis you can use to analyze the statute? Note that how you characterize the right or interest asserted against the statute is very important. Could you characterize the right or interest here so it would be the sort of liberty protected by *Lochner*?

What is the harm? What is the trait? How would you describe the statute: is it over-inclusive, under-inclusive, or both? Why?

Now, if you wish, look at how the Court decided the case of *Weaver v. Palmer Bros. Co.* (1926).

The Brandeis Brief

In cases like *Lochner*, with the Court reaching an independent decision on the wisdom of state economic regulation, presentation of the facts was particularly important. Louis Brandeis, a future Supreme Court Justice, pioneered a new and highly factual approach to arguing these cases (the "Brandeis Brief") in *Muller v. Oregon* (1908). In *Muller*, the Court upheld a statute limiting working hours for women, distinguishing *Lochner* on gender lines. In addition to traditional legal argument, Brandeis presented masses of legislative, economic, and sociological data in his brief. The Court commented on the data:

> It may not be amiss, in the present case, before examining the constitutional question, to notice the course of legislation, as well as expressions of opinion from other than judicial sources. In the brief filed by Mr. Louis D. Brandeis for the defendant in error is a very copious collection of all these matters, an epitome of which is found in the margin.

The Court noted in a footnote:

> The following legislation of the states imposes restriction in some form or another upon the hours of labor that may be required of women: [citing statutes from Massachusetts, Rhode Island, Louisiana, Connecticut, Maine, New Hampshire, Maryland, Virginia, Pennsylvania, New York, Nebraska, Washington, Colorado, New Jersey, Oklahoma, North Dakota, South Dakota, Wisconsin, and South Carolina].
>
> In foreign legislation Mr. Brandeis calls attention to these statutes: [citing statutes from Great Britain, France, Switzerland, Austria, Holland, Italy, and Germany]. Then follow extracts from over ninety reports of committees, bureaus of statistics, commissioners of hygiene, inspectors of factories, both in this country and in Europe, to the effect that long hours of labor are dangerous for women, primarily because of their special physical organization. The matter is discussed in these reports in different aspects, but all agree as to the danger. It would, of course, take too much space to give these reports in detail. Following them are extracts from similar reports discussing the general benefits of short hours from an economic aspect of the question. In many of these reports individual instances are given tending to support the general conclusion. Perhaps the general scope and character of all these reports may be summed up in what an inspector for Hanover says: "The reasons for the reduction of the working day to ten hours—

(a) the physical organization of women, (b) her maternal functions, (c) the rearing and education of the children, (d) the maintenance of the home—are all so important and so far reaching that the need for such reduction need hardly be discussed."

After the footnote, the Court continued:

> The legislation and opinions referred to in the margin may not be, technically speaking, authorities, and in them is little or no discussion of the constitutional question presented to us for determination, yet they are significant of a widespread belief that woman's physical structure, and the functions she performs in consequence thereof, justify special legislation restricting or qualifying the conditions under which she should be permitted to toil. Constitutional questions, it is true, are not settled by even a consensus of present public opinion, for it is the peculiar value of a written constitution that it places in unchanging form limitations upon legislative action, and thus gives a permanence and stability to popular government which otherwise would be lacking. At the same time, when a question of fact is debated and debatable, and the extent to which a special constitutional limitation goes is affected by the truth in respect to that fact, a widespread and long continued belief concerning it is worthy of consideration. We take judicial cognizance of all matters of general knowledge.

* * *

We will return to the question of judicial attitudes toward women when we reach equal protection. However, note how the *Muller* Court distinguished *Lochner*:

> That woman's physical structure and the performance of maternal functions place her at a disadvantage in the struggle for subsistence is obvious. This is especially true when the burdens of motherhood are upon her. Even when they are not, by abundant testimony of the medical fraternity continuance for a long time on her feet at work, repeating this from day to day, tends to injurious effects upon the body, and, as healthy mothers are essential to vigorous offspring, the physical well-being of woman becomes an object of public interest and care in order to preserve the strength and vigor of the race.
>
> Still again, history discloses the fact that woman has always been dependent upon man. He established his control at the outset by superior physical strength, and this control in various forms, with diminishing intensity, has continued to the present....

B. The History of Economic Substantive Due Process, Part II

The Progressive Era

The "Progressive" presidents, Theodore Roosevelt (Republican) and Woodrow Wilson (Democrat), favored more government regulation of the economy, regulation of working conditions, and income taxes on upper income earners. Theodore Roosevelt in particular was highly critical of Court decisions that found reform legislation unconstitutional—such as that protecting workers or banning products made with child labor from interstate commerce. In 1908, Roosevelt endorsed William Howard Taft to succeed him. In 1912, Roosevelt thought Taft had betrayed Progressivism and he challenged Taft for the Republican nomination. Roosevelt lost, but then ran as a third party Progressive candidate. He outpolled Taft in the election, but lost to Woodrow Wilson.

Roosevelt spelled out some basic Progressive ideas in the 1912 campaign:

> The only way in which our people can increase their power over the big corporation that does wrong, the only way in which they can protect the working man in his conditions of work and life, the only way in which the people can prevent children working in industry or secure women an eight-hour day in industry, or secure compensation for men killed or crippled in industry, is by extending, instead of limiting, the power of government. There was once a time in history when the limitation of governmental power meant increasing liberty for the people. In the present day the limitation of governmental power, of governmental action, means the enslavement of the people by the great corporations who can only be held in check through the extension of governmental power.

Theodore Roosevelt, "Address at San Francisco, Sept. 14, 1912," in William H. Harbaugh, ed. *The Writings of Theodore Roosevelt*, 288–91 (1967).

In his autobiography, Roosevelt wrote:

> [A] simple and poor society can exist as a democracy on a basis of sheer individualism. But a rich and complex industrial society cannot so exist; for some individuals, and especially those artificial individuals called corporations, become so very big that the ordinary individual is utterly dwarfed beside them, and cannot deal with them on terms of equality.

Theodore Roosevelt, *An Autobiography* 276 (1913). Roosevelt's younger cousin, Franklin Roosevelt, embraced many of his ideas and decided to follow in Theodore's political footsteps. Like Theodore, he was assistant Secretary of the Navy, Governor of New York, and eventually, President of the United States.

The 1920s and 1930s

The Roaring Twenties saw a return to "normalcy" following the First World War. After eight years of Wilson, Republicans recaptured the White House. They reduced the regulatory and anti-trust enforcement of the Progressive era. Labor unions declined. Many more businesses merged and formed organizations such as public utility holding companies and investment trusts. The top personal income tax rate was reduced from 73% to 25% and other taxes were cut as well. Though a few enjoyed great prosperity, many did not. Small farmers, in particular, suffered. The top 1% of Americans owned 49% of U.S. wealth. Buying on credit expanded. The era ended with the stock market crash of 1929 and the beginning of the Great Depression.

During the 1920s and early 1930s, the Court again struck down state and federal economic regulations. Indeed, the Court struck down more legislation during the 1920s than any prior decade. From 1900 to 1937 the Court often interpreted the *federal* commerce power narrowly, limiting the power of Congress to address the economic conditions spawned by industrialization. In *Hammer v. Dagenhart* (1918), for example, the Court struck down a *federal* statute that attempted to ban child labor. The narrow reading of the Commerce Clause ended with *NLRB v. Jones & Laughlin Steel* (1937). The following is a list of some cases from that era:

1. *Coppage v. Kansas* (1915). The Court struck down a state statute prohibiting employers from conditioning employment on an employee's promise never to join a union.

2. *Bunting v. Oregon* (1917). The Court upheld maximum hour legislation for men without mentioning *Lochner*.

3. *Adkins v. Children's Hospital* (1923). The Court invalidated a federal minimum wage statute for women and minors in the District of Columbia as violating the Due Process Clause of the 5th Amendment.

4. *Meyer v. Nebraska* (1923). The Court struck down a state statute prohibiting the teaching of a foreign language to a child below the eighth grade. It recognized that "liberty" includes non-economic rights. This case will later become associated with personal privacy.

5. *Pierce v. Society of Sisters* (1925). The Court extended the rationale of *Meyer*, invalidating a state statute requiring children to go only to public (as opposed to parochial) schools.

6. *Nebbia v. New York* (1934). The Court rejected a due process attack on a state minimum price statute for milk.

7. *Morehead v. New York ex rel. Tipaldo* (1936). The Court held that a state statute providing a minimum wage for women workers was a violation of the Due Process Clause.

8. *West Coast Hotel Co. v. Parrish* (1937). The Court (5–4) upheld a state minimum wage law for women, overturning *Adkins v. Children's Hospital*.

Franklin D. Roosevelt

In October 1929, the stock market—which had been at an all time high—crashed. Many investors lost virtually their entire savings. The collapse of the stock market was followed by a general financial panic. Businesses and banks failed. Depositors—worried about the safety of their deposits—made runs on banks, withdrawing their funds and causing more banks to fail. Unemployment soared, eventually reaching 25% of the work force. Many Americans kept their jobs but worked for reduced wages. For those with jobs, wages dropped to 40% of their pre-depression level. By 1932, national income was less than 50% of its 1929 level. Homeowners and farmers were unable to pay mortgages; and banks foreclosed on many homes and farms.

In 1932, Franklin Roosevelt was elected president. His inauguration in 1933 marked the start of the New Deal. Roosevelt served until 1944, though New Deal reforms had largely ended by 1938. The New Deal was characterized by far more active government intervention in the economy. Roosevelt was pragmatic and not highly ideological. He said he would try one thing, and if that did not work, he would try another. One important piece of New Deal legislation was the National Industrial Recovery Act (NIRA), pursuant to which industry and labor established codes of fair competition that limited competition, set maximum hours and minimum wages, and guaranteed the right of labor to organize. But in a series of cases, the Court struck down much New Deal legislation. In *Schechter Poultry Corp. v. United States* (1935), the Court held the NIRA exceeded the power of Congress to regulate commerce and that Congress had unconstitutionally delegated its legislative power. *See also Carter v. Carter Coal* (1936) (Court invalidates Bituminous Coal Act) and *United States v. Butler* (1936) (Court invalidates Agricultural Adjustment Act).

The Court's decisions threatened the survival of the New Deal. Re-nominated in 1936, Roosevelt promised to continue New Deal reforms like Social Security and wage and hour legislation that he said protected the interests of most Americans. Roosevelt struck some basic themes in his 1936 acceptance speech:

> The age of machinery, of railroads, of steam and electricity; the telegraph and the radio; mass production, mass distribution—all of these combined to bring

forward a new civilization and with it a problem for those who sought to remain free.

For out of this modern civilization economic royalists carved new dynasties. New Kingdoms were built upon concentration of control over material things. Through new uses of corporations, banks, and securities, new machinery of industry and agriculture, of labor and capital—all undreamed of by the fathers—the whole structure of modern life was impressed into this royal service.

There was no place among this royalty for our many thousands of small business men and merchants who sought to make a worthy use of the American system of initiative and profit. They were no more free than the worker or the farmers ...

For too many of us the political equality we once had was meaningless in the face of economic inequality. A small group had concentrated into their own hands an almost complete control over other people's property, other people's money, other people's lives. For too many of us life was no longer free; liberty no longer real; men could no longer follow the pursuit of happiness

Against economic tyranny such as this, the American citizen could only appeal to the organized power to government....

The royalists I have spoken of—the royalists of the economic order have conceded that political freedom was the business of the government, but they have maintained that economic slavery was nobody's business.... [T]hey denied that the government could do anything to protect the citizen in his right to work and his right to live....

Roosevelt was re-elected in 1936 by a large majority. On February 7, 1937 he sent to Congress a plan to expand the membership of the Court (it had been expanded and contracted before in American history). His opponents dubbed it the "Court packing plan." Although Roosevelt's Court expansion plan failed, thereafter the Court changed direction and upheld basic New Deal legislation, a change one wag named "the switch in time that saved nine." Moreover, Roosevelt soon had the opportunity to appoint new members of the Court—four by 1939. The doctrine of economic substantive due process and the related narrow reading of the power of Congress over commerce went into a long decline.

A "second New Deal" followed the destruction of the NIRA in *Schechter*. Roosevelt's second term continued public works in order to give work to the unemployed. The government continued to regulate banks and continued federal deposit insurance. It regulated the stock market and agricultural production. The National Labor Relations Act guaranteed labor the right to organize. Unemployment insurance protected workers from unemployment and social security provided income for the aged. National legislation set minimum wage and maximum hours. Congress also enacted a progressive income tax with high rates for upper brackets. For a time, the New Deal engaged in aggressive antitrust enforcement, a practice that ended with American entry into World War II. Ultimately, while the New Deal regulated business labor practices, it did little to stem the tide of corporate consolidation.

The battle over economic substantive due process raised an issue that appears again and again in American constitutional law—the proper role of the judiciary in a democracy. How should we protect basic rights of individuals (however they should be defined) from the democratic process? Roosevelt raised this issue in a 1937 speech on what his opponents labeled his "court packing" plan.

Fireside Chat on the "Court Packing" Bill
March 9, 1937

Tonight, sitting at my desk in the White House, I make my first radio report to the people in my second term of office....

In 1933 you and I knew that we must never let our economic system get completely out of joint again—that we could not afford to take the risk of another great depression.

We also became convinced that the only way to avoid a repetition of those dark days was to have a government with power to prevent and to cure the abuses and the inequalities which had thrown that system out of joint.

We then began a program of remedying those abuses and inequalities—to give balance and stability to our economic system—to make it bomb-proof against the causes of 1929.

Today we are only part-way through that program and recovery is speeding up to a point where the dangers of 1929 are again becoming possible, not this week or month perhaps, but within a year or two.

National laws are needed to complete that program. Individual or local or state effort alone cannot protect us in 1937 any better than ten years ago.

It will take time—and plenty of time—to work out our remedies administratively even after legislation is passed. To complete our program of protection in time, therefore, we cannot delay one moment in making certain that our National Government has power to carry through.

Four years ago action did not come until the eleventh hour. It was almost too late....

The American people have learned from the depression. For in the last three national elections an overwhelming majority of them voted a mandate that the Congress and the President begin the task of providing that protection—not after long years of debate, but now.

The Courts, however, have cast doubts on the ability of the elected Congress to protect us against catastrophe by meeting squarely our modern social and economic conditions.

We are at a crisis, a crisis in our ability to proceed with that protection. It is a quiet crisis. There are no lines of depositors outside closed banks. But to the far-sighted it is far-reaching in its possibilities of injury to America.

I want to talk with you very simply tonight about the need for present action in this crisis—the need to meet the unanswered challenge of one-third of a nation ill-nourished, ill-clad, ill-housed.

Last Thursday I described the American form of Government as a three-horse team provided by the Constitution of the American people so that their field might be plowed. The three horses are, of course, the Congress, the Executive and the Courts. Two of the horses, the Congress and the Executive, are pulling in unison today; the third is not. Those who have intimated that the President of the United States is trying to drive that team, overlook the simple fact that the President, as Chief Executive, is himself one of the three horses.

It is the American people themselves who are in the driver's seat. It is the American people themselves who want the furrow plowed.

It is the American people themselves who expect the third horse to pull in unison with the other two.

I hope that you have re-read the Constitution of the United States in these past few weeks. Like the Bible, it ought to be read again and again.

It is an easy document to understand when you remember that it was called into being because the Articles of Confederation under which the original thirteen States tried to operate after the Revolution showed the need of a National Government with power enough to handle national problems. In its Preamble, the Constitution states it was intended to form a more perfect Union and promote the general welfare; and the powers given to the Congress to carry out those purposes can best be described by saying that they were all the powers needed to meet each and every problem which then had a national character and which could not be met by merely local action.

But the framers went further. Having in mind that in succeeding generations many other problems then undreamed of would become national problems, they gave to the Congress the ample broad powers "to levy taxes … and provide for the common defense and general welfare of the United States."

That, my friends, is what I honestly believe to have been the clear and underlying purpose of the patriots who wrote a Federal Constitution to create a National Government with national power, intended as they said, "to form a more perfect union … for ourselves and our posterity."

For nearly twenty years there was no conflict between the Congress and the Court. Then, in 1803, Congress passed a statute which the Court said violated an express provision of the Constitution. The Court claimed the power to declare it unconstitutional and did so declare it. But a little later the Court itself admitted that it was an extraordinary power to exercise and through Mr. Justice Washington laid down this limitation upon it. He said: "It is but a decent respect due to the wisdom, the integrity and the patriotism of the Legislative body, by which any law is passed, to presume in favor of its validity until its violation of the Constitution is proved beyond all reasonable doubt."

But since the rise of the modern movement for social and economic progress through legislation, the Court has more and more often and more and more boldly asserted a power to veto laws passed by the Congress and by State Legislatures in complete disregard of this original limitation, which I have just read.

In the last four years the sound rule of giving statutes the benefit of all reasonable doubt has been cast aside. The Court has been acting not as a judicial body, but as a policy-making body.

When the Congress has sought to stabilize national agriculture, to improve the conditions of labor, to safeguard business against unfair competition, to protect our national resources, the majority of the Court has been assuming the power to pass on the wisdom of these Acts of the Congress—and to approve or disapprove the public policy written into these laws.

That is not only my accusation. It is the accusation of most distinguished Justices of the present Supreme Court. I have not the time to quote to you all the language used by dissenting Justices in many of these cases. But in the case holding the Railroad Retirement Act unconstitutional, for instance, Chief Justice Hughes said in a dissenting opinion that the majority opinion was "a departure from sound principles," and placed "an unwarranted limitation upon the commerce clause." And three other Justices agreed with him.

In the case holding the Triple A unconstitutional, Justice Stone said of the majority opinion that it was a "tortured construction of the Constitution." And two other Justices agreed with him.

In the case holding the New York Minimum Wage Law unconstitutional, Justice Stone said that the majority were actually reading into the Constitution their own "personal economic predilections," and that if the legislative power is not left free to choose the methods of solving the problems of poverty, subsistence and health of large numbers in the community, then "government is to be rendered impotent." And two other Justices agreed with him.

In the face of these dissenting opinions, there is no basis for the claim made by some members of the Court that something in the Constitution has compelled them regretfully to thwart the will of the people.

In the face of such dissenting opinions, it is perfectly clear that as Chief Justice Hughes has said: "We are under a Constitution, but the Constitution is what the Judges say it is."

The Court, in addition to the proper use of its judicial functions, has improperly set itself up as a third House of the Congress—a super-legislature, as one of the Justices has called it—reading into the Constitution words and implications which are not there, and which were never intended to be there.

We have therefore, reached the point as a Nation where we must take action to save the Constitution from the Court and the Court from itself. We must find a way to take an appeal from the Supreme Court to the Constitution itself. We want a Supreme Court which will do justice under the constitution—not over it. In our Courts we want a government of laws and not of men.

I want—as all Americans want—an independent judiciary as proposed by the framers of the constitution. That means a Supreme Court that will enforce the Constitution as written—that will refuse to amend the Constitution by the arbitrary exercise of judicial power—amendment, in other words, by judicial say-so. It does not mean a judiciary so independent that it can deny the existence of facts which are universally recognized....

Forces that Shape Constitutional Law

Many factors influence the direction of the Court. A major one is the legal and political philosophy of those who appoint the Justices. From 1932 to 1968, Democrats dominated the presidency. The sole Republican was Dwight Eisenhower (1952–60), a moderate. A central concern of the Democratic administrations was that New Deal economic legislation not be declared unconstitutional by the Court. All of the Roosevelt and Truman (and indeed Eisenhower) appointees gave substantial deference to the decisions of the legislature on most economic matters. None of the Roosevelt Justices was inclined to return to the heightened scrutiny of economic legislation that characterized the *Lochner*-era.

In another example, Richard Nixon and subsequent Republican presidents were critical of the constitutional criminal procedure decisions of the Warren Court. The Justices Presidents Nixon and Reagan appointed substantially limited those decisions.

Of course, Justices serve long after the presidents who have appointed them depart; they often face new and unforeseen problems and their views can change over time. A change in national administration does not, of course, produce an immediate change in the Court. Long term political shifts, however, tend to be reflected in the Court. This observation is not to say that the law or constitutional law is merely politics. Judges are shaped by their training as lawyers and by the values of the culture in which they live. Their training and their notion of the appropriate judicial function constrain their decisions. Justices sometimes fail to fulfill the hopes of the Presidents who appoint them, especially on issues that were not salient at the time they were appointed.

The rise and demise of *Lochner*-era jurisprudence can be viewed in light of the new judicial philosophy that became dominant during and after the New Deal. Changes in doctrine occurred across a range of doctrinal categories. For example, the New Deal Court and later Courts abandoned tough due process and equal protection scrutiny of most economic legislation and at the same time expanded the ability of Congress to regulate commerce. In short, the Court allowed the political branches to take the steps the voters had overwhelmingly supported in 1936 (Roosevelt carried all but two states) and to which voters continued to adhere. Minimum wage, maximum hours, worker safety, child labor, social security, unemployment insurance and a host of other reforms were, the Court decided, within the power of the Congress or state legislatures. In some cases, such as state discrimination against interstate commerce, the Court continued to exercise tough scrutiny. But this scrutiny still allowed broad policy discretion for the legislature. One can easily draw the wrong lesson from all this—that judicial decisions are "merely politics." But it is equally mistaken to assume that powerful political and social movements do not influence the course of the law.

A second question is raised by these events. Would the Court be as deferential to the legislature on matters involving personal, non-economic rights as it was on most economic matters? Over the course of the past sixty years, the Court has often closely scrutinized government regulations that allegedly infringed a variety of non-economic rights. The *Lochner*-era Court, faced with criticism that it was only really protecting business, began to expand its protection to other human rights. Later cases continued this trend. For example, from the 1930s through the 1960s, the Court extended the protections of the federal Bill of Rights to the states, expanded the protection for free speech and press, and struck down legislation forbidding access to birth control devices and later, during the Burger Court era, abortion. The ban on birth control devices was struck down as a violation of the penumbras of the Bill of Rights. The ban on abortion was struck down as a violation of the liberty component of the Due Process Clause. These actions in turn provoked political protest. The Justice Department under Presidents Reagan and George H.W. Bush was especially critical of the Court's expansive reading of personal privacy. Indeed, the ultimate direction of the law on abortion may depend on the outcome of the recent presidential election. Should that be the case?

Finally, these materials raise basic questions about constitutional change. The Constitution contains a process for amendment in Article V. The Articles of Confederation also had a provision for amendment. But as Bruce Ackerman has noted in *We The People: Transformations* (1998), again and again in American history, basic constitutional changes have occurred that did not follow the constitutional provision for amendment. (One example, according to Ackerman, was the ratification of the Constitution itself. Another was the New Deal Court's treatment of the Commerce Clause. The New Deal Justices did not see it that way, however. They thought they were returning to a broad understanding of the commerce power enunciated by John Marshall.) As Ackerman sees it, these changes were legitimated by a constitutional "moment" of profound public discussion of the basic issue and a series of very substantial electoral victories in which the proposed changes were ratified and accepted by all sides. Ackerman then contends these constitutional changes should be accepted as constitutional amendments subject to change only in another equally dramatic constitutional moment.

What do you think? Should Roosevelt have pushed for constitutional amendments to authorize the New Deal? Should the Court return to heightened scrutiny of economic legislation? While few Justices seem inclined to return to *Lochner*-era jurisprudence, at least under the Due Process Clause, what became accepted New Deal jurisprudence also had had little support on the Court before Franklin Roosevelt's election.

The Demise of Economic Rights as "Liberty" Subject to Heightened Scrutiny

From 1900 to 1937 the Court was often hostile to the use of congressional power under the Commerce Clause to address the economic conditions spawned by industrialization and the Great Depression. The Court was often also hostile to *state* attempts to regulate the workplace, striking reform legislation as a violation of the 14th Amendment Due Process Clause. In *NLRB v. Jones & Laughlin Steel Corp.* (1937), however, the Court significantly expanded congressional power under the Commerce Clause. The Court also rejected claims that the National Labor Relations Act violated the liberty of employers and employees under the 5th Amendment Due Process Clause. In passing the act, Congress had specifically found:

> The inequality of bargaining power between employees who do not possess full freedom of association or actual liberty of contract, and employers who are organized in the corporate or other forms of ownership association substantially burdens and affects the flow of commerce, and tends to aggravate recurrent business depressions, by depressing wage rates and the purchasing power of wage earners in industry and by preventing the stabilization of competitive wage rates and working conditions within and between industries.

> Experience has proved that protection by law of the right of employees to organize and bargain collectively safeguards commerce from injury, impairment, or interruption, and promotes the flow of commerce by removing certain recognized sources of industrial strife and unrest, by encouraging practices fundamental to the friendly adjustment of industrial disputes arising out of differences as to wages, hours, or other working conditions, and by restoring equality of bargaining power between employers and employees.

Though Congress explicitly attempted to equalize bargaining power between employers and employees (an aim the Court had earlier often treated as impermissible under the Due Process Clause), the Court upheld the National Labor Relations Act against a due process challenge.

In *United States v. Carolene Products Co.* (1938), the Court issued another watershed opinion construing "liberty" under the Due Process Clause for economic substantive due process. While announcing the Court's decision not to apply heightened scrutiny of economic legislation, Justice Stone suggested in Footnote 4 that there were other interests that the Court would scrutinize closely.

The *Carolene Products* Court considered a federal statute that prohibited the sale of evaporated milk to which coconut oil had been added. (The product was similar to modern non-dairy creamer.) The statute did not, however, regulate the sale of oleomargarine to which coconut oil had been added. The defendant's first line of attack was that the statute exceeded Congress' authority under the commerce power. The lower court accepted that argument, citing *Hammar v. Dagenhart* (1918). Consistent with its deferential approach to congressional exercise of its commerce power, the Court rejected that argument. The defendant also argued that the statute violated the Due Process Clause of the 5th Amendment since the sale of margarine containing coconut oil was allowed. The

Illinois Supreme Court, in *People v. Carolene Products Co.* (Ill. 1931), had invalidated a similar state statute on this ground. While the cases in these materials so far have concerned the 14th Amendment Due Process Clause, the standard for due process analysis is essentially similar for both the 5th and 14th Amendments.

United States v. Carolene Products Co.
304 U.S. 144 (1938)

[Majority: Hughes (C.J.), Brandeis, Stone, Roberts, and Black. Concurring: Butler. Dissenting: McReynolds.]

Mr. Justice Stone delivered the opinion of the Court.

The question for decision is whether the "Filled Milk Act" of Congress of March 4, 1923 which prohibits the shipment in interstate commerce of skimmed milk compounded with any fat or oil other than milk fat, so as to resemble milk or cream, transcends the power of Congress to regulate interstate commerce or infringes the 5th Amendment. [The Court summarily disposed of the Commerce Clause attack.] ...

[W]e might rest decision [concerning the 5th Amendment] wholly on the presumption of constitutionality. But affirmative evidence also sustains the statute. In twenty years evidence has steadily accumulated of the danger to the public health from the general consumption of foods which have been stripped of elements essential to the maintenance of health. The Filled Milk Act was adopted by Congress after committee hearings, in the course of which eminent scientists and health experts testified. An extensive investigation was made of the commerce in milk compounds in which vegetable oils have been substituted for natural milk fat, and of the effect upon the public health of the use of such compounds as a food substitute for milk. Both [congressional] committees concluded, as the statute itself declares, that the use of filled milk as a substitute for pure milk is generally injurious to health and facilitates fraud on the public.

There is nothing in the Constitution which compels a legislature, either national or state, to ignore such evidence, nor need it disregard the other evidence which amply supports the conclusions of the Congressional committees that the danger is greatly enhanced where an inferior product, like appellee's, is indistinguishable from a valuable food of almost universal use, thus making fraudulent distribution easy and protection of the consumer difficult....

[T]he existence of facts supporting the legislative judgment is to be presumed, for regulatory legislation affecting ordinary commercial transactions is not to be pronounced unconstitutional unless in the light of the facts made known or generally assumed it is of such a character as to preclude the assumption that it rests upon some rational basis within the knowledge and experience of the legislators. [Footnote 4, set out *infra*, occurs here.] The present statutory findings affect appellee no more than the reports of the Congressional committees; and since in the absence of the statutory findings they would be presumed, their incorporation in the statute is no more prejudicial than surplusage.

Where the existence of a rational basis for legislation whose constitutionality is attacked depends upon facts beyond the sphere of judicial notice, such facts may properly be made the subject of judicial inquiry, *Borden's Farm Products Co. v. Baldwin* (1934), and the constitutionality of a statute predicated upon the existence of a particular state of facts may be challenged by showing to the court that those facts have ceased to exist. *Chastleton Corporation v. Sinclair* (1924). Similarly we recognize that the constitutionality of a statute, valid on its face, may be assailed by proof of facts tending to show that the statute as applied to a particular article is without support in reason because the article, although within the prohibited class, is so different from others of the class as to be without the reason for the prohibition....

But by their very nature such inquiries, where the legislative judgment is drawn in question, must be restricted to the issue whether any state of facts either known or which could reasonably be assumed affords support for it. Here the demurrer challenges the validity of the statute on its face and it is evident from all the considerations presented to Congress, and those of which we may take judicial notice, that the question is at least debatable whether commerce in filled milk should be left unregulated, or in some measure restricted, or wholly prohibited. As that decision was for Congress, neither the finding of a court arrived at by weighing the evidence, nor the verdict of a jury can be substituted for it....

Reversed.

Carolene Products' Footnote Four

Carolene Products is more famous for its Footnote 4 than for the holding of the case. Only three Justices joined the third part of the opinion, in which the footnote was located. The footnote read as follows:

> There may be narrower scope for operation of the presumption of constitutionality when legislation appears on its face to be within a specific prohibition of the Constitution, such as those of the first ten Amendments, which are deemed equally specific when held to be embraced within the 14th. See *Stromberg v. California* (1931); *Lovell v. Griffin* (1938).
>
> It is unnecessary to consider now whether legislation which restricts those political processes which can ordinarily be expected to bring about repeal of undesirable legislation, is to be subjected to more exacting judicial scrutiny under the general prohibitions of the 14th Amendment than are most other types of legislation. On restrictions upon the right to vote, see *Nixon v. Herndon* (1927); *Nixon v. Condon* (1932); on restraints upon the dissemination of information, see *Near v. Minnesota* (1931); *Grosjean v. American Press Co.* (1936); *Lovell v. Griffin*; on interferences with political organizations, see *Stromberg v. California*; *Fiske v. Kansas* (1927); *Whitney v. California* (1927); *Herndon v. Lowry* (1937) ...; and see Holmes, J., in *Gitlow v. New York* (1925); as to prohibition of peaceable assembly, see *De Jonge v. Oregon* (1937).
>
> Nor need we enquire whether similar considerations enter into the review of statutes directed at particular religious, *Pierce v. Society of Sisters* (1925), or national, *Meyer v. Nebraska* (1923), or racial minorities, *Nixon v. Herndon; Nixon v. Condon;* [or] whether prejudice against discrete and insular minorities may be a special condition, which tends seriously to curtail the operation of those political processes ordinarily to be relied upon to protect minorities, and which may call for a correspondingly more searching judicial inquiry. Compare *McCulloch v. Maryland* (1819); *South Carolina State Highway Department v. Barnwell Bros.* (1938).

Carolene Products: Questions

1. Does this case suggest that the Court will continue to protect certain interests or liberties even as it begins to defer to governmental regulation of economic matters? What types of issues does it suggest should be subjected to heightened judicial scrutiny?

2. After the Court repudiated a broad reading of substantive due process as applied to economic legislation, what test did it use to see if such laws violated due process? Is there a difference between what the Court says the test is and the way it applies it?
3. How likely is it that a plaintiff will succeed in a due process attack on social or economic legislation under the test articulated in *Carolene Products*?
4. What does the Court mean by *rational basis*? Could legislation be supported by a simply conceivable basis? Must the legislature have even thought of it?
5. Why is the Court so reluctant to review ordinary economic legislation? Is this reluctance appropriate?

Williamson v. Lee Optical: Background

In *Day-Brite Lighting v. Missouri* (1952), the Court rejected a federal constitutional challenge to a state statute requiring employers to allow employees time away from their jobs to vote without loss of pay. However, in *Heimgaertner v. Benjamin Electric Mfg. Co.* (Ill. 1955), the Illinois Supreme Court struck down a similar statute under the Due Process Clause of the Illinois constitution. The state court refused to follow *Day-Brite*:

> Although the decision eliminates the Federal aspects of the problems surrounding such regulations, it serves to reaffirm that it is for each State to determine if its legislature is empowered to enact such a statute and to determine if the means selected to further the public welfare bear a real and substantial relation to the objects sought to be obtained. It is the duty of each State to pass upon the validity of its own legislation and, if no Federal question is involved, the United States Supreme Court will adopt and follow the decision of the State court.

Williamson v. Lee Optical (1955) is representative of the modern Court's approach to most due process challenges to economic legislation. One exception to this low level review is challenges to regulations of advertising, which the Court now says implicate the 1st Amendment. At the time the *Williamson* decision was rendered, commercial speech was not considered constitutionally protected.

As you consider the statutory prohibition in *Williamson* on making lenses for glasses without a prescription from a licensed ophthalmologist or optometrist, analyze the tightness of the fit between the state's ends and means, using the ideas of rationality, under-inclusiveness, and over-inclusiveness. What is the harm? What is the trait? Do all of those with the trait cause the harm?

Williamson v. Lee Optical of Oklahoma, Inc.
348 U.S. 483 (1955)

[Majority: Warren, Black, Reed, Frankfurter, Douglas, Burton, Clark, and Minton.]

Mr. Justice Douglas delivered the opinion of the Court.

This suit was instituted in the District Court to have an Oklahoma law declared unconstitutional and to enjoin state officials from enforcing it for the reason that it allegedly violated various provisions of the Federal Constitution....

The District Court held unconstitutional portions of three sections of the Act. First, it held invalid under the Due Process Clause of the 14th Amendment the portions of §2 which make it unlawful for any person not a licensed optometrist or ophthalmologist to fit lenses to a face or to duplicate or replace into frames lenses or other optical appliances, except upon written prescriptive authority of an Oklahoma licensed ophthalmologist or optometrist.

An ophthalmologist is a duly licensed physician who specializes in the care of the eyes. An optometrist examines eyes for refractive error, recognizes (but does not treat) diseases of the eye, and fills prescriptions for eyeglasses. The optician is an artisan qualified to grind lenses, fill prescriptions, and fit frames.

The effect of §2 is to forbid the optician from fitting or duplicating lenses without a prescription from an ophthalmologist or optometrist. In practical effect, it means that no optician can fit old glasses into new frames or supply a lens, whether it be a new lens or one to duplicate a lost or broken lens, without a prescription. The District Court conceded that it was in the competence of the police power of a State to regulate the examination of the eyes. But it rebelled at the notion that a State could require a prescription from an optometrist or ophthalmologist "to take old lenses and place them in new frames and then fit the completed spectacles to the face of the eyeglass wearer." It held that such a requirement was not "reasonably and rationally related to the health and welfare of the people." The court found that through mechanical devices and ordinary skills the optician could take a broken lens or a fragment thereof, measure its power, and reduce it to prescriptive terms. The court held that "Although on this precise issue of duplication, the legislature in the instant regulation was dealing with a matter of public interest, the particular means chosen are neither reasonably necessary nor reasonably related to the end sought to be achieved." It was, accordingly, the opinion of the court that this provision of the law violated the Due Process Clause by arbitrarily interfering with the optician's right to do business....

The Oklahoma law may exact a needless, wasteful requirement in many cases. But it is for the legislature, not the courts, to balance the advantages and disadvantages of the new requirement. It appears that in many cases the optician can easily supply the new frames or new lenses without reference to the old written prescription. It also appears that many written prescriptions contain no directive data in regard to fitting spectacles to the face. But in some cases the directions contained in the prescription are essential, if the glasses are to be fitted so as to correct the particular defects of vision or alleviate the eye condition. The legislature might have concluded that the frequency of occasions when a prescription is necessary was sufficient to justify this regulation of the fitting of eyeglasses. Likewise, when it is necessary to duplicate a lens, a written prescription may or may not be necessary. But the legislature might have concluded that one was needed often enough to require one in every case. Or the legislature may have concluded that eye examinations were so critical, not only for correction of vision but also for detection of latent ailments or diseases, that every change in frames and every duplication of a lens should be accompanied by a prescription from a medical expert. To be sure, the present law does not require a new examination of the eyes every time the frames are changed or the lenses duplicated. For if the old prescription is on file with the optician, he can go ahead and make the new fitting or duplicate the lenses. But the law need not be in every respect logically consistent with its aims to be constitutional. It is enough that there is an evil at hand for correction, and that it might be thought that the particular legislative measure was a rational way to correct it.

The day is gone when this Court uses the Due Process Clause of the 14th Amendment to strike down state laws, regulatory of business and industrial conditions, because they may be unwise, improvident, or out of harmony with a particular school of thought. We emphasize again what Chief Justice Waite said in *Munn v. State of Illinois* (1877), "For protection against abuses by legislatures the people must resort to the polls, not to the courts."...

[T]he District Court [also] held unconstitutional, as violative of the Due Process Clause of the 14th Amendment, the provision of §4 of the Oklahoma Act which reads as follows:

> No person, firm, or corporation engaged in the business of retailing merchandise to the general public shall rent space, sublease departments, or otherwise permit any person purporting to do eye examination or visual care to occupy space in such retail store.

It seems to us that this regulation is on the same constitutional footing as the denial to corporations of the right to practice dentistry. *Semler v. Oregon State Board of Dental Examiners* (1935). It is an attempt to free the profession, to as great an extent as possible, from all taints of commercialism. It certainly might be easy for an optometrist with space in a retail store to be merely a front for the retail establishment. In any case, the opportunity for that nexus may be too great for safety, if the eye doctor is allowed inside the retail store. Moreover, it may be deemed important to effective regulation that the eye doctor be restricted to geographical locations that reduce the temptations of commercialism. Geographical location may be an important consideration in a legislative program which aims to raise the treatment of the human eye to a strictly professional level. We cannot say that the regulation has no rational relation to that objective and therefore is beyond constitutional bounds....

FCC v. Beach Communications: Background

The Burger, Rehnquist, and Roberts courts have been quite deferential in their review of economic legislation not implicating an incorporated right when it is challenged as a violation of substantive due process. (Note that a different result may occur under the dormant Commerce, the interstate Privileges and Immunities, the Takings, or the Contract Clauses.) In *U.S. R.R. Retirement Bd. v. Fritz* (1980), the Court upheld a statute which failed to accomplish the goal its congressional sponsors had represented to Congress that it would achieve. However, the statute did accomplish *other* goals. The Court said that counsel for the government was free to argue that the statute was rational if counsel could think of *any* goals the statute accomplished, even if the legislature had not considered them at the time of passage. *Fritz* is referred to repeatedly in the following case, *FCC v. Beach Communications*, Inc. (1993).

While *Fritz* and *FCC v. Beach Communications* are both 5th Amendment due process cases, the Court discusses the cases in equal protection terms. The standards of equal protection have been read into the Due Process Clause of the 5th Amendment. The level of scrutiny for either clause is virtually identical when the Court is reviewing a similar topic (*i.e.*, both Clauses use deferential review for economic legislation, both Clauses use strict scrutiny for fundamental rights, etc.).

FCC v. Beach Communications, Inc.
508 U.S. 307 (1993)

[Majority: Thomas, Rehnquist (C.J.), White, Blackmun, O'Connor, Scalia, Kennedy, and Souter. Concurring: Stevens.]

Mr. Justice Thomas delivered the opinion of the Court....

[*Beach Communications* involved a challenge to a provision of §602(7)(B) of the Cable Communications Policy Act of 1984. Under the Act, operators of typical cable television systems must apply for a franchise from the city in which they operate. However, apartment buildings which use a satellite to receive a signal and then distribute the programs to their tenants (satellite master antenna television or "SMATV" systems) may operate without a license. This exception does not apply if the satellite owner's transmission lines (cables) interconnect separately owned and managed buildings or if its lines use or cross any public right-of-way. Beach Communications contended that this qualification had no relevance whatsoever to whether or not a satellite owner should be forced to purchase a franchise and that there was no rational basis for distinguishing between facilities covered by the franchise requirement and those exempted from the franchise requirement.]

II. Whether embodied in the 14th Amendment or inferred from the 5th, equal protection is not a license for courts to judge the wisdom, fairness, or logic of legislative choices. In areas of social and economic policy, a statutory classification that neither proceeds along suspect lines nor infringes fundamental constitutional rights must be upheld against equal protection challenge if there is any reasonably conceivable state of facts that could provide a rational basis for the classification. See [e.g.] *United States Railroad Retirement Bd. v. Fritz* (1980). Where there are "plausible reasons" for Congress' action, "our inquiry is at an end." *Id.* This standard of review is a paradigm of judicial restraint. "The Constitution presumes that, absent some reason to infer antipathy, even improvident decisions will eventually be rectified by the democratic process and that judicial intervention is generally unwarranted no matter how unwisely we may think a political branch has acted." *Vance v. Bradley* (1979).

On rational-basis review, a classification in a statute such as the Cable Act comes to us bearing a strong presumption of validity, see *Lyng v. Int'l Union* (1988), and those attacking the rationality of the legislative classification have the burden "to negative every conceivable basis which might support it," *Lehnhausen v. Lake Shore Auto Parts Co.* (1973). Moreover, because we never require a legislature to articulate its reasons for enacting a statute, it is entirely irrelevant for constitutional purposes whether the conceived reason for the challenged distinction actually motivated the legislature. *United States Railroad Retirement Bd. v. Fritz.* Thus, the absence of "'legislative facts'" explaining the distinction "[o]n the record," has no significance in rational-basis analysis. See *Nordlinger v. Hahn* (1992) (equal protection "does not demand for purposes of rational-basis review that a legislature or governing decision maker actually articulate at any time the purpose or rationale supporting its classification"). In other words, a legislative choice is not subject to courtroom fact-finding and may be based on rational speculation unsupported by evidence or empirical data.

These restraints on judicial review have added force "where the legislature must necessarily engage in a process of line-drawing." *United States Railroad Retirement Bd. v. Fritz.* Defining the class of persons subject to a regulatory requirement—much like classifying governmental beneficiaries—"inevitably requires that some persons who have an almost equally strong claim to favored treatment be placed on different sides of the line, and the fact [that] the line might have been drawn differently at some points is a matter for legislative, rather than judicial, consideration." The distinction at issue here represents such a line.... This necessity renders the precise coordinates of the resulting legislative judgment virtually unreviewable, since the legislature must be allowed leeway to approach a perceived problem incrementally....

III. [T]here are plausible rationales ... for regulating cable facilities serving separately owned and managed buildings. The assumptions underlying these rationales may be erroneous, but the very fact that they are "arguable" is sufficient, on rational-basis review, to "immuniz[e]" the congressional choice from constitutional challenge. *Vance v. Bradley.*

[The Court suggested two conceivable rationales. First it was possible that common ownership was indicative of systems for which the costs of regulation would outweigh the benefits to consumers. Legislators could rationally assume that such systems would typically be limited in size or would share some other attribute affecting their impact on cable viewers' welfare such that regulators could safely ignore them. The Court's second conceivable basis for the statutory distinction was concern about the danger of monopoly power. It was conceivable that the first SMATV operator installing a dish on one building in a block of separately owned buildings would have a significant cost advantage in competing for the remaining subscribers.]

The judgment of the Court of Appeals is reversed.

Justice Stevens, concurring in the judgment....

[Footnote to Stevens' opinion:] The Court states that a legislative classification must be upheld "if there is any reasonably conceivable state of facts that could provide a rational basis for the classification," and that "[w]here there are 'plausible reasons' for Congress' action, 'our inquiry is at an end.'" In my view, this formulation sweeps too broadly, for it is difficult to imagine a legislative classification that could not be supported by a "reasonably conceivable state of facts." Judicial review under the "conceivable set of facts" test is tantamount to no review at all.

I continue to believe that when Congress imposes a burden on one group, but leaves unaffected another that is similarly, though not identically, situated, "the Constitution requires something more than merely a 'conceivable' or 'plausible' explanation for the unequal treatment." *United States Railroad Retirement Bd. v. Fritz* (1980) (Stevens, J., concurring in judgment). In my view, when the actual rationale for the legislative classification is unclear, we should inquire whether the classification is rationally related to "a legitimate purpose that we may *reasonably presume* to have motivated an impartial legislature." *Id.* (emphasis added).

* * *

Along with the (incorporated) Takings Clause, the Due Process Clause has been used to invalidate state economic regulation in the narrow area of punitive damages. In *BMW of North America, Inc. v. Gore* (1996), the Court struck down what it considered to be a grossly excessive award of punitive damages as a violation of due process. The new BMW that Gore purchased had a minor defect and was repainted before he bought it, but Gore was not told of the repainting. When he discovered the facts, Gore sued BMW and recovered four thousand dollars in actual damages and four million dollars in punitive damages. The Alabama Supreme Court reduced the punitive damages to two million dollars. The Supreme Court, in a 5–4 opinion, held the award excessive as a violation of due process. It concluded that the jury's punitive damages verdict could not be supported by the fact that similar conduct had occurred in other states. Alabama was limited to vindicating the rights of its own citizens. The Court also said that due process requires fair notice, not only that conduct *could* be punished, but also of the *possible severity* of the punishment. Because the punishment was so grossly excessive, the Court held that BMW was denied fair notice. The factors the Court considered in holding the verdict to be grossly excessive included the Court's judgment that BMW's conduct was not reprehensible, the 500–1 ratio between the actual damages and the punitive damages, and the great difference between the criminal penalty Alabama imposed for such conduct and the civil punishment BMW received. The dissenters contended that the issues regarding punitive damages should be left to the states.

Modern Economic Legislation Hypothetical

The State of Nebraska sets maximum fees for employment agencies. Instantjobs specializes in employment for attorneys, doctors, engineers, and other professionals. Its fee is 25% of the employee's first year net salary. The Nebraska statute sets the maximum fee at 10% for a period not to exceed six months. The purpose of the statute, as expressed by the legislature, is to prevent excessive prices and exploitation of a vulnerable group—the unemployed. In 1999, Nebraska obtained an injunction against Instantjobs forbidding it from charging fees in excess of the state maximum price. Instantjobs and Sam South, a recent law school graduate, challenge the statute as a violation of their liberty interests under the Due Process Clause.

1. What are the steps of analysis?
2. What amendment will Instantjobs and South cite?
3. What argument will they make?
4. What kind of due process protection are they invoking?
5. What cases might they cite?
6. What cases will be cited by the state?
7. How should the case be resolved?

IV. The Origins of Substantive Protection for Non-Economic Rights

Justice James McReynolds was one of the economic libertarian Justices who often voted to strike down Progressive and New Deal legislation based on his understanding of freedom of contract or private property rights. In *Nebbia v. New York* (1934), one of the cases signaling the end of economic substantive due process, he strenuously dissented from the Court's decision upholding the New York milk price support law. He said in part:

> Regulation to prevent recognized evils in business has long been upheld as permissible legislative action. But fixation of the price at which "A," engaged in an ordinary business, may sell, in order to enable "B," a producer, to improve his condition, has not been regarded as within legislative power. This is not regulation, but management, control, dictation—it amounts to the deprivation of the fundamental right which one has to conduct his own affairs honestly and along customary lines. The argument advanced here would support general prescription of prices for farm products, groceries, shoes, clothing, all the necessities of modern civilization, as well as labor, when some legislature finds and declares such action advisable and for the public good. This Court has declared that a State may not by legislative fiat convert a private business into a public utility.... And if it be now ruled that one dedicates his property to public use whenever he embarks on an enterprise which the Legislature may think it desirable to bring under control, this is but to declare that rights guaranteed by the Constitution exist only so long as supposed public interest does not require their extinction. To adopt such a view, of course, would put an end to liberty under the Constitution....
>
> [This statute] takes away the liberty of 12 million consumers to buy a necessity of life in an open market. It ... burdens ... those already seriously impoverished with the alleged immediate design of affording special benefits to others.... A superabundance [of milk may exist]; but no child can purchase from a willing storekeeper below the figure appointed by three men at headquarters!

The two cases that follow, *Meyer v. Nebraska* (1923) and *Pierce v. Society of Sisters* (1925), were written by Justice McReynolds and have served as a basis for the modern expansion of substantive due process rights in the area of privacy and autonomy. They were the first cases in which the Court invoked the 14th Amendment's Due Process Clause to invalidate statutes that infringed non-economic liberties. We have just traced the demise of freedom of contract as a liberty right. Is there a principled basis under the Due Process Clause to distinguish between personal privacy and economic liberty? If there is, what is it?

In *Meyer*, the Court nullified a Nebraska law that prohibited the teaching of foreign languages in elementary schools. The statute was similar to laws enacted in twenty-one other states during and shortly after the First World War in an effort to promote "Americanism" and to ensure the assimilation of ethnic enclaves, especially the large and often insular German-American communities that were particularly numerous in the Middle West. The constitutionality of the Nebraska statute was challenged by Robert T. Meyer, a teacher in a Lutheran parochial school in rural Nebraska. Meyer continued his German lesson when the county attorney visited his classroom one day in 1920 even though he knew that the county attorney did not want to create trouble with the local German community and that he would not prosecute him if he did not catch him in the act of teaching German. As Meyer explained to his attorney, "I had my choice. I knew that, if I changed into English, he would say nothing. If I went on in German, he would arrest me. I told myself that I must not flinch. And I did not flinch. I went on in German." Meyer believed that he had a religious duty to teach German because the school was affiliated with a congregation that conducted its services in German.

Convicted of violating the law and fined $25, Meyer unsuccessfully appealed to the Supreme Court of Nebraska and then carried the case to the U.S. Supreme Court. Although Meyer and the Lutheran denomination that challenged the law contended that the statute infringed religious freedom, the Nebraska Supreme Court rejected a religious liberty argument under the state constitution, and the plaintiffs could not invoke the Free Exercise Clause of the 1st Amendment because it had not yet been incorporated into state law. Since the Court in previous cases had invoked the Due Process Clause of the 14th Amendment only to protect economic liberties, Meyer claimed an economic right to teach German and the denomination argued that the economic value of its large network of parochial schools would be diminished or destroyed if the schools could not teach German. Similarly, parents who joined the litigation relied upon the doctrine of liberty of contract to argue that they had a right to enter into contracts with schools to teach the German language to their children. In accepting these arguments, the Court's holding in *Meyer* seems to rely primarily if not wholly upon economic grounds, but its *dictum* declares that due process embraces an expansive array of personal liberties. *Meyer* therefore commenced the Court's modern role as a guardian of personal rights. In his *Carolene Products* footnote, Justice Stone cited *Meyer* in support of his suggestion that the Court might exercise a higher level of scrutiny in reviewing statutes directed at particular national groups than it does in reviewing economic legislation.

Meyer provided the doctrinal basis for *Pierce*, in which the Court unanimously invalidated an Oregon statute that required all children to attend public school. The Oregon law, which would have the had the effect of eliminating all full-time parochial and private elementary and secondary schools, was part of a nationwide movement for compulsory public education that reflected a resurgent nativism and hostility toward ethnic Americans, especially those who were Roman Catholic or Lutheran. The Ku Klux Klan strongly supported this movement and was instrumental in the enactment of the Oregon statute. Although the Court in *Pierce* once again relied in part upon the economic interests of schools, teachers, and parents, the Court also held that the statute interfered with the right of parents to direct the education of their children. In declaring that the statute "unreasonably interferes with the liberty of parents and guardians to direct the upbringing and education of children under their control," the Court explained that "[t]he child is not the mere creature of the State; those who nurture him and direct his destiny have the right, coupled with the high duty, to recognize and prepare him for additional obligations." The Court re-affirmed this principle two years later in striking down a Hawaiian law restricting the teaching of Asian languages, *Farrington v. Tokushige* (1927).

Even though the Court in *Meyer* and *Pierce* did not rely upon the religious liberty concerns that were so close to the hearts of the opponents of the statutes because it had not yet incorporated any part of the Bill of Rights into state law, these decisions may have hastened the process by which the Bill of Rights was nationalized. Only one week after the Court decided *Pierce*, the Court's decision in *Gitlow v. New York* (1925) began the process of nationalization by stating in dictum that the free speech clause of the 1st Amendment was binding on the states. The Court's use of the specific provisions of the Bill of Rights to invalidate intrusions on personal liberties has been less controversial than its use of substantive due process because the provisions of the Bill of Rights are more specific and therefore at least theoretically provide less opportunity for judicial discretion.

The *Meyer, Pierce,* and *Tokushige* cases also are important because they were among the first cases in which ethnic and religious minorities organized to protect their liberties, and they provided a prototype for the civil rights movements of the 1950s and 1960s.*

Meyer v. Nebraska
262 U.S. 390 (1923)

[Majority: McReynolds, Taft (C.J.), McKenna, Van Devanter, Brandeis, Butler, and Sanford. Dissenting: Holmes and Sutherland.]

Mr. Justice McReynolds delivered the opinion of the Court.

The [Nebraska Supreme Court] ... held that the statute ... did not conflict with the 14th Amendment, but was a valid exercise of the police power. The following excerpts from the [Nebraska] opinion sufficiently indicate the reasons advanced to support the conclusion.

> The salutary purpose of the statute is clear. The legislature had seen the baneful effects of permitting foreigners, who had taken residence in this country, to rear and educate their children in the language of their native land. The result of that condition was found to be inimical to our own safety. To allow the children of foreigners, who had emigrated here, to be taught from early childhood the language of the country of their parents was to rear them with that language as their mother tongue. It was to educate them so that they must always think in that language, and, as a consequence, naturally inculcate in them the ideas and sentiments foreign to the best interests of this country. The statute, therefore, was intended not only to require that the education of all children be conducted in the English language, but that, until they had grown into that language and until

---

* For a historical and legal analysis of *Meyer, Pierce,* and *Tokushige,* see William G. Ross, *Forging New Freedoms: Nativism, Education, and the Constitution, 1917–1927* (University of Nebraska Press, 1994).

it had become a part of them, they should not in the schools be taught any other language. The obvious purpose of this statute was that the English language should be and become the mother tongue of all children reared in this state. The enactment of such a statute comes reasonably within the police power of the state....

[After quoting from the state supreme court decision, the Supreme Court opinion continued:]

While this Court has not attempted to define with exactness the liberty thus guaranteed [by the Due Process Clause of the 14th Amendment], the term has received much consideration and some of the included things have been definitely stated. Without doubt, it denotes not merely freedom from bodily restraint but also the right of the individual to contract, to engage in any of the common occupations of life, to acquire useful knowledge, to marry, establish a home and bring up children, to worship God according to the dictates of his own conscience, and generally to enjoy those privileges long recognized at common law as essential to the orderly pursuit of happiness by free men. [Citing, among others] *Slaughter-House Cases* (1873); *Allgeyer v. Louisiana* (1897); *Lochner v. New York* (1905); *Twining v. New Jersey* (1908); *Adkins v. Children's Hospital* (1923).

The established doctrine is that this liberty may not be interfered with, under the guise of protecting the public interest, by legislative action which is arbitrary or without reasonable relation to some purpose within the competency of the State to effect. Determination by the legislature of what constitutes proper exercise of police power is not final or conclusive but is subject to supervision by the courts....

Practically, education of the young is only possible in schools conducted by especially qualified persons who devote themselves thereto. The calling always has been regarded as useful and honorable, essential, indeed, to the public welfare. Mere knowledge of the German language cannot reasonably be regarded as harmful. Heretofore it has been commonly looked upon as helpful and desirable. Plaintiff in error taught this language in school as part of his occupation. His right thus to teach and the right of parents to engage him so to instruct their children, we think, are within the liberty of the Amendment.

The challenged statute forbids the teaching in school of any subject except in English; also the teaching of any other language until the pupil has attained and successfully passed the eighth grade, which is not usually accomplished before the age of twelve. The Supreme Court of the State has held that "the so-called ancient or dead languages" are not "within the spirit or the purpose of the act." Latin, Greek, Hebrew are not proscribed; but German, French, Spanish, Italian and every other alien speech are within the ban....

For the welfare of his Ideal Commonwealth, Plato suggested a law which should provide: "That the wives of our guardians are to be common, and their children are to be common, and no parent is to know his own child."...

In order to submerge the individual and develop ideal citizens, Sparta assembled the males at seven into barracks and intrusted their subsequent education and training to official guardians. Although such measures have been deliberately approved by men of great genius, their ideas touching the relation between individual and State were wholly different from those upon which our institutions rest; and it hardly will be affirmed that any legislature could impose such restrictions upon the people of a State without doing violence to both letter and spirit of the Constitution....

No emergency has arisen which renders knowledge by a child of some language other than English so clearly harmful as to justify its inhibition with the consequent infringement of rights long freely enjoyed. We are constrained to conclude that the statute as applied is arbitrary and without reasonable relation to any end within the competency of the State.

As the statute undertakes to interfere only with teaching which involves a modern language, leaving complete freedom as to other matters, there seems no adequate foundation for the suggestion that the purpose was to protect the child's health by limiting his mental activities. It is well known that proficiency in a foreign language seldom comes to one not instructed at an early age, and experience shows that this is not injurious to the health, morals or understanding of the ordinary child.

The judgment of the court below must be reversed and the cause remanded for further proceedings not inconsistent with this opinion....

Mr. Justice Holmes, dissenting.

We all agree, I take it, that it is desirable that all the citizens of the United States should speak a common tongue, and therefore that the end aimed at by the statute is a lawful and proper one. The only question is whether the means adopted deprive teachers of the liberty secured to them by the 14th Amendment. It is with hesitation and unwillingness that I differ from my brethren with regard to a law like this but I cannot bring my mind to believe that in some circumstances, and circumstances existing it is said in Nebraska, the statute might not be regarded as a reasonable or even necessary method of reaching the desired result. The part of the act with which we are concerned deals with the teaching of young children. Youth is the time when familiarity with a language is established and if there are sections in the State where a child would hear only Polish or French or German spoken at home I am not prepared to say that it is unreasonable to provide that in his early years he shall hear and speak only English at school. But if it is reasonable it is not an undue restriction of the liberty either of teacher or scholar. No one would doubt that a teacher might be forbidden to teach many things, and the only criterion of his liberty under the Constitution that I can think of is "whether, considering the end in view, the statute passes the bounds of reason and assumes the character of a merely arbitrary fiat." ... I think I appreciate the objection to the law but it appears to me to present a question upon which men reasonably might differ and therefore I am unable to say that the Constitution of the United States prevents the experiment being tried....

Buck v. Bell

274 U.S. 200 (1927)

[Majority: Holmes, Taft (C.J.), Van Devanter, McReynolds, Brandeis, Sutherland, Sanford, and Stone. Dissenting: Butler.]

Mr. Justice Holmes delivered the opinion of the Court.

This is a writ of error to review a judgment of the Supreme Court of Appeals of the State of Virginia, affirming a judgment of the Circuit Court of Amherst County, by which the defendant in error, the superintendent of the State Colony for Epileptics and Feeble Minded, was ordered to perform the operation of salpingectomy upon Carrie Buck, the plaintiff in error, for the purpose of making her sterile. The case comes here upon the contention that the statute authorizing the judgment is void under the 14th Amendment as denying to the plaintiff in error due process of law and the equal protection of the laws.

Carrie Buck is a feeble minded white woman who was committed to the State Colony above mentioned in due form. She is the daughter of a feeble minded mother in the same institution, and the mother of an illegitimate feeble minded child. She was eighteen years old at the time of the trial of her case in the Circuit Court in the latter part of 1924. An Act of Virginia approved March 20, 1924 recites that the health of the patient and the welfare of society may be promoted in certain cases by the sterilization of mental defectives, under careful safeguard, etc.; that the sterilization may be effected in males by vasectomy and in females by salpingectomy, without serious pain or substantial danger to life; that the Commonwealth is supporting in various institutions many defective persons who if now discharged would become a menace but if incapable of procreating might be discharged with safety and become self-supporting with benefit to themselves and to society; and that experience has shown that heredity plays an important part in the transmission of insanity, imbecility, etc. The statute then enacts that whenever the superintendent of certain institutions including the above named State Colony shall be of opinion that it is for the best interest of the patients and of society that an inmate under his care should be sexually sterilized, he may have the operation performed upon any patient afflicted with hereditary forms of insanity, imbecility, etc., on complying with the very careful provisions by which the act protects the patients from possible abuse....

The attack is not upon the procedure but upon the substantive law. It seems to be contended that in no circumstances could such an order be justified. It certainly is contended that the order cannot be justified upon the existing grounds. The judgment finds the facts that have been recited and that Carrie Buck "is the probable potential parent of socially inadequate offspring, likewise afflicted, that she may be sexually sterilized without detriment to her general health and that her welfare and that of society will be promoted by her sterilization," and thereupon makes the order. In view of the general declarations of the Legislature and the specific findings of the Court obviously we cannot say as matter of law that the grounds do not exist, and if they exist they justify the result. We have seen more than once that the public welfare may call upon the best citizens for their lives. It would be strange if it could not call upon those who already sap the strength of the State for these lesser sacrifices, often not felt to be such by those concerned, in order to prevent our being swamped with incompetence. It is better for all the world, if instead of waiting to execute degenerate offspring for crime, or to let them starve for their imbecility, society can prevent those who are manifestly unfit from continuing their kind. The principle that sustains compulsory vaccination is broad enough to cover cutting the Fallopian tubes. *Jacobson v. Massachusetts* (1905). Three generations of imbeciles are enough.

But, it is said, however it might be if this reasoning were applied generally, it fails when it is confined to the small number who are in the institutions named and is not applied to the multitudes outside. It is the usual last resort of constitutional arguments to point out shortcomings of this sort. But the answer is that the law does all that is needed when it does all that it can, indicates a policy, applies it to all within the lines, and seeks to bring within the lines all similarly situated so far and so fast as its means allow. Of course so far as the operations enable those who otherwise must be kept confined to be returned to the world, and thus open the asylum to others, the equality aimed at will be more nearly reached.

Judgment affirmed.

Mr. Justice Butler dissents.

Buck Revisited

According to Professor Stephen Jay Gould, the movement for compulsory sterilization began in earnest in the 1890s. The laws typically provided for sterilization of persons in the custody of the state and could be used on those judged insane, idiotic, or imbecilic; on convicted rapists; or on criminals recommended for sterilization by a board of experts. By the 1930s more than thirty states had passed such laws. About 20,000 people had been forcibly sterilized by 1935. Carrie Buck, an eighteen-year-old white woman, was the first person selected for sterilization under a recently passed Virginia sterilization statute. She had scored a mental age of nine, and her mother of about eight on an early and primitive version of the I.Q. test applied to her. The theory justifying sterilization was that deficiencies were genetic and inherited. The state therefore also relied on the asserted mental deficiency of Carrie's daughter who was a bit over six months old when examined. An expert witness for the state began his history of the Buck family by explaining, "These people belong to the shiftless, ignorant and worthless class of anti-social whites of the South."

More than 4,000 people had been sterilized up to 1970 in the same hospital where Carrie's operation had been performed. The director of the hospital who in 1980 discovered the records of the sterilizations, searched for Carrie Buck and found her alive and well in Charlottesville. Her sister who was also still alive had also been sterilized, but had been told the operation was to remove her appendix. She was appalled to learn that the covert sterilization operation had prevented her and her husband from having the children they had wanted more than anything else in life. When scholars and experts visited Carrie they discovered that she was a woman of normal intelligence. Mental health professionals who examined her found her to be neither mentally ill nor retarded. Carrie had originally been confined to the mental hospital based on the testimony of her foster parents—without even the evidence of the crude intelligence test of that day. According to Gould, the reason for her commitment was moral—she was the mother of an illegitimate child. After much detective work Gould also discovered the school records for Carrie's allegedly mentally defective daughter. The child had been adopted, but died at age 8. Her school records showed her to be a well behaved student who "performed adequately, although not brilliantly, in her academic subjects." *See* Stephen Jay Gould, *Carrie Buck's Daughter*, 2 Const. Comm. 331 (1985). In 2002, the Governor of Virginia formally apologized for the state's extensive sterilization program.

Consider again Carrie's sterilization case. Consider how the various theories of substantive due process that we will soon see might apply to Carrie's case.

Skinner v. Oklahoma: Background

After *Carolene Products* (1938), the Court was extremely reluctant to engage in anything that might appear to be "Lochnerizing" under the Due Process Clause. As Justice Douglas said in *Williamson v. Lee Optical* (1955): "The day is gone when this Court uses the Due Process Clause of the 14th Amendment to strike down state laws, regulatory of business and industrial conditions, because they may be unwise, improvident, or out of harmony with a particular school of thought."

The *Slaughter-House Cases* (1873) had rejected the butchers' due process and equal protection challenges as well as their privileges or immunities challenge. However, just as the *Lochner*-era Court had moved from the Privileges or Immunities Clause to the Due Process Clause to uphold challenges to what it perceived as governmental overreaching, the Court in the 1940's and 1950's also looked elsewhere. With the Privileges or Immunities and Due Process Clauses rendered dormant, the Court "rediscovered" the Equal Protection Clause.

The following case, *Skinner v. Oklahoma* (1942), involves the use of heightened scrutiny of a statute implicating reproductive rights. Challenges to statutes affecting voting rights were similarly subjected to equal protection, rather than due process, analysis. *See, e.g., Reynolds v. Sims* (1964) (reapportionment case). The voting cases will be discussed in the equal protection materials.

Skinner v. Oklahoma ex rel. Williamson
316 U.S. 535 (1942)

[Majority: Stone (C.J.), Roberts, Black, Reed, Frankfurter, Douglas, Murphy, Byrnes, and Jackson. Concurring: Stone (C.J.) and Jackson.]

Mr. Justice Douglas delivered the opinion of the Court.

This case touches a sensitive and important area of human rights. Oklahoma deprives certain individuals of a right which is basic to the perpetuation of a race—the right to have offspring. Oklahoma has decreed the enforcement of its law against petitioner, overruling his claim that it violated the 14th Amendment. Because that decision raised grave and substantial constitutional questions, we granted the petition for certiorari.

The statute involved is Oklahoma's Habitual Criminal Sterilization Act. That Act defines an "habitual criminal" as a person who, having been convicted two or more times for crimes "amounting to felonies involving moral turpitude," either in an Oklahoma court or in a court of any other State, is thereafter convicted of such a felony in Oklahoma and is sentenced to a term of imprisonment in an Oklahoma penal institution. Machinery is provided for the institution by the Attorney General of a proceeding against such a person in the Oklahoma courts for a judgment that such person shall be rendered sexually sterile. Notice, an opportunity to be heard, and the right to a jury trial are provided. The issues triable in such a proceeding are narrow and confined. If the court or jury finds that the defendant is an "habitual criminal" and that he "may be rendered sexually sterile without detriment to his or her general health," then the court "shall render judgment to the effect that said defendant be rendered sexually sterile" by the operation of vasectomy in case of a male, and of salpingectomy in case of a female. Only one other provision of the Act is material here and that is § 195, which provides that "offenses arising out of the violation of the prohibitory laws, revenue acts, embezzlement, or political offenses, shall not come or be considered within the terms of this Act."

Petitioner was convicted in 1926 of the crime of stealing chickens, and was sentenced to the Oklahoma State Reformatory. In 1929 he was convicted of the crime of robbery with firearms and was sentenced to the reformatory. In 1934 he was convicted again of robbery with firearms, and was sentenced to the penitentiary. He was confined there in 1935 when the Act was passed. In 1936 the Attorney General instituted proceedings against him. Petitioner in his answer challenged the Act as unconstitutional by reason of the 14th Amendment. A jury trial was had.... A judgment directing that the operation of vasectomy be performed on petitioner was affirmed by the Supreme Court of Oklahoma by a five to four decision....

We do not stop to point out all of the inequalities in this Act. A few examples will suffice. In Oklahoma grand larceny is a felony. Larceny is grand larceny when the property taken exceeds $20 in value. Embezzlement is punishable "in the manner prescribed for feloniously stealing property of the value of that embezzled." Hence, he who embezzles property worth more than $20 is guilty of a felony. A clerk who appropriates over $20 from his employer's till and a stranger who steals the same amount are thus both guilty of felonies. If the latter repeats his act and is convicted three times, he may be sterilized. But the clerk is not subject to the pains and penalties of the Act no matter how large his embezzlements nor how frequent his convictions. A person who enters a chicken coop and steals chickens commits a felony; and he may be sterilized if he is thrice convicted. If, however, he is a bailee of the property and fraudulently appropriates it, he is an embezzler. Hence, no matter how habitual his proclivities for embezzlement are and no matter how often his conviction, he may not be sterilized. Thus, the nature of the two crimes is intrinsically the same and they are punishable in the same manner. Furthermore, the line between them follows close distinctions—distinctions comparable to those highly technical ones which shaped the common law as to "trespass" or "taking."...

It was stated in *Buck v. Bell* (1927) that the claim that state legislation violates the equal protection clause of the 14th Amendment is "the usual last resort of constitutional arguments." Under our constitutional system the States in determining the reach and scope of particular legislation need not provide "abstract symmetry." They may mark and set apart the classes and types of problems according to the needs and as dictated or suggested by experience. It was in that connection that Mr. Justice Holmes, speaking for the Court in *Bain Peanut Co. v. Pinson* (1931), stated, "We must remember that the machinery of government would not work if it were not allowed a little play in its joints."... Thus, if we had here only a question as to a State's classification of crimes, such as embezzlement or larceny, no substantial federal question would be raised. For a State is not constrained in the exercise of its police power to ignore experience which marks a class of offenders or a family of offenses for special treatment. Nor is it prevented by the equal protection clause from confining "its restrictions to those classes of cases where the need is deemed to be clearest." As stated in *Buck v. Bell*, "... the law does all that is needed when it does all that it can, indicates a policy, applies it to all within the lines, and seeks to bring within the lines all similarly situated so far and so fast as its means allow."

But the instant legislation runs afoul of the equal protection clause, though we give Oklahoma that large deference which the rule of the foregoing cases requires. We are dealing here with legislation which involves one of the basic civil rights of man. Marriage and procreation are fundamental to the very existence and survival of the race. The power to sterilize, if exercised, may have subtle, far-reaching and devastating effects. In evil or reckless hands it can cause races or types which are inimical to the dominant group to wither and disappear. There is no redemption for the individual whom the law touches. Any experiment which the State conducts is to his irreparable injury. He is forever deprived of a basic liberty. We mention these matters not to reexamine the scope of the police power of the States. We advert to them merely in emphasis of our view that strict scrutiny of the classification which a State makes in a sterilization law is essential, lest unwittingly or otherwise invidious discriminations are made against groups or types of individuals in violation of the constitutional guaranty of just and equal laws. The guaranty of "equal protection of the laws is a pledge of the protection of equal laws." *Yick Wo v. Hopkins* (1886). When the law lays an unequal hand on those who have committed intrinsically the same quality of offense and sterilizes one and not the other, it has made as an invidious a discrimination as if it had selected a particular race or nationality for oppressive treatment. *Yick Wo v. Hopkins*.

Sterilization of those who have thrice committed grand larceny, with immunity for those who are embezzlers, is a clear, pointed, unmistakable discrimination. Oklahoma makes no attempt to say that he who commits larceny by trespass or trick or fraud has biologically inheritable traits which he who commits embezzlement lacks. Oklahoma's line between larceny by fraud and embezzlement is determined, as we have noted, "with reference to the time when the fraudulent intent to convert the property to the taker's own use" arises. *Riley v. State* (Okla. Crim. App. 1938). We have not the slightest basis for inferring that that line has any significance in eugenics nor that the inheritability of criminal traits follows the neat legal distinctions which the law has marked between those two offenses. In terms of fines and imprisonment, the crimes of larceny and embezzlement rate the same under the Oklahoma code. Only when it comes to sterilization are the pains and penalties of the law different. The equal protection clause would indeed be a formula of empty words if such conspicuously artificial lines could be drawn....

Mr. Chief Justice Stone concurring. [Omitted.]

Mr. Justice Jackson concurring. [Omitted.]

Robinson v. California

The Court also looked to the 8th Amendment as a justification for heightened scrutiny. In *Robinson v. California* (1962), the Court invalidated a state statute that made it a crime for a person to be addicted to narcotics. The Court, per Justice Stewart, held that it was "cruel and unusual" to punish a person for his *status* as an addict, rather than for the *possession* of illegal drugs (*i.e.*, under the statute, an "addict" who did not possess drugs could be sentenced to jail). Justice White dissented:

> Finally, I deem this application of "cruel and unusual punishment" so novel that I suspect the Court was hard put to find a way to ascribe to the Framers of the Constitution the result reached today rather than to its own notions of ordered liberty. If this case involved economic regulation, the present Court's allergy to substantive due process would surely save the statute and prevent the Court from imposing its own philosophical predilections upon state legislatures or Congress. I fail to see why the Court deems it more appropriate to write into the Constitution its own abstract notions of how best to handle the narcotics problem, for it obviously cannot match either the States or Congress in expert understanding.

Rochin v. California

There was one significant case during the period after *Carolene Products* in which the Court did look to the 14th Amendment Due Process Clause to strike down legislation as an infringement on liberty: *Rochin v. California* (1952). The case involved Due Process and evidence used in a criminal prosecution. There were no dissents and *Lochner v. New York* (1905) was never explicitly mentioned.

Rochin involved a state prosecution for the possession of two capsules of morphine. The evidence was "acquired" by forcibly pumping the stomach of the defendant after he had swallowed the capsules in an effort to hide them from the police. The Court, per Justice Frankfurter, reversed the conviction, holding:

> [T]he proceedings by which this conviction was obtained do more than offend some fastidious squeamishness or private sentimentalism about combatting crime too energetically. This is conduct that shocks the conscience. Illegally breaking into the privacy of the petitioner, the struggle to open his mouth and remove what was there, the forcible extraction of his stomach's contents — this course of proceeding by agents of government to obtain evidence is bound to offend even hardened sensibilities. They are methods too close to the rack and the screw to permit of constitutional differentiation.

Justices Black and Douglas concurred, relying on incorporation of the 5th Amendment's ban on self-incrimination.

V. Liberty and Sexual Privacy

Poe v. Ullman: Background

In 1961, the Court considered for the first time, in *Poe v. Ullman*, the constitutionality of a state statute prohibiting the use of contraceptives, even by married couples. The Court dismissed the case on ripeness grounds, but Justice Harlan dissented from the dismissal and reached the merits of the challenge.

How does Justice Harlan justify striking down statutes banning birth control for married couples? What is his methodology? Put another way, Justice Harlan finds rights that are "implicit in ordered liberty" in the Due Process Clause. How does he determine what is implicit?

Poe v. Ullman
367 U.S. 497 (1961)

[Majority: Frankfurter, Warren (C.J.), Clark, and Whitaker. Concurring: Brennan. Dissenting: Black, Douglas, Harlan, and Stewart.]

Mr. Justice Harlan, dissenting.

I am compelled, with all respect, to dissent from the dismissal of these appeals. In my view the course which the Court has taken does violence to established concepts of "justiciability," and unjustifiably leaves these appellants under the threat of unconstitutional prosecution. Regrettably, an adequate exposition of my views calls for a dissenting opinion of unusual length....

I consider that this Connecticut legislation, as construed to apply to these appellants, violates the 14th Amendment. I believe that a statute making it a criminal offense for *married couples* to use contraceptives is an intolerable and unjustifiable invasion of privacy in the conduct of the most intimate concerns of an individual's personal life.... Since both the contentions draw their basis from no explicit language of the Constitution, and have yet to find expression in any decision of this Court, I feel it desirable at the outset to state the framework of Constitutional principles in which I think the issue must be judged.

I. In reviewing state legislation, whether considered to be in the exercise of the State's police powers, or in provision for the health, safety, morals or welfare of its people, it is clear that what is concerned are "the powers of government inherent in every sovereignty." Only to the extent that the Constitution so requires may this Court interfere with the exercise of this plenary power of government. But precisely because it is the Constitution alone which warrants judicial interference in sovereign operations of the State, the basis of judgment as to the Constitutionality of state action must be a rational one, approaching the text which is the only commission for our power not in a literalistic way, as if we had a tax statute before us, but as the basic charter of our society, setting out in spare but meaningful terms the principles of government. *McCulloch v. Maryland* (1819). But as inescapable as is the rational process in Constitutional adjudication in general, nowhere is it more so than in giving meaning to the prohibitions of the 14th Amendment and, where the Federal Government is involved, the 5th Amendment, against the deprivation of life, liberty or property without due process of law.

It is but a truism to say that this provision of both Amendments is not self-explanatory....

Due process has not been reduced to any formula; its content cannot be determined by reference to any code. The best that can be said is that through the course of this Court's decisions it has represented the balance which our Nation, built upon postulates of respect for the liberty of the individual, has struck between that liberty and the demands of organized society. If the supplying of content to this Constitutional concept has of necessity been a rational process, it certainly has not been one where judges have felt free to roam where unguided speculation might take them. The balance of which I speak is the balance struck by this country, having regard to what history teaches are the traditions from which it developed as well as the traditions from which it broke. That tradition is a living thing. A decision of this Court which radically departs from it could not long survive, while a decision which builds on what has survived is likely to be sound. No formula could serve as a substitute, in this area, for judgment and restraint.

It is this outlook which has led the Court continuingly to perceive distinctions in the imperative character of Constitutional provisions, since that character must be discerned from a particular provision's larger context. And inasmuch as this context is one not of words, but of history and purposes, the full scope of the liberty guaranteed by the Due Process Clause cannot be found in or limited by the precise terms of the specific guarantees elsewhere provided in the Constitution. This "liberty" is not a series of isolated points pricked out in terms of the taking of property; the freedom of speech, press, and religion; the right to keep and bear arms; the freedom from unreasonable searches and seizures; and so on. It is a rational continuum which, broadly speaking, includes a freedom from all substantial arbitrary impositions and purposeless restraints, and which also recognizes, what a reasonable and sensitive judgment must, that certain interests require particularly careful scrutiny of the state needs asserted to justify their abridgment. Cf. *Skinner v. Oklahoma* (1942), *Bolling v. Sharpe* (1954)....

Each new claim to Constitutional protection must be considered against a background of Constitutional purposes, as they have been rationally perceived and historically developed. Though we exercise limited and sharply restrained judgment, yet there is no "mechanical yard-stick," no "mechanical answer." The decision of an apparently novel claim must depend on grounds which follow closely on well-accepted principles and criteria. The new decision must take "its place in relation to what went before and further [cut] a channel for what is to come." The matter was well put in *Rochin v. California* (1952):

> The vague contours of the Due Process Clause do not leave judges at large. We may not draw on our merely personal and private notions and disregard the limits that bind judges in their judicial function. Even though the concept of due process of law is not final and fixed, these limits are derived from considerations that are fused in the whole nature of our judicial process.... These are considerations deeply rooted in reason and in the compelling traditions of the legal profession.

On these premises I turn to the particular Constitutional claim in this case....

III. Precisely what is involved here is this: the State is asserting the right to enforce its moral judgment by intruding upon the most intimate details of the marital relation with the full power of the criminal law. Potentially, this could allow the deployment of all the incidental machinery of the criminal law, arrests, searches and seizures; inevitably, it must mean at the very least the lodging of criminal charges, a public trial, and testimony as to the corpus delicti. Nor could any imaginable elaboration of presumptions, testimonial privileges, or other safeguards, alleviate the necessity for testimony as to the mode and manner of the married couples' sexual relations, or at least the opportunity for the accused to make denial of the charges. In sum, the statute allows the State to enquire into, prove and punish married people for the private use of their marital intimacy.

This, then, is the precise character of the enactment whose Constitutional measure we must take. The statute must pass a more rigorous Constitutional test than that going merely to the plausibility of its underlying rationale. This enactment involves what, by common understanding throughout the English-speaking world, must be granted to be a most fundamental aspect of "liberty," the privacy of the home in its most basic sense, and it is this which requires that the statute be subjected to "strict scrutiny."

That aspect of liberty which embraces the concept of the privacy of the home receives explicit Constitutional protection at two places only. These are the 3rd Amendment, relating to the quartering of soldiers, and the 4th Amendment, prohibiting unreasonable searches and seizures. While these Amendments reach only the Federal Government, this Court has held in the strongest terms, and today again confirms, that the concept of "privacy" embodied in the 4th Amendment is part of the "ordered liberty" assured against state action by the 14th Amendment....

Perhaps the most comprehensive statement of the principle of liberty underlying these aspects of the Constitution was given by Mr. Justice Brandeis, dissenting in *Olmstead v. United States* (1928):

> The protection guaranteed by the (4th and 5th) Amendments is much broader in scope. The makers of our Constitution undertook to secure conditions favorable to the pursuit of happiness. They recognized the significance of man's spiritual nature, of his feelings and of his intellect. They knew that only a part of the pain, pleasure and satisfactions of life are to be found in material things. They sought to protect Americans in their beliefs, their thoughts, their emotions and their sensations. They conferred, as against the government, the right to be let alone—the most comprehensive of rights and the right most valued by civilized men. To protect that right, every unjustifiable intrusion by the government upon the privacy of the individual whatever the means employed, must be deemed a violation of the 4th Amendment....

I think the sweep of the Court's decisions, under both the 4th and 14th Amendments, amply shows that the Constitution protects the privacy of the home against all unreasonable intrusion of whatever character. "[These] principles ... affect the very essence of constitutional liberty and security. They reach farther than (a) concrete form of the case ... before the court, with its adventitious circumstances; they apply to all invasions on the part of the government and its employees of the sanctity of a man's home and the privacies of life...." *Boyd v. United States* (1886). "The security of one's privacy against arbitrary intrusion by the police—which is at the core of the 4th Amendment—is basic to a free society." *Wolf v. Colorado* (1949).

It would surely be an extreme instance of sacrificing substance to form were it to be held that the Constitutional principle of privacy against arbitrary official intrusion comprehends only physical invasions by the police....

Certainly the safeguarding of the home does not follow merely from the sanctity of property rights. The home derives its pre-eminence as the seat of family life. And the integrity of that life is something so fundamental that it has been found to draw to its protection the principles of more than one explicitly granted Constitutional right.... This same principle is expressed in the *Pierce v. Society of the Sisters* (1925) and *Meyer v. State* of *Nebraska* (1923) cases. These decisions ... "have respected the private realm of family life which the state cannot enter."

Of this whole "private realm of family life" it is difficult to imagine what is more private or more intimate than a husband and wife's marital relations. We would indeed be straining at a gnat and swallowing a camel were we to show concern for the niceties of property law involved in our recent decision, under the 4th Amendment, in *Chapman v. United States* (1961), and yet fail at least to see any substantial claim here.

Of course, just as the requirement of a warrant is not inflexible in carrying out searches and seizures, so there are countervailing considerations at this more fundamental aspect of the right involved. "[T]he family ... is not beyond regulation," and it would be an absurdity to suggest either that offenses may not be committed in the bosom of the family or that the home can be made a sanctuary for crime. The right of privacy most manifestly is not an absolute. Thus, I would not suggest that adultery, homosexuality, fornication and incest are immune from criminal enquiry, however privately practiced. So much has been explicitly recognized in acknowledging the State's rightful concern for its people's moral welfare. But not to discriminate between what is involved in this case and either the traditional offenses against good morals or crimes which, though they may be committed anywhere, happen to have been committed or concealed in the home, would entirely misconceive the argument that is being made.

Adultery, homosexuality and the like are sexual intimacies which the State forbids altogether, but the intimacy of husband and wife is necessarily an essential and accepted feature of the institution of marriage, an institution which the State not only must allow, but which always and in every age it has fostered and protected. It is one thing when the State exerts its power either to forbid extra-marital sexuality altogether, or to say who may marry, but it is quite another when, having acknowledged a marriage and the intimacies inherent in it, it undertakes to regulate by means of the criminal law the details of that intimacy.

In sum, even though the State has determined that the use of contraceptives is as iniquitous as any act of extra-marital sexual immorality, the intrusion of the whole machinery of the criminal law into the very heart of marital privacy, requiring husband and wife to render account before a criminal tribunal of their uses of that intimacy, is surely a very different thing indeed from punishing those who establish intimacies which the law has always forbidden and which can have no claim to social protection....

Since, as it appears to me, the statute marks an abridgment of important fundamental liberties protected by the 14th Amendment, it will not do to urge in justification of that abridgment simply that the statute is rationally related to the effectuation of a proper state purpose. A closer scrutiny and stronger justification than that are required....

But conclusive, in my view, is the utter novelty of this enactment. Although the Federal Government and many States have at one time or other had on their books statutes forbidding or regulating the distribution of contraceptives, none, so far as I can find, has made the *use* of contraceptives a crime. Indeed, a diligent search has revealed that no nation, including several which quite evidently share Connecticut's moral policy, has seen fit to effectuate that policy by the means presented here.

Though undoubtedly the States are and should be left free to reflect a wide variety of policies, and should be allowed broad scope in experimenting with various means of promoting those policies, I must agree with Mr. Justice Jackson that "There are limits to the extent to which a legislatively represented majority may conduct ... experiments at the expense of the dignity and personality" of the individual. *Skinner v. Oklahoma*. In this instance these limits are, in my view, reached and passed....

Griswold v. Connecticut: Background

1. How is *Lochner v. New York* (1905) used by Justices Douglas and Black in *Griswold v. Connecticut*?
2. How does the majority opinion reach its result? What is a *penumbra*? Since the Court had applied most guarantees of the Bill of Rights to the states at the time of *Griswold*, presumably the penumbras of these rights would apply as well. However, incorporation of the 3rd Amendment, cited by Justice Douglas, has yet to be considered by the Court.
3. Why doesn't Justice Douglas simply base his opinion on the word "liberty" in the Due Process Clause of the 14th Amendment? Does the word "liberty" appear in the opinion? Why or why not? How does Justice Douglas treat the *Meyer v. Nebraska* (1923) decision—i.e., what constitutional text does he imply it is expounding? Is he re-interpreting the meaning of this precedent?
4. What do you think of the argument based on the 9th Amendment in Justice Goldberg's opinion? Does the logic of the dissent allow the state to limit families to one child, or to none, as Justice Goldberg suggests?
5. Why do Justices Harlan and White concur only in the judgment? How do their approaches differ from the others?

Griswold v. Connecticut
381 U.S. 479 (1965)

[Majority: Douglas, Goldberg, Warren (C.J.), Clark, and Brennan. Concurring: Goldberg, Harlan, and White. Dissenting: Black and Stewart.]

Mr. Justice Douglas delivered the opinion of the Court.

Appellant Griswold is Executive Director of the Planned Parenthood League of Connecticut. Appellant Buxton is a licensed physician and a professor at the Yale Medical School who served as Medical Director for the League at its Center in New Haven—a center open and operating from November 1 to November 10, 1961, when appellants were arrested.

They gave information, instruction, and medical advice to married persons as to the means of preventing conception. They examined the wife and prescribed the best contraceptive device or material for her use. Fees were usually charged, although some couples were serviced free.

The statutes whose constitutionality is involved in this appeal are §§ 53-32 and 54-196 of the General Statutes of Connecticut. The former provides:

> Any person who uses any drug, medicinal article or instrument for the purpose of preventing conception shall be fined not less than fifty dollars or imprisoned not less than sixty days nor more than one year or be both fined and imprisoned.

Section 54-196 provides:

Any person who assists, abets, counsels, causes, hires or commands another to commit any offense may be prosecuted and punished as if he were the principal offender.

The appellants were found guilty as accessories and fined $100 each, against the claim that the accessory statute as so applied violated the 14th Amendment. The Appellate [courts] affirmed....

Coming to the merits, we are met with a wide range of questions that implicate the Due Process Clause of the 14th Amendment. Overtones of some arguments suggest that *Lochner v. New York* (1905) should be our guide. But we decline that invitation as we did in [among others] *West Coast Hotel Co. v. Parrish* (1937); *Williamson v. Lee Optical Co.* (1955). We do not sit as a super-legislature to determine the wisdom, need, and propriety of laws that touch economic problems, business affairs, or social conditions. This law, however, operates directly on an intimate relation of husband and wife and their physician's role in one aspect of that relation.

The association of people is not mentioned in the Constitution nor in the Bill of Rights. The right to educate a child in a school of the parents' choice—whether public or private or parochial—is also not mentioned. Nor is the right to study any particular subject or any foreign language. Yet the 1st Amendment has been construed to include certain of those rights.

By *Pierce v. Society of Sisters* (1925), the right to educate one's children as one chooses is made applicable to the States by the force of the 1st and 14th Amendments. By *Meyer v. Nebraska* (1923), the same dignity is given the right to study the German language in a private school. In other words, the State may not, consistently with the spirit of the 1st Amendment, contract the spectrum of available knowledge. The right of freedom of speech and press includes not only the right to utter or to print, but the right to distribute, the right to receive, the right to read (*Martin v. City of Struthers* (1943)) and freedom of inquiry, freedom of thought, and freedom to teach (see *Wieman v. Updegraff* (1952))—indeed the freedom of the entire university community. *Sweezy v. New Hampshire* (1957). Without those peripheral rights the specific rights would be less secure. And so we reaffirm the principle of the *Pierce* and the *Meyer* cases.

In *NAACP v. Alabama* (1958) we protected the "freedom to associate and privacy in one's associations," noting that freedom of association was a peripheral 1st Amendment right.... In other words, the 1st Amendment has a penumbra where privacy is protected from governmental intrusion. In like context, we have protected forms of "association" that are not political in the customary sense but pertain to the social, legal, and economic benefit of the members. *NAACP v. Button* (1963)....

[W]hile [the freedom to associate] is not expressly included in the 1st Amendment its existence is necessary in making the express guarantees fully meaningful.

The foregoing cases suggest that specific guarantees in the Bill of Rights have penumbras, formed by emanations from those guarantees that help give them life and substance. Various guarantees create zones of privacy. The right of association contained in the penumbra of the 1st Amendment is one, as we have seen. The 3rd Amendment in its prohibition against the quartering of soldiers "in any house" in time of peace without the consent of the owner is another facet of that privacy. The 4th Amendment explicitly affirms the "right of the people to be secure in their persons, houses, papers, and effects, against unreasonable searches and seizures." The 5th Amendment in its Self-Incrimination Clause enables the citizen to create a zone of privacy which government may not force him to surrender to his detriment. The Ninth Amendment provides: "The enumeration in the Constitution, of certain rights, shall not be construed to deny or disparage others retained by the people."

The 4th and 5th Amendments were described in *Boyd v. United States* (1886), as protection against all governmental invasions "of the sanctity of a man's home and the privacies of life." We recently referred in *Mapp v. Ohio* (1961), to the 4th Amendment as creating a "right to privacy, no less important than any other right carefully and particularly reserved to the people."

We have had many controversies over these penumbral rights of "privacy and repose." See *Skinner v. Oklahoma* (1942). These cases bear witness that the right of privacy which presses for recognition here is a legitimate one.

The present case, then, concerns a relationship lying within the zone of privacy created by several fundamental constitutional guarantees. And it concerns a law which, in forbidding the *use* of contraceptives rather than regulating their manufacture or sale, seeks to achieve its goals by means having a maximum destructive impact upon that relationship. Such a law cannot stand in light of the familiar principle, so often applied by this Court, that a "governmental purpose to control or prevent activities constitutionally subject to state regulation may not be achieved by means which sweep unnecessarily broadly and thereby invade the area of protected freedoms." *NAACP v. Alabama*. Would we allow the police to search the sacred precincts of marital bedrooms for telltale signs of the use of contraceptives? The very idea is repulsive to the notions of privacy surrounding the marriage relationship.

We deal with a right of privacy older than the Bill of Rights—older than our political parties, older than our school system. Marriage is a coming together for better or for worse, hopefully enduring, and intimate to the degree of being sacred. It is an association that promotes a way of life, not causes; a harmony in living, not political faiths; a bilateral loyalty, not commercial or social projects. Yet it is an association for as noble a purpose as any involved in our prior decisions.

Reversed.

Mr. Justice Goldberg, whom The Chief Justice and Mr. Justice Brennan join, concurring.

I agree with the Court that Connecticut's birth-control law unconstitutionally intrudes upon the right of marital privacy, and I join in its opinion and judgment. Although I have not accepted the view that "due process" as used in the 14th Amendment includes all of the first eight Amendments, I do agree that the concept of liberty protects those personal rights that are fundamental, and is not confined to the specific terms of the Bill of Rights. My conclusion that the concept of liberty is not so restricted and that it embraces the right of marital privacy though that right is not mentioned explicitly in the Constitution[1] is supported both by numerous decisions of this Court, referred to in the Court's opinion, and by the language and history of the Ninth Amendment. In reaching the conclusion that the right of marital privacy is protected, as being within the protected penumbra of specific guarantees of the Bill of Rights, the Court refers to the Ninth Amendment.... I add these words to emphasize the relevance of that Amendment to the Court's holding....

The language and history of the Ninth Amendment reveal that the Framers of the Constitution believed that there are additional fundamental rights, protected from governmental infringement....

---

1. This Court ... has never held that the Bill of Rights or the 14th Amendment protects only those rights that the Constitution specifically mentions by name....

The Ninth Amendment reads, "The enumeration in the Constitution, of certain rights, shall not be construed to deny or disparage others retained by the people."... It was proffered to quiet expressed fears that a bill of specifically enumerated rights could not be sufficiently broad to cover all essential rights and that the specific mention of certain rights would be interpreted as a denial that others were protected....

While this Court has had little occasion to interpret the 9th Amendment,[2] "[i]t cannot be presumed that any clause in the constitution is intended to be without effect." *Marbury v. Madison* (1803). In interpreting the Constitution, "real effect should be given to all the words it uses." The 9th Amendment to the Constitution may be regarded by some as a recent discovery and may be forgotten by others, but since 1791 it has been a basic part of the Constitution which we are sworn to uphold. To hold that a right so basic and fundamental and so deep-rooted in our society as the right of privacy in marriage may be infringed because that right is not guaranteed in so many words by the first eight amendments to the Constitution is to ignore the 9th Amendment and to give it no effect whatsoever. Moreover, a judicial construction that this fundamental right is not protected by the Constitution because it is not mentioned in explicit terms by one of the first eight amendments or elsewhere in the Constitution would violate the 9th Amendment, which specifically states that "[t]he enumeration in the Constitution, of certain rights shall not be *construed* to deny or disparage others retained by the people" (emphasis added)....

I do not mean to imply that the 9th Amendment is applied against the States by the 14th. Nor do I mean to state that the 9th Amendment constitutes an independent source of rights protected from infringement by either the States or the Federal Government. Rather, the 9th Amendment shows a belief of the Constitution's authors that fundamental rights exist that are not expressly enumerated in the first eight amendments and an intent that the list of rights included there not be deemed exhaustive....

While the 9th Amendment—and indeed the entire Bill of Rights—originally concerned restrictions upon federal power, the subsequently enacted 14th Amendment prohibits the States as well from abridging fundamental personal liberties.... In sum, the 9th Amendment simply lends strong support to the view that the "liberty" protected by the 5th and 14th Amendments from infringement by the Federal Government or the States is not restricted to rights specifically mentioned in the first eight amendments....

The entire fabric of the Constitution and the purposes that clearly underlie its specific guarantees demonstrate that the rights to marital privacy and to marry and raise a family are of similar order and magnitude as the fundamental rights specifically protected.

Although the Constitution does not speak in so many words of the right of privacy in marriage, I cannot believe that it offers these fundamental rights no protection. The fact that no particular provision of the Constitution explicitly forbids the State from disrupting the traditional relation of the family—a relation as old and as fundamental as our entire civilization—surely does not show that the Government was meant to have the power to do so. Rather, as the 9th Amendment expressly recognizes, there are fundamental personal rights such as this one, which are protected from abridgment by the Government though not specifically mentioned in the Constitution....

The logic of the dissents would sanction federal or state legislation that seems to me even more plainly unconstitutional than the statute before us. Surely the Government,

---

2. This Amendment has been referred to as *The Forgotten Ninth Amendment*, in a book with that title by Bennett B. Patterson (1955). As far as I am aware, until today this Court has referred to the 9th Amendment only [5 times].

absent a showing of a compelling subordinating state interest, could not decree that all husbands and wives must be sterilized after two children have been born to them. Yet by their reasoning such an invasion of marital privacy would not be subject to constitutional challenge because, while it might be "silly," no provision of the Constitution specifically prevents the Government from curtailing the marital right to bear children and raise a family.... [I]f upon a showing of a slender basis of rationality, a law outlawing voluntary birth control by married persons is valid, then, by the same reasoning, a law requiring compulsory birth control also would seem to be valid. In my view, however, both types of law would unjustifiably intrude upon rights of marital privacy which are constitutionally protected.

In a long series of cases this Court has held that where fundamental personal liberties are involved, they may not be abridged by the States simply on a showing that a regulatory statute has some rational relationship to the effectuation of a proper state purpose....

The State, at most, argues that there is some rational relation between this statute and what is admittedly a legitimate subject of state concern—the discouraging of extra-marital relations. It says that preventing the use of birth-control devices by married persons helps prevent the indulgence by some in such extra-marital relations. The rationality of this justification is dubious, particularly in light of the admitted widespread availability to all persons in the State of Connecticut, unmarried as well as married, of birth-control devices for the prevention of disease, as distinguished from the prevention of conception. But, in any event, it is clear that the state interest in safeguarding marital fidelity can be served by a more discriminately tailored statute, which does not, like the present one, sweep unnecessarily broadly, reaching far beyond the evil sought to be dealt with and intruding upon the privacy of all married couples....

In sum, I believe that the right of privacy in the marital relation is fundamental and basic—a personal right "retained by the people" within the meaning of the 9th Amendment. Connecticut cannot constitutionally abridge this fundamental right, which is protected by the 14th Amendment from infringement by the States. I agree with the Court that petitioners' convictions must therefore be reversed.

Mr. Justice Harlan, concurring in the judgment.

I fully agree with the judgment of reversal, but find myself unable to join the Court's opinion. The reason is that it seems to me to evince an approach to this case very much like that taken by my Brothers Black and Stewart in dissent, namely: the Due Process Clause of the 14th Amendment does not touch this Connecticut statute unless the enactment is found to violate some right assured by the letter or penumbra of the Bill of Rights.

In other words, what I find implicit in the Court's opinion is that the "incorporation" doctrine may be used to *restrict* the reach of 14th Amendment Due Process. For me this is just as unacceptable constitutional doctrine as is the use of the "incorporation" approach to *impose* upon the States all the requirements of the Bill of Rights as found in the provisions of the first eight amendments and in the decisions of this Court interpreting them....

[T]he proper constitutional inquiry in this case is whether this Connecticut statute infringes the Due Process Clause of the 14th Amendment because the enactment violates basic values "implicit in the concept of ordered liberty," *Palko v. Connecticut* (1937). For reasons stated at length in my dissenting opinion in *Poe v. Ullman* (1961), I believe that it does. While the relevant inquiry may be aided by resort to one or more of the provisions of the Bill of Rights, it is not dependent on them or any of their radiations. The Due Process Clause of the 14th Amendment stands, in my opinion, on its own bottom....

Mr. Justice White, concurring in the judgment.

In my view this Connecticut law as applied to married couples deprives them of "liberty" without due process of law, as that concept is used in the 14th Amendment. I therefore concur in the judgment of the Court reversing these convictions under Connecticut's aiding and abetting statute....

There is no serious contention that Connecticut thinks the use of artificial or external methods of contraception immoral or unwise in itself, or that the anti-use statute is founded upon any policy of promoting population expansion. Rather, the statute is said to serve the State's policy against all forms of promiscuous or illicit sexual relationships, be they premarital or extramarital, concededly a permissible and legitimate legislative goal....

I wholly fail to see how the ban on the use of contraceptives by married couples in any way reinforces the State's ban on illicit sexual relationships....

At most the broad ban is of marginal utility to the declared objective. A statute limiting its prohibition on use to persons engaging in the prohibited relationship would serve the end posited by Connecticut in the same way, and with the same effectiveness, or ineffectiveness, as the broad anti-use statute under attack in this case. I find nothing in this record justifying the sweeping scope of this statute....

Mr. Justice Black, with whom Mr. Justice Stewart joins, dissenting.

I agree with my Brother Stewart's dissenting opinion. And like him I do not to any extent whatever base my view that this Connecticut law is constitutional on a belief that the law is wise or that its policy is a good one....

The Court talks about a constitutional "right of privacy" as though there is some constitutional provision or provisions forbidding any law ever to be passed which might abridge the "privacy" of individuals. But there is not. There are, of course, guarantees in certain specific constitutional provisions which are designed in part to protect privacy at certain times and places with respect to certain activities. Such, for example, is the 4th Amendment's guarantee against "unreasonable searches and seizures." But I think it belittles that Amendment to talk about it as though it protects nothing but "privacy." ...

One of the most effective ways of diluting or expanding a constitutionally guaranteed right is to substitute for the crucial word or words of a constitutional guarantee another word or words, more or less flexible and more or less restricted in meaning. This fact is well illustrated by the use of the term "right of privacy" as a comprehensive substitute for the 4th Amendment's guarantee against "unreasonable searches and seizures." "Privacy" is a broad, abstract and ambiguous concept which can easily be shrunken in meaning but which can also, on the other hand, easily be interpreted as a constitutional ban against many things other than searches and seizures....[1] I like my privacy as well as the next one, but I am nevertheless compelled to admit that government has a right to invade it unless prohibited by some specific constitutional provision....

---

1. The phrase "right to privacy" appears first to have gained currency from an article written by Messrs. Warren and (later Mr. Justice) Brandeis in 1890 which urged that States should give some form of tort relief to persons whose private affairs were exploited by others. *The Right to Privacy*, 4 Harv. L. Rev. 193.... Observing that "the right of privacy ... presses for recognition here," today this Court, which I did not understand to have power to sit as a court of common law, now appears to be exalting a phrase which Warren and Brandeis used in discussing grounds for tort relief, to the level of a constitutional rule....

This brings me to the arguments made by my Brothers Harlan, White and Goldberg.... I discuss the due process and 9th Amendment arguments together because on analysis they turn out to be the same thing—merely using different words to claim for this Court and the federal judiciary power to invalidate any legislative act ... it considers to be arbitrary, capricious, unreasonable, or oppressive, or on this Court's belief that a particular state law under scrutiny has no "rational or justifying" purpose, or is offensive to a "sense of fairness and justice." If these formulas based on "natural justice" ... are to prevail, they require judges to determine what is or is not constitutional on the basis of their own appraisal of what laws are unwise or unnecessary.... I do not believe that we are granted ... the power to make laws ... a power which was specifically denied to federal courts by the convention that framed the Constitution.

Of the cases on which my Brothers White and Goldberg rely so heavily, undoubtedly the reasoning of two of them supports their result here ... *Meyer v. Nebraska* (1923) [and] *Pierce v. Society of Sisters* (1925). *Meyer* held unconstitutional, as an "arbitrary" and unreasonable interference with the right of a teacher to carry on his occupation and of parents to hire him, a state law forbidding the teaching of modern foreign languages to young children in the schools.[2] And in *Pierce*, relying principally on *Meyer*, Mr. Justice McReynolds said that a state law requiring that all children attend public schools interfered unconstitutionally with the property rights of private school corporations because it was an "arbitrary, unreasonable, and unlawful interference" which threatened "destruction of their business and property." Without expressing an opinion as to whether either of those cases reached a correct result in light of our later decisions applying the 1st Amendment to the States through the 14th, I merely point out that the reasoning stated in *Meyer* and *Pierce* was the same natural law due process philosophy which many later opinions repudiated, and which I cannot accept....

My Brother Goldberg has adopted the recent discovery[3] that the 9th Amendment as well as the Due Process Clause can be used by this Court as authority to strike down all state legislation which this Court thinks violates "fundamental principles of liberty and justice," or is contrary to the "traditions and [collective] conscience of our people." ... [O]ne would certainly have to look far beyond the language of the 9th Amendment to find that the Framers vested in this Court any such awesome veto powers over lawmaking.... [F]or a period of a century and a half no serious suggestion was ever made that the 9th Amendment ... could be used as a weapon of federal power to prevent state legislatures from passing laws they consider appropriate to govern local affairs....

I realize that many good and able men have eloquently spoken and written, sometimes in rhapsodical strains, about the duty of this Court to keep the Constitution in tune with the times. The idea is that the Constitution must be changed from time to time and that this Court is charged with a duty to make those changes. For myself, I must with all deference reject that philosophy. The Constitution makers knew the need for change and provided for it. Amendments suggested by the people's elected representatives can be submitted to the people or their selected agents for ratification. That method of change was

---

2. In *Meyer*, in the very same sentence quoted in part by my Brethren in which he asserted that the Due Process Clause gave an abstract and inviolable right "to marry, establish a home and bring up children," Mr. Justice McReynolds asserted also that the Due Process Clause prevented States from interfering with "the right of the individual to contract."

3. See Patterson, *The Forgotten Ninth Amendment* (1955). Mr. Patterson urges that the Ninth Amendment be used to protect unspecified "natural and inalienable rights." P. 4. The Introduction by Roscoe Pound states that "there is a marked revival of natural law ideas throughout the world. Interest in the Ninth Amendment is a symptom of that revival."

good for our Fathers, and being somewhat old-fashioned I must add it is good enough for me.... I had thought that we had laid that [*Lochner v. New York* (1905)] formula, as a means for striking down state legislation, to rest once and for all in cases like *West Coast Hotel Co. v. Parrish* (1937)....

The late Judge Learned Hand, after emphasizing his view that judges should not use the due process formula suggested in the concurring opinions today or any other formula like it to invalidate legislation offensive to their "personal preferences," made the statement, with which I fully agree, that:

> For myself it would be most irksome to be ruled by a bevy of Platonic Guardians, even if I knew how to choose them, which I assuredly do not.

So far as I am concerned, Connecticut's law as applied here is not forbidden by any provision of the Federal Constitution as that Constitution was written, and I would therefore affirm.

Mr. Justice Stewart, whom Mr. Justice Black joins, dissenting.

Since 1879 Connecticut has had on its books a law which forbids the use of contraceptives by anyone. I think this is an uncommonly silly law.... But we are not asked in this case to say whether we think this law is unwise, or even asinine. We are asked to hold that it violates the United States Constitution. And that I cannot do....

What provision of the Constitution ... make[s] this state law invalid? The Court says it is the right of privacy "created by several fundamental constitutional guarantees." With all deference, I can find no such general right of privacy in the Bill of Rights, in any other part of the Constitution, or in any case ever before decided by this Court.

At the oral argument in this case we were told that the Connecticut law does not "conform to current community standards." But it is not the function of this Court to decide cases on the basis of community standards.... If, as I should surely hope, the law before us does not reflect the standards of the people of Connecticut, the people of Connecticut can freely exercise their true 9th and 10th Amendment rights to persuade their elected representatives to repeal it. That is the constitutional way to take this law off the books.

* * *

For articles on the 9th Amendment and less textually explicit rights under the 14th Amendment, see 56 *Drake L. Rev. No.* 4 (2008).

Griswold v. Connecticut: Notes

1. Robert Bork was a Professor at Yale Law School and subsequently a federal circuit judge and unsuccessful nominee to the United States Supreme Court. He wrote an article criticizing *Griswold* in 1971, two years before the Court—relying on *Griswold's* reasoning—decided *Roe v. Wade* (1973):

    > In *Griswold* a husband and wife assert that they wish to have sexual relations without fear of unwanted children. The law impairs their sexual gratifications. The State [asserts] that the majority finds the use of contraceptives immoral. Knowledge that it takes place and that the State makes no effort to inhibit it causes the majority anguish, impairs [the majority's] gratifications....
    >
    > [The case is not covered] specifically or by obvious implication in the Constitution. Unless we can distinguish forms of gratification, the only course for a principled Court is to let the majority have its way in both cases.... There is no

principled way to decide that one man's gratifications are more deserving of respect than another's.... There is no way of deciding these matters other than by reference to some system of moral or ethical values that has no objective or intrinsic validity of its own and about which men can and do differ....

It follows, of course, that broad areas of constitutional law ought to be reformulated.

Robert H. Bork, *Neutral Principles and Some First Amendment Problems*, 47 Ind. L.J. 1, 9–11 (1971).

2. *A Note on Method.* At this point it is apparent that legislation impinging on fundamental rights will receive strict scrutiny. Mere economic legislation typically receives low level rational basis review. The problem, of course, is to identify which rights are fundamental and which are not. What methods are available for identifying fundamental rights? The Court often uses various justifications. It appeals to the textual basis of rights in the Bill of Rights, to precedent, to reasoned judgment, to analogy from prior cases, to the penumbras of the Bill of Rights, to inherent liberties of Americans, to ethical aspirations, and to history and tradition.

Two types of justification are essentially different. Appeals to history and tradition may—and appeals to social consensus clearly do—look at what values the majority has traditionally accepted or has now come to accept. An inherent rights or natural rights approach looks to basic human rights, whether the majority accepts them or not. There are paradoxes connected to each approach.

3. The Supreme Court confronted another contraceptive case before addressing the even more volatile issue of abortion. In *Eisenstadt v. Baird* (1972), the defendant Baird had distributed contraceptive foam after a birth control lecture. The party who received the contraceptive was unmarried. Baird was convicted under a Massachusetts statute barring the distribution of contraceptives. The Court based its decision on equal protection analysis and found the statute lacked rationality. (Here, commentators suggest, we see a new type of rational basis analysis emerging, one far different from low level rational basis. We will later explore this sort of "rational basis with bite" as a separate level of scrutiny.)

Eisenstadt v. Baird
405 U.S. 438 (1972)

[Majority: Brennan, Douglas, Stewart, and Marshall. Concurring: Douglas, White, and Blackmun. Dissenting: Burger (C.J.).]

Mr. Justice Brennan delivered the opinion of the Court....

If the Massachusetts statute cannot be upheld as a deterrent to fornication or as a health measure, may it, nevertheless, be sustained simply as a prohibition on contraception? The Court of Appeals analysis "led inevitably to the conclusion that, so far as morals are concerned, it is contraceptives per se that are considered immoral—to the extent that *Griswold* will permit such a declaration." The Court of Appeals went on to hold:

> To say that contraceptives are immoral as such, and are to be forbidden to unmarried persons who will nevertheless persist in having intercourse, means that such persons must risk for themselves an unwanted pregnancy, for the child, illegitimacy, and for society, a possible obligation of support. Such a view of morality is not only the very mirror image of sensible legislation; we consider that it

conflicts with fundamental human rights. In the absence of demonstrated harm, we hold it is beyond the competency of the state.

We need not and do not, however, decide that important question in this case because, whatever the rights of the individual to access to contraceptives may be, the rights must be the same for the unmarried and the married alike.

If under *Griswold v. Connecticut* (1965) the distribution of contraceptives to married persons cannot be prohibited, a ban on distribution to unmarried persons would be equally impermissible. It is true that in *Griswold* the right of privacy in question inhered in the marital relationship. Yet the marital couple is not an independent entity with a mind and heart of its own, but an association of two individuals each with a separate intellectual and emotional makeup. If the right of privacy means anything, it is the right of the *individual*, married or single, to be free from unwarranted governmental intrusion into matters so fundamentally affecting a person as the decision whether to bear or beget a child. See *Stanley v. Georgia* (1969). See also *Skinner v. Oklahoma* (1942); *Jacobson v. Massachusetts* (1905).

On the other hand, if *Griswold* is no bar to a prohibition on the distribution of contraceptives, the State could not, consistently with the Equal Protection Clause, outlaw distribution to unmarried but not to married persons. In each case the evil, as perceived by the State, would be identical, and the underinclusion would be invidious. Mr. Justice Jackson, concurring in *Railway Express Agency v. New York* (1949), made the point:

> The framers of the Constitution knew, and we should not forget today, that there is no more effective practical guaranty against arbitrary and unreasonable government than to require that the principles of law which officials would impose upon a minority must be imposed generally. Conversely, nothing opens the door to arbitrary action so effectively as to allow those officials to pick and choose only a few to whom they will apply legislation and thus to escape the political retribution that might be visited upon them if larger numbers were affected. Courts can take no better measure to assure that laws will be just than to require that laws be equal in operation.

Although Mr. Justice Jackson's comments had reference to administrative regulations, the principle he affirmed has equal application to the legislation here. We hold that by providing dissimilar treatment for married and unmarried persons who are similarly situated, Massachusetts General Laws Ann., c. 272, §§ 21 and 21A, violate the Equal Protection Clause.

The judgment of the Court of Appeals is affirmed.

[Concurring and dissenting opinions omitted.]

Roe v. Wade: Background

1. How does the Court justify its decision in *Roe v Wade* (1973)? What authority does it cite? What part of the Constitution does the Court rely upon in reaching its decision?
2. How does the Court decide if the fetus is a "person" within the meaning of the 14th Amendment? What difference would it make if the Court did find the fetus to be a person?
3. The Court finds that interests are possessed by the pregnant woman, the state, and the viable fetus. What are each party's interests?

4. The majority's trimester approach has been criticized for being closer to a legislative standard than a judicial standard. Is this criticism appropriate? Do the trimester dates have significance *in their own right* or merely as dates that represent the points, in 1973, at which certain interests shift? Would the ability of evolving medical technology to make younger and younger fetuses viable call for the reversal of *Roe*, or merely an ongoing reformulation of the trimester approach consistent with the *Roe* balancing of interests?

5. How do the dissenting opinions deal with the majority approach? Is the criticism of the dissenting opinions, by implication at least, broader than the actual *Roe* decision?

6. After the decision in *Roe*, assume that technology marches on. Assume that fetuses and fertilized eggs can now be raised in artificial wombs. The operation to remove the fetus or fertilized egg and transplant it into an artificial womb is no more risky than abortion. In all cases where women wish to terminate their pregnancy after viability the law of the State of Florida forbids abortions but allows fetuses to be raised in artificial wombs, at state expense, and to be held for adoption by foster parents. Florida defines viability as the moment the sperm unites with the egg. Is the Florida statute constitutional? Why? Would your answers change if, under state law, natural parents could be required to pay child support to adoptive parents, though at a much reduced rate in recognition of the existence of the adoptive family's obligation and ability to support the child?

7. In his concurrence, Justice Stewart, a dissenter in *Griswold*, cites *Ferguson v. Skrupa* (1963). The Court in *Ferguson* had unanimously rejected a challenge to a Kansas statute that prohibited anyone but lawyers from engaging in the business of "debt adjusting." The Court repeatedly stated that it would not strike legislation merely because it thought it unwise, invoking *Lochner* as an example of inappropriate judicial behavior.

Roe v. Wade
410 U.S. 113 (1973)

[Majority: Blackmun, Burger (C.J.), Douglas, Brennan, Stewart, Marshall, and Powell. Concurring: Burger (C.J.), Douglas, and Stewart. Dissenting: White and Rehnquist.]

Mr. Justice Blackmun delivered the opinion of the Court.

This Texas federal appeal and its Georgia companion, *Doe v. Bolton* (1973), present constitutional challenges to state criminal abortion legislation. The Texas statutes under attack here are typical of those that have been in effect in many States for approximately a century. The Georgia statutes, in contrast, have a modern cast and are a legislative product that, to an extent at least, obviously reflects the influences of recent attitudinal change, of advancing medical knowledge and techniques, and of new thinking about an old issue.

We forthwith acknowledge our awareness of the sensitive and emotional nature of the abortion controversy, of the vigorous opposing views, even among physicians, and of the deep and seemingly absolute convictions that the subject inspires. One's philosophy, one's experiences, one's exposure to the raw edges of human existence, one's religious training, one's attitudes toward life and family and their values, and the moral standards one establishes and seeks to observe, are all likely to influence and to color one's thinking and conclusions about abortion.

In addition, population growth, pollution, poverty, and racial overtones tend to complicate and not to simplify the problem.

Our task, of course, is to resolve the issue by constitutional measurement, free of emotion and of predilection. We seek earnestly to do this, and, because we do, we have inquired into, and in this opinion place some emphasis upon, medical and medical-legal history and what that history reveals about man's attitudes toward the abortion procedure over the centuries. We bear in mind, too, Mr. Justice Holmes' admonition in his now-vindicated dissent in *Lochner v. New York* (1905):

> [The Constitution] is made for people of fundamentally differing views, and the accident of our finding certain opinions natural and familiar, or novel, and even shocking, ought not to conclude our judgment upon the question whether statutes embodying them conflict with the Constitution of the United States.

I. The Texas statutes that concern us here are Arts. 1191–1194 and 1196 of the State's Penal Code. These make it a crime to "procure an abortion," as therein defined, or to attempt one, except with respect to "an abortion procured or attempted by medical advice for the purpose of saving the life of the mother." Similar statutes are in existence in a majority of the States....

V. The principal thrust of appellant's attack on the Texas statutes is that they improperly invade a right, said to be possessed by the pregnant woman, to choose to terminate her pregnancy. Appellant would discover this right in the concept of personal "liberty" embodied in the 14th Amendment's Due Process Clause; or in personal marital, familial, and sexual privacy said to be protected by the Bill of Rights or its penumbras, see *Griswold v. Connecticut* (1965), *Eisenstadt v. Baird* (1972).... Before addressing this claim, we feel it desirable briefly to survey, in several aspects, the history of abortion, for such insight as that history may afford us, and then to examine the state purposes and interests behind the criminal abortion laws.

VI. [R]estrictive criminal abortion laws ... derive from statutory changes effected, for the most part, in the latter half of the 19th century....

[T]hus ... at common law, at the time of the adoption of our Constitution, and throughout the major portion of the 19th century ... a woman enjoyed a substantially broader right to terminate a pregnancy than she does in most States today....

VII. Three reasons have been advanced to explain historically the enactment of criminal abortion laws in the 19th century and to justify their continued existence.

It has been argued occasionally that these laws were the product of a Victorian social concern to discourage illicit sexual conduct. Texas, however, does not advance this justification in the present case, and it appears that no court or commentator has taken the argument seriously....

A second reason is concerned with abortion as a medical procedure. When most criminal abortion laws were first enacted, the procedure was a hazardous one for the woman....

Modern medical techniques have altered this situation. Appellants and various amici refer to medical data indicating that abortion in early pregnancy, that is, prior to the end of the first trimester, although not without its risk, is now relatively safe. Mortality rates for women undergoing early abortions, where the procedure is legal, appear to be as low as or lower than the rates for normal childbirth. Consequently, any interest of the State in protecting the woman from an inherently hazardous procedure, except when it would be equally dangerous for her to forgo it, has largely disappeared. Of course, important state interests in the areas of health and medical standards do remain. The State has a legitimate interest in seeing to it that abortion, like any other medical procedure, is performed under circumstances that insure maximum safety for the patient. This interest obviously extends at least to the performing physician and his staff, to the facilities involved, to the availability of after-care, and to adequate provision for any complication or emergency that might arise. The prevalence of high mortality rates at illegal "abortion mills" strengthens, rather than weakens, the State's interest in regulating the conditions under which abortions are performed. Moreover, the risk to the woman increases as her pregnancy continues. Thus, the State retains a definite interest in protecting the woman's own health and safety when an abortion is proposed at a late stage of pregnancy.

The third reason is the State's interest—some phrase it in terms of duty—in protecting prenatal life. Some of the argument for this justification rests on the theory that a new human life is present from the moment of conception. The State's interest and general obligation to protect life then extends, it is argued, to prenatal life. Only when the life of the pregnant mother herself is at stake, balanced against the life she carries within her, should the interest of the embryo or fetus not prevail. Logically, of course, a legitimate state interest in this area need not stand or fall on acceptance of the belief that life begins at conception or at some other point prior to live birth. In assessing the State's interest, recognition may be given to the less rigid claim that as long as at least *potential* life is involved, the State may assert interests beyond the protection of the pregnant woman alone.

Parties challenging state abortion laws have sharply disputed in some courts the contention that a purpose of these laws, when enacted, was to protect prenatal life. Pointing to the absence of legislative history to support the contention, they claim that most state laws were designed solely to protect the woman. Because medical advances have lessened this concern, at least with respect to abortion in early pregnancy, they argue that with respect to such abortions the laws can no longer be justified by any state interest. There is some scholarly support for this view of original purpose. The few state courts called upon to interpret their laws in the late 19th and early 20th centuries did focus on the State's interest in protecting the woman's health rather than in preserving the embryo and fetus. Proponents of this view point out that in many States, including Texas, by statute or judicial interpretation, the pregnant woman herself could not be prosecuted for self-abortion or for cooperating in an abortion performed upon her by another. They claim that adoption of the "quickening" distinction through received common law and state statutes tacitly recognizes the greater health hazards inherent in late abortion and impliedly repudiates the theory that life begins at conception.

It is with these interests, and the weight to be attached to them, that this case is concerned.

VIII. The Constitution does not explicitly mention any right of privacy. In a line of decisions, however, going back perhaps as far as *Union Pacific R. Co. v. Botsford* (1891), the Court has recognized that a right of personal privacy, or a guarantee of certain areas or zones of privacy, does exist under the Constitution. In varying contexts, the Court or individual Justices have, indeed, found at least the roots of that right in the 1st Amendment, *Stanley v. Georgia* (1969); in the 4th and 5th Amendments, *Terry v. Ohio* (1968); in the penumbras of the Bill of Rights, *Griswold v. Connecticut*; in the 9th Amendment, *id.*, (Goldberg, J., concurring); or in the concept of liberty guaranteed by the first section of the 14th Amendment, see *Meyer v. Nebraska* (1923). These decisions make it clear that only personal rights that can be deemed "fundamental" or "implicit in the concept of ordered liberty," *Palko v. Connecticut* (1937), are included in this guarantee of personal privacy. They also make it clear that the right has some extension to activities relating to marriage, *Loving v. Virginia* (1967); procreation, *Skinner v. Oklahoma* (1942); contraception, *Eisenstadt v. Baird*; family relationships, *Prince v. Massachusetts* (1944); and child rearing and education, *Pierce v. Society of Sisters* (1925) [and] *Meyer v. Nebraska*.

This right of privacy, whether it be founded in the 14th Amendment's concept of personal liberty and restrictions upon state action, as we feel it is, or, as the District Court determined, in the 9th Amendment's reservation of rights to the people, is broad enough to encompass a woman's decision whether or not to terminate her pregnancy. The detriment that the State would impose upon the pregnant woman by denying this choice altogether is apparent. Specific and direct harm medically diagnosable even in early pregnancy may be involved. Maternity, or additional offspring, may force upon the woman a distressful life and future. Psychological harm may be imminent. Mental and physical health may be taxed by child care. There is also the distress, for all concerned, associated with the unwanted child, and there is the problem of bringing a child into a family already unable, psychologically and otherwise, to care for it. In other cases, as in this one, the additional difficulties and continuing stigma of unwed motherhood may be involved. All these are factors the woman and her responsible physician necessarily will consider in consultation.

On the basis of elements such as these, appellant and some amici argue that the woman's right is absolute and that she is entitled to terminate her pregnancy at whatever time, in whatever way, and for whatever reason she alone chooses. With this we do not agree. Appellant's arguments that Texas either has no valid interest at all in regulating the abortion decision, or no interest strong enough to support any limitation upon the woman's sole determination, are unpersuasive. The Court's decisions recognizing a right of privacy also acknowledge that some state regulation in areas protected by that right is appropriate. As noted above, a State may properly assert important interests in safeguarding health, in maintaining medical standards, and in protecting potential life. At some point in pregnancy, these respective interests become sufficiently compelling to sustain regulation of the factors that govern the abortion decision. The privacy right involved, therefore, cannot be said to be absolute. In fact, it is not clear to us that the claim asserted by some amici that one has an unlimited right to do with one's body as one pleases bears a close relationship to the right of privacy previously articulated in the Court's decisions. The Court has refused to recognize an unlimited right of this kind in the past. *Jacobson v. Massachusetts* (1905) (vaccination); *Buck v. Bell* (1927) (sterilization).

We, therefore, conclude that the right of personal privacy includes the abortion decision, but that this right is not unqualified and must be considered against important state interests in regulation.

We note that those federal and state courts that have recently considered abortion law challenges have reached the same conclusion. A majority, in addition to the District Court in the present case, have held state laws unconstitutional, at least in part, because of vagueness or because of overbreadth and abridgment of rights.

Although the results are divided, most of these courts have agreed that the right of privacy, however based, is broad enough to cover the abortion decision; that the right, nonetheless, is not absolute and is subject to some limitations; and that at some point the state interests as to protection of health, medical standards, and prenatal life, become dominant. We agree with this approach.

Where certain "fundamental rights" are involved, the Court has held that regulation limiting these rights may be justified only by a "compelling state interest," *Kramer v. Union Free School District* (1969); and that legislative enactments must be narrowly drawn to express only the legitimate state interests at stake. *Griswold v. Connecticut*.

In the recent abortion cases, cited above, courts have recognized these principles. Those striking down state laws have generally scrutinized the State's interests in protecting health and potential life, and have concluded that neither interest justified broad limitations on the reasons for which a physician and his pregnant patient might decide that she should have an abortion in the early stages of pregnancy. Courts sustaining state laws have held that the State's determinations to protect health or prenatal life are dominant and constitutionally justifiable.

IX. The District Court held that the [state] failed to meet [its] burden of demonstrating that the Texas statute's infringement upon Roe's rights was necessary to support a compelling state interest, and that, although the [state] presented "several compelling justifications for state presence in the area of abortions," the statutes outstripped these justifications and swept "far beyond any areas of compelling state interest." [Roe] and [the state] both contest that holding. [Roe], as has been indicated, claims an absolute right that bars any state imposition of criminal penalties in the area. [The state] argues that the State's determination to recognize and protect prenatal life from and after conception constitutes a compelling state interest. As noted above, we do not agree fully with either formulation.

IX-A. The [state] and certain amici argue that the fetus is a "person" within the language and meaning of the 14th Amendment. In support of this, they outline at length and in detail the well-known facts of fetal development. If this suggestion of personhood is established, [Roe's] case, of course, collapses, for the fetus' right to life would then be guaranteed specifically by the Amendment. [Roe] conceded as much on reargument. On the other hand, the [state] conceded on reargument that no case could be cited that holds that a fetus is a person within the meaning of the 14th Amendment.

The Constitution does not define "person" in so many words. Section 1 of the 14th Amendment contains three references to "person." The first, in defining "citizens," speaks of "persons born or naturalized in the United States." The word also appears both in the Due Process Clause and in the Equal Protection Clause. "Person" is used in other places in the Constitution: in the listing of qualifications for Representatives and Senators, Art, I, § 2, cl. 2, and § 3, cl. 3; in the Apportionment Clause, Art. I, § 2, cl. 3; in the Migration and Importation provision, Art. I, § 9, cl. 1; in the Emoulument Clause, Art, I, § 9, cl. 8; in the Electors provisions, Art. II, § 1, cl. 2, and the superseded cl. 3; in the provision outlining qualifications for the office of President, Art. II, § 1, cl. 5; in the Extradition provisions, Art. IV, § 2, cl. 2, and the superseded Fugitive Slave Clause 3; and in the 5th, 12th, and 22nd Amendments, as well as in §§ 2 and 3 of the 14th Amendment. But in nearly all these instances, the use of the word is such that it has application only postnatally. None indicates, with any assurance, that it has any possible prenatal application.[1]

---

1. When Texas urges that a fetus is entitled to 14th Amendment protection as a person, it faces a dilemma. Neither in Texas nor in any other State are all abortions prohibited. Despite broad proscription, an exception always exists. The exception contained in Art. 1196, for an abortion procured or attempted by medical advice for the purpose of saving the life of the mother, is typical. But if the fetus is a person who is not to be deprived of life without due process of law, and if the mother's condition is the sole determinant, does not the Texas exception appear to be out of line with the Amendment's command? There are other inconsistencies between 14th Amendment status and the typical abortion statute. It has already been pointed out ... that in Texas the woman is not a principal or an accomplice with respect to an abortion upon her. If the fetus is a person, why is the woman not a principal or an accomplice? Further, the penalty for criminal abortion specified by Art. 1195 is significantly less than the maximum penalty for murder prescribed by Art. 1257 of the Texas Penal Code. If the fetus is a person, may the penalties be different?

All this, together with our observation that throughout the major portion of the 19th century prevailing legal abortion practices were far freer than they are today, persuades us that the word "person," as used in the 14th Amendment, does not include the unborn....

This conclusion, however, does not of itself fully answer the contentions raised by Texas, and we pass on to other considerations.

IX-B. The pregnant woman cannot be isolated in her privacy. She carries an embryo and, later, a fetus, if one accepts the medical definitions of the developing young in the human uterus. See *Dorland's Illustrated Medical Dictionary* 478–79, 547 (24th ed. 1965). The situation therefore is inherently different from marital intimacy, or bedroom possession of obscene material, or marriage, or procreation, or education, with which *Eisenstadt* and *Griswold, Stanley, Loving, Skinner* and *Pierce* and *Meyer* were respectively concerned. As we have intimated above, it is reasonable and appropriate for a State to decide that at some point in time another interest, that of health of the mother or that of potential human life, becomes significantly involved. The woman's privacy is no longer sole and any right of privacy she possesses must be measured accordingly.

Texas urges that, apart from the 14th Amendment, life begins at conception and is present throughout pregnancy, and that, therefore, the State has a compelling interest in protecting that life from and after conception. We need not resolve the difficult question of when life begins. When those trained in the respective disciplines of medicine, philosophy, and theology are unable to arrive at any consensus, the judiciary, at this point in the development of man's knowledge, is not in a position to speculate as to the answer.

It should be sufficient to note briefly the wide divergence of thinking on this most sensitive and difficult question. There has always been strong support for the view that life does not begin until live birth. This was the belief of the Stoics. It appears to be the predominant, though not the unanimous, attitude of the Jewish faith. It may be taken to represent also the position of a large segment of the Protestant community, insofar as that can be ascertained; organized groups that have taken a formal position on the abortion issue have generally regarded abortion as a matter for the conscience of the individual and her family. As we have noted, the common law found greater significance in quickening. Physicians and their scientific colleagues have regarded that event with less interest and have tended to focus either upon conception, upon live birth, or upon the interim point at which the fetus becomes "viable," that is, potentially able to live outside the mother's womb, albeit with artificial aid. Viability is usually placed at about seven months (28 weeks) but may occur earlier, even at 24 weeks. The Aristotelian theory of "mediate animation," that held sway throughout the Middle Ages and the Renaissance in Europe, continued to be official Roman Catholic dogma until the 19th century, despite opposition to this "ensoulment" theory from those in the Church who would recognize the existence of life from the moment of conception. The latter is now, of course, the official belief of the Catholic Church. As one amicus brief discloses, this is a view strongly held by many non-Catholics as well, and by many physicians. Substantial problems for precise definition of this view are posed, however, by new embryological data that purport to indicate that conception is a "process" over time, rather than an event, and by new medical techniques such as menstrual extraction, the "morning-after" pill, implantation of embryos, artificial insemination, and even artificial wombs.

In areas other than criminal abortion, the law has been reluctant to endorse any theory that life, as we recognize it, begins before live birth or to accord legal rights to the unborn except in narrowly defined situations and except when the rights are contingent upon life birth. For example, the traditional rule of tort law denied recovery for prenatal injuries even though the child was born alive. That rule has been changed in almost every jurisdiction. In most States, recovery is said to be permitted only if the fetus was viable, or at least quick, when the injuries were sustained, though few courts have squarely so held. In a recent development, generally opposed by the commentators, some States permit the parents of a stillborn child to maintain an action for wrongful death because of prenatal injuries. Such an action, however, would appear to be one to vindicate the parents' interest.... In short, the unborn have never been recognized in the law as persons in the whole sense.

X. In view of all this, we do not agree that, by adopting one theory of life, Texas may override the rights of the pregnant woman that are at stake. We repeat, however, that the State does have an important and legitimate interest in preserving and protecting the health of the pregnant woman, whether she be a resident of the State or a non-resident who seeks medical consultation and treatment there, and that it has still another important and legitimate interest in protecting the potentiality of human life. These interests are separate and distinct. Each grows in substantiality as the woman approaches term and, at a point during pregnancy, each becomes "compelling."

With respect to the State's important and legitimate interest in the health of the mother, the "compelling" point, in the light of present medical knowledge, is at approximately the end of the first trimester. This is so because of the now-established medical fact, referred to above..., that until the end of the first trimester mortality in abortion may be less than mortality in normal childbirth. It follows that, from and after this point, a State may regulate the abortion procedure to the extent that the regulation reasonably relates to the preservation and protection of maternal health. Examples of permissible state regulation in this area are requirements as to the qualifications of the person who is to perform the abortion; as to the licensure of that person; as to the facility in which the procedure is to be performed, that is, whether it must be a hospital or may be a clinic or some other place of less-than-hospital status; as to the licensing of the facility; and the like.

This means, on the other hand, that, for the period of pregnancy prior to this "compelling" point, the attending physician, in consultation with his patient, is free to determine, without regulation by the State, that, in his medical judgment, the patient's pregnancy should be terminated. If that decision is reached, the judgment may be effectuated by an abortion free of interference by the State.

With respect to the State's important and legitimate interest in potential life, the "compelling" point is at viability. This is so because the fetus then presumably has the capability of meaningful life outside the mother's womb. State regulation protective of fetal life after viability thus has both logical and biological justifications. If the State is interested in protecting fetal life after viability, it may go so far as to proscribe abortion during that period, except when it is necessary to preserve the life or health of the mother.

Measured against these standards, Art. 1196 of the Texas Penal Code, in restricting legal abortions to those "procured or attempted by medical advice for the purpose of saving the life of the mother," sweeps too broadly. The statute makes no distinction between abortions performed early in pregnancy and those performed later, and it limits to a single reason, "saving" the mother's life, the legal justification for the procedure. The statute, therefore, cannot survive the constitutional attack made upon it here....

XI. To summarize and to repeat:

1. A state criminal abortion statute of the current Texas type, that excepts from criminality only a *life-saving* procedure on behalf of the mother, without regard to pregnancy stage and without recognition of the other interests involved, is violative of the Due Process Clause of the 14th Amendment.

(a) For the stage prior to approximately the end of the first trimester, the abortion decision and its effectuation must be left to the medical judgment of the pregnant woman's attending physician.

(b) For the stage subsequent to approximately the end of the first trimester, the State, in promoting its interest in the health of the mother, may, if it chooses, regulate the abortion procedure in ways that are reasonably related to maternal health.

(c) For the stage subsequent to viability, the State in promoting its interest in the potentiality of human life may, if it chooses, regulate, and even proscribe, abortion except where it is necessary, in appropriate medical judgment, for the preservation of the life or health of the mother.

2. The State may define the term "physician," as it has been employed in the preceding paragraphs of this Part XI of this opinion, to mean only a physician currently licensed by the State, and may proscribe any abortion by a person who is not a physician as so defined.

In *Doe v. Bolton* [the companion case to *Roe*], procedural requirements contained in one of the modern abortion statutes are considered. That opinion and this one, of course, are to be read together.[2]

This holding, we feel, is consistent with the relative weights of the respective interests involved, with the lessons and examples of medical and legal history, with the lenity of the common law, and with the demands of the profound problems of the present day. The decision leaves the State free to place increasing restrictions on abortion as the period of pregnancy lengthens, so long as those restrictions are tailored to the recognized state interests. The decision vindicates the right of the physician to administer medical treatment according to his professional judgment up to the points where important state interests provide compelling justifications for intervention. Up to those points, the abortion decision in all its aspects is inherently, and primarily, a medical decision, and basic responsibility for it must rest with the physician. If an individual practitioner abuses the privilege of exercising proper medical judgment, the usual remedies, judicial and intra-professional, are available....

Mr. Justice Stewart, concurring.

In 1963, this Court, in *Ferguson v. Skrupa* (1963), purported to sound the death knell for the doctrine of substantive due process....

Barely two years later, in *Griswold v. Connecticut* (1965), the Court held a Connecticut birth control law unconstitutional. In view of what had been so recently said in *Skrupa*, the Court's opinion in *Griswold* understandably did its best to avoid reliance on the Due Process Clause of the 14th Amendment as the ground for decision. Yet, the Connecticut law did not violate any provision of the Bill of Rights, nor any other specific provision of the Constitution. So it was clear to me then, and it is equally clear to me now, that the *Griswold* decision can be rationally understood only as a holding that the Connecticut statute substantively invaded the "liberty" that is protected by the Due Process Clause of

---

2. Neither in this opinion nor in *Doe v. Bolton*, do we discuss the father's rights, if any exist in the constitutional context, in the abortion decision. No paternal right has been asserted in either of the cases....

the 14th Amendment. As so understood, *Griswold* stands as one in a long line of pre-*Skrupa* cases decided under the doctrine of substantive due process, and I now accept it as such....

The Constitution nowhere mentions a specific right of personal choice in matters of marriage and family life, but the "liberty" protected by the Due Process Clause of the 14th Amendment covers more than those freedoms explicitly named in the Bill of Rights....

[While the state's interests are] amply sufficient to permit a State to regulate abortions as it does other surgical procedures, and perhaps sufficient to permit a State to regulate abortions more stringently or even to prohibit them in the late stages of pregnancy ... these state interests cannot constitutionally support the broad abridgment of personal liberty worked by the existing Texas law....

Mr. Chief Justice Burger, concurring. [Omitted.]

Mr. Justice Douglas, concurring. [Omitted.]

Mr. Justice White, with whom Mr. Justice Rehnquist joins, dissenting.

At the heart of the controversy in these cases are those recurring pregnancies that pose no danger whatsoever to the life or health of the mother but are, nevertheless, unwanted for any one or more of a variety of reasons—convenience, family planning, economics, dislike of children, the embarrassment of illegitimacy, etc. The common claim before us is that for any one of such reasons, or for no reason at all, and without asserting or claiming any threat to life or health, any woman is entitled to an abortion at her request if she is able to find a medical advisor willing to undertake the procedure.

The Court for the most part sustains this position....

With all due respect, I dissent. I find nothing in the language or history of the Constitution to support the Court's judgment. The Court simply fashions and announces a new constitutional right for pregnant mothers and, with scarcely any reason or authority for its action, invests that right with sufficient substance to override most existing state abortion statutes. The upshot is that the people and the legislatures of the 50 States are constitutionally disentitled to weigh the relative importance of the continued existence and development of the fetus, on the one hand, against a spectrum of possible impacts on the mother, on the other hand. As an exercise of raw judicial power, the Court perhaps has authority to do what it does today; but in my view its judgment is an improvident and extravagant exercise of the power of judicial review that the Constitution extends to this Court.

The Court apparently values the convenience of the pregnant woman more than the continued existence and development of the life or potential life that she carries. Whether or not I might agree with that marshaling of values, I can in no event join the Court's judgment because I find no constitutional warrant for imposing such an order of priorities on the people and legislatures of the States. In a sensitive area such as this, involving as it does issues over which reasonable men may easily and heatedly differ, I cannot accept the Court's exercise of its clear power of choice by interposing a constitutional barrier to state efforts to protect human life and by investing women and doctors with the constitutionally protected right to exterminate it. This issue, for the most part, should be left with the people and to the political processes the people have devised to govern their affairs.

It is my view, therefore, that the Texas statute is not constitutionally infirm because it denies abortions to those who seek to serve only their convenience rather than to protect their life or health....

Mr. Justice Rehnquist, dissenting.

The Court's opinion brings to the decision of this troubling question both extensive historical fact and a wealth of legal scholarship. While the opinion thus commands my respect, I find myself nonetheless in fundamental disagreement with those parts of it that invalidate the Texas statute in question, and therefore dissent....

II. I have difficulty in concluding, as the Court does, that the right of "privacy" is involved in this case. Texas, by the statute here challenged, bars the performance of a medical abortion by a licensed physician on a plaintiff such as Roe. A transaction resulting in an operation such as this is not "private" in the ordinary usage of that word. Nor is the "privacy" that the Court finds here even a distant relative of the freedom from searches and seizures protected by the 4th Amendment to the Constitution, which the Court has referred to as embodying a right to privacy. *Katz v. United States* (1967).

If the Court means by the term "privacy" no more than that the claim of a person to be free from unwanted state regulation of consensual transactions may be a form of "liberty".... I agree with ... Justice Stewart that "liberty" embraces more than the rights found in the Bill of Rights. But that liberty is not guaranteed absolutely against deprivation, only against deprivation without due process of law. The test traditionally applied in the area of social and economic legislation is whether or not a law such as that challenged has a rational relation to a valid state objective.... If the Texas statute were to prohibit an abortion even where the mother's life is in jeopardy, I have little doubt that such a statute would lack a rational relation to a valid state objective....

The Court eschews the history of the 14th Amendment in its reliance on the "compelling state interest" test. But the Court adds a new wrinkle to this test by transposing it from the legal considerations associated with the Equal Protection Clause of the 14th Amendment to this case arising under the Due Process Clause of the 14th Amendment. Unless I misapprehend the consequences of this transplanting of the "compelling state interest test," the Court's opinion will accomplish the seemingly impossible feat of leaving this area of the law more confused than it found it.

While the Court's opinion quotes from the dissent of Mr. Justice Holmes in *Lochner v. New York* (1905), the result it reaches is more closely attuned to the majority opinion of Mr. Justice Peckham in that case. As in *Lochner* and similar cases applying substantive due process standards to economic and social welfare legislation, the adoption of the compelling state interest standard will inevitably require this Court to examine the legislative policies and pass on the wisdom of these policies in the very process of deciding whether a particular state interest put forward may or may not be "compelling." The decision here to break pregnancy into three distinct terms and to outline the permissible restrictions the State may impose in each one, for example, partakes more of judicial legislation than it does of a determination of the intent of the drafters of the 14th Amendment.

The fact that a majority of the States reflecting, after all the majority sentiment in those States, have had restrictions on abortions for at least a century is a strong indication, it seems to me, that the asserted right to an abortion is not "so rooted in the traditions and conscience of our people as to be ranked as fundamental," *Snyder v. Massachusetts* (1934). Even today, when society's views on abortion are changing, the very existence of the debate is evidence that the "right" to an abortion is not so universally accepted as the appellant would have us believe....

By the time of the adoption of the 14th Amendment in 1868, there were at least 36 laws enacted by state or territorial legislatures limiting abortion....

The only conclusion possible from this history is that the drafters did not intend to have the 14th Amendment withdraw from the States the power to legislate with respect to this matter....

A. The Evolution of Privacy Holdings from *Griswold* to *Casey*

Griswold v. Connecticut (1965): "[T]he foregoing cases suggest that specific guarantees in the Bill of Rights have penumbras, formed by emanations from those guarantees that help give them life and substance.... Various guarantees create zones of privacy.... We deal with a right of privacy older than the Bill of Rights. [Marriage]...."

Eisenstadt v. Baird (1972): "[A] marital couple is not an independent entity with a mind and heart of its own, but an association of two individuals.... If the right to privacy means anything, it is the right of the *individual*, married or single, to be free from unwarranted governmental intrusion into matters so fundamentally affecting a person as the decision whether to bear or beget a child."

Roe v. Wade (1973): "The right of privacy [whether in the 14th Amendment's 'personal liberty' or the 9th Amendment] is broad enough to encompass a woman's decision whether or not to terminate her pregnancy."

Village of Belle Terre v. Boraas (1974). The Court rejected a challenge to a zoning ordinance that forbade more than two unrelated persons from living together in one dwelling. Only one member of the Court was willing to say such a prohibition implicated the right to privacy. The majority opinion stated: "[This case] involves no 'fundamental' right guaranteed by the Constitution, such as ... any rights of privacy, cf. *Griswold v. Connecticut*.... It is said, however, that if two unmarried people can constitute a 'family,' there is no reason why three or four may not. But every line drawn by a legislature leaves some out that might well have been included. That exercise of discretion, however, is a legislative, not a judicial, function."

Moore v. City of East Cleveland (1977). In a 4–1–4 split, the Court narrowly sustained a challenge to a zoning statute prohibiting grandchildren from living with their grandmother. Justice White's dissent attacked the substantive due process approach of the plurality opinion:

> Although the Court regularly proceeds on the assumption that the Due Process Clause has more than a procedural dimension, we must always bear in mind that the substantive content of the Clause is suggested neither by its language nor by preconstitutional history; that content is nothing more than the accumulated product of judicial interpretation of the 5th and 14th Amendments. This is not to suggest, at this point, that any of these cases should be overruled, or that the process by which they were decided was illegitimate, or even unacceptable, but only to underline Mr. Justice Black's constant reminder to his colleagues that the Court has no license to invalidate legislation which it thinks merely arbitrary or unreasonable.

Maher v. Roe (1977). The Court rejected a challenge to a state refusal to provide medicaid funding for nontherapeutic abortions: "[*Roe v. Wade* (1973)] did not declare an unqualified right to an abortion. [Rather], the right protects the woman [only] from unduly burdensome interference with her freedom to decide whether to terminate her pregnancy."

Harris v. McRae (1980). The Court rejected a challenge to a state refusal to provide medicaid funding for therapeutic abortions: "It is evident that a woman's interest in protecting her health was an important theme in *Roe* [*v. Wade*]. But ... it simply does not follow that a woman's freedom of choice carries with it a constitutional entitlement to the financial resources to avail herself of the full range of protected choices."

Bowers v. Hardwick (1986). The Court rejected a challenge to a state sodomy statute, considering only its effect on homosexuals:

> This case does not require a judgment on whether laws against sodomy between consenting adults in general, or between homosexuals in particular, are wise or desirable.... The issue presented is whether the Federal Constitution confers a fundamental right upon homosexuals to engage in sodomy and hence invalidates the laws of the many States that still make such conduct illegal and have done so for a very long time. The case also calls for some judgment about the limits of the Court's role in carrying out its constitutional mandate.

Michael H. v. Gerald D. (1989). The Court rejected a challenge to a state statute that denied a biological parent the opportunity to overcome the presumption that a child is the product of a marital union, thereby denying him visitation rights. (The child had been conceived during an adulterous relationship.): "[T]he legal issue in the present case reduces to whether the relationship between persons in the situation of Michael and Victoria has been treated as a protected family unit under the historic practices of our society, or whether on any other basis it has been accorded special protection."

Webster v. Reproductive Health Services (1989). Court upheld Missouri statute that, among other provisions, banned performance of abortions in any public hospitals except to save a woman's life. The George H.W. Bush administration, as amicus curiae, asked the Court to overrule *Roe v. Wade*. The plurality opinion of Chief Justice Rehnquist, joined by Justices Kennedy and White, held in part:

> The experience of the Court in applying *Roe v. Wade* (1973) in later cases suggests to us that there is wisdom in not unnecessarily attempting to elaborate the abstract differences between a "fundamental right" to abortion, as the Court described it in *Akron v. Akron Center for Reproductive Health, Inc.* (1983), a "limited fundamental constitutional right," which Justice Blackmun today treats *Roe* [*v. Wade*] as having established, or a liberty interest protected by the Due Process Clause, which we believe it to be....

> Both appellants and the United States as *amicus curiae* have urged that we overrule our decision in *Roe v. Wade*.... The facts of the present case, however, differ from those at issue in *Roe*.... This case therefore affords us no occasion to revisit the holding of *Roe*, which was that the Texas statute unconstitutionally infringed the right to an abortion derived from the Due Process Clause, and we leave it undisturbed. To the extent indicated in our opinion, we would modify and narrow *Roe* and succeeding cases.

Justice O'Connor concurred, holding that regulations should be forbidden only if they place an "undue burden" on the woman's right to seek an abortion.

Planned Parenthood of Southeastern Pennsylvania v. Casey (1992). The Court considered challenges to a variety of abortion regulations. Once again, the issue produced a fractured Court. The per curiam plurality opinion, by Justices O'Connor, Kennedy, and Souter, was joined in the following part of the opinion by Justices Blackmun and Stevens:

Roe's essential holding, the holding we reaffirm, has three parts. First is a recognition of the right of the woman to choose to have an abortion before viability and to obtain it without undue interference from the State. Before viability, the State's interests are not strong enough to support a prohibition of abortion or the imposition of a substantial obstacle to the woman's effective right to elect the procedure. Second is a confirmation of the State's power to restrict abortions after fetal viability, if the law contains exceptions for pregnancies which endanger a woman's life or health. And third is the principle that the State has legitimate interests from the outset of the pregnancy in protecting the health of the woman and the life of the fetus that may become a child. These principles do not contradict one another; and we adhere to each.

Planned Parenthood v. Casey: Background and Questions

1. What are the tests for regulation of abortion suggested in *Casey*—by the lead opinion, by the two concurring Justices, and by the dissent?
2. Whose analysis of stare decisis is more sound, that of Justices O'Connor, Kennedy, and Souter or that of Justices Rehnquist and Scalia? Why?
3. Whose application of the undue burden test to the issue of the 24-hour waiting period is more sound, the plurality's or Justice Stevens'? Why?
4. Whose analysis of the comparison of *Roe/Casey*, *Lochner/West Coast Hotel*, and *Plessy/Brown* is more sound? Why?
5. Is it beneficial or harmful to a society to have a contentious moral issue removed from the scope of ordinary legislation? Does lobbying for a constitutional amendment provide the judicial "losers" an adequate forum?
6. Would your answer to the constitutionality of the artificial womb statute hypothetical be affected by the decision in *Casey*? How might you use *Casey* on this question?

Robert Bork (whose comment on *Griswold v. Connecticut* (1965) you read earlier) was, in turn, a private lawyer, professor at the Yale Law School, and the Solicitor General of the United States. In 1982, President Ronald Reagan appointed Bork to the U.S. Court of Appeals for the District of Columbia. In July, 1987, Ronald Reagan nominated him to replace Lewis Powell on the Supreme Court. Most believed he would vote to overturn *Roe v. Wade* (1973). Judge Bork was defeated in a bitterly contested nomination fight.

Anthony M. Kennedy was eventually nominated and confirmed for Powell's seat. In *Casey*, the Bush administration as *amicus curiae* again asked the Court to overrule *Roe*, and four Justices voted to do so. However, Justice Kennedy voted with Justices O'Connor and Souter to retain, they said, *Roe*'s central premise. Justice Kennedy joined Justice O'Connor, in spite of having joined Chief Justice Rehnquist's opinion in *Webster v. Reproductive Health Services* (1989).

Planned Parenthood of Southeastern Pennsylvania v. Casey
505 U.S. 833 (1992)

[Majority (Parts I, II, III, V-A, V-C, and VI): O'Connor, Kennedy, Souter, Blackmun, and Stevens. Plurality (Part V-E): O'Connor, Kennedy, Souter, and Stevens. Plurality (Parts IV, V-B, and V-D): O'Connor, Kennedy, and Souter. Concurring (in part): Stevens. Dissenting: Rehnquist (C.J.), White, Scalia, and Thomas.]

Joint opinion of Justices O'Connor, Kennedy and Souter.

I. Liberty finds no refuge in a jurisprudence of doubt. Yet 19 years after our holding that the Constitution protects a woman's right to terminate her pregnancy in its early stages, *Roe v. Wade* (1973), that definition of liberty is still questioned. [T]he United States, as it has done in five other cases in the last decade, again asks us to overrule *Roe*.

At issue in these cases are five provisions of the Pennsylvania Abortion Control Act of 1982, as amended in 1988 and 1989.... The Act requires that a woman seeking an abortion give her informed consent prior to the abortion procedure, and specifies that she be provided with certain information at least 24 hours before the abortion is performed. For a minor to obtain an abortion, the Act requires the informed consent of one of her parents, but provides for a judicial bypass option if the minor does not wish to or cannot obtain a parent's consent. Another provision of the Act requires that, unless certain exceptions apply, a married woman seeking an abortion must sign a statement indicating that she has notified her husband of her intended abortion. The Act exempts compliance with these three requirements in the event of a "medical emergency," which is defined in §3203 of the Act.... [T]he Act [also] imposes certain reporting requirements on facilities that provide abortion services....

[The District Court] held all the provisions at issue here unconstitutional.... The Court of Appeals upheld all of the regulations except for the husband notification requirement....

After considering the fundamental constitutional questions resolved by *Roe*, principles of institutional integrity, and the rule of stare decisis, we are led to conclude this: the essential holding of *Roe v. Wade* should be retained and once again reaffirmed.

... *Roe*'s essential holding, the holding we reaffirm, has three parts. First is a recognition of the right of the woman to choose to have an abortion before viability and to obtain it without undue interference from the State. Before viability, the State's interests are not strong enough to support a prohibition of abortion or the imposition of a substantial obstacle to the woman's effective right to elect the procedure. Second is a confirmation of the State's power to restrict abortions after fetal viability, if the law contains exceptions for pregnancies which endanger the woman's life or health. And third is the principle that the State has legitimate interests from the outset of the pregnancy in protecting the health of the woman and the life of the fetus that may become a child. These principles do not contradict one another; and we adhere to each....

II.... Neither the Bill of Rights nor the specific practices of States at the time of the adoption of the 14th Amendment marks the outer limits of the substantive sphere of liberty which the 14th Amendment protects....

The inescapable fact is that adjudication of substantive due process claims may call upon the Court in interpreting the Constitution to exercise that same capacity which by tradition courts always have exercised: reasoned judgment. Its boundaries are not susceptible of expression as a simple rule. That does not mean we are free to invalidate state policy choices with which we disagree; yet neither does it permit us to shrink from the duties of our office....

Men and women of good conscience can disagree, and we suppose some always shall disagree, about the profound moral and spiritual implications of terminating a pregnancy, even in its earliest stage. Some of us as individuals find abortion offensive to our most basic principles of morality, but that cannot control our decision. Our obligation is to define the liberty of all, not to mandate our own moral code. The underlying constitutional issue is whether the State can resolve these philosophic questions in such a definitive way that a woman lacks all choice in the matter, except perhaps in those rare circumstances in which the pregnancy is itself a danger to her own life or health, or is the result of rape or incest....

Our law affords constitutional protection to personal decisions relating to marriage, procreation, contraception, family relationships, child rearing, and education.... These matters, involving the most intimate and personal choices a person may make in a lifetime, choices central to personal dignity and autonomy, are central to the liberty protected by the 14th Amendment. At the heart of liberty is the right to define one's own concept of existence, of meaning, of the universe, and of the mystery of human life. Beliefs about these matters could not define the attributes of personhood were they formed under compulsion of the State.

These considerations begin our analysis of the woman's interest in terminating her pregnancy but cannot end it, for this reason: though the abortion decision may originate within the zone of conscience and belief, it is more than a philosophic exercise. Abortion is a unique act. It is an act fraught with consequences for others: for the woman who must live with the implications of her decision; for the persons who perform and assist in the procedure; for the spouse, family, and society which must confront the knowledge that these procedures exist, procedures some deem nothing short of an act of violence against innocent human life; and, depending on one's beliefs, for the life or potential life that is aborted. Though abortion is conduct, it does not follow that the State is entitled to proscribe it in all instances. That is because the liberty of the woman is at stake in a sense unique to the human condition and so unique to the law. The mother who carries a child to full term is subject to anxieties, to physical constraints, to pain that only she must bear. That these sacrifices have from the beginning of the human race been endured by woman with a pride that ennobles her in the eyes of others and gives to the infant a bond of love cannot alone be grounds for the State to insist she make the sacrifice. Her suffering is too intimate and personal for the State to insist, without more, upon its own vision of the woman's role, however dominant that vision has been in the course of our history and our culture. The destiny of the woman must be shaped to a large extent on her own conception of her spiritual imperatives and her place in society....

[I]n some critical respects the abortion decision is of the same character as the [constitutionally protected] decision to use contraception.... We have no doubt as to the correctness of those decisions. They support the reasoning in *Roe* relating to the woman's liberty because they involve personal decisions concerning not only the meaning of procreation but also human responsibility and respect for it....

While we appreciate the weight of the arguments made on behalf of the State in the cases before us, arguments which in their ultimate formulation conclude that *Roe* should be overruled, the reservations any of us may have in reaffirming the central holding of *Roe* are outweighed by the explication of individual liberty we have given combined with the force of stare decisis. We turn now to that doctrine.

III–A. ... [W]hen this Court reexamines a prior holding, its judgment is customarily informed by a series of prudential and pragmatic considerations designed to test the consistency of overruling a prior decision with the ideal of the rule of law, and to gauge the respective costs of reaffirming and overruling a prior case....

III-A-1. Although *Roe* has engendered opposition, it has in no sense proven "unworkable," see *Garcia v. San Antonio Metropolitan Transit Authority* (1985), representing as it does a simple limitation beyond which a state law is unenforceable.... [T]he required determinations fall within judicial competence....

III-A-2. [F]or two decades of economic and social developments, people have organized intimate relationships and made choices that define their views of themselves and their places in society, in reliance on the availability of abortion in the event that contraception should fail. The ability of women to participate equally in the economic and social life of the Nation has been facilitated by their ability to control their reproductive lives....

III-A-3. No evolution of legal principle has left *Roe*'s doctrinal footings weaker than they were in 1973....

Roe stands at an intersection of two lines of decisions.... [In the *Griswold v. Connecticut* (1965) line], *Roe* is clearly in no jeopardy, since subsequent constitutional developments have neither disturbed, nor do they threaten to diminish, the scope of recognized protection accorded to the liberty relating to intimate relationships, the family, and decisions about whether or not to beget or bear a child.

Roe, however, may be seen not only as an exemplar of *Griswold* liberty but as a rule (whether or not mistaken) of personal autonomy and bodily integrity, with doctrinal affinity to cases recognizing limits on governmental power to mandate medical treatment or to bar its rejection. If so, our cases since *Roe* accord with *Roe*'s view that a State's interest in the protection of life falls short of justifying any plenary override of individual liberty claims. *Cruzan v. Director, Mo. Dept. of Health* (1990).

Finally, one could classify *Roe* as sui generis. If the case is so viewed, then there clearly has been no erosion of its central determination. The original holding ... was expressly affirmed by a majority of six in 1983 and by a majority of five in 1986. More recently, in *Webster v. Reproductive Health Services* (1989), although two of the present authors questioned the trimester framework in a way consistent with our judgment today ... a majority of the Court either decided to reaffirm or declined to address the constitutional validity of the central holding of *Roe v. Wade*....

Even on the assumption that the central holding of *Roe* was in error, that error would go only to the strength of the state interest in fetal protection, not to the recognition afforded by the Constitution to the woman's liberty....

The soundness of this prong of the *Roe* analysis is apparent from a consideration of the alternative. If indeed the woman's interest in deciding whether to bear and beget a child had not been recognized as in *Roe*, the State might as readily restrict a woman's right to choose to carry a pregnancy to term as to terminate it, to further asserted state interests in population control, or eugenics, for example....

III-A-4. [D]ivergences from the factual premises of 1973 have no bearing on the validity of *Roe*'s central holding, that viability marks the earliest point at which the State's interest in fetal life is constitutionally adequate to justify a legislative ban on nontherapeutic abortions.... Whenever it may occur, the attainment of viability may continue to serve as the critical fact, just as it has done since *Roe* was decided; which is to say that no change in *Roe*'s factual underpinning has left its central holding obsolete, and none supports an argument for overruling it.

III-A-5. ... Within the bounds of normal stare decisis analysis, then, ... the stronger argument is for affirming *Roe*'s central holding, with whatever degree of personal reluctance any of us may have, not for overruling it.

III-B. In a less significant case, stare decisis analysis could, and would, stop at the point we have reached. But the sustained and widespread debate *Roe* has provoked calls for some comparison between that case and others of comparable dimension that have responded to national controversies and taken on the impress of the controversies addressed. Only two such decisional lines from the past century present themselves for examination, and in each instance the result reached by the Court accorded with the principles we apply today.

The first example is that line of cases identified with *Lochner v. New York* (1905), which imposed substantive limitations on legislation limiting economic autonomy in favor of health and welfare regulation, adopting, in Justice Holmes's view, the theory of laissez-faire.... *West Coast Hotel Co. v. Parrish* (1937), signaled the demise of *Lochner* by overruling *Adkins v. Children's Hospital* (1923). In the meantime, the Depression had come and, with it, the lesson that seemed unmistakable to most people by 1937, that the interpretation of contractual freedom protected in *Adkins* rested on fundamentally false factual assumptions about the capacity of a relatively unregulated market to satisfy minimal levels of human welfare.... The facts upon which the earlier case had premised a constitutional resolution of social controversy had proven to be untrue, and history's demonstration of their untruth not only justified but required the new choice of constitutional principle that *West Coast Hotel* announced.... [T]he clear demonstration that the facts of economic life were different from those previously assumed warranted the repudiation of the old law.

The second comparison that 20th century history invites is with the cases employing the separate-but-equal rule for applying the 14th Amendment's equal protection guarantee. They began with *Plessy v. Ferguson* (1896), [which] reject[ed] the argument that racial separation enforced by the legal machinery of American society treats the black race as inferior....

The Court in *Brown* [*v. Board of Education* (1954)], observ[ed] that whatever may have been the understanding in *Plessy*'s time of the power of segregation to stigmatize those who were segregated with a "badge of inferiority," it was clear by 1954 that legally sanctioned segregation had just such an effect.... Society's understanding of the facts upon which a constitutional ruling was sought in 1954 was thus fundamentally different from the basis claimed for the decision in 1896. While we think *Plessy* was wrong the day it was decided, we must also recognize that the *Plessy* Court's explanation for its decision was so clearly at odds with the facts apparent to the Court in 1954 that the decision to reexamine *Plessy* was on this ground alone not only justified but required....

In constitutional adjudication as elsewhere in life, changed circumstances may impose new obligations, and the thoughtful part of the Nation could accept each decision to overrule a prior case as a response to the Court's constitutional duty....

Because neither the factual underpinnings of *Roe*'s central holding nor our understanding of it has changed (and because no other indication of weakened precedent has been shown), the Court could not pretend to be reexamining the prior law with any justification beyond a present doctrinal disposition to come out differently from the Court of 1973. To overrule prior law for no other reason than that would run counter to the view repeated in our cases, that a decision to overrule should rest on some special reason over and above the belief that a prior case was wrongly decided.

III-C. The examination of the conditions justifying the repudiation of *Adkins* by *West Coast Hotel* and *Plessy* by *Brown* is enough to suggest the terrible price that would have been paid if the Court had not overruled as it did. In the present cases, however, ... the terrible price would be paid for overruling.... [O]verruling *Roe*'s central holding would not only reach an unjustifiable result under principles of stare decisis, but would seriously weaken the Court's capacity to exercise the judicial power and to function as the Supreme Court of a Nation dedicated to the rule of law....

The Court's power lies ... in its legitimacy, a product of substance and perception....

The Court must take care to speak and act in ways that allow people to accept its decisions on the terms the Court claims for them, as grounded truly in principle, not as compromises with social and political pressures having, as such, no bearing on the principled choices that the Court is obliged to make....

The need for principled action to be perceived as such is implicated to some degree whenever this, or any other appellate court, overrules a prior case....

Where ... the Court decides a case in such a way as to resolve the sort of intensely divisive controversy reflected in *Roe* and those rare, comparable cases, its decision has a dimension that the resolution of the normal case does not carry. It is the dimension present whenever the Court's interpretation of the Constitution calls the contending sides of a national controversy to end their national division by accepting a common mandate rooted in the Constitution.

The Court is not asked to do this very often, having thus addressed the Nation only twice in our lifetime, in the decisions of *Brown* and *Roe*. But when the Court does act in this way, its decision requires an equally rare precedential force to counter the inevitable efforts to overturn it.... [O]nly the most convincing justification ... could suffice to demonstrate that a later decision overruling the first was anything but a surrender to political pressure, and an unjustified repudiation of the principle on which the Court staked its authority in the first instance. So to overrule under fire in the absence of the most compelling reason to reexamine a watershed decision would subvert the Court's legitimacy beyond any serious question....

A decision to overrule *Roe*'s essential holding under the existing circumstances would address error, if error there was, at the cost of both profound and unnecessary damage to the Court's legitimacy, and to the Nation's commitment to the rule of law. It is therefore imperative to adhere to the essence of *Roe*'s original decision, and we do so today.

IV.... [Although] much criticism has been directed at *Roe*['s linedrawing], a criticism that always inheres when the Court draws a specific rule from what in the Constitution is but a general standard[,].... [L]iberty must not be extinguished for want of a line that is clear....

We conclude the line should be drawn at viability, so that before that time the woman has a right to choose to terminate her pregnancy. We adhere to this principle for two reasons. First, ... stare decisis....

[S]econd[,] the concept of viability ... is the time at which there is a realistic possibility of maintaining and nourishing a life outside the womb, so that the independent existence of the second life can in reason and all fairness be the object of state protection that now overrides the rights of the woman.... The viability line also has, as a practical matter, an element of fairness. In some broad sense it might be said that a woman who fails to act before viability has consented to the State's intervention on behalf of the developing child.

The woman's right to terminate her pregnancy before viability is the most central principle of *Roe v. Wade*. It is a rule of law and a component of liberty we cannot renounce.

On the other side of the equation is the interest of the State in the protection of potential life.... The weight to be given this state interest, not the strength of the woman's interest, was the difficult question faced in *Roe*. We do not need to say whether each of us, ... as an original matter, would have concluded, as the *Roe* Court did, that its weight is insufficient to justify a ban on abortions prior to viability even when it is subject to certain exceptions.... [T]he immediate question is not the soundness of *Roe*'s resolution of the issue, but the precedential force that must be accorded to its holding. And we have concluded that the essential holding of *Roe* should be reaffirmed.

Yet it must be remembered that *Roe v. Wade* speaks with clarity in establishing not only the woman's liberty but also the State's "important and legitimate interest in potential life." That portion of the decision in *Roe* has been given too little acknowledgment and implementation by the Court in its subsequent cases [which] decided that any regulation touching upon the abortion decision must survive strict scrutiny, to be sustained only if drawn in narrow terms to further a compelling state interest. Not all of the cases decided under that formulation can be reconciled with the holding in *Roe* itself that the State has legitimate interests in the health of the woman and in protecting the potential life within her. In resolving this tension, we choose to rely upon *Roe*, as against the later cases.

The trimester framework no doubt was erected to ensure that the woman's right to choose not become so subordinate to the State's interest in promoting fetal life that her choice exists in theory but not in fact. We do not agree, however, that the trimester approach is necessary to accomplish this objective. A framework of this rigidity was unnecessary and in its later interpretation sometimes contradicted the State's permissible exercise of its powers.

Though the woman has a right to choose to terminate or continue her pregnancy before viability, it does not at all follow that the State is prohibited from taking steps to ensure that this choice is thoughtful and informed. Even in the earliest stages of pregnancy, the State may enact rules and regulations designed to encourage her to know that there are philosophic and social arguments of great weight that can be brought to bear in favor of continuing the pregnancy to full term and that there are procedures and institutions to allow adoption of unwanted children as well as a certain degree of state assistance if the mother chooses to raise the child herself....

We reject the trimester framework, which we do not consider to be part of the essential holding of *Roe*. Measures aimed at ensuring that a woman's choice contemplates the consequences for the fetus do not necessarily interfere with the right recognized in *Roe*, although those measures have been found to be inconsistent with the rigid trimester framework announced in that case.... The trimester framework suffers from these basic flaws: in its formulation it misconceives the nature of the pregnant woman's interest; and in practice it undervalues the State's interest in potential life, as recognized in *Roe*....

The fact that a law which serves a valid purpose, one not designed to strike at the right itself, has the incidental effect of making it more difficult or more expensive to procure an abortion cannot be enough to invalidate it. Only where state regulation imposes an undue burden on a woman's ability to make this decision does the power of the State reach into the heart of the liberty protected by the Due Process Clause....

[T]he Court's experience applying the trimester framework has led to the striking down of some abortion regulations which in no real sense deprived women of the ultimate decision. Those decisions went too far because the right recognized by *Roe* is a right "to be free from unwarranted governmental intrusion into matters so fundamentally affecting a person as the decision whether to bear or beget a child." *Eisenstadt v. Baird* (1972). Not all governmental intrusion is of necessity unwarranted; and that brings us to the other basic flaw in the trimester framework: even in *Roe*'s terms, in practice it undervalues the State's interest in the potential life within the woman....

Before viability, *Roe* and subsequent cases treat all governmental attempts to influence a woman's decision on behalf of the potential life within her as unwarranted. This treatment is, in our judgment, incompatible with the recognition that there is a substantial state interest in potential life throughout pregnancy.

The very notion that the State has a substantial interest in potential life leads to the conclusion that not all regulations must be deemed unwarranted. Not all burdens on the right to decide whether to terminate a pregnancy will be undue. In our view, the undue burden standard is the appropriate means of reconciling the State's interest with the woman's constitutionally protected liberty....

A finding of an undue burden is a shorthand for the conclusion that a state regulation has the purpose or effect of placing a substantial obstacle in the path of a woman seeking an abortion of a nonviable fetus. A statute with this purpose is invalid because the means chosen by the State to further the interest in potential life must be calculated to inform the woman's free choice, not hinder it. And a statute which, while furthering the interest in potential life or some other valid state interest, has the effect of placing a substantial obstacle in the path of a woman's choice cannot be considered a permissible means of serving its legitimate ends. To the extent that the opinions of the Court or of individual Justices use the undue burden standard in a manner that is inconsistent with this analysis, we set out what in our view should be the controlling standard.... In our considered judgment, an undue burden is an unconstitutional burden.... Understood another way, we answer the question, left open in previous opinions discussing the undue burden formulation, whether a law designed to further the State's interest in fetal life which imposes an undue burden on the woman's decision before fetal viability could be constitutional. The answer is no.

Some guiding principles should emerge.... Regulations which do no more than create a structural mechanism by which the State, or the parent or guardian of a minor, may express profound respect for the life of the unborn are permitted, if they are not a substantial obstacle to the woman's exercise of the right to choose. Unless it has that effect on her right of choice, a state measure designed to persuade her to choose childbirth over abortion will be upheld if reasonably related to that goal. Regulations designed to foster the health of a woman seeking an abortion are valid if they do not constitute an undue burden.

Even when jurists reason from shared premises, some disagreement is inevitable. That is to be expected in the application of any legal standard which must accommodate life's complexity. We do not expect it to be otherwise with respect to the undue burden standard. We give this summary:

(a) To protect the central right recognized by *Roe v. Wade* while at the same time accommodating the State's profound interest in potential life, we will employ the undue burden analysis as explained in this opinion. An undue burden exists, and therefore a provision of law is invalid, if its purpose or effect is to place a substantial obstacle in the path of a woman seeking an abortion before the fetus attains viability.

(b) We reject the rigid trimester framework of *Roe v. Wade*. To promote the State's profound interest in potential life, throughout pregnancy the State may take measures to ensure that the woman's choice is informed, and measures designed to advance this interest will not be invalidated as long as their purpose is to persuade the woman to choose childbirth over abortion. These measures must not be an undue burden on the right.

(c) As with any medical procedure, the State may enact regulations to further the health or safety of a woman seeking an abortion. Unnecessary health regulations that have the purpose or effect of presenting a substantial obstacle to a woman seeking an abortion impose an undue burden on the right.

(d) Our adoption of the undue burden analysis does not disturb the central holding of *Roe v. Wade*, and we reaffirm that holding. Regardless of whether exceptions are made for particular circumstances, a State may not prohibit any woman from making the ultimate decision to terminate her pregnancy before viability.

(e) We also reaffirm *Roe*'s holding that "subsequent to viability, the State in promoting its interest in the potentiality of human life may, if it chooses, regulate, and even proscribe, abortion except where it is necessary, in appropriate medical judgment, for the preservation of the life or health of the mother."

These principles control our assessment of the Pennsylvania statute, and we now turn to the issue of the validity of its challenged provisions.

V-A. [The Court upholds a narrow statutory definition of the type of "medical emergency" that could justify an abortion under the Pennsylvania legislation after the first trimester, upholds an informed consent requirement that requires a woman to be told a great deal of information relating to fetal development, and upholds the requirement that this information be delivered only by a physician. The latter two holdings overrule earlier cases decided under *Roe*.] ...

V-B. Our analysis of Pennsylvania's 24-hour waiting period between the provision of the information deemed necessary to informed consent and the performance of an abortion under the undue burden standard requires us to reconsider the premise behind the decision in *Akron*[*v. Akron Reproductive Health* (1983) (*Akron I*)] invalidating a parallel requirement. In *Akron I* we said: "Nor are we convinced that the State's legitimate concern that the woman's decision be informed is reasonably served by requiring a 24-hour delay as a matter of course." We consider that conclusion to be wrong. The idea that important decisions will be more informed and deliberate if they follow some period of reflection does not strike us as unreasonable, particularly where the statute directs that important information become part of the background of the decision. The statute, as construed by the Court of Appeals, permits avoidance of the waiting period in the event of a medical emergency and the record evidence shows that in the vast majority of cases, a 24-hour delay does not create any appreciable health risk. In theory, at least, the waiting period is a reasonable measure to implement the State's interest in protecting the life of the unborn, a measure that does not amount to an undue burden.

Whether the mandatory 24-hour waiting period is nonetheless invalid because in practice it is a substantial obstacle to a woman's choice to terminate her pregnancy is a closer question. The findings of fact by the District Court indicate that because of the distances many women must travel to reach an abortion provider, the practical effect will often be a delay of much more than a day because the waiting period requires that a woman seeking an abortion make at least two visits to the doctor. The District Court also found that in many instances this will increase the exposure of women seeking abortions to "the harassment and hostility of anti-abortion protestors demonstrating outside a clinic." As a result, the District Court found that for those women who have the fewest financial resources, those who must travel long distances, and those who have difficulty explaining their whereabouts to husbands, employers, or others, the 24-hour waiting period will be "particularly burdensome."

These findings are troubling in some respects, but they do not demonstrate that the waiting period constitutes an undue burden. We do not doubt that, as the District Court held, the waiting period has the effect of "increasing the cost and risk of delay of abortions," but the District Court did not conclude that the increased costs and potential delays amount to substantial obstacles. Rather, applying the trimester framework's strict prohibition of all regulation designed to promote the State's interest in potential life before viability, the District Court concluded that the waiting period does not further the state "interest in maternal health" and "infringes the physician's discretion to exercise sound medical judgment." Yet, as we have stated, under the undue burden standard a State is permitted to enact persuasive measures which favor childbirth over abortion, even if those measures do not further a health interest. And while the waiting period does limit a physician's discretion, that is not, standing alone, a reason to invalidate it. In light of the construction given the statute's definition of medical emergency by the Court of Appeals, and the District Court's findings, we cannot say that the waiting period imposes a real health risk.

We also disagree with the District Court's conclusion that the "particularly burdensome" effects of the waiting period on some women require its invalidation. A particular burden is not of necessity a substantial obstacle. Whether a burden falls on a particular group is a distinct inquiry from whether it is a substantial obstacle even as to the women in that group. And the District Court did not conclude that the waiting period is such an obstacle even for the women who are most burdened by it. Hence, on the record before us, and in the context of this facial challenge, we are not convinced that the 24-hour waiting period constitutes an undue burden.

We are left with the argument that the various aspects of the informed consent requirement are unconstitutional because they place barriers in the way of abortion on demand. Even the broadest reading of *Roe*, however, has not suggested that there is a constitutional right to abortion on demand. Rather, the right protected by *Roe* is a right to decide to terminate a pregnancy free of undue interference by the State.... The informed consent requirement is not an undue burden on that right.

V-C. Section 3209 of Pennsylvania's abortion law provides, except in cases of medical emergency, that no physician shall perform an abortion on a married woman without receiving a signed statement from the woman that she has notified her spouse that she is about to undergo an abortion. The woman has the option of providing an alternative signed statement certifying that her husband is not the man who impregnated her; that her husband could not be located; that the pregnancy is the result of spousal sexual assault which she has reported; or that the woman believes that notifying her husband will cause him or someone else to inflict bodily injury upon her. A physician who performs an abortion on a married woman without receiving the appropriate signed statement will have his or her license revoked, and is liable to the husband for damages.

[The Court here listed the extensive factual findings of The District Court regarding the extent and severity of spousal abuse, including marital rape and murder.] ...

In well-functioning marriages, spouses discuss important intimate decisions such as whether to bear a child. But there are millions of women in this country who are the victims of regular physical and psychological abuse at the hands of their husbands. Should these women become pregnant, they may have very good reasons for not wishing to inform their husbands of their decision to obtain an abortion. Many may have justifiable fears of physical abuse, but may be no less fearful of the consequences of reporting prior abuse to the Commonwealth of Pennsylvania. Many may have a reasonable fear that notifying their husbands will provoke further instances of child abuse; these women are not exempt from § 3209's notification requirement. Many may fear devastating forms of psychological abuse from their husbands, including verbal harassment, threats of future violence, the destruction of possessions, physical confinement to the home, the withdrawal of financial support, or the disclosure of the abortion to family and friends. These methods of psychological abuse may act as even more of a deterrent to notification than the possibility of physical violence, but women who are the victims of the abuse are not exempt from § 3209's notification requirement. And many women who are pregnant as a result of sexual assaults by their husbands will be unable to avail themselves of the exception for spousal sexual assault, § 3209(b)(3), because the exception requires that the woman have notified law enforcement authorities within 90 days of the assault, and her husband will be notified of her report once an investigation begins, § 3128(c). If anything in this field is certain, it is that victims of spousal sexual assault are extremely reluctant to report the abuse to the government; hence, a great many spousal rape victims will not be exempt from the notification requirement imposed by § 3209.

The spousal notification requirement is thus likely to prevent a significant number of women from obtaining an abortion. It does not merely make abortions a little more difficult or expensive to obtain; for many women, it will impose a substantial obstacle. We must not blind ourselves to the fact that the significant number of women who fear for their safety and the safety of their children are likely to be deterred from procuring an abortion as surely as if the Commonwealth had outlawed abortion in all cases....

This conclusion is in no way inconsistent with our decisions upholding parental notification or consent requirements. Those enactments, and our judgment that they are constitutional, are based on the quite reasonable assumption that minors will benefit from consultation with their parents and that children will often not realize that their parents have their best interests at heart. We cannot adopt a parallel assumption about adult women....

There was a time, not so long ago, when a different understanding of the family and of the Constitution prevailed. In *Bradwell v. State* (1873), three Members of this Court reaffirmed the common-law principle that "a woman had no legal existence separate from her husband, who was regarded as her head and representative in the social state; and, notwithstanding some recent modifications of this civil status, many of the special rules of law flowing from and dependent upon this cardinal principle still exist in full force in most States." Only one generation has passed since this Court observed that "woman is still regarded as the center of home and family life," with attendant "special responsibilities" that precluded full and independent legal status under the Constitution. These views, of course, are no longer consistent with our understanding of the family, the individual, or the Constitution....

The husband's interest in the life of the child his wife is carrying does not permit the State to empower him with this troubling degree of authority over his wife.... A State may not give to a man the kind of dominion over his wife that parents exercise over their children....

Women do not lose their constitutionally protected liberty when they marry....

V-D. We next consider the parental consent provision. [The Court upheld this requirement.] ...

V-E. Under the recordkeeping and reporting requirements of the statute, every facility which performs abortions is required to file a report stating its name and address as well as the name and address of any related entity, such as a controlling or subsidiary organization. In the case of state-funded institutions, the information becomes public. [These requirements were upheld by the Court.]

VI. Our Constitution is a covenant running from the first generation of Americans to us and then to future generations. It is a coherent succession. Each generation must learn anew that the Constitution's written terms embody ideas and aspirations that must survive more ages than one. We accept our responsibility not to retreat from interpreting the full meaning of the covenant in light of all of our precedents. We invoke it once again to define the freedom guaranteed by the Constitution's own promise, the promise of liberty....

Justice Stevens, concurring in part and dissenting in part.

The portions of the Court's opinion that I have joined are more important than those with which I disagree....

I. [I accept] what is implicit in the Court's analysis, namely, a reaffirmation of *Roe*'s [1973] explanation of why the State's obligation to protect the life or health of the mother must take precedence over any duty to the unborn. The Court in *Roe* carefully considered, and rejected, the State's argument "that the fetus is a 'person' within the language and meaning of the 14th Amendment." ... Accordingly, an abortion is not "the termination of life entitled to 14th Amendment protection." From this holding, there was no dissent; indeed, no Member of the Court has ever questioned this fundamental proposition. Thus, as a matter of federal constitutional law, a developing organism that is not yet a "person" does not have what is sometimes described as a "right to life." This has been and, by the Court's holding today, remains a fundamental premise of our constitutional law governing reproductive autonomy....

II. Sections 3205(a)(2)(i)-(iii) of the Pennsylvania statutes are unconstitutional. Those sections require a physician or counselor to provide the woman with a range of materials clearly designed to persuade her to choose not to undergo the abortion. While the Commonwealth is free, pursuant to § 3208 of the Pennsylvania law, to produce and disseminate such material, the Commonwealth may not inject such information into the woman's deliberations just as she is weighing such an important choice....

III. The 24-hour waiting period ... raises even more serious concerns. Such a requirement arguably furthers the Commonwealth's interests in two ways, neither of which is constitutionally permissible.

First, it may be argued that the 24-hour delay is justified by the mere fact that it is likely to reduce the number of abortions, thus furthering the Commonwealth's interest in potential life. But such an argument would justify any form of coercion that placed an obstacle in the woman's path. The Commonwealth cannot further its interests by simply wearing down the ability of the pregnant woman to exercise her constitutional right.

Second, it can more reasonably be argued that the 24-hour delay furthers the Commonwealth's interest in ensuring that the woman's decision is informed and thoughtful. But there is no evidence that the mandated delay benefits women or that it is necessary to enable the physician to convey any relevant information to the patient. The mandatory delay thus appears to rest on outmoded and unacceptable assumptions about the decisionmaking capacity of women....

In the alternative, the delay requirement may be premised on the belief that the decision to terminate a pregnancy is presumptively wrong. This premise is illegitimate.... States may not presume that a woman has failed to reflect adequately merely because her conclusion differs from the State's preference. A woman who has, in the privacy of her thoughts and conscience, weighed the options and made her decision cannot be forced to reconsider all, simply because the State believes she has come to the wrong conclusion.

Part of the constitutional liberty to choose is the equal dignity to which each of us is entitled. A woman who decides to terminate her pregnancy is entitled to the same respect as a woman who decides to carry the fetus to term. The mandatory waiting period denies women that equal respect.

IV. In my opinion, a correct application of the "undue burden" standard leads to the same conclusion concerning the constitutionality of these requirements. A state-imposed burden on the exercise of a constitutional right is measured both by its effects and by its character: A burden may be "undue" either because the burden is too severe or because it lacks a legitimate, rational justification.

The 24-hour delay requirement fails both parts of this test. The findings of the District Court establish the severity of the burden that the 24-hour delay imposes on many pregnant women. Yet even in those cases in which the delay is not especially onerous, it is, in my opinion, "undue" because there is no evidence that such a delay serves a useful and legitimate purpose....

The counseling provisions are similarly infirm. Whenever government commands private citizens to speak or to listen, careful review of the justification for that command is particularly appropriate....

Accordingly, while I disagree with Parts IV, V-B, and V-D of the joint opinion, I join the remainder of the Court's opinion.

Justice Blackmun, concurring in part, concurring in the judgment in part, and dissenting in part.

I join Parts I, II, III, V-A, V-C, and VI of the joint opinion of Justices O'Connor, Kennedy, and Souter.

Three years ago four Members of this Court appeared poised to "cas[t] into darkness the hopes and visions of every woman in this country" who had come to believe that the Constitution guaranteed her the right to reproductive choice.... All that remained between the promise of *Roe* (1973) and the darkness of the plurality was a single, flickering flame.... But now, just when so many expected the darkness to fall, the flame has grown bright.

I do not underestimate the significance of today's joint opinion. Yet I remain steadfast in my belief that the right to reproductive choice is entitled to the full protection afforded by this Court before *Webster*[*v. Reproductive Health Services* (1989)]. And I fear for the darkness as four Justices anxiously await the single vote necessary to extinguish the light.

I. Make no mistake, the joint opinion of Justices O'Connor, Kennedy, and Souter is an act of personal courage and constitutional principle....

What has happened today should serve as a model for future Justices and a warning to all who have tried to turn this Court into yet another political branch.

In striking down the Pennsylvania statute's spousal notification requirement, the Court has established a framework for evaluating abortion regulations that responds to the social context of women facing issues of reproductive choice.... And in applying its test, the Court remains sensitive to the unique role of women in the decisionmaking process....

[W]hile I believe that the joint opinion errs in failing to invalidate the other regulations, I am pleased that the joint opinion has not ruled out the possibility that these regulations may be shown to impose an unconstitutional burden. The joint opinion makes clear that its specific holdings are based on the insufficiency of the record before it. I am confident that in the future evidence will be produced to show that "in a large fraction of the cases in which [these regulations are] relevant, [they] will operate as a substantial obstacle to a woman's choice to undergo an abortion."

II-B. ... The Court has [previously] held that limitations on the right of privacy are permissible only if they survive "strict" constitutional scrutiny—that is, only if the governmental entity imposing the restriction can demonstrate that the limitation is both necessary and narrowly tailored to serve a compelling governmental interest. *Griswold v. Connecticut* (1965). We have applied this principle specifically in the context of abortion regulations. *Roe v. Wade*....

Roe's requirement of strict scrutiny as implemented through a trimester framework should not be disturbed. No other approach has gained a majority, and no other is more protective of the woman's fundamental right. Lastly, no other approach properly accommodates the woman's constitutional right with the State's legitimate interests.

II-C. Application of the strict scrutiny standard results in the invalidation of all the challenged provisions. Indeed, as this Court has invalidated virtually identical provisions in prior cases, stare decisis requires that we again strike them down....

III. ... If there is much reason to applaud the advances made by the joint opinion today, there is far more to fear from the Chief Justice's opinion.

The Chief Justice's criticism of *Roe* follows from his stunted conception of individual liberty. While recognizing that the Due Process Clause protects more than simple physical liberty, he then goes on to construe this Court's personal-liberty cases as establishing only a laundry list of particular rights, rather than a principled account of how these particular rights are grounded in a more general right of privacy.... This constricted view is reinforced by the Chief Justice's exclusive reliance on tradition as a source of fundamental rights.... Given the Chief Justice's exclusive reliance on tradition, people using contraceptives seem the next likely candidate for his list of outcasts.

Even more shocking than the Chief Justice's cramped notion of individual liberty is his complete omission of any discussion of the effects that compelled childbirth and motherhood have on women's lives....

Under his standard, States can ban abortion if that ban is rationally related to a legitimate state interest—a standard which the United States calls "deferential, but not toothless." Yet when pressed at oral argument to describe the teeth, the best protection that the Solicitor General could offer to women was that a prohibition, enforced by criminal penalties, *with no exception for the life of the mother*, "could raise very serious questions." Perhaps, the Solicitor General offered, the failure to include an exemption for the life of the mother would be "arbitrary and capricious." If, as the Chief Justice contends, the undue burden test is made out of whole cloth, the so-called "arbitrary and capricious" limit is the Solicitor General's "new clothes."

Even if it is somehow "irrational" for a State to require a woman to risk her life for her child, what protection is offered for women who become pregnant through rape or incest?...

But, we are reassured, there is always the protection of the democratic process. While there is much to be praised about our democracy, our country since its founding has recognized that there are certain fundamental liberties that are not to be left to the whims of an election. A woman's right to reproductive choice is one of those fundamental liberties. Accordingly, that liberty need not seek refuge at the ballot box.

IV. In one sense, the Court's approach is worlds apart from that of the Chief Justice and Justice Scalia. And yet, in another sense, the distance between the two approaches is short—the distance is but a single vote.

I am 83 years old. I cannot remain on this Court forever, and when I do step down, the confirmation process for my successor well may focus on the issue before us today. That, I regret, may be exactly where the choice between the two worlds will be made.

Chief Justice Rehnquist, with whom Justice White, Justice Scalia, and Justice Thomas join, concurring in the judgment in part and dissenting in part.

The joint opinion, following its newly minted variation on stare decisis, retains the outer shell of *Roe v. Wade* (1973), but beats a wholesale retreat from the substance of that case. We believe that *Roe* was wrongly decided, and that it can and should be overruled consistently with our traditional approach to stare decisis in constitutional cases. We would adopt the approach of the plurality in *Webster v. Reproductive Health Services* (1989) ... and uphold the challenged provisions of the Pennsylvania statute in their entirety.

I.... Although they reject the trimester framework that formed the underpinning of *Roe*, Justices O'Connor, Kennedy, and Souter adopt a revised undue burden standard to analyze the challenged regulations. We conclude, however, that such an outcome is an unjustified constitutional compromise, one which leaves the Court in a position to closely scrutinize all types of abortion regulations despite the fact that it lacks the power to do so under the Constitution....

We have held that a liberty interest protected under the Due Process Clause of the 14th Amendment will be deemed fundamental if it is "implicit in the concept of ordered liberty." *Palko v. Connecticut* (1937). Three years earlier, in *Snyder v. Massachusetts* (1934), we referred to a "principle of justice so rooted in the traditions and conscience of our people as to be ranked as fundamental." These expressions are admittedly not precise, but our decisions implementing this notion of "fundamental" rights do not afford any more elaborate basis on which to base such a classification.

In construing the phrase "liberty" incorporated in the Due Process Clause of the 14th Amendment, we have recognized that its meaning extends beyond freedom from physical restraint.... But a reading of these opinions makes clear that they do not endorse any all-encompassing "right of privacy."

In *Roe v. Wade*, the Court recognized a "guarantee of personal privacy" which "is broad enough to encompass a woman's decision whether or not to terminate her pregnancy." We are now of the view that, in terming this right fundamental, the Court in *Roe* read the earlier opinions upon which it based its decision much too broadly. Unlike marriage, procreation, and contraception, abortion "involves the purposeful termination of a potential life." *Harris v. McRae* (1980). The abortion decision must therefore "be recognized as sui generis, different in kind from the others that the Court has protected under the rubric of personal or family privacy and autonomy." One cannot ignore the fact that a woman is not isolated in her pregnancy, and that the decision to abort necessarily involves the destruction of a fetus.

Nor do the historical traditions of the American people support the view that the right to terminate one's pregnancy is "fundamental." ...

II. The joint opinion['s] discussion of the principle of stare decisis appears to be almost entirely dicta, because [it] does not apply that principle in dealing with *Roe*. *Roe* decided that a woman had a fundamental right to an abortion. The joint opinion rejects that view. *Roe* decided that abortion regulations were to be subjected to "strict scrutiny" and could be justified only in the light of "compelling state interests." The joint opinion rejects that view. *Roe* analyzed abortion regulation under a rigid trimester framework, a framework which has guided this Court's decisionmaking for 19 years. The joint opinion rejects that framework....

Decisions following *Roe*, such as *Akron v. Akron Center for Reproductive Health, Inc.* (1983) and *Thornburgh v. American College of Obstetricians & Gynecologists* (1986) are frankly overruled in part under the "undue burden" standard expounded in the joint opinion....

In our view, authentic principles of stare decisis do not require that any portion of the reasoning in *Roe* be kept intact.... Erroneous decisions in such constitutional cases are uniquely durable, because correction through legislative action, save for constitutional amendment, is impossible. It is therefore our duty to reconsider constitutional interpretations that "depar[t] from a proper understanding" of the Constitution....

In the end, ... the joint opinion's argument is based solely on generalized assertions about the national psyche, on a belief that the people of this country have grown accustomed to the *Roe* decision over the last 19 years and have "ordered their thinking and living around" it. As an initial matter, one might inquire how the joint opinion can view the "central holding" of *Roe* as so deeply rooted in our constitutional culture, when it so casually uproots and disposes of that same decision's trimester framework. Furthermore, at various points in the past, the same could have been said about this Court's erroneous decisions that the Constitution allowed "separate but equal" treatment of minorities, see *Plessy v. Ferguson* (1896), or that "liberty" under the Due Process Clause protected "freedom of contract," see *Adkins v. Children's Hospital* (1923); *Lochner v. New York* (1905). The "separate but equal" doctrine lasted 58 years after *Plessy*, and *Lochner*'s protection of contractual freedom lasted 32 years. However, the simple fact that a generation or more had grown used to these major decisions did not prevent the Court from correcting its errors in those cases, nor should it prevent us from correctly interpreting the Constitution here.

Apparently realizing that conventional stare decisis principles do not support its position, the joint opinion advances a belief that retaining a portion of *Roe* is necessary to protect the "legitimacy" of this Court....

[T]he joint opinion goes on to state that when the Court "resolve[s] the sort of intensely divisive controversy reflected in *Roe* and those rare, comparable cases," its decision is exempt from reconsideration under established principles of stare decisis in constitutional cases....

[Distinguishing] cases which are "intensely divisive" ... from those that are not ... is entirely subjective....

It appears to us very odd indeed that the joint opinion chooses as benchmarks two cases in which the Court chose *not* to adhere to erroneous constitutional precedent, but instead enhanced its stature by acknowledging and correcting its error, apparently in violation of the joint opinion's "legitimacy" principle. See *West Coast Hotel Co. v. Parrish* (1937); *Brown v. Board of Education* (1954).... Public protests should not alter the normal application of stare decisis, lest perfectly lawful protest activity be penalized by the Court itself.

Taking the joint opinion on its own terms, we doubt that its distinction between *Roe*, on the one hand, and *Plessy* and *Lochner*, on the other, withstands analysis....

But the [joint] opinion contends that the Court was entitled to overrule *Plessy* and *Lochner* in those cases, despite the existence of opposition to the original decisions, only because both the Nation and the Court had learned new lessons in the interim. This is at best a feebly supported, post hoc rationalization for those decisions....

When the Court finally recognized its error in *West Coast Hotel*, it did not engage in the post hoc rationalization that the joint opinion attributes to it today; it did not state that *Lochner* had been based on an economic view that had fallen into disfavor, and that it therefore should be overruled. Chief Justice Hughes in his opinion for the Court simply recognized what Justice Holmes had previously recognized in his *Lochner* dissent, that "[t]he Constitution does not speak of freedom of contract."... [T]he theme of the opinion is that the Court had been mistaken as a matter of constitutional law when it embraced "freedom of contract" 32 years previously....

[As for *Brown*,] adherence to *Roe* today under the guise of "legitimacy" would seem to resemble more closely adherence to *Plessy* on the same ground. Fortunately, the Court did not choose that option in *Brown*, and instead frankly repudiated *Plessy*. The joint opinion concludes that such repudiation was justified only because of newly discovered evidence that segregation had the effect of treating one race as inferior to another. But it can hardly be argued that this was not urged upon those who decided *Plessy*, as Justice Harlan observed in his dissent that the law at issue "puts the brand of servitude and degradation upon a large class of our fellow-citizens, our equals before the law." *Plessy v. Ferguson*. It is clear that the same arguments made before the Court in *Brown* were made in *Plessy* as well. The Court in *Brown* simply recognized, as Justice Harlan had recognized beforehand, that the 14th Amendment does not permit racial segregation. The rule of *Brown* is not tied to popular opinion about the evils of segregation; it is a judgment that the Equal Protection Clause does not permit racial segregation, no matter whether the public might come to believe that it is beneficial. On that ground it stands, and on that ground alone the Court was justified in properly concluding that the *Plessy* Court had erred.

There is also a suggestion in the joint opinion that the propriety of overruling a "divisive" decision depends in part on whether "most people" would now agree that it should be overruled.... How such agreement would be ascertained, short of a public opinion poll, the joint opinion does not say. But surely even the suggestion is totally at war with the idea of "legitimacy" in whose name it is invoked. The Judicial Branch derives its legitimacy, not from following public opinion, but from deciding by its best lights whether legislative enactments of the popular branches of Government comport with the Constitution. The doctrine of stare decisis is an adjunct of this duty, and should be no more subject to the vagaries of public opinion than is the basic judicial task....

[T]he joint opinion forgets that there are two sides to any controversy.... The decision in *Roe* has engendered large demonstrations, including repeated marches on this Court and on Congress, both in opposition to and in support of that opinion. A decision either way on *Roe* can therefore be perceived as favoring one group or the other. But this perceived dilemma arises only if one assumes, as the joint opinion does, that the Court should make its decisions with a view toward speculative public perceptions. If one assumes instead, as the Court surely did in both *Brown* and *West Coast Hotel*, that the Court's legitimacy is enhanced by faithful interpretation of the Constitution irrespective of public opposition, such self-engendered difficulties may be put to one side....

The end result of the joint opinion's paeans of praise for legitimacy is the enunciation of a brand new standard for evaluating state regulation of a woman's right to abortion—the "undue burden" standard. As indicated above, *Roe v. Wade* adopted a "fundamental right" standard under which state regulations could survive only if they met the requirement of "strict scrutiny." While we disagree with that standard, it at least had a recognized basis in constitutional law at the time *Roe* was decided. The same cannot be said for the "undue burden" standard, which is created largely out of whole cloth by the authors of the joint opinion. It is a standard which even today does not command the support of a majority of this Court. And it will not, we believe, result in the sort of "simple limitation," easily applied, which the joint opinion anticipates. In sum, it is a standard which is not built to last....

[T]his standard is based even more on a judge's subjective determinations than was the trimester framework.... Because the undue burden standard is plucked from nowhere, the question of what is a "substantial obstacle" to abortion will undoubtedly engender a variety of conflicting views. For example, in the very matter before us now, the authors of the joint opinion would uphold Pennsylvania's 24-hour waiting period, concluding that a "particular burden" on some women is not a substantial obstacle. But the authors would at the same time strike down Pennsylvania's spousal notice provision, after finding that in a "large fraction" of cases the provision will be a substantial obstacle. And, while the authors conclude that the informed consent provisions do not constitute an "undue burden," Justice Stevens would hold that they do....

The sum of the joint opinion's labors in the name of stare decisis and "legitimacy" is this: *Roe v. Wade* stands as a sort of judicial Potemkin Village, which may be pointed out to passers-by as a monument to the importance of adhering to precedent. But behind the facade, an entirely new method of analysis, without any roots in constitutional law, is imported to decide the constitutionality of state laws regulating abortion. Neither stare decisis nor "legitimacy" are truly served by such an effort.

We have stated above our belief that the Constitution does not subject state abortion regulations to heightened scrutiny. Accordingly, we think that the correct analysis is that set forth by the plurality opinion in *Webster*. A woman's interest in having an abortion is a form of liberty protected by the Due Process Clause, but States may regulate abortion procedures in ways rationally related to a legitimate state interest....

[The remainder of the dissent found all of the Pennsylvania statutes constitutional.]

Justice Scalia, with whom The Chief Justice, Justice White, and Justice Thomas join, concurring in the judgment in part and dissenting in part....

The States may, if they wish, permit abortion on demand, but the Constitution does not *require* them to do so. The permissibility of abortion, and the limitations upon it, are to be resolved like most important questions in our democracy: by citizens trying to persuade one another and then voting....

[T]he issue in these cases [is] not whether the power of a woman to abort her unborn child is a "liberty" in the absolute sense; or even whether it is a liberty of great importance to many women. Of course it is both. The issue is whether it is a liberty protected by the Constitution of the United States. I am sure it is not. I reach that conclusion not because of anything so exalted as my views concerning the "concept of existence, of meaning, of the universe, and of the mystery of human life." Rather, I reach it for the same reason I reach the conclusion that bigamy is not constitutionally protected—because of two simple facts: (1) the Constitution says absolutely nothing about it, and (2) the longstanding traditions of American society have permitted it to be legally proscribed.[1] ...

---

1. The Court's suggestion, that adherence to tradition would require us to uphold laws against interracial marriage is entirely wrong. Any tradition in that case was contradicted *by a text*—an Equal Protection Clause that explicitly establishes racial equality as a constitutional value. See *Loving v. Virginia* (1967) ("In the case at bar, ... we deal with statutes containing racial classifications, and the fact of equal application does not immunize the statute from the very heavy burden of justification which the 14th Amendment has traditionally required of state statutes drawn according to race"); see also ... (Stewart, J., concurring in judgment). The enterprise launched in *Roe v. Wade* (1973), by contrast, sought to *establish*—in the teeth of a clear, contrary tradition—a value found nowhere in the

[A]pplying the rational basis test, I would uphold the Pennsylvania statute in its entirety. I must, however, respond to a few of the more outrageous arguments in today's opinion, which it is beyond human nature to leave unanswered....

"[R]easoned judgment" does not begin by begging the question, as *Roe v. Wade* (1973) and subsequent cases unquestionably did by assuming that what the State is protecting is the mere "potentiality of human life." The whole argument of abortion opponents is that what the Court calls the fetus and what others call the unborn child *is a human life*. Thus, whatever answer *Roe* came up with after conducting its "balancing" is bound to be wrong, unless it is correct that the human fetus is in some critical sense merely potentially human. There is of course no way to determine that as a legal matter; it is in fact a value judgment....

The emptiness of the "reasoned judgment" that produced *Roe* is displayed in plain view by the fact that ... the best the Court can do to explain how it is that the word "liberty" must be thought to include the right to destroy human fetuses is to rattle off a collection of adjectives that simply decorate a value judgment and conceal a political choice.... But it is obvious to anyone applying "reasoned judgment" that the same adjectives can be applied to many forms of conduct that this Court (including one of the Justices in today's majority, see *Bowers v. Hardwick* (1986)) has held are *not* entitled to constitutional protection—because, like abortion, they are forms of conduct that have long been criminalized in American society. Those adjectives might be applied, for example, to homosexual sodomy, polygamy, adult incest, and suicide, all of which are equally "intimate" and "deep[ly] personal" decisions involving "personal autonomy and bodily integrity," and all of which can constitutionally be proscribed because it is our unquestionable constitutional tradition that they are proscribable. It is not reasoned judgment that supports the Court's decision; only personal predilection....

The shortcomings of *Roe* did not include lack of clarity: Virtually all regulation of abortion before the third trimester was invalid. [Now] ... the joint opinion ... calls upon federal district judges to apply an "undue burden" standard as doubtful in application as it is unprincipled in origin....

The rootless nature of the "undue burden" standard ... is further reflected in the fact that the joint opinion finds it necessary expressly to repudiate the more narrow formulations used in Justice O'Connor's earlier opinions. Those opinions stated that a statute imposes an "undue burden" if it imposes "absolute obstacles or severe limitations on the abortion decision," *Akron v. Akron Center for Reproductive Health* (1983) (*Akron* I).... (dissenting opinion).... Justice O'Connor has also abandoned (again without explanation) the view she expressed in *Planned Parenthood v. Ashcroft* (1983) (dissenting opinion), that a medical regulation which imposes an "undue burden" could nevertheless be upheld if it "reasonably relate[s] to the preservation and protection of maternal health," In today's version, even health measures will be upheld only "*if they do not constitute an undue burden.*"

[W]hat is remarkable about the joint opinion's fact-intensive analysis is that it does not result in any measurable clarification of the "undue burden" standard. Rather, the approach of the joint opinion is, for the most part, simply to highlight certain facts in the record that apparently strike the three Justices as particularly significant in estab-

---

constitutional text. There is, of course, no comparable tradition barring recognition of a "liberty interest" in carrying one's child to term free from state efforts to kill it. For that reason, it does not follow that the Constitution does not protect childbirth simply because it does not protect abortion....

lishing (or refuting) the existence of an undue burden; after describing these facts, the opinion then simply announces that the provision either does or does not impose a "substantial obstacle" or an "undue burden." ... We do not know whether the same conclusions could have been reached on a different record, or in what respects the record would have had to differ before an opposite conclusion would have been appropriate. The inherently standardless nature of this inquiry invites the district judge to give effect to his personal preferences about abortion. By finding and relying upon the right facts, he can invalidate, it would seem, almost any abortion restriction that strikes him as "undue"—subject, of course, to the possibility of being reversed by a court of appeals or Supreme Court that is as unconstrained in reviewing his decision as he was in making it....

The Court's reliance upon stare decisis can best be described as contrived.... I confess never to have heard of this new, keep-what-you-want-and-throw-away-the-rest version....

Under *Roe*, requiring that a woman seeking an abortion be provided truthful information about abortion before giving informed written consent is unconstitutional, if the information is designed to influence her choice. *Thornburgh v. American College* (1986); *Akron I* (1983). Under the joint opinion's "undue burden" regime (as applied today, at least) such a requirement is constitutional.

Under *Roe*, requiring that information be provided by a doctor, rather than by nonphysician counselors, is unconstitutional. *Akron I*. Under the "undue burden" regime (as applied today, at least) it is not....

Under *Roe*, requiring detailed reports that include demographic data about each woman who seeks an abortion and various information about each abortion is unconstitutional. *Thornburgh*. Under the "undue burden" regime (as applied today, at least) it generally is not.

"Where, in the performance of its judicial duties, the Court decides a case in such a way as to resolve the sort of intensely divisive controversy reflected in *Roe*, its decision has a dimension that the resolution of the normal case does not carry. It is the dimension present whenever the Court's interpretation of the Constitution calls the contending sides of a national controversy to end their national division by accepting a common mandate rooted in the Constitution."

The Court's description of the place of *Roe* in the social history of the United States is unrecognizable. Not only did *Roe* not ... *resolve* the deeply divisive issue of abortion; it did more than anything else to nourish it, by elevating it to the national level where it is infinitely more difficult to resolve. National politics were not plagued by abortion protests, national abortion lobbying, or abortion marches on Congress before *Roe v. Wade* was decided....

Roe's mandate for abortion on demand destroyed the compromises of the past, rendered compromise impossible for the future, and required the entire issue to be resolved uniformly, at the national level. At the same time, *Roe* created a vast new class of abortion consumers and abortion proponents by eliminating the moral opprobrium that had attached to the act. ("If the Constitution guarantees abortion, how can it be bad?"—not an accurate line of thought, but a natural one.) Many favor all of those developments, and it is not for me to say that they are wrong. But to portray *Roe* as the statesmanlike "settlement" of a divisive issue, a jurisprudential Peace of Westphalia that is worth preserving, is nothing less than Orwellian. *Roe* fanned into life an issue that has inflamed our national politics in general, and has obscured with its smoke the selection of Justices to this Court in particular, ever since. And by keeping us in the abortion-umpiring business, it is the perpetuation of that disruption, rather than of any *Pax Roeana*, that the Court's new majority decrees....

I am as distressed as the Court is ... about the "political pressure" directed to the Court.... The Court would profit, I think, from giving less attention to the *fact* of this distressing phenomenon, and more attention to the *cause* of it [:] a new mode of constitutional adjudication that relies not upon text and traditional practice to determine the law, but upon what the Court calls "reasoned judgment" which turns out to be nothing but philosophical predilection and moral intuition.

As long as this Court thought (and the people thought) that we Justices were doing essentially lawyers' work up here—reading text and discerning our society's traditional understanding of that text—the public pretty much left us alone. Texts and traditions are facts to study, not convictions to demonstrate about. But if ... our pronouncement of constitutional law rests primarily on value judgments, then a free and intelligent people's attitude towards us can be expected to be (*ought* to be) quite different. The people know that their value judgments are quite as good as those taught in any law school—maybe better. If, indeed, the "liberties" protected by the Constitution are, as the Court says, undefined and unbounded, then the people *should* demonstrate, to protest that we do not implement *their* values instead of *ours*. Not only that, but confirmation hearings for new Justices *should* deteriorate into question-and-answer sessions in which Senators go through a list of their constituents' most favored and most disfavored alleged constitutional rights, and seek the nominee's commitment to support or oppose them. Value judgments, after all, should be voted on, not dictated; and if our Constitution has somehow accidently committed them to the Supreme Court, at least we can have a sort of plebiscite each time a new nominee to that body is put forward. Justice Blackmun not only regards this prospect with equanimity, he solicits it....

B. The Language of "Fundamental Rights" versus "Liberty Interests"

In examining how the court's methodology evolved from *Roe* (1973) to *Casey* (1992), note the use of the "fundamental rights" language in *Roe* and its marked absence in *Casey*. The plurality opinion in *Casey* says *Roe* has not been overruled. Do you agree? First look at the following excerpt from Justice Blackmun's majority opinion in *Roe*:

> The Constitution does not explicitly mention any right of privacy. In a line of decisions, however, going back perhaps as far as *Union Pacific R. Co. v. Botsford* (1891), the Court has recognized that a right of personal privacy, or a guarantee of certain areas or zones of privacy, does exist under the Constitution....
>
> These decisions make it clear that only personal rights that can be deemed "fundamental" or "implicit in the concept of ordered liberty," *Palko v. Connecticut* (1937), are included in this guarantee of personal privacy.
>
> This right of privacy, whether it be founded in the 14th Amendment's concept of personal liberty and restrictions upon state action, as we feel it is, or, as the District Court determined, in the 9th Amendment's reservation of rights to the people, is broad enough to encompass a woman's decision whether or not to terminate her pregnancy.
>
> Where certain "fundamental rights" are involved, the Court has held that regulation limiting these rights may be justified only by a "compelling state interest,"

Kramer v. Union Free School District (1969); *Shapiro v. Thompson* (1969); *Sherbert v. Verner* (1963), and that legislative enactments must be narrowly drawn to express only the legitimate state interests at stake. *Griswold v. Connecticut* (1965); *Aptheker v. Secretary of State* (1964); *Cantwell v. Connecticut* (1940); see *Eisenstadt v. Baird* (1972) (White, J., concurring in result).

Now consider the following excerpt from the plurality opinion of Justices O'Connor, Kennedy, and Souter in *Casey*. What is the significance of this change in approach?

Numerous forms of state regulation might have the incidental effect of increasing the cost or decreasing the availability of medical care, whether for abortion or any other medical procedure. The fact that a law which serves a valid purpose, one not designed to strike at the right itself, has the incidental effect of making it more difficult or more expensive to procure an abortion cannot be enough to invalidate it. Only where state regulation imposes an undue burden on a woman's ability to make this decision does the power of the State reach into the heart of the liberty protected by the Due Process Clause....

A finding of an undue burden is a shorthand for the conclusion that a state regulation has the purpose or effect of placing a substantial obstacle in the path of a woman seeking an abortion of a nonviable fetus. A statute with this purpose is invalid because the means chosen by the State to further the interest in potential life must be calculated to inform the woman's free choice, not hinder it. And a statute which, while furthering the interest in potential life or some other valid state interest, has the effect of placing a substantial obstacle in the path of a woman's choice cannot be considered a permissible means of serving its legitimate ends. To the extent that the opinions of the Court or of individual Justices use the undue burden standard in a manner that is inconsistent with this analysis, we set out what in our view should be the controlling standard.... In our considered judgment, an undue burden is an unconstitutional burden.... Understood another way, we answer the question, left open in previous opinions discussing the undue burden formulation, whether a law designed to further the State's interest in fetal life which imposes an undue burden on the woman's decision before fetal viability could be constitutional.... The answer is no.

Some guiding principles should emerge. What is at stake is the woman's right to make the ultimate decision, not a right to be insulated from all others in doing so. Regulations which do no more than create a structural mechanism by which the State, or the parent or guardian of a minor, may express profound respect for the life of the unborn are permitted, if they are not a substantial obstacle to the woman's exercise of the right to choose.... Unless it has that effect on her right of choice, a state measure designed to persuade her to choose childbirth over abortion will be upheld if reasonably related to that goal. Regulations designed to foster the health of a woman seeking an abortion are valid if they do not constitute an undue burden.

Even when jurists reason from shared premises, some disagreement is inevitable.... That is to be expected in the application of any legal standard which must accommodate life's complexity. We do not expect it to be otherwise with respect to the undue burden standard. We give this summary:

(a) To protect the central right recognized by *Roe v. Wade* while at the same time accommodating the State's profound interest in potential life, we will employ the undue burden analysis as explained in this opinion. An undue burden exists, and therefore a provision of law is invalid, if its purpose or effect is to place a substantial obstacle in the path of a woman seeking an abortion before the fetus attains viability.

(b) We reject the rigid trimester framework of *Roe v. Wade*. To promote the State's profound interest in potential life, throughout pregnancy the State may take measures to ensure that the woman's choice is informed, and measures designed to advance this interest will not be invalidated as long as their purpose is to persuade the woman to choose childbirth over abortion. These measures must not be an undue burden on the right.

(c) As with any medical procedure, the State may enact regulations to further the health or safety of a woman seeking an abortion. Unnecessary health regulations that have the purpose or effect of presenting a substantial obstacle to a woman seeking an abortion impose an undue burden on the right.

(d) Our adoption of the undue burden analysis does not disturb the central holding of *Roe v. Wade*, and we reaffirm that holding. Regardless of whether exceptions are made for particular circumstances, a State may not prohibit any woman from making the ultimate decision to terminate her pregnancy before viability.

(e) We also reaffirm *Roe's* holding that "subsequent to viability, the State in promoting its interest in the potentiality of human life may, if it chooses, regulate, and even proscribe, abortion except where it is necessary, in appropriate medical judgment, for the preservation of the life or health of the mother." *Roe v. Wade*. These principles control our assessment of the Pennsylvania statute, and we now turn to the issue of the validity of its challenged provisions.

* * *

In *Casey*, Justices O'Connor, Souter, and Kennedy do not discuss the level of scrutiny required by undue burden analysis. They reject *Roe's* classification of the right to an abortion as a fundamental right. Is the plurality using some form of heightened scrutiny similar to rational basis with bite? By *heightened* scrutiny, we mean any form of scrutiny more exacting than low level rational basis. At any rate, the decisional method seems to employ a form of ad hoc balancing in which the plurality considers the totality of the circumstances and weighs the degree of interference with the woman's liberty interest in deciding whether or not to beget a child against the state's interest in promoting potential life.

The following section considers partial birth abortion. In *Stenberg v. Carhart* (2000), the Court, citing *Casey*, struck down a Nebraska ban on the procedure. Justice O'Connor joined the majority. In 2006, Justice Alito replaced Justice O'Connor. In *Gonzales v. Carhart* (2007), the *Stenberg* dissenters, joined by Justice Alito, upheld a federal partial birth abortion ban. The *Gonzales* opinion also cites *Casey*. Was the Court's test clear after *Roe*? Was the Court's test clear after *Casey*? Is it clear after *Gonzales*?

"Partial Birth" Abortion

Gonzales v. Carhart: Background

Following the Court's refusal to flatly overrule *Roe v. Wade* (1973) in *Planned Parenthood v. Casey* (1992), a number of organizations opposed to abortion stopped lobbying for statutes that banned abortion outright, but sought to get legislatures to pass statutes placing additional (but arguably not undue) burdens on the right to obtain an abortion. Opponents sought a variety of additional restrictions. Some of these included imposing new regulations on abortion clinics, where the increased costs had the potential to drive them out of business.

Another restriction was an attack on a procedure its opponents named "partial birth abortion." This restriction was aimed at one type of late term abortion procedure, medically known as "intact dilation and extraction." In *Stenberg v. Carhart* (2000), the Court, voting 5–4, struck down a Nebraska ban. Justice Breyer wrote for the Court, joined by Justices Ginsburg, O'Connor, Stevens, and Souter. Chief Justice Rehnquist and Justices Kennedy, Scalia, and Thomas dissented.

Approximately 90% of abortions performed in the United States occur during the first trimester (before 12 weeks). The predominant procedure during this time period is "vacuum aspiration." This method uses suction to remove the embryo (first eight weeks) or fetus, empty the contents of the uterus, and clean the uterine wall.

Virtually all of the remaining 10% of abortions occur during the second trimester prior to viability (12 to approximately 20 weeks, although viability can vary up to 27 weeks). The predominant procedure during this time period is "dilation and evacuation," known as "D & E." Because of the larger size of the fetus, this procedure involves dilating the cervix and removing the fetus. Because of the size and development of the fetus, vacuum aspiration will not work. The physician must physically remove the fetus. This procedure usually involves dismembering the fetus within the uterus and removing the pieces.

"Intact dilation and extraction" ("D & X") was developed as a modification of the D & E procedure. An intact D & X occurs when the physician removes the fetus in one piece. However, in order to have the fetus pass through the birth canal, the physician must first collapse the fetus' skull by piercing the skull and aspirating its contents. If the fetus has a breech presentation (feet first), the physician removes the fetus up to the head, and then collapses the skull. Its proponents believed it to be safer than a D & E for the woman because the fetus was not dismembered. It was publicized in a monograph published by W. Martin Haskell, M.D., in 1992. Shortly afterward, Congressman Charles Canady (R-Fla.) and his staff came up with the term "partial-birth abortion" in an effort to publicize what they considered to be the gruesome nature of the procedure. Abortion opponents then began introducing legislation to ban the procedure at both the state and federal level.

At this time, under *Roe* and *Casey*, the unfettered right to choose an abortion only existed in the case of *pre-viable* fetuses. After viability, abortion procedures were permitted only if necessary to preserve the life or health of the mother.

By the time of the opinion in *Stenberg* (2000), thirty states had passed statutes of some type attempting to regulate "partial-birth" abortions. The Nebraska statute read as follows:

> No partial birth abortion shall be performed in this state, unless such procedure is necessary to save the life of the mother whose life is endangered by a physical disorder, physical illness, or physical injury, including a life-endangering physical condition caused by or arising from the pregnancy itself.

Neb. Rev. Stat. Ann. s. 28-328(1).

The statute defined "partial birth abortion" as:

> an abortion procedure in which the person performing the abortion partially delivers vaginally a living unborn child before killing the unborn child and completing the delivery.

Neb. Rev. Stat. Ann. s. 28-326(9).

It further defined "partially delivers vaginally a living unborn child before killing the unborn child" to mean

> deliberately and intentionally delivering into the vagina a living unborn child, or a substantial portion thereof, for the purpose of performing a procedure that the person performing such procedure knows will kill the unborn child and does kill the unborn child.

The statute was a felony, carrying a possible penalty of up to 20 years in prison, a fine of up to $25,000, and automatic revocation of a physician's medical license.

The *Stenberg* Court struck down the statute as violating the principles set forth in *Roe* and *Casey*. Justice Breyer began the majority opinion as follows:

> Three established principles determine the issue before us. We shall set them forth in the language of the joint opinion in *Casey*. First, before "viability ... the woman has a right to choose to terminate her pregnancy." *Id.* (joint opinion of O'Connor, Kennedy, and Souter, JJ.). Second, "a law designed to further the State's interest in fetal life which imposes an undue burden on the woman's decision before fetal viability" is unconstitutional. An "undue burden is ... shorthand for the conclusion that a state regulation has the purpose or effect of placing a substantial obstacle in the path of a woman seeking an abortion of a nonviable fetus." Third, "'subsequent to viability, the State in promoting its interest in the potentiality of human life may, if it chooses, regulate, and even proscribe, abortion except where it is necessary, in appropriate medical judgment, for the preservation of the life or health of the mother.'" (Quoting *Roe v. Wade.*)

The Court first held that the absence of a "necessary ... for the ... health of the mother" exception invalidated the statute, even post-viability. While the state had contended that D & E was not reached by the language of the statute and was available to those needing late-term abortions, the trial judge had concluded that the evidence showed that D & X was a safer procedure in some instances. The United States Supreme Court emphasized that

> The word "necessary" in *Casey's* phrase "necessary, in appropriate medical judgment, for the preservation of the life or health of the mother," cannot refer to an absolute necessity or to absolute proof. Medical treatments and procedures are often considered appropriate (or inappropriate) in light of estimated comparative health risks (and health benefits) in particular cases. Neither can that phrase require unanimity of medical opinion. Doctors often differ in their estimation of comparative health risks and appropriate treatment. And *Casey's* words "appropriate medical judgment" must embody the judicial need to tolerate responsible differences of medical opinion—differences of a sort that the American Medical Association and American College of Obstetricians and Gynecologists' statements together indicate are present here.... [W]here substantial medical authority supports the proposition that banning a particular abortion procedure could endanger women's health, *Casey* requires the statute to include a health exception....

Besides failing to have a health exception, the Court also held that the statute constituted an "undue burden" on a woman's right to choose because the vagueness of the statute allowed it to be read to prohibit D & E's as well as D & X's (it criminalized delivering a "substantial portion" of the fetus into the birth canal).

Justice Stevens (joined by Justice Ginsburg) concurred, writing:

Although much ink is spilled today describing the gruesome nature of late-term abortion procedures, that rhetoric does not provide me a reason to believe that the procedure Nebraska here claims it seeks to ban is more brutal, more gruesome, or less respectful of "potential life" than the equally gruesome procedure Nebraska claims it still allows.... [T]he notion that either of these two equally gruesome procedures performed at this late stage of gestation is more akin to infanticide than the other, or that the State furthers any legitimate interest by banning one but not the other, is simply irrational.

Justice O'Connor concurred, stating that she would uphold a statute that banned D & X's if: 1) it explicitly exempted D & E's, and 2) provided a "health of the mother" exception to the ban. She wrote in part:

First, the Nebraska statute is inconsistent with *Casey* because it lacks an exception for those instances when the banned procedure is necessary to preserve the health of the mother. Importantly, Nebraska's own statutory scheme underscores this constitutional infirmity. As we held in *Casey*, prior to viability "the woman has a right to choose to terminate her pregnancy." After the fetus has become viable, States may substantially regulate and even proscribe abortion, but any such regulation or proscription must contain an exception for instances "'where it is necessary, in appropriate medical judgment, for the preservation of the life or health of the mother.'" Nebraska has recognized this constitutional limitation in its separate statute generally proscribing postviability abortions. See *Neb. Rev. Stat. Ann.* § 28-329. That statute provides that "no abortion shall be performed after the time at which, in the sound medical judgment of the attending physician, the unborn child clearly appears to have reached viability, *except when necessary to preserve the life or health of the mother.*" (emphasis added). Because even a postviability proscription of abortion would be invalid absent a health exception, Nebraska's ban on previability partial-birth abortions, under the circumstances presented here, must include a health exception as well, since the State's interest in regulating abortions before viability is "considerably weaker" than after viability. The statute at issue here, however, only excepts those procedures "necessary to save the life of the mother whose life is endangered by a physical disorder, physical illness, or physical injury." Neb. Rev. Stat. Ann. § 28-328(1). This lack of a health exception necessarily renders the statute unconstitutional.

Contrary to the assertions of Justice Kennedy and Justice Thomas, the need for a health exception does not arise from "the individual views of Dr. Carhart and his supporters." Rather, as the majority explains, where, as here, "a significant body of medical opinion believes a procedure may bring with it greater safety for some patients and explains the medical reasons supporting that view," then Nebraska cannot say that the procedure will not, in some circumstances, be "necessary to preserve the life or health of the mother." Accordingly, our precedent requires that the statute include a health exception.

Justice Ginsburg (joined by Justice Stevens) also concurred:

I write separately only to stress that amidst all the emotional uproar caused by an abortion case, we should not lose sight of the character of Nebraska's "partial birth abortion" law. As the Court observes, this law does not save any fetus from destruction, for it targets only "a method of performing abortion."... Seventh Circuit Chief Judge Posner correspondingly observed, regarding similar bans in Wisconsin and Illinois, that the law prohibits the D&X procedure "not because the procedure kills the fetus, not because it risks worse complications for the woman than alternative procedures would do, not because it is a crueler or more painful or more disgusting method of terminating a pregnancy." *Hope Clinic v. Ryan* (7th Cir. 1999) (dissenting opinion). Rather, Chief Judge Posner commented, the law prohibits the procedure because the State legislators seek to chip away at the private choice shielded by *Roe v. Wade*, even as modified by *Casey*. [A]s stated by Chief Judge Posner, "if a statute burdens constitutional rights and all that can be said on its behalf is that it is the vehicle that legislators have chosen for expressing their hostility to those rights, the burden is undue." *Hope Clinic.*

Justice Kennedy, who had co-authored the joint opinion in *Casey* with Justices O'Connor and Souter, dissented. He maintained that the statute survived *Casey*. He argued that the Court should have accepted Nebraska's contention that the statute did not reach D & E's, that D & E's provided a safe alternative to D & X's, and that the state should be allowed to express its moral disapproval of a medical procedure with debatable merits. Chief Justice Rehnquist joined the dissent.

Justice Scalia also dissented, calling for the overruling of *Roe* and *Casey*:

> I am optimistic enough to believe that, one day, *Stenberg v. Carhart* will be assigned its rightful place in the history of this Court's jurisprudence beside *Korematsu v. United States* (1944) and *Dred Scott v. Sandford* (1857). The method of killing a human child—one cannot even accurately say an entirely unborn human child—proscribed by this statute is so horrible that the most clinical description of it evokes a shudder of revulsion. And the Court must know (as most state legislatures banning this procedure have concluded) that demanding a "health exception"—which requires the abortionist to assure himself that, in his expert medical judgment, this method is, in the case at hand, marginally safer than others (how can one prove the contrary beyond a reasonable doubt?)—is to give live-birth abortion free rein.... In my dissent in *Casey*, I wrote that the "undue burden" test made law by the joint opinion created a standard that was "hopelessly unworkable in practice." ... *Casey* must be overruled.

Following *Stenberg*, abortion opponents in Congress re-introduced a federal partial-birth abortion ban. Sponsors attached a set of "Findings of Fact" to the statute, eventually signed into law as the Partial-Birth Abortion Ban Act of 2003. They contended that the Court in *Stenberg* had been constrained in its decision by factual findings made during the litigation in the lower courts and hoped that new congressional findings, particularly regarding the "fact" that D & X was "never" medically necessary, would insulate the statute from judicial attack. A proposed amendment that would have struck the findings on the grounds that they were in fact erroneous was defeated in Committee on a party line vote.

The sponsors also defeated, again on a party line vote, proposed amendments to include a health exception to the scope of the ban. D & X opponents argued that physicians' use of a health exception justification (particularly *mental* health) could not be tightly controlled by the government, essentially allowing continued open access to the procedure.

The Act was promptly challenged. The lower federal courts struck the statute down as inconsistent with *Stenberg*, *Casey*, and *Roe*. Many of the congressional findings were created to support the proposition that the D & X procedure is never medically necessary to protect the health of a woman, thereby rendering the nonexistence of a health exception to the ban moot. While every finding of fact was not considered by each lower court, virtually all of these "facts" were found to be clearly erroneous by a least one court in light of the congressional record and subsequent testimony heard during the litigation. The challenge eventually made its way to the Supreme Court, where Joseph Alito had replaced the recently retired Sandra Day O'Connor.

Gonzales v. Carhart
550 U. S. 124 (2007)

[Majority: Kennedy, Roberts (C.J.), Scalia, Thomas, Alito. Concurring: Thomas, Kennedy. Dissenting: Ginsburg, Breyer, Stevens, Souter.]

Mr. Justice Kennedy delivered the opinion of the Court.

These cases require us to consider the validity of the Partial-Birth Abortion Ban Act of 2003 (Act), 18 U. S. C. § 1531, a federal statute regulating abortion procedures.... Compared to the state statute at issue in *Stenberg v. Carhart* (2000), the Act is more specific concerning the instances to which it applies and in this respect more precise in its coverage. We conclude the Act should be sustained against the objections lodged by the broad, facial attack brought against it....

I-A. The Act proscribes a particular manner of ending fetal life, so it is necessary here, as it was in *Stenberg*, to discuss abortion procedures in some detail....

Abortion methods vary depending to some extent on the preferences of the physician and, of course, on the term of the pregnancy and the resulting stage of the unborn child's development. Between 85 and 90 percent of the approximately 1.3 million abortions performed each year in the United States take place in the first three months of pregnancy, which is to say in the first trimester.... The Act does not regulate these procedures.

Of the remaining abortions that take place each year, most occur in the second trimester. The surgical procedure referred to as "dilation and evacuation" or "D&E" is the usual abortion method in this trimester....

A doctor must first dilate the cervix at least to the extent needed to insert surgical instruments into the uterus and to maneuver them to evacuate the fetus ... A doctor often begins the dilation process by inserting osmotic dilators, such as laminaria (sticks of seaweed), into the cervix....

After sufficient dilation the surgical operation can commence. The woman is placed under general anesthesia or conscious sedation. The doctor, often guided by ultra-sound, inserts grasping forceps through the woman's cervix and into the uterus to grab the fetus. The doctor grips a fetal part with the forceps and pulls it back through the cervix and vagina, continuing to pull even after meeting resistance from the cervix. The friction causes the fetus to tear apart. For example, a leg might be ripped off the fetus as it is pulled through the cervix and out of the woman. The process of evacuating the fetus piece by piece continues until it has been completely removed. A doctor may make 10 to 15 passes with the forceps to evacuate the fetus in its entirety, though sometimes removal is completed with fewer passes. Once the fetus has been evacuated, the placenta and any remaining fetal material are suctioned or scraped out of the uterus. The doctor examines the different parts to ensure the entire fetal body has been removed.

Some doctors, especially later in the second trimester, may kill the fetus a day or two before performing the surgical evacuation. They inject digoxin or potassium chloride into the fetus, the umbilical cord, or the amniotic fluid. Fetal demise may cause contractions and make greater dilation possible. Once dead, moreover, the fetus' body will soften, and its removal will be easier. Other doctors refrain from injecting chemical agents, believing it adds risk with little or no medical benefit.

The abortion procedure that was the impetus for the numerous bans on "partial-birth abortion," including the Act, is a variation of this standard D&E.... For discussion purposes this D&E variation will be referred to as intact D&E. The main difference between the two procedures is that in intact D&E a doctor extracts the fetus intact or largely intact with only a few passes. There are no comprehensive statistics indicating what percentage of all D&Es are performed in this manner....

In an intact D&E procedure the doctor extracts the fetus in a way conducive to pulling out its entire body, instead of ripping it apart. One doctor, for example, testified:

> "If I know I have good dilation and I reach in and the fetus starts to come out and I think I can accomplish it, the abortion with an intact delivery, then I use my forceps a little bit differently. I don't close them quite so much, and I just gently draw the tissue out attempting to have an intact delivery, if possible."

Rotating the fetus as it is being pulled decreases the odds of dismemberment....

[Dr. Martin Haskell has explained the next step as follows:]

> "At this point, the right-handed surgeon slides the fingers of the left [hand] along the back of the fetus and "hooks" the shoulders of the fetus with the index and ring fingers (palm down).

> "While maintaining this tension, lifting the cervix and applying traction to the shoulders with the fingers of the left hand, the surgeon takes a pair of blunt curved Metzenbaum scissors in the right hand. He carefully advances the tip, curved down, along the spine and under his middle finger until he feels it contact the base of the skull under the tip of his middle finger.

> "[T]he surgeon then forces the scissors into the base of the skull or into the foramen magnum. Having safely entered the skull, he spreads the scissors to enlarge the opening.

> "The surgeon removes the scissors and introduces a suction catheter into this hole and evacuates the skull contents. With the catheter still in place, he applies traction to the fetus, removing it completely from the patient."

This is an abortion doctor's clinical description. Here is another description from a nurse who witnessed the same method performed on a 26½-week fetus and who testified before the Senate Judiciary Committee:

> "'Dr. Haskell went in with forceps and grabbed the baby's legs and pulled them down into the birth canal. Then he delivered the baby's body and the arms—everything but the head. The doctor kept the head right inside the uterus....'"The baby's little fingers were clasping and un-clasping, and his little feet were kicking. Then the doctor stuck the scissors in the back of his head, and the baby's arms jerked out, like a startle reaction, like a flinch, like a baby does when he thinks he is going to fall.

> "'The doctor opened up the scissors, stuck a high-powered suction tube into the opening, and sucked the baby's brains out. Now the baby went completely limp....

> "'He cut the umbilical cord and delivered the placenta. He threw the baby in a pan, along with the placenta and the instruments he had just used.'"

Dr. Haskell's approach is not the only method of killing the fetus once its head lodges in the cervix, and "the process has evolved" since his presentation. Another doctor, for example, squeezes the skull after it has been pierced "so that enough brain tissue exudes to allow the head to pass through." Still other physicians reach into the cervix with their forceps and crush the fetus' skull. Others continue to pull the fetus out of the woman until it disarticulates at the neck, in effect decapitating it. These doctors then grasp the head with forceps, crush it, and remove it.

I-B. After Dr. Haskell's [D & X] procedure received public attention, with ensuing and increasing public concern, bans on "partial birth abortion" proliferated. By the time of the *Stenberg* decision, about 30 States had enacted bans designed to prohibit the procedure....

The Act responded to *Stenberg* in two ways. First, Congress made factual findings. Congress determined that this Court in *Stenberg* "was required to accept the very questionable findings issued by the district court judge," § 2(7), 117 Stat. 1202, notes following 18 U. S. C. § 1531, ¶ (7) (Congressional Findings), but that Congress was "not bound to accept the same factual findings," ¶ (8). Congress found, among other things, that "[a] moral, medical, and ethical consensus exists that the practice of performing a partial-birth abortion ... is a gruesome and inhumane procedure that is never medically necessary and should be prohibited." Id., ¶ (1)....

I-C. The Court of Appeals for the Eighth Circuit addressed only the lack of a health exception. The court began its analysis with what it saw as the appropriate question — "whether 'substantial medical authority' supports the medical necessity of the banned procedure." This was the proper framework, according to the Court of Appeals, because "when a lack of consensus exists in the medical community, the Constitution requires legislatures to err on the side of protecting women's health by including a health exception." ...

I-D. The District Court in *Planned Parenthood* concluded the Act was unconstitutional "because it (1) pose[d] an undue burden on a woman's ability to choose a second trimester abortion; (2) [was] unconstitutionally vague; and (3) require[d] a health exception as set forth by ... *Stenberg*."

The Court of Appeals for the Ninth Circuit agreed. Like the Court of Appeals for the Eighth Circuit, it concluded the absence of a health exception rendered the Act unconstitutional. The court interpreted *Stenberg* to require a health exception unless "there is consensus in the medical community that the banned procedure is never medically necessary to preserve the health of women." *Planned Parenthood Federation of America v. Ashcroft* (9th Cir. 2006). Even after applying a deferential standard of review to Congress' factual findings, the Court of Appeals determined "substantial disagreement exists in the medical community regarding whether" the procedures prohibited by the Act are ever necessary to preserve a woman's health. *Id.*

The Court of Appeals concluded further that the Act placed an undue burden on a woman's ability to obtain a second-trimester abortion. The court found the textual differences between the Act and the Nebraska statute struck down in *Stenberg* insufficient to distinguish D&E and intact D&E. *Id.* As a result, according to the Court of Appeals, the Act imposed an undue burden because it prohibited D&E....

II. The principles set forth in the joint opinion in *Planned Parenthood of Southeastern Pa. v. Casey* (1992), did not find support from all those who join the instant opinion. Whatever one's views concerning the *Casey* joint opinion, it is evident a premise central to its conclusion — that the government has a legitimate and substantial interest in preserving and promoting fetal life — would be repudiated were the Court now to affirm the judgments of the Courts of Appeals....

We assume the following principles for the purposes of this opinion. Before viability, a State "may not prohibit any woman from making the ultimate decision to terminate her pregnancy." (plurality opinion).

It also may not impose upon this right an undue burden, which exists if a regulation's "purpose or effect is to place a substantial obstacle in the path of a woman seeking an abortion before the fetus attains viability." On the other hand, "[r]egulations which do no more than create a structural mechanism by which the State, or the parent or guardian of a minor, may express profound respect for the life of the unborn are permitted, if they are not a substantial obstacle to the woman's exercise of the right to choose." *Id. Casey*, in short, struck a balance. The balance was central to its holding. We now apply its standard to the cases at bar.

III. We begin with a determination of the Act's operation and effect. A straightforward reading of the Act's text demonstrates its purpose and the scope of its provisions: It regulates and proscribes, with exceptions or qualifications to be discussed, performing the intact D&E procedure.... In this litigation the Attorney General does not dispute that the Act would impose an undue burden if it covered standard D&E.

We conclude that the Act is not void for vagueness, does not impose an undue burden from any overbreadth, and is not invalid on its face. [The Court rejects the vagueness challenges and notes that the crime includes a knowledge requirement.]

III-C. We next determine whether the Act imposes an undue burden, as a facial matter, because its restrictions on second-trimester abortions are too broad. A review of the statutory text discloses the limits of its reach. The Act prohibits intact D&E; and, notwithstanding respondents' arguments, it does not prohibit the D&E procedure in which the fetus is removed in parts.

The Act prohibits a doctor from intentionally performing an intact D&E. The dual prohibitions of the Act, both of which are necessary for criminal liability, correspond with the steps generally undertaken during this type of procedure. First, a doctor delivers the fetus until its head lodges in the cervix, which is usually past the anatomical landmark for a breech presentation. See 18 U. S. C. § 1531(b)(1)(A). Second, the doctor proceeds to pierce the fetal skull with scissors or crush it with forceps. This step satisfies the overt-act requirement because it kills the fetus and is distinct from delivery. See § 1531(b)(1)(B). The Act's intent requirements, however, limit its reach to those physicians who carry out the intact D&E after intending to undertake both steps at the outset.

The Act excludes most D&Es in which the fetus is removed in pieces, not intact. If the doctor intends to remove the fetus in parts from the outset, the doctor will not have the requisite intent to incur criminal liability....

[The Court distinguishes the Nebraska statute struck down in *Stenberg* which was interpreted to include other D&E procedures.]

[T]he Act departs in material ways from the statute in *Stenberg*. It adopts the phrase "delivers a living fetus," § 1531(b)(1)(A), instead of "'delivering ... a living unborn child, or a substantial portion thereof.'"... D&E does not involve the delivery of a fetus because it requires the removal of fetal parts that are ripped from the fetus as they are pulled through the cervix.

The identification of specific anatomical landmarks to which the fetus must be partially delivered also differentiates the Act from the statute at issue in *Stenberg*. § 1531(b)(1)(A). The Court in *Stenberg* interpreted "'substantial portion'" of the fetus to include an arm or a leg. The Act's anatomical landmarks, by contrast, clarify that the removal of a small portion of the fetus is not prohibited. The landmarks also require the fetus to be delivered so that it is partially "outside the body of the mother." § 1531(b)(1)(A). To come within the ambit of the Nebraska statute, on the other hand, a substantial portion of the fetus only had to be delivered into the vagina; no part of the fetus had to be outside the body of the mother before a doctor could face criminal sanctions....

The canon of constitutional avoidance, finally, extinguishes any lingering doubt as to whether the Act covers the prototypical D&E procedure. "'[T]he elementary rule is that every reasonable construction must be resorted to, in order to save a statute from unconstitutionality.'" It is true this longstanding maxim of statutory interpretation has, in the past, fallen by the wayside when the Court confronted a statute regulating abortion. The Court at times employed an antagonistic "'canon of construction under which in cases involving abortion, a permissible reading of a statute [was] to be avoided at all costs.'" ... *Casey* put this novel statutory approach to rest. *Stenberg* (Kennedy, J., dissenting). *Stenberg* need not be interpreted to have revived it. We read that decision instead to stand for the uncontroversial proposition that the canon of constitutional avoidance does not apply if a statute is not "genuinely susceptible to two constructions."...

Contrary arguments by the respondents are unavailing. Respondents look to situations that might arise during D&E, situations not examined in *Stenberg*. They contend—relying on the testimony of numerous abortion doctors—that D&E may result in the delivery of a living fetus beyond the Act's anatomical landmarks in a significant fraction of cases. This is so, respondents say, because doctors cannot predict the amount the cervix will dilate before the abortion procedure. It might dilate to a degree that the fetus will be removed largely intact. To complete the abortion, doctors will commit an overt act that kills the partially delivered fetus. Respondents thus posit that any D&E has the potential to violate the Act, and that a physician will not know beforehand whether the abortion will proceed in a prohibited manner. This reasoning, however, does not take account of the Act's intent requirements, which preclude liability from attaching to an accidental intact D&E. If a doctor's intent at the outset is to perform a D&E in which the fetus would not be delivered to either of the Act's anatomical land-marks, but the fetus nonetheless is delivered past one of those points, the requisite and prohibited scienter is not present....

IV. ... The question is whether the Act, measured by its text in this facial attack, imposes a substantial obstacle to late-term, but pre-viability, abortions. The Act does not on its face impose a substantial obstacle, and we reject this further facial challenge to its validity....

IV-A. ... The Act proscribes a method of abortion in which a fetus is killed just inches before completion of the birth process. Congress stated as follows: "Implicitly approving such a brutal and inhumane procedure by choosing not to prohibit it will further coarsen society to the humanity of not only newborns, but all vulnerable and innocent human life, making it increasingly difficult to protect such life." Congressional Findings (14)(N). The Act expresses respect for the dignity of human life.

Congress was concerned, furthermore, with the effects on the medical community and on its reputation caused by the practice of partial-birth abortion. The findings in the Act explain:

> "Partial-birth abortion ... confuses the medical, legal, and ethical duties of physicians to preserve and promote life, as the physician acts directly against the physical life of a child, whom he or she had just delivered, all but the head, out of the womb, in order to end that life."

Congressional Findings (14)(J). There can be no doubt the government "has an interest in protecting the integrity and ethics of the medical profession."

Casey reaffirmed these governmental objectives. The government may use its voice and its regulatory authority to show its profound respect for the life within the woman. A central premise of the opinion was that the Court's precedents after Roe had "undervalue[d] the State's interest in potential life." *Casey* (plurality opinion). The plurality opinion indicated "[t]he fact that a law which serves a valid purpose, one not designed to strike at the right itself, has the incidental effect of making it more difficult or more expensive to procure an abortion cannot be enough to invalidate it." *Id.* This was not an idle assertion. The three premises of *Casey* must coexist. *Id.* The third premise, that the State, from the inception of the pregnancy, maintains its own regulatory interest in protecting the life of the fetus that may become a child, cannot be set at naught by interpreting *Casey's* requirement of a health exception so it becomes tantamount to allowing a doctor to choose the abortion method he or she might prefer. Where it has a rational basis to act, and it does not impose an undue burden, the State may use its regulatory power to bar certain procedures and substitute others, all in furtherance of its legitimate interests in regulating the medical profession in order to promote respect for life, including life of the unborn.

The Act's ban on abortions that involve partial delivery of a living fetus furthers the Government's objectives. No one would dispute that, for many, D&E is a procedure itself laden with the power to devalue human life. Congress could nonetheless conclude that the type of abortion proscribed by the Act requires specific regulation because it implicates additional ethical and moral concerns that justify a special prohibition. Congress determined that the abortion methods it proscribed had a "disturbing similarity to the killing of a newborn infant," Congressional Findings (14)(L), and thus it was concerned with "draw[ing] a bright line that clearly distinguishes abortion and infanticide." Congressional Findings (14)(G) The Court has in the past confirmed the validity of drawing boundaries to prevent certain practices that extinguish life and are close to actions that are condemned. *Washington v. Glucksberg* (1997) found reasonable the State's "fear that permitting assisted suicide will start it down the path to voluntary and perhaps even involuntary euthanasia."

Respect for human life finds an ultimate expression in the bond of love the mother has for her child. The Act recognizes this reality as well. Whether to have an abortion requires a difficult and painful moral decision. *Casey*. While we find no reliable data to measure the phenomenon, it seems unexceptionable to conclude some women come to regret their choice to abort the infant life they once created and sustained. Severe depression and loss of esteem can follow.

In a decision so fraught with emotional consequence some doctors may prefer not to disclose precise details of the means that will be used, confining themselves to the required statement of risks the procedure entails. From one standpoint this ought not to be surprising. Any number of patients facing imminent surgical procedures would prefer not to hear all details, lest the usual anxiety preceding invasive medical procedures become the more intense. This is likely the case with the abortion procedures here in issue. See, e.g., *Nat. Abortion Federation v. Gonzales* (2nd Cir. 2006) ("Most of [the plaintiffs'] experts acknowledged that they do not describe to their patients what [the D&E and intact D&E] procedures entail in clear and precise terms.")

It is, however, precisely this lack of information concerning the way in which the fetus will be killed that is of legitimate concern to the State. *Casey* ("States are free to enact laws to provide a reasonable framework for a woman to make a decision that has such profound and lasting meaning"). The State has an interest in ensuring so grave a choice is well informed. It is self-evident that a mother who comes to regret her choice to abort must struggle with grief more anguished and sorrow more profound when she learns, only after the event, what she once did not know: that she allowed a doctor to pierce the skull and vacuum the fast-developing brain of her unborn child, a child assuming the human form.

It is a reasonable inference that a necessary effect of the regulation and the knowledge it conveys will be to encourage some women to carry the infant to full term, thus reducing the absolute number of late-term abortions. The medical profession, furthermore, may find different and less shocking methods to abort the fetus in the second trimester, thereby accommodating legislative demand. The State's interest in respect for life is advanced by the dialogue that better informs the political and legal systems, the medical profession, expectant mothers, and society as a whole of the consequences that follow from a decision to elect a late-term abortion.

It is objected that the standard D&E is in some respects as brutal, if not more, than the intact D&E, so that the legislation accomplishes little. What we have already said, however, shows ample justification for the regulation. Partial-birth abortion, as defined by the Act, differs from a standard D&E because the former occurs when the fetus is partially outside the mother to the point of one of the Act's anatomical landmarks. It was reasonable for Congress to think that partial-birth abortion, more than standard D&E, "undermines the public's perception of the appropriate role of a physician during the delivery process, and perverts a process during which life is brought into the world." Congressional Findings (14)(K)....

IV-B. The Act's furtherance of legitimate government interests bears upon, but does not resolve, the next question: whether the Act has the effect of imposing an unconstitutional burden on the abortion right because it does not allow use of the barred procedure where "'necessary, in appropriate medical judgment, for [the] preservation of the ... health of the mother.'"...

Respondents presented evidence that intact D&E may be the safest method of abortion, for reasons similar to those adduced in *Stenberg*. Abortion doctors testified, for example, that intact D&E decreases the risk of cervical laceration or uterine perforation because it requires fewer passes into the uterus with surgical instruments and does not require the removal of bony fragments of the dismembered fetus, fragments that may be sharp....

These contentions were contradicted by other doctors who testified in the District Courts and before Congress. They concluded that the alleged health advantages were based on speculation without scientific studies to support them. They considered D&E always to be a safe alternative.

There is documented medical disagreement whether the Act's prohibition would ever impose significant health risks on women....

The question becomes whether the Act can stand when this medical uncertainty persists. The Court's precedents instruct that the Act can survive this facial attack. The Court has given state and federal legislatures wide discretion to pass legislation in areas where there is medical and scientific uncertainty.

This traditional rule is consistent with *Casey*, which confirms the State's interest in promoting respect for human life at all stages in the pregnancy ... The law need not give abortion doctors unfettered choice in the course of their medical practice, nor should it elevate their status above other physicians in the medical community. In *Casey* the controlling opinion held an informed-consent requirement in the abortion context was "no different from a requirement that a doctor give certain specific information about any medical procedure." ...

Medical uncertainty does not foreclose the exercise of legislative power in the abortion context any more than it does in other contexts. The medical uncertainty over whether the Act's prohibition creates significant health risks provides a sufficient basis to conclude in this facial attack that the Act does not impose an undue burden.

The conclusion that the Act does not impose an undue burden is supported by other considerations. Alternatives are available to the prohibited procedure.... If the intact D&E procedure is truly necessary in some circumstances, it appears likely an injection that kills the fetus is an alternative under the Act that allows the doctor to perform the procedure....

The Court retains an independent constitutional duty to review factual findings where constitutional rights are at stake. See *Crowell v. Benson* (1932) ("In cases brought to enforce constitutional rights, the judicial power of the United States necessarily extends to the independent determination of all questions, both of fact and law, necessary to the performance of that supreme function").

As respondents have noted, and the District Courts recognized, some recitations in the Act are factually incorrect. Whether or not accurate at the time, some of the important findings have been superseded. Two examples suffice. Congress determined no medical schools provide instruction on the prohibited procedure. Congressional Findings (14)(B), in notes following 18 U. S. C. §1531. The testimony in the District Courts, however, demonstrated intact D&E is taught at medical schools. Congress also found there existed a medical consensus that the prohibited procedure is never medically necessary. Congressional Findings (1). The evidence presented in the District Courts contradicts that conclusion. Uncritical deference to Congress' factual findings in these cases is inappropriate.

On the other hand, relying on the Court's opinion in *Stenberg*, respondents contend that an abortion regulation must contain a health exception "if 'substantial medical authority supports the proposition that banning a particular procedure could endanger women's health.'" As illustrated by respondents' arguments and the decisions of the Courts of Appeals, *Stenberg* has been interpreted to leave no margin of error for legislatures to act in the face of medical uncertainty.

A zero tolerance policy would strike down legitimate abortion regulations, like the present one, if some part of the medical community were disinclined to follow the proscription. This is too exacting a standard to impose on the legislative power, exercised in this instance under the Commerce Clause, to regulate the medical profession. Considerations of marginal safety, including the balance of risks, are within the legislative competence when the regulation is rational and in pursuit of legitimate ends. When standard medical options are available, mere convenience does not suffice to displace them; and if some procedures have different risks than others, it does not follow that the State is altogether barred from imposing reasonable regulations....

V. The considerations we have discussed support our further determination that these facial attacks should not have been entertained in the first instance. In these circumstances the proper means to consider exceptions is by as-applied challenge. The Government has acknowledged that pre-enforcement, as-applied challenges to the Act can be maintained.

This is the proper manner to protect the health of the woman if it can be shown that in discrete and well-defined instances a particular condition has or is likely to occur in which the procedure prohibited by the Act must be used. In an as-applied challenge the nature of the medical risk can be better quantified and balanced than in a facial attack....

What that burden consists of in the specific context of abortion statutes has been a subject of some question....

As the previous sections of this opinion explain, respondents have not demonstrated that the Act would be unconstitutional in a large fraction of relevant cases. *Casey*. We note that the statute here applies to all instances in which the doctor proposes to use the prohibited procedure, not merely those in which the woman suffers from medical complications. It is neither our obligation nor within our traditional institutional role to resolve questions of constitutionality with respect to each potential situation that might develop....

The Act is open to a proper as-applied challenge in a discrete case....

Respondents have not demonstrated that the Act, as a facial matter, is void for vagueness, or that it imposes an undue burden on a woman's right to abortion based on its overbreadth or lack of a health exception. For these reasons the judgments of the Courts of Appeals for the Eighth and Ninth Circuits are reversed. It is so ordered.

Justice Thomas, with whom Justice Scalia joins, concurring....

I write separately to reiterate my view that the Court's abortion jurisprudence, including *Planned Parenthood of Southeastern Pa. v.* Casey (1992) and *Roe v.* Wade (1973), has no basis in the Constitution....

Justice Ginsburg, with whom Justice Stevens, Justice Souter, and Justice Breyer join, dissenting....

Taking care to speak plainly, the *Casey* Court restated and reaffirmed *Roe's* essential holding. First, the Court addressed the type of abortion regulation permissible prior to fetal viability. It recognized "the right of the woman to choose to have an abortion before viability and to obtain it without undue interference from the State." Second, the Court acknowledged "the State's power to restrict abortions after fetal viability, if the law contains exceptions for pregnancies which endanger the woman's life or health." Third, the Court confirmed that "the State has legitimate interests from the outset of the pregnancy in protecting the health of the woman and the life of the fetus that may become a child."

In reaffirming *Roe*, the *Casey* Court described the centrality of "the decision whether to bear ... a child," *Eisenstadt v. Baird* (1972), to a woman's "dignity and autonomy," her "personhood" and "destiny," her "conception of ... her place in society." Of signal importance here, the *Casey* Court stated with unmistakable clarity that state regulation of access to abortion procedures, even after viability, must protect "the health of the woman." *Id*.

Seven years ago, in *Stenberg v. Carhart* (2000), the Court invalidated a Nebraska statute criminalizing the performance of a medical procedure that, in the political arena, has been dubbed "partial-birth abortion."[1] With fidelity to the *Roe-Casey* line of precedent,

---

1. The term "partial-birth abortion" is neither recognized in the medical literature nor used by physicians who perform second-trimester abortions. See *Planned Parenthood Federation of Am. v. Ashcroft* (ND Cal. 2004), aff'd (CA9 2006). The medical community refers to the procedure as either dilation & extraction (D&X) or intact dilation and evacuation (intact D&E). See *Stenberg v. Carhart* (2000).

the Court held the Nebraska statute unconstitutional in part because it lacked the requisite protection for the preservation of a woman's health.

Today's decision is alarming. It refuses to take *Casey* and *Stenberg* seriously. It tolerates, indeed applauds, federal intervention to ban nationwide a procedure found necessary and proper in certain cases by the American College of Obstetricians and Gynecologists (ACOG). It blurs the line, firmly drawn in *Casey*, between pre-viability and post-viability abortions. And, for the first time since *Roe*, the Court blesses a prohibition with no exception safeguarding a woman's health....

I-A. As *Casey* comprehended, at stake in cases challenging abortion restrictions is a woman's "control over her [own] destiny." "There was a time, not so long ago," when women were "regarded as the center of home and family life, with attendant special responsibilities that precluded full and independent legal status under the Constitution." *Id.* Those views, this Court made clear in *Casey*, "are no longer consistent with our understanding of the family, the individual, or the Constitution." Women, it is now acknowledged, have the talent, capacity, and right "to participate equally in the economic and social life of the Nation." Their ability to realize their full potential, the Court recognized, is intimately connected to "their ability to control their reproductive lives." Thus, legal challenges to undue restrictions on abortion procedures do not seek to vindicate some generalized notion of privacy; rather, they center on a woman's autonomy to determine her life's course, and thus to enjoy equal citizenship stature....

In keeping with this comprehension of the right to reproductive choice, the Court has consistently required that laws regulating abortion, at any stage of pregnancy and in all cases, safeguard a woman's health. We have thus ruled that a State must avoid subjecting women to health risks not only where the pregnancy itself creates danger, but also where state regulation forces women to resort to less safe methods of abortion. Indeed, we have applied the rule that abortion regulation must safeguard a woman's health to the particular procedure at issue here—intact dilation and evacuation (D&E).

In *Stenberg*, we expressly held that a statute banning intact D&E was unconstitutional in part because it lacked a health exception. We noted that there existed a "division of medical opinion" about the relative safety of intact D&E, but we made clear that as long as "substantial medical authority supports the proposition that banning a particular abortion procedure could endanger women's health," a health exception is required. We explained:

> The word 'necessary' in *Casey's* phrase 'necessary, in appropriate medical judgment, for the preservation of the life or health of the [pregnant woman],' cannot refer to an absolute necessity or to absolute proof. Medical treatments and procedures are often considered appropriate (or inappropriate) in light of estimated comparative health risks (and health benefits) in particular cases. Neither can that phrase require unanimity of medical opinion. Doctors often differ in their estimation of comparative health risks and appropriate treatment. And *Casey's* words 'appropriate medical judgment' must embody the judicial need to tolerate responsible differences of medical opinion....

Thus, we reasoned, division in medical opinion "at most means uncertainty, a factor that signals the presence of risk, not its absence." "[A] statute that altogether forbids [intact D&E].... consequently must contain a health exception." See also id. (O'Connor, J., concurring) ("Th[e] lack of a health exception necessarily renders the statute unconstitutional.")...

I-B. More important, Congress claimed there was a medical consensus that the banned procedure is never necessary. Congressional Findings (1). But the evidence "very clearly demonstrate[d] the opposite."

Similarly, Congress found that "[t]here is no credible medical evidence that partial-birth abortions are safe or are safer than other abortion procedures." Congressional Findings (14)(B) ... But the congressional record includes letters from numerous individual physicians stating that pregnant women's health would be jeopardized under the Act, as well as statements from nine professional associations, including ACOG, the American Public Health Association, and the California Medical Association, attesting that intact D&E carries meaningful safety advantages over other methods ... No comparable medical groups supported the ban. In fact, "all of the government's own witnesses disagreed with many of the specific congressional findings."

I-C. ... During the District Court trials, "numerous" "extraordinarily accomplished" and "very experienced" medical experts explained that, in certain circumstances and for certain women, intact D&E is safer than alternative procedures and necessary to protect women's health....

Intact D&E, plaintiffs' experts explained, provides safety benefits over D&E by dismemberment for several reasons: First, intact D&E minimizes the number of times a physician must insert instruments through the cervix and into the uterus, and thereby reduces the risk of trauma to, and perforation of, the cervix and uterus—the most serious complication associated with non-intact D&E. Second, removing the fetus intact, instead of dismembering it in utero, decreases the likelihood that fetal tissue will be retained in the uterus, a condition that can cause infection, hemorrhage, and infertility. Third, intact D&E diminishes the chances of exposing the patient's tissues to sharp bony fragments sometimes resulting from dismemberment of the fetus. Fourth, intact D&E takes less operating time than D&E by dismemberment, and thus may reduce bleeding, the risk of infection, and complications relating to anesthesia....

The trial courts concluded, in contrast to Congress' findings, that "significant medical authority supports the proposition that in some circumstances, [intact D&E] is the safest procedure."

The District Courts' findings merit this Court's respect.... Nevertheless, despite the District Courts' appraisal of the weight of the evidence, and in undisguised conflict with *Stenberg*, the Court asserts that the Partial-Birth Abortion Ban Act can survive "when ... medical uncertainty persists."... This assertion is bewildering. Not only does it defy the Court's longstanding precedent affirming the necessity of a health exception, with no carve-out for circumstances of medical uncertainty; it gives short shrift to the records before us, carefully canvassed by the District Courts. Those records indicate that "the majority of highly-qualified experts on the subject believe intact D&E to be the safest, most appropriate procedure under certain circumstances."

The Court acknowledges some of this evidence, but insists that, because some witnesses disagreed with the ACOG and other experts' assessment of risk, the Act can stand. In this insistence, the Court brushes under the rug the District Courts' well-supported findings that the physicians who testified that intact D&E is never necessary to preserve the health of a woman had slim authority for their opinions. They had no training for, or personal experience with, the intact D&E procedure, and many performed abortions only on rare occasions. Even indulging the assumption that the Government witnesses were equally qualified to evaluate the relative risks of abortion procedures, their testimony could not erase the "significant medical authority support[ing] the proposition that in some circumstances, [intact D&E] would be the safest procedure."

II-A. The Court offers flimsy and transparent justifications for upholding a nationwide ban on intact D&E sans any exception to safeguard a women's health. Today's ruling, the Court declares, advances "a premise central to [*Casey's*] conclusion"—i.e., the Government's "legitimate and substantial interest in preserving and promoting fetal life." But the Act scarcely furthers that interest: The law saves not a single fetus from destruction, for it targets only a method of performing abortion. In short, the Court upholds a law that, while doing nothing to "preserv[e] ... fetal life," bars a woman from choosing intact D&E although her doctor "reasonably believes [that procedure] will best protect [her]."

As another reason for upholding the ban, the Court emphasizes that the Act does not proscribe the non-intact D&E procedure. But why not, one might ask. Non-intact D&E could equally be characterized as "brutal," involving as it does "tear[ing] [a fetus] apart" and "ripp[ing] off" its limbs, "[T]he notion that either of these two equally gruesome procedures ... is more akin to infanticide than the other, or that the State furthers any legitimate interest by banning one but not the other, is simply irrational." *Stenberg* (Stevens, J., concurring).

Delivery of an intact, albeit non-viable, fetus warrants special condemnation, the Court maintains, because a fetus that is not dismembered resembles an infant. But so, too, does a fetus delivered intact after it is terminated by injection a day or two before the surgical evacuation, or a fetus delivered through medical induction or cesarean, Yet, the availability of those procedures—along with D&E by dismemberment—the Court says, saves the ban on intact D&E from a declaration of unconstitutionality. Never mind that the procedures deemed acceptable might put a woman's health at greater risk.

Ultimately, the Court admits that "moral concerns" are at work, concerns that could yield prohibitions on any abortion. "Congress could ... conclude that the type of abortion proscribed by the Act requires specific regulation because it implicates additional ethical and moral concerns that justify a special prohibition."). Notably, the concerns expressed are untethered to any ground genuinely serving the Government's interest in preserving life. By allowing such concerns to carry the day and case, overriding fundamental rights, the Court dishonors our precedent....

Revealing in this regard, the Court invokes an anti-abortion shibboleth for which it concededly has no reliable evidence: Women who have abortions come to regret their choices, and consequently suffer from "[s]evere depression and loss of esteem." Because of women's fragile emotional state and because of the "bond of love the mother has for her child," the Court worries, doctors may withhold information about the nature of the intact D&E procedure. The solution the Court approves, then, is not to require doctors to inform women, accurately and adequately, of the different procedures and their attendant risks. Instead, the Court deprives women of the right to make an autonomous choice, even at the expense of their safety.

This way of thinking reflects ancient notions about women's place in the family and under the Constitution — ideas that have long since been discredited. Compare, e.g., *Muller v. Oregon* (1908) ("protective" legislation imposing hours-of-work limitations on women only held permissible in view of women's "physical structure and a proper discharge of her maternal funct[ion]"); *Bradwell v. State* (1873) (Bradley, J., concurring) ("Man is, or should be, woman's protector and defender. The natural and proper timidity and delicacy which belongs to the female sex evidently unfits it for many of the occupations of civil life.... The paramount destiny and mission of woman are to fulfil[l] the noble and benign offices of wife and mother."), with *United States v. Virginia* (1996) (State may not rely on "overbroad generalizations" about the "talents, capacities, or preferences" of women; "[s]uch judgments have ... impeded ... women's progress toward full citizenship stature throughout our Nation's history"); *Califano v. Goldfarb* (1977) (gender-based Social Security classification rejected because it rested on "archaic and overbroad generalizations" "such as assumptions as to [women's] dependency").

Though today's majority may regard women's feelings on the matter as "self-evident," this Court has repeatedly confirmed that "[t]he destiny of the woman must be shaped ... on her own conception of her spiritual imperatives and her place in society." ...

II-B. In cases on a "woman's liberty to determine whether to [continue] her pregnancy," this Court has identified viability as a critical consideration. "[T]here is no line [more workable] than viability," the Court explained in *Casey*, for viability is "the time at which there is a realistic possibility of maintaining and nourishing a life outside the womb, so that the independent existence of the second life can in reason and all fairness be the object of state protection that now overrides the rights of the woman.... In some broad sense it might be said that a woman who fails to act before viability has consented to the State's intervention on behalf of the developing child."

Today, the Court blurs that line, maintaining that "[t]he Act [legitimately] appl[ies] both pre-viability and post-viability because ... a fetus is a living organism while within the womb, whether or not it is viable outside the womb." Instead of drawing the line at viability, the Court refers to Congress' purpose to differentiate "abortion and infanticide" based not on whether a fetus can survive outside the womb, but on where a fetus is anatomically located when a particular medical procedure is performed.

One wonders how long a line that saves no fetus from destruction will hold in face of the Court's "moral concerns." The Court's hostility to the right *Roe* and *Casey* secured is not concealed. Throughout, the opinion refers to obstetrician-gynecologists and surgeons who perform abortions not by the titles of their medical specialties, but by the pejorative label "abortion doctor." A fetus is described as an "unborn child," and as a "baby;" second-trimester, previability abortions are referred to as "late-term;" and the reasoned medical judgments of highly trained doctors are dismissed as "preferences" motivated by "mere convenience," Instead of the heightened scrutiny we have previously applied, the Court determines that a "rational" ground is enough to uphold the Act. And, most troubling, *Casey*'s principles, confirming the continuing vitality of "the essential holding of *Roe*," are merely "assume[d]" for the moment, rather than "retained" or "reaffirmed."

III-A. ... Without attempting to distinguish *Stenberg* and earlier decisions, the majority asserts that the Act survives review because respondents have not shown that the ban on intact D&E would be unconstitutional "in a large fraction of relevant cases." But *Casey* makes clear that, in determining whether any restriction poses an undue burden on a "large fraction" of women, the relevant class is not "all women," nor "all pregnant women," nor even all women "seeking abortions." Rather, a provision restricting access to abortion, "must be judged by reference to those [women] for whom it is an actual rather than an irrelevant restriction," Thus the absence of a health exception burdens all women for whom it is relevant—women who, in the judgment of their doctors, require an intact D&E because other procedures would place their health at risk.... It makes no sense to conclude that this facial challenge fails because respondents have not shown that a health exception is necessary for a large fraction of second-trimester abortions, including those for which a health exception is unnecessary: The very purpose of a health exception is to protect women in exceptional cases....

IV.... Though today's opinion does not go so far as to discard *Roe* or *Casey*, the Court, differently composed than it was when we last considered a restrictive abortion regulation, is hardly faithful to our earlier invocations of "the rule of law" and the "principles of stare decisis." Congress imposed a ban despite our clear prior holdings that the State cannot proscribe an abortion procedure when its use is necessary to protect a woman's health. Although Congress' findings could not withstand the crucible of trial, the Court defers to the legislative override of our Constitution-based rulings. A decision so at odds with our jurisprudence should not have staying power.

In sum, the notion that the Partial-Birth Abortion Ban Act furthers any legitimate governmental interest is, quite simply, irrational ... In candor, the Act, and the Court's defense of it, cannot be understood as anything other than an effort to chip away at a right declared again and again by this Court—and with increasing comprehension of its centrality to women's lives. When "a statute burdens constitutional rights and all that can be said on its behalf is that it is the vehicle that legislators have chosen for expressing their hostility to those rights, the burden is undue."

C. Abortion Politics

As the *Casey* opinions state, the abortion controversy has continued to be a subject of great political significance. The following excerpts appeared in the platforms of the Democratic and Republican parties.

From the 2004 Democratic Party Platform

We will defend the dignity of all Americans against those who would undermine it. Because we believe in the privacy and equality of women, we stand proudly for a woman's right to choose, consistent with *Roe v. Wade*, and regardless of her ability to pay. We stand firmly against Republican efforts to undermine that right. At the same time, we strongly support family planning and adoption incentives. Abortion should be safe, legal, and rare.

From the 2004 Republican Party Platform

As a country, we must keep our pledge to the first guarantee of the Declaration of Independence. That is why we say the unborn child has a fundamental individual right to life which cannot be infringed. We support a human life amendment to the Constitution and we endorse legislation to make it clear that the 14th Amendment's protections apply to unborn children. Our purpose is to have legislative and judicial protection of that right against those who perform abortions. We oppose using public revenues for abortion and will not fund organizations which advocate it. We support the appointment of judges who respect traditional family values and the sanctity of innocent human life.

From the 2008 Democratic Party Platform

The Democratic Party strongly and unequivocally supports *Roe v. Wade* and a woman's right to choose a safe and legal abortion, regardless of ability to pay, and we oppose any and all efforts to weaken or undermine that right. The Democratic Party also strongly supports access to comprehensive affordable family planning services and age-appropriate sex education which empower people to make informed choices and live healthy lives. We also recognize that such health care and education help reduce the number of unintended pregnancies and thereby also reduce the need for abortions.

The Democratic Party strongly supports a woman's decision to have a child by ensuring access to and availability of programs for pre- and post-natal health care, parenting skills, income support, and caring adoption programs. We oppose the current Administration's consistent attempts to undermine a woman's ability to make her own life choices and obtain reproductive health care, including birth control. We will end health insurance discrimination against contraception and provide compassionate care to rape victims.

From the 2008 Republican Party Platform

[W]e assert the inherent dignity and sanctity of all human life and affirm that the unborn child has a fundamental individual right to life which cannot be infringed. We support a human life amendment to the Constitution, and we endorse legislation to make clear that the 14th Amendment's protections apply to unborn children. We oppose using public revenues to promote or perform abortion and will not fund organizations which advocate it.

We have made progress. The Supreme Court has upheld prohibitions against the barbaric practice of partial-birth abortion.... We must protect girls from exploitation and statutory rape through a parental notification requirement. We all have a moral obligation to assist, not to penalize, women struggling with the challenges of an unplanned pregnancy. At its core, abortion is a fundamental assault on the sanctity of innocent human life.... We salute those who provide them alternatives, including pregnancy care centers, and we take pride in the tremendous increase in adoptions that has followed Republican legislative initiatives.

D. Substantive Due Process after *Roe*

The year after *Roe* (1973) the Court considered two cases addressing the scope of personal privacy under the 14th Amendment. In the first case, *Cleveland Board of Education v. LaFleur* (1974), the Court invalidated policies imposing mandatory maternity leave on pregnant teachers regardless of their health. The Court stated:

> This Court has long recognized that freedom of personal choice in matters of marriage and family life is one of the liberties protected by the Due Process Clause of the 14th Amendment. *Roe v. Wade* (1973); *Loving v. Virginia* (1967); *Griswold v. Connecticut* (1965); *Pierce v. Society of Sisters* (1925); *Meyer v. Nebraska* (1923). See also *Prince v. Massachusetts* (1944); *Skinner v. Oklahoma* (1942). As we noted in *Eisenstadt v. Baird* (1972), there is a right "to be free from unwarranted governmental intrusion into matters so fundamentally affecting a person as the decision whether to bear or beget a child."
>
> By acting to penalize the pregnant teacher for deciding to bear a child, overly restrictive maternity leave regulations can constitute a heavy burden on the exercise of these protected freedoms. Because public school maternity leave rules directly affect "one of the basic civil rights of man," *Skinner v. Oklahoma*, the Due Process Clause of the 14th Amendment requires that such rules must not needlessly, arbitrarily, or capriciously impinge upon this vital area of a teacher's constitutional liberty....

However, the Court summarily rejected a challenge to a zoning ordinance that forbade more than two unrelated persons from living together in one dwelling. *Village of Belle Terre v. Boraas* (1974). Only one member of the court was willing to say such a prohibition implicated the right to privacy. The Court stated:

> [This case] involves no "fundamental" right guaranteed by the Constitution, such as ... any rights of privacy, cf. *Griswold v. Connecticut*.
>
> It is said, however, that if two unmarried people can constitute a "family," there is no reason why three or four may not. But every line drawn by a legislature leaves some out that might well have been included. That exercise of discretion, however, is a legislative, not a judicial, function.

VI. Liberty and the Family

Moore v. City of East Cleveland: Background

1. What precedent does the Court grapple with in *Moore v. City of East Cleveland* (1977)? How does it deal with it? How successful is the distinction?
2. Does *Moore* reveal any potential limitations on the Court's decision in *Roe v. Wade* (1973)?
3. Should the liberty interest in the Due Process Clause be construed to include liberties that are less explicitly stated in the text, such as a right to birth control, abortion, or the right of a grandmother to have her grandson live with her after the death of the child's parents?
4. What fundamental problems with the Court's due process jurisprudence does Justice White suggest?
5. How does the Court go about judging the constitutionality of the ordinance in *Moore*? What method does it use to evaluate the state's asserted purpose for the ordinance? Why does it find that the ordinance falls short?

Moore v. City of East Cleveland
431 U.S. 494 (1977)

[Plurality: Powell, Brennan, Marshall, and Blackmun. Concurring: Brennan, Marshall, and Stevens. Dissenting: Burger (C.J.), Stewart, White, and Rehnquist.]

Mr. Justice Powell announced the judgment of the Court.

[Inez Moore lived in her East Cleveland, Ohio, home with her son, Dale Moore, Sr., and two grandsons Dale, Jr., and John Moore, Jr. (who were first cousins). John had come to live with his grandmother after his mother's death. An East Cleveland housing ordinance limited occupancy of a dwelling unit to members of a single family, but defined "family" in such a way that appellant's household did not qualify. Appellant was convicted of a criminal violation of the ordinance. Her conviction was upheld on appeal over her claim that the ordinance violated her right to privacy. The city contended that the ordinance should be sustained under *Village of Belle Terre v. Boraas* (1974), which upheld an ordinance imposing limits on the types of groups that could occupy a single dwelling unit.]

East Cleveland's housing ordinance, like many throughout the country, limits occupancy of a dwelling unit to members of a single family. § 1351.02. But the ordinance contains an unusual and complicated definitional section that recognizes as a "family" only a few categories of related individuals, § 1341.08. Because her family, living together in her home, fits none of those categories, appellant stands convicted of a criminal offense. The question in this case is whether the ordinance[1] violates the Due Process Clause of the 14th Amendment.

---

1. [The crucial section of the ordinance provides]: "'Family'" means a number of individuals related to the nominal head of the household or to the spouse of the nominal head of the household living as a single housekeeping unit in a single dwelling unit, but limited to the following:

    (a) Husband or wife of the nominal head of the household. (b) Unmarried children of the nominal head of the household or of the spouse of the nominal head of the household,

I.... In early 1973, Mrs. Moore received a notice of violation from the city, stating that John was an "illegal occupant" and directing her to comply with the ordinance. When she failed to remove him from her home, the city filed a criminal charge. Mrs. Moore moved to dismiss, claiming that the ordinance was constitutionally invalid on its face. Her motion was overruled, and upon conviction she was sentenced to five days in jail and a $25 fine. The Ohio Court of Appeals affirmed after giving full consideration to her constitutional claims, and the Ohio Supreme Court denied review. We noted probable jurisdiction....

II. The city argues that our decision in *Village of Belle Terre v. Boraas*, requires us to sustain the ordinance attacked here. Belle Terre, like East Cleveland, imposed limits on the types of groups that could occupy a single dwelling unit. Applying the constitutional standard announced in this Court's leading land-use case, *Euclid v. Ambler Realty Co.* (1926), we sustained the Belle Terre ordinance on the ground that it bore a rational relationship to permissible state objectives.

But one overriding factor sets this case apart from *Belle Terre*. The ordinance there affected only *unrelated* individuals. It expressly allowed all who were related by "blood, adoption, or marriage" to live together, and in sustaining the ordinance we were careful to note that it promoted "family needs" and "family values." East Cleveland, in contrast, has chosen to regulate the occupancy of its housing by slicing deeply into the family itself. This is no mere incidental result of the ordinance. On its face it selects certain categories of relatives who may live together and declares that others may not. In particular, it makes a crime of a grandmother's choice to live with her grandson in circumstances like those presented here.

When a city undertakes such intrusive regulation of the family, neither *Belle Terre* nor *Euclid* governs; the usual judicial deference to the legislature is inappropriate. "This Court has long recognized that freedom of personal choice in matters of marriage and family life is one of the liberties protected by the Due Process Clause of the 14th Amendment." *Cleveland Board of Education v. LaFleur* (1974).... A host of cases, tracing their lineage to *Meyer v. Nebraska* (1923), and *Pierce v. Society of Sisters* (1925), have consistently acknowledged a "private realm of family life which the state cannot enter." *Prince v. Massachusetts* (1944). See, e.g., *Roe v. Wade* (1973), ... *Griswold v. Connecticut* (1965), ... *Poe v. Ullman* (1961) (Harlan, J., dissenting), *Skinner v. Oklahoma* (1942). Of course, the family is not beyond regulation. See *Prince v. Massachusetts*. But when the government intrudes on choices concerning family living arrangements, this Court must examine carefully the importance of the governmental interests advanced and the extent to which they are served by the challenged regulation.

When thus examined, this ordinance cannot survive. The city seeks to justify it as a means of preventing overcrowding, minimizing traffic and parking congestion, and avoiding an undue financial burden on East Cleveland's school system. Although these are legitimate goals, the ordinance before us serves them marginally, at best. For example, the ordinance permits any family consisting only of husband, wife, and unmarried children to live together, even if the family contains a half dozen licensed drivers, each with his or her own

provided, however, that such unmarried children have no children residing with them. (c) Father or mother of the nominal head of the household or of the spouse of the nominal head of the household. (d) Notwithstanding the provisions of subsection (b) hereof, a family may include not more than one dependent married or unmarried child of the nominal head of the household or of the spouse of the nominal head of the household and the spouse and dependent children of such dependent child. For the purpose of this subsection, a dependent person is one who has more than fifty percent of his total support furnished for him by the nominal head of the household and the spouse of the nominal head of the household. (e) A family may consist of one individual.

car. At the same time it forbids an adult brother and sister to share a household, even if both faithfully use public transportation. The ordinance would permit a grandmother to live with a single dependent son and children, even if his school-age children number a dozen, yet it forces Mrs. Moore to find another dwelling for her grandson John, simply because of the presence of his uncle and cousin in the same household. We need not labor the point. Section 1341.08 has but a tenuous relation to alleviation of the conditions mentioned by the city.

III. The city would distinguish the cases based on *Meyer* and *Pierce*. It points out that none of them "gives grandmothers any fundamental rights with respect to grandsons," and suggests that any constitutional right to live together as a family extends only to the nuclear family—essentially a couple and their dependent children.

To be sure, these cases did not expressly consider the family relationship presented here. They were immediately concerned with freedom of choice with respect to childbearing, or with the rights of parents to the custody and companionship of their own children, or with traditional parental authority in matters of child rearing and education. But unless we close our eyes to the basic reasons why certain rights associated with the family have been accorded shelter under the 14th Amendment's Due Process Clause, we cannot avoid applying the force and rationale of these precedents to the family choice involved in this case.

Understanding those reasons requires careful attention to this Court's function under the Due Process Clause. Mr. Justice Harlan described it eloquently:

> Due process has not been reduced to any formula; its content cannot be determined by reference to any code. The best that can be said is that through the course of this Court's decisions it has represented the balance which our Nation, built upon postulates of respect for the liberty of the individual, has struck between that liberty and the demands of organized society. If the supplying of content to this Constitutional concept has of necessity been a rational process, it certainly has not been one where judges have felt free to roam where unguided speculation might take them. The balance of which I speak is the balance struck by this country, having regard to what history teaches are the traditions from which it developed as well as the traditions from which it broke. That tradition is a living thing. A decision of this Court which radically departs from it could not long survive, while a decision which builds on what has survived is likely to be sound. No formula could serve as a substitute, in this area, for judgment and restraint.

> [T]he full scope of the liberty guaranteed by the Due Process Clause cannot be found in or limited by the precise terms of the specific guarantees elsewhere provided in the Constitution. This 'liberty' is not a series of isolated points pricked out in terms of the taking of property; the freedom of speech, press, and religion; the right to keep and bear arms; the freedom from unreasonable searches and seizures; and so on. It is a rational continuum which, broadly speaking, includes a freedom from all substantial arbitrary impositions and purposeless restraints, ... and which also recognizes, what a reasonable and sensitive judgment must, that certain interests require particularly careful scrutiny of the state needs asserted to justify their abridgment. *Poe v. Ullman* (dissenting opinion).

Substantive due process has at times been a treacherous field for this Court. There *are* risks when the judicial branch gives enhanced protection to certain substantive liberties without the guidance of the more specific provisions of the Bill of Rights. As the history of the *Lochner* era demonstrates, there is reason for concern lest the only limits to such judicial intervention become the predilections of those who happen at the time to be Members of this Court. That history counsels caution and restraint. But it does not counsel abandonment, nor does it require what the city urges here: cutting off any protection of family rights at the first convenient, if arbitrary boundary—the boundary of the nuclear family.

Appropriate limits on substantive due process come not from drawing arbitrary lines but rather from careful "respect for the teachings of history [and] solid recognition of the basic values that underlie our society." *Griswold v. Connecticut* (Harlan, J., concurring). Our decisions establish that the Constitution protects the sanctity of the family precisely because the institution of the family is deeply rooted in this Nation's history and tradition. It is through the family that we inculcate and pass down many of our most cherished values, moral and cultural.

Whether or not such a household is established because of personal tragedy, the choice of relatives in this degree of kinship to live together may not lightly be denied by the State. *Pierce* struck down an Oregon law requiring all children to attend the State's public schools, holding that the Constitution "excludes any general power of the State to standardize its children by forcing them to accept instruction from public teachers only."... By the same token the Constitution prevents East Cleveland from standardizing its children and its adults by forcing all to live in certain narrowly defined family patterns.

Reversed.

Mr. Justice Brennan, with whom Mr. Justice Marshall joins, concurring.

I join the plurality's opinion. I agree that the Constitution is not powerless to prevent East Cleveland from prosecuting as a criminal and jailing a 63-year-old grandmother for refusing to expel from her home her now 10-year-old grandson who has lived with her and been brought up by her since his mother's death when he was less than a year old. I do not question that a municipality may constitutionally zone to alleviate noise and traffic congestion and to prevent overcrowded and unsafe living conditions, in short to enact reasonable land-use restrictions in furtherance of the legitimate objectives East Cleveland claims for its ordinance. But the zoning power is not a license for local communities to enact senseless and arbitrary restrictions which cut deeply into private areas of protected family life. East Cleveland may not constitutionally define "family" as essentially confined to parents and the parents' own children. The plurality's opinion conclusively demonstrates that classifying family patterns in this eccentric way is not a rational means of achieving the ends East Cleveland claims for its ordinance, and further that the ordinance unconstitutionally abridges the "freedom of personal choice in matters of ... family life [that] is one of the liberties protected by the Due Process Clause of the 14th Amendment." *Cleveland Board of Education v. LaFleur* (1974)....

"*If any freedom not specifically mentioned in the Bill of Rights enjoys a "preferred position" in the law it is most certainly the family.*"... [The] plurality recognizes today, that the choice of the "extended family" pattern is within the "freedom of personal choice in matters of ... family life [that] is one of the liberties protected by the Due Process Clause of the 14th Amendment."...

Mr. Justice Stevens, concurring in the judgment. [Omitted.]

Mr. Chief Justice Burger, dissenting. [Omitted.]

Mr. Justice Stewart, with whom Mr. Justice Rehnquist joins, dissenting.

In *Village of Belle Terre v. Boraas* (1974), the Court considered a New York village ordinance that restricted land use within the village to single-family dwellings. That ordinance defined "family" to include all persons related by blood, adoption, or marriage who lived and cooked together as a single-housekeeping unit; it forbade occupancy by any group of three or more persons who were not so related. We held that the ordinance was a valid effort by the village government to promote the general community welfare, and that it did not violate the 14th Amendment or infringe any other rights or freedoms protected by the Constitution.

The present case brings before us a similar ordinance of East Cleveland, Ohio, one that also limits the occupancy of any dwelling unit to a single family, but that defines "family" to include only certain combinations of blood relatives. The question presented, as I view it, is whether the decision in *Belle Terre* is controlling, or whether the Constitution compels a different result because East Cleveland's definition of "family" is more restrictive than that before us in the *Belle Terre* case....

In my view, the appellant's claim that the ordinance in question invades constitutionally protected rights of association and privacy is in large part answered by the *Belle Terre* decision. The argument was made there that a municipality could not zone its land exclusively for single-family occupancy because to do so would interfere with protected rights of privacy or association. We rejected this contention, and held that the ordinance at issue "involve[d] no 'fundamental' right guaranteed by the Constitution, such as ... the right of association, *NAACP v. Alabama* (1958); or any rights of privacy, cf. *Griswold v. Connecticut* (1965)."...

The *Belle Terre* decision thus disposes of the appellant's contentions to the extent they focus not on her blood relationships with her sons and grandsons but on more general notions about the "privacy of the home." Her suggestion that every person has a constitutional right permanently to share his residence with whomever he pleases, and that such choices are "beyond the province of legitimate governmental intrusion," amounts to the same argument that was made and found unpersuasive in *Belle Terre*....

The appellant [contends] ... that the East Cleveland ordinance intrudes upon "the private realm of family life which the state cannot enter." *Prince v. Massachusetts* (1944). Several decisions of the Court have identified specific aspects of what might broadly be termed "private family life" that are constitutionally protected against state interference. See, e.g., *Roe v. Wade* (1973) (woman's right to decide whether to terminate pregnancy); *Loving v. Virginia* (1967) (freedom to marry person of another race); *Griswold v. Connecticut*.

Although the appellant's desire to share a single-dwelling unit also involves "private family life" in a sense, that desire can hardly be equated with any of the interests protected in the cases just cited. The ordinance about which the appellant complains did not impede her choice to have or not to have children, and it did not dictate to her how her own children were to be nurtured and reared. The ordinance clearly does not prevent parents from living together or living with their unemancipated offspring.

But even though the Court's previous cases are not directly in point, the appellant contends that the importance of the "extended family" in American society requires us to hold that her decision to share her residence with her grandsons may not be interfered with by the State. This decision, like the decisions involved in bearing and raising children, is said to be an aspect of "family life" also entitled to substantive protection under the Constitution. Without pausing to inquire how far under this argument an "extended family" might extend, I cannot agree. When the Court has found that the 14th Amendment placed a substantive limitation on a State's power to regulate, it has been in those rare cases in which the personal interests at issue have been deemed "'implicit in the concept of ordered liberty.'" See *Roe v. Wade*, quoting *Palko v. Connecticut* (1937). The interest that the appellant may have in permanently sharing a single kitchen and a suite of contiguous rooms with some of her relatives simply does not rise to that level. To equate this interest with the fundamental decisions to marry and to bear and raise children is to extend the limited substantive contours of the Due Process Clause beyond recognition....

Mr. Justice White, dissenting.

The 14th Amendment forbids any State to "deprive any person of life, liberty, or property, without due process of law."...

I. Mr. Justice Black ... recognized that the 14th Amendment had substantive as well as procedural content. But believing that its reach should not extend beyond the specific provisions of the Bill of Rights, see *Adamson v. California* (1947) (dissenting opinion), he never embraced the idea that the Due Process Clause empowered the courts to strike down merely unreasonable or arbitrary legislation, nor did he accept Mr. Justice Harlan's [opposing] view. See *Griswold v. Connecticut* (1965) (Black, J., dissenting) (Harlan, J., concurring in judgment). Writing at length in dissent in *Poe v. Ullman* (1961). Mr. Justice Harlan stated the essence of his position as follows:

> This "liberty" is not a series of isolated points pricked out in terms of the taking of property; the freedom of speech, press, and religion; the right to keep and bear arms; the freedom from unreasonable searches and seizures; and so on. It is a rational continuum which, broadly speaking, includes a freedom from all substantial arbitrary impositions and purposeless restraints ... and which also recognizes, what a reasonable and sensitive judgment must, that certain interests require particularly careful scrutiny of the state needs asserted to justify their abridgment.

This construction was far too open ended for Mr. Justice Black. For him, *Meyer v. Nebraska* (1923), and *Pierce v. Society of Sisters* (1925), as substantive due process cases, were as suspect as *Lochner v. New York* (1905), *Coppage v. Kansas* (1915), and *Adkins v. Children's Hospital* (1923). In his view, *Ferguson v. Skrupa* (1963) should have finally disposed of them all. But neither *Meyer* nor *Pierce* has been overruled, and recently there have been decisions of the same genre—*Roe v. Wade* (1973), *Loving v. Virginia* (1967) [striking down a Virginia statute that banned inter-racial marriage]; *Griswold v. Connecticut* and *Eisenstadt v. Baird* (1972).... [A]ll [of these decisions] represented substantial reinterpretations of the Constitution.

Although the Court regularly proceeds on the assumption that the Due Process Clause has more than a procedural dimension, we must always bear in mind that the substantive content of the Clause is suggested neither by its language nor by preconstitutional history; that content is nothing more than the accumulated product of judicial interpretation of the 5th and 14th Amendments. This is not to suggest, at this point, that any of these cases should be overruled, or that the process by which they were decided was illegitimate or even unacceptable, but only to underline Mr. Justice Black's constant reminder to his colleagues that the Court has no license to invalidate legislation which it thinks merely arbitrary or unreasonable. And no one was more sensitive than Mr. Justice Harlan to any suggestion that his approach to the Due Process Clause would lead to judges "roaming at large in the constitutional field." *Griswold v. Connecticut*. No one proceeded with more caution than he did when the validity of state or federal legislation was challenged in the name of the Due Process Clause.

This is surely the preferred approach. That the Court has ample precedent for the creation of new constitutional rights should not lead it to repeat the process at will. The Judiciary, including this Court, is the most vulnerable and comes nearest to illegitimacy when it deals with judge-made constitutional law having little or no cognizable roots in the language or even the design of the Constitution.... [T]he Court should be extremely reluctant to breathe still further substantive content into the Due Process Clause so as to strike down legislation adopted by a State or city to promote its welfare. Whenever the Judiciary does so, it unavoidably pre-empts for itself another part of the governance of the country without express constitutional authority.

II. Accepting the cases as they are and the Due Process Clause as construed by them, however, I think it evident that the threshold question in any due process attack on legislation, whether the challenge is procedural or substantive, is whether there is a deprivation of life, liberty, or property. With respect to "liberty," the statement of Mr. Justice Harlan in *Poe v. Ullman* most accurately reflects the thrust of prior decisions—that the Due Process Clause is triggered by a variety of interests, some much more important than others. These interests have included a wide range of freedoms in the purely commercial area such as the freedom to contract and the right to set one's own prices and wages. *Meyer v. Nebraska*, took a characteristically broad view of "liberty":

> While this Court has not attempted to define with exactness the liberty thus guaranteed, the term has received much consideration and some of the included things have been definitely stated. Without doubt, it denotes not merely freedom from bodily restraint but also the right of the individual to contract, to engage in any of the common occupations of life, to acquire useful knowledge, to marry, establish a home and bring up children, to worship God according to the dictates of his own conscience, and generally to enjoy those privileges long recognized at common law as essential to the orderly pursuit of happiness by free men.

As I have said, *Meyer* has not been overruled nor its definition of liberty rejected. The results reached in some of the cases cited by *Meyer* have been discarded or undermined by later cases, but those cases did not cut back the definition of liberty espoused by earlier decisions. They disagreed only, but sharply, as to the protection that was "due" the particular liberty interests involved. See, for example, *West Coast Hotel Co. v. Parrish* (1937), overruling *Adkins v. Children's Hospital*....

II. It would not be consistent with prior cases to restrict the liberties protected by the Due Process Clause to those fundamental interests "implicit in the concept of ordered liberty." *Palko v. Connecticut* (1937), from which this much-quoted phrase is taken, is not to the contrary. *Palko* was a criminal case, and the issue was thus not whether a protected liberty interest was at stake but what protective process was "due" that interest. The Court used the quoted standard to determine which of the protections of the Bill of Rights was due a criminal defendant in a state court within the meaning of the 14th Amendment. Nor do I think the broader view of "liberty" is inconsistent with or foreclosed by the dicta in *Roe v. Wade*, and *Paul v. Davis* (1976). These cases at most assert that only fundamental liberties will be given substantive protection; and they may be understood as merely identifying certain fundamental interests that the Court has deemed deserving of a heightened degree of protection under the Due Process Clause.

It seems to me that Mr. Justice Douglas was closest to the mark in *Poe v. Ullman*, when he said that the trouble with the holdings of the "old Court" was not in its definition of liberty but in its definition of the protections guaranteed to that liberty—"not in entertaining inquiries concerning the constitutionality of social legislation but in applying the standards that it did."

The term "liberty" is not, therefore, to be given a crabbed construction. I have no more difficulty than Mr. Justice Powell apparently does in concluding that appellant in this case properly asserts a liberty interest within the meaning of the Due Process Clause. The question is not one of liberty vel non. Rather, there being no procedural issue at stake, the issue is whether the precise interest involved the interest in having more than one set of grandchildren live in her home is entitled to such substantive protection under the Due Process Clause that this ordinance must be held invalid.

III. Looking at the doctrine of "substantive" due process as having to do with the possible invalidity of an official rule of conduct rather than of the procedures for enforcing that rule, I see the doctrine as taking several forms under the cases, each differing in the severity of review and the degree of protection offered to the individual. First, a court may merely assure itself that there is in fact a duly enacted law which proscribes the conduct sought to be prevented or sanctioned. In criminal cases, this approach is exemplified by the refusal of courts to enforce vague statutes that no reasonable person could understand as forbidding the challenged conduct. There is no such problem here.

Second is the general principle that "liberty may not be interfered with, under the guise of protecting the public interest, by legislative action which is arbitrary or without reasonable relation to some purpose within the competency of the State to effect." *Meyer v. Nebraska*. This means-end test appears to require that any statute restrictive of liberty have an ascertainable purpose and represent a rational means to achieve that purpose, whatever the nature of the liberty interest involved. This approach was part of the substantive due process doctrine prevalent earlier in the century, and it made serious inroads on the presumption of constitutionality supposedly accorded to state and federal legislation. But with *Nebbia v. New York* (1934), and other cases of the 1930's and 1940's such as *West Coast Hotel Co. v. Parrish* (1937), the courts came to demand far less from and to accord far more deference to legislative judgments. This was particularly true with respect to legislation seeking to control or regulate the economic life of the State or Nation. Even so, "while the legislative judgment on economic and business matters is 'well-nigh conclusive'..., it is not beyond judicial inquiry." *Poe v. Ullman* (Douglas, J., dissenting). No case that I know of, including *Ferguson v. Skrupa* (1963), has announced that there is some legislation with respect to which there no longer exists a means-ends test as a matter of substantive due process law. This is not surprising, for otherwise a protected liberty could be infringed by a law having no purpose or utility whatsoever. Of course, the current approach is to deal more gingerly with a state statute and to insist that the challenger bear the burden of demonstrating its unconstitutionality; and there is a broad category of cases in which substantive review is indeed mild and very similar to the original thought of *Munn v. Illinois* (1877), that "if a state of facts could exist that would justify such legislation," it passes its initial test.

There are various "liberties," however, which require that infringing legislation be given closer judicial scrutiny, not only with respect to existence of a purpose and the means employed, but also with respect to the importance of the purpose itself relative to the invaded interest. Some interest would appear almost impregnable to invasion, such as the freedoms of speech, press, and religion, and the freedom from cruel and unusual punishments. Other interests, for example, the right of association, the right to vote, and various claims sometimes referred to under the general rubric of the right to privacy, also weigh very heavily against state claims of authority to regulate. It is this category of interests which, as I understand it, Mr. Justice Stewart refers to as "implicit in the concept of ordered liberty." Because he would confine the reach of substantive due process protection to interests such as these and because he would not classify in this category the asserted right to share a house with the relatives involved here, he rejects the due process claim.

Given his premise, he is surely correct. Under our cases, the Due Process Clause extends substantial protection to various phases of family life, but none requires that the claim made here be sustained. I cannot believe that the interest in residing with more than one set of grandchildren is one that calls for any kind of heightened protection under the Due Process Clause. To say that one has a personal right to live with all, rather than some, of one's grandchildren and that this right is implicit in ordered liberty is, as my Brother Stewart says, "to extend the limited substantive contours of the Due Process Clause beyond recognition." The present claim is hardly one of which it could be said that "neither liberty nor justice would exist if (it) were sacrificed." *Palko v. Connecticut.*

Mr. Justice Powell would apparently construe the Due Process Clause to protect from all but quite important state regulatory interests any right or privilege that in his estimate is deeply rooted in the country's traditions. For me, this suggests a far too expansive charter for this Court.... What the deeply rooted traditions of the country are is arguable; which of them deserve the protection of the Due Process Clause is even more debatable. The suggested view would broaden enormously the horizons of the Clause; and, if the interest involved here is any measure of what the States would be forbidden to regulate, the courts would be substantively weighing and very likely invalidating a wide range of measures that Congress and state legislatures think appropriate to respond to a changing economic and social order.

Mrs. Moore's interest in having the offspring of more than one dependent son live with her qualifies as a liberty protected by the Due Process Clause; but, because of the nature of that particular interest, the demands of the Clause are satisfied once the Court is assured that the challenged proscription is the product of a duly enacted or promulgated statute, ordinance, or regulation and that it is not wholly lacking in purpose or utility....

* * *

The Court revisited the issue of grandparents' rights in *Troxel v. Granville* (2000). In a plurality decision, the Court struck down a Washington statute that allowed third parties (often grandparents) to gain visitation with children, even over the objection of a fit parent, if it were in the best interest of the child. The Court was concerned about the overbreadth of the statute, which seemed not to give appropriate deference to a parent's right to raise a child. While the various opinions were fragmented, a majority of the Court appeared to continue to recognize a fundamental right in parents to raise their children and a liberty interest in grandparents to have contact with their grandchildren.

Michael H. v. Gerald D: Background and Questions

1. In *Michael H. v. Gerald D* (1989), what methodology does Justice Scalia follow with reference to fundamental rights under the Due Process Clause? What does he find to be the source of fundamental rights that are less explicit in the text? Does his method limit the class of fundamental rights? What is the position of the Court on this point? Does protection of minority rights in *Michael H.* ultimately depend on the values of the majority? Is there a sense in which that is always so?

2. Why do Justices O'Connor and Kennedy refuse to join Justice Scalia in footnote 3? [The notes have been renumbered. The original number is 6.]

3. What, according to Justice Scalia, is the function of fundamental rights of the sort he explicates in footnote 3?

4. Why and how does Justice Scalia propose to limit the judicial recognition of fundamental rights that are less explicitly textual? Does he have valid concerns? Is his resolution correct?

5. Does his methodology logically apply to other constitutional clauses as well, for example to the Equal Protection Clause of the 14th Amendment? Under that clause the Court struck down state imposed segregation. Was that decision correct? Why?

Michael H. v. Gerald D.
491 U.S. 110 (1989)

[Plurality: Scalia, Rehnquist (C.J.). Concurring: Stevens. Concurring (in part): O'Connor and Kennedy. Dissenting: Brennan, White, Marshall, and Blackmun.]

Justice Scalia announced the judgment of the Court and delivered an opinion, in which the Chief Justice joins, and in all but footnote [3] of which O'Connor and Kennedy join.

[Gerald was married to Carole. During the marriage, Carole had an affair with Michael and conceived a child, Victoria. At various times during the marriage, Carole left Gerald and she and Victoria lived with Michael. As a result, Victoria developed psychological bonds with both Michael and Gerald. At the time of this litigation, Carole had decided to resume the marriage, and she and Victoria were living with Gerald. Michael and Victoria wanted to continue to visit one another, a desire opposed by Carole and Gerald. The issue in the case was whether Michael was entitled to a judicial hearing to decide if it were in Victoria's best interest to continue visitation. Michael's right to this hearing depended on whether he had a liberty interest in visitation with his child.]

Under California law, a child born to a married woman living with her husband is presumed to be a child of the marriage. The presumption of legitimacy may be rebutted only by the husband or wife, and then only in limited circumstances. The instant appeal presents the claim that this presumption infringes upon the due process rights of a man who wishes to establish his paternity of a child born to the wife of another man, and the claim that it infringes upon the constitutional right of the child to maintain a relationship with her natural father....

III. [I]t is necessary to clarify what [Michael H.] sought and what he was denied. California law, like nature itself, makes no provision for dual fatherhood. Michael was seeking to be declared the father of Victoria. The immediate benefit he evidently sought to obtain from that status was visitation rights....

Michael contends as a matter of substantive due process that, because he has established a parental relationship with Victoria, protection of Gerald's and Carole's marital union is an insufficient state interest to support termination of that relationship. This argument is, of course, predicated on the assertion that Michael has a constitutionally protected liberty interest in his relationship with Victoria.

It is an established part of our constitutional jurisprudence that the term "liberty" in the Due Process Clause extends beyond freedom from physical restraint. See, e.g., *Pierce v. Society of Sisters* (1925); *Meyer v. Nebraska* (1923). Without that core textual meaning as a limitation, defining the scope of the Due Process Clause "has at times been a treacherous field for this Court," giving "reason for concern lest the only limits to ... judicial intervention become the predilections of those who happen at the time to be Members of this Court." *Moore v. East Cleveland* (1977)....

In an attempt to limit and guide interpretation of the Clause, we have insisted not merely that the interest denominated as a "liberty" be "fundamental" (a concept that, in isolation, is hard to objectify), but also that it be an interest traditionally protected by our society.[1] As we have put it, the Due Process Clause affords only those protections "so rooted in the traditions and conscience of our people as to be ranked as fundamental." *Snyder v. Massachusetts* (1934) (Cardozo, J.). Our cases reflect "continual insistence upon respect for the teachings of history [and] solid recognition of the basic values that underlie our society...." *Griswold v. Connecticut* (1965) (Harlan, J., concurring in judgment).

This insistence that the asserted liberty interest be rooted in history and tradition is evident, as elsewhere, in our cases according constitutional protection to certain parental rights.... As Justice Powell stated for the plurality in *Moore v. East Cleveland*: "Our decisions establish that the Constitution protects the sanctity of the family precisely because the institution of the family is deeply rooted in this Nation's history and tradition."

Thus, the legal issue in the present case reduces to whether the relationship between persons in the situation of Michael and Victoria has been treated as a protected family unit under the historic practices of our society, or whether on any other basis it has been accorded special protection. We think it impossible to find that it has. In fact, quite to the contrary, our traditions have protected the marital family (Gerald, Carole, and the child they acknowledge to be theirs) against the sort of claim Michael asserts[2]....

What Michael asserts here is a right to have himself declared the natural father and thereby to obtain parental prerogatives. What he must establish, therefore, is not that our society has traditionally allowed a natural father in his circumstances to establish paternity, but that it has traditionally accorded such a father parental rights, or at least has not traditionally denied them. Even if the law in all States had always been that the entire world could challenge the marital presumption and obtain a declaration as to who was the natural father, that would not advance Michael's claim. Thus, it is ultimately irrelevant, even for purposes of determining current social attitudes towards the alleged substantive right Michael asserts, that the present law in a number of States appears to allow the natural father—including the natural father who has not established a relationship with the child—the theoretical power to rebut the marital presumption.... What counts is whether the States in fact award substantive parental rights to the natural father of a child conceived within, and born into, an extant marital union

---

1. We do not understand what Justice Brennan has in mind by an interest "that society traditionally has thought important ... without protecting it." ... The protection need not take the form of an explicit constitutional provision or statutory guarantee, but it must at least exclude (all that is necessary to decide the present case) a societal tradition of enacting laws denying the interest. Nor do we understand why our practice of limiting the Due Process Clause to traditionally protected interests turns the Clause "into a redundancy." ... Its purpose is to prevent future generations from lightly casting aside important traditional values—not to enable this Court to invent new ones.

2. Justice Brennan insists that in determining whether a liberty interest exists we must look at Michael's relationship with Victoria in isolation, without reference to the circumstance that Victoria's mother was married to someone else when the child was conceived, and that that woman and her husband wish to raise the child as their own.... We cannot imagine what compels this strange procedure of looking at the act which is assertedly the subject of a liberty interest in isolation from its effect upon other people—rather like inquiring whether there is a liberty interest in firing a gun where the case at hand happens to involve its discharge into another person's body. The logic of Justice Brennan's position leads to the conclusion that if Michael had begotten Victoria by rape, that fact would in no way affect his possession of a liberty interest in his relationship with her.

that wishes to embrace the child. We are not aware of a single case, old or new, that has done so. This is not the stuff of which fundamental rights qualifying as liberty interests are made.[3] ...

We do not accept Justice Brennan's criticism that this result "squashes" the liberty that consists of "the freedom not to conform." It seems to us that reflects the erroneous view that there is only one side to this controversy—that one disposition can expand a "liberty" of sorts without contracting an equivalent"liberty" on the other side. Such a happy choice is rarely available. Here, to provide protection to an adulterous natural father is to deny protection to a marital father, and vice versa. If Michael has a "freedom not to conform" (whatever that means), Gerald must equivalently have a "freedom to conform." One of them will pay a price for asserting that "freedom"—Michael by being unable to act as father of the child he has adulterously begotten, or Gerald by being unable to preserve the integrity of the traditional family unit he and Victoria have established. Our disposition does not choose between these two "freedoms," but leaves that to the people

---

3. Justice Brennan criticizes our methodology in using historical traditions specifically relating to the rights of an adulterous natural father, rather than inquiring more generally "whether parenthood is an interest that historically has received our attention and protection." ... There seems to us no basis for the contention that this methodology is "nove[l]." ... For example, in *Bowers v. Hardwick* (1986), we noted that at the time the 14th Amendment was ratified all but 5 of the 37 States had criminal sodomy laws, that all 50 of the States had such laws prior to 1961, and that 24 States and the District of Columbia continued to have them; and we concluded from that record, regarding that very specific aspect of sexual conduct, that "to claim that a right to engage in such conduct is 'deeply rooted in this Nation's history and tradition' or 'implicit in the concept of ordered liberty' is, at best, facetious." ... In *Roe v. Wade* (1973), we spent about a fifth of our opinion negating the proposition that there was a longstanding tradition of laws proscribing abortion....

We do not understand why, having rejected our focus upon the societal tradition regarding the natural father's rights vis-a-vis a child whose mother is married to another man, Justice Brennan would choose to focus instead upon "parenthood." Why should the relevant category not be even more general—perhaps "family relationships"; or "personal relationships"; or even "emotional attachments in general"? Though the dissent has no basis for the level of generality it would select, we do: We refer to the most specific level at which a relevant tradition protecting, or denying protection to, the asserted right can be identified. If, for example, there were no societal tradition, either way, regarding the rights of the natural father of a child adulterously conceived, we would have to consult, and (if possible) reason from, the traditions regarding natural fathers in general. But there is such a more specific tradition, and it unqualifiedly denies protection to such a parent.

One would think that Justice Brennan would appreciate the value of consulting the most specific tradition available, since he acknowledges that "[e]ven if we can agree ... that 'family' and 'parenthood' are part of the good life, it is absurd to assume that we can agree on the content of those terms and destructive to pretend that we do." ... Because such general traditions provide such imprecise guidance, they permit judges to dictate rather than discern the society's views. The need, if arbitrary decisionmaking is to be avoided, to adopt the most specific tradition as the point of reference—or at least to announce, as Justice Brennan declines to do, some other criterion for selecting among the innumerable relevant traditions that could be consulted—is well enough exemplified by the fact that in the present case Justice Brennan's opinion and Justice O'Connor's opinion ... which disapproves this footnote, both appeal to tradition, but on the basis of the tradition they select reach opposite results. Although assuredly having the virtue (if it be that) of leaving judges free to decide as they think best when the unanticipated occurs, a rule of law that binds neither by text nor by any particular, identifiable tradition is no rule of law at all.

Finally, we may note that this analysis is not inconsistent with the result in cases such as *Griswold v. Connecticut*, or *Eisenstadt v. Baird* (1972). None of those cases acknowledged a longstanding and still extant societal tradition withholding the very right pronounced to be the subject of a liberty interest and then rejected it. Justice Brennan must do so here. In this case, the existence of such a tradition, continuing to the present day, refutes any possible contention that the alleged right is "so rooted in the traditions and conscience of our people as to be ranked as fundamental," *Snyder v. Massachusetts* (1934), or "implicit in the concept of ordered liberty," *Palko v. Connecticut* (1937).

of California. Justice Brennan's approach chooses one of them as the constitutional imperative, on no apparent basis except that the unconventional is to be preferred.

IV.... The judgment of the California Court of Appeal is Affirmed.

Justice O'Connor, with whom Justice Kennedy joins, concurring in part.

I concur in all but footnote [3] of Justice Scalia's opinion. This footnote sketches a mode of historical analysis to be used when identifying liberty interests protected by the Due Process Clause of the 14th Amendment that may be somewhat inconsistent with our past decisions in this area. See *Griswold v. Connecticut* (1965)*; Eisenstadt v. Baird* (1972). On occasion the Court has characterized relevant traditions protecting asserted rights at levels of generality that might not be "the most specific level" available.... See *Loving v. Virginia* (1967); *Turner v. Safley* (1987); cf. *United States v. Stanley* (1987) (O'Connor, J., concurring in part and dissenting in part). I would not foreclose the unanticipated by the prior imposition of a single mode of historical analysis. *Poe v. Ullman* (1961) (Harlan, J., dissenting).

Justice Stevens, concurring in the judgment. [Omitted]

Justice Brennan, with whom Justice Marshall and Justice Blackmun join, dissenting....

I. Once we recognized that the "liberty" protected by the Due Process Clause of the 14th Amendment encompasses more than freedom from bodily restraint, today's plurality opinion emphasizes, the concept was cut loose from one natural limitation on its meaning. This innovation paved the way, so the plurality hints, for judges to substitute their own preferences for those of elected officials. Dissatisfied with this supposedly unbridled and uncertain state of affairs, the plurality casts about for another limitation on the concept of liberty.

It finds this limitation in "tradition." Apparently oblivious to the fact that this concept can be as malleable and as elusive as "liberty" itself, the plurality pretends that tradition places a discernible border around the Constitution. The pretense is seductive; it would be comforting to believe that a search for "tradition" involves nothing more idiosyncratic or complicated than poring through dusty volumes on American history. Yet, as Justice White observed in his dissent in *Moore v. East Cleveland* (1977): "What the deeply rooted traditions of the country are is arguable." Indeed, wherever I would begin to look for an interest "deeply rooted in the country's traditions," one thing is certain: I would not stop (as does the plurality) at Bracton, or Blackstone, or Kent, or even the American Law Reports in conducting my search. Because reasonable people can disagree about the content of particular traditions, and because they can disagree even about which traditions are relevant to the definition of "liberty," the plurality has not found the objective boundary that it seeks....

It is ironic that an approach so utterly dependent on tradition is so indifferent to our precedents. Citing barely a handful of this Court's numerous decisions defining the scope of the liberty protected by the Due Process Clause to support its reliance on tradition, the plurality acts as though English legal treatises and the American Law Reports always have provided the sole source for our constitutional principles. They have not. Just as common-law notions no longer define the "property" that the Constitution protects, see *Goldberg v. Kelly* (1970), neither do they circumscribe the "liberty" that it guarantees. On the contrary, "'[l]iberty' and 'property' are broad and majestic terms. They are among the '[g]reat [constitutional] concepts ... purposely left to gather meaning from experience.... [T]hey relate to the whole domain of social and economic fact, and the statesmen who founded this Nation knew too well that only a stagnant society remains unchanged.'" *Board of Regents of State Colleges v. Roth* (1972).

It is not that tradition has been irrelevant to our prior decisions. Throughout our decisionmaking in this important area runs the theme that certain interests and practices—freedom from physical restraint, marriage, childbearing, childrearing, and others—form the core of our definition of "liberty." Our solicitude for these interests is partly the result of the fact that the Due Process Clause would seem an empty promise if it did not protect them, and partly the result of the historical and traditional importance of these interests in our society. In deciding cases arising under the Due Process Clause, therefore, we have considered whether the concrete limitation under consideration impermissibly impinges upon one of these more generalized interests.

Today's plurality, however, does not ask whether parenthood is an interest that historically has received our attention and protection; the answer to that question is too clear for dispute. Instead, the plurality asks whether the specific variety of parenthood under consideration—a natural father's relationship with a child whose mother is married to another man—has enjoyed such protection.

If we had looked to tradition with such specificity in past cases, many a decision would have reached a different result. Surely the use of contraceptives by unmarried couples, *Eisenstadt v. Baird* (1972), or even by married couples, *Griswold v. Connecticut* (1965); the freedom from corporal punishment in schools, *Ingraham v. Wright* (1977); the freedom from an arbitrary transfer from a prison to a psychiatric institution, *Vitek v. Jones* (1980); and even the right to raise one's natural but illegitimate children, *Stanley v. Illinois* (1972), were not "interest[s] traditionally protected by our society," at the time of their consideration by this Court. If we had asked, therefore, in *Eisenstadt*, *Griswold*, *Ingraham*, *Vitek*, or *Stanley* itself whether the specific interest under consideration had been traditionally protected, the answer would have been a resounding "no." That we did not ask this question in those cases highlights the novelty of the interpretive method that the plurality opinion employs today.

The plurality's interpretive method is more than novel; it is misguided. It ignores the good reasons for limiting the role of "tradition" in interpreting the Constitution's deliberately capacious language. In the plurality's constitutional universe, we may not take notice of the fact that the original reasons for the conclusive presumption of paternity are out of place in a world in which blood tests can prove virtually beyond a shadow of a doubt who sired a particular child and in which the fact of illegitimacy no longer plays the burdensome and stigmatizing role it once did.... [B]y describing the decisive question as whether Michael's and Victoria's interest is one that has been "traditionally protected by our society," rather than one that society traditionally has thought important (with or without protecting it), and by suggesting that our sole function is to "discern the society's views," the plurality acts as if the only purpose of the Due Process Clause is to confirm the importance of interests already protected by a majority of the States. Transforming the protection afforded by the Due Process Clause into a redundancy mocks those who, with care and purpose, wrote the 14th Amendment....

II. The plurality's reworking of our interpretive approach is all the more troubling because it is unnecessary....

The better approach ... is to ask whether the specific parent-child relationship under consideration is close enough to the interests that we already have protected to be deemed an aspect of "liberty" as well. On the facts before us, therefore, the question is not what "level of generality" should be used to describe the relationship between Michael and Victoria, see ante, n. [3], but whether the relationship under consideration is sufficiently substantial to qualify as a liberty interest under our prior cases....

Justice White, with whom Justice Brennan joins, dissenting. [Omitted.]

Substantive Due Process and Less Textually Explicit Rights

In *Michael H. v. Gerald D.*(1989), Justice Scalia conceded that there is not a "core textual meaning" to the "liberty" found in the 14th Amendment's Due Process Clause. In order to limit judicial discretion, he contends that the clause should protect individuals only if their behavior falls within the "most specific level at which a relevant tradition protecting, or denying protection to, the asserted right can be identified." What is the role of judicial reasoning by analogy to prior cases in this standard? Does history provide clear and crisp answers?

Recall the text of the 9th Amendment: "The enumeration in the Constitution, of certain rights, shall not be construed to deny or disparage others retained by the people." Reconsider also the remarks of Senator Howard, speaking to the Senate on behalf of the Committee that drafted the 14th Amendment. In speaking of the scope of the new Privileges or Immunities Clause, he makes reference to Justice Washington's discussion of Article IV, §2, in *Corfield v. Coryell* (1823). He then continues:

> Such is the character of the privileges and immunities spoken of in the second section of the 4th article of the Constitution. To these privileges and immunities, whatever they may be—for they are not and cannot be fully defined in their entire extent and precise nature—to these should be added the personal rights guaranteed and secured by the first eight amendments of the Constitution; such as the freedom of speech and of the press; the right of the people peaceably to assemble and petition the Government for a redress of grievances....

What does Senator Howard mean when he says that these rights "are not and cannot be fully defined in their entire extent and precise nature"? What should a court do with such rights? Should it do anything? What rights does the 9th Amendment "retain" for the people?

What problems are avoided by Justice Scalia's approach? What problems are created?

VII. Liberty and Sexual Autonomy: Restrictions on Private Sexual Behavior

Historically states regulated sexual practices under their police powers. Fornication, sodomy, adultery, and statutory rape statutes are common examples. Should recognition of greater privacy rights in the marital relationship lead to greater privacy rights for those engaging in non-traditional practices? The Supreme Court in *Bowers v. Hardwick* (1986) rejected a challenge by a homosexual to a Georgia statute that criminalized sodomy. Since *Bowers*, several states have invalidated sodomy statutes under their state constitutions—including, ironically, Georgia. *See e.g., Powell v. State* (Ga. 1998); *Gryczan v. State* (Mont. 1997); *Kentucky v. Wasson* (Ky. 1992).

A. Liberty and Sodomy: *Bowers*

Bowers v. Hardwick: Background

1. What is the narrow holding of *Bowers v. Hardwick* (1986)? What clause of the Constitution is the Court considering?
2. What is the implication of the decision for currently recognized fundamental rights that are not explicitly set out in the text of the Constitution?
3. What is the significance of the Court's decision for future claims based on *asserted* fundamental rights not explicitly set out in the text?
4. What is the basis for the claim in the dissenting opinions in *Bowers* that the conduct is protected by the right to privacy?
5. Assume that after *Bowers*, a heterosexual unmarried couple is apprehended engaging in oral sex. They are prosecuted and convicted under the North Carolina Crime Against Nature statute and sentenced to six years in prison. Is the statute valid as applied in this case? Would it make any difference if the couple were married?
6. What methods and tests are used by the majority in its examination of the claim of a fundamental right to sexual privacy in *Bowers*? How does it decide if Mr. Hardwick has a fundamental right to sexual privacy? What methodology is followed by the dissent? How does the majority in *Kentucky v. Wasson*, *infra*, approach this issue?

* * *

In 1982, Hardwick (the respondent) was charged with violating the Georgia sodomy statute. The statute holds in relevant part: "A person commits the offense of sodomy when he performs or submits to any sexual act involving the sex organs of one person and the mouth or anus of another...." The penalty ranges from one to twenty years in prison.

The charge arose when a police officer came to Hardwick's apartment to serve a warrant in an unrelated case. A guest let the officer in and told him Hardwick was in the bedroom. When the officer opened the bedroom door he found Hardwick and another man having oral sex. The officer charged Hardwick.

The district attorney elected not to prosecute. Hardwick nonetheless filed a civil action seeking to have the statute declared unconstitutional. The 11th Circuit agreed with him and the Supreme Court granted review. The District Court also dismissed a challenge by a heterosexual couple on ripeness grounds. This ruling was not appealed to the Supreme Court.

The following is an excerpt from an interview with Michael Hardwick reprinted with the permission of The Free Press, A Division of Simon & Schuster Adult Publishing Group from *The Courage of Their Convictions: Sixteen Americans Who Fought Their Way to the Supreme Court*, by Peter Irons. Copyright © 1988 by Peter Irons.

> I had been working for about a year, in a gay bar that was getting ready to open up a discotheque. I was there one night until seven o'clock in the morning, helping them put in insulation. When I left, I went up to the bar and they gave me a beer. I was kind of debating whether I wanted to leave, because I was pretty exhausted, or stay and finish the beer. I decided to leave, and I opened the door and threw the beer bottle into this trash can by the front door of the bar. I wasn't really in the mood for the beer.

Just as I did that I saw a cop drive by. I walked about a block, and he turned around and came back and asked me where the beer was. I told him I had thrown it in the trash can in front of the bar. He insisted I had thrown the beer bottle right as he pulled up. He made me get in the car and asked what I was doing. I told him that I worked there, which immediately identified me as a homosexual, because he knew it was a homosexual bar. He was enjoying *his* position as opposed to *my* position.

After about twenty minutes of bickering he drove me back so I could show him where the beer bottle was. There was no way of getting out of the back of a cop car. I told him it was in the trash can and he said he couldn't see it from the car. I said, "Fine, just give me a ticket for drinking in public." He was just busting my chops because he knew I was gay.

Anyway, the ticket had a court date on the top and a date in the center and they didn't coincide; they were one day apart. Tuesday was the court date, and the officer had written Wednesday on top of the ticket. So Tuesday, two hours after my court date, he was at my house with a warrant for my arrest. This was Officer Torick. This was unheard of, because it takes forty-eight hours to process a warrant. What I didn't realize, and didn't find out until later, was that he had personally processed a warrant for the first time in ten years. So I think there is reason to believe that he had it out for me.

I wasn't there when he came with the warrant. I got home that afternoon and my roommate said there was a cop here with a warrant. I said, That's impossible; my court date isn't until tomorrow. I went and got my ticket and realized the court date was Tuesday, not Wednesday. I asked my roommate if he'd seen the warrant and he said he hadn't. So I went down to the county clerk and showed him the discrepancy on the ticket. He brought it before the judge, and he fined me $50. I told the county clerk the cop had already been at my house with a warrant and he said that was impossible. He wrote me a receipt just in case I had any problems with it further down the road. That was that, and I thought I had taken care of it and everything was finished, and I didn't give it much thought.

Three weeks went by, and my mom had come up to visit me. I came home one morning after work at 6:30 and there were three guys standing in front of my house. I cannot say for sure that they had anything to do with this, but they were very straight, middle thirties, civilian clothes. I got out of the car, turned around, and they said "Michael" and I said yes, and they proceeded to beat the hell out of me. Tore all the cartilage out of my nose, kicked me in the face, cracked about six of my ribs. I passed out. I don't know how long I was unconscious. When I came to, all I could think of was, God, I don't want my mom to see me like this!

I managed to crawl up the stairs into the house, into the back bedroom. What I didn't realize was that I'd left a trail of blood all the way back. My mom woke up, found this trail of blood, found me passed out, and just freaked out. I assured her that everything was okay, that it was like a fluke accident, these guys were drunk or whatever. They weren't drunk, they were ruffians, and they knew who I was. I convinced her everything was okay and she left to go visit a friend in Pennsylvania.

I had a friend come in a few days later who was from out of town, in Atlanta to apply for a government job. He waited for me to get off work. That night at work, another friend of mine had gotten really drunk, and I took his car keys, put him in a cab, and sent him to my house, so he was passed out on the couch in the living room. He did not hear me and my friend come in. I retired with my friend. He had left the front door open, and Officer Torick came into my house about 8:30 in the morning. He had a warrant that had not been valid for three weeks and that he didn't bother to call in and check on. Officer Torick came in and woke up the guy who was passed out on my couch, who didn't know I was there and had a friend with me.

Officer Torick then came to my bedroom. The door was cracked, and the door opened up and I looked up and there was nobody there. I just blew it off as the wind and went back to what I was involved in, which was mutual oral sex. About thirty-five seconds went by and I heard another noise and looked up, and this officer is standing in my bedroom. He identified himself when he realized I had seen him. He said, "My name is Officer Torick. Michael Hardwick, you are under arrest." I said, "For what? What are you doing in my bedroom?" He said, "I have a warrant for your arrest." I told him the warrant isn't any good. He said, "It doesn't matter, because I [am] acting under good faith."

I asked Torick if he would leave the room so we could get dressed and he said, "There's no reason for that, because I have already seen you in your most intimate aspect." He stood there and watched us get dressed, and then he brought us over to a substation. We waited in the car for about twenty-five minutes, handcuffed to the back floor. Then he brought us in and made sure everyone in the holding cells and guard and people who were processing us knew I was in there for "cocksucking" and that I should be able to get what I was looking for. The guards were having a real good time with that.

Bowers v. Hardwick
478 U.S. 186 (1986)

[Majority: White, Burger (C.J.), Powell, Rehnquist, and O'Connor. Concurring: Burger (C.J.) and Powell. Dissenting: Blackmun, Stevens, Brennan, and Marshall.]

Justice White delivered the opinion of the Court....

This case does not require a judgment on whether laws against sodomy between consenting adults in general, or between homosexuals in particular, are wise or desirable. It raises no question about the right or propriety of state legislative decisions to repeal their laws that criminalize homosexual sodomy, or of state-court decisions invalidating those laws on state constitutional grounds. The issue presented is whether the Federal Constitution confers a fundamental right upon homosexuals to engage in sodomy and hence invalidates the laws of the many States that still make such conduct illegal and have done so for a very long time. The case also calls for some judgment about the limits of the Court's role in carrying out its constitutional mandate.

We first register our disagreement with the Court of Appeals and with respondent that the Court's prior cases have construed the Constitution to confer a right of privacy that extends to homosexual sodomy and for all intents and purposes have decided this case. The reach of this line of cases was [recently] sketched in *Carey v. Population Services International* (1977): *Pierce v. Society of Sisters* (1925) and *Meyer v. Nebraska* (1923) were described as dealing with child rearing and education; *Prince v. Massachusetts* (1944) with family relationships; *Skinner v. Oklahoma* (1942) with procreation; *Loving v. Virginia* (1967) with marriage; *Griswold v. Connecticut* (1965) and *Eisenstadt v. Baird* (1972) with contraception; and *Roe v. Wade* (1973) with abortion. The latter three cases were interpreted as construing the Due Process Clause of the 14th Amendment to confer a fundamental individual right to decide whether or not to beget or bear a child.

Accepting the decisions in these cases and the above description of them, we think it evident that none of the rights announced in those cases bears any resemblance to the claimed constitutional right of homosexuals to engage in acts of sodomy that is asserted in this case. No connection between family, marriage, or procreation on the one hand and homosexual activity on the other has been demonstrated, either by the Court of Appeals or by respondent. Moreover, any claim that these cases nevertheless stand for the proposition that any kind of private sexual conduct between consenting adults is constitutionally insulated from state proscription is unsupportable. Indeed, the Court's opinion in *Carey* twice asserted that the privacy right, which the *Griswold* line of cases found to be one of the protections provided by the Due Process Clause, did not reach so far.

Precedent aside, however, respondent would have us announce, as the Court of Appeals did, a fundamental right to engage in homosexual sodomy. This we are quite unwilling to do. It is true that despite the language of the Due Process Clauses of the 5th and 14th Amendments, which appears to focus only on the processes by which life, liberty, or property is taken, the cases are legion in which those Clauses have been interpreted to have substantive content, subsuming rights that to a great extent are immune from federal or state regulation or proscription. Among such cases are those recognizing rights that have little or no textual support in the constitutional language. *Meyer*, *Prince*, and *Pierce* fall in this category, as do the privacy cases from *Griswold* to *Carey*.

Striving to assure itself and the public that announcing rights not readily identifiable in the Constitution's text involves much more than the imposition of the Justices' own choice of values on the States and the Federal Government, the Court has sought to identify the nature of the rights qualifying for heightened judicial protection. In *Palko v. Connecticut* (1937), it was said that this category includes those fundamental liberties that are "implicit in the concept of ordered liberty," such that "neither liberty nor justice would exist if [they] were sacrificed." A different description of fundamental liberties appeared in *Moore v. East Cleveland* (1977) (opinion of Powell, J.), where they are characterized as those liberties that are "deeply rooted in this Nation's history and tradition."

It is obvious to us that neither of these formulations would extend a fundamental right to homosexuals to engage in acts of consensual sodomy. Proscriptions against that conduct have ancient roots. See generally *Survey on the Constitutional Right to Privacy in the Context of Homosexual Activity*, 40 U. Miami L. Rev. 521, 525 (1986). Sodomy was a criminal offense at common law and was forbidden by the laws of the original 13 States when they ratified the Bill of Rights. In 1868, when the 14th Amendment was ratified, all but 5 of the 37 States in the Union had criminal sodomy laws. In fact, until 1961, all 50 States outlawed sodomy, and today, 24 States and the District of Columbia continue to provide criminal penalties for sodomy performed in private and between consenting adults. Against this background, to claim that a right to engage in such conduct is "deeply rooted in this Nation's history and tradition" or "implicit in the concept of ordered liberty" is, at best, facetious.

Nor are we inclined to take a more expansive view of our authority to discover new fundamental rights imbedded in the Due Process Clause. The Court is most vulnerable and comes nearest to illegitimacy when it deals with judge-made constitutional law having little or no cognizable roots in the language or design of the Constitution. That this is so was painfully demonstrated by the face-off between the Executive and the Court in the

1930's, which resulted in the repudiation of much of the substantive gloss that the Court had placed on the Due Process Clauses of the 5th and 14th Amendments. There should be, therefore, great resistance to expand the substantive reach of those Clauses, particularly if it requires redefining the category of rights deemed to be fundamental. Otherwise, the Judiciary necessarily takes to itself further authority to govern the country without express constitutional authority. The claimed right pressed on us today falls far short of overcoming this resistance.

Respondent, however, asserts that the result should be different where the homosexual conduct occurs in the privacy of the home. He relies on *Stanley v. Georgia* (1969), where the Court held that the 1st Amendment prevents conviction for possessing and reading obscene material in the privacy of one's home: "If the 1st Amendment means anything, it means that a State has no business telling a man, sitting alone in his house, what books he may read or what films he may watch."

Stanley did protect conduct that would not have been protected outside the home, and it partially prevented the enforcement of state obscenity laws; but the decision was firmly grounded in the 1st Amendment. The right pressed upon us here has no similar support in the text of the Constitution, and it does not qualify for recognition under the prevailing principles for construing the 14th Amendment. Its limits are also difficult to discern. Plainly enough, otherwise illegal conduct is not always immunized whenever it occurs in the home. Victimless crimes, such as the possession and use of illegal drugs, do not escape the law where they are committed at home. *Stanley* itself recognized that its holding offered no protection for the possession in the home of drugs, firearms, or stolen goods. And if respondent's submission is limited to the voluntary sexual conduct between consenting adults, it would be difficult, except by fiat, to limit the claimed right to homosexual conduct while leaving exposed to prosecution adultery, incest, and other sexual crimes even though they are committed in the home. We are unwilling to start down that road.

Even if the conduct at issue here is not a fundamental right, respondent asserts that there must be a rational basis for the law and that there is none in this case other than the presumed belief of a majority of the electorate in Georgia that homosexual sodomy is immoral and unacceptable. This is said to be an inadequate rationale to support the law. The law, however, is constantly based on notions of morality, and if all laws representing essentially moral choices are to be invalidated under the Due Process Clause, the courts will be very busy indeed. Even respondent makes no such claim, but insists that majority sentiments about the morality of homosexuality should be declared inadequate. We do not agree, and are unpersuaded that the sodomy laws of some 25 States should be invalidated on this basis.

Accordingly, the judgment of the Court of Appeals is Reversed.

Chief Justice Burger, concurring.

I join the Court's opinion, but I write separately to underscore my view that in constitutional terms there is no such thing as a fundamental right to commit homosexual sodomy.

As the Court notes, the proscriptions against sodomy have very "ancient roots." Decisions of individuals relating to homosexual conduct have been subject to state intervention throughout the history of Western civilization. Condemnation of those practices is firmly rooted in Judeao-Christian moral and ethical standards. Homosexual sodomy was a capital crime under Roman law. See Code Theod. 9.7.6; Code Just. 9.9.31. See also D. Bailey, *Homosexuality and the Western Christian Tradition* 70–81 (1975). During the English Reformation when powers of the ecclesiastical courts were transferred to the King's Courts, the first English statute criminalizing sodomy was passed. 25 Hen. VIII, ch. 6. Blackstone described "the infamous crime against nature" as an offense of "deeper malignity" than rape, a heinous act "the very mention of which is a disgrace to human nature," and "a crime not fit to be named." 4 W. Blackstone, *Commentaries*. The common law of England, including its prohibition of sodomy, became the received law of Georgia and the other Colonies. In 1816 the Georgia Legislature passed the statute at issue here, and that statute has been continuously in force in one form or another since that time. To hold that the act of homosexual sodomy is somehow protected as a fundamental right would be to cast aside millennia of moral teaching.

This is essentially not a question of personal "preferences" but rather of the legislative authority of the State. I find nothing in the Constitution depriving a State of the power to enact the statute challenged here.

Justice Powell, concurring.

I join the opinion of the Court. I agree with the Court that there is no fundamental right—i.e., no substantive right under the Due Process Clause—such as that claimed by respondent Hardwick, and found to exist by the Court of Appeals. This is not to suggest, however, that respondent may not be protected by the 8th Amendment of the Constitution. The Georgia statute at issue in this case, Ga. Code Ann. § 16-6-2 (1984), authorizes a court to imprison a person for up to 20 years for a single private, consensual act of sodomy. In my view, a prison sentence for such conduct—certainly a sentence of long duration—would create a serious 8th Amendment issue. Under the Georgia statute a single act of sodomy, even in the private setting of a home, is a felony comparable in terms of the possible sentence imposed to serious felonies such as aggravated battery, § 16-5-24, first-degree arson, § 16-7-60, and robbery, § 16-8-40.

In this case, however, respondent has not been tried, much less convicted and sentenced. Moreover, respondent has not raised the 8th Amendment issue below. For these reasons this constitutional argument is not before us.

Justice Blackmun, with whom Justice Brennan, Justice Marshall, and Justice Stevens join, dissenting.

This case is no more about "a fundamental right to engage in homosexual sodomy," as the Court purports to declare, than *Stanley v. Georgia* (1969), was about a fundamental right to watch obscene movies, or *Katz v. United States* (1967), was about a fundamental right to place interstate bets from a telephone booth. Rather, this case is about "the most comprehensive of rights and the right most valued by civilized men," namely, "the right to be let alone." *Olmstead v. United States* (1928) (Brandeis, J., dissenting).

The statute at issue, Ga. Code Ann. § 16-6-2 (1984), denies individuals the right to decide for themselves whether to engage in particular forms of private, consensual sexual activity. The Court concludes that § 16-6-2 is valid essentially because "the laws of ... many States ... still make such conduct illegal and have done so for a very long time." But the fact that the moral judgments expressed by statutes like § 16-6-2 may be "'natural and familiar ... ought not to conclude our judgment upon the question whether statutes embodying them conflict with the Constitution of the United States.'" *Roe v. Wade* (1973), quoting *Lochner v. New York* (1905) (Holmes, J., dissenting). Like Justice Holmes, I believe that "[i]t is revolting to have no better reason for a rule of law than that so it was laid down in the time of Henry IV. It is still more revolting if the grounds upon which it was laid down have vanished long since, and the rule simply persists from blind imitation of the past." Holmes, *The Path of the Law*, 10 Harv. L. Rev. 457, 469 (1897). I believe we must analyze Hardwick's claim in the light of the values that underlie the constitutional right to privacy. If that right means anything, it means that, before Georgia can prosecute its citizens for making choices about the most intimate aspects of their lives, it must do more than assert that the choice they have made is an "'abominable crime not fit to be named among Christians.'" *Herring v. State* (Ga. 1904).

I.... A fair reading of the statute and of the complaint clearly reveals that the majority has distorted the question this case presents.

First, the Court's almost obsessive focus on homosexual activity is particularly hard to justify in light of the broad language Georgia has used. Unlike the Court, the Georgia Legislature has not proceeded on the assumption that homosexuals are so different from other citizens that their lives may be controlled in a way that would not be tolerated if it limited the choices of those other citizens. Rather, Georgia has provided that "[a] person commits the offense of sodomy when he performs or submits to any sexual act involving the sex organs of one person and the mouth or anus of another." Ga. Code Ann. § 16-6-2(a) (1984). The sex or status of the persons who engage in the act is irrelevant as a matter of state law. In fact, to the extent I can discern a legislative purpose for Georgia's 1968 enactment of § 16-6-2, that purpose seems to have been to broaden the coverage of the law to reach heterosexual as well as homosexual activity. I therefore see no basis for the Court's decision to treat this case as an "as applied" challenge to § 16-6-2 or for Georgia's attempt, both in its brief and at oral argument, to defend § 16-6-2 solely on the grounds that it prohibits homosexual activity. Michael Hardwick's standing may rest in significant part on Georgia's apparent willingness to enforce against homosexuals a law it seems not to have any desire to enforce against heterosexuals. But his claim that § 16-6-2 involves an unconstitutional intrusion into his privacy and his right of intimate association does not depend in any way on his sexual orientation....

II. "Our cases long have recognized that the Constitution embodies a promise that a certain private sphere of individual liberty will be kept largely beyond the reach of government." *Thornburgh v. American College of Obstetricians & Gynecologists* (1986). In construing the right to privacy, the Court has proceeded along two somewhat distinct, albeit complementary, lines. First, it has recognized a privacy interest with reference to certain decisions that are properly for the individual to make. E.g., *Roe v. Wade*; *Pierce v. Society of Sisters* (1925). Second, it has recognized a privacy interest with reference to certain places without regard for the particular activities in which the individuals who occupy them are engaged. The case before us implicates both the decisional and the spatial aspects of the right to privacy.

II-A. The Court concludes today that none of our prior cases dealing with various decisions that individuals are entitled to make free of governmental interference "bears any resemblance to the claimed constitutional right of homosexuals to engage in acts of sodomy that is asserted in this case." While it is true that these cases may be characterized by their connection to protection of the family, see *Roberts v. United States Jaycees* (1984), the Court's conclusion that they extend no further than this boundary ignores the warning in *Moore v. East Cleveland* (1977) (plurality opinion), against "clos[ing] our eyes to the basic reasons why certain rights associated with the family have been accorded shelter under the 14th Amendment's Due Process Clause." We protect those rights not because they contribute, in some direct and material way, to the general public welfare, but because they form so central a part of an individual's life. "[T]he concept of privacy embodies the 'moral fact that a person belongs to himself and not others nor to society as a whole.'" *Thornburgh v. American College of Obstetricians & Gynecologists* (1986) (Stevens, J., concurring). And so we protect the decision whether to marry precisely because marriage "is an association that promotes a way of life, not causes; a harmony in living, not political faiths; a bilateral loyalty, not commercial or social projects." *Griswold v. Connecticut* (1965). We protect the decision whether to have a child because parenthood alters so dramatically an individual's self-definition, not because of demographic considerations or the Bible's command to be fruitful and multiply. Cf. *Thornburgh v. American College of Obstetricians & Gynecologists* (Stevens, J., concurring). And we protect the family because it contributes so powerfully to the happiness of individuals, not because of a preference for stereotypical households. Cf. *Moore v. East Cleveland.* The Court recognized in *Roberts* that the "ability independently to define one's identity that is central to any concept of liberty" cannot truly be exercised in a vacuum; we all depend on the "emotional enrichment from close ties with others."

Only the most willful blindness could obscure the fact that sexual intimacy is "a sensitive, key relationship of human existence, central to family life, community welfare, and the development of human personality," *Paris Adult Theatre I v. Slaton* (1973). The fact that individuals define themselves in a significant way through their intimate sexual relationships with others suggests, in a Nation as diverse as ours, that there may be many "right" ways of conducting those relationships, and that much of the richness of a relationship will come from the freedom an individual has to choose the form and nature of these intensely personal bonds.

In a variety of circumstances we have recognized that a necessary corollary of giving individuals freedom to choose how to conduct their lives is acceptance of the fact that different individuals will make different choices.... The Court claims that its decision today merely refuses to recognize a fundamental right to engage in homosexual sodomy; what the Court really has refused to recognize is the fundamental interest all individuals have in controlling the nature of their intimate associations with others.

II-B. The behavior for which Hardwick faces prosecution occurred in his own home, a place to which the 4th Amendment attaches special significance. The Court's treatment of this aspect of the case is symptomatic of its overall refusal to consider the broad principles that have informed our treatment of privacy in specific cases. Just as the right to privacy is more than the mere aggregation of a number of entitlements to engage in specific behavior, so too, protecting the physical integrity of the home is more than merely a means of protecting specific activities that often take place there....

The Court's interpretation of the pivotal case of *Stanley v. Georgia* is entirely unconvincing. *Stanley* held that Georgia's undoubted power to punish the public distribution of constitutionally unprotected, obscene material did not permit the State to punish the private possession of such material. According to the majority here, *Stanley* relied entirely on the 1st Amendment, and thus, it is claimed, sheds no light on cases not involving printed materials. But that is not what *Stanley* said. Rather, the *Stanley* Court anchored its holding in the 4th Amendment's special protection for the individual in his home....

The central place that *Stanley* gives Justice Brandeis' dissent in *Olmstead* [*v. United States*], a case raising no 1st Amendment claim, shows that *Stanley* rested as much on the Court's understanding of the 4th Amendment as it did on the 1st...."The right of the people to be secure in their ... houses," expressly guaranteed by the 4th Amendment, is perhaps the most "textual" of the various constitutional provisions that inform our understanding of the right to privacy, and thus I cannot agree with the Court's statement that "[t]he right pressed upon us here has no ... support in the text of the Constitution." Indeed, the right of an individual to conduct intimate relationships in the intimacy of his or her own home seems to me to be the heart of the Constitution's protection of privacy.

III.... In light of the state of the record, I see no justification for the Court's attempt to equate the private, consensual sexual activity at issue here with the "possession in the home of drugs, firearms, or stolen goods" to which *Stanley* refused to extend its protection.... Nothing in the record before the Court provides any justification for finding the activity forbidden by § 16-6-2 to be physically dangerous, either to the persons engaged in it or to others.[1]

The core of petitioner's defense of § 16-6-2, however, is that respondent and others who engage in the conduct prohibited by § 16-6-2 interfere with Georgia's exercise of the "'right of the Nation and of the States to maintain a decent society,'" *Paris Adult Theatre I v. Slaton*, quoting *Jacobellis v. Ohio* (1964) (Warren, C.J., dissenting). Essentially, petitioner argues, and the Court agrees, that the fact that the acts described in § 16-6-2 "for hundreds of years, if not thousands, have been uniformly condemned as immoral" is a sufficient reason to permit a State to ban them today.

I cannot agree that either the length of time a majority has held its convictions or the passions with which it defends them can withdraw legislation from this Court's scrutiny. See, e.g., *Roe v. Wade*; *Loving v. Virginia* (1967); *Brown v. Board of Education* (1954).[2] ... It is precisely because the issue raised by this case touches the heart of what makes individuals what they are that we should be especially sensitive to the rights of those whose choices upset the majority....

IV. It took but three years for the Court to see the error in its analysis in *Minersville School District v. Gobitis* (1940), and to recognize that the threat to national cohesion posed by a refusal to salute the flag was vastly outweighed by the threat to those same values posed by compelling such a salute. See *West Virginia Board of Education v. Barnette* (1943). I can only hope that here, too, the Court soon will reconsider its analysis and conclude that depriving individuals of the right to choose for themselves how to conduct their intimate relationships poses a far greater threat to the values most deeply rooted in our Nation's history than tolerance of nonconformity could ever do. Because I think the Court today betrays those values, I dissent.

---

1. Although I do not think it necessary to decide today issues that are not even remotely before us, it does seem to me that a court could find simple, analytically sound distinctions between certain private, consensual sexual conduct, on the one hand, and adultery and incest (the only two vaguely specific "sexual crimes" to which the majority points), on the other. For example, marriage, in addition to its spiritual aspects, is a civil contract that entitles the contracting parties to a variety of governmentally provided benefits. A State might define the contractual commitment necessary to become eligible for these benefits to include a commitment of fidelity and then punish individuals for breaching that contract. Moreover, a State might conclude that adultery is likely to injure third persons, in particular, spouses and children of persons who engage in extramarital affairs. With respect to incest, a court might well agree with respondent that the nature of familial relationships renders true consent to incestuous activity sufficiently problematical that a blanket prohibition of such activity is warranted. Notably, the Court makes no effort to explain why it has chosen to group private, consensual homosexual activity with adultery and incest rather than with private, consensual heterosexual activity by unmarried persons or, indeed, with oral or anal sex within marriage.

2. The parallel between *Loving* and this case is almost uncanny. There, too, the State relied on a religious justification for its law. There, too, defenders of the challenged statute relied heavily on the fact that when the 14th Amendment was ratified, most of the States had similar prohibitions. There, too, at the time the case came before the Court, many of the States still had criminal statutes concerning the conduct at issue. Yet the Court held, not only that the invidious racism of Virginia's law violated the Equal Protection Clause, but also that the law deprived the Lovings of due process by denying them the "freedom of choice to marry" that had "long been recognized as one of the vital personal rights essential to the orderly pursuit of happiness by free men."

Justice Stevens, with whom Justice Brennan and Justice Marshall join, dissenting....

I. Our prior cases make two propositions abundantly clear. First, the fact that the governing majority in a State has traditionally viewed a particular practice as immoral is not a sufficient reason for upholding a law prohibiting the practice; neither history nor tradition could save a law prohibiting miscegenation from constitutional attack. Second, individual decisions by married persons, concerning the intimacies of their physical relationship, even when not intended to produce offspring, are a form of "liberty" protected by the Due Process Clause of the 14th Amendment. *Griswold v. Connecticut* (1965). Moreover, this protection extends to intimate choices by unmarried as well as married persons. *Carey v. Population Services International* (1977); *Eisenstadt v. Baird* (1972)....

Paradoxical as it may seem, our prior cases thus establish that a State may not prohibit sodomy within "the sacred precincts of marital bedrooms," *Griswold*, or, indeed, between unmarried heterosexual adults. *Eisenstadt*....

II. If the Georgia statute cannot be enforced as it is written—if the conduct it seeks to prohibit is a protected form of liberty for the vast majority of Georgia's citizens—the State must assume the burden of justifying a selective application of its law. Either the persons to whom Georgia seeks to apply its statute do not have the same interest in "liberty" that others have, or there must be a reason why the State may be permitted to apply a generally applicable law to certain persons that it does not apply to others.

The first possibility is plainly unacceptable. Although the meaning of the principle that "all men are created equal" is not always clear, it surely must mean that every free citizen has the same interest in "liberty" that the members of the majority share. From the standpoint of the individual, the homosexual and the heterosexual have the same interest in deciding how he will live his own life, and, more narrowly, how he will conduct himself in his personal and voluntary associations with his companions. State intrusion into the private conduct of either is equally burdensome.

The second possibility is similarly unacceptable. A policy of selective application must be supported by a neutral and legitimate interest—something more substantial than a habitual dislike for, or ignorance about, the disfavored group. Neither the State nor the Court has identified any such interest in this case. The Court has posited as a justification for the Georgia statute "the presumed belief of a majority of the electorate in Georgia that homosexual sodomy is immoral and unacceptable." But the Georgia electorate has expressed no such belief—instead, its representatives enacted a law that presumably reflects the belief that *all sodomy* is immoral and unacceptable....

Justice Powell's Reconsideration

In 1990, following his retirement from the Supreme Court, former Justice Lewis Powell, when asked how he could reconcile his vote in *Roe v. Wade* (1973) with his vote in *Bowers*, responded: "I think I probably made a mistake in that one. I do think it was inconsistent in a general way with *Roe*. When I had the opportunity to reread the opinions a few months later, I thought the dissent had the better of the arguments." He added: "My vote was the deciding vote that made the decision 5–4." *New York Law Journal*, Oct. 26, 1990, p.1.

In the following case, the Kentucky Supreme Court, in a 4–3 decision, reached a result contrary to *Bowers* under the Kentucky constitution.

B. Liberty and Sodomy: *Bowers* Repudiated

Kentucky v. Wasson
842 S.W.2d 487 (Ky. 1992)

Leibson, Justice.

Appellee, Jeffrey Wasson, is charged with having solicited an undercover Lexington policeman to engage in deviate sexual intercourse. KRS 510.100 punishes "deviate sexual intercourse with another person of the same sex" as a criminal offense, and specifies "consent of the other person shall not be a defense." Nor does it matter that the act is private and involves a caring relationship rather than a commercial one. It is classified as a Class A misdemeanor.

[Wasson] is actually charged [with solicitation].... The issue here is whether KRS 510.100, which defines the underlying criminal offense, is constitutional....

Both courts below decided the issues solely on state constitutional law grounds, and our decision today, affirming the judgments of the lower courts, is likewise so limited. Federal constitutional protection under the Equal Protection Clause was not an issue reached in the lower courts and we need not address it. *Bowers v. Hardwick* (1986) held federal constitutional protection of the right of privacy was not implicated in laws penalizing homosexual sodomy. We discuss *Bowers* in particular, and federal cases in general, not in the process of construing the United States Constitution or federal law, but only where their reasoning is relevant to discussing questions of state law....

Lexington police were conducting a downtown undercover operation. Their modus operandi was to drive to a certain parking area, in plain clothes with microphones on their persons, and try to engage in conversation with persons passing by to see whether they would be solicited for sexual contact. The taped conversation between the undercover officer and Wasson covered approximately 20–25 minutes, toward the end of which Wasson invited the officer to "come home" to his residence. The officer then prodded Wasson for details, and Wasson suggested sexual activities which violated KRS 510.100. There was no suggestion that sexual activity would occur anyplace other than in the privacy of Wasson's home. The sexual activity was intended to have been between consenting adults. No money was offered or solicited.

Seven expert witnesses testified in support of Wasson's case: (1) a cultural anthropologist testified about the presence of homosexuals in every recorded human culture, including societies where they were rejected and those where they have been tolerated or even welcomed; (2) a Presbyterian minister discussed Biblical references, providing a modern interpretation that these references were not an indictment of homosexuals as such, but rather statements against aggression, inhospitality and uncaring relationships; (3) a social historian testified about the presence of homosexuals throughout the history of the United States, despite what was at times exceptionally strict punishment for homosexual acts; (4) a sociologist and sex researcher (a co-author of the Kinsey Report on homosexual behavior) testified that studies indicated "'homosexuality' is just as deep-rooted as 'heterosexuality,'" that it is not a choice and there is no "cure" for it, and that sexual acts prohibited to homosexuals by KRS 510.100, oral and anal sex, are practiced widely by heterosexuals; (5) a psychologist testified that homosexuality is no longer classified as a personality disorder by either the American Psychological Association or the American Psychiatric Association, and further, rather than being in and of themselves either harmful or pathological, the sexual acts outlawed by KRS 510.100 are a necessary adjunct to their sex life; (6) a therapist from a comprehensive care treatment center in Lexington, with fourteen years' experience counseling homosexual clients, testified that the statute criminalizing their sexual activities has an adverse impact on homosexuals and interferes with efforts to provide therapy to those who may need it; and (7) the Professor of Medicine at the University of Louisville, Chief of the Infectious Diseases section, testified at length about the origins and spread of AIDS, expressing the opinion that the statute in question offers no benefit in preventing the spread of the disease and can be a barrier to getting accurate medical histories, thus having an adverse effect on public health efforts.

The testimony from Wasson's expert witnesses is further substantiated by extensive citations to medical and social science literature and treatises supplied in Amicus Curiae Briefs filed by national and state associations of psychologists and clinical social workers, various national and state public health associations, and organizations covering a broad spectrum of religious denominations.

The Commonwealth, on the other hand, presented no witnesses and offers no scientific evidence or social science data. Succinctly stated, its position is that the majority, speaking through the General Assembly, has the right to criminalize sexual activity it deems immoral, without regard to whether the activity is conducted in private between consenting adults and is not, in and of itself, harmful to the participants or to others; that, if not in all instances, at least where there is a Biblical and historical tradition supporting it, there are no limitations in the Kentucky Constitution on the power of the General Assembly to criminalize sexual activity these elected representatives deem immoral.

The Commonwealth maintains that the United States Supreme Court's decision in *Bowers v. Hardwick* is dispositive of the right to privacy issue; that the "Kentucky Constitution did not intend to confer any greater right to privacy than was afforded by the U.S. Constitution." Turning to the equal protection argument raised by a statute which criminalizes oral or anal intercourse between persons of the same sex, but not between persons of different sexes, which was not addressed in the *Bowers* case, the Commonwealth argues there is "a rational basis for making such a distinction." To support this argument the Commonwealth takes bits and pieces from the testimony of Wasson's expert witnesses out of context and disregards their overwhelming evidence to the contrary. The thrust of the argument advanced by the Commonwealth as a rational basis for criminalizing consensual intercourse between persons of the same sex, when the same acts between persons of the opposite sex are not punished, is that the level of moral indignation felt by the majority of society against the sexual preference of homosexuals justifies having their legislative representatives criminalize these sexual activities. The Commonwealth believes that homosexual intercourse is immoral, and that what is beyond the pale of majoritarian morality is beyond the limits of constitutional protection....

A significant part of the Commonwealth's argument rests on the proposition that homosexual sodomy was punished as an offense at common law, that it has been punished by statute in Kentucky since 1860, predating our Kentucky Constitution. Indeed, in *Bowers v. Hardwick*, the United States Supreme Court takes note of the original Kentucky statute codifying the common law found at 1 Ky. Rev. Stat., Ch. 28, Art. IV, § 11 (1860). This, of course, would lend credence to the historical and traditional basis for punishing acts of sodomy, but for the fact that "sodomy" as defined at common law and in this 1860 statute is an offense significantly different from KRS 510.100, limited to *anal* intercourse between *men*. Unlike the present statute our common law tradition punished *neither oral copulation nor any form of deviate sexual activity between women*. The definitive Kentucky case on the subject is *Commonwealth v. Poindexter* (Ky. 1909), summarizing the common law and statutory background, and holding: "A penetration of the mouth is not sodomy."...

Thus the statute in question here punishes conduct which has been historically and traditionally viewed as immoral, but much of which has never been punished as criminal....

For reasons that follow, we hold the guarantees of individual liberty provided in our 1891 Kentucky Constitution offer greater protection of the right of privacy than provided by the Federal Constitution as interpreted by the United States Supreme Court, and that the statute in question is a violation of such rights; and, further, we hold that the statute in question violates rights of equal protection as guaranteed by our Kentucky Constitution.

I. RIGHTS OF PRIVACY

No language specifying "rights of privacy," *as such*, appears in either the Federal or State Constitution. The Commonwealth recognizes such rights exist, but takes the position that, since they are implicit rather than explicit, our Court should march in lock step with the United States Supreme Court in declaring when such rights exist. Such is not the formulation of federalism. On the contrary, under our system of dual sovereignty, it is our responsibility to interpret and apply our state constitution independently. We are not bound by decisions of the United States Supreme Court when deciding whether a state statute impermissibly infringes upon individual rights guaranteed in the State Constitution so long as state constitutional protection does not fall below the federal *floor*, meaning the minimum guarantee of individual rights under the United States Constitution as interpreted by the United States Supreme Court. *Oregon v. Hass* (1975). The holding in *Oregon v. Hass* is: "[A] State is free *as a matter of its own law* to impose greater restrictions on police activity than those this [United States Supreme] Court holds to be necessary upon federal constitutional standards."

Contrary to popular belief, the Bill of Rights in the United States Constitution represents neither the primary source nor the maximum guarantee of state constitutional liberty. Our own constitutional guarantees against the intrusive power of the state do not derive from the Federal Constitution. The adoption of the Federal Constitution in 1791 was preceded by state constitutions developed over the preceding 15 years, and, while there is, of course, overlap between state and federal constitutional guarantees of individual rights, they are by no means identical. State constitutional law documents and the writings on liberty were more the source of federal law than the child of federal law....

Thus, while we respect the decisions of the United States Supreme Court on protection of individual liberty, and on occasion we have deferred to its reasoning, certainly we are not bound to do so, and we should not do so when valid reasons lead to a different conclusion.

We are persuaded that we should not do so here for several significant reasons. First, there are both textual and structural differences between the United States Bill of Rights and our own, which suggest a different conclusion from that reached by the United States Supreme Court is more appropriate. More significantly, Kentucky has a rich and compelling tradition of recognizing and protecting individual rights from state intrusion in cases similar in nature, found in the Debates of the Kentucky Constitutional Convention of 1890 and cases from the same era when that Constitution was adopted. The judges recognizing that tradition in their opinions wrote with a direct, firsthand knowledge of the mind set of the constitutional fathers, upholding the right of privacy against the intrusive police power of the state. This tradition is formulated in ringing terms in the opinion of this Court in *Commonwealth v. Campbell* (Ky. 1909), [and other cited cases].

Kentucky cases recognized a legally protected right of privacy based on our own constitution and common law tradition long before the United States Supreme Court first took notice of whether there were any rights of privacy inherent in the Federal Bill of Rights....

[S]tate constitutional jurisprudence in this area is not limited by the constraints inherent in federal due process analysis. Deviate sexual intercourse conducted in private by consenting adults is not beyond the protections of the guarantees of individual liberty in our Kentucky Constitution simply because "proscriptions against that conduct have ancient roots." *Bowers v. Hardwick*. Kentucky constitutional guarantees against government intrusion address substantive rights....

The Commonwealth has stressed that there was no discussion of the right of privacy at the 1890 Kentucky Constitutional Convention, but that is only partly true. The meaning of Sections One and Two as they apply to personal liberty is found in the remarks of J. Proctor Knott of Marion County (see Official Report of the Proceedings and Debates in the 1890 Convention, E. Polk Johnson, Vol. 1, p. 718): "[T]hose who exercise that power in organized society with any claim of justice, derive it from the people themselves. That with the whole of such power residing in the people, the people as a body rest under the highest of all moral obligations to protect each individual in the rights of life, liberty, and the pursuit of happiness, *provided that he shall in no wise injure his neighbor in so doing*" (emphasis added). See also *Comments of Delegate J.A. Brents from Clinton County. Debates*, Vol. 1, p. 614–18, concluding "majorities cannot and ought not exercise arbitrary power over the minority."

The leading case on this subject is *Commonwealth v. Campbell*. At issue was an ordinance that criminalized possession of intoxicating liquor, even for "private use." Our Court held that the Bill of Rights in the 1891 Constitution prohibited state action thus intruding upon the "inalienable rights possessed by the citizens" of Kentucky.

Our Court interpreted the Kentucky Bill of Rights as defining a right of privacy, even though the constitution did not say so in that terminology:

> Man in his natural state has the right to do whatever he chooses and has the power to do. When he becomes a member of organized society, under governmental regulation, he surrenders, of necessity, all of his natural right the exercise of which is, or may be, injurious to his fellow citizens. This is the price that he pays for governmental protection, but it is not within the competency of a free government to invade the sanctity of the absolute rights of the citizen any further than the direct protection of society requires.... It is *not within the competency of government to invade the privacy of a citizen's life and to regulate his conduct in matters in which he alone is concerned*, or to prohibit him any liberty the exercise of which will not directly injure society. *Id.* Let a man therefore be ever so abandoned in his principles, or vicious in his practice, provided he keeps his wickedness to himself, and does not offend against the rules of public decency, he is out of the reach of human laws. *Id.*

The Court concludes: "The theory of our government is to allow the largest liberty to the individual commensurate with the public safety, or, as it has been otherwise expressed, that government is best which governs least. Under our institutions there is no room for that inquisitorial and protective spirit which seeks to regulate the conduct of men in matters in themselves indifferent, and to make them conform to a standard, not of their own choosing, but the choosing of the lawgiver...."

The right of privacy has been recognized as an integral part of the guarantee of liberty in our 1891 Kentucky Constitution since its inception. The *Campbell* case is overwhelming affirmation of this proposition:

> [W]e are of the opinion that it never has been within the competency of the Legislature to so restrict the liberty of this citizen, and certainly not since the adoption of the present [1891] Constitution. The Bill of Rights, which declares that among the inalienable rights possessed by the citizens is that of seeking and pursuing their safety and happiness, and that the absolute and arbitrary power over the lives, liberty, and property of freeman exists nowhere in a republic, not even in the largest majority, would be but an empty sound if the Legislature could prohibit the citizen the right of owning or drinking liquor, when in so doing he did not offend the laws of decency by being intoxicated in public....

At the time *Campbell* was decided, the use of alcohol was as much an incendiary moral issue as deviate sexual behavior in private between consenting adults is today. Prohibition was the great moral issue of its time. It was addressed both in the 1891 Constitution and in the 19th Amendment of the United States Constitution. In 1907, in *Board of Trustees of Town of New Castle v. Scott* (Ky. 1907), Chief Justice O'Rear passionately attacked the evil of alcohol in a pro-prohibition ruling interpreting § 61 of the Kentucky Constitution, which provides for local option elections. He stated: "There is yet another view of the subject which we must assume was in the mind of the Convention. The liquor traffic had then [in 1891] come to be regarded as one of the most serious evils of the age, if not the most sinister menace to society that was known.... No other subject had been more clearly settled upon as being within the legitimate exercise of the police power of the state than the regulation of the sale and use of intoxicating liquors." *Id.*

Notwithstanding their strong views that drinking was immoral, this same Court with these same judges, including Judge O'Rear, in the *Campbell* case recognized that private possession and consumption of intoxicating liquor was a liberty interest beyond the reach of the state....

The clear implication is that immorality in private which does "not operate to the detriment of others," is placed beyond the reach of state action by the guarantees of liberty in the Kentucky Constitution....

In the area of civil law, Kentucky has been in the forefront in recognizing the right of privacy. In 1909, our Court stepped outside traditional libel law and recognized invasion of privacy as a tort in *Foster-Milburn Co. v. Chinn* (Ky. App. 1909). Then in 1927, in *Brents v. Morgan* (Ky. App. 1927) our Court defined this emerging right as "the right to be left alone, that is, the right of a person to be free from unwarranted publicity, or the right to live without unwarranted interference by the public about matters with which the public is not necessarily concerned."

> The right of privacy is incident to the person and not to property.... It is considered as a natural and an absolute or pure right springing from the instincts of nature. It is of that class of rights which every human being has in his natural state and which he did not surrender by becoming a member of organized society. The fundamental rights of personal security and personal liberty, include the right of privacy, the right to be left alone.... The right to enjoy life [Ky. Const., § 1, first subpart] in the way most agreeable and pleasant, and the right of privacy is nothing more than a right to live in a particular way. *Id.*...

In the *Campbell* case our Court quoted at length from the "great work" *On Liberty* of the 19th century English philosopher and economist, John Stuart Mill. We repeat the quote in part: "The only part of the conduct of anyone, for which he is amenable to society, is that which concerns others. In the part which merely concerns himself, his independence is, of right, absolute.... The principle requires liberty of taste and pursuits; of framing the plan of our life to suit our own character; of doing as we like, subject to such consequences as may follow; without impediment from our fellow creatures, so long as what we do does not harm them, even though they should think our conduct foolish, perverse, or wrong."

Mill's premise is that "physical force in the form of legal penalties," i.e., criminal sanctions, should not be used as a means to improve the citizen. The majority has no moral right to dictate how everyone else should live. Public indignation, while given due weight, should be subject to the overriding test of rational and critical analysis, drawing the line at harmful consequences to others. Modern legal philosophers who follow Mill temper this test with an enlightened paternalism, permitting the law to intervene to stop self-inflicted harm such as the result of drug taking, or failure to use seat belts or crash helmets, not to enforce majoritarian or conventional morality, but because the victim of such self-inflicted harm becomes a burden on society. See *Introduction to Jurisprudence*, 4th ed, p. 59 (1979) by Lord Lloyd of Hampstead.

Based on the *Campbell* opinion, and on the Comments of the 1891 Convention Delegates, there is little doubt but that the views of John Stuart Mill, which were then held in high esteem, provided the philosophical underpinnings for the reworking and broadening of protection of individual rights that occurs throughout the 1891 Constitution.

We have recognized protection of individual rights greater than the federal floor in a number of cases.... In so doing we stated: "We have decided this case solely on the basis of our Kentucky Constitution.... We find it unnecessary to inject any issues raised under the United States Constitution or the United States Bill of Rights in this matter."....

We view the United States Supreme Court decision in *Bowers v. Hardwick* as a misdirected application of the theory of original intent. To illustrate: as a theory of majoritarian morality, miscegenation was an offense with ancient roots. It is highly unlikely that protecting the rights of persons of different races to copulate was one of the considerations behind the 14th Amendment. Nevertheless, in *Loving v. Virginia* (1967), the United States Supreme Court recognized that a contemporary, enlightened interpretation of the liberty interest involved in the sexual act made its punishment constitutionally impermissible.

According to *Bowers v. Hardwick*, "until 1961, all 50 States outlawed sodomy, and today, 25 States and District of Colombia continue to provide criminal penalties for sodomy performed in private and between consenting adults." In the space of three decades half the states decriminalized this conduct, some no doubt in deference to the position taken by the American Law Institute in the Model Penal Code, §213.2: "Section 213.2 of the Model Code makes a fundamental departure from prior law in excepting from criminal sanctions deviate sexual intercourse between consenting adults." American Law Institute, *Model Penal Code and Commentaries*, Part II, 1980 Ed., pp. 362–63.

> The usual justification for laws against such conduct is that, even though it does not injure any identifiable victim, it contributes to moral deterioration of society. One need not endorse wholesale repeal of all 'victimless' crimes in order to recognize that legislating penal sanctions solely to maintain widely held concepts of morality and aesthetics is a costly enterprise. It sacrifices personal liberty, not because the actor's conduct results in harm to another citizen but only because it is inconsistent with the majoritarian notion of acceptable behavior. In the

words of the *Wolfenden Report*, the decisive factor favoring decriminalization of laws against private homosexual relations between consenting adults is "the importance which society and the law ought to give to individual freedom of choice and action in matters of private morality." *Id.* at 371–72.

Two states by court decisions hold homosexual sodomy statutes of this nature unconstitutional for reasons similar to those stated here: New York in *People v. Onofre* (N.Y. 1980); and Pennsylvania in *Commonwealth v. Bonadio* (Pa. 1980). There are two other states where lower courts have ruled such statutes unconstitutional: *Texas v. Morales* (Tex. App. 1992); *Michigan Organization for Human Rights v. Kelly* (Mich., Wayne Cnty. Cir. Ct. 1990). Thus our decision, rather than being the leading edge of change, is but a part of the moving stream.

The *Bonadio* case from Pennsylvania is particularly noteworthy because of the common heritage shared by the Kentucky Bill of Rights of 1792 and the Pennsylvania Bill of Rights of 1790....

[The remainder of the Court's discussion, including its discussion of equal protection under the Kentucky Constitution, is omitted.]

For the reasons stated, we affirm the decision of the Fayette Circuit Court, and the judgment on appeal from the Fayette District Court [and invalidate the statute].

Lambert, Justice, dissenting.

The issue here is not whether private homosexual conduct should be allowed or prohibited. The only question properly before this Court is whether the Constitution of Kentucky denies the legislative branch a right to prohibit such conduct. Nothing in the majority opinion demonstrates such a limitation on legislative prerogative.

To justify its view that private homosexual conduct is protected by the Constitution of Kentucky, the majority has found it necessary to disregard virtually all of recorded history, the teachings of the religions most influential on Western Civilization [here the dissent dropped a footnote citing Leviticus 20:13; Romans 1:26–27], the debates of the delegates to the Constitutional Convention, and the text of the Constitution itself. Rather than amounting to a decision based upon precedent as is suggested, this decision reflects the value judgment of the majority and its view that public law has no right to prohibit the conduct at issue here.

The majority concedes that "'proscriptions against that conduct [sodomy] have ancient roots.'" It fails, however, to describe the depth of such roots as was done in *Bowers v. Hardwick* (1986): "Sodomy was a criminal offense at common law which was forbidden by the laws of the original 13 States when they ratified the Bill of Rights." Chief Justice Burger elaborated upon the historical condemnation of sodomy as follows:

> Decisions of individuals relating to homosexual conduct have been subject to state intervention throughout the history of Western Civilization. Condemnation of those practices is firmly rooted in Judeao-Christian moral and ethical standards. Homosexual sodomy was a capital crime under Roman law. During the English Reformation when powers of the ecclesiastical courts were transferred to the King's Courts, the first English statute criminalizing sodomy was passed. Blackstone described "the infamous crime against nature" as an offense of "deeper malignity" than rape, a heinous act "the very mention of which is a disgrace to human nature" and "a crime not fit to be named."... To hold that the act of homosexual sodomy is somehow protected as a fundamental right would be to cast aside millennia of moral teaching.

The history and traditions of this Commonwealth are fully in accord with the Biblical, historical and common law view. Since at least 1860, sodomy has been a criminal offense in Kentucky and this fact was well known to the delegates at the time of the 1890 Constitutional Convention.

Embracing "state constitutionalism," a practice in vogue among many state courts as a means of rejecting the leadership of the Supreme Court of the United States, the majority has declared its independence from even the influence of this nation's highest court. The majority cannot, however, escape the logic and scholarship of *Bowers* which reached the conclusion that nothing in the Due Process Clause of the United States Constitution prevented a state from punishing sodomy as a crime. While I do not advocate the view that state courts should march in lock step with the Supreme Court of the United States, on those occasions when state courts depart from that Court's reasoned interpretations, it should be for compelling reasons, usually text or tradition, and only in clearly distinguishable circumstances, none of which are present here.

The majority also concedes that the debates of the Kentucky Constitutional Convention of 1890 contain no mention of a right of privacy or a right to engage in homosexual sodomy. It rationalizes this fact by indicating that the concept was not articulated until publication of an article by Warren and Brandeis in the Harvard Law Review on December 15, 1890. According to the majority, the delegates to the Constitutional Convention intended to create such a right but lacked the verbal skills to devise a phrase so complicated as "right of privacy." For whatever reason, the debates contain only the most limited and inexplicit reference to any concept which could be translated into privacy....

[The rest of this dissenting opinion and the other dissents are omitted.]

Lawrence v. Texas
539 U.S. 558 (2003)

[Majority: Kennedy, Stevens, Souter, Ginsburg, and Breyer. Concurring: O'Connor. Dissenting: Scalia, Rehnquist (C.J.), and Thomas.]

Justice Kennedy delivered the opinion of the Court.

Liberty protects the person from unwarranted government intrusions into a dwelling or other private places. In our tradition the State is not omnipresent in the home. And there are other spheres of our lives and existence, outside the home, where the State should not be a dominant presence. Freedom extends beyond spatial bounds. Liberty presumes an autonomy of self that includes freedom of thought, belief, expression, and certain intimate conduct. The instant case involves liberty of the person both in its spatial and more transcendent dimensions.

I. The question before the Court is the validity of a Texas statute making it a crime for two persons of the same sex to engage in certain intimate sexual conduct.

In Houston, Texas, officers of the Harris County Police Department were dispatched to a private residence in response to a reported weapons disturbance. They entered an apartment where one of the petitioners, John Geddes Lawrence, resided. The right of the police to enter does not seem to have been questioned. The officers observed Lawrence and another man, Tyron Garner, engaging in a sexual act. The two petitioners were arrested, held in custody over night, and charged and convicted before a Justice of the Peace.

The complaints described their crime as "deviate sexual intercourse, namely anal sex, with a member of the same sex (man)." The applicable state law is Tex. Penal Code Ann.

§ 21.06(a) (2003). It provides: "A person commits an offense if he engages in deviate sexual intercourse with another individual of the same sex." The statute defines "[d]eviate sexual intercourse" as follows:

(A) any contact between any part of the genitals of one person and the mouth or anus of another person; or

(B) the penetration of the genitals or the anus of another person with an object....

The petitioners were adults at the time of the alleged offense. Their conduct was in private and consensual.

II. We conclude the case should be resolved by determining whether the petitioners were free as adults to engage in the private conduct in the exercise of their liberty under the Due Process Clause of the 14th Amendment to the Constitution. For this inquiry we deem it necessary to reconsider the Court's holding in *Bowers v. Hardwick* (1986).

There are broad statements of the substantive reach of liberty under the Due Process Clause in earlier cases; but the most pertinent beginning point is our decision in *Griswold v. Connecticut* (1965).

In *Griswold* the Court invalidated a state law prohibiting the use of drugs or devices of contraception and counseling or aiding and abetting the use of contraceptives. The Court described the protected interest as a right to privacy and placed emphasis on the marriage relation and the protected space of the marital bedroom.

After *Griswold* it was established that the right to make certain decisions regarding sexual conduct extends beyond the marital relationship. In *Eisenstadt v. Baird* (1972), the Court invalidated a law prohibiting the distribution of contraceptives to unmarried persons. The case was decided under the Equal Protection Clause, but with respect to unmarried persons, the Court went on to state the fundamental proposition that the law impaired the exercise of their personal rights. It quoted from the statement of the Court of Appeals finding the law to be in conflict with fundamental human rights, and it followed with this statement of its own:

It is true that in *Griswold* the right of privacy in question inhered in the marital relationship.... If the right of privacy means anything, it is the right of the *individual*, married or single, to be free from unwarranted governmental intrusion into matters so fundamentally affecting a person as the decision whether to bear or beget a child.

The opinions in *Griswold* and *Eisenstadt* were part of the background for the decision in *Roe v. Wade* (1973).... *Roe* recognized the right of a woman to make certain fundamental decisions affecting her destiny and confirmed once more that the protection of liberty under the Due Process Clause has a substantive dimension of fundamental significance in defining the rights of the person.

In *Carey v. Population Services Int'l.* (1977), the Court confronted a New York law forbidding sale or distribution of contraceptive devices to persons under 16 years of age. Although there was no single opinion for the Court, the law was invalidated. Both *Eisenstadt* and *Carey*, as well as the holding and rationale in *Roe*, confirmed that the reasoning of *Griswold* could not be confined to the protection of rights of married adults. This was the state of the law with respect to some of the most relevant cases when the Court considered *Bowers.*

The facts in *Bowers* had some similarities to the instant case. A police officer, whose right to enter seems not to have been in question, observed Bowers, in his own bedroom, engaging in intimate sexual conduct with another adult male. The conduct was in violation of a Georgia statute making it a criminal offense to engage in sodomy....

The Court began its substantive discussion in *Bowers* as follows: "The issue presented is whether the Federal Constitution confers a fundamental right upon homosexuals to engage in sodomy and hence invalidates the laws of the many States that still make such conduct illegal and have done so for a very long time." That statement, we now conclude, discloses the Court's own failure to appreciate the extent of the liberty at stake. To say that the issue in *Bowers* was simply the right to engage in certain sexual conduct demeans the claim the individual put forward, just as it would demean a married couple were it to be said marriage is simply about the right to have sexual intercourse. The laws involved in *Bowers* and here are, to be sure, statutes that purport to do no more than prohibit a particular sexual act. Their penalties and purposes, though, have more far-reaching consequences, touching upon the most private human conduct, sexual behavior, and in the most private of places, the home. The statutes do seek to control a personal relationship that, whether or not entitled to formal recognition in the law, is within the liberty of persons to choose without being punished as criminals.

This, as a general rule, should counsel against attempts by the State, or a court, to define the meaning of the relationship or to set its boundaries absent injury to a person or abuse of an institution the law protects. It suffices for us to acknowledge that adults may choose to enter upon this relationship in the confines of their homes and their own private lives and still retain their dignity as free persons. When sexuality finds overt expression in intimate conduct with another person, the conduct can be but one element in a personal bond that is more enduring. The liberty protected by the Constitution allows homosexual persons the right to make this choice.

Having misapprehended the claim of liberty there presented to it, and thus stating the claim to be whether there is a fundamental right to engage in consensual sodomy, the *Bowers* Court said: "Proscriptions against that conduct have ancient roots." In academic writings, and in many of the scholarly *amicus* briefs filed to assist the Court in this case, there are fundamental criticisms of the historical premises relied upon by the majority and concurring opinions in *Bowers*. We need not enter this debate in the attempt to reach a definitive historical judgment, but the following considerations counsel against adopting the definitive conclusions upon which *Bowers* placed such reliance.

At the outset it should be noted that there is no longstanding history in this country of laws directed at homosexual conduct as a distinct matter. Beginning in colonial times there were prohibitions of sodomy derived from the English criminal laws passed in the first instance by the Reformation Parliament of 1533. The English prohibition was understood to include relations between men and women as well as relations between men and men. 19th-century commentators similarly read American sodomy, buggery, and crime-against-nature statutes as criminalizing certain relations between men and women and between men and men.... Thus early American sodomy laws were not directed at homosexuals as such but instead sought to prohibit nonprocreative sexual activity more generally. This does not suggest approval of homosexual conduct. It does tend to show that this particular form of conduct was not thought of as a separate category from like conduct between heterosexual persons.

Laws prohibiting sodomy do not seem to have been enforced against consenting adults acting in private. A substantial number of sodomy prosecutions and convictions for which there are surviving records were for predatory acts against those who could not or did not consent, as in the case of a minor or the victim of an assault.... Instead of targeting relations between consenting adults in private, 19th-century sodomy prosecutions typically involved relations between men and minor girls or minor boys, relations between adults involving force, relations between adults implicating disparity in status, or relations between men and animals.

To the extent that there were any prosecutions for the acts in question, 19th-century evidence rules imposed a burden that would make a conviction more difficult to obtain even taking into account the problems always inherent in prosecuting consensual acts committed in private. Under then-prevailing standards, a man could not be convicted of sodomy based upon testimony of a consenting partner, because the partner was considered an accomplice. A partner's testimony, however, was admissible if he or she had not consented to the act or was a minor, and therefore incapable of consent. The rule may explain in part the infrequency of these prosecutions. In all events that infrequency makes it difficult to say that society approved of a rigorous and systematic punishment of the consensual acts committed in private and by adults. The longstanding criminal prohibition of homosexual sodomy upon which the *Bowers* decision placed such reliance is as consistent with a general condemnation of nonprocreative sex as it is with an established tradition of prosecuting acts because of their homosexual character....

[F]ar from possessing "ancient roots," American laws targeting same-sex couples did not develop until the last third of the 20th century. The reported decisions concerning the prosecution of consensual, homosexual sodomy between adults for the years 1880–1995 are not always clear in the details, but a significant number involved conduct in a public place.

It was not until the 1970's that any State singled out same-sex relations for criminal prosecution, and only nine States have done so.... [Arkansas, Kansas, Kentucky, Missouri, Montana, Nevada, Oklahoma and Tennessee.] Post-*Bowers* even some of these States did not adhere to the policy of suppressing homosexual conduct. [Citing four state decisions finding the statutes violated *state* constitutions and action by the Nevada legislature.] Over the course of the last decades, States with same-sex prohibitions have moved toward abolishing them.... [Citing the same authorities noted above.]

In summary, the historical grounds relied upon in *Bowers* are more complex than the majority opinion and the concurring opinion by Chief Justice Burger indicate. Their historical premises are not without doubt and, at the very least, are overstated.

It must be acknowledged, of course, that the Court in *Bowers* was making the broader point that for centuries there have been powerful voices to condemn homosexual conduct as immoral. The condemnation has been shaped by religious beliefs, conceptions of right and acceptable behavior, and respect for the traditional family. For many persons these are not trivial concerns but profound and deep convictions accepted as ethical and moral principles to which they aspire and which thus determine the course of their lives. These considerations do not answer the question before us, however. The issue is whether the majority may use the power of the State to enforce these views on the whole society through operation of the criminal law. "Our obligation is to define the liberty of all, not to mandate our own moral code." *Planned Parenthood of Southeastern Pa. v. Casey* (1992).

Chief Justice Burger joined the opinion for the Court in *Bowers* and further explained his views as follows: "Decisions of individuals relating to homosexual conduct have been subject to state intervention throughout the history of Western civilization. Condemnation of those practices is firmly rooted in Judeo-Christian moral and ethical standards." As with Justice White's assumptions about history, scholarship casts some doubt on the sweeping nature of the statement by Chief Justice Burger as it pertains to private homosexual conduct between consenting adults. In all events we think that our laws and traditions in the past half century are of most relevance here. These references show an emerging awareness that liberty gives substantial protection to adult persons in deciding how to conduct their private lives in matters pertaining to sex. "[H]istory and tradition are the starting point but not in all cases the ending point of the substantive due process inquiry." *County of Sacramento v. Lewis* (1998) (Kennedy, J., concurring).

This emerging recognition should have been apparent when *Bowers* was decided. In 1955 the American Law Institute promulgated the Model Penal Code and made clear that it did not recommend or provide for "criminal penalties for consensual sexual relations conducted in private." It justified its decision on three grounds: (1) The prohibitions undermined respect for the law by penalizing conduct many people engaged in; (2) the statutes regulated private conduct not harmful to others; and (3) the laws were arbitrarily enforced and thus invited the danger of blackmail. In 1961 Illinois changed its laws to conform to the Model Penal Code. Other States soon followed.

In *Bowers* the Court referred to the fact that before 1961 all 50 States had outlawed sodomy, and that at the time of the Court's decision 24 States and the District of Columbia had sodomy laws. Justice Powell pointed out that these prohibitions often were being ignored, however. Georgia, for instance, had not sought to enforce its law for decades. ("The history of nonenforcement suggests the moribund character today of laws criminalizing this type of private, consensual conduct.")

The sweeping references by Chief Justice Burger to the history of Western civilization and to Judeo-Christian moral and ethical standards did not take account of other authorities pointing in an opposite direction. A committee advising the British Parliament recommended in 1957 repeal of laws punishing homosexual conduct. *Wolfenden Report* (1963). Parliament enacted the substance of those recommendations 10 years later.

Of even more importance, almost five years before *Bowers* was decided the European Court of Human Rights considered a case with parallels to *Bowers* and to today's case.... The court held that the laws proscribing the conduct were invalid under the European Convention on Human Rights. *Dudgeon v. United Kingdom* (Eur. Ct. H. R. 1981). Authoritative in all countries that are members of the Council of Europe (21 nations then, 45 nations now), the decision is at odds with the premise in *Bowers* that the claim put forward was insubstantial in our Western civilization.

In our own constitutional system the deficiencies in *Bowers* became even more apparent in the years following its announcement. The 25 States with laws prohibiting the relevant conduct referenced in the *Bowers* decision are reduced now to 13, of which 4 enforce their laws only against homosexual conduct. In those States where sodomy is still proscribed, whether for same-sex or heterosexual conduct, there is a pattern of nonenforcement with respect to consenting adults acting in private. The State of Texas admitted in 1994 that as of that date it had not prosecuted anyone under those circumstances. *State v. Morales* (Tex. App. 1992).

Two principal cases decided after *Bowers* cast its holding into even more doubt. In *Casey*, the Court reaffirmed the substantive force of the liberty protected by the Due Process Clause. The *Casey* decision again confirmed that our laws and tradition afford constitutional protection to personal decisions relating to marriage, procreation, contraception, family relationships, child rearing, and education. In explaining the respect the Constitution demands for the autonomy of the person in making these choices, we stated as follows:

> These matters, involving the most intimate and personal choices a person may make in a lifetime, choices central to personal dignity and autonomy, are central to the liberty protected by the 14th Amendment. At the heart of liberty is the

right to define one's own concept of existence, of meaning, of the universe, and of the mystery of human life. Beliefs about these matters could not define the attributes of personhood were they formed under compulsion of the State.

Persons in a homosexual relationship may seek autonomy for these purposes, just as heterosexual persons do. The decision in *Bowers* would deny them this right.

The second post-*Bowers* case of principal relevance is *Romer v. Evans* (1996). There the Court struck down class-based legislation directed at homosexuals as a violation of the Equal Protection Clause. *Romer* invalidated an amendment to Colorado's constitution which named as a solitary class persons who were homosexuals, lesbians, or bisexual either by "orientation, conduct, practices or relationships," and deprived them of protection under state antidiscrimination laws. We concluded that the provision was "born of animosity toward the class of persons affected" and further that it had no rational relation to a legitimate governmental purpose.

As an alternative argument in this case, counsel for the petitioners and some *amici* contend that *Romer* provides the basis for declaring the Texas statute invalid under the Equal Protection Clause. That is a tenable argument, but we conclude the instant case requires us to address whether *Bowers* itself has continuing validity. Were we to hold the statute invalid under the Equal Protection Clause some might question whether a prohibition would be valid if drawn differently, say, to prohibit the conduct both between same-sex and different-sex participants.

Equality of treatment and the due process right to demand respect for conduct protected by the substantive guarantee of liberty are linked in important respects, and a decision on the latter point advances both interests. If protected conduct is made criminal and the law which does so remains unexamined for its substantive validity, its stigma might remain even if it were not enforceable as drawn for equal protection reasons. When homosexual conduct is made criminal by the law of the State, that declaration in and of itself is an invitation to subject homosexual persons to discrimination both in the public and in the private spheres. The central holding of *Bowers* has been brought in question by this case, and it should be addressed. Its continuance as precedent demeans the lives of homosexual persons.

The stigma this criminal statute imposes, moreover, is not trivial. The offense, to be sure, is but a class C misdemeanor, a minor offense in the Texas legal system. Still, it remains a criminal offense with all that imports for the dignity of the persons charged. The petitioners will bear on their record the history of their criminal convictions. Just this Term we rejected various challenges to state laws requiring the registration of sex offenders. *Smith v. Doe* (2003); *Connecticut Dept. of Public Safety v. Doe* (2003). We are advised that if Texas convicted an adult for private, consensual homosexual conduct under the statute here in question the convicted person would come within the registration laws of a least four States were he or she to be subject to their jurisdiction. This underscores the consequential nature of the punishment and the state-sponsored condemnation attendant to the criminal prohibition. Furthermore, the Texas criminal conviction carries with it the other collateral consequences always following a conviction, such as notations on job application forms, to mention but one example.

The foundations of *Bowers* have sustained serious erosion from our recent decisions in *Casey* and *Romer*. When our precedent has been thus weakened, criticism from other sources is of greater significance. In the United States criticism of *Bowers* has been substantial and continuing, disapproving of its reasoning in all respects, not just as to its historical assumptions. See, *e.g.*, C. Fried, *Order and Law: Arguing the Reagan Revolution—*

A Firsthand Account 81–84 (1991); R. Posner, *Sex and Reason* 341–50 (1992). The courts of five different States have declined to follow it in interpreting provisions in their own state constitutions parallel to the Due Process Clause of the 14th Amendment.

To the extent *Bowers* relied on values we share with a wider civilization, it should be noted that the reasoning and holding in *Bowers* have been rejected elsewhere. The European Court of Human Rights has followed not *Bowers* but its own decision in *Dudgeon v. United Kingdom* (2001). Other nations, too, have taken action consistent with an affirmation of the protected right of homosexual adults to engage in intimate, consensual conduct. The right the petitioners seek in this case has been accepted as an integral part of human freedom in many other countries. There has been no showing that in this country the governmental interest in circumscribing personal choice is somehow more legitimate or urgent.

The doctrine of *stare decisis* is essential to the respect accorded to the judgments of the Court and to the stability of the law. It is not, however, an inexorable command. In *Casey* we noted that when a Court is asked to overrule a precedent recognizing a constitutional liberty interest, individual or societal reliance on the existence of that liberty cautions with particular strength against reversing course. ("Liberty finds no refuge in a jurisprudence of doubt.") The holding in *Bowers*, however, has not induced detrimental reliance comparable to some instances where recognized individual rights are involved. Indeed, there has been no individual or societal reliance on *Bowers* of the sort that could counsel against overturning its holding once there are compelling reasons to do so. *Bowers* itself causes uncertainty, for the precedents before and after its issuance contradict its central holding.

The rationale of *Bowers* does not withstand careful analysis. In his dissenting opinion in *Bowers* Justice Stevens came to these conclusions:

> Our prior cases make two propositions abundantly clear. First, the fact that the governing majority in a State has traditionally viewed a particular practice as immoral is not a sufficient reason for upholding a law prohibiting the practice; neither history nor tradition could save a law prohibiting miscegenation from constitutional attack. Second, individual decisions by married persons, concerning the intimacies of their physical relationship, even when not intended to produce offspring, are a form of "liberty" protected by the Due Process Clause of the 14th Amendment. Moreover, this protection extends to intimate choices by unmarried as well as married persons.

Justice Stevens' analysis, in our view, should have been controlling in *Bowers* and should control here.

Bowers was not correct when it was decided, and it is not correct today. It ought not to remain binding precedent. *Bowers* should be and now is overruled.

The present case does not involve minors. It does not involve persons who might be injured or coerced or who are situated in relationships where consent might not easily be refused. It does not involve public conduct or prostitution. It does not involve whether the government must give formal recognition to any relationship that homosexual persons seek to enter. The case does involve two adults who, with full and mutual consent from each other, engaged in sexual practices common to a homosexual lifestyle. The petitioners are entitled to respect for their private lives. The State cannot demean their existence or control their destiny by making their private sexual conduct a crime. Their right to liberty under the Due Process Clause gives them the full right to engage in their conduct without intervention of the government. "It is a promise of the Constitution that there is a realm of personal liberty which the government may not enter." *Casey*. The Texas statute furthers no legitimate state interest which can justify its intrusion into the personal and private life of the individual.

Had those who drew and ratified the Due Process Clauses of the 5th Amendment or the 14th Amendment known the components of liberty in its manifold possibilities, they might have been more specific. They did not presume to have this insight. They knew times can blind us to certain truths and later generations can see that laws once thought necessary and proper in fact serve only to oppress. As the Constitution endures, persons in every generation can invoke its principles in their own search for greater freedom.

The judgment of the Court of Appeals for the Texas Fourteenth District is reversed, and the case is remanded for further proceedings not inconsistent with this opinion.

Justice O'Connor, concurring in the judgment.

The Court today overrules *Bowers v. Hardwick* (1986). I joined *Bowers*, and do not join the Court in overruling it. Nevertheless, I agree with the Court that Texas' statute banning same-sex sodomy is unconstitutional. Rather than relying on the substantive component of the 14th Amendment's Due Process Clause, as the Court does, I base my conclusion on the 14th Amendment's Equal Protection Clause.

The Equal Protection Clause of the 14th Amendment "is essentially a direction that all persons similarly situated should be treated alike." *Cleburne v. Cleburne Living Center, Inc.* (1985); see also *Plyler v. Doe* (1982). Under our rational basis standard of review, "legislation is presumed to be valid and will be sustained if the classification drawn by the statute is rationally related to a legitimate state interest." *Cleburne*.

Laws such as economic or tax legislation that are scrutinized under rational basis review normally pass constitutional muster, since "the Constitution presumes that even improvident decisions will eventually be rectified by the democratic processes." *Cleburne*.... We have consistently held, however, that some objectives, such as "a bare ... desire to harm a politically unpopular group," are not legitimate state interests. *Department of Agriculture v. Moreno* (1973). See also *Cleburne*; *Romer v. Evans* (1996). When a law exhibits such a desire to harm a politically unpopular group, we have applied a more searching form of rational basis review to strike down such laws under the Equal Protection Clause.

We have been most likely to apply rational basis review to hold a law unconstitutional under the Equal Protection Clause where, as here, the challenged legislation inhibits personal relationships. In *Moreno*, for example, we held that a law preventing those households containing an individual unrelated to any other member of the household from receiving food stamps violated equal protection because the purpose of the law was to "'discriminate against hippies.'" ...

The statute at issue here makes sodomy a crime only if a person "engages in deviate sexual intercourse with another individual of the same sex." Sodomy between opposite-sex partners, however, is not a crime in Texas. That is, Texas treats the same conduct differently based solely on the participants. Those harmed by this law are people who have a same-sex sexual orientation and thus are more likely to engage in behavior prohibited by § 21.06.

The Texas statute makes homosexuals unequal in the eyes of the law by making particular conduct-and only that conduct-subject to criminal sanction....

And the effect of Texas' sodomy law is not just limited to the threat of prosecution or consequence of conviction. Texas' sodomy law brands all homosexuals as criminals, thereby making it more difficult for homosexuals to be treated in the same manner as everyone else. Indeed, Texas itself has previously acknowledged the collateral effects of the law, stipulating in a prior challenge to this action that the law "legally sanctions discrimination against [homosexuals] in a variety of ways unrelated to the criminal law," including in the areas of "employment, family issues, and housing." *State v. Morales* (Tex. App. 1992)....

This case raises a different issue than *Bowers*: whether, under the Equal Protection Clause, moral disapproval is a legitimate state interest to justify by itself a statute that bans homosexual sodomy, but not heterosexual sodomy. It is not. Moral disapproval of this group, like a bare desire to harm the group, is an interest that is insufficient to satisfy rational basis review under the Equal Protection Clause. Indeed, we have never held that moral disapproval, without any other asserted state interest, is a sufficient rationale under the Equal Protection Clause to justify a law that discriminates among groups of persons.

Moral disapproval of a group cannot be a legitimate governmental interest under the Equal Protection Clause because legal classifications must not be "drawn for the purpose of disadvantaging the group burdened by the law." [*Romer v. Evans* (1996).] ...

Texas argues, however, that the sodomy law does not discriminate against homosexual persons. Instead, the State maintains that the law discriminates only against homosexual conduct. While it is true that the law applies only to conduct, the conduct targeted by this law is conduct that is closely correlated with being homosexual. Under such circumstances, Texas' sodomy law is targeted at more than conduct....

Indeed, Texas law confirms that the sodomy statute is directed toward homosexuals as a class. In Texas, calling a person a homosexual is slander *per se* because the word "homosexual" "impute[s] the commission of a crime." The State has admitted that because of the sodomy law, *being* homosexual carries the presumption of being a criminal. Texas' sodomy law therefore results in discrimination against homosexuals as a class in an array of areas outside the criminal law. In *Romer* we refused to sanction a law that singled out homosexuals "for disfavored legal status." The same is true here. The Equal Protection Clause "'neither knows nor tolerates classes among citizens.'"

A State can of course assign certain consequences to a violation of its criminal law. But the State cannot single out one identifiable class of citizens for punishment that does not apply to everyone else, with moral disapproval as the only asserted state interest for the law. The Texas sodomy statute subjects homosexuals to "a lifelong penalty and stigma. A legislative classification that threatens the creation of an underclass ... cannot be reconciled with" the Equal Protection Clause. *Plyler v. Doe* (1982).

Whether a sodomy law that is neutral both in effect and application, see *Yick Wo v. Hopkins* (1886), would violate the substantive component of the Due Process Clause is an issue that need not be decided today. I am confident, however, that so long as the Equal Protection Clause requires a sodomy law to apply equally to the private consensual conduct of homosexuals and heterosexuals alike, such a law would not long stand in our democratic society....

That this law as applied to private, consensual conduct is unconstitutional under the Equal Protection Clause does not mean that other laws distinguishing between heterosexuals and homosexuals would similarly fail under rational basis review. Texas cannot assert any legitimate state interest here, such as national security or preserving the traditional institution of marriage....

Justice Scalia, with whom The Chief Justice and Justice Thomas join, dissenting.

"Liberty finds no refuge in a jurisprudence of doubt." *Planned Parenthood of Southeastern Pa. v. Casey* (1992). That was the Court's sententious response, barely more than a decade ago, to those seeking to overrule *Roe v. Wade* (1973). The Court's response today, to those who have engaged in a 17-year crusade to overrule *Bowers v. Hardwick* (1986), is very different. The need for stability and certainty presents no barrier.

Most of the rest of today's opinion has no relevance to its actual holding—that the Texas statute "furthers no legitimate state interest which can justify" its application to petitioners under rational-basis review. (Overruling *Bowers* to the extent it sustained Georgia's anti-sodomy statute under the rational-basis test.) Though there is discussion of "fundamental proposition[s]," and "fundamental decisions," nowhere does the Court's opinion declare that homosexual sodomy is a "fundamental right" under the Due Process Clause; nor does it subject the Texas law to the standard of review that would be appropriate (strict scrutiny) if homosexual sodomy *were* a "fundamental right." Thus, while overruling the *outcome* of *Bowers*, the Court leaves strangely untouched its central legal conclusion: "[R]espondent would have us announce ... a fundamental right to engage in homosexual sodomy. This we are quite unwilling to do." *Bowers*. Instead the Court simply describes petitioners' conduct as "an exercise of their liberty"—which it undoubtedly is—and proceeds to apply an unheard-of form of rational-basis review that will have far-reaching implications beyond this case.

I. I begin with the Court's surprising readiness to reconsider a decision rendered a mere 17 years ago in *Bowers*. I do not myself believe in rigid adherence to *stare decisis* in constitutional cases; but I do believe that we should be consistent rather than manipulative in invoking the doctrine. Today's opinions in support of reversal do not bother to distinguish—or indeed, even bother to mention—the paean to *stare decisis* coauthored by three Members of today's majority in *Planned Parenthood v. Casey*....

Today's approach to *stare decisis* invites us to overrule an erroneously decided precedent (including an "intensely divisive" decision) *if*: (1) its foundations have been "eroded" by subsequent decisions; (2) it has been subject to "substantial and continuing" criticism; and (3) it has not induced "individual or societal reliance" that counsels against overturning. The problem is that *Roe* itself—which today's majority surely has no disposition to overrule—satisfies these conditions to at least the same degree as *Bowers*.

(1) A preliminary digressive observation with regard to the first factor: The Court's claim that *Planned Parenthood v. Casey* "casts some doubt" upon the holding in *Bowers* (or any other case, for that matter) does not withstand analysis. As far as its holding is concerned, *Casey* provided a *less* expansive right to abortion than did *Roe, which was already on the books when Bowers was decided*. And if the Court is referring not to the holding of *Casey*, but to the dictum of its famed sweet-mystery-of-life passage ("'At the heart of liberty is the right to define one's own concept of existence, of meaning, of the universe, and of the mystery of human life'"): That [passage] "casts some doubt" upon either the totality of our jurisprudence or else (presumably the right answer) nothing at all. I have never heard of a law that attempted to restrict one's "right to define" certain concepts; and if the passage calls into question the government's power to regulate *actions based on* one's self-defined "concept of existence, etc.," it is the passage that ate the rule of law.

I do not quarrel with the Court's claim that *Romer v. Evans* (1996) "eroded" the "foundations" of *Bowers*' rational-basis holding. But *Roe* and *Casey* have been equally "eroded" by *Washington v. Glucksberg* (1997), which held that *only* fundamental rights which are "'deeply rooted in this Nation's history and tradition'" qualify for anything other than rational basis scrutiny under the doctrine of "substantive due process." *Roe* and *Casey*, of course, subjected the restriction of abortion to heightened scrutiny without even attempting to establish that the freedom to abort *was* rooted in this Nation's tradition.

(2) *Bowers*, the Court says, has been subject to "substantial and continuing [criticism], disapproving of its reasoning in all respects, not just as to its historical assumptions." Exactly what those nonhistorical criticisms are, and whether the Court even agrees with them, are left unsaid, although the Court does cite two books. Of course, *Roe* too (and

by extension *Casey*) had been (and still is) subject to unrelenting criticism, including criticism from the two commentators cited by the Court today.

(3) That leaves, to distinguish the rock-solid, unamendable disposition of *Roe* from the readily overrulable *Bowers*, only the third factor. "[T]here has been," the Court says, "no individual or societal reliance on *Bowers* of the sort that could counsel against overturning its holding...." It seems to me that the "societal reliance" on the principles confirmed in *Bowers* and discarded today has been overwhelming. Countless judicial decisions and legislative enactments have relied on the ancient proposition that a governing majority's belief that certain sexual behavior is "immoral and unacceptable" constitutes a rational basis for regulation....

What a massive disruption of the current social order, therefore, the overruling of *Bowers* entails. Not so the overruling of *Roe*, which would simply have restored the regime that existed for centuries before 1973, in which the permissibility of and restrictions upon abortion were determined legislatively State-by-State. *Casey*, however, chose to base its *stare decisis* determination on a different "sort" of reliance. "[P]eople," it said, "have organized intimate relationships and made choices that define their views of themselves and their places in society, in reliance on the availability of abortion in the event that contraception should fail." *Casey*. This falsely assumes that the consequence of overruling *Roe* would have been to make abortion unlawful. It would not; it would merely have *permitted* the States to do so. Many States would unquestionably have declined to prohibit abortion, and others would not have prohibited it within six months (after which the most significant reliance interests would have expired). Even for persons in States other than these, the choice would not have been between abortion and childbirth, but between abortion nearby and abortion in a neighboring State.

To tell the truth, it does not surprise me, and should surprise no one, that the Court has chosen today to revise the standards of *stare decisis* set forth in *Casey*. It has thereby exposed *Casey*'s extraordinary deference to precedent for the result-oriented expedient that it is.

II. Having decided that it need not adhere to *stare decisis*, the Court still must establish that *Bowers* was wrongly decided and that the Texas statute, as applied to petitioners, is unconstitutional.

Texas Penal Code Ann. §21.06(a) (2003) undoubtedly imposes constraints on liberty. So do laws prohibiting prostitution, recreational use of heroin, and, for that matter, working more than 60 hours per week in a bakery. But there is no right to "liberty" under the Due Process Clause, though today's opinion repeatedly makes that claim. ("The liberty protected by the Constitution allows homosexual persons the right to make this choice"); ("'These matters ... are central to the liberty protected by the 14th Amendment'"); ("Their right to liberty under the Due Process Clause gives them the full right to engage in their conduct without intervention of the government")....

Our opinions applying the doctrine known as "substantive due process" hold that the Due Process Clause prohibits States from infringing *fundamental* liberty interests, unless the infringement is narrowly tailored to serve a compelling state interest. *Glucksberg*. We have held repeatedly, in cases the Court today does not overrule, that *only* fundamental rights qualify for this so-called "heightened scrutiny" protection—that is, rights which are "'deeply rooted in this Nation's history and tradition,'".... All other liberty interests may be abridged or abrogated pursuant to a validly enacted state law if that law is rationally related to a legitimate state interest.

Bowers held, first, that criminal prohibitions of homosexual sodomy are not subject to heightened scrutiny because they do not implicate a "fundamental right" under the Due Process Clause. Noting that "[p]roscriptions against that conduct have ancient roots," that "[s]odomy was a criminal offense at common law and was forbidden by the laws of the original 13 States when they ratified the Bill of Rights," and that many States had retained their bans on sodomy, *Bowers* concluded that a right to engage in homosexual sodomy was not "'deeply rooted in this Nation's history and tradition.'"

The Court today does not overrule this holding. Not once does it describe homosexual sodomy as a "fundamental right" or a "fundamental liberty interest," nor does it subject the Texas statute to strict scrutiny. Instead, having failed to establish that the right to homosexual sodomy is "'deeply rooted in this Nation's history and tradition,'" the Court concludes that the application of Texas's statute to petitioners' conduct fails the rational-basis test, and overrules *Bowers*' holding to the contrary. "The Texas statute furthers no legitimate state interest which can justify its intrusion into the personal and private life of the individual."

I shall address that rational-basis holding presently. First, however, I address some aspersions that the Court casts upon *Bowers*' conclusion that homosexual sodomy is not a "fundamental right"—even though, as I have said, the Court does not have the boldness to reverse that conclusion.

III. The Court's description of "the state of the law" at the time of *Bowers* only confirms that *Bowers* was right. The Court points to *Griswold v. Connecticut* (1965). But that case *expressly disclaimed* any reliance on the doctrine of "substantive due process," and grounded the so-called "right to privacy" in penumbras of constitutional provisions *other than* the Due Process Clause. *Eisenstadt v. Baird* (1972), likewise had nothing to do with "substantive due process"; it invalidated a Massachusetts law prohibiting the distribution of contraceptives to unmarried persons solely on the basis of the Equal Protection Clause. Of course, *Eisenstadt* contains well known dictum relating to the "right to privacy," but this referred to the right recognized in *Griswold*—a right penumbral to the *specific* guarantees in the Bill of Rights, and not a "substantive due process" right.

Roe v. Wade recognized that the right to abort an unborn child was a "fundamental right" protected by the Due Process Clause. The *Roe* Court, however, made no attempt to establish that this right was "'deeply rooted in this Nation's history and tradition'"; instead, it based its conclusion that "the 14th Amendment's concept of personal liberty ... is broad enough to encompass a woman's decision whether or not to terminate her pregnancy" on its own normative judgment that anti-abortion laws were undesirable. We have since rejected *Roe*'s holding that regulations of abortion must be narrowly tailored to serve a compelling state interest, and thus, by logical implication, *Roe*'s holding that the right to abort an unborn child is a "fundamental right."

After discussing the history of antisodomy laws, the Court proclaims that, "it should be noted that there is no longstanding history in this country of laws directed at homosexual conduct as a distinct matter." This observation in no way casts into doubt the "definitive [historical] conclusion," on which *Bowers* relied: that our Nation has a longstanding history of laws prohibiting *sodomy in general*—regardless of whether it was performed by same-sex or opposite-sex couples....

It is (as *Bowers* recognized) entirely irrelevant whether the laws in our long national tradition criminalizing homosexual sodomy were "directed at homosexual conduct as a distinct matter." Whether homosexual sodomy was prohibited by a law targeted at same-sex sexual relations or by a more general law prohibiting both homosexual and heterosexual sodomy, the only relevant point is that it *was* criminalized—which suffices to establish that homosexual sodomy is not a right "deeply rooted in our Nation's history and tradition." The Court today agrees that homosexual sodomy was criminalized and thus does not dispute the facts on which *Bowers actually* relied.

Next the Court makes the claim, again unsupported by any citations, that "[l]aws prohibiting sodomy do not seem to have been enforced against consenting adults acting in private." The key qualifier here is "acting in private"—since the Court admits that sodomy laws *were* enforced against consenting adults (although the Court contends that prosecutions were "infrequent"). I do not know what "acting in private" means; surely consensual sodomy, like heterosexual intercourse, is rarely performed on stage. If all the Court means by "acting in private" is "on private premises, with the doors closed and windows covered," it is entirely unsurprising that evidence of enforcement would be hard to come by. (Imagine the circumstances that would enable a search warrant to be obtained for a residence on the ground that there was probable cause to believe that consensual sodomy was then and there occurring.) Surely that lack of evidence would not sustain the proposition that consensual sodomy on private premises with the doors closed and windows covered was regarded as a "fundamental right," even though all other consensual sodomy was criminalized. There are 203 prosecutions for consensual, adult homosexual sodomy reported in the West Reporting system and official state reporters from the years 1880–1995. There are also records of 20 sodomy prosecutions and 4 executions during the colonial period. *Bowers'* conclusion that homosexual sodomy is not a fundamental right "deeply rooted in this Nation's history and tradition" is utterly unassailable.

Realizing that fact, the Court instead says: "[W]e think that our laws and traditions in the past half century are of most relevance here. These references show *an emerging awareness* that liberty gives substantial protection to adult persons in deciding how to conduct their private lives *in matters pertaining to sex.*" (emphasis added). Apart from the fact that such an "emerging awareness" does not establish a "fundamental right," the statement is factually false. States continue to prosecute all sorts of crimes by adults "in matters pertaining to sex": prostitution, adult incest, adultery, obscenity, and child pornography. Sodomy laws, too, have been enforced "in the past half century," in which there have been 134 reported cases involving prosecutions for consensual, adult, homosexual sodomy. In relying, for evidence of an "emerging recognition," upon the American Law Institute's 1955 recommendation not to criminalize "'consensual sexual relations conducted in private,'" the Court ignores the fact that this recommendation was "a point of resistance in most of the states that considered adopting the Model Penal Code."

In any event, an "emerging awareness" is by definition not "deeply rooted in this Nation's history and tradition[s]," as we have said "fundamental right" status requires. Constitutional entitlements do not spring into existence because some States choose to lessen or eliminate criminal sanctions on certain behavior. Much less do they spring into existence, as the Court seems to believe, because *foreign nations* decriminalize conduct. The *Bowers* majority opinion *never* relied on "values we share with a wider civilization," but rather rejected the claimed right to sodomy on the ground that such a right was not "'deeply rooted in *this Nation's* history and tradition,'" (emphasis added). *Bowers'* rational-basis holding is likewise devoid of any reliance on the views of a "wider civilization." The Court's discussion of these foreign views (ignoring, of course, the many countries that have retained criminal prohibitions on sodomy) is therefore meaningless dicta. Dangerous dicta, however, since "this Court ... should not impose foreign moods, fads, or fashions on Americans." *Foster v. Florida* (2002) (Thomas, J., concurring in denial of certiorari).

IV. I turn now to the ground on which the Court squarely rests its holding: the contention that there is no rational basis for the law here under attack. This proposition is so out of accord with our jurisprudence—indeed, with the jurisprudence of *any* society we know—that it requires little discussion.

The Texas statute undeniably seeks to further the belief of its citizens that certain forms of sexual behavior are "immoral and unacceptable," *Bowers*—the same interest furthered by criminal laws against fornication, bigamy, adultery, adult incest, bestiality, and obscenity. *Bowers* held that this *was* a legitimate state interest. The Court today reaches the opposite conclusion. The Texas statute, it says, "furthers *no legitimate state interest* which can justify its intrusion into the personal and private life of the individual." The Court embraces instead Justice Stevens' declaration in his *Bowers* dissent, that "the fact that the governing majority in a State has traditionally viewed a particular practice as immoral is not a sufficient reason for upholding a law prohibiting the practice." This effectively decrees the end of all morals legislation. If, as the Court asserts, the promotion of majoritarian sexual morality is not even a *legitimate* state interest, none of the above-mentioned laws can survive rational-basis review.

V. Finally, I turn to petitioners' equal-protection challenge, which no Member of the Court save Justice O'Connor embraces: On its face § 21.06(a) applies equally to all persons. Men and women, heterosexuals and homosexuals, are all subject to its prohibition of deviate sexual intercourse with someone of the same sex. To be sure, § 21.06 does distinguish between the sexes insofar as concerns the partner with whom the sexual acts are performed: men can violate the law only with other men, and women only with other women. But this cannot itself be a denial of equal protection, since it is precisely the same distinction regarding partner that is drawn in state laws prohibiting marriage with someone of the same sex while permitting marriage with someone of the opposite sex.

The objection is made, however, that the antimiscegenation laws invalidated in *Loving v. Virginia* (1967), similarly were applicable to whites and blacks alike, and only distinguished between the races insofar as the *partner* was concerned. In *Loving*, however, we correctly applied heightened scrutiny, rather than the usual rational-basis review, because the Virginia statute was "designed to maintain White Supremacy." A racially discriminatory purpose is always sufficient to subject a law to strict scrutiny, even a facially neutral law that makes no mention of race. No purpose to discriminate against men or women as a class can be gleaned from the Texas law, so rational-basis review applies. That review is readily satisfied here by the same rational basis that satisfied it in *Bowers*-society's belief that certain forms of sexual behavior are "immoral and unacceptable." This is the same justification that supports many other laws regulating sexual behavior that make a distinction based upon the identity of the partner—for example, laws against adultery, fornication, and adult incest, and laws refusing to recognize homosexual marriage....

Justice O'Connor simply decrees application of "a more searching form of rational basis review" to the Texas statute. The cases she cites do not recognize such a standard, and reach their conclusions only after finding, as required by conventional rational-basis analysis, that no conceivable legitimate state interest supports the classification at issue. Nor does Justice O'Connor explain precisely what her "more searching form" of rational-basis review consists of. It must at least mean, however, that laws exhibiting "'a ... desire to harm a politically unpopular group,'" are invalid *even though* there may be a conceivable rational basis to support them.

This reasoning leaves on pretty shaky grounds state laws limiting marriage to opposite-sex couples. Justice O'Connor seeks to preserve them by the conclusory statement that "preserving the traditional institution of marriage" is a legitimate state interest. But "preserving the traditional institution of marriage" is just a kinder way of describing the State's *moral disapproval* of same-sex couples. Texas's interest in § 21.06 could be recast in similarly euphemistic terms: "preserving the traditional sexual mores of our society." In the jurisprudence Justice O'Connor has seemingly created, judges can validate laws by characterizing them as "preserving the traditions of society" (good); or invalidate them by characterizing them as "expressing moral disapproval" (bad).

Today's opinion is the product of a Court, which is the product of a law-profession culture, that has largely signed on to the so-called homosexual agenda, by which I mean the agenda promoted by some homosexual activists directed at eliminating the moral opprobrium that has traditionally attached to homosexual conduct. I noted in an earlier opinion the fact that the American Association of Law Schools (to which any reputable law school *must* seek to belong) excludes from membership any school that refuses to ban from its job-interview facilities a law firm (no matter how small) that does not wish to hire as a prospective partner a person who openly engages in homosexual conduct.

One of the most revealing statements in today's opinion is the Court's grim warning that the criminalization of homosexual conduct is "an invitation to subject homosexual persons to discrimination both in the public and in the private spheres." It is clear from this that the Court has taken sides in the culture war, departing from its role of assuring, as neutral observer, that the democratic rules of engagement are observed. Many Americans do not want persons who openly engage in homosexual conduct as partners in their business, as scoutmasters for their children, as teachers in their children's schools, or as boarders in their home. They view this as protecting themselves and their families from a lifestyle that they believe to be immoral and destructive. The Court views it as "discrimination" which it is the function of our judgments to deter. So imbued is the Court with the law profession's anti-anti-homosexual culture, that it is seemingly unaware that the attitudes of that culture are not obviously "mainstream"; that in most States what the Court calls "discrimination" against those who engage in homosexual acts is perfectly legal; that proposals to ban such "discrimination" under Title VII have repeatedly been rejected by Congress.

Let me be clear that I have nothing against homosexuals, or any other group, promoting their agenda through normal democratic means. Social perceptions of sexual and other morality change over time, and every group has the right to persuade its fellow citizens that its view of such matters is the best. That homosexuals have achieved some success in that enterprise is attested to by the fact that Texas is one of the few remaining States that criminalize private, consensual homosexual acts. But persuading one's fellow citizens is one thing, and imposing one's views in absence of democratic majority will is something else. I would no more *require* a State to criminalize homosexual acts—or, for that matter, display *any* moral disapprobation of them—than I would *forbid* it to do so. What Texas has chosen to do is well within the range of traditional democratic action, and its hand should not be stayed through the invention of a brand-new "constitutional right" by a Court that is impatient of democratic change. It is indeed true that "later generations can see that laws once thought necessary and proper in fact serve only to oppress," and when that happens, later generations can repeal those laws. But it is the premise of our system that those judgments are to be made by the people, and not imposed by a governing caste that knows best.

One of the benefits of leaving regulation of this matter to the people rather than to the courts is that the people, unlike judges, need not carry things to their logical conclusion. The people may feel that their disapprobation of homosexual conduct is strong enough to disallow homosexual marriage, but not strong enough to criminalize private homosexual acts—and may legislate accordingly. The Court today pretends that it possesses a similar freedom of action, so that we need not fear judicial imposition of homosexual marriage, as has recently occurred in Canada (in a decision that the Canadian Government has chosen not to appeal). At the end of its opinion—after having laid waste the foundations of our rational-basis jurisprudence—the Court says that the present case "does not involve whether the government must give formal recognition to any relationship that homosexual persons seek to enter." Do not believe it. More illuminating than this bald, unreasoned disclaimer is the progression of thought displayed by an earlier passage in the Court's opinion, which notes the constitutional protections afforded to "personal decisions relating to *marriage*, procreation, contraception, family relationships, child rearing, and education," and then declares that "[p]ersons in a homosexual relationship may seek autonomy for these purposes, just as heterosexual persons do." Today's opinion dismantles the structure of constitutional law that has permitted a distinction to be made between heterosexual and homosexual unions, insofar as formal recognition in marriage is concerned. If moral disapprobation of homosexual conduct is "no legitimate state interest" for purposes of proscribing that conduct; and if, as the Court coos (casting aside all pretense of neutrality), "[w]hen sexuality finds overt expression in intimate conduct with another person, the conduct can be but one element in a personal bond that is more enduring"; what justification could there possibly be for denying the benefits of marriage to homosexual couples exercising "[t]he liberty protected by the Constitution"? Surely not the encouragement of procreation, since the sterile and the elderly are allowed to marry. This case "does not involve" the issue of homosexual marriage only if one entertains the belief that principle and logic have nothing to do with the decisions of this Court. Many will hope that, as the Court comfortingly assures us, this is so....

Justice Thomas, dissenting. [Omitted].

C. Homosexuality and Politics

The legal status of homosexuals continues to be a hotly debated issue. Below are the relevant excerpts from the 2004 and 2008 platforms of the Democratic and Republican parties.

From the 2004 Democratic Party Platform

We support full inclusion of gay and lesbian families in the life or our nation and seek equal responsibilities, benefits, and protections for these families. In our country, marriage has been defined at the state level for 200 years, and we believe it should continue to be defined there. We repudiate President Bush's divisive effort to politicize the Constitution by pursuing a "Federal Marriage Amendment." Our goal is to bring Americans together, not drive them apart.

From the 2004 Republican Party Platform

We strongly support President Bush's call for a Constitutional amendment that fully protects marriage, and we believe that neither federal or state judges nor bureaucrats should force states to recognize other living arrangements as equivalent to marriage. We believe, and the social science confirms, that the well-being of children is best accomplished in the environment of the home, nurtured by their mother and father anchored by the bonds of marriage. We further believe that legal recognition and the accompanying benefits afforded couples should be preserved for that unique and special union of one man and one woman which has historically been called marriage.

From the 2008 Democratic Party Platform

We believe in the essential American ideal that we are not constrained by the circumstances of birth but can make of our lives what we will.... Democrats will fight to end discrimination based on race, sex, ethnicity, national origin, language, religion, sexual orientation, gender identity, age, and disability in every corner of our country, because that's the America we believe in....

We all have to do our part to lift up this country, and that means changing hearts and changing minds, and making sure that every American is treated equally under the law.... We support the full inclusion of all families, including same-sex couples, in the life of our nation, and support equal responsibility, benefits, and protections. We will enact a comprehensive bipartisan employment non-discrimination act. We oppose the Defense of Marriage Act and all attempts to use this issue to divide us.

From the 2008 Republican Party Platform

Republicans recognize the importance of having in the home a father and a mother who are married. The two-parent family still provides the best environment of stability, discipline, responsibility, and character. Children in homes without fathers are more likely to commit a crime, drop out of school, become violent, become teen parents, use illegal drugs, become mired in poverty, or have emotional or behavioral problems.

Republicans have been at the forefront of protecting traditional marriage laws, both in the states and in Congress. A Republican Congress enacted the Defense of Marriage Act, affirming the right of states not to recognize same-sex "marriages" licensed in other states. Unbelievably, the Democratic Party has now pledged to repeal the Defense of Marriage Act, which would subject every state to the redefinition of marriage by a judge without ever allowing the people to vote on the matter.

D. The Constitutional Status of Gay Marriage*

The battle over gay marriage has been raging for nearly forty years. *Baker v. Nelson* (Minn. 1971) is considered by many to be the "first" gay marriage case. In that case a male couple applied for a marriage license in Minnesota. Ultimately, on a "marriage for procreation" rationale, the Minnesota appellate courts denied the plaintiffs' claims. The Minnesota court also rejected federal Due Process and Equal Protection claims, stating simply, "We do not find support for [these arguments] in any decision of the United States Supreme Court."

In December 1990, two lesbian couples and one gay couple applied for marriage licenses at the Hawaii State Department of Health. The applications were denied, and the plaintiffs sued. In *Baehr v. Lewin* (Ha. 1993), the Supreme Court of Hawaii ruled that the Hawaii legislature must either present a "compelling state interest" for denying same-sex couples marriage licenses or must allow same-sex marriage. On remand in 1996, a trial judge found that the state of Hawaii could not justify its discrimination. While an appeal from the trial judge's ruling was pending, the Hawaii legislature proposed a constitutional amendment providing that "the legislature has the power to reserve marriage to opposite-sex couples." The voters of Hawaii approved that amendment in 1998 by a more than two-to-one margin.

While the Hawaii appeal was pending, in March 1998, an Alaska state trial court ruled that the choice of a marital partner is fundamental and cannot be interfered with by the state absent a compelling reason. In the court's words, "[T]he choice of a life partner is personal, intimate, and subject to the protection of the right of privacy." *Brause v. Bu-*

---

* © Shannon Gilreath, 2010.

reau of Vital Statistics (Alaska Super. Ct. 1998). As in Hawaii, in November 1998, the Alaska electorate approved a state constitutional amendment requiring that all marriages be "between one man and one woman."

Between 1995 and 2001, after the Hawaii and Alaska litigation, 34 states enacted laws expressly providing that marriage be limited to one man and one woman and also providing that those states would not recognize same-sex marriages from other states. In 1996, Congress passed the Defense of Marriage Act ("DOMA") (codified at 1 U.S.C. § 7 and 28 U.S.C. § 1738C), which provided that no state was obliged to recognize a same-sex marriage from another state.

In spite of these setbacks, the struggle for gay marriage continued. In 1997 three same-sex couples (Stan Baker and Peter Harrigan, Beck and Stacy Jolles, and Lois Farnham and Holly Puterbaugh) brought suit against the State of Vermont and their towns for denying them marriage licenses. On December 20, 1999, the Vermont Supreme Court in *Baker v. Vermont* (Vt. 1999) unanimously held that denying the benefits of marriage to same-sex couples in Vermont violated the state constitution's "common benefits clause." The court directed the Vermont legislature to address the problem by either granting same-sex couples marriage rights or by creating a new institution that would assure same-sex couples the same rights and responsibilities under state law as married couples. In response, the Vermont legislature passed, and Governor Dean signed, "An Act Relating to Civil Unions." The act created a "civil union" status for same-sex couples. It granted couples in civil unions all of the rights and responsibilities under Vermont law that married couples enjoyed.

In 2003, the Massachusetts Supreme Judicial Court decided the case of *Goodridge v. Dept. of Public Health* (Ma. 2003). The *Goodridge* court held that lesbian and gay citizens of Massachusetts must be given the same civil marriage rights as their heterosexual counterparts. The court rejected the state's proffered reasons for reserving marriage for opposite-sex couples: procreation, optimal child rearing, and conservation of scarce financial resources. The defendants also claimed that gay relationships were unstable and undeserving of legal recognition. However, the court noted that the relationships of the four plaintiff couples had lasted for an average of fourteen years. Two of the couples were raising children and, in one instance, a partner had become the soul caregiver and provider when her partner was stricken with cancer.

The Massachusetts court noted that same sex couples were deprived of many statutory benefits extended to married couples. These included: joint state income tax filing, tenancy by the entirety, extension of the benefit of homestead protection to one's spouse and children, automatic rights to inherit property of a deceased spouse who does not leave a will, rights of elective share and of dower, entitlement to wages owed to a deceased employee, eligibility to continue certain businesses of a deceased spouse, the right to share the medical policy of one's spouse, 39-week continuation of health coverage for the spouse of a person who is laid off or dies; preferential options under the state's pension system; preferential benefits in the state's medical program; access to veterans' spousal benefits and preferences; financial protections for spouses of certain state employees killed in performance of duty; equitable division of marital property on divorce; temporary and permanent alimony rights; right to separate support during a separation that does not result in divorce; and the right to bring claims for wrongful death, loss of consortium, funeral and burial expenses, and punitive damages resulting from tort actions.

While the *Goodridge* court said it employed a "rational basis" standard of review, it apparently used something like "rational basis with bite." In spite of a presumably deferential standard of review, the Court still found the state's justifications wanting. Under the Massachusetts constitution, for due process claims, rational basis requires that statutes bear a real and substantial relation to the public health, safely, morals, or some other phase of the general welfare. For equal protection, rational basis requires that an impartial law maker could logically believe that the classification would serve a legitimate public interest that transcends the harm to members of the disadvantaged class. See Mary L. Bonauto, Goodridge *in Context*, 40 Harvard Civil Rights-Civil Liberties Law Review 1, 39–40 (2005). Applying these standards, the court held that the state could not meet its burden of justification. The court also rejected a proffered legislative compromise that would have created civil unions instead of extending the right to marriage.

On May 17, 2004, the fiftieth anniversary of *Brown v. Board*, Cambridge, Massachusetts issued the first legally authorized marriage license to a same-sex couple. Thousands of gay couples have married and continue to marry legally in Massachusetts. In 2004, gays also sought to open marriage across the country and a number of locales complied. San Francisco, California, Sandoval, New Mexico, and New Paltz, New York all began issuing licenses. Oregon's Multnomah County (which includes Portland) granted some three thousand marriage licenses. State courts halted all of these efforts to expand marriage.

As noted, successful efforts for gay marriage have often been followed by a backlash, and that was so after the Massachusetts decision as well. The forward march of the marriage equality movement, coupled with concerns about the constitutionality of DOMA, led to a push for state constitutional amendments banning gay marriage, as well as a federal amendment. Twenty-four states amended their constitutions expressly to ban same-sex marriage or were considering such a move in *Goodridge's* wake. In the November 2004 elections, constitutional amendments to ban same-sex marriage passed in every state (11 total) in which they appeared on the ballot. Some went beyond prohibiting "marriage" and prohibited granting gay couples rights such as those enjoyed by married couples—, which might arguably include even domestic partner health benefits granted by private firms. For example, Ohio's amendment went beyond marriage to prohibit "legal status for relationships of unmarried individuals that intend to approximate the design, qualities, significance or effect of marriage."

In the 2006 mid-term elections, seven more states added amendments banning same-sex marriage. However, Arizona became the first state in which a proposed amendment banning same-sex marriage was defeated by voters, 51% to 49%. State amendments have been challenged under federal Due Process and Equal Protection. See, *e.g.*, *Citizens for Equal Protection v. Bruning* (8th Cir., 2006). For a general discussion see Shannon Gilreath, *Sexual Politics: The Gay Person in America Today*, University of Akron Press (2006).

Despite set backs, progress continued. On April 20, 2005, the Connecticut legislature became the first state legislature to provide civil union rights for gay citizens in the absence of a judicial mandate. Prompted by its state Supreme Court (*Lewis v. Harris* (N.J. 2006)), the New Jersey legislature passed a statute creating civil unions, effective in 2007. New Hampshire did likewise, effective 2008. Oregon allowed domestic partnerships, effective 2007.

In 2008, in the landmark *In re Marriage Cases*, the California Supreme Court held that California's bifurcated system of partnership recognition (marriage for straights, domestic partnerships for gays) affronted a fundamental right to marry found in the privacy and due process provisions of the state constitution. The court held that designation of same-sex relationships by a different name than straight relationships denied same-sex partners "one of the core elements" of the right to marry: the right to the "same dignity, respect, and stature as that accorded to all other officially recognized family relationships" in California. The court also held that the state's dual system violated equal protection under the California constitution. In so doing, the court for the first time declared sexual orientation a suspect classification under California law. Gay couples began legally marrying in California in June, 2008, although the right to marry was overturned by a state constitutional amendment, Proposition 8, passed by a narrow margin in the November 2008 elections.

Recent gay rights victories on the partnership front have made the question of interstate recognition of same-sex relationships more pressing and complicated. The attorney general of Rhode Island opined that same-sex marriages would be recognized as valid for purposes of state benefits. The New Jersey attorney general opined that same-sex relationships that are the legal equivalent of New Jersey's civil union would be recognized as a civil union in that state. In 2008, the governor of New York directed state agencies to ensure that same-sex marriages validly performed in other states be respected under New York state law, although same-sex couples may not marry in New York.

Other nations now recognize gay marriage or other forms of legal partnership. The Netherlands (2000), Belgium (2003), Canada (2005), Spain (2005), South Africa (2006), and Norway (2008) provide for same-sex marriage. Other nations, including the United Kingdom, France, Germany, Croatia, Denmark, Finland, Hungary, Iceland, Luxembourg, Mexico, New Zealand, Portugal, Sweden, and Switzerland provide varying degrees of legal recognition for same-sex couples, including partnership registration, civil unions, and common law marriage status. Legislation currently considered in Columbia and Cuba portends sweeping gay rights recognition, including same-sex partnership recognition.

The first half of 2009 saw a whirlwind of activity on the marriage equality front. On April 3, 2009, the Iowa Supreme Court ruled unanimously that a state law limiting marriage to opposite-sex couples violated the equality guarantee of the Iowa constitution. (See *Varnum v. Brien* (Iowa 2009) excerpted below). Also in April, Vermont was again a leader (having enacted the first civil union law in the nation in 2000), this time successfully enacting marriage equality by legislative initiative and without a judicial mandate. The law was enacted by a legislative supermajority override of a veto by Republican governor Jim Douglas. Connecticut enacted a marriage equality law in direct response to the Connecticut Supreme Court's decision on October 28, 2008 (*Kerrigan v. Comm. of Public Health*), holding that state laws restricting marriage *qua* marriage (Connecticut had created civil unions for same-sex couples by legislative initiative in 2005) to opposite-sex couples violated state constitutional equal protection guarantees. The Maine legislature enacted and the governor signed, in May, a bill legalizing same-sex marriage in that state, but Maine voters repealed the law in a referendum. In June 2009, the governor of New Hampshire signed a law opening marriage to same-sex couples in that state.

Many of these legislative victories were hard-won, and elsewhere there were setbacks. In *Strauss v. Horton* (Cal., 2009) the California Supreme Court upheld Proposition 8, the measure approved by voters in November 2008 to define marriage as a union of a man and woman and effectively to overturn *In re Marriage Cases*, in which the same court had mandated marriage equality in the state. The court however upheld all marriages between same-sex partners that occurred while *In re Marriage Cases* was still the state's law. In addition, both Arizona and Florida voters passed the anti-marriage amendments on the November '08 ballot in their states. Twenty-nine states (Alabama, Alaska, Arkansas, Arizona, California, Colorado, Florida, Georgia, Idaho, Kansas, Kentucky, Louisiana, Michigan, Mississippi, Missouri, Montana, Nebraska, North Dakota, Ohio, Oklahoma, Oregon, South Carolina, South Dakota, Tennessee, Texas, Utah, Virginia, Wisconsin, and Wyoming) now have constitutional amendments specifically defining marriage as a union between a man and a woman. Hawaii's state constitutional amendment has the same effect, although it does not technically define marriage, reading instead that the Hawaii legislature has "the power to reserve marriage to opposite-sex couples." Maine, by referendum, overturned the state's gay marriage law. In Iowa, a referendum is being considered that would overturn marriage equality.

Finally, steps short of full equality have been taken in several jurisdictions. The Washington, D.C. city council voted in May to recognized same-sex marriage performed elsewhere. The state of Washington expanded its Domestic Partnership Law purportedly to extend all the right and responsibilities of marriage (but not the name) to same-sex couples who register as domestic partners under state law. Colorado has enacted a Designated Beneficiary Agreement Act that took effect July 1, 2009. The new law provides a limited set of rights to unmarried Coloradans (both same-sex and opposite sex) who designate each other beneficiaries.

* * *

The excerpt that follows is the decision of the Iowa Supreme Court on the gay marriage issue.

Varnum v. Brien
763 N.W.2d 862 (Iowa 2009)

Justice Cady, delivered the opinion of the court.

I. This lawsuit is a civil rights action by twelve individuals who reside in six communities across Iowa. Like most Iowans, they are responsible, caring, and productive individuals. They maintain important jobs, or are retired, and are contributing, benevolent members of their communities. They include a nurse, business manager, insurance analyst, bank agent, stay-at-home parent, church organist and piano teacher, museum director, federal employee, social worker, teacher, and two retired teachers. Like many Iowans, some have children and others hope to have children. Some are foster parents....

The twelve plaintiffs comprise six same-sex couples who live in committed relationships. Each maintains a hope of getting married one day, an aspiration shared by many throughout Iowa....

As other Iowans have done in the past when faced with the enforcement of a law that prohibits them from engaging in an activity or achieving a status enjoyed by other Iowans, the twelve plaintiffs turned to the courts to challenge the statute. They seek to declare the marriage statute unconstitutional so they can obtain the array of benefits of marriage enjoyed by heterosexual couples, protect themselves and their children, and demonstrate to one another and to society their mutual commitment....

III. The framers of the Iowa Constitution knew, as did the drafters of the United States Constitution, that "times can blind us to certain truths and later generations can see that laws once thought necessary and proper in fact serve only to oppress," and as our constitution "endures, persons in every generation can invoke its principles in their own search for greater freedom" and equality. See *Lawrence v. Texas* (2003)....

IV-A. The primary constitutional principle at the heart of this case is the doctrine of equal protection. The concept of equal protection is deeply rooted in our national and state history, but that history reveals this concept is often expressed far more easily than it is practiced....

In the first reported case of the Supreme Court of the Territory of Iowa, *In re Ralph* (Iowa 1839), we refused to treat a human being as property to enforce a contract for slavery and held our laws must extend equal protection to persons of all races and conditions. This decision was seventeen years before the United States Supreme Court infamously decided *Dred Scott v. Sandford* (1856), which upheld the rights of a slave owner to treat a person as property. Similarly, in *Clark v. Board of Directors* (Iowa 1868), and *Coger v. North West. Union Packet Co.* (Iowa 1873), we struck blows to the concept of segregation long before the United States Supreme Court's decision in *Brown v. Board of Education* (1954). Iowa was also the first state in the nation to admit a woman to the practice of law, doing so in 1869.... In each of those instances, our state approached a fork in the road toward fulfillment of our constitution's ideals and reaffirmed the "absolute equality of all" persons before the law as "the very foundation principle of our government." See *Coger*.

So, today, this court again faces an important issue that hinges on our definition of equal protection. This issue comes to us with the same importance as our landmark cases of the past. The same-sex-marriage debate waged in this case is part of a strong national dialogue centered on a fundamental, deep-seated, traditional institution that has excluded, by state action, a particular class of Iowans. This class of people asks a simple and direct question: How can a state premised on the constitutional principle of equal protection justify exclusion of a class of Iowans from civil marriage?...

IV-B. The foundational principle of equal protection is expressed in article I, §6 of the Iowa Constitution, which provides: "All laws of a general nature shall have a uniform operation; the general assembly shall not grant to any citizen or class of citizens, privileges or immunities, which, upon the same terms shall not equally belong to all citizens."...

IV-E. The County initially points out that §595.2 does not explicitly refer to "sexual orientation" and does not inquire into whether either member of a proposed civil marriage is sexually attracted to the other. Consequently, it seizes on these observations to support its claim that the statute does not establish a classification on the basis of sexual orientation because the same-sex civil marriage ban does not grant or withhold the benefits flowing from the statute based on sexual preference. Instead, the County argues, §595.2 only incidentally impacts disparately upon gay and lesbian people....

It is true the marriage statute does not expressly prohibit gay and lesbian persons from marrying; it does, however, require that if they marry, it must be to someone of the opposite sex. Viewed in the complete context of marriage, including intimacy, civil marriage with a person of the opposite sex is as unappealing to a gay or lesbian person as civil marriage with a person of the same sex is to a heterosexual. Thus, the right of a gay or lesbian person under the marriage statute to enter into a civil marriage only with a person of the opposite sex is no right at all.... Instead, a gay or lesbian person can only gain the same rights under the statute as a heterosexual person by negating the very trait that defines gay and lesbian people as a class—their sexual orientation. *In re Marriage Cases* (Cal. 2008). The benefit denied by the marriage statute—the status of civil marriage for same-sex couples—is so "closely correlated with being homosexual" as to make it apparent the law is targeted at gay and lesbian people as a class. See *Lawrence* (O'Connor,

J., concurring) (reviewing criminalization of homosexual sodomy and concluding that "[w]hile it is true that the law applies only to conduct, the conduct targeted by this law is conduct that is closely correlated with being homosexual. Under such circumstances, [the] sodomy law is targeted at more than conduct. It is instead directed toward gay persons as a class.")... Thus, we proceed to analyze the constitutionality of the statute based on sexual orientation discrimination.

[The court determined that classifications based on sexual orientation required some level of heightened scrutiny under the Iowa Constitution, but as they held that the marriage statute in question would not withstand intermediate scrutiny, they did not have to determine whether to employ strict scrutiny.] ...

IV-H-2. [T]he question we must answer is whether excluding gay and lesbian people from civil marriage is substantially related to any important governmental objective.

IV-H-3. The County has proffered a number of objectives supporting the marriage statute. These objectives include support for the "traditional" institution of marriage, the optimal procreation and rearing of children, and financial considerations....

IV-H-3-a. The governmental objective identified by the County—to maintain the traditional understanding of marriage—is simply another way of saying the governmental objective is to limit civil marriage to opposite-sex couples. Opposite-sex marriage, however, is the classification made under the statute, and this classification must comply with our principles of equal protection. Thus, the use of traditional marriage as both the governmental objective and the classification of the statute transforms the equal protection analysis into the question of whether restricting marriage to opposite-sex couples accomplishes the governmental objective of maintaining opposite-sex marriage.

This approach is, of course, an empty analysis. It permits a classification to be maintained "'for its own sake.'" *Kerrigan v. Comm. of Public Health* (Conn. 2008) [quoting *Romer v. Evans* (1996)]. Moreover, it can allow discrimination to become acceptable as tradition and helps to explain how discrimination can exist for such a long time. If a simple showing that discrimination is traditional satisfies equal protection, previous successful equal protection challenges of invidious racial and gender classifications would have failed. Consequently, equal protection demands that "'the classification ([that is], the exclusion of gay [persons] from civil marriage) must advance a state interest that is separate from the classification itself.'" ...

IV-H-3-c. The County also proposes that government endorsement of traditional civil marriage will result in more procreation. It points out that procreation is important to the continuation of the human race, and opposite-sex couples accomplish this objective because procreation occurs naturally within this group. In contrast, the County points out, same-sex couples can procreate only through assisted reproductive techniques, and some same-sex couples may choose not to procreate. While heterosexual marriage does lead to procreation, the argument by the County fails to address the real issue in our required analysis of the objective: whether *exclusion* of gay and lesbian individuals from the institution of civil marriage will result in *more* procreation? If procreation is the true objective, then the proffered classification must work to achieve that objective....

[T]he sole conceivable avenue by which exclusion of gay and lesbian people from civil marriage could promote more procreation is if the unavailability of civil marriage for same-sex partners caused homosexual individuals to "become" heterosexual in order to procreate within the present traditional institution of civil marriage. The briefs, the record, our research, and common sense do not suggest such an outcome....

IV-H-3-d. A fourth suggested rationale supporting the marriage statute is "promoting stability in opposite sex relationships." While the institution of civil marriage likely encourages stability in opposite-sex relationships, we must evaluate whether *excluding* gay and lesbian people from civil marriage encourages stability in opposite-sex relationships. The County offers no reasons that it does, and we can find none....

State government can have no religious views, either directly or indirectly, expressed through its legislation. *Knowlton v. Baumhover* (Iowa 1918). This proposition is the essence of the separation of church and state. As a result, civil marriage must be judged under our constitutional standards of equal protection and not under religious doctrines or the religious views of individuals. This approach does not disrespect or denigrate the religious views of many Iowans who may strongly believe in marriage as a dual-gender union, but considers, as we must, only the constitutional rights of all people, as expressed by the promise of equal protection for all. We are not permitted to do less and would damage our constitution immeasurably by trying to do more....

IV-I. A religious denomination can still define marriage as a union between a man and a woman, and a marriage ceremony performed by a minister, priest, rabbi, or other person ordained or designated as a leader of the person's religious faith does not lose its meaning as a sacrament or other religious institution. The sanctity of all religious marriages celebrated in the future will have the same meaning as those celebrated in the past. The only difference is *civil* marriage will now take on a new meaning that reflects a more complete understanding of equal protection of the law. This result is what our constitution requires....

VIII. Liberty and the "Right" to Die

A person in a "persistent vegetative state" is one who has no brain function and must be kept alive by medical intervention. Many people desire to be allowed to die in such a situation. In *Cruzan v. Director, Missouri Department of Health* (1990), the Court addressed the issue of whether a state could require the higher civil proof standard of "clear and convincing evidence," rather than the usual "preponderance of the evidence," in hearings to determine whether such a patient (who had not made a living will) wished to refuse treatment. *Cruzan* is referred to repeatedly in *Glucksberg v. Washington* (1997), *infra*.

Nancy Cruzan was a young woman who had been profoundly injured in an automobile collision and was in a persistent vegetative state. She was kept alive by tubes that provided food and water. Missouri had a "living will" statute that allowed people to avoid extraordinary life sustaining care in such cases. In cases where a person had not made a living will, their families were required to prove the patient's desire by the higher civil proof standard of clear and convincing evidence. Nancy Cruzan had not made a living will. Her parents wanted to stop her treatment, but a trial judge found that they failed to prove Nancy's intent by the higher burden of proof. The Court, in an opinion by Chief Justice Rehnquist, upheld the standard.

The Court characterized the patient's interest as a "liberty interest" rather than a "fundamental right":

> Although many state courts have held that a right to refuse treatment is encompassed by a generalized constitutional right of privacy, we have never so held.

We believe this issue is more properly analyzed in terms of a 14th Amendment liberty interest. See *Bowers v. Hardwick* (1986).

The Court held that "for purposes of this case, we assume that the United States Constitution would grant a competent person a constitutionally protected right to refuse life-saving hydration and nutrition," but ruled that Missouri "may *legitimately* seek to safeguard the personal element of this choice through the imposition of heightened evidentiary requirements." The Court then listed reasons why the legislation was rational.

The Court summarized its approach as follows:

> The 14th Amendment provides that no State shall "deprive any person of life, liberty, or property, without due process of law." The principle that a competent person has a constitutionally protected liberty interest in refusing unwanted medical treatment may be inferred from our prior decisions. In *Jacobson v. Massachusetts* (1905), for instance, the Court balanced an individual's liberty interest in declining an unwanted smallpox vaccine against the State's interest in preventing disease. Decisions prior to the incorporation of the 4th Amendment into the 14th Amendment analyzed searches and seizures involving the body under the Due Process Clause and were thought to implicate substantial liberty interests. See, *e.g., Breithaupt v. Abram* (1957) ("As against the right of an individual that his person be held inviolable ... must be set the interests of society....")

> Just this Term, in the course of holding that a State's procedures for administering antipsychotic medication to prisoners were sufficient to satisfy due process concerns, we recognized that prisoners possess "a significant liberty interest in avoiding the unwanted administration of antipsychotic drugs under the Due Process Clause of the 14th Amendment." *Washington v. Harper* (1990) ("The forcible injection of medication into a nonconsenting person's body represents a substantial interference with that person's liberty"). Still other cases support the recognition of a general liberty interest in refusing medical treatment. *Vitek v. Jones* (1980) (transfer to mental hospital coupled with mandatory behavior modification treatment implicated liberty interests); *Parham v. J.R.* (1979) ("[A] child, in common with adults, has a substantial liberty interest in not being confined unnecessarily for medical treatment").

> But determining that a person has a "liberty interest" under the Due Process Clause does not end the inquiry; "whether respondent's constitutional rights have been violated must be determined by balancing his liberty interests against the relevant state interests." *Youngberg v. Romeo* (1982).

Justice O'Connor joined the opinion, but concurred. She noted:

> I also write separately to emphasize that the Court does not today decide the issue whether a State must also give effect to the decisions of a surrogate decisionmaker. In my view, such a duty may well be constitutionally required to protect the patient's liberty interest in refusing medical treatment. Few individuals provide explicit oral or written instructions regarding their intent to refuse medical treatment should they become incompetent.... Delegating the authority to make medical decisions to a family member or friend is becoming a common method of planning for the future....

Justice Scalia also concurred:

> While I agree with the Court's analysis today, and therefore join in its opinion, I would have preferred that we announce, clearly and promptly, that the federal

courts have no business in this field; that American law has always accorded the State the power to prevent, by force if necessary, suicide—including suicide by refusing to take appropriate measures necessary to preserve one's life; that the point at which life becomes "worthless," and the point at which the means necessary to preserve it become "extraordinary" or "inappropriate," are neither set forth in the Constitution nor known to the nine Justices of this Court any better than they are known to nine people picked at random from the Kansas City telephone directory....

Justices Brennan, Blackmun, and Marshall dissented, arguing that one "has a fundamental right to be free of unwanted artificial nutrition and hydration, which right is not outweighed by any interests of the State, and ... the improperly biased procedural obstacles imposed by the Missouri Supreme Court impermissibly burden that right." Justice Stevens also dissented: "The Court ... permits the State's abstract, undifferentiated interest in the preservation of life to overwhelm the best interests of Nancy Beth Cruzan, interests which would, according to an undisputed finding, be served by allowing her guardians to exercise her constitutional right to discontinue medical treatment." Justice Stevens found this interest would not satisfy rational basis review.

Washington v. Glucksberg: Background and Questions

1. Why does the Court in *Cruzan v. Director* (1990) and *Washington v. Glucksberg* (1997), analyze the right to die as a liberty interest and not as a fundamental right? What is the difference between the analysis used to evaluate a challenge involving a liberty interest versus a fundamental right?

2. Why would Justices O'Connor and Kennedy join Chief Justice Rehnquist's opinion in *Glucksberg* after refusing to join Justice Scalia's footnote 6 in *Michael H.*? What is the difference in approach?

3. What is the dispute between Justice Souter and Chief Justice Rehnquist in *Glucksberg*? What are the implications of the difference in their approaches?

4. How would a conclusion that plaintiffs in *Michael H.*, *Cruzan*, and *Glucksberg* were asserting a fundamental right have affected the reasoning in those cases?

5. In *Glucksberg*, the Court refers to a companion case, *Vacco v. Quill* (1997). In *Vacco*, the Court, using rational basis analysis, rejected an equal protection challenge to New York's prohibition on assisting suicide.

6. After *Cruzan* and *Glucksberg*, assume that State X requires proof of desire to die in circumstances like those of *Cruzan* by proof beyond a reasonable doubt. Is this requirement constitutional? Assume another state requires execution of a written and witnessed living will. Is this requirement constitutional?

7. Consider the following hypothetical. Dr. Herb is a homeopathic physician in the state of Virginia. He was trained and licensed as an M.D. and then went to Europe for further training in homeopathic medicine. Homeopathic physicians treat illnesses by prescribing very small doses of medicines that would produce similar symptoms to the patient's problem if given to a healthy individual. For example, it is the medical system that pioneered treating malaria with quinine. The system is recognized in three states and in many European countries. Homeopathic practice was largely suppressed in this country for many years through the efforts of the medical establishment.

A proceeding is brought to bar Dr. Herb from practicing medicine. Evidence indicates that none of his patients were harmed and some were helped. The statute permits barring doctors who deviate from standards of acceptable and prevailing medical practice. One of Dr. Herb's patients, Dr. Groat—herself an M.D.—is being treated by him for a gastrointestinal disorder. She saw 12 doctors before Doctor Herb and experienced no improvement. Under Doctor Herb's care she has improved, but is still under treatment. She contends that the action against Dr. Herb violates her right to privacy. What result? Why?

On what clause of the Constitution will Dr. Groat rely? What is the first question to ask in analyzing Dr. Groat's privacy claim? What factors are relevant to analyzing that question? How does the answer to that question affect the rest of the analysis? How does level of scrutiny fit in?

Washington v. Glucksberg
521 U.S. 702 (1997)

[Majority: Rehnquist (C.J.), O'Connor, Scalia, Kennedy, and Thomas. Concurring: O'Connor, Stevens, Souter, Ginsburg, and Breyer.]

Chief Justice Rehnquist delivered the opinion of the Court.

The question presented in this case is whether Washington's prohibition against "caus[ing]" or "aid[ing]" a suicide offends the 14th Amendment to the United States Constitution. We hold that it does not.

It has always been a crime to assist a suicide in the State of Washington. In 1854, Washington's first Territorial Legislature outlawed "assisting another in the commission of self-murder." Today, Washington law provides: "A person is guilty of promoting a suicide attempt when he knowingly causes or aids another person to attempt suicide." Wash. Rev. Code §9A.36.060(1) (1994). "Promoting a suicide attempt" is a felony, punishable by up to five years' imprisonment and up to a $10,000 fine. §§9A.36.060(2) and 9A.20.021(1)(c). At the same time, Washington's Natural Death Act, enacted in 1979, states that the "withholding or withdrawal of life-sustaining treatment" at a patient's direction "shall not, for any purpose, constitute a suicide." Wash. Rev. Code §70.122.070(1)....

The plaintiffs asserted "the existence of a liberty interest protected by the 14th Amendment which extends to a personal choice by a mentally competent, terminally ill adult to commit physician-assisted suicide." Relying primarily on *Planned Parenthood v. Casey* (1992), and *Cruzan v. Director, Missouri Dept. of Health* (1990), the District Court agreed, and concluded that Washington's assisted-suicide ban is unconstitutional because it "places an undue burden on the exercise of [that] constitutionally protected liberty interest."...

[The 9th Circuit Court of Appeals, sitting en banc, affirmed and] emphasized our *Casey* and *Cruzan* decisions. The court also discussed what it described as "historical" and "current societal attitudes" toward suicide and assisted suicide, and concluded that "the Constitution encompasses a due process liberty interest in controlling the time and manner of one's death—that there is, in short, a constitutionally-recognized 'right to die.'" After "[w]eighing and then balancing" this interest against Washington's various interests, the court held that the State's assisted-suicide ban was unconstitutional "as applied to terminally ill competent adults who wish to hasten their deaths with medication prescribed by their physicians."... We granted certiorari, and now reverse.

I. We begin, as we do in all due process cases, by examining our Nation's history, legal traditions, and practices. See, e.g., *Casey*; *Cruzan*; *Moore v. East Cleveland* (1977) (plurality opinion) (noting importance of "careful 'respect for the teachings of history'"). In almost every State—indeed, in almost every western democracy—it is a crime to assist a suicide.[1] The States' assisted-suicide bans are not innovations. Rather, they are long-standing expressions of the States' commitment to the protection and preservation of all human life.... [S]ee *Stanford v. Kentucky* (1987) ("[T]he primary and most reliable indication of [a national] consensus is ... the pattern of enacted laws"). Indeed, opposition to and condemnation of suicide—and, therefore, of assisting suicide—are consistent and enduring themes of our philosophical, legal, and cultural heritages.

More specifically, for over 700 years, the Anglo-American common-law tradition has punished or otherwise disapproved of both suicide and assisting suicide.... [The Court reviews English, American colonial, and American history.] ...

Though deeply rooted, the States' assisted-suicide bans have in recent years been re-examined and, generally, reaffirmed. Because of advances in medicine and technology, Americans today are increasingly likely to die in institutions, from chronic illnesses. Public concern and democratic action are therefore sharply focused on how best to protect dignity and independence at the end of life, with the result that there have been many significant changes in state laws and in the attitudes these laws reflect. Many States, for example, now permit "living wills," surrogate health-care decision making, and the withdrawal or refusal of life-sustaining medical treatment. At the same time, however, voters and legislators continue for the most part to reaffirm their States' prohibitions on assisting suicide.

The Washington statute at issue in this case was enacted in 1975 as part of a revision of that State's criminal code. Four years later, Washington passed its Natural Death Act, which specifically stated that the "withholding or withdrawal of life-sustaining treatment ... shall not, for any purpose, constitute a suicide" and that "[n]othing in this chapter shall be construed to condone, authorize, or approve mercy killing...." (Wash. Rev. Code §§ 70.122.070(1), 70.122.100 (1994)). In 1991, Washington voters rejected a ballot initiative which, had it passed, would have permitted a form of physician-assisted suicide. Washington then added a provision to the Natural Death Act expressly excluding physician-assisted suicide....

Thus, the States are currently engaged in serious, thoughtful examinations of physician-assisted suicide and other similar issues....

Attitudes toward suicide itself have changed since [the 13th century], but our laws have consistently condemned, and continue to prohibit, assisting suicide. Despite changes in medical technology and notwithstanding an increased emphasis on the importance of end-of-life decisionmaking, we have not retreated from this prohibition. Against this backdrop of history, tradition, and practice, we now turn to respondents' constitutional claim.

II. The Due Process Clause guarantees more than fair process, and the "liberty" it protects includes more than the absence of physical restraint. *Collins v. Harker Heights* (1992) (Due Process Clause "protects individual liberty against 'certain government actions regardless of the fairness of the procedures used to implement them'"). The Clause also provides heightened protection against government interference with certain fundamental rights and liberty interests....

But we "have always been reluctant to expand the concept of substantive due process because guideposts for responsible decisionmaking in this unchartered area are scarce

---

1. [Court noted that 44 states, the District of Columbia, and several western European countries prohibit or condemn assisted suicide.]

and open-ended." By extending constitutional protection to an asserted right or liberty interest, we, to a great extent, place the matter outside the arena of public debate and legislative action. We must therefore "exercise the utmost care whenever we are asked to break new ground in this field," lest the liberty protected by the Due Process Clause be subtly transformed into the policy preferences of the members of this Court.

Our established method of substantive-due-process analysis has two primary features: First, we have regularly observed that the Due Process Clause specially protects those fundamental rights and liberties which are, objectively, "deeply rooted in this Nation's history and tradition," [or "so rooted in the traditions and conscience of our people as to be ranked as fundamental",] and "implicit in the concept of ordered liberty," such that "neither liberty nor justice would exist if they were sacrificed." Second, we have required in substantive-due-process cases a "careful description" of the asserted fundamental liberty interest. Our Nation's history, legal traditions, and practices thus provide the crucial "guideposts for responsible decisionmaking", "that direct and restrain our exposition of the Due Process Clause." ...

Justice Souter, relying on Justice Harlan's dissenting opinion in *Poe v. Ullman* (1961), would largely abandon this restrained methodology, and instead ask "whether [Washington's] statute sets up one of those 'arbitrary impositions' or 'purposeless restraints' at odds with the Due Process Clause of the 14th Amendment." In our view, however, the development of this Court's substantive-due-process jurisprudence, described briefly [above], has been a process whereby the outlines of the "liberty" specially protected by the 14th Amendment—never fully clarified, to be sure, and perhaps not capable of being fully clarified—have at least been carefully refined by concrete examples involving fundamental rights found to be deeply rooted in our legal tradition. This approach tends to rein in the subjective elements that are necessarily present in due-process judicial review. In addition, by establishing a threshold requirement—that a challenged state action implicate a fundamental right—before requiring more than a reasonable relation to a legitimate state interest to justify the action, it avoids the need for complex balancing of competing interests in every case.

Turning to the claim at issue here, the Court of Appeals stated that "[p]roperly analyzed, the first issue to be resolved is whether there is a liberty interest in determining the time and manner of one's death," or, in other words, "[i]s there a right to die?" Similarly, respondents assert a "liberty to choose how to die" and a right to "control of one's final days," and describe the asserted liberty as "the right to choose a humane, dignified death," and "the liberty to shape death." As noted above, we have a tradition of carefully formulating the interest at stake in substantive-due-process cases. For example, although *Cruzan* is often described as a "right to die" case, we were, in fact, more precise: We assumed that the Constitution granted competent persons a "constitutionally protected right to refuse lifesaving hydration and nutrition." The Washington statute at issue in this case prohibits "aid[ing] another person to attempt suicide," and, thus, the question before us is whether the "liberty" specially protected by the Due Process Clause includes a right to commit suicide which itself includes a right to assistance in doing so.

We now inquire whether this asserted right has any place in our Nation's traditions. Here, as discussed [above], we are confronted with a consistent and almost universal tradition that has long rejected the asserted right, and continues explicitly to reject it today, even for terminally ill, mentally competent adults. To hold for respondents, we would have to reverse centuries of legal doctrine and practice, and strike down the considered policy choice of almost every State....

According to respondents, our liberty jurisprudence, and the broad, individualistic principles it reflects, protects the "liberty of competent, terminally ill adults to make end-of-life decisions free of undue government interference." The question presented in this case, however, is whether the protections of the Due Process Clause include a right to commit suicide with another's assistance. With this "careful description" of respondents' claim in mind, we turn to *Casey* and *Cruzan*.

In *Cruzan*, we considered whether Nancy Beth Cruzan, who had been severely injured in an automobile accident and was in a persistive vegetative state, "ha[d] a right under the United States Constitution which would require the hospital to withdraw life-sustaining treatment" at her parents' request…."[W]e assume[d] that the United States Constitution would grant a competent person a constitutionally protected right to refuse lifesaving hydration and nutrition." We concluded that, notwithstanding this right, the Constitution permitted Missouri to require clear and convincing evidence of an incompetent patient's wishes concerning the withdrawal of life-sustaining treatment….

[T]he Court of Appeals concluded [below] that "*Cruzan*, by recognizing a liberty interest that includes the refusal of artificial provision of life-sustaining food and water, necessarily recognize[d] a liberty interest in hastening one's own death."

The right assumed in *Cruzan*, however, was not simply deduced from abstract concepts of personal autonomy. Given the common-law rule that forced medication was a battery, and the long legal tradition protecting the decision to refuse unwanted medical treatment, our assumption was entirely consistent with this Nation's history and constitutional traditions. The decision to commit suicide with the assistance of another may be just as personal and profound as the decision to refuse unwanted medical treatment, but it has never enjoyed similar legal protection. Indeed, the two acts are widely and reasonably regarded as quite distinct. In *Cruzan* itself, we recognized that most States outlawed assisted suicide — and even more do today — and we certainly gave no intimation that the right to refuse unwanted medical treatment could be somehow transmuted into a right to assistance in committing suicide.

Respondents also rely on *Casey*.… In reaching [its] conclusion, the opinion discussed in some detail this Court's substantive-due-process tradition of interpreting the Due Process Clause to protect certain fundamental rights and "personal decisions relating to marriage, procreation, contraception, family relationships, child rearing, and education," and noted that many of those rights and liberties "involv[e] the most intimate and personal choices a person may make in a lifetime."

The Court of Appeals, found *Casey* "highly instructive" and "almost prescriptive" for determining "'what liberty interest may inhere in a terminally ill person's choice to commit suicide'":

> Like the decision of whether or not to have an abortion, the decision how and when to die is one of "the most intimate and personal choices a person may make in a lifetime," a choice "central to personal dignity and autonomy." …

That many of the rights and liberties protected by the Due Process Clause sound in personal autonomy does not warrant the sweeping conclusion that any and all important, intimate, and personal decisions are so protected, and *Casey* did not suggest otherwise.

The history of the law's treatment of assisted suicide in this country has been and continues to be one of the rejection of nearly all efforts to permit it. That being the case, our decisions lead us to conclude that the asserted "right" to assistance in committing suicide is not a fundamental liberty interest protected by the Due Process Clause. The Constitution also requires, however, that Washington's assisted-suicide ban be rationally related to legitimate government interests.… This requirement is unquestionably met here. As the court below recognized,[2] Washington's assisted-suicide ban implicates a number of state interests....

We need not weigh exactly the relative strengths of these various interests. They are unquestionably important and legitimate, and Washington's ban on assisted suicide is at least reasonably related to their promotion and protection. We therefore hold that [the ban] does not violate the 14th Amendment, either on its face or "as applied to competent, terminally ill adults who wish to hasten their deaths by obtaining medication prescribed by their doctors."[3]

Throughout the Nation, Americans are engaged in an earnest and profound debate about the morality, legality, and practicality of physician-assisted suicide. Our holding permits this debate to continue, as it should in a democratic society. The decision of the en banc Court of Appeals is reversed, and the case is remanded for further proceedings consistent with this opinion.

Justice Souter, concurring in the judgment....

[This statute punishes a] doctor who accede[s] to a dying patient's request for a drug to be taken by the patient to commit suicide. The question is whether the statute sets up one of those "arbitrary impositions" or "purposeless restraints" at odds with the Due Process Clause of the 14th Amendment. *Poe v. Ullman* (1961) (Harlan, J., dissenting). I conclude that the statute's application to the doctors has not been shown to be unconstitutional, but I write separately to give my reasons for analyzing the substantive due process claims as I do, and for rejecting this one....

I. [T]he State argues that the interest asserted by the doctors is beyond constitutional recognition because it has no deep roots in our history and traditions. But even aside from that, without disputing that the patients here were competent and terminally ill, the State insists that recognizing the legitimacy of doctors' assistance of their patients as contemplated here would entail a number of adverse consequences that the Washington Legislature was entitled to forestall. The nub of this part of the State's argument is not that such patients are constitutionally undeserving of relief on their own account, but that any attempt to confine a right of physician assistance to the circumstances presented by these doctors is likely to fail....

The State thus argues that recognition of the substantive due process right at issue here would jeopardize the lives of others outside the class defined by the doctors' claim, creating risks of irresponsible suicides and euthanasia, whose dangers are concededly within the State's authority to address.

---

2. The court identified and discussed six state interests: (1) preserving life; (2) preventing suicide; (3) avoiding the involvement of third parties and use of arbitrary, unfair, or undue influence; (4) protecting family members and loved ones; (5) protecting the integrity of the medical profession; and (6) avoiding future movement toward euthanasia and other abuses.

3. Justice Stevens states that "the Court does conceive of respondents' claim as a facial challenge—addressing not the application of the statute to a particular set of plaintiffs before it, but the constitutionality of the statute's categorical prohibition...." We emphasize that we today reject the Court of Appeals' specific holding that the statute is unconstitutional "as applied" to a particular class. Justice Stevens agrees with this holding, but would not "foreclose the possibility that an individual plaintiff seeking to hasten her death, or a doctor whose assistance was sought, could prevail in a more particularized challenge." Our opinion does not absolutely foreclose such a claim. However, given our holding that the Due Process Clause of the 14th Amendment does not provide heightened protection to the asserted liberty interest in ending one's life with a physician's assistance, such a claim would have to be quite different from the ones advanced by respondents here.

II.... [Plaintiffs make a substantive due process claim.] The persistence of substantive due process in our cases points to the legitimacy of the modern justification for such judicial review found in Justice Harlan's dissent in *Poe*, on which I will dwell further on, while the acknowledged failures of some of these cases [e.g., *Lochner v. New York* (1905)] point with caution to the difficulty raised by the present claim....

III. My understanding of unenumerated rights in the wake of the *Poe* dissent and subsequent cases avoids the absolutist failing of many older cases without embracing the opposite pole of equating reasonableness with past practice described at a very specific level. That understanding begins with a concept of "ordered liberty," comprising a continuum of rights to be free from "arbitrary impositions and purposeless restraints," *Poe* (Harlan, J., dissenting).

> Due Process has not been reduced to any formula; its content cannot be determined by reference to any code. The best that can be said is that through the course of this Court's decisions it has represented the balance which our Nation, built upon postulates of respect for the liberty of the individual, has struck between that liberty and the demands of organized society. If the supplying of content to this Constitutional concept has of necessity been a rational process, it certainly has not been one where judges have felt free to roam where unguided speculation might take them. The balance of which I speak is the balance struck by this country, having regard to what history teaches are the traditions from which it developed as well as the traditions from which it broke. That tradition is a living thing. A decision of this Court which radically departs from it could not long survive, while a decision which builds on what has survived is likely to be sound. No formula could serve as a substitute, in this area, for judgment and restraint....

After the *Poe* dissent, as before it, this enforceable concept of liberty would bar statutory impositions even at relatively trivial levels when governmental restraints are undeniably irrational as unsupported by any imaginable rationale. See, e.g., *United States v. Carolene Products Co.* (1938) (economic legislation "not ... unconstitutional unless ... facts ... preclude the assumption that it rests upon some rational basis"). Such instances are suitably rare. The claims of arbitrariness that mark almost all instances of unenumerated substantive rights are those resting on "certain interests requir[ing] particularly careful scrutiny of the state needs asserted to justify their abridgment." *Skinner v. Oklahoma* (1942); *Bolling v. Sharpe* (1954); that is, interests in liberty sufficiently important to be judged "fundamental."... In the face of an interest this powerful a State may not rest on threshold rationality or a presumption of constitutionality, but may prevail only on the ground of an interest sufficiently compelling to place within the realm of the reasonable a refusal to recognize the individual right asserted....

This approach calls for a court to assess the relative "weights" or dignities of the contending interests, and to this extent the judicial method is familiar to the common law. Common law method is subject, however, to two important constraints in the hands of a court engaged in substantive due process review. First, such a court is bound to confine the values that it recognizes to those truly deserving constitutional stature, either to those expressed in constitutional text, or those exemplified by "the traditions from which [the Nation] developed," or revealed by contrast with "the traditions from which it broke." *Poe* (Harlan, J., dissenting). "'We may not draw on our merely personal and private notions and disregard the limits ... derived from considerations that are fused in the whole nature of our judicial process ... [,] considerations deeply rooted in reason and in the compelling traditions of the legal profession.'" *Id.*

The second constraint, again, simply reflects the fact that constitutional review, not judicial lawmaking, is a court's business here. The weighing or valuing of contending interests in this sphere is only the first step, forming the basis for determining whether the statute in question falls inside or outside the zone of what is reasonable in the way it resolves the conflict between the interests of state and individual. It is no justification for judicial intervention merely to identify a reasonable resolution of contending values that differs from the terms of the legislation under review. It is only when the legislation's justifying principle, critically valued, is so far from being commensurate with the individual interest as to be arbitrarily or pointlessly applied that the statute must give way. Only if this standard points against the statute can the individual claimant be said to have a constitutional right.

The *Poe* dissent thus reminds us of the nature of review for reasonableness or arbitrariness and the limitations entailed by it. But the opinion cautions against the repetition of past error in another way as well, more by its example than by any particular statement of constitutional method: it reminds us that the process of substantive review by reasoned judgment, is one of close criticism going to the details of the opposing interests and to their relationships with the historically recognized principles that lend them weight or value.

Although the *Poe* dissent disclaims the possibility of any general formula for due process analysis (beyond the basic analytic structure just described), Justice Harlan of course assumed that adjudication under the Due Process Clauses is like any other instance of judgment dependent on common-law method, being more or less persuasive according to the usual canons of critical discourse. When identifying and assessing the competing interests of liberty and authority, for example, the breadth of expression that a litigant or a judge selects in stating the competing principles will have much to do with the outcome and may be dispositive. As in any process of rational argumentation, we recognize that when a generally accepted principle is challenged, the broader the attack the less likely it is to succeed. The principle's defenders will, indeed, often try to characterize any challenge as just such a broadside, perhaps by couching the defense as if a broadside attack had occurred. So the Court in *Dred Scott* (1857) treated prohibition of slavery in the Territories as nothing less than a general assault on the concept of property.

Just as results in substantive due process cases are tied to the selections of statements of the competing interests, the acceptability of the results is a function of the good reasons for the selections made. It is here that the value of common-law method becomes apparent, for the usual thinking of the common law is suspicious of the all-or-nothing analysis that tends to produce legal petrification instead of an evolving boundary between the domains of old principles. Common-law method tends to pay respect instead to detail, seeking to understand old principles afresh by new examples and new counterexamples. The "tradition is a living thing," *Poe* (Harlan, J., dissenting), albeit one that moves by moderate steps carefully taken. "The decision of an apparently novel claim must depend on grounds which follow closely on well-accepted principles and criteria. The new decision must take its place in relation to what went before and further [cut] a channel for what is to come." *Id.* Exact analysis and characterization of any due process claim is critical to the method and to the result.

So, in *Poe*, Justice Harlan viewed it as essential to the plaintiffs' claimed right to use contraceptives that they sought to do so within the privacy of the marital bedroom. This detail in fact served two crucial and complementary functions, and provides a lesson for today. It rescued the individuals' claim from a breadth that would have threatened all state regulation of contraception or intimate relations; extramarital intimacy, no matter how privately practiced, was outside the scope of the right Justice Harlan would have recognized in that case. It was, moreover, this same restriction that allowed the interest to be valued as an aspect of a broader liberty to be free from all unreasonable intrusions into the privacy of the home and the family life within it, a liberty exemplified in constitutional provisions such as the 3rd and 4th Amendments, in prior decisions of the Court involving unreasonable intrusions into the home and family life, and in the then-prevailing status of marriage as the sole lawful locus of intimate relations.

On the other side of the balance, the State's interest in *Poe* was not fairly characterized simply as preserving sexual morality, or doing so by regulating contraceptive devices. Just as some of the earlier cases went astray by speaking without nuance of individual interests in property or autonomy to contract for labor, so the State's asserted interest in *Poe* was not immune to distinctions turning (at least potentially) on the precise purpose being pursued and the collateral consequences of the means chosen. It was assumed that the State might legitimately enforce limits on the use of contraceptives through laws regulating divorce and annulment, or even through its tax policy, but not necessarily be justified in criminalizing the same practice in the marital bedroom, which would entail the consequence of authorizing state enquiry into the intimate relations of a married couple who chose to close their door.

The same insistence on exactitude lies behind questions, in current terminology, about the proper level of generality at which to analyze claims and counter-claims, and the demand for fitness and proper tailoring of a restrictive statute is just another way of testing the legitimacy of the generality at which the government sets up its justification.[1] We may therefore classify Justice Harlan's example of proper analysis in any of these ways: as applying concepts of normal critical reasoning, as pointing to the need to attend to the levels of generality at which countervailing interests are stated, or as examining the concrete application of principles for fitness with their own ostensible justifications. But whatever the categories in which we place the dissent's example, it stands in marked contrast to earlier cases whose reasoning was marked by comparatively less discrimination, and it points to the importance of evaluating the claims of the parties now before us with comparable detail. For here we are faced with an individual claim not to a right on the part of just anyone to help anyone else commit suicide under any circumstances, but to the right of a narrow class to help others also in a narrow class under a set of limited circumstances. And the claimants are met with the State's assertion, among others, that rights of such narrow scope cannot be recognized without jeopardy to individuals whom the State may concededly protect through its regulations.

IV-A. Respondents claim that a patient facing imminent death, who anticipates physical suffering and indignity, and is capable of responsible and voluntary choice, should have a right to a physician's assistance in providing counsel and drugs to be administered by the patient to end life promptly. They accordingly claim that a physician must have the corresponding right to provide such aid, contrary to the provisions of Wash. Rev. Code § 9A.36.060 (1994). I do not understand the argument to rest on any assumption that rights either to suicide or to assistance in committing it are historically based as such. Respondents, rather, acknowledge the prohibition of each historically, but rely on the fact

---

1. The dual dimensions of the strength and the fitness of the government's interest are succinctly captured in the so called "compelling interest test," under which regulations that substantially burden a constitutionally protected (or "fundamental") liberty may be sustained only if "narrowly tailored to serve a compelling state interest." How compelling the interest and how narrow the tailoring must be will depend, of course, not only on the substantiality of the individual's own liberty interest, but also on the extent of the burden placed upon it....

that to a substantial extent the State has repudiated that history. The result of this, respondents say, is to open the door to claims of such a patient to be accorded one of the options open to those with different, traditionally cognizable claims to autonomy in deciding how their bodies and minds should be treated....

IV-A-1. ... It is, indeed, in the abortion cases that the most telling recognitions of the importance of bodily integrity and the concomitant tradition of medical assistance have occurred....

The analogies between the abortion cases and this one are several. Even though the State has a legitimate interest in discouraging abortion, the Court recognized a woman's right to a physician's counsel and care. Like the decision to commit suicide, the decision to abort potential life can be made irresponsibly and under the influence of others, and yet the Court has held in the abortion cases that physicians are fit assistants. Without physician assistance in abortion, the woman's right would have too often amounted to nothing more than a right to self-mutilation, and without a physician to assist in the suicide of the dying, the patient's right will often be confined to crude methods of causing death, most shocking and painful to the decedent's survivors.

There is, finally, one more reason for claiming that a physician's assistance here would fall within the accepted tradition of medical care in our society, and the abortion cases are only the most obvious illustration of the further point. While the Court has held that the performance of abortion procedures can be restricted to physicians, the Court's opinion in *Roe v. Wade* (1973) recognized the doctors' role in yet another way. For, in the course of holding that the decision to perform an abortion called for a physician's assistance, the Court recognized that the good physician is not just a mechanic of the human body whose services have no bearing on a person's moral choices, but one who does more than treat symptoms, one who ministers to the patient.... Its value is surely as apparent here as in the abortion cases....

IV-B. The State has put forward several interests to justify the Washington law as applied to physicians treating terminally ill patients, even those competent to make responsible choices: protecting life generally, discouraging suicide even if knowing and voluntary, and protecting terminally ill patients from involuntary suicide and euthanasia, both voluntary and nonvoluntary.

It is not necessary to discuss the exact strengths of the first two claims of justification in the present circumstances, for the third is dispositive for me. That third justification is different from the first two, for it addresses specific features of respondents' claim, and it opposes that claim not with a moral judgment contrary to respondents', but with a recognized state interest in the protection of nonresponsible individuals and those who do not stand in relation either to death or to their physicians as do the patients whom respondents describe. The State claims interests in protecting patients from mistakenly and involuntarily deciding to end their lives, and in guarding against both voluntary and involuntary euthanasia. Leaving aside any difficulties in coming to a clear concept of imminent death, mistaken decisions may result from inadequate palliative care or a terminal prognosis that turns out to be error; coercion and abuse may stem from the large medical bills that family members cannot bear or unreimbursed hospitals decline to shoulder. Voluntary and involuntary euthanasia may result once doctors are authorized to prescribe lethal medication in the first instance, for they might find it pointless to distinguish between patients who administer their own fatal drugs and those who wish not to, and their compassion for those who suffer may obscure the distinction between those who ask for death and those who may be unable to request it. The argument is that a progression would occur, obscuring the line between the ill and the dying, and between the responsible and the unduly influenced, until ultimately doctors and perhaps others would abuse a limited freedom to aid suicides by yielding to the impulse to end another's suffering under conditions going beyond the narrow limits the respondents propose. The State thus argues, essentially, that respondents' claim is not as narrow as it sounds, simply because no recognition of the interest they assert could be limited to vindicating those interests and affecting no others. The State says that the claim, in practical effect, would entail consequences that the State could, without doubt, legitimately act to prevent.

The mere assertion that the terminally sick might be pressured into suicide decisions by close friends and family members would not alone be very telling. Of course that is possible, not only because the costs of care might be more than family members could bear but simply because they might naturally wish to see an end of suffering for someone they love. But one of the points of restricting any right of assistance to physicians would be to condition the right on an exercise of judgment by someone qualified to assess the patient's responsible capacity and detect the influence of those outside the medical relationship.

The State, however, goes further, to argue that dependence on the vigilance of physicians will not be enough. First, the lines proposed here (particularly the requirement of a knowing and voluntary decision by the patient) would be more difficult to draw than the lines that have limited other recently recognized due process rights. Limiting a state from prosecuting use of artificial contraceptives by married couples posed no practical threat to the State's capacity to regulate contraceptives in other ways that were assumed at the time of *Poe* to be legitimate; the trimester measurements of *Roe* and the viability determination of *Casey* were easy to make with a real degree of certainty. But the knowing and responsible mind is harder to assess. Second, this difficulty could become the greater by combining with another fact within the realm of plausibility, that physicians simply would not be assiduous to preserve the line. They have compassion, and those who would be willing to assist in suicide at all might be the most susceptible to the wishes of a patient, whether the patient was technically quite responsible or not. Physicians, and their hospitals, have their own financial incentives, too, in this new age of managed care. Whether acting from compassion or under some other influence, a physician who would provide a drug for a patient to administer might well go the further step of administering the drug himself; so, the barrier between assisted suicide and euthanasia could become porous, and the line between voluntary and involuntary euthanasia as well. The case for the slippery slope is fairly made out here, not because recognizing one due process right would leave a court with no principled basis to avoid recognizing another, but because there is a plausible case that the right claimed would not be readily containable by reference to facts about the mind that are matters of difficult judgment, or by gatekeepers who are subject to temptation, noble or not.

Respondents propose an answer to all this, the answer of state regulation with teeth. Legislation proposed in several States, for example, would authorize physician-assisted suicide but require two qualified physicians to confirm the patient's diagnosis, prognosis, and competence; and would mandate that the patient make repeated requests witnessed by at least two others over a specified timespan; and would impose reporting requirements and criminal penalties for various acts of coercion.

But at least at this moment there are reasons for caution in predicting the effectiveness of the teeth proposed. Respondents' proposals, as it turns out, sound much like the guidelines now in place in the Netherlands, the only place where experience with physician-assisted suicide and euthanasia has yielded empirical evidence about how such regulations might affect actual practice. Dutch physicians must engage in consultation before proceeding, and must decide whether the patient's decision is voluntary, well considered, and stable, whether the request to die is enduring and made more than once, and whether the patient's future will involve unacceptable suffering. There is, however, a substantial dispute today about what the Dutch experience shows. Some commentators marshall evidence that the Dutch guidelines have in practice failed to protect patients from involuntary euthanasia and have been violated with impunity.... This evidence is contested.... The day may come when we can say with some assurance which side is right, but for now it is the substantiality of the factual disagreement, and the alternatives for resolving it, that matter. They are, for me, dispositive of the due process claim at this time.

I take it that the basic concept of judicial review with its possible displacement of legislative judgment bars any finding that a legislature has acted arbitrarily when the following conditions are met: there is a serious factual controversy over the feasibility of recognizing the claimed right without at the same time making it impossible for the State to engage in an undoubtedly legitimate exercise of power; facts necessary to resolve the controversy are not readily ascertainable through the judicial process; but they are more readily subject to discovery through legislative factfinding and experimentation. It is assumed in this case, and must be, that a State's interest in protecting those unable to make responsible decisions and those who make no decisions at all entitles the State to bar aid to any but a knowing and responsible person intending suicide, and to prohibit euthanasia. How, and how far, a State should act in that interest are judgments for the State, but the legitimacy of its action to deny a physician the option to aid any but the knowing and responsible is beyond question.

The capacity of the State to protect the others if respondents were to prevail is, however, subject to some genuine question, underscored by the responsible disagreement over the basic facts of the Dutch experience. This factual controversy is not open to a judicial resolution with any substantial degree of assurance at this time. It is not, of course, that any controversy about the factual predicate of a due process claim disqualifies a court from resolving it. Courts can recognize captiousness, and most factual issues can be settled in a trial court. At this point, however, the factual issue at the heart of this case does not appear to be one of those. The principal enquiry at the moment is into the Dutch experience, and I question whether an independent front-line investigation into the facts of a foreign country's legal administration can be soundly undertaken through American courtroom litigation. While an extensive literature on any subject can raise the hopes for judicial understanding, the literature on this subject is only nascent. Since there is little experience directly bearing on the issue, the most that can be said is that whichever way the Court might rule today, events could overtake its assumptions, as experimentation in some jurisdictions confirmed or discredited the concerns about progression from assisted suicide to euthanasia.

Legislatures, on the other hand, have superior opportunities to obtain the facts necessary for a judgment about the present controversy. Not only do they have more flexible mechanisms for fact finding than the Judiciary, but their mechanisms include the power to experiment, moving forward and pulling back as facts emerge within their own jurisdictions. There is, indeed, good reason to suppose that in the absence of a judgment for respondents here, just such experimentation will be attempted in some of the States.

I do not decide here what the significance might be of legislative footdragging in ascertaining the facts going to the State's argument that the right in question could not be confined as claimed. Sometimes a court may be bound to act regardless of the institutional preferability of the political branches as forums for addressing constitutional claims. Now, it is enough to say that our examination of legislative reasonableness should consider the fact that the Legislature of the State of Washington is no more obviously at fault than this Court is in being uncertain about what would happen if respondents prevailed today. We therefore have a clear question about which institution, a legislature or a court, is relatively more competent to deal with an emerging issue as to which facts currently unknown could be dispositive. The answer has to be, for the reasons already stated, that the legislative process is to be preferred. There is a closely related further reason as well.

One must bear in mind that the nature of the right claimed, if recognized as one constitutionally required, would differ in no essential way from other constitutional rights guaranteed by enumeration or derived from some more definite textual source than "due process." An unenumerated right should not therefore be recognized, with the effect of displacing the legislative ordering of things, without the assurance that its recognition would prove as durable as the recognition of those other rights differently derived. To recognize a right of lesser promise would simply create a constitutional regime too uncertain to bring with it the expectation of finality that is one of this Court's central obligations in making constitutional decisions.

Legislatures, however, are not so constrained. The experimentation that should be out of the question in constitutional adjudication displacing legislative judgments is entirely proper, as well as highly desirable, when the legislative power addresses an emerging issue like assisted suicide. The Court should accordingly stay its hand to allow reasonable legislative consideration. While I do not decide for all time that respondents' claim should not be recognized, I acknowledge the legislative institutional competence as the better one to deal with that claim at this time.

Justice O'Connor, concurring.

Death will be different for each of us. For many, the last days will be spent in physical pain and perhaps the despair that accompanies physical deterioration and a loss of control of basic bodily and mental functions. Some will seek medication to alleviate that pain and other symptoms.

The Court frames the issue in [this case] as whether the Due Process Clause of the Constitution protects a "right to commit suicide which itself includes a right to assistance in doing so," and concludes that our Nation's history, legal traditions, and practices do not support the existence of such a right. I join the Court's opinions because I agree that there is no generalized right to "commit suicide." But respondents urge us to address the narrower question whether a mentally competent person who is experiencing great suffering has a constitutionally cognizable interest in controlling the circumstances of his or her imminent death. I see no need to reach that question in the context of the facial challenges to the New York and Washington laws at issue here. ("The Washington statute at issue in this case prohibits 'aid[ing] another person to attempt suicide,'... and, thus, the question before us is whether the 'liberty' specially protected by the Due Process Clause includes a right to commit suicide which itself includes a right to assistance in doing so"). The parties and amici agree that in these States a patient who is suffering from a terminal illness and who is experiencing great pain has no legal barriers to obtaining medication, from qualified physicians, to alleviate that suffering, even to the point of causing unconsciousness and hastening death. In this light, even assuming that we would recognize such an interest, I agree that the State's interests in protecting those who are not truly competent or facing imminent death, or those whose decisions to hasten death would not truly be voluntary, are sufficiently weighty to justify a prohibition against physician-assisted suicide....

Justice Stevens, concurring in the judgments.

The Court ends its opinion with the important observation that our holding today is fully consistent with a continuation of the vigorous debate about the "morality, legality, and practicality of physician-assisted suicide" in a democratic society. I write separately to make it clear that there is also room for further debate about the limits that the Constitution places on the power of the States to punish the practice.

I.... The value to others of a person's life is far too precious to allow the individual to claim a constitutional entitlement to complete autonomy in making a decision to end that life. Thus, I fully agree with the Court that the "liberty" protected by the Due Process Clause does not include a categorical "right to commit suicide which itself includes a right to assistance in doing so."

But just as our conclusion that capital punishment is not always unconstitutional did not preclude later decisions holding that it is sometimes impermissibly cruel, so is it equally clear that a decision upholding a general statutory prohibition of assisted suicide does not mean that every possible application of the statute would be valid. A State, like Washington, that has authorized the death penalty and thereby has concluded that the sanctity of human life does not require that it always be preserved, must acknowledge that there are situations in which an interest in hastening death is legitimate. Indeed, not only is that interest sometimes legitimate, I am also convinced that there are times when it is entitled to constitutional protection....

Justice Ginsburg, concurring in the judgments. [Omitted.]

Justice Breyer, concurring in the judgments. [Omitted.]

Justice Souter's History of Substantive Due Process

As a final review, you might want to read Justice Souter's history of substantive due process in his *Glucksberg* concurrence:

II. When the physicians claim that the Washington law deprives them of a right falling within the scope of liberty that the 14th Amendment guarantees against denial without due process of law,[1] they are not claiming some sort of procedural defect in the process through which the statute has been enacted or is administered. Their claim, rather, is that the State has no substantively adequate justification for barring the assistance sought by the patient and sought to be offered by the physician. Thus, we are dealing with a claim to one of those rights sometimes described as rights of substantive due process and sometimes as unenumerated rights, in view of the breadth and indeterminacy of the "due process" serving as the claim's textual basis. The doctors accordingly arouse the skepticism of those who find the Due Process Clause an unduly vague or oxymoronic warrant for judicial review of substantive state law, just as they also invoke two centuries of American constitutional practice in recognizing unenumerated, substantive limits on governmental action. Although this practice has neither rested on any single textual basis nor expressed a consistent theory (or, before *Poe v. Ullman* (1961), a much articulated one), a brief overview of its history is instructive on two counts. The persistence of substantive due process in our cases points to the legitimacy of the modern justification for such ju-

---

1. The doctors also rely on the Equal Protection Clause, but that source of law does essentially nothing in a case like this that the Due Process Clause cannot do on its own.

dicial review found in Justice Harlan's dissent in *Poe*,[2] on which I will dwell further on, while the acknowledged failures of some of these cases point with caution to the difficulty raised by the present claim.

Before the ratification of the 14th Amendment, substantive constitutional review resting on a theory of unenumerated rights occurred largely in the state courts applying state constitutions that commonly contained either Due Process Clauses like that of the 5th Amendment (and later the 14th) or the textual antecedents of such clauses, repeating Magna Carta's guarantee of "the law of the land." On the basis of such clauses, or of general principles untethered to specific constitutional language, state courts evaluated the constitutionality of a wide range of statutes.

Thus, a Connecticut court approved a statute legitimating a class of previous illegitimate marriages, as falling within the terms of the "social compact," while making clear its power to review constitutionality in those terms. *Goshen v. Stonington* (1822). In the same period, a specialized court of equity, created under a Tennessee statute solely to hear cases brought by the state bank against its debtors, found its own authorization unconstitutional as "partial" legislation violating the state constitution's "law of the land" clause. *Bank of the State v. Cooper* (Tenn. 1831). And the middle of the 19th century brought the famous *Wynehamer* case, invalidating a statute purporting to render possession of liquor immediately illegal except when kept for narrow, specified purposes, the state court finding the statute inconsistent with the state's due process clause. *Wynehamer v. People* (1856). The statute was deemed an excessive threat to the "fundamental rights of the citizen" to property. See generally, E. Corwin *Liberty Against Government* (1948) (discussing substantive due process in the state courts before the Civil War); T. Cooley, *Constitutional Limitations*.

Even in this early period, however, this Court anticipated the developments that would presage both the Civil War and the ratification of the 14th Amendment, by making it clear on several occasions that it too had no doubt of the judiciary's power to strike down legislation that conflicted with important but unenumerated principles of American government. In most such instances, after declaring its power to invalidate what it might find inconsistent with rights of liberty and property, the Court nevertheless went on to uphold the legislative acts under review. See, e.g., *Calder v. Bull* (1798) (opinion of Chase, J.). But in *Fletcher v. Peck* (1810), the Court went further. It struck down an act of the Georgia legislature that purported to rescind a sale of public land ab initio and reclaim title for the State, and so deprive subsequent, good-faith purchasers of property conveyed by the original grantees. The Court rested the invalidation on alternative sources of authority: the specific prohibitions against bills of attainder, ex post facto laws, laws impairing contracts in Article I, § 10, of the Constitution; and "general principles which are common to our free institutions," by which Chief Justice Marshall meant that a simple deprivation of property by the State could not be an authentically "legislative" act.

Fletcher was not, though, the most telling early example of such review. For its most salient instance in this Court before the adoption of the 14th Amendment was, of course, the case that the Amendment would in due course overturn, *Dred Scott v. Sandford* (1857). Unlike *Fletcher*, *Dred Scott* was textually based on a Due Process Clause (in the 5th Amend-

---

2. The status of the Harlan dissent in *Poe v. Ullman* (1961) is shown by the Court's adoption of its result in *Griswold v. Connecticut* (1965), and by the Court's acknowledgment of its status and adoption of its reasoning in *Planned Parenthood of Southeastern Pa. v. Casey* (1992)....

ment, applicable to the national government), and it was in reliance on that Clause's protection of property that the Court invalidated the Missouri Compromise. This substantive protection of an owner's property in a slave taken to the territories was traced to the absence of any enumerated power to affect that property granted to the Congress by Article I of the Constitution, the implication being that the Government had no legitimate interest that could support the earlier congressional compromise. The ensuing judgment of history needs no recounting here.

After the ratification of the 14th Amendment, with its guarantee of due process protection against the States, interpretation of the words "liberty" and "property" as used in Due Process Clauses became a sustained enterprise, with the Court generally describing the due process criterion in converse terms of reasonableness or arbitrariness. That standard is fairly traceable to Justice Bradley's dissent in the *Slaughter-House Cases* (1873), in which he said that a person's right to choose a calling was an element of liberty (as the calling, once chosen, was an aspect of property) and declared that the liberty and property protected by due process are not truly recognized if such rights may be "arbitrarily assailed." After that, opinions comparable to those that preceded *Dred Scott* expressed willingness to review legislative action for consistency with the Due Process Clause even as they upheld the laws in question. See, e.g., *Bartemeyer v. Iowa* (1874); *Munn v. Illinois* (1877); *Railroad Comm'n Cases* (1886); *Mugler v. Kansas* (1887). See generally Corwin, *Liberty Against Government* (surveying the Court's early 14th Amendment cases and finding little dissent from the general principle that the Due Process Clause authorized judicial review of substantive statutes).

The theory became serious, however, beginning with *Allgeyer v. Louisiana* (1897), where the Court invalidated a Louisiana statute for excessive interference with 14th Amendment liberty to contract, and offered a substantive interpretation of "liberty," that in the aftermath of the so-called *Lochner* Era has been scaled back in some respects, but expanded in others, and never repudiated in principle. The Court said that 14th Amendment liberty includes "the right of the citizen to be free in the enjoyment of all his faculties; to be free to use them in all lawful ways; to live and work where he will; to earn his livelihood by any lawful calling; to pursue any livelihood or avocation; and for that purpose to enter into all contracts which may be proper, necessary and essential to his carrying out to a successful conclusion the purposes above mentioned." "[W]e do not intend to hold that in no such case can the State exercise its police power," the Court added, but "[w]hen and how far such power may be legitimately exercised with regard to these subjects must be left for determination to each case as it arises."

Although this principle was unobjectionable, what followed for a season was, in the realm of economic legislation, the echo of *Dred Scott*. *Allgeyer* was succeeded within a decade by *Lochner v. New York* (1905), and the era to which that case gave its name, famous now for striking down as arbitrary various sorts of economic regulations that post-New Deal courts have uniformly thought constitutionally sound. Compare, e.g., *Lochner* (finding New York's maximum-hours law for bakers "unreasonable and entirely arbitrary") and *Adkins v. Children's Hospital of D.C.* (1923) (holding a minimum wage law "so clearly the product of a naked, arbitrary exercise of power that it cannot be allowed to stand under the Constitution of the United States"), with *West Coast Hotel Co. v. Parrish* (1937) (overruling *Adkins* and approving a minimum-wage law on the principle that "regulation which is reasonable in relation to its subject and is adopted in the interests of the community is due process"). As the parentheticals here suggest, while the cases in the *Lochner* line routinely invoked a correct standard of constitutional arbitrariness review, they harbored the spirit of *Dred Scott* in their absolutist implementation of the standard they espoused.

Even before the deviant economic due process cases had been repudiated, however, the more durable precursors of modern substantive due process were reaffirming this Court's obligation to conduct arbitrariness review, beginning with *Meyer v. Nebraska* (1923). Without referring to any specific guarantee of the Bill of Rights, the Court invoked precedents from the *Slaughter-House Cases* through *Adkins* to declare that the 14th Amendment protected "the right of the individual to contract, to engage in any of the common occupations of life, to acquire useful knowledge, to marry, establish a home and bring up children, to worship God according to the dictates of his own conscience, and generally to enjoy those privileges long recognized at common law as essential to the orderly pursuit of happiness by free men." The Court then held that the same 14th Amendment liberty included a teacher's right to teach and the rights of parents to direct their children's education without unreasonable interference by the States, with the result that Nebraska's prohibition on the teaching of foreign languages in the lower grades was "arbitrary and without reasonable relation to any end within the competency of the State." See also *Pierce v. Society of Sisters* (1925) (finding that a statute that all but outlawed private schools lacked any "reasonable relation to some purpose within the competency of the State"); *Palko v. Connecticut* (1937) ("even in the field of substantive rights and duties the legislative judgment, if oppressive and arbitrary, may be overridden by the courts." "Is that [injury] to which the statute has subjected [the appellant] a hardship so acute and shocking that our polity will not endure it? Does it violate those fundamental principles of liberty and justice which lie at the base of all our civil and political institutions?")

After *Meyer* and *Pierce*, two further opinions took the major steps that lead to the modern law. The first was not even in a due process case but one about equal protection, *Skinner v. Oklahoma* (1942), where the Court emphasized the "fundamental" nature of individual choice about procreation and so foreshadowed not only the later prominence of procreation as a subject of liberty protection, but the corresponding standard of "strict scrutiny," in this Court's 14th Amendment law. *Skinner*, that is, added decisions regarding procreation to the list of liberties recognized in *Meyer* and *Pierce* and loosely suggested, as a gloss on their standard of arbitrariness, a judicial obligation to scrutinize any impingement on such an important interest with heightened care. In so doing, it suggested a point that Justice Harlan would develop, that the kind and degree of justification that a sensitive judge would demand of a State would depend on the importance of the interest being asserted by the individual. *Poe.*

The second major opinion leading to the modern doctrine was Justice Harlan's *Poe* dissent just cited, the conclusion of which was adopted in *Griswold v. Connecticut* (1965), and the authority of which was acknowledged in *Planned Parenthood of Southeastern Pa. v. Casey* (1992).... The dissent is important for three things that point to our responsibilities today. The first is Justice Harlan's respect for the tradition of substantive due process review itself, and his acknowledgement of the Judiciary's obligation to carry it on. For two centuries American courts, and for much of that time this Court, have thought it necessary to provide some degree of review over the substantive content of legislation under constitutional standards of textual breadth. The obligation was understood before *Dred Scott* and has continued after the repudiation of *Lochner*'s progeny, most notably on the subjects of segregation in public education, *Bolling v. Sharpe* (1954), interracial marriage, *Loving v. Virginia* (1967), marital privacy and contraception, *Carey v. Population Services Int'l* (1977); *Griswold v. Connecticut*, abortion, *Planned Parenthood of Southeastern Pa. v. Casey* (joint opinion of O'Connor, Kennedy, and Souter, JJ.); *Roe v. Wade* (1973), personal control of medical treatment, *Cruzan v. Director, Mo. Dept. of Health* (1990) (O'Connor, J., concurring), and physical confinement, *Foucha v. Louisiana* (1992). This enduring tradition of American constitutional practice is, in Justice Harlan's view, nothing more than what is required by the judicial authority and obligation to construe constitutional text and review legislation for conformity to that text. See *Marbury v. Madison* (1803). Like many judges who preceded him and many who followed, he found it impossible to construe the text of due process without recognizing substantive, and not merely procedural, limitations. "Were due process merely a procedural safeguard it would fail to reach those situations where the deprivation of life, liberty or property was accomplished by legislation which by operating in the future could, given even the fairest possible procedure in application to individuals, nevertheless destroy the enjoyment of all three." *Poe*. The text of the Due Process Clause thus imposes nothing less than an obligation to give substantive content to the words "liberty" and "due process of law."

Following the first point of the *Poe* dissent, on the necessity to engage in the sort of examination we conduct today, the dissent's second and third [points] implicitly address those cases, already noted, that are now condemned with virtual unanimity as disastrous mistakes of substantive due process review. The second of the dissent's lessons is a reminder that the business of such review is not the identification of extratextual absolutes but scrutiny of a legislative resolution (perhaps unconscious) of clashing principles, each quite possibly worthy in and of itself, but each to be weighed within the history of our values as a people. It is a comparison of the relative strengths of opposing claims that informs the judicial task, not a deduction from some first premise. Thus informed, judicial review still has no warrant to substitute one reasonable resolution of the contending positions for another, but authority to supplant the balance already struck between the contenders only when it falls outside the realm of the reasonable.

IX. The Takings Clause

The 5th Amendment prohibits the taking of private property for public use without just compensation to the owner. The prohibition against taking private property has been incorporated into the Due Process Clause of the 14th Amendment. Originally, the clause seems to have been understood to be limited to physical appropriation (through the exercise of eminent domain), and perhaps invasion, of property by the government. A *regulation* that diminished the value of property was not understood to be a taking. William Michael Treanor, *The Original Understanding of the Takings Clause and the Political Process*, 95 Col. L. Rev. 782, 802 (1995). But see, Richard Epstein, *History Lean: The Reconciliation of Private Property and Representative Government*, 95 Col. L. Rev. 523 (1995) and Richard Epstein, *Takings: Private Property and the Power of Eminent Domain* (1985).

Historically, the government had been given great deference in the exercise of its police powers for the public good. But on occasion, the Court has found legislative regulations that dramatically affect the value of property to violate either the Due Process or the Takings Clauses.

In *Dred Scott v. Sandford* (1857), a slave sought his freedom because of his residence in a free state and a federal territory. The Court held that free blacks could not be American citizens, denying them any constitutional protections. *Dred Scott* also held that the

5th Amendment prevented Congress from banning slavery in the federal territories. The following is an excerpt from *Dred Scott*:

> [T]he rights of property are united with the rights of person, and placed on the same ground by the 5th Amendment to the Constitution, which provides that no person shall be deprived of life, liberty, and property, without due process of law. And an act of Congress which deprives a citizen of the United States of his liberty or property, merely because he came himself or brought his property into a particular Territory of the United States, and who had committed no offence against the laws, could hardly be dignified with the name of due process of law.
>
> Upon these considerations, it is the opinion of the court that the act of Congress which prohibited a citizen from holding and owning property of this kind in the territory of the United States north of the line therein mentioned, is not warranted by the Constitution, and is therefore void; and that neither Dred Scott himself, nor any of his family, were made free by being carried into this territory; even if they had been carried there by the owner, with the intention of becoming a permanent resident.

The Republican Party contended that the 5th Amendment required exactly the opposite. Republicans argued that no one could be deprived of liberty without due process. Since slaves would be held in federal territory without benefit of trial, their slavery would be illegal.

For a time after *Dred Scott*, the courts showed greater deference to the police powers of the states. For example, in *Munn v. Illinois* (1877), the Court rejected a challenge to a statute limiting the price private grain silo operators could charge because their business affected the public interest. In *Mugler v. Kansas* (1887), the Court ruled that the forced closure of a brewery did not constitute a taking. The Court held in part:

> [I]t is contended that, as the primary and principal use of beer is as a beverage; as their respective breweries were erected when it was lawful to engage in the manufacture of beer for every purpose; as such establishments will become of no value as property, or, at least, will be materially diminished in value, if not employed in the manufacture of beer for every purpose; the prohibition upon their being so employed is, in effect, a taking of property for public use without compensation, and depriving the citizen of his property without due process of law. In other words, although the state, in the exercise of her police powers, may lawfully prohibit the manufacture and sale, within her limits, of intoxicating liquors to be used as a beverage, legislation having that object in view cannot be enforced against those who, at the time, happen to own property, the chief value of which consists in its fitness for such manufacturing purposes, unless compensation is first made for the diminution in the value of their property, resulting from such prohibitory enactments....
>
> The present case must be governed by principles that do not involve the power of eminent domain, in the exercise of which property may not be taken for public use without compensation. A prohibition simply upon the use of property for purposes that are declared, by valid legislation, to be injurious to the health, morals, or safety of the community, cannot, in any just sense, be deemed a taking or an appropriation of property for the public benefit. Such legislation does not disturb the owner in the control or use of his property for lawful purposes, nor restrict his right to dispose of it, but is only a declaration by the state that

its use by any one, for certain forbidden purposes, is prejudicial to the public interests. Nor can legislation of that character come within the 14th Amendment, in any case, unless it is apparent that its real object is not to protect the community, or to promote the general well-being, but, under the guise of police regulation, to deprive the owner of his liberty and property, without due process of law. The power which the states have of prohibiting such use by individuals of their property as will be prejudicial to the health, the morals, or the safety of the public, is not and, consistently with the existence and safety of organized society, cannot be—burdened with the condition that the state must compensate such individual owners for pecuniary losses they may sustain, by reason of their not being permitted, by a noxious use of their property, to inflict injury upon the community. The exercise of the police power by the destruction of property which is itself a public nuisance, or the prohibition of its use in a particular way, whereby its value becomes depreciated, is very different from taking property for public use, or from depriving a person of his property without due process of law. In the one case, a nuisance only is abated; in the other, unoffending property is taken away from an innocent owner.

It is true that, when the defendants in these cases purchased or erected their breweries, the laws of the state did not forbid the manufacture of intoxicating liquors. But the state did not thereby give any assurance, or come under an obligation, that its legislation upon that subject would remain unchanged. Indeed, as was said in *Stone v. Mississippi* (1879), the supervision of the public health and the public morals is a governmental power, "continuing in its nature," and "to be dealt with as the special exigencies of the moment may require;" and that, "for this purpose, the largest legislative discretion is allowed, and the discretion cannot be parted with any more than the power itself." So in *Beer Co. v. Massachusetts* (1877): "If the public safety or the public morals require the discontinuance of any manufacture or traffic, the hand of the legislature cannot be stayed from providing for its discontinuance by any incidental inconvenience which individuals or corporations may suffer."

In *Pennsylvania Coal Co v. Mahon* (1922), the Court considered a statute which prohibited a mining company from utilizing its mineral rights under a piece of property if the subsurface mining might cause the ground to sink. The Court held the statute passed the point of regulation and was, therefore, a taking. [Note, however, that a modern version of this statute was recently upheld by a 5–4 vote. *Keystone Bituminous Coal Association v. Debenedictis* (1987)]. Until *Pennsylvania Coal*, the Takings Clause was not understood to apply to regulatory takings, as opposed to physical takings or invasions of property by government.

The *Pennsylvania Coal* decision allowed the courts to review a wide range of legislative action involving property rights. The balancing test the Court embraced—a regulation was invalid if it "went too far"—was similar to the substantive due process test that allowed the courts to scrutinize decisions by democratically elected branches involving "freedom of contract." See William Michael Treanor, *The Original Understanding of the Takings Clause and the Political Process*, 95 Col. L. Rev. 782, 802 (1995). The point at which a "reasonable" exercise of the police powers (*e.g.*, zoning) becomes confiscatory is a subtle one.

The following case, *Miller v. Schoene*, shows substantial deference to government regulation and the police power. Compare the discussion of common law nuisances in the following two cases.

Miller v. Schoene
276 U.S. 272 (1928)

[In the 1920s, the state of Virginia had a large and prosperous apple industry. Red cedar trees could harbor a fungus that did not endanger the cedars but destroyed apple blooms and threatened the apple crop. While red cedars were sometimes used for lumber, they were generally of little economic value. Faced with danger to the apple crop, the Virginia legislature provided that infected cedar trees should be cut down.]

Mr. Justice Stone delivered the opinion of the Court.

Acting under the Cedar Rust Act of Virginia, the state entomologist, ordered the [Millers] to cut down a large number of ornamental red cedar trees growing on their property, as a means of preventing the communication of a rust or plant disease with which they were infected to the apple orchards in the vicinity. [The Virginia Circuit Court] affirmed the order and allowed [the Millers] $100 to cover the expense of removal of the cedars. Neither the judgment of the court nor the statute as interpreted allows compensation for the value of the standing cedars or the decrease in the market value of the realty caused by their destruction whether considered as ornamental trees or otherwise. But they save to [the Millers] the privilege of using the trees when felled....

On the evidence we may accept the conclusion of the Supreme Court of Appeals that the state was under the necessity of making a choice between the preservation of one class of property and that of the other wherever both existed in dangerous proximity. It would have been none the less a choice if, instead of enacting the present statute, the state, by doing nothing, had permitted serious injury to the apple orchards within its borders to go on unchecked. When forced to such a choice the state does not exceed its constitutional powers by deciding upon the destruction of one class of property in order to save another which, in the judgment of the legislature, is of greater value to the public. It will not do to say that the case is merely one of a conflict of two private interests and that the misfortune of apple growers may not be shifted to cedar owners by ordering the destruction of their property; for it is obvious that there may be, and that here there is, a preponderant public concern in the preservation of the one interest over the other. And where the public interest is involved preferment of that interest over the property interest of the individual, to the extent even of its destruction, is one of the distinguishing characteristics of every exercise of the police power which affects property. *Mugler v. Kansas* (1887), *Hadacheck v. Los Angeles* (1915) [law barring operation of brick mill in residential area held not to be a taking]; *Euclid v. Ambler Realty Co.* (1926) [zoning regulation that diminished value of property held not to be a taking].

We need not weigh with nicety the question whether the infected cedars constitute a nuisance according to the common law; or whether they may be so declared by statute. For where, as here, the choice is unavoidable, we cannot say that its exercise, controlled by considerations of social policy which are not unreasonable, involves any denial of due process. The injury to property here is no more serious, nor the public interest less, than in *Hadacheck v. Los Angeles*....

* * *

In 1926, four years after *Pennsylvania Coal*, the Court first considered and upheld zoning laws in *Euclid v. Ambler Realty Co.* The *Euclid* Court declined to extend its *Pennsylvania Coal* holding to zoning, even though the zoning in *Euclid* caused a 75% decline in the market value of the zoned property. More than fifty years later, in *Penn Central Trans-*

portation Co. v. New York (1978), the Court did extend its regulatory takings analysis to zoning.

In *Penn Central*, the Court held that landmark preservation, as a type of zoning, was not a taking based on the facts of that case, but might be in another setting. As interpreted in later cases, the Court established a three-factor test to decide if a regulation which did not deprive a landowner of substantially all value should be considered a taking: the economic impact of the regulation, the extent to which it interferes with investment-backed expectations, and the character of the governmental action. In contrast, where a regulation deprives a landowner of virtually all the value of the property, the Court will apply a per se rule and find a taking.

The latter problem was addressed in *Lucas v. South Carolina Coastal Council* (1992). As you read *Lucas*, consider the methodology that the Court uses to determine whether this exercise of the police power is reasonable or unreasonable. Is *Lucas* consistent with *Mugler v. Kansas* (1887) or with *Miller v. Schoene* (1928)? Are the Justices consistent in their approaches to the importance of original understanding or history and tradition in the recent takings and substantive due process decisions? How does the majority approach square with *Lochner v. New York* (1905), *United States v. Carolene Products* (1938), and *Williamson v. Lee Optical* (1955)?

Lucas v. South Carolina Coastal Council
505 U.S. 1003 (1992)

[Majority: Scalia, Rehnquist (C.J.), White, O'Connor, and Thomas. Concurring: Kennedy. Dissenting: Blackmun and Stevens. Separate Statement: Souter.]

Justice Scalia delivered the opinion of the Court.

In 1986, petitioner David H. Lucas paid $975,000 for two residential lots on the Isle of Palms in Charleston County, South Carolina, on which he intended to build single-family homes. In 1988, however, the South Carolina Legislature enacted the Beachfront Management Act, which had the direct effect of barring petitioner from erecting any permanent habitable structures on his two parcels.... A state trial court found that this prohibition rendered Lucas's parcels "valueless." This case requires us to decide whether the Act's dramatic effect on the economic value of Lucas's lots accomplished a taking of private property under the 5th and 14th Amendments requiring the payment of "just compensation."...

I-A. ... In the late 1970's, Lucas and others began extensive residential development of the Isle of Palms, a barrier island situated eastward of the city of Charleston. Toward the close of the development cycle for one residential subdivision known as "Beachwood East," Lucas in 1986 purchased the two lots at issue in this litigation for his own account. No portion of the lots, which were located approximately 300 feet from the beach, qualified as a "critical area" under the 1977 Act; accordingly, at the time Lucas acquired these parcels, he was not legally obliged to obtain a permit from the Council in advance of any development activity. His intention with respect to the lots was to do what the owners of the immediately adjacent parcels had already done: erect single-family residences. He commissioned architectural drawings for this purpose.

The Beachfront Management Act brought Lucas's plans to an abrupt end. Under that 1988 legislation, the Council was directed to establish a "baseline" connecting the landward-most "point[s] of erosion ... during the past forty years" in the region of the Isle of Palms that includes Lucas's lots. In action not challenged here, the Council fixed this baseline landward of Lucas's parcels. That was significant, for under the Act construction of occupiable improvements was flatly prohibited seaward of a line drawn 20 feet landward of, and parallel to, the baseline. The Act provided no exceptions.

I-B. Lucas promptly filed suit.... Lucas contended that the Act's complete extinguishment of his property's value entitled him to compensation regardless of whether the legislature had acted in furtherance of legitimate police power objectives. Following a bench trial, the court agreed....

The Supreme Court of South Carolina reversed....

III-A. Prior to Justice Holmes' exposition in *Pennsylvania Coal Co. v. Mahon* (1922), it was generally thought that the Takings Clause reached only a "direct appropriation" of property or the functional equivalent of a "practical ouster of [the owner's] possession." Justice Holmes recognized in *Mahon*, however, that if the protection against physical appropriations of private property was to be meaningfully enforced, the government's power to redefine the range of interests included in the ownership of property was necessarily constrained by constitutional limits. If, instead, the uses of private property were subject to unbridled, uncompensated qualification under the police power, "the natural tendency of human nature [would be] to extend the qualification more and more until at last private property disappear[ed]." These considerations gave birth in that case to the oft-cited maxim that, "while property may be regulated to a certain extent, if regulation goes too far it will be recognized as a taking."

Nevertheless, our decision in *Mahon* offered little insight into when, and under what circumstances, a given regulation would be seen as going "too far" for purposes of the 5th Amendment. In 70-odd years of succeeding "regulatory takings" jurisprudence, we have generally eschewed any "'set formula'" for determining how far is too far, preferring to "engag[e] in ... essentially ad hoc, factual inquiries." *Penn Central Transportation Co. v. New York City* (1978) (quoting *Goldblatt v. Hempstead* (1962)). We have, however, described at least two discrete categories of regulatory action as compensable without case-specific inquiry into the public interest advanced in support of the restraint. The first encompasses regulations that compel the property owner to suffer a physical "invasion" of his property. In general (at least with regard to permanent invasions), no matter how minute the intrusion, and no matter how weighty the public purpose behind it, we have required compensation. For example, in *Loretto v. Teleprompter Manhattan CATV Corp.* (1982), we determined that New York's law requiring landlords to allow television cable companies to emplace cable facilities in their apartment buildings constituted a taking even though the facilities occupied at most only one and one half cubic feet of the landlords' property.... See also *United States v. Causby* (1946) (physical invasions of airspace); cf. *Kaiser Aetna v. United States* (1979) (imposition of navigational servitude upon private marina).

The second situation in which we have found categorical treatment appropriate is where regulation denies all economically beneficial or productive use of land.... As we have said on numerous occasions, the 5th Amendment is violated when land-use regulation "does not substantially advance legitimate state interests *or denies an owner economically viable use of his land.*" *Agins v. City of Tiburon* (1980).[1]

---

1. Regrettably, the rhetorical force of our "deprivation of all economically feasible use" rule is greater than its precision, since the rule does not make clear the "property interest" against which the loss of value is to be measured. When, for example, a regulation requires a developer to leave 90% of a rural tract in its natural state, it is unclear whether we would analyze the situation as one in which the owner has been deprived of all economically beneficial use of the burdened portion of the tract, or as one in which the owner has suffered a mere diminution in value of the tract as a whole. (For an extreme—and, we think, unsupportable—view of the relevant calculus, see *Penn Central Trans-*

We have never set forth the justification for this rule. Perhaps it is simply, as Justice Brennan suggested, that total deprivation of beneficial use is, from the landowner's point of view, the equivalent of a physical appropriation. See *San Diego Gas & Electric Co. v. San Diego* (1981) (dissenting opinion). "[F]or what is the land but the profits thereof[?]" 1 E. Coke, *Institutes*, ch. 1, §1 (1st Am. ed. 1812). Surely, at least, in the extraordinary circumstance when no productive or economically beneficial use of land is permitted, it is less realistic to indulge our usual assumption that the legislature is simply "adjusting the benefits and burdens of economic life," *Penn Central Transportation Co. v. New York City,* in a manner that secures an "average reciprocity of advantage" to everyone concerned, *Pennsylvania Coal Co. v. Mahon*. And the *functional* basis for permitting the government, by regulation, to affect property values without compensation—that "Government hardly could go on if to some extent values incident to property could not be diminished without paying for every such change in the general law,"—does not apply to the relatively rare situations where the government has deprived a landowner of all economically beneficial uses.

On the other side of the balance, affirmatively supporting a compensation requirement, is the fact that regulations that leave the owner of land without economically beneficial or productive options for its use—typically, as here, by requiring land to be left substantially in its natural state—carry with them a heightened risk that private property is being pressed into some form of public service under the guise of mitigating serious public harm....

The many statutes on the books, both state and federal, that provide for the use of eminent domain to impose servitudes on private scenic lands preventing developmental uses, or to acquire such lands altogether, suggest the practical equivalence in this setting of negative regulation and appropriation....

We think, in short, that there are good reasons for our frequently expressed belief that when the owner of real property has been called upon to sacrifice all economically beneficial uses in the name of the common good, that is, to leave his property economically idle, he has suffered a taking.[2]

---

portation Co. v. New York City, where the state court examined the diminution in a particular parcel's value produced by a municipal ordinance in light of total value of the takings claimant's other holdings in the vicinity.) Unsurprisingly, this uncertainty regarding the composition of the denominator in our "deprivation" fraction has produced inconsistent pronouncements by the Court. Compare *Pennsylvania Coal Co. v. Mahon* (law restricting subsurface extraction of coal held to effect a taking), with *Keystone Bituminous Coal Assn. v. DeBenedictis* (1987) (nearly identical law held not to effect a taking).... The answer to this difficult question may lie in how the owner's reasonable expectations have been shaped by the State's law of property—i.e., whether and to what degree the State's law has accorded legal recognition and protection to the particular interest in land with respect to which the takings claimant alleges a diminution in (or elimination of) value. In any event, we avoid this difficulty in the present case, since the "interest in land" that Lucas has pleaded (a fee simple interest) is an estate with a rich tradition of protection at common law, and since the South Carolina Court of Common Pleas found that the Beachfront Management Act left each of Lucas's beachfront lots without economic value.

2. Justice Stevens criticizes the "deprivation of all economically beneficial use" rule as "wholly arbitrary," in that "[the] landowner whose property is diminished in value 95% recovers nothing," while the landowner who suffers a complete elimination of value "recovers the land's full value." Post. This analysis errs in its assumption that the landowner whose deprivation is one step short of complete is not entitled to compensation. Such an owner might not be able to claim the benefit of our categorical formulation, but, as we have acknowledged time and again, "[t]he economic impact of the regulation on the claimant and ... the extent to which the regulation has interfered with distinct investment-backed expectations" are keenly relevant to takings analysis generally. *Penn Central Transportation Co. v. New York City*.... It is true that in at least *some* cases the landowner with 95% loss will get nothing, while the landowner with total loss will recover in full. But that occasional result is no more strange than the gross disparity between the landowner whose premises are taken for a high-

III-B. The trial court found Lucas's two beachfront lots to have been rendered valueless by respondent's enforcement of the coastal-zone construction ban. Under Lucas's theory of the case, which rested upon our "no economically viable use" statements, that finding entitled him to compensation. Lucas believed it unnecessary to take issue with either the purposes behind the Beachfront Management Act, or the means chosen by the South Carolina Legislature to effectuate those purposes. The South Carolina Supreme Court, however, thought otherwise. In its view, the Beachfront Management Act was no ordinary enactment, but involved an exercise of South Carolina's "police powers" to mitigate the harm to the public interest that petitioner's use of his land might occasion. By neglecting to dispute the findings enumerated in the Act or otherwise to challenge the legislature's purposes, petitioner "concede[d] that the beach/dune area of South Carolina's shores is an extremely valuable public resource; that the erection of new construction, inter alia, contributes to the erosion and destruction of this public resource; and that discouraging new construction in close proximity to the beach/dune area is necessary to prevent a great public harm." In the court's view, these concessions brought petitioner's challenge within a long line of this Court's cases sustaining against Due Process and Takings Clause challenges the State's use of its "police powers" to enjoin a property owner from activities akin to public nuisances. See *Mugler v. Kansas* (1887) (law prohibiting manufacture of alcoholic beverages); *Hadacheck v. Sebastian* (1915) (law barring operation of brick mill in residential area); *Miller v. Schoene* (1928) (order to destroy diseased cedar trees to prevent infection of nearby orchards); *Goldblatt v. Hempstead* (1962) (law effectively preventing continued operation of quarry in residential area).

It is correct that many of our prior opinions have suggested that "harmful or noxious uses" of property may be proscribed by government regulation without the requirement of compensation. For a number of reasons, however, we think the South Carolina Supreme Court was too quick to conclude that that principle decides the present case. The "harmful or noxious uses" principle was the Court's early attempt to describe in theoretical terms why government may, consistent with the Takings Clause, affect property values by regulation without incurring an obligation to compensate—a reality we nowadays acknowledge explicitly with respect to the full scope of the State's police power. See, e.g., *Penn Central Transportation Co.* (where State "reasonably conclude[s] that 'the health, safety, morals, or general welfare' would be promoted by prohibiting particular contemplated uses of land," compensation need not accompany prohibition); see also *Nollan v. California Coastal Comm'n* (1987) ("Our cases have not elaborated on the standards for determining what constitutes a 'legitimate state interest[,]' [but] [t]hey have made clear ... that a broad range of governmental purposes and regulations satisfy these requirements"). We made this very point in *Penn Central Transportation Co.*, where, in the course of sustaining New York City's landmarks preservation program against a takings challenge, we rejected the petitioner's suggestion that *Mugler* and the cases following it were premised on, and thus limited by, some objective conception of "noxiousness":

---

way (who recovers in full) and the landowner whose property is reduced to 5% of its former value by the highway (who recovers nothing). Takings law is full of these "all-or-nothing" situations. Justice Stevens similarly misinterprets our focus on "developmental" uses of property (the uses proscribed by the Beachfront Management Act) as betraying an "assumption that the only uses of property cognizable under the Constitution are *developmental* uses." We make no such assumption. Though our prior takings cases evince an abiding concern for the productive use of, and economic investment in, land, there are plainly a number of noneconomic interests in land whose impairment will invite exceedingly close scrutiny under the Takings Clause. See, e.g., *Loretto v. Teleprompter Manhattan CATV Corp.* (interest in excluding strangers from one's land).

[T]he uses in issue in *Hadacheck, Miller,* and *Goldblatt* were perfectly lawful in themselves. They involved no 'blameworthiness, ... moral wrongdoing or conscious act of dangerous risk-taking which induce[d society] to shift the cost to a pa[rt]icular individual.' Sax, *Takings and the Police Power,* 74 Yale L.J. 36, 50 (1964). These cases are better understood as resting not on any supposed 'noxious' quality of the prohibited uses but rather on the ground that the restrictions were reasonably related to the implementation of a policy—not unlike historic preservation—expected to produce a widespread public benefit and applicable to all similarly situated property.

"Harmful or noxious use" analysis was, in other words, simply the progenitor of our more contemporary statements that "land-use regulation does not effect a taking if it 'substantially advance[s] legitimate state interests.'" *Nollan v. California Coastal Commission.*

The transition from our early focus on control of "noxious" uses to our contemporary understanding of the broad realm within which government may regulate without compensation was an easy one, since the distinction between "harm-preventing" and "benefit-conferring" regulation is often in the eye of the beholder. It is quite possible, for example, to describe in *either* fashion the ecological, economic, and esthetic concerns that inspired the South Carolina Legislature in the present case. One could say that imposing a servitude on Lucas's land is necessary in order to prevent his use of it from "harming" South Carolina's ecological resources; or, instead, in order to achieve the "benefits" of an ecological preserve. Whether one or the other of the competing characterizations will come to one's lips in a particular case depends primarily upon one's evaluation of the worth of competing uses of real estate. See Restatement (Second) of Torts §822, Comment g, p. 112 (1979) ("Practically all human activities unless carried on in a wilderness interfere to some extent with others or involve some risk of interference"). A given restraint will be seen as mitigating "harm" to the adjacent parcels or securing a "benefit" for them, depending upon the observer's evaluation of the relative importance of the use that the restraint favors.... Whether Lucas's construction of single-family residences on his parcels should be described as bringing "harm" to South Carolina's adjacent ecological resources thus depends principally upon whether the describer believes that the State's use interest in nurturing those resources is so important that *any* competing adjacent use must yield.[3]

When it is understood that "prevention of harmful use" was merely our early formulation of the police power justification necessary to sustain (without compensation) *any* regulatory diminution in value; and that the distinction between regulation that "prevents harmful use" and that which "confers benefits" is difficult, if not impossible, to discern on an objective, value-free basis; it becomes self-evident that noxious-use logic cannot serve as a touchstone to distinguish regulatory "takings"—which require compensation—from regulatory deprivations that do not require compensation. A fortiori the legislature's recitation of a noxious-use justification cannot be the basis for departing from our categorical rule that total regulatory takings must be compensated. If it were, departure would virtually always be allowed. The South Carolina Supreme Court's approach would essentially nullify *Mahon*'s affirmation of limits to the noncompensable exercise of

---

3. In Justice Blackmun's view, even with respect to regulations that deprive an owner of all developmental or economically beneficial land uses, the test for required compensation is whether the legislature has recited a harm-preventing justification for its action.... Since such a justification can be formulated in practically every case, this amounts to a test of whether the legislature has a stupid staff. We think the Takings Clause requires courts to do more than insist upon artful harm-preventing characterizations.

the police power. Our cases provide no support for this: None of them that employed the logic of "harmful use" prevention to sustain a regulation involved an allegation that the regulation wholly eliminated the value of the claimant's land.

Where the State seeks to sustain regulation that deprives land of all economically beneficial use, we think it may resist compensation only if the logically antecedent inquiry into the nature of the owner's estate shows that the proscribed use interests were not part of his title to begin with. This accords, we think, with our "takings" jurisprudence, which has traditionally been guided by the understandings of our citizens regarding the content of, and the State's power over, the "bundle of rights" that they acquire when they obtain title to property. It seems to us that the property owner necessarily expects the uses of his property to be restricted, from time to time, by various measures newly enacted by the State in legitimate exercise of its police powers; "[a]s long recognized, some values are enjoyed under an implied limitation and must yield to the police power." *Pennsylvania Coal Co. v. Mahon.* And in the case of personal property, by reason of the State's traditionally high degree of control over commercial dealings, he ought to be aware of the possibility that new regulation might even render his property economically worthless (at least if the property's only economically productive use is sale or manufacture for sale). See *Andrus v. Allard* (1979) (prohibition on sale of eagle feathers). In the case of land, however, we think the notion pressed by the Council that title is somehow held subject to the "implied limitation" that the State may subsequently eliminate all economically valuable use is inconsistent with the historical compact recorded in the Takings Clause that has become part of our constitutional culture.[4]

Where "permanent physical occupation" of land is concerned, we have refused to allow the government to decree it anew (without compensation), no matter how weighty the asserted "public interests" involved, *Loretto v. Teleprompter Manhattan CATV Corp.*— though we assuredly *would* permit the government to assert a permanent easement that was a pre-existing limitation upon the landowner's title. Compare *Scranton v. Wheeler* (1900) (interests of "riparian owner in the submerged lands ... bordering on a public navigable water" held subject to Government's navigational servitude), with *Kaiser Aetna v. United States* (1979) (imposition of navigational servitude on marina created and rendered navigable at private expense held to constitute a taking). We believe similar treatment must be accorded confiscatory regulations, i.e., regulations that prohibit all economically beneficial use of land: Any limitation so severe cannot be newly legislated or decreed (without compensation), but must inhere in the title itself, in the restrictions that background principles of the State's law of property and nuisance already place upon land ownership. A law or decree with such an effect must, in other words, do no more than duplicate the result that could have been achieved in the courts — by adjacent landowners (or other uniquely affected persons) under the State's law of private nuisance, or by the State under its complementary power to abate nuisances that affect the public generally, or otherwise.

On this analysis, the owner of a lakebed, for example, would not be entitled to compensation when he is denied the requisite permit to engage in a landfilling operation that

---

4. [J]ustice Blackmun ... argu[es] that our description of the "understanding" of land ownership that informs the Takings Clause is not supported by early American experience. That is largely true, but entirely irrelevant. The practices of the States *prior* to incorporation of the Takings and Just Compensation Clauses ... were out of accord with *any* plausible interpretation of those provisions. Justice Blackmun is correct that early constitutional theorists did not believe the Takings Clause embraced regulations of property at all ... but even he does not suggest (explicitly, at least) that we renounce the Court's contrary conclusion in *Mahon*. Since the text of the Clause can be read to encompass regulatory as well as physical deprivations ... we decline to do so as well.

would have the effect of flooding others' land. Nor the corporate owner of a nuclear generating plant, when it is directed to remove all improvements from its land upon discovery that the plant sits astride an earthquake fault. Such regulatory action may well have the effect of eliminating the land's only economically productive use, but it does not proscribe a productive use that was previously permissible under relevant property and nuisance principles. The use of these properties for what are now expressly prohibited purposes was *always* unlawful, and (subject to other constitutional limitations) it was open to the State at any point to make the implication of those background principles of nuisance and property law explicit. See Michelman, *Property, Utility, and Fairness, Comments on the Ethical Foundations of "Just Compensation" Law*, 80 Harv. L. Rev. 1165, 1239–41 (1967). When, however, a regulation that declares "off-limits" all economically productive or beneficial uses of land goes beyond what the relevant background principles would dictate, compensation must be paid to sustain it.[5]

The "total taking" inquiry we require today will ordinarily entail (as the application of state nuisance law ordinarily entails) analysis of, among other things, the degree of harm to public lands and resources, or adjacent private property, posed by the claimant's proposed activities, see, e.g., Restatement (Second) of Torts §§ 826, 827, the social value of the claimant's activities and their suitability to the locality in question, see, e.g., *id.*, §§ 828(a) and (b), 831, and the relative ease with which the alleged harm can be avoided through measures taken by the claimant and the government (or adjacent private landowners) alike, see, e.g., *id.*, §§ § 827(e), 828(c), 830. The fact that a particular use has long been engaged in by similarly situated owners ordinarily imports a lack of any common-law prohibition (though changed circumstances or new knowledge may make what was previously permissible no longer so, see *id.*, § 827, Comment g). So also does the fact that other landowners, similarly situated, are permitted to continue the use denied to the claimant.

It seems unlikely that common-law principles would have prevented the erection of any habitable or productive improvements on petitioner's land; they rarely support prohibition of the "essential use" of land, *Curtin v. Benson* (1911). The question, however, is one of state law to be dealt with on remand. We emphasize that to win its case South Carolina must do more than proffer the legislature's declaration that the uses Lucas desires are inconsistent with the public interest, or the conclusory assertion that they violate a common-law maxim such as *sic utere tuo ut alienum non laedas*. Instead, as it would be required to do if it sought to restrain Lucas in a common-law action for public nuisance, South Carolina must identify background principles of nuisance and property law that prohibit the uses he now intends in the circumstances in which the property is presently found. Only on this showing can the State fairly claim that, in proscribing all such beneficial uses, the Beachfront Management Act is taking nothing.[6] ...

---

5. Of course, the State may elect to rescind its regulation and thereby avoid having to pay compensation for a permanent deprivation. See *First English Evangelical Lutheran Church v. County of Los Angeles* (1987). But "where the [regulation has] already worked a taking of all use of property, no subsequent action by the government can relieve it of the duty to provide compensation for the period during which the taking was effective."

6. Justice Blackmun decries our reliance on background nuisance principles at least in part because he believes those principles to be as manipulable as we find the "harm prevention"/"benefit conferral" dichotomy. There is no doubt some leeway in a court's interpretation of what existing state law permits—but not remotely as much, we think, as in a legislative crafting of the reasons for its confiscatory regulation. We stress that an affirmative decree eliminating all economically beneficial uses may be defended only if an *objectively reasonable application* of relevant precedents would exclude those beneficial uses in the circumstances in which the land is presently found.

Justice Kennedy, concurring in the judgment....

The South Carolina Court of Common Pleas found that petitioner's real property has been rendered valueless by the State's regulation. The finding appears to presume that the property has no significant market value or resale potential. This is a curious finding, and I share the reservations of some of my colleagues about a finding that a beach-front lot loses all value because of a development restriction.... Accepting the finding as entered, it follows that petitioner is entitled to invoke the line of cases discussing regulations that deprive real property of all economic value. See *Agins v. City of Tiburon* (1980).

The finding of no value must be considered under the Takings Clause by reference to the owner's reasonable, investment-backed expectations. *Kaiser Aetna v. United States* (1979), *Penn Central* (1978). The Takings Clause, while conferring substantial protection on property owners, does not eliminate the police power of the State to enact limitations on the use of their property. *Mugler v. Kansas* (1887). The rights conferred by the Takings Clause and the police power of the State may coexist without conflict. Property is bought and sold, investments are made, subject to the State's power to regulate. Where a taking is alleged from regulations which deprive the property of all value, the test must be whether the deprivation is contrary to reasonable, investment-backed expectations.

There is an inherent tendency towards circularity in this synthesis, of course; for if the owner's reasonable expectations are shaped by what courts allow as a proper exercise of governmental authority, property tends to become what courts say it is. Some circularity must be tolerated in these matters, however ... [t]he definition ... is not circular in its entirety. The expectations protected by the Constitution are based on objective rules and customs that can be understood as reasonable by all parties involved.

In my view, reasonable expectations must be understood in light of the whole of our legal tradition. The common law of nuisance is too narrow a confine for the exercise of regulatory power in a complex and interdependent society. *Goldblatt v. Hempstead* (1962). The State should not be prevented from enacting new regulatory initiatives in response to changing conditions, and courts must consider all reasonable expectations whatever their source. The Takings Clause does not require a static body of state property law; it protects private expectations to ensure private investment. I agree with the Court that nuisance prevention accords with the most common expectations of property owners who face regulation, but I do not believe this can be the sole source of state authority to impose severe restrictions. Coastal property may present such unique concerns for a fragile land system that the State can go further in regulating its development and use than the common law of nuisance might otherwise permit.

The Supreme Court of South Carolina erred, in my view, by reciting the general purposes for which the state regulations were enacted without a determination that they were in accord with the owner's reasonable expectations and therefore sufficient to support a severe restriction on specific parcels of property. The promotion of tourism, for instance, ought not to suffice to deprive specific property of all value without a corresponding duty to compensate. Furthermore, the means, as well as the ends, of regulation must accord with the owner's reasonable expectations. Here, the State did not act until after the property had been zoned for individual lot development and most other parcels had been improved, throwing the whole burden of the regulation on the remaining lots. This too must be measured in the balance. See *Pennsylvania Coal Co. v. Mahon* (1922)....

Justice Blackmun, dissenting....

I-C. The South Carolina Supreme Court['s] ... decision rested on two premises that until today were unassailable—that the State has the power to prevent any use of property it finds to be harmful to its citizens, and that a state statute is entitled to a presumption of constitutionality....

If the state legislature is correct that the prohibition on building in front of the setback line prevents serious harm, then, under this Court's prior cases, the Act is constitutional. "Long ago it was recognized that all property in this country is held under the implied obligation that the owner's use of it shall not be injurious to the community, and the Takings Clause did not transform that principle to one that requires compensation whenever the State asserts its power to enforce it." *Keystone Bituminous Coal Assn. v. DeBenedictis* (1987). The Court consistently has upheld regulations imposed to arrest a significant threat to the common welfare, whatever their economic effect on the owner. See, e.g., *Goldblatt v. Hempstead* (1962); *Euclid v. Ambler Realty Co.* (1926); *Mugler v. Kansas* (1887).

Petitioner never challenged the legislature's findings that a building ban was necessary to protect property and life....

Nothing in the record undermines the General Assembly's assessment that prohibitions on building in front of the setback line are necessary to protect people and property from storms, high tides, and beach erosion. Because that legislative determination cannot be disregarded in the absence of such evidence, see, e.g., *Euclid v. Ambler Realty Co.* (1926); *O'Gorman & Young, Inc. v. Hartford Fire Ins. Co.* (1931) (Brandeis, J.), and because its determination of harm to life and property from building is sufficient to prohibit that use under this Court's cases, the South Carolina Supreme Court correctly found no taking....

III. ... We only recently have reaffirmed that claimants have the burden of showing a state law constitutes a taking. See *Keystone Bituminous Coal*. See also *Goldblatt* (citing "the usual presumption of constitutionality" that applies to statutes attacked as takings).

Rather than invoking these traditional rules, the Court decides the State has the burden to convince the courts that its legislative judgments are correct....

IV. ... [The Court] takes the opportunity to create a new scheme for regulations that eliminate all economic value. From now on, there is a categorical rule finding these regulations to be a taking unless the use they prohibit is a background common-law nuisance or property principle....

IV-A. ... If one fact about the Court's takings jurisprudence can be stated without contradiction, it is that "the particular circumstances of each case" determine whether a specific restriction will be rendered invalid by the government's failure to pay compensation. *United States v. Central Eureka Mining Co.* (1958). This is so because although we have articulated certain factors to be considered, including the economic impact on the property owner, the ultimate conclusion "necessarily requires a weighing of private and public interests." *Agins v. City of Tiburon* (1992). When the government regulation prevents the owner from any economically valuable use of his property, the private interest is unquestionably substantial, but we have never before held that no public interest can outweigh it. Instead the Court's prior decisions "uniformly reject the proposition that diminution in property value, standing alone, can establish a 'taking.'" *Penn Central Transp. Co. v. New York City* (1978).

This Court repeatedly has recognized the ability of government, in certain circumstances, to regulate property without compensation no matter how adverse the financial effect on the owner may be. More than a century ago, the Court explicitly upheld the right of States to prohibit uses of property injurious to public health, safety, or welfare without paying compensation: "A prohibition simply upon the use of property for purposes that are declared, by valid legislation, to be injurious to the health, morals, or safety of the community, cannot, in any just sense, be deemed a taking or an appropriation of property." *Mugler v. Kansas* (1887). On this basis, the Court upheld an ordinance effectively prohibiting operation of a previously lawful brewery, although the "establishments will become of no value as property." ...

In *First English Evangelical Lutheran Church of Glendale v. County of Los Angeles* (1987), the owner alleged that a floodplain ordinance had deprived it of "all use" of the property. The Court remanded the case for consideration whether, even if the ordinance denied the owner all use, it could be justified as a safety measure. And in *Keystone Bituminous Coal*, the Court summarized over 100 years of precedent: "[T]he Court has repeatedly upheld regulations that destroy or adversely affect real property interests."

The Court recognizes that "our prior opinions have suggested that 'harmful or noxious uses' of property may be proscribed by government regulation without the requirement of compensation," but seeks to reconcile them with its categorical rule by claiming that the Court never has upheld a regulation when the owner alleged the loss of all economic value. Even if the Court's factual premise were correct, its understanding of the Court's cases is distorted. In none of the cases did the Court suggest that the right of a State to prohibit certain activities without paying compensation turned on the availability of some residual valuable use. Instead, the cases depended on whether the government interest was sufficient to prohibit the activity, given the significant private cost.

These cases rest on the principle that the State has full power to prohibit an owner's use of property if it is harmful to the public. "[S]ince no individual has a right to use his property so as to create a nuisance or otherwise harm others, the State has not 'taken' anything when it asserts its power to enjoin the nuisance-like activity." *Keystone Bituminous Coal*. It would make no sense under this theory to suggest that an owner has a constitutionally protected right to harm others, if only he makes the proper showing of economic loss.

IV-B. Ultimately even the Court ... agrees that there cannot be a categorical rule for a taking based on economic value that wholly disregards the public need asserted. Instead, the Court decides that it will permit a State to regulate all economic value only if the State prohibits uses that would not be permitted under "background principles of nuisance and property law."

Until today, the Court explicitly had rejected the contention that the government's power to act without paying compensation turns on whether the prohibited activity is a common-law nuisance.... Instead the Court has relied in the past, as the South Carolina court has done here, on legislative judgments of what constitutes a harm....

Even more perplexing, however, is the Court's reliance on common-law principles of nuisance in its quest for a value-free takings jurisprudence. In determining what is a nuisance at common law, state courts make exactly the decision that the Court finds so troubling when made by the South Carolina General Assembly today: they determine whether the use is harmful. Common-law public and private nuisance law is simply a determination whether a particular use causes harm.... There is nothing magical in the reasoning of judges long dead. They determined a harm in the same way as state judges and legislatures do today. If judges in the 18th and 19th centuries can distinguish a harm from a benefit, why not judges in the 20th century, and if judges can, why not legislators? There simply is no reason to believe that new interpretations of the hoary common-law nuisance doctrine will be particularly "objective" or "value free." Once one abandons the level of generality of *sic utere tuo ut alienum non laedas* one searches in vain, I think, for anything resembling a principle in the common law of nuisance.

IV-C. Finally, the Court justifies its new rule that the legislature may not deprive a property owner of the only economically valuable use of his land, even if the legislature finds it to be a harmful use, because such action is not part of the "long recognized" "understandings of our citizens." These "understandings" permit such regulation only if the use is a nuisance under the common law. Any other course is "inconsistent with the historical compact recorded in the Takings Clause." It is not clear from the Court's opinion where our "historical compact" or "citizens' understanding" comes from, but it does not appear to be history....

Although, prior to the adoption of the Bill of Rights, America was replete with land-use regulations describing which activities were considered noxious and forbidden ... the 5th Amendment's Takings Clause originally did not extend to regulations of property, whatever the effect.[1] ... Most state courts agreed with this narrow interpretation of a taking....

Even when courts began to consider that regulation in some situations could constitute a taking, they continued to uphold bans on particular uses without paying compensation, notwithstanding the economic impact, under the rationale that no one can obtain a vested right to injure or endanger the public....

In addition, state courts historically have been less likely to find that a government action constitutes a taking when the affected land is undeveloped....

With similar result, the common agrarian conception of property limited owners to "natural" uses of their land prior to and during much of the 18th century....

Nor does history indicate any common-law limit on the State's power to regulate harmful uses even to the point of destroying all economic value. Nothing in the discussions in Congress concerning the Takings Clause indicates that the Clause was limited by the common-law nuisance doctrine....

In short, I find no clear and accepted "historical compact" or "understanding of our citizens" justifying the Court's new takings doctrine.... If the Court decided that the law of a later period provides the background principles, then regulation might be compensable, but the Court would have to confront the fact that legislatures regularly determined which uses were prohibited, independent of the common law, and independent of whether the uses were lawful when the owner purchased. What makes the Court's analysis unworkable is its attempt to package the law of two incompatible eras and peddle it as historical fact....

Justice Stevens, dissenting....

II. ... In my opinion, the Court is doubly in error. The categorical rule the Court establishes is an unsound and unwise addition to the law and the Court's formulation of the exception to that rule is too rigid and too narrow....

The Categorical Rule

We have frequently—and recently—held that, in some circumstances, a law that renders property valueless may nonetheless not constitute a taking....

---

1. James Madison, author of the Takings Clause, apparently intended it to apply only to direct, physical takings of property by the Federal Government....

In addition to lacking support in past decisions, the Court's new rule is wholly arbitrary. A landowner whose property is diminished in value 95% recovers nothing, while an owner whose property is diminished 100% recovers the land's full value....

Moreover, because of the elastic nature of property rights, the Court's new rule will also prove unsound in practice. In response to the rule, courts may define "property" broadly and only rarely find regulations to effect total takings. This is the approach the Court itself adopts in its revisionist reading of venerable precedents. We are told that—notwithstanding the Court's findings to the contrary in each case—the brewery in *Mugler v. Kansas* (1887), the brickyard in *Hadacheck v. Sebastian* (1915), and the gravel pit in *Goldblatt v. Hempstead* (1962) all could be put to "other uses" and that, therefore, those cases did not involve total regulatory takings.[1]

On the other hand, developers and investors may market specialized estates to take advantage of the Court's new rule. The smaller the estate, the more likely that a regulatory change will effect a total taking. Thus, an investor may, for example, purchase the right to build a multifamily home on a specific lot, with the result that a zoning regulation that allows only single-family homes would render the investor's property interest "valueless." In short, the categorical rule will likely have one of two effects: Either courts will alter the definition of the "denominator" in the takings "fraction," rendering the Court's categorical rule meaningless, or investors will manipulate the relevant property interests, giving the Court's rule sweeping effect. To my mind, neither of these results is desirable or appropriate, and both are distortions of our takings jurisprudence.

Finally, the Court's justification for its new categorical rule is remarkably thin. The Court mentions in passing three arguments in support of its rule; none is convincing. First, the Court suggests that "total deprivation of feasible use is, from the landowner's point of view, the equivalent of a physical appropriation." This argument proves too much. From the "landowner's point of view," a regulation that diminishes a lot's value by 50% is as well "the equivalent" of the condemnation of half of the lot. Yet, it is well established that a 50% diminution in value does not by itself constitute a taking. See *Euclid v. Ambler Realty Co.* (1926) (75% diminution in value). Thus, the landowner's perception of the regulation cannot justify the Court's new rule.

Second, the Court emphasizes that because total takings are "relatively rare" its new rule will not adversely affect the government's ability to "go on."... This argument proves too little. Certainly it is true that defining a small class of regulations that are *per se* takings will not greatly hinder important governmental functions—but this is true of *any* small class of regulations. The Court's suggestion only begs the question of why regulations of *this* particular class should always be found to effect takings.

Finally, the Court suggests that "regulations that leave the owner ... without economically beneficial ... use ... carry with them a heightened risk that private property is being pressed into some form of public service."... I agree that the risks of such

---

1. Of course, the same could easily be said in this case: Lucas may put his land to "other uses"—fishing or camping, for example—or may sell his land to his neighbors as a buffer. In either event, his land is far from "valueless." This highlights a fundamental weakness in the Court's analysis: its failure to explain why only the impairment of "*economically* beneficial or productive use"..., of property is relevant in takings analysis. I should think that a regulation arbitrarily prohibiting an owner from continuing to use her property for bird watching or sunbathing might constitute a taking under some circumstances; and, conversely, that such uses are of value to the owner. Yet the Court offers no basis for its assumption that the only uses of property cognizable under the Constitution are *developmental* uses.

singling out are of central concern in takings law. However, such risks do not justify a per se rule for total regulatory takings. There is no necessary correlation between "singling out" and total takings: A regulation may single out a property owner without depriving him of all of his property ... and it may deprive him of all of his property without singling him out, see, e.g., *Mugler v. Kansas*; *Hadacheck v. Sebastian*. What matters in such cases is not the degree of diminution of value, but rather the specificity of the expropriating act. For this reason, the Court's third justification for its new rule also fails.

In short, the Court's new rule is unsupported by prior decisions, arbitrary and unsound in practice, and theoretically unjustified. In my opinion, a categorical rule as important as the one established by the Court today should be supported by more history or more reason than has yet been provided.

The Nuisance Exception

Like many bright-line rules, the categorical rule established in this case is only "categorical" for a page or two in the U.S. Reports....

Mugler v. Kansas held that a statewide statute that prohibited the owner of a brewery from making alcoholic beverages did not effect a taking, even though the use of the property had been perfectly lawful and caused no public harm before the statute was enacted. We squarely rejected the rule the Court adopts today....

Under our reasoning in *Mugler*, a State's decision to prohibit or to regulate certain uses of property is not a compensable taking just because the particular uses were previously lawful. Under the Court's opinion today, however, if a State should decide to prohibit the manufacture of asbestos, cigarettes, or concealable firearms, for example, it must be prepared to pay for the adverse economic consequences of its decision. One must wonder if government will be able to "go on" effectively if it must risk compensation "for every such change in the general law." ...

The Court's holding today effectively freezes the State's common law, denying the legislature much of its traditional power to revise the law governing the rights and uses of property. Until today, I had thought that we had long abandoned this approach to constitutional law. More than a century ago we recognized that "the great office of statutes is to remedy defects in the common law as they are developed, and to adapt it to the changes of time and circumstances." *Munn v. Illinois* (1877). As Justice Marshall observed about a position similar to that adopted by the Court today:

> If accepted, that claim would represent a return to the era of *Lochner v. New York* (1905) when common-law rights were also found immune from revision by State or Federal Government. Such an approach would freeze the common law as it has been constructed by the courts, perhaps at its 19th-century state of development. It would allow no room for change in response to changes in circumstance. The Due Process Clause does not require such a result.

PruneYard Shopping Center v. Robins (1980) (concurring opinion).

Arresting the development of the common law is not only a departure from our prior decisions; it is also profoundly unwise. The human condition is one of constant learning and evolution—both moral and practical. Legislatures implement that new learning; in doing so they must often revise the definition of property and the rights of property owners. New appreciation of the significance of endangered species, see, e.g., *Andrus v. Allard* (1979); the importance of wetlands ... and the vulnerability of coastal lands ... shapes our evolving understandings of property rights.

Of course, some legislative redefinitions of property will effect a taking and must be compensated—but it certainly cannot be the case that every movement away from common law does so.... The rule that should govern a decision in a case of this kind should focus on the future, not the past.

The Court's categorical approach rule will, I fear, greatly hamper the efforts of local officials and planners who must deal with increasingly complex problems in land-use and environmental regulation....

Viewed more broadly, the Court's new rule and exception conflict with the very character of our takings jurisprudence. We have frequently and consistently recognized that the definition of a taking cannot be reduced to a "set formula" and that determining whether a regulation is a taking is "essentially [an] ad hoc, factual inquir[y]." *Penn Central Transportation Co. v. New York City* (1978). This is unavoidable, for the determination whether a law effects a taking is ultimately a matter of "fairness and justice," *Armstrong v. United States* (1960), and "necessarily requires a weighing of private and public interests," *Agins v. City of Tiburon* (1992). The rigid rules fixed by the Court today clash with this enterprise: "fairness and justice" are often disserved by categorical rules.

III. It is well established that a takings case "entails inquiry into [several factors:] the character of the governmental action, its economic impact, and its interference with reasonable investment-backed expectations." *PruneYard*. The Court's analysis today focuses on the last two of these three factors: The categorical rule addresses a regulation's "economic impact," while the nuisance exception recognizes that ownership brings with it only certain "expectations." Neglected by the Court today is the first and, in some ways, the most important factor in takings analysis: the character of the regulatory action.

The Just Compensation Clause "was designed to bar Government from forcing some people alone to bear public burdens which, in all fairness and justice, should be borne by the public as a whole."... We have, therefore, in our takings law frequently looked to the *generality* of a regulation of property.

For example, in the case of so-called "developmental exactions," we have paid special attention to the risk that particular landowners might "b[e] singled out to bear the burden" of a broader problem not of his own making. *Nollan[v. California Coastal Comm'n* (1987)]; see also *Pennell v. San Jose* (1988). Similarly, in distinguishing between the Kohler Act (at issue in *Mahon*) and the Subsidence Act (at issue in *Keystone*), we found significant that the regulatory function of the latter was substantially broader.... Perhaps the most familiar application of this principle of generality arises in zoning cases. A diminution in value caused by a zoning regulation is far less likely to constitute a taking if it is part of a general and comprehensive land-use plan, see *Euclid v. Ambler Realty Co.*; conversely, "spot zoning" is far more likely to constitute a taking, see *Penn Central*.

The presumption that a permanent physical occupation, no matter how slight, effects a taking is wholly consistent with this principle. A physical taking entails a certain amount of "singling out."... In analyzing takings claims, courts have long recognized the difference between a regulation that targets one or two parcels of land and a regulation that enforces a statewide policy....

In considering Lucas' claim, the generality of the Beachfront Management Act is significant. The Act does not target particular landowners, but rather regulates the use of the coastline of the entire State.... Moreover, the Act did not single out owners of undeveloped land. The Act also prohibited owners of developed land from rebuilding if their structures were destroyed.... In short, the South Carolina Act imposed substantial burdens on owners of developed and undeveloped land alike. This generality indicates that the Act is not an effort to expropriate owners of undeveloped land....

The impact of the ban on developmental uses must also be viewed in light of the purposes of the Act....

In view of all of these factors, even assuming that petitioner's property was rendered valueless, the risk inherent in investments of the sort made by petitioner, the generality of the Act, and the compelling purpose motivating the South Carolina Legislature persuade me that the Act did not effect a taking of petitioner's property.

Accordingly, I respectfully dissent.

Statement of Justice Souter. [Omitted.]

Lucas v. South Carolina Coastal Council: **Notes**

Justice Stevens' critique in *Lucas* of the expansive use of categorical analysis in takings cases seems to have gained the support of the majority of the Court. In *Tahoe-Sierra Preservation Council, Inc. v. Tahoe Regional Planning Agency* (2002), the Supreme Court rejected a takings claim arising from a series of "temporary" moratoria on development. The plaintiffs alleged that the moratoria deprived their property of all economic use during the pendency of the moratoria and that, consistent with *Lucas*, this loss should constitute a taking per se. Justice Stevens delivered the opinion of the Court and was joined by Justices O'Connor, Kennedy, Souter, Ginsburg, and Breyer. Chief Justice Rehnquist dissented, joined by Justices Scalia and Thomas. Justice Thomas also dissented, joined by Justice Scalia. The dissenters argued for application of categorical analysis.

Justice Stevens' narrow interpretation of *Lucas* suggests that the categorical analysis of *Lucas* is limited to its facts. Unless a piece of property permanently lost all of its value, categorical analysis should be rejected in favor of the three-part balancing approach of *Penn Central*. The Court stated:

> [W]e still resist the temptation to adopt per se rules in our cases involving partial regulatory takings, preferring to examine "a number of factors" rather than a simple "mathematically precise" formula.

A year prior to *Tahoe-Sierra* in *Palazzolo v. Rhode Island* (2001), another regulatory takings case, the Court found a diminution of value of 93.7%, yet applied the Penn Central balancing test. Professor Tom Roberts concludes that after *Tahoe-Sierra* the *Lucas* approach seems to be in decline:

> The parameters placed on *Lucas* mean that it will rarely apply. With *Tahoe-Sierra* limiting *Lucas* to permanent regulations that deprive property of all value and *Palazzolo* holding a 93.7% loss insufficient to trigger *Lucas*, "all" pretty much means "all."

Thomas E. Roberts, *An Analysis of* Tahoe-Sierra *and Its Help and Hindrance in Understanding the Concept of a Temporary Regulatory Taking*, 25 U. Haw. L. Rev. 417, 425 (2003). Following the *Lucas* litigation, a neighboring landowner offered the state $350,000 to buy one of the lots as a buffer, promising not to build on it. Professor Roberts concludes that if the *Lucas* case were retried today, it would therefore be subjected to *Penn Central* balancing.

* * *

In *Kelo v. City of New London* (2005), the Court ruled 5–4 that a city could use its power of eminent domain to take property and sell it for private development as part of a comprehensive urban renewal project. While the result sparked controversy, the result was consistent with earlier precedent that had held that property could be taken for a public "purpose" as well as a literal public "use."

Decades of economic decline led a state agency to designate New London, Connecticut a "distressed municipality" in 1990. Subsequently, state and local officials targeted New London, and in particular the Fort Trumbull neighborhood, for economic revitalization. The New London Development Corporation (NLDC), a private nonprofit entity, was created to oversee the project. The State authorized a $5.35 million bond issue to support the NLDC's planning activities and a $10 million bond issue toward the creation of a Fort Trumbull State Park. The NDLC eventually developed an integrated development plan focused on 90 acres in the Fort Trumbull area. The centerpiece of the plan was to be a $300 million research facility that Pfizer Inc. committed to build. The development plan included such things as a waterfront conference hotel, marinas, a riverwalk, residences, a U.S. Coast Guard Museum, and research and development office space. The plan's purposes were to create jobs, generate tax revenue, and make the City more attractive to developers.

After the plan was approved, the City Council authorized the NDLC to purchase the property or to acquire property by exercising eminent domain in the City's name. Much of the land was purchased, except for the land of the Plaintiffs. None of the Plaintiffs' properties were blighted or otherwise in poor condition. The NDLC condemned the Plaintiffs' land when they refused to sell. The Plaintiffs then filed suit in state court, claiming that the taking of their property violated the public use restriction of the 5th Amendment (as incorporated by the 14th).

The 5th Amendment provides: "[N]or shall private property be taken for public use, without just compensation." Prior to *Kelo*, the Court had upheld an urban redevelopment plan of a blighted area that was challenged by the owner of non-blighted property within the area of the plan. *Berman v. Parker* (1954). It had also upheld a decision by Hawaii to force landlords to sell their property to their tenants because the undue concentration of land ownership in Hawaii adversely skewed the real estate market. *Hawaii Housing Authority v. Midkiff* (1984). Justice Stevens, speaking for the majority in *Kelo*, noted:

> Two polar propositions are perfectly clear. On the one hand, it has long been accepted that the sovereign may not take the property of A for the sole purpose of transferring it to another private party B, even though A is paid just compensation. On the other hand, it is equally clear that a State may transfer property from one private party to another if future "use by the public" is the purpose of the taking; the condemnation of land for a railroad with common-carrier duties is a familiar example. Neither of these propositions, however, determines the disposition of this case.
>
> As for the first proposition, the City would no doubt be forbidden from taking petitioners' land for the purpose of conferring a private benefit on a particular private party. See *Midkiff* (1984) ("A purely private taking could not withstand the scrutiny of the public use requirement; it would serve no legitimate purpose of government and would thus be void"). Nor would the City be allowed to take property under the mere pretext of a public purpose, when its actual purpose was to bestow a private benefit. The takings before us, however, would be executed pursuant to a "carefully considered" development plan. The trial judge and all the members of the Supreme Court of Connecticut agreed that there was no evidence of an illegitimate purpose in this case. Therefore, as was true of the statute

challenged in *Midkiff*, the City's development plan was not adopted "to benefit a particular class of identifiable individuals."

On the other hand, this is not a case in which the City is planning to open the condemned land—at least not in its entirety—to use by the general public. Nor will the private lessees of the land in any sense be required to operate like common carriers, making their services available to all comers. But although such a projected use would be sufficient to satisfy the public use requirement, this "Court long ago rejected any literal requirement that condemned property be put into use for the general public." *Id*....

The disposition of this case therefore turns on the question whether the City's development plan serves a "public purpose." Without exception, our cases have defined that concept broadly, reflecting our longstanding policy of deference to legislative judgments in this field....

Given the comprehensive character of the plan, the thorough deliberation that preceded its adoption, and the limited scope of our review, it is appropriate for us, as it was in *Berman*, to resolve the challenges of the individual owners, not on a piecemeal basis, but rather in light of the entire plan. Because that plan unquestionably serves a public purpose, the takings challenged here satisfy the public use requirement of the 5th Amendment.

To avoid this result, petitioners urge us to adopt a new bright-line rule that economic development does not qualify as a public use.... Clearly, there is no basis for exempting economic development from our traditionally broad understanding of public purpose.

Alternatively, petitioners maintain that for takings of this kind we should require a "reasonable certainty" that the expected public benefits will actually accrue. Such a rule, however, would represent an even greater departure from our precedent. "When the legislature's purpose is legitimate and its means are not irrational, our cases make clear that empirical debates over the wisdom of takings—no less than debates over the wisdom of other kinds of socioeconomic legislation—are not to be carried out in the federal courts." *Midkiff*.

In affirming the City's authority to take petitioners' properties, we do not minimize the hardship that condemnations may entail, notwithstanding the payment of just compensation. We emphasize that nothing in our opinion precludes any State from placing further restrictions on its exercise of the takings power. Indeed, many States already impose "public use" requirements that are stricter than the federal baseline. Some of these requirements have been established as a matter of state constitutional law, while others are expressed in state eminent domain statutes that carefully limit the grounds upon which takings may be exercised.

Justice Kennedy supplied the fifth vote to the majority. He concurred:

This is not the occasion for conjecture as to what sort of cases might justify a more demanding standard, but it is appropriate to underscore aspects of the instant case that convince me no departure from *Berman* and *Midkiff* is appropriate here. This taking occurred in the context of a comprehensive development plan meant to address a serious city-wide depression, and the projected economic benefits of the project cannot be characterized as de minimus. The identity of most of the private beneficiaries were unknown at the time the city formulated its plans. The city complied with elaborate procedural requirements that facilitate review of the record and inquiry into the city's purposes. In sum, while there may be categories of cases in which the transfers are so suspicious, or the procedures employed so prone to abuse, or the purported benefits are so trivial or implausible, that courts should presume an impermissible private purpose, no such circumstances are present in this case.

Justice O'Connor, joined by Chief Justice Rehnquist and Justices Scalia and Thomas, dissented:

> Under the banner of economic development, all private property is now vulnerable to being taken and transferred to another private owner, so long as it might be upgraded—i.e., given to an owner who will use it in a way that the legislature deems more beneficial to the public—in the process. To reason, as the Court does, that the incidental public benefits resulting from the subsequent ordinary use of private property render economic development takings "for public use" is to wash out any distinction between private and public use of property—and thereby effectively to delete the words "for public use" from the Takings Clause of the 5th Amendment.

The 5–4 division in this case is likely to encourage further litigation challenging local government's use of the taking power.

* * *

As we have seen, *Dred Scott* (1857) held that a statute outlawing slavery in the Missouri Territory deprived territorial slave owners of their property without due process of law. *Dred Scott* did not invoke the Takings Clause, probably because the clause was understood to be limited to appropriations or physical invasions—not regulations. In this sense, *Dred Scott* was a substantive due process case akin to *Lochner*. How would you compare *Dred Scott* and *Lucas*?

As of 1998, takings cases had involved either a physical invasion of property or virtually complete elimination of the owner's right to use his property. In *Eastern Enterprises v. Apfel* (1998), four members of the Court held that the Takings Clause prohibited retroactive regulatory legislation that imposed what the Justices thought was a "severe, disproportionate, and extremely retroactive burden." See generally William Church, *The Eastern Enterprises Case: A New Vigor for Judicial Review*, 2000 Wis. L. Rev. 547.

Eastern Enterprises was an energy company that beginning in 1929 had been extensively involved in coal mining. In 1965, it transferred its coal business to a wholly owned subsidiary, and continued to earn profits from that company until it was sold in 1987.

Coal miners had long suffered from occupational diseases and injuries and inadequate medical care. Beginning in the 1950s, the United Mine Workers negotiated labor contracts that provided health care for miners, and later for their families, through health care funds administered by trustees. The funds were originally funded out of a royalty on coal sold from mines with union contracts. Until 1978, these health care plans provided for medical coverage only to the extent of the funds available from the royalties. In 1978, a new agreement obligated signatories to make sufficient contributions to maintain benefits as long as they were in the coal business. As medical costs escalated, companies began to withdraw from the coal business, leaving a smaller group of remaining signatories to absorb the increasing costs. Retired miners were faced with loss of health benefits.

Congress intervened and enacted a tax on coal to be used to pay for miners' health benefits. This plan was vetoed by President George H. W. Bush, as violating his "no new taxes" pledge. Congress then passed the Coal Act of 1992. The Act required those companies that had, at one time, employed miners who were now retired, to contribute to the ongoing health costs of those retirees. Eastern, now out of the coal business, objected and filed suit to avoid liability.

Eastern had signed union agreements providing for miners' health costs between 1947 and 1964, but none of these agreements had fixed benefits; rather, the benefits were derived from contributions from royalties on coal sold. In spite of some statements by coal company and government officials that retired miners would always be protected, nothing had contractually obligated companies to provide lifetime care for miners or their families. However, the congressional act applied to Eastern as a former participant and it sued seeking to avoid the large expenses involved. Eastern argued that it had never contractually promised to pay lifetime health care benefits for the retired miners and therefore, the Coal Act, as applied to Eastern, constituted both a taking and a violation of substantive due process. Four Justices (O'Connor, Rehnquist, Scalia, and Thomas) held the Act was a taking. They concluded that the Act imposed a severe retroactive liability on a limited class of parties that could not have anticipated the liability and that the extent of the liability was substantially disproportionate to Eastern's involvement in the coal industry.

Justice Kennedy concurred but found the congressional act was not a taking but a violation of substantive due process. Justice Kennedy wrote:

> Our cases do not support the plurality's conclusion that the Coal Act takes property. The Coal Act imposes a staggering financial burden on the petitioner, Eastern Enterprises, but it regulates the former mine owner without regard to property. It does not operate upon or alter an identified property interest, and it is not applicable to or measured by a property interest. The Coal Act does not appropriate, transfer, or encumber an estate in land (e.g., a lien on a particular piece of property), a valuable interest in an intangible (e.g., intellectual property), or even a bank account or accrued interest. The law simply imposes an obligation to perform an act, the payment of benefits. The statute is indifferent as to how the regulated entity elects to comply or the property it uses to do so. To the extent it affects property interests, it does so in a manner similar to many laws; but until today, none were thought to constitute takings. To call this sort of governmental action a taking as a matter of constitutional interpretation is both imprecise and, with all due respect, unwise.
>
> As the role of Government expanded, our experience taught that a strict line between a taking and a regulation is difficult to discern or to maintain. This led the Court in *Pennsylvania Coal Co. v. Mahon* (1922), to try to span the two concepts when specific property was subjected to what the owner alleged to be excessive regulation. "The general rule at least is, that while property may be regulated to a certain extent, if regulation goes too far it will be recognized as a taking." The quoted sentence is, of course, the genesis of the so-called regulatory takings doctrine. See *Lucas v. South Carolina Coastal Council* (1992) ("Prior to Justice Holmes's exposition in *Pennsylvania Coal Co. v. Mahon*, it was generally thought that the Takings Clause reached only a 'direct appropriation' of property or the functional equivalent of a 'practical ouster of [the owner's] possession'". Without denigrating the importance the regulatory takings concept has assumed in our law, it is fair to say it has proved difficult to explain in theory and to implement in practice. Cases attempting to decide when a regulation becomes a taking are among the most litigated and perplexing in current law. See *Penn Cen-*

tral Transp. Co. v. New York City (1978) ("The question of what constitutes a 'taking' for purposes of the 5th Amendment has proved to be a problem of considerable difficulty"); *Kaiser Aetna v. United States* (1979) (the regulatory taking question requires an "essentially ad hoc, factual inquir[y]").

Until today, however, one constant limitation has been that in all of the cases where the regulatory taking analysis has been employed, a specific property right or interest has been at stake. After the decision in *Pennsylvania Coal Co. v. Mahon*, we confronted cases where specific and identified properties or property rights were alleged to come within the regulatory takings prohibition: air rights for high-rise buildings, *Penn Central*; zoning on parcels of real property, e.g., *MacDonald, Sommer & Frates v. Yolo County* (1986); trade secrets, *Ruckelshaus v. Monsanto Co.* (1984); right of access to property, e.g., *PruneYard Shopping Center v. Robins* (1980); right to affix on structures, *Loretto v. Teleprompter Manhattan CATV Corp.* (1982); right to transfer property by devise or intestacy, e.g., *Hodel v. Irving* (1987); creation of an easement, *Dolan v. City of Tigard* (1994); right to build or improve, *Lucas*; liens on real property, *Armstrong v. United States* (1960); right to mine coal, *Keystone Bituminous Coal Assn. v. DeBenedictis* (1987); right to sell personal property, *Andrus v. Allard* (1979); and the right to extract mineral deposits, *Goldblatt v. Hempstead* (1962). The regulations in the cited cases were challenged as being so excessive as to destroy, or take, a specific property interest. The plurality's opinion disregards this requirement and, by removing this constant characteristic from takings analysis, would expand an already difficult and uncertain rule to a vast category of cases not deemed, in our law, to implicate the Takings Clause.

* * *

Several academic commentators have been less gentle than Justice Kennedy in their descriptions of the Court's takings jurisprudence, describing it as a mess. E.g., Daniel A. Farber, *Public Choice and Just Compensation*, 9 Const. Comm. 279 (1992); cf, William Michael Treanor, *The Original Understanding of the Takings Clause and the Political Process*, 95 Col. L. Rev. 782 (1995).

Four other Justices in the *Eastern Enterprises* case held there was not a taking. In a dissenting opinion written by Justice Breyer, they agreed with Justice Kennedy that the claim should be evaluated under economic substantive due process to determine if the arrangement was "fundamentally unfair." They found it was not, and therefore found no due process violation. These Justices said the claim of arbitrary retroactive means to accomplish the congressional goal implicated the "fair application of law, which ... hearkens back to the Magna Carta." They insisted they were not "resurrect[ing] the long-discredited substantive notions of 'freedom of contract.'" Still, the test of "fundamental fairness" (perhaps limited to retroactive legislation) seems more similar to heightened rational basis scrutiny (rational basis with bite) than the low level rational basis which was announced by the Court in the years of and following the New Deal Court.

These dissenters found the statute fair because it applied only to miners Eastern had employed whose labor had benefitted Eastern when they were younger and healthier; because Eastern created the working conditions that often caused the health problems; because Eastern had contributed to a promise of health care which, while not contractually binding, led the miners to have a reasonable expectation of protection; and because even after it sold its mines to a wholly owned subsidiary, Eastern continued until the late 1980s to reap profits from the mines.

The conflict between an expansive reading of the Takings Clause and a possible resurrection of economic substantive due process arose again in *Stop the Beach Renourishment v. Florida Department of Environmental Protection* (2010). The constitutional issue in *Stop the Beach Renourishment* involves whether or not judicial decisions which unexpectedly change the law and thereby adversely affect private property values are subject to a takings challenge in the same way that legislative or executive conduct is. The facts of the case involved a decision by the Florida Supreme Court determining ownership boundaries to beachfront property that had increased in size as the result of a beach renourishment project. Common law property doctrine distinguishes between sand which is incrementally added to a beach by natural forces such as storms, ocean currents, etc., and sand which is suddenly added by man. The case has significant federalism implications, because recognizing that judicial behavior is subject to the Takings Clause could create an avalanche of litigation as courts routinely develop common law property rules that can adversely affect ownership rights.

All members of the Court agreed that the decision below was consistent with prior Florida law and that the property owners should lose. However, Chief Justice Roberts and Justices Scalia, Thomas, and Alito went on to say that they would extend the Takings Clause to judicial decisions. Justice Kennedy, as he had done in *Eastern Enterprises*, again said that an arbitrary change in reasonable expectations regarding property rights would be subject to a due process challenge. Justice Sotomayor joined this opinion. Justices Breyer and Ginsburg said that since all members of the Court had agreed that the Florida Supreme Court's opinion was consistent with prior case law that the Court should not even address the takings issue.

* * *

One thing is especially worthy of note as we conclude this chapter on due process analysis. The *Lochner* Court, the *Lochner* dissenters, the New Deal Court, and the Justices of the current Court often refer to "rational basis" as the test when evaluating economic legislation. But of course, the words "rational basis," as used by Justice Peckham in *Lochner* (1905) and Justice Douglas in *Williamson v. Lee Optical* (1955), have very different meanings. This fact shows why understanding constitutional law requires the understanding of constitutional history and the eras in which the Court functions.

As you consider the ebb and flow of judicial activism in the area of substantive due process, recall the excerpt from Chapter 8 of Mark Twain's *Life on the Mississippi* set out in Chapter 2 of this casebook.

Index

Abortion, 858–912 See also *Liberty interests*
  Partial birth, 892–910
  Platforms, Democratic and Republican on, 910–911
  Trimester approach, 858, 876, 883
  Undue burden approach, 877, 888
Ackerman, Bruce, 156, 825
Adams, John, 314, 340, 468, 469, 485, 486, 500, 793
Adams, John Quincy, 466
Adequate and Independent State Ground, 309, 349, 351–357
  Clear statement, examples of, 355–356
  Graphic portrayal of (chart), 356–357
  Supreme Court review (chart), 312
Advisory Opinions, 309, 311, 350, 353, 366, 367
Age Discrimination, see also *State sovereign immunity*302
Airbags, state tort action and preemption, 522–535
Amar, Akhil Reed, 37, 686, 721, 729, 756, 757
American Independent Party, 735, 790
Amnesty Act, 634
Andrews, George, 733
Anthony, Susan B., 634
Appointments Clause, 478
Article III, §2, as interpreted in *Dred Scott*, 645
Article IV, §2, Interstate Privileges and Immunities Clause
  Interpreted with 14th Amendment in *Slaughter-House Cases*, 696–698
  Limit on states, 610–620, 627, 628,
  Post-14th Amendment ratification case on, 686

  "Privileges" and "immunities" used in 14th Amendment, 632
  Protection for temporary visitors from out of state, 641
Articles of Confederation, 3, 5, 23, 72, 154, 156, 225, 233, 243, 275, 280, 558, 631, 635, 651–653, 656, 657, 697, 765, 823, 825
  Failure of, 19, 34, 89, 194, 202–204, 220, 273, 328, 375, 407, 427, 435, 480, 506, 527, 531, 532, 534–536, 538, 605, 716, 717, 804, 807, 883, 942, 946, 1001
Aynes, Richard, 706, 721, 756, 757
Bailey, Fred Arthur, 709
Balanced Budget Act of 1997, 462–464
Balkin, Jack M., 28
Bank of the United States, 35, 61, 64, 65, 67–70, 76, 79, 339, 341, 343
Barnett, Randy, 115
Berger, Raoul, 40, 45, 686, 721
Bicameralism, 458, 459
Bill of Rights
  Arguments against adoption of, 632
  Drafting, 632
  Madison's protection for freedom of the press, rights of conscience, and jury trial as a limit on the states in original draft, 632
Bill of Rights, application to the states, see also *Fourteenth Amendment, Incorporation, Privileges or Immunities, Warren Court*, Chapter 7
  Bingham, John, on application to states, 625, 667, 670–672, 682–684, 721, 756, 757, 766
  Georgia Supreme Court, 641, 745
  Historical debate over incorporation, 720
  Howard, Jacob on, 677, 681, 756, 766

Bill of Rights, *continued*
   Not entirely incorporated as limits on states, 730
   Specific provisions, 32, 103, 246, 836, 853, 914, 917
   Warren Court, 732–737
Bingham, John, 163, 625, 655, 661, 664–666, 721, 756, 757, 766
   Dred Scott, 655–657
   On prototype of the Amendment, 666–667, 670–672
   On the final version of the Amendment, 676–677, 682–684
   Privileges and immunities of citizens of the U.S., 661, 683–684
   Reasons for modification of 14th Amendment, 682–683
Birth control, 252, 537, 721, 730, 735, 789, 795, 799, 825, 844, 852, 856, 865, 910, 912
Bivens Doctrine, 382
Black, Charles L., Jr., 34
Black Codes, 625, 662–664, 685, 687, 720, 760
Blackstone, William, 245, 743, 792, 794
Bobbit, Philip, 34
Bond, James, 686
Bork, Robert, 30, 171, 477, 739, 740, 855, 856, 870
Brady Act, 273, 276–280, 282, 283, 305
Bromall, John H., 675
Brown, Ernest J., 115
Buchanan, James, 644
Buck, Carrie, 838–840
Burnside, Ambrose, 660
Bush, George H.W., 180, 251, 366, 825, 869, 870
Bush, George W., 251, 367, 368, 398, 471, 473, 475, 476, 535, 740, 959
Calhoun, John C., 68, 69
Central Intelligence Agency, 384, 388, 395
Citizenship Clause of 14th Amendment, 644, 654
Civil Rights Act of 1866, 663–664, 688, 720, 759, 766
   and Fourteenth Amendment, 34, 632, 682, 686, 706, 721, 757, 765
   constitutionality, 664
   veto by Andrew Johnson, 664

Civil Rights Act of 1964, 164, 171–173, 176, 179, 189
Civil Rights Laws, 163, 195, 688–690, 731, 737
   Civil Rights Act of 1866, 664, 688, 720, 759, 766
   Reconstruction Acts, 688–690
Clark, Walter, 142
Clinton, William J., Impeachment of, 40
Colfax Massacre, 707, 755
Commerce Clause and congressional power, 97–224
   Aggregation, 190, 199, 934
   Concurrent state power, 98–101, 127, 251, 515, 520
   Direct/indirect distinction [Carter], 150 [Wickard], 167
   Effect on interstate commerce, 126, 127, 144, 151, 161, 162, 168, 178–180, 185, 187–189, 201, 207–212, 216, 221, 550, 606
   Excluding products from interstate commerce, 130, 135, 199
   Great Society and, 170
   Late 19th/Early 20th century view, 134–150
   Marshall Court's interpretation of, 103–113
   Medical marijuana, 199, 201, 203, 205, 206, 208, 211–214, 216, 306
   Modern view (graphic portrayals), 97–103, 199
   Motive for legislation, "pretext," 76, 136–137, 160
   Navigation and, 105, 106, 111, 119, 120, 148, 222
   New Deal Court and, 36, 97, 628, 735, 821, 825, 1009, 1010
   Pre-New Deal, 151
   Preemption of state law by federal statute or rule, 509–539
   Preemptive effect of, 110, 116, 118, 122, 199
   Racial discrimination and, 164, 171, 175, 176, 179, 189, 635, 736, 739, 760, 789, 798
   Regulation of interstate commerce, 123, 124, 130, 135, 138, 142, 145, 148, 154, 160, 161, 184, 185, 206, 207, 209, 215,

216, 270, 276, 548, 550, 556, 574, 599, 609, 610
Slavery and federal power, 116
State regulation of commerce, congressional authorization of, 122–123
Stream of commerce theory, 126
Compromise of 1850, 633, 644
Compromise of 1877, 634, 708, 738, 788
Concurrent State and Federal Power, 98–99
Congress
Qualifications for members, 86, 95, 370, 374
Congressional powers in general
Affirmative limits, see also *10th Amendment, Bill of Rights*, 98, 100, 102–103
Commerce, see *Commerce Clause and congressional power*
Delegated Powers, 5, 8
Implied Powers, 61, 64, 65, 67, 72, 73, 80, 113, 146, 232, 260, 444–446, 450, 485, 630, 631
Structural limits, e.g., 185–187, 273, 286
Taxing and Spending Power, 62, 225, 226, 393, 394, 398, 400–402
Treaty Power, 41, 62, 113, 225, 236–238, 244
War Power, 10, 62, 80, 106, 116, 155, 192, 225, 232–236, 260, 375, 396, 466, 467, 630, 631, 634, 639, 678
Constitution of the United States of America, 6–20
Constitutional Arguments, 3, 34–38, 37–39, 81, 82, 221, 252, 286, 331, 369, 495, 636–637
Contextual, 35, 114–116,
Ethical aspirations, 37
Historical, generally (6 types), 36–37
Precedent, 35,
Public Policy, 37
Structure and relationship, 35
Constitutional Change, theory of, 61
Constitutional Ratifying Convention, 32, 36, 42, 43, 48, 49, 54–56, 64–66, 84, 86, 114, 156, 214, 286, 292, 295, 298, 360, 371, 379, 395, 457, 485, 490, 492, 558, 631–633, 939, 940, 943, 944
Constitutional questions, statutory construction as a means of avoiding, 218–219

Continental Congress, Second, 5
Cooley, T., 983
Corwin, E., 983
Court Reform Plans, 143, 836
Crosskey, W.W., 114, 721
Curtis, Charles, 34
Curtis, Michael Kent, 34, 156, 314, 632, 661, 685, 686, 721, 757 n 1., 765, 765, 766
Declaration of Independence, 5, 22, 27, 37, 48, 233, 295, 345, 367, 647, 648, 653, 654, 657, 658, 674, 747, 787, 793, 910
Interpreted by Abraham Lincoln in relation to African-Americans, 657–658
Delegated powers, see *Congressional powers, limits on delegated powers*
De Tocqueville, Alexis, 21, 22, 241, 729, 791
Dew, Charles B., 709
Dillon, John Forrest, 139
Dormant Commerce Clause, 98–100, 118, 398, 507, 509, 540–610
Alternatives, state regulations that do not discriminate or burden interstate commerce, e.g., 548–549
Conservation, environmental aims, e.g., 583, 590, 595
Discrimination against out of staters or commerce from out of state, e.g. 545–549, 557–560
Discrimination by cities or counties, 573, 575 n.3
Doctrine challenged, 409
Extra-territorial regulation, 507, 599
Garbage, state ban on out-of state, 583
Graphic portrayal (chart), 544
Market participant exception, 507, 600, 614
Undue burden on interstate commerce, 554, 574
Wine, discrimination against out of state wine, 557
Douglas, Stephen, 22, 27, 344, 657
Dual Sovereignty, relationship between state and national power
10th Amendment, 101–103
Bank of the United States, 35, 61, 64–81, 339, 341
Commerce Clause, 97–125

Dual Sovereignty, *continued*
  Roosevelt, Franklin, 31, 143, 153, 155, 164, 251, 467, 628, 732, 736–738, 741, 789, 819, 820, 826
  Taxing and Spending Power, 225–232
  Treaty Power, 236–246
  War Power, 10, 232–236, 260, 375, 396, 466, 467, 630, 631, 634, 639, 678
Due Process Clause, see *Economic Substantive Due Process, Substantive Due Process*
  Application of Bill of Rights to states, see generally, 627–783.
Due Process, Substantive, generally, 142–143, 157–158, 206, 596, 628, 791–1010
  Abortion, 858–912
  Assisted suicide, 902, 970, 971, 973, 974, 979–982
  Balancing, ad hoc, 798, 892
  Birth control, see also *abortion, sterilization*, 844–857
  Categorical analysis, 798, 800, 1004
  Chronological overview, 625, 633, 785, 787
  Economic substantive due process, 628, 799–834, 867, 1004–1010
  Education, choices, 872, 910
  End or purpose of statute, constitutional legitimacy, 798
  Family matters, 774, 866, 872, 911, 913, 915
  Fundamental rights and liberty interests, e.g., 796–799, 800 (chart), 890–892
  Graphic portrayal, substantive due process model, 800
  Harm/Trait [End/Means] diagram, 797
  History, 787–790, 799–990, 818–827, 982–986
  Narrow view, for non-economic rights, e.g., 880, n. 327
  Non-economic rights, less textually explicit, generally, 834–986
  Penumbras, 848–850
  Privacy, evolution of holdings from *Griswold* to *Casey*, 868–870
  Scrutiny, 796–800
  Sexual autonomy, privacy, in general, 926–967
  Sodomy (oral or anal sex), 36, 37, 355, 763, 790, 869, 888, 926, 927–960, 966
  Stare decisis, e.g., 870–890
  Sterilization, 789, 838–843, 861
  Stomach pumping for drugs, 843
Dukakis, Michael, 366
Dworkin, Ronald, 28
East, John, 359, 741
Economic substantive due process, 628, 785, 790, 799, 817, 818, 821, 825, 826, 829, 834, 843, 867, 924, 1009, 1010
  Brandeis brief, 785, 817
  Carolene Products footnote, 785, 791, 828, 835
  Court expansion, Franklin D. Roosevelt, 151–156, 820–824
  Demise of, in federal law, 826–833
  Dred Scott v. Sandford, 25, 340, 343, 510, 625, 633, 643, 645, 696, 764, 792, 896, 965, 983, 986
  Economic liberty, *Lochner* and progressive approaches compared, 802–804
  Scrutiny (economic liberty) 826–833
  Takings, generally, 986–1010
Eldridge, Charles, 667
Eleventh Amendment, 284–304
  Federal causes of action against states in state court (see also state sovereign immunity), 284–304
  Waiver of immunity, 297
  14th Amendment, §5, 302–303
Elliot, Thomas, 673
Ellis, Elmer, 139
Emancipation Proclamation, 466, 467
Emergency Price Control Act of 1942, 282
Enforcement Act of 1870, 688–689
Enumerated Powers, generally, e.g., 67, 71, 72, 81, 109, 272
Epstein, Richard, 986
Ethics in Government Act of 1978, 477
Exclusive federal power, 97–101, 117, 122, 124, 127, 251
Executive power, scope, 439, 440–479
Executive privilege or immunities, 479–506
  Civil immunity and official duties, 483
  Civil immunity and unofficial acts, 497
  Immunity from criminal prosecution, 479

Impeachment, 3, 6, 7, 11, 12, 40–59, 141, 240, 316, 377–380, 459, 467, 477, 479, 485, 487, 489–492, 501, 506
  Military or diplomatic secrets, 479, 481, 482
  Presumptive privilege of confidentiality, 479, 482
Executive seizure of domestic commercial facilities, 445–454
Extradition Act of 1793, 519
Fair Labor Standards Act, 158–162
Fair Labor Standards Act and State Employees, 253–273, 286–304.
Fairman, Charles, 721, 726
Fallon, Richard, 34, 37
Farber, Daniel A., 1009
Farnsworth, John, 674
Farrelly, David, 140
Federalist/Anti-Federalist Debate, 633
Federalist Papers, e.g., xxxvii, 41, 49, 214
Federalists (on Bill of Rights), 632
Fifteenth Amendment, 687, 688, 695
Finkelman, Paul, 64, 115, 116
First Amendment, see *Freedom of Expression* (Volume 2), *Bill of Rights, application to states*, 29, 84, 97, 252, 315, 330, 336, 339, 369, 390, 391, 626, 635, 721, 732–737, 740, 741, 772, 824, 935
Flack, Horace, 720
Forbath, William E., 141
Fourteenth Amendment, see also *Bingham, John, Black Codes, Howard, Jacob*
  Bill of Rights 14th Amendment, 267, 359, 628, 635, 637, 643, 664, 665, 672, 685, 686, 691, 707, 709, 715, 720, 721, 723, 726, 727, 732, 756, 760, 761, 771, 780, 850, 930
  Congressional debate, 485, 660, 664
  Drafting/framing of, 661–684
  Final version, 534, 625, 642, 665, 666, 672, 681
  Historical background, 84, 627–684
  Limit only on federal government, 102, 637
  Modification, 85, 689, 893, 968
  Prototype, 346, 664–667, 672, 836
Fourteenth Amendment, early interpretation of, 682–716
  As protection for constitutional rights of citizens of United States, in *Slaughter-House* dissent, 703–706
  Language interpreted in *Slaughter-House Cases* 697–700
  Privileges or immunities of citizens in the several states, 610–620, 686
  Privileges or immunities of citizens of United States, 16, 612, 628, 632, 644, 658, 661, 665, 673, 674, 676, 678, 679, 682, 683, 691, 697, 704, 706, 710, 720, 726, 754, 764, 765, 767, 787
Free blacks, citizenship, 643–657
  Bingham, John, 163, 625, 655, 661, 664–666, 721, 756, 757, 766
  Lincoln, Abraham, 22, 23, 27, 309, 343, 346, 347, 465, 470, 625, 634, 644, 655, 657
Fundamental rights, see, generally, e.g., 796–800, 848–858
Fusionists (Populist-Republicans), Reconstruction political coalition of, 708–709
Gallup Poll, on protection for the accused, 736
Garrison, William Lloyd, 633
Gay marriage, 786, 960–967
Gay rights, 910, 959
General warrants, 45, 250, 787, 793
Gillman, Howard, 125, 801
Goebel, Julius, 115
Goldwater, Barry, 29, 171, 709, 739, 789
Gould, Stephen J., 839
Graham, Billy, 733
Graham, Howard Jay, 721
Great Depression, 164, 260, 789, 819, 822, 826
Gun Control Act of 1968, 273
Habeas Corpus, 9, 122, 153, 240, 359–362, 432, 449, 467, 475, 476, 514, 632, 641, 676, 687, 694, 699, 705, 706, 732
Hale, Robert, 667
Hamilton, Alexander, 41, 43, 44, 48, 55, 64–66, 85, 197, 225, 280, 287, 294, 379, 633
  Congressional taxing and spending power, 225–232, 393, 398, 401
Hamilton, J.G. de Roulhac, 688
Handicapped (disability) discrimination, see also *State sovereign immunity*, 303

Harbaugh, W.H., 129
Hardwick, Michael, 927, 929, 933
Harrington, James, 21
Hart, H.L.A., 34
Hart, Henry M., 115
Hart, Roswell, 672
Helms, Jesse, 362
Helper, Hinton, 633, 659, 661, 662
High Crimes and Misdemeanors, 12, 40, 43–46, 49, 50, 52–54, 56, 59, 377, 491
Hill, David, 139
History and tradition, generally, e.g., 912–915
    Strictly limiting less textually-explicit rights (or not doing so), e.g., 923 n.3, 924, 929–930, 935, 947–948, 956
Hobbes, Thomas, 792
Holmes, Oliver Wendell, 24
Homosexuality, 926–967
Hotchkiss, Giles, 672
Howard, Jacob, 677, 756, 766
Huhn, Wilson, 34, 38
Humphrey, Hubert, 736, 740
Hutchison, Ann, 719
Immigration and Nationality Act, 454, 460
Impeachment, Clinton, 3, 40, 49, 50, 58, 506
Impending Crisis, The, see also *Helper, Hinton*, 633, 659, 661
Implied executive powers, e.g., 445–464, 468–471, 475–476
Implied powers, e.g., 71–76
Income tax of 1894, 61, 139
Incompatibility Clause, 389, 412
Incorporation Doctrine, e.g., 655–732
    Approaches to, 97, 125, 140, 626, 730, 799, 990
    Civil Rights, Bill of, 171, 626, 635, 663, 664, 672, 675, 676, 681, 720, 738–740
    Meese, Edwin, 359, 731
    Roberts Court approach to, 753–762
    Warren Court approach to, 390, 626, 721, 735, 741
Incorporation timeline, 633–635
Independent counsel, see also *Appointments, Separation of powers*, 476–479
Interstate Commerce, see *Commerce Clause, Dormant Commerce Clause*, 544
Irons, Peter, 927

Jackson, Andrew, 68, 329, 339, 343, 344
Jay, John, 41, 366, 633
Jefferson, Thomas, 41, 48, 66, 68, 80, 336, 341, 366, 485, 486, 500, 503
Johnson, Andrew, 51, 634, 662, 664
Johnson, Lyndon, presidency of, civil rights gains during, liv, 171, 736, 740
Johnson, William, 117, 340
Jones, Paula, 479, 497, 505, 506
Judiciary Act of 1789, 309, 312, 315, 317, 329–331, 335, 341, 358–360, 362, 514, 633
Judiciary
    American Judicial System, a graphic portrayal, 309, 312
Judicial Review, see also *Supremacy Clause*
    Adequate and independent state ground doctrine, 309, 349
    Appellate Jurisdiction, 12, 312, 316–319, 324, 325, 329, 332–335, 338, 339, 341, 357–363
    Congressional control, 88, 234, 260, 309, 357, 358, 363, 447, 460, 461
    Constitution, Article III, 29, 42, 284, 287, 293, 316, 328, 357, 363, 392, 395, 396, 399, 400, 406, 645
    Creation of a federal court system, 299
    Judiciary Act of 1789, 309, 312–318, 328–331, 335, 339, 341, 358–360, 362, 514, 633
    Jurisdiction stripping bills, 163–163
    Lincoln, Abraham, 22, 23, 27, 309, 343, 346, 347, 465, 470, 625, 634, 644, 655, 657
    Marbury v. Madison, political setting, 309, 313
    Marshall Court, brief history, 339–343
    Original Jurisdiction, 12, 312, 315–319, 324, 325, 328, 329, 332, 333, 357, 358
    Southern Manifesto, 309, 347, 348
    Treaties, 11–13, 41, 42, 94, 233, 237, 238, 243, 244, 311, 316, 331, 333–336, 338, 340, 343, 349, 357, 366, 444, 459, 467, 630, 667, 699, 765
Justices of the U.S. Supreme Court, lxxi–lxxvii
Justiciability, see also, *Standing*
    Advisory Opinions, 309, 311, 350, 353, 366, 367, 502

Generally, 364–432
Mootness, 310, 311, 430–436
Political questions, 309, 311, 314, 323, 367, 368, 370, 467
Ripeness, 310, 311, 387, 412, 419, 430–432, 844, 927
Standing, 45, 141, 193, 195, 309–311, 346, 350, 355, 359, 364, 369–371, 373–376, 386–420, 422–434, 456, 462, 490, 570, 578–580, 744, 746–748, 758, 761, 764, 775, 879, 928, 929, 933, 989, 998

Kaczorowski, Robert J., 706
Kansas-Nebraska Act, 633, 644
King, Rufus, 65, 114, 193, 233
Klarman, Michael, 27, 31
Korean War, 444, 466
Ku Klux Klan, 163, 687, 835
Latham, George, 677
Legislative Veto, 451, 457, 459–462, 568, 963
 Bi-cameralism, 458–459
 Presentment Clause, 53, 462–464
 Separation of powers, 32, 276, 363, 366, 368, 370, 391–393, 437, 443, 448, 457, 460, 465, 476, 478, 480–482, 484–486, 490, 496, 501–504
Lessig, Lawrence, 33
Levellers, 792
Levinson, Sanford, 28
Liberator, The, 633
Limits on delegated powers, 249
 Bill of Rights, generally, 271
 Structure of the Constitution, 34, 52, 88, 94, 103, 112, 251, 273, 275, 279, 286–292, 300, 302, 305, 341, 501, 742
Limits on state power, 118, 261, 266, 268, 273, 274, 277, 278, 285, 301, 302, 507–623, 628, 631, 709–782
 Article I, 10,10
 Dormant Commerce Clause, see generally, 540–610
 Privileges and Immunities Clause of Article IV, 507, 541, 610–614, 620, 625, 627, 628, 640, 661, 665, 754, 787
 Supremacy Clause, 99, 118, 205, 243, 267, 274, 282, 283, 289, 293, 363, 524, 529, 533, 541, 594, 627, 630

Lincoln, Abraham, 22, 23, 27, 309, 343, 346, 347, 465, 470, 625, 634, 644, 655, 657
 Assassination, 164, 634, 789
 Election as President, 740
 On Declaration of Independence, 345
 On Dred Scott, 309, 343, 345, 625, 645, 655, 983
 Prosecution of Clement Vallandigham, 660
Lincoln-Douglas Debates, 22, 343, 346, 657
Linde, Hans, 629
Line Item Veto, 462–465
Louisiana Purchase, 154, 644
Lovejoy, Elijah, 658, 659
Lovejoy, Owen, 659
LSD, U.S. Army experiments on soldiers, 381–386
Lumpkin, Joseph Henry, 641–642
Madison, James, 41, 43, 48, 54, 64, 65, 67, 68, 84, 214, 225, 250, 267, 268, 271, 315, 372, 379, 398, 403, 457, 509, 632, 633, 748, 1000
 And Bill of Rights, 250, 632
 And *Federalist Papers*, 49, 214
 Appointment Clause, 478, 756
 Bank of United States, 35, 61, 64, 65, 67–70, 76, 79, 339, 341, 343
 Madisonian Compromise, 274
Marshall, John, 29, 31, 68, 69, 89, 140, 156, 174, 258, 314, 328, 329, 341, 469, 633, 713, 732, 825
Martin, Elbert, 659
Mason, George, 43, 54, 271, 372, 748
Meese, Edwin, 359, 731
Members of Congress, qualifications, 85, 86, 374, 376
Methods of Interpretation, generally, 21–38
Missouri Compromise, 154, 340, 633, 644, 645, 984
 As violating 5th Amendment, 650–651
National emergency and executive power, 445–454, 465–471, 473–476
Natural law, 66, 289, 294–297, 299, 679, 718, 787, 792, 793, 854, 858, 922
Necessary and Proper Clause, 35, 65, 67, 68, 75, 81, 189, 207, 209, 212–217, 227, 235, 244, 245, 276, 289, 341, 471, 606
Nelson, Grant, 115

Nelson, William E., 686
New Deal, see also *Commerce Clause* and *Roosevelt, Franklin D.*
  Political realignment and Commerce Clause, 143–170
New York Journal, 936
Ninth Amendment, 849–851, 854
  Arthur Goldberg on 850–851
  Hugo Black on, 854
Non-delegation doctrine, 439–444
  Executive lawmaking, 442, 461
  Intelligible principle, 440–444
Northwest Ordinance, 644
Nuremberg Code, 383
"Original Meaning," controversy over, 61, 114
Partisan entrenchment, 28, 29
Paul, Arnold M., 139
Pennoyer, Sylvester, 141
Perry, Michael, 34, 686
Pledge of Allegiance, 363, 366
Poland, Luke, 665, 676
  Arguments on 14th Amendment, 676
Political Questions, 309, 311, 314, 323, 367, 368, 370, 467
  Generally, 322, 323, 367–386
  Impeachment trials, 44, 376–381, 459
  Reapportionment, 368, 841
Popper, Karl, on economic liberty, 804
Popular sovereignty, 22–24, 38, 49, 92, 156, 157, 295, 630, 791
Populist Party, 708, 709
Populists, 129, 139, 140, 142, 143, 708, 709, 788, 801, 802, 807
  Reaction to Court decisions, 139–141, See also, 141–143
Positive Law, 29, 167, 681, 792–794
Powe, Lucas A., 732
Prather, H. Leon, Sr., 709
Preemption, 100, 118, 306, 509–540
  Commerce Clause (graphic portrayal), 100
  Conflict preemption, 521, 535
  Express preemption, 521, 535, 536
  Implied preemption, 509, 535
Presentment Clause, 53, 462–464
Presser, Stephen, 40
Privacy, right to, see *Due Process, substantive,* non-economic rights, 834–986

Privileges and Immunities Clause of Article IV, 507, 541, 610–614, 620, 625, 627, 628, 640, 661, 665, 754, 787
  After ratification of 14th Amendment, 625, 636, 682, 801, 984
  And NAFTA, 620, 621
  Bar admission for out-of-staters, 615–620
  Current doctrinal approach, 611–614
  Discrimination, type forbidden by, see generally, 543–610
  Fourteenth Amendment clause distinguished, 612
  General introduction, 56
  Graphic portrayal, 309, 312, 613, 614
  Interests protected, 268, 429, 610, 750, 820, 916, 918, 922, 924, 925, 949
  State power limited, 608, 628, 631
  Washington, Bushrod, 611, 640, 787
"Privileges" and "Immunities, (14th Amendment)
  14th Amendment background (word usage), 658–661
  1830s, 21, 658
  Black, Hugo, 719, 726, 732
  Civil War, 659–660
  Congressional debate on abolition, 660
  Lumpkin, Joseph Henry, 641
  Madison, James (privilege used to describe Bill of Rights liberties), 632
  Prosecution of Clement Vallandigham, 660
Privileges or Immunities, see also *Bill of Rights, application to states, Fourteenth Amendment, early interpretation of*
  Bingham, John, 163, 625, 655, 661, 664–666, 721, 756, 757, 766
  Black, Hugo, 719, 726, 732
  Bradley, Joseph P., in Slaughter-House dissent, 706
  Changed language in 14th Amendment, 666 (early version), 678, 681
  Field, Stephen J., in Slaughter-House dissent, 701–702
  Frankfurter, Felix, in Adamson concurrence (ignoring the words and focusing only on due process), 717
  Harlan, John M. (II), in Duncan dissent (rejecting incorporation), 728

INDEX 1019

Historical linguistics, 658–661
Howard, Jacob, 677, 756, 766
Twining, 626, 710, 711, 713, 715, 717–719, 721, 725, 756, 758, 837
Progressives, 61, 129, 141–143, 601, 801, 802
  Response to judicial activism, 61
Pushaw, Robert J., Jr., 115
Rauch, Basil, 143
Reagan, Ronald, 29, 62, 180, 359, 731, 739–741, 790, 870
  Second Inaugural Address, 62, 180
Reconstruction
  Civil rights statutes arise out of, 688–690
  Context, 686–688,
  End of in Mississippi, 687
Reeve, Henry, 22, 729
Rehnquist Court, 179–218, 304–307
Rivers, Mendel, 733
Roosevelt, Franklin D., 155, 820
  1936 nomination speech, 143
  Constitution as a Layman's Document, 153
  Court expansion ("packing") plan, 821
  New Deal, 143–170
Roosevelt, Theodore, 129, 142, 143, 452, 601, 710, 818, 819
  Laissez-faire, opposition to, 819
  On corporate power, 819
  Recall of judicial decisions, 142
Ross, Michael A., 690
Ross, William G., 143, 836
Schwartz, Bernard, 250
Scott, Dred, 25, 27, 140, 309, 340, 343–347, 510, 625, 633, 643–646, 649, 651, 654–657, 664, 696, 764, 787, 792, 896, 965, 976, 983–987, 1007
Scott, Sir Walter, 28
Scrutiny, see this topic under *Commerce Clause, Due Process, substantive Dormant Commerce Clause, Equal Protection, Freedom of Expression, Privileges and Immunities Clause*, 796–800
Sedition Act of 1798, 313
Separation of powers, 454–462, 476–479
Sherman Act, 127, 140, 149, 162, 167, 191, 201, 269, 807
Sherman, John, 681
Sixth Amendment, 240–241, 722–729

Slaves, fugitive, 510, 511, 514, 519, 631
Special prosecutor, see *Independent counsel*
Standing, 386–432
  Associations, 418–419, 579
  Cause in fact, 415, 418
  Citizen, 388–405
  Congressional power to confer, 428–430
  Establishment Clause claims, 390–405
  Injury, personal, cognizable, 310, 404, 405, 412, 413
  Personal (cognizable) injury requirement, 416–418
  Redressability, 310, 402, 415, 422, 423
  Ripeness, 310, 311, 387, 412, 419, 430–432, 844, 927
  Taxpayer, 388–405
  Third party standing, 424–428
Stanton, Elizabeth Cady, 634
State Action, see also *State Action* in Index to Volume 2
  Cities & Counties, 625, 685
  14th Amendment, text of, 16
State constitutions, protection for rights under, 629
State intergovernmental immunity, 247, 252
  Enforcement of federal programs by state officials, e.g., 273–284
  Generally, 252–304
  States, as subject to federal regulatory programs, 252–304
State sovereign immunity, generally, 252–304, see also *Eleventh Amendment*
  Age discrimination, 302, 305, 425
  Commerce power, 252, 253–272, 286–304
  English origins, 758
  Handicapped (disability) discrimination, 252, 264
  Patent powers, 285, 302
  Private suits, 284, 286–293, 296, 485, 502
  Waiver, 288, 297, 302, 465
Sterilization, 789, 839–843, 861
Stevens, Thaddeus, 667, 673, 757, 768
Story, Joseph, 45, 93, 340, 464, 510
Strict Construction, 104, 105, 251

Judicial restraint and deference to Congress, 251
Original meaning, 27, 28, 33, 36, 40, 61, 114, 115, 156, 214, 251, 252, 629, 658, 661, 664, 737, 762, 764, 769, 778
Warren Court, 29, 84, 97, 252, 315, 330, 336, 339, 369, 390, 391, 626, 635, 721, 732–737, 740, 741, 772, 824, 935
Sunstein, Cass, 33
Supremacy Clause, e.g., limit on states, 25, 405, 628, 635, 636, 711, 720, 722, 730, 741, 769, 808
Taft-Hartley Act, 446
Taft, William Howard, 140, 818
Takings Clause, 35, 252, 786, 833, 986, 988, 991, 993–995, 997, 998, 1000, 1007–1010
Taney, Roger B., 69, 340
Tenth Amendment, 249–252
Delegated powers, 64–239
Independent limit on federal power, 102
Reserved powers, 69, 83, 86, 88, 91–94, 98, 102, 103, 137, 147, 162, 211, 214, 228, 230, 237, 250, 259, 273, 668
Truism, 102, 162, 251, 254, 259, 844
Territories, 116, 154, 155, 242, 274, 343, 344, 466, 472, 473, 512, 519, 560, 625, 643–645, 649, 765, 976, 984, 987
Congressional power limited, 151, 160, 470
Free blacks and slaves, 768
Thirteenth Amendment, xlii, xliv, 156, 164, 172, 544, 631, 634, 664, 688, 766, 768
Thompson, E.P., 729
Thurmond, Strom, 171, 739, 740
Treanor, William Michael, 986, 988, 1009
Tribe, Lawrence, 49–59,
Truman, Harry, 444, 736, 738
Tucker, St. George, *A Dissertation on Slavery*, 625, 655
Turner, Nat, 633
Twain, Mark, 62, 169, 1010
United States Constitution, background, 351

Urofsky, Melvin I., 141
Vallandigham, Clement, 660
Vietnam War, 471, 734, 736, 740, 789
Voting Rights Act of 1965, 635, 736, 740, 789
Wages, regulation, 114, 142, 160, 261, 802
Wallace, George, 735, 736, 740, 790
War on Poverty, 32, 736, 789
War Powers, see also *Executive power, scope*, 232–236
Generally, Congressional Power, 232–236
Generally, Executive Power, 439
War Powers Resolution, 437, 460, 461, 471, 473, 475
Warren Court, 29, 84, 97, 252, 315, 330, 336, 339, 369, 390, 391, 626, 635, 721, 732–737, 740, 741, 772, 824, 935
Protection of freedom of speech, 32, 629, 792
Protection of impoverished and granting access to justice, 734, 735
Substantially increasing number of Bill of Rights liberties limiting states, 732
Washington, Bushrod, 617
Washington, George, 42, 48, 49, 366, 633
Watergate, 226, 477, 479, 489
Weaver, James, 788, 801
Webster, Daniel, 660
Westin, Alan, 140
Westlaw oral argument briefs and transcripts, 82
Wharton, Vernon, 687
Wiecek, William M., 721
Wildenthal, Bryan H., 706, 721, 757
Wilkes, John, 371
Wilson, James, 65, 194, 267, 268, 288, 501, 660
Wilson, Woodrow, 818, 819
Woodhull, Victoria, 634
Woodward, C. Vann, 709
Worth, Daniel, 633, 661